REPRESENTATIVE AMERICAN DRAMAS

NATIONAL AND LOCAL

REPRESENTATIVE AMERICAN DRAMAS

NATIONAL AND LOCAL

EDITED, WITH INTRODUCTIONS

BY

MONTROSE J. MOSES *onas 1878 -*

STUDENTS' EDITION

BOSTON
LITTLE, BROWN, AND COMPANY
1931

Copyright, 1925,

By Little, Brown, and Company.

All rights reserved

TO
ALFRED R. McINTYRE
IN FRIENDSHIP

PREFACE

It has not been an easy matter to assemble the present collection of plays. The difficulty has been commensurate with the abundant material at hand of an isolated character from which to choose. There is no gainsaying the fact that the American Drama, during recent decades, has so vastly improved in its technical expression that there is a wide area of well-worth-while plays one cannot pass by lightly or discard without hesitation. I often wonder what the student of the near future will do in his endeavor to cover the growing field with conscientious thoroughness. For, even now, barring the historical perspective which I have tried to suggest in my former collection of plays under the title, "Representative Plays by American Dramatists" (Dutton), if one begins with playwrights within the immediate memory of theatregoers — who are still not so very ancient — a lengthy list of authors, both native and worthy of consideration, confronts one.

I may, therefore, say that the fifteen plays which are offered in the present collection have been chosen with some forethought, some object in view. The American Drama is still held under suspicion by certain editors whose motives and points of view may be perfectly sincere, if not wholly sound. For the three-volume edition of the "Cambridge History of American Literature" two chapters were written covering the entire field of playwriting in this country from the beginning to "the very hour." But, when an abridgment of these volumes was made, the editors omitted the Drama altogether, following in the wake of Professor Barrett Wendell and other conservatives. Their reason for so doing was perfectly right on their part — if their position was justifiable. They claimed that the American Drama had not so far — despite its vigorous activity — produced one figure commensurate in importance with Emerson, Poe, and Whitman; not one figure that impelled extensive or intensive analysis.

This is true. Even Eugene O'Neill, whom we are likely to turn to daily in our desperate claim that we are doing something worthy in the theatre, should not, at the present, be subjected to a judgment which might suggest a tone of finality. The American Drama has heretofore advanced, not through the work of preponderately great figures, but through unconscious group experiment in certain forms : there were writers of Indian plays, of semi-historical plays, of plays in which the Yankee type and the frontiersman are their chief claim to our present interest. Coming to the immediate present, what challenges our consideration is, not this or that man who has happened to write a successful farce, but what, for instance, are the characteristics of the American farce, which has a native life of its own, and for which there is a formula. The one-volume abridgment of the "Cambridge History of American Literature" lacks a chapter, it seems to me, which takes the entire range of American Drama from this angle.

It is with such a viewpoint in mind, therefore, that the present Editor has approached this collection of American plays. He has not gone back into historical perspective, for he feels that he has already sufficiently covered that range in his three-volume edition of American Plays. But he has started at a time in the modern development when there were evident a break with old models and a statement of the newest spirit of the then Eighteen-Nineties. He has not taken Charles Hoyt because he thought him any better than Edward Harrigan in the handling of a certain type of farce. Hoyt in this volume represents a species of raciness against which it is both profitable and justifiable to place the raciness of "Dulcy." There was another reason for using "A Texas Steer"; so far as I know not one of Hoyt's popular farces has as yet appeared in print, except in the typed copies left to five libraries in accordance with Mr. Hoyt's will. It has ever been my desire to make available unpublished texts. And, for that reason, it is evident why David Belasco's "The Girl of the Golden West" is included. It has been foreshortened in the magazines, with excerpts; it has been novelized; librettoes have been made available to the opera-goer; but the text complete is here given for the first time.

A significant spirit of change is to be detected in playwriting for those who read this anthology through. Since the days of Hoyt the theatre has made strides somewhat akin to those of the Seven-Leagued Boots. Bronson Howard, in his lifetime, recognized the absurd pattern which he was made, through theatrical convention, to follow. He almost laughs at himself in his illuminating lecture, "The Autobiography of a Play" (Dramatic Museum of Columbia University, 1914), and now we shake our heads at his plays, for they are so creaky, so imperfectly made on the model of the well-made play, so lacking in literary distinction. The cruel out-of-dateness of the literary product often obscures the worthiness of such a figure as Mr. Howard in the theatre. He gave the impulse to modern American dramatic creativeness, and has been left far behind.

When Hoyt is read — and I have left some of the crudenesses in the text for the purpose of showing the advance we have made in the sheer technique of movement — it will be clearly seen that where current life enters so strongly into the content of the play — absurd and slapstick as it may seem, — the vitality of type preserves some of its old appeal. The same thing would have been observed had we given an example of Harrigan's Irish fun. Such plays have no literary pretensions. Hoyt was all in the acting, and the current news reports of a Hoyt opening used to be built on excuses that the web was so flimsy, so dependent on the actor — yet, withal, so relished by the crowded houses that brought to Hoyt his fortune. I sometimes wonder whether such plays might not be revived with profit: their current event may be out of date, but the types persist, just as the Yankee type remains. Weber and Fields have faded into "Potash and Perlmutter", the one-time popular minstrel has faded into Al Jolson and Jazz. It is significant thus to recall our literary and art antecedents. There were certain elements in Eugene O'Neill's "Desire Under the Elms" which made me think of the best realistic moments in the plays of James A. Herne. With W. D. Howells, Mr. Herne stands the forerunner of American realism, just as surely as Howard may be regarded as the Father of the American Dramatist. Unfortunately, Mr. Herne wrote at a time when a love of sentimental melodrama was uppermost in fashion. Yet, dropped into "Shore Acres" were immaculate rhythms of life, just as they were to be found in "Griffith Davenport" and "Margaret Fleming." I do not think that Owen Davis's "The Detour" is as far away from Herne as it is from Mr. Davis's own early blood-curdlers, "Tony, the Bootblack" and "Nellie, the Beautiful Cloak-Model." In fact, there is some common blood tinge between "Shore Acres" and O'Neill and Davis.

In the present collection, there is no violent break between yesterday and to-day, although one might feel it who read first Percy MacKaye's "The Scarecrow" and then O'Neill's "The Emperor Jones." Methods of playwriting change slowly, and it is worth while to note the shifts in emphasis, from dramatist to dramatist. One asks, "How West is 'The Girl of the Golden West'?" and then contrasts with it the sociological treatment of Hatcher Hughes' "Hell-Bent for Heaven" and the atmospheric and character treatment of Lulu Vollmer's "Sun-Up." But if, between Belasco and these, one should put William Vaughn Moody's "The Great Divide", the chasm becomes understandable. Even now we are rightly picking flaws in the Moody play which was once generally hailed as *the American Drama*. Because it is so easily available, it has been omitted from this collection.

On the other hand, "The Piper" has been included for two reasons: it represents an official recognition of the American dramatist abroad, and it occupies a position as positive as Moody's "The Great Divide": it was spoken of generally at the time as a forerunner in this country of a poetic drama revival: a renaissance on the stage of poetry.

I have included Clyde Fitch and Augustus Thomas in this collection because they were such distinct pioneers for the playwrights of the immediate present. They made the road easier for Rachel Crothers and James Forbes; they dealt with subjects interesting to Americans and of a timely nature; they showed in their writing the value of good dialogue, the necessity for good structure. They attempted, at least, even if the commercial manager, with whom they dealt, frustrated their faint endeavors, to put some thought, some smattering of philosophy into their stories. It is accessory largely, and slim thinking, that have dated them so completely. But their importance in the structure of American Drama cannot be gainsaid.

James Forbes gave to the stage some excellent character studies, written in the conventional manner, but with an understanding of the stage and of certain condition. On that score, "The Chorus Lady" or "The Show Shop" might have been a consistent choice. But Mr. Forbes went to France during the War, and, when he came back, he wrote "The Famous Mrs. Fair", and it shows a change — a significant one — in Mr. Forbes, rather than in the character of his playwriting. Miss Crothers, on the other hand, in "Nice People", reveals herself a stage technician not quite sure of her types, yet fully aware of changing social condition, and trying, in the old manner, to keep up with it, as Lewis Beach has done in "The Goose Hangs High."

Of the other plays, this may be said: Harry James Smith's "Mrs. Bumpstead-Leigh" is chosen as an example of farcical elements mingled with high comedy; the Megrue-Hackett farce, "It Pays to Advertise", is an excellent example of the impelling outward power of American light farce-comedy. The field of farce is so excellently full that the choice might have been given to any of the pieces which measure the physical standard set by "It Pays to Advertise." One might enjoy equally as well "Seven Days" or "Officer 666", for there are in them both the same tension, the same high speed, — qualities smiled over yet always praised by the foreign press.

The new phases in playwriting are excellently exemplified by O'Neill's "The Emperor Jones" and Elmer Rice's "The Adding Machine", in which originality of thought, vividness of character, and incisive criticism are wrought to a fine emotional pitch and done with pronounced artistic integrity. While they are apparently based on European models, they are in accord with the *mood* of the American people in their fragmentary progressiveness, and they have received cordial acceptance abroad.

"Dulcy" and "The Show-Off" are representative of that locality in American drama, difficult to understand very far away from the locality which brought them to light. By this I do not mean that they are not a distinct contribution : they are more than an addition to the richness of American comedy ; they are poignantly tragic in their fundamental note, which shows how deeply the playwrights have gauged and sounded the limitations of certain American social strata. I cannot yet get over the fact that not more people wept over Miss Crothers's "Expressing Willie" than laughed over it, *Willie* to me was so profoundly a tragic character. The same is to be said about "Dulcy" and "The Show-Off."

In this Table of Contents there are to be noted several interesting phases which put the American Drama on a footing different from the American Drama of the past. Sporadically, in the days of Howard and Fitch, our native drama crossed the ocean, sadly changed in content and in name. "Saratoga" became "Brighton", and, when Fitch's "The Truth" was played in London by Miss Marie Tempest, the scene — once shifted from New York to Baltimore, — was shifted from London to Brighton. For several decades the exporting of American plays to Europe has been on the increase. This matter of change to suit new conditions still goes on : "Friendly Enemies" becomes "Uncle Sam" ; and American slang is quickly converted into the London equivalent. I have seen English editions of American plays where there were changes not confined to the U's in favor, labor and honor, but to other points which took away from the — shall we say flavour — of the piece, destroyed its native integrity. Recently, we have had on the New York stage John Galsworthy's "Old English", as typically English as "The Show-Off" is American. There are no changes in slang, no shiftings in locality. Its literary features are preserved. Does it mean that the American Drama is still regarded as a commodity by the managers who purvey it ; that, sold across the box-office sill, it must be cut according to specification? [1] Eugene O'Neill has not thus been touched. He is given "as is", and the reason for it is, no doubt, that he is conscious of his literary worth ; and that worth is something beyond locality, beyond the box-office, — something universal.

By their very nature there are certain American plays which are typically American, and, as such, should not be made English. Contrast "It Pays to Advertise" with A. A. Milne's "The Great Broxopp", — practically the same theme. The latter play was given in America unchanged — and rightly so. It failed — and rightly so — because we advertize in our way, the English in theirs. There is nothing more intensely interesting than the study of national characteristics and their points of contact here and there. French drama — apart from the French drama of broad philosophic and poetic content — has never bitten into the American Theatre because the individual attitude of the French is so different from ours. "The Show-Off" did not meet with ready welcome from London ; it becomes the furor in Amsterdam, Holland. "The Emperor Jones" does not appeal to the French, even though we thought their African possessions would make it understandable. There is an interesting thesis here for some sociological student eager for a literary topic.

---

[1] Mr. Kelly informs me, however, that "The Show-Off" was given in London without any changes in his text, except the substitution of "cinema" for "movie", and "gramaphone" for "Victrola."

The modern American Drama, however, is not unknown abroad. It travels and is variously received. How it is received, the points upon which it is condemned, the directions in which it is praised — these matters should be of concern to us. In another direction, the drama is having a broader contact. It is a present-day shame that the country at large is no longer considered important hunting ground for the American theatre-manager. The old-time extensive theatrical circuits are deserted. Economic reasons have forced the manager to give up all but a small territory. Disorganized stock, independent Little Theatre groups, an occasional braving of the road by some individual actor — and the theatre-loving people outside the large cities of the present limited theatrical circuit are left to shift for themselves. They take to the reading of plays. But in addition they seek the moving-picture both for their theatre and for their novel. "The Famous Mrs. Fair" is on the screen. So is "Dulcy." And it is easy to make a bibliography of many other American plays in celluloid. The only difficulty is that the character of the play is often lost, though its content becomes the foundation for the scenario. Its incidents are spread out over a large area in a technique all its own.

The student is therefore advised to go back to the printed play. Clyde Fitch's "Beau Brummell" on the screen may be a better canvas, but it is not Clyde Fitch. Different by far is the fate of the novelist in celluloid. I would not advise a class in drama to get its knowledge of a play by first seeing the moving-picture of it. But I believe the screen version of Robert Louis Stevenson's "Treasure Island" or of Joseph Hergesheimer's "Java Head", or of the pictorial "Robin Hood" might drive readers to the original. Not so many years ago, a successful play was immediately novelized. We do not turn to the novel to study the play. Now American Drama is screened. The play form is a different matter.

The present Table of Contents shows the encouraging strength of the American Drama, — its vitality, its growing technique, its vivid characterization, its refreshing satire. It indicates the dramatist making capital out of native characteristics. It does not show him preponderately pledged to any angle of vision; he is interested in all things, and a little shy — we'll put it at that — when it comes to revealing his innermost convictions. He is experimental. But is that experiment in an original vein? Would O'Neill have written "The Emperor Jones", Rice "The Adding Machine", Kaufmann and Connelly their "Beggar on Horseback" if Andreyeff had not done "The Life of Man" and Karel Capek his "R. U. R."? This does not take away in the least from the dexterity with which the plays just mentioned were done. In them one sees sources of national hope. It may be that the short scene method is a national outlet for us. It's a dangerous form, for one can become as hazy in a shift of scene as in an intensive adherence to one scene alone. The recent production of John Howard Lawson's "Processional", where our jazz panorama of life is inexpertly unfolded, shows that the form has to be very skillfully handled to hold tensely, as it does — even though the handling be none too firm — in "The Emperor Jones" and "The Adding Machine."

In the sense that Fitch and Forbes and Davis and Thomas have contented themselves with adhering to the old form, they are of the old order. The other men are frankly experimental. Eugene O'Neill naïvely declares that it is an easy matter to create "Anna Christies", but a different and far more interesting matter to write "Hairy Apes." Elsewhere I state the case of Expressionism. Here I merely indicate reasons for the selection of the plays.

Despite the many limitations which the critic is enforced to recognize in American

Drama, from season to season, its live quality is its alertness to experiment. Hardly a year passes that some excellent example of dramatic writing does not come to the front — no matter how difficult it may seem for the Pulitzer Prize Committee to make its annual award. Many of these plays rightly find their way into print and are worthy of the most careful study, for they are representative of certain phases of outlook and interest, certain advances in technique, certain openings of new fields of unworked material and unusual character. On the score of any one writer having stamped his quality definitely in mind — excepting O'Neill — having something to say in which he profoundly believes, the editors of "The Cambridge History of American Literature" are justified in their omission. But this anthology will, I hope, persuade those who read it that there are real character, real humor, real satire and high comedy, real imagination, and real structure in the American play. It may be that the next step in drama will not be Expressionism. None the less will O'Neill and Rice have to be read, as here represented. It may be that our satire will take a new turn, but "Dulcy" is none the less a contribution — and an actable one, I may say for the benefit of the future Repertory Theatre. O'Neill, no matter what his growth, has created something big in "Emperor Jones." "The Scarecrow" is no mean companion for Hawthorne. And so on through the Table of Contents. Since I believe these plays must be read and studied several decades from now, I believe they are representative of the present, both in their national and local meaning — and, what is more, in certain qualities which make some of them of universal significance.

So obviously are many of the plays in this volume experimental both in content and form that they take on a most impersonal value. As we have noted many times in our discussion of the American Theatre, there is ample creativeness going on, but this creativeness seems somehow to be attached to movements, to artistic theories, rather than to personal interest or conviction. There is apparent an extravagance of effort on the part of many dramatists, who write one successful play and then disappear from the field or else follow with a play of different calibre, and of casual though none the less interesting intention.

For that reason, when a young dramatist has created well, and his play represents a high-water mark in the special form he has adopted, because it interests him for the moment, there does not seem to be any particular reason for prefacing one significant play with a life story which, as far as the theatre is concerned, is just about to be lived, and which has no apparent connection with the play itself. In the discussion of Hatcher Hughes's "Hell-Bent for Heaven", for example, the important thing to understand in the appreciation of his play is, not that he teaches at Columbia University — for that has no particular bearing on the play in question — but that he has been to the mountains and understands the peculiar civilization of the mountain poor white. He is merely representative of a host of others who are beginning to be alive to the presence of an untouched civilization which, as seen in Lulu Vollmer's "Sun-Up" and Percy MacKaye's "This Fine-Pretty World", is showing its rich soil flavor and its inherent dramatic content. The entrance of the folk drama into our theatre has been encouraged by such men as Professor Frederick Koch, one-time Professor at the University of North Dakota and now at the University of North Carolina, who has tried to demonstrate the value of writing drama in community fashion and of awakening in young students an understanding of the drama of their own immediate locality. For drama that is not of pure imagination is built of the life the playwright knows best; and even in imagination, the philosophy and symbol must be sustained by a view of life that has some personal connection.

I have, therefore, thought it best to reserve the statistical facts and biographical details of the more recent dramatists for the bibliographical section of the book. All that is necessary to know about Mr. Kaufmann and Mr. Connelly is that they have had a typical newspaper training, and that their play was born of the "column" of F. P. A., as a sort of literary father to "Dulcy." To those who witnessed Elmer Rice's "On Trial", it was only necessary to learn that he had studied law, but the more interesting thing to fathom was the application of moving-picture technique to the theatre — the cutback scene which was a novelty. His "The Adding Machine" attaches itself to a problem not personal, but artistic — the application of Expressionism to a social philosophy not wholly convincing, but none the less effective. When one is told that Mr. Kelly came to the theatre through vaudeville, it seems to me that such fact is alone necessary to show for the present. There may come a time when these men will have created enough, and related it sufficiently to their own lives, to make the lives necessary for more full analysis of their work than the mere biographical note which accompanies each individual bibliography.

In the working out of this book, the Editor has had the assistance of many to whom thanks and credit are a pleasure to give. The Table of Contents shows my gratefulness to authors; the copyright to their publisher or their agent. The Hoyt Estate has been gracious in letting me have "A Texas Steer"; Mr. Belasco, always eager in his interest, has overcome for my sake his unwillingness to have his plays published for the present; the owners of the Fitch copyright have accorded with my desire to use "The City." Through the courtesy of Samuel French and their managing director, Mr. T. R. Edwards, I have been given access to several plays. And, finally, through the eager desire on the part of the many authors to contribute to the richness of the contents, I am justified in feeling that this Anthology has a place in the scheme of things. In my Introductions and Bibliographies I have given credit to those I have quoted. Reading the collection afresh, I am gratefully reminded of the many pleasant hours I have spent in the theatre witnessing these plays which, in print, prove to be "cold but sure friends."

MONTROSE J. MOSES.

New York, January 26, 1925.

CONTENTS

Contents

A TEXAS STEER

(1894)

By Charles H. Hoyt

CHARLES HOYT

LITTLE has been written about Charles Hoyt and Edward Harrigan. And it is only very recently that Weber and Fields have had their just deserts given them. They created three types of entertainment, typically native, that were contributions — not literary, but strictly for the stage; more or less evanescent, but intriguing to the memory, if we are to judge by the affectionate way in which Hoyt and Harrigan and Hart are mentioned in autobiographical reminiscences. Every now and then I come across such a comment as this from Mr. Harrigan, published in *Harper's Weekly* for February 2, 1889:

> At the outset of my career I found that whenever I tried to portray a type, I was warmly applauded by the audience, and praised by the press the next day. This, in all probability, is what gave me a decided bent, and has confined all my work to certain fields. It began with the New York "boy", the Irish-American, and our African brother. As these grew in popularity, I added the other prominent types which go to make up life in the metropolis, and in every other large city of the Union and Canada. . . . This system has given my pieces their peculiar polyglot character.
>
> Though I use type and never individuals, I try to be as realistic as possible. Not only must the costuming and accessories be correct, but the speech or dialect, the personal "make-up", the vices and virtues, habits and customs, must be equally accurate in their similarity to the facts. Each drama is a series of photographs of life to-day in the Empire City. As examples, the bar-room in one of the Mulligan series was copied from a saloon in Roosevelt Street, the opium den in "Investigation" from a "joint" in Pell Street, and the "dive" in "Waddy Googan" from an establishment in the neighborhood of the Bowery.
>
> If I have given undue prominence to the Irish and Negro, it is because they form almost the most salient features of Gotham humanity, and also because they are the two races who care the most for song and dance. There are at least three hundred organizations in New York like the Mulligan Guards, and probably fifty like The Full Moons.

Reading this, one is impressed that in such entertainment, only one step removed from variety, realism, as practiced on the American stage, had its roots. There was a certain music-hall, vaudeville looseness to the form of such production, and the lack of literary style has buried it as soon as it left the stage. Weber and Fields were together called by Professor Brander Matthews the Aristophanes of America, but they have nothing to show for their entertainment. It was a fleeting form. But there is a line of relationship between Harrigan and Hoyt and George M. Cohan, just as there is between the minstrels and Al Jolson. There is a connection also between the realism of Harrigan, as emphasized above, and the realism of David Belasco. There is a relationship between the active principle of a Hoyt farce, and the later type of farce-comedy which I have represented by Megrue and Hackett's "It Pays to Advertise." But there was also a "time spirit" about Harrigan and Hoyt that should be preserved.

3

The critics of the period treated Hoyt sharply; they never failed to indicate that a Hoyt farce was a theatre event that always kept audiences in gales of merriment; but they regarded his plays usually as a sort of "dance and song" accomplishment.

But in many ways Hoyt's plays were pioneer as well as contemporaneous. He capitalized the "movements" of his day, treated them with a newspaper deftness which was closely akin to the way contemporaneousness thrusts its way into musical comedy. Hoyt did not merely utilize occasional comments on ways and manners of the "reformer" of his day; he wrote entire plays on these subjects. The sporting craze, politics, the temperance movement, the militia, woman's rights all came under his treatment. Unfortunate that they were oftentimes obscured by a frivolous manner which tended to discount them. Through a certain faithful handling of detail, he established the worth of his farce; he likewise made a market for such entertainment. Without Hoyt's farces, the dramatic period of the Eighteen-Nineties would have been very much the poorer.

The bare details of Mr. Hoyt's life are given in the Bibliography. The more thorough study of his plays is reserved for the new edition of my "The American Dramatist", shortly to be published. I hope that, in selecting "A Texas Steer", the first of the Hoyt farces to be printed, I have paved the way for a more serious consideration of his work. The files of the Boston *Post* need to be searched for his comments on contemporary drama; the records of the New Hampshire Legislature need to be read to see how far he entered into the machinery of politics. A "Life" of Charles Hoyt has yet to be written. I quote a letter received from Mr. Harlan C. Pearson, secretary to the present Governor of New Hampshire. It shows the relish there is in the subject of Hoyt's plays for the student who undertakes it. He writes:

Although a Democrat in politics, living in a two-to-one Republican town, Charlestown, he was twice elected to the legislature by substantial majorities, being a member of the House in 1893 and again in 1895. The legislature, also, was Republican, but he was given important committee assignments, on Banks and State Library, in 1893, and on the chief committee of all, Judiciary, in 1895. At the latter session, he was the candidate of his party for Speaker of the House. He had a conspicuous seat in what we call "Statesmen's Row", in the Hall of Representatives, next to his long-time friend, the late James O. Lyford, chairman of the State Bank Commission.

Mr. Hoyt was not a bitter partisan, and he did not care much for the routine work of the legislature; but he did like many of the men he met there, and he entered into the social life of the session with enjoyment, making countless friends. At each session, he brought a production of one of his plays from the Park Theatre in Boston entire to Concord, for an afternoon performance, in compliment to his fellow-members of the legislature, company and scenery making the trip by special train so that the usual evening performance could be given in Boston. I think the two pieces thus given were "A Contented Woman" and "A Black Sheep." . . .

In 1893, under the auspices of the Committee on State Library, of which Mr. Hoyt was a member, the State dedicated a new State library building, with a reception to the Governor, Hon. John B. Smith, and his lady. But Mr. Hoyt brought to town for the occasion for the first time his beautiful young wife, Caroline Miskel, and the Governor's wife was almost forgotten in the furore the Blue Grass Beauty occasioned.

Come up to New Hampshire, and I can tell you where you can go to the original sources for the most interesting stories of his boyhood here in Concord, of his summer home in Charlestown, of the real "Mink" Jones, and others of his characters. How interesting a figure he was, and how he lightened and livened the American stage, the present generation little knows.

Hoyt's structure was faulty; it was so articulated that many of his plays could be easily whipped into success, if they lagged at any point. The American Drama was largely adaptable to change in those days. In my early theatregoing, I remember many evenings spent in the theatre, within earshot of manager and playwright, watching the play for "points", for "laughs", and discussing wherein their plan of attack had failed, and wherein the dialogue would have to be changed at rehearsal on the morrow. The literary drama is of a different shape. It is more of a growth. But I doubt whether some of this literary drama, as written to-day by the more technically mature playwright, is any the more reflective of native life than Hoyt's farces.

The Lambs Club, of which Mr. Hoyt was a member, should see that such a record as I suggest be made of a phase of the American Theatre which was original and thoroughly native. If they do not do it, steps should be made to reorganize the Dunlap Society, which in the past has done such service in gathering data of the early theatre. Harrigan and Herne need to be studied carefully, for their services are fading from memory and their plays are not available for the library. The printing of "A Texas Steer", as it was left in manuscript by Mr. Hoyt, it seems to me, is a valuable contribution. It should lead to the further opening of a rich field.

According to Mr. Hoyt's will, the eighth clause directed his executors to have printed five copies each of the plays composed by him, and "when so printed and properly bound, shall be an *edition de luxe* and shall be entitled 'The Dramatic Works of Charles H. Hoyt'", and distributed as follows:

One copy to the Town Library of the town of Charlestown, State of New Hampshire;
One copy to the "Lambs" Library;
One copy to the Library of the Actor's Fund;
One copy to the Tilden Library;
One copy to be retained by Frank McKee.

The plays, handsomely bound, are typewritten copies, based upon theatre manuscripts. The present Editor secured a version of "A Texas Steer", through the courtesy of Sanger & Jordan, after arrangements had been made with the remaining Executor of the Hoyt Estate, to publish it in the present collection. A comparison of this copy with the play in the New York Public Library (called the Tilden Library above) showed so many variations, not only in small bits of dialogue, but in the final scene, that the Editor has deemed it wise to indicate some of these differences. He has likewise retained some of the technical stage directions so as to emphasize how constantly movement, in the Hoyt farce, was employed for humorous effect. The abbreviation N. Y. P. L., means the New York Public Library.

A TEXAS STEER

OR

"MONEY MAKES THE MARE GO"

By CHARLES H. HOYT

"A Texas Steer" is a collection of saws and instances supposed to bear more or less directly upon the extraordinary possibility of American politics, and the development of statesmanship of the average type. The author does not claim that his treatment of the subject is exhaustive and profound; he will not insist that it is absolutely truthful, but he hopes that, as far as it goes, it will be found amusing.

SYNOPSIS

WHERE'S WHERE

The Prologue — Texas. The door-yard of Mr. Brander's house. The Congressman-elect.

THE REST OF IT IN WASHINGTON

ACT   I. — *Private reception-room at the Arlington. The Congressman arrives at the Capital.*

ACT II. — *Ante-room and dining-room of Mr. Brander's apartments at the Arlington. The Congressman investigated.*

ACT III. — *Mr. Brander's parlors. The Congressman vindicated.*

NOTE.   — *Sufficient time is supposed to elapse between Acts I and II for the Brander family to get acquainted with the town.*

WHO'S WHO

MAVERICK BRANDER, *a Texas cattle king* . . . . . . Will Mandeville

CAPTAIN FAIRLEIGH BRIGHT, U.S.A. ⎫ . . . . Charles Hallock

MAJOR YELL, *lawyer* . . . . . ⎬ *Members of Farmers'* . James C. Marlowe

COLONEL BRAGG, *faro dealer* . . . ⎭ *Alliance* . . . . Harry J. Turner

COLONEL BLOW, *bar tender* . . . . G. D. Cunningham

OTHELLO MOORE, *private waiter at the Arlington Hotel* . . John T. Craven

BRASSY GALL, ESQ., *member of third house* . . . . . . H. D. Byers

COLONEL K. N. PEPPER, *a retired army officer* . . . . . G. D. Cummins

CHRISTOPHER COLUMBUS, JR., FISHBACK, *a colored statesman* Will H. Bray

KNOTT INNITT, *Brander's private secretary* . . . . . Edward Craven

SERGEANT-AT-ARMS . . . . Jay Binkly

ANATOLE, *a valet* . . . . H. D. Byers

A. WHITTAKER BELLOWS, *a Senator* . . . . Robert Mack

LIEUTENANT GREEN, U.S.A. . . . . Edward Craven

GREEN WOODHEAD, *a Judge* . . . . Charles Bradford

LOWE DODGE, *an artist* . . . . Morris Fenton

CRAB ⎫ *field hands* . . . . ⎰ George Ovey

MINK ⎭ . . . . ⎱ Jay Binkly

SAM ROW, *boy at the Arlington Hotel* . . . . George Ovey

MRS. BRANDER, *the cattle king's wife* . . . . Miss Lizzie Duroy

MRS. MAJOR CAMPBELL, *whose husband is stationed in Texas* Miss Thora Ode-Gard

DIXIE STYLE, *an orphan from Indiana* . . . . . . Miss Adelaide Sawyer

BOSSY, *Brander's pet* . . . . Charlotte Crane

Street band, waiters, Indians, Greasers, and general riff-raff of a frontier town, etc., by artists peculiarly adapted to their various rôles.

A TEXAS STEER

ACT I [1]

Exterior of BRANDER'S *house centre, above third entrance. Music at rise. Lights all up. At rise shouts in distance, "Mink."* MINK [*Negro*] *enters with old saddle from left fourth entrance, goes to bench, L. H. When* MINK *about half way down stage,* CRAB [*Negro*] *enters right third entrance, running and shouting.*

CRAB [*excited*]. Mars Brander's elected shuah! Can't be no possible doubt of it! I voted for him!

MINK [*left*]. Huh! 'Spose you tink yo' vote elected him. How much did yo' get fo' votin' fo' him?

CRAB [*centre*]. I got five dollars. How much did yo' git?

MINK. Didn't get nuffin'!

CRAB. Didn't get nuffin'? What yo' tinkin' of? You's de only man dat voted fo' him that didn't get paid. Yo's a fool!

[MINK *puts saddle on bench*]

MINK [*crossing to* CRAB]. Fool! See heah, nigger — yo' don't know what yo's talkin' about. Don' yo' tink I know dar was money to be had? Majah Yell, he offered me five dollars fo' my vote, but I said, "No, sah! I'm not dat sort o' a man, sah! Do yo' tink I'd barter my right o' sufferin' fo' a mess o' potash, sah!! No, sah! If de cullad vote is to be a article of commerce, sah, de race will go to de dogs, sah!" I wouldn't tech a cent ob his money, sah! [*Crossing to bench*] The best I'd do was to let him buy me a par ob boots.

BRIGHT [*off right*]. Come along, Green.

[MINK *picks up saddle quick*]

CRAB [*runs up stage to gate right*]. Dar's Captain Bright come over from de fort.

[MINK, *up stage, behind* CRAB, *looks off right*]

MINK. And somebody with him! Go and take car ob de gemman's hosses. [*Exit* CRAB *right fourth entrance*] Spec' he'll know if Mars Brander is elected.

[*Enter* BRIGHT *right fourth entrance, with* GREEN. *As they enter,* MINK *takes off hat.* GREEN *enters first, crosses to bench left,* BRIGHT *crosses to centre,* MINK *down right*]

BRIGHT [*to* GREEN]. You'll learn to be careful of those prickly pears in time. [*To* MINK] Mink, is Miss Bossy at home?

MINK [*right*]. She done gone to de post-office, sah!

BRIGHT. We'll wait. Go and tell Mrs. Brander we're here. [*Exit* MINK *into house. Turning to* GREEN] Make yourself at home, Green. Don't mind tearing your clothes. It's nothing. Make yourself comfortable.

GREEN [*arranging clothes, etc.*]. In Texas! Never! I dare say, Captain Bright, Texas is all right when you get used to it, but I'm afraid I never shall. Such social festivities as lynching bees don't appeal to my taste as much as Germans at the British Legation. Since you like Texas so much, I wish they would let you stay here and let me remain in Washington, instead of sending me to relieve you. [*Lights cigarette — sits*]

BRIGHT [*centre*]. Oh, you'll get used to it, and then you'll like it.

GREEN. No, I never shall get used to it. I don't understand the way they do things here at all. Now, take this congressional election — why, it seems to have been a perfect farce.

[1] Called a prologue in the Synopsis of Scenes.

11

[*Enter* MINK *from house,* — *exits right third*]

BRIGHT. No more so than such elections are everywhere. The bosses named their man and the people elected him, just as they do in New York. [*Crosses to bench left*] There was a difference in the detail of doing it, just as there's a difference between New York and Texas, but their principle was just the same.

GREEN. But I understand that this Mr. Brander, who has just been elected, didn't want to be elected, and doesn't know he *is* elected.

BRIGHT [*placing foot on end of bench*]. Listen, old man, and I'll explain. You see, this old Mr. Brander is a very rich man. What with cattle and land and mining interests in Mexico, he's worth several million dollars, but, of course, he's lived here in Texas all his life, while he has been making it, and he is — not to put too fine a point on it — a pretty rough old man. But money has its influence on its possessors, even on a Texas frontier. And his wife and daughter are really refined, nice people. They are the leaders of what society there is in this town — and we have only had one lady at the Fort — the wife of Major Campbell. She and Miss Brander have been great friends. So naturally, during the two years I've been stationed at the Fort here, I've been at their house a great deal. [*Turns to centre*]

GREEN. And naturally you fell in love with the daughter.

BRIGHT. Old man, I don't know you very well — [*Crosses, turning to* GREEN] But as a brother officer I think I can speak freely with you. Bossy and I are engaged.

GREEN [*rising*]. And she the heiress to several millions! Old man, I congratulate you. [*Offers hand; both shake;* GREEN *sits*]

BRIGHT. Thanks. [*Sits on bench*] But, you see, we haven't thought it best to tell her father yet. And then came this order transferring me to Washington, and that was likely to separate us. And now I'm coming to the story of this election.

GREEN. I see. You wanted her to go to Washington.

BRIGHT. Yes. Bossy always had social ambitions. She was brought up here on the frontier, but she has known Mrs. Campbell and the other people who have been to the Fort, and from them she has learned to realize that out beyond there is a great world, and that in it, money talks; and she felt that in that world she could and ought to be somebody. And she talked this to her mother till she got the old lady all stirred up, and then they went for the old man; they wanted him to run for Congress and take them to Washington where his position and money would put them on a society footing, and Bossy would be near me.

GREEN. But I suppose the old man didn't hanker after society triumphs.

BRIGHT. Well, hardly! He knows how to swear and he did. Then he got mad and started off to visit some mines he owns, away down in Mexico. He vowed he'd stay there where he could not hear from them, or they from him, till election was over; and he has. [*Rises and goes to centre*]

GREEN. But still he's elected!

BRIGHT. We judge so from the way the returns come in. You see, Bossy and I were bound he should go to Congress. There are political bosses on the frontier as well as anywhere else. The Boss here is a lawyer, named Major Yell. He's an infernal rascal and everybody knows it. He couldn't be elected fence viewer himself. But he runs the district just the same, and names the man every time.

GREEN. And you got Yell interested to elect old Brander?

BRIGHT. Interested! Should say he was! Bossy is allowed to draw on her father's bank account when he's away and she promised Yell she'd furnish all the money necessary if he'd get her father elected and make him serve. The returns, as far as received, indicate the old man's election, though there was some opposition — and I'll trust Yell to make him serve.

MRS. BRANDER [*inside house*]. Don't let those cakes burn.

BRIGHT. Sh! Here comes Mrs. Brander.

[*Enter* MRS. BRANDER *from house centre.* BRIGHT *goes to her as she advances.* GREEN *rises, lifts cap, bows*]

MRS. BRANDER [*centre*]. Oh, Captain! You're here! Are the returns all in?

BRIGHT [*left centre*]. Not quite; but they are all right as far as heard from. Mrs. Brander, let me introduce to you

Lieutenant Green, who has been sent to relieve me at the Fort. [*Turns up stage*]

MRS. BRANDER [*centre*]. How do you do, sir? [*Crosses to* GREEN] First visit to Texas, I judge? [*Looking at him*]

GREEN [*left*]. Yes, ma'am.

MRS. BRANDER. It's a great place for you army officers. Two years here, chasing horse-thieves and fighting Indians will make a man of you.

[*Cheers heard in distance. Enter* FISH-BACK *right fourth entrance, excited.* BRIGHT *rushes down right*]

FISHBACK [*during this speech all look at him, without moving*]. Mrs. Brander, Major Yell says he'd give million head ob cattle if he had a caliope to make the boundless plains re-echo with the glad tidings, that in spite of oratory, sentimentality, civil service reform and claptrap surging upon us like a mighty sea, the grand principle, the corner-stone of American politics remains unmoved. The mighty dollar still rules the roost. The longest pole knocks the persimmon. Victory for the rock! The sea ceaseth and it sufficeth us. [*Turns, runs up stage. Shouts off*] I'll be with you gentlemen — I'm coming.

[*Exit right fourth, excited and very quick.* MRS. BRANDER *looks after him.* BRIGHT *straddles stump of tree, back to audience;* GREEN *throws himself on bench, astonished*]

GREEN [*slowly*]. What did that creature say?

BRIGHT [*turns to* GREEN]. How do you suppose I know?

MRS. BRANDER [*turns to both*]. He must have meant that Mr. Brander's elected! I distinctly heard him say so! [*Goes up stage*]

BRIGHT [*on stump of tree*]. You were very fortunate.

GREEN. For mercy's sake, who is it? What is it?

BRIGHT [*laughing*]. That! Why, that's the leading colored politician of this district. Yell used him to corral the negro vote. Promised him, if Mr. Brander was elected, they'd get him appointed minister to Dahomey.

GREEN. Good heavens! Will they appoint it — him to an office?

BRIGHT. Never! But Yell had to promise him to get his influence. Now election's over, Yell will throw him out.

[*More cheers off right*]

MRS. BRANDER [*coming down centre*]. Hear that! It must mean Mr. Brander's elected! There can't be a doubt of it! Nobody would refuse to vote for Mr. Brander!

BRIGHT [*rising*]. Well, I'm not so sure of that. But I don't think many would refuse to vote for him when they could get five dollars apiece for doing so.

MRS. BRANDER [*crossing to* BRIGHT]. Well, haven't they all got five dollars apiece for doing so? Didn't we give Mr. Yell fifty thousand dollars? There ain't more than six thousand voters in the whole district, he tells me; that's five dollars for every vote. Mr. Brander must be unanimously elected!

BRIGHT. Oh, no! You forget that Major Yell probably took half that money to pay him for his trouble.

MRS. BRANDER. That's so. I forgot that. Perhaps Mr. Brander only got half the votes after all, and it's a tie. Oh, I do wish Bossy would get here. She's down the post-office now, waiting the returns.

[*Music, loud cheering heard outside. Then* BOSSY *rushes in from right fourth entrance and down centre.* GREEN *rises at her entrance*]

BOSSY [*centre*]. Hooray! We got there with both feet! Scooped their checks, reds, whites and blues. Pike County's with us, and we win.

MRS. BRANDER and BRIGHT. We win!

BOSSY. The other folks thought they had us there. They had two thousand niggers all rounded up and ready to corral. But when Major Yell jumped in among 'em with those five dollar bills, they stampeded and never stopped running till they were all on our range, and then Yell had his brand on 'em in no time. Six hundred majority for Dad and they say Yell cleared ten thousand dollars on the job.

[*All hold picture at end of speech.* BOSSY *kisses* MRS. BRANDER *and then crosses to* BRIGHT *right corner*]

MRS. BRANDER [*centre*]. Never mind what he cleared. [GREEN *begins to bow to* BOSSY] He got your father elected, and that's the important point. [*Turns left to go up stage — sees* GREEN *bowing to* BOSSY. *Suddenly*] Excuse my rudeness, Lieutenant Green, let me introduce my daughter. BOSSY. [*Takes* BOSSY'S *hand and passes her to center.* MRS.

BRANDER *turns to* BRIGHT *and sits on stump right.* BRIGHT *right corner*]

BOSSY [*centre, turns to him suddenly and then hesitates*]. Sh! I didn't see there was a stranger here or I wouldn't have been so free.

[GREEN *advances to* BOSSY]

GREEN. No apology is necessary.

BOSSY [*offering hand to him*]. You must excuse us for being a little on the rampage to-day. You see, the fact is, my father has just been elected to Congress.

GREEN [*left*]. It is a great honor and he must feel proud of it.

BOSSY [*left centre*]. Well, I don't know how much honored he'll feel when he finds his votes cost him about five dollars apiece; but he'll have the satisfaction of knowing that he came by his election honestly. He paid all it was worth for it.

MRS. BRANDER. Yes.

BOSSY. And there's no reason why he shouldn't feel perfectly independent in Congress. For he's under no obligation to anybody. Every man who voted for him has got his pay in advance. I believe that's the true way to elect Congressmen.

[*Loud cheering outside right. Then* YELL *speaks.* BOSSY *rushes up stage centre*]

YELL [*off right*]. Don't let the band have any liquor. They play bad enough now.

[MRS. BRANDER *rises*]

BOSSY [*looking off right*]. Why, it's Major Yell! Come in, Major, come in.

[YELL *enters right fourth.* BOSSY *takes his hand and drags him down centre*]

YELL [*centre*]. Hooray! Mrs. Brander, sound the hen-gag and let the eagle scream! [*Picture*]

MRS. BRANDER [*not sarcastic*]. We should be pleased to do as you desire, Major Yell, but, the fact is, we don't keep an eagle and we haven't such a thing as a hen-gag in the house.

YELL. I refer to the great American eagle — that proud bird of freedom, who raises his head in the waters of the Arctic Ocean and wags his tail in the Gulf of Mexico.

BOSSY. Major Yell, shake hands with Lieutenant Green. [*Goes up stage.* BRIGHT *follows her and joins her*]

YELL [*crosses to* GREEN *and shakes hands*]. Hope I see you, sir. — Sorry I didn't meet you ten hours befo', sir. I'd have voted you for old Brander, sir. [*Turns to centre.* MRS. BRANDER *sits on stump*]

GREEN. As much as I would have been pleased to vote for the Honorable Mr. Brander, I fear that it would have been impossible, as I am not a resident of Texas.

YELL [*turning to* GREEN]. Bless you, sir! That wouldn't have made any difference. [*Places hands on* GREEN'S *shoulder*] Think I couldn't have voted as good looking a man as you, sir? Why, I put through three Chinamen and an Indian that was half negro. We ain't particular out here in Texas! [*Turns to centre. Takes* BOSSY'S *hands*]

GREEN. But they, at least, live here.

YELL. No — died here, though. After they voted, some of the boys, in a spirit of fun, lynched them for illegal voting —

GREEN. Horrible!!

YELL. Well, I dunno. They voted illegally and the purity of the ballot must be preserved. I haven't much sympathy with the Chinese. They've done my washing lately. But, see here — I've only a moment to stay and I've got news for you. [BOSSY *right centre.* — BRIGHT *right corner*] The old man is on his way home.

ALL [*excited*]. On his way home?

YELL. Yes; Col. Bragg, who has just come in, passed him up here about twelve miles. His wagon broke down and the old man was tearing mad, but he'll get in before night. And we're going to have the boys out to give him a reception.

[BRIGHT *goes to gate right*]

BOSSY. I think I'll get out till he's had time to hear the news and cool off. [*Business of walking up stage*]

MRS. BRANDER. Stop, Bossy! Don't go and leave me to face him alone. Oh no! Don't!

BOSSY [*stops left centre — then down left centre*]. That would be rough! But say, I'm afraid he won't accept.

YELL [*centre*]. Leave that to me! I'm going to take a delegation of prominent citizens out to meet him and to notify him of his election and congratulate him. They are all business men, and when they urge him, you bet he'll accept. Say, it would be a good idea to have some refreshments for the procession when we get back.

BOSSY. That's so — they will need refreshments. I'll send over to the brewery right off. [*Turns up stage. Enter* FISHBACK *right fourth entrance, rushes to* YELL, *seizes hand and shakes it heartily*]

FISHBACK. E pluribus unum, Majah Yell. E pluribus unum! [*Picture*]

YELL [*left centre*]. What do you mean, a cock-tail?

FISHBACK. I mean, sah, that the rising sun ob destiny casts its glorious rays on our State, sah; gilding with the glittering gleams of future glory the destiny of Texas. He approacheth! And de next minister to Dahomy, followed by his cohorts, goes forth to welcome him. In other words, I've got the entire colored population out to meet Mr. Brander. Come, sah. Let the Damon an' Pythias of politics, arm in arm, lead the way.

YELL [*looks around and then about to kick* FISHBACK]. Go along! I'll be with you.

FISHBACK. You place the whole responsibility in me — very well, sah! [*Rushes up stage*] I'll be with you gentlemen, I'm coming. [*Rushes off right fourth entrance*]

YELL. I'm about due to let that nigger know that election's over and I can't see him — [1] [*Starts up stage*]

BOSSY [*crossing to* MRS. BRANDER]. Say, mother, you go and send some of the boys over to the brewery to get some beer.

MRS. BRANDER [*rising and going to house*]. How much shall they get?

BOSSY [*right centre*]. It's a crowd of politicians — bring the brewery.

MRS. BRANDER [*on steps of house*]. Oh, I shall be so glad when it's all over. [*Exit into house*]

[*Enter* MRS. CAMPBELL, *with two flags from house left fourth entrance, running*]

MRS. CAMPBELL. Bossy! Bossy! I've heard the news — I've — [*Sees* GREEN *left and* BRIGHT *right*] Oh, good morning, gentlemen.

BRIGHT *and* GREEN [*raising caps*]. Good morning, Mrs. Campbell.

BOSSY [*going to her centre*]. Hullo! What have you got, Liz?

MRS. CAMPBELL [*centre*]. Flags! I made my husband let me bring them over to decorate your house. We must give your father a grand reception. [*Hands a flag to* BOSSY]

BOSSY. Liz, you're a thoroughbred.

BRIGHT. Allow us. [*Crossing to* BOSSY, *takes flag from her.* GREEN *crosses, takes flag from* MRS. CAMPBELL. *Both go to house and place flags on porch over door*]

MRS. CAMPBELL. It's all the Major could let me have. You'd better put them over the porch. [*Crosses to left corner,* BOSSY *to right corner*]

GREEN [*handing flag to* BRIGHT]. Do these Southerners like to see that flag flying?

BRIGHT [*arranging flags*]. Well, if you doubt it, just try hauling it down.

MRS. CAMPBELL [*crossing to centre*]. There! It isn't much, but it's better than nothing.

[GREEN *goes to stump*]

BOSSY [*crossing to centre*]. It's great! And, by the way, Liz, you haven't said you're glad we won the fight.

MRS. CAMPBELL. Well, of course I'm glad. But I've just begun to realize that in a month you'll be in Washington and I'll be here alone. [*To* GREEN, *crossing to stump.* GREEN *places handkerchief on stump.* MRS. CAMPBELL *sits.* BOSSY *crosses to bench left, sits.* BRIGHT *goes to back of bench left*] Think of it, Lieutenant Green — I'm the only woman at the Fort, and the only feminine friend, during the hideous six months that my husband has been stationed in Texas, has been Bossy. Oh, Bossy, what will I do without you?

BOSSY. Oh, Liz — don't you fret; as soon as we are fixed in Washington, I'll invite you on to visit us.

MRS. CAMPBELL. Will you? Well, I'll be there. And say, Bossy, you'll have to get ready right away for your departure. I hope you'll get along all right in Washington.

BRIGHT. That shall be my care. You know I leave to-morrow. I shall have apartments all engaged for them at the Arlington, and be on hand to

[1] In copy, N. Y. P. L., the following additional dialogue:
Now must I go and whoop up the boys for the reception. [*Turning back laughing*] Say, I've got a band for the parade. Three I-talians. Play right smart, too; only trouble is, the fellow that plays the horn can't march and play too. But I'll fix that. Don't you worry, Mrs. Brander — we'll make him accept. [*Exit centre*]

receive them; and I'll take Mr. Brander up to the house. By the way, your father buys his clothes of Mose Shomberg, doesn't he?

BOSSY. Yes. Why?

BRIGHT. Well, Mose Shomberg is all right, but his clothes are not just the thing for Washington. We'll have to manage some way for your father to have some decent clothes to wear there.

BOSSY. That's so. How you do think of everything.

BRIGHT. I'll tell you what! You give me a suit of his old clothes to take to Washington with me, and I'll have my tailor make a suit from the measurements. I'll have them ready when he gets there, and we'll find some way to get him to wear them.

MRS. CAMPBELL. You'd better be thinking of some way of getting him to Washington. [*Quartette heard in the distance*] From what he said when he went away to Mexico, I don't believe he'll accept the office.

BOSSY. Yes, he will — Yell and I have got that all fixed.

GREEN [*hearing Quartette*]. What's that?

BOSSY. It's the darky boys bringing the beer over from the brewery.

[MRS. CAMPBELL *goes up to fence, and looks off right*]

GREEN [*goes up to gate*]. How pretty it sounds. Listen!

[*Quartette grows louder.* — *Boys enter right fourth entrance, bring beer kegs, singing, and then exeunt left fourth entrance. For encore return to centre, sing and exeunt left.* BOSSY *calls Quartette for each encore, then she resumes seat*]

[BRIGHT *goes up stage. After first song,* MRS. CAMPBELL *goes to porch;* GREEN *to stump centre*]

MRS. CAMPBELL [*after singing is over, rising and going to house*]. There's the refreshments. I will go and help your mother get some cups ready. [*Pauses and looks at* BOSSY *and* BRIGHT, *who are*

deep in conversation. Then turns to GREEN] Come, Lieutenant Green! Learn Texas ways and make yourself useful by helping me.

GREEN [*going to her*]. With pleasure. [*Offers arm. She laughs and runs into house. He follows*]

[BRIGHT *looks toward house, then crosses to right, looks off, then down right centre, and holds his arms open for* BOSSY. BOSSY *looks about, then turns, sees* BRIGHT *with his arms opened for her, looks down, then rushes to him, kisses him*]

[BRIGHT [1] [*with arms about* BOSSY]. Oh, Bossy, isn't it great?

BOSSY. Why, it's out of sight! They can't stop us now, can they?

BRIGHT. I don't see *how* they can.

BOSSY. Say — how soon do we have to go to Washington?

BRIGHT. Oh, in about a month.

BOSSY. A month! Oh, I wish we were going to start this very minute. It just seems as though I couldn't wait to get there. And you're going to-morrow! Oh, what'll I do for a whole month? I'll go crazy! Say, dear, can't you wait till we go?

BRIGHT. I wish I could. But you know, an army officer must go where he is sent.

BOSSY. Well, I'm not stuck on your going to Washington a whole month alone.

BRIGHT. Why not?

BOSSY. Oh, nothing much. Only you've been out in this country a good long time, and, when you get to Washington and see a lot of those society girls, maybe you'll forget all about us.

BRIGHT. Bossy, you know I'd rather have my own little wild prairie rosebud than all the hot-house flowers that ever bloomed. Do I deserve to have you think that I could forget you?

BOSSY. No, Fairleigh, you don't, and I take it all back. But if I should get there and find you weren't glad to see me, I'd be all broke up.

BRIGHT. Well, you needn't have any fear.

---

[1] In place of dialogue between heavy brackets, N. Y. P. L. the copy has the following:

BRIGHT. Well, little girl, we've been through a great deal, but we've accomplished our object. Your father's elected, and it's all right. He'll have to accept. In a month you will be in Washington — you will see the great world of which you have dreamed so much — for which you have so longed.

BOSSY. Yes, dear — and I feel like a bird just

getting out of a cage. Oh, I do so want to be something besides a Texas ranch girl. And I shall have you with me to teach me and show me everything, and I — I — [*Rises and rushes to centre*] Oh, I feel so happy, I just want to get right out in the prairie and holler "Whoop!"

[*Cheers and music in distance.* BOSSY *rushes up stage — looks off, then rushes up to door, opens it, and calls.* BRIGHT *looks off right, then exits*]

Bossy. A month's an awful long time, though — isn't it?

Bright. It seems long to think of it. But with all you've got to do to get ready, the time will pass very quickly. We'll soon be together again, then you will see the great world of which you have dreamed so much — for which you have so longed.

Bossy. And I feel like a bird just getting out of a cage. Oh, I do so want to be something besides a Texas ranch girl. And I shall have you with me to teach me and show me everything, and I — I — [*Rushes to left*] Oh, I feel so happy, I just want to get right out on the prairie and holler! "Whoop!"] [*Cheers and music in the distance. Enter* Fishback *from right third, excited and running. He rushes to* Bossy, *trying to tell her something, then rushes to house and calls,* "Mrs. Brander", *and then dances excitedly about, doing nothing, yet trying to do everything.* Bossy *rushes up stage, looks off, then rushes up to door, opens it and calls.* Bright *looks off right, then on porch. Cheers near by*] Mamma! Liz! Here they come!

[*Enter* Mrs. Brander *and* Mrs. Campbell *and* Green. *Cheers outside continue. Mob enters, cheering*]

[*Enter two men, then two musicians, wheelbarrow with hand-organ and man playing it —* Yell, Bragg *and* Blow; *then mob, then* Brander *on wagon seat, carried by four men who move to centre. Part of procession crosses to left, passing in front of porch, and part down stage to right. Four men, bearing* Brander, *move to centre of stage in front of porch, face to audience.* Yell *is left centre,* Bragg *right centre,* Blow *right, band right, comes round left, and back of* Brander. *All cheering and waving hats; at sign from* Yell *noise stops. Red fire right third entrance*]

Yell. Three cheers for the Honorable Maverick Brander! [*All cheer. Band plays*]

Brander [*centre, on wagon seat*]. What's the meaning of this damn nonsense? Why have I been yanked off o' my wagon and brought home in triumph?

Bragg [*right corner*]. Mr. Brander, you have been made the victim of a great honor. Three cheers for the Honorable Maverick Brander. [*All cheer and band plays*]

Brander. Stop that infernal band. [*Band stopped by* Yell] I see it all. You have taken advantage of my absence! You've elected me to Congress.

Yell. We have. Three cheers for the Honorable Maverick Brander. [*All cheer. Band plays*]

Brander. Stop your noise! I'm an honest man! What do I want in Congress?

Yell. *We* want a few honest men there.

Brander. Well, I won't be the one to go first. [*Throwing wreath off head, jumps off wagon seat and goes to right corner to drive crowd off*] So you get out of my dooryard, all of you.

Yell [*left*]. You won't go to Congress?

Brander. No, sir! [*Turning to centre*]

Yell [*left centre*]. See here, Mr. Maverick Brander, the people of the district have elected you to represent them in Congress! If you think you're too good to represent us, just declare yourself. [*Covers him with revolver*]

Omnes [*covering* Brander *with revolvers*]. Declare yourself!

Brander [*after taking in situation*]. Gentlemen, I'll serve.

[*All cheer — band plays*]

CURTAIN

[*Encore: Picture:* Bossy *on stool centre placing wreath on* Brander's *head, who is right of her.* Mrs. Brander *at left centre.* Bright, Green *and* Mrs. Campbell *all around* Brander. Yell *left,* Bragg *and* Blow *right,* Fishback *right of* Brander. *When curtain up,* Fishback *rushes to* Brander, *grabs his hand*]

Fishback. Mr. Brander, shake hands with the minister to Dahomy!

[Yell *and* Blow *fall on stump. Negroes about*]

CURTAIN

ACT II

SCENE. — *Private Parlor, Arlington Hotel, Washington.* OTHELLO *discovered, arranging room.* SAM *enters with salver and card.*

SAM [*handing card*]. Here's a card and it's for Mr. Brander.

OTHELLO [*coming down stage, reads card*]. Minister to Dahomy? He's a new one on me. What's he like?

SAM [*up at door*]. He's a culled person — so black I thought you'd have to light a lamp. Said he'd have to see Mr. Brander at once.

OTHELLO. M'm! Well, Mr. Brander's out. But de proprietor told me dat dese Texas folks what's got dis yer suite o' rooms ain't tame yet and I was to look out fo' 'em. Reckon I'd better see dis yer chap. Let him in.

[OTHELLO *goes to looking-glass and arranges his collar, etc.*]

SAM [*opens door*]. You can come in.

[*Enter* FISHBACK *left centre. Looks at* SAM, *then goes down stage, meets* OTHELLO, *who has turned from glass to centre. Two coons size each other up.* — SAM *exits left centre.*

OTHELLO [*right centre*]. What can I do fo' you, sah?

FISHBACK [*left centre*]. What can yo' do fo' me? Nuffin, sah! I'm hyar, sah, to see my particular friend, Mr. Brander. De man I made a Congressman, sah.

OTHELLO. Mars Brander's out.

FISHBACK. Out, sah! Do yo' tink yo' can spring dat old gag on me, sah? Yo' know who I am, sah?

OTHELLO. No, sah.

FISHBACK. Den yo'd better, sah! I'm de next Minister to Dahomy, sah! And I wants to see Mr. Brander at once, sah! I've been here fo' fo' days waitin' fo' him to git ter town, sah! [*Places cane, coat and hat on table, then sits in chair*] I can't wait any longer.

OTHELLO. You'll have to wait till he comes in. You'd better call again, sah! [*Goes to* FISHBACK]

FISHBACK [*rising*]. See here! I've been gettin' dat fo' fo' days, sah! [*Puts on hat, picks up coat, then cane*] I will call again, sah! And if I don't find him in, sah, I'll hold you pusonally responsible, sah! [*Goes up half way to door, stops and turns to* OTHELLO]

Pusonally responsible to me, sah! De Minister to Dahomy! [*Grabs door open and exits*]

OTHELLO [*centre*]. Somebody's been stringin' dat fellow. [*Going to door left centre*] I must keep an eye on him. [*Rolling up cuffs*] Or he'll be troublesome. [*Exit left centre*]

MRS. BRANDER [*enters right second entrance, goes to looking-glass, looks at herself through eye-glasses*]. Very neat and becoming. Bossy, ain't you most ready? [*Crossing to sofa left, book in hand*]

BOSSY [*off right*]. Almost, ma! I'm looking for my fan! [*Enters right second entrance, in gorgeous raiment*] How's these duds? [*Crosses to centre*]

MRS. BRANDER. Oh, Bossy, how I wish the folks in Texas could see you now! They'd be proud of you.

BOSSY. You bet! But where's Captain and Dad? [*Goes to looking-glass right centre*]

MRS. BRANDER [*sitting on sofa*]. They ain't home yet. Say, Bossy, it was right good of Captain Bright to have these rooms all engaged and ready for us, and to take charge of your father as soon as he got here.

BOSSY. He's a trump! [*Enter* BRIGHT *left centre; goes to table centre, and sits left, very quick*] Why, what's the matter? [BOSSY *goes to table*]

BRIGHT. Bossy, I have walked up Pennsylvania Avenue with your father.

BOSSY [*right centre*]. Well, where is he?

BRIGHT. I lost him. [*Falls into chair, left centre of table*]

MRS. BRANDER [*on sofa*]. Lost him!

[BOSSY *falls into chair right of table*]

BRIGHT. Yes; he saw a man up the street he thought was from Texas and bolted after him! I couldn't stop him.

MRS. BRANDER. Oh, but he may get lost!

BRIGHT. I'll risk him, he'll come in all right. [*To* BOSSY] By the way, I had a tailor make a new suit for your father from the measurements of that old suit of his you sent me. He doesn't guarantee a perfect fit, as the style is somewhat different, but 'twill do for a few days.

BOSSY. Is it done?

BRIGHT. Yes, and the sooner we get him into it, the better. I've engaged a valet for your father as I promised, and he'll be here soon and bring the clothes.[1] [*Crash.* BRANDER *heard outside quarrelling with someone back of door*] I think your father has come in. [*Shudders*]

BRANDER [*outside*]. Tell that fellow my name's Brander! I'm from Texas, and he can find me at any time he wants me.

[*Enter left centre with revolver and hat. Goes to centre, looks right and left.* MRS. BRANDER *and* BOSSY *turn to him.* BRIGHT *also turns to him*]

ALL. What's the matter?

BRANDER [*centre*]. Matter! I came into the hotel and says I, "I want to go to my room!" A boy standing in a little office-like place says, "Step in here!" and when I did, he shut an iron bar door behind me that fastened with a spring lock, and then the floor began to rise up under me! I dunno what his game was, but I pulled my gun on him and says I, "You let me out o' here." He sees I meant business and he did it. [*Places hat and revolver on table centre.* MRS. BRANDER *sits left.* BOSSY *turns to* BRIGHT, BRANDER *crosses to left*] Then that fresh clerk tried to give me some talk about it, and I just told him who I was and left him.

[*Enter* OTHELLO *left centre.* BRANDER *sits on sofa*]

OTHELLO [*goes to* BRANDER *with sign*]. 'Scuse me — de clerk sent me up with this, sah. [*Hangs sign on gas. Exits laughing*]

BRANDER [*rising and going to centre, reads sign*]. "Don't blow out the gas!" I'll have trouble with that clerk. [*Picks up hat and goes to door*]

[BRIGHT[2] [*quick*]. Stop, Mr. Brander! [*Starts for* BRANDER, *crosses to him behind table.* BRANDER *turns near door.* BRIGHT *takes revolver from him*] Leave this affair with me. [*Goes to table, places revolver on it. Takes sign from gas fixture*] Did you catch that Texas man? [*Behind table*]]

BRANDER [*coming to centre*]. He wasn't from Texas. He was from Maine. Here with a Wild West show playing scout. Say, I've got to change my personal appearance. Everybody

here thinks I'm with a Wild West show — whatever that is. Keep asking me for passes — especially these boys in this hotel.

[BRIGHT *crosses to fireplace, throws sign into it; then crosses to* MRS. BRANDER *and sits beside her on sofa*]

BOSSY [*going to* BRIGHT, *aside*]. How lucky! [*Aloud*] We thought of that, Dad, so the Captain had some made for you; and he's engaged a valet for you, too.

BRANDER. What's that?

BOSSY. Why, a valet is — is — a valet. All Congressmen have them, so you must.

[*Enter* OTHELLO]

OTHELLO. Your man, sah!

BRIGHT. Come in, Anatole. [*Enter* ANATOLE *with clothes on arm.* OTHELLO *exits.* ANATOLE *stands at head of sofa*] Mr. Brander, this is your new valet.

[BRANDER *turns and, extending hand, goes to* ANATOLE]

BRANDER. Hope I see you!

[BRIGHT *jumps up quick, crosses over, takes* BRANDER's *hand. Then* BRANDER *turns to* BOSSY. BRIGHT *turns to* ANATOLE]

BRIGHT. Did you bring the clothes?

ANATOLE [*crossing to* BRANDER]. Dey all ees here.

BOSSY [*right centre*]. Dad, put 'em on and see how you'll look.

BRANDER [*centre*]. Well, I reckon I'd better. I can't be taken all the time for a Wild West. [BRIGHT *motions to* ANATOLE *to go.* ANATOLE *starts to go.* BRANDER *gives him look, then takes clothes from him, goes to door.* ANATOLE *follows him closely. When at door* BRANDER *turns and looks at him. Pause*] Where are you going?

ANATOLE. To your room, sir.

BRANDER. But, don't you know I'm going to change my clothes?

ANATOLE. Oh, yes, but I suppose I could assist you, sir.

BRANDER. Assist me? Do you think I've got so I can't put my clothes on? [*Pause*]

BOSSY [*right centre*]. But that's what he's hired for, Dad.

[1] In N. Y. P. L. copy, the following addition:
BRANDER [*outside door left centre*]. I don't want any trouble but I won't be imposed upon!

[2] Between the heavy brackets, N. Y. P. L. copy has the following:

[*Starts to go. Picks up revolver*]

BRIGHT [*taking down sign, tears it up*] Stop, Mr. Brander. Did you catch that Texas man?
BRANDER [*coming back, puts revolver on table*]. He wasn't from . . .

BRANDER. I won't have it; I'll put the clothes on, but I'm hanged if I'll do it before a perfect stranger. [*Exit*]

BRIGHT [*to* ANATOLE — *up stage right*]. Wait in the ante-room. We'll want you presently. [*Exit* ANATOLE *left centre*]

BOSSY [*crossing to centre*]. Say, speaking of clothes, don't you think me and ma are ragged out pretty well for folks right off a ranch? [*Business with train of dress.* MRS. BRANDER *rises and displays her dress*]

BRIGHT [*turning and seeing her dress for first time. Not enthusiastic*]. Why — why — of course —

BOSSY. We had them made in San Ton[1] for a surprise for you.

BRIGHT. Yes — yes —

BOSSY [*crossing to right, parades her dress*]. Knock 'em out when we go in the dining-room, eh?

[MRS. BRANDER *sits on sofa again*]

BRIGHT. No doubt of it. But, Bossy, don't you think that dress is a little too — er — elaborate to wear into a public dining-room? You've got on a great many diamonds, you know.

BOSSY [*turning to* BRIGHT]. You bet I know it, and, what's more, I know that Dad owns 80,000 head of cattle, and when they see me, I mean they shall know it. [*Crash off left*] Dad's dressing. [*Goes to looking-glass*]

BRIGHT [*crossing to sofa, looks at* BOSSY]. She'll learn. What book is that, Mrs. Brander, that seems to take so much of your time?

MRS. BRANDER. The rules of Washington society. I have been looking up our social duties. — It seems we call on almost everybody first. I don't understand it. At home a Congressman is a great man, but in Washington he doesn't seem to be anybody.

BOSSY. I wish Dad would hurry — I'm as hungry as a bear. [*Crash left*]

MRS. BRANDER. I think he's doing the best he can.

BRIGHT [*aside*]. She mustn't be seen in that hideous dress. [*Aloud*] Bossy, don't you think we had better have lunch served in this room?

BOSSY [*surprised*]. What! Not go to the dining-room, after putting all of my pretty new things on?

BRIGHT. Well — well — you see — your father is a little new to Washington, and — it might be pleasanter — for him to dine in private.

BOSSY. Very well. [*Crosses to sofa*] Ma, don't you want to go into your room and put some more powder on your nose?

MRS. BRANDER [*rising and crossing to right quickly*]. Dear me, do I need it? [*Exit*]

[BOSSY *goes to fireplace and rings electric bell. Then goes to sofa, sits, picks up paper and reads.* OTHELLO *enters as soon as* MRS. BRANDER *is off, and goes to head of sofa.* BRIGHT *turns to looking-glass*]

BOSSY. Have lunch for four fetched up here to this room right away.

[BRIGHT *turns and looks*]

OTHELLO. Will you order it?

BOSSY. Why, I did just order it! Oh, you mean what! Anything that's filling! [BRIGHT *goes to right*] And you can get it quick. I'm so hungry I could eat a mule stuffed with fire-crackers.

[BRIGHT *falls into chair right of table.* OTHELLO *goes to door quickly; then turns and laughs loud.* BRIGHT *jumps up, turns and gives him a look.* OTHELLO *turns and exits quickly.* BRIGHT *then crosses to centre*]

BRIGHT. Bossy, don't you think —

BOSSY. Think what?

BRIGHT. You ought to be a little more careful in the way you speak to the waiters?

BOSSY. Why, what did I say to him?

BRIGHT. Bring something "filling."

BOSSY. Why, he understood it, didn't he?

BRIGHT. Of course he understood it!

BOSSY. Well, that's all I wanted, and it's more than he'd have done if I'd tried to tell him from one of those French bills of fare. [*Suddenly rising and going to* BRIGHT] Say, I thought your sister was going to come and call on us to-day?

BRIGHT [*aside*]. I'd forgotten that. I must go and tell her not to come. [*Turns away to right a little*]

BOSSY [*looking at him*]. What's that?

BRIGHT [*turns to her*]. I — I say I'll go over to our house after her now.

BOSSY. Bring her to lunch. Hurry, too — I'm starved. [*Pushes him over to left*]

---

[1] Meaning San Antonio.

BRIGHT [*going to door left centre*]. I will be back in fifteen minutes. [*Aside*] Oh, if my sister ever saw her in that dress! [*At door.* BOSSY *turns to him*]

BOSSY. Good-bye, dear. [*Fixing mouth for kiss*]

BRIGHT [*looks, then goes to her quickly*]. Good — oh! [*Kisses her*] Good-bye! [*Exits*]

BOSSY [*going to looking-glass*]. Well, even if we don't go down to dinner, his sister'll see my pretty dress anyway. [*Goes up stage to door*]

BRANDER [*outside*]. Will you come on? [*Backs on fully dressed, except one shoe he's trying to get on, and exits right center. Crash off right.* MRS. BRANDER *enters right second, goes to him quickly*]

BOSSY [*rushing to him*]. Father, what's the matter?

BRANDER [*enters, assisted by* MRS. BRANDER]. This infernal shoe! I left the shoes until the last because they looked tight, and, after I got this collar on, I was in a clinch — couldn't do a thing. Well, how do I look?

MRS. BRANDER. Very distinguished. You'll make a sensation when you appear at the Capitol.

BRANDER. I'm afraid I will.

BOSSY [*crossing to sofa*]. You look lovely, Dad.

[*Enter* OTHELLO]

OTHELLO. Card, sah! [*Shoves salver under* BRANDER'S *nose.* BRANDER *starts suddenly, then takes card, but looking at* OTHELLO *suspiciously*]

BRANDER [*reads*]. Knott Innitt. Who's he? [*Looks at* OTHELLO *suspiciously*]

MRS. BRANDER. He may have important business. Perhaps we'd better retire to the parlor. [*Starts off for door, then turns suddenly*] Where's my book of etiquette? [*Grabs book from chair and exits*]

BRANDER [*to* OTHELLO]. Send him up.

[OTHELLO *exits*]

BOSSY [*crosses in front of* BRANDER. *At door*]. Be on your dignity, Dad, and impress him! [*Turns and stumbles over her train, then exits*]

BRANDER. Impress him? Oh, yes, I'll impress him! [*Goes up to long mir-*

ror, *looks himself over*] I'm a sight! It's a shame, too, after the time I had getting into these cussed things! Brander, old man, if they saw you in Texas now, you'd get shot. [*Turns and sees revolver on table*] Oh, there's my old reliable — that looks good — I mustn't forget that! [*Business of finding pocket for it*] What sort of a fool made that for a pistol pocket? [*Pushes revolver into it, sits on chair right of table*]

[*Enter* OTHELLO]

OTHELLO. Mr. Innitt!

[*Enter* INNITT; *hands hat to* OTHELLO, *who exits*]

BRANDER. Take a seat.

INNITT [*at table*]. Have I the honor to address the famous Mr. Brander?

BRANDER. Didn't know I was famous. [*Looks at clothes*] I haven't been out on the street [1] since I put them on. Never mind my being famous. I suppose you have some business with me. Get at it at once, sir.

INNITT [*placing chair left centre*]. Yes, sir. This is your first visit to Washington, I am told. You don't know what sort of a place it is.

BRANDER. Oh, yes I do! I'd only been here six hours, and they'd buncoed me out of more than a hundred dollars.

INNITT [*crossing to him*]. It's a very trying place for a stranger. That is what I called to see you about. [*Sits on table*] It is the custom for Congressmen to have private secretaries. The secretary knows the ropes and can show his employer the town, give him all the fun he wants, and bring him home in the morning. [*Crosses to chair he has placed left centre, and sits*] Now, sir, I've called to see if I couldn't secure the position of your private secretary.

BRANDER. Oh, you did! Well, sir, I don't doubt you know all the disreputable resorts, but I didn't come to Washington to see the town and be brought home in the morning. I came for business.

[INNITT.[2] You didn't? [*Moves his chair over to* BRANDON *and then sits*] Well, what did you come for?

BRANDER. I came for business!]

INNITT. Oh, if it's money you're

---

[1] Following "I haven't been out on the street yet", N. Y. P. L. copy has:

INNITT. Nevertheless, you are famous, sir. We have all heard of you.

BRANDER. Well, sir, never mind my being famous. I suppose you have some business with me. Get at it at once, sir.

[2] Between brackets is typical omission from N. Y. P. L. copy.

after, I can be just as useful. I know all the lobbyists and can arrange all your business with them. Why, I've no doubt I could get you five thousand dollars for advocating the land-grant for the Northern Texas Transportation Co. They're here with lots of money to get the bill through.

BRANDER. And do you think I'd support that bill? Why, it's an infernal robbery of the settlers!

INNITT. Oh, well! What of that? [1] [You get your five thousand dollars, don't you?] You are too sensitive, Mr. Brander. You won't give a thought to such trifles as that after you've been in Congress a session.

BRANDER. But, sir! That bill would rob me of eighty thousand acres of cattle range!

INNITT. Oh! Then, of course your conscientious scruples against the bill are justified. As you say, the scheme is an infernal outrage and must be squelched. Of course you'll make a speech against it.

BRANDER. Me make a speech! Well, if I could I would; but I couldn't get up a speech to save my life.

INNITT. My dear sir, nobody expects you to. All you've got to do is to stand up and read one.

BRANDER. Well, I've got to have it to read.

INNITT. Of course; but what's your private secretary for — if he doesn't write your speeches for you? It's not the gift of eloquence, but a good private secretary that makes the orator.

BRANDER. Oh, I see. And I'm to stand up like a snivelling parrot and just read what you've given me. [BRANDER *has been annoyed with revolver. Takes it out of pocket.* INNITT *yells and gets behind chair he's been sitting in*]

INNITT. Don't! Don't!! Don't!!! [BRANDER *rises, crosses over to* INNITT'S *chair and looks at* INNITT *behind it*] Don't shoot! Don't shoot!!

[BRANDER *crosses back to his chair*]

BRANDER [*laughing*]. Shoot! I've no intention of shooting. It was in my way, that's all. Sit down.

INNITT [*rising from behind chair*]. Is that all?

BRANDER [*placing revolver on table*]. That's all!

INNITT [*crossing to* BRANDER]. And you didn't intend to shoot?

BRANDER [*laughing*]. Why, no!

INNITT [*fresh*]. Say, old man, you want to be careful how you monkey with that revolver. If anyone had seen you, they'd have thought you a d——d fool. [*Sits in chair again*]

BRANDER [*sits in his chair right of table*]. Young man, is it a regular thing for Congressmen to have a private secretary?

INNITT. All the great orators do.

BRANDER. And you can write a speech showing up that steal?

INNITT. I can write a speech on any side of any question.

BRANDER. What has become of your conscience, sir?

INNITT. I've lived in Washington all my life.

[BRANDER *rises, takes* INNITT'S *hand; he also rises*]

BRANDER. Don't say another word. I see very well that you're an infernal rascal. But I don't suppose you're any worse than any of the rest of them hereabout, and you may be useful to me. I'll make some inquiries about you, and if I find that you are as smart a rascal as you claim to be —

INNITT. You'll find me right in line!

BRANDER. You may consider yourself engaged. [*Rises*]

[2] [INNITT. When shall I begin with you?

BRANDER. This minute. I expect you to save me from fifty sharpers between this and bed-time.

INNITT. I'll do it. I'll have my trunk sent over here at once. [*Goes to door; when at door, turns*] For the present, Mr. Brander, good-bye.] Say, we'll own this town before we get through. [*Exits*]

BRANDER. What a town! I guess this fellow's right. I do need a private secretary who knows the ropes.

[*Enter* OTHELLO *with salver. Down to* BRANDER *left centre*]

OTHELLO. Mars Brander, dars a card fo' you, sah!

[BRANDER *takes card*]

---

[1] Between brackets is typical omission from N. Y. P. L. copy.
[2] In N. Y. P. L. copy, the following takes place of dialogue between heavy brackets:

INNITT. Thank you, sir. [*Going to door*] I'll not disappoint you, sir. Good day, sir. [*At door, turns*]

BRANDER [*reading from card*]. Minister to Dahomy! [*Turning to* OTHELLO] Who's he? [*Suspiciously*]

OTHELLO. Dunno, sah! A culled person, sah! Says he's your most intimate friend, sah!

BRANDER. A nigger says he's my most intimate friend! [*Turning to* OTHELLO, *gives him a look*] Are you sure he said that, or did you dream it?

OTHELLO. He said it, sah!

BRANDER. He's no friend of mine — I don't even know who he is. But I'll see him. [*Crosses to right, looking at card.* OTHELLO *goes and opens door*]

OTHELLO. De Minister to Dahomy.

[*Enter* FISHBACK, *looks at* OTHELLO, *then goes to* BRANDER *quickly.* OTHELLO *exits*]

FISHBACK. Mars Brander, hyar I is.

BRANDER [*turning to him*]. What! Why, it's — why, what are you doing here?

FISHBACK. What am I doing here, sah? Why, I'm here after my appointment, sah, as de Minister to Dahomy, sah. I should like it to-day, sah, as I have arranged to start to Dahomy to-morrow, sah. [*Pose*]

BRANDER [*looks hard at* FISHBACK]. What are you talking about?

FISHBACK. Talking about? Why, my appointment as Minister to Dahomy, sah. Major Yell promised me, sah, if I'd frow de culled vote fo' yo', sah, you'd have me appointed Minister to Dahomy. I'm hyah, sah!

BRANDER.[1] You want to be Minister to Dahomy?

FISHBACK. Yes, sah!

BRANDER. Well, where is Dahomy?

FISHBACK. Dunno, sah. But I know it's an office with a salary, sah — I want it, sah. [*Pause*]

BRANDER. Well, I don't know how to get it for you, sir. [*Goes to chair right of table*]

FISHBACK. Then why did you promise it, sah?

BRANDER [*turns to him*]. I promised it? I didn't! But I am willing you should have the office if it will get you out of Texas. You go and find out how to go to work to get it, and perhaps I'll help you. [*Sits right of table*]

FISHBACK. Me, sah? Why, sah, I expects you to attend to all that, sah.

BRANDER. Oh, you do? Well, I shan't do it!

FISHBACK. Very well, sah. Then I will, sah. [*Goes toward door*] But remember, sah, I expects it to be suah thing. [*At door*] Do you think I'd better postpone starting fo' Dahomy to-morrow, sah?

BRANDER. Yes, I think you had.

FISHBACK. Very well, sah — see you later. [*Exits*]

BRANDER [*when* FISHBACK *is off, closes book and rises*] The first of the office-seekers!

[OTHELLO *enters suddenly and quietly*]

OTHELLO. Hist! [BRANDER *turns. Then* OTHELLO *closes curtains on arch; crosses to right, closes curtains, then to left and closes curtains; then to fireplace, puts blower on grate; then* OTHELLO *and* BRANDER *at table centre, raise table-cloth together in front; then raise heads and look at each other.* OTHELLO *takes* BRANDER's *arm and brings him gently down stage a little.* OTHELLO *looks about, then speaks*] Lady to see you, sah! [*Pause*]

BRANDER. Lady to see me? Well, what are you closing the doors for? What makes you whisper?

OTHELLO. Why, sah, when we announce to a Congressman that thar's a lady to see him, we always take pains that his family doesn't hear him.

BRANDER. H'm! What a town! Let her come in. [*Goes to looking-glass, arranges collar, etc.* OTHELLO *goes to door, opens it.* DIXIE *enters slowly*]

OTHELLO [*at door*]. First day in Washington, too! [*Exits*]

[BRANDER *turns from glass and starts down stage, stately; suddenly sees* DIXIE *standing left centre. He starts, abashed; then recovers himself*]

BRANDER. Well, young woman, what can I do for you?

DIXIE. I came to ask a favor.

BRANDER [*puts hand in pocket and goes toward her*]. How much!

DIXIE. Oh! Mr. Brander, you wrong me — I haven't come to ask for money.

BRANDER. Don't want money? [*Places chair in front of table*] Sit right down! [DIXIE *sits*] You don't belong here! Are you a stranger here, too?

---

[1] Scene here varies slightly in wording from N. Y. P. L. copy.

DIXIE. I am, sir — all alone here in this great big city, where everybody takes advantage of you. [*Pause*]

BRANDER [1] [*looks, — then moves lips as if swearing. Then places his chair opposite to hers and sits*]. What can I do for you?

DIXIE. Oh, thank you, Mr. Brander, you are so kind! I am an orphan and very poor. Now, before my poor dear papa died, he invented a powder for keeping moths out of clothing. It was his intention of making a present of his invention to his country — but he died. [*Weeps*]

BRANDER. There! There! Don't cry — no doubt he's better off.

DIXIE. I don't know — probably he is. Our home was in Indiana. But forgive me, Mr. Brander, for being so silly — [*dries eyes*] as to cry. Poor papa left us very poor, — all we have is this wonderful invention. Now, some of papa's friends have organized a company to manufacture the powder. All we want is to get a bill through Congress directing its use on the Government storehouses.

BRANDER. Oh, I see.

DIXIE. And I came here to Washington to see about it, and I didn't know who to go to, and they told me what a real good man you were, and I thought perhaps you might tell me what to do, or perhaps you might want to introduce the bill yourself?

BRANDER. Why, certainly I will. I don't know much about this business, but I reckon I'll learn. You just bring along the bill and I'll introduce it. [*Rises, turns to right.* DIXIE *rises, catches hold of his hands. He turns to her*]

DIXIE. Will you? Oh, thank you! I'll bring the bill up to-morrow, and tell you all about what to do. [*Goes to door, opens it*] Now you won't forget, will you?

BRANDER. No, I won't forget.

DIXIE [*coming down stage*]. Mr. Brander, do you know — [*Hesitates*]

BRANDER. Well?

DIXIE. I didn't expect to see such a nice looking gentleman as you. [*Very naively*]

BRANDER. Did you expect to see a gorilla?

DIXIE. Oh, no. But I didn't expect to see such a handsome, elegant

gentleman. [*Starts to go, then stops*] Mr. Brander, may I ask another favor?

BRANDER. I suppose so. [*Puts hand in pocket, but suddenly withdraws it. — Aside*] Hang it! She didn't want money. [*Aloud*] What is it?

DIXIE. When my mama was a very little girl, not even as old as I am, she told me a very great man, Daniel Webster, kissed her, and she was very proud of it, and used to tell me of it. Now, would you be willing to kiss me?

BRANDER [*starts and looks about*]. Would I?

DIXIE. I should be so proud of it!

BRANDER [*going to her slowly. Looks at door right*]. Well — I — hang it! I would just as soon kiss you as not, but I've got a wife and I reckon you'd better not brag about it till I'm dead as Daniel Webster is.

DIXIE. Oh, certainly not. Say, Mr. Brander, you don't think I'm fresh, do you?

BRANDER. Oh, no! [*Catches her face, kisses her, then goes to right corner*]

DIXIE [*going to door, then pauses*]. Oh, Mr. Brander, thank you so much. Now I'll go, for I know a statesman's time is very valuable. You won't forget about the bill, will you? [*At door*] Good-bye, Mr. Brander. I'm so much obliged to you for that kiss. [*Pose*]

BRANDER [*emphatically*]. Don't mention it! [*Exit* DIXIE] This being a Congressman isn't so bad, after all!

[*Enter* BOSSY]

BOSSY. Well, Dad, how goes it? How are the clothes?

BRANDER [*at sofa*]. Well, I can't say I like 'em yet.

[OTHELLO *and* FISHBACK *in excited debate outside*]

FISHBACK. Get out o' my way. I will see him!

BOSSY. What's that?

BRANDER. What's the trouble?

FISHBACK. Let me alone! I will see Mars Brander!

[*The above lines are spoken all together. Then* OTHELLO *and* FISHBACK *rush into room*, FISHBACK *first —* OTHELLO *follows.* FISHBACK *rushes down to* BRANDER *at sofa, excited.* OTHELLO *remains at table behind* FISHBACK. BOSSY *right centre*]

---

[1] Slight change in wording from N. Y. P. L. copy.

BRANDER [*standing in front of sofa*]. What's the matter?

FISHBACK. Mattah, sah! Mattah! There's no such position as Minister to Dahomy! [*Bossy laughs and falls into chair.* BRANDER *falls on sofa laughing.* OTHELLO *laughs heartily*] That's what's the mattah! What do yo' say to dat, sah?

BRANDER. No such position?

FISHBACK. No, sah! Never was, sah! It's been disrepresented to me, sah! Now, what do yo' say to dat?

BRANDER [*seated*]. Well, if there's no such office, of course you can't get it.

FISHBACK. But what becomes of me, sah?

BRANDER. I don't know!

FISHBACK [*excited*]. Don't know! Don't know! See here, Mars Maverick Brander, I was promised an office for electing you, and I want it, sah! Are you one o' those pests o' society who repudiate their political obligations, sah? Do you propose to get me that office, sah?

BRANDER [*angry*]. No, I don't! I never promised you an office. And I won't get you one! You're not fit to hold one!

FISHBACK. I don't get it! I don't get it! Then I'll attend to de mattah myself, sah. [*Starts for door, and then back*] I'll ask no further favor from you, sah. [*Starts to go, then back*] But remember, sah, I made you, sah, and I'll unmake you, sah. When de next 'lection comes, sah, I'll have you licked out of your boots, sah.

BRANDER [*jumping up quick*]. Kick him down stairs!

[OTHELLO *grabs* FISHBACK *by collar and yanks him up to door*]

OTHELLO. Right dis way fo' Dahomy! [*Picture*]

FISHBACK. Don't do dat! Don' do dat! I'll go! I'll go! [OTHELLO *releases him*] Mr. Brander, when I came to Washington, I didn't expect to be treated like this, sah!

[OTHELLO *suddenly grabs him and throws him off.* OTHELLO *follows. Crash heard outside*]

BRANDER [*sits on sofa*]. Yell had no business to promise that fellow an office.

BOSSY. Well, Dad, we wanted those negro votes and that was the only way to get them.

[*Enter* OTHELLO *with salver. Goes to head of sofa*]

OTHELLO [*out of breath*]. He won't be allowed in the hotel again, sah. And here's more cards fo' yo', sah.

BRANDER. Bossy, read the cards.

[OTHELLO *hands her cards and puts arm-chair right of centre table*]

BOSSY [*reads*]. Col. Ebenezer Pepper — Col. Brassy Gall [1] — Othello, do you know anything about them?

OTHELLO. Yes'm — I know de gem-men.

BRANDER. What sort of men are they?

OTHELLO. Well, sah, dey's always been so liberal to me pussonally dat I'd rather not express my opinion ob 'em, sah.

BRANDER. More Washington men, eh? Had we better see them, Bossy?

BOSSY. May as well.

BRANDER [*rising — crossing to right*]. Show them in. [OTHELLO *exits*] My girl, sit down. [*Bossy sits right corner.* BRANDER *gets sight of himself in glass*] If either of these fellows makes fun of my personal appearance, I'll shoot him. [*Sits right of table*]

[*Enter* OTHELLO]

OTHELLO [*at door*]. Col. Gall and Col. Pepper.

[*Enter* GALL *and* PEPPER. *Business of* OTHELLO *taking hats from them*]

GALL [*rushing down to* BRANDER, *grabs* BRANDER'S *hands*]. My dear Mr. Brander, I'm delighted to see you, sir — delighted, my dear boy. [*To* OTHELLO] Wait, my son — [*To* BRANDER] Delighted, my dear boy. Let me introduce Col. Pepper, my particular friend, Col. Pepper, of the United States Army, retired. Col. Pepper occupies rooms in the hotel, right above yours. Col. Pepper, the Hon. Maverick Brander. By Jove! It's a pleasure to make two such men friends for life. Pepper, old fellow, you know all about Capt. Brander; and, of course, Brander, you don't need to be told that Col. Pepper here was a hero of both battles of Bull Run. The first man on each occasion to arrive in Washington after the de-

---

[1] This delightful thrust, in N. Y. P. L. copy, has been omitted from the "stock copy": instead, it reads "probably two gentlemen from Kentucky."

feat. Shake hands, gentlemen, shake. [BRANDER *crosses to* PEPPER. *Both shake hands. Then up stage, crosses to right, then down right*] That's right! [*Sees* BOSSY] Ah, this lady, Mr. Brander's daughter. [*Grabs* BOSSY'S *hand and shakes it*] How do you do? [*Drags her over to* PEPPER] Pepper, old man, this is young Miss Brander — a chip of the old block, sir. Has all her father's sterling qualities. Shake hands with Col. Pepper. [*They shake hands.* PEPPER "*chucks*" BOSSY *under the chin.* BOSSY *draws away*] There! [BOSSY *up stage after handshake.* GALL *centre*]

BRANDER. If you don't think I'm too curious, I'd like to ask a question.

GALL. Certainly — a hundred — if you wish.

BRANDER. Who the devil are you?

GALL. What!

PEPPER [*perhaps pantomime*]. What! It can't be, sir, that you don't know Col. Brassy Gall? Why, blast it, this comes near being a personal insult to me! [*Goes up stage very angry.* BOSSY *jumps to right,* OTHELLO *to left.* PEPPER *glares at both severely*]

GALL. Pepper, old fellow, be calm. My dear Major Brander, you must have heard of me! Why, you know, the finest race-horse in the country is named for me.

BRANDER. Never heard of the horse or you either.

GALL. But I've held office.

BRANDER. That's nothing in your favor. I tell you, sir, I never heard of you.

BOSSY [*right*]. I heard of a man once by the name of Gall. They said he was the greatest liar alive! [*Backs up stage a little, laughing*]

GALL [*crossing to* BRANDER]. That's me! I knew you'd heard of me! Now we know each other — sit down. [*Pushes* BRANDER *into chair right of table, very affectionately. Then motions to* BOSSY *to be seated. She sits right*] Permit me to order some refreshments. Son, a bottle and cigars. [OTHELLO *starts to go, stops when* GALL *speaks*] Better make that two bottles and a box of perfectos. [*Exit* OTHELLO. PEPPER *down to sofa and sits*] Now, my dear Major Brander, I suppose you'd like to know why we called. My friend Col. Pepper here is a retired army officer. The army lost one of its brightest ornaments when he retired from active service; which he did, sir, just

the time when war with England was imminent; and it is believed that war was averted because of the reluctance of the Government to engage in it unless Col. Pepper went to the front.

BOSSY. No object in having the war if they couldn't get him killed off.

[*Enter* OTHELLO *with tray, bottles, cigars, etc., and places all on table. Pours out wine, hands* BOSSY *and* PEPPER *each a glass. Places glasses for* BRANDER *and* GALL *on table*]

GALL [*laughing*]. Ha! ha! Very good! Of course, you didn't mean it. But it's good. But let me continue. [*Sits*] Though out of active service, the Colonel's patriotic soul thirsts to be of benefit to his country; so he has concluded to let the Government have a piece of land he owns at Red Dog in the Panhandle. Land, sir, which he bought from an Indian Chief for two blankets and an old gun. This land he proposes to build a court-house on. All he wants is for Congress to appropriate $20,000 to buy the land. Now, you're just the man to do him a service by getting Congress to do this. Yes, General Brander, it's your opportunity to stamp your name on the pages of history as a patriot. [*Rising and taking up glass* OTHELLO *has placed for him*] Gentlemen, before we discuss the case further, let's imbibe. [*All take their glasses and rise*] There is nothing assists a statesman's mind like a glass of good wine — even those from prohibition states place great dependence on it. Here, drink — come on, Pepper — to the health of the Statesman from Texas. [*They drink and then all sit*] Now a cigar. [GALL *sits and lights cigar.* OTHELLO *serves cigars and refills* BRANDER'S *glass*] You'll tackle this matter of this new building?

BRANDER. What! A $20,000 building at Red Dog! Why, Red Dog is nothing but a camp of horse thieves in a desert.

GALL [*seated*]. What! Red Dog! One of the finest towns in Texas! All it needs is some good society and a little more rain.

BRANDER. Some good society and a little more rain — that's all Hell needs. [*Pause*]

PEPPER [*suddenly rising as if to go*]. Come, Colonel, let's go.

GALL [*rising and stopping* PEPPER]. Certainly not! General Brander is just right. He wants to know what he's about. I assure you, Governor, since you've been to Red Dog it has grown to be a beautiful town and climate has changed, too — it rains there now twice a week, regularly. So, of course, you'll vote for the bill. [*Taking out small book with pencil*] I've made a little memorandum and I'll now get you to O.K. it — that you pledge yourself to support our bill. [BRANDER *signs same.* GALL *takes book after signing*] And you've done your judgment credit, too — great credit! Now, Pepper, we can go. [PEPPER *crosses to* GALL — *both lock arms and go up stage a little; then both turn*] Gov. Brander, remember you are to consider yourself one of my intimate friends. [*Repeats business and gradually gets to door*] Find them good cigars?

[BOSSY *and* BRANDER *rise and look at* GALL *and* PEPPER]

BRANDER. Very.

GALL. Son, leave the box here for Gov. Brander. [*Repeats arm business*] Good-day, Governor. Good-day, Miss Brander. [*Shakes* BOSSY'S *hand*] Come on, Colonel. Don't forget us, Governor.

BRANDER. Oh no — call again.

GALL. I'll do it, and take dinner with you. [*Exit with* PEPPER]

BRANDER [*turns to* BOSSY]. That fellow is rather fresh, but I like him. He's got a hearty, liberal way with him. Money's no object to him, BOSSY — [*Crossing*] I begin to like being a Congressman.

OTHELLO [*gathering glasses on tray*]. Mars Brander, shall I have de wine charged to de room, or will you pay for it?

BRANDER. Why, that man that just went out, Gall — he pays for it.

OTHELLO [*back of table*]. But he didn't, and it's de custom to charge what's sent to de room to de man what occupies de room.

BRANDER [*looks at* OTHELLO]. Did Gall know that?

OTHELLO. Ob course, sah.

BRANDER. Where can this fellow Gall be found? [*Grabs hat and pistol, exits*]

BOSSY [*to* OTHELLO]. If Dad catches him, he'll be sorry.

OTHELLO. I reckon dey won't have no trouble, ma'am.

[*Enter* BRIGHT. OTHELLO *exits.* BOSSY *runs to* BRIGHT, *both meeting centre*]

BOSSY. Oh, I'm so glad you've got here. Where is your sister?

BRIGHT. Oh — er — she's got such a headache, she begged to be excused.

BOSSY [*turns away a little*]. Oh, I'm awfully sorry. I've only got mama to talk to, and she don't do anything but read that old book of etiquette. [*Turns to him*] And you don't seem like you used to, and I'm so lonesome. [*Suddenly*] Say, can't you take us around to see the President?

BRIGHT. I — I — [*Looking at her dress*] I — I — don't think he receives to-day.

BOSSY [*persistent*]. Well, then, let's go and see the Capitol.

BRIGHT. Oh, we'll see that when the session begins.

BOSSY. Well, can't we go to some show?

BRIGHT. There's nothing in town worth seeing.

BOSSY [*crossing to left*]. You don't seem to want to take us anywhere.

BRIGHT [*following her a little*]. Why, yes, I do. But don't you think you'd better get a little used to the city?

[BOSSY.[1] But how can I get used to the city if you don't take me out and show it to me?

BRIGHT. Yes — but for a day or two, you might look out the window.

BOSSY. What! Fairleigh Bright, I'm from Texas, but I'm not a fool! I begin to see.

BRIGHT. Bossy, I — I — Do you remember what you said to me the day your father was elected?

BOSSY. What was it?

BRIGHT. You said, "I shall have you with me to teach me and show me everything" —

BOSSY. And now you want to teach me before anybody sees me! I understand now why your sister had a headache.

BRIGHT. Bossy, don't misunderstand me — but don't you think —]

BOSSY. I think and I know — I've been watching you ever since we got to Washington and I know just how you feel. You're ashamed of Dad — and you're ashamed of me — [*pathetically*] you're ashamed of me — [*Falls on sofa crying*] I know we're green — awful green — all we know is cattle. We do

---

[1] The dialogue between heavy brackets omitted from N. Y. P. L. copy.

very well in Texas, but here where you've got society friends we make you mortified.

BRIGHT [*going to her and leaning over her*]. My dear girl — I'm sure —

BOSSY [*rising determinedly and crossing to centre*]. So am I sure, and I don't blame you. Dad, I know, has his odd little ways, but I am not ashamed of my father — [*Crosses a little toward door*] I'm sure we can get along somehow. [*Turns to him,* BRIGHT *standing near end of sofa*] We are very much obliged to you for all your kindness to us, and we won't trouble you any more. [*Goes to door*] Some day, when we learn the ways of society, come and see us. Good morning. [*Exits*]

BRIGHT [1] [*looks after her dumbfounded*]. Well, what's happened now? Bossy! Bossy! [*Starts after her*] Why, she's given me my congé. [*Piqued*] All right, ma'am, I'll go. If you can get along without me, I can get along without you. [*Up to door*] When you want to see me again, you'll send for me. [*Jams hat on viciously, thrusts hands in pockets, exits angrily*]

[*Enter* MRS. BRANDER, *looks about up stage*]

MRS. BRANDER. There's nobody here. Bossy, come in! [*Enter* BOSSY, *goes to chair right of table*] What was the matter with Captain, Bossy? [*Goes to right corner chair and sits*]

BOSSY [*crying*]. We were not stylish enough for him. You saw how he looked when he got back from his walk with Dad to-day. And when he looked at you he shuddered — and when I fixed myself all up to please him, he thought I looked jay, — and — [*sobbing, falls in chair right of centre table*] wouldn't let me go down to dinner. [*Weeps*]

MRS. BRANDER. Don't cry, Bossy — he'll come back.

BOSSY [*suddenly rising*]. No he won't — I won't let him! But — [*Crossing to* MRS. BRANDER] You wait! If we don't know everything, we'll learn, and we'll get there — you bet! [*Grabs book of etiquette, sits at table and studies hard*]

MRS. BRANDER [*rising and looking in glass*]. Well, if he saw anything to

object to in this dress, he must be a fool.

[*Enter* BRANDER. *Throws hat on table. Has lighted cigar and is smoking*]

BRANDER [*back of table. Looks at what* BOSSY *is reading*] What! Bossy, you reading that book of etiquette? [*Goes to front of table*]

MRS. BRANDER [*near chair*]. She's come to realize the need of it. Capt. Bright has shown her. [*Sits*]

BOSSY. That he is ashamed of us — we are so green. [*Rising*]

BRANDER. Ashamed of us?

BOSSY. It's so, Dad! I — I found it out and sent him away. [*Weeps on his breast*]

BRANDER. Ashamed of us? I don't know as I blame him — as far as I am concerned. And maybe your mother is a few chips shy. But you! Why, he couldn't be ashamed of you. But if he's hurt your feelings by pretending to, I'll — [*Starts to turn left*]

BOSSY [*stopping him, catches his arm*]. No, don't do that, Dad. I'll fix him — the time will come when he'll be proud to be seen with us! Then you see if he gets the chance to be. [*Enter* OTHELLO, *with tray, dishes, tablecloth, etc., and, during following lines, arranges dishes, on table*] Oh, Dad, did you find that man, Gall? [*Sits on sofa*]

BRANDER [*smoking cigar*]. Yes, down in the bar-room.

BOSSY. What did he say about the wine?

BRANDER. Why, he was as pleasant as could be. Explained that it was an oversight. We had another bottle and parted friends.

BOSSY. Did he pay for the bottle?

BRANDER. No — I did!

BOSSY. And did he pay for that sent to this room?

BRANDER. No. Say, come to think of it, well — I'll be damned — he's done me again! This town is one grand swindle! There's that cigar he gave me! Brown paper stuffed with an inferior article of flannel. [*Throws cigar on stage*] Give me something to take the taste out of my mouth. [OTHELLO *starts for door*] Here! These grapes will do. [*Walks to table, picks up olive and partly eats it; then spits*

---

[1] In N. Y. P. L. copy, speech runs as follows:
BRIGHT [*starting after her*]. Bossy, Bossy! [*Pauses centre*] Perhaps she's right. Texas and Washington are different. I don't think I could

stand another day about town with her father. And, well — she gave me my congé. [*Exits left centre. Enter* MRS. BRANDER, *looks about stage*] *it out*] Great grief!¹ What sort of grapes do you call those?

OTHELLO [*back of table turns when* BRANDER *picks up olive*]. Beg pardon, sah! Them's no grapes — them's olives!

BRANDER. Olives! Well, give me something to take away the taste of the olives! Where's that cigar? [*Looks about, finds it, picks it up and goes to smoking*] Now hurry up with the food.

OTHELLO [*going to door*]. I'll go for the soup now, sah! [*Exits*]

MRS. BRANDER [*rises, and goes to right second entrance*]. Bossy, don't you want to wash your hands before we eat? [*Exits*]

BOSSY. Call me, Dad, the minute the victuals come. I'm starved. [*Exits*]

BRANDER. Starved! My stomach's a howling wilderness!

[*Enter* OTHELLO, *very quickly*]

OTHELLO. Hist! [*At door*, BRANDER *turns and looks at him*. OTHELLO *goes to curtains, closes them*]

BRANDER. Is it the same one? [*He has turned quick as a flash to curtains on arch, and closes them; then turns to* OTHELLO, *who has gone to back of sofa. Picture. Both look at each other*]

OTHELLO. Yes, sah!

BRANDER. Let her in.

[OTHELLO *goes to door, opens it.* DIXIE, *followed by* TOUGH, *enters, very quickly and excitedly. She goes to centre, speaks as soon as she enters*]

DIXIE. Oh, Mr. Brander, I'm in such trouble! This man — [*pointing to* TOUGH]

BRANDER [*turning to her*]. What's he done?

DIXIE. Do you see that thing he's got? It's an instantaneous photograph machine, and when you kissed me —

BRANDER [*nervous*]. Yes?

DIXIE. He was hiding out in the hall, and I must have left the door open, for he got a picture of us.

BRANDER. My grief!

DIXIE. And he came and said if I didn't give him a hundred dollars for the negative, he'd show it to Mrs. Brander.

BRANDER. Holy smoke!

DIXIE. And she wouldn't understand it, and what would she think of me?

BRANDER. You!! What would she think of me!!! [*Crossing to* TOUGH] Is the whole business in that box? [DIXIE *near table, looks off*]

TOUGH [*holding up negative*]. Yes. There's the negative! See it?

BRANDER [*looking at it*]. Yes, I see. [*Produces money*] Here's your hundred. [*Gives money*] Give that to me. Now, get out!

[TOUGH *exits.* BRANDER *crosses to right, looking at negative*]

DIXIE [*centre, when* BRANDER *right*]. Mr. Brander, I hope you don't blame me for this affair?

BRANDER [*looking at* DIXIE]. Oh, no. [DIXIE *starts to door; and is half way up stage*] Say, stop! [DIXIE *stops.* BRANDER *takes her hand*] Tell me one thing. Did it cost Daniel Webster a hundred dollars to kiss your mother?

QUICK CURTAIN

[*Encore picture.* — BRANDER *at door left centre with hat on, satchel in hand, holding trunk with right hand;* MRS. BRANDER *and* BOSSY *looking at him in surprise*]

BRANDER. You can stay here, but I'm going back to Texas.

CURTAIN

ACT III

SCENE. — *Ante-room, in* BRANDER'S *apartments, Arlington Hotel. Folding door centre, arches right and left first entrance.* SAM *and* INNITT *enter at rise. Music.*

INNITT [*crossing to centre*]. You say Mr. Gall wants to see me; where is he?

SAM. Coming, sah! [*Exits*]

INNITT. It's wonderful how this fellow Gall manages to ingratiate himself with people. He seems to come pretty near being boss of the Brander outfit. [*Enter* GALL]

GALL. Oh, you're here, Mr. Innitt! You go up to the Capitol and in Mr. Brander's desk in the committee-room you'll find a map of Texas showing the land we want to take. Bring it over quick. I want to show it to Senator Bellows to-night.

---

¹ "A thousand devils!" in N. Y. P. L. copy.

INNITT. Oh! Mr. Gall, doesn't it strike you that you're giving orders pretty freely? I'm Mr. Brander's private secretary — not yours.

GALL. My boy, you won't be anybody's private secretary if you talk like that.

INNITT [*crossing to sofa*]. Well, I can't say that I care much. [*Sits*] Brander simply makes an errand-boy of me! I'd have resigned six months ago only I have hoped Miss Bossy —

GALL [*bursts into laughter*]. What, you too! Why do you think she'd ever marry you?

INNITT. Girls have been known to elope with their coachmen.

GALL. Not the kind of girls she is. Besides, there's only two men of the lot stand any chance. If she marries to please her mother, she'll take this Italian Count, Frechetti, the old woman's so stuck on. If she pleases herself, she'll marry this Army fellow, Bright.

INNITT [*rising and going to him*]. Bright! Why, they never speak!

GALL. True! But I saw him on the Avenue yesterday look at her as she drove by with Frechetti, and I never saw a fiercer look on a man's face. And the way she looked right at him, and didn't see him, was a beautiful effort. My boy, he's the love of her life. You ain't in it a little bit! [INNITT *looks at* GALL] So get her out of your head and hurry after that map. [INNITT *exits.* GALL *crosses to right corner*] I wonder if there's a man in Washington who isn't in love with this Texas girl! [*Enter* OTHELLO, *goes to folding doors and opens them, showing dining-room with table prepared for dinner*] Ah! Othello, everything right for the supper party?

OTHELLO. Yes, sah! Take a look at the table, sah! Fine a supper for a small party, sah, as ever was served in this house, sah. [*Closes doors*]

GALL. The table looks very nice. These Branders have changed some since they came to Washington, Othello!

OTHELLO. Yes, sah!

GALL. Do you remember the first meal they ate in the house?

OTHELLO. Reckon I do, sah!

GALL. That was the day, I believe, that Mr. Brander fed you the burning omelette. [*Laughs*]

OTHELLO. Yes, sah! Same day, sah, that you ordered the wine and fo'got to pay fo' it, sah! [*Laughs*]

GALL. Othello, you've got too good a memory. You ought to use some of your leisure time learning how to forget things. [*Exits*]

OTHELLO. Learning how to fo'get. [*Crosses to left*] Fo'getting is professional service, an' I expects to be paid fo' it. [*Exits.* Enter MRS. BRANDER, *followed by* MRS. CAMPBELL]

MRS. BRANDER. I think everything is correct! The service in this house is excellent, but, if Mr. Brander is elected again, we shall buy or build a house; we are tiring of the confinement of hotel life. You see, there are only six rooms [MRS. CAMPBELL *begins to count on fingers*] in this suite, and — What are you counting on your fingers?

MRS. CAMPBELL. I was counting the rooms in your house in Texas. You only had five. [*Crossing to* MRS. BRANDER]

MRS. BRANDER. Texas and Washington are two different places, Mrs. Campbell. [MRS. CAMPBELL *goes back to sofa and sits*] We had no occasion there to entertain Senators, Judges and Foreign Ministers. I don't see what Texas has to do with it, anyway. I never mention Texas except to refer to the fact that Mr. Brander has 80,000 head of cattle there. [BOSSY *enters*] You see, Texas is — is —

BOSSY. Texas is a mighty good State to be from. [*Pause.* BOSSY *crosses to* MRS. CAMPBELL. MRS. BRANDER *crosses to right*]

MRS. CAMPBELL [*seated*]. That's so, Bossy, and it was awfully good of you to give me a chance to be from it for a visit to you. You remember how your father objected to coming here?

BOSSY. Don't I?

MRS. CAMPBELL. And now he tells me he likes Washington and is going to try to get a re-election!

MRS. BRANDER [*rises and goes to right first entrance*]. Yes, and dear me! I must go and find him. He may have forgotten that we have a dinner party to-day — he's so absorbed in that game of poker. [*Exits*]

MRS. CAMPBELL. It's a poker party he has in his room, is it?

BOSSY. Yes. Poker is one of the things he did not have to learn after we came from Texas.

MRS. CAMPBELL. Pardon me, Bossy, for saying so, but it does seem so funny to see you here and know you are one of the leaders of Washington society. Honestly, dear, I was afraid you'd be the laughing-stock of the whole town when you came here.

BOSSY. [Oh, indeed!

MRS. CAMPBELL. Tell me the secret of your getting on so well.] [1]

BOSSY. Six million dollars!

MRS. CAMPBELL. I don't understand —

BOSSY. Why, people discovered we were rich before they found out anything else about us, and, I tell you, money'll cover more sins than charity! Everything we did was right. When Dad raised a row, it was charming eccentricity; when I talked slang, it was refreshing, chic. I did make some awful breaks, though —

MRS. CAMPBELL. Breaks?

BOSSY. Why, you know! Displays of ignorance! A dude who belonged to the British Legation got mashed on Dad's millions before we'd been here a week; found out I rode, made me a present of a saddle.

MRS. CAMPBELL. Well?

BOSSY. A side saddle, of course, and I looked at it and said I, "Where's the other stirrup?"

MRS. CAMPBELL. Good heavens!

BOSSY. Oh! It was all right! Everybody thought I said it to be funny. It was quoted as a joke. And when Dad got acquainted up at the Capitol, he found that, instead of his being the only "Yap", as he calls it, in Congress, there were about two hundred other members from just as far back in the woods as he was. Why, he says that some of those Indiana Congressmen, when they came here, were afraid of the cars. [_Rising and going to centre_]

MRS. CAMPBELL. So he wasn't conspicuous as a "Yap"?

BOSSY. No, and we kept our eyes and our ears open and, what we didn't know, we managed to learn. Whatever else may be said of us Texans, there's nothing slow about us. Oh, we're right in the line of good society now, you'll see. We've got a Senator and a Judge of the Superior Court to dine with us to-night.

MRS. CAMPBELL. And, by the way, Captain Bright —

BOSSY [_turning to her_]. He — oh,

I forgot you don't know that affair's all off.

MRS. CAMPBELL. Why, I thought —

BOSSY. I know. But you see, Texas and Washington are two different places. A Captain is all very well on the frontier, but he doesn't cut much of a figure among the officers in Washington. [_Turns away a little_]

MRS. CAMPBELL [_rising and going to her_]. And is that why you dropped him, Bossy? It isn't like you.

BOSSY [_crossing to sofa with_ MRS. CAMPBELL]. Well, no, it isn't. The truth is, when we arrived in Washington he thought we were so jay he got ashamed of us, and I found it out and got mad at him and shook him!

MRS. CAMPBELL [_sitting on sofa_]. And you haven't seen him since? [_Looks at newspaper she carries_]

BOSSY [_sits on sofa_]. Oh, yes! I've seen him every day — on the Avenue, when we've been out driving — of course, though, we never bow.

MRS. CAMPBELL [_reading paper_]. Well, you won't even see him again for some time. I [2] just saw a paragraph in the _Army and Navy Gazette_ only a moment ago — [_sees article_] here it is. — It says that Captain Bright has been ordered to San Francisco. He leaves Wednesday night — that's the day after to-morrow.

BOSSY [_turns quickly and crosses to_ MRS. CAMPBELL]. Ordered to San Francisco?

MRS. CAMPBELL. Yes. [_Handing_ BOSSY _paper_]

BOSSY. How far away is that?

MRS. CAMPBELL. About three thousand miles.

BOSSY. Indeed? Liz — [_sits beside_ MRS. CAMPBELL] do you think he'll call on you to say good-bye before he goes?

MRS. CAMPBELL. Well, hardly; especially in view of his position toward you.

BOSSY. Oh, I don't mind your inviting him to call here, if you'd like to see him.

MRS. CAMPBELL. Thank you, Bossy, but he's probably quite forgotten me by this time, and, besides, he'll be too busy preparing for his journey to call.

BOSSY [_rising slowly and crossing to_

---

[1] Dialogue between heavy brackets not in N. Y. P. L. copy.

[2] In the N. Y. P. L. copy, the expression varies thus:

I noticed by the _Army and Navy Gazette_ that he has been ordered to San Francisco. He starts, I think, day after to-morrow.

centre]. Ye — yes, three thousand miles! That's an awful long way, isn't it? [*Turns back to audience and looks through crevice of centre doors to hide tears*]

BRANDER [*off*]. I tell you, wife, I'm all dressed! We quit playing poker an hour ago. [*Enters*] Well, Mrs. Campbell, how are you? [*Crossing to her; she rises and takes his hand*]

MRS. CAMPBELL. Oh! I'm beginning to feel quite at home. Been playing poker, eh? So you still cling to your old Texas habits.

BRANDER. Some of them. Play poker and drink whiskey. But I've given up carrying a gun, and I think, too, I've improved on my drinking habits.

[BOSSY *crosses to chair right*]

MRS. CAMPBELL. How so?

BRANDER. The liquor I drink now is of a better quality. [*Motions to her to sit.* MRS. CAMPBELL *sits on sofa*]

BOSSY [*sits right*]. What made you stop playing poker so soon?

BRANDER.[1] [Well, I was in a position where it was best for me to get out!

BOSSY. Broke?

BRANDER. No; had all the money there was in the crowd.]

MRS. CAMPBELL. And you're not anxious to go back to Texas? I should think you'd want to look after your ranch.

BRANDER. I'm looking after it here. [*Pause. She seems surprised*] This is the place to make money off a Texas ranch. I've learned a thing or two, Mrs. Campbell, since I saw you in Texas. And one is, that Texas land, worth six dollars an acre to pasture cattle on, is worth fifty to mortgage with railroad bonds. I'm mortgaging mine. [*Sits on sofa*]

MRS. CAMPBELL. Then you really like being in Congress?

BRANDER. Yes. I don't know how it is, but, after a man has once held office, he never wants to give it up. [*Pause*] And besides, he's never good for anything else afterwards.[2] [*Pause*] What

I want, though, is to be a Senator. I tell you, the Senate is the best Club in America to belong to.

MRS. CAMPBELL. But you'll have to go back to Texas to look after your election, won't you?

BRANDER. Yes, I suppose so, and I may have some trouble in getting re-elected.

MRS. CAMPBELL. Why, you had no trouble last election!

BRANDER. Nobody knew anything about me then — couldn't say anything against me. But now I've got a record for them to find fault with. [*Rises and crosses to centre*] But Gall is going down to Texas with me to help run my campaign. You don't know who Brassy Gall is?

MRS. CAMPBELL. I've only heard the name.

BOSSY [*seated*]. He's the man I wrote you about, that came to our room the first day we were here and ordered a lot of wine and stuff.

MRS. CAMPBELL. Oh, I remember how I laughed over it. [*To* BRANDER] And are you and he friends?

BRANDER. He's my right hand man.

MRS. CAMPBELL. How did that come about?

BRANDER. Mutual interests. Gall has charge of lobbying our railroad bill. He's smarter'n chained lightning. Why, he's the feller that stuffed the ballot-boxes in the 19 Arkansas district. He's just the man to run my campaign. We've begun it already, too! Why, I've sent an agricultural report to every voter in my district.

BOSSY. It's a great scheme and it's cheap.

BRANDER. You see, the Government prints the report and, being a Congressman, I can send them by mail for nothing. I've sent about two tons of them to Texas already.[3]

[*Enter* MRS. BRANDER]

MRS. BRANDER. Bossy! Father! Here's the Senator and his wife. [*Exits*]

BOSSY. Come on, Dad. [*Exits*]

[MRS. CAMPBELL *rises and crosses to right as soon as* MRS. BRANDER

---

[1] Instead of the dialogue between brackets, the N. Y. P. L. copy has the following:
BRANDER. Why, I had all the money there was in the crowd.

[2] In N. Y. P. L. copy, the following is added:
About the most pitiable creature on earth is an ex-Congressman.

[3] In N. Y. P. L. copy, the following is added:
MRS. CAMPBELL. And do the voters read the reports?
BRANDER. Never! But it makes them proud to have their Congressman remember them,

speaks first word. When about to go off, BRANDER, *who is at centre, crosses to right and on his speaking she stops. Both near right first entrance,* MRS. CAMPBELL *with face to audience*]

BRANDER. Little woman, I've been watching you ever since you got here yesterday. You find us changed, don't you? It's a great change! And maybe you liked us just as much when we were only plain Texas folks.

MRS. CAMPBELL [*turning and putting hand out to him*]. Why, Mr. Brander, I —

BRANDER [*taking her hand*]. Don't say a word. But when you think, think this: Most Congressmen come here meaning to do right. But when they take an innocent, honest man right from the country and send him to Congress, they put him in a damned hard spot!

[*Exit* MRS. CAMPBELL. BRANDER *about to follow when* OTHELLO *enters.* BRANDER *stops on hearing him*]

OTHELLO. Mars Brander, has yo' a minute to spar', sah?

BRANDER [*at door*]. My guests are waiting. What is it?

OTHELLO. Deys a poor cullud man here, sah, wants to see yo', sah!

BRANDER [*about to go*]. Oh, some other time.

OTHELLO. Mars Brander, he seems in trouble, sah! He seems so miserable, sah! I couldn't help pitying him to dat extent, sah! dat I came very near giving him half a dollah, sah! As a favor to me, sah, would you just say a word to him?

BRANDER [*turns, goes to chair right, and sits*]. Yes! But be quick!

OTHELLO [*goes to left first entrance*] Come in! [*Enter* FISHBACK, *very dilapidated. Exit* OTHELLO]

FISHBACK [*crossing to left centre*].

Mars Brander, your humble servant, sah!

BRANDER. What can I do for you?

FISHBACK. Mars Brander, doesn't yo' remember me, sah?

BRANDER. Why — you're that darkey from my district, Fishback. You still in Washington?

FISHBACK. Yes, sah.

BRANDER. Why, what have you been doing to yourself?

FISHBACK. Seeking office, sah.

BRANDER. I remember. You came here to be appointed Minister to — Minister to —

FISHBACK. Dahomy, sah! Fo' I got through, sah, I was willing to get a job firin' de boilers at de Capitol, sah — and I couldn't git dat. I found out, sah, except when dey want his vote, de politicians has no use fo' de cullud man.

BRANDER. So you didn't get a Government job?

FISHBACK. Only a month in de chain-gang, sah.

BRANDER. Did you get that? Well, you have had a hard time.[1] [*Very quiet*] Why don't you go home to Texas? I'll help you.

FISHBACK. Mars Brander, I'se just like all de rest ob 'em. I come hyah fo' an office, and I'm ashamed to go home without it.

BRANDER [*rising and crossing to* FISHBACK]. That's it! Well, here's some money for you — get yourself a suit of clothes and come up to the Capitol to-morrow. We'll see if we can find you a job. Go now — I'm busy. [*Turns as if to go*]

FISHBACK [*takes money, about to thank him.* BRANDER *motions him to stop, very kindly though.* FISHBACK *bursts into tears*] You'll find me waitin' on de steps of de Capitol, sah. [*Exits*]

[BRANDER *turns and looks after* FISHBACK, *then turns slowly and goes to right first entrance; looks again* [2]]

[1] Instead of this line, the N. Y. P. L. copy has:
FISHBACK. Office seeking is mighty poor business, sah, fo' white man as well as culled, sah. I've seen, sah, bright smart men who had done service for his party and come here expectin' his reward at once. He stopped at de best hotel and takes de theatres. I sees him again. He hasn't got de office. He's stoppin' at a cheaper hotel and he give de theatre de go-by. And de next time I sees him he's at a way down cheaper hotel; his clothes getting shabby and dars a care-worn look on his face. And den it's a boarding-house and a bite at de free lunch counters, and den it's a bench in de

park, and, some night when he's blue and discouraged, and all tired out, sah, and hasn't no bed to sleep in, sah, he just goes and finds his rest down dar in de Potomac. Mars Brander, dis great beautiful city with its grand and its bro'd streets, its sunshine and its glitter, is one big graveyard of broken hearts, sah; de hearts ob de men who have come hyar to seek office. [*Turns away*]

[2] There follows here, in N. Y. P. L. copy:
BRANDER. Poor fellow! Well, he's got this office-seeking business sized up mighty near right. [*Exits*]

[*Enter* OTHELLO]

OTHELLO. Walk in, gemmen. [*Enter* YELL, BRAGG *and* BLOW *with satchels, looking about*] Dis yer's Mars Brander's ante-room. [*Three Texans stand in a row, exchange looks and then look at* OTHELLO]

YELL. What's that?

OTHELLO. Mars Brander's ante-room. [*Texans look at each other and then at* OTHELLO]

YELL [*putting hand in pocket*]. How much?

OTHELLO [*surprised*]. Fifty cents! [*Crosses to them and takes money. Crosses back*] This is finding something!

BRAGG. Now, when do we get in the game?

OTHELLO [*looks at* BRAGG. *Pause*]. Right away, sah! You wants to see Mars Brander. I'll have to ask each of yo' gemmen fo' a card. [*Texans repeat business of look*]

BLOW. You want a card from each of us? Is that it?

OTHELLO. Yes, sah. To take to Mars Brander. [*Three Texans look and each produces a pack of cards and give one to* OTHELLO. BLOW *puts satchel down in front of him.* OTHELLO *crosses to them and takes cards, as each speaks*]

BLOW. There's the Jack of Hearts —

BRAGG. There's the ten o' clubs —

YELL. That's little Casino. Take them right along now.

OTHELLO [*after getting cards, going to right first entrance*]. Yes, sah. Say, I reckon you gemmen's straight from Texas. [*Exits*]

YELL. We play cards down in Texas, but this is carrying poker further'n ever I see it done before. [*Texans turn about, business exact, and raise coat-tails so as to show pistols in back pockets, backs to audience*]

BLOW. Brander's got things powerful gaudy! [*All turn to audience*]

YELL [*turning to footlights*]. Mebbe we ain't up to this sort o' thing.

BRAGG [*to* BLOW]. Have you got the comb? [*Feeling for comb*]

BLOW. Yes. [*Gives comb.* BRAGG *combs whiskers; hands it to* YELL, *who repeats business, then hands it to* BLOW. *Same business.* BRANDER, *followed by* GALL, *enters with three cards. Then* YELL *gets comb and begins to comb moustache*]

BRANDER. The Jack o' —, the ten o' clubs — [*looking at cards*] and the two of — [*looks up, sees Texans*] Suffering Ireland!

GALL [*to* BRANDER]. Well, who the —

BRANDER [*to* GALL, *aloud*]. Why, it's the boys, — Yell, Bragg and Blow! [*Crossing over to them and extending hand. They look at hand and then put hands behind them. Movement exact*] Why, boys, how came you here?

YELL. Mr. Brander, we are here on a very serious errand.

BRANDER. Why, what's the matter?

YELL. The matter is that election's coming on pretty soon and the people of your district are particular to have a representative whose heart beats warmly for his native land. Now, we've heard of your favoring Land Grant Bills and such things. It may be all right, but we don't know; so — your constituents have sent us here as a committee to investigate your course, and then give them the straight steer about voting for you again!

BRANDER [*aside*]. Here's a treat I didn't expect. [*Aside to* GALL] What am I to do?

GALL [*quick*]. Do? Tell 'em to go ahead and investigate. Give 'em a grand bluff. [BRANDER *presses* GALL'S *hand and advances to Texans who have been conversing among themselves*]

YELL [*turning to* BRANDER]. Well, sir?

BRANDER [*aloud*]. Gentlemen, I am glad to have you investigate my course to the fullest extent. And if I don't satisfy you, I want you to go back to Texas and steer them all against me.[1]

[*Texans turn to each other and nod approval of what* BRANDER *has said.* BRANDER *turns to* GALL *quickly on seeing Texans turn away*]

GALL [*advancing to* BRANDER]. That's the idea. Now jolly 'em and put 'em under obligations to you quick.

BRANDER [*turns to Texans*]. And, by the way, gentlemen, while you are here investigating me, you will consider yourselves my guests. Here, Sam. [SAM *enters near door*] Go to the office and order three elegant rooms for these gentlemen, and charge to me. [*Exit* SAM] Gentlemen, be seated. [*Texans sit*] Now, gentlemen, we'll begin this in-

---

[1] Slight variation from N. Y. P. L. copy.

vestigation right. Othello! [OTHELLO *enters and crosses to* BRANDER] Give us a drink! [*Whispers*] Whiskey!

[OTHELLO *opens door and passes into dining-room.* GALL *and* BRANDER *exchange looks all through scene*]

BRAGG [*seated on sofa, aside to* BLOW *and* YELL]. That sounds Texas-like.

BLOW [*to* YELL *and* BRAGG]. I don't believe he's got out of his good old Texas ways yet, after all.

BRANDER [*to Texans*]. Have a pleasant trip here?

BLOW. Yes, only I wanted to kill a conductor and Yell wouldn't let me.

BRAGG. He made us all agree before we started, not to kill a man till we got back to Texas.

[*Enter* OTHELLO *with five glasses from dining-room, three large and two small glasses, all on tray*]

OTHELLO [*to* BRANDER]. Here you are, sah.

[GALL *takes up small glass as* BRANDER *does. Both look at large glasses*]

BRANDER. Well, you know your business. [GALL *in right corner*]

OTHELLO [*aside to* BRANDER]. Reckon I do, sah — I put red pepper in theirs, sah.

[BRANDER *crosses to right, then turns to Texans*]

BRANDER. Step this way, gentlemen. [*Texans rise and cross to* OTHELLO] Drink with me! [*They pick up glasses, smell and drink.* BRANDER *and* GALL *also drink.* OTHELLO *gathers glasses after all drink, and then exits, closing doors*]

YELL [*after drink*]. That's the best whiskey I've had since I left Texas — burns the throat right out of you.

BRAGG [*to* YELL *and* BLOW]. I was afraid he was going to insult us with champagne.

[*Enter* SAM]

SAM. De gemmen's rooms am ready, and your wife says your guests am all here and waitin' fo' yo' to come to dinner.

YELL. Dinner! That's good! I haven't eaten since breakfast. Come on, Brander! We're with you. [*Starts to go*]

BRANDER [*apologetically stopping them*]. Well, boys, I've got a little dinner-party here to-night — a Judge of the Supreme Court and a Senator.

YELL. Oh, that's all right. We won't mind 'em a bit. Will we, boys?

BLOW *and* BRAGG. No!!

BRANDER. That's nice, but I thought, as you were just off the cars, you'd like to go to your rooms and wash up. Sam, show the gentlemen to their rooms.

[SAM *picks up satchel, starts to go*]

YELL [*drawing revolver quick*]. Drop that! [SAM *drops satchel quick. Pause*] That's the third boy that's tried to get away with that bag in this house.

[GALL *and* BRANDER *exchange looks*]

BRANDER [*laughing*]. Why, he only wants to carry it for you. [BRAGG *looks at* BRANDER, *opens bag, takes out bottle, hands it to* YELL *and gives grip to* BOY.[1] SAM *takes it and steps up stage. Texans exeunt*] Sam, explain to them what they're tackling before you put them in the elevator.

[GALL *goes to folding doors*]

SAM. Oh, they're been in it all right, sah. Only Col. Bragg said 'twas a shame to make one small boy pull three heavy men up. [*Exits*]

BRANDER [*crossing, sinks on sofa*]. I have done wrong, here, but I haven't deserved this.

[*Enter* BOSSY, *crosses to* BRANDER]

BOSSY. Dad, I saw 'em — I was coming to call you. What'll we do with 'em? [*Puts arms about his neck.* GALL *exits, leaving doors open*]

BRANDER. My daughter, for once your poor father is stumped. It won't do to get 'em mad if I want to be re-elected; they hold up the district by the tail. We've got to entertain 'em! I don't know as the Judge and the Senator will ever forgive me for introducing 'em, but it's got to be done. [*Goes to centre doors*]

---

[1] In copy, N. Y. P. L., before Texans exeunt, there is this speech:

YELL. Come on, boys. [*They move to door*] Say, Brander, don't you sit down to dinner without us. [*Exeunt Texans*]

Bossy.[1] [But it's enough to make one die with shame at being from Texas.

Brander. My daughter, don't say that! No Texan has cause to blush for his State. If Massachusetts had her Warren and her Putnam, Texas had her Houston and her Crockett. The men who fell at Lexington and Bunker Hill were no braver, truer patriots than those who died at San Jacinto and The Alamo. The history of Texas is the story of one long battle for freedom, written in the blood of her heroes. Don't blush for your State, my daughter — be proud of it!

Bossy. You're right, Dad! But I wish the present population would stop celebrating those victories.

Brander. We'll keep 'em as quiet as we can. My grief! What will your mother say — [*Passes through into dining-room and closes folding-doors after him*]]

Bossy [*falls on sofa*]. Poor mama! [*Lays back and laughs*]

[*Enter* Mrs. Brander]

Mrs. Brander [*crossing to centre*]. Oh, Bossy! Bossy! Has it driven you to hysterics? Oh, my child! What will the Senator think! We are disgraced forever! [*Weeps*]

Bossy [*rising and going to her*]. There! There! Mama, don't you fret!

Mrs. Brander. Oh, but they're bad enough anyway, and I suppose they'll all get drunk.

Bossy. Mother, we must make the best of it! Come [*crosses*] and entertain our guests. [*Exits*]

Mrs. Brander. I've an idea! If I only had somebody to get them drunk! [*Enter* Innitt *with map*] Here, Mr. Innitt, you'll do!

Innitt. Do what?

Mrs. Brander. Get them drunk!

Innitt. Get who drunk?

Mrs. Brander. Those three Texas men who just went out.

Innitt. But I've got to —

Mrs. Brander. Never mind what you've got to do — I'll take that map. You take this money and get those three men drunk. [*Pushing him gradually to left first entrance*] Get them so full they won't be able to stand up. Then have them put to bed. Get them so drunk

they can't get up stairs to dinner. Can you do it?

Innitt. I can, ma'am.

Mrs. Brander. Then hurry, get them paralyzed. [*Exit* Innitt] Well, I reckon I know how to get out of a scrape as well as the rest of them. Mr. Brander will have to admit that I've managed this very cleverly. [*Exits*]

[*Enter* Brander *and* Gall *through centre doors. They talk fast and move quickly.* Brander *first,* Gall *follows and closes centre doors*]

Brander [*as he enters*]. It isn't the dinner-party that worries me. As long as they're sober, they won't do anything very bad. It's the investigation that worries me. It's a condition and not a theory that confronts us. I haven't done anything very wicked here, but they may kick about our railroad bill. Now, what are we to do?

Gall. We'll jolly 'em — give 'em a good time! Tell 'em what we've a mind to and send 'em home hooraying for Brander! That's the way investigating committees are always handled.

Brander. But can't we do something to square me with them? Make 'em think I'm — er — what I ought to be?

Gall. That's easy enough! I'll make a little speech after dinner that will make them think you're a second Daniel Webster![2]

[3][Brander [*starts*]. I wouldn't do that!

Gall. Why? Haven't you been trying to follow in the footsteps of Daniel Webster?

Brander. Yes, but it's mighty hard to strike Daniel's gait — [*Pause*] Perhaps I haven't succeeded. [Gall *turns up stage*]

[*Enter* Mrs. Brander]]

Mrs. Brander [*crossing to* Brander]. Father, come in the parlor. You needn't worry a bit about those men. I've attended to them.

Brander. What have you done?

Mrs. Brander. I've sent Mr. Innitt to get them drunk.

Brander. What!

Mrs. Brander. Yes, so drunk that they will have to go right to bed. They

---

[1] Dialogue between brackets omitted from N. Y. P. L. copy.

[2] Add speech from N. Y. P. L. copy:
Brander. Yes. But say — nothing about my kissing that girl, you know.

Gall. Well, hardly. [*Turns up stage*]

[3] Between brackets omitted from N. Y. P. L. copy.

won't be able to come to dinner. Wasn't I smart to think of it?

BRANDER. Well, you have gone and been and done it! Now we shall have a sweet time!

MRS. BRANDER. You won't hear from them again to-night. [*Texans yell off left first entrance.* BRANDER *looks off left and then goes to head of sofa*] Mercy on me!

[MRS. BRANDER *crosses. Enter three Texans, jolly, followed by* INNITT, *very full. He staggers to centre. Three Texans fall on sofa.* GALL *right corner*]

INNITT. Mrs. B-br-ander — I've done 'em up for you — I've — I've — [*Falls senseless*]

BRANDER. Mother, you go into that parlor and look after your visitors.

MRS. BRANDER [*exiting*]. I always knew that Innitt was a fool.

BRANDER [*crosses to door*]. Othello, here! [*Enter* OTHELLO, *opening doors*] Take this man up and put him to bed. [OTHELLO *picks* INNITT *up*]

INNITT [*to Texans*]. Say, boys — [*Sings*] "She's my sweetheart —" [*All sing*] "I'm her beau —" [OTHELLO *drags* INNITT *off, then doors close*]

YELL [*on sofa*]. Say, Brander, who is that fellow?

BRANDER. He! He's nobody! He's a paper-bag filled with wind. [*Pause*]

BLOW. No, he ain't filled with wind!

YELL.[1] [He's filled with about two quarts of whiskey! I never see a man with such a wolfish appetite for liquor. Why, another hour of such pouring her in would have got us drunk.]

BRANDER. Well, gentlemen, the Senator and Judge are waiting — come. Let me have the pleasure of showing them what kind of men I have the honor to represent. [*Three Texans rise and cross stage to right.* BRANDER *stands centre and watches them.* GALL *up stage looking on. Three Texans bow as they pass* BRANDER. *Exeunt. Then* BRANDER *and* GALL *walk down stage slowly, looking at each other. Then* BRANDER *crosses to* GALL, *takes his arm, and both walk to exit*] Gall, we've got a pleasant evening before us. [*Exit*]

[*Enter* OTHELLO *followed by* SERGEANT. OTHELLO *crosses to centre.* SERGEANT *remains near sofa*]

SERGEANT. I am the Sergeant-at-arms of the House. I must see Mr. Brander at once.

OTHELLO. Dey's got a dinner-party, sah. Just sitting down. [*Loud laugh from Texans back of doors*]

SERGEANT. I'm very sorry, but I've got to disturb him. [OTHELLO *opens folding-doors, disclosing dining-room. Leaves doors open.* SERGEANT *sits on sofa. Texans yell.* OTHELLO *goes to* BRANDER *and whispers to him. He rises and goes to* SERGEANT, *at cue*] Seem to be enjoying themselves. It ought to be worth fifty dollars to Brander not to be found.

[*Enter* BRANDER. OTHELLO *closes doors,* SERGEANT *rises*]

BRANDER. What is it, Sergeant?

SERGEANT. Call of the House, sir. No quorum at the evening session — Am sent to bring members in. Sorry to disturb you, sir.

BRANDER. You needn't be. [*Loud laugh back of door*] I'm glad to get away. [*Texans laugh*] I've got three drunken Texans in there. [*Exit* SERGEANT *laughing*] Here, Sam! [*Enter* SAM] Sam, go in and tell Gall to explain that I am sent for on a call of the House. [*Texans laugh.* SAM *throws folding-doors wide open. Then goes and whispers to* GALL. BRANDER *crosses to arch*][2] This is one of the times I don't mind answering the call of duty. [*Exits*]

[*At table:* MRS. BRANDER, BLOW, BOSSY, YELL, SENATOR'S WIFE, BRAGG, MRS. CAMPBELL, GALL, JUDGE, SENATOR]

OTHELLO [*back of* YELL]. Game, sir?

YELL [*at table*]. What's that?

OTHELLO. Game, sir?

YELL. After dinner.

GALL [*rising at left end of table*]. My friends, pardon me for interrupting the progress of the feast, but I am called on to make an apology.

YELL. Don't do it! Fight! Fight! [*Jumping up and offering knife to* GALL. *Characters all rise. Ad lib. talk. All excited*]

---

[1] Not in N. Y. P. L. copy.
[2] The latter part of this speech is omitted from N. Y. P. L. copy.

GALL. Let me explain. Mr. Brander is obliged to leave us. The House of Representatives is now in session and feels that it cannot get along without him, so he has been sent for. While we shall miss his presence here, it must be a source of pride to you gentlemen from Texas, that your representative is in so much demand. [*Texans yell and business with dishes*] And, gentlemen from Texas, while I am on my feet, let me say a word to you. Gentlemen, we are glad to have you here — you are welcome! [YELL *rises, throws celery out of large glass, picks up decanter, fills glass and then drinks. Texans yell all through this business till* YELL *drinks*] Gentlemen, things have not always been thus. The time was that we regarded Texas as the refuge of the criminal and the home of the coyote and cactus. But since Mr. Brander has been here, our eyes have been opened. [*Renewed applause*] We have learned to appreciate the greatness and future glory of Texas. [*Wild applause*] He has taught us that Texas is the coming Empire State. [*Applause*] Gentlemen, thanks to the efforts of Mr. Brander, Texas is becoming the center of commerce, the home of science, literature and the arts. [*Wild applause*]

YELL [*rising, drunk, with glass in hand*]. Three cheers for literature! [*Texans rise and cheer*] Go on!

GALL [*Wild applause*]. And mark my words, gentlemen, in five years, and maybe less, New York will go to Texas for their fashions.

YELL. Hooray for Texas fashions!

THREE TEXANS. Hooray! Hooray! Hooray! Whoop! [*They draw revolvers and fire them in air. Everybody else at table goes under table and looks out front*]

QUICK CURTAIN

ACT IV

SCENE. — BRANDER'S *sitting-room, the next morning.* MRS. BRANDER, MRS. CAMPBELL *and* BOSSY *discovered.* BOSSY *writing at desk;* MRS. CAMPBELL *snoozing on lounge. They evidently haven't been to sleep or in bed.* MRS. BRANDER *seated with newspaper.*

MRS. BRANDER [*reading newspaper*]. Oh, what a night!

MRS. CAMPBELL. I'm afraid things are not pleasant up at the Senator's. His wife will have something to say about his running away and leaving her.

BOSSY. Well, there's one consolation! We'll never have to entertain that stupid old Judge at dinner again.

MRS. BRANDER. No! And we'll never be able to get anybody else to dine with us. Of course, the story is all over Washington by this time. Here's a full account of it in the *Post*. I'm afraid Count Frechetti will never ask you to marry him now.

BOSSY. Then some good comes out of this racket anyway.

MRS. BRANDER. Bossy, if you talk that way about the Count, you'll drive me crazy!

BRANDER [*outside*]. Bring me up an absinthe frappé. [*Enters very quickly, putting hat and coat on chair*] Hello! Up all ready?

MRS. BRANDER [*turns back to him*]. Up! We haven't been to bed!

MRS. CAMPBELL. Have you just got home?

BRANDER. Yes; all night session!

MRS. CAMPBELL. Was it exciting?

BRANDER [*sinking in chair*]. Exciting! Had nineteen calls of the yeas and nays. I'm dead!

MRS. BRANDER [*rising*]. Don't talk about being dead, and exciting sessions! You should have seen the one we had here! [*Crossing*] Those miserable wretches — [*Up stage*]

BOSSY [*goes to* BRANDER, *puts arm about his neck, letter in hand*]. Got to firing pistols, Dad!

BRANDER. And then I suppose the party broke up?

BOSSY. Yes, all broke up.

[*Enter* OTHELLO]

OTHELLO. Two letters by messengers, marked "Important." [*Hands them to* BOSSY *and goes up to door.* BOSSY *hands them to* BRANDER]

BRANDER. One from Senator Bellows, one from Judge Woodhead. Let's see which one I'll read first.

BOSSY. The Senator's, Dad.

BRANDER [*opens letter, reads*]. "Maverick Brander, Sir: I presume you consider it's a very pretty joke to invite respectable gentlemen and timid ladies to your house, introduce them to the society of drunken desperadoes, and then run away, leaving these unhappy people to the mercy of your rum-maddened brutes. [*Looks*. MRS. BRANDER *falls into chair*] I, sir, fail to see the exquisite humor of the proceedings. I do not object to your dashing out the spoonful of goose grease that has for years served you for brains — [*Looks*] in a frantic effort to be funny, but I won't be made the target for your squirt-gun of wit. Permit me to say that I consider you're a rum-benumbed, an opium-dazed bunco sharp, and that you are only permitted to live because they can't find a graveyard mean enough to bury you in. Yours, with profound contempt, G. Whittaker Bellows." That's a nice letter to get.

MRS. BRANDER [*rising*]. Mercy! What language! [*Crosses to right*]

BOSSY. What does the Judge say, Dad?

BRANDER. I don't care to read it. [*Crosses to fireplace and puts both notes in fire*]

OTHELLO [*up at door*]. Any answer, sah?

BRANDER [*turns to* OTHELLO]. Yes; send word to each man that I'll kick him — the whole length of the Capitol.

[BOSSY *crosses to sofa and sits, letter in lap*]

OTHELLO. Yes, sah! [*Exits*]

BRANDER. That settles it. [*Turning*] The Senator'll vote against our bill and the Judge will injunct us. That'll be nice! Where are the visiting Statesmen now? [*Goes to chair, centre*]

BOSSY [*on sofa*]. Gall took them upstairs to put them to bed. [*Drops letter;* MRS. CAMPBELL *picks it up and hands it to her*]

BRANDER [*standing*]. Were they drunk?

BOSSY. Paralyzed!

[BRANDER *sits. Enter* OTHELLO]

OTHELLO [*down to sofa*]. Messenger boy you wanted is here, ma'am.

BOSSY [*gives letter*]. Send him with this.

OTHELLO. Mars Brander, your cullud friend is outside — wants to see you.

BRANDER. Let him in. [OTHELLO *opens door. Enter* FISHBACK, *who bows to ladies.* OTHELLO *remains up at door*] Well, are you all right?

FISHBACK. All right! Should say I was, sah! Dat note you gave me to de head janitor, sah, commanded respec'ful attention, sah. I have received my appointment, sah, and assume the duties

of my official position, sah, to-morrow. I just dropped in so as to allow you to congratulate me, sah, and to say, sah, dat at any time, sah, de services an' favahs pertaining to my department are at your command, sah.

BOSSY [*on sofa*]. What is your department?

FISHBACK. I have the general supervision of de dumping of de waste baskets. It's a mighty impo'tant office. I'll fill it, I trust, with credit to our district. As I said afore, Mars Brander, de department is always at your service, sah. Ladies, your servant. Mars Brander, good-day, sah. 'Scuse me for hastening back to de Capitol, sah, for I should hate to have anything go wrong during my absence. [*Exits*]

OTHELLO [*at door*]. Mars Brander, Col. Pepper, de gemman as has de rooms above, wants to see you, sah.

BRANDER [*picks up paper*]. Hang Pepper! Tell him I don't want to see him.

OTHELLO. But, Mars Brander, he's been wounded, sah — shot, sah, by your friends from Texas. [*All rise suddenly*] He wants to see you about it.

BRANDER [*drops paper*]. What! Have they tried to add murder to their list of crimes?

MRS. BRANDER. I thought they had agreed not to kill a man till they got back to Texas.

BRANDER [*turning*]. I may as well find out what this is. Is he able to come down?

OTHELLO. Yes, sah! He's been laying fo' yo', sah. He's outside the door.

BRANDER. Let him in. [OTHELLO *opens door.* PEPPER *enters, brought in by two men, on stretcher. He lies on stomach. Head to audience*] Good-morning, sir.

PEPPER. No, sir — nothing of the sort, sir — you see before you a wounded man, sir. This is the only position that I'm able to assume, sir. I have your infernal gang to thank for this, sir.

BRANDER. Well, sir, what was the affair anyway? What was the quarrel?

PEPPER [*raising head a little*]. Quarrel! Cuss it, sir, there was no quarrel. I was seated alone in my own room, sir, seated in a cane-bottom chair, when this devilish fusillade began beneath me. [*Drops head*]

BRANDER. And the bullets went through the floor?

PEPPER [*raising head*]. And through

the chair. [*Drops head*] Heavens! To think that I should have gone through the Mexican and Civil Wars, unscathed, to be wounded now! And that, too, in the back. See here, sir, I've got to occupy this absurd position, sir, for two weeks — for two weeks more, I've got to eat off the mantel. [*Drops head*] Now, sir, what do you propose to do for me?

BRANDER. I know only of one thing I can do.

PEPPER. What's that?

BRANDER [*takes revolver from pocket. Turns, points it at* PEPPER]. Put you out of your misery.

PEPPER [*rolls off of stretcher*]. Let me out! Let me out! [*Jumps up and runs out, followed by men with bier. Women all laugh.* BOSSY *falls on sofa,* MRS. BRANDER *on chair*]

BRANDER.[1] That will drive me to drink! I'm going downstairs to get my head rubbed. [*Exits*]

MRS. BRANDER. Well, I'm going to my room. [*Exits*]

MRS. CAMPBELL [*crossing to* BOSSY]. Bossy, I don't want to be curious, but I accidentally saw the address of that note you sent by messenger.

BOSSY. To Captain Bright? Yes, I have written him asking him to call here. He is to leave to-day for San Francisco, you know, and there is something I want to say to him before he goes. Something I have only learned within the last few hours.

[*Enter* OTHELLO *with card*]

OTHELLO. Card, ma'm.

[BOSSY *crosses,* MRS. CAMPBELL *takes and looks at card*]

BOSSY. Why! It's Captain Bright! How quick he got here.

OTHELLO. He was in the office, ma'am, when your note went down, and the clerk knew him and gave it to him.

BOSSY. Ask him to come up.

[*Exit* OTHELLO]

MRS. CAMPBELL. Bossy, don't you want a touch of rouge before he comes up? We've been up all night, you know.

BOSSY. No! I don't care how I look. I'm not going to try to make a mash on the Captain.

MRS. CAMPBELL. Well, he'll not see me looking like this. He'll think I've been to the French Ball. [*Knock*] MRS. CAMPBELL *goes quickly*] There he is, and I haven't got a bit on my face yet. [*Exits. Knock*]

BOSSY [*turns a little as if to prepare herself*]. He's there. Come in!

[*Enter* OTHELLO]

OTHELLO. Captain Bright!

[BRIGHT *enters, goes down stage.* OTHELLO *exits*]

BRIGHT [*bows*]. Good-morning, Miss Brander.

BOSSY [*very formal*]. Good-morning. Captain Bright. [*Changing and crossing to him, cordially extending hand*] I'm right glad to see you. Sit down. [*He moves to chair left centre,* BOSSY *to chair right centre*]

BRIGHT. Thank you. [BOSSY *sits, then* BRIGHT. *Pause*] Well?

BOSSY. Well, I suppose you're rather surprised at receiving my note?

BRIGHT. I should hardly be surprised at anything that Miss Brander might do, though I'll confess that an invitation to call was the last thing that I expected to receive from her.

BOSSY [*looking up*]. And the last thing that you did receive from her.

BRIGHT [*looking up*]. Yes — Well —

BOSSY. Well, Captain Bright, I will be frank with you —

BRIGHT. Now you put me on my guard.

BOSSY. Indeed?

BRIGHT. When a lady says she is going to be frank with you, look out for deception.

BOSSY. Did you learn that at West Point?

BRIGHT. No, at a summer hotel nearby. Well —

BOSSY. Well — I will cut it short, as Dad says, for I know you leave, Captain, for the West to-night, and your time must be valuable. Captain Bright, you and I were once — [*Turns away a little, still seated*]

BRIGHT [*rising and going to her*]. I'll say it for you — lovers.

BOSSY. We were engaged —

BRIGHT [*turns away a little*]. It's the same thing.

PEPPER [*looks in door*]. You'll sweat for this.

BRANDER [*turns to* PEPPER]. You get out. [*Exit* PEPPER] This will drive me to drink, etc.

---

[1] N. Y. P. L. copy reads here:
BRANDER [*going to centre, laughs*]. That's the end of him, I reckon.

BOSSY. Sometimes — in our case we thought it was.

BRIGHT [*over her at back of chair*]. Miss Brander, do you doubt that I loved you?

BOSSY [*rising*]. Not while we were in Texas. [*Crossing to right, and then turning to him*] It's all passed and gone now, and we can afford to laugh at it.

BRIGHT. Yes! It's very amusing, when you come to think of it.

BOSSY. The breaking of our engagement broke no hearts.

BRIGHT. *You* are looking very well.

BOSSY [*crossing to chair*]. And you're rather stouter, I think.

BRIGHT. Well —

BOSSY [*at back of chair*]. Well — when I saw the announcement that you were going so far away, when I thought that we might not meet again, it seemed too bad that we shouldn't part friends.

BRIGHT. It might be as well, if we're to be three thousand miles apart! We certainly can't derive much pleasure from quarrelling.

BOSSY. And don't you think it's right nice for folks who have been lovers to be friends afterwards?

BRIGHT. I don't know. It deprives them of the pleasure of hating each other.

BOSSY [*sitting in chair*]. I hadn't thought of that.

BRIGHT [*going to her*]. Do you realize what a comfort it is at times to nurse a sense of injury? [*Turns away a little*]

BOSSY [*rising and advancing*]. That brings me to what I wish to say. I never should have sent for you to come here to-day had I not felt I owed you an apology for an injury. [BRIGHT *turns to her*] And I only came to a realizing sense of it to-day. [*Turns away a little*]

BRIGHT. I do not comprehend?

BOSSY [*turns to him*]. I'll make you! If you remember, we parted because, when you got us to Washington, you found us a mortifying burden — you were ashamed of us!

BRIGHT. Miss Brander, I am sorry you asked me here to renew *that* subject. I —

BOSSY. Oh! I'm not going to reproach you for it, but to confess my error.

BRIGHT. Then you feel you were mistaken?

BOSSY. Oh, no, I don't! I was right! You were ashamed —

BRIGHT. Miss Brander —

BOSSY [*going to him*]. Now, be honest — weren't you ashamed to be seen with me, the gawky Texas girl? Now, tell the truth!

BRIGHT. Well — I would have preferred taking you on a side street to parading the Avenue.

BOSSY. That's right. Thank you for telling me the truth! You were ashamed of me, and I was mad. And that's where I was wrong. [*Turns away to right*]

BRIGHT. Oh, you were perfectly justified.

BOSSY. Pardon me — I wasn't, Captain Bright. I've just had an experience — visitors from Texas — do you understand me now?

BRIGHT. I'm not sure.

BOSSY. Messrs. Yell, Bragg and Blow. I regret to say they are still our guests. And what I want to say to you is this: If I was one-half — even one-tenth the burden, the source of shame and misery to you that they have been to us, your feelings were more than excusable, and I had no right to be angry with you. And I ask you to forgive me. Here — this is right on the level — will you shake hands and be friends?

BRIGHT [*taking her hand*]. Why, of course — being friends is awfully monotonous, but since you don't insist on being a sister to me, I won't complain. [*Crossing. Serious*] Oh, confound it! I can't joke! When I think what we might have been, if I hadn't been such a fool!

BOSSY [*moves to chair right centre*]. We might not have been friends! [*Sits*]

BRIGHT. Well, I have only myself to blame, and there is no use crying over what can't be helped.

BOSSY. No — no — [*Suddenly*] Say, you ain't engaged to anybody else, are you?

BRIGHT. No, and never will be! [*Goes to her suddenly*] Bossy, I can't say what I want to. You are a belle and an heiress, and I'm a mere Captain — but some day I may be a General — [*Goes to left corner*]

BOSSY [*angry*]. Have you stopped to consider how slow promotion is in our Army? Would you want a girl to wait till she is a withered old maid — that is — [*Catches herself and drops head*]

BRIGHT [*going to her, leaning over her*]. Bossy, would you forgive a man for making a fool of himself?

BOSSY. A woman who couldn't do that at least once a week should never marry.

[1] [BRIGHT. And you forgive me?

BOSSY. Yes!

BRIGHT. Bossy!] [BOSSY *rises, turns and looks at him. He advances, catches her in his arms, embraces and kisses her.* BOSSY *then drops her head on his shoulder*]

BOSSY. Say, we've been losing time. [BRIGHT *kisses her again*] Say, we must have Dad go right up to the War Department and get your orders to go West changed.

BRANDER [*outside*]. Want soda-water, do they? Give 'em prussic acid. [*Enters*]

BOSSY [*running up to* BRANDER]. Here he is! Oh, Dad, you're just in time. There's something you must do right off for me. Go to the War Department and get Captain Bright a month's leave of absence.

BRANDER [*coming down stage with* BOSSY]. What for?

BOSSY. Why, you see, we are going to be friends — we are going to be married — I mean — er — [*Turns away*]

BRANDER. What!

BOSSY. Oh, don't blame him, Dad — I proposed to him.

BRIGHT. Well, hardly! [*Turning up stage to right*]

BOSSY. Yes, I did. I'm not going to deny it. But I had to, or he'd have gone off to California.

BRANDER. But why didn't he propose to you? Was he afraid?

BOSSY. Oh, he was delicate about it because we're well fixed. He is brave enough!

BRANDER. Let him prove it! Let him go and break the news to your mother!

BRIGHT [*up stage*]. I'll do so at once. [*Exits*]

BRANDER. She'll be disappointed, after setting her heart on that I-talian Count.

BOSSY. Are you, Dad?

BRANDER [*going to her and taking her hands*]. Why, I'm an American, I am, and an American son-in-law's good enough for me! And I don't like I-talians, anyway — call him Lord, Duke or Count. To my mind a greaser is a greaser just the same. [*Wild scream off*

right] He has told your mother. Maybe he needs help. [*Exits*]

BOSSY [*going to piano*]. Well, I've done a pretty good day's work, and it isn't twelve o'clock yet. [*Begins to play on piano. Enter* GALL]

GALL. Miss Brander, where's your father? The Statesmen are coming to see him.

BOSSY. He's in the parlor.

[*Exit* GALL. BOSSY *still seated at piano. Enter* YELL, BRAGG *and* BLOW. YELL *goes to sofa and falls on it.* BRAGG *to chair and falls on it.* BLOW *to chair and falls on it.* BOSSY *looks at them, then begins to play "We've all been there before." Three Texans look at her, then groan, take off their hats and throw them on floor. Movement together*]

BOSSY [*still playing*]. Good-morning, gentlemen. Don't you feel well?

BRAGG [*looking up*]. Well! My head feels like a cat in a dish of stewed tomatoes.[2]

BOSSY [*playing waltz*]. And you, Colonel Yell?

YELL [*gruff and snappy*]. I've got a deep, dark red taste in my mouth. Ugh!

BLOW. Boys, we've been carrying too much sail for our ballast.

[BOSSY *plays waltz. At each run on piano, Texans raise heads suddenly, look at her, shudder, groan, then drop heads. This repeated three times before* YELL'S *speech*]

YELL. Miss Bossy, do you play the piano very much?

BOSSY. I practice about two hours every morning. [*Runs. Texans same business*]

YELL. What time did you begin?

BOSSY [*same business*]. About ten minutes ago. Aren't you fond of music?

BLOW [*despairingly*]. Oh, yes!

BOSSY. Wouldn't you like to sing us a song?

BLOW [*looks up suddenly*]. Sing? [*Shudders*]

BOSSY. Oh, do! We'd all love to hear you sing. Col. Bragg, don't you want to hear him sing?

BRAGG [*helplessly*]. Yes; I want him to sing. [*Puts out foot and draws cuspidor to him*]

---

[1] Not in N. Y. P. L. copy.
[2] In N. Y. P. L. copy, the line reads: "feels like two eggs in a handkerchief."

Bossy. There! Colonel Blow, the gentlemen want you to sing — you can't refuse. What shall he sing, Colonel?

Yell. I don't give a damn what he sings! [Bossy *begins to play*]

Bragg. Sing "Home, Sweet Home" — that's where I wish I was.

Yell. Yes; pianos ain't plenty there.

[*Enter* Innitt, *very pale, with towel about his head.*[1] *Several letters in his hand. He crosses very slowly, looks at Texans — then* Bossy *does run on piano.* Innitt *throws letters in the air, claps hand to mouth, and runs off*]

[*Enter* Gall *and* Brander. Gall *looks at Texans and laughs, and calls* Brander's *attention to them; then exits.* Brander *laughs, touches* Bossy, *then motions her to stop playing, then goes to chair.* Bossy *stops playing and follows him down stage*]

Brander. Good-morning, gentlemen. How is the investigation proceeding? [*Texans all look at him and then turn away*]

Yell. Investigation! Brander, old man, don't taunt us. We feel bad enough — we're ashamed.

Brander. Ashamed!

Yell. Yes, sir; that's the word. There's no time when a man feels so ashamed of himself as when he's just getting over a drunk.

Blow. He thinks everybody is on to him.

Brander [*laughing*]. Nonsense! laugh at it! [*All look at him and turn away*]

Yell. Bye and bye, maybe — not now.

Bragg. It ain't our place to laugh.

Brander [*placing chair and sitting*]. Well, boys, the day is waning. What would you like to investigate first? [Bossy *stands behind* Brander]

Blow. The time-table.

Bragg. We want to know when the next train starts for Texas.

Bossy. For Texas?

Yell. We're going home.

Brander. But you haven't investi-

gated me at all, yet. It amounts to nothing!

Yell. I reckon it amounts to as much as most investigations do! [*Rises*] Mr. Brander, people come to Washington with the idea that they are going to regulate the whole business, and when they get here, they find that they were damn fools for coming. [*Sits on sofa*]

Bragg. Twelve hours here have done us up. If you've stood it two years! —

Blow. And kept out of jail —

Yell. You've done well!!

Brander [*taking papers from pocket*]. By the way, about the railroad matter. There's a certificate for 100 shares for each of you! [*Hands papers to* Bossy, *who hands one to each of Texans, and then goes up stage centre*] As stockholders, you'll be able to understand the matter better.

[*Enter* Gall, *closes door*]

Yell. That's all we need to know about it. We're satisfied.

Blow. We're ready to start for home.

Gall [*at door*]. I'm afraid you can't get away! That man you shot last night —

[Bossy *down stage centre quick*]

Three Texans [*rising suddenly and turning to* Gall]. What!

[*Enter* Mrs. Brander, *followed by* Bright]

Yell. We didn't shoot anyone!

Gall [*coming down left a little*]. Yes, you did. The man in the room above. He knows you're in this room, and he's outside the door with three officers waiting to arrest you.

[Gall *goes to window, centre;* Bossy *to door.* Brander *falls into chair. Three Texans sink into chairs*][2]

Bossy [*crosses to* Brander]. Dad, we must save them. We need them in Texas.[3] [Bossy *turns to centre*] Couldn't we disguise them in women's clothes?

Brander. No, that won't do. [*Voices heard outside*]

---

[1] Only part of this stage direction in N. Y. P. L. copy.

[2] Here the N. Y. P. L. copy has:
Mrs. Brander. What's that? Arrest them here in our room? Oh, now we are disgraced forever. [*Sits*]

[3] The close of the play as found in the manuscript copy in N. Y. P. L. is as follows:

GALL [*at door*]. There's Pepper in the hallway now. I'll lock the door. [*Locks door*] Is there any other way out of these rooms?

MRS. BRANDER. There's a window in my maid's room that opens into the back hallway. They can crawl through that window, go down the back stairs to the kitchen, and out through the alley where they dump the rubbish.

BRANDER. That's it! Gall, take them out that way. [GALL *crosses to right third entrance*] You've got just thirty minutes to get them to the depot.

GALL. This way, gentlemen.

BRANDER [*rising*]. It can be done. After being two years in Congress, I guess I know how to dodge people I don't want to see.

[BOSSY *turns to centre*]

BOSSY. Couldn't we disguise them in women's clothes?

BRANDER [*crossing to centre*]. No. Jeff Davis tried that game and it didn't work.

[BRAGG *crosses to* MRS. BRANDER. *Enter* OTHELLO *very quickly*]

OTHELLO [*at door*]. Collector from the Post-Office!

[*Enter* COLLECTOR]

COLLECTOR [*down left centre*]. Came for those sacks of mail, sir. Our wagon's at the door.

BRANDER [*centre*]. By Jove! An idea! Gall. [GALL *comes down stage*] I've got three sacks of agricultural reports in my library. Go, dump them and bring the sacks to me. [*Exit* GALL *very quickly*] Pepper [*outside door*]. It's room 99 — Brander's room — [*Knocks at door, and keeps knocking until door is opened*]

BOSSY [*goes to door*]. Dad, here comes Pepper and the officers.

BRANDER [*to* OTHELLO]. Othello, lock that door! [OTHELLO *does so quickly*] Don't let them in.

[*Enter* GALL *and* BRIGHT *with sacks*]

GALL [*speaks as he enters, putting sacks on stage*]. Here's the sacks.

[BRIGHT *in right corner with one sack.* GALL *next to him, with another, and* OTHELLO, *who comes to* GALL *as soon as he enters, takes third sack and places it next to* GALL'S. *All are placed in a row on stage right.* BRAGG *is in right corner with* BOSSY. MRS. BRANDER *door left third entrance,* COLLECTOR *near fireplace,* BRANDER *left centre. Everybody must move very quickly, a constant talk kept up until* PEPPER *enters.* BLOW *and* YELL *on sofa left*]

BRANDER [*to* Texans]. Boys, get into those sacks. [BLOW *and* YELL *rise indignantly*] Don't stop to argue. Get in — it's your only chance.

YELL. What! Southern Gentlemen hide in sacks!

[MRS. BRANDER *goes to sofa left*]

BRANDER. Yes, or Southern Gentlemen'll go to jail. Othello, help them!

[YELL, BRAGG *and* BLOW *rush for sacks.* BRAGG *goes to* BRIGHT'S *sack,* BLOW *to* GALL'S *and* YELL *to* OTHELLO'S. *Business of getting into them in a great hurry, and finally fastened sacks, entirely hid from view, standing in a row. Knocking. Ad lib. talk all through this, as follows*]

BOSSY [*excited*]. There they are, Dad!

BRANDER [*goes to door*]. Who's there?

PEPPER [*outside*]. Me, sir!!

BRANDER [*looking to see if sacks are ready*]. Who's me?

PEPPER [*outside*]. Col. Pepper! And officers of the law. We demand admittance.

BRANDER. You can't come in.

PEPPER. We will come in! [*Knocks very loud*] Let us in or we'll break down the door. [*Knocks hard*]

BRANDER. Get away from that door.

GALL [*must speak this line regardless of cue — speaks when Texans are in sacks, hid from view*]. Here's your men!

[OTHELLO *goes to door left third entrance*]

BRANDER [*to* COLLECTOR]. There's your mail. It's in your possession.

PEPPER [*beating door*]. Open this door, or I'll break it down.

BRANDER. Othello, let them in. [OTHELLO *unlocks door quickly.* PEPPER, *followed by* OFFICERS, *enters very quickly, a policeman remaining outside of door which is left open.* BRANDER *says while* PEPPER *is entering*] And now to squelch Pepper and the officers of the law. [PEPPER *by this time is down, the* OFFICERS *left centre.* GALL *crosses to sofa,* BRANDER *moving toward* PEPPER] What the devil do you mean? [PEPPER *retreats a little*]

OFFICER. I have a police justice's warrant for the arrest of the three men who are here.

[*Texans move in sack*]

PEPPER. There they are! They're hid in those bags. I can see 'em move. Take 'em.

[OFFICER *advances*]

BRANDER. Stop! [OFFICER *stops*] Seize United States Mail at your peril! [*Picture*]

PEPPER [*to* OFFICER, *after pause*]. Open those bags.

OFFICER [*to* PEPPER]. Excuse me. I only represent a Police Court. I've no authority to open United States mail-bags. [*Goes to door*]

PEPPER [*excited, to* OFFICER, *as he goes up stage*] You pig! You fool! You zebra!!! [OFFICER *laughs and exits.* To BRANDER] I'll get even with you for this yet! [*Rushes out*]

BRANDER [*to* COLLECTOR]. Mr. Collector, take your mail. [*Hands money*] Handle it carefully!

[BRANDER *crosses to* MRS. BRANDER *left.* COLLECTOR *goes to* BRAGG, BRIGHT, *and* BOSSY *in right corner*]

BRAGG [*in sack*]. But say! When do we get out of these bags?

BRANDER [*going centre*]. When you're across the river — you're safe, then. But boys, one word before you leave. You're going back to Texas to give the voters of my district a steer. What's that steer to be?

YELL [*putting his head out of bag*]. That you're the ablest and the best man in Congress, and we're all for your re-election.

CURTAIN

PEPPER [*outside*]. Break open the door.

BLOW [*crosses to right*]. Boys, we'd better move.

YELL. Boys, this is a proud moment. We came in the front door and up the elevator. We sneak down the back stairs and out through the alley where they dump the rubbish. Washington is a rough town for a stranger. Come along, boys.

BRANDER. But, boys, one word before you leave! You're going back to Texas to give the voters of my district a steer. What's that steer to be?

YELL. That you're a second Daniel Webster, and we're all for your re-election.

CURTAIN

END OF PLAY

THE GIRL OF THE GOLDEN WEST

(1905)

By David Belasco

DAVID BELASCO

DAVID BELASCO has told his own story of the writing of "The Girl of the Golden West." Here is a part of it which explains how he based one of the most effective situations in the play on happenings in real life. He writes:

It was from my father that I first got the idea which afterwards so well served me in "The Girl of the Golden West", — the incident of the Sheriff and the blood dripping on his handkerchief. The experience occurred during the Caribee mine period. My father and his friend, Shannon, with several others, had a hut together. There had been a heavy snow, so for a while they had to give up all idea of prospecting. Food was growing very scarce, until finally the twenty-four huts that constituted the expedition could boast of but three or four loaves of bread, one bottle of whisky, a scant supply of bear meat, and some straggling fish. The miners were apt to be careless, and the food supply became so low that it was necessary to form a committee to guard the precious stores. A Sheriff and a commission of deputies made a law that any one taking more than was handed to him should be shot without trial. Thus things went on for a few weeks. A poor fellow from Philadelphia who was in camp had had the blues for months before this, and had made every effort to start for home. In the midst of the famine he was taken with the hunger fever, and when the boys told him that he was very low he cried out that he did not want to die. So one night he sneaked over to the box, and stole a bit of bread and beef and some gold dust. Then he fled from camp. The next day he was missed, and the loss in the chest discovered. The Sheriff immediately went after him. Instinctively the poor fellow must have felt that he was being followed, for he doubled on his own tracks, and came back to the hut. My father was playing poker at the time, and presently heard a shot outside. The missing man staggered into the room, and fell at the feet of the players. "Humphrey," he gasped, "for the sake of my wife, don't let them do me up. Save me!" My father told him to get out or be plugged, and he pulled his gun from his belt. But at the same time my father did not say anything when the fellow crawled upstairs into the loft. Hot upon this came the Sheriff, asking all sorts of questions, but never a guiding answer did he receive from the players. Then he joined the game, just as he did in "The Girl of the Golden West", my father living an eternity while the man was above them. They let the Sheriff win so as to make him feel good, and the game finally broke up. As he held his hand out to my father for a good-night shake a drop of blood fell upon his arm. A blanched face looked down through the rafters, a hand clutched nervously at a shirt, now deep-stained in red. The Sheriff gazed at the tell-tale spot on his arm, and smiled cynically as one can afford to do who is master of such a situation.

"Did you fellows know he was up there?" he asked, taking his gun from his pocket.

There was nothing to be said; the facts were against it. The victim was caught. There was no staying the hand of the law; one could see this very well as the Sheriff gripped his gun and drew himself up to his full height. Standing there, his gaunt shadow thrown against the wall, his white face etched deep with marks of hardship and of toil, he poked the muzzle of his gun between the rafters and fired. He had done his job, and so he left without another word.

Now, the morning after "The Girl of the Golden West" opened, one or two critics declared that I did not know the times; they said that my gambler, so distinctively played by Frank Keenan, was a caricature, that he was taken from prints rather than from life. Why, I know the period of 'Forty-nine as I know my alphabet, and there are things in my "The Girl of the Golden West" truer than many of the incidents in Bret Harte.

With this situation in mind, an all-pervading love of California in his heart, and the immediate necessity of finding a new rôle for Blanche Bates, Mr. Belasco set forth on romantic adventure in the land he loved best and knew best. There streamed into his brain myriad touches — realistic, picturesque, suffused with atmosphere — which would give the play cumulative interest and give the audience a superficial sense of the period. The structure of "The Girl of the Golden West" is that of a man who knows the theatre and the value of detail; who knows whether certain trickery will get across the footlights with sufficient plausibility to be accepted rather than challenged by the spectator. In the writing of his plays, any of them, Mr. Belasco has never saved himself as a stage-manager; rather he has challenged his own ingenuity, relished difficult problems like the gambling scene in "The Girl" or *Peter* after death in "The Return of Peter Grimm."

The play, therefore, grew with the cadence of Blanche Bates's voice in mind. "The lines just crackle," he wrote her. "There are some beautiful speeches in the play — very 'Batesesque'," he added. Romance and realism not only dominated the play but the investiture of it. Just as in "Madame Butterfly" and "The Darling of the Gods" and "The Rose of the Rancho" he sought to make the moon and the stars, the sun and the flowers exude the time and the place, so now he resorted to moving scenery to carry an audience up the mountain side. He tells us how for long, weary hours he practiced with his stage electricians to give not alone sunlight, but California sunlight to his scene. He tells us, in respect to his other plays, how similarly he has toiled to be true to that Nature, in whom he believes implicitly, and whom he tries to copy.

"The Girl of the Golden West" was given at the Belasco Theatre, Pittsburgh, on October 3, 1905, and on November 14 it came to New York. It was an instantaneous success. In January, 1907, Puccini reached New York for the special purpose of selecting a play typically American as a libretto for a new opera. His choice wavered for an instant between two Belasco productions, "The Rose of the Rancho" and "The Girl of the Golden West." The outcome of his decision was to be seen in "La Fanciulla del West", given its première at the Metropolitan Opera House on December 10, 1910, with Emmy Destinn as the *Girl*, Caruso as the *road-agent* and Pasquale Amato as *Jack Rance*. Those who wish an interesting exposition of Belasco's methods as a stage-manager and director will find much profit by turning to his book, "The Theatre Through Its Stage Door", and reading how he brought realism home to a group of opera people — all speaking a different language, all with the acting methods of the singer rather than of the player that Belasco wanted them to be — and how they responded to his drilling in the spirit of true artists. I have heard actors who have been under his direction tell of the effect of his teaching upon them in after years. And the results speak for themselves.

This is the first time the text of "The Girl of the Golden West" has been published. It has been specially prepared by Mr. Belasco for this collection.

Elsewhere, in my "Representative Plays by American Dramatists", I have written on Mr. Belasco, and I have an essay on his work in "The American Dramatist." In the Bibliography to the present collection, the essential facts of his life are given. That life has been a long and serviceable one in the American Theatre. It has stretched from the so-called "Golden Period of Acting" to the present "Revolutionary Period", which is trying to break entirely from the old theatre. In his day Mr. Belasco was regarded as an innovator : he was the Peter Pan among the older managers, and that Peter Pan quality has not deserted him yet. From the earliest days of his experience as a stage-manager he has experimented, and always for the external novelty of the theatre. Others followed in his wake and copied him; but he does not seem to have gone far afield for his technical ideas; they were evolved in his own studio, talking with others; they were evolved in his workshop beneath stage, where — like Thomas Edison — he spent weary hours of the early morning in shades of incandescence. To him, the new methods that have come into the theatre are not surprising; he claims he has practised them all in his California days, in his Madison Square Theatre days, in the days when his large spectacular productions were the talk of the town because of their lavish pictorial value. Some came from abroad preaching no footlights; Belasco smiled his inscrutable smile. Others came with their impressionistic treatment of Nature; Belasco seemed hurt, not because of himself, but because he loved Nature so well.

Always his life is that of the theatre; he does not go far afield from the work at hand; when he has an evening away from a production, he is at the theatre, looking in unusual quarters for new acting material. He finds it where others have not looked; his insight, which is almost uncanny, sees the acting possibilities. Such a prophet is not a prophet in his own country. Belasco has been scolded while others of less importance have been allowed to go unscathed. But he has not been shaken from his purpose : and his purpose has not been unworthy. It is true it smacks of the showman's ability to "put it across", but that is not to be deplored; its vitality is that it does not pall, and that it holds interest. Belasco smiles at the innovations which the reformer makes; he has seen the iconoclast in the theatre before, and has seen the theatre return to normal. As a stage-manager, as a director of acting, he has not staled; he has merely elected to remain conservative, true to his old loves, firm in his belief that for all its problems, its psycho-sociological implications, the theatre is a form of entertainment, and the spectator is entitled to all the resources that the theatre can offer to make that entertainment thorough. He interprets that entertainment in terms of the heart, and he is at perfect liberty to adhere to this interpretation if he wants. Personally, I believe that he has missed a great element in the theatre by not giving more attention to the head, to those signs of the time whereby new interests are allowed their dramatic life, and new methods are used for what they are worth. It is this one-sided adherence to past accomplishment, which detracted from his production of "The Merchant of Venice"; the echo of other days is the only way in which Mr. Belasco shows that he is not of this day and generation.

The theatre has claimed him in three directions : dramatist, producer, and director. In early years he was also an actor. The dramatist part of him has had only limited sway : comparatively few plays in these later years have borne his name. But nearly all the plays he has produced have gone through the mill of his studio, been livened by his touch. There is not a phase of the theatre he does not know. His productions are personal : by that I mean that every detail comes under his observation. Everything concentrates in him. He reads extensively if not always to his profit; he knows the drama of the world and has sympathy with it. But I still believe — and he and I have argued it out — that he distrusts a too rich inner content to a play. He seeks drama of emotion, not of ideas. He distrusts

the work of art that cannot be manipulated.   James Huneker, in a rather illuminating essay on Belasco, in the *Theatre Arts Magazine* for October, 1921, says:

He demands the consoling veils of illusion to cover the nakedness of the human
soul.   If a man loves the classic English school of portraiture and landscape, the
suave mellow tones of Sir Joshua Reynolds, the fragile grace and delicious melting
hues of Gainsborough, the humid glory of the clouds in a Constable country scene,
shall we quarrel with him for not preferring Manet or Degas?   Mr. Belasco admires
Ibsen, and he appreciates the skill and sincerity of Degas and Manet.   But he sticks
to his Reynolds and Constable and Gainsborough.   Other days, other ways.

A man of seventy-two, with a full background, a memory of rare traditions, of
changing conditions — making theatre history as he progresses from year to year,
never losing his enthusiasm for the theatre, his feeling of obligation as a producer,
his feeling of faith in the new material he undertakes to train, David Belasco is
a picturesque figure in the theatre to-day.   The younger generation regard him with
distrust; but they treasure any praise he may give them.   They never wish to
coöperate with him, but to break away from him.   They follow the current, believing
in its ultimate goal.   He stands and watches for the current to change, to return
upon itself.   But he is canny, he is astute.   If he uses something old, he tells you it
is old.   "Let's grant that the realistic melodrama is old-fashioned," he practically
said to his audience the opening night of a new play, "The Dove", a Mexican gringo
story — "but, after all these 'R.U.R'S' and 'Adding Machines', in your heart of
hearts, don't you like to be thrilled, without having your brain question?"   It is
the old Belasco hypnotizing his audience — just as at rehearsal he inoculates his
players with his own enthusiasm and his own sensory intuition.   I am sure this has
its place in the theatre, just as long as there is a public for it.   And to judge by the
eagerness with which a Belasco production is followed, the relish of the screen for
his plays, the desire of the actor to be under his guidance — there is still room
for a David Belasco for many years to come.   He is the one man in the American
Theatre to-day who, because of ceaseless devotion to the Play, the Playhouse, and
Player, as he sees them, deserved the decoration which the French Government
bestowed upon him in 1924, for his services to the theatre at large.

THE GIRL OF THE GOLDEN WEST

A PLAY IN FOUR ACTS

By DAVID BELASCO

"In those strange days, people coming from God knows where, joined forces in that far western land; and according to the rude custom of the camp became known as 'St. Louis Joe', 'Noo Orleans Bill', 'Handsome Jack', 'Ace-high Jim', etc.; and here, their real names lost and unrecorded, they struggled, laughed, gambled, cursed, killed, loved, and worked out their strange destinies in a manner incredible to us of to-day. Of one thing only are we sure — they lived!"

Early History of California.

FIRST PICTURE.   *In the Sierras.   A glimpse of the home of the Girl on Cloudy Mountain.*

SECOND PICTURE.   *At the foot of Cloudy Mountain, showing the Girl's place of business: the Polka Saloon.*

ACT   I. — *In the Polka Saloon.   Midnight.*
                "The Girl and the Stranger."

ACT II. — *In the home of the Girl, one o'clock in the morning.*
                "Two people who came from nothing."

ACT III. — *The dance-hall of the Polka.   A few days later.   Nine o'clock in the morning.*
                "No star is ever lost we once have seen,
                We always may be what we might have been."

ACT IV. — *The boundless prairies of the West.   At the dawn of a day about a week later.*
                "Oh, my beautiful West!
                Oh, my California!"

Original Cast of THE GIRL OF THE GOLDEN WEST.   First produced at the New Belasco Theatre, Pittsburgh, Penn., — October 3, 1905, and in New York, at the Belasco Theatre, November 14, 1905.

THE GIRL	Blanche Bates
WOWKLE, *an Indian Squaw*	Harriet Sterling
DICK JOHNSON	Robert Hilliard
JACK RANCE	Frank Keenan
SONORA SLIM	John W. Cope
TRINIDAD JOE	James Kirkwood
NICK	Thomas J. McGrane
THE SIDNEY DUCK	Horace James
JIM LARKENS	Fred. Maxwell
"HAPPY" HALLIDAY	Richard Hoyer
"HANDSOME" CHARLIE	Clifford Hipple
DEPUTY SHERIFF	T. Hayes Hunter
BILLY JACKRABBIT, *an Indian*	J. H. Benrime
ASHBY	J. Al. Sawtelle
JOSÉ CASTRO	Roberto Deshen
RIDER OF THE PONY EXPRESS	Lowell Sherman
JAKE WALLACE, *a travelling-camp minstrel*	Ed. A. Tester
BUCKING BILLY	A. M. Beattie
THE LOOKOUT	Fred. Sidney
A FARO-DEALER	William Wild
THE RIDGE BOY	Ira M. Flick
JOE	H. L. Wilson
CONCERTINA PLAYER	Ignazie Biondi

Citizens of the Camp and Boys of the Ridge

THE GIRL OF THE GOLDEN WEST

THE CAST

THE GIRL

WOWKLE, *the fox, Billie's Squaw*

DICK JOHNSON, *a stranger*   (*Ramerrez, the Road-Agent*)

JACK RANCE, *gambler and sheriff*

SONORA SLIM

TRINIDAD JOE

NICK, *bartender at the "Polka"*

THE SIDNEY DUCK, *a faro-dealer*

JIM LARKENS

HAPPY HALLIDAY

HANDSOME CHARLIE

DEPUTY SHERIFF

BILLY JACKRABBIT, *an Indian*

ASHBY, *Wells-Fargo Agent*

JOSÉ CASTRO, *ex-padroña of the bull-fights and horse-breaker, now with Ramerrez' Band*

RIDER OF THE PONY EXPRESS

JAKE WALLACE, *a traveling-camp minstrel*

BUCKING BILLY, *from Watson's*

THE LOOKOUT

A FARO-DEALER

THE BOY FROM THE RIDGE

JOE

CONCERTINA PLAYER

Citizens of the Camp and Boys of the Ridge

TIME.   *During the days of the gold fever, 1849–50*

PLACE.   *Cloudy Mountain, California, a mining camp*

THE GIRL OF THE GOLDEN WEST

ACT I

*The two scenes, which precede the dia-
logue of the play, are not drawn in
detail but are merely a few lines and
lights to show the steep snow-tipped
Sierras, the trail, the silent California
night, deep ravines, and cabins of
the miners of '49 hid amongst the
manzanitas and pines; in fact, the
scene represents a little world by itself, drawn in a few crude strokes,
to explain more than the author could
tell in a thousand pages.*

*The curtain rises to a glimpse of Cloudy
Mountain, in the Sierras. The
peak is white, the sky above very blue,
and the moon, which seems strangely
near, shines on the steep trail leading
up to the cabin of the Girl. A lamp,
placed in the cabin window by
WOWKLE, the squaw, shows that the
Girl has not yet come home from her
place of business, the Polka Saloon.*

*This scene shifts to an exterior view of the
Polka Saloon and the miners' cabins
at the foot of Cloudy Mountain. The
cheerful glow of kerosene lamps, the
rattle of poker chips, and an occasional "whoop", show that life in the
Polka is in full swing. The strains
of "Dooda Day" are heard from
within, the singer accompanying
himself on the concertina:*

"Camp town ladies, sing this song,
　Dooda! Dooda!
Camptown race track, five miles long,
　Dooda! Dooda! Day.
G'wine to run all night,
G'wine to run all day,
Bet my money on a bob-tail nag,
Somebody bet on the bay."

*As the scene shifts to the interior of the
Polka, we see a large square bar-
room, built of rough pine boards. A
pair of scales for weighing gold-dust,
and a dice-box used to "shake for
drinks", are on the bar. Behind*
*the bar on a shelf are liquors, cigars,
and chewing tobacco.*

*The till contains one and two bit pieces,
Mexican dollars, and slugs of gold
($50). The safe is made out of
an empty whiskey keg. Boxes and
cans of provisions lie on the floor,
and strings of red peppers hang
from the rude rafters. A stuffed
grizzly bear graces the scene, a small
green parasol in one paw, a battered
old silk hat on its head. An odd
collection of hats and caps are stuck
on the prongs of a pair of elk antlers
on the wall, and several saddles lie
on the floor under the antlers.*

*The furniture is composed of pine chairs,
a faro table, a poker table, and an
old whittled desk at which the miners
write their rare letters to those at home.*

*A $5000 reward for the road-agent, Ramer-
rez, or information leading to his
capture, signed by Wells-Fargo, is
tacked to the back of the door. The
platform on which a camp minstrel
is singing "Dooda Day" is protected
by a piece of sheet iron which the
musician can lift as a shield to ward
off stray bullets in case of a sudden
quarrel. The room is heated by a
blazing pine log fire in an adobe fireplace. A square opening in the wall
leads to the dance-hall left; a ladder,
resting against a balcony over the bar,
enables the bartender to ascend in case
of trouble and cast a quick glance over
both rooms.*

*As the interior of the barroom is disclosed,
SONORA SLIM, a tall, lanky miner
with an emphatic manner, and
TRINIDAD JOE, his partner, are playing at faro. The dealer is "SID",
an Australian known as "SIDNEY
DUCK", fat, greasy, unctuous, and
cowardly. He is an expert at fancy
shuffling. His even voice is heard
from time to time, murmuring below*

the dialogue, as the game goes on. A case-keeper and lookout complete the group at the faro table. BILLY JACKRABBIT, *a full-blooded Indian, lazy, shifty and beady-eyed, wearing moccasins, odds and ends of a white man's costume, and a quantity of brass jewelry, is watching the game. He frequents the barroom, picking up cigar butts, and occasionally, when the opportunity presents itself, steals a drink.*

HANDSOME CHARLIE, *a big picturesque miner, is drinking at the bar with* HAPPY HALLIDAY, *a long-legged fellow, high-booted and spurred.* NICK, *the bartender, is busy during the act carrying drink into the dance-hall and returning to those in the barroom. He wears 'Frisco trousers, very high-heeled boots, a flashy necktie, a gay velvet vest. He combs his hair over his forehead in a cowlick.*

SONORA [*joining the singer who is accompanying himself on the concertina*]. "Dooda! Dooda! Day!" [*To the faro-dealer*] What did that last eight do?
SID. Lose.
SONORA. Well, let the tail go with the hide.

[NICK, *who has entered, sets a few fresh candles about and gives a drink to the concertina player who goes into the dance-hall*]

TRINIDAD. How many times did the ace win?
SID. Three times.
BILLY JACKRABBIT. Give Billy Jack-rabbit four two dolla — Mexican — chips.

[SIDNEY *gives some chips to the* INDIAN. *As the music starts in the dance-hall, and the shuffling of feet is heard,* HAPPY, *unable to resist, gives a long whoop*]

HAPPY. Root hog or die!

[*With another whoop, he joins the dancers.* HANDSOME *would follow him, but decides to remain to take another drink*]

SONORA [*suspiciously*]. See here, gamboleer Sid, you're too lucky.
TRINIDAD. You bet! More chips, Australiar.

[SID *gives some chips to* TRINIDAD. *The proprietor of a wheel-of-fortune, which is set up in the dance-hall, is heard to call in a professional voice*]

PROPRIETOR OF THE WHEEL-OF-FORTUNE. And round goes the wheel!
HAPPY'S VOICE [*heard above the music*]. Git, you loafer!

[*A muffled shot is heard. The music stops abruptly*]

A VOICE [*from the dance-hall*]. Missed!

[NICK *hastens off, not forgetting to take a bottle and glasses with him. During the excitement,* BILLY JACKRABBIT *steals four cigars from a box on the bar*]

THE PROPRIETOR OF THE WHEEL-OF-FORTUNE. The lone star now rises!

[*The music continues and* NICK *re-enters, giving the* INDIAN *a suspicious glance.* BILLY JACKRABBIT *decides to take himself off for a short time*]

NICK [*explaining as loud whoops are heard*]. Boys from the Ridge — cuttin' up in the dance-hall. Hy're you, Jim?

[JIM LARKENS, *shabby and despondent, a miner who has not struck it rich, returns* NICK's *greeting, gets paper, a pen and ink from the bar, and sits at the desk to write the usual sad letter to his family in the East*]

SONORA [*looking towards the dancers with disgust*]. I don't dance with men for partners. When I chassay, Trinidad, I want a femi*nine* piece of flesh and blood — with garters on!
TRINIDAD. You bet!
SONORA. I say, Nick. [*Going up to the bar, confidentially*] Has the Girl said anything more about me to-day?
NICK [*lying as usual*]. Well, you got the first chance.
SONORA [*grinning*]. Yes? Cigars for the boys.

[NICK *brings a box of cigars to the faro table, and the men smoke*]

VOICE OF THE FIDDLER [*calling in time to the dance music*].
"First lady swing with the right hand gent,
 With the left hand gent, with the right hand gent,
First lady swing with the left hand gent,
And — lady in the centre, and gents all around!"

[*During this, two men from the rival mining-camp at the Ridge, enter — dancing up to the bar*]

SID. Hello, boys! 'Ow's things at the Ridge?

ONE OF THE RIDGE MEN [*defiantly*]. Wipes this camp off the map.

[*All jump to their feet, save SID. The insult calls for immediate punishment*]

SONORA. What?

TRINIDAD. Say it again!

[NICK *persuades the Ridge boys to retire to avert bloodshed, and they disappear with a final defiant whoop as* JAKE WALLACE, *a favorite camp minstrel, who journeys from one camp to another, is heard in the road outside, playing on his banjo and singing*]

JAKE WALLACE.
"Wait for the wagon — wait for the wagon —
Wait for the wagon and we'll all take a ride.
Wait for the wagon, and we'll all take a ride."

NICK [*announcing in extravagant style*]. Aw! Here he is, boys — just up from the Ridge — Jake Wallace, the camp favorite!

[JAKE WALLACE *enters, carrying a banjo, his face half blackened. He wears a long minstrel's duster over his heavy coat, flapping shoes, and a "stove-pipe" hat. He is the typical camp minstrel*]

SONORA. Howdy, Jake!

HANDSOME. Hello, Jake, old man! How be you?

TRINIDAD, SID *and the* CASE-KEEPER. Hello, Jake!

JAKE [*nods, smiling, seats himself on the musician's stand, in the musician's chair*]. Hello, boys! My first selection, friends, will be, "The little —"

SONORA. Aw — give us "Old Dog Tray", Jake.

[JAKE *tunes up*]

TRINIDAD [*apart to* NICK]. Nick, have you saw the Girl?

NICK [*confidentially*]. Well, I gave her your message. You've got the best chance.

[*Digs him playfully in the ribs and winks at him*]

TRINIDAD. Whiskey for everybody.

[NICK *sets out whiskey and glasses, and the men drink*]

JAKE [*strikes a chord, announcing impressively*]. "Old Dog Tray, or Echoes from Home."

[*During the song,* BILLY JACKRABBIT, *who has followed* JAKE *on, sits on the floor playing solitaire. The miners continue to gamble*]

"How often do I picture
Them old folks down to home;
And often wonder if they think of me!"

[JIM LARKENS, *dropping his letter in the box on the floor, chokes back a sob*]

SONORA. Slug's worth of chips.

[SID *gives chips to* SONORA]

JAKE.
"Would angel mother know me,
If back there I did roam?
Would old dog Tray remember me?"

[*The singer pauses to take a drink from* NICK]

Now, boys!

[*All join in the chorus, keeping time with their feet*]

ALL.
"Oh, mother, angel mother, are you a-waitin' there,
Beside the littul cottage on the lea?"

JAKE [*alone*]. "On the lea —"

ALL.
"How often would she bless me, all in them days so fair —
Would old dog Tray remember me?"

SONORA. "Remember me!"

[LARKENS *breaks down and sobs. All stop playing and turn in their chairs, looking at him*]

Why, Jim . . .

LARKENS. Say, boys, — I'm homesick and I'm broke, and I don't give a damn who knows it. I want to go home again. . . . I'm tired o' drillin' rocks. . . . I want to be out in the fields again. . . . I want to see the grain growin'. . . . I want the dirt in the furrows at home. . . . I want old Pennsylvany. . . . I want my folks. . . . I'm done! I'm done! I'm done!

[*He sobs on the bar, his face buried in his hands*]

JAKE [*quite used to these scenes*].
"Oh, mother, angel mother, are you a-waitin' —"
SONORA [*motions* JAKE *to stop singing.* JAKE, *understanding, smilingly makes a gesture as though touching an imaginary hat brim, and collects his money*]. Here, Jake. [*Tosses a coin to* JAKE] Boys, Jim Larkens allows he's goin' back East. Chip in. [*The miners and gamblers throw money on the table. When the cash is handed to* SONORA, *he gives it to* LARKENS] Here you are, Jim.
JIM [*deeply touched*]. Thank you, boys — thank you.

[*Crying, he stumbles out of the room*]

TRINIDAD [*who has suddenly made a lunge at* SID'S *card box*]. That ain't a square deal — he's cheating!

[BILLY JACKRABBIT *picks up a chair, and holds it up to protect himself;* JAKE WALLACE *hides behind the shield. The lookout steals out as though in league with* SID. NICK *re-enters with a large tray of whiskey glasses.* HANDSOME *and the gambler seize* SID *and bring him down in front of the table*]

SONORA. Lift his hand!
TRINIDAD. Hist his arms! [*Taking up the deck of cards and throwing it on the table*] There!
SONORA. String him up!
TRINIDAD. You bet!
SID [*whining*]. For 'eaven's sike!
NICK. Chicken lifter!
TRINIDAD. String him!
SID. Oh, boys! Boys!
RANCE [*who has come in, stands impassively watching the scene. He is the cool, waxen, deliberate gambler. His hands, almost feminine in their whiteness, are as waxen as his face. He has a very black moustache. He wears the beaver hat of the times, and an immaculate suit of broadcloth. His boots are highly polished, long and narrow with high heels, his trousers strapped over them. He wears a white puffed shirt, with a diamond stud held by side chains, and a large diamond flashes on his hand. He smokes the Spanish cigarros*]. Well, gentlemen, what's this?
SONORA. Ah! Here's Jack Rance.

TRINIDAD [*threatening* SID]. The Sheriff!
RANCE. What's the matter with the cyards?

[*He takes out his handkerchief, delicately unfolding it, and flicks it over his boots*]

SONORA. The Sidney Duck's cheated.
TRINIDAD. String him! [*To* SID] Come on, — you!
RANCE. Wait a minute. Don't be hasty, gentlemen. I've got something to say about this. I don't forget, although I am Sheriff of Manzanita County, that I'm running four games. It's men like him cast reflections on square-minded sporting men like myself; and worse — he casts reflections on the Polka, the establishment of the one decent woman in Cloudy.
NICK [*indignant*]. You bet!
SONORA. A lady, damn it! [*Turning on* SID] You lily-covered skunk!
TRINIDAD. String him up!
HANDSOME. Come on!

[*There is a general movement towards* SID]

RANCE. Hold on! Hold on! After all, gents, what's death? A kick and you're off. I've thought of a worse punishment. Give him his coat. [HANDSOME *gives a coat to* SID, *who puts it on*] Stand him over here. [SID *is pushed forward*] Hand me the deuce of spades. [SONORA *gives* RANCE *the card.* RANCE *takes a pin from* SID'S *cravat, and pins the card over* SID'S *heart*] I place it over his heart as a warning. He can't leave the camp, and he never plays cyards again. Handsome, pass the word to the boys.

[HANDSOME *goes into the dance-hall to spread the news*]

SID [*sniffs imploringly*]. Ow — now! Don't say that! Don't say that!
NICK [*pointing to the door*]. Git! Git!

[SID *leaves the room hurriedly, followed by* BILLY JACKRABBIT, *who is never quite comfortable when the* SHERIFF *is laying down the law.* JAKE WALLACE, *one eye on the would-be lynchers, is softly playing* "*Pop Goes the Weasel*"]

RANCE [*coolly, as though nothing had occurred*]. Well, gentlemen, a little

game of poker, just for social recreation?
Nick, chips.

SONORA. Ha! I'm your Injun!

[*Goes to the poker table as* NICK *brings down the poker chips*]

TRINIDAD [*joining* RANCE]. That's me!

[*But before the game can proceed, a* DEPUTY SHERIFF *enters, a gaunt, hollow cheeked, muscular man, with a heavy, sweeping moustache, his hair in a cowlick — wearing a pale, faded beaver hat and a heavy overcoat, his pistol and powder flask in his belt*]

DEPUTY [*to* RANCE]. Sheriff, Ashby, of Wells-Fargo, just rode in with his posse.

RANCE. Ashby? Why, what's he doing here?

DEPUTY. He's after Ramerrez.

RANCE. Ramerrez? Oh, that polite road-agent that's been visitin' the other camps?

DEPUTY. Yes, they say he has just turned into our county.

[NICK *gives the* DEPUTY *a drink*]

SONORA [*apprehensively*]. What? Our county?

[ASHBY *enters, — a man to remember, — nervous, dogged, white and closely-cropped hair, very black eyebrows — thin lips. He wears 'Frisco clothing, which shows the wear and tear of the road. He is suave in his greetings, but quick in action and speech. He is never sober, never drunk, but continually drinking*]

ASHBY [*greeting* RANCE]. Hello, Sheriff!

RANCE. Boys, Mr. Ashby, of Wells-Fargo.

[ASHBY *shakes hands with* TRINIDAD *and* SONORA, *then makes for the bar*]

ASHBY. Hello, Nick!

NICK. Hello, Ash!

ASHBY [*to the* DEPUTY]. How are you, sir? [DEPUTY *returns* ASHBY'S *greeting and passes off, as* ASHBY *shakes hands warmly with* NICK] Nick, give us a drink.

NICK. Sure.

[*Takes four glasses and a bottle of whiskey to the poker table and then hastens off into the dance-hall*]

ASHBY. Everybody'll have the same.
[*The camp minstrel joins the group as*

RANCE *pours the whiskey*] Well, gentlemen, I trust the Girl who runs the Polka is well?

SONORA. Fine as silk, Mr. Ashby. How long you been chasin' up this here road agent?

ASHBY. Oh, he only took to the road three months ago. Wells-Fargo have had me and a posse busy ever since. He's a wonder.

SONORA. Must be, to evade *you*.

ASHBY. Yes, I can smell a road-agent in the wind; but, Rance, I expect to get that fellow right here in your county.

RANCE. Is this Ramerrez a Spaniard?

ASHBY. No, can't prove it. Heads a crew of greasers and Spaniards. His name's assumed.

RANCE. They say he robs you like a gentleman.

ASHBY [*lifting his glass*]. Well, look out for the greasers up the road!

[*All drink*]

RANCE. We don't let 'em pass through here.

ASHBY. Well, boys, I've had a long ride. Wake me up when the Pony Express goes through.

[*Takes off his coat, goes up to a table, and, setting a bottle of whiskey in a convenient spot, lies down on the table*]

NICK [*bringing in a kettle of hot water and glasses containing whiskey and lemon*]. Regards of the Girl. Hot whiskey with lemming extract.

[*He pours the hot water into the glasses*]

RANCE [*accepting a glass*]. Gentlemen, the Girl! The only girl in the Camp — the girl I mean to make Mrs. Jack Rance!

[NICK *catches* SONORA'S *eye, also* TRINIDAD'S]

SONORA. That's a joke, Rance. She makes you look like a Chinaman.

RANCE [*rising, at white heat*]. You prove that!

SONORA. In what particular spot will you have it?

[*Instantly* RANCE'S *right hand creeps towards his pistol as* SONORA, *anticipating his movement, has reached for his weapon. TRINIDAD runs to the bar and drops behind it as* NICK *crouches out of sight at one end of it. JAKE WALLACE hides behind the shield*]

NICK [*seeing* THE GIRL *coming in through the dance-hall*]. The Girl. . . . [*Coaxingly*] Aw — take your drinks.

[TRINIDAD *and* JAKE *venture to peep out. The quarrel is over*]

RANCE. Ha! Ha! Ha! Once more, friends, — the Girl!

ALL. The Girl!

[*They drink.* ASHBY *snores peacefully*]

[THE GIRL *enters. The character of* THE GIRL *is rather complex. Her utter frankness takes away all suggestion of vice — showing her to be unsmirched, happy, careless, untouched by the life about her. Yet she has a thorough knowledge of what the men of her world generally want. She is used to flattery — knows exactly how to deal with men — is very shrewd — but quite capable of being a good friend to the camp boys*]

[HANDSOME *follows her and stands leaning against the bar, watching her admiringly*]

GIRL. Hello, boys! How's everything? Gettin' taken care of?

SONORA [*who melts whenever he sees her*]. Hello, Girl!

GIRL. Hello, Sonora!

TRINIDAD. Hello, Girl!

GIRL. Hello, Trin.

SONORA. Mix me a prairie oyster.

GIRL. I'll fix you right up, Sonora. [*As shots are heard in the dance-hall*] Say, Nick — you quiet things down. [NICK *leaves the room*] They've had about enough. Look here, Sonora: before I crack this egg, I'd like to state that eggs is four bits apiece — only two hens left. [*Giving a little push to* HANDSOME, *who has been leaning on the bar*] Oh, run away, Handsome.

[HANDSOME *sits, watching* THE GIRL]

SONORA. Crack the egg — I'll stand it.

NICK [*re-entering, grinning, pouring out a drink, going to* THE GIRL]. Regards of Blond Harry.

GIRL [*taking it*]. Here: give it to me — [*pouring it back into the bottle*] — and say it hit the spot.

NICK [*whispering*]. Say, Min: throw around a few kind words — good for the bar.

GIRL [*good-naturedly*]. Oh, you! [*Exit* NICK *to deliver* THE GIRL'S *message to* BLOND HARRY] Ha! Ha! [*As* ASHBY *awakens*] Hello, Mr. Ashby!

ASHBY [*rousing and gallantly picking up his glass, goes to the bar to toast* THE GIRL]. Compliments of Wells-Fargo!

GIRL. Thank you. [*Shaking* SONORA'S *drink*] You see we live high shouldered here in Cloudy.

SONORA. You bet!

ASHBY. What cigars have you?

GIRL. Regalias, Auroras and Eurekas.

ASHBY. Any'll do.

NICK [*entering hurriedly*]. Man jest come in threatin' to shoot up the furniture.

GIRL [*quietly, giving* ASHBY *a cigar*]. Who is it?

NICK. Old man Watson.

GIRL. Leave him shoot. He's good for it.

VOICE [*from the inner room*]. Nick! Nick!

[NICK *hastens off as several shots are heard. In the excitement,* BILLY JACKRABBIT, *who has re-entered, quietly steals down to the faro table and drains a glass of whiskey which has been left standing there*]

GIRL. Here, you Billy Jackrabbit: what are you doing? Did you marry my squaw yet?

BILLY JACKRABBIT. Not so much married squaw yet.

GIRL. No so much married? Come here, you thieving redskin — [BILLY JACKRABBIT *goes up to the bar*] with a pocketful of my best cigars! [*She takes the cigars from him*] You git up to my cabin and marry my squaw before I get there. Git! [BILLY JACKRABBIT *goes out*] With a papoose six months old — it's awful! Here, Sonora: [*bringing him the drink*] here's your prairie oyster. Hello, Rance!

RANCE. Hello, Girl!

SONORA. Here, Girl: clear the slate out of that. [*Giving her a bag of gold-dust*]

NICK [*re-entering with a bottle*]. Say, they's a fellow in there wants to know if we can help out on provisions.

GIRL. Sure. What does he want?

NICK. Bread.

[*Putting the cigar-box and bottle back on the shelf*]

GIRL [*behind the bar*]. Bread! Does he think we're runnin' a bakery?

NICK. Then he asked for sardines.

GIRL. Sardines! Great Gilead! You tell him we have nothing but straight provisions here: we got pickled oysters, smoking tobacco, an' the best whiskey he ever saw.

NICK. Yes'm.

TRINIDAD. You bet!

GIRL. Sonora. [*Gives him his change. Cleaning the slate on which she keeps the record of the drinks*] Mr. Ashby, — change. [*She hands* ASHBY *some coins*]

ASHBY [*throws the money back on the bar*]. Keep the change. Buy a ribbon at the Ridge. Compliments of Wells-Fargo.

GIRL [*sweeping it into the drawer*]. Thank you.

SONORA. Girl: [*going up to the bar*] buy *two* ribbons at the Ridge. [*Throwing down a stack of silver dollars on the bar and facing* ASHBY. *Insinuatingly*] Fawn's *my* color! . . .

GIRL. Thank you.

RANCE. Play cyards.

ASHBY [*changing — raising his finger warningly*]. You, Girl! You must bank with us oftener, and then if this road-agent, Ramerrez, should drop in, you won't lose so much.

SONORA. The devil!

TRINIDAD [*thoughtfully*]. Ha!

GIRL. Oh, go on! I keep the specie in an empty keg now, but personally I've took to banking in my stocking.

NICK [*who has brought in an armful of wood and mended the fire*]. Say, we've got an awful pile this month — makes me sort o' nervous. Why, Sonora alone has got ten thousand in that keg fer safe keepin'. [*Pointing to a keg at the end of the bar*]

ASHBY. And Ramerrez' band everywhere!

GIRL. Bet if a road-agent come in here, I could offer him a drink an' he'd treat me like a perfect lady.

SONORA. You bet he would, the darned old halibut!

NICK. Tobacco.

GIRL. Solace of Honeydew?

NICK. Dew. [*He takes it and is about to exit when the* DEPUTY *enters wildly*]

DEPUTY. Boys! Boys! Pony Express!

[*The sound of the approaching pony has grown louder, and now stops quickly*]

DRIVER OF THE PONY EXPRESS [*heard off*]. Hello!

[NICK *runs out*]

DEPUTY'S VOICE [*outside*]. Hello!

DRIVER OF THE PONY EXPRESS [*unseen, speaking through the open door as though on horseback*]. Big hold-up last night at the Forks.

TRINIDAD. Hold-up?

DRIVER OF THE PONY EXPRESS. Ramerrez!

[*Enter* NICK *with several letters and one newspaper. He gives the mail to* THE GIRL *and goes to the bar*]

SONORA. Ramerrez!

ASHBY [*to* THE GIRL]. You see?

DRIVER OF THE PONY EXPRESS [*still out of sight*]. Look sharp! There's a greaser in the trail.

RANCE. A greaser? Deputy, go find him.

GIRL [*looking over the mail*]. Sonora, you got a newspaper.

[SONORA *receives it joyously*]

DRIVER OF THE PONY EXPRESS. So long!

ASHBY [*going to the door — calls*]. Pony Express: I want you.

HANDSOME [*leaning over* SONORA — *enviously*]. Sonora's got a newspaper.

SONORA. Yes — damn thing's two months old.

HANDSOME [*wistfully*]. Still, he *did* get a newspaper.

[*The* DRIVER *of the Pony Express enters, coming quickly towards* ASHBY. *He is a thin young fellow of twenty — his skin deeply tanned by the wind — smooth-faced but unshaven. His clothing is weather-beaten and faded by wind, rain, dust and alkali. A leather patch is stitched over the seat of his breeches. His shabby leather gloves proclaim hard service. He is booted and spurred, and has a pistol in his belt. He carries a mail pouch*]

ASHBY. You drop mail at the greaser settlement?

DRIVER OF THE PONY EXPRESS. Yes, sir — tough place.

ASHBY. Know a girl there named Nina Micheltoreña?

GIRL [*laughs*]. Nina Micheltoreña? Oh, they all know her. Whoo! She's one of them Cachuca girls, with droopy Spanish eyes. Oh, ask the boys about her! [*She slaps* HANDSOME *and* TRINIDAD *on the back*]

[*The music starts in the dance-hall and* THE GIRL *runs off to see that her patrons are enjoying the evening.* HANDSOME, SONORA *and* TRINIDAD *follow her off*]

ASHBY [*to the* DRIVER OF THE PONY EXPRESS]. Hold her letters.

DRIVER OF THE PONY EXPRESS. Yes, sir. [*He hastens off to ride to the next camp*]

ASHBY [*to* RANCE]. Sheriff: I expect to see this Nina Micheltoreña to-night — here — in the Polka.

RANCE. You do? Well, the boys better look out for their watches. I met that lady once.

ASHBY. She wrote about that five thousand reward I offered for Ramerrez.

RANCE. What! She's after that? [*Shuffling the cards*]

ASHBY. She knows something. [*Getting his coat. To* THE GIRL *who has re-entered and gone behind the bar*] Well, I'll have a look at that greaser up the road. He may have his eye on the find in that stocking of yours.

GIRL [*good-naturedly*]. You be darned!

[ASHBY *goes out*]

RANCE. Say, Minnie —

GIRL [*polishing glasses*]. H'm?

RANCE. Will you marry me?

GIRL. Nop.

RANCE [*going to the bar*]. Why not?

GIRL. 'Cause you got a wife in Noo Orleans — or so the mountain breezes say.

RANCE. Give me some cigars.

GIRL [*handing him cigars from a certain box*]. Them's your kind, Jack.

RANCE [*putting the cigars in his case*]. I'm stuck on you.

GIRL [*lightly*]. Thank you.

RANCE. I'm going to marry you.

GIRL. Think so?

RANCE. H'm . . . [*Lighting a cigar*]

GIRL. They ain't a man here goin' to marry me.

NICK [*entering hurriedly*]. One good cigar.

GIRL [*handing a cigar to* NICK]. Here's your poison. Three bits. [*To* RANCE] Why, look at 'em! There's Handsome: got two wives I know of somewhere East — [*Turning suddenly to* NICK] Who's that cigar for?

NICK. Tommy!

GIRL. Give it back. He don't know a good cigar when he's smoking it. [*She puts the cigar back in the box, takes another and hands it to* NICK] Same

price. [NICK *goes off with the cigar*] And Trin with a widder in Sacramento; and you — Ha! Not one of you travellin' under your own name.

NICK [*comes back, grinning*]. One whiskey.

GIRL [*pouring out the whiskey and giving it to* NICK]. Here you be.

NICK. With water.

GIRL [*putting the bottle back*]. No, no, you don't: no fancy drinks here.

NICK. Feller just rode in from the Crossin' — says he wants it with water.

GIRL. He'll take it straight, or git!

NICK. But he won't git.

GIRL. You send him to me — I'll curl his hair for him!

NICK. Yes'm. [*Exit*]

RANCE [*earnestly*]. Give you a thousand dollars on the spot for a kiss.

GIRL. Some men invite bein' played.

RANCE. Well, what are men made for? [*Putting down a gold piece*]

GIRL [*taking it*]. That's true.

RANCE. You can't keep on running this place alone — it's getting too big for you. Too much money circulating through the Polka. You need a man behind you. Marry me.

GIRL. Nop.

RANCE. My wife won't know it.

GIRL. Nop.

RANCE. Now, see here, Min —

GIRL [*firmly*]. No — take it straight, Jack — nop! Ah, come along: start your game again, Jack. Come along. [*Going to the faro table,* RANCE *following her*] Whoop la! Mula! Good Lord, look at that faro table!

RANCE. Listen: we may not have another chance.

GIRL. Look here, Jack: let's have it right now. I run this Polka alone because I like it. My father taught me the business, and — well, don't worry about me — I can look after myself. I carry my little wepping — [*touching her pocket to show that she has a pistol*] I'm independent — I'm happy — the Polka's paying an' — ha! — it's all bully! Say, what the devil do you mean proposin' to me with a wife in Noo Orleans? Now, this is a respectable saloon — an' I don't want no more of that talk.

RANCE. I didn't say nothin'.

GIRL [*tidying the faro table*]. Push me that queen. [RANCE *slowly hands the card to her and, going to the table, leans thoughtfully against a chair*] Thank you, Jack. No offence, Jack;

but I got other idees of married life from what you have.

RANCE. Aw! Nonsense!

GIRL [*leaning against the faro table, facing* RANCE]. I dunno about that. You see I had a home once, and I ain't forgot it. A home up over our little saloon in Soledad. Ha! I ain't forgot my father an' mother an' what a happy married couple they was. Lord! How they loved each other — it was beautiful!

SID [*entering, snivelling*]. Ow, Miss...

GIRL. Say — I've heard about you — you git! [SID *hastily takes his departure.* To RANCE] I can see mother now ... fussin' over father an' pettin' him, an' father dealin' faro — Ah, but he was square ... and me, a kid as little as a kitten, under the table sneakin' chips for candy. Talk about married life! That was a little heaven. I guess everybody's got some remembrance of their mother tucked away. I always see mine at the faro table with her foot snuggled up to Dad's an' the light of lovin' in her eyes. Ah, she was a lady! No; [*getting up from the table and going behind the bar*] I couldn't share that table an' the Polka with any man — unless there was a heap o' carin' back of it. I couldn't, Jack, I couldn't.

RANCE [*restraining his anger*]. Oh, the boys were right! I *am* a Chinaman! [*Following her up to the bar*]

GIRL. No, you're not, Jack.

RANCE [*following her*]. But once when I rode in here, it was nothing but Jack — Jack — Jack — Jack — Jack Rance! God! I nearly got you then.

GIRL [*with playful sarcasm*]. Did you?

RANCE. Then you went on that trip to Sacramento and Monterey ... and you changed. ... Who's the man?

GIRL. Ha! Ha! Ha! Ha!

RANCE. One of them high-toned Sacramento shrimps? [*As she laughs*] Do you think he'd have *you*?

GIRL [*suddenly serious*]. What's the matter with me? Anythin' about me a high-toned gent would object to? Look here, Jack Rance, ain't I always been a perfect lady?

RANCE. Oh, Heaven knows your character's all right. [*He goes back to the faro table*]

GIRL [*sarcastically*]. Well, that ain't your fault. Adios. [*She starts to leave the room, then pauses and looks at him*] Jack ... [*As he will not look at her, she turns again to go into the dance-hall, but, looking off, she sees an unexpected guest and exclaims in surprise*] H'mp! Utopia! [*She goes behind the bar*]

[MR. JOHNSON *enters the room from the dance-hall. He is a young man of about 30 — smooth-faced, tall. His clothing is bought in fashionable Sacramento. He is the one man in the place who has the air of a gentleman. At first acquaintance, he bears himself easily but modestly, yet at certain moments there is a devil-may-care recklessness about him. He is, however, the last man in the world one would suspect of being the road-agent, Ramerrez*]

JOHNSON. Where's the man who wanted to curl my hair?

[RANCE *turns to look at the stranger*]

GIRL [*who remembers* JOHNSON *as a man she met on the road to Monterey*]. Hello — er — stranger. [JOHNSON *looks at* THE GIRL]

RANCE. We're not much on strangers here.

JOHNSON. I'm the man who wanted water in his whiskey.

GIRL. You, eh? [*To* NICK *who comes back with a bottle and glasses*] Oh, — er — Nick, this gentleman takes his whiskey as he likes it.

NICK. Moses!

JOHNSON [*coming to the bar*]. In the presence of a lady — I will take — nothing. [*Bows to her with formality*] Pardon me, but you seem to be almost at home here.

[NICK *laughs softly*]

GIRL [*amused*]. Who — me? [*Leaning on the bar*]

NICK [*laughing*]. Why, she's the Girl who runs the Polka. [*He passes off, still laughing*]

JOHNSON [*staring at* THE GIRL]. You?

GIRL. Yep.

JOHNSON [*meditating*]. The Girl who runs the Polka. ...

[*There is a merry twinkle in* THE GIRL's *eye as she looks at* JOHNSON, *but he is disconcerted. This news interferes with* MR. JOHNSON's *plans*]

GIRL. Yes.

RANCE. You're from the Crossing,

the bartender said. I don't remember you.

JOHNSON. You're mistaken: I said that I rode over from the Crossing. [*Turning to* THE GIRL *again*] So you are the Girl?

GIRL. Yes.

RANCE [*aggressively*]. No strangers allowed in this camp.

[*A pause*]

[THE GIRL *and* JOHNSON *speak in such low tones that* RANCE *is unable to hear them*] Perhaps you're off the road.

[*A pause*]

[THE GIRL *and* JOHNSON *are still talking*] [*Sneeringly*]

Men often get mixed up when they're visiting Nina Micheltoreña on the back trail.

GIRL. Rance!

JOHNSON [*sharply to* RANCE]. I merely stopped in to rest my horse — and perhaps try a game of — [*coming to the table*] er — poker. [*Picking up a pack of cards*]

GIRL. Nick, bring in his saddle.

[*As* NICK *goes for the saddle,* RANCE *rises, annoyed*]

RANCE. A game, eh? I haven't heard your name, young man.

GIRL [*laughs*]. Oh! Names out here!

JOHNSON. My name's Johnson. [*Throwing down the cards*]

GIRL [*cynically*]. Is — how much?

JOHNSON. Of Sacramento.

GIRL. Of — how much? [*Coming down to* JOHNSON *and shaking hands — not believing a word he says*] I admire to know you, Mr. Johnson, of Sacramento.

JOHNSON. Thank you.

RANCE [*angrily*]. Say, Minnie, — I —

GIRL [*aside to* RANCE, *lightly*]. Oh, — set down. [*Turning to* JOHNSON *as* RANCE *indignantly sits on the end of the faro table*] Say, do you know what I think of you? I think you staked out a claim in a etiquette book. So you *think* you can play poker?

JOHNSON. That's my conviction.

GIRL. Out of every fifty men who *think* they can play, one ain't mistaken.

JOHNSON [*following* THE GIRL *to the bar*]. You may be right.

GIRL. Say, try a cigar.

JOHNSON. Thank you.

GIRL. Best in the house — my compliments.   [*She lights a match*]

JOHNSON. Thank you — you're very kind. [*In a lower tone*] So you remember me?

GIRL. If you remember me.

RANCE [*muttering to himself, glancing over his shoulder*]. What the devil are they talking about, anyway?

JOHNSON. I met you on the road to Monterey —

GIRL. Goin' an' comin'. You passed me up a bunch of wild syringa over the wheel. You asked me to go a-berryin', but I didn't see it.

JOHNSON. I noticed that.

GIRL. And when you went away, you said — [*embarrassed*] Oh, I dunno ...

JOHNSON. Yes, you do — yes, you do. I said: "I'll think of you all the time!" Well, I've thought of you ever since.

GIRL. Ha! Somehow I kinder thought you might drop in, but as you didn't . . . of course [*with a sense of propriety*] it wasn't my place to remember you — first.

JOHNSON. But I didn't know where you lived . . . I —

GIRL [*confidentially*]. I got a special bottle here. Best in the house. Will you?

JOHNSON. Why —

GIRL [*gets a bottle and a glass*]. My compliments.

JOHNSON. You are *very* kind. Thanks.

[RANCE *rises and, going up to the bar, proceeds to dash the glass to the floor as* MR. JOHNSON *is about to take it*]

RANCE [*livid*]. Look here, Mr. Johnson: your ways are offensive to me — damned offensive. My name's Rance — Jack Rance. Your business here — your business! [*Calling*] Boys! Boys! Come in! [TRINIDAD, HANDSOME, SONORA *and* HAPPY *come in*] There's a man here who won't explain his business — he —

SONORA, TRINIDAD, HAPPY, HANDSOME [*at the same time*]. What? Won't he? Oh, we'll see! Guess we'll make him.

GIRL. Wait a minute. I know him.

THE BOYS [*as one man*]. Eh?

GIRL [*to* RANCE]. Yes, I didn't tell you, but I know him.

RANCE [*to himself*]. The Sacramento shrimp, by God!

GIRL [*comes from behind the bar*].
Boys: I vouch to Cloudy for Mr.
Johnson.

[*All the men except* RANCE *salute* JOHN-
SON, *who makes a sweeping gesture*]

JOHNSON. Boys . . .
THE BOYS. Hello, Johnson.
SONORA. Boys: Rance ain't runnin'
the Polka yet.

[*A waltz is played as* NICK *enters*]

NICK [*to* THE GIRL]. The boys from
the Ridge invites you to dance with
them.
JOHNSON. May I have the honor of
a waltz?

[TRINIDAD, SONORA *and* HANDSOME
are overcome by the manners of
JOHNSON]

NICK. Moses! [*Retreats to the
dance-hall*]
GIRL. Me waltz? Me? Ha! Oh,
I can't waltz. Ha! — but I can polky.
JOHNSON. Then may I have the
pleasure of the next polka?
SONORA [*to the boys*]. He's too flip.
GIRL. Oh, I dunno. Makes me feel
kind o' foolish, — you know — kind
o' retirin' like a elk in summer.
JOHNSON [*amused*]. Yes, they *are*
retiring.
GIRL [*unconsciously wipes her hands
on her dress*]. Well . . . I don't like
everybody's hand on the back of my
waist; but somehow — [*She looks at*
RANCE *recklessly.* JOHNSON *offers her
his arm. Unused to this formality,
she looks at his proffered arm two or
three times, half ashamed, then she looks
at the boys, who stand watching her with
twinkling eyes*] Oh, Lord, must I?
[*Then making up her mind*] Oh, come
along.
JOHNSON. Thanks.
GIRL [*dances off with* JOHNSON, *calling
to the* FIDDLER]. A polky!

[*In the dance-hall they are acclaimed by
loud whoops*]

SONORA [*to* RANCE]. Chink!
RANCE. Ha! Ha! Cleaned out, by
God! by a high-toned, fine-haired dog
named Johnson. Well, I'll be damned!
[*As* NICK *comes in with a saddle*] What's
that?
NICK. Johnson's saddle.
RANCE [*knocking the saddle out of*
NICK'S *hands*]. You know, Nick —

I've got a great notion to walk out of
this door, and —
NICK [*scenting the loss of a good cus-
tomer*]. Aw, she's only kiddin' him. [*He
removes the saddle to a place of safety*]
ASHBY [*outside*]. Boys!
RANCE. What's that?
TRINIDAD. Why, that's —
NICK. That's Ashby.
ASHBY [*outside*]. Come on — you!
TRINIDAD. What's the matter?
THE DEPUTY SHERIFF [*is heard to
call*]. Run him in.

[*He enters with* ASHBY *and several men.
They bring in* JOSÉ CASTRO. BILLY
JACKRABBIT *follows them on*]

[CASTRO *is an oily, greasy, unwashed
Mexican greaser of a low type. His
clothing is partly Mexican. He is
yellow, sullen, wiry, hard-faced,
tricky and shifty-eyed. He has the
curved legs of a man who lives on a
broncho*]

[ASHBY *is completely transformed. His
hat is on the back of his head, his
hair is ruffled and falls over his
forehead in straggling locks; his
coat is thrown open and his face is
savage and pitiless*]

ASHBY. The greaser in the trail.
RANCE [*takes* CASTRO *by the hair,
throwing him over and forcing his head
back*]. Here, you — give us a look
at your face.
ASHBY. Nick, come — give us a
drink. [*Going to the bar*]
RANCE. Tie him up.

[BILLY JACKRABBIT *goes to the fireplace,
gets the lariat as* RANCE *pushes
CASTRO to the floor*]

ASHBY [*inviting all to drink*]. Come
on, boys.

[*The boys, with the exception of* SONORA,
join ASHBY *at the bar*]

CASTRO [*seeing* JOHNSON'S *saddle on
the floor — to himself*]. Ramerrez' . . .
[*He pauses — overcome*] Taken . . .
ASHBY [*to* SONORA, *who is watching*
THE GIRL *dance*]. Say, my friend,
don't you drink?
SONORA. Oh, occasionally. [*He joins*
ASHBY]
RANCE [*looking off at* THE GIRL].
Polkying!

[NICK *lets down the pelts which screen off
the dance-hall, as* BILLY JACKRABBIT

and the DEPUTY *throw* CASTRO *into
a chair.* CASTRO, *who has caught a
glimpse of* JOHNSON *dancing with*
THE GIRL, *is relieved*]

ASHBY [*having tasted his drink —
going to* CASTRO]. Come now, tell us
what your name is.
HAPPY. You bet!
ASHBY. Speak up! Who are you?
SONORA *and* HANDSOME. Speak up!
What's your name?

[RANCE, *eying* CASTRO, *sits at the faro
table, his legs crossed*]

CASTRO. José Castro, ex-padroña of
the bull-fights.
RANCE. But the bull-fights are at
Monterey. Why do you come to this
place?
CASTRO. To tell the Señor Sheriff
I know where ees — Ramerrez.

[*The men would surround* CASTRO *to
question him, but* RANCE *motions
to them to stand back*]

RANCE. You lie! [*Raises his hand
for silence*]
CASTRO. Nay, plaanty Mexican
vaquero — my friends Peralta — Velle-
jos — all weeth Ramerrez — so I know
where ees.
RANCE [*pointing at him quickly to
take him off his guard*]. You're one of
his men yourself!
CASTRO [*quickly with childlike inno-
cence*]. No — no . . .
RANCE [*pointing to* ASHBY]. That's
Ashby — the man that pays out that
reward you've heard of. Where is
Ramerrez' camp?
CASTRO. Come weeth me one mile,
and, by the soul of my mother, — the
blessed Maria Saltaja, — we weel put
a knife into hees back.
RANCE. One mile, eh?
SONORA. If I thought . . .
RANCE. Where is this trail?
CASTRO. Up the Madroña Canyada.
A MAN [*entering from the dance-hall*].
Hello, boys! What's —
ALL [*warning the new-comer to silence*].
Sh! Git! Git out! Shut up! Git!
RANCE. Go on.
CASTRO. Ramerrez can be taken, if
many men come weeth me . . . forty
minute there and back —
RANCE. What do you think?
ASHBY. Curious . . . This is the
second warning we have had from here.
RANCE [*to* ASHBY]. This Nina

Micheltoreña's letter to you? You
say she is coming here to-night? [*As*
ASHBY *nods*] Looks as though he was
known around here.
ASHBY. All the same, I wouldn't go.
SONORA. What! Risk losin' him?
RANCE. Boys, we'll take the chance.
[*He rises*]
NICK. Want a drink? [*He goes up
to the bar, clearing off the bottles and
glasses*]

[ASHBY *has gone out. The men put on
their overcoats, hats, etc., and prepare to leave in search of the road-
agent. They exclaim:* "Ready,
Sheriff!" "Come on, boys!"
"Come on, Happy!" "Careful,
boys!" etc.]

RANCE [*at the open door, sniffing the
air*]. I don't like the smell of the air.
Snow.   [*He goes out*]
DEPUTY. Load up.
TRINIDAD. Get out the horses.
HAPPY. We'll git this road-agent.
SONORA [*as he passes* CASTRO]. Come
on, you oily, garlic-eating, red-peppery,
dog-trottin' sun-baked son of a skunk!

[*The men hasten off, followed by* BILLY
JACKRABBIT, *leaving* CASTRO, NICK
and the DEPUTY *in the barroom*]

DEPUTY. Come on, you!
CASTRO [*his teeth chattering*]. One
dreenk — I freeze —
DEPUTY. Give him a drink, Nick.
Watch him.   [*He goes out*]
NICK [*contemptuously*]. What'll you
have?
CASTRO [*rises*]. Geeve me —
[*Loudly, suddenly facing the dance-hall
and speaking so that his voice may be
heard by* JOHNSON] aguardiente.
NICK. Set down!

[CASTRO, *looking off, seeing that* JOHN-
SON *has seen him, sits, as* JOHNSON
hastens on from the dance-hall]

JOHNSON. So — you did bring my
saddle in, eh, Nick?
CASTRO [*in a low voice*]. Ramerrez!
. . . Master . . .
JOHNSON. Don't talk . . .
CASTRO. I let them take me, ac-
cording to your beeding.
JOHNSON [*looking toward* NICK].
Careful, José . . . [*Puts the saddle on
the table*]
NICK [*coming down with a drink for
José, who bolts it*]. Here.

Voices [*from the dance-hall*]. Nick! Nick!

Nick. Oh — the Ridge boys goin'. [*Goes back to the bar with the glasses — then speaks to* Johnson] Say — keep your eye on him a minute, will you?

Johnson. Certainly. You tell the Girl you pressed me into service, will you? [*Touches his pistol pocket*]

Nick. Sure. Say, she's taken an awful fancy to you.

Johnson. No!

Nick. Yes. Drop in often — great bar.

Johnson. It certainly is. [Nick *hastens off*] Ha! Ha! Ha! [*To* Castro] Go on . . .

Castro. Bueno! Our men lie in the bushes near, I lead the sheriff far off . . . then I slip away. Queeckly rob thes place now and fly. It is death for you to linger. Ashby ees here.

Johnson [*without looking*]. Ashby! Wait a minute. [*As* Nick *sticks in his head to cast a watchful glance at* Castro] All right, Nick. Yes, everything's all right. [Nick *goes out again as a cachuca is gaily played*]

Castro. By to-morrow twilight, you must be safe in your rancho.

Johnson. No — we'll raid on.

Castro. An hundred men on your track —

Johnson. One minute's start of the devil does me, José.

Castro. I fear the woman, Nina Micheltoreña . . . teeribly I fear. Close at hand . . . knowing all . . . fresh from your four weeks' quarrel with her . . . still loving you.

Johnson. Loving me? Oh, no. Like you, Nina loved the spoils, not me. No, I raid on.

Sonora [*heard outside*]. Bring along the greaser, Dep.

[*The boys are heard off stage and the glare of torches is seen through the windows*]

Deputy [*heard outside*]. All right.

Castro [*to* Johnson]. We start. Queeckly geeve the signal.

Girl [*calling in the dance-hall*]. Good-night, boys — good-night. [*The music ends*] Remember me to the Ridge.

Voices of the Ridge Boys [*off stage*]. You bet! So long! Whoop! Whooppee!

Castro. All gone. Only the woman there — and her servant. . . . Antonio waits your signal.

Deputy [*entering*]. Come on.

Castro. Adios.

Johnson. Adios.

Deputy. Come on.

[*He drags* Castro *off. We hear the boys moving away.* Johnson *takes up his saddle*]

Girl [*entering from the dance-hall*]. Nick, you can put the lights out. [Nick *puts out the candle over the table*] Put the lights out here, too. Oh, you ain't goin'?

Johnson. Not yet, no, but . . .

Girl. I'm glad of that. Don't it feel funny here? It's kind of creepy. I suppose that's because I never remember seeing the bar so empty before. [*Putting a chair in place*]

Nick [*putting out the candle on the mantelpiece*]. I'm goin' to close the shutters. [*He closes the shutters*]

Girl [*crossing to the table*]. What for — so early?

Nick [*in a half whisper*]. Well, you see, the boys is out huntin' Ramerrez — and they's too much money here.

Girl. Oh, all right. Cash in. Don't put the head on the keg. I ain't cashed in m'self yet.

Nick [*rolling out the keg*]. Say, Min . . .

Girl. Huh?

Nick [*looking uneasily at the keg, and then darting a glance towards* Johnson]. Know anything about — him?

Girl. Oh, sure.

Nick. All right, eh?

Girl. Yes. [Nick *blows out the lights at the door, and goes into the empty dance-hall*] Well, Mr. Johnson: it seems to be us a-keepin' house here to-night, don't it?

Johnson. Strange how things come about. . . . Strange to be looking everywhere for you, and to find you at last at the Polka. [*Sitting on the table*]

Girl. Anything wrong with the Polka?

Johnson. Well, it's hardly the place for a young woman like you.

Girl. How so?

Johnson. It's rather unprotected, and —

Girl. Oh, pshaw! I said to Ashby only to-night: "I bet if a road-agent come in here, I could offer him a drink an' he'd treat me like a perfect lady." Say, won't you take something? [*Going back of the bar for a bottle*]

JOHNSON. No, thank you. I'd like to ask you a question.

GIRL. I know what it is — every stranger asks it, but I didn't think *you* would. It's this: am I decent? Yep, I am — you bet!

JOHNSON. Oh, Girl: I'm not blind — that was not the question.

GIRL [*leaning over the bar, looking at him*]. Dear me suz!

JOHNSON. What I meant to say was this: I am sorry to find you here almost at the mercy of the passer-by . . . where a man may come, may drink, may rob you if he will; and where I daresay more than one has even laid claim to a kiss.

GIRL. They's a good many people claimin' things they never git. [*She is putting her money in a cigar-box*] I've got my first kiss to give.

JOHNSON [*studying her*]. You're clever. Been here long?

GIRL. Yep.

JOHNSON. Live in the Polka?

GIRL. Nop.

JOHNSON. Where do you live?

GIRL. Cabin up the mountain a little ways.

JOHNSON. You're worth something better than this.

GIRL. What's better'n this? I ain't boastin', but if keepin' this saloon don't give me a sort of position round here, I dunno what does. Ha! Look here: say, you ain't one of them exhorters, are you, from the missionaries' camp?

JOHNSON. My profession has its faults, but I am not an exhorter.

GIRL. You know I can't figger out jest exactly what you are.

JOHNSON. Try.

GIRL [*getting a chair from behind the poker table*]. Well — you ain't one of us.

JOHNSON. No?

GIRL. Oh, I can tell — I can spot my man every time. I tell you, keepin' saloon is a great educator. [*Sitting*] I dunno but what it's a good way to bring up girls. They git to know things. Now, I'd trust you.

JOHNSON. You would trust me?

GIRL. Notice I danced with you to-night?

JOHNSON. Yes.

GIRL. I seen from the first you was the real article.

JOHNSON. I beg pardon.

GIRL. Why, that was a compliment I handed to you.

JOHNSON. Oh . . .

GIRL [*confidentially*]. Your kind don't prevail much here . . . I can tell — I got what you call a quick eye.

JOHNSON. I'm afraid that men like me — prevail, as you say, almost everywhere.

GIRL. Go on! What are you giving me? Of course they don't. Ha! Before I went on that trip to Monterey, I thought Rance here was the genu*ine* thing in a gent — but the minute I kind o' glanced over you on the road — I — I seen he wasn't. Say — take your whiskey — and water. [*She rises*]

JOHNSON. No.

GIRL [*calling*]. Nick? [*Changing her mind*] No, I'll help you to a drink myself.

JOHNSON. No, thank you.

GIRL [*leaning against the bar, studying him*]. Say, I've got you figgered out: you're awful good, or awful bad. . . .

JOHNSON [*half amused*]. Now what do you mean by that?

GIRL. Well, so good that you're a teetotaler — or so bad that you're tired of life an' whiskey.

JOHNSON [*rising and going up to her*]. On the contrary, although I'm not good — I've lived, and I've liked life pretty well, and I am not tired of it: it's been bully! [*Leaning on the bar*] So have you liked it, Girl, only you haven't lived — you haven't lived. [*He attempts to take* THE GIRL'S *hand, but she retreats*] Not with *your* nature. You see, I've got a quick eye, too.

[NICK *enters slowly and prepares to seat himself in a chair back of the poker table*]

GIRL. Nick, git! [NICK *casts an inquisitive glance at the pair and hastens out*] Say, what do you mean by — I haven't lived?

JOHNSON [*insinuatingly, half under his breath*]. Oh, you know.

GIRL. No, I don't.

JOHNSON. Yes, you do.

GIRL. Well, say it's an even chance I do and an even chance I don't.

JOHNSON [*in a low voice*]. I mean life for all it's worth . . . to the utmost . . . to the last drop in the cup . . . so that it atones for what's gone before, or may come after.

GIRL. No, I don't believe I do know what you mean by them words. Is it a — [*She crosses to the poker table and sits down on her revolver which is in her pocket. She rises hastily*] Oh, Lord! Excuse me — I set on my gun. [*Impulsively*] I can't pass you on the road. I take your dust. Look here: I'm goin' to make you an offer.

JOHNSON. An offer?

GIRL. It's this: if ever you need to be staked —

JOHNSON. Eh?

GIRL. Which of course you don't, — name your price — jest for the style I'll git from you an' the deportment.

JOHNSON. Deportment? Me?

NICK [*re-entering*]. Oh, er — I'd like to say —

GIRL [*annoyed*]. Oh!

[NICK *goes off hurriedly*]

JOHNSON. Well, I never heard before that my society was so desirable. Apart from the financial aspect of the matter — I —

GIRL [*admiringly, half to herself*]. Ain't that great? Ain't that great? Oh, you got to let me stand treat. [*Calls*] Nick? [*She slips down from the table where she has been seated*]

JOHNSON. No, really. Say, Girl: you're like finding some new kind of flower.

GIRL. You know the reason I made you that offer is — we're kind of rough up here, but we're reaching out. Now, I take it that what we're all put on this earth for — every one of us — is to rise ourselves up in the world — to reach out.

JOHNSON [*with a change of manner*]. That's true — that's true. I venture to say there isn't a man who hasn't thought seriously about that. I have. If only a man knew how to reach out for something he hardly dare even hope for. It's like trying to catch the star shining just ahead.

GIRL. That's the cheese. You've struck it.

[NICK *enters*]

NICK. I *have* been a-tryin' to say —

GIRL. What *is* it, Nick?

NICK. I jest seen an ugly lookin' greaser outside a winder.

GIRL [*going up to the door*]. A greaser? Let me look.

JOHNSON [*who knows that it is his man, awaiting the signal — speaking with an air of authority*]. I wouldn't.

GIRL. Why not?

NICK. I'll bolt all the winders. [*He goes off*]

[*A whistle is heard outside.* JOHNSON *recognizes the signal*]

GIRL. Don't that sound horrid? [*Getting behind the counter*] I'm awful glad you're here. Nick's so nervous. He knows what a lot of money I've got. Why, there's a little fortune right in that keg.

JOHNSON [*crossing over to the keg and looking at it*]. In that keg?

GIRL. The boys sleep round it nights.

JOHNSON. But when they're gone — isn't that a careless place to leave it?

GIRL [*coming down to the keg*]. Oh, they'd have to kill me before they got it.

JOHNSON. I see — it's *your* money.

GIRL. No, it belongs to the boys.

JOHNSON. Oh, that's different. Now, I wouldn't risk my life for that.

GIRL [*putting the bags of gold-dust in the keg, and closing the keg and standing with her foot on it*]. Oh, yes, you would — yes, you would — if you seen how hard they got it. When I think of it — I — I nearly cry. You know there's something awful pretty in the way the boys hold out before they strike it — awful pretty — in the face of rocks and clay and alkali. Oh, Lord, what a life it is, anyway! Why, they eat dirt — an' they sleep dirt, an' they breathe dirt till their backs are bent, their hands twisted, their souls warped; they're all wind-swept an' blear-eyed — an' some of 'em just lie down in their own sweat beside the sluices, an' they don't never rise again. I've seen 'em there. I got some money of old Brownie's. [*Pointing to the keg*] He was lyin' out in the sun on a pile of clay two weeks ago an' I guess the only clean thing about him was his soul — an' he was quittin' — quittin' right there on the clay — an' quittin' hard. . . . [*Remembering the scene with horror*] Oh, he died — jest like a dog . . . you wanted to shoot him to help him along quicker. Before he went, he sez: "Girl, give it to my old woman," and he — left. She'll git it. [*Slight pause*] An' that's what aches you. They ain't one of these men working for themselves alone. The Almighty never put it in no man's heart to make a beast or pack-horse of himself — except for some woman, or some child. Ain't it wonderful? Ain't it wonderful, that instinct, ain't it? — What a man'll do when it comes to a woman.

Ain't it wonderful? Yep, the boys use me as a — ha — sort of lady bank. [*She wipes her eyes*] You bet I'll drop down dead before anyone'll get a dollar of theirs outer the Polka!

JOHNSON [*after a short pause*]. That's right. [*Taking* THE GIRL'S *hand*] I'm with you. I'd like to see anyone get that. [*They shake hands over the keg — not heroically, but very simply*] Girl, you make me wish I could talk more with you, but I can't. By daybreak I must be a long way off. I'm sorry. I should have liked to call at your cabin.

GIRL [*wistfully*]. Must you be movin' — so — soon?

JOHNSON. I'm only waiting till the posse gets back and you're safe. [*Listening*] There. . . . They're coming now. . . .

GIRL. I'm awful sorry you got to go. I was goin' to say: [*rolling the keg up stage, she takes a lantern off the bar and sets it on the keg*] if you didn't have to go so soon, I'd like to have you come up to the cabin to-night, and we would talk of reaching out up there. You see, the boys will come back here. . . . We close the Polka at one — any time after that.

JOHNSON. I — I should ride on now — but — I'll come.

GIRL. Oh, good! [*Giving the lantern to* JOHNSON] You can use this lantern. It's the straight trail up — you can't miss it. Say, don't expect too much of me — I've only had thirty-two dollars' worth of education. [*Her voice breaks, her eyes fill with tears*] P'raps if I'd had more — why, you can't tell what I might have been. Say, that's a turrible thought, ain't it? What we — might have been? And I know it when I look at you.

JOHNSON [*touched*]. God knows it is! What we might have been — and *I* know it when I look at *you*, Girl — I know it — when I look at you.

GIRL [*wipes away a tear*]. You bet! [*Suddenly collapses, burying her face on her arm on the bar, sobbing, speaking through her tears*] Oh, 'tain't no use — I'm ignorant — I don't know nothin' and I never knowed it till to-night. The boys always told me I knowed so much — but they're such damned liars.

JOHNSON [*comes up and leans on the bar. Earnestly, with a suggestion of tears in his voice*]. Don't you care — you're all right, Girl — you're all right.

Your heart's all right — that's the main thing. As for your looks, — to me you've got the face of an angel. I — I'll just take a glance at my horse. [*He takes up his saddle, crosses to the door, then turns back. To himself*] Johnson, what the devil's the matter with you? [*He goes out hastily, carrying the lantern and slamming the door behind him*]

[THE GIRL *stands immovable for a moment, then calls suddenly*]

GIRL. Nick! Nick! [NICK *enters quickly. She turns her face away, wiping off a tear*] You run over to the Palmetter rest'rant an' tell 'em to send me up two charlotte rusks an' a lemming turnover — jest as quick as they can — right up to the cabin for supper.

[NICK *goes off*]

Ha! [*She crosses to the poker table and sits on the edge, the light above shining down on her face. Strumming on a guitar and mandolin is heard as though the musicians were tuning up for the boys*] He says . . . He says . . . [*sentimentally*] I have the face of an angel. [*A little pause, then turning her face away*] Oh, Hell!

CURTAIN

ACT II

"Two people who came from nothing."

SCENE. — *The home of* THE GIRL *on Cloudy Mountain. One o'clock in the morning.*

The interior of the cabin has but one room, square, and made of logs. It is half papered as though the owner had bought wall-paper in camp and the supply had given out.

There is but one door, and that leads to the trail. This door, in the centre at back, is double boarded and fastened by a heavy bar. It opens on a rough vestibule, built to keep out the storms and cold.

The windows, at which are calico curtains, are provided with heavy wooden shutters and bars. The barred door and windows give an air of security to the room as though it could be made into a little fortress.

The furniture is rather primitive. A bed, screened off by calico curtains, stands at the right side of the room.

Below the bed is a bureau covered by a Navajo blanket on which a few crude toilet articles are set about. A cheap black framed mirror, decorated with strings of Indian beads and white cambric roses, hangs over the bureau. A wash-stand, backed by a "splasher" of white oilcloth, is near the bed. On the opposite side of the room, a pine wardrobe, rudely painted by a miner, contains most of THE GIRL'S clothing. A sunbonnet and shawl hang on a peg driven into the side of the wardrobe. A gay hat-box from Monterey and a small basket grace the top of the wardrobe. A calico curtain covers a few garments hanging on pegs. In an angle, formed by a fireplace, is a row of shelves, holding tin cups, Indian baskets, two plates, a tin can, knives, forks and spoons. A rocking-chair, made of a barrel, set on rockers and dyed with blueing, is embellished with calico cushions and an anti-macassar. There are four other chairs in the room. A pine table is almost in the centre of the room. It is covered with a red cloth and over this a white table-cloth. Three dishes are on the table; one contains the charlotte "rusks", one the "lemming" turnover, and the other holds biscuit and chipped beef. A sugar bowl with brown sugar is placed in the centre of the table. A fire burns in a fireplace which has an iron hood, a big back log and a smaller log in front. A pile of wood lies on the floor close at hand. A kettle hangs over the fire and a coffee-pot is set on a log. A few china ornaments, a bunch of winter berries stuck in a glass jar, and a bottle of whiskey with two glasses, are on the mantel. A box is nailed on the wall to form a bookshelf for a few well-worn old books. A wolf skin and moccasins are in front of the bureau, a large bear-skin rug is on the floor opposite the fireplace. A few pictures taken from "Godey's Lady's Book", one or two old prints, and a large sombrero hat hang on the wall. A horse-shoe over the door and the head of a small antelope, an old pair of snowshoes over the window and a lady's night-dress on a peg, complete the decorations in the lower part of the room. Above is a loft reached by a ladder which is swung up out of the

way. By standing on a chair and reaching up, the ladder may be pulled down to the floor. Some old trunks and a few little boxes are neatly piled on the floor of the loft. Blankets screen off one end of the attic. A lamp hangs from an arm (swinging from the loft above) and shines down on the table. The winter is now beginning, and, although there is no evidence of snow in the early part of the act, the cabin windows are heavily frosted. When the curtain rises, the scene is lighted by the lamps and the glow from the fireplace. The moon is shining brightly through the window.

At the rise of the curtain, WOWKLE, a squaw, is seated on the floor, singing, her papoose on her back. She is dressed in a long cloth skirt, a short red calico skirt hanging over it. She wears moccasins. Her hair is parted in the middle and drawn into two tight little blue-black braids, crossed in the back, low in the neck. She wears a number of glass bead necklaces and small silver hoops in her ears. She is young, beady-eyed, sweet-faced, and rather plump, — the lax, uncorseted, voluptuous type of squaw. She is perfectly good-natured, at times quizzical, but utterly unreliable and without any ideas of morality.

[BILLY JACKRABBIT enters]

BILLY JACKRABBIT. Ugh!

WOWKLE. Ugh! [As BILLY JACKRABBIT comes towards WOWKLE, he sees the food on the table, looks at it greedily, picks up a plate and is about to stick his finger into the contents] Charlotte rusk — Palmetto rest'rant. Not take.

BILLY JACKRABBIT [putting the plate back on the table]. H'm . . . H'm . . . Me honest.

WOWKLE. Huh! [BILLY stoops and picks up a piece of paper to which some of the food (which has been wrapped in it) still clings. He rubs his fingers over the paper and licks them during the following conversation]

BILLY JACKRABBIT [grunting, sitting down beside WOWKLE]. Send me up from Polka — say p'raps me marry you . . . . Huh?

WOWKLE [impassively]. Me don't know.

[Pause]

BILLY JACKRABBIT. Me don't know.

[*A slight pause. They are sitting side by side on the floor — unlike lovers — just two Indians*] Me marry you, how much me got give fatha — Huh?

WOWKLE [*indifferently with a black look*]. Huh! Me don't know.

BILLY JACKRABBIT. Me don't know. [*Pause*] Me give fatha four dolla — [*indicating with his fingers — licking one as he speaks*] — and one blanket.

WOWKLE. Betta me keep um blanket for baby.

BILLY JACKRABBIT [*grunts*]. Me give fatha three dolla and baby.

WOWKLE. We keep um baby.

BILLY JACKRABBIT. Tawakawa. [*Tearing off a piece of the sticky paper and handing it to* WOWKLE]

WOWKLE. Toanimbutuc. [BILLY *offers to let the baby lick the paper, but* WOWKLE *draws the child away*] Aie! Missionary woman at Battla Ridge him say marry first — then baby.

BILLY JACKRABBIT [*who has licked the paper clean, and is now smoking his pipe*]. Huh!

WOWKLE. Me say baby first . . . him say all right, but marry — get plenty bead.

BILLY JACKRABBIT [*eying her beads and giving his pipe to* WOWKLE *who takes a puff*]. You sing hymn for get those bead?

WOWKLE. Me sing — [*singing softly but in a fairly high pitched voice with a slight nasal quality of tone*] "My days are as um grass —"

BILLY JACKRABBIT [*recognizing the air, gives a grunt and joins in with* WOWKLE].

"Or as um faded flowa — Um wintry winds sweep o'er um plain, We pe'ish in — um — ow-a —"

[*Taking his pipe from* WOWKLE] By Gar, to-morrow we go missionary — sing like Hell — get whiskey. [*Rises*] "pe'ish in um ow-a"

[*He goes up to the door and stands there*] Al-right — go missionary to-morrow — get marry — huh?

WOWKLE. Billy Jackrabbit: [*she rises*] p'haps me not stay marry with you for long time.

BILLY JACKRABBIT [*unimpressed*]. Huh! How long — seven monse?

WOWKLE. Six monse.

BILLY JACKRABBIT [*taking a red handkerchief from his pocket, and sticking it between the papoose and the board*]. Um . . . for baby. [*Nudging*

WOWKLE *with his elbow*] You come soon?

WOWKLE. Girl eat suppa first — me come.

BILLY JACKRABBIT [*nudging her again — then going into the vestibule*]. Huh! Girl come.

[THE GIRL *appears outside the door, holding up a lantern. There is a certain suppressed excitement in her manner as she enters, yet she shows a new thoughtfulness and speaks quietly. She looks about as though to see what effect this little cabin will have on* JOHNSON]

GIRL. Turn up the lamps — quick. [*She hangs her lantern on the outer door.* WOWKLE *turns up the lamp on the table*] Hello, Jackrabbit: fixed it?

BILLY JACKRABBIT. Me fix.

GIRL [*who is seated*]. That's good. Now git! [*Rising — going to the table*] Wowkle: it's for two to-night.

WOWKLE. Ugh!

GIRL. Yep.

WOWKLE. Come   anotha? Neva before come anotha.

GIRL. Never you mind. He's coming — he's coming: Pick up the room. What time is it, Wowkle? [*She has hung up her coat and now shakes* WOWKLE. WOWKLE *gets plates, cups, etc.*] Wowkle, what did you do with them red roses?

WOWKLE. Ugh. [*Pointing to the bureau*]

GIRL. Good. [*She finds the roses and arranges them in her hair*] No offense — but I want you to put your best foot forward [*takes a pistol out of her pocket and puts it on the lower end of the bureau*] when you're waitin' on table to-night. This here comp'ny of mine is a man of idees. Oh, he knows everything — sort of a damn-me style. Wowkle, how's the papoose? Father really proposed to you?

WOWKLE. Yep — get marry.

GIRL [*taking a ribbon from a drawer*]. Here: you can have that to fix the baby up for the weddin'. Hurry, Wowkle. I'm going to put them on, [*she sits on the floor and puts on a pair of new slippers which she has taken from the bottom drawer*] — if I can git 'em on. Remember what fun I made of you when you took up with Billy Jackrabbit? "What for?" sez I. Well, perhaps you was right. Perhaps it's nice to have someone you really care for —

who really belongs to you. Perhaps there ain't so much in the saloon business for a woman, after all — an' you don't know what livin' really is. Ah, Wowkle: it's nice to have someone you can talk to, someone you can turn your heart inside out to — [*As a knock sounds on the window*] Oh, Lord! here he is, Wowkle!

[*She tries to conceal herself behind the foot of the bed — one slipper in her hand. SID opens the window and peers in*]

WOWKLE. Ugh!

GIRL [*disgusted at seeing SID*]. What are you doin' here, you Sidney Duck? You git!

SID. Beg pardon, Miss. I know men ain't allowed up here.

GIRL. No.

SID. But I'm in grite trouble. The boys are 'ot. They missed that road-agent, Ramerrez — and now they're tiking it out on me. [*Sniffs*] If you'd only speak a word for me, Miss.

GIRL. No! Wowkle, shut the winder.

SID [*pleading*]. Ow, don't be 'ard on me.

GIRL. Now, look here: they's one kind of men [*gesticulating with a slipper*] I can't stand — a cheat and a thief, an' you're it. You're no better than that road-agent, Ramerrez. [*Putting on the other slipper*] Wowkle, close the winder. Close the winder.

SID. Public 'ouse jide! [*He slams the window and disappears*]

GIRL. I got 'em on! [*Rising with difficulty*] Say, Wowkle: do you think he'll like 'em? How do they look? Gosh! They're tight. Say, Wowkle: I'm going the whole hog. [*She has taken a lace shawl from the bureau drawer and puts it on; then she sprinkles some perfumery over a large lace handkerchief and starts to draw on a pair of one-button gloves*] Look here, Wowkle: does it look like an effort?

WOWKLE [*understanding at last*]. H'm! Two plate . . .

[*There is a knock on the door. THE GIRL hastily adjusts her belt, pulls up her stocking and opens the door*]

JOHNSON [*surprised*]. Hello!

GIRL [*embarrassed*]. Hello, Mr. Johnson . . .

JOHNSON [*noticing her gloves*]. Are you — going out?

GIRL. Yes — no — I don't know. Oh, come on in.

JOHNSON [*setting his lantern on the table*]. Thank you. [*Attempting to put his arms round her*]

WOWKLE. Ugh!

[*She shuts the door which JOHNSON left open*]

JOHNSON [*eying WOWKLE*]. I beg your pardon. I didn't see —

GIRL. You stop jest where you are, Mr. Johnson.

JOHNSON. I — I apologize. But seeing you standing there, and looking into your lovely eyes — well, the temptation to take you in my arms was so great — that I — I took it.

[*WOWKLE, blowing out JOHNSON's lantern, goes into the cupboard with her papoose*]

THE GIRL. You must be in the habit of taking things, Mr. Johnson. I seen you on the road to Monterey, goin' an' comin' — I seen you once since, and passed a few words with you; but that don't give you no excuse to begin this sort of game. Besides, you might have prospected a bit first, anyway.

JOHNSON. I see how wrong I was. May I take off my coat? [*She does not answer*] Thank you. [*He lays his coat on a chair*] What a bully little place you have here — awfully snug. And I've found you again! Oh, the luck! [*Holding out his hands*] Friends, Girl?

GIRL [*withholding her hand*]. Are you sorry?

JOHNSON. No, I'm not sorry.

GIRL [*bashfully — half to herself*]. That damn-me style! Well, look here: [*going towards the chair at the table*] down to the saloon to-night, you said you always got what you wanted. Well, of course I've got to admire you for that — I guess women always do admire men for gettin' what they want. But if huggin' me is included, cut it out, Mr. Johnson.

JOHNSON [*facing her across the table*]. That was a lovely day, Girl, on the road to Monterey, wasn't it?

GIRL. Was it? Oh, take a chair an' set down.

JOHNSON. Thanks. [*But he does not sit*]

GIRL. Say, look here: I been thinkin' . . . You didn't come to the saloon to see me to-night. What brought you?

JOHNSON. It was Fate.

GIRL. Was it Fate — or — the back trail?

JOHNSON [*coming to the table and attempting to embrace* THE GIRL]. It was Fate.

GIRL [*retreating to a corner*]. Wowkle: git the coffee. Oh, Lord, take a chair.

[*Starts up to place a chair near the table, but* JOHNSON *intercepts her before she can pick up his coat which lies across the back of the chair*]

JOHNSON. Careful, please! Careful!

GIRL [*peering at the revolvers in his coat pockets*]. How many guns do you carry?

JOHNSON [*hangs his coat on the peg*]. Oh, several — when travelling through the country.

GIRL [*apprehensively*]. Set down.

[*He sits*]

JOHNSON. Ha! It must be strange, living all alone way up here in the mountain. Isn't it lonely?

GIRL. Lonely? Mountains lonely? Ha! Besides — [*sitting in the barrel rocking-chair*] I got a little pinto, an' I'm all over the country on him — finest little horse you ever throwed a leg over. If I want to, I can ride right down into the summer at the foothills, with miles of Injun pinks just a-laffin' — an' tiger lilies as mad as blazes. There's a river there, too — the Injuns call it a 'water road' — an' I can git on that an' drift an' drift, an' I smell the wild syringa on the banks — M'm! And if I git tired o' that, I can turn my horse up grade an' gallop right into the winter an' the lonely pines an' firs a-whisperin' an' a-sighin'. Oh, my mountains! My beautiful peaks! My Sierras! God's in the air here, sure. You can see Him layin' peaceful hands on the mountain tops. He seems so near, you want to let your soul go right on up.

JOHNSON [*who has been listening, nodding his head slightly in appreciation*]. When you die, you won't have far to go, Girl.

GIRL [*after a pause*]. Wowkle, git the coffee.

[THE GIRL *and* JOHNSON *sit at the table.* WOWKLE *pours the coffee into the*

cups, and sets the pot back in the fireplace]

JOHNSON. But when it's cold up here — very cold and it snows?

GIRL. Oh, the boys come up an' dig me out of my front door — ha — like — a — [*spearing a biscuit with her fork*]

JOHNSON. Little rabbit, eh?

GIRL. I git dug out nearly every day when the mines is shet down an' the Academy opens.

JOHNSON [*in surprise*]. Academy? Here? Who teaches in your Academy?

GIRL. Me. I'm her. I'm teacher.

JOHNSON. You teach? Oh —

GIRL. Yep, I learn m'self — [*putting sugar in* JOHNSON'S *coffee*] an' the boys at the same time. But, of course, Academy's suspended when they's a blizzard on —

JOHNSON [*seeing that she is continuing to put sugar in his coffee*]. Hold on . . . hold on . . .

GIRL. — 'Cause no girl could git down the mountain then.

JOHNSON. Is it so very severe here when there's a blizzard on?

GIRL. Oh, Lordy! They come in a minute — all of a sudden — and you don't know where you are. It's awful! [*Offering a dish with an air of pride*] Charlotte Rusks!

JOHNSON [*surprised*]. No!

GIRL. And lemming turnovers!

JOHNSON. Well!

GIRL. Will you have one?

JOHNSON. You bet! Thank you. Let me send you some little souvenir of to-night — something you'd love to read in your course of teaching at the Academy. What have you been reading lately?

GIRL. Oh, it's an awful funny book, about a couple. He was a classic an' his name was Dant.

JOHNSON. He was a classic, and his name was Dant. Oh, Dante! Yes, I know. And did you find it funny? Dante funny?

GIRL. I roared. You see, he loves a lady — [*Rising to get the book*]

JOHNSON. Beatrice —

GIRL. How?

JOHNSON. Go on.

GIRL. He loves a lady. It made me think of it what you said down to the saloon to-night about livin' so you didn't care what come after. Well, he made up his mind — this Dant — Dantee — that one hour of happiness with her was worth the whole da — [*correcting herself*] outfit that come after. He was willin' to sell out his chances for sixty minutes with her. Well, I jest put the book down and hollered!

JOHNSON. Of course you did. All the same, you knew he was right.

GIRL. I didn't. [*Putting the book back on the shelf*]

JOHNSON. You did.

GIRL. Didn't.

JOHNSON. You did.

GIRL. Didn't.

JOHNSON. You know he was right!

GIRL. I don't.

JOHNSON. Yes, you do. You do.

GIRL. I don't. That a feller could so wind himself up as to say: [*sitting at the table*] "Jest give me one hour of your sassiety — time ain't nothin' — nothin' ain't nothin' — only to be a da — darn fool over you." Ain't it funny to feel like that? Yet I suppose there are folks who feel like that; folks that love into the grave, and into death — and after. Golly! It jest lifts you right up by your boot-straps to think of it, don't it?

JOHNSON [*looks at her intently, not smiling. One can see that he is fascinated*]. It does have that effect.

GIRL. Yet p'raps he was ahead of the game. Ha — I dunno. Oh, say, I just love this conversation with you. I love to hear you talk. You give me idees. Wowkle, bring the candle. [WOWKLE *gives the candle to* JOHNSON] Say, look here: one of your real Havanas.

[WOWKLE *knows now that* JOHNSON *is the chosen man. She eyes him with great curiosity*]

JOHNSON. No, I —

GIRL [*handing him the cigar*]. Go on.

JOHNSON [*looking her through and through, his eyes half closed*]. Thank you. How I would love to know you, Girl!

GIRL. You do know me.

JOHNSON [*lights his cigar*]. Not well enough.

GIRL. What's your drift?

JOHNSON. To know you as Dante knew the lady. To say: "One hour for me — one hour — worth the world"

GIRL. He didn't git it, Mr. Johnson. [*Drinking her coffee*]

JOHNSON. All the same, there are women we can die for . . .

GIRL. How many times have you died?

JOHNSON [*lays the cigar down on the table*]. That day on the road to Monterey, I said: "Just that one woman for me." [*Taking* THE GIRL'S *hand*] I wanted to kiss you then.

[*She rises, pulls her hand away and starts to clear the table*]

GIRL. Wowkle, hist the winder. [WOWKLE *goes to the window and stands there*] Mr. Johnson: some men think so much of kisses, that they don't never want a second kiss from the same girl.

JOHNSON. That depends on whether they love her or not. All loves are not alike.

GIRL. No, but they all have the same aim — to git her, if they can.

JOHNSON. You don't know what love is.

GIRL. Nop, I don't. My mother used to say, Mr. Johnson, "Love's a tickling sensation at the heart that you can't scratch." [JOHNSON *rises and goes up to the door, laughing heartily*] We'll let it go at that.

JOHNSON [*turns to embrace* THE GIRL]. Oh, Girl, you're bully!

[WOWKLE *clears the table*]

GIRL [*retreating*]. Look out or you'll muss my roses.

JOHNSON. Hadn't you better take them off, then?

GIRL. Give a man an inch, an' he'll be at Sank Hosey before you know it.

JOHNSON [*following* THE GIRL]. Is there anyone else?

GIRL [*taking off her roses*]. A man always says: "Who was the first one?" But the girl says: "Who'll be the next one?"

JOHNSON. But the time comes when there never will be a next one.

GIRL. No? [*Takes off one of her gloves, blows into it and puts it in the bureau drawer*]

JOHNSON. No.

GIRL. I'd hate to stake my pile on that! Git to your wigwam, Wowkle.

[*She takes off the other glove.* WOWKLE, *who has put the dishes in a pail, grunts, hangs the papoose on her back and puts on her blanket*]

JOHNSON. Must I go, too?

GIRL. Mm — not just yet. You can stay — a — a hour or two longer.

JOHNSON. Yes? Well, I'm like Dante: I want the world in that hour, because I'm afraid the door of this little paradise may be shut to me afterwards. Let's say that this is my one hour — the hour that gives me that kiss.

GIRL. Go long . . .

[WOWKLE *has reached the door and opened it. A gust of wind, and a little snow blows in. The wind has been rising for some time, but* THE GIRL *and* JOHNSON *have not noticed it*]

WOWKLE. Ugh — come snow.

[THE GIRL *and* JOHNSON *do not hear her. All through the following scene, they are so engrossed in each other, that they don't notice* WOWKLE]

GIRL [*to* JOHNSON]. You go to grass.

JOHNSON [*embracing her — trying to kiss her*]. Listen . . .

WOWKLE. Ugh! It snow . . . See . . .

GIRL. Why, if I let you have one, you'd take two.

JOHNSON. No, I wouldn't.

WOWKLE. Very bad.

JOHNSON. I swear I wouldn't.

WOWKLE. Ugh! [*She is disgusted and goes out closing the door*]

GIRL [*retreating*]. Oh, please . . .

JOHNSON [*steps back a little and stands with his arms open*]. One kiss — only one.

GIRL. 'Tain't no use. I lay down my hand to you. [*She runs into his arms*]

JOHNSON [*embracing and kissing her*]. I love you!

[*The wind blows the snow against the windows. The vestibule doors slam. The curtains of the bed flap in the wind. A small basket on the wardrobe blows down. A flower-pot topples over. The blankets in the loft flap. The lamps flicker. Suddenly the wind dies down. The clock on the mantel strikes two. The wind begins to rise again.* THE GIRL *and* JOHNSON *are absolutely oblivious to the storm. After a little pause* JOHNSON *speaks, still holding her in his arms*]

What's your name, Girl — your real name?

GIRL. Min — Minnie. My father's name was Smith.

JOHNSON. Oh, Minnie Sm—

GIRL. But 'twasn't his right name.

JOHNSON. No?

GIRL. His right name was Falconer —

JOHNSON. Minnie Falconer. That's a pretty name. [*He kisses her hand*]

GIRL. I think that was it, — I ain't sure. That's what he said it was. I ain't sure of anything — only — jest you. [*She snuggles closer*]

JOHNSON. I've loved you ever since I first saw you. . . . So you're sure of me — sure. [*He gently puts her away, remembering what he is*] You turn your head away, Girl, and don't you listen to me, for I'm not worth you. Don't you listen. You just say, "No — no — no!" [*He turns away*]

GIRL. Say, I know I ain't good enough for you, but I'll try hard. If you see anything better in me, why don't you bring it out? I've loved you ever since I saw you first . . . 'cause I knowed that you was the right man.

JOHNSON [*conscience-smitten*]. The right man. Ha, ha!

GIRL. Don't laugh.

JOHNSON [*seriously*]. I'm not laughing.

GIRL. Of course, every girl kind o' looks ahead.

JOHNSON. Yes.

GIRL. And figgers about — bein' — Well — Oh, you know —

JOHNSON. Yes, I know. [*He is standing so that she cannot see his face*]

GIRL. She figgers about being settled . . . and when the right one comes — why, she knows him — just as we both knew each other standin' in the road to Monterey. I said that day: "He's good — he's grand — he can have me!"

JOHNSON [*meditatively, with longing — turning to her*]. I could have you . . . [*With sudden resolve*] I have looked into your heart, Girl, and into my own, and now I realize what this means for us both — for you, Girl, for you — and knowing that it seems hard to say good-bye — as I should . . . and must . . . and will. [*He kisses her, then turns to go*]

GIRL. What do you mean?

JOHNSON [*collecting himself*]. I mean it's hard to go — and leave you here. The clock reminded me that long before this, I should have been on the way.

I shouldn't have come up here at all. God bless you, dear, — I love you as I never thought I could.

GIRL [*troubled*]. But it ain't for long you're goin'?

JOHNSON. For long? [*Resolving not to tell her the truth*] No — no; but I've got to go now while I have the courage. [*Taking her face in his hands — kissing her*] Oh, Girl! Girl! [*Kissing her hands*] Good-bye . . . [*Getting his hat and coat and opening door, he looks out*] Why, it's snowing!

[*As the door opens, all the sounds of the storm-swept woods are heard — the whispering and rocking of the storm-tossed pines, and the winds howling through a deep cañon. THE GIRL runs up and closes the outside and inside doors, goes to the window, pulls back the curtain, wipes the frost from the window-pane, trying to peer out*]

GIRL. Snowing . . . It's the first snow this winter. You can't see an inch ahead. That's the way we git it up here. Look! Look!

JOHNSON [*looking through the window*]. This means — No . . . it can't mean that I can't leave Cloudy to-night. I must.

GIRL [*turning to him*]. Leave Cloudy? You couldn't keep to the trail. It means you can't git off this mountain to-night.

JOHNSON [*thinking of the posse*]. But I must!

GIRL. You can't leave this room to-night — you couldn't find your way three feet from this door — you, a stranger. . . . You don't know the trail anyway, unless you can see it.

JOHNSON [*apprehensively*]. But I can't stay here.

GIRL. Why not? It's all right. The boys'll come up an' dig us out to-morrow or day after. Plenty of food here — and you can have my bed.

JOHNSON. I couldn't think of taking it.

GIRL. I never use it cold nights. I always roll up in my rug in front of the fire. [*Amused*] Think of it storming all this time, an' we didn't know it!

JOHNSON [*pre-occupied — gravely*]. But people coming up and finding me here, might . . .

GIRL. Might what?

[*Two shots, fired in quick succession, are heard in the distance at the foot of the mountain*]

JOHNSON. What's that? . . . What's that?

GIRL. Wait . . . [*More shots are heard in the distance, fired at intervals*] They've got a road-agent . . . It's the posse. Perhaps they've got Ramerrez or one of his band. [*JOHNSON rushes to the window, vainly trying to look out*] Whoever it is, they're snowed in — couldn't git away. [*Another shot is heard*] I guess that time another thief crept into camp. [*Meaning eternity*]

JOHNSON [*wincing*]. Poor devil! But, of course — as you say — he's only a thief.

GIRL [*who has thrown her pillow in front of the fire*]. I ain't sorry for him.

JOHNSON [*after a slight pause*]. You're right! [*Then, as though he had made up his mind, he takes down his overcoat and puts it on*] Girl, I've been thinking . . . I've got to go — I've got to go. I have very important business at dawn — imperative.

GIRL. Ever sample one of our mountain blizzards? In five minutes you wouldn't know where you was. Your important business would land you at the bottom of a cañon — about twenty feet from here. You say you believe in Fate: well, it's caught up with you. You got to stay here.

[*She puts the tablecloth in the cupboard as though putting the house in order for the night*]

JOHNSON. Well, it is Fate — my Fate — [*throwing down his coat*] that has always made it easy for me to do the thing I shouldn't do. As you say, Girl, if I can't go, I can't . . . [*looking at her intently*] but I know now as I stand here, that I'll never give you up.

GIRL [*not quite understanding*]. Why, what do you mean?

JOHNSON [*deliberately — speaking above the crying of the wind*]. I mean . . . suppose we say that's an omen — [*pointing as though to the falling snow*] that the old trail is blotted out and there's a fresh road. . . . Would you take it with me, a stranger — who says: "From this day I mean to be all that you would have me"? Would you take it with me? Far away from here — and — forever?

GIRL. Well, show me the girl who would want to go to Heaven alone. [*JOHNSON kisses her hand*] I'll sell out the saloon. I'll go anywhere with you — you bet!

JOHNSON. You know what that means, don't you?

[*He sits by the table, looking at* THE GIRL]

GIRL. Oh, yes. They's a little Spanish Mission Church here . . . I pass it 'most every day. I can look in an' see the light burnin' before the Virgin — an' all the saints standin' round with glassy eyes an' faded satin slippers — an' I often thought: what'd they think if I was to walk right in to be made — well, some man's wife. That's a great word, ain't it — wife? It makes your blood like pin-points thinkin' about it. There's somethin' kind o' holy about love, ain't there? Say: did you ever ask any other woman to marry you?

[*She sits down on the floor, leaning towards* JOHNSON, *in his arms*]

JOHNSON. No.

GIRL. Oh, I'm glad! Ah — take me — I don't care where — as long's it's with you. Jest take me.

JOHNSON. So help me Heaven, I'm going to, Girl. You're worth something better than me, Girl; but they say love works miracles every hour: it weakens the strong and strengthens the weak. With all my soul I love you. . . . [*He notices that she is dozing*] Why, Minnie . . . Minnie . . .

GIRL [*waking with a start*]. I wasn't asleep . . . I'm jest happy an' let down, that's all. Say, I'm awful sorry — I've got to say good-night.

JOHNSON. Good-night. [*He kisses her*]

[*They rise*]

GIRL. That's your bed over there.

JOHNSON. I hate to take it. Hadn't you better take the bed and let me sleep by the fire?

GIRL. Nop. [*She moves the barrel rocking-chair away from the fireplace*]

JOHNSON. Are you sure you will be more comfortable there?

GIRL. You bet I will — don't worry.

JOHNSON. Very well. [*He throws his coat and hat on the bed*]

GIRL [*as she spreads rugs on the floor in front of the fire*]. This beats a bed any time. There's one thing — [*reaching up and pulling down a quilt from the loft*] — you don't have to make it up in the morning. [*She puts a lighted candle on the hearth, blows out the lamps on the mantel, the stand and the bureau. She climbs up on the table, turns down the hanging lamp, steps to the floor, notices that she has turned it too low, glances at* JOHNSON, *making sure that he does not see her, gets up on the table again, turns the wick higher, then goes into the wardrobe where she makes her toilet for the night*] Now, you can talk to me from your bunk, and I'll talk to you from mine.

JOHNSON. Good-night.

GIRL. Good-night.

JOHNSON [*starts to go to bed — turns quickly — listens — then goes towards the bed — pauses — runs to the door and listens. His face is full of resolve. He shows the desperado's ability to meet all emergencies. He speaks quietly — in fact, the scene between these two, from this moment until the door is opened, must be done in the lowest audible tones — to convey the impression that those outside do not hear*]. What's that?

GIRL. That's snow slidin'. . . Good-night.

JOHNSON. God bless you, Girl. Thank you. [*He goes behind the curtains of the bed. A pause*] H'm . . . there *is* something out there . . . sounded like someone calling.

GIRL. That's only the wind. [*She comes out of the wardrobe*] It's gettin' colder, ain't it? [*She sits on the floor, takes off her slippers and puts on moccasins, then rises and comes down to the fire, arranges the rugs and pillow, says a brief prayer, lies down and tucks herself in*] Good-night again.

JOHNSON. Good-night.

GIRL [*lifting up her head*]. Say, what's your first name?

JOHNSON. Dick.

GIRL [*sentimentally*]. So long, Dick.

[*She snuggles down again in the folds of the rug*]

JOHNSON. So long, Girl.

GIRL [*half rising*]. Say, Dick, are you sure you don't know that Nina Micheltoreña?

JOHNSON [*after a slight pause*]. Sure.

GIRL [*with a satisfied air*]. Good-night. [*She lies down again*]

JOHNSON. Good-night.

[*Suddenly a voice is heard to call and some one knocks on the door*]

[THE GIRL *rises and sets the candle on the table*]

[JOHNSON *throws open the curtains and pulls his revolvers from his pockets*]

GIRL. There *is* some one calling.

NICK. Hello!

GIRL. Listen! What could that —
JOHNSON [*in a low voice*]. Don't
answer.
GIRL. Who can it be?
JOHNSON. You can't let anybody in
here — they wouldn't understand.
GIRL. Understand what?

[*She goes to the window. It never occurs
to her that the situation is com-
promising*]

JOHNSON. Sh!
GIRL. It's the posse. How did
they ever risk it in this blizzard?
What can they want?
JOHNSON [*low, but very distinctly,
above the rising wind, his hands on his
pistols*]. Don't answer.
NICK [*voice outside*]. Min! Minnie!
Girl!
GIRL [*calling off through the door*].
What do you want? [*Turning quickly
to* JOHNSON] What did you say?
JOHNSON. Don't let them in.
SONORA'S VOICE. Are you all right,
Girl?
GIRL [*calling loudly through the door*].
Yes, Sonora, I'm all right. [*Turning
again to* JOHNSON] Jack Rance is
there . . . If he was to see you here —
he's that jealous — I'd be afraid of
him. [*Listening at the door*] And Ash-
by's there and —
JOHNSON [*now sure that they are after
him*]. Ashby!
NICK [*outside*]. We want to come in.
JOHNSON. No.
GIRL [*glibly, calling*]. You can't
come in. [*To* JOHNSON] What will I
say?
JOHNSON [*quietly*]. You've gone to
bed.
GIRL. Oh, yes. [*To* NICK, *outside*]
I've gone to bed — I'm in bed now.
ASHBY [*outside*]. We've come to
warn you.
GIRL. They've come to warn me.
NICK [*outside*]. Ramerrez . . .
GIRL [*calling through door*]. What?
NICK. Ramerrez is on the trail.
GIRL. Ramerrez is on the trail.
[*To* JOHNSON] I got to let 'em in.
[JOHNSON *gets behind the curtains of the
bed where he is entirely concealed*] I
can't keep 'em out such a night. [*Call-
ing to men outside*] Come on in, boys.
[*She opens the door, and the men enter —*
RANCE *first*]

[RANCE, *wearing a luxurious fur overcoat, his trousers tucked into his*

high-heeled boots, goes to the candle,
warming his hands over it, taking
off his gloves, brushing the snow off
with his handkerchief. SONORA,
wearing a buffalo overcoat, cap,
ear muffs and high boots, comes
down to the fireplace. ASHBY follows with a lighted lantern; he
is dressed as before, but wears an
overcoat over the one in which he
first appeared. NICK comes down
to* THE GIRL, *then crosses to the fire;
he has pieces of blanket tied round
his legs and feet. RANCE turns
up the wick of the hanging lamp.
All are snow-covered*]

SONORA [*as he goes to the fireplace*].
Ow! Glad you are safe. I'm froze!
[*He stamps his feet and rubs his hands
together*]
NICK. The Polka has had a narrow
squeak, Girl.
GIRL [*seated*]. Why, what's the mat-
ter, Nick?
RANCE [*suspiciously*]. It takes you a
long time to get up, — and you don't
seem to have so much on you, either.
GIRL [*indignantly*]. Well, upon my
— [*She rises and, picking up a rug
from the floor, wraps it round her knees
and sits. The wind rises and falls,
crying in the cañons*]
SONORA. We thought sure you was in
trouble. My breath jest stopped . . .
GIRL. Me — in trouble?
RANCE. See here — that man Johnson —
SONORA. Fellow you was dancin'
with —
RANCE [*with a grimace of pleasure,
spreading his stiffened fingers before
the blaze*]. Your polkying friend John-
son is Ramerrez.
GIRL [*blankly*]. What'd you say?
ASHBY. I warned you. Bank with
us oftener.
GIRL [*dazed*]. What did you say?
RANCE. We say — Johnson was a —
GIRL. What?
RANCE. Are you deaf? The fellow
you've been polkying with is the man
that has been asking people to hold
up their hands.
GIRL [*lightly, yet positively*]. Go on!
You can't hand me out that.
RANCE. You don't believe it yet, eh?
GIRL [*imitating his "yet"*]. No, I
don't believe it yet, eh! I know he
isn't.
RANCE. Well, he *is* Ramerrez, and

he *did* come to the Polka to rob it.

GIRL. But he didn't rob it.

SONORA. That's what gits me — he didn't.

GIRL. I should think it would git you.

ASHBY. We've got his horse.

SONORA. I never knew one of these men to separate from his horse.

RANCE. Oh, well, if we've got his horse, with this storm on, we've got him. The last seen of Johnson he was heading this way. You seen anything of him?

GIRL. Heading this way?

SONORA. So Nick said.

[THE GIRL *gives* NICK *a glance*]

NICK. He was. Sid says he saw him, too.

RANCE. But the trail ends here — and if she hasn't seen him — [*he looks at* THE GIRL] — where was he going?

[NICK *spying* JOHNSON'S *cigar, recognizes it as one of their rare dollar Havanas.* THE GIRL'S *eyes follow* NICK'S *glance. Unseen by* RANCE, *there is a glance between* NICK *and* THE GIRL]

NICK [*to himself*]. Oh, my God!

SONORA [*answering* RANCE'S *question*]. Yes, where was he going?

[RANCE *looks at* THE GIRL, *now intercepting* NICK'S *glance*]

NICK. Well, I thought I seen him — I couldn't swear to it. You see, it was so dark. Oh, that Sidney Cove's a liar, anyway. [NICK *puts the tell-tale cigar in his pocket, looking furtively about to make sure that he is not seen*]

ASHBY. He's snowed under. Something scared him off, an' he lit off without his horse.

GIRL [*sitting down*]. Ha! How do you know that man is a road-agent?

SONORA [*warming his hands and breathing on his fingers*]. Well, two greasers jest now was pretty positive of it before they quit.

GIRL [*with scorn*]. Greasers! Oh!

RANCE. But the woman knew him — she knew him. [*Sitting on the table*]

GIRL [*quietly, for the first time impressed*]. The woman? What'd you say?

SONORA. It was the woman who first told us that Ramerrez was here — to rob the Polka.

RANCE. She's down at the Palmetto now.

ASHBY. It will cost us the reward.

RANCE. But Ramerrez is trapped.

GIRL. Who is this woman?

RANCE [*as though to excite her jealousy*]. Why, the woman from the back trail — that damn —

GIRL. Nina Micheltoreña?

RANCE. H'm, h'm.

GIRL. Then she knows him. She *does* know him . . . [*She rises again*]

RANCE. He was the sort of man who polkas with you first — then cuts your throat.

GIRL [*turning on* RANCE]. It's my throat, ain't it?

RANCE. Well, I'll be —

NICK [*going to* RANCE *and speaking to him in a low voice*]. Say, she's cut up because she vouched for him. Don't rub it in.

GIRL. Nina Micheltoreña . . . How did she know it?

SONORA. Why, from what she said —

RANCE. She's his girl. She's —

GIRL. His girl?

RANCE. Yes, she gave us his picture — [*taking a picture from his pocket, and turning it over*] — with " Love " on the back.

GIRL [*takes the picture, looks at it, and laughs*]. Nina Micheltoreña, eh? Ha! I'm sorry I vouched for him, Mr. Ashby.

RANCE. Ah!

GIRL [*so that* ASHBY *shall not suspect*]. I suppose they had one of them little lovers' quarrels that made her tell you, eh? He's the kind of man that sort o' polkys with every girl he meets. Ha! Ha! Ha! Ha!

RANCE. What are you laughing at?

GIRL [*turning to* RANCE *again*]. Oh, nothing — only it's kind o' damn funny how things come out, — ain't it? Took in! Nina Micheltoreña! Nice company he keeps. One of them Cachuca girls with eye-lashes at half mast, ha! And she sold him out — for money. Ah, you're a better guesser than I am, Jack.

RANCE [*grimly*]. Yes.

GIRL. Well, it's gittin' late. Thank you. Good-night, boys.

SONORA. Hell, boys! Come on and let a lady go to bed. Good-night, Girl.

[*He goes to the door, followed by the other men,* ASHBY *following* SONORA, *then* RANCE *and, last,* NICK. *When the door opens, all the lamps flicker in the wind*]

GIRL. Good-night, Sonora. Good-night, Mr. Ashby. Good-night, Jack.

SONORA. Lordy! Will we ever git down again?

NICK [*as the others are outside, looking at her meaningly*]. You want *me* to stay?

GIRL [*going to the door*]. No. Good-night. [*The men all go off calling "good-night", etc.* THE GIRL *shuts the door, and stands with her back against it. With a change of manner, her eyes blazing*] Come out of that — step out there! [JOHNSON *appears between the curtains of the bed*] You came here to rob me.

JOHNSON [*quietly*]. I didn't.

GIRL [*viciously*]. You lie!

JOHNSON. I don't.

GIRL. You do.

JOHNSON. I — I admit that every circumstance points to —

GIRL. Stop! Don't you give me any more of that Webster dictionary talk — but git to cases. If you didn't come here to steal — you came to the Polka to rob it, didn't you?

JOHNSON [*with sudden determination*]. Yes, I did, but when I knew it was you who — [*He goes towards her*]

GIRL. Wait! Wait! [JOHNSON *pauses*] Don't you take a step — look out, or I'll — A road-agent . . . a road-agent! . . . Well, ain't it my luck? Wouldn't anybody know to look at me that a gentleman wouldn't fall my way? A road-agent . . . Oh! Oh! Oh! [*Then with a revulsion of feeling*] You can git now — git! You — you thief! You imposer on a decent woman. I ought to have told the boys — but I wasn't goin' to let on I could be so took in. I wasn't goin' to be the joke of the world, with you behind the curtain, an' me eatin' charlotte rusks and lemming turnovers and a-polkering with a road-agent. Ha! But now you can git! Now you can git! [*She sits on the table, looking straight before her as though to forget the sight of the man*]

JOHNSON [*in a low voice*]. One word — only one word. . . . I'm not going to say anything in defense of myself. It's all true — everything is true, except that I would have stolen from you. I am called Ramerrez — I have robbed — I am a vagabond — a vagabond by birth — a cheat and a swindler by profession. I'm all that — and my father was all that before me. I was born, brought up, educated, thrived on thieves' money — but until six months

ago, when he died, I didn't know it. I lived in Monterey — Monterey where we met. I lived decently. I wasn't the thing I am to-day. I only learned the truth when he died and left me with a rancho and a band of thieves — nothing else — nothing for us all — and I . . . I was my father's son — no excuse . . . it was in me — in the blood . . . I took to the road. I didn't mind much after — the first time. I only drew the line at killing. I wouldn't have that. And that's the man I am — the blackguard I am. [*With feeling*] But, so help me God, from the moment I kissed you to-night, I meant to change. I meant to change.

GIRL [*sniffling*]. The devil you did!

JOHNSON [*advancing a step*]. I did, believe me — I did. I meant to go straight and take you with me — but honestly . . . when I could do it honestly. I meant to work for you. Every word you said to me to-night about being a thief, cut me like a knife. Over and over again, I said to myself: "She must never know." Now . . . [*A slight pause*] Well, — I've finished.

GIRL. Is that all?

JOHNSON. No. Yes. What's the use? That's all.

GIRL [*half crying*]. Well, there's jest one thing you've overlooked explainin', Mr. Johnson. It shows jest exactly what you are. It wasn't so much bein' a road-agent I got against you — it's this: you kissed me. You kissed me. You got my first kiss.

JOHNSON. Yes, damn me!

GIRL. You said you'd been thinkin' of me ever since you saw me at Monterey — an' all the time you'd walked straight off and been kissing that other woman. You've got a girl. It's that I've got against you. It's my first kiss I've got against you. It's that damned Nina Micheltoreña that I can't forgive. But now you can git — you can git! [*Rushing to the door and opening it*] If they kill you, so much the better. I don't care — I don't care — I don't care!

JOHNSON. You're right. You're right. By God! You're right. [*He takes out a pistol, but, not much caring whether he lives or dies, he looks at the pistol, then puts it back in his pocket and goes out empty-handed — his head bowed*]

GIRL. That's the end of that — that's the end of that. [*She goes to the door, closes it*] I don't care — I don't care. I'll be like the rest of the women I've seen. I'll give that Nina Micheltoreña cards and spades. [*Wipes her nose*] There'll be another huzzy around here. [*At that moment, we hear a shot outside, close at hand*] They've got him . . . [*With a bravado toss of her head*] Well, I don't care — I don't care.

[JOHNSON *falls against the door outside.* THE GIRL, *with a revulsion of feeling, rushes to the door, opens it, and he staggers in, her arms about him.* JOHNSON *leans against the wall.* THE GIRL *closes the door*]

JOHNSON [*holding his hand to his right side*]. . . . Don't lock the door . . . I'm going out again . . . I'm going out . . . [*He swings round, lurches and nearly falls as* THE GIRL *pushes him onto a chair*] Don't bar the door. Open it . . . Open it . . . By God! I won't hide behind a woman.

GIRL [*leaning over* JOHNSON]. I love you an' I'm goin' to stand by you. You asked me to go away with you. [*Crosses for the whiskey bottle and a glass*] You get out of this, an' I will. If you can't save your own soul — [*There is a rap on the window.* RANCE *is peering through, but he cannot see* JOHNSON. THE GIRL *sets down the bottle and glass and pauses. She looks up at the ladder to the loft, gets on a chair and lets it down.* RANCE *goes from the window to the door*] — I'm goin' to save it for you. You're the man that had my first kiss. Go up there! [*In a lower voice, never pausing, she urges* JOHNSON *to the loft*]

JOHNSON [*his handkerchief pressed to his side*]. No — no — no — no — Not here.

GIRL. Do you want them to see you in my cabin? Hurry . . . Hurry . . .

JOHNSON. No — No —

[*There is a rap on the door. She gives him a push, and with an effort* JOHNSON *gradually climbs up the ladder, reeling as he goes*]

GIRL. Yes, you can do it — you can — you're the man I love. You've got to show me the man that's in you. Go on. . . . Go on. . . . [*There is a second rap on the door*] Just a step — a step.

JOHNSON. I can't . . . I can't. [*He reaches the loft, collapses, falling to his knees. He lies on the floor of the loft, one*

outstretched hand holding the handkerchief. THE GIRL *swings the ladder up*]

GIRL [*looks up, calls softly*]. You can. Don't move. [*There is another rap on the door*] The cracks are wide — take that handkerchief away. [*He draws the handkerchief out of sight*] That's it. [*There is another knock.* THE GIRL *calls off*] Yes, yes, in a minute. [*In a whisper to* JOHNSON] Don't move. [*The door opens and* RANCE *appears. He slams the door behind him*] Well, what do you want now? You can't come in here, Jack Rance.

RANCE. No more Jack Rance. It's the Sheriff after Mr. Johnson.

GIRL. What?

RANCE. I saw him coming in here. [*He cocks his revolver*]

GIRL. It's more than I did — [RANCE *glances at the bed, opening the curtains*] and the door was barred. Do you think I want to shield a man who tried to rob me? If you doubt my word, go on — search the place; but that ends your acquaintance with the Polka. Don't you ever speak to me again — we're through!

RANCE. Wait a minute . . . What's that? [*He listens — the wind is calling. After a slight pause,* RANCE *comes down to the table.* THE GIRL *is leaning against the bureau.* RANCE *uncocks his revolver, puts it in the holster, takes off his hat, shakes the water from it, and drops it on the table. His eyes never leave* THE GIRL'S *face*] I saw someone standing outside — there — [*he crosses to the fireplace*] against the white snow. [*Taking off his overcoat*] I fired. [*Shaking the coat*] I could have sworn it was a man.

GIRL. Go on — go on — finish your search, — then never speak to me again.

RANCE [*seeing that he has gone too far — turning to her*]. Say, I — I don't want to quarrel with you.

GIRL. Go on — go on — and then leave a lady to herself to git to bed. Go on and git it over. [*She goes up to the bureau, her back to* RANCE]

RANCE. I'm crazy about you. I could have sworn I saw — You know it's just you for me — just you — and damn the man you like better! I — I — Even yet I — I can't — [*starting to put on his coat*] get over the queer look on your face when I told you who that man really was. You dón't love him, do you? [*A pause. He throws* the coat down on the floor and advances towards her] Do you?

GIRL [*lightly*]. Who? Me? [*With a forced laugh, she eyes* RANCE *disdainfully*]

RANCE [*his feelings somewhat relieved, takes a step towards her*]. Say, was your answer to-night final about marrying me?

GIRL [*coyly, flirting with him*]. I might think it over, Jack. [*With another somewhat artificial laugh*]

RANCE. Minnie . . . [*Coming close to her*] I love you . . . [*Putting his arms about her, kissing her*] I love you. [*She struggles to escape from him, and, picking up the bottle from the table, raises it to strike him, then sinks to the floor, sobbing*]

GIRL [*nervously*]. Oh, my God, I —

[RANCE *stands looking down at her*]

RANCE [*with the nasty laugh of a man whose vanity is hurt*]. Ha! Ha! Ha! God! I — I didn't think it was that bad, — I didn't. I am much obliged to you. Thank you. [*Taking his cap from the table and going up towards the door*] Good-night. [*Taking up his coat and starting to put it on*] Good-night. Much obliged. Can't you — can't you even say good-night? [*He has his coat in his left hand, his cap in his right.* THE GIRL *rubs her hands on her dress and comes reluctantly towards him. He drops his cap*]

GIRL. Yes. Good-night, Jack Rance. Good-night, Jack Rance, I — [*As he holds out his hand, a drop of blood from the loft falls on it*]

RANCE [*slowly, after a pause*]. Look at my hand . . . [*pulls out his handkerchief and wipes his hand*] . . . my hand. [*Looking at the blood*] That's blood.

GIRL. Yes, I must have scratched you just now. I'm awful sorry.

RANCE. There's no scratch there. There isn't a mark. [*More blood falls on the outstretched hand, holding the handkerchief*]

GIRL [*quickly*]. Yes, but there will be in the morning, Jack. You'll see in the morning.

RANCE [*looks towards the loft. Placing his hand on his pistol, he puts his handkerchief in his pocket*]. He's up there.

GIRL [*holding his hand which grasps the revolver*]. No, he isn't, Jack. No, he isn't. No, he —

RANCE. You go straight to the devil.

[*He picks up a chair to climb up — then sees the ladder*]

GIRL [*trying to stop* RANCE]. No, he isn't, Jack. Not there, Jack. Not there, Jack. He is not there — [*Drawing down the ladder*]

RANCE. Mr. Johnson, come down.

GIRL. Wait a minute, Jack . . . Wait a minute . . .

RANCE [*as* JOHNSON *moves towards the top of the ladder*]. Come down, or I'll —

GIRL. Wait jest a minute, Jack — jest a minute . . .

RANCE [*his revolver levelled at* JOHNSON]. Come down here!

[*Step by step,* JOHNSON *comes down the ladder, his eyes fastened on* RANCE. THE GIRL *stands watching* JOHNSON. JOHNSON'S *hands, which are up, slowly fall, and, with unseeing eyes, he lurches to the chair behind the table, falls forward, his head resting on the table — unconscious, half in the shadow.* RANCE *puts his revolver in the holster*]

GIRL. Don't you see he can't hold up his hands? Oh, Jack, don't make him. Don't you see he can't? Oh, Jack, don't make him. No, no, wait, Jack, jest a minute — wait!

RANCE [*leaning over* JOHNSON]. Wait a minute? What for? [*Laughs — a low, unctuous laugh*] So you dropped into the Polka, Mr. Johnson, to play me a little game of poker to-night? Ha! Ha! Ha! Funny how things change about in an hour or two. You think you can play poker? That's your conviction, is it? Ha! Ha! Ha! Well, you can play freeze-out as to your chances, Mr. Johnson, of Sacramento! It's shooting or the tree. Speak up — which will you have?

GIRL [*who has picked up her pistol — in a low voice, quiet but tense*]. You better stop that laughing, or you'll finish it in some other place where things ain't quite so funny. [*Something in her voice strikes* RANCE *and he stops laughing*] He doesn't hear you. He's out of it. But me — me — I hear you — I ain't out of it. You're a gambler — he was, too — so am I. [*Having engaged* RANCE'S *attention, she throws the pistol back into the drawer*] I live on chance money — drink money — card money — saloon money. We're gamblers — we're all gamblers! [*Lean-*

ing over towards RANCE] You asked me to-night if my answer to you was final. Now's your chance! I'll play you a game — straight poker. It's two out of three for me. Hatin' the sight of you — it's the nearest chance you'll ever git for me.

RANCE. Do you mean —

GIRL. With the wife in Noo Orleans — all right. If you're lucky, you git him an' me; but if you lose, this man settin' between us is mine — mine to do with as I please — an' you shut up and lose like a gentleman.

RANCE [*looking in her eyes*]. You must be crazy about him.

GIRL [*briefly*]. That's my business.

RANCE Do you know you're talking to the Sheriff?

GIRL. I'm talkin' to Jack Rance, the gambler.

RANCE [*quietly and coolly*]. You're right. [*Standing upright*] And I'm just fool enough to take you up. [*Looks for a chair*] Ah! [*Brings the chair down, placing it before the table*] You and the cards have got into my blood. I'll take you. [*He pulls off the table-cover and throws it on the floor*]

GIRL. Your word?

RANCE. I can lose like a gentleman. [*She starts to draw back her hand, but he grasps it*] But, my God! I'm hungry for you — and, if I'm lucky, I'll take it out on you so long as God lets you breathe.

GIRL [*draws away from him*]. Fix the lamp. [RANCE, *his eyes still on her, reaches up to the lamp, does not find it at first, looks up, turns up the wick*] Wait jest a minute — jest a minute. [*She goes into the wardrobe with the candle*]

RANCE. What are you waiting for? [*He takes a pack of cards from his pocket, sits at the table and shuffles them*]

GIRL [*in the closet*]. I'm jest gettin' the cards, an' kind o' — steadyin' my nerves.

RANCE. I've got a deck here.

GIRL [*coming out of the wardrobe, blowing out the candle, and throwing it on the floor*]. We'll use a fresh deck. [*Laying a fresh pack of cards on the table*] There's a good deal dependin' on this, Jack Rance. [THE GIRL *sits*. RANCE *looks at her, then lays aside his own cards and takes hers*] Are you — ready?

RANCE. Ready? Yes, I'm ready. Cut for deal. [*She cuts.* RANCE *shuffles.*] This is a case of show-down.

GIRL. Show-down.

RANCE. Cut. [*Begins to deal*] The best two out of three.

GIRL. Best two out of three.

RANCE [*as he glances over the cards he has drawn — in a low voice — colloquially*]. What do you see in him?

GIRL. What do you see in me, Jack? [*Taking up her cards*] What have you got?

RANCE. King high.

GIRL. King high.

RANCE [*showing her the hand*]. Jack next.

GIRL [*showing her hand to* RANCE]. Queen next.

RANCE. You've got it. [*Throws down his hand. She shuffles*] You've made a mistake on Johnson.

GIRL [*dealing*]. If I have, Jack, it's my mistake. What have you got?

RANCE. One pair — aces. [*Showing her the cards*]

GIRL. Nothing. [*Throwing down her cards*]

RANCE [*shuffles the cards*]. We're even. We're even.

GIRL. It's the next hand that tells, Jack, ain't it?

RANCE. Yes.

GIRL. I'm awful sorry it's the next hand that tells. I — I — want to say that no matter how it comes out —

RANCE. Cut.

[*She cuts the cards and he picks them up and deals*]

GIRL. — that I'll always think of you the best I can, and I want you to do the same for me.

RANCE. You heard what I said.

GIRL [*starts to draw her cards towards her. He reaches across, places his hand over hers and over the cards*]. Yes.

RANCE. But I have got a feeling that I win — that in one minute I'll hold you in my arms. [*He spreads out his cards, still holding her hand and looking at her. Then, as though resolved to face the consequences, he looks at his cards. She is leaning forward and her hand is being drawn towards him. As he sees his cards, he smiles.* THE GIRL *collapses with a shudder. He leans forward. Very calmly*] I win.

GIRL [*very anxiously*]. Think so?

RANCE. Three Kings and it's the last hand. [*Showing his cards to* THE GIRL]

GIRL. Oh, Jack, quick — get me something — I'm fainting!

Rance [*throws the cards face down on the table*] Where? Where?

Girl. There.

Rance [*finds the bottle, but not the glass*]. Oh, yes, here it is — here's the bottle. Where's a glass? Where's that damn glass?

[*As* Rance *turns away, she puts her cards in the bosom of her dress and draws five cards from her stocking*]

Girl. Hurry . . . Hurry . . .

Rance [*dropping the bottle, turning and leaning forward as if to impress her, his arm round her neck*]. You're fainting because you've lost.

Girl [*rises, laying down her hand on the table*]. No, Jack — it's because I've won — three aces and a pair! [*He looks at her hand. There is a slight pause*]

Rance. Good-night. [*Always the gambler, he picks up his hat and coat and goes*]

[The Girl *drops the cards and takes* Johnson *in her arms*]

CURTAIN

ACT III

Scene. — *The interior of a typical mining-camp dance-hall of the period. The walls are of rough boards nailed across upright beams.*

The mines are closed on account of the weather, and the hall is decorated in honor of the opening of the "Academy." Garlands of pine and wreaths of red berries hang over the doors and windows. Yellow curtains hang at the windows. Eagles' wings, as well as wings of smaller birds, are tacked to the wall. Antlers (on which the miners hang their hats when the "Academy" is in session) are fastened to the wall, also birds' wings and a motto, painted on an old weather-beaten piece of wood, "Live and Learn." A stuffed game-cock and a candle lamp with a reflector are over a door at right. A horseshoe is fastened over the door to the exterior. A lamp hangs from the centre of the ceiling, and stuck in its cheap iron brackets are flags whose stars indicate the number of States of that period. At the back, towards the right, is a platform on which the

teacher's home-made desk stands. *It is decorated with a garland of pine. A bunch of red and white berries, a ruler, chalk, a whiskey bottle, glass and bell are on the desk. A box is used for the teacher's seat. A blackboard is at the back, standing on the floor and resting against the table. An old sheet-iron stove, heavily dented, is below the desk. The fire is burning brightly. The stove has an iron railing fastened to the base, on which the miners rest their feet. The stove-pipe goes up through the ceiling. Whittled benches are arranged about the room and two or three chairs.* Sonora's *coat is lying on a chair, and* Trinidad's *jacket is on the bench against the wall at back. Doors lead to the bar-room, which we saw in the first act, and a glimpse of the bar is shown. Fastened to the frame of one of these doors is a large hand, rudely painted, the index finger pointing to the words, "To the bar!" A red curtain cuts off the balcony on this same side of the room. Another door, on the opposite side of the room, leads to a lean-to in which there is a door leading to the exterior. A door at back opens directly upon the trail, and, when this door is ajar, one sees the snow-covered country and the green firs of Cloudy Mountain heavily weighted by snow. It is a bright winter's morning.*

At the rise of the curtain, Jack Rance *is sitting near the fire, — worn, pale and waxen. He has not slept, and his eyes are red and half closed as he sits thinking. He is no longer immaculate in dress, — his necktie is partly undone, his waist-coat is unfastened, his boots unpolished, his hair is ruffled and his cigar (in his hand) has gone out.* Nick, *standing near the foot of the platform, seems troubled as he looks through the window as though towards* The Girl's *cabin.*

Nick. I'd be willin' to lose the profits of the bar, if we could git back to a week ago, before Johnson walked into this room. [*He pours out a drink*]

Rance [*showing feeling*]. Johnson! By — [*taking off his hat*] — week — a week . . . A week in her cabin — nursed and kissed . . .

Nick [*remonstrating*]. Oh, say, Rance!

Rance. You bet she kissed him,

Nick. It was all I could do to keep from telling the whole camp he was up there.

Nick. But you didn't. If I hadn't been let into the game by the Girl, I'd a-thought you were a level Sheriff, looking for him. Rance, you're my deal of a perfect gent.

Rance. What did she see in that Sacramento shrimp to love?

Nick [*puts his foot on a chair, hands the drink to* Rance]. Well, you see, I figger it out this way, boss: love's like a drink that gits a-holt on you, and you can't quit . . . it's a turn of the head, or a touch of the hands, or it's a half sort of smile — and you're doped — doped with a feelin' like strong liquor runnin' through your veins — [Rance *drops the hand which holds the glass*] an' there ain't nothin' on earth can break it up, once you've got the habit. That's love. I've got it — you've got it — the boys've got it — the Girl's got it — the whole damn world's got it! It's all the Heaven there is on earth, and, in nine cases out of ten, it's Hell. [*There is a pause*]

[Rance, *deep in thought, lets his glass tip and his whiskey drip to the floor.* Nick *touches* Rance's *arm, points to the whiskey.* Rance *takes out his watch, glances at it, hands the glass back to* Nick, *who goes towards the door leading to the bar*]

Rance. Well, Nick, her road-agent's got off by now. [*Looking at his watch*]

Nick. Left Cloudy at three o'clock this morning — five hours off.

[Rance *takes out a match, strikes it on the stove, then lights his cigar*]

[*Suddenly we hear a voice calling*]

Rider of the Pony Express [*outside*]. Hello!

Nick. Pony Express! Got through at last!   [*Goes to the bar-room*]

[*The* Rider of the Pony Express *comes in from the bar-room, muffled up to his eyes*]

Rider of the Pony Express. Hello, boys! [*Giving a letter to the* Deputy Sheriff, *who comes in from the lean-to*] Letter for Ashby. Well, boys, how'd you like bein' snowed in for a week?

Rance. Ashby ain't up yet. Dep: call Ashby.

[The Deputy Sheriff *goes off at the left*]

Rider of the Pony Express [*at the stove*]. Boys: there's a rumor up at the Ridge that you all let Ramerrez freeze, an' missed a hangin'. Say: they're roaring at you, boys. So long!

[Sonora *and* Trinidad, *who have appeared from the bar-room, give the* Rider *a hard glance as he goes out through the bar*]

Sonora [*calling after the* Pony Express Rider]. Wait! Says you to the boys at the Ridge as you ride by — the Academy at Cloudy is open to-day — says you — full blast.

[*We hear a door slam as the* Rider *goes on his way*]

Trinidad [*calling after the* Rider]. Whoopee! Whoop! They ain't got no Academy at the Ridge.

Nick [*bringing in whiskey for* Trinidad *and* Sonora]. Here, Sonora.

Rance [*with a sneer*]. Academy! Ha! Ha! Academy!

Sonora. What's the matter with you, Rance, anyway? We began this Academy game together — we boys an' the Girl — an' there's a — [*spits on the floor*] — pretty piece of sentiment back of it. She's taught some of us our letters and —

Trinidad. He's wearin' mournin' because Johnson didn't fall alive into his hands.

Sonora. Is that it?

Trinidad [*to* Rance]. Ain't it enough that he must be lyin' dead down some cañon with his mouth full of snow?

Sonora. You done all you could to git him. The boys is all satisfied he's dead.

[Nick *gives* Sonora *a sharp look, then turns guiltily to* Rance]

Rance [*rising, walking about restlessly*]. Yes — he's dead. The matter with *me* is, I'm a "Chink." [*He goes up to the window and glances out*]

All. Ha! Ha! Ha! Ha!

Rance. Boys: it's all up with the Girl and me.

Trinidad [*self-consciously*]. Throwed him!

Sonora [*in a low voice to* Nick, *who has picked up the empty glasses and is standing near the window*]. As sure's you live, she's throwed him over for me.

[Nick *hastily leaves the room with the glasses — coming back at once*]

TRINIDAD [*singing in his glee*]. "Will old dog Tray remember me."

SONORA [*crossing to the door at the left*]. The percession will now form to the Academy wood-pile, to finish splittin' wood for teacher.

TRINIDAD *and* SONORA [*singing*]. "Old dog Tray remember me."

SONORA [*chuckling to himself*]. For me! [*They go out to the lean-to*]

DEPUTY [*entering excitedly*]. Ashby's out with a posse. [RANCE *turns quickly*] Got off just after three this morning. [*Closes the door*]

NICK. What?

RANCE [*aside to* NICK, *with much excitement*]. He's after Johnson!

NICK. Help yourself, Dep.

[THE DEPUTY *goes into the bar-room*]

RANCE. Ashby's after Johnson! He was watching that horse — took him ten minutes to saddle up. Johnson has ten minutes' start. [*Hopefully*] Oh, God! [*Going towards the bar*] They'll never get him. Johnson's a wonder on the road. You got to take your hat off to the damn cuss. [*He passes off*]

[*We hear the whoop of approaching miners coming to school*]

[SONORA *enters with an armful of wood, which he puts on the floor near the stove*]

[TRINIDAD *enters, runs to the door at the back and opens it, then puts on his jacket*]

[THE DEPUTY *strolls in from the bar*]

SONORA. Boys gatherin' for school.

[HANDSOME, HAPPY, JOE, *a gambler, and a miner, come into the room, playing leap-frog as they enter, talking and laughing. Their boots are covered with snow.* HAPPY *goes up to the teacher's desk and picks up a book tied in a red handkerchief*]

HAPPY. Here, Trin, — here's the book.

[*He throws it to* TRINIDAD, *who throws it to* SONORA, SONORA *to* JOE, JOE *to* HANDSOME, HANDSOME *to* SONORA]

[BUCKING BILLY, *a new scholar from Watson's Camp, comes in*]

THE DEPUTY SHERIFF. Sh, boys! Noo scholer from Watson's. [*Indicating* BUCKING BILLY]

[BILLY *is a large, awkward miner, wearing an overcoat, muffler and top boots with brass tips. He carries a dinner pail which contains a sandwich and whiskey flask. He has a slate under his arm*]

SONORA [*as all stare at* BILLY]. Did you ever play lame soldier, m' friend?

BUCKING BILLY. No.

SONORA. We'll play it after school. You'll be the stirrup. [*To the others — with a wink*] We'll initiate him.

NICK [*up at the window*]. Boys, boys, here she is.

HAPPY [*looking out of the window*]. Here comes the Girl.

SONORA. Fix the seats.

[*All save* NICK, TRINIDAD *and one miner hasten off*]

TRINIDAD [*confidentially*]. Here, Nick: you don't think to-day'd be a good time to put the splice question to her?

NICK [*dubiously*]. I wouldn't rush her. You got plenty of time.

[*He hangs the blackboard on the wall.* SONORA *enters with a cask. The* MINER *gets another cask,* HANDSOME *enters with a plank, which he lays across the two casks. This forms a long table for the students.* SONORA *picks up his coat, which is lying on a chair, and puts it on hurriedly.* HAPPY, *the* DEPUTY, *and the* MINER *arrange more benches*]

TRINIDAD. Hurry up, boys — hurry up! Git everything in order.

[THE GIRL *enters. She is carrying a small book of poems. The men take off their hats*]

BOYS [*all speaking together*]. Hello, teacher!

GIRL. Hello!

[SONORA *crosses to* THE GIRL *and hands her a bunch of berries*]

TRINIDAD. Hello, teacher! [*He hands her an orange*]. From 'Frisco.

HAPPY [*comes down with a bunch of berries which he gives to* THE GIRL]. Regards!

[NICK *takes off her moccasins*]

GIRL [*quietly*]. Hello, boys! How's everything? [*With a guilty look, she glances from one to another, to see if they suspect her*]

HANDSOME. Bully!

SONORA. Say — we missed you. Never knew you to desert the Polka for a whole week before.

GIRL [*who has gone up to the desk*]. No, I — I — [*She lays the berries and the orange on the desk*]

HAPPY. Academy's opened.

GIRL. Yes . . . I see . . . [*She takes off her gloves*]

SONORA. Here's a noo pupil — Bucking Billy from Watson's.

[BUCKING BILLY *comes forward*]

GIRL. How do you do, Bucking Billy?

BUCKING BILLY [*shyly*]. How do!

GIRL [*starting and looking out of the window*]. What's that?

NICK. Log fell in the stove.

GIRL. Oh . . . [*Pulling herself together*] I guess I'm kind of nervous to-day.

[*She exchanges glances with* NICK *as she takes off her coat and hands it to him*]

SONORA. No wonder. Road-agent's been in camp . . . and we missed a hangin'. I can't get over that!

GIRL. Well, come on, boys, and let me see your hands. [*Emphatically*] Let me see them! [*After looking at the outstretched hands*] Git in there and wash them.

SONORA. Yes'm. Been blackenin' my boots. [*He points to his boots*]

GIRL. Yes, and look at them boots — and them boots — and them boots! Git in there, the whole lot of you, and clean up — and leave your whiskey behind. [*The boys go into the lean-to. Untying the strings of her cap, she takes if off and hands it to* NICK] Have you heard anything? Did he git away safe?

NICK. Yes.

GIRL. I was watchin' an' I seen him go . . . but suppose he don't git through . . . suppose . . .

NICK. He'll git through, sure. We'll hear he's out of this country before you know it. [*He hangs up* THE GIRL's *wraps*]

[RANCE *enters*]

GIRL. Jack Rance: I want to thank you.

RANCE. Oh, don't thank me that he got away. [*In a low voice*] It was them three aces and the pair you held.

GIRL [*in confidence*]. About them three aces — I want to say —

RANCE. But he better keep out of my country.

[THE GIRL *and* RANCE *look intently at one another*]

GIRL. Yes . . .

[*She rings the bell. The boys enter.* RANCE *sits down by the stove, paying no attention to the others.* HAPPY *enters, carrying the slates which are in a very bad condition — some have no frames, some have very little slate left — one or two have sponges hanging to the frames on strings, and all have slate-pencils fastened to the frames.* HAPPY *gives out the slates as the others march by*]

HAPPY. Come along, boys — git your slates.

TRINIDAD. Whoop!

GIRL. Trin, you're out of step, there. Git in step, Happy. [*The boys all march forward in the manner of school children. As each one gets his slate, he takes his seat.* THE GIRL *sits back of her desk on the platform. With a sickly laugh, trying to take interest in the scholars*] Now, boys: what books have we left over from last year?

HAPPY [*rising*]. Why, we scared up jest one whole book left — and the name of it is —

SONORA [*taking the book out of his pocket, and reading the title*]. "Old Joe Miller's Jokes."

GIRL. That will do nicely.

SONORA [*rising*]. Now, boys, before we begin, I propose no drawin' of weppings, drinkin' or swearin' in school hours. The conduct of certain members wore on teacher last term. I don't want to mention no names — but I want Handsome and Happy to hear what I'm sayin'. Is that straight?

ALL. You bet it is!

GIRL [*timidly*]. Last year you led off with an openin' address, Jack. [*She looks at him timidly*]

ALL. Yes! Yes! Yes! Yes! Go on, Sheriff!

TRINIDAD. Let her go, Jack. [*There is a pause.* RANCE *looks at* THE GIRL, *then turns away*]

RANCE. I pass.

GIRL [*quickly and with anxiety*]. Then Sonora?

SONORA [*embarrassed at being called upon to make a speech*]. Oh, Hell! I —

ALL. Sh! Sh! Sh! Go on! Go on! Go on!

SONORA [*abashed*]. I didn't mean that, of course. [*As he rises, he shifts his tobacco and unconsciously spits on* BUCKING BILLY's *new boots.* BUCKING BILLY *moves away*] I look upon this place as somethin' more than a place to set around an' spit on the stove. I claim they's culture in the air of California — an' we're here to buck up again' it an' hook on.

ALL. Hear! Hear! Hear!

[*Several of the men pound upon the desks enthusiastically*]

SONORA. With these few remarks, I — I set.

GIRL [*with deep feeling*]. Once more we meet together. There's been a lot happened of late that has learned me that — [RANCE *turns slightly in his seat.* NICK *looks at* RANCE, RANCE *at* THE GIRL] perhaps — I don't know so much as I thought I did — and I can't learn you much more. But if you're willin' to take me for what I am, — jest a woman who wants everybody to be all they ought to be, — why I'm willin' to rise up with you, an' help reach out [HANDSOME *raises his hand*] an' — What is it, Handsome?

HANDSOME. Whiskey, teacher. I want it so bad! Just one drink 'fore we start.

[*The boys all stand up, raising their hands and calling:* "Teacher." THE GIRL *puts her fingers in her ears*]

GIRL. No! . . . And now jest a few words on the subject of not settin' in judgment on the errin' — [*the boys all sit down again*] a subjeck near my heart.

[*The* SIDNEY DUCK *opens the door. The card is still pinned on his coat*]

ALL [*at sight of the* SIDNEY DUCK]. Git! Git!

[SID *is about to retreat*]

GIRL. Boys! Boys! I was jest gittin' to you, Sid, as I promised. Come in.

[SID *enters*]

SONORA. What — here? Among gentlemen? Git!

ALL. Eh? What? Git! Git!

TRINIDAD. Why, this fellow's a —

GIRL. I know — I know . . . but of late a man in trouble has been on my mind —

ALL. Eh?

GIRL [*catching* RANCE's *eye*]. Sid — of course, Sid —

ALL. Oh . . .

GIRL. — and I fell to thinkin' of the Prodigal Son — he done better at last, didn't he?

SONORA. I never heard that he was a card sharp.

TRINIDAD. No.

GIRL [*overcome with guilt — swallowing nervously*]. But suppose there was a moment in Sid's life when he felt called upon to find an extra ace. [*There is a slight pause*] Can't we forgive him? He says he's sorry. Sid?

SID. Oh, yes, Miss, I'm sorry. Course if I 'adn't got caught, things would 'a been different. I'm sorry.

GIRL. Sid, you git your chance. [*The boys mutter.* THE GIRL *takes the card off* SID's *coat*] Now go and set down. [THE GIRL *sits*]

[HAPPY *strikes* SID *as he attempts to sit*]

HAPPY. Git out of here!

GIRL. Happy! Happy! [SONORA, *as* SID *passes him, puts out his foot and trips him*] Sonora!

[SID *sits on a stool in a corner. Everyone moves away as far as possible*]

TRINIDAD [*rises*]. Say, Girl: you mean to say that honesty ain't the best policy? Supposin' my watch had no works, an' I was to sell it to the Sheriff for one hundred dollars. Would you have much respect for me?

GIRL. If you could do it, I'd have more respect for you than for the Sheriff.

[*The two Indians,* BILLY JACKRABBIT *and* WOWKLE, *enter quietly and sit on the bench by the wall under the blackboard. They take no part, but listen stupidly.* WOWKLE *has the papoose on her back*]

RANCE [*rising*]. Well, being Sheriff, I'm careful about the company I keep. I'll set in the bar. Cheats — [*looking at* SID] or road-agents aren't jest in my line. [*He turns and starts to go*] I walk in the open road, with my head up — [THE GIRL *looks down*] and my face to the sun; and wherever I've pulled up, you'll remark I've always played square and stood by the cyards. [*He pauses in the doorway*]

GIRL [*sitting*]. I know — I know — an' that's the way to travel — in the straight road. But if ever I don't travel that road — or — you —

NICK. You always will, you bet!

ALL. You bet she will! You bet!

GIRL. But if I don't — I hope there'll be someone to lead me back to the right road. Cause remember. Rance: some of us are lucky enough to be born good — others have to be elected.

[RANCE *goes out*]

SONORA [*touched*]. That's eloquence.

[SID *sobs.* HAPPY *takes out a bottle of whiskey and puts it to his lips. The boys all reach for it.* THE GIRL *takes the bottle away*]

GIRL. Give me that and set down. [*The boys sit down obediently.* THE GIRL *goes back to her desk, hands the bottle to* NICK *and sits.* NICK *puts the bottle on the shelf of the desk*] Now, if somebody can sing "My Country 'Tis" — Academy's opened. Sonora?

SONORA. No — I can't sing.

[*The boys all try to make each other sing. While they are chafing each other,* WOWKLE *and* BILLY JACKRABBIT *rise and sing*]

BILLY JACKRABBIT *and* WOWKLE. "My country 'tis of thee, Sweet land of liberty, Of thee I sing!"

SONORA. Well, if that ain't sarkism!

BILLY JACKRABBIT *and* WOWKLE. "Land where our fathers died". . .

SONORA [*quickly during the pause between the two lines*]. You bet they died hard!

INDIANS.
"Land of the Pilgrim's pride, From every mountain-side Let freedom ring!"

[*When the song is ended, the* INDIANS *sit down again*]

GIRL. Thank you, Billy and Wowkle. Now, them that can read, read.

TRINIDAD. This is us! Old Joe Miller!

SONORA [*reading from the book*]. "Can Feb-u-ary March? No, but — A-pril May."

GIRL. Now, Trin. [*As* TRINIDAD *laboriously reads the ancient joke,* SID *who has noticed* BUCKING BILLY'S *dinner-pail, reaches out with his feet, pulls the pail over to him, helps himself to food and a small flask of whiskey. He pushes the pail back and starts to eat and drink, glancing at the others furtively to see if he has been caught*] Now, then, boys, we mustn't forget our general infla — information. Trin, who killed Abel?

TRINIDAD [*in a surprised tone — thinking of some local character*]. Why, I didn't know he was dead.

GIRL. Bucking Billy: you count up to ten.

BUCKING BILLY [*rising*]. 1, 2, 3, 4 —

SONORA. Pretty good! I didn't think he knowed that much.

BUCKING BILLY. 5, 6, 7, 8, 9, 10, Jack, Queen — [*Everybody laughs.* BUCKING BILLY *suddenly discovers that his pail has been opened*] Somebody stole my lunch!

SONORA [*rising*]. Who?

BUCKING BILLY. Him! [*Pointing to* SID]

ALL. Put him out! Git out! Put him out!

GIRL. Boys! Boys!

[SONORA, TRINIDAD *and* HANDSOME *throw* SID *out and return to their seats*]

[THE GIRL *looks out through the window for a moment, then turns and opens a book*] I will read you a little verse from a book of pomes. "No star is ever lost we once have seen, We always may be what we might have been."

[*She rests her hand on the desk and breaks down, sobbing quietly.* NICK *rises and goes to her*]

SONORA. Why, what's the —

ALL. Why — what's —

GIRL. Nothin' . . . nothin' . . . Only it jest came over me that we mustn't be hard on sinners and . . . [*Breaking down completely*] Oh, boys . . . I'll be leavin' you soon — how can I do it? How can I do it?

SONORA. What?

TRINIDAD. What did she say?

SONORA. What'd you say? [*Going to her*] Why, what's the matter?

GIRL [*raising her head*]. Nothin' — nothin' — only I jest remembered I've promised to leave Cloudy soon, an' perhaps we — might never be together again — you an' me an' the Polka. Oh, it took me jest like that — when I seen your dear old faces — your dear, plucky old faces — an' reelized that — [*She drops her head on the desk again*]

[RANCE *enters*]

SONORA [*after a pause*]. What! You leavin' us?

HAPPY. Leavin' us?

NICK [*softly, that the others do not hear*] Careful, Girl, careful!

GIRL. It's bound to happen soon.

SONORA. Why, I don't quite understand. Great Gilead! We done anythin' to offend you?

GIRL. Oh, no, no!

SONORA. Tired of us? Ain't we got — [*casting about for a word*] style enough for you?

HAPPY [*rising*]. Be you goin' to show them Ridge boys we're petered out an' culture's a dead dog here?

TRINIDAD. Ain't we your boys no more?

SONORA [*with sentiment, looking like a large, fat cherub*]. Ain't I your boy? Why, what is it, Girl? Has anybody — tell me — perhaps —

GIRL [*raising her head and drying her eyes*]. We won't say no more about it. Let's forgit it. Only — when I go away — I want to leave the key of my cabin with old Sonora here. And I want you all to come up sometimes, an' to think of me as the Girl who loved you all, an' somewhere is wishin' you well — an' — I want to think of little Nick here runnin' my bar, an' not givin' the boys too much whiskey. [*Putting her hand on NICK's shoulder*]

SONORA. Hold on! They's jest one reason for a girl to leave her home an' friends . . . only one. Some other fellow away from here — that she — she likes better than she does any of us. Is that it?

GIRL [*raising her head again*]. Likes in a different way, — yes.

HAPPY. Well, so help me!

[SONORA *goes sadly back to his seat. The boys form a pathetic picture*]

TRINIDAD. Sure you ain't makin' a mistake?

GIRL. Mistake? No, no, boys — no mistake. Oh, boys: if you knew — [*She rises, hesitates a moment, then goes to them*] Trin . . . [*Putting hands on TRINIDAD's shoulder*] Ah, Sonora . . . [*She kisses* SONORA *on the cheek, turns and exits into the bar-room, sobbing*]

SONORA. Boys, Academy's busted . . .

[*There is a pause*]

RANCE [*sitting down in front of the stove*]. Ha! Ha! Ha! Well, the right man has come at last. Take your medicine, gentlemen.

SONORA. Rance, who's the man?

RANCE [*casually*]. Oh, — Johnson.

TRINIDAD. Holy —!

SONORA. Great —!

TRINIDAD *and* SONORA. You lie!

[*During the following speeches, some of the boys move the benches and desks back against the walls.* BUCKING BILLY *and the* MINER *leave*]

RANCE. Ask Nick.

[TRINIDAD *and* SONORA *look at* NICK]

SONORA. Why, you told me I had the first chance.

TRINIDAD. He told me the same thing.

SONORA. Well, for a first class liar!

TRINIDAD. You bet!

SONORA. But Johnson's dead. [*Suddenly, after a short pause*] He got away . . .

RANCE [*shaking the ashes from his cigar*]. Yes, he got away . . .

[*There is a pause as they realize the situation.* SONORA *comes to* RANCE, *followed by* TRINIDAD *and* HAPPY]

SONORA. Jack Rance: I call on you, as Sheriff, for Johnson. He was in your county.

HAPPY. You hustle up an' run a bridle through your pinto's teeth, or your boom for re-election's over, you lily-fingered gambler!

TRINIDAD [*shaking his fist at* RANCE]. You bet!

RANCE [*coolly*]. Oh — I — don't know as I give a —

TRINIDAD. No talk! We want —

ALL [*save* RANCE *and* NICK]. Johnson!

[ASHBY's *voice is heard outside*]

ASHBY. Boys!

NICK. Why, that's —

RANCE. That's Ashby! Oh, if — [*In his face is the hope of* JOHNSON's *capture. To* ASHBY, *who is still outside*] You've got him?

[ASHBY *enters, his face cool, triumphant. He stands near the door. The* DEPUTY *hastens out. This entire, scene is played easily and naturally — no suggestion of dramatic emphasis*]

ASHBY. Yes — we've got him!

SONORA. Not —

ASHBY. Johnson.

[*All look at each other with meaning glances.* NICK *alone is sorry that* JOHNSON *is caught*]

TRINIDAD. Alive?

ASHBY. You bet!

RANCE [*with a short, brutal laugh — the veneer of the gambler disappearing*]. Well, I didn't do it. I didn't do it. Now he be damned! [JOHNSON *enters his arms bound, pale, but with the courage of a man who is accustomed to risking his life. He is followed by the* DEPUTY] There's an end of him. How do you do, Mr. Johnson? I think, Mr. Johnson, about five minutes will do for you.

[TRINIDAD *takes out his watch*]

JOHNSON. I think so.

SONORA [*sarcastically*]. So this is the gentleman the girl loves?

RANCE. That's the gentleman.

[THE GIRL's *voice is heard outside*]

GIRL. Nick? Boys? [NICK *holds the door open.* THE GIRL *appears on the threshold of the bar-room.* ASHBY *steps between* THE GIRL *and* JOHNSON, *so that* THE GIRL *does not see him*] I forgot . . . it's recess. They can have a drink now. [*She moves away from the door*]

JOHNSON. Lock that door, Nick.

[NICK *shuts the door to the bar and locks it*]

RANCE. Why the hell —

JOHNSON. Please!

SONORA [*threateningly*]. Why, you —

RANCE [*to* SONORA]. You keep out of this. I handle the rope — I pick the tree.

SONORA. Then hurry.

TRINIDAD. You bet!

[ASHBY *nods in approval*]

SONORA. Come on.

[*There is a general movement towards the door leading to the trail*]

RANCE. Deputy?

[*The* DEPUTY *comes forward*]

JOHNSON. One minute . . .

RANCE. Be quick, then.

JOHNSON. It's true . . . I love the Girl.

RANCE [*brutally*]. Well — you won't in a minute. You — [*He makes a movement to strike him*]

JOHNSON. Oh, I don't care what you do to me. I'm prepared for death. That's nothing new. The man who travels my path faces death every day — for a drink of water or ten minutes' sleep. You've got me, and I wouldn't care . . . but for the Girl.

TRINIDAD. You've jest got three minutes.

SONORA. Yes.

JOHNSON. I don't want her to know my end. That would be an awful thought — that I died out there, close at hand. She couldn't stay here after that — she couldn't, boys, she couldn't.

RANCE [*briefly*]. That's understood.

JOHNSON. I'd like her to think that I got away — went East — and changed my way of living. So you jest drag me a long way from here before you . . . and when she grows tired of looking for letters that never come, she will say: "He has forgotten me," and that will be about enough for her to remember. She loved me before she knew what I was . . . and you can't change love in a minute.

RANCE [*striking him in the face*]. Why, you . . .

JOHNSON. I don't blame you! Strike me again — strike me! Hanging is too good for me. Damn me, body and soul — damn me! Why couldn't I have let her pass? Oh, by God, I'm sorry I came her way; but it's too late now — it's too late! [*He bows his head*]

[*There is a pause*]

RANCE. Is that your last word? [JOHNSON *does not answer*] That your last word? [TRINIDAD *snaps his fingers to indicate that time is up*] Dep.

[*The* DEPUTY *comes to* JOHNSON. RANCE *moves away, but* NICK *steps to* JOHNSON's *side*]

NICK. Good-bye, sir . . .

JOHNSON. Good-bye, Nick. You tell the Girl — no, don't say anything.

HAPPY. Come on, you!

[*They start to go*]

NICK [*his voice trembling*]. Boys: when Alliger was hanged, Rance let

The Girl of the Golden West

him see his sweetheart. I think — considerin' as how she ain't goin' to see no more of Mr. Johnson here — an' knowin' the Girl's feelin's, — I think she ought to have a chance to —

ALL. No! No! No!

RANCE. No!

JOHNSON. I've had my chance — inside of ten minutes I'll be dead, and it will be all your way. Couldn't you let me? I thought I'd have the courage not to ask, but — Oh, couldn't you?

[NICK goes to the door as though hearing some sound]

NICK. Here's the Girl, boys.

RANCE. No!

JOHNSON. All right. Thank you, Nick.

NICK. You must excuse Rance for bein' so small a man as to deny the usual courtesies, but he ain't quite himself.

JOHNSON. Come, boys, come.

[He starts for the door left. SONORA pushes him back. The DEPUTY and one of the miners step between JOHNSON and the door]

RANCE. Wait a minute. [There is a pause. JOHNSON slowly turns to face RANCE] I don't know that I'm so small a man as to deny the usual courtesies, since you put it that way. I always have extended them. But we'll hear what you have to say — that's our protection; and it might interest some of us to hear what the Girl will have to say to you, Mr. Johnson. After a week in her cabin, there may be more to know than —

JOHNSON [in a low voice]. Why, you damned —

[NICK moves towards RANCE]

NICK. Rance, you —

[The boys all look at RANCE angrily, showing that they resent his words]

SONORA. Now, Rance, you stop that!

RANCE. We'll hear every word he has to say.

SONORA. You bet! He puts up nothin' noo on us.

ASHBY [looking at his watch]. Well, boys, you've got him safe — I can't wait. I'm off. [He goes off]

[THE GIRL'S voice is heard outside the bar-room door]

GIRL. Nick? Nick?

NICK. Here's the Girl, boys.

RANCE. Deputy . . . [He unties JOHNSON]. Circle around to the bar, boys. Trin, put a man at that door. Sonora, put a couple of men at those windows. [SONORA, HAPPY, the DEPUTY and the GAMBLER go outside. HANDSOME and TRINIDAD go into the lean-to. NICK stands at the bar-room door] Johnson, if you can't think of something pleasant to tell the Girl, lie to her.

JOHNSON. I'll let her think I came back to see her again. She needn't know it's the last time.

[THE GIRL'S voice is heard outside]

GIRL. Nick? Nick?

[RANCE leaves the room. TRINIDAD, HANDSOME and RANCE can be seen to pass the windows. JOHNSON steps behind the door. NICK unbars the bar-room door and THE GIRL enters]

GIRL. What you got the door barred for, Nick? [Looking round] Where are the boys?

NICK. Well, you see, the boys — the boys — has — has —

GIRL. Has what?

NICK [as though struck by a bright idea]. Has gone.

GIRL. Gone where?

NICK. Why, to the Palmetter. Oh, say, Girl — [He crosses over to her and puts his hands on her shoulders] I like you. You've been my religion — the bar an' you. You don't never want to leave us. Why, I'd drop dead for you!

GIRL [somewhat surprised and touched]. Nick! [She goes up to her desk as JOHNSON knocks on the door left]

JOHNSON [appearing]. Girl! [He holds out his arms to her]

GIRL. You? You? Look outside and —

[NICK closes the door, bars and holds it]

JOHNSON. Don't say a word.

GIRL [in JOHNSON's arms]. You shouldn't have come back.

JOHNSON. I had to — to say good-bye once more.

NICK [lying with effort]. It's all right — it's all right. [During NICK's speech, THE GIRL draws the curtains] The boys — why, the boys — they are good for quite a little bit yet. Don't git nervous. I'll give you warning.

[NICK *steps into the bar*]

JOHNSON. Don't be afraid, Girl.

GIRL. But you can't go now without being seen.

JOHNSON [*with a smile*]. Yes — there's one way out of Cloudy — and I'm going to take it.

GIRL [*attempting to move from him*]. Then go! Go!

JOHNSON. Just remember that I am sorry for the past — and don't forget me.

GIRL. Forgit you? How could —

JOHNSON. I mean . . . till we meet.

GIRL [*apprehensively*]. Did he call?

JOHNSON. No. He will — he'll warn me . . . Don't forget me.

GIRL. Every day that dawns I'll wait for a message from you. I'll feel you wanting me. Every night, I'll say: "To-morrow" — and every to-morrow I'll say: "To-day!" For you've changed the whole world for me. I can't let you go . . . but I must. Dick — Oh, I'm afraid! [*She hides her head on* JOHNSON's *shoulder*]

JOHNSON. You mustn't be afraid. In a few minutes, I shall be quite free.

GIRL. And you'll make a little home for me where you're goin' — soon — with you? [*She is overcome.* JOHNSON *merely nods*] A strange feelin' has come over me. A feelin' to hold you, to cling to you — not to let you go. Somethin' in my heart says, "Don't let him go."

JOHNSON. Girl, it's been worth life just to know you. You've brought me nearer Heaven. You — to love a man like me! [*He covers his face with his hands, breaks down and sobs*]

GIRL. Don't say that. Don't! Suppose you was only a road-agent — an' I was a saloon-keeper: we both came out of nothin' an' we met, but, through loving, we're goin' to reach things now — that's us! We had to be lifted up like this, to be saved.

[NICK *enters. As he opens the door, the boys are seen outside, but* THE GIRL *has her back to them*]

NICK. It's all clear now. [NICK *backs off, closing the door again*]

JOHNSON. Good-bye.

GIRL [*in* JOHNSON's *arms*]. You act as though he was never goin' to meet again, an' we are, ain't we?

JOHNSON. Why, surely — we are.

GIRL. I want you to think of me here jes' waitin'. You was the first . . . there'll never be anyone but you. All that mother was to father, *I'm* goin' to be to you. You're the man I'd want settin' across the table, if they was a little kid like I was, playin' under it. I can't say more than that! Only — you — you will — you must get through safe — and, well, think of me here jes' waitin' . . . jes' waitin' . . . jes' waitin' . . .

[*He stands looking at her. After a little pause, she puts her face in his arm and weeps*]

JOHNSON. Oh, Girl, Girl! That first night I went to your cabin — I saw you kneeling — praying. Say that in your heart again just for me — now. Perhaps I believe it — perhaps I don't. I hope I do. I want to. But say it — say it, Girl — just for the luck of it. Say it. [*He kneels at her feet, his head bowed.* THE GIRL *prays silently, crossing herself before she begins, and, at the end of the prayer, they embrace.* SONORA *opens the door quietly*] God bless you! Good-bye . . . Good-bye, Girl!

[SONORA *is followed by the rest of the boys,* RANCE *being the last to enter.* JOHNSON, *looking over* THE GIRL's *shoulder, sees the boys. He kisses her hands affectionately*]

GIRL. Good-bye . . .

JOHNSON! Girl! Girl! [*He goes off left*]

GIRL. He's gone — Nick. [*Sobbing, she makes a movement to follow* JOHNSON, *then goes to* NICK *and sobs in his arms. Suddenly she sees the men*]

NICK [*soothingly*]. Girl! Girl!

GIRL [*in alarm*]. You — you knew . . . You all knew . . . You had him — you had him all the time . . . An' you're goin' to kill him — but you sha'n't! [*Running over to the door left, she throws herself against it — her back to it, then sobs convulsively*] No! You sha'n't kill him — you sha'n't — you sha'n't!

SONORA [*advances*]. Girl . . . the boys an' me ain't perhaps reelized jest what Johnson stood for to you, Girl — an', hearin' what you said, an' seein' you prayin' over the cuss —

RANCE. Damned cuss!

SONORA. Yes, the damned cuss, I got an idee maybe God's back of this here game.

GIRL [*with much anxiety*]. You're not goin' to pull the rope on him?

RANCE [*to the men*]. You mean I am to set him free?

GIRL [*a gleam of hope in her heart*]. You set him free?

RANCE. I let him go?

SONORA. That's our verdict, an' we're prepared to back it up.

GIRL. Dick — Dick — you're free! [*She rushes out and her voice is heard outside*]. You're free! You're free!

[*There is a pause. The men stand silently looking at each other*]

NICK. The Polka won't never be the same, boys — the Girl's gone.

CURTAIN

ACT IV

The boundless prairies of the West.

On the way East, at the dawn of a day about a week later.

"Oh, my beautiful West!
Oh, my California!"

The scene is a great stretch of prairie. In the far background are foothills with here and there a suggestion of a winding trail leading to the West. The foliage is the pale green of sage brush, — the hills the deeper green of pine and hemlock. In the foreground is a little tepee made of two blankets on crossed sticks. The tepee is built against a grass mound and is apparently only a rude shelter for the night. Back of the tent is an old tree stump which stands out distinctly against the horizon. Here and there are little clumps of grass, bushes and small mounds of earth and rocks. A log fire is burning to the left of the tepee, a Mexican saddle lies beside the fire.

As the curtain rises, the stage is in darkness. JOHNSON is lying on the grass, leaning against his saddle, smoking a cigarette. THE GIRL is inside the tepee. Gradually the dawn begins to break. As the scene becomes visible, THE GIRL pushes aside the blanket and appears in the opening.

GIRL. Dick, are you awake?

JOHNSON [*turning to her*]. Another day . . . the dawn is breaking.

GIRL [*looking towards the unseen hills in the distance*]. Another day . . . Look back . . . the foothills are growing fainter — every dawn — farther away. Some night when I am going to sleep, I'll turn — and they won't be there — red and shining. That was the promised land.

JOHNSON [*rising*]. We must look ahead, Girl, not backwards. The promised land is always ahead.

[*A glimmer of the rising sun is seen on the foliage of the foothills*]

GIRL. Always ahead . . . Yes, it must be. [*She comes out of the tepee and goes up the path*] Dick: all the people there in Cloudy — how far off they seem now — like shadows in a dream. Only a few days ago, I clasped their hands; I saw their faces — their dear faces! And now they are fading. In this little, little while, I've lost them . . . I've lost them. [*There are tears in her voice*]

JOHNSON. Through you, all my old life has faded away. *I* have lost that.

GIRL. Look! [*Pointing to the left as she notices the sunrise*] The dawn is breaking in the East — far away — fair and clear.

JOHNSON. A new day . . . Trust me. [*Stretching out his hands to her*] Trust me. . . . A new life!

GIRL. A new life. [*Putting her hands in his*] Oh, my mountains — I'm leaving you — Oh, my California, I'm leaving you — Oh, my lovely West — my Sierras! — I'm leaving you! — Oh, my — [*turning to JOHNSON, going to him and resting in his arms*] — my home.

CURTAIN

THE WITCHING HOUR

(1907)

By Augustus Thomas

AUGUSTUS THOMAS

Since the early days when Augustus Thomas first turned his attention to the theatre, there has been no one who has contributed more to the healthy amusement of the public than he. He is the product of the playhouse of his own time, a little less amenable to the wishes of the Frohmans than Clyde Fitch, but filling a position of importance among the dramatists of the Frohman era. He began, after his first dramas, to write a series of racy comedies that have in them a simple flavor which was native in atmosphere and familiarly good-natured in temper. He had a reportorial eye — having been himself a newspaper man; he viewed his problems predominately from the masculine angle, which inevitably made him, in the critical estimation of the press, a contrast to the more detailed and feminine approach of Clyde Fitch. But his range of observation was more limited, and his psychology was less subtle than Fitch's. Looking over his long list of plays, and remembering the stage presentation of many of them; reading some of them in closer study of their technique, Mr. Thomas's development in finesse resulted in a style which was distinctive. And to this was added a mastery of stage detail that carried many a play of slim content a long way toward success.

This technique in later years has been excellently analyzed by Mr. Thomas in a series of introductions to many of his plays, explaining the origin of many of his plots, their growth and expansion, and their claim to worthiness as dramatic material. He has followed this examination further in his entertaining volume of reminiscences, "The Print of My Remembrance." Here one is told how long he carried in his mind many subjects which he first worked up as one-act plays, afterwards to be changed into the full length dramas. "Alabama", "The Harvest Moon", "The Witching Hour", "As a Man Thinks", "Rio Grande" and "The Copperhead" were thus transformed.

Mr. Thomas has lived in the midst of the newspaper and show business, and in addition has had wide contacts of a political nature. He has had every opportunity for studying the point of view of the man about town, of the man on the street. "The Witching Hour" is full of those touches which are a close reading of that daily human nature which makes so many of his plays excellent transcripts of the hour.

A number of his plays have moved in cycles of interest, as measured by the response of the box-office. His "state" comedies: "Alabama", "In Mizzoura", "Arizona", "Colorado", "Rio Grande" are related in shape and in intent. The best of them, theatrically, is "Arizona." "The Earl of Pawtucket" — a good, wholesome, amusing farce — was the forerunner of "Delancey" and "The Embassy Ball." And his interest in psychopathic cases, beginning with "The Witching Hour", passed into "The Harvest Moon" and "As a Man Thinks." Personally, I have remembered with particular pleasure the breeziness of "Mrs. Leffingwell's Boots" and the New York metropolitan flavor of "The Other Girl."

Knowing his theatre as closely and as thoroughly as Clyde Fitch, Mr. Thomas has rehearsed his plays unerringly, chosen his actors with foresight, and oftentimes written his plays with definite actors in mind. The managers left to him, as they did to Fitch, those details of casting which in both dramatists helped to enrich their plays as theatre commodities, and usually gave finished and satisfying results.

Mr. Thomas's attitude toward the theatre has always been that of the theatre; but his excellent grasp of stagecraft has given to many of his plays a certain polish very near literature. When he has used themes that required set psychological intrigue, coupled with external action, he has not only well utilized the cumulative value of psychological interest, but has also paved the way in his dialogue for explanation of a partially scientific character. This opened him to the accusation of being preachy at times, as he tended to be in certain speeches of "The Witching Hour", and "The Harvest Moon", but very noticeably in "As a Man Thinks" — the rôle of *Doctor Seelig*. But in the latter play, where the dialogue is excellently fluent, his technique reached its most precise height, even though the play suffered because of a plethora of themes and a division of interest on the part of his audience.

Mr. Thomas was of the theatre of the period of the Eighteen-Nineties. He was steeped in the Frohman era, even though, with "The Witching Hour", he turned from Frohman to Lee Shubert for production. It seems strange that there was any doubt about the advisability of using such a theme as underlies this play. Yet on the advice of Daniel Frohman, his brother Charles went against his own decision to use the play, and let it pass to another. But, in the Eighteen-Nineties, telepathy and other problems of psychic phenomena were just beginning to be thought of by the public, through such writers as Hudson who, in 1893, published his "Law of Psychic Phenomena." At an earlier period, in 1888, Mr. Thomas had been the publicity man for Washington Irving Bishop, a thought-reader, who had turned his "power" to the showman's uses. And his interest from then on in the subject resulted in more intent study on his part and the trial of a one-act piece, in 1890, called "A Constitutional Point." The manager, A. M. Palmer, at that time thought the subject too abstruse for the theatre-going public. It was this play that later became the second act of "The Witching Hour." Both Mr. Palmer and Mr. Thomas were then associated, the former as manager, the latter as "house" dramatist for the Madison Square Theatre. The plot of this sketch came from a reportorial experience.

Through arrangement with The Lambs Club, Mr. Thomas tried out his one-act playlet to sound the temper of his audience. From the Lambs Club, therefore, came "The Witching Hour." It will be recalled that James Forbes's "The Chorus Lady" had originally been a Lambs Club entertainment. Although I do not believe Eugene Walter's "The Easiest Way" was thus tried out, I know that it too began its career as a one-act sketch, entitled "All the Way from Denver."

How the longer play evolved from the sketch is a story Mr. Thomas has outlined in an Introduction written for the Samuel French acting version of "The Witching Hour." His forewords to other plays as well — "Oliver Goldsmith", "The Earl of Pawtucket", "Mrs. Leffingwell's Boots," and "In Mizzoura" — throw much light on the habits of a playwright's mind, — a playwright of the Frohman period. "Things began to click and drop into place," he says, in one of these explanations. Here then a dramatist gives lessons in playwriting. The student cannot pass them by, any more than he should ignore Bronson Howard's enlightening "Autobiography of a Play." Mr. Thomas is a good raconteur; without effort he makes his points. The American well-made play stands revealed.

In 1922, Mr. Thomas became the executive chairman of the Producing Managers, Association; through his agency it was hoped to bring more coördination among theatre men. It was believed that he would do for the theatre what Will Hays is attempting to do for the moving-picture industry; what Judge Landis has been struggling to do for baseball. The Association has been disbanded because of division, due to the organized stand of actors through the Equity Association. It was an economic struggle where the actors had a justifiable position. To the very last Mr. Thomas served the cause of the theatre as he interpreted it. But he was not serving in the capacity of dramatist. And it is Mr. Thomas, the dramatist, who here concerns us. Of late years he has created little.

"The Witching Hour" was presented at the Hackett Theatre, in New York, on November 18, 1907. Of contemporary criticism, Walter P. Eaton's estimate is worthy of quotation:

Swallow the pill or not as you like, scoff or not as your scepticism or credulity dictates at the telepathy, there still remains in "The Witching Hour" a human story, crisply, naturally, strongly told; there still remains the medicinal effect of a mild hypnotism applied with no little philosophic and psychologic insight in the last act, not the shallow, or bromide, philosophy of the usual drama; there still remains the imaginative skill displayed in the weaving through the warp of concrete facts the woof of airy things and things intangible. Mr. Thomas has surely added nothing to science; he may even have exceeded what science and common sense allow him of hypnotic and telepathic phenomena. But this at least he has done, and done well; he has reached down through the crust of the commonplace for the dim fires that smolder beneath, and in a drama of truth and power he has set a coal from those fires to glow unceasingly. His attempt was audacious, fine; his achievement deserving of a fine reward.

Thus, in 1907, we welcomed a piece of sincerity in a plethora of native theatricalism; we enjoyed pseudo-intellectualism where there was not much intellect at all in the native product.

THE WITCHING HOUR

A DRAMA IN FOUR ACTS

———

By AUGUSTUS THOMAS

Revised 1916 by AUGUSTUS THOMAS

COPYRIGHT, 1916,

BY AUGUSTUS THOMAS

THE WITCHING HOUR

Original Company in Mr. Shubert's production at the Hackett Theatre, New York,
November 18, 1907
In order of their first appearance.

Jo	S. E. Hines
Jack Brookfield	John Mason
Tom Denning	Freeman Barnes
Harvey	T. P. Jackson
Mrs. Alice Campbell	Ethel Winthrop
Mrs. Helen Whipple	Jennie A. Eustace
Viola	Adelaide Nowak
Clay Whipple	Morgan Coman
Frank Hardmuth	George Nash
Lew Ellinger	William Sampson
Justice Prentice	Russ Whytal
Justice Henderson	E. J. Walton
Servant	W. Butterfield
Colonel Bayley	Harry Hadfield
Mr. Emmett	Mr. Fawnsgaines

THE WITCHING HOUR

ACT I

SCENE. — *The library and card-room at* "JACK BROOKFIELD'S", *Louisville.*

There is a large doorway center, at the back, that lets into a hallway, in which the bannister of a stairway that descends to the street level is seen. A second and smaller doorway is near the front in the wall to the left of the stage. This doorway leads to the dining-room. The second plan of the left wall is occupied by a fireplace and mantel, surmounted by a marine painting. The fireplace is surrounded by a garde au feu *club seat.*

The rest of the left wall, as well as the rear wall on both sides of the center door and all of the right wall, is fitted with bookcases about five feet high, in which are books handsomely bound.

The walls above these bookcases are hung with heavy brocaded Genoese velvet of a deep maroon in color and loosely draped. The ceiling is of hard wood, gilded. On the wall velvet, at proper intervals, are paintings by celebrated modern artists. Some of these paintings are fitted with hooded electric lights. Such a fitting is above a noticeable Corot, which hangs to the right of the center door.

A dark-red rug of luxuriant thickness is on the floor. The furniture is simple, massive, and Colonial in type. It consists of a heavy sofa above the fireplace and running at right angles to the wall. A heavy table fitted with books is in the center, a smaller table for cards is at the stage, right. Chairs are at both tables.

Above the center door is a marble bust of Minerva, surmounted by a bronze raven, lacquered black, evidently illustrating Poe's poem. The Antommarchi death-mask of Napoleon in bronze hangs on the dark wood fireplace. A bronze mask of Bee-

thoven is on one of the bookcases and on another is a bust of Dante. A bronze Sphinx is on another bookcase.

The room is lighted by a standing lamp at the back and by the glow from the fire-place. Over the table, center, is suspended an electric lamp in a large bronze shade. This lamp, while not lighted, is capable of being turned on by a push button, which depends from it.

On the table, center, is a large paper-cutter made of an ivory tusk.

Empty stage. After pause, sound of laughter and dishes, left.

[*Enter* JO, *sleek negro of Pullman car variety, by stairway and center door. He goes to door, left, and pauses — laughter ceases*]

JO.   Massar Brookfield.
JACK [*outside left*].   Well, Jo?
JO.   Mr. Denning, sah.
JACK.   Ask Mr. Denning to come up.
JO.   Yes, sah. [*Exit center. More talk and laughter, left*]

[JACK *enters left. He walks to center on way toward main door. Pauses. Returns, left*]

JACK [*at door left*].   Lew! I say — Lew — you ladies excuse Mr. Ellinger a moment?
HELEN, ALICE, VIOLA [*outside*].   Oh — yes, certainly.

[*Enter* LEW ELLINGER, *from dining-room, left*]

LEW.   See me?
JACK.   Tom Denning's here — he expects a game. My sister and Mrs. Whipple object to the pasteboards — so don't mention it before them.
LEW.   Not a word — but, Tom —?
JACK.   I'll attend to Tom.
LEW.   Good. [*Starts back to dining-room*]

107

[*Enter* Tom Denning, *right center, he is fat, indolent type*]

Tom. Hello, Lew. [Lew *stops and turns.* Jack *motions him out and* Lew *goes*] What you got to-night? Young Rockefeller?

Jack. Some ladies.

Tom [*grinning*]. What —

Jack [*sternly*]. My sister and her daughter — and a lady friend of theirs.

Tom [*disappointed*]. No game?

Jack. Not until they go.

Tom [*getting a peek off into dining-room*]. Oh — chafing dish.

Jack. They've been to the opera. — I had Harvey brew them some terrapin.

Tom [*complaining*]. My luck! [*His hands hang limp*]

Jack. No, I think there's some left. [*Pause*] I'm going to take a long chance and introduce you, Tom, only don't say anything about poker before the ladies.

Tom. Thought you said your sister —

Jack. I did.

Tom. Well, she's on, isn't she?

Jack. But she doesn't like it — and my niece — my *niece* doesn't like it.

[*Enter* Harvey, *old negro servant, from dining-room, left*]

Harvey. I'se made some coffee, Mars Jack. You have it in the dining-room or heah, sah?

Jack [*going*]. I'll ask the ladies.

Tom. How are you, Harvey?

Harvey [*bowing*]. Mars Denning —

Jack [*who has paused at door, left*]. Got some terrapin for Mr. Denning, Harvey?

Harvey. Yas, sah. [*To* Tom] Yas, sah.

[*Exit* Jack, *left*]

Tom. They left some of the rum, too, I hope.

Harvey. Couldn't empty my ice-box in one evening, Mars Denning. [*Starts off. Pause*] De ladies getting up. [*Stands up stage in front of fire.* Tom *goes right. A pause. Enter* Jack]

Jack. The ladies will have their coffee in here, Harvey.

Harvey. Yes, sah.

[*Enter* Alice. *She is smartly gowned and is energetic*]

Jack. Alice — this is my friend, Mr. Denning — my sister — Mrs. Campbell.

Alice. Mr. Denning.

[*Enter* Helen *and* Viola. Helen *is thoroughly feminine in type, and is young-looking for the mother of a boy of twenty —* Viola *is an athletic Kentucky girl*]

Helen. I never take coffee even after dinner and at this hour — never!

[*Exit* Harvey]

Jack. Mrs. Whipple, may I present Mr. Denning?

Helen. Mr. Denning.

Tom. Good-evening!

Jack. My niece, Miss Viola Campbell.

Tom. How are you?

[Viola *bows*]

Jack. Mr. Denning's just left the *foundry* and he's very hungry.

Tom. And thirsty —

Jack [*pushing him toward dining-room*]. Yes, and thirsty. Uncle Harvey's going to save his life.

Tom. Ha, ha! Excuse me! [*Exit*]

Alice. The foundry? [*Sits right of table*]

Jack. Never did a day's work in his life. That's Tom Denning.

Viola [*on sofa at fireplace*]. Tom Denning's the name of the big race-horse.

Jack. Yes — he's *named after* the race-horse.

Helen [*on sofa, beside* Viola]. What does he do?

Jack. His father — father's in the packing business — Kansas City; this fellow has four men *shoveling* money away from him so he can breathe. [*Starts toward dining-room*]

Alice [*in amused protest*]. Oh, Jack!

Jack. Yes — I'm one of them — you'll find cigarettes in that box.

Alice. Jack! [*Rises*]

Jack [*apologizing*]. Not *you*, Alice, but —

Viola [*protesting*]. Well, certainly not for *me*, Uncle Jack?

Jack. Of course, not you. —

Helen. Thank you, Mr. Brookfield!

Alice [*joining* Jack]. My dear brother, you confuse the Kentucky ladies with some of your Eastern friends.

Jack. Careful, Alice. *Helen* lived in the East twenty years, remember.

Helen. But even my *husband* didn't smoke.

Jack. No?

Helen. *Never* — in his life —

JACK. In his *life?* Why make such a pessimistic distinction?

[HELEN *turns away right*]

ALICE. Jack! [*After a look to* HELEN] How can you say a thing like that?

JACK. *She's* the man's widow — *I've* got to say it if any one does. [*Enter* HARVEY, *with coffee*] Mr. Denning's got his tortoise, Uncle Harvey?

HARVEY [*offering tray to* HELEN]. He's got the same as we all had, Mars Jack. Yas, sah. [*Laughs*]

HELEN. None, thank you.

[HARVEY *moves on*]

JACK. I'll take it, Uncle Harvey, I think three or four of them'll help this head of mine.

ALICE [*taking coffee*]. Why don't you let Viola cure your headache?

VIOLA [*taking coffee*]. Yes, Uncle Jack.

JACK. No, the coffee'll fix it, I'm sure.

[*Exit* HARVEY]

VIOLA. Sit here while you drink it.

JACK. No — no, Viola. It isn't enough for that. I'll conserve your mesmeric endowment for a real occasion. [*Swallows coffee in one mouthful*]

VIOLA. Goodness! Just to please me?

JACK [*shaking head*]. Don't want to spoil your awful stories. [*Exit to dining-room*]

HELEN. Is Viola a magnetic healer, too? [*Sits right of table*]

VIOLA [*takes a book, and returns to sofa, carrying also the large ivory tusk paper-cutter*]. Oh, no.

ALICE [*sitting left of table*]. Yes — a remarkable one.

VIOLA. Only headaches, Mrs. Whipple. Those I *crush* out of my victims.

HELEN. I remember Jack used to have a wonderful ability that way as a young man.

VIOLA. He says only with the girls.

ALICE. We know better, don't we?

HELEN. Yes.

VIOLA. Well, for myself, I'd rather have Uncle Jack sit by me than any regular physician I ever saw.

HELEN. You mean if you were ill?

VIOLA. Of course.

ALICE. You must be very clear with Mrs. Whipple on that point, Viola, because she used to prefer your Uncle Jack to sit by her, even when she wasn't ill.

HELEN [*to* VIOLA]. But especially when ill, my dear. [*To* ALICE] And has he quit it?

ALICE. Yes — you know Jack went into politics for a while.

HELEN. Did he?

ALICE. *Local* politics — yes — something about the police didn't please him and then he quit all of his curative work.

HELEN. Why?

ALICE. Well, in politics, I believe there's something unpleasant about the word "heeler."

HELEN. Oh!

VIOLA. Entirely different spelling, however.

HELEN. Our English language is so elastic in that way.

ALICE. Yes, the papers joked about his magnetic touch. The word "touch" is used offensively also. So Jack dropped the whole business.

HELEN. And Viola inherits the ability?

ALICE. Well, if one can inherit ability from an uncle.

HELEN. From a family.

ALICE. That's even more generous, but Viola is like Jack in every way in which a girl may resemble a man. Horses and boats and every kind of personal risk — and —

VIOLA [*rises*]. I'm *proud* of it.

ALICE. And Jack spoils her?

VIOLA. Am I spoiled? [*Goes to back of table*]

ALICE. He couldn't love her more if he were her father —

[*Enter* CLAY, *left, a boy of twenty*]

CLAY [*pausing at door*]. May I come in?

VIOLA. Certainly.

CLAY. Isn't this a jolly room, mother?

HELEN. Beautiful.

CLAY [*waving hand above*]. And the sleeping apartments are what I take pride in. Private bath to every bedroom, reading lamps just over the pillows —

VIOLA. Haven't you seen the house, Mrs. Whipple?

HELEN. Not above this floor.

ALICE. Would it interest you? [*Rises and goes left*]

HELEN. Very much.

ALICE [*at door of dining-room*]. Jack —

JACK [*outside*]. Yes —

ALICE [*to* HELEN]. Will I do as your guide?

HELEN [*rises*]. Oh, yes.

[*Enter* JACK, *left*]

ALICE. I want to show Helen over the house.

JACK. Do.

ALICE. The rooms are empty?

JACK. Empty, of course.

ALICE. Don't be too indignant, they're not always empty. [*To* HELEN] In *Jack's* house one is liable to find a belated pilgrim in any room.

HELEN [*laughing*]. And a lady walking in unannounced would be something of a surprise, wouldn't she?

JACK. Well — two ladies would, certainly.

ALICE. Jack!

JACK. My dear sister — they *would*. Hard lines when the reputation of a man's house isn't respected by his own sister — ha! [*Exit left, with mock indignation*]

HELEN [*smiling*]. The same Jack.

ALICE. Intensified and confirmed! [*Pausing at door*] Will you come, too, Viola?

VIOLA. No, thank you, mother.

[HELEN *looks at* ALICE. *She and* ALICE *exeunt left center*]

CLAY. What was Frank Hardmuth saying to you?

VIOLA. When?

CLAY. At supper — and in the box at the theater, too?

VIOLA. Oh — Frank Hardmuth — nobody pays any attention to him.

CLAY. I thought *you* paid a great deal of attention to what he was saying.

VIOLA. In the same theater party a girl's got to listen — or leave the box.

CLAY. Some persons listen to the opera.

VIOLA. I told him that was what I wanted to do.

CLAY. Was he making love to you, Viola?

VIOLA. I shouldn't call it that.

CLAY. Would anybody else have called it that if they'd overheard it?

VIOLA. I don't think so.

CLAY. Won't you tell me what it was about?

VIOLA. I don't see why you ask.

CLAY. I asked because he seemed so

much in earnest — and because *you* seemed so much in earnest.

VIOLA. Well?

CLAY. And Frank Hardmuth's a fellow that'll stand watching. [*Looks off left*]

VIOLA [*smiling*]. He stood a good deal to-night.

CLAY. I mean that he's a clever lawyer and would succeed in making a girl commit herself in some way to *him* before she knew it.

VIOLA. I think that depends more on the way the *girl* feels.

CLAY. Well — I don't want you to listen to Frank Hardmuth under the idea that he's the only chance in Kentucky.

VIOLA. Why, Clay Whipple —

CLAY. You know very well *I've* been courting you myself, Viola, don't you?

VIOLA. You haven't. You've been coming round like a big boy.

CLAY [*follows right*]. Have I gone with any other girl — anywhere?

VIOLA. I don't know. [*Sits right*]

CLAY. And I've spoken to your Uncle Jack about it.

VIOLA. To Uncle Jack?

CLAY. Yes.

VIOLA [*rises*]. Nobody told you to speak to Uncle Jack.

CLAY. Mother did.

VIOLA. *Your* mother?

CLAY. Yes. Mother's got regular old-fashioned ideas about boys and young ladies and she said, "if you think Viola *likes* you, the *honorable* thing to do is to speak to her guardian first."

VIOLA. Oh! — you *thought* that, did you?

CLAY. I certainly did.

VIOLA. I can't imagine why.

CLAY. I thought that because you're Jack Brookfield's niece, and nobody of his blood would play a game that isn't fair.

VIOLA. I wish you wouldn't always throw that up to me. [*Goes to sofa*] 'Tisn't our fault if Uncle Jack's a sporting man. [*Sits*]

CLAY [*following*]. Why, Viola, I was praising him. I think your Uncle Jack the gamest man in Kentucky.

VIOLA. Nor that either. I don't criticise my Uncle Jack, but he's a lot better man than just a fighter or a cardplayer. I love him for his big heart.

CLAY. So do I. If I'd thought you cared I'd have said you were too much like him at heart to let a fellow come a-courtin' if you meant to refuse him — and that was all that was in my mind when I asked about Frank Hardmuth — and I don't care what Hardmuth said either, if it wasn't personal that way.

VIOLA. Frank Hardmuth's nothing to me.

CLAY. And he won't be? [*Pause*] Will he —? [*Pause*] Say that. Because I'm awfully in love with you.

VIOLA. Are you?

CLAY. You bet I am. Just Tom-fool heels over head in love with you.

VIOLA. You never said so.

CLAY. Mother said a boy in an architect's office had better wait till he was a partner — but I can't wait, Viola, if other fellows are pushing me too hard.

VIOLA [*rises*]. Uncle Jack says you are a regular architect if there ever was one.

CLAY. It's what *you* think that makes the difference to me.

VIOLA. Well, I think — [*Pause*] — Uncle Jack certainly *knows*.

CLAY. And an architect's just as good as a lawyer.

VIOLA. Every bit.

CLAY. Viola. [*Takes her in his arms*]

VIOLA. Now — I don't *mind* tellin' you — he was speakin' for himself — Frank Hardmuth.

CLAY. By Jove — on this very night.

VIOLA. Yes.

CLAY. Seems like the Hand of Providence that I was here. Let's sit down. *They sit*] You've got confidence in me, haven't you?

VIOLA. Yes — I've always said to mother — Clay Whipple'll make his mark some day — I should say I *had* confidence in you.

CLAY. Huh. [*Laughs*] Of course the *big* jobs *pay*. Things like insurance buildings — but my heart's in domestic architecture — and if you don't laugh at me, I'll *tell* you something.

VIOLA. Laugh at you — about your work and your ambition! Why, Clay!

CLAY. I do most of the domestic interiors for the firm already — and whenever I plan a second floor or a stair-case I can see *you* plain as day walkin' through the rooms — or saying good-night over the banisters.

VIOLA. Really? [CLAY *nods*] You mean in your mind?

CLAY. No, with my eyes. Domestic architecture's the most poetic work a man can get into outside of *downright* poetry itself.

VIOLA. It must be if you can *see* it all that way.

CLAY. Every room — I can see your short sleeves as you put your hands on the banisters — and sometimes you push up your front hair with the back of your hand that way — [*Brushes his forehead*]

VIOLA. Oh, this — [*repeats the gesture*] — all girls do that.

CLAY. But not just the same way as you do it. Yes, sir! I can see every little motion *you* make.

VIOLA. Whenever you care to think about me.

CLAY. Bless you, no — that's the trouble of it.

VIOLA. What trouble?

CLAY. The pictures of you — don't come just when I *want* them to come — and they don't go when I want them to go — especially in the dark.

VIOLA. Why, how funny.

CLAY. Sometimes I've had to light the gas in order to go to sleep.

VIOLA. Why, I never heard of anything like that.

CLAY. Well, it happens with me often. I designed this room for your Uncle Jack — but before I put a brush in my color-box I saw this very Genoese velvet and the picture frames in their places — and that Corot right there — I've got kind of a superstition about that picture.

VIOLA [*rises*]. A superstition! [*Regards the Corot*]

CLAY. I said to Jack, have anything else you want on the other walls, but right there I want you to put a Corot that I've seen at a dealer's in New York — and he did it.

VIOLA. Uncle Jack generally has his own way about pictures.

CLAY. I only mean that he approved my taste in the matter — but my idea of this house really started *with* — and grew around that canvas of Corot's.

VIOLA. Then it isn't always *me* that you see?

CLAY. Always you when I think about a real house, you bet — a house for *me* — and you'll be there, won't you? [*Takes her in his arms*]

VIOLA. Will I?

CLAY. Yes — say, "I will."

VIOLA. I will.

[*Re-enter* ALICE *and* HELEN]

ALICE [*astonished*]. Viola!

[VIOLA *goes left*]

CLAY. I've asked her — mother.

ALICE. Helen, you knew?

HELEN. Yes.

CLAY [*to* ALICE]. And I asked Jack, too.

ALICE. You mean —

CLAY. We're engaged — if you say it's all right.

ALICE. And you — Viola?

VIOLA [*nodding*]. Yes —

ALICE [*going to chair left of table*]. Well, if Jack's been consulted and you *all* know of it — I should make a very hopeless minority.

CLAY. Why any minority?

ALICE. Only the necessary considerations. [*To* HELEN] Clay's prospects — his youth.

VIOLA. Why, he designs most of the work for his firm now.

CLAY. That is, dwellings.

HELEN. I should advise waiting — myself — until Clay is in the firm — [*To* CLAY] And I did advise delay in speaking to Viola herself.

CLAY. I'd 'a' waited, mother, only Frank Hardmuth proposed to Viola *to-night!*

ALICE. To-night?

VIOLA. At the opera.

ALICE. One isn't safe anywhere.

CLAY. You wouldn't want *him!* So you do consent, don't you?

ALICE. I think your mother and I should talk it over.

CLAY. Well, it's a thing a fellow doesn't usually ask his mother to arrange, but — [*Pause*]

VIOLA. You mean privately?

ALICE. Yes.

CLAY. We can go to the billiard room, I suppose?

VIOLA. Come on.

CLAY [*at the center door with* VIOLA]. You know, mother — how I feel about it. [*Exit with* VIOLA *left center*]

HELEN. I supposed you had guessed it. [*Sits right of table*]

ALICE. I had — but when the moment arrives after all, it's such a surprise that a mother can't act naturally.

HELEN. Clay is really very trustworthy for his years.

ALICE. There's only one thing to discuss. I haven't mentioned it because — well, because I've seen so little of you since it began and because the fault is in my own family.

HELEN. Fault?

ALICE. Yes — Jack's fault — [*Pause*] Clay is playing.

HELEN. You mean —

ALICE. Here with Jack's friends.

HELEN. Clay gambling!

ALICE [*wincing*]. I don't quite get used to the word, though we've had a lifetime of it — [*sits left of table*] — gambling.

HELEN. I shouldn't have thought Jack would do that — with *my* boy.

ALICE. Jack hasn't our feminine viewpoint, Helen — and, besides, Jack is calloused to it.

HELEN. You should have talked to Jack yourself.

ALICE. Talked to him? I did much more — that is, as much more as a sister dependent on a brother for support could do. You know Jack really *built* this place for me and Viola.

HELEN. I'd thought so — yes.

ALICE. Viola is the very core of Jack's heart — well, we both left the house and went into our little apartment and are there now. A woman can't do much more than that and still take her living from a man, can she?

HELEN. No —

ALICE. And it hurt him — hurt him past any idea.

HELEN. You did that because my Clay was — was playing here?

ALICE. Not entirely Clay — everybody! [*Pause — a distant burst of laughter comes from the men in the dining-room*] There isn't a better-hearted man nor an abler one in the State than Jack Brookfield, but I had my daughter to consider. There were two nights under our last city government when nothing but the influence of Frank Hardmuth kept the police from coming to this house and arresting everybody — think of it.

HELEN. Dreadful —

ALICE. Now, that's something Helen, that I wouldn't tell a soul but you. *Viola* doesn't know it — but Jack's card-playing came between you and him years ago and you — may know it. [*Rises and looks toward dining-room*] You may even have some influence with Jack.

HELEN. I — ah, no.

ALICE. Yes — this supper to-night was Jack's idea for you. The box at the opera for you.

HELEN. Why, Jack didn't even sit with us.

ALICE. Also — for you — Jack

Brookfield is a more notable character in Louisville to-day than he was twenty-two years ago. His company would have made you the subject of unpleasant comment. That's why he left us alone in the box.

HELEN. Isn't it a pity — a terrible pity! [*Laughter off left.* HELEN *rises*]

[*Enter* HARDMUTH, JACK, DENNING, *and* LEW. HARDMUTH *is the aggressive prosecutor*]

HARDMUTH. I tell the gentlemen we've left the ladies to themselves long enough, Mrs. Campbell.

ALICE. *Quite* long enough, Mr. Hardmuth.

DENNING. Where's the young lady? Jack's niece?

HELEN. In the billiard room, I believe.

DENNING [*to* HELEN, *disappointed*]. Oh — Jack's been telling us what a great girl she is.

HARDMUTH. Some of us knew that without being told.

DENNING. And she's wonderfully like you — wonderfully.

HELEN. You compliment me —

JACK. Are you under the impression you're speaking to Viola's mother?

DENNING. Ain't I?

JACK. This lady is Mrs. Whipple.

DENNING. Oh, Clay's mother? HELEN *bows*] Well, your boy, Mrs. Whipple, plays in the hardest luck of all the people I ever sat next to.

HELEN. You mean —

JACK [*interrupting and putting his arm about* DENNING]. You depreciate yourself, Tom. There's no hard luck in merely sitting next to you.

DENNING. Ha, ha.

HELEN [*to* ALICE]. I think Clay and I should be going.

JACK [*consulting his watch*]. Oh, no — only a little after twelve and no one ever goes to sleep here before two. [*To* DENNING] I told you to keep still about card games.

DENNING. I meant unlucky at billiards. *They're* all right, ain't they?

JACK. Oh — [*Walks away impatiently*]

DENNING. Let's go and see the young lady play billiards with Clay. *To* ALICE] I can see now your daughter resembles you. [*Moves up with* ALICE *toward door.* LEW *follows*]

JACK. Shall we join them?

HELEN. I'd like it.

[JACK *and* HELEN *start up*]

HARDMUTH. Jack! Just a minute.

JACK [*to* HELEN]. Excuse me —

DENNING [*to* ALICE *as they go*]. No, Kansas City's my *home*, but I don't live there. [*Exit with* ALICE]

JACK. Be right in, Lew. [*Exit* HELEN *with* LEW] Well, Frank —

HARDMUTH. I took advantage of your hospitality, old man, to-night.

JACK. Advantage?

HARDMUTH. Yes — I've been talking to your niece.

JACK. Oh!

HARDMUTH. Proposed to her.

JACK. Yes —

HARDMUTH. Yes —

[*Enter* JO *from downstairs*]

JO. A gentleman called you on the telephone, sah.

JACK [*regarding watch*]. Who?

JO. Judge Brennus — name sounds like. Holding the wire, sah.

JACK. I don't know any Judge Brennus.

JO. Says you don't know him, sah, but he's got to leave town in the mornin' and he'd be very much obliged if you'd see him to-night.

JACK. Did you tell him we were dark to-night?

JO. He didn't want no game. It's about a picture — a picture *you've* got.

JACK. A picture?

JO. He wants to look at it.

[JACK *looks at* HARDMUTH]

HARDMUTH. It's a blind.

JACK [*consulting watch*]. Well, this is a good night to work a blind on me. [*To* JO] Tell the gentleman I'll be up for half an hour.

JO. Yes, sah. [*Exit*]

JACK. So you proposed to Viola?

HARDMUTH. Yes. How do you feel about that?

JACK. You know the story of the barkeeper asking the owner, "Is Grady good for a drink?" — "Has he had it?" — "He has." — "He is."

HARDMUTH. Just that way, eh? [JACK *nods*] Well — she hasn't answered me.

JACK [*musing*]. Mm —

HARDMUTH. And under those conditions, how's Grady's credit with you?

JACK. Well, Frank, on any *ordinary* proposition you're aces with me. You know that.

HARDMUTH [*seated right of table*]. But for the girl?

JACK. It's different.

HARDMUTH. Why?

JACK. She's only nineteen — you know.

HARDMUTH. My sister married at eighteen.

JACK. I mean *you're* thirty-five.

HARDMUTH. That's not an unusual difference.

JACK. Not an impossible difference, but I think unusual — and rather unadvisable.

HARDMUTH. That's what *you* think.

JACK. That's what I think.

HARDMUTH. But suppose the lady is willing to give that handicap? [*Pause* — JACK *shrugs his shoulder*] What then?

JACK. Let's cross that bridge when we come to it.

HARDMUTH. You mean *you'd* still drag a little?

JACK [*pause*]. Do you think Viola likes you well enough to say yes?

HARDMUTH. Let's cross *that* bridge when we come to it.

JACK. We have come to that one, Frank. There's another man in the running and I think she likes him.

HARDMUTH. You mean young Whipple? [*Rises, goes to fireplace*] Well, he took second money in the box party to-night — at the supper table, too. I'll agree to take care of him if you're with *me.*

JACK [*at table, center*]. I think he's your biggest opposition.

HARDMUTH. But you. Can I count on *you* in the show-down?

JACK [*Pause. Sits right of table*]. If Viola didn't care enough for you, Frank, to accept you in spite of everything, I shouldn't try to influence her in your favor.

[*Enter* LEW, *center, from left*]

LEW. I think a bum game of billiards is about as thin an entertainment for the outsiders as "Who's got the button."

HARDMUTH [*meeting* LEW *up left center*]. I've got a little business, Lew, with Jack for a minute.

LEW. Well, I can sit in by the bottle can't I? [*Moves toward dining-room*]

JACK. Help yourself, Lew.

LEW. Such awful "stage waits" while they chalk their cues. [*Exit left*]

HARDMUTH. But you wouldn't try to influence her against me.

JACK [*pause*]. She's about the closest thing to me there *is* — that niece of mine.

HARDMUTH [*pause*]. Well?

JACK. I'd protect her happiness to the limit of my ability.

HARDMUTH. If she likes me — or should come to like me — enough — her — happiness would be with *me*, wouldn't it? [*Sits again*]

JACK. She might think so.

HARDMUTH. Well?

JACK. But she'd be mistaken. It would be a mistake, old chap.

HARDMUTH. I know twenty men — twelve to fifteen years older than their wives — all happy — wives happy, too.

JACK. 'Tisn't just that.

HARDMUTH. What is it?

JACK. She's a fine girl — that niece of mine — not a blemish.

HARDMUTH. Well —

JACK. I want to see her get the best — the very best — in family — position — character —

HARDMUTH. Anything against the Hardmuths? [JACK *shakes head*] I'm assistant district attorney — and next trip I'll be *the* district attorney.

JACK. I said character.

HARDMUTH. Character?

JACK. Yes.

HARDMUTH. You mean there's anything against my reputation?

JACK. No — I mean character pure and simple — I mean the moral side of you!

HARDMUTH. Well, by God!

JACK. You see, I'm keeping the *girl* in mind all the time.

HARDMUTH. *My morals!*

JACK. Let's say your moral fiber.

HARDMUTH [*rises*]. Well, for richness this beats anything I've struck. Jack Brookfield talking to me about my moral fiber! [*Goes toward fire*]

JACK. You asked for it.

HARDMUTH [*returns aggressively*]. Yes — I did, and now I'm going to ask for the show-down. What do you mean by it?

JACK [*with fateful repression*]. I mean — as long as you've called attention to the "richness" of Jack Brookfield talking to you on the subject — that Jack Brookfield is a professional gambler — people get from Jack Brookfield just what he promises — a square game. Do you admit that?

HARDMUTH. I admit that. Go on.

JACK [*rises, front of table*]. You're the

assistant prosecuting attorney for the city of Louisville; the people *don't* get from you just what *you* promised — not by a jugful —

HARDMUTH. I'm the *assistant* prosecuting attorney, remember — I promised to assist in prosecution, not to institute it.

JACK. I expect technical defense, old man, but this was to be a show-down.

HARDMUTH. Let's have it — I ask for particulars.

JACK. Here's one. You *play* in my house and you know it's against the law that you've sworn to support.

HARDMUTH. I'll support the law whenever it's invoked. Indict me and I'll plead guilty.

JACK. This evasion is what I mean by lack of moral fiber.

HARDMUTH. Perhaps we're a little shy somewhere on mental fiber.

JACK. You make me say it, do you, Frank? Your duty, at least, is to keep secret the information of your office; contrary to that duty you've betrayed the secrets of your office to warn me and other men of this city when their game was in danger from the police.

HARDMUTH. You *throw* that up to me?

JACK [*sits on left end of table*]. Throw nothing — you asked for it.

HARDMUTH. I stand by my friends.

JACK. Exactly — and you've taken an oath to stand by the people.

HARDMUTH. Do you know any sure politician that doesn't stand by his friends?

JACK. Not one.

HARDMUTH. Well, there!

JACK. But, I don't know any sure politician that I'd tell my niece to marry.

HARDMUTH. That's a little too fine-haired for me! [*Turns to fire*]

JACK. I think it is.

HARDMUTH [*returns*]. I'll bet you a thousand dollars I'm the next prosecuting attorney of this city.

JACK. I'll take half of that if you can place it. I'll bet even money you're anything in politics that you go after for the next ten years.

HARDMUTH. Then I don't understand your kick.

JACK. But I'll give odds that the time'll come when you're way up there — full of honor and reputation and pride — that somebody'll drop to you, Frank, and flosh! *You* for the down and outs.

HARDMUTH. Rot!

JACK. It's the same in every game in the world — the crook either gets too gay or gets too slow, or both, and the "come on" sees him make the pass. I've been pallbearer for three of the slickest men that ever shuffled a deck in Kentucky — just a little *too* slick, that's all — and they've always got it when it was hardest for the family.

HARDMUTH. So that'll be my finish, will it?

JACK. Sure.

HARDMUTH [*going back of table*]. You like the moral fiber of this Whipple kid?

JACK. I don't know. [*Crosses to fireplace*]

HARDMUTH. Weak as dishwater.

JACK. I don't think so.

HARDMUTH. I'll do him at any game you name.

JACK. He's only a boy — you should.

HARDMUTH. I'll do him at this game.

JACK. What game?

HARDMUTH. The girl! I thought I could count on you because — well, for the very tips you hold against me; but you're only her uncle, old man, after all. [*Swaggers down right*]

JACK. That's all.

HARDMUTH. And if she says "yes" —

JACK [*comes to front of table. Pause. The men confront each other*]. Frank! Some day the truth'll come out — as to who murdered the governor-elect of this State.

HARDMUTH. Is there any doubt about that?

JACK. Isn't there?

HARDMUTH. The man who fired that shot's in jail.

JACK. I don't want my niece mixed up in it.

HARDMUTH [*angrily*]. What do you mean by that? [*Enter* HELEN, *center. An awkward pause*] The young people still playing?

HELEN. Yes.

HARDMUTH. I'll look 'em over. [*Exit*]

HELEN. Won't you come, too?

JACK. I'd rather stay here with you.

HELEN. That gentleman that called after supper —

JACK. Mr. Denning —

HELEN. Yes. He seems to take pleasure in annoying Clay —

JACK [*seriously*]. Yes — I know that side of Denning! [*Goes to door of dining-room*] Lew!

LEW. Yes.

JACK. I wish you'd go into the billiard room and look after Tom Denning.

LEW [*entering left*]. What's he doing?

[JACK *turns to* HELEN]

HELEN [*to* JACK]. Commenting humorously — hiding the chalk and so on.

LEW [*as he goes up*]. Lit up a little I suppose.

JACK [*nodding*]. Just "ride herd" on him.

[*Exit* LEW]

HELEN [*going left to sofa*]. He doesn't seem much of a gentleman, this Mr. Denning.

JACK. He wasn't expected to-night.

HELEN. Is he one of your "clients"?

JACK [*smiling*]. One of my "*clients*."

HELEN. Clay meets him here?

JACK. Yes — *has* met him here.

HELEN. I didn't think you'd do that — Jack — with *my* boy.

JACK. Do what?

HELEN. Gamble.

JACK [*smiling*]. It's no gamble with your boy, Helen — sure thing. He hasn't won a dollar!

HELEN. I'm glad you're able to smile over it.

JACK. Perhaps it would be more humorous to you if he'd won.

HELEN. If he plays — I'd rather see him win, of course.

JACK [*beside sofa*]. That's what put me in the *business* — winning. The thing that makes every gambler stick to it is winning occasionally. I've never let your boy get up from the table a dollar to the good ₹nd because he *was* your boy.

HELEN. Why let him play at all?

JACK. He'll play somewhere till he gets sick of it — or marries.

HELEN. Will marriage cure it?

JACK. It would have cured me — but you didn't see it that way.

HELEN. You made your choice.

JACK. I asked you to trust me — you wanted some ironclad pledge — well, my dear Helen — that wasn't the best way to handle a fellow of spirit. [*Goes front of table*]

HELEN. So *you* chose the better way?

JACK. No choice — I stood pat — that's all.

HELEN. And wasted your life.

JACK [*sitting on edge of table*]. That depends on how you look at it. You married a doctor who wore himself out

in the Philadelphia hospitals. I've had three meals a day — and this place — and — a pretty fat farm and a stable with some good blood in it — and —

HELEN [*coming to him*]. And every one of them, Jack, is a monument to the worst side of you.

JACK [*stands and takes her hands; he smiles*]. Prejudice, my dear Helen. You might say that if I'd earned these things in some respectable business combination that starved out all its little competitors — but I've simply furnished a fairly expensive entertainment — to eminent citizens — looking for rest.

HELEN. I know all the arguments of your — profession — Jack, and I don't pretend to answer them any more than I answer the arguments of reckless women who claim that they are more commendable than their sisters who make loveless marriages.

JACK [*goes to chair, right*]. I'm not flattered by the implied comparison — still —

HELEN. I only feel sure that anything which the majority of good people condemn is wrong. [*Sits left of table*]

JACK [*sits right of table*]. I'm sorry —

HELEN. I'd be glad if you meant that — but you're not sorry.

JACK. I *am* sorry — I'm sorry not to have public respect — as long as you think it's valuable.

HELEN. I amuse you — don't I?

JACK [*elbows on knees*]. Not a little bit — but you make me blue as the devil, if that's any satisfaction.

HELEN. I'd be glad to make you blue as the devil, Jack, if it meant discontent with what you're doing — if it could make you do better.

JACK. I'm a pretty old leopard to get nervous about my spots.

HELEN. Why are you blue?

JACK. You.

HELEN. In what way?

JACK. I had hoped that twenty years of charitable deeds had made you also charitable in your judgment.

HELEN. I hope it has.

JACK. Don't seem to ease up on my specialty.

HELEN. You called your conduct "wild oats" twenty years ago.

JACK. It was — but I found such an excellent market for my wild oats that I had to stay in that branch of the grain business. Besides, it has been partly your fault, you know.

[HELEN *plays with the ivory paper-knife, balancing it on the front edge of table*]

HELEN. Mine?

JACK. Your throwing me over for my wild oats — put it up to me to prove that they were a better thing than you thought.

HELEN. Well — having demonstrated that —

JACK. Here we are —

HELEN. Yes — here we are.

JACK. Back in the old town. Don't you think it would be rather a pretty finish, Helen, if despite all my — my leopard's spots — and despite that — [*pause*] — that Philadelphia episode of yours —

HELEN. You call twenty years of marriage episodic.

JACK. I call any departure from the main story episodic.

HELEN. And the main story is —

JACK. You and I —

HELEN. Oh —

[*Paper-knife falls to floor* — JACK *rises and picks it up, stands in front of table left hand on* HELEN'S — *his right gesticulating with paper-knife*]

JACK. Wouldn't it be a pretty finish if you took my hand and I could walk right up to the camera and say, "I told you so" —? You know I always felt that you were coming back.

HELEN. Oh, did you?

JACK [*playfully, and going right center*]. Had a candle burning in the window every night.

HELEN. You're sure it wasn't a red light?

JACK [*remonstrating*]. Dear Helen! have some poetry in your composition. Literally "red light" of course — but the real flame was here — [*hand on breast*] — a flickering hope that somewhere — somehow — somewhen I should be at rest — with the proud Helen that loved and — rode away.

HELEN [*almost accusingly*]. I — believe — you.

JACK. Of course you believe me.

HELEN. You had a way, Jack — when you were a boy at college, of making me write to you.

JACK. Had I? [*Goes back of table*]

HELEN. You know you had; at nights — about this hour — I'd find it impossible to sleep until I'd got up and written to you — and two days later I'd get from you a letter that had crossed mine on the road. I don't believe the word "telepathy" had been coined then — but I guessed something of the force — and all these years, I've felt it — nagging! Nagging!

JACK. Nagging?

HELEN. Yes — I could keep you out of my waking hours — out of my thought — but when I surrendered myself to sleep the *call* would come — and I think it was rather cowardly of you, really.

JACK [*back of table*]. I plead guilty to having thought of you, Helen — lots — and it was generally when I was alone — late — my — clients gone. This room —

"Whose lights are fled,
Whose garlands dead,
And all but he departed."

HELEN. And as you say — here we are.

JACK. Well, what of my offer? Shall we say to the world — "We told you so?" What of my picturesque finish?

HELEN. You know my ideas — you've known them twenty-two years.

JACK. No modification?

HELEN. None!

JACK. I'll be willing to sell the tables. [*Points above to second floor*] And — well — I don't think I could get interested in this bridge game that the real good people play — would you object to a gentleman's game of "draw" now and then?

HELEN. You called it a gentleman's game in those days.

JACK. No leeway at all?

HELEN. No compromise, Jack — no —

JACK. M — [*Pause*] I trust you won't consider my seeming hesitation uncomplimentary?

HELEN. Not unprecedented, at least.

JACK. You see it opens up a new line of thought — and — [*Passes his hand over forehead*]

HELEN [*rising in sympathy*]. And you have a headache, too, — it isn't kind I'm sure.

[*Enter* Jo, *right center*]

JACK. Oh, nothing — nothing. [*To* Jo] Well?

Jo. That gentleman, sah, about the picture.

JACK. I'll see him. [*Exit* Jo]

HELEN. A caller?

JACK. Won't be a minute — don't go away, because I think we can settle this question to-night, you and I.

HELEN. Please don't put me in the light of waiting for an answer.

JACK. Dear Helen — we're both past that — aren't we? If I can only be sure that I could be worthy of you. I'm the one that's waiting for an answer — from my own weak character and rotten irresolution.

[JACK *goes with* HELEN *to door, center, kisses her hand. She goes;* JACK *retains her hand as long as possible and when he lets it go, it falls limply to* HELEN'S *side as she disappears*]

They say cards make a fellow superstitious. [*Pause*] Well — I — guess they do —

[*Enter* JO *and* JUSTICE PRENTICE. PRENTICE *wears overcoat, carries cane and silk hat*]

Judge de Brennus?

PRENTICE [*after amused look at* JO]. Justice Prentice. [*Exit* JO]

JACK. Oh, Justice Prentice! Good-evening!

PRENTICE. You are Mr. Brookfield?

JACK. Yes.

PRENTICE. I shouldn't have attempted so late a call but that a friend pointed you out to-night at the opera, Mr. Brookfield, and said that your habit was — well —

JACK. Not to retire immediately?

PRENTICE. Yes.

JACK. Will you be seated?

PRENTICE. I'm only passing through the city. I called to see a Corot that I understand you bought from Knoedler.

JACK. That's it.

PRENTICE. Oh — thank you. [*Starts*] You don't object to my looking at it?

JACK. Not at all. [*Touches button, light shows on picture*]

PRENTICE [*after regard*]. That's it. [*Pause*] I thought at one time that I would buy this picture.

JACK. You know it, then?

PRENTICE. Yes. [*Pause*] Are you particularly attached to it, Mr. Brookfield?

JACK [*sitting*]. I think not irrevocably. [*Takes pad of paper and figures mechanically*]

PRENTICE. Oh. [*Pause, during which the* JUSTICE *looks at the picture*] Do I understand that is what you paid

for it, or what you intend to ask me for it?

[JACK *starts*]

JACK. What?

PRENTICE. Sixty-five hundred.

JACK [*astonished*]. I didn't speak the price, did I?

PRENTICE. Didn't you — oh. [*Pause*] I couldn't pay that amount.

JACK [*puzzled*]. That's its price — however.

PRENTICE. I regret I didn't buy it from the dealer when I had my chance. [*Looks about at other pictures on back wall*] I couldn't have given it so beautiful a setting, Mr. Brookfield, nor such kindred — but it would not have been friendless — [*At fireplace*] That's a handsome marine.

JACK. Yes.

PRENTICE. Pretty idea I read recently in an essay of Dr. Van Dyke's. His pictures were for him his windows by which he looked out from his study onto the world. [*Pause*] Yes?

JACK. Quite so.

PRENTICE [*regarding a picture over dining-room door*]. Mm — Washington!

JACK [*again astonished*]. What?

PRENTICE. My home is Washington — I thought you asked me?

JACK. No, I didn't.

PRENTICE. I beg your pardon —

JACK [*front of table, aside*]. But I'm damned if I wasn't *just* going to ask him.

PRENTICE [*viewing other pictures*]. And the phases of your world, Mr. Brookfield, have been very prettily multiplied.

JACK. Thank you — may I offer you a cigar? [*Opens box on table*]

PRENTICE. Thank you, I won't smoke.

JACK. Or a glass of wine?

PRENTICE. Nothing. I'll return to the hotel — first asking you again to excuse my untimely call.

JACK. I wish you'd sit down awhile.

PRENTICE. But I didn't know until I'd missed it from Knoedler's how large a part of my world — my dream world — I had been looking at through this frame. [*Regards the Corot again*]

JACK. Well, if it's a sentimental matter, Mr. Justice, we might talk it over.

PRENTICE. I mustn't submit the sentimental side of it, Mr. Brookfield, and where I have so — so intruded.

JACK. That's the big side of anything for me — the sentimental.

PRENTICE. I'm sure of it — and I mustn't take advantage of that knowledge.

JACK. You're sure of it?

PRENTICE. Yes.

JACK. Is that my reputation?

PRENTICE. I don't know your reputation.

JACK. Then, how are you sure of it?

PRENTICE [*impressively*]. Oh — I see you — and — well, we have *met*.

JACK. [*Pause*] Ah —

PRENTICE. Good-night. [*Going up*]

JACK. One moment. [*Pause*] You said your address was Washington?

PRENTICE. Yes.

JACK. You thought at the time I was about to ask you that question?

PRENTICE. I thought you *had* asked it.

JACK. And you thought a moment before I had said sixty-five hundred for the picture?

PRENTICE. Yes.

JACK. Do you often — pick answers that way?

PRENTICE. Well, I think we all do — at times.

JACK. We all do?

PRENTICE. Yes — but we speak the answers only as we get older and less attentive and mistake a person's thought for his spoken word.

JACK. A person's thought?

PRENTICE. Yes.

JACK. Do you mean you know what I think?

PRENTICE [*returning to table*]. I hadn't meant to claim any monopoly of that power. It's my opinion that every one reads the thoughts of others — that is, some of the thoughts.

JACK. Every one?

PRENTICE. Oh, yes.

JACK. That *I* do?

PRENTICE [*regarding him*]. I should say *you* more generally than the majority of men.

JACK. There was a woman said something like that to me not ten minutes ago.

PRENTICE. A woman would be apt to be conscious of it.

JACK. You really believe that — that stuff? [*Sits left of table*]

PRENTICE. Oh, yes — and I'm not a pioneer in the belief. The men who declare the stuff most stoutly are scientists who have given it most attention.

JACK. How do they prove it?

PRENTICE. They *don't* prove it — that is, not universally. Each man must do that for himself, Mr. Brookfield.

JACK. How —

PRENTICE. [*Pause. Smiles*] Well, I'll tell you all I know of it. [*Becoming serious*] Every thought is active — that is, born of a desire — and travels from us — or it is born of the desire of some one else and comes to us. We send them out — or we take them in — that is all.

JACK. How do we know which we are doing?

PRENTICE. If we are idle and empty-headed, our brains are the playrooms for the thought of others — frequently rather bad. If we are active, whether benevolently or malevolently, our brains are workshops — *power-houses*. I was passively regarding the pictures; your active idea of the price — registered, that's all — so did your wish to know where I was from.

JACK. You say "*our* brains" — do you still include mine?

PRENTICE. Yes.

JACK. You said mine more than the majority of men's.

PRENTICE. I think so.

JACK. Why hasn't this whatever it is — effect — happened to me, then?

PRENTICE. It has.

JACK. [*Pause*] Why didn't I know it?

PRENTICE. Vanity? Perhaps.

JACK. Vanity?

PRENTICE. Yes — often some — friend has broached some independent subject and you have said, "I was just about to speak of that myself."

JACK. Very often, but —

PRENTICE. Believing the idea was your own — your vanity shut out the probably proper solution — that it was his.

JACK. Well, how, then, does a man tell which of his thoughts are his own?

PRENTICE. It's difficult. Most of his idle ones are not. When we drift we are with the current. To go against it or to make even an eddy of our own we must swim — Most everything less than that is hopeless.

JACK [*smiling*]. Well — I haven't been exactly helpless.

PRENTICE. No one would call you so, Mr. Brookfield. [*Going*] You have a strong psychic — a strong hypnotic ability.

JACK [*smiling*]. You think so?

PRENTICE. I know it.

JACK. This business? [*Makes slight pass after manner of the professional hypnotist*]

PRENTICE [*smiling*]. That business for the beginner, yes —

JACK. You mean that I could hypnotize anybody?

PRENTICE. Many persons — yes — but I wouldn't do it if I were you —

JACK. Why not?

PRENTICE. Grave responsibility.

JACK. In what way?

PRENTICE. [*Pause. Smiles*] I'll send you a book about it — if I may.

JACK. Instructions?

PRENTICE. And cautions — yes — [*Goes up to picture again*] If you tire of your Corot, I'd be glad to hear from you.

JACK. Why couldn't I save postage by just *thinking* another price?

PRENTICE. The laws on contracts haven't yet recognized that form of tender.

[*Enter* TOM, *left center. He laughs and shows signs of drink*]

TOM. I say, Jack — here's the greatest joke you ever saw — [*Sees the* JUSTICE] Oh, excuse me.

[*Enter* LEW, *following*]

LEW. That won't do, Tom. — [*To* JACK] Excuse me, Jack, but I had to get him out of there.

JACK. I'll go downstairs with you, Mr. Justice. [*Exit with the* JUSTICE]

TOM. Who's that old bird?

LEW. You'll offend Jack if you're not careful, Tom. You've got half a jag now.

TOM. J' ever see anything's as funny as that? He don't like my scarf-pin — ha, ha — well, I don't like it — but my valet put it on me and what's the difference —

[*Enter left* HARDMUTH]

HARDMUTH. What was that?

TOM. My scarf-pin!

HARDMUTH. Scarf-pin?

TOM. Yes — he pushed me away from him and I said "what's matter." He said "I don't like your scarf-pin" — ha, ha — I said "don't? I don't like your face."

LEW. Very impolite with the ladies there.

HARDMUTH. Why should he criticize Tom's scarf-pin?

TOM. 'Zactly. I said "I can change my scarf-pin — but I don't like your face."

[*Enter* CLAY *from dining-room excitedly*]

CLAY. Where's Jack?

LEW. Saying good-night to some old gentleman below.

TOM [*interposing as* CLAY *starts up left center*]. And I don't like your face.

CLAY. That's all right, Mr. Denning. [*Tries to pass*] Excuse me.

TOM [*with scarf-pin in hand*]. Excuse me. What's the matter with that scarf-pin?

CLAY. It's a cat's-eye and I don't like them, that's all — I don't like to look at them.

LEW. Let him alone, Tom.

TOM. Damn 'f'ee ain't scared o' it, ha, ha! [*Pushing pin in front of* CLAY'S *face*]

CLAY [*greatly excited*]. Don't do that.

HARDMUTH [*sneering*]. 'T won't bite you, will it?

CLAY [*averts his face*]. Go away, I tell you.

TOM. [*Holds* CLAY *with left hand. Has pin in right*] 'T will bite him — bow — wow — wow —

CLAY. Don't, I tell you — don't.

TOM [*still holding him*]. Bow — wow — wow —

LEW. Tom!

HARDMUTH [*laughing*]. Let them alone.

CLAY. Go away.

TOM. Bow — wow —

[*Enter* JACK]

JACK. What's the matter here?

TOM [*pursuing* CLAY]. Wow —

[CLAY *in frenzy swings the large ivory paper-knife from table, blindly strikes* TOM, *who falls*]

JACK. Clay!

CLAY [*horrified*]. He pushed that horrible cat's-eye right against my face.

JACK. What cat's eye?

HARDMUTH [*picks up the pin which* DENNING *has dropped*]. Only playing with him — a scarf-pin.

LEW [*kneeling by* DENNING]. He's out, Jack.

[*Enter* JO]

CLAY. I didn't mean to hurt him; really I didn't mean that.

HARDMUTH [*taking the paper-knife from* CLAY]. The hell you didn't. You could kill a bull with that ivory tusk.

JACK. Put him on the window seat — give him some air.

[*Enter* ALICE, *left center*]

ALICE. Jack, we're going now — all of us.

[*Enter* HARVEY *left*]

JACK [*turning to* ALICE]. Wait a minute. [*To* Jo] Help Mr. Ellinger there.

[Jo, LEW, *and* HARVEY *carry off* TOM *into the dining-room*]

ALICE. What is it?

JACK. An accident — keep Helen and Viola out of these rooms.

ALICE. Hadn't we better go? Clay is with us.

CLAY. I can't go just now, Mrs. Campbell — [*Looks off*] I hope it isn't serious — I didn't mean to hurt him, really. [*Exit left*]

ALICE. A quarrel?

[LEW *enters and waves hand, meaning "All over"*]

HARDMUTH [*with paper-knife*]. A murder!

[*Enter* HELEN *and* VIOLA]

VIOLA. What's the matter?

[*Enter* CLAY]

CLAY [*in panic and up right center. To* HELEN]. Oh, mother, I've killed him.

HELEN [*taking* CLAY *in her arms*]. Killed him — whom?

HARDMUTH. Tom Denning.

CLAY. But I never meant it — Jack; I just struck — struck wild.

HARDMUTH. With this.

HELEN. With that! Oh, my boy!

JACK. That will do! Everybody — Lew, telephone Dr. Monroe it's an emergency case and to come in dressing-gown and slippers. [*Exit* LEW, *right center*] Alice, I know you're not afraid of a sick man — or — that sort of thing. Help me and Jo. [*Leads* ALICE, *left. She braces herself*] Viola, you take Mrs. Whipple upstairs and wait there.

HARDMUTH [*starting up right*]. I'll notify the police.

HELEN. Oh!

JACK [*interposing*]. *Stop!* You'll stay just where you are!

HARDMUTH. You tryin' to hide this thing?

JACK. The doctor'll tell us exactly what this thing is. And then the boy'll have the credit himself *of notifying the police.*

CURTAIN

ACT II

SCENE. — *The library-living room of* JUSTICE PRENTICE, *Washington, D. C.*

The walls of this room are bookcases glassed quite to the ceiling, and filled with books mostly in sheepskin binding. This array is broken by a large bay window at the back, center, which is equipped with a window seat, and by two doors near the front of the stage, one on the right and one on the left.

At the left is also a fireplace with a log fire. In the upper left-hand corner of the room there is a buffet, fitted with glasses and decanters. A dark rug is on the floor.

The furniture of the room is dark oak in Gothic. It consists of a table and three chairs at the center, sofa and smaller table up right. The smaller table holds a lamp.

Over the buffet there is a small canvas by Rousseau showing a sunset.

JUSTICE PRENTICE *and* JUDGE HENDERSON *are playing chess.*

HENDERSON. Checkmate in three moves.

PRENTICE. I don't see that.

HENDERSON. Well, Knight to —

PRENTICE. Yes, yes, I see. Checkmate in three moves. That's one game each. Shall we play another?

HENDERSON. Let us look at the enemy. [*Draws watch*] By Jove! Quarter of twelve. I guess Mrs. Henderson will be expecting me soon. [*Pause*] I'll play a rubber with you, and its result shall decide your position on the Whipple case.

PRENTICE. Why, Mr. Justice, I'm surprised at you. A United States Supreme Court decision — shaped by a game of chess. We'll be down to the level of intelligent jurymen soon — flipping pennies for the verdict.

HENDERSON. And a very good method in just such cases as this. Well, if you won't play — [*rises*] — I'll have to go.

PRENTICE [*rises*]. Not without another toddy.

HENDERSON. Yes.

PRENTICE [*at sideboard up left*]. Oh, no. Come now, don't you like this liquor?

HENDERSON. Immensely. Where did you say you got it?

PRENTICE. Kentucky. One lump?

HENDERSON. Only one!

PRENTICE. My old home, sir — and a bit of lemon?

HENDERSON. A piece of the peel — yes.

PRENTICE. They make it there.

HENDERSON. I'll pour the water. [*Pours*]

PRENTICE. There, there, don't drown me.

HENDERSON. My folks were Baptists, you see. What do you say it costs you?

PRENTICE. Fifty cents a gallon.

HENDERSON. What!! I think I'll take water. [*Puts down glass*]

PRENTICE. That's what it cost me. Its value I don't know. An old friend sends it to me. Fifty cents for express.

HENDERSON. Oh!

PRENTICE. That's different, isn't it?

HENDERSON [*recovers glass*]. Very!

PRENTICE. He makes it down there. Why, it's in the same county in which this Whipple murder occurred.

HENDERSON. How about that point? We might as well admit it and remand the case.

PRENTICE. No. There's no constitutional point involved.

HENDERSON. A man's entitled to an open trial.

PRENTICE. Well, Whipple had it.

HENDERSON. No, he didn't. They wouldn't admit the public.

PRENTICE. Oh, come, now; the court-room was crowded and the Judge refused admission to others — only when there was danger of the floor breaking.

HENDERSON. But, my dear Mr. Justice, that would have been all right to limit the attendance —

PRENTICE. Well, that's all he did.

HENDERSON. Only he did it by having the sheriff issue tickets of admission. That placed the attendance entirely in the control of the prosecution and the defense is right in asking a rehearing.

PRENTICE. Oh, nonsense! Justice is a little too slow in my old State and I'm impatient with technical delays.

It is two years since they openly assassinated the governor-elect and the guilty man is still at large.

HENDERSON. Why should the killing of Scovill bear on this case!

PRENTICE. It bears on me. I'm concerned for the fair fame of Kentucky.

HENDERSON. Well, if you won't, you won't, and there's an end of it. [*Rings call bell*]

PRENTICE. Have another?

HENDERSON. Not another drop. [*Enter* SERVANT] Get my coat!

PRENTICE. A nightcap.

SERVANT. I beg pardon, sir.

PRENTICE. Speaking to the Justice.

[*Exit* SERVANT]

HENDERSON. No, I mustn't. Mrs. Henderson filed her protest against my coming home loaded and I've got to be moderate.

PRENTICE. Well, if you won't, you won't.

HENDERSON [*front of table, picks up book*]. Hello! Reading the Scriptures in your old age?

PRENTICE. It does look like a Bible, doesn't it? That's a flexible binding I had put on a copy of Bret Harte. I admire him very much.

HENDERSON. I like some of his stuff.

PRENTICE. When I get home from the Capitol and you prosy lawyers, I'm too tired to read Browning and those heavy guns, so I take Bret Harte — very clever, I think; I was reading before you came — [*takes book*] — "A Newport Romance." Do you know it?

HENDERSON. I don't think I do.

PRENTICE. It's about an old house at Newport — that's haunted — a young girl in the colonial days died of a broken heart in this house, it seems. Her sweetheart sailed away and left her — and here's the way Bret Harte tells of her coming back. [HENDERSON *sits*] Oh, I'm not going to read all of it to you — only one verse. [*Looks at book.* — *Pause*] Oh, I forgot to tell you that when this chap left the girl he gave her a little bouquet — understand? That's a piece of material evidence necessary to this summing up. [HENDERSON *nods*. PRENTICE *reads*]

"And ever since then when the clock strikes two,
 She walks unbidden from room to room,

And the air is filled, that she passes
through,
With a subtle, sad perfume.

The delicate odor of mignonette,
The ghost of a dead-and-gone bouquet,
Is all that tells of her story ; yet
Could she think of a sweeter way?"

Isn't that charming, eh?

HENDERSON. A very pretty idea.

PRENTICE. Beautiful to have a perfume suggest her. I suppose it appeals to me especially because I used to know a girl who was foolishly fond of mignonette.

HENDERSON. Well, you don't believe in that stuff, do you?

PRENTICE. What stuff?

HENDERSON. That Bret Harte stuff — the dead coming back — ghosts and so forth?

PRENTICE. Yes, in one way I do. I find as I get older, Judge, that the things of memory become more real every day — every day. Why, there are companions of my boyhood that I haven't thought of for years — that seem to come about me — more tangible, or as much so as they were in life.

HENDERSON. Well, how do you account for that? Spiritualism?

PRENTICE. Oh, no. It's Time's perspective.

HENDERSON. Time's perspective?

PRENTICE. Yes. [*Pause*] I'll have to illustrate my meaning. [*Indicates a painting*] Here's a sunset by Rousseau. I bought it in Paris last summer. Do you see what an immense stretch of land there is in it?

HENDERSON. Yes.

PRENTICE. A bird's-eye view of that would require a chart reaching to the ceiling. But see Rousseau's perspective. The horizon line isn't two inches from the base.

HENDERSON. Well?

PRENTICE [*returns to table*]. Well, my dear Judge, that is the magic in the perspective of Time. My boyhood's horizon is very near to my old eyes now. The dimmer they grow, the nearer it comes, until I think sometimes that when we are through with it all — we go out almost as we entered — little children.

HENDERSON. [*Pause*] That's a very beautiful painting, Judge — a Russell, you say?

PRENTICE. A Rousseau.

HENDERSON. Oh —

PRENTICE. Yes — cost me three thousand only, and a funny thing about it : the canvas just fitted into the top of my steamer trunk, and it came through the custom-house without a cent of duty. I completely forgot it.

HENDERSON. Your memory isn't so retentive, then, as it seems?

PRENTICE. Not on those commercial matters. [*Enter* SERVANT *with coat. In crossing front of table to* HENDERSON, *the coat knocks a miniature from the table to the floor*] You dropped your tobacco-box, I guess, Mr. Justice.

HENDERSON [*examines pocket*]. No.

SERVANT [*picks up miniature*]. It was this picture, sir.

PRENTICE. My gracious — my gracious! It might have been broken.

SERVANT. Oh, it often falls when I'm dusting, sir.

PRENTICE. Oh, does it? Well, I'll put it away. [*Exit* SERVANT] An ivory miniature by Wimar. I prize it highly — old-fashioned portrait, see! Gold back.

HENDERSON. A beautiful face.

PRENTICE [*eagerly*]. Isn't it? Isn't it? [*Looks over* HENDERSON's *shoulder*]

HENDERSON. Very. What a peculiar way of combing the hair — long, and over the ears.

PRENTICE. The only becoming way women ever wore their hair. I think the scrambly style they have now is disgraceful.

HENDERSON. Your mother?

PRENTICE. Dear, no, a young girl I used to know. Oh, don't smile, she's been dead a good thirty years — married and had a large family.

HENDERSON. Very sweet — very sweet, indeed.

PRENTICE. Isn't it? [*Enter* SERVANT] Well?

SERVANT. Card, sir.

PRENTICE. Gentleman here? [*Takes card*]

SERVANT. Yes, sir.

PRENTICE. I'll see him. [*Exit* SERVANT]

HENDERSON. Call?

PRENTICE. Yes. The man owns a picture that I've been trying to buy — a Corot.

HENDERSON. Oh — another of these perspective fellows?

PRENTICE. Yes — his call doesn't surprise me, for he's been in my mind all day.

HENDERSON. Seems to be in a hurry for the money — coming at midnight.

PRENTICE. I set him the example — besides, midnight is just the shank of the evening for Mr. Brookfield. He's supposed to be a sporting man — ahem. [*Enter* SERVANT *and* JACK, JACK *is paler and less physical than in first act*] Good-evening.

JACK. You remember me, Mr. Justice?

PRENTICE. Perfectly, Mr. Brookfield — this is Justice Henderson.

HENDERSON. Mr. Brookfield.

JACK. Pleased to meet you, Mr. Justice. [*To* PRENTICE] I hope I'm not intruding.

HENDERSON. I'm just going, Mr. Brookfield. [*To* PRENTICE] To-morrow?

PRENTICE. To-morrow!

HENDERSON [*at door, inquiringly*]. No constitutional point about it? Eh?

PRENTICE. None.

HENDERSON. Good-night.

PRENTICE. Good-night. [*To* JACK] Have a chair.

JACK. Thank you. [*Stands by chair left of table*]

PRENTICE [*toward buffet*]. I've some medicine here that comes directly from your city.

JACK. I don't think I will — if you'll excuse me.

PRENTICE. Ah — [*Pause. Smiles*] Well, have you brought the picture?

JACK. The picture is still in Louisville — I — I'm in Washington with my niece.

PRENTICE. Yes?

JACK. And — a lady friend of hers. They're very anxious to meet you, Mr. Justice.

PRENTICE. Ah. [*Pause*] Well — I go to the Capitol at noon to-morrow and —

JACK. To-night! — They're leaving the city to-morrow — as you were when I had the pleasure of receiving you.

PRENTICE. I remember.

JACK [*with watch*]. They were to come after me in five minutes if I didn't return; and those five minutes, Mr. Justice, I hoped you would give to me.

PRENTICE. With pleasure. [*Sits right of table*]

JACK [*plunging at once into his subject*]. Those two books you sent me —

PRENTICE. Yes?

JACK. I want to thank you for them again — and to ask you how far you go

— with the men that wrote them — especially the second one. Do you believe that book?

PRENTICE. Yes.

JACK. You do?

PRENTICE. I do. I know the man who wrote it — and I believe him.

JACK. Did he ever do any of his stunts for you — that he writes about?

PRENTICE. He didn't call them "stunts," but he has given me many demonstrations of his ability — and mine.

JACK. For example?

PRENTICE. For example? He asked me to think of him steadily at some unexpected time, and to think of some definite thing. A few days later — this room — two o'clock in the morning — I concentrated my thoughts — I mentally pictured him going to his telephone and calling me.

JACK. And did he do it?

PRENTICE. No — [*pause*] — but he came here at my breakfast hour and told me that at two o'clock he had waked and risen from his bed — and walked to his 'phone in the hallway with an *impulse* to call me — and then had stopped — because he had no message to deliver and because he thought his imagination might be tricking him.

JACK. You hadn't given him any tip, such as asking how he'd slept?

PRENTICE. None. Five nights after that I repeated the experiment.

JACK. Well?

PRENTICE. That time he called me.

JACK. What did he say?

PRENTICE. He said, "Old man, you ought to be in bed asleep; and not disturbing honest citizens," which was quite true.

JACK. By Jove, it's a devilish creepy business, isn't it?

PRENTICE. Yes.

JACK. And if it's so —

PRENTICE. And it is so.

JACK. Pay a man to be careful what he thinks — eh?

PRENTICE. It will very well pay your type of man to do so.

JACK. I don't want to be possessed by any of these bughouse theories; but I'll be blamed if a few things haven't happened to me, Mr. Justice, since you started me on this subject.

PRENTICE. Along this line?

JACK. Yes. [*Pause*] And I've tried the other side of it, too.

PRENTICE. What other side?

JACK. The mesmeric business. [*Pause. Makes passes*] I can do it.

PRENTICE. Then I, should say, Mr. Brookfield, that for you the obligation for clean and unselfish thinking was doubly imperative.

JACK. Within this last year I've put people — well — practically asleep in a chair and I've made them tell me what a boy was doing — a mile away — in a jail.

PRENTICE. I see no reason to call clairvoyance a "bughouse" theory.

JACK. I only know that I do it.

PRENTICE. Yes — you have the youth for it — the glorious strength. Does it make any demand on your vitality?

JACK [*passes hand over his eyes*]. I've fancied that a headache to which I'm subject is more frequent — that's all.

PRENTICE. But you find the ability — the power — increases — don't you?

JACK. Yes — in the last month I've put a man into a hypnotic sleep with half a dozen waves of the hand. [*Makes pass*]

PRENTICE. Why any motion?

JACK. Fixes his attention, I suppose.

PRENTICE [*shaking head*]. Fixes your attention. When in your own mind your belief is sufficiently trained, you won't need this. [*Another slight pass*]

JACK. I won't?

PRENTICE. No.

JACK. What'll I do?

PRENTICE. Simply think. [*Pause*] You have a headache, for example.

JACK. I have a headache for a fact. [JACK *again passes hand over eyes and forehead*]

PRENTICE. Well — some persons could cure it by rubbing your forehead.

JACK. I know that.

PRENTICE. Others could cure it by the passes of the hypnotist. Others by simply willing that it should — [*Pause*] — be cured.

JACK. Well, that's where I can't follow you — and your friend the author.

PRENTICE. You simply think your headache.

JACK. I know it aches.

PRENTICE. I think it doesn't.

JACK [*astonished*]. What?

PRENTICE. I — think — it doesn't.

JACK [*pauses*]. Well, just this moment, it doesn't but — [*pause*] — isn't

that — simply mental excitement — won't it come back?

PRENTICE. It won't come back to-day.

JACK. That's some comfort. The blamed things have made it busy for me since I've been studying this business.

PRENTICE. It is a two-edged sword—

JACK. You mean it's bad for a man who tries it?

PRENTICE. I mean that it constantly opens to the investigator new mental heights, higher planes — and every man, Mr. Brookfield, is ill in some manner who lives habitually on a lower level — than the light he sees.

[*Enter* SERVANT]

SERVANT. Two ladies, sir.

PRENTICE. Your friends?

JACK. I think so.

[PRENTICE *and* JACK *look at* SERVANT]

SERVANT. Yes, sir.

PRENTICE. Ask them up.

[*Exit* SERVANT]

JACK. Thank you.

PRENTICE [*rises*]. I'll put away Judge Henderson's glass.

JACK. They're Kentucky ladies, Mr. Justice.

PRENTICE [*indicating* JACK]. But I don't want any credit for a hospitality I haven't earned.

JACK. I see.

(*Enter* SERVANT *with* HELEN *and* VIOLA.) My niece, Miss Campbell.

PRENTICE. Miss Campbell.

JACK. And —

HELEN. One moment, Jack; I prefer to introduce myself.

PRENTICE. Won't you be seated, ladies?

[*Exit* SERVANT. HELEN *sits right of table.* VIOLA *goes to the window-seat.* JACK *stands up center*]

HELEN. You are not a married man, Justice Prentice?

PRENTICE. I am not.

HELEN. But you have the reputation of being a very charitable one.

PRENTICE [*sits left of table*]. That's pleasant to hear — what charity do you represent?

HELEN. None. I hardly know how to tell you my object.

PRENTICE. It's a personal matter, is it?

JACK [*back of table*]. Yes, a very personal matter.

PRENTICE. Ah!

HELEN. I have here an autograph book —

PRENTICE [*to* JACK]. I usually sign my autograph for those who wish it — at the —

HELEN. I did not come for an autograph, Justice Prentice; I have brought one.

PRENTICE. Well, I don't go in for that kind of thing very much. I have no collection — my taste runs more toward —

HELEN. The autograph I have brought is one of yours, written many years ago. It is signed to a letter. Will you look at it? [*Opens an autograph book and gives small folded and old lace handkerchief from book to* VIOLA, *who joins her*]

PRENTICE. With pleasure. [*Takes book*] Is this the letter? Ah — [*Reads*] "June 15, 1860." Dear me, that's a long time ago. [*Reads*] "My dear Margaret, the matter passed satisfactorily — A mere scratch. Boland apologized. — Jim." What is this?

HELEN. A letter from you.

PRENTICE. And my dear Margaret — 1860. Why, this letter — was it written to Margaret?

HELEN. To Margaret Price —

PRENTICE. Is it possible — well — well. [*Pauses*] I wonder if what we call coincidences are ever mere coincidences. Margaret Price! Her name was on my lips a moment ago.

JACK. Really, Mr. Justice?

PRENTICE [*to* JACK]. Yes. Did you know Margaret Price?

JACK. Yes. [*Looks at* HELEN — PRENTICE'S *gaze follows*]

HELEN. She was my mother —

PRENTICE. Margaret Price was —

HELEN. Was my mother.

PRENTICE. Why, I was just speaking of her to Justice Henderson whom you saw go out. Her picture dropped from the table here. [*Gets it*] This miniature, Margaret Price gave it to me herself. And you are her daughter?

HELEN. Yes, Justice Prentice.

PRENTICE. Yes, I can see the likeness. At twenty you must have looked very like this miniature. [*Passes miniature to* HELEN]

HELEN [*as* JACK *and* VIOLA *look at miniature*]. I have photographs of myself that are very like this. [*To* PRENTICE] And you were speaking of her just now.

PRENTICE. Not five minutes ago. — But be seated, please. [VIOLA *sits again at window*] I'm very delighted to have you call.

HELEN. Even at such an hour?

PRENTICE. At any hour. Margaret Price was a very dear friend of mine; and to think, you're her daughter. And this letter 1860 — what's this?

HELEN. Oh, don't touch that. It will break. It's only a dry spray of mignonette, pinned to the note when you sent it.

PRENTICE [*musingly*]. A spray of mignonette.

HELEN. My mother's favorite flower, and perfume.

PRENTICE. I remember. Well, well, this is equally astonishing.

JACK. Do you remember the letter, Mr. Justice?

PRENTICE. Perfectly.

JACK. And the circumstances it alludes to?

PRENTICE. Yes. It was the work of a romantic boy. I — I was very fond of your mother, Mrs. — by the way, you haven't told me your name.

HELEN. Never mind that now. Let me be Margaret Price's daughter for the present.

PRENTICE. Very well. Oh, this was a little scratch of a duel — they've gone out of fashion now, I'm thankful to say.

HELEN. Do you remember the cause of this one?

PRENTICE. Yes; Henry Boland had worried Margaret some way. She was frightened, I think, and fainted.

HELEN. And you struck him?

PRENTICE. Yes, and he challenged me.

HELEN. I've heard mother tell it. Do you remember what frightened her?

PRENTICE. I don't believe I do. Does the letter say?

HELEN. No. Try to think.

PRENTICE. Was it a snake or a toad?

HELEN. No — a jewel.

PRENTICE. A jewel? I remember now — a — a — cat's-eye. A cat's-eye jewel, wasn't it?

HELEN [*with excitement*]. Yes, yes, yes. [*Weeping*]

PRENTICE. My dear madam, it seems to be a very emotional subject with you.

HELEN. It is. I've hoped so you would remember it. On the cars I was praying all the way you would remember it. And you do — you do.

PRENTICE. I do.

VIOLA [*comes to* HELEN]. Compose yourself, dear. Remember what depends on it.

PRENTICE. It is evidently something in which I can aid you.

HELEN. It is — and you will?

PRENTICE. There is nothing I would not do for a daughter of Margaret Price. You are in mourning, dear lady; is it for your mother?

HELEN. For my son.

PRENTICE [*to* JACK]. How long has he been dead?

HELEN. He is not dead. Justice Prentice, my boy — the grandson of Margaret Price — is under a sentence of death.

PRENTICE. Sentence of death?

HELEN. Yes. I am the mother of Clay Whipple —

PRENTICE [*rises*]. But, madam —

HELEN. He is to die. I come —

PRENTICE [*retreats towards second door*]. Stop! You forget yourself. The case of Whipple is before the Supreme Court of the United States. I am a member of that body — I cannot listen to you.

HELEN. You must.

PRENTICE. You are prejudicing his chances. [*To* JACK] You are making it *necessary* for me to rule against him. [*To* HELEN] My dear madam, for the sake of your boy, do not do this. It is unlawful — without dignity or precedent. [*To* JACK] If the lady were not the mother of the boy I should call your conduct base —

VIOLA. But she is his mother.

HELEN [*following*]. And Justice Prentice, I am the daughter of the woman you loved.

PRENTICE. I beg you to be silent.

JACK. Won't you hear us a moment?

PRENTICE. I cannot. I dare not — I must leave you. [*Going*]

VIOLA. Why?

PRENTICE. I have explained — the matter is before the court. For me to hear you would be corrupt.

HELEN. I won't talk of the question before your court. That our attorneys tell us, is a constitutional point.

PRENTICE. That is its attitude.

HELEN. I will not talk of that. I wish to speak of this letter.

JACK. You can listen to that, can't you, Mr. Justice?

PRENTICE. Do you hope for its influence indirectly?

HELEN. No; sit down, Justice Prentice, and compose yourself. I will talk calmly to you.

PRENTICE. My dear madam, my heart bleeds for you. [*To* JACK] Her agony must be past judicial measurement.

JACK. Only God knows, sir!

[HELEN *sits at table;* VIOLA *stands by her side;* PRENTICE *sits by the fire;* JACK *remains standing*]

HELEN. [*Pause*] Justice Prentice.

PRENTICE. Mrs. Whipple.

HELEN. You remember this letter — you have recalled the duel. You remember — thank God — its cause?

PRENTICE. I do.

HELEN. You know that my mother's aversion to that jewel amounted almost to an insanity?

PRENTICE. I remember that.

HELEN. I inherited that aversion. When a child, the sight of one of them would throw me almost into convulsions.

PRENTICE. Is it possible?

HELEN. It is true. The physicians said I would outgrow the susceptibility, and in a measure I did so. But I discovered that Clay had inherited the fatal dislike from me.

JACK. You can understand that, Mr. Justice?

PRENTICE. Medical jurisprudence is full of such cases. Why should we deny them? Is nature faithful only in physical matters? You are like this portrait. Your voice *is* that of Margaret Price. Nature's behest should have also embraced some of the less apparent possessions, I think.

JACK. We urged all that at the trial, but they called it invention.

PRENTICE. Nothing seems more probable to me.

HELEN. Clay, my boy, had that dreadful and unreasonable fear of the jewel. I protected him as far as possible, but one night over a year ago, some men — companions — finding that the sight of this stone annoyed him, pressed it upon his attention. He did not know, Justice Prentice, he was not responsible. It was insanity, but he struck his tormentor and the blow resulted in the young man's death.

PRENTICE. Terrible — terrible!

HELEN. My poor boy is crushed with the awful deed. He is not a murderer. He was never that, but they have sentenced him, Justice Prentice — he — is to die. [*Rises impulsively*]

JACK [*catching her*]. Now — now — my dear Helen, compose yourself.

VIOLA [*embracing her*]. You promised.

HELEN. Yes, yes, I will. [VIOLA *leads* HELEN *aside*]

PRENTICE. All this was ably presented to the trial court, you say?

JACK. By the best attorneys.

PRENTICE. And the verdict?

JACK. Still was guilty. But, Mr. Justice, the sentiment of the community has changed very much since then. We feel that a new trial would result differently.

HELEN. When our lawyers decided to go to the Supreme Court, I remembered some letters of yours in this old book. Can you imagine my joy when I found the letter was on the very point of this inherited trait on which we rested our defense?

JACK. We have ridden twenty-four hours to reach you. The train came in only at ten o'clock.

HELEN. You — you are not powerless to help me. What is an official duty to a mother's love? To the life of her boy?

PRENTICE. My dear, dear madam, that is not necessary — believe me. This letter comes very properly under the head of new evidence. [*To* JACK] The defendant is entitled to a rehearing on that.

HELEN. Justice Prentice! Justice Prentice! [*Turns again to* VIOLA]

VIOLA. There — there — [*Comforts* HELEN]

PRENTICE. Of course that isn't before us, but when we remand the case on this constitutional point —

HELEN. Then you will — you will remand it?

PRENTICE [*prevaricating*]. Justice Henderson had convinced me on the point as you called. So I think there is no doubt of the decision.

HELEN. You can never know the light you let into my heart.

[VIOLA *returns lace handkerchief to book which* HELEN *opens for the purpose, closing it again on handkerchief*]

PRENTICE. What is that perfume? Have you one about you?

HELEN. Yes, on this handkerchief.

PRENTICE. What is it?

HELEN. Mignonette.

PRENTICE. Mignonette.

HELEN. A favorite perfume of mother's. This handkerchief of hers was in the book with the letter.

PRENTICE. Indeed.

HELEN. Oh, Justice Prentice, do you think I can save my boy?

PRENTICE [*to* JACK]. On the rehearing I will take pleasure in testifying as to this hereditary aversion — and what I knew of its existence in Margaret Price.

JACK. May I tell the lawyers so?

PRENTICE. No. They will learn it in the court to-morrow. They can stand the suspense. I am speaking comfort to the mother's heart.

HELEN. Comfort. It is life!

PRENTICE [*to* JACK]. Say nothing of this call, if you please. Nothing to anyone.

JACK. We shall respect your instructions, Mr. Justice. My niece, who has been with Mrs. Whipple during this trouble, is the fiancée of the boy who is in jail.

PRENTICE. You have my sympathy, too, my dear.

VIOLA. Thank you. [*Goes to* PRENTICE *and gives him her hand*]

PRENTICE. And now good-night.

VIOLA. Good-night. [*Goes to door where* JACK *joins her*]

HELEN. Good-night, Justice Prentice. You must know my gratitude — words cannot tell it.

[*Exit* VIOLA]

PRENTICE. Would you do me a favor?

HELEN. Can you ask it? [JACK *waits at the door*]

PRENTICE. If that was the handkerchief of Margaret Price, I'd like to have it.

[*With a moment's effort at self-control,* HELEN *gives* PRENTICE *the handkerchief. She does not dare to speak, but turns to* JACK *who leads her out.* PRENTICE *goes to the table and takes up the miniature. A distant bell strikes two*]

Margaret Price. People will say that she has been in her grave thirty years, but I'll swear her spirit was in this room to-night and directed a decision of the Supreme Court of the United

States. [*Noticing the handkerchief which he holds, he puts it to his lips*]

"The delicate odor of mignonette,
  The ghost of a dead-and-gone bouquet,
Is all that tells of her story ; yet
  Could she think of a sweeter way?"

CURTAIN

ACT III

SCENE. — *Same as Act I*

JACK *in chair right of table with elbows on knees apparently in deep thought.*

[*Enter* HARVEY, *left*]

HARVEY.   Mars Jack.

JACK.   Well, Uncle Harvey?

HARVEY.   'Scuse me, sah, when you wants to be alone, but I'se awful anxious, myself. Is dey any word from the court-house?

JACK.   None, Uncle Harvey.

HARVEY.   'Cause Jo said Missus Campbell done come in, an' I thought she'd been to the trial, you know.

JACK.   She has. You're not keeping anything from me, Uncle Harvey.

HARVEY.   'Deed, no, sah. Ah jes' like to ask you, Mars Jack, if I'd better have de cook fix sumpun' to eat — maybe de other ladies comin' too?

JACK.   Yes, Uncle Harvey, but whether they'll want to eat or not'll depend on what word comes back with the jury.

HARVEY.   Yes, sah. [*Exit   left*] [*Enter* ALICE, *right center*]

ALICE [*in astonishment and reproach*]. Jack — [*She comes down left*]

JACK.   Well —

ALICE.   Why are you here?

JACK.   Well — I live here.

ALICE.   But I thought you'd gone to Helen and Viola.

JACK.   No.

ALICE.   You should do so, Jack. Think of them alone when that jury returns — as it may at any moment — with its verdict.

JACK.   The lawyers are there and Lew Ellinger is with them.

ALICE.   But Helen — Helen needs you.

JACK.   I may be useful here.

ALICE.   How?

JACK.   There's one man on that jury that I think is a friend.

ALICE.   One man?

JACK.   Yes.

ALICE.   Out of a jury of twelve.

JACK.   One man can stop the other eleven from bringing in an adverse verdict — and this one is with us.

ALICE.   Would your going to Helen and Viola in the court-house stop his being with us?

JACK.   Perhaps not, but it would stop my being with him.

ALICE.   What? [*Looks about*] I don't understand you.

JACK.   Justice Prentice told me that he could sit alone in his room and make another man get up and walk to the telephone and call him by simply thinking steadily of that other man.

ALICE.   Superstitious people imagine anything.

JACK.   Imagine much — yes — but this isn't imagination.

ALICE.   It's worse — Jack. I call it spiritualism.

JACK.   Call it anything you like — spiritualism — or socialism — or rheumatism — it's there. I know nothing about it scientifically, but I've tried it on and it works, my dear Alice, it works.

ALICE.   You've tried it on?

JACK.   Yes.

ALICE.   With whom?

JACK.   With you.

ALICE.   I don't know it if you have.

JACK.   That is one phase of its terrible subtlety.

ALICE.   When did you try it on?

JACK [*inquiringly*]. That night, a month ago, when you rapped at my door at two o'clock in the morning and asked if I was ill in any way.

ALICE.   I was simply nervous about you.

JACK.   Call it "nervousness" if you wish to — but that was an experiment of mine — a simple experiment.

ALICE.   Oh!

JACK.   Two Sundays ago you went up to the church door — hesitated, and turned home again.

ALICE.   Lots of people do that.

JACK.   I don't ask you to take stock in it, but that was another experiment of mine. The thing appeals to me. I can't help Helen by being at the court-house, but, as I'm alive and my name's Jack Brookfield, I do believe that my thought reaches that particular juryman.

ALICE.   That's lunacy, Jack, dear.

JACK [*rises and walks*]. Well, call it

"lunacy." I don't insist on "rheumatism."

ALICE. Oh, Jack, the boy's life is in the balance. Bitter vindictive lawyers are prosecuting him, and I don't like my big strong brother, who used to meet men and all danger face to face, treating the situation with silly mind-cure methods — hidden alone in his rooms. I don't like it.

JACK. You can't acquit a boy of murder by having a strong brother thrash somebody in the court-room. If there was anything under the sun I could do with my physical strength, I'd do it; but there isn't. Now, why not try this? Why not, if I believe I can influence a juryman by my thought, — why not try?

[ALICE *turns away. Enter* Jo, *right center*]

Well?

Jo. Mistah Hardmuth.

ALICE [*astonished*]. Frank Hardmuth?

Jo. Yes.

JACK. Here's one of the "bitter vindictive" men you want me to meet face to face. You stay here while I go and do it. [*Starts up*] [*Enter* HARDMUTH]

HARDMUTH. Excuse me, but I can't wait in an anteroom.

JACK. That'll do, Jo. [*Exit* Jo]

HARDMUTH. I want to see you alone.

JACK [*to* ALICE]. Yes —

ALICE [*going*]. What do you think it is?

JACK. Nothing to worry over. [*Conducts her to door left. Exit* ALICE]

HARDMUTH [*threateningly*]. Jack Brookfield.

JACK. Well? [*Confronts* HARDMUTH]

HARDMUTH. I've just seen Harvey Fisher — of the *Courier*.

JACK. Yes.

HARDMUTH. He says you've hinted at something associating me with the shooting of Scovill.

JACK. Right.

HARDMUTH. What do you mean?

JACK. I mean, Frank Hardmuth, that you shan't hound this boy to the gallows without reckoning with me and the things I know of you.

HARDMUTH. I'm doing my duty as a prosecuting attorney.

JACK. You are, and a great deal more — you're venting a personal hatred.

HARDMUTH. That hasn't anything to do with this insinuation you've handed to a newspaper man, an insinuation for which anybody ought to kill you.

JACK. I don't deal in " insinuations." It was a charge.

HARDMUTH. A statement?

JACK. A charge! You understand English — a specific and categorical charge.

HARDMUTH. That I knew Scovill was to be shot.

JACK. That you knew it? No. That you planned it and arranged and *procured* his assassination.

HARDMUTH [*in low tone*]. If the newspapers print that, I'll kill you — damn you, I'll kill you.

JACK. I don't doubt your willingness. And they'll print it — if they haven't done so already — and if they don't print it, by God, I'll print it myself and *paste it on the fences*.

HARDMUTH [*weakening*]. What have I ever done to you, Jack Brookfield, except to be your friend?

JACK. You've been much too friendly. With this murder on your conscience, you proposed to take to yourself, as wife, my niece, dear to me as my life. As revenge for her refusal and mine, you've persecuted through two trials the boy she loved, and the son of the woman whose thought regulates the pulse of my heart, an innocent, unfortunate boy. In your ambition you've reached out to be the governor of this State, and an honored political party is seriously considering you for that office to-day.

HARDMUTH. That Scovill story's a lie — a political lie. I think you mean to be honest, Jack Brookfield, but somebody's strung you.

JACK. Wait! The man that's now hiding in Indiana — a fugitive from your feeble efforts at extradition — sat upstairs drunk and desperate — his last dollar on a case card. I pitied him. If a priest had been there he couldn't have purged his soul cleaner than poor Raynor gave it to me. If *he* put me on, am I strung?

HARDMUTH [*frightened*]. Yes, you are. I can't tell you why, because this jury is out and may come in any moment and I've got to be there, but I can square it. So help me God, I can square it.

JACK. You'll have to square it.

[*Enter* ALICE, *left, followed by* PRENTICE]

ALICE. Jack. [*Indicates* PRENTICE]

PRENTICE. Excuse me, I —

HARDMUTH. Oh — Justice Prentice.

JACK. Mr. Hardmuth — the State's attorney.

PRENTICE. I recognize Mr. Hardmuth. I didn't salute him because I resent his disrespectful treatment of myself during his cross-examination.

HARDMUTH. Entirely within my rights as a lawyer and —

PRENTICE. Entirely — and never within the opportunities of a gentleman.

HARDMUTH. Your side foresaw the powerful effect on a local jury of any testimony by a member of the Supreme Court, and my wish to break that —

PRENTICE. Was quite apparent, sir, — quite apparent, — but the testimony of every man is entitled to just such weight and consideration as that man's character commands. But it is not that disrespect which I resent. I am an old man — That I am unmarried — childless — without a son to inherit the vigor that time has reclaimed, is due to — a sentiment that you endeavored to ridicule, Mr. Hardmuth, a sentiment which would have been sacred in the hands of any true Kentuckian, which I am glad to hear you are not.

JACK. That's all.

HARDMUTH. Perhaps not. [*Exit*]

PRENTICE. My dear Mr. Brookfield, that man certainly hasn't seen this newspaper?

JACK. No — but he knows it's coming.

PRENTICE. When I urged you as a citizen to tell anything you knew of the man, I hadn't expected a capital charge.

ALICE. What is it, Jack, — what have you said?

JACK [*to* ALICE. *Hands paper*]. All in the headlines — read it. [*To* PRENTICE] That enough for your purpose, Justice Prentice?

PRENTICE. I never dreamed of an attack of that — that magnitude — Enough!

ALICE. Why — why did you do this, Jack?

JACK. Because I'm your big strong brother — and I had the information.

PRENTICE. It was necessary, Mrs. Campbell, — necessary.

ALICE. Why necessary?

JACK. My poor sister, you don't think. If that jury brings in a verdict of guilty — what then?

ALICE. What then? I don't know.

JACK. An appeal to the governor — for clemency.

ALICE. Well?

JACK. Then we delay things until a new governor comes in. But suppose that new governor is Hardmuth himself.

ALICE. How can the new governor be Hardmuth?

PRENTICE. Nothing can stop it if he gets the nomination, and the convention is in session at Frankfort to-day with Mr. Hardmuth's name in the lead.

JACK [*indicating paper*]. I've served that notice on them and they won't dare nominate him. That is, I think they won't.

ALICE. But to charge him with murder?

PRENTICE. The only thing to consider there is, — have you your facts?

JACK. I have.

PRENTICE. Then it was a duty and you chose the psychological moment for its performance. "With what measure you mete — it shall be measured to you again." I have pity for the man whom that paper crushes, but I have greater pity for the boy he is trying to have hanged. [*Goes to* ALICE] You know, Mrs. Campbell, that young Whipple is the grandson of an old friend of mine.

ALICE. Yes, Justice Prentice, I know that.

[*Enter* JO, *right center, followed by* HELEN *and* VIOLA]

JO. Mars Jack!

JACK [*turning*]. Yes?

HELEN. Oh, Jack! — [*Comes down to* JACK. VIOLA *goes to* ALICE]

JACK. What is it? [*Catches and supports* HELEN]

VIOLA. The jury returned and asked for instructions.

JACK. Well.

HELEN. There's a recess of an hour.

VIOLA. The court wishes them locked up for the night, but the foreman said the jurymen were all anxious to get to their homes and he felt an agreement could be reached in an hour.

PRENTICE. Did he use exactly those words — "to their homes"?

VIOLA. "To their homes" — yes.

PRENTICE [*smiling at* JACK]. There you are.

HELEN. What, Jack?

JACK. What?

PRENTICE. Men with vengeance or severity in their hearts would hardly say they're "anxious to get to their homes." They say "the jury is anxious to get away," or "to finish its work."

HELEN. Oh, Justice Prentice, you pin hope upon such slight things.

PRENTICE. That is what hope is for, my dear Mrs. Whipple; the frail chances of this life.

VIOLA. And now, Uncle Jack, Mrs. Whipple ought to have a cup of tea and something to eat.

HELEN. Oh, I couldn't — we must go back at once.

VIOLA. Well, I could — I — I must.

ALICE. Yes — you must — both of you. [*Exit to dining-room*]

VIOLA [*returning to* HELEN]. You don't think it's heartless, do you?

HELEN. You dear child. [*Kisses her*]

VIOLA. You come, too.

HELEN [*refusing*]. Please. [*Exit* VIOLA. HELEN *sinks to sofa*]

JACK. And now, courage, my dear Helen; it's almost over.

HELEN. At the other trial the jury delayed — just this way.

PRENTICE. Upon what point did the jury ask instruction?

HELEN. Degree.

PRENTICE. And the court?

HELEN. Oh, Jack, the judge answered — guilty in the first degree, or not guilty.

PRENTICE. That all helps us.

HELEN. It does?

JACK. Who spoke for the jury?

HELEN. The foreman — and one other juryman asked a question.

JACK. Was it the man in the fourth chair — first row?

HELEN [*inquiringly*]. Yes —?

JACK. Ah.

HELEN. Why?

JACK. I think he's a friend, that's all.

HELEN. I should die, Jack, if it wasn't for your courage. You won't get tired of it — will you — and forsake my poor boy — and me?

JACK [*encouragingly*]. What do you think?

HELEN. All our lawyers are kindness itself, but — but — you — Jack — you somehow —

[*Enter* VIOLA]

VIOLA. Oh, Uncle Jack — here's a note our lawyer asked me to give to you — I forgot it until this minute.

JACK. Thank you. [*Takes note*]

VIOLA. Please try a cup of tea.

HELEN. No — no — Viola. [*Exit* VIOLA] What is it, Jack? Are they afraid?

JACK. It's not about the trial at all. [*Hands note to* PRENTICE]

HELEN. Really?

JACK. Yes.

HELEN. But why don't you show it to us, then?

JACK [PRENTICE *returns note*]. I will — if my keeping it gives you so much alarm as that. [*Turns on the large drop light and stands under it*] Colonel Bayley says — "Dear Jack, I've seen the paper; Hardmuth will shoot on sight."

HELEN [*quickly to* JACK'S *side*]. Oh, Jack, if anything should happen to you —

JACK. "Anything" is quite as likely to happen to Mr. Hardmuth.

HELEN. But not even that — my boy has killed a man — and — you — Jack — you — well, you just mustn't let it happen, that's all.

JACK. I mustn't let it happen because — ?

HELEN. Because — I — couldn't bear it.

[JACK *lifts her hand to his face and kisses it. Enter* ALICE]

ALICE. What was the letter, Jack?

JACK [*hands letter to* ALICE *as he passes, leading* HELEN *to door*]. And, now I'll agree to do the best I can for Mr. Hardmuth if you'll take a cup of tea and a biscuit.

HELEN. There isn't time.

JACK. There's plenty of time if the adjournment was for an hour.

ALICE [*in alarm*]. Jack!

JACK. Eh — [*Turns to* ALICE]. Wait one minute. [*Goes on to door with* HELEN] Go.

[*Exit* HELEN]

ALICE [*as* JACK *returns*]. He threatens your life.

JACK. Not exactly. Simply Colonel Bayley's opinion that he will shoot on sight.

ALICE [*impatiently*]. Oh —

JACK. That is a difference, you know.

[*Enter* Jo]

Jo. Mr. Ellinger, sah.

[*Enter* LEW]

LEW [*briskly*]. Hello, Jack.

[*Exit* JO]

JACK. Well, Lew?

LEW [*with newspaper*]. Why that's the damnedest thing — [*To* ALICE] I beg your pardon.

ALICE. Don't, please — some manly emphasis is a real comfort, Mr. Ellinger.

LEW. That charge of yours against Hardmuth is raisin' more h-h-high feeling than anything that ever happened.

JACK. I saw the paper.

LEW. You didn't see this — it's an extra. [*Reads*] "The charge read to the convention in night session at Frankfort — Bill Glover hits Jim Macey on the nose — DeVoe of Carter County takes Jim's gun away from him. The delegation from Butler get down to their stomachs and crawl under the benches — some statesmen go through the windows. Convention takes recess till morning. Local sheriff swearin' in deputies to keep peace in the barrooms." — That's all you've done.

JACK [*to* ALICE]. Good! [*To* PRENTICE] Well, they can't nominate Mr. Hardmuth now.

LEW [*to* ALICE]. I been hedgin' — I told the fellows I'd bet Jack hadn't said it.

JACK. Yes — I did say it.

LEW. In just those words —? [*Reads*] "The poor fellow that crouched back of a window sill and shot Kentucky's governor deserves hanging less than the man whom he is shielding — the man who laid the plot of assassination. The present prosecuting attorney by appointment — Frank Allison Hardmuth." Did you say that?

JACK. Lew, that there might be no mistake — I wrote it. [LEW *whistles;* JACK *takes the paper and scans it*]

LEW. Is it straight?

JACK. Yes. [*Pushes hanging button and turns off the large drop*]

LEW. He *was* in the plot to kill the governor?

JACK. He organized it.

LEW. Well, what do you think of that? And now he's runnin' for governor himself — a murderer!

JACK. Yes.

LEW [*to* PRENTICE]. And for six months he's been houndin' every fellow in Louisville that sat down to a game of cards. [JACK *nods*] The damned rascal's nearly put me in the poorhouse.

JACK. Poor old Lew!

LEW [*to* PRENTICE]. Why, before I could get to that court-house to-day I had to take a pair of scissors that I used to cut coupons with and trim the whiskers off o' my shirt cuffs. [*To* JACK] How long have you known this?

JACK. Ever since the fact.

PRENTICE. Mm —

LEW. Why do you spring it only now?

JACK. Because until now I lacked the character and the moral courage. I spring it now by the advice of Justice Prentice to reach that convention at Frankfort.

LEW. Well, you reached them.

PRENTICE. The convention was only a secondary consideration with me — my real object was this jury with whom Mr. Hardmuth seemed too powerful.

LEW. Reach the jury?

JACK [*enthusiastically*]. The jury? Why, of course, — the entire jury, — and I was hoping for one man —

LEW. Why, they don't see the papers — the jury won't get a line of this.

JACK. I think they will.

LEW. You got 'em fixed?

JACK. Fixed? No.

LEW. Then how will they see it?

PRENTICE [*firmly and slowly to* LEW, *who is half dazed*]. How many people in Louisville have already read that charge as you have read it?

LEW. Thirty thousand, maybe, but —

PRENTICE. And five hundred thousand in the little cities and the towns. Do you think, Mr. Ellinger, that all those minds can be at white heat over that knowledge and none of it reach the thought of those twelve men? Ah, no —

JACK. To half a million good Kentuckians to-night Frank Hardmuth is a repulsive thing — and that jury's faith in him — is dead.

LEW. [*Pause*] Why, Jack, old man, you're dippy.

[ALICE *turns away wearily, agreeing with* LEW]

PRENTICE. Then, Mr. Ellinger, I am dippy, too.

[ALICE *turns back*]

LEW. You mean you think the jury gets the public opinion — without anybody tellin' them or their reading it.

PRENTICE. Yes. [*Pause.* LEW *looks stunned*] In every widely discussed trial the defendant is tried not alone by his twelve peers, but by the entire community.

LEW. Why, blast it! The community goes by what the newspaper says!

PRENTICE. That is often the regrettable part of it — but the fact remains.

JACK. And that's why you asked me to expose Frank Hardmuth?

PRENTICE. Yes.

LEW. Well, the public will think you did it because he closed your game.

JACK. Hardmuth didn't close my game.

LEW. Who did?

JACK [*pointing to* PRENTICE]. This man.

PRENTICE [*to* JACK]. Thank you.

LEW. How the he — er — heaven's name did he close it?

JACK. He gave my self-respect a slap on the back and I stood up. [*Exit*]

LEW [*thoroughly confused. Pause*]. Stung! [*Turns to* PRENTICE]. So you are responsible for these — these new ideas of Jack's?

PRENTICE. In a measure. Have the ideas apparently hurt Mr. Brookfield?

LEW. They've put him out of business — that's all.

PRENTICE. Which business?

LEW. Why, this house of his.

PRENTICE. I see. But his new ideas? Don't you like them, Mr. Ellinger?

LEW. I love Jack Brookfield — love him like a brother — but I don't want even a brother askin' me if I'm sure I've "thought it over" when I'm startin' to take the halter off for a pleasant evenin'. Get my idea?

PRENTICE. I begin to.

LEW. In other words — I don't want to take my remorse first. It dampens the fun. The other day a lady at the races said, "We've missed you, Mr. Ellinger." And I said, "Have you? — Well I'll be up this evening," and I'm pressing her hand and hanging on to it till I'm afraid I'll get the carriage grease on my coat — feelin' only about thirty-two, you know; then I turn round and Jack has those sleepy lamps on me — and "bla" — [*Turns and sinks onto sofa*]

PRENTICE. And you don't go?

LEW [*bracing up*]. I do go — as a

matter of self-respect — but I don't make a hit. I'm thinking so much more about those morality ideas of Jack's than I am about the lady that it cramps my style and we never get past the weather, and "when did you last hear from So-and-so?" [*Rises*] I want to reform all right. I believe in reform. But first I want to have the fun of fallin' and fallin' hard.

JO [*distant and outside*]. 'Fore God, Mars Clay!

CLAY. Jo, is my mother here?

ALICE [*entering left*]. Why, that's Clay.

[*Voices off continue together and approach*]

LEW [*to* PRENTICE]. It's the boy.

ALICE. His mother! [*Starts to call* HELEN, *then falters in indecision*] Oh! [*The outside voices grow louder*]

PRENTICE. Acquittal!

[*Enter* CLAY, *followed by* COLONEL BAYLEY, *his attorney*]

ALICE. Clay, Clay!

CLAY. Oh, Mrs. Campbell.

ALICE *embraces him. Enter* JACK, HELEN, *and* VIOLA *from the dining-room*]

JACK [*seeing* CLAY *and speaking back to* HELEN]. Yes.

HELEN [*as she enters*]. My boy!

CLAY. Mother!

[*They embrace.* CLAY *slips to his knee with his face hidden in* HELEN's *lap, repeating her name.* HELEN *standing sways and is caught by* JACK. CLAY *noting this weakness rises and helps support her*]

JACK [*rousing her*]. He's free, Helen, he's free.

CLAY. Yes, mother, I'm free.

[VIOLA, *who has crossed back of* CLAY *and* HELEN, *weeps on shoulder of* ALICE, *who comforts her*]

HELEN. My boy, my boy!

[VIOLA *looks at them.* HELEN *sees* VIOLA *and turns* CLAY *toward her.* CLAY *takes* VIOLA *in his arms*]

CLAY. Viola, my brave sweetheart!

VIOLA. It's really over?

CLAY. Yes.

JACK. It's a great victory, Colonel.

BAYLEY. Thank you.

JACK. If ever a lawyer made a good

fight for a man's life, you did. Helen, Viola, you must want to shake this man's hand.

VIOLA. I could have thrown my arms around you when you made that speech.

BAYLEY [*laughing*]. Too many young fellows crowding into the profession as it is.

HELEN [*taking his hand*]. Life must be sweet to a man who can do so much good as you do.

BAYLEY. I couldn't stand it, you know, if it wasn't that my ability works both ways.

[*Enter* HARVEY, *left*]

HARVEY. Mars Clay.

CLAY. Harvey! Why, dear old Harvey. [*Half embraces* HARVEY *and pats him affectionately*]

HARVEY. Yes, sah. Could — could you eat anything, Mars Clay?

CLAY. Eat anything! Why, I'm starvin', Harvey.

HARVEY. Ha, ha. Yes, sah. [*Exit quickly*]

CLAY. But you with me, mother — and Viola.

HELEN. My boy! Colonel! [*Turns to* BAYLEY. *Exeunt* CLAY, VIOLA, HELEN, BAYLEY, *and* ALICE *to dining-room*]

JACK [*alone with* PRENTICE. *Picks up* BAYLEY'*s letter; takes hold of push button over head*]. Mr. Justice — I shall never doubt you again.

PRENTICE. Mr. Brookfield, never doubt yourself.

[*Enter* HARDMUTH. *He rushes down toward dining-room and turns back to* JACK *who is under the lamp with his hand on its button*]

HARDMUTH. You think you'll send me to the gallows, but, damn you, you go first yourself. [*Thrusts a derringer against* JACK'*s body*]

JACK. Stop! [*The big light flashes on above* HARDMUTH'*s eyes. At* JACK'*s* "Stop", PRENTICE *inclines forward with eyes on* HARDMUTH *so that there is a double battery of hypnotism on him. A pause*] You can't shoot — that — gun. You can't pull the trigger. [*Pause*] You can't — even — hold — the — gun. [*Pause. The derringer drops from* HARDMUTH'*s hand*] Now, Frank, you can go.

HARDMUTH [*recoiling slowly*]. I'd like to know — how in hell you did that — to me.

CURTAIN

ACT IV

SCENE. — *Same as Act III. All lights on including big electric.*

CLAY *and* VIOLA *seated on sofa near the fire-place.*

VIOLA. I must really say good-night and let you get some sleep.

CLAY. Not before Jack gets home. Our mothers have considerately left us alone together. They'll just as considerately tell us when it's time to part.

VIOLA. *My* mother said it was time half an hour ago.

CLAY. Wait till Jack comes in.

[*Enter* JO]

JO. Mars Clay?

CLAY. Well, Jo?

JO. Dey's another reporter to see you, sah?

VIOLA. Send him away — Mr. Whipple won't see any more reporters.

CLAY [*rises*]. Wait a minute — who is he? [*Jo hands card*] I've got to see this one, Viola.

VIOLA [*complaining*]. Why "got to"?

CLAY. He's a friend — I'll see him, Jo.

JO. Yas, sah — [*Exit*]

VIOLA [*rises*]. You've said that all day — they're all friends.

CLAY. Well, they are — but this boy especially. It was fine to see you and mother and Jack when I was in that jail — great — but you were there daytimes. This boy spent hours on the other side of the bars helping me pass the awful nights. I tell you — death-cells would be pretty nearly hell if it wasn't for the police reporters — ministers ain't in it with 'em.

[*Enter* EMMETT, *a reporter*]

EMMETT. Good-evening.

CLAY. How are you, Ned? You know Miss Campbell?

EMMETT [*bowing*]. Yes.

VIOLA. Good-evening.

CLAY. Have a chair.

EMMETT. Thank you. [*Defers to* VIOLA *who sits first on sofa. Pause*] This is different. [*Looks around the room*]

CLAY. Some.

EMMETT. Satisfied? The way we handled the story?

CLAY. Perfectly. You were just bully, old man.

EMMETT [*to* VIOLA]. That artist of ours is only a kid — and they work him to death on the "Sunday" — so — [*Pause. To* CLAY] You understand.

CLAY. Oh — I got used to the — pictures a year ago.

EMMETT. Certainly. [*Pause*] Anything you want to say?

VIOLA. For the paper?

EMMETT. Yes.

CLAY. I think not.

[*Enter* HELEN *and* ALICE *from diningroom.* EMMETT *rises*]

HELEN. Clay, dear — [*Pause*] Oh —

CLAY. You met my mother?

EMMETT. No —

CLAY. Mother — this is Mr. Emmett of whom I've told you so often.

HELEN. Oh — the good reporter.

EMMETT [*to* CLAY]. Gee! That'd be a wonder if the gang heard it. [*Taking* HELEN's *hand as she offers it*] We got pretty well acquainted — yes'm.

CLAY [*introducing* ALICE]. Mrs. Campbell.

ALICE. Won't you sit down, Mr. Emmett?

EMMETT. Thank you. I guess we've covered everything, but the chief wanted me to see your son — [*turns to* CLAY] and see if you'd do the paper a favor?

CLAY. If possible — gladly —

EMMETT. I don't like the assignment because — well, for the very reason that it was handed to me — and that is because we're more or less friendly.

[*Enter* JACK *right center in fur coat with cap and goggles in hand*]

JACK. Well, it's a wonderful night outside.

ALICE. You're back early.

JACK. Purposely. [*To* EMMETT] How are you?

EMMETT [*rising*]. Mr. Brookfield.

JACK. I thought you girls might like a little run in the moonlight before I put in the machine.

HELEN. Mr. Emmett has some message from his editor.

JACK. What is it?

EMMETT. There's a warrant out for Hardmuth — you saw that?

VIOLA. Yes, we saw that. [*Goes to* JACK]

JACK. To-night's paper —

EMMETT. If they get him and he comes to trial and all that, it'll be the biggest trial Kentucky ever saw.

CLAY. Well?

EMMETT. Well — the paper wants you to agree to report it for them — the trial — there'll be other papers after you, of course.

VIOLA. Oh, no —

EMMETT. Understand, Clay, I'm not asking it. [*To* VIOLA] I'm here under orders just as I'd be at a fire or a bread riot.

CLAY [*demurring*]. And — of course — you understand, don't you?

EMMETT. Perfectly — and I told the chief myself you wouldn't see it.

CLAY. Paper's been too friendly for me to assume any — any —

JACK. Unnecessary dignity —

CLAY. Exactly — but — I just couldn't, you see —

EMMETT [*going*]. Oh, leave it to me — I'll let 'em down easy.

CLAY. Thank you.

EMMETT. You expect to be in Europe or —

CLAY. But I don't.

[JACK *removes fur coat, puts it on chair up right center*]

VIOLA. We're going to stay right here in Louisville —

CLAY. And work out my — my own future among the people who know me.

EMMETT. Of course — Europe's just to stall off the chief — get him on to some other dope —

HELEN (*rising*). But ——

JACK [*interrupting*]. It's all right.

HELEN [*to* JACK]. I hate to begin with a falsehood.

EMMETT. Not your son — me — Saw some copy on our telegraph desk, Mr. Brookfield, that'd interest you.

JACK. Yes.

EMMETT. Or maybe you know of it? Frankfort —

JACK. No.

EMMETT. Some friend named you in the caucus.

JACK. What connection?

EMMETT. Governor.

VIOLA [*to* EMMETT]. Uncle Jack?

EMMETT. Yes'm — that is, for the nomination.

JACK. It's a joke.

EMMETT. Grows out of these Hardmuth charges, of course.

JACK. That's all.

EMMETT. Good-night — [*Bows*] Mrs. Whipple — ladies — [*Exit*]

CLAY [*going to door with* EMMETT]. You'll make that quite clear, won't you?

EMMETT [*outside*]. I'll fix it.

CLAY [*returning*]. If it wasn't for the notoriety of it, I'd like to do that. [*Sits right of table*]

HELEN [*reproachfully*]. My son!

JACK. Why would you like to do it?

CLAY. To get even. I'd like to see Hardmuth suffer as he made me suffer. I'd like to watch him suffer and write of it.

JACK. That's a bad spirit to face the world with, my boy.

CLAY. I hate him. [*Goes to* VIOLA]

JACK. Hatred is heavier freight for the shipper than it is for the consignee.

CLAY. I can't help it.

JACK. Yes, you can help it. Mr. Hardmuth should be of the utmost indifference to you. To hate him is weak.

VIOLA. Weak?

JACK. Yes, weak-minded. Hardmuth was in love with you at one time — he hated Clay. He said Clay was as weak as dishwater — [*to* CLAY] — and you were at that time. You've had your lesson — profit by it. Its meaning was self-control. Begin now if you're going to be the custodian of this girl's happiness.

HELEN. I'm sure he means to, Jack.

JACK. You can carry your hatred of Hardmuth and let it embitter your whole life — or you can drop it — so — [*Drops a book on table*] The power that any man or anything has to annoy us we give him or it by our interest. Some idiot told your great-grandmother that a jewel with different colored strata in it was "bad luck" — or a "hoodoo" — she believed it, and she nursed her faith that passed the lunacy on to your grandmother.

HELEN. Jack, don't talk of that, please.

JACK. I'll skip one generation — but I'd like to talk of it.

ALICE [*rising, comes to* HELEN]. Why talk of it?

JACK. It was only a notion, and an effort of will can banish it.

CLAY. It was more than a notion.

JACK. Tom Denning's scarf-pin which he dropped there [*indicates floor*] was an exhibit in your trial — Judge Bayley returned it to me to-day. [*Puts hand in pocket*]

VIOLA. I wish you wouldn't, Uncle Jack. [*Turns away*]

JACK [*to* CLAY]. You don't mind, do you?

CLAY. I'd rather not look at it — to-night.

JACK. You needn't look at it. I'll hold it in my hand and you put your hands over mine.

ALICE. I really don't see the use in this experiment, Jack.

JACK [*with* CLAY'S *hand over his*]. That doesn't annoy you, does it?

CLAY. I'm controlling myself, sir — but I feel the influence of the thing all through and through me.

HELEN. Jack.

[VIOLA *turns away in protest*]

JACK. Down your back, isn't it, and in the roots of your hair — tingling —?

CLAY. Yes.

HELEN. Why torture him?

JACK. Is it torture?

CLAY [*with brave self-control*]. I shall be glad when it's over.

JACK [*severely*]. What rot! That's only my night-key — look at it. I haven't the scarf-pin about me.

CLAY. Why make me think it was the scarf-pin?

JACK. To prove to you that it's only thinking — that's all. Now, be a man — the cat's-eye itself is in that table drawer. Get it and show Viola that you're not a neuropathic idiot. You're a child of *the everlasting God* and nothing on the earth or under it can harm you in the slightest degree. [CLAY *opens drawer and takes pin*] That's the spirit — look at it — [*pushes* CLAY'S *hand up to his face*] I've made many a young horse do that to an umbrella. Now give it to me. [*To* VIOLA] You're not afraid of it.

VIOLA. Why, of course I'm not.

JACK [*putting pin on her breast*]. Now, if you want my niece, go up to that hoodoo like a man. [CLAY *embraces* VIOLA]

HELEN. Oh, Jack, do you think that will last?

JACK. Which — indifference to the hoodoo or partiality to my niece?

CLAY. They'll both last.

JACK. Now, my boy, drop your hatred of Hardmuth as you drop your fear of the scarf-pin. Don't look back — your life's ahead of you. Don't mount for the race over-weight.

[*Enter* Jo, *right center*]

Jo. Mr. Ellinger.

[*Enter* Lew]

Lew. I don't intrude, do I?

Jack. Come in.

Lew [*to* Ladies]. Good-evening. Ah, Clay. [*Shakes hands with* Clay] Glad to see you looking so well. Glad to see you in such good company. [*To* Jack, *briskly*] I've got him.

Jack. Got whom?

Lew. Hardmuth. [*To* Ladies] Detectives been hunting him all day, you know.

Helen. He's caught, you say?

Lew. No — but I've treed him — [*to* Jack] — and I thought I'd just have a word with you before passing the tip. [*To* Ladies] He's nearly put me in the poorhouse with his raids and closing laws, and I see a chance to get even.

Jack. In what way?

Lew. They've been after him nearly twenty-four hours — morning paper's going to offer a reward for him, and I understand the State will also. If I had a little help I'd hide him for a day or two and then surrender him for those rewards.

Jack. Where is Hardmuth? [*Sits at table*]

Lew. Hiding.

Jack [*writing a note*]. Naturally.

Lew. You remember Big George?

Jack. The darkey?

Lew. Yes — used to be on the door at Phil Kelly's?

Jack. Yes.

Lew. He's there. In Big George's cottage — long story — Big George's wife — that is, she — well, his wife — used to be pantry maid for Hardmuth's mother. When they raided Kelly's game, Big George pretended to turn State's evidence, but he really hates Hardmuth like a rattler — so it all comes back to me. You see, if I'd win a couple of hundred at Kelly's I used to slip George a ten going out. Your luck always stays by you if you divide a little with a nigger or a humpback — and in Louisville it's easier to find a nigger — so —

Jack. He's there now?

Lew. Yes. He wants to get away. He's got two guns and he'll shoot before he gives up — so I'd have to con him some way. George's wife is to open the door to Kelly's old signal, you remember — [*raps*] — one knock, then two, and then one.

Jack. Where is the cottage?

Lew. Number 7 Jackson Street — little dooryard — border of arbor-vitæ on the path.

Jack. One knock — then two — and then one — [*Rises with note written*]

Lew. What you gonta do?

Jack. Send for him.

Lew. Who you gonta send?

Jack. That boy there.

Clay. Me?

Jack. Yes.

Helen. Oh, no — no.

Jack. And my niece.

Viola. What! To arrest a man?

Jack [*to* Clay]. My machine is at the door. Give Hardmuth this note. He'll come with you quietly. Bring him here. We'll decide what to do with him after that.

Alice. I can't allow Viola on such an errand.

Jack. When the man she's promised to marry is going into danger —

Viola. If Mr. Hardmuth will come for that note — why can't I deliver it?

Jack. You may — if Clay'll let you.

Clay [*quietly taking note as* Jack *offers it to* Viola]. I'll hand it to him.

Jack. I hope so. [*Gives goggles and coat*] Take these — remember — one rap, then two, then one.

Clay. I understand — number seven —?

Lew. Jackson Street.

Alice. I protest.

Helen. So do I.

Jack [*to* Clay *and* Viola]. You're both of age. I ask you to do it. If you give Hardmuth the goggles, nobody'll recognize him and with a lady beside him you'll get him safely here.

Clay. Come. [*Exit with* Viola]

Lew [*following to door*]. I ought to be in the party.

Jack. No — you stay here.

Alice. That's scandalous.

Jack. But none of us will start the scandal, will we?

Helen. Clay knows nothing of that kind of work — a man with two guns — think of it.

Jack. After he's walked barehanded up to a couple of guns a few times, he'll quit fearing men that are armed only with a scarf-pin.

Helen [*hysterically*]. It's cruel to keep constantly referring to that — that

— mistake of Clay's — I want to forget it.

JACK [*going to* HELEN. *Tenderly*]. The way to forget it, my dear Helen, is not to guard it as a sensitive spot in your memory, but to grasp it as the wise ones grasp a nettle — crush all its power to harm you in one courageous contact. We think things are calamities and trials and sorrows — only names. They are spiritual gymnastics and have an eternal value when once you front them and make them crouch at your feet. Say once for all to your soul and thereby to the world — "Yes, my boy killed a man — because I'd brought him up a half-effeminate, hysterical weakling, but he's been through the fire and I've been through the fire, and we're both the better for it."

HELEN. I can say that truthfully, but I don't want to make a policeman of him, just the same. [*Exit to dining-room*]

ALICE [*following*]. Your treatment's a little too heroic, Jack. [*Exit*]

LEW. Think they'll fetch him?

JACK [*sits left of table*]. Yes.

LEW. He'll come, of course, if he does, under the idea that you'll help him when he gets here.

JACK. Yes.

LEW. Pretty hard double-cross, but he deserves it. I've got a note of fifteen thousand to meet to-morrow, or damn it, I don't think I'd fancy this man-huntin'. I put up some Louisville-Nashville bonds for security, and the holder of the note'll be only too anxious to pinch 'em.

JACK. You can't get your rewards in time for that.

LEW. I know — and that's one reason I come to you, Jack. If you see I'm in a fair way to get a reward —

JACK. I'll lend you the money, Lew.

LEW. Thank you. [JACK *takes check-book and writes*] I thought you would. If I lose those bonds they'll have me selling programs for a livin' at a grand stand. You see, I thought hatin' Hardmuth as you do, and your reputation bein' up through that stuff to the papers —

JACK. There. [*Gives check*]

LEW. Thank you, old man. I'll hand this back to you in a week.

JACK [*rises*]. You needn't.

LEW. What?

JACK. You needn't hand it back. It's only fifteen thousand and you've

lost a hundred of them at poker in these rooms.

LEW. Never belly-ached, did I?

JACK. Never — but you don't owe me that fifteen.

LEW. Rot! I'm no baby — square game, wasn't it?

JACK. Perfectly.

LEW. And I'll sit in a square game any time I get a chance.

JACK. I know, Lew, all about that.

LEW. I'll play you for this fifteen right now. [*Displays check*]

JACK. No. [*Walks aside*]

LEW. Ain't had a game in three weeks — and, besides, I think my luck's changin'? When Big George told me about Hardmuth I took George's hand before I thought what I was doin' — and you know what shakin' hands with a nigger does just before any play.

JACK [*resisting* LEW'S *plea*]. No, thank you, Lew.

LEW. My money's good as anybody else's, ain't it?

JACK. Just as good, but —

LEW. It ain't a phoney check, is it? [*Examines check*]

JACK. The check's all right.

LEW [*taunting*]. Losing your nerves?

JACK. No [*pause*] — suppose you shuffle those and deal a hand. [*Indicates small table, right*]

LEW. That's like old times; what is it — stud-horse or draw? [*Sits at table*]

JACK [*goes to fireplace*]. Draw if you say so.

LEW. I cut 'em?

JACK. You cut them.

LEW [*dealing two poker hands*]. Table stakes — check goes for a thousand.

JACK. That suits me.

LEW [*taking his own cards*]. Sit down.

JACK [*at other side of room looking into fire*]. I don't need to sit down just yet.

LEW. As easy as that, am I?

JACK. Lew!

LEW. Yes?

JACK. [*Pause*] Do you happen to have three queens?

[LEW *looks at* JACK, *then carefully at back of his own cards, then at the deck*]

LEW. Well, I can't see it.

JACK. No use looking — they're not marked.

LEW. Well, I shuffled 'm all right.

JACK. Yes.

Lew. And cut'm? [Jack *nods*] Couldn't 'a' been a cold deck?

Jack. No.

Lew. Then, how did you know I had three queens?

Jack. I didn't know it. I just thought you had.

Lew. Can you do it again?

Jack. I don't know. Draw one card.

Lew [*drawing one card from deck*]. All right.

Jack. [*Pause*] Is it the ace of hearts?

Lew. It is.

Jack. Mm — turns me into a rotter, doesn't it? [*Comes gloomily to the big table*]

Lew. Can you do that every time?

Jack. I never tried it until to-night — that is, consciously. I've always had luck and I thought it was because I took chances on a game — same as any player — but that don't look like it, does it?

Lew. Beats me.

Jack. And what a monster it makes of me — these years I've been in the business.

Lew. You say you didn't know before?

Jack. I didn't know it — no — but — some things have happened lately that have made me think it might be so; that jury yesterday — some facts I've had from Justice Prentice. Telepathy of a very common kind — and I guess it's used in a good many games, old man, we aren't on to.

Lew. Well — have you told anybody?

Jack. No.

Lew [*excitedly*]. Good! [*Rises and comes to* Jack] Now, see here, Jack, if you can do that right along I know a game in Cincinnati where it'd be like takin' candy from children.

Jack. Good God! you're not suggesting that I keep it up?

Lew. Don't over-do it — no — [*Pause*] Or you show me the trick and, *I'll* collect all right.

Jack [*slowly*]. Lew — [*Pause*] Some of the fellows I've won from in this house have gone over to the park and blown their heads off.

Lew. Some of the fellows anybody wins from in any house go somewhere and blow their heads off.

Jack. True — [*Pause*]

Lew. Three queens — before the draw — well, you could 'a' had me all

right — and you won't tell me how you do it?

Jack. I don't know how I do it; the thought just comes to my mind stronger than any other thought.

Lew [*reprovingly*]. God A'mighty gives you a mind like that and you won't go with me to Cincinnati. [*Goes to card table; studies cards*]

[*Enter* Jo]

Jo. Justice Prentice, sah.

Jack. Ask him to step up here.

Jo. Yes, sah. [*Exit*]

Jack [*goes to door, left*]. Alice — Helen — Justice Prentice has called; I'd like you to join us.

Lew. Can the old man call a hand like that, too?

Jack. I'm sure he could.

Lew. And — are there others?

Jack. I believe there are a good many others who unconsciously have the same ability.

Lew. Well, it's a God's blessin' there's a sucker born every minute. I'm a widow and an orphan 'longside o' that. [*Throws cards in disgust onto table*]

[*Enter* Alice *and* Helen]

Alice. Been losing, Mr. Ellinger?

Lew. Losing? I just saved fifteen thousand I was gonta throw 'way like sand in a rathole. I'm a babe eatin' spoon victuals and only gettin' half at that.

[*Enter* Prentice, *right center*]

Jack. Good-evening.

Prentice. Good-evening. [*Shakes hands with* Alice *and* Helen]

Jack. I stopped at your hotel, Mr. Justice, but you were out.

[*Enter* Viola, *right center*]

Alice [*anxiously*]. Viola.

Helen. Where's Clay?

Viola. Downstairs. Good-evening.

Prentice. Good-evening.

Jack [*to others*]. Pardon. [*To* Viola] Did the — gentleman come with you?

Viola. Yes.

[Lew *flutters and shows excitement*]

Jack. Won't you ask Clay, my dear, to take him through the lower hall and into the dining-room until I'm at liberty?

Viola. Certainly. [*Exit*]

PRENTICE. I am keeping you from other appointments?

JACK. Nothing that can't wait.

PRENTICE. I am leaving for Washington in the morning.

JACK. We'll all be at the train to see you off.

PRENTICE. That's good, because I should like to say good-bye to — to the young people — I can see them there — I shan't see you then, Mr. Ellinger — [*Goes to* LEW, *who stands at card table*]

LEW. Good-bye, Judge — you — you've given me more of a "turn over" than you know.

PRENTICE. Really?

LEW. I'd 'a' saved two hundred thousand dollars if I'd 'a' met you thirty years ago.

PRENTICE. Well, that's only about six thousand a year, isn't it?

LEW. That's so — and, damn it, I have lived. [*Smiles — looks dreamily into the past*]

PRENTICE. Good-night. [*Exit* PRENTICE]

JACK. Good-night — good-night.

ALICE. Is that Hardmuth in there? [*Points to dining-room*]

JACK. Yes.

ALICE. I don't want to see him.

JACK. Very well, dear, I'll excuse you.

ALICE [*going*]. Come, Helen.

JACK [*at door, left*]. Come in. [*To* HELEN, *who is going with* ALICE] Helen! I'd like *you* to stay.

HELEN. Me?

JACK. Yes.

[*Exit* ALICE, *left center. Enter* CLAY, HARDMUTH, *and* VIOLA *from dining-room.* VIOLA *lays automobile coat on sofa.* HARDMUTH *bows to* HELEN. HELEN *bows*]

Your mother has just left us, Viola. You'd better join her.

VIOLA. Very well.

JACK [*taking her hand as she passes him*]. And I want you to know — I appreciate very much, my dear, your going on this errand for me — you're the right stuff. [*Kisses her. Exit* VIOLA, *left center. To* HARDMUTH] You're trying to get away?

HARDMUTH. This your note?

JACK. Yes.

HARDMUTH. You say you'll help me out of the State?

JACK. I will.

HARDMUTH. When?

JACK. Whenever you're ready.

HARDMUTH. I'm ready now.

JACK. Then I'll help you now.

LEW. Now?

JACK. Yes.

HELEN. Doesn't that render you liable in some way, Jack, to the law?

JACK. Yes — but I've been liable to the law in some way for the last twenty years. [*To* CLAY] You go down and tell the chauffeur to leave the machine and walk home. I'm going to run it myself and I'll turn it in.

CLAY. Yes, sir. [*Exit right center*]

HARDMUTH. You're going to run it yourself?

JACK. Yes.

HARDMUTH. Where to?

JACK. Across the river, if that's agreeable to you — or any place you name.

HARDMUTH. Is anybody — *waiting* for you — across the river?

JACK. No.

HARDMUTH [*again with note*]. This is all on the level?

JACK. Completely.

LEW. Why, I think you mean that.

JACK. I do.

LEW [*aggressively*]. But I've got something to say, haven't I?

JACK. I hope not.

LEW [*quitting*]. If you're in earnest, of course. But I don't see your game.

JACK. I'm not fully convinced of Mr. Hardmuth's guilt.

LEW. Why, he's running away?

[*Enter* CLAY]

HARDMUTH. I know what a case they'd make against me, but I'm not guilty in any degree.

JACK. I want to do this thing for you, Frank — don't make it too difficult by any lying. When I said I wasn't fully convinced of your guilt, my reservation was one you wouldn't understand. [*To* CLAY] He gone?

CLAY. Yes.

JACK. My coat and goggles?

CLAY. Below in the reception-room.

JACK. Thank you. I wish now you'd go to Viola and her mother and keep them wherever they are.

CLAY. All right. [*Exit*]

JACK [*to* HARDMUTH]. Hungry? [*Touches push button*]

HARDMUTH. No, thank you.

JACK. Got money?

HARDMUTH. Yes.

[*Enter* Jo, *right center*]

JACK. Jo, take Mr. Hardmuth below

and lend him one of the fur coats. [*To* HARDMUTH] I'll join you immediately.

[*Exit* HARDMUTH *with* Jo]

HELEN. What does it all mean, Jack?

JACK. Lew, I called that ace of hearts, didn't I?

LEW. And the three queens.

JACK. Because the three queens and the ace were in your mind.

LEW. I don't see any other explanation.

JACK. Suppose, instead of the cards there'd been in your mind a well-developed plan of assassination — the picture of a murder —

LEW. Did you drop to him that way?

JACK. No. Raynor told me all I know of Hardmuth — but here's the very *hell* of it. Long before Scovill was killed I thought he deserved killing and I thought it *could* be done just — as — it — was done.

HELEN. Jack!

JACK. I never breathed a word of it to a living soul, but Hardmuth planned it exactly as I dreamed it — and by God, a guilty thought is almost as criminal as a guilty deed. I've always had a considerable influence over that poor devil that's running away to-night, and I'm not sure that before the Judge of both of us the guilt isn't mostly mine.

HELEN. That's morbid, Jack, dear, perfectly morbid.

JACK. I hope it is — we'll none of us ever know — in this life — but we can all of us — [*Pause*]

LEW. What?

JACK. Live as if it were true. [*Change of manner to brisk command*] I'm going to help him over the line — the roads are watched, but the police won't suspect me and they won't suspect Lew — and all the less if there's a lady with us — [*To* LEW] Will you go?

LEW. The limit.

JACK. Get a heavy coat from Jo.

LEW. Yes. [*Exit*]

JACK [*alone with* HELEN]. You know you said I used to be able to make you write to me when I was a boy at College?

HELEN. Yes.

JACK. And you were a thousand miles away — while this fellow — Hardmuth — was just at my elbow half the time.

HELEN. It can't help you to brood over it.

JACK. It can help me to know it, and make what amend I can. Will you go with me while I put this poor devil over the line?

HELEN [*taking* VIOLA'S *fur coat*]. Yes, I'll go with you.

JACK. Helen, you stood by your boy in a fight for his life.

HELEN. Didn't you?

JACK. Will you stand by *me* while I make my fight?

HELEN [*giving her hand*]. You've made your fight, Jack, and you've *won*.

[JACK *kisses her hand, which he reverently holds in both of his*]

CURTAIN

THE CITY

(1910)

By Clyde Fitch

CLYDE FITCH

SHORTLY after the death of Clyde Fitch, on September 4, 1909, there began that levelling process by which a man is placed in value. Though the papers carried editorials which were measure of the public interest in America's most popular dramatist, nothing that was written about him at the time augured well for the future of his plays on the stage. They could not gainsay the keenness of his observation, the almost uncanny understanding of feminine foibles, which constituted so large a share of the humor of his comedies. But they would not grant that such a vision as he possessed did more than skim the surface. If he saw deeply, the light manner of his treatment was no evidence of that probity.

Nevertheless, these critics, eager to be off with the old and on with the new, could not but credit Clyde Fitch with certain positive benefits brought to the American Theatre. They could not but recognize that his plays were written in a dialogue that had literary rhythms, whereas the old dialogue had been disjointed and impossible to read, if not to speak. They could not but credit him with that thoroughness of planning which let no detail of outward arrangement escape him, though his idea might be decimated to such a degree that it became almost lost in the glitter of cleverness.

Long before his death, one heard the slogan usually applied to Fitch: popular, prolific, and prosperous. It was a difficult slogan to combat, because in every respect it was true. The greatest handicap to Fitch was that the theatre — the theatre as it was in the period of Charles Frohman — made him all three, and kept him that, leaving him no time to give expression to that which he yearned to do, to work out carefully that which, in his home life, so separated from the stage, he had pondered well and thought out earnestly. I am not saying that the theatre made him entirely what he was, but it did not encourage him to be anything else. It cornered him so that he was forced to promise a play in ten days or three weeks; it brought him inferior German and French dramas and asked him to convert them into thirty per cent. of the original and seventy per cent. of himself; it brought "star" after "star" and asked him to tailor for them. And he did all this with volatile spirit, with fresh imagination, with a certain joyful love of the theatre itself.

From his boyhood — during the Amherst days — he had been a clever manipulator of stage effect; he had been a constant attendant of the theatre. His college monthly had abetted a rather facile pen. And from his surroundings, fostered by a loving mother, he had been trained in love of a rather decorative art — which always gave to his possessions a distinctly decorative and foreign atmosphere. The theatre made greedy use of these tendencies in the man, and, though lean years punctuated his onward course, it might be said of Clyde Fitch that through a comparatively short life — he was only forty-nine when he was stricken at Chalôns-sur-Marne — he worked for the theatre as no other American playwright has ever worked. Jones and Pinero in England were doing deeper work, more consistent in their narrative, more logical in the development of their situations, more substance in their characterization. But Fitch was — as public interest then ran — covering a wider area of superficial interests. With his love of "white-washing", Jones could be guessed at almost before his new plays were seen; with his interest in feminine psychology, Pinero surpassed Jones in his power of story interest. Fitch, to a lesser degree, was creating well and with a certain literary flavor.

But the American theatre was different from the English theatre of the Eighteen-Nineties : and it was a long time before the theatre-manager in America was willing to experiment with the purely intellectual drama. Fitch was interested in that drama : I have myself talked with him about those "revolutionists" who were the forerunners of the most modern continental dramatists. His constant trips abroad, where he saturated himself with the plays of the moment, brought him in contact with those first experimental efforts in France and in Germany which were to lead to such startling changes in the technique of the theatre, and in the dramatists' habits of mind.

But the unfortunate thing about Fitch abroad was that he always went to the theatre as a sort of emissary of Charles Frohman : he was always on the alert for something suitable for America. And the Americans of that period wanted the lighter play : they did not even know the Shaw of the Fabian era, and Ibsen was just beginning — through the rare habit of special performances — to seep into the New York playhouse.

I say advisedly the New York playhouse, for the entire career of Clyde Fitch was dependent on the theatre as run by the manager on Broadway, and the actor who was reared in the warmth of its incandescence. Fitch was not the type of man who could ever have written a play that was outside his social sympathy. By this I do not mean that rural life did not interest him, that police courts did not have for him a dramatic interest. But he saw life as he ran, not as he went for it. And with an alert mind ever ready for those isolated characteristics which mark a city life, he fused what he saw into pictures of the period : but they were New York pictures, ever so lightly sketched, ever so gently dealt with, ever so unerringly used for their momentary dramatic effect. It would have been better for the future of Clyde Fitch if he had not been so deft in his handling of such detail; if he had not been so expertly apt in his uses of the familiar, if he had not been so clever in repartee.

His mind was ever alert for these details, and the quick existence he lived in America and Europe only accentuated and encouraged such a response. Having won for himself a certain distinction for stage management, this reputation distracted him often in the writing of a play. The cleverness of a deck scene in "The Stubbornness of Geraldine", the laughable eccentricities of a company of Cook's tourists around the Apollo Belvedere in "The Girl with the Green Eyes", the tail-end of a funeral in "The Climbers", the apartment life eccentricities in "Girls", these were at the same time the weakness and the excellence of Clyde Fitch. They were the things which distracted him because he saw their stage possibilities, and perhaps in certain instances their applicableness to the individual style of a particular actor.

Looking over the many notices that were written at the time of his death, one cannot fail to find, in spite of the preponderant treatment of him lightly, certain

emphasis on characteristics which are the enduring marks entitling Clyde Fitch
to permanence in the history of the American Theatre. Some said he humanized
the American stage, others said that he stood alone in the skill with which he probed
the feminine point of view, still others remarked his widening of the field of theatre
treatment. The critic of the *Boston Transcript* wrote discriminatingly :

In Mr. Fitch's earlier days managers, actors and even audiences mistrusted the
ability of American playwrights and the interest of plays of American life. Most
of all they were suspicious of the comedy of American manners and incidents of the
hour. It was such pieces that Mr. Fitch wished to write, that he wrote best, and he
had almost single-handed to prove by his own skill and example that they could
be written interestingly, amusingly, even significantly ; that players of reputation
could venture themselves safely in them ; that a secure public would quickly recognize and like them. The comedy of American manners was indeed neglected, frail,
and struggling when Mr. Fitch began to write. He has left it firm in its place on
the stage, assured of an intelligent public, a significant, capable and promising part
of our rising drama. He died almost young ; but with the comedy of American
manners he was already an example and incentive to a new generation.

The rapid strides that have taken place in the development of world drama since
1909 make a very wide gap between the things theatrical of the Frohman era and
the period of the Theatre Guild. And Fitch was typically of the Frohman era, as
were Jones and Pinero — for they wrote often by prescription also. There is
nothing that dates a man quicker than technique, there is nothing that tempts a
man writing for the stage more than what the stage has to offer him in the way of a
production. Just as for many years after the death of Clyde Fitch we looked in
vain for some successor who would follow in his wake, treating of the same atmosphere with the same deftness and wit, so to-day we are likely to find it difficult to
get a more incisive study of character than that he put into the one play of his
which had international reputation — England, France, Germany, Italy and elsewhere — "The Truth."
I have been interested to notice in the fifteen years which have elapsed since his
death how readily we have allowed Fitch to slip from our consideration — illustrating our extravagance in matters pertaining to the stage. Outside the moving-picture
field, I have seen but two revivals of his plays : a very smudgy performance of
"Beau Brummell" and a rather slow-paced revival of "The Truth." Yet I believe
that one only has to forget the youthful radiance of Ethel Barrymore to relish
"Captain Jinks of the Horse Marines" ; and I am still a believer in the excellent
melodrama of "The Woman in the Case." Though there are certain romantic
weakenings in his historical dramas, I feel that there is still in "Barbara Frietchie"
something of theatre value, and there is a decided picturesque flavor to "Beau
Brummell", for all its old-fashioned structure.
The attitude that has been shown by some toward his recently published "Letters" measures the unfairness of some of this neglect, and yet the inevitable reason
for it. Fitch's plays still read well, though in them one feels the preponderance
of repartee, and a most uncanny understanding of their acting possibilities. The
technique that he used he understood well ; he studied it on and off the stage ; he
argued it with his managers and his players ; he made it fit the stage scene, even
as he fitted the stage scene to re-inforce his play. But he scarcely ever wrote about
it. If one could get a verbatim report of the many talks he had with Robert
Herrick about play making, as they tramped the deck of the ocean liner or walked

on the terrace at Taormina, one might then determine how seriously he took his craft.   But Frohman demanded — and he had been brought to accede to the demand — that this technique be handled in accord with the stage as it was then. Frohman was scared of a preponderance of ideas.   American audiences stayed away from plays of ideas — and Fitch was a dramatist of his time.   That is the tragedy of up-to-dateness.   Had Eugene O'Neill lived in those days — when there were no independent groups — he could scarcely have made headway.   Even the publishing of plays was just beginning to be recognized as necessary and profitable. And it was the eager way in which Fitch's plays were read that made him a pioneer in that direction also.

A dramatist must be produced, otherwise he is a playwright in potentiality only. Fitch was scarcely that.   He was the dramatist of the hour, and the one man whom the managers could turn to, after they had seen the amount of unsound, unwork-manlike material submitted to them by other native authors.   Sometimes, in their limited vision, they would pass by such excellent attempts to escape the for-mula as were to be found in Eugene Walter's "Paid in Full", Edward Sheldon's "The Nigger", and Charles Kenyon's "Kindling"; these were plays of the younger generation in those days, before Clyde Fitch had entirely passed from stage con-sideration.   But they would never let Fitch escape.

Of course, he could not escape certain limitations of his own.   He was never violently shaken by the themes he dealt with, until it came time for him to write "The City": and then it was more a personal desire in him to counteract the con-tinual fusillade hurled by the critics that he could not handle masculine character and had no real strength of conviction.   His strongest conviction was that he could do just such a thing, and he set about the task with unbounded energy — an energy made all the more significant since it sapped him of his vitality and left him unable to withstand the onslaughts of an operation for appendicitis.

His letters of this period show the almost morbid intensity with which he went about answering these critics of his.   Living most of the time in the country, coming continually to the city, determining in his mind the future life which he had planned for himself in the village of Katonah, New York, only added to the contrast in his mind of the country and the city.   National investigations of public men in their relation to Wall Street, the virile figure of Roosevelt were as grist to his mill.   He thought hotly, rather than clearly about the matter.   And he hit upon an emotional theme which the Greeks alone knew how to use, and which he now wove into a realistic play.

All of his friends at this time kept pace with the progress of this absorbing drama. He wrote by day, he read by night; he sat by the roadside, while a tire was being changed, and wrote; he ate his meals on the terrace, and wrote; he always carried with him his composition books, to add here and cut out there, if the idea struck him.   The typical Clyde Fitch at work, but somehow this time with a newer tension, a more dangerous tension, considering his state of health.   For Fitch was literally worn out by the demands of the theatre of his time.   These details are all sketched in the volume of letters which reveal more of the man than his method. A rapid assemblying of cast, a quick preparation of two finished acts, one act in the rough taken with him aboard the steamer, a rapid witness of stage successes in London, and a rapid consummation of contracts abroad.   Then a rush to the steamer by motor homeward bound, and the hand of Death upon him at Chalôns-sur-Marne.

I have just read over again the press notices of "The City", given at the Lyric Theatre, New York, on December 21, 1909. They are astounding in the measurement of how completely Clyde Fitch answered his critics. They tell a story of hysterical audiences, grown ill from raw sensation, — they acknowledge that they were wrong and he right. He did not take time to prove the tenableness of his thesis regarding the effect of city life upon character; he piled upon his accusers all the power he could assemble by unerring technical structure, he accumulated his incidents — instead of unerringly interlocking these incidents by the cold logic of his theme — into a climax which left shuddering people in their chairs, and a contagious roar of response when the curtain fell. To my mind — disagreeable as it is — "The City" will always stand as a symbol of the strength in Clyde Fitch which the régime of Charles Frohman — and that means the managers also who were Frohman's contemporaries — would not allow him to develop. "The City" does not escape the cleverness of the early pieces: the superficial sentiment — too deeply ingrained in dramatists of the day to approach the poignancy of Ibsen's "A Doll's House" and Shaw's "Candida", now considered so dated by the younger generation! But it has terrific power, and this power is maintained no less by skilled technique than by the inherent horror of its main situation.

There is not a critic who did not comment on and disapprove of the language employed at certain moments in "The City." They were shocked, not alone at the daring situation, which was horrible in the extreme, but at the vulgarity of suggestion. On another point they were rather ready to scoff, and that was at the use of the "set" speech, where all the intent of the play was stated in terms that were the dramatist's rather than the character's.

What an audience will stand has widened in its boundaries since that evening, and, on the re-reading of "The City", I could not but ponder over the language of O'Neill's "The Hairy Ape", and the crude awfulness of his "The First Man", wherein the birth agony is made a dramatic asset. There is perhaps more than melodramatic purpose in such scenes as O'Neill puts upon the stage, though there are moments in "Desire Under the Elms" when the strangling of an infant, and such details, for the artistic value of the play, might just as well be omitted.

It is my belief that, except for the melodramatic effectiveness of the scene, in that abhorrent discovery of *Hannock's*, the dramatist lost the thread of his deeper purpose in the play. Indirectly the scene was to have an effect on young *Rand*, but its main use was theatrical rather than spiritual. O'Neill's purposes are spiritual and more fundamental. They are more organic. Though I doubt whether at times they are any more in artistic taste.

I am inclined to place Fitch fairly high in the scale of American Drama as it now is, and has been in the past, because he was a truthful observer. But the rapidity of that observation, the resting of it on too many superficial elements made him often depart from his main theme — as he did, for example, in "The City." Others might — and did — improve on him. But he gave to the American Theatre, in the Frohman period, its greatest incentive to Truth. He might not have been encouraged by the Frohman era in Idea. Hence, being a man of the theatre, conforming to the theatre, Idea became secondary, a slender thread which often broke. One can therefore understand this excerpt from his lecture on "The Play and the Public", delivered before the students of Professor William Lyon Phelps, at Yale, and elsewhere. He wrote:

Be truthful, and then nothing can be too big, nothing should be too small, so long as it is here, and *there!* Apart from the question of literature, apart from the question of art, reflect the real thing with true observation and with sincere feeling for what it is and what it represents, and that is art and literature in a modern play. If you inculcate an idea in your play, so much the better for your play and for you — and for your audience. In fact, there is small hope for your play *as* a play if you haven't some small idea in it somewhere and somehow, even if it is hidden — it is sometimes better for you if it is hidden, but it must of course be integral.

In truth it was too often hidden. But that was the fault of his theatrical era, which made him the most popular playwright of his time.

THE CITY

A MODERN PLAY OF AMERICAN LIFE IN THREE ACTS

By CLYDE FITCH

Act I. — Middleburg, New York. *The Library in the* Rand *House.*

Act II. — New York City. *The Library in the* Rand *House*
Several Years Later.

Act III. — The Same.
A Few Hours Later.

Originally produced at the Lyric Theatre, New York, December 21, 1909, with the following cast:

GEORGE D. RAND	A. H. Stuart
GEORGE D. RAND, JR.	Walter Hampden
MRS. RAND	Eva Vincent
TERESA RAND	Lucile Watson
CICELY RAND	Mary Nash
ALBERT F. VORHEES	George Howell
ELEANOR VORHEES	Helen Holmes
GEORGE FREDERICK HANNOCK	Tully Marshall
DONALD VAN VRANKEN	Edward Emery
SUSAN	Jane Gail
JOHN	John Jex
FOOT	Fred Courtenay

THE PERSONS IN THE PLAY

George D. Rand

George D. Rand, Jr.

Mrs. Rand

Teresa Rand

Cicely Rand

Albert F. Vorhees

Eleanor Vorhees

George Frederick Hannock

Donald Van Vranken

Susan, *maidservant in Middleburg*

John, *the coachman in Middleburg*

Foot, *butler in New York*

THE CITY

ACT I

SCENE. — *At the* RANDS'. *The library of a substantial house in Middleburg. Front doors open out into the "front hall." It is furnished in a "set" of rosewood furniture, upholstered in brown and red figured velvet. The walls are covered with dark maroon wall-paper, with framed photographs of Thorwaldsen's "Four Seasons," and over the mantel there is an engraving of "Washington Crossing the Delaware." A rocking-chair and an armchair are in front of the grate fire. Lace curtains and heavy curtains are draped back from two French windows that look out on a covered piazza. There are a desk, a bookcase with glass doors, a "centre table" on which stands a double, green-shaded "Student's lamp," a few novels, and some magazines. Near the bookcase is a stand holding a "Rogers' Group." There are jars and bowls filled with flowers everywhere.*

RAND *enters with the New York evening papers, The Post, The Sun; he half yawns, half sighs with fatigue. He starts to make his armchair ready before the fire; stops and goes over to his desk, where he finds a letter which he dislikes, recognizing the handwriting.*

RAND [*angry*]. Yes, still keeping it up, the young blackguard! [*He tears the letter in two, and throws it into the fire without reading it. He watches it burn a second, lighting a cigar; then takes his papers, makes himself comfortable in his chair before the fire, and starts to read. After a second,* MRS. RAND *and* CICELY, *a very pretty girl of about seventeen, enter.* MRS. RAND *carries a pitcher of water, scissors, and a newspaper.* CICELY *has her arms full of yellow tulips and a big bowl*]

MRS. RAND. Why, father! Aren't you home early? Teresa's train won't be in for an hour or so yet. [MRS. RAND, *filling the bowl with water, spreads the newspaper on the table; then cuts off the stems, and hands the flowers one by one to* CICELY, *who arranges them*]

RAND. I felt tired to-day, Molly. My head bothers me!

MRS. RAND [*going to him with affection and solicitude*]. Why don't you lie down? [*She lays her hand on his head*] You haven't any fever. [*She kisses his forehead*] You're just over-tired! [*He pats her hand affectionately, and holds it*] When are you going to give up business entirely, darling, and leave it all to George?

RAND. Never, I'm afraid, dear. [*Letting go her hand*] I've tried to face the idea, but the idleness appalls me.

CICELY. Mother, have you the scissors?

MRS. RAND. Yes, dear. [*Joins her, and continues with the flowers*]

RAND. Besides, *George* is too restless, too discontented yet, for me to trust him with my two banks! He's got the New York bee in his bonnet.

CICELY [*glances at her mother before she speaks*]. Oh! We all have that, father, — except you.

RAND. And mother!

CICELY. Humph! Mother's just as bad as the rest of us. Only she's afraid to say so. [*Smiling*] Go on, mother, own up you've got villiageitis and city-phobia!

MRS. RAND [*smiling*]. I dare, only I don't want to bother your father!

RAND. That's the effect of George, — and Teresa. I've noticed all the innuendos in her letters home. Europe's spoiled the girl! The New York school started the idea, but I hoped travel would cure her, and instead —!

MRS. RAND. Wait till you see her.

Remember, in spite of letters, what a year may have done for her. Oh, I'm so eager to see her! What a long hour this is! [*The telephone bell rings out in the hall.* MRS. RAND *goes out and is heard saying,* "Hello! Yes, who is it? Oh, is it you, Katherine?"]

RAND [*reading his paper*]. Who's that talking to your mother?

CICELY. One of Middleburg's Social Queens, Mrs. Mulholland — known in our society as the lady who can wear a décolleté gown, cut in accordance with the Middleburg limit, and not look as if she'd dressed in a hurry and forgotten her collar!

[RAND *laughs*]

MRS. RAND [*off stage*]. Really! I should think she was much too old to be so advanced in the styles as that!

CICELY. The flowers are lovely all over the house. Father, you ought to see them! They came from a New York florist. [MRS. RAND *off stage:* "Good-by. See you at five"] Our man here hadn't anything but ferns and aniline-dyed pinks.

MRS. RAND [*reënters*]. Kate Mulholland called up to tell me Mary Carterson's mother-in-law is visiting her from South Norwalk, and went down street this morning wearing one of those new washtub hats, — and she's sixty, if she isn't over! She was born in 1846, — at least she *used* to be!

RAND [*still reading*]. When do you expect your crowd to come this afternoon?

CICELY. Crowd? [*She laughs derisively*] The only thing that can get a crowd in Middleburg is a fire or a funeral!

MRS. RAND. As we expect Teresa at four, I asked everybody to come in at five. But you know, father, "*everybody*" in Middleburg isn't *many!*

CICELY. Not many — nor *much!*

RAND. You have the best the town affords, and it's good old stock!

CICELY. I'm afraid Tess'll think it's rather tame for a girl who has been presented at *two European courts!*

MRS. RAND. Yes, I'm afraid she'll find it awfully dull. Don't you think, father, we could go to New York, if only for the winter months?

RAND. Don't tell me *you're* ambitious, too?

MRS. RAND. Well, I've done all, in a social way, a woman can in Middleburg, and I want to do more.

CICELY. You can't tell the difference in Middleburg between a smart afternoon tea and a Mother's Meeting, or a Sunday-school teacher's conclave, or a Lenten Sewing Circle, or a Fair for the Orphan Asylum, or any other like "Event"! It's always the same old people and the same old thing! Oh, Lord, we live in a cemetery!

RAND. Molly, wouldn't you rather be *it* in Middleburg — than *nit* in the City?

MRS. RAND. But with your influence and our friends, — we'd take letters, — I would soon have the position your wife was entitled to in the City, too.

CICELY. I don't care a darn about the position, if I can only have something to do, and something to see! Who wants to smell newmown hay, if he can breathe in gasoline on Fifth Avenue instead! Think of the theatres! the crowds! *Think* of being able to go out on the street and *see some one you didn't know even by sight! !*

RAND [*laughs, amused*]. Molly! How can *you* deceive yourself? A banker from a small country town would give you about as much position as he could afford to pay for on the West Side, above Fifty-ninth Street.

MRS. RAND. But, *George* said you'd been asked to join a big corporation in New York, which would make the family's everlasting fortune, and social position beside.

RAND [*looks up, angry*]. George had no right telling you that. I told him only in confidence. What is this anyway, — a family conspiracy?

CICELY. No, it is the American legation shut up in Peking, longing for a chance to escape from social starvation.

RAND [*thoroughly irritated*]. Now listen! This has got to stop, once and for all! So long as I'm the head of this family, it's going to *keep its head* and not lose it! And our home is *here*, and *will be here*, if to hold it I have to die in harness.

MRS. RAND [*going to him affectionately*]. Father, don't be angry! You know *your will is law* with all of us. And so long as you want it, we'll stay right here.

CICELY. Giving teas to the wallflower brigade, and dinners to the Bible class! And our cotillion favors will be articles appropriate for the missionaries' boxes! Oh, Lord!

RAND. Mother, Cicely has convinced me of *one thing*.

CICELY [*delighted*]. Not really! Good! What?

RAND. *You* go to no *finishing school* in *New York!* You get *finished* all you're going to, right here in Middleburg. New York would completely turn your head!

CICELY. Well, don't worry; Middleburg will "*finish*" me all right! Good and strong! Maybe New York would turn your head, but Middleburg turns my — [*She is going to say "stomach", but her mother interrupts*]

MRS. RAND. Cicely!

[*Enter* GEORGE. *He is a handsome, clean-cut young American, of about twenty-seven*]

GEORGE. Hello, everybody!

RAND [*surprised*]. Hello, George! What's the matter? It's only half past four! Nothing happened in the office?

GEORGE. Nothing! *All day!* That's why I am here. I thought I'd be in good time for Tess; and, so far as missing anything *really doing in the office* is concerned, I could have left at ten this morning — [*adds half aside*] or almost any morning, *in this* — *our city!*

CICELY. Look out! The word "*city*" is a red rag to a bull with father, to-day! And it's for good in the graveyard! I'm going to dress. Thank the Lord, I've actually got somebody new to look smart for, if it's only my sister! [*Yawns and starts to go*]

RAND. Who's coming to your tea party?

CICELY [*as she goes out*]. All the names are on the tombstones in the two churchyards, plus Miss Carterson's mother-in-law from South Norwalk!

MRS. RAND. I must dress, too. [*Going over to* RAND] Dear, aren't you going to change your coat, and help me?

RAND. Oh, Molly, don't ask me to bore myself with your old frumps!

MRS. RAND. *I have to!* And I don't know that *I* take any more interest than *you* do in what sort of a hat Mary Carterson's mother is wearing! But if it were in New York —

RAND [*sneers*]. Stop! I meant what I said — let's drop that!

MRS. RAND. All right, — I didn't say anything!

GEORGE. Look here, father, — mother's right.

RAND [*interrupting*]. No, *you* do the "*looking*", George, — and straight *in my eyes!* [*He does so.*] Your mother's wrong, but it isn't *her* fault, — it's *you* children.

MRS. RAND [*remonstrating*]. Now, father —

GEORGE. But we're *not children*, and that's the mistake you make! *I'm* twenty-seven.

MRS. RAND. Yes, father, you forget, — George is twenty-seven!

GEORGE. I'm no longer a *boy!*

RAND. Then why did you tell your mother about this offer I had from New York, when I told you it was absolutely *confidential!* And a *man* in business knows what the word "*confidential*" means.

MRS. RAND. It was *my* fault; *I* wormed it out of George!

GEORGE. Nonsense, mother! [*To his father*] I told, because I thought you needed a good, big hump, and I believed, if all of us put our shoulders to it, we could move you.

RAND. Out of Middleburg?

GEORGE. Yes!

RAND. *Into New York?*

GEORGE. Yes!

RAND. Listen, George, —

GEORGE [*going on*]. What position is there for a fellow like me in a hole like this?

[RAND *tries to interrupt*]

MRS. RAND [*stops him*]. No, father, let George have his say out!

RAND. All right! Come on, George, we'll have it out now, — but this must *settle it!*

GEORGE. You grew up with this town. You and Middleburg reached your prime together, — so she's good enough for you. Besides, you are *part of it*, so you haven't any point of view, — you're too close!

RAND. What's good enough for your father ought to be good enough for you.

MRS. RAND. That's true, George.

GEORGE. *Grandfather Rand* was a real estate dealer in East Middleburg, with an income of about two thousand a year. I notice *your father's limit* wasn't good enough for you!

RAND. No, but *my* father turned me loose, without a cent, to make my own way! *Your* father will leave you the *richest man in your town*, — with the best established name, with two banks as safe as Gibraltar behind you!

GEORGE. But, I tell you, Middleburg and her banks are just as picayune to *me*, in comparison with the *City* and a *big career there*, as *East Middleburg and real estate* were to *you* in *1860!*

RAND. Good God, how little you know of the struggle and fight *I* went through!

GEORGE. No, sir! Good God —

RAND [*interrupting*]. Don't swear before your father. I don't like it!

GEORGE. Well — what *you* don't realize is that *I* am just starving after a big fight and a big struggle — for even bigger stakes than *you* fought for! I'm my father's own son — [*Going up to him with a sudden impulse of pride and affection, and putting his arm about his shoulder*] Accept this great city chance, father! There's millions in it, *and no fight!* They're offering the position to you on a gold plate. All I'll ask of you afterward is to launch me. Give me a start; the rest will be up to me! All I'll ask you to do then is *watch*.

RAND. No, I'm too old now.

MRS. RAND. Now *I* must join in! It's ridiculous you calling yourself too old. Besides, it reflects on me! [*Smiling*] Men and women of our age in the City dress and act just as young as their children, more or less. *Old age* has gone out of fashion! There's no such thing, except in dull little *country towns!*

GEORGE. Exactly! That's just what stagnation in the small place does for you. Come to the City, father! It'll give you a new lease of life!

RAND. No, I *don't want* to!

GEORGE. I wouldn't have the selfish courage to go on persuading you, if I didn't feel you'd be *glad of it in the end.* And besides, you're *one* against *all the rest* of us, — Mother, Teresa, Cicely — we're all choking here, dying of exasperation, *dry-rotting* for *not enough to do!*

RAND. Not at all! It's only amusement and excitement you children are after, and you've inoculated your mother with the germ.

MRS. RAND. No! If I'm restless and dissatisfied here, it's my own fault. I sympathize with Teresa having to come back to this, after New York and all Europe. I'm tired, myself, of our humdrum, empty existence. I'm tired of being the leading woman in a society where there's nobody to lead! I'm tired of the narrow point of view here! I'm tired of living to-day on yesterday's news, and wearing styles adapted to what Middleburg will stand for! I sympathize with Cicely. I want her to have a chance with the *real* world — not our expurgated edition! I know what she means when she says the quiet of the country gets on her nerves! that the birds keep her awake! that she longs for the rest of a cable-car and the lullaby of a motor-bus! Yes, I want the City for myself, but even more for my children, and most of all for George to make a name and career for himself!

RAND. You've all got an exaggerated idea of the importance of the City. This country isn't *made* or run by New York or its half dozen sisters! It's in the smaller towns, — and spread all over the country, — that you find the bone and sinew of the United States!

GEORGE. But for a young man to make a career for himself — I don't mean in business only, — in politics, in —

RAND [*interrupting*]. You don't need the *City!* What's the matter with here?

GEORGE. Look at what Bert Vorhees has done, going to New York! He's going to be District Attorney, they say. And how long has he been there? Five or six years! I had a long talk with Eleanor Vorhees when she was here last month; it's wonderful what Bert's accomplished! And look at Eleanor herself! By George, she's the finest girl I've even seen!

RAND. Still, did Lincoln need New York? Did Grant? Did a metropolis turn out McKinley, or have anything to do with forming the character and career of Grover Cleveland? You're cheating yourself, if you're honest in your talk with me! All you want of the City is what you can get out of it, — not what you can do for it!

GEORGE. No, you judge from your own point of view! Middleburg makes you look through the wrong end of the opera-glass. You *can't* judge from *my* point of view.

RAND. When you're *my* age, if you've kept as abreast of the times as I have, you'll be lucky. But if you're in New York, you won't have had time. There, you'll know one thing to perfection — but only one — where your interests are centered! All city men specialize — they have to *get* success, and *keep* it! Every walk in life, there, is a marathon! But the worst of it is, the goal isn't stationary. It's like the horizon, — no man can reach it!

GEORGE. But why blame the City?

RAND. Because the City turns ambition into selfish greed! There, no matter what you get, you want more! And when you've got more, at God knows what price sometimes, it's not enough! There's no such thing as being satisfied! First, you want to catch up with your neighbor; then you want to pass him; and then you die disappointed if you haven't left him out of sight!

MRS. RAND. I'm afraid your father's determined. And forty years with him has taught me two things, — first, when he *is* determined, you might just as well realize it in the beginning; and second, in the end you're sure to *be glad he was!*

RAND. Thank you, Molly. And I was never more determined than I am this time.

MRS. RAND [*with a sigh of half-amused resignation*]. Then I'll go and put on the dress I got in New York, which the dressmaker said I'd made her spoil in order that my neighbors at home shouldn't say I'd gone out of my senses. [*She exits*]

GEORGE. Well father, if *you* won't leave, let me go away! Let me go to the City on my own account. Bert Vorhees has been urging me to come for over a year. He says politics in the City are crying for just such new, clean men as me. He wants me to help *him;* that, in itself, is a big opening. I won't ask for any help from you. Just let me go, as *your father* let *you* go, to work out, myself, my own salvation!

RAND. Your own damnation it would be! No, sir, you stay here as long as I live and have any power over or influence with you.

GEORGE. Suppose *I'm* stubborn as *you* are, and go, even if it has to be against your will.

RAND. Look here, boy! You're trained in my methods, for my job. Those methods are all right for Middleburg, where I'm known and respected. No one has been to this town more, in a civic way, than I have. The Park Street Congregational Church couldn't have been built, nor halfway supported

as it has been, without my help; and I could go on for some length, if I liked, in much the same sort of strain. What *I* do in this town is *right.* But the public libraries of Middleburg wouldn't help me in the City, nor the Park Street Church be a sufficient guarantee for my banking methods, to let me risk myself in the hornet's nest New York is at present.

GEORGE [*almost laughing at the idea*]. You don't mean you would be afraid of any investigation —?

RAND. *Here,* no! I've always kept to the right side of the line, but I've kept very close, and the line may be *drawn* differently here. My conscience is clear, George, but my common sense is a good watch-dog.

[*The* MAIDSERVANT *enters*]

MAIDSERVANT. Here's a man says he has an appointment with you, sir.

RAND [*startled and a little angry*]. *No one* has an appointment with me!

MAIDSERVANT. Well, I didn't know!

[*Enter* HANNOCK, *during the speech. The* MAIDSERVANT *looks a little alarmed at what she has done, as she goes out*]

HANNOCK [*very hard*]. I told you, in the letter I sent here to-day, I was going to call this afternoon.

RAND. I destroyed that letter without reading it, — as I have the last half dozen you've sent me.

HANNOCK. That's what made it necessary for me to call in person!

[GEORGE *looks from one to the other, dumfounded*]

GEORGE. Father?

RAND [*to* HANNOCK, *referring to* GEORGE]. This is my son. I'm glad he is here, to be a witness. Go ahead! I take it, as you seem to be *in the business,* you've made yourself acquainted with the *law of blackmail!*

HANNOCK. I know what you've already told me — but I don't give a damn! I've got nothing to lose, and nothing to get, except money, from you. *You won't jail me,* anyway, for you know a trial here would ruin *you,* no matter what happened to me!

GEORGE. Here, you —!

RAND [*taking a step forward*]. No, George! Keep your temper. This man says I ruined his mother — [*In great shame and emotion*]

GEORGE [*to* HANNOCK]. You *liar!*

HANNOCK. Then why did he give her a regular allowance till she died? and why did he keep on giving to me? — for a while!

RAND. George, I feel badly. Get me some whiskey and water. [GEORGE *hurries out.* RAND, *in rising anger*] I kept on giving to you, till I found out you were a sot and a degenerate blackguard — a drug fiend and a moral criminal. I kept on helping you after three houses of correction had handled you, and one prison! *Then I stopped!* What was the use, — money was only helping you on!

HANNOCK. Still, for my mother's sake, you can't let me *starve!* You oughtn't to have torn up those letters; then you'd have had the blackmail in writing. I told you, if you didn't give me what I want, I'd print your letters to my mother right here in this town. The anti-saloon paper, that hates you for not joining its movement, would be glad to get them and show you up for a God damn whited sepulchre!

RAND [*quiet, controlling himself by a terrific effort*]. And suppose that didn't frighten me!

HANNOCK. I've just got on to something bigger yet, I can use by way of a lever! The two years you had me working in the bank, I kept my eyes open. If it hadn't been for the yellow streak in me, I guess I'd have made a banker, all right. I liked it, and I seem to catch on to things sorter by instinct. You were the *big thing*, and I watched and studied your methods to make 'em mine!

RAND. Well?

HANNOCK. Yes! "Well", by God! I guess you realize just as plain as I do that those very methods in New York, that have been raising hell with the insurance companies and all sorts of corporations, aren't a patch on some of *your deals* I know of! And I tell you, if there should be a State investigation in Middleburg, you'd go under as sure as I stand here; and if I had to go to prison, I'd stand a sure chance of passing you in the yard some day — wearing the same old stripes yourself.

RAND [*in a paroxysm of rage*]. It's a lie! It's a lie! Just to get money out of me! I told you, before you began, you'd come to blackmail! [*He chokes*]

HANNOCK. Well, you know how to prove it! Have me arrested; charge me with it; and *let the whole thing be thrashed out!* [*A second's pause*] Aw — you don't dare. You know you don't!

[*Enter* CICELY, *looking girlishly lovely in a fresh white dress and corncolored sash.*

CICELY. Father, aren't you going to dress — and help us?

[HANNOCK *looks at* CICELY, *admiring her*]

RAND. Excuse me, Cicely, I'm engaged just now.

CICELY. I beg your pardon. [*She goes out*]

HANNOCK [*following her with his eyes*]. She's growing into a lovely girl, your daughter! It would be a pity — [*He speaks in broken sentences*]

RAND [*giving in*]. How much do you want?

HANNOCK. I want two thousand dollars.

RAND. For how long?

HANNOCK. *For as long as it lasts!*

RAND [*with a reaction*]. No, I won't do it! You'll gamble, or squander this in some low way, and be back before the week's out! What's the use! I can't keep this up for ever!

HANNOCK [*bringing a pistol out of his pocket, quickly*]. Do you see that? [*He puts it on the desk*]

RAND [*greatly frightened*]. Good God!

HANNOCK. Don't be frightened! It's not for *you*. I'm no murderer! It's for myself.

RAND [*suffering from shock*]. How do you mean?

HANNOCK [*taking up the pistol, and handling it almost affectionately*]. I'm never without it. And when I can't get anything more out of you, when I'm clean empty, — not a crust, or drink, or drug to be had, — then I'll take this friend to my heart, so — [*Placing pistol over his heart*]

RAND [*frightened, calls feebly*]. George!

HANNOCK. Oh, not yet! [*Taking pistol from his chest*] I'm not ready yet. But remember, when you've signed your last check for me, *you will be responsible for this.* [*He touches the pistol; then hides it quickly in his pocket, as* GEORGE *enters with whiskey and water*]

GEORGE. I'm sorry to take so long, but I had to persuade mother not to come with me, when she heard you were faint. And I thought you wouldn't want —

RAND. Yes, quite right — [*He drinks, excitedly, tremblingly, feebly*]

GEORGE [*to* HANNOCK]. You can see my father is ill; surely, ordinary human feeling will make you realize to-day is no time for you to —

RAND [*interrupting*]. It's all right, George. Hannock and I have had it out while you were gone. [*Writing a check*] We understand each other now!

HANNOCK. I've made my position quite clear to your father.

RAND [*giving* HANNOCK *the check*]. Here — and for God's sake try to behave yourself! [*Looking at him intently, with a strange, almost yearning look, as if he really cared whether* HANNOCK *behaved himself or not*] Try to do right!

HANNOCK. Thanks for your advice *and money!* [*To* GEORGE] Good-by!

RAND. Good-by!

[GEORGE *only nods his head, looking at* HANNOCK *with unconcealed dislike.* HANNOCK *goes out.* RAND *sinks on his arms, his head falling on the table.* GEORGE *goes to him in alarm*]

GEORGE. Father!

RAND. I'm not well. I've felt dizzy all day. It was more than I could stand!

GEORGE. I don't approve of your giving him money! Till you once take a firm stand, there'll never be any let up.

RAND. But I owe it to him, George! I owe it to him.

GEORGE. Nonsense! What sort of a woman was his mother?

RAND. She was a dressmaker in East Middleburg; hadn't a very good reputation. I doubt very much if what he says is *true.*

GEORGE. *Well then?*

RAND. Yes, but more than he knows *is true!* — and worse!

GEORGE. How do you mean?

RAND. Yes, the whole thing is more than I can carry any longer! I'm too old! Your younger shoulders must help me bear it, George. It breaks my heart to tell you, and shames me, George, but I must unburden myself. Besides, I need help — I need advice! And besides, you'll see how you can't go away and leave me alone here! [*He rises in fear and excitement*] I'm your father, and you've got to stand by me

and help me! I can't stand alone any longer!

GEORGE. Father! [*He goes to him*]

RAND. Promise me, George, promise me you won't leave me here! You'll stand by me!

GEORGE. Yes, father, *I promise you!*

RAND [*sinks back exhausted into his chair. A second's pause*]. That man who just left here don't know it, but — [*He stops from dread and shame of finishing*]

GEORGE. But what?

RAND. I'm his father!

GEORGE [*astounded*]. That *fellow's?*

RAND. *That* fellow's!

GEORGE. *Then of course he knows it!*

RAND. No, it would be a stronger lever for money than any he has used, and he doesn't hesitate to use the strongest he can find — or *invent!* In return for the financial arrangement I made with her, his mother swore he should never know. As a matter of fact, she was anxious, for her own sake, to keep it quiet. She moved to Massachusetts, passed herself off as a widow, and married a man named Hannock, there; but he died, and so back she came, passing off this boy, *here*, as Hannock's son! [*He groans*] What a story for a father to own up to, before a son like you. [*After a second's pause*]

GEORGE. Don't think of that! *Don't mind me!* After all, I'm a twentieth century *son*, you know, and *New York at heart!*

RAND. Of course your mother's never dreamed. *That* I couldn't bear —

GEORGE. That's right. Mother's not me, — she's *nineteenth century* and Middleburg!

RAND. Now, you see I do owe this young man something. I can't shut my eyes to it!

GEORGE. Yes. I'm even wondering, father, if you don't owe him — the *truth!*

RAND. No, no, I couldn't trust him with it!

GEORGE. *Still*, father, don't *you owe it to him?* Even more than money! And don't you suppose he suspects it, anyway?

RAND. No, and he *mustn't know.* He'd tell *everybody!* It would be my ruin; and your mother? — break her heart, — and for what good?

GEORGE [*with a sudden idea*]. Father, why not come to the City and escape him?

RAND. Escape him! He'd follow! That's his hunting ground! When you came back home from college, I'd had him in the bank a couple of years. But I didn't want you two to meet, so I got him a good place in Boston. But in six months he'd lost it, and was mixed up in some scrape in New York! No! Remember, George, you gave me your promise you wouldn't leave me! You'll stay with me here. We must take care of this man, of course, for our own sakes, as well as his. I am his father!

GEORGE. And I'm his brother, and Cicely and Tess are his sisters! It's hard lines on him! I can't help feeling, father, we owe him a good deal.

RAND. You'll stand by me — so long as I live. [*Excitedly*] Promise me solemnly!

GEORGE. I have promised you, father.

RAND. And, if anything should ever happen to *me*, you'd look after — Hannock, wouldn't you, George?

GEORGE. Yes, father. I consider you — we — owe Hannock a future!

RAND. But you'll keep my secret — promise me that, too!

GEORGE. I give you my word of honor, father.

RAND [*half collapses and sways*]. I feel so badly again! I — I'm going to my room to lie down. Don't let them disturb me till supper-time. [GEORGE *goes to help him out.* RAND *smiles, though with an effort*] No, no! I'm not so far gone as all that, — not yet a while, boy, not quite yet —! [*Goes out alone*]

GEORGE [*coming back*]. Who'd have thought it! Who'd have thought it! Father! [*A heavy fall is heard in the hall outside.* GEORGE *looks up, and then starts on, but stops and lifts his head suddenly to listen. A look of fright and dread is on his face. Then he turns to the door and walks into the hall. A moment after, off stage, he cries,* "Father!"]

[*The following scene takes place off stage*]

MRS. RAND [*in a voice of excitement*]. What was it? Father? Did he faint? [*Calling*] James! *James*, bring me water, *quick!*

GEORGE. I'll telephone for the doctor. I'll get Dr. Hull from across the street. He'll be the quickest. [*Passes by the door from Left to Right. The telephone bell is heard. The* MAIDSER-

VANT *hurries past the door with water*] Hello. Give me sixteen —

MRS. RAND [*to* MAIDSERVANT]. Is John in the kitchen having his supper?

MAIDSERVANT. Yes, ma'am.

GEORGE. Hello?

MRS. RAND. Tell him to come here to help us carry Mr. Rand into the parlor, and you come right back.

MAIDSERVANT. Yes, ma'am. [*She goes hurriedly past the door from Left to Right, as* GEORGE *is talking*]

GEORGE [*at 'phone, off stage*]. Is that you, Dr. Hull? Can you come right over? Father — looks to me like a stroke! Good-by. [*Rings telephone bell, and passes before the door on his way from Right to Left*]

MRS. RAND. I've sent for John. I thought between us we could carry him. [MAIDSERVANT *passes through hall from Right to Left*] Susan, get a pillow from upstairs, and put it on the sofa in the parlor, and send Miss Cicely.

MAIDSERVANT. Yes, ma'am.

[*Before doorway,* JOHN *passes from Right to Left*]

GEORGE. Here, John! Father's very ill. John, we want to get him on to the sofa in the parlor.

CICELY. What's the matter? What is it, mother?

MRS. RAND. We don't know ourselves, dear, but we're waiting for Dr. Hull.

GEORGE. You hold his head up, mother. And John — that's right!

MRS. RAND. Give me the pillow, Susan, — help me.

GEORGE. Cicely, go into the library, close the door, and wait for me. As soon as the doctor comes — [*Front doorbell rings outside*]

MRS. RAND. There he is! Susan, go to the door.

[*Enter* CICELY. *She closes the door behind her, frightened, and leans against it, listening*]

CICELY [*whispers*]. He's dead, — I know it, — he's *dead!* [*She carefully opens the door on a crack to listen. She sees* MAIDSERVANT] Susan! [MAID-SERVANT *approaches in the hall beyond the half open door*] Was it the doctor?

MAIDSERVANT [*in doorway*]. Yes, Miss.

CICELY. What did he say?

MAIDSERVANT. I don't know, Miss. I didn't go in the room.

JOHN [*appearing in the hall*]. Susan! [*Whispers*]

CICELY. What is it, John? What does the doctor say?

JOHN [*embarrassed*]. I — I — don't know, Miss. Mr. George'll tell you. He wants you, Susan, to telephone to his aunt, Mrs. Loring, and ask her to have word 'phoned round to the guests for this afternoon not to come. You're to say Mr. Rand has been taken suddenly ill, and will she come over at once.

MAIDSERVANT. All right. [*She goes*]

CICELY. Poor papa! He isn't dead, then?

[SUSAN *is heard ringing the 'phone*]

JOHN. Mr. George'll tell you. [*He goes off*]

MAIDSERVANT. Hello! Give me thirty-one, please.

[GEORGE *comes into the room to* CICELY]

CICELY. How is he?

GEORGE. Cicely!

CICELY [*frightened*]. What?

MAIDSERVANT [*heard outside*]. Is that Mrs. Loring, please — this is Susan —

[GEORGE *shuts the hall door; he puts his arm around* CICELY]

GEORGE. Cicely, father's dead.

CICELY. Oh, George! [*Bursts into tears*]

GEORGE [*putting his arms around her again*]. Cicely, dear, don't cry, little girl! Go upstairs to mother; she wants you. And stay with her till Aunt Nellie comes —

CICELY [*crying*]. Oh, poor mother, poor mother! [CICELY *goes out, leaving door open*]

MAIDSERVANT [*off stage at the telephone*]. Yes, ma'am. Good-by.

GEORGE. Susan?

MAIDSERVANT [*in the doorway*]. Yes, sir?

GEORGE. If any strangers come to the door to ask questions, tell them nothing. Do you know Mr. Straker?

MAIDSERVANT. No, sir.

GEORGE. Well, he's on the evening newspaper here. He's sure to hear we've put off our little party, and come around to find out. If any one asks, never mind who, — you know nothing except that Mr. Rand was taken suddenly sick. That's all. You don't know how, or what it is. You understand?

MAIDSERVANT. Yes, sir.

GEORGE. All right. [*Nods to her to go. She goes out. He walks over to the desk and looks where his father sat and stood*] Why, it was only a minute ago he was there, talking with me! It doesn't seem possible — that now — he's dead — dead — [*he wipes the tears out of his eyes, and gives a long sigh; sinks in the seat*] gone for good out of this life! I don't understand it! What does it all mean? [*He is staring straight ahead of him. Suddenly a thought comes to him and takes possession of him*] I know one thing it *means for me!* — [*He rises and stands straight.*] It means New York. [*There is a tapping on the glass of the window. He doesn't hear it at first. It is* TERESA, *outside, tapping. She taps again. He looks up and sees her*] Tess!! [*He hurries to the window and opens it*] Tess! [*Embraces her enthusiastically*]

TERESA. I thought I'd stroll in and surprise you! It's the same old room! — [*smiling around, as she recognizes things*] not a thing changed! — nor in the town, either, from the smelly old barn of a depot — past the same gay houses with the empty old iron urns, right up to *ours*, — bigger and uglier than all the rest! Nothing's changed! And oh, George, how can I live here? I'll never be able to stand it! I can't do it! I know I can't do it! [*Kisses him again*]

GEORGE. Tess! You won't have to! We're going to live in New York!

TERESA. George!! What do you mean?

GEORGE. We're going to live in the City!

TERESA. Oh, George! You don't know how much that means to me! I can be married in New York, then!

GEORGE [*amazed*]. Married!

TERESA. Sh! That's my surprise! Heavens, how hard it's been to keep it out of my letters! I met him first in Egypt, and then he joined us at Nice, at Paris, and in London, and *there* he proposed.

GEORGE. But who?

TERESA. I just told you!

GEORGE [*smiling*]. No, you didn't!

TERESA. Oh! Donald Van Vranken.

GEORGE. Don Van Vranken?

TERESA. Yes! Think what my position will be in New York!

GEORGE. But Tess! He's the fastest fellow going! He's notorious!

Look at the scandals that have been more or less public property about him. It's the last one that drove him abroad, afraid of the witness bench!

▸ TERESA. Oh, you can't believe everything you hear! He's a handsome darling, and I love him, and he loves me, — so don't worry!

GEORGE. But I can't help worrying! Your happiness isn't safe with a man like Don Van Vranken.

TERESA. Oh, come, you haven't been away from Middleburg enough! Here, *maybe*, the husbands do go to the altar like Easter lilies! But in the City, you don't marry a man for what he has or hasn't been; you marry him for what he is and what you hope he's going to be! But I did dread a wedding here — with his people and friends! How in the world did you *persuade* father?

[*A second's pause, as* GEORGE *suddenly comes back with a terrific shock*]

GEORGE. Good God! I forgot! I've some awful news!

TERESA. Mother —!

GEORGE. No, — father.

TERESA. What? — not —?

GEORGE. Yes. To-day, — just a little while ago! Suddenly — in a second! His heart gave out — I was talking with him two minutes before.

TERESA. Oh, poor mother! Where is she? Let me go to her!

GEORGE. She's up in her room.

TERESA. Mother! — [*As she goes out in great distress, she is heard again in the distance*] Mother!!

GEORGE [*stands where she left him — alone — his head bowed. He straightens up, and lifts his head; and his face flushes with the uncontrolled impulses of youth and ambition. With a voice of suppressed excitement, full of emotion, and with a trembling ring of triumph, he says*] The CITY . . . !

THE CURTAIN FALLS

ACT II

SCENE. — *Several years later. The library in the* RANDS' *house in New York. The walls are panelled in light walnut. Two French windows, with the sun shining in, are on the left. There are small doors, Right and Left Centre, opening into other* rooms. *Between the bookcases, which occupy most of the wall space, are marble busts, standing in deep niches. There are flowers about. The sofa, chairs, hangings, and cushions are of golden yellow brocade, except one big armchair, upholstered in red, standing in front of the open wood fire. A Sargent portrait is built in over the mantel. A small typewriting table is at one side. Almost in the centre of the room, with chairs grouped near it, is a long carved table, with all the desk fittings of a luxurious but busy man; there is also a bunch of violets on it, in a silver goblet — and at present it is strewn with papers, etc.*

[FOOT *is arranging the fire. There is a knock at the door.* HANNOCK *enters. He comes in, in evident and only partly suppressed, nervous excitement. He wears a white flower in his buttonhole*]

HANNOCK. Hello, Foot. Is Mr. Rand out?

FOOT. Yes, sir. [*Rises, having finished the fire*]

HANNOCK. He left no message for me?

FOOT. Yes, sir. He left some papers on the desk, which he said he'd like you to go over carefully, at once, and two letters he wanted you to answer.

HANNOCK. All right. Get me a package of longish papers, with an elastic band around them, in my overcoat in the hall.

FOOT. Yes, sir.

HANNOCK. Has the stenographer been here?

FOOT. Yes, but he's gone; said he couldn't wait any longer, as he has an appointment.

HANNOCK [*angry; making nervous, irritable movements*]. He'll be sorry! I'll see to it he loses Mr. Rand's job, that's all, if he don't knuckle down to me!

FOOT. Yes, sir. It's none of my business, but Mr. Rand didn't like your being late. He said you knew it was an important day for him, and he couldn't understand it.

HANNOCK. He'll understand all right when I explain! It's an *important* day for me too!

FOOT [*eagerly*]. Is he going to get the nomination for governor, sir?

HANNOCK. Nothing surer! — except his election. That'll be a knock-out, and then you'll see us both forging ahead.

FOOT. I'm sure I wish you luck, sir.

HANNOCK. Thanks! Oh, yes, I shall tie my fortune up to Mr. Rand's!

FOOT. Yes, sir — [*He goes out*]

HANNOCK. Yes, sir, [*imitating* FOOT] — *damned "important"* day for me, too! Phew! [*A great sigh, showing he is carrying something big on his mind*] I wonder just how he'll take it? I wish it was over. [*He goes to the type-writing table, rummages in a drawer, takes out a little box, containing a hypodermic needle, and tries it; then, putting it to his arm just above the wrist, he presses it, half grinning and mumbling to himself, — looking furtively over his shoulder fearing an interruption. Just as he finishes, the door opens.* CICELY *half comes in. She is in hat, gloves, etc.*

CICELY [*half whispering*]. You're back first. [*He nods, hiding the hypodermic needle*] I've just this minute come in, and I didn't meet a soul. I've sent for Eleanor Vorhees — she's the best.

[*Enter* TERESA *hurriedly, in great and angry emotional excitement, pushing past* CICELY]

TERESA. Good morning, Cicely. Where's George?

CICELY. Give it up! [*Following her in*]

HANNOCK. He'll be in soon, Mrs. Van Vranken. He's an appointment with Mr. Vorhees.

[*Enter* FOOT]

FOOT. I can't find any papers with an elastic band, sir.

HANNOCK [*irritated*]. Oh, well, perhaps there wasn't a band! Use your *common sense!* I'll look myself. [*To the ladies*] Excuse me. [*Goes out, followed by* FOOT]

CICELY. What's the matter with you, Tess? Don on the loose again?

TERESA. I don't know and I don't care! I've *left* him.

CICELY. *Left your husband!* — for good? Honest? Or has *he* left you?

TERESA. What do you mean by that? That's a nice thing for my sister to say!

CICELY. My dear! — even donkeys — I mean sisters — have ears, — and you must know how every one has been talking about you and Jimmy Cairns!

TERESA. Well, if I can't depend upon my own family, I don't suppose I can expect my husband to protect me.

CICELY. After all, what can Don say? He can't find any fault with *you!*

TERESA. Exactly! — and I went to him, perfectly calm and reasonable, and said very sweetly: "Don, I'm going to divorce you. We needn't have any disagreeable feeling about it, or any scandal. I will simply bring the divorce, mentioning this woman" —

CICELY. Mrs. Judly?

TERESA. Of course — but doing it as quietly as possible, behind closed doors, or with sealed papers, or whatever they call it. Only, of course he must give me the children!

CICELY. Oh! — and he refused?

TERESA. *Absolutely refuses,* — and to let me get the divorce as I propose! He will only agree to a legal separation, the children's time to be divided between us. That's all he'll stand for.

CICELY. Let him agree to what he likes! You've got your case, all right. You could prove everything you want to, couldn't you?

TERESA [*getting angry*]. Yes, but he — Oh, the beast! — he dares to *threaten!* If I attempt to do this, he'll bring a counter suit, mentioning Mr. Cairns!

CICELY. Tess!

TERESA. You see! He ties my hands!

CICELY. But not if he couldn't —

TERESA. Sh-h! Let's talk about something else. I don't want that horrid Hannock to know anything. I despise him!

CICELY [*on the defensive*]. I don't know why!

TERESA. Well, I'm not alone in my feelings. I don't know any one who *likes* him.

CICELY. Yes, you do, because *I'm* one.

TERESA. He always affects me like a person who would listen at keyholes!

CICELY. Some day you'll be very sorry you said that.

[HANNOCK *reënters*]

HANNOCK. Mr. Vorhees is here with Miss Vorhees.

CICELY. I asked Eleanor to come. [*She goes out to greet them*]

TERESA [*to* HANNOCK]. Let me know the minute Mr. Rand comes in. [*She goes out.* HANNOCK *takes up letters on desk which are for him to answer, goes to the typewriting table, and sits down to write, reading over to himself one of the letters — mumbling the words. He laughs to himself]*

HANNOCK. Ha! And I suppose he thinks this is legitimate business! — that *this sort of a deal* goes hand in hand with his "clean record", with his "white politics", with the Vorhees "good government." Humph! "Teddy, Jr." is a good nickname for him, — I guess not! The *public* would put George Rand in the Roosevelt class with a vengeance, wouldn't they! — if they were on to this one piece of manipulation! Following in father's footsteps, all right, and going popper one better! That's what! And he *pretends* to think his methods are on the level! All the same, I guess he is just as square as the rest of 'em. You can't tell me Vorhees isn't feathering *his nest* good! You bet *I'm* on to Vorhees! [*He looks up, half startled*] Damn it, when am I going to stop talking in my sleep when I'm wide awake? [*Looking at the place on his arm, and smoothing it over*] Too much of the needle, I guess!

[*Enter* SERVANT *with* VORHEES. SERVANT *goes out*]

VORHEES. Good morning, Hannock.

HANNOCK. Good morning, Mr. Vorhees. You're ten minutes early for your appointment, sir.

VORHEES. Mr. Rand is generally ready ahead of time. I thought I'd probably find him.

HANNOCK. He isn't here yet. I *hope* he gets the nomination for governor!

VORHEES. Well, I'm inclined to think it's all *up to him* now, Hannock, and that to-day will decide.

HANNOCK. Isn't it wonderful how far he's got in barely five years!

VORHEES. Well, it was Rand's good luck — to come along at the right psychological moment — the party tired of the political gambler, the manipulator. We wanted a candidate with just the freshness, the force and stability of a *small town's bringing up*. The whole of Middleburg, no matter what the party, will come forward unanimously, and speak for their young fellow townsman. His family is the boast of the place! His father's name stands for everything that's best and finest in public and private life, and, when George took hold in New York, with all the political vitality and straightforward vigor of his blood and bringing up, and not only helped along *our reforms*, but *created new ones of his own*, giving his time and his strength and his money to the public good! Well, you know what the man in the street's been calling him for a year now?

HANNOCK [*with a covert sneer*]. "Teddy, Jr.!"

VORHEES. Yes, "Teddy, Jr." That idea ought to land him in Albany, all right!

HANNOCK [*with the bare suggestion of a bully's manner*]. I hope, Mr. Vorhees, I haven't been altogether overlooked in all the enthusiasm.

VORHEES [*with a big drop*]. How do you mean?

HANNOCK. Well, I've been George Rand's right hand, you know! I've done my share of the work. Where do *I* come in on the *reward* end?

VORHEES [*strongly*]. I *really* don't understand you.

HANNOCK [*smiling, but serious and determined, and speaking deliberately*]. What do *I* get out of it?

VORHEES [*after a pause*]. You get a damned lot of pride in the man you've had the honor of serving, that's what you get!

HANNOCK [*angry at the snub, and suspicious that he is to be thrown down*]. And a hell of a lot of good that'd do me! Look here, Mr. Vorhees, I might as well have my say out now! If George Rand wants to be elected Governor of New York, he and his electors have got to square me!

VORHEES. Why, you talk like a fool — or a scoundrel!

HANNOCK. Well, never mind what I talk *like;* I know what I'm talking *about*, and I say there's something good in the way of a job coming to his confidential secretary out of "*Gov.*" Rand's election!

[VORHEES *half laughs, half sneers, but still is slightly disturbed.* GEORGE *enters*]

GEORGE. Hello! Am I late? Sorry!

VORHEES. No, I'm early. Well!! Can we have our talk?

GEORGE [*smiling at himself*]. I believe I'm nervous! Go ahead! Fire your first gun! [*Takes a chair.* HANNOCK *also sits*]

VORHEES [*with a glance toward* HANNOCK]. I'll wait, if you have any business to discuss with Mr. Hannock.

GEORGE. No, nothing in a hurry; that's all right, go on —

VORHEES. Well, if you don't mind, I'd like to talk with *you privately*.

GEORGE. Certainly. Would you mind, Hannock, waiting in —

VORHEES [*interrupting; to* HANNOCK]. Eleanor's in the drawing-room. Cicely sent for her; wants her advice, I believe, about something or other, *very important!* [*Guying the latter with a smile*]

GEORGE. Well, suppose you go to my room, Hannock, and use the desk there.

HANNOCK [*in a hard voice, reluctant to leave them*] Very good. [*Rises, takes papers, and starts to go*]

VORHEES [*with the tone of a final good-by*]. Good morning, Hannock.

HANNOCK. Good morning, sir. [*Stops at the door*] If I wanted to speak with you later on to-day, after I've had a talk with Mr. Rand, could I call you up on the 'phone, and make an appointment?

VORHEES. Certainly.

HANNOCK [*in a satisfied voice*]. Thank you. [*Goes out*]

GEORGE. Well?

VORHEES. How do you *feel?* Eager, eh?

GEORGE. That depends on what I'm going to get! I'm eager, all right, if you've come to tell me what I want to hear!!

VORHEES. You're *warm*, as the children say!

GEORGE. What wouldn't I give — that was honest to give — for this chance, not just to *talk*, not to *boast*, not to *promise*, only —

VORHEES [*interrupting him*]. Exactly! That's exactly what we want — the man behind the gun in *front of the gun!* We don't want a Fourth of July orator *only*, in the Capitol! We want a man who'll be *doing something*, George!

GEORGE [*enthusiastically*]. Every minute!!

VORHEES. We can hire a human phonograph to do the talking. The party's full of them!

GEORGE. I want to make *my name mean*, in this *whole country*, what *father's* meant in *that small*, up-State town we came from!!

VORHEES. Your name can take care of itself. Don't think of any glory *you're* going to get! You'll get most by keeping busy for the good of the State, for the welfare of the people —

GEORGE [*eagerly, not waiting for* VORHEES *to finish*]. I know! But I'm going to show the gods and the demigods, the rabble and the riffraff, that one good lesson we've learned from the success of the last administration is that the real leader of a party must be its independent choice, and not its tool.

VORHEES [*approving*]. Right!

GEORGE. Machine politics are a *back number*. The public has got on to the engine, and smashed the works!

VORHEES. Man is greater than a machine, because God's soul is in him.

GEORGE. Yes, and what I'm going to show is that the soul of a political party is the uncompromising honesty of its leader.

VORHEES. Don't always be emphasizing the leader; — let it go at the *party's* honesty! You're inclined, George, to over-emphasize the personal side of it! It's E Pluribus *Unum*, not E Pluribus *me*-um!

GEORGE. All right, all right! Only, don't forget that I've got an inordinate ambition, and you're dangling in front of my eyes the talisman that may land me, God knows how high!

VORHEES. Well, come back to earth! Now, I've come here with the nomination in one hand —

[GEORGE *draws a long, excited breath*]

GEORGE. And a *string* in the other?

VORHEES. Yes.

GEORGE. Well, give it to us!

VORHEES. The Committee decided it was up to me! I've known you as a boy. You're going to marry my sister. We're brothers practically. I can speak frankly, without giving any offence — that's sure, isn't it?

GEORGE. Nothing surer!

VORHEES. It's just this! Of course the minute you're nominated, our political opponents will get busy! The muckrakes are all ready!

GEORGE. You bet they are, and the searchlights haven't any Foolish Virgins in charge of them. They're trimmed, all right, and filled with *gasoline!*

VORHEES [*very seriously*]. You can stand it, George?

GEORGE. I can.

VORHEES. You've got a wonderful

popularity, and the Committee believes in you, but it wants your word confirming its confidences, — that's all.

GEORGE. That's the least it can ask.

VORHEES. Is there anything in your life that isn't absolutely above board, George? No skeleton in your heart, or your *cupboard?* It's safe for us to put you up? You're sure not a particle of the mud they'll rake can stick?

GEORGE. Not a particle.

VORHEES. Look back a little. Sometimes I think you're a little *too* cocksure of yourself. No man can be, absolutely, till he's been tried in the furnace, and you haven't been, yet. But we're getting the fires ready! [*Smiles*] You're all right at heart, I'm sure of it. Nobody in this world believes more in you than I do, — [*again smiling*] except, perhaps, you yourself. But there's nothing, nothing that could be ferreted out? You know they'll dig, and dig, and dig!!

GEORGE. But I give you my word of honor, so help me God, I've never done a dishonest or dishonorable act, or an act —

VORHEES [*interrupting*]. In business?

GEORGE [*hesitates just one moment*]. You know what my father stood for, — and my business methods *he* taught me. I've gone ahead of him, of course, — gone on with the times, — but on the road father blazed for me! I've not deviated from a single principle.

VORHEES. Good! I know what George Rand, Sr., stood for in Middleburg! That's good enough for me. And in your private life? Oh, this is just going through the form; personally, I'd stake my life on your answer, and Eleanor's instinct would have kept her ₊om loving you.

GEORGE. I was brought up in a small town, in the old-fashioned family life that's almost ancient history in the bigger cities. I loved my father and my mother, and their affection meant everything to me. From their influence, I went under Eleanor's. You needn't have one worry about my private life.

VORHEES. Of course I knew you were clean and above board, but different men have differeṇt ideas about some things.

GEORGE. Listen, — I'm no little tin god! I'm as full of faults as the next man, but I'm not afraid to own up my mistakes; I'm not afraid to tell the truth to my own disadvantage; I'm not afraid to stand or fall by my sincere conviction! In a word, I'm game to be put to any test you or the party want to put me, and I'll stand straight as I know how, so long as there's a drop or a breath of life in me!

VORHEES. Then that's all! And unofficially — *unofficially* — I can tell you, barring the unexpected accident, the nomination is yours! [*Holding out his hand, he grips* GEORGE'S *in his*]

GEORGE. *Isn't it great?* *It's wonderful!* Oh, God, if *I* can only do it big!

VORHEES. You mean *do it well!*

GEORGE [*taken aback only for a second*]. Er — yes, of course — same thing! — Do half I dream of and want to!

VORHEES [*smiling*]. Well — I'm taking any bets!

GEORGE. I owe the whole business to you, you know, and *I* know it!

VORHEES. Nonsense! With that overwhelming ambition of yours! Perhaps I taught you your *primer* of politics, your *grammar* of public life; that's all — except that I'm a *damned proud* teacher!!!

[*Enter* FOOT]

FOOT. Mr. Van Vranken must see you at once, sir, — says it's very urgent.

GEORGE. All right.

VORHEES. Say in two or three minutes.

FOOT. Yes, sir. [*Goes out*]

VORHEES. There is just one more thing before I can go.

GEORGE. What?

VORHEES. Nothing that really concerns you, though it may cause you some inconvenience. The Committee thinks you'd better get rid of your secretary.

GEORGE [*astounded*]. *Hannock?*

VORHEES. Yes, — he's no good!

GEORGE. No good?

VORHEES. A damn rotten specimen. We've found out enough about him to make sure we don't want him mixed up with us in *any way* in the election.

GEORGE. You — you take me off my feet!

VORHEES. If you want more detailed information, ask any detective with tenderloin experience.

GEORGE. I've never liked him. I can't say I've really trusted him. And yet I laid my prejudice to a personal source.

VORHEES. He's dishonest besides.

You can't have him in a confidential position. You couldn't help getting tarred with some of his pitch!

GEORGE. But are you sure of what you say?

VORHEES. Sure! Why, just now, here, he showed me the hoof of a black-mailer.

GEORGE [*looks up quickly*]. *At that again!*

VORHEES. How do you mean "*again*"?

GEORGE. Explain to *me* what *you* mean.

VORHEES. Oh, he didn't get far — we were interrupted! He put out a feeler, which was very like a *demand*, as to what he was going to get out of this election.

GEORGE [*carelessly, and not very loudly*]. He needn't think I'm *father!*

VORHEES [*not understanding*]. What's that?

GEORGE. You leave Hannock to me. I'll take care of *him!*

VORHEES. You'll *discharge* him? [*A pause*]

GEORGE. No, — I can't.

VORHEES [*astonished*]. How do you mean, — "can't?"

GEORGE. I couldn't turn him out, if he insists on staying.

VORHEES. *Why not?*

GEORGE [*a short second's pause*]. That I cannot tell you —

VORHEES. Look here, George! What hold has this man got on you?

GEORGE. On me personally none. But I owe him a certain duty, and in a way he could do harm to —

VORHEES. I thought you said you had no skeleton?

GEORGE. It isn't in *my* closet, but it concerns those that are nearest and dearest to me.

VORHEES. Then you must risk sacrificing them, if you want the position.

GEORGE. I'd have to sacrifice a memory, too, — and I haven't the right!

VORHEES. If I went to the Committee, and said to them — Rand refuses to dismiss Hannock; doesn't deny he may be a scoundrel; owns up, in fact, that his family is in some way in the man's power; says he himself is not; but still he doesn't dismiss him, — do you believe for a minute the Committee will go on with your nomination?

GEORGE. No! For God's sake don't tell the Committee anything of the sort!

Perhaps I can handle Hannock — beg him off!

VORHEES. I don't like the sound of that. There's one thing about you I'm afraid of, George. You're one of those men who think wrong means are justified by right ends; — unsafe and dishonest policy!

GEORGE. I tell you he can't hurt *me*, George Rand — [*after a second*] "Jr."

VORHEES. That don't do for the Committee. You can't handle mud and not —

GEORGE [*interrupting*]. Very well, then if I can't buy him off, I *will* dismiss him! And the others must face the music! There's too much at stake for the future, to over-consider the past.

VORHEES. All right!

[*Enter* VAN VRANKEN, *excited and angry; perhaps he's had a little too much to drink*]

VAN VRANKEN. Look here!

GEORGE. Good morning, Don.

VORHEES. Good morning.

GEORGE. I'm very busy now.

VAN VRANKEN [*with a jeer*]. I won't interrupt you long!

VORHEES. Would you like *me* to hunt up Eleanor and Cicely, and come back later?

VAN VRANKEN. Oh, you might as well stop. You're as good as in the family, now. You'll be sure to be asked to put *your* oar in!

GEORGE. Sit down, Don, and cool off!

VAN VRANKEN. I haven't time. I'm on the way to my lawyer! I understand my wife's here. Has she talked with you?

GEORGE. No. I've been busy with Vorhees.

VAN VRANKEN. I know — the governship! Well, your sister'll put a spoke in that wheel, if you don't side with *me!*

GEORGE. What do you mean?

VAN VRANKEN. She threatens to take my children from me by bringing a suit for divorce, — mentioning Nellie Jud — Mrs. Judly.

GEORGE. Well, can you blame her?

VAN VRANKEN. It's a pity you haven't gone out, once in a while, into the society that bores you so, and kept your ears open.

GEORGE. What for?

VAN VRANKEN. You'd have heard a whisper, or caught a look that would have kept you from being surprised at what I'm going to tell you.

GEORGE. What?

VAN VRANKEN. If your sister starts a suit against me, bringing in Nellie's — Mrs. Judly's — name, I'll bring a *counter suit* against her, naming Jim *Cairns!*

GEORGE. You drunken liar! [*Going for him.* VORHEES *holds* GEORGE *back*]

VAN VRANKEN. You didn't *know* I could win. I wouldn't put such a stumbling block in the way of my little daughter's happiness!

GEORGE. Liar!! [*Struggles to free himself*]

VORHEES. No, George! Even *I've* heard enough to wonder something of it hasn't come your way.

VAN VRANKEN [*thickly, whiningly*]. All I ask for is a noiseless, dignified separation, — that's all I want, and God, I want that bad! Legal or not, as *she* wishes, — only she's got to agree to cut out Cairns. I give her this chance for my little daughter's sake, — not for hers! But in another day, maybe, it'll be too late. I get my children six months of the year, and she the other six. I ask no more than I give, — that's fair! I'd like my complete freedom as well as she. So far as love goes, it's a pretty even thing between us! And when the children are grown up, and settled in life, she can do what she damn pleases, and good luck to her!

VORHEES. I've heard the gossip, Van Vranken, but you know enough of our world to realize half that gets about, gets about wrong.

GEORGE. Granted Tess has been *foolish.* That's bad *enough,* God knows! Still — I can't *believe* worse than that! *I grew up with her, — I know her!*

VAN VRANKEN. You knew her before she came to New York. She hadn't developed yet, in that *mud*hole you all lived in! There's no 'smoke without —

GEORGE. Yes, there is! There's a smoldering that never breaks into a flame! And you know, Don, you've given every reason for Tess's heart to smolder, yes, and burn, too — though I don't believe it. While we're about it, let's finish the whole ugly business here, now. You're a drunkard, and your best friends are the most depraved crew in town, — a crowd that is used individually as markers to tally off each smart scandal that crops up. It never

occurred to you, before you married Tess, that you would be faithful to her afterwards; and you didn't disappoint yourself.

VAN VRANKEN. What right had she to be disappointed? I never made any bluff or pose, and you all fought the match! She married me with her eyes open.

GEORGE. You had the glamour of the City about you. Tess was a *real* woman, full of good and bad; she was ready to be what the man she loved would make of her. And, poor girl, she married *you!*

VORHEES. Well, all that's done. What about the present? Van Vranken is right in saying any divorce scandal would endanger your election. We might lose the entire Catholic vote, and the support of the anti-divorce party, — both of which we're banking on. And besides, one of the strongest planks of our platform is the Sanctity of the Home! We're putting you up as the representative of the great section of the country which stands for the Purity of Family Life. We'd have to drop that platform, or be ridiculed off the face of the earth. And it doesn't seem right in any way to me! And it's not up *to you* to suffer for your sister. [*To* VAN VRANKEN] If we persuade Mrs. Van Vranken to a dignified separation such as you want —

VAN VRANKEN. And she gives her promise to call off Cairns —!

GEORGE [*quickly*]. Tess will be as anxious to stop gossip, when she hears its extent, as you. I'll take that on *my* shoulders.

[VAN VRANKEN *looks at him, and half smiles cynically at his confidence*]

VORHEES. Very well! Will you, Van Vranken, be willing to hush the whole business up?

VAN VRANKEN. Glad to!

VORHEES. Live on with Mrs. Van Vranken in your house as if nothing had happened?

VAN VRANKEN. No! Not by a damned sight!

VORHEES. Come, don't be a yellow dog. Do all or nothing.

VAN VRANKEN. She left my house of her own accord, and I've sworn she shall never put her foot in it again.

VORHEES. Oh, well, what's an oath more or less to you! It will be only till after the election! Rand's nomination is practically settled on —

Van Vranken. Oh, I see! Why didn't you say that at first? I've nothing personal against Rand.

Vorhees. I'm sure Mrs. Van Vranken, on her side, will do all she can to protect his interests.

Van Vranken. I suppose I'll have to give in —

Vorhees. *Good!*

George. I'll see her now, if she's in the house.

Vorhees [*to* Van Vranken]. I will communicate something to you, after Rand has seen your wife.

Van Vranken. Very good. She took both the children when she left this morning. One child must go back with me now.

Vorhees. *Both must go back*, to-day, and Mrs. Van Vranken, herself, — to live under your roof till after the election.

Van Vranken. That's true! Of course! All right! God, it'll be a *hell* of a life! However, there'll be an end of it to look forward to! Good-by.

Vorhees and George. Good-by.

[*Enter* Teresa *and* Mrs. Rand. Mrs. Rand *is very altered. Her hair is dressed fashionably, etc., and, instead of the sweet, motherly woman she was, in Act I, she is now a rather overdressed, nervous-looking woman, ultra-smart, but no longer comfortable-looking and happy*]

Teresa [*as she enters*]. George!

Mrs. Rand. George!

[*They both stop short, as they see* Van Vranken. *He bows to* Teresa; *she only glares at him*]

Van Vranken [*to* Mrs. Rand]. Good morning.

Mrs. Rand [*looking at him, — outraged and angry*]. You *wicked* man!

[Van Vranken *is somewhat taken aback; from her, he turns and looks at the two men; he raises his eyebrows, smiles, shrugs his shoulders, and slouches out indifferently*]

Vorhees. I must go, too.

Teresa. Good morning, Bert.

Vorhees. Good morning, Tess. How do you do, Mrs. Rand.

Mrs. Rand. I don't know where I am, Bert. I never felt the need of Mr. Rand more than to-day!

George. Bert, will you have to tell the Committee about this? Won't it queer my nomination?

Vorhees. Not if Tess will do what we expect. I'll leave you to explain to her. [*Moving as to go*]

George. No, — stay, Bert!

Mrs. Rand. George! Tess couldn't possibly tell you everything she wants to, before Bert.

Teresa. Oh, don't worry, mother. I guess *Don* hasn't left much for me to tell! Besides, Bert's a lawyer. I'd like his advice. [*To* George] Don gave you his version, didn't he?

George. Listen! My whole future is at stake, and it's in *your* hands!

Teresa. Nonsense! My hands are full of my own troubles.

Mrs. Rand [*to nobody in particular, and nobody pays any attention to her*] What a tragedy!

Vorhees. George is right. His nomination for governor was decided on, this morning, provided he had an open chance. If you make a scandal now, he'll lose the nomination, sure, — and if not, what's worse, the election!

Teresa. You are trying to influence me against what I want to do, through George. I will never live with Don again!

George. Won't you? Only till after the election?

Teresa. No! I intend to begin proceedings for a divorce to-day.

George. But Don *offers* you a legal separation, and to share the children.

Teresa. That's done purposely to keep me *tied*, so I couldn't marry again! I want the children all the time, and I want my freedom!

George. But you know what he threatens to do?

Teresa. *He won't dare!*

Vorhees. That's not his reputation in New York.

Mrs. Rand [*at random*]. If she only wouldn't decide at once — all of a sudden. That's where women always slip up!

Teresa. Did he pretend he wanted me to come back?

George [*smiling in spite of himself*]. No, but we persuaded him to be willing.

Vorhees. For George's sake, till after the election, on one condition —

Teresa [*quickly*]. *What* condition?

Vorhees. That you agree to the sort of separation he planned.

George. And promise to put an end, once for all, to the Cairns gossip.

TERESA. Just what I told you! The whole thing with him is only a mean spirit of revenge! He would sacrifice the children and me and everything else, to keep me from being happy with Jim.

GEORGE [*surprised at the apparent confession*]. Do you mean you *do* love Cairns?

TERESA. Yes.

MRS. RAND [*breaking in*]. No, she doesn't mean that! She doesn't love him *now*, but she *will*, if she gets her divorce.

GEORGE [*to* TERESA]. What you really want to divorce Don for, then, is not because of Mrs. Judly, but so you can marry Cairns?

TERESA. Exactly.

VORHEES [*looking at his watch*]. I must go. [*To* GEORGE] The Committee will be waiting now for me.

MRS. RAND [*mortified*]. You've shocked Bert, Tess.

VORHEES [*smiling*]. Oh, no, I've a report to make before George's nomination can be official, and I don't see, now, just how I'm going to make that report exactly as I wish.

GEORGE. You mean on account of *Tess!*

TERESA. I'll make any sacrifice I can for George, except my own personal happiness. That, I haven't the right to sacrifice, because that belongs half to some one else.

GEORGE. You go on and call me up by telephone when you get there. I'll have had a longer talk with Tess, and I may have something different to say to you.

VORHEES. All right. [*Going to* TERESA]

TERESA. I shall want you for my lawyer, Bert.

VORHEES. Thanks. That isn't exactly in my line, but I hope you won't *need* a lawyer. Do what you can for George, won't you?

TERESA. Of course.

[MRS. RAND *goes out with* VORHEES]

MRS. RAND [*as they go out*]. Bert, you mustn't get a wrong impression from what Tess said, will you? She's her father's own daughter, and you know a Rand *couldn't* do a really wrong thing; it's not in the blood.

GEORGE. Now, look here, Tess! On one side is a great career and me, and a dignified life for you, with independence and the happiness and the love and

respect of your children; on the other is probable failure for me, and worse than failure for you. Don'll do what he says, and if he wins his suit, you'll lose *both* children and everything else you ought to care about —

TERESA. Except Jim!

GEORGE. Would he make up for anything?

TERESA. Everything!

GEORGE. Even the children?

TERESA [*almost breaking down*]. How can I say that? You know I wouldn't have to give up my children!

GEORGE. Ten chances to one you'd have to.

TERESA. I don't believe any judge would give *Don* the children in preference to *me.*

GEORGE. Believe me, it'll be taking awful chances.

TERESA. All life is that. [*She turns aside, crying quietly*]

GEORGE [*going over to her*]. Tess! But you don't realize what this nomination means to me — more than anything in the world! I want it with every nerve and sinew in my body, with every thought in my brain, with every ambition I've got! Just let me get this one big thing in my hands, and nothing *shall stop me!* I'll climb on up the ladder of achievement and fame, and I'll take you all up with me! Remember our boy and girl days, Tess, in Middleburg. We were never selfish, you and I, with each other. It used to be a fight between us as to which should give up. Don't go back on me this time. You've got it in your power to give me a *great* boost, or push the whole scaffolding of my career from under my feet. For the love of God, stand by me to-day!

TERESA. It's your future against my future! Why should you expect me to sacrifice mine for yours? We aren't children now, and this isn't Middleburg. I love you very much, but not in that old-fashioned way.

GEORGE. But has any one in this world the right to absolutely ignore everybody else, and think only of one's self?

TERESA. It sounds to me *exactly* like *what you're doing!*

GEORGE. I suppose I do sound like a selfish brute; but I can't help feeling that what I ask of you, if six for me, is half a dozen for you, too, in the end.

TERESA. If Don'll give me a full divorce, I'll do anything for you — live with the beast *two years*, if necessary, and not see Jim all that time. But don't ask me to give up *Jim* — [*with motion again*] because I love him, and I won't, I couldn't; if I said I would, I'd lie!

GEORGE. But Don won't give you what you want, and if you insist, he'll do what *he* says — divorce you, with a filthy scandal!

TERESA. The *hour after* the divorce was granted, Jim Cairns and I would be married.

GEORGE. Listen! Would you do *this?* Deceive *me* now?

TERESA. How?

GEORGE. Well — agree to what Don asks —

TERESA. Never!

GEORGE. Wait! After the election, you might change your mind. Whatever course you took then, wouldn't interfere with me.

TERESA. Does that seem to you quite square? Isn't it a good deal like breaking your word?

GEORGE. Has Don done much else beside *break* his since he answered "I will" with you to the Bishop in the chancel?

TERESA. His word was cracked before I knew him! But I wasn't thinking of Don and me. Aren't you playing trick on the party that is putting its trust in you?

GEORGE. I don't see it! If your divorce comes out after my election, it needn't affect the party. My acts will be speaking for themselves, then. I intend to be square in office, and to succeed or fail by that standard. I don't mind a failure, *doing the right thing*, what I can't stand is failure *doing nothing* with having had my chance!

TERESA. I see; a sort of the-end-justifying-the-means principle.

GEORGE. Not exactly, because I don't see anything wrong. It's just election tactics! the others'd do it; we must fight them with their weapons.

TERESA [*rather cunningly*]. Will you tell Bert Vorhees?

GEORGE [*after a second's pause*]. No.

TERESA. *That's just what I mean!* It's something father wouldn't do.

GEORGE. He *wouldn't!* Why, father's whole business success was due to his not letting his left hand know what his right hand was after, but to square things in the end by a good division! — one third to the left hand on the basis that the *right hand* had done *all the work!* And you know what father's name stood for — the very criterion of business honor!

TERESA. Well, George, suppose I do it. I'm in no position to criticise, anyway. I'll go back till you're elected, and pretend I'm going to carry out Don's plan.

GEORGE. Thank you, Tess. [*But the enthusiasm is gone*]

TERESA. Only, somehow it doesn't coincide with my idea of what I *thought* you were being and striving for. Maybe you're on your way up the ladder, but you, at the same time, are coming down from the pedestal I'd put you on, to join me at the bottom of *mine*.

[*There is a moment's pause, both looking straight ahead, not liking to look into each other's eyes. Enter* HANNOCK]

HANNOCK. Excuse me, Mr. Rand. Mr. Vorhees is on the 'phone.

TERESA [*quickly, to* GEORGE]. I'll tell him. Then you won't have to *lie*, if he asks any difficult questions.

GEORGE. I wouldn't lie; I'd just beg anything I don't want to answer — and tell Eleanor to be sure and let me see her before she goes.

TERESA [*very serious*]. I wonder if *she'd* approve of this little plot of ours? I wish it didn't seem contemptible to me!

GEORGE [*hurt and showing a hint of shame for the first time*]. For God's sake, Tess, don't suggest such a thing! Eleanor is the one thing in the world I wouldn't give up to get this election.
[TERESA *looks at him meaningly as she goes out*]
What did you mean by looking for personal graft out of this election just now, with Mr. Vorhees?

HANNOCK. I was showing my hand, that's all. I was calling the pot! It's time!

GEORGE. You don't know the men you're dealing with!

HANNOCK [*looking* GEORGE *squarely and meaningly in the face*]. I know one of them better than he knows himself!

GEORGE. Listen, Hannock! That day my father died, I promised myself and his memory I'd look after you, and look after you well — not like a dependent on father's charity —

HANNOCK [*interrupts*]. Damned unwilling charity — he was *afraid* —

GEORGE. We won't go into the story of your mother — [HANNOCK *winces*] I've tried to treat you as I would a — brother who was unlucky — somebody I was *glad* to give a hand to —

HANNOCK [*interrupting*]. Well, haven't I made good? What complaints have you —

GEORGE [*going on*]. You've been of the greatest service to me in every way. There's no question about that! But it's time for us now to open a new pack, and each go his own way —

HANNOCK [*thunderstruck*]. What's that you say?

GEORGE. I'm going to offer you a fixed yearly income, — a sum we'll agree on, — and you're to get a job elsewhere, that's all —

HANNOCK [*dry and ugly*]. Is it!

GEORGE. What do you say?

HANNOCK. Oh, I've got a hell of a lot to say!

GEORGE. Cut it down to yes or no, and we'll discuss the amount of the income!

HANNOCK. *No!!!* You haven't got to give half of what I expect to get out of the present situation.

GEORGE [*angry, but controlled*]. If you don't look out, you'll get *nothing*.

HANNOCK [*sneers*]. Pah! Just wait till I begin to open your eyes for you! For instance, how about the New Brunswick deal?

GEORGE. *What about* it? [*On the defensive*]

HANNOCK. As crooked as anything that's ever been in "high finance"! [*With a sneer*]

GEORGE. What do you mean? You knew that deal from the very beginning — you knew every step I took in it?

HANNOCK. Yes, *I* did! I notice you kept the transaction pretty quiet from everybody else.

GEORGE. It was nobody else's business. My father taught me that —

HANNOCK [*not listening out*]. *Yes!* — and he taught you a lot of *other* things, too! But you go farther than he would have dared.

GEORGE. That's enough!

HANNOCK. What's the difference between your deal, and the Troy business that sent Pealy to State's Prison?

GEORGE. Every difference!

HANNOCK [*triumphantly*]. *Is* there? *Think* a minute! [*A second's pause*] You gambled with your partner's money: Pealy gambled with his bank's.

GEORGE. It wasn't my *partner's* money; it was the *firm's*.

HANNOCK. But you were the only one who knew what was being done with it.

GEORGE. My partner got his fair share, didn't he?

HANNOCK. Yes, but you got the *unfair!* You got paid pretty high for your "*influence*." Nobody else had any chance to sell theirs! If that isn't taking money under false pretences, if it isn't using funds you haven't the right to use, — there was a miscarriage of justice in the Pealy case, that's all.

GEORGE. But —!

HANNOCK. Go over the two deals with *Vorhees*, if you don't believe *me!* Show *him* the differences between the Brunswick Transaction and the Pealy case, — if he can *see* any!

[*Enter* ELEANOR, *breezily, enthusiastically*]

ELEANOR. Good morning! [*She sees* HANNOCK; *her manner changes to a cold one*] Good morning, Mr. Hannock.

HANNOCK. Good morning, Miss Vorhees. Excuse me!

[*He passes* MISS VORHEES, *and goes out as he goes, with his back to them, he is seen taking out from his pocket his hypodermic needle, and a small bottle, — and, by then, he is out;* ELEANOR *and* GEORGE *silently follow him with their eyes*]

ELEANOR [*turning*]. What *is* it about him?

GEORGE [*kisses her*]. You don't like him either?

ELEANOR. I *detest* him! What Cicely can see in him I —

GEORGE [*quietly*]. Cicely?

ELEANOR. Yes, I've come to-day as a go-between — between you and Cicely —

GEORGE. Ha! Cicely's clever enough to know how to get what she wants from me. She has only to use you —

ELEANOR. She's in love with your secretary.

GEORGE [*not taking it in*]. What?

ELEANOR. Cicely and Mr. Hannock are in love with each other —

GEORGE [*aghast*]. Impossible —

ELEANOR. I know; I felt the same as you do. I detest him; he's no match for Cicely — I feel instinctively the last man in the world for her.

GEORGE. Even *not* that —

ELEANOR. But Cicely insists. They wish to marry.

GEORGE. Never!

ELEANOR. She guessed you would be against it. She says we none of us like Hannock, and nobody's fair to him; and so she begged me to persuade you. She asked me to remember how much *I* loved *you*, and what *our* marriage meant to *us*. You see, I couldn't refuse! But I'm afraid I'm not a very good go-between; my heart isn't in it!

GEORGE [*hardly hearing* ELEANOR]. It's beyond believing! [*He touches the bell with decision*] I must talk to Cicely now, before she sees Hannock again.

ELEANOR. Wouldn't it be better without me? She might resent your refusing and giving your reasons before me.

[*Enter* FOOT]

GEORGE. Ask Miss Cicely to come here at once, please.

FOOT. Yes, sir. [*He goes out*]

GEORGE. Perhaps it *would* be better.

ELEANOR. George, it doesn't make any difference to *you* that Hannock has no family or position? Cicely thinks you're prejudiced against him because his mother was a milliner or dressmaker — or something —

GEORGE. Of course that makes no difference to me —

ELEANOR. And you wouldn't be influenced against a man by your personal feeling, where your sister's happiness was concerned, would you? [*He makes his head*] If you don't *know* anything against Hannock, you'll let him have a *chance* to prove himself worthy of Cicely, won't you?

GEORGE. Eleanor, it can't be! Don't ask me any questions, but believe me, nothing could make such a thing possible, — personal prejudice and any other kind aside! I want you to help me pull Cicely through it. I may even ask you to take Cicely into your house for a while. Would you do this for me? Teresa and Don, you know, would be no comfort, and, on the other hand, would set her a bad example, and fan every little rebellious flame in her!

ELEANOR. Of course, I'll do whatever I possibly can, dear. This is the very sort of thing I want to *share* with you, if I can't take it *entirely* off your shoulders.

[*Enter* CICELY]

CICELY [*half defiant, half timid and hopeful*]. Well?

ELEANOR [*going. To* CICELY, *speaking tenderly*]. I won't go home yet. I'll wait for you upstairs.

CICELY. Humph! *Thank* you; I know what *that* means!

[ELEANOR *goes out*]

GEORGE. My dear girl, it isn't possible that you care for Hannock?

CICELY [*determined*]. Yes, *very much!*

GEORGE. Well, even that may be, but still not in the way you think.

CICELY. *I love him!* Oh, I knew you'd be against it! Nobody cares for him in this house!

GEORGE [*quickly*]. And that's *why* you do! You're *sorry* for him, my dear girl! It's *pity*, not *love!*

CICELY [*increasing her resentment and determination*]. Nothing of the sort! He doesn't need my pity in any way.

GEORGE. It's just as I would feel toward a girl who seemed to me to be ignored.

CICELY. Abused! As good as *insulted here*, by everybody!

GEORGE. You *think* so, and your sympathy is aroused, — but that's not love.

CICELY. You don't know what you're talking about!

GEORGE. Yes, I do, — better than you. You've never been in love in your life, and so you mistake something, that is probably like a sisterly affection for this man, for the other thing.

CICELY. *Ridiculous!*

GEORGE. You don't know the difference now —

CICELY. Nonsense!

GEORGE. But you'll realize it some day when the right man comes along —

CICELY [*satirically*]. I hope not! It would be awkward, as *I shall be married* to Fred Hannock.

GEORGE. No, you'll never be married to Hannock!

CICELY. *You're* not my father!

GEORGE. But I represent him, and I tell you you must give up this idea —

CICELY [*interrupting angrily*]. And I tell you I won't! Good-by! [*Starting to go*]

GEORGE. Wait a minute. [*Rings bell*] You can't marry this man. He isn't good enough for you!

CICELY. Humph!

GEORGE. Or for any self-respecting woman to marry, as far as that goes.

CICELY. Your opinion as to whom I shall marry, or not, means absolutely nothing to me.

GEORGE. Very well, I'll go even farther. I'll tell you that, even if both my reasons for disapproving of Hannock were done away with, — still, I say for you to marry him is *impossible*, and I, as your elder brother, *representing your father*, forbid it.

[*Enter* FOOT]

FOOT. Yes, sir?

GEORGE. Ask Mr. Hannock to come here.

FOOT. Yes, sir. [*Goes out*]

GEORGE. I shall tell him, *before you*, anything between him and you is absolutely impossible, — that I forbid it, and that he is dismissed from my service.

CICELY. Then I will go with him, if he wants me to. Do you think I'm going to have *him* lose his position and everything *through me*, and not stick to him?

GEORGE [*with tension*]. *Sorry for him!* That's all it is! *Sorry for him!*

CICELY. *It's not* — and you can forbid now till doomsday. I'm my own mistress, and I shall do as I *darn please!* I shall marry the man I want to, in spite of you — and the whole family, if necessary, — but I wanted to give you the chance to stand by me — [*Her voice falters, and she turns away; she cries*] I felt you *wouldn't*, but I wanted you to, and that's why — I've come here now — and let you — humiliate me — in this — way. I wanted my own brother to sympathize with me, to help me. Everybody will follow your lead!

GEORGE [*goes to her, and puts his arms about her*]. Cis! I can't tell you how sorry I am! Not since father died have I felt as I do now. I've nothing to gain or lose except your affection, dear girl, and your happiness, so you can believe me when I say this marriage *can't* be — [*She pushes his arm away and faces him*]

CICELY [*literal and absolutely unconvinced or frightened*]. *Why* not?

GEORGE. I *can't* tell you.

CICELY. Well, you know me well enough to realize such reasoning with me is a waste of breath.

GEORGE [*suffering*]. I want to *spare* you —

CICELY. *What?* It doesn't seem to me you're *sparing* me much!

GEORGE. But listen — Vorhees just now told me — Hannock isn't on the level, — he isn't *honest!*

CICELY. I won't take Bert Vorhees word for that! Fred's been your right-hand man here for four years and over. Have you ever found him doing a single dishonest thing? I'm sure you haven't, or you wouldn't have kept him. I don't know why you did *anyway!* It was perfectly evident you didn't like him!

[HANNOCK *enters*]

GEORGE [*quickly, before he is fully in the room, and going to the door*]. Hannock, please excuse me. Will you wait one minute in the hall?

HANNOCK [*in the doorway. He looks questioningly at* CICELY. *She nods her head*]. Certainly. [*He goes out*]

GEORGE [*intensely, with his hand on the knob, holding the door closed behind him*]. Listen to me, for God's sake! You're my *sister*, I'm your *brother*. Have I ever showed that I did anything but love you?

CICELY. No, that's why I hoped —

GEORGE [*interrupting, almost beside himself*]. But it can't be!! Won't you trust me, — *won't* you? Let me tell Hannock, without going any deeper into it, that — you realize the marriage can't be; that you and he mustn't meet again! You can say what kind thing you —

CICELY [*flashing*]. Never!! You ought to know me better than to propose any such thing! [*She moves toward the door*]

GEORGE [*with a movement to stop her*]. For your *own* sake, for *his* sake, for *mother's*, for *everybody's* — trust me and —

CICELY [*looking him directly in the face after a second's silence, speaks with the note of finality*]. Listen! I married Fred Hannock this morning!

[GEORGE *looks at her, his eyes dilating. There is a pause*]

GEORGE [*in horror*]. What!!

CICELY. I *married* Fred Hannock half an hour ago. We walked home from the church, separately. He went to his work, and I sent for Eleanor.

GEORGE [*in a voice of terrible but suppressed rage, goes to the door, throws it open with violence, and calls loudly*]. Come in!

HANNOCK *enters quietly, expecting a fight or a scene; he is on the defensive and not in any way frightened*]

GEORGE [*controlling himself by a big effort*]. Is this *true*, what my sister says, that behind my back you've been making love to her —

CICELY [*interrupting him*]. I *never* said that!

GEORGE. That you've repaid all that I've done for you, and all my father did, by taking advantage of our kindness and your position here to run off with —

CICELY [*interrupting*]. I was as anxious to run off as he —

GEORGE. But why wasn't I told? Why do it secretly? [*To* HANNOCK] Why didn't you go about it in the square, open way, unless you *knew* you were doing wrong?

HANNOCK. I knew you'd fight it for all you were worth, and I wasn't going to run any risk of losing her!

CICELY. But you wouldn't have! My brother would have wasted his words then, as much as he is now —

HANNOCK. I was afraid — any fool in my place could see how I've really stood in this family. The only friend I had in the house, or who ever came to it, was *she!* [*With a wave of his hand toward* CICELY]

GEORGE. And that's *why!* Can't you see it? Don't you know the difference between *pity* and *love?*

CICELY. I love *him* and *he knows it;* — *don't* you, Fred?

HANNOCK. Yes, I *do know it!* As well as I know your brother only kept me here because — [*turning to* GEORGE] you were afraid of me!

GEORGE. *Afraid of you?*

HANNOCK. Yes! Do you suppose I didn't guess your father must have told you I was on to him in the bank!

GEORGE. Leave the dead alone! You've got your hands full with the *living!*

HANNOCK. Well, I know my business well enough to realize that once Cicely and I were married, you'd have to make the best of it!

GEORGE. Never! I tell you this marriage is *no* marriage!

CICELY *and* HANNOCK *exclaim in derision*]

CICELY. What's the use of talking any more about it? We aren't getting anywhere! It's *done* — and George has *got* to make the best of it!

GEORGE. I tell you it can't be! Will you take my word, Hannock?

HANNOCK. No! [*Laughs loudly*]

GEORGE. Then, I must go ahead without you! You're dismissed. Do you hear? You're *discharged* from my employ!

HANNOCK [*getting very angry, but controlled*]. You take care!

GEORGE [*continues determinedly*]. You'll leave this house to-day. I'll give you an hour to pack up and get out, and you'll never lay your eyes on this girl again.

CICELY. If he goes now, I'll go with him. I'm his wife!

GEORGE. You *won't go* with him!

HANNOCK. Who'll prevent her?

GEORGE. *I will!*

HANNOCK [*in a blaze*]. Try it!!

CICELY. I've just promised to love, honor and obey him — and if he says to come, I'll go!

GEORGE [*slowly but strongly*]. He *won't say it.*

HANNOCK. I *do* say it! Come on, Cicely! But if you want to come back, you can, because, before I'm through with your brother, I'll get him down on to his knees, begging me to come back, and I won't come *without you!*

GEORGE [*going to the door and holding it open*]. Cicely, will you wait in here with Eleanor for a few minutes?

HANNOCK. Oh, we can speak out before her! I want my wife to know the truth about everything! I don't intend to be the goat in this family any longer!

GEORGE. Well, you can tell Cicely, afterward, what I'm going to tell you, if you like. God keep me from ever having to tell her! [*After a look straight at* HANNOCK, *he looks at* CICELY *very seriously. She responds to his look, impressed by it, and turns her eyes to* HANNOCK. *Neither quite understands, but each feels the depth of seriousness in* GEORGE's *attitude*]

HANNOCK [*doggedly to* CICELY]. Go on.

CICELY [*to* HANNOCK]. I'll wait there for you. Don't do anything without me. I'm so sorry my brother takes this attitude! Don't think it can influence *me*, any more than the disgraceful way you've always been treated here has; *nothing* they say can change *me* toward you, Fred! [*She leaves them*]

GEORGE. I didn't *want* to have to tell you this. I'd rather almost die than have to tell Cicely! I must break faith with father, but of course he'd be the first to ask me to. I must dig out a skeleton that is rotting in its closet — that's the trouble! I must do this, and a lot more, if you make me, and give *you* a couple of blows which will come pretty near to knocking you out, if you've anything at all of a man in you. And every bit of it can be spared *everybody*, if you'll go away and let Cicely — divorce you.

HANNOCK. Well, I *won't!*

GEORGE. Because you won't give up Cicely?

HANNOCK. Exactly. I love her better than anything, — money, comfort, happiness, everything you can think of, — so go on, fire your last gun, and let's get through with it! My wife —

GEORGE [*with excitement*]. She *isn't* your wife! — [HANNOCK *looks at him and sneers.* GEORGE'S *rage at* HANNOCK *is only governed by the tragedy of the whole thing*] Your *marriage wasn't any marriage!*

HANNOCK [*a little frightened, and very angry now*]. What do you mean? —

GEORGE [*looks towards the door where* CICELY *has gone, and, with difficulty, manages to control his voice, as he lowers it*]. Cicely is your *sister!*

HANNOCK [*with a cry*]. Cicely is *what?*

GEORGE. *Your sister!*

HANNOCK [*sees "red", and goes nearly mad*]. You're a God damn liar!

GEORGE. It's the truth —

HANNOCK [*out of his mind, with an insane laugh*]. You're a liar! [CICELY, *alarmed, opens the door to come in.* HANNOCK *shouts at her angrily, in an ugly voice*] You go back! — and shut the door! Do *you hear!* Get *out of this room!*

GEORGE [*strong, but more kind*]. Wait in the room till I call you.

HANNOCK [*brokenly — ugly*]. I don't want her hanging round here now! This is none of her business, none o' hers!

GEORGE [*speaks toward the doorway*]. Eleanor, I don't want Cicely to hear what we're saying.

ELEANOR [*answering*]. Very good. [*She is seen shutting the door*]

HANNOCK [*making guttural sounds, and unable to pronounce the words clearly*]. Hugh — hugh — hah! — You'd play any game to get rid of me,

wouldn't you? But you can't fool me like that!! [*He sits in a chair, mumbling to himself incoherently every other minute, working his hands, his mouth and his chin wet with saliva*]

GEORGE. That day I saw you first, just before he died, my father told me.

HANNOCK. I don't believe it!

GEORGE. He made me promise two things: — that I wouldn't tell you — never! — and that I would look out for you.

HANNOCK. I don't *believe it!*

GEORGE. That's why your mother got her allowance, — and to buy her silence —

HANNOCK. I don't *believe it!* [*Laughing and weeping*]

GEORGE. Now, you see why you must leave here to-day — leave New York! Why there was no marriage this morning and never can be! Why —

HANNOCK [*his mind deranged, rises unevenly; he is loud, partly incoherent and his face is twitching and distorted, his hands clutching and clenching, his whole body wracked and trembling, but still strong, with a nervous madman's strength*]. It's all a *lie* — to separate Cicely from me!

GEORGE [*goes to him and sees the change*]. Hannock!

HANNOCK. I'll never believe it!

GEORGE [*taking him by the shoulder*] Have you gone out of your mind!

HANNOCK. I'll never give her up!

GEORGE. *What!! I tell you, she's your sister!*

HANNOCK. And I say *I don't believe it! I love* her, she *loves* me. I won't give her up!!

GEORGE. *Yes, you will!!*

HANNOCK. *I won't!* Do you think I'd give her up to some other fellow to hold in his arms! For some other man to *love* and *take care of!!* You're crazy! She said if I said come, she'd go with me, and I'll say it!! [*He starts toward the door.* GEORGE *takes hold of him to stop him from calling her*]

GEORGE. Wait! If you don't give her up now, after what I've told you *and leave here* before she comes out of that room, I'll have to do the only thing left, — *tell her!*

HANNOCK [*furious*]. No, you won't! You sha'n't tell her! It isn't *true!* And if it was, by God, she sha'n't know it! It *would separate* us!

GEORGE [*horrified at what this means*]

*alls sternly and with determination].
Cicely!

HANNOCK [*wildly*]. Don't you dare to
ell her that lie!

ELEANOR [*opening the door*]. You
*w*ant Cicely to come in?

GEORGE. Yes.

ELEANOR *turns away from the door,
leaving it open behind her.* CICELY
*appears, and enters, — leaving the
door open*]

HANNOCK. There isn't any lie too
*b*ig for him to make up to separate us!
I'm going! Will you come with me?

CICELY. Of course!

GEORGE. Cicely! Are you strong?
Are you brave? You must hear something *unbelievably terrible!*

HANNOCK [*holding out his hand beg-
gingly*]. Come along, don't listen to
him! [*She makes a movement toward
HANNOCK*]

GEORGE. You *can't!* [*Taking hold
of her*]

CICELY. I *will!* Leave go of me!
[*Struggling desperately*]

GEORGE [*puts his arms about her, and
holds her in his arms — her back to him*].
My poor child, he's your —

[HANNOCK, *without warning, pulls out a
pistol from his hip pocket, and shoots
her dead in* GEORGE'S *arms*]

ELEANOR [*calls, in fright*]. George!!

GEORGE. Cicely! [*He holds her in
his arms, and carries her over to sofa.
Calls brokenly*] Cicely!

[ELEANOR *enters quickly, and goes to them*]

ELEANOR [*in horror as she sees*]. Oh!

GEORGE. Take her.

[ELEANOR *takes* CICELY *tenderly from
him*]

HANNOCK. Now, you nor nobody
else can separate us! [*Lifts the pistol to
his heart to shoot, feeling for the place he
showed in Act I.* GEORGE *springs forward and gets hold of him and the pistol
before he can shoot*]

GEORGE. No! *That's too good for
you!* That's too easy! By God, you've
got to *pay.*

[*Enter* FOOT *in excitement*]

FOOT. Excuse me, sir, I heard —

GEORGE. All right. Telephone for
the police. Is she breathing, Eleanor?
[ELEANOR *shakes her head*] Oh, God!
[*Bowing his head, emotion surges up in

him.* HANNOCK, *in this movement of
weakness, almost frees himself and almost
gets hold of the pistol*]

ELEANOR [*who is watching, cries out in
alarm*]. George! George, be careful!
[GEORGE *pulls himself together too
quickly for him, and prevents* HANNOCK.
FOOT *starts to go.* To FOOT] Help me;
it won't take you a moment!

GEORGE. No! Foot, I know I can
trust you. [*Giving him the pistol*] Keep
this, yourself, and don't let him get out
of the room.

FOOT. Yes, sir. [*Takes the pistol,
and stands before* HANNOCK. GEORGE
goes to CICELY, *and takes her in his arms*]

GEORGE. Poor little woman! little
sister! Why did this have to be! I
wonder if *this* is what they call the sins
of the fathers? [*He carries her out of
the room, Left, followed by* ELEANOR.
HANNOCK, *the moment they are gone,
makes a movement.* FOOT *at once covers
him with the pistol*]

HANNOCK. Give *me* that pistol!

FOOT. No, sir.

HANNOCK. Name your own *price!*

FOOT. Miss Cicely's life back, sir!

HANNOCK. *You're* against me too,
are you! Every one's against *me!*

[GEORGE *comes back*]

GEORGE [*taking the pistol from* FOOT].
Thank you. Now, telephone, and ask
them to be quick, please.

FOOT. Shall I come back, sir?

GEORGE. No, I think this job had
better be mine. [*Looking hard at* HAN-
NOCK]

HANNOCK [*quickly*]. I won't try to
get away, — I give you my word of
honor.

GEORGE. Your word of honor! [*To
FOOT*] When you've telephoned, go to
Miss Vorhees.

FOOT. Yes, sir.

GEORGE. Ask her to keep my mother
and Mrs. Van Vranken from coming
here.

FOOT. Yes, sir. [*Goes out*]

HANNOCK [*makes a move for* GEORGE].
Give me that gun! [*There is a short
struggle.* GEORGE *breaks from* HAN-
NOCK, *and, crossing to the table, lays the
pistol on it.* HANNOCK *makes a tricky
attempt to get to it quickly, but is caught by
GEORGE, who holds him. The following
scene takes place with* GEORGE *keeping
hold of* HANNOCK, *who sometimes struggles and sometimes tries to break, sud-*

denly or craftily, away from GEORGE'S *grip, and at other times remains quiescent*] You're a damn fool! Don't you see it's the easiest way all around for us? I've got to die anyway.

GEORGE. But not that way. That's too easy for you!

HANNOCK. Well, it's easier for you, too, with me out of the way! There's no arrest, no trial, no scandal! Nobody'll know I was her brother; nobody'll know about your father! Think what it'll save your mother! Think what it'll save you! Think what it'll save everybody!

GEORGE. Including *you*, — and you don't deserve to be saved *anything!*

HANNOCK. Still, even *I* am your own blood! For God's sake, go on, let me! All you have to do is to turn your back a minute — it won't take *two!* Please! Think of *her* — what it'll save her memory!

GEORGE. No!

HANNOCK. Then for your mother's sake! How can *she* go through a trial and all *that* means!

GEORGE. Your work in the next room is worse than any trial for her to bear.

HANNOCK. Think of yourself, of the election! What will my trial do to your election?

GEORGE. I'm not thinking of my election now, — I'm thinking of that little, still figure lying in the next room!

HANNOCK [*emotionally, almost crying*]. There'd have been two, if you hadn't stopped me! For the love of God, give me the gun —

GEORGE. No! *You've got to sit in the chair!*

HANNOCK [*with an ugly change*]. Well, you'll get *your* punishment, too, — don't you forget that!! I know how eaten up with ambition you are! And every single wish nearest to your heart will die just as dead as I do, if you let me go to trial!

GEORGE. What do you think you're doing?

HANNOCK. If I have to pay *my* price, I'll make you pay *yours*. And you'll be dead, publicly and politically, before I go into the condemned cell.

GEORGE. You're crazy, and that's the only thing that may save you, if *Matteawan* is salvation!

HANNOCK. I knew your father was dishonest, and I told him that day; I guess it killed him. And I've watched you, and tempted you, and helped you go on with his methods! Every bit of this will come out in my trial. I'll get a clever enough lawyer to manage *that*. And you'll lose, not only your ambition, but your position in the world, and one more thing besides, — *the woman you're in love with!* For that kind of a high-browed moral crank wouldn't stand for one half *you* stand for in business, and when she finds out how deceived she's been in you, if I know human nature, she won't have that much love left for you — [*Snapping his fingers*] And *she'll find out*, and they'll *all know!* — *your* party and the *other* party! That election'll be a hell of a walkover for the other side!

[ELEANOR *enters*]

GEORGE. What is it, Eleanor? I don't want you here.

HANNOCK [*half aside, with a half jeer, and a half smile*]. Hah!

ELEANOR. Excuse me. Bert wants you on the telephone. Shall I answer?

GEORGE. Yes, please. [HANNOCK *begins to steal behind, toward the pistol*] Does mother know?

ELEANOR. Yes, and she's very plucky. But I'm surprised how full she is of the desire for revenge! [GEORGE *turns and sees* HANNOCK, *and quickly but quietly intercepts him, and stands with his hand on the pistol*] She wants Hannock punished! She's watching for the police!

GEORGE. They ought to be here soon, now.

ELEANOR. Teresa is with me. She feels it terribly. [*Goes out*]

HANNOCK. Do you realize how completely you'll be done for, if you don't let me do it? The New Brunswick business isn't a patch on some of your other deals I know about!

GEORGE. I've never done a thing in business that couldn't stand the strictest overhauling.

HANNOCK. If you believe that, you're bigger fool than I thought! *I'd* rather be a *crook* than a *fool*, any day! Quick, before she comes from the telephone! Turn your back; walk to the door there! It's easily explained; — you're not to blame!

GEORGE. *No!*

HANNOCK [*hysterically*]. If you *don't*, I'll explain now, *before her*, where and how your stand in business is rotten, and your dealings crooked, — and you *can begin to take* your medicine!

GEORGE. I dare you!

[ELEANOR *comes back*]

ELEANOR. Bert wants me to tell you it's settled, — your nomination — and he adds, "*good luck!*"

GEORGE. Did you tell him about —?

ELEANOR. No — I — I told him to come here as soon as he could.

GEORGE. All right.

[ELEANOR *starts to go*]

HANNOCK [*excitedly*]. Wait a minute, Miss Vorhees!

GEORGE. No, Eleanor, go back, please!

HANNOCK [*quickly*]. This man, who thinks he has it on me, is afraid to have you hear the truth about himself. That's why he don't want you to stay.

GEORGE [*to* ELEANOR]. Stay!

HANNOCK. You think George Rand stands for honesty, and the square deal in the business world! Well, he does, but *it's a lie!* And if he wasn't paying up to the hilt — East, West, North and South — to protect himself, everybody in this country would know what we, on the inside, do!

ELEANOR. George, unless you'd really rather I stayed, I don't want to hear what he has to say about you.

HANNOCK [*quickly*]. I don't blame you for not wanting to hear about the suicide of Henry Bodes! [*To* GEORGE] Do you know who killed Bodes? *You did!*

GEORGE. The man's out of his mind still, Eleanor.

HANNOCK. Am I? Bodes was on to your Copper Pit scheme, and *saw it succeed* — so he tried one like it, and it failed!

GEORGE. Was that *my* fault?

HANNOCK. Yes! It was your example set him on, and do you think your scheme was legitimate?

GEORGE. So help me God, I *do!*

HANNOCK. Then why, when it failed, did Bodes kill himself? He wasn't *broke!* It wasn't *money* that drove him to it! It was *shame*, because his scheme was *crooked*, just as yours was. Success covered it, but failure showed it up.

ELEANOR. Don't ask me to listen to this any longer! [*She goes out.* GEORGE *watches her go, but* HANNOCK *only gives a quick glance after her*]

HANNOCK. Bodes was one of your sweet, weak family men, who can't stand on disgrace!

GEORGE. Disgrace!!

HANNOCK. Ask Vorhees, — and about the New Brunswick case! And get him to *tell you the truth!*

GEORGE [*half to himself*]. Good God! If there is something in all this?

HANNOCK. What are you paying Elmer Caston ten thousand a year for?

GEORGE. For his legal services!

HANNOCK. Rot! The firm's never used him —

GEORGE. But keeping him on our pay list keeps him from working against us.

HANNOCK. Hush money!

GEORGE. No!

HANNOCK. *Why* were all these Amsterdam tunnel bonds made over to Parker Jennings?

GEORGE. He helped us get the bill passed!

HANNOCK. *Ask Vorhees* if he wouldn't put that down in the expense-book under the name of Blackmail.

GEORGE. No!

HANNOCK. Ask Vorhees!

GEORGE. You can't alter the diplomacy of the business world — calling it by ugly names.

HANNOCK. No, I can't, but *Roosevelt did!*

GEORGE. If you think I'm afraid of what you —

HANNOCK. Oh, come! Stop bluffing! If you don't realize I know what I'm talking about, I'll go on. I know at least *five* separate deals of yours so damned crooked, if any *one* of them were made public you'd be out of business over night, and out of the country, if you know your job. [*He waits. No answer.* GEORGE *is weighing the truth or the lie of what he is saying. He evidently sees some truth in it*] And I've got proof of what I say! Every proof! I've got copies of letters and telegrams, when I couldn't get the originals. I've got shorthand reports of private telephone conversations. I've got data enough for fifty trials, if it should come to that. I've been preparing for a deal of my own *with you* ever since I came to you! Only — God! [*He is moved as he thinks of* CICELY] I didn't think it would be trying to get rid of my life! I'd planned to make you finance a big game for me!

GEORGE. If what you say is true — and I don't know but what some of it may be, — then it's good-by to everything for me, and it'll be about all I'm worth having come to me.

HANNOCK. That's it! Even Middleburg'll be too small for you, if I show you up! But you know what'll shut my lips tight! Gimme the gun —

GEORGE [*quickly*]. No.

HANNOCK [*pleadingly*]. You've *everything* to get, and *nothing* to lose by it!

GEORGE. Yes, I have something to lose! — what rag of honor I've got left!

HANNOCK. No! Think a minute — if *I'm* out of the way? There's no real scandal — your father's old story — *our* father's old story — isn't even known by *your mother*. I shot Cicely, and killed myself, — it's an ordinary story. I was drunk or crazy — she wouldn't have me. Any story you want to make up, and there'll not be a murmur against Cicely, then! But can you see the papers if the *real story comes out!!* All over this country, and all the countries, it'll be telegraphed and pictured and revelled in. It'll even get into the cinematograph shows in Europe — with some low down girl masquerading as Cicely.

GEORGE. Stop! *Stop!*

HANNOCK. And the story will come out, if I go to trial. I'll stop at nothing to take it out of you. Whether you believe or not what I say about your business methods, you take my word for it, my arrest will put a quietus on your election, and *finish you*, not only in a political career, but any old career at all!

GEORGE. What a finish! What a finish of all I hoped to do and be!

HANNOCK. And — you'll lose the woman who's just left this room. Whether all *her brother's* high-browed talk is bunkum or not, even *I* know *hers* is serious; and if she finds you've deceived her all the time, that your high ideals are *fake* —!

GEORGE [*interrupts, crying, in an agony, half to himself*]. They're not! They're not! God knows, nobody's been more deceived in me than I've been myself!

HANNOCK. Well, you know she won't stand for it. A girl like — her heart couldn't stomach it! Go on, bring me to trial and lose everything you've banked on for a career! Lose your business standing, lose your best friends, lose the woman you want, and raise the rottenest scandal for your family, for your mother, to bear, and your little sister's memory to go foul under! Do

it all, and be damned to you!! [*He falls on his knees with exhaustion*]

GEORGE. My God, how can I?

HANNOCK [*whining, pleading*]. All you have to do, to save every mother's son of us, is to let me do what the law'll do anyway! Leave that pistol where I can get it, and walk half a dozen steps away. That's all you need do! [*He sees* GEORGE *hesitate*] It's *all* or nothing for you!! It's the finish or the beginning! Are you ready and willing to be down and out, and go through the hell my living'll mean for you? [*He sees* GEORGE *weaken more*] You'll be Governor! Sure, you'll marry Miss Vorhees! You'll find all the proofs I told you about in my safty deposit box at the Manhattan. And there'll be only *white* flowers and pity on the new little grave! It'll be your *chance* to prove by the future that you were made of the right stuff at heart, after all!

[GEORGE *puts down the pistol not far from* HANNOCK'S *reach, and starts to walk away with a set face — suffering.* HANNOCK *makes a slow, silent step towards the pistol, but, before he can get it,* GEORGE *turns and recovers it, with a terrific revulsion of feeling. He seizes the pistol and throws it through the big glass window*]

GEORGE. No! I haven't the right! You must take your punishment as it comes, and I *must take mine!* [*He suddenly breaks down; tears fill his throat and pour from his eyes.* HANNOCK *is crouching and drivelling on the floor*] This is my *only chance to show I can be on the level!* That I *can be straight*, when it's plain what *is* the right thing to do! God help me *do it!*

[*The door opens and a* POLICEMAN *enters with* FOOT, *as*

THE CURTAIN FALLS

ACT III

SCENE. — *Same room as Act II, only seen from another point of view. The mantel is now Right and the windows Back. Left is the wall not seen before. Later the same day.* VORHEES *and* GEORGE *are seated at the desk before a mass of business papers. There is a tall whiskey-and-soda glass, nearly empty, and a plate with the remnants of some sandwiches, beside* GEORGE. *The shades of the windows are drawn, but it is still daylight.* GEORGE *looks crushed, mentally and physically, but is calm and immovable.* VORHEES *looks stern and disappointed. There is a pause; neither men move.*

GEORGE. That's all? [VORHEES *nods his head.* GEORGE *drinks, and gathers up the papers*] What's to be done with these papers? Are they Hannock's or mine?

VORHEES. They have only to do with *your* affairs. Hannock hadn't any right to them! In any case, you don't pretend to deny anything these papers prove. Destroy them!

GEORGE. But — [*Getting up all the papers, except some of his own, which he separates and leaves on the desk*]

VORHEES. I doubt if, when it comes to the point, Hannock will go into all this business! He will have had months to cool down, and his hands will be full enough. [*He gives* GEORGE *a couple of papers he has had in his hand, and motions to the fireplace*] Here! don't wash your dirty linen; *burn* it!

[GEORGE *goes to the fireplace with a mass of papers, and burns them*]

GEORGE [*as the papers burn*]. Has Eleanor gone home?

VORHEES. Yes, but she promised your mother to come back later and stop over-night with her.

GEORGE. I wonder if she'd be willing to see me?

VORHEES. Yes, because I'm sure she didn't believe Hannock.

GEORGE. Tess can stay with mother. There'll be no need of her pretending to go back to Don, now.

VORHEES. *Pretending!*

GEORGE. Yes. That's something else I did, — persuaded Tess to make Don believe she'd come back in accordance with his conditions. But it was agreed between us she was to break her word to him, *after the election!* [*He burns his last batch of papers*]

VORHEES. It's a pity you can't burn that, too! I'd have staked my reputation on your being absolutely on the level! How I have been taken in by you!

GEORGE. I know, it sounds ridiculous, and I don't expect you to understand it; but I've been taken in by myself, too! Shall I write my withdrawal

from the nomination, or will you take a verbal message?

VORHEES. Write it. It will make less for me to say by way of explanation. [GEORGE *goes to the desk and writes*] I'm sorry, I'm sorry, George. I *know* what it means to you!

GEORGE. Somehow now, it doesn't seem so much, after all; I suppose that's Cicely — poor little girl — poor little girl, — and — Eleanor. [*He adds the last, almost in a whisper*]

VORHEES. You're a *young* man, George! You've got a good chance yet to make good, and it's all up to you!

GEORGE. I know that —

VORHEES. I suppose you won't want to go back to Middleburg?

GEORGE. No! No!! For everybody's sake! But, *would it have* been wrong — leave *me out of it*, — to have saved *father's memory*, to have saved mother — could I have let him do it?

VORHEES. You know you couldn't!

GEORGE. Yes, and anyway, I didn't. Why can't I forget it!

VORHEES. Oh, it'll be many a day before you *deserve* to forget it!

GEORGE. But, will *you* ever have any confidence in me? Can any one ever believe in me again? [*Buries his face in his hands, and groans*]

VORHEES. *I can.* Whether I *do* or not, is entirely up to you.

GEORGE. You're sure of that?

VORHEES [*takes his hand and shakes it*]. Sure.

GEORGE. And Eleanor?

VORHEES. Well — there's no use in my lying about it. If I know her, you must give up all idea of marrying her. Eleanor's husband must be a man she can *look up* to. That's a necessity of her nature — she can't help it. But I *do* believe she'll *help you* with *her friendship*. If you don't go back to Middleburg, where will you go?

GEORGE. Here! I stay *right here!*

VORHEES [*surprised*]. Here! It'll be *hard*.

GEORGE. I suppose it will!

VORHEES. How will you start?

GEORGE. First, make a clean breast to my partners! Give back all the money I've made in ways which you've proved to me are illegal. Publish every form of graft I've benefited by, for the sake of future protection! Resign from all —

VORHEES. It's gigantic! It's colossal! *Can* you *do* it?

GEORGE [*simply*]. I can try. I'm going to have a go at it, anyway!

VORHEES. The Press! Among your professional associates — here and all over the State — it'll be hell for you to go through!

GEORGE. I know it! I know it! But to get back where I want to be — if I ever can! I've got to fight it out right here, and make good *here*, or not at all. I don't care what it costs me!

TERESA [*opening the door*]. May I come in?

GEORGE. Yes, come in, Tess. Where's mother?

TERESA. She's locked herself in her room. She's *turned against me* in the most extraordinary manner! Says my influence over Cicely is at the bottom of everything! [*She begins to cry*] She goes so far as to say, if I'd behaved like a decent woman, she doesn't believe this would have happened! I didn't care what other people believe of me, but this I didn't bargain for! I have been unfaithful to Don in my heart — and in my mind, perhaps, — but that's all —

GEORGE. I always felt it, Tess!

TERESA. Can't you persuade mother?

GEORGE. *Bert could*, because he represents the outside world.

TERESA. But you know Bert. He wouldn't persuade her, unless he believed in me himself.

VORHEES. That's true, and I'll go talk with her now, if Mrs. Rand will see me. [*He goes toward door*]

TERESA [*deeply moved, and grateful*]. *Thank* you!

VORHEES. That's all right. [*He goes out*]

TERESA. George, I don't know — but everything, even Jimmy Cairns, seems so little now, in comparison with *Cicely — dead*, — the bottom fallen out of everything!

GEORGE. Even worse than that, for me. I've given up the nomination.

TERESA. I'm sorry! Did Bert feel you had to?

GEORGE. No more than I did. You won't have to act a lie for me after all, Tess.

TERESA. I'm glad! I know, if Eleanor Vorhees knew I was doing it —

GEORGE. She's going to know it, — and that I'm a liar! She's going to know much worse things than that! Everybody's going to know them, I guess! Father was a crook in business,

— that's the ugly, unvarnished fact, — and I've been a worse one! But I'd rather she'd learn these things from me, — what Hannock hasn't already told her — rather than she learned them outside.

TERESA. But George! George!! Don't you realize you'll lose her?

GEORGE. Well, I've lost everything else, except —

TERESA. Except what?

GEORGE. Except that! After all, I don't believe, way down at the bottom, I'm not fundamentally straight! I mean to give myself, all by myself, a chance to prove it! I know there are lots of "good men" who are born crooks. I want to see if I'm not a crook who was born good!

[VORHEES *reënters*]

VORHEES. It's all right. They've told Mrs. Rand she can go in and see Cicely now, and she wants you to go with her.

TERESA [*holds his hand in her two, for a moment*]. Thank you! [*She goes out*]

VORHEES. And give me that paper you wrote. The sooner we get that off our hands, the better. [GEORGE *takes up the paper and, reading it over to himself, goes slowly to* VORHEES, *and gives it to him*]

VORHEES. Too bad, old man, too bad! But it *can't* be helped.

GEORGE. I know! [VORHEES *starts to go*] Bert, — Eleanor hasn't come yet?

VORHEES. No. Are you sure you want to see her, or shall I first —

GEORGE. No, leave it to me! I'd rather. I don't want a loophole, anywhere, for her thinking me a coward. I want to make a clean breast of it all! That's what I'm after, — a clean breast, no matter what the doing it costs me!

VORHEES. You're right. [*About to go*]

[*Enter* FOOT]

FOOT. A gentleman from a newspaper, sir.

GEORGE. Will you see him, Bert?

VORHEES. Yes. [*To* FOOT] You refer all the reporters to me. You know my address?

FOOT. Yes, sir.

VORHEES [*to* FOOT]. Say no one here can be seen. [*To* GEORGE] I'll see you early to-morrow.

GEORGE. Thank you. I'd like your

help in laying out a plan of action. Of course I shan't do anything till after — [*He hesitates, and raises his head and eyes to upstairs*]

VORHEES. I wouldn't. [*Goes out*]

[FOOT *exits.* GEORGE *stands alone in the room, a picture of utter dejection, of ruin and sorrow, but with a bulldog look all the while, — the look of a man who is licked, beaten, but not dead yet. He stands immovable almost — in complete silence. Slowly and softly, the door opens.* VAN VRANKEN *looks in. He speaks in a sullen, hushed, and somewhat awed voice. He is pale; all evidence of drinking and excitement are gone*]

VAN VRANKEN. George?

GEORGE [*in a monotonous voice*]. Hello, Don — you know?

VAN VRANKEN. I just heard. It's *true?* [GEORGE, *with a set face and stern lips, nods his head firmly, still standing.* VAN VRANKEN *collapses in a chair*] God! Poor Cicely!

GEORGE. Tough, isn't it? [*With a great sigh*]

VAN VRANKEN. I was having an awful time, George, with Mrs. Judly. She was giving it to me good for being willing to patch it up, temporarily, with Tess! She *didn't care about you!* I've come to the conclusion she don't care about anybody, anyway, but herself. Her brother telephoned it from his Club, and *she* — [*his anger rises*] had the rottenness to say she believed there was something between Hannock and Cicely. That was more than I could stand for! God knows I'm as bad as they make them, but, with that little girl dead like that — to think such a thing, let alone say it — I don't know! — It took it out of me, somehow! It didn't seem to me it was the time to have a low quarrel between two people like us! It made us seem so beastly small! Death's such an awful — such a big — I suppose I'll feel differently to-morrow — but to-day — now — George, I *couldn't* stand for it! She kicked me out, and I give you my word of honor I'm glad she did!

GEORGE [*not deeply impressed, but civil*]. As you say, you'll feel differently to-morrow.

VAN VRANKEN. Very likely! Still, I've got these few decent hours, anyway, to put on your sister's grave. [*A pause.* GEORGE *sits*]

GEORGE. I've given up running for governor.

VAN VRANKEN [*surprised*]. Because —?

GEORGE. No. You'll hear all the reasons soon enough. The point for the moment is, you and Tess needn't fake any further — living together.

VAN VRANKEN [*thoughtfully*]. I see. [*After a pause*] George —?

GEORGE. What?

VAN VRANKEN. Could I see Cicely?

GEORGE [*hesitating*]. Tess is there.

VAN VRANKEN [*after a moment*]. Then, perhaps I'd better not go —?

GEORGE. I think I *would*, if I were you.

[VAN VRANKEN *looks at* GEORGE *questioningly.* TERESA *enters*]

TERESA [*quietly*]. Don — [*Her voice fills; she turns aside, and hastily wipes her eyes*]

VAN VRANKEN [*moved*]. I was going upstairs.

TERESA. Not now! Mother and I have just left. They've come to — [*She stops, and again turns aside*]

VAN VRANKEN. Where are the children?

TERESA. Home!

VAN VRANKEN. "Home"? [*Very meaningly*]

TERESA. At the house.

VAN VRANKEN. Oh, Tess! — I'm — I'm not fit to take care of them! You'd better take them both, Tess, but let me see them off and on —

TERESA. I'm going back now with you, Don.

VAN VRANKEN. You needn't. I take it all back, Tess. You can have your own way entirely. Leave Mrs. Judly out of it, — that's all I'll ask. Outside that, I'll fix it easy for you.

TERESA. Thank you, Don, [*after a second's pause*] but, if you don't mind, I'd rather go back with you for the present, anyway. It seems to me, between us, we've pretty well spoiled everything except — well, — perhaps, in thinking of the children's happiness we might find something for ourselves! What do you say?

VAN VRANKEN. It's worth a try — so long as you're willing!

[*Enter* MRS. RAND *in a flurry*]

MRS. RAND. Has any one thought to send for a dressmaker? [*Nobody answers*] Did *you* think of it, Teresa?

TERESA. No, I'm afraid I didn't.

MRS. RAND [*her eyes filling*]. I haven't the remotest idea what's the thing to wear! In Middleburg, I'd have known, — but here, I'm always wrong! If I'd had my way, I'd never have taken off my crepe veil for your father, and now *I wish I hadn't!* [*She sees* DON] Oh! I didn't see you, Don. Have you come to beg Tess's pardon? Has this terrible thing reformed you?

VAN VRANKEN. I don't know, mother, how much reform is possible, but I came to tell Tess I'm ashamed — [*He and* TERESA *exchange a look of almost sympathy, — at least, all antagonism has gone from them*]

MRS. RAND. I confess, if I were Tess I could never forgive you! *Her father* spoiled me for that sort of thing!

GEORGE. Tess isn't thinking now only of herself.

MRS. RAND. Oh, why did we ever come here! That was the first and *great mistake!* I haven't had a happy moment since I left their father's and my old home!

TERESA. Mother! Mother!!

MRS. RAND. It's the truth, — I haven't! I've never been anything, in New York, but a fizzle! I've been snubbed right and left by the people I wanted to know! I'm lonesome for my church, and if I died I wouldn't have a handful of people at my funeral!

GEORGE. But you're going to *live*, mother, and you'll see we'll make you happy yet!

MRS. RAND. Not here! You can't do it yourself! Bert says you have given up running for governor, and Tess says everything's off between you and Eleanor. I don't have to be told how disappointed and unhappy you are, and Tess's made a miserable mess of it! And now, Cicely, the baby of you all! — killed, like this! [*She breaks down into hysterical sobbing*] It's more than I can bear! I tell you, children, I can't bear it! And it's all thanks to coming *here!!* This is what we get for not doing what your father wished. Why didn't we stay home? I amounted to something there. I had as much sense as my neighbors. I could hold my own! Here, I've been made to understand I was such a nonentity — that I've grown actually to be the fool they believe me! Oh, what the City has done for the whole of us!

TERESA. Yes, you're right, mother.

I was happy too, till I came here. It was the City that taught me to make the worst of things, instead of the best of them.

GEORGE [*gently*]. No, Tess — let's be honest with ourselves to-day. After all, it's our own fault —

VAN VRANKEN. I agree with Tess! She and I, in a small town, would have been happy always! I'd not have been tempted like I am here — I couldn't have had the chances —

GEORGE [*rising and speaking with the fulness of conviction*]. *No!* You're all wrong! Don't blame the City. It's not her fault! It's our own! What the City does is to bring out what's strongest in us. If at heart we're good, the good in us will win! If the bad is strongest, God help us! Don't blame the City! *She* gives the man his opportunity; it is up to *him* what he makes of it! A man can live in a small town all his life, and deceive the whole place and *himself* into thinking he's got all the virtues, when at heart he's a hypocrite! But the village gives him no chance to find it out, to prove it to his fellows — the small town is too easy! *But the City!!!* A man goes to the gates of the City and knocks! — New York or Chicago, Boston or San Francisco, no matter *what* city so long as it's big, and busy, and selfish, and self-centred. And she comes to her gates and takes him in, and she stands him in the middle of her market place — where Wall Street and Herald Square and Fifth Avenue and the Bowery, and Harlem, and Forty-second Street all meet, and there she strips him naked of all his disguises — and all his hypocrisies, — and she paints his ambition on her fences, and lights up her skyscrapers with it! — what *he wants* to be and *what he thinks he is!* — and then she says to him, Make good if you can, or to Hell with you! And what is in him comes out to clothe his nakedness, and to the City he can't lie! *I know*, because *I tried!* [*A short pause*]

[FOOT *enters*]

FOOT. Miss Vorhees.

GEORGE. Ask her to come in here.

[TERESA *rises quickly*]

TERESA. Don, I think —

VAN VRANKEN. I've a taxi outside.

MRS. RAND. All this time, and that clock going on every minute!

TERESA [*to* MRS. RAND]. Mother, if you want to see us after dinner, telephone. [*Kisses her*]

MRS. RAND. What about our clothes?

TERESA. I'll attend to everything in the morning. [TERESA *and* DON *go out together*]

MRS. RAND. I think I'd rather be alone with you, George, to-night, if the things are off between you and Eleanor. At a time like this, there is no excuse for her going back on you —

GEORGE. Hush, mother! You don't understand. She has every excuse. I'll tell you about it afterward.

MRS. RAND. No, tell her for me not to stop. I wanted her, because I thought she loved you — and was to be one of us — that's all! [*Enter* ELEANOR] Thank you for coming back, Eleanor, but good night. George will explain. [*She goes out*]

ELEANOR. What is the matter with your mother? and Teresa? And Bert seemed strange, too, when I met him outside. What have I done?

GEORGE. Nothing, Eleanor.

ELEANOR [*realizing what it may mean*]. They think I believed what Hannock said? That anything he would say against *you* could for *one* moment mean anything to *me!*

GEORGE. You didn't believe Hannock?

ELEANOR. Not for one second! That's why I left the room.

GEORGE. You'd better have stayed.

ELEANOR. Why?

GEORGE. Because he told the truth!

ELEANOR. How do you mean?

GEORGE. Everything he told me here, this afternoon, was true.

ELEANOR. Not when *I* was here! When I was here, he was calling you a thief, and a cheat, and a liar!

GEORGE. He was right!

ELEANOR. No! I don't understand you!

GEORGE. Your brother understands — and I've withdrawn my name from the nomination! I'm giving up all the things it seemed to me I wanted most, — and *you*, most of all, Eleanor! I thought I minded losing the others, but in comparison with what I feel now!!! *You loved* me because I was honest!

ELEANOR. Not *because*, — but, of course, if you were not *honest* —

GEORGE. Well, I'm not — I'm *not!*

ELEANOR. *You are!* I know you are!

GEORGE. No! I've lied and tricked and cheated in business, and I've got to pay for it!

ELEANOR. And all this you did *deliberately?*

GEORGE. The only excuse I have, if you can call it an excuse, is that I didn't realize what I was doing! I did what others I had been taught to respect, to pattern on, did before me, — what others were doing around me! I accepted cheating for business diplomacy. I explained lying as the commercial code! I looked on stealing as legitimate borrowing! But I was a grown man, and in possession of my senses, and I had no real excuse! Eleanor, I've been a *business "crook"*, in a big way, perhaps, but still a *"crook"*, and I'm not good enough for *you!* [*A pause*]

ELEANOR. What are you going to do?

GEORGE. Give up all the positions I haven't any right to fill. Pay back interest I hadn't any right to get, and money I hadn't any right to use! Give up principal I gained on somebody else's risk than my own! Begin all over again at the bottom, but on the *level*, and climb, only if I can do it on the square!

ELEANOR. I understand! I understand it all, now! You've done wrong?

GEORGE. Yes.

ELEANOR. Oh, so wrong, but you're owning all up, and *giving* all up!

GEORGE. Yes.

ELEANOR. You aren't being pressed to?

GEORGE. Of course I could fight it, but what's the use? *It's true!* Now *I realize that*, I can't own up fast enough! I can't begin over again soon enough! I can't eat or sleep or take a long breath even, till I'm on the level again with myself. Even at the price of *you!* But I'll make you believe in me again, Eleanor, — you'll see, if we live long enough!

ELEANOR. We don't have to live *any longer* for that.

GEORGE. In what way?

ELEANOR. The man who has done wrong, and can own it up, — face life all over again empty-handed, emptying his own hands of his own accord, turn his back on everything he counted on and lived for, because it is the right thing to do, and because — leaving the world out of it — he *had to be honest with himself!* — that — George — is the man I look up to ten times more than the one who was *born* good and lived good because he never was tempted to enjoy the spoils of going wrong! It's the man whom it costs something to be good, — that's what makes real character! And to me — [*she goes up to him, and puts her hand on his arm*] you, here, *to-day*, are twice the man you were yesterday! You needed a test, though we didn't know it! And at the same time we found that out, you had to go through it; and thank God, your real self has triumphed! *To-day* you *are* the man I loved yesterday!

GEORGE [*looking away*]. Now, I know what those people mean who say a man gets all the *Hell* that's coming to him *in this world*, — [*looking at her*] — and *all the Heaven, too!*

THE CURTAIN FALLS

THE SCARECROW

(1910)

By Percy MacKaye

PERCY MACKAYE

PERCY MACKAYE graduated from Harvard in 1897. Since then his life has been one continuous devotion to his profession of poet and dramatist. He brought to the theatre the training he had received under Professor Baker, of Harvard; and the influences of his father, Steele MacKaye, whose work in the theatre of his day was of a strikingly pioneer character. It is this pioneer tendency which the father seems to have passed on to his son. For, in the twenty-eight intervening years from Harvard until now, Percy MacKaye has pressed the claims of many new movements, and put some of them into successful execution. The dominant characteristic of him is his complete absorption in each new enterprise; his visioning of the huge possibilities of everything by which his attention is caught. In no way are these various interests isolated, however. Percy MacKaye has never been one to leave these various essayals of his in new fields unattached. He has had a consuming desire to serve the masses, to give to the people a large mold into which they might pour their civic love and pride, and through which they might find an outlet for certain common instincts. It is a curious anomaly — this thirst to serve mankind, and the inability to give expression in terms the masses could understand. Percy MacKaye, as a playwright, has always appealed to me as one who in expression was farthest removed from the crowd. And for that reason, I believe, he has suffered undue isolation in the theatre, however much his plays may have been produced.

If there is a civic consciousness in the theatre to-day, the honor is due to Percy MacKaye. He has preached the gospel in a voice that reflected the fervor of his father, when, in his last days, he preached faith in his Spectatorium for the Chicago World's Fair. I do not believe that his attitude has changed much since the time he wrote "The Civic Theatre" as a plea for the redemption of Leisure. He has always taken his work in the broad sense of being a citizen artist, one ready to make communities conscious of beauty, one eager to open up the rich veins of local inheritance, and show to the masses material at their very doorstep. In review, I recall his communal dramas, his masques and pageant-rituals which gave such an impetus to outdoor pageantry in this country: the Saint-Gaudens Masque-Prologue, "The Canterbury Pilgrims" at Gloucester, "A Masque of Labor" at Pittsburg, "Sanctuary, A Bird Masque", the Civic Masque of "Saint Louis", a Civic Ritual: "The New Citizenship", "Caliban by the Yellow Sands", which called into play all the arts of the theatre in commemoration of Shakespeare. Community singing at Christmas time has received his attention in "The Evergreen Tree"; during the War he contributed a Masque of the Red Cross, entitled "The Roll Call"; and, with Harry Barnhart, he carried over the impulse for community singing which had been trained and directed during the Great War in a so-called dramatic service, "The Will of Song."

These will show that Percy MacKaye has put into practice what he preached so eloquently, if not always clearly. He has wanted the theatre to be the centre of

191

expressive life; around it he has seen in his mind an entire social structure concentrate. To him, art on a national scale of distribution would mean a defter, more sensitive craftsmanship, a better citizenship, a countercurrent to the machine-made world of a pressing industrialism. So far, Mr. MacKaye's persistent pleadings for the theatre to occupy such a community value have not resulted in what he had hoped for. The Government still remains deaf to the suggestion that there be a portfolio of Fine Arts added to the President's Cabinet. While innovation in the theatre itself has come from other directions than those realized by Mr. MacKaye when he wrote his books, "The Playhouse and the Play" and "The Civic Theatre", this does not detract from the claim, however, that, in the uplifting of the theatre from the purely speculative field, Mr. MacKaye did some of the ploughing and a great deal of the planting.

This social fervor has not been without its well-founded historical sense. Too long has the American scene been neglected by the American playwright : I do not mean scene in the local sense but in the historic. It took an Englishman, John Drinkwater, to write plays in the spirit of historical chronicles about Lincoln and Lee. The history of Clyde Fitch in "Nathan Hale" and "André" was a slim thread on which to hang romantic situation not sustained always by fact. Gillette's "Secret Service" and Howard's "Shenandoah" gave the outward excitement of well-known fact, without the substance of character. MacKaye's civic consciousness has run more deeply into history, and whatever may be said of the dramatic value of his "Washington, The Man Who Made Us", his consistent and persistent passion for citizenship, his realization of national background gave a certain distinction to the piece.

The national background prompted him, no doubt, in his choice of "The Scarecrow" for theme, and in the writing of his "Yankee Fantasies." And the work he is now engaged in, after a sojourn among the mountaineers of Kentucky, is simply another phase of an endeavor to discover to ourselves the richness of something worth preservation, worth protecting from the inroads of a benumbing industrialism. The introductory matter to his interesting play, "This Fine-Pretty World", shows how the passing years have deepened MacKaye's passion for serving humanity. It shows, likewise, a beautiful poetic ear and eye, more consistently worked out than in any of his other plays. For here, in the midst of a civilization which antedates, in its temperament, its customs, its dialect, the period of colonization, there dwell Americans of the purest origin. Mr. MacKaye pleads their cause with the same fervor that he has pleaded for all humanity. Seriousness of purpose, however, is delightfully tempered by native humor and human beauty of character that make of this play a document profoundly valuable. The play itself is as worthy of reading as the notes MacKaye and his wife gathered on that trip South, which I trust some day he will be impelled to publish.

The realization of a life devoted to art is uppermost in Mr. MacKaye's mind. The events since his graduation from Harvard crowd in upon him. He writes about these events with a gusto and a picturesqueness that reveal the intense enthusiasm with which he approaches all his work. This work is interpreted, not in personal terms, but in relation to what it will later develop into for others. Just as his Kentucky Mountain experience opened vistas of possibilities for a lost people who have something to contribute to civilization, so, when MacKaye was elected to a fellowship of Poetry by Miami University, Oxford, Ohio, he became all enthusiastic about the relation university life should have to the creative arts. Through his enthusiasm one begins to imagine the world at last quick to the necessity of art. In this respect his has been a unique voice just at a period when the American Theatre needed such a voice to oppose the tide of box-office commercialism.

In a small pamphlet, which is a sketch of his life and a full bibliography of his work, Mr. MacKaye writes thus:

Many changeful vistas of those tasks glimmer in remembrance: Early stage rehearsals of "The Canterbury Pilgrims", with a recalcitrant milk-white donkey, all four legs frozen, budgeless with his burden, the dismayed soubrette *Wife of Bath*. — Midwinter, in the little town of Dublin, N. H.; a man-model against a dusky curtain: Abbott Thayer, the artist-inventor, intent, excited, testing (in 1906!) his new "camouflage" principles to create a stained-glass vision of Charlemange for the Sothern-Marlowe production of my play "Jeanne d'Arc." — The battlefield of Ticonderoga: a raised platform: speeches from President Taft, Secretary Root, Ambassador Jusserand: tourists, farmers, hundreds of up-peering faces, as I read to them of "soldier and saint and sagamore" in my poem of old Champlain. — Opening night of my Greek tragedy in New York (across the street from "The Merry Widow", also having its première): the net scene between *Sappho* and her slave lover *Phaon:* enter from the wings a brindled, unsalaried cat, who slinks between the lovers toward the temple: "Never mind, old fellow", whispers William Vaughn Moody, who sits next me, "it's a tortoise-shell cat!" — Behind the scenes at "The Scarecrow": half a dozen stage-hands furiously puffing corn-cob pipes, to keep the *Devil* supplied with brimstone for *Lord Ravensbane:* one stage-hand horned, and hairy to the waist, to portray the "dummy" in the magic mirror. — The Metropolitan Opera House, crammed to the ceiling: Peary, just returned from the North Pole: the clamorous ovation: a few tingling moments of silence in which to voice that consummation of the centuries in a poem, Governor Hughes introducing me: the thrilling response and its memory.— Again the Metropolitan, and again the *Wife of Bath*, but this time a German singer in my "Canterbury" opera and deKoven's, 1917: From a box Ambassador Gerard has just read President Wilson's proclamation of our entrance into the World War: the German orchestra has just played (for the first time ever) "The Star-Spangled Banner": curtain rises on Third Act: the *Wife of Bath* begins an aria, sways, sings more faintly, falls in a swoon — and is carried offstage (soon after to be interned as a German spy): end of that performance!— Snowy quiet on the lonely hills of Cornish, N. H.: midnight: a lit candle: paper, pencil, and work: a snug wood-fire: a little mouse climbs up the candle, nibbling close to the flame: we eye each other: he wonders: so do I.— Night again: Two hundred thousand human beings massed on a summer hillside near St. Louis, like clover-tops in a moonlit field: across a gleaming of water, the magic world of my Masque in full production: the *Pioneers* and the *Earth-Spirits* shine in their wrestling, half-naked: *Gold* and his followers are drowned: the human clover field rustles, rumbles, roars like a million bee-swarms. — Carnegie Hall, New York: demurer crowds: black coats on the platform: amongst them one white head with hand tilting forward the left ear: Edison receiving his gold medal: he doesn't hear my poem, but discusses it afterward, telling me reminiscently how he and my father had sat up all night, many's the time, discussing each other's inventions.— Dawn in the Harvard Stadium, after an all-night rehearsal of "Caliban": the glow in the forty-foot plaster dome of *Prospero's* visions is a misty rose color; but so also — a misty rose — is that sky there at 3.30 A.M.: the two dome lights commingle: the dawns are blended.

This quoted paragraph recalls other phases of Percy MacKaye's career as poet and dramatist: it suggests his numberless volumes of earnest poetry, his occasional odes, like the one for the Lincoln Centenary. It suggests further his collaboration with the composer, F. S. Converse, in the preparation of such operas as "The Immigrants" and "Sinbad, the Sailor." And deKoven's name must also be linked with his in the folk-opera, "Rip Van Winkle." The mention of his father recalls the biography which the son has prepared of Steele MacKaye, relating him with the innovations which bid fair to-day to revolutionize the form of the theatre.

There is, of course, the side of Percy MacKaye which is purely the playwright, the writer of dramas for the theatre itself. I have selected "The Scarecrow" for use in this collection, fully realizing that it has heretofore been used by two other anthologists. It has not been my desire to repeat the work of others. But "The Scarecrow" is the one play of Mr. MacKaye's which has the dramatic value of the theatre, and the one play which fits in with the spirit and mood of the present collection: since it has the American background, and since, likewise, it is an interesting study of how a dramatist may base a play on the work of another — Hawthorne, in this instance — and make it so completely his own. As a theatregoer, I recall most of MacKaye's dramas as they made their way to the stage. I remember the "Canterbury Pilgrims" as the Coburn Company played it in the open. "Jeanne d'Arc" was spoiled for me by the romance which the poet chose to treat, rather than the historical picturesqueness of facts as they were. "Mater" had about it an irony which nearly brought it to popular success. "A Thousand Years Ago" showed MacKaye's aliveness to new forces in the theatre which one detected in Reinhardt's "Sumûrun", when it was first brought to this country. The two may therefore be regarded as the forerunners of the modern methods as used by Jones, Simonson and Geddes in their decorations and their atmospheric treatment.

There are other plays and other facts which will be noted in the bibliography. They will show MacKaye's community of interest with his fellow-craftsman to be very sincere, very generous. In the introductions to his various published plays he always shows a thoroughness of intent and a complete mastery of the student quality of his material. One reads his "A Garland to Sylvia", and what he has to say about it with a certain sense of its autobiographical value. When the time comes to write a biography of this serious worker in the theatre, whatever strictures the critic may find in the work of MacKaye, he will find the positive merits of the enthusiastic citizen outweighing the aristocratic aloofness of the poet. His rhythms are not those of the crowd. And that is one of the misfortunes of a dramatist so eager to awaken a humanity he loves.

"The Scarecrow" was first produced by the Harvard Dramatic Club, December 7, 1909. It was given its professional première in New York, under the management of Henry B. Harris, with Frank Reicher and Edmund Breese, at the Garrick Theatre, January 17, 1911, and held the boards on the road for two years. In England it was produced at Bristol, November 30, 1914. Under the title of "Die Vogelscheuche", translated by Walther Fischer, it was produced under the direction of Max Reinhardt at the Deutsches Theater, Berlin, with Rudolph Schildkraut. In 1910, it was translated into French, "L'Epouvantail", by Charles-Marie Garnier, of the Sorbonne. The play has likewise been given in Russia. It was published in 1908, in the first edition of which there was a preface, explaining Mr. Mackaye's attitude toward his material.

Noting the differences between the original and his play, Mr. MacKaye emphasizes in this foreword that the *Scarecrow* of Hawthorne "is the imaginative epitome or symbol of human charlatanism, with special emphasis upon the coxcombery of fashionable society." The other characters are thus treated in accord with this idea, the whole story being "a satire upon a restricted artificial phase of society." But to the dramatist, the nature of Hawthorne's theme "is susceptible of an application far less restricted, a development far more universal, than such satire. This wider issue once or twice in his sketch he seems to have touched upon, only immediately to ignore again. Thus, in the very last paragraph, *Mother Rigby* exclaims:

Poor *Feathertop!* I could easily give him another chance and send him forth again to-morrow. But no! *His feelings are too tender — his sensibilities too deep.*' In these words, spoken in irony, Hawthorne ends his narrative with an undeveloped aspect of his theme, which constitutes the starting-point of the conception of my play : the aspect, namely, of the essential *tragedy of the ludicrous.* . . . The scarecrow *Feathertop* is ridiculous as the emblem of a superficial fop; the scarecrow *Ravensbane* is pitiful, as the emblem of human bathos."

This entirely new aspect makes of "The Scarecrow" more than a dramatization, though it gratefully acknowledges Hawthorne as the source.

THE SCARECROW

OR

THE GLASS OF TRUTH

A TRAGEDY OF THE LUDICROUS

By PERCY MACKAYE

𝕿𝖔

MY MOTHER

IN MEMORY OF AUSPICIOUS

"COUNTINGS OF THE CROWS"

BY OLD NEW ENGLAND CORN-FIELDS

DRAMATIS PERSONÆ

JUSTICE GILEAD MERTON

GOODY RICKBY ("*Blacksmith Bess*")

LORD RAVENSBANE ("*Marquis of Oxford, Baron of Wittenberg, Elector of Worms, and Count of Cordova*"), *their hypothetical son*

DICKON, *a Yankee improvisation of the Prince of Darkness*

RACHEL MERTON, *niece of the Justice*

MISTRESS CYNTHIA MERTON, *sister of the Justice*

RICHARD TALBOT, *Esquire, betrothed to Rachel*

SIR CHARLES REDDINGTON, *Lieutenant Governor*

MISTRESS REDDINGTON ⎱ *his daughters*
AMELIA REDDINGTON ⎰

CAPTAIN BUGBY, *the Governor's Secretary*

MINISTER DODGE

MISTRESS DODGE, *his wife*

REV. MASTER RAND, *of Harvard College*

REV. MASTER TODD, *of Harvard College*

MICAH, *a servant of the Justice*

TIME.   *Late Seventeenth Century*

PLACE.   *A town in Massachusetts*

THE SCARECROW

ACT I

The interior of a blacksmith shop. Right centre, a forge. Left, a loft, from which are hanging dried cornstalks, hay, and the yellow ears of cattle-corn. Back centre, a wide double door, closed when the curtain rises. Through this door — when later it is opened — is visible a New England landscape in the late springtime: a distant wood; stone walls, high elms, a well-sweep; and, in the near fore-ground, a ploughed field, from which the green shoots of early corn are just appearing. The blackened walls of the shop are covered with a miscel-laneous collection of old iron, horse-shoes, cart wheels, etc., the usual ap-purtenances of a smithy. In the right-hand corner, however, is an array of things quite out of keep-ing with the shop proper: musical instruments, puppets, tall clocks, and fantastical junk. Conspicuous amongst these articles is a large stand-ing mirror, framed grotesquely in old gold and curtained by a dull stuff, embroidered with peaked caps and crescent moons.

Just before the scene opens, a hammer is heard ringing briskly upon steel. As the curtain rises there is discov-ered, standing at the anvil in the flickering light of a bright flame from the forge, a woman — powerful, ruddy, proud with a certain masterful beauty, white-haired as though pre-maturely, bare-armed to the elbows, clad in a dark skirt (above her ankles), a loose blouse, open at the throat; a leathern apron and a workman's cap. The woman is GOODY RICKBY. *On the anvil she is shaping a piece of iron. Beside her stands a frame-work of iron formed like the ribs and backbone of a man. For a few moments she continues to ply her hammer, amid a shower of sparks,* till suddenly the flame on the forge dies down.

GOODY RICKBY. Dickon! More flame.

A VOICE [*above her*]. Yea, Goody.

[*The flame in the forge spurts up high and suddenly*]

GOODY RICKBY. Nay, not so fierce.

THE VOICE [*at her side*]. Votre par-don, madame. [*The flame subsides*] Is that better?

GOODY RICKBY. That will do. [*With her tongs, she thrusts the iron into the flame; it turns white-hot*] Quick work; nothing like brimstone for the smithy trade. [*At the anvil, she begins to weld the iron rib on to the framework*] There, my beauty! We'll make a stout set of ribs for you. I'll see to it this year that I have a scarecrow can outstand all the nor'easters that blow. I've no notion to lose my corn-crop this summer. [*Outside, the faint cawings of crows are heard. Putting down her tongs and hammer,* GOODY RICKBY *strides to the double door, and flinging it wide open, lets in the gray light of dawn. She looks out over the fields and shakes her fist*] So, ye're up before me and the sun, are ye? [*Squinting against the light*] There's one! Nay, two. Aha!
One for sorrow,
Two for mirth —
Good! This time we'll have the laugh on our side. [*She returns to the forge, where again the fire has died out*] Dickon! Fire! Come, come, where be thy wits?

THE VOICE [*sleepy from the forge*]. 'Tis early, dame.

GOODY RICKBY. The more need — [*Takes up her tongs*]

THE VOICE [*screams*]. Ow!

GOODY RICKBY. Ha! Have I got thee? [*From the blackness of the forge she pulls out with her tongs, by the right ear, the figure of a devil, horned and tailed. In general aspect, though he resembles a mediæval familiar demon, yet the suggestions of a goatish beard, a shrewdly humorous smile, and (when he speaks) the slightest of nasal drawls, remotely simulate a species of Yankee rustic.* GOODY RICKBY *substitutes her fingers for the tongs]* Now, Dickon!

DICKON. *Deus!* I haven't been nabbed like that since St. Dunstan tweaked my nose. Well, sweet Goody?

GOODY RICKBY. The bellows!

DICKON *[going slowly to the forge]*. Why, 'tis hardly dawn yet. Honest folks are still abed. It makes a long day.

GOODY RICKBY *[working, while* DICKON *plies the bellows]*. Aye, for your black pets, the crows, to work in. That's why I'm at it early. You heard 'em. We must have this scarecrow of ours out in the field at his post before sunrise. *[Finishing]* So, there! Now, Dickon boy, I want that you should —

DICKON *[whipping out a note-book and writing]*. Wait! Another one! "I want that you should —"

GOODY RICKBY. What's that you're writing?

DICKON. The phrase, Goody dear; the construction. Your New England dialect is hard for a poor cosmopolitan devil. What with *ut* clauses in English and Latinized subjunctives — You want that I should — Well?

GOODY RICKBY. Make a masterpiece. I've made the frame strong, so as to stand the weather; *you* must make the body lifelike so as to fool the crows. Last year I stuck up a poor sham and after a day they saw through it. This time, we must make 'em think it's a real human crittur.

DICKON. To fool the philosophers is my specialty, but the crows — hm!

GOODY RICKBY. Pooh! That staggers thee!

DICKON. Madame Rickby, prod not the quick of my genius. I am Phidias, I am Raphael, I am the Lord God! — You shall see — *[Demands with a gesture]* Yonder broom-stick.

GOODY RICKBY *[fetching him a broom from the corner]*. Good boy!

DICKON *[straddling the handle]*. Haha! gee up! my Salem mare. *[Then, pseudo-philosophically]* A broomstick — that's for imagination! *[He begins to construct the scarecrow, while* GOODY

RICKBY, *assisting, brings the constructive parts from various nooks and corners*. We are all pretty artists, to be sure, Bessie. Phidias, he sculptures the gods; Raphael, he paints the angels; the Lord God, he creates Adam; and Dickon — fetch me the poker — aha, Dickon! What doth Dickon? He nullifies 'em all; he endows the Scarecrow — A poker: here's his conscience. There's two fine legs to walk on, — imagination and conscience. Yonder flails now! The ideal — the *beau idéal*, dame — that's what we artists seek. The apotheosis of scarecrows! And pray, what's a scarecrow? Why, the anthithesis of Adam. — "Let there be candles!" quoth the Lord God, sitting in the dark. "Let there be candle-extinguishers," saith Dickon. "I am made in the image of my maker," quoth Adam. "Look at yourself in the glass," saith Goodman Scarecrow. *[Taking two implements from* GOODY RICKBY*]* Fine! fine! here are flails — one for wit, t'other for satire. *Sapristi!* with two such arms, my lad, how thou wilt work thy way in the world!

GOODY RICKBY. You talk as if you were making a real mortal, Dickon.

DICKON. To fool a crow, Goody, I must fashion a crittur that will first deceive a man.

GOODY RICKBY. He'll scarce do that without a head. *[Pointing to the loft]* What think ye of yonder Jack-o'-lantern? 'Twas made last Hallowe'en.

DICKON. Rare, my Psyche! We shall collaborate. Here! *[Running up the ladder, he tosses down a yellow hollowed pumpkin to* GOODY RICKBY, *who catches it. Then rummaging forth an armful of cornstalks, ears, tassels, dried squashes, gourds, beets, etc., he descends and throws them in a heap on the floor]* Whist! the anatomy.

GOODY RICKBY *[placing the pumpkin on the shoulders]*. Look!

DICKON. O Johannes Baptista! What wouldst thou have given for such a head! I helped Salome to cut his off, dame, and it looked not half so appetizing on her charger. Tut! Copernicus wore once such a pumpkin, but it is rotten. Look at his golden smile! Hail, Phœbus Apollo!

GOODY RICKBY. 'Tis the finest scarecrow in town.

DICKON. Nay, poor soul, 'tis but a skeleton yet. He must have a man's heart in him. *[Picking a big red beet from among the cornstalks, he places it under the left side of the ribs]* Hush! Dost thou hear it *beat?*

GOODY RICKBY. Thou merry rogue!

DICKON. Now for the lungs of him. *[Snatching a small pair of bellows from a peg on the wall]* That's for eloquence! He'll preach the black knaves a sermon on theft. And now — *[Here, with* GOODY RICKBY's *help, he stuffs the framework with the gourds, corn, etc., from the loft, weaving the husks about the legs and arms]* here goes for digestion and inherited instincts! More corn, Goody. Now he'll fight for his own flesh and blood!

GOODY RICKBY *[laughing]*. Dickon, I am proud of thee.

DICKON. Wait till you see his peruke. *[Seizing a feather duster made of crow's feathers]* Voici! Scalps of the enemy! *[Pulling them apart, he arranges the feathers on the pumpkin, like a gentleman's wig]* A rare conqueror!

GOODY RICKBY. Oh, you beauty!

DICKON. And now a bit of comfort for dark days and stormy nights. *[Taking a piece of corn-cob with the kernels on it, Dickon makes a pipe, which he puts into the* SCARECROW's *mouth]* So! There Goody! I tell thee, with yonder brand-new coat and breeches of mine — those there in my cupboard! — we'll make him a lad to be proud of. *[Taking the clothes, which* GOODY RICKBY *brings — a pair of fine scarlet breeches and a gold-embroidered coat with ruffles of lace — he puts them upon the scarecrow. Then, eyeing it like a connoisseur. makes a few finishing touches]* Why, dame, he'll be a son to thee.

GOODY RICKBY. A son? Ay, if I had but a son!

DICKON. Why, here you have him. *[To the* SCARECROW] Thou wilt scare the crows off thy mother's cornfield — wont my pretty? And send 'em all over t'other side the wall — to her dear neighbour's, the Justice Gilead Merton's.

GOODY RICKBY. Justice Merton! Nay, if they'd only peck his eyes out, instead of his corn.

DICKON *[grinning]*. Yet the Justice was a dear friend of "Blacksmith Bess."

GOODY RICKBY. Ay, "Blacksmith Bess!" If I hadn't had a good stout arm when he cast me off with the babe, I might have starved for all his worship cared.

DICKON. True, Bessie; 'twas a scurvy trick he played on thee — and on

me, that took such pains to bring you together — to steal a young maid's heart —

GOODY RICKBY. And then toss it away like a bad penny to the gutter! And the child — to die! *[Lifting her hammer in rage]* Ha! if I could get the worshipful Justice Gilead into my power again — *[Drops the hammer sullenly on the anvil]* But no! I shall beat my life away on this anvil, whilst my justice clinks his gold, and drinks his port to a fat old age. Justice! Ha — justice of God!

DICKON. Whist, dame! Talk of angels and hear the rustle of their relatives.

GOODY RICKBY *[turning, watches outside a girl's figure approaching]*. His niece — Rachel Merton! What can she want so early? Nay, I mind me; 'tis the mirror. She's a maid after our own hearts, boy, — no Sabbath-go-to-meeting airs about *her!* She hath read the books of the *magi* from cover to cover, and paid me good guineas for 'em, though her uncle knows naught on't. Besides, she's in love, Dickon.

DICKON *[indicating the* SCARECROW]. Ah? With *him?* Is it a rendezvous?

GOODY RICKBY *[with a laugh]*. Pff! Begone!

DICKON *[shakes his finger at the* SCARECROW]. Thou naughty rogue! *[Then, still smiling slyly, with his head placed confidentially next to the* SCARECROW's *ear, as if whispering, and with his hand pointing to the maiden outside,* DICKON *fades away into air.* RACHEL *enters, nervous and hesitant.* GOODY RICKBY *makes her a courtesy, which she acknowledges by a nod, half absent-minded]*

GOODY RICKBY. Mistress Rachel Merton — so early! I hope your uncle, our worshipful Justice, is not ill?

RACHEL. No, my uncle is quite well. The early morning suits me best for a walk. You are — quite alone?

GOODY RICKBY. Quite alone, mistress. *[Bitterly]* Oh, folks don't call on Goody Rickby — except on business.

RACHEL *[absently, looking round in the dim shop]*. Yes — you must be busy. Is it — is it here?

GOODY RICKBY. You mean the —

RACHEL *[starting back, with a cry]*. Ah! who's that?

GOODY RICKBY *[chuckling]*. Fear not, mistress; 'tis nothing but a scarecrow. I'm going to put him in my corn-field yonder. The crows are so pesky this year.

RACHEL [*draws her skirts away with a shiver*]. How loathsome!

GOODY RICKBY [*vastly pleased*]. He'll do!

RACHEL. Ah, here! — This is *the* mirror?

GOODY RICKBY. Yea, mistress, and a wonderful glass it is, as I told you. I wouldn't sell it to most comers, but seeing how you and Master Talbot —

RACHEL. Yes; that will do.

GOODY RICKBY. You see, if the town folks guessed what it was, well — You've heard tell of the gibbets on Salem hill? There's not many in New England like you, Mistress Rachel. You know enough to approve some miracles — outside the Scriptures.

RACHEL. You are quite sure the glass will do all you say? It — never fails?

GOODY RICKBY. Ay, now, mistress, how could it? 'Tis the glass of truth — [*insinuatingly*] the glass of true lovers. It shows folks just as they are; no shams, no varnish. If your sweetheart be false, the glass will reveal it. If a wolf should dress himself in a white sheep's wool, this glass would reflect the black beast inside it.

RACHEL. But what of the sins of the soul, Goody? Vanity, hypocrisy, and — and inconstancy? Will it surely reveal them?

GOODY RICKBY. I have told you, my young lady. If it doth not as I say, bring it back and get your money again. Trust me, sweeting, 'tis your only mouse-trap for a man. Why, an old dame hath eyes in her heart yet. If your lover be false, this glass shall pluck his fine feathers!

RACHEL [*with aloofness*]. 'Tis no question of that. I wish the glass to — to amuse me.

GOODY RICKBY [*laughing*]. Why, then, it shall amuse you. Try it on some of your neighbours.

RACHEL. You ask a large price for it.

GOODY RICKBY [*shrugs*]. I run risks. Besides, where will you get another?

RACHEL. That is true. Here, I will buy it. That is the sum you mentioned, I believe? [*She hands a purse to* GOODY RICKBY, *who opens it and counts over some coins*]

GOODY RICKBY. Let see; let see.

RACHEL. Well?

GOODY RICKBY. Good: 'tis good. Folks call me a witch, mistress. Well — harkee — a witch's word is as good as

a justice's gold. The glass is yours — with my blessing.

RACHEL. Spare yourself that, dame. But the glass: how am I to get it? How will you send it to me — quietly?

GOODY RICKBY. Trust me for that. I've a willing lad that helps me with such errands; a neighbour o' mine. [*Calls*] Ebenezer!

RACHEL [*startled*]. What! is he here?

GOODY RICKBY. In the hay-loft. The boy's an orphan; he sleeps there o' times. Ebenezer!

[*A raw, dishevelled country boy appears in the loft, slides down the ladder, and shuffles up sleepily*]

THE BOY. Evenin'.

RACHEL [*drawing* GOODY RICKBY [*aside*]. You understand; I desire no comment about this purchase.

GOODY RICKBY. Nor I, mistress, be sure.

RACHEL. Is he —?

GOODY RICKBY [*tapping her forehead significantly*]. Trust his wits who hath no wit; he's mum.

RACHEL. Oh!

THE BOY [*gaping*]. Job?

GOODY RICKBY. Yea, rumple-head! His job this morning is to bear yonder glass to the house of Justice Merton — the big one on the hill; to the side door. Mind, no gabbing. Doth he catch?

THE BOY [*nodding and grinning*]. 'E swallows.

RACHEL. But is the boy strong enough?

GOODY RICKBY. Him? [*Pointing to the anvil*] Ebenezer!

[*The boy spits on his palms, takes hold of the anvil, lifts it, drops it again, sits on it, and grins at the door, just as* RICHARD TALBOT *appears there, from outside*]

RACHEL. Gracious!

GOODY RICKBY. Trust him. He'll carry the glass for you.

RACHEL. I will return home at once, then. Let him go quietly to the side door, and wait for me. Good morning. [*Turning, she confronts* RICHARD]

RICHARD. Good morning.

RACHEL. Richard! — Squire Talbot, you — you are abroad early.

RICHARD. As early as Mistress Rachel. Is it pardonable? I caught sight of you walking in this direction, so I thought it wise to follow, lest — [*Looks hard at* GOODY RICKBY]

RACHEL. Very kind. Thanks. I've done my errand. Well; we can return together. [*To* GOODY RICKBY] You will make sure that I receive the — the article.

GOODY RICKBY. Trust me, mistress. [*Courtesying*] Squire Talbot! the honour, sir?

RICHARD [*bluntly, looking from one to the other*]. What article?

[RACHEL *ignores the question and starts to pass out.* RICHARD *frowns at* GOODY RICKBY, *who stammers*]

GOODY RICKBY. Begging your pardon, sir?

RICHARD. What article? I said. [*After a short, embarrassed pause: more sternly*] Well?

GOODY RICKBY. Oh, the article! Yonder old glass, to be sure, sir. A quaint piece, your honour.

RICHARD. Rachel, you haven't come here at sunrise to buy — that thing?

RACHEL. Verily, "that thing" and at sunrise. A pretty time for a pretty purchase. Are you coming?

RICHARD [*in a low voice*]. More witchcraft nonsense? Do you realize this is serious?

RACHEL. Oh, of course. You know I am desperately mystical, so pray let us not discuss it. Good-by.

RICHARD. Rachel, just a moment. If you want a mirror, you shall have the prettiest one in New England. Or I will import you one from London. Only — I beg of you — don't buy stolen goods.

GOODY RICKBY. Stolen goods?

RACHEL [*aside to* RICHARD]. Don't! don't!

RICHARD. At least, articles under suspicion. [*To* GOODY RICKBY] Can you account for this mirror — how you came by it?

GOODY RICKBY. I'll show ye! I'll show ye! Stolen — ha!

RICHARD. Come, old swindler, keep your mirror, and give this lady back her money.

GOODY RICKBY. I'll damn ye both, I will! — Stolen!

RACHEL [*imploringly*]. Will you come?

RICHARD. Look you, old Rickby; this is not the first time. Charm all the broomsticks in town, if you like; bewitch all the tables and saucepans and mirrors you please; but gull no more money out of young girls. Mind you!

We're not so enterprising in this town as at Salem; but — *it may come to it!* So look sharp! I'm not blind to what's going on here.

GOODY RICKBY. Not blind, Master Puritan? Oho! You can see through all my counterfeits, can ye? So! you would scrape all the wonder out'n the world, as I've scraped all the meat out'n my punkin-head yonder! Aha! wait and see! Afore sundown, I'll send ye a nut to crack, shall make your orthodox jaws ache. Your servant, Master Deuteronomy!

RICHARD [*to* RACHEL, *who has seized his arm*]. We'll go.

[*Exeunt* RICHARD *and* RACHEL]

GOODY RICKBY [*calls shrilly after them*]. Trot away, pretty team; toss your heads. I'll unhitch ye and take off your blinders.

THE SLOUCHING BOY [*capering and grimacing in front of the mirror, shrieks with laughter*]. Ohoho!

GOODY RICKBY [*returning, savagely*]. Yes, yes, my fine lover! I'll pay thee for "stolen goods" — I'll pay thee. [*Screams*] Dickon! Stop laughing.

THE BOY. O Lord! O Lord!

GOODY RICKBY. What tickles thy mirth now?

THE BOY. For to think as the soul of an orphan innocent, what lives in a hayloft, should wear horns.

[*On looking into the mirror, the spectator perceives therein that the reflection of the slouching boy is the horned demon figure of* DICKON, *who performs the same antics in pantomime within the glass as the boy does without*]

GOODY RICKBY. Yea; 'tis a wise devil that knows his own face in the glass. But hark now! Thou must find me a rival for this cock-squire, — dost hear? A rival, that shall steal away the heart of his Mistress Rachel.

DICKON. And take her to church?

GOODY RICKBY. To church or to Hell. All's one.

DICKON. A rival! [*Pointing at the glass*] How would *he* serve — in there? Dear Ebenezer! Fancy the deacons in the vestry, Goody, and her uncle, the Justice, when they saw him escorting the bride to the altar, with his tail round her waist!

GOODY RICKBY. Tut, tut! Think it over in earnest, and meantime take her the glass. Wait, we'd best fold it up small, so as not to attract notice on the road. [DICKON, *who has already drawn the curtains over the glass, grasps one side of the large frame*, GOODY RICKBY *the other*] Now! [*Pushing their shoulders against the two sides, the frame disappears and* DICKON *holds in his hand a mirror about a foot square, of the same design*] So! Be off! And mind, a rival for Richard!

DICKON.
For Richard a rival,
Dear Goody Rickby
Wants Dickon's connival:
Lord! What can the trick be?

[*To the* SCARECROW] By-by, Sonny; take care of thy mother. [DICKON *slouches out with the glass, whistling*]

GOODY RICKBY. Mother! Yea, if only I had a son — the Justice Merton's and mine! If the brat had but lived now to remind him of those merry days, which he has forgotten. Zooks, wouldn't I put a spoke in his wheel! But no such luck for me! No such luck! [*As she goes to the forge, the stout figure of a man appears in the doorway behind her. Under one arm he carries a large book, in the other hand a gold-headed cane. He hesitates, embarrassed*]

THE MAN. Permit me, Madam.

GOODY RICKBY [*turning*]. Ah, him! — Justice Merton!

JUSTICE MERTON [*removing his hat, steps over the sill, and lays his great book on the table; then with a supercilious look, he puts his hat firmly on again*]. Permit me, dame.

GOODY RICKBY. You! [*With confused, affected hauteur, the* JUSTICE *shifts from foot to foot, flourishing his cane. As he speaks*, GOODY RICKBY, *with a shrewd, painful expression, draws slowly backward toward the door left, which opens into an inner room. Reaching it, she opens it part way, stands facing him, and listens*]

JUSTICE MERTON. I have had the honour — permit me — to entertain suspicions; to rise early, to follow my niece, to meet just now Squire Talbot, an excellent young gentleman of wealth, if not of fashion; to hear his remarks concerning — hem! — you, dame! to call here — permit me — to express myself and inquire —

GOODY RICKBY. Concerning your waistcoat? [*Turning quickly, she snatches an article of apparel which hangs on the inner side of the door, and holds it up*]

JUSTICE MERTON [*starting, crimson*] Woman!

GOODY RICKBY. You left it behind — the last time.

JUSTICE MERTON. I have not the honour to remember —

GOODY RICKBY. The one I embroidered?

JUSTICE MERTON. 'Tis a matter —

GOODY RICKBY. Of some two and twenty years. [*Stretching out the narrow width of the waistcoat*] Will you try it on now, dearie?

JUSTICE MERTON. Unconscionable Un-un-unconscionable witch!

GOODY RICKBY. Witchling — thou used to say.

JUSTICE MERTON. Pah! pah! I forget myself. Pride, permit me, goeth before a fall. As a magistrate, Rickby, I have already borne with you long. The last straw, however, breaks the camel's back.

GOODY RICKBY. Poor camel!

JUSTICE MERTON. You have soiled, you have smirched, the virgin reputation of my niece. You have inveigled her into notions of witchcraft; already the neighbours are beginning to talk. 'Tis a long lane which hath no turning, saith the Lord. Permit me — as a witch, thou art judged. Thou shalt hang.

A VOICE [*behind him*]. And me too?

JUSTICE MERTON [*turns about and stares*]. I beg pardon.

THE VOICE [*in front of him*]. Not at all.

JUSTICE MERTON. Did — did somebody speak?

THE VOICE. Don't you recognize my voice? *Still and small*, you know. If you will kindly let me out, we can chat.

JUSTICE MERTON [*turning fiercely on* GOODY RICKBY]. These are thy sorceries. But I fear them not. The righteous man walketh with God. [*Going to the book which lies on the table*] Satan, I ban thee! I will read from the Holy Scriptures! [*Unclasping the Bible, he flings open the ponderous covers. —* DICKON *steps forth in smoke*]

DICKON. Thanks; it was stuffy in there.

JUSTICE MERTON [*clasping his hands*]. Dickon!

DICKON [*Moving a step nearer on the table*]. Hillo, Gilly! Hillo, Bess!

JUSTICE MERTON. Dickon! No! No!

DICKON. Do ye mind Auld Lang

Syne — the chorus that night, Gilly?
[*Sings*]

> Gil-ead, Gil-ead, Gil-ead
> Merton,
> He was a silly head, silly head,
> Certain,
> When he forgot to steal a bed-
> Curtain!

Encore, now!

JUSTICE MERTON. No, no, be merciful! I will not harm her; she shall not hang: I swear, I swear it! [DICKON *disappears*] I swear — ah! Is he gone? Witchcraft! Witchcraft! I have witnessed it. 'Tis proved on thee, slut. I swear it: thou shalt hang. [*Exit wildly*]

GOODY RICKBY. Ay, Gilead! I shall hang *on!* Ahaha! Dickon, thou angel! Ah, Satan! Satan! For a son now!

DICKON [*reappearing*]. *Videlicet,* in law — a bastard. *N'est ce pas?*

GOODY RICKBY. Yea, in law and in justice, I should-a had one now. Worse luck that he died.

DICKON. One and twenty years ago? [GOODY RICKBY *nods*] Good; he should be of age now. One and twenty — a pretty age, too, for a rival. Haha! — For arrival? — Marry, he shall arrive, then; arrive and marry and inherit his patrimony — all on his birthday! Come, to work!

GOODY RICKBY. What rant is this?

DICKON. Yet, Dickon, it pains me to perform such an anachronism. All this Mediævalism in Massachusetts! — These old-fashioned flames and alchemic accompaniments, when I've tried so hard to be a native American product; it jars. But *che vuole!* I'm naturally middle-aged. I haven't been really myself, let me think, — since 1492!

GOODY RICKBY. What art thou mooning about?

DICKON [*still impenetrable*]. There was my old friend in Germany, Dr. Johann Faustus; he was nigh such a bag of old rubbish when I made him over. Ain't it trite! No, you can't teach an old dog like me new tricks. Still, a scarecrow! that's decidedly local color. Come then; a Yankee masterpiece! [*Seizing* GOODY RICKBY *by the arm, and placing her before the scarecrow, he makes a bow and wave of introduction*] Behold, madam, your son — illegitimate; the future affianced of Mistress Rachel Merton, the heirelect, through matrimony, of Merton House,

— Gilead Merton second; Lord Ravensbane! Your lordship — your mother.

GOODY RICKBY. Dickon! Can you do it?

DICKON. I can — try.

GOODY RICKBY. You will create him for me? — [*wickedly*] and for Gilead!

DICKON. I will — for a kiss.

GOODY RICKBY [*about to embrace him*]. Dickon!

DICKON [*dodging her*]. Later. Now, the waistcoat.

GOODY RICKBY [*handing it*]. Rare! rare! He shall go wooing in't — like his father.

DICKON [*shifting the* SCARECROW's *gold-trimmed coat, slips on the embroidered waistcoat and replaces the coat*] Stand still, Jack! So, my macaroni. *Perfecto!* Stay — a walking-stick!

GOODY RICKBY [*wrenching a spoke out of an old rickety wheel*]. Here: the spoke for Gilead. He used to take me to drive in the chaise it came out of.

DICKON [*placing the spoke as a cane, in the scarecrow's sleeve, views him with satisfaction*]. *Sic!* There, Jacky! *Filius fit non nascitur.* — Sam Hill! My Latin is stale. "In the beginning, was the — gourd!" Of these thy modest ingredients may thy spirit smack! [*Making various mystic passes with his hands,* DICKON *in tones, now deep and solemn, now with fanciful shrill rapidity, this incantation:*]

> Flail, flip;
> Broom, sweep;
> *Sic itur!*
> Cornstalk
> And turnip, talk!
> Turn crittur!
>
> Pulse, beet;
> Gourd, eat;
> *Ave* Hellas!
> Poker and punkin,
> Stir the old junk in:
> Breathe, bellows!
>
> Corn-cob,
> And crow's feather,
> And the job:
> Jumble the rest o' the rubbish together;
> Dovetail and tune 'em.
> *E pluribus unum!*

[*The* SCARECROW *remains stock still*] The devil! Have I lost the hang of it? Ah! Hullo! He's dropped his pipe.

What's a dandy without his 'baccy! [*Restoring the corn-cob pipe to the* SCARE-CROW'S *mouth*] 'Tis the life and breath of him. So; hand me yon hazel switch, Goody. [*Waving it*] Presto!

> Brighten, coal,
> I' the dusk between us!
> Whiten, soul!
> *Propinquit Venus!*

[*A whiff of smoke puffs from the* SCARE-CROW'S *pipe*] *Sic! Sic! Jacobus!* [*Another whiff*] Bravo! [*The whiffs grow more rapid and the thing trembles*]

GOODY RICKBY. Puff! puff, manny, for thy life!

DICKON. *Fiat, fœtus!* — Huzza! *Noch einmal!* Go it! [*Clouds of smoke issue from the pipe, half fill the shop, and envelop the creature, who staggers.[1]*]

GOODY RICKBY. See! See his eyes!

DICKON [*beckoning with one finger*]. *Veni, fili! Veni!* Take'ee first step, *bambino!* — Toddle!

[*The* SCARECROW *makes a stiff lurch forward and falls sidewise against the anvil, propped half-reclining against which he leans rigid, emitting fainter puffs of smoke in gasps*]

GOODY RICKBY [*screams*]. Have a care! He's fallen.

DICKON. Well done, Punkin Jack! Thou shalt be knighted for that! [*Striking him on the shoulder with the hazel rod*] Rise, Lord Ravensbane!

[*The* SCARECROW *totters to his feet, and makes a forlorn rectilinear salutation*]

GOODY RICKBY. Look! He bows. — He flaps his flails at thee. He smiles like a tik-doo-loo-roo!

DICKON [*with a profound reverence, backing away*]. Will his lordship deign to follow his tutor?

[*With hitches and jerks, the* SCARECROW *follows Dickon*]

GOODY RICKBY. O Lord! Lord! the style o' the broomstick!

DICKON [*holding ready a high-backed chair*]. Will his lordship be seated and rest himself?

[*Awkwardly the* SCARECROW *half falls into the chair; his head sinks sideways, and his pipe falls out.* DICKON

snatches it up instantly and restores it to his mouth]

Puff! Puff, *puer;* 'tis thy life. [*The* SCARECROW *puffs again*] Is his lordship's tobacco refreshing?

GOODY RICKBY. Look now! The red colour in his cheeks. The beet-juice is pumping, oho!

DICKON [*offering his arm*]. Your lordship will deign to receive an audience? [*The* SCARECROW *takes his arm and rises*] The Marchioness of Rickby, your lady mother, entreats leave to present herself.

GOODY RICKBY [*Courtesying low*]. My son!

DICKON [*holding the pipe, and waving the hazel rod*]. *Dicite!* Speak! [*The* SCARECROW, *blowing out his last mouthful of smoke, opens his mouth, gasps, gurgles, and is silent*] *In principio erat verbum!* Accost thy mother! [*The* SCARECROW, *clutching at his side in a struggle for coherence, fixes a pathetic look of pain on* GOODY RICKBY]

THE SCARECROW. Mother!

GOODY RICKBY [*with a scream of hysterical laughter, seizes both* DICKON'S *hands and dances him about the forge*]. O Beelzebub! I shall die!

DICKON. Thou hast thy son. [DICKON *whispers in the* SCARECROW'S *ear, shakes his finger, and exit*]

GOODY RICKBY. He called me "mother." Again, boy, again.

THE SCARECROW. From the bottom of my heart — mother.

GOODY RICKBY. "The bottom of his heart" — Nay, thou killest me.

THE SCARECROW. Permit me, madam!

GOODY RICKBY. Gilead! Gilead himself! Waistcoat, "permit me", and all: thy father over again, I tell thee.

THE SCARECROW [*with a slight stammer*]. It gives me — I assure you — lady — the deepest happiness.

GOODY RICKBY. Just so the old hypocrite spoke when I said I'd have him. But thou hast a sweeter deference, my son.

[*Reënter* DICKON; *he is dressed all in black, save for a white stock, — a suit of plain elegance*]

DICKON. Now, my lord, your tutor is ready.

---

[1] Here the living actor through a trap, concealed by the smoke, will substitute himself for the elegantly clad effigy. His make-up, of course, will approximate to the latter, but the grotesque contours of his expression gradually, throughout the remainder of the act, become refined and sublimated till, at the *finale*, they are of a lordly and distinguished caste.

THE SCARECROW [*to* GOODY RICKBY]. I have the honour — permit me — to wish you — good morning. [*Bows and takes a step after* DICKON, *who, taking a three-cornered cocked hat from a peg, goes toward the door*]

GOODY RICKBY. Whoa! Whoa, Jack! Whither away?

DICKON [*presenting the hat*]. Deign to reply, sir.

THE SCARECROW. I go — with my tutor — Master Dickonson — to pay my respects — to his worship — the Justice — Merton — to solicit — the hand — of his daughter — the fair Mistress — Rachel. [*With another bow*] Permit me.

GOODY RICKBY. Permit ye? God speed ye! Thou must teach him his tricks, Dickon.

DICKON. Trust me, Goody. Between here and Justice Merton's, I will play the mother-hen, and I promise thee, our bantling shall be as stuffed with compliments as a callow chick with caterpillars. [*As he throws open the big doors, the cawing of crows is heard again*] Hark! your lordship's retainers acclaim you on your birthday. They bid you welcome to your majority. Listen! "Long live Lord Ravensbane! Caw!"

GOODY RICKBY. Look! Count 'em, Dickon.

One for sorrow,
Two for mirth,
Three for a wedding,
Four for a birth —

Four on 'em! So! Good luck on thy birthday! And see! There's three on 'em flying into the Justice's field.

— Flight o' the crows
Tells how the wind blows! —

A wedding! Get ye gone. Wed the girl, and sting the Justice. Bless ye, my son!

THE SCARECROW [*with a profound reverence*]. Mother — believe me — to be — your ladyship's — most devoted — and obedient — son.

DICKON [*prompting him aloud*]. Ravensbane.

THE SCARECROW [*donning his hat, lifts his head in hauteur, shakes his lace ruffle over his hand, turns his shoulder, nods slightly, and speaks for the first time with complete mastery of his voice*]. Hm! Ravensbane! [*With one hand in the arm of* DICKON, *the other twirling his*

cane (*the converted chaise-spoke*), *wreathed in halos of smoke from his pipe, the fantastical figure hitches elegantly forth into the daylight, amid louder acclamations of the crows*]

ACT II

The same morning. Justice Merton's parlour, furnished and designed in the style of the early colonial period. On the right wall, hangs a portrait of the JUSTICE *as a young man; on the left wall, an old-fashioned looking-glass. At the right of the room stands the Glass of Truth, draped — as in the blacksmith shop — with the strange, embroidered curtain.*

In front of it are discovered RACHEL *and* RICHARD; RACHEL *is about to draw the curtain.*

RACHEL. Now! Are you willing?

RICHARD. So you suspect me of dark, villainous practices?

RACHEL. No, no, foolish Dick.

RICHARD. Still, I am to be tested; is that it?

RACHEL. That's it.

RICHARD. As your true lover.

RACHEL. Well, yes.

RICHARD. Why, of course, then, I consent. A true lover always consents to the follies of his lady-love.

RACHEL. Thank you, Dick; I trust the glass will sustain your character. Now; when I draw the curtain —

RICHARD [*staying her hand*]. What if I be false?

RACHEL. Then, sir, the glass will reflect you as the subtle fox that you are.

RICHARD. And you — as the goose?

RACHEL. Very likely. Ah! but, Richard dear, we mustn't laugh. It may prove very serious. You do not guess — you do not dream all the mysteries —

RICHARD [*shaking his head, with a grave smile*]. You pluck at too many mysteries; sometime they may burn your fingers. Remember our first mother Eve!

RACHEL. But this is the glass of truth; and Goody Rickby told me —

RICHARD. Rickby, forsooth!

RACHEL. Nay, come; let's have it over. [*She draws the curtain, covers her eyes, steps back by* RICHARD'S *side, looks at the glass, and gives a joyous cry*] Ah! there you are, dear! There we are, both of us — just as we have always seemed to each other, true. 'Tis proved. Isn't it wonderful?

RICHARD. Miraculous! That a mirror bought in a blacksmith shop, before sunrise, for twenty pounds, should prove to be actually — a mirror!

RACHEL. Richard, I'm so happy.

[*Enter* JUSTICE MERTON *and* MISTRESS MERTON]

RICHARD [*embracing her*]. Happy, art thou, sweet goose? Why, then, God bless Goody Rickby.

JUSTICE MERTON. Strange words from you, Squire Talbot.

[RACHEL *and* RICHARD *part quickly;* RACHEL *draws the curtain over the mirror;* RICHARD *stands stiffly*]

RICHARD. Justice Merton! Why, sir, the old witch is more innocent, perhaps, than I represented her.

JUSTICE MERTON. A witch, believe me, is never innocent. [*Taking their hands, he brings them together and kisses* RACHEL *on the forehead*] Permit me, young lovers. I was once young myself, young and amorous.

MISTRESS MERTON [*in a low voice*]. Verily!

JUSTICE MERTON. My fair niece, my worthy young man, beware of witchcraft.

MISTRESS MERTON. And Goody Rickby, too, brother?

JUSTICE MERTON. That woman shall answer for her deeds. She is proscribed.

RACHEL. Proscribed? What is that?

MISTRESS MERTON [*examining the mirror*]. What is this?

JUSTICE MERTON. She shall hang.

RACHEL. Uncle, no! Not merely because of my purchase this morning.

JUSTICE MERTON. Your purchase?

MISTRESS MERTON [*pointing to the mirror*]. That, I suppose.

JUSTICE MERTON. What! you purchased that mirror of her? You brought it here?

RACHEL. No, the boy brought it; I found it here when I returned.

JUSTICE MERTON. What! From her! You purchased it? From her shop? From her infamous den, into my parlour! [*To* MISTRESS MERTON] Call the servant. [*Himself calling*] Micah! This instant, this instant — away with it! Micah!

RACHEL. Uncle Gilead, I bought —

JUSTICE MERTON. Micah, I say! Where is the man?

RACHEL. Listen, Uncle. I bought it with my own money.

JUSTICE MERTON. Thine own money! Wilt have the neighbours gossip? Wilt have me, thyself, my house, suspected of complicity with witches? [*Enter* MICAH] Micah, take this away.

MICAH. Yes, sir; but, sir —

JUSTICE MERTON. Out of my house!

MICAH. There be visitors.

JUSTICE MERTON. Away with —

MISTRESS MERTON [*touching his arm*]. Gilead!

MICAH. Visitors, sir; gentry.

JUSTICE MERTON. Ah!

MICAH. Shall I show them in, sir?

JUSTICE MERTON. Visitors! In the morning? Who are they?

MICAH. Strangers, sir. I should judge they be very high gentry; lords, sir.

ALL. Lords!

MICAH. At least, one on 'em, sir. The other — the dark gentleman — told me they left their horses at the inn, sir.

MISTRESS MERTON. Hark! [*The faces of all wear suddenly a startled expression*] Where is that unearthly sound?

JUSTICE MERTON [*listening*]. Is it in the cellar?

MICAH. 'Tis just the dog howling, madam. When he spied the gentry he turned tail and run below.

MISTRESS MERTON. Oh, the dog!

JUSTICE MERTON. Show the gentlemen here, Micah. Don't keep them waiting. [*Exit* MICAH] A lord! [*To* RACHEL] We shall talk of this matter later. — A lord! [*Turning to the small glass on the wall, he arranges his peruke and attire*]

RACHEL [*to* RICHARD]. What a fortunate interruption! But, dear Dick! I wish we needn't meet these strangers now.

RICHARD. Would you really rather we were alone together? [*They chat aside, absorbed in each other*]

JUSTICE MERTON. Think of it, Cynthia, a lord!

MISTRESS MERTON [*dusting the furniture hastily with her handkerchief*]. And such dust!

RACHEL [*to* RICHARD]. You know, dear, we need only be introduced, and then we can steal away together.

[*Reënter* MICAH]

MICAH [*announcing*]. Lord Ravensbane: Marquis of Oxford, Baron of Wittenberg, Elector of Worms, and Count of Cordova; Master Dickonson.

[*Enter* RAVENSBANE *and* DICKON]

JUSTICE MERTON. Gentlemen, permit me, you are excessively welcome. I am deeply gratified to meet —

DICKON. Lord Ravensbane, of the Rookeries, Somersetshire.

JUSTICE MERTON. Lord Ravensbane — his lordship's most truly honoured.

RAVENSBANE. Truly honoured.

JUSTICE MERTON [*turning to* DICKON]. His lordship's —?

DICKON. Tutor.

JUSTICE MERTON [*checking his effusiveness*]. Ah, so!

DICKON. Justice Merton, I believe.

JUSTICE MERTON. Of Merton House. — May I present — permit me, your lordship — my sister, Mistress Merton.

RAVENSBANE. Mistress Merton.

JUSTICE MERTON. And my — and my — [*under his breath*]. Rachel! [RACHEL *remains with a bored expression behind* RICHARD] — my young neighbour, Squire Talbot, Squire Richard Talbot of — of —

RICHARD. Of nowhere, sir.

RAVENSBANE [*nods*]. Nowhere.

JUSTICE MERTON. And permit me, Lord Ravensbane, my niece — Mistress Rachel Merton.

RAVENSBANE [*Bows low*]. Mistress Rachel Merton.

RACHEL [*courtesies*]. Lord Ravensbane. [*As they raise their heads, their eyes meet and are fascinated.* DICKON *just then takes* RAVENSBANE'S *pipe and fills it*]

RAVENSBANE. Mistress Rachel!

RACHEL. Your lordship!

[DICKON *returns the pipe*]

MISTRESS MERTON. A pipe! Gilead! — in the parlour! [JUSTICE MERTON *frowns silence*]

JUSTICE MERTON. Your lordship — ahem! — has just arrived in town?

DICKON. From London, via New Amsterdam.

RICHARD [*aside*]. Is he staring at *you?* Are you ill, Rachel?

RACHEL [*indifferently*]. What?

JUSTICE MERTON. Lord Ravensbane honours my humble roof.

DICKON [*touches* RAVENSBANE'S *arm*]. Your lordship — "roof."

RAVENSBANE [*starting, turns to* MERTON]. Nay, sir, the roof of my father's oldest friend bestows generous hospitality upon his only son.

JUSTICE MERTON. Only son — ah, yes! Your father —

RAVENSBANE. My father, I trust, sir, has never forgotten the intimate companionship, the touching devotion, the unceasing solicitude for his happiness which you, sir, manifested to him in the days of his youth.

JUSTICE MERTON. Really, your lordship, the — the slight favours which — hem! some years ago, I was privileged to show your illustrious father —

RAVENSBANE. Permit me! — Because, however, of his present infirmities — for I regret to say that my father is suffering a temporary aberration of mind —

JUSTICE MERTON. You distress me!

RAVENSBANE. My lady mother has charged me with a double mission here in New England. On my quitting my home, sir, to explore the wideness and the mystery of this world, my mother bade me be sure to call upon his worship, the Justice Merton; and deliver to him, first, my father's remembrances; and secondly, my mother's epistle.

DICKON [*handing to* JUSTICE MERTON *a sealed document*]. Her ladyship's letter, sir.

JUSTICE MERTON [*examining the seal with awe speaks aside to* MISTRESS MERTON]. Cynthia! — a crested seal!

DICKON. His lordship's crest, sir: rooks rampant.

JUSTICE MERTON [*embarrassed, breaks the seal*]. Permit me.

RACHEL [*looking at* RAVENSBANE]. Have you noticed his bearing, Richard: what personal distinction! what inbred nobility! Every inch a true lord!

RICHARD. He may be a lord, my dear, but he walks like a broomstick.

RACHEL. How dare you! [*Turns abruptly away; as she does so, a fold of her gown catches in a chair*]

DICKON [*to* JUSTICE MERTON]. A word, sir.

JUSTICE MERTON [*glancing up from the letter*]. I am astonished — overpowered!

RAVENSBANE. Mistress Rachel — permit me. [*Stooping, he extricates the fold of her gown*]

RACHEL. Oh, thank you. [*They go aside together*]

RICHARD [*to* MISTRESS MERTON]. So

Lord Ravensbane and his family are old friends of yours?

MISTRESS MERTON [*monosyllabically*]. I never heard the name before, Richard.

RICHARD. Why! but I thought that your brother, the Justice —

MISTRESS MERTON. The Justice is reticent.

RICHARD. Ah!

MISTRESS MERTON. Especially concerning his youth.

RICHARD. Ah!

RAVENSBANE [*to* RACHEL, *taking her hand after a whisper from* DICKON]. Believe me, sweet lady, it will give me the deepest pleasure.

RACHEL. Can you really tell fortunes?

RAVENSBANE. More than that; I can bestow them.

JUSTICE MERTON [*to* DICKON]. But is her ladyship really serious? An offer of marriage!

DICKON. Pray read it again, sir.

JUSTICE MERTON [*reads*].

"To the Worshipful, the Justice Gilead
  "Merton,
  "Merton House.

"My Honourable Friend and Benefactor:

  "With these brief lines I commend to you our son" — *our* son!

DICKON. She speaks likewise for his young lordship's father, sir.

JUSTICE MERTON. Ah! of course. [*Reads*] "In a strange land, I intrust him to you as to a father." Honoured, believe me! "I have only to add my earnest hope that the natural gifts, graces, and inherited fortune" — ah — !

DICKON. Twenty thousand pounds — on his father's demise.

JUSTICE MERTON. Ah! — "fortune of this young scion of nobility will so propitiate the heart of your niece, Mistress Rachel Merton, as to cause her to accept his proffered hand in matrimony"; — but — but — but Squire Talbot is betrothed to — well, well, we shall see; "in matrimony, and thus cement the early bonds of interest and affection between your honoured self and his lordship's father; not to mention, dear sir, your worship's ever grateful and obedient admirer,

"ELIZABETH,
  "Marchioness of R."

Of R.! of R.! Will you believe me, my dear sir, so long is it since my travels in England — I visited at so many

— hem! noble estates — permit me, it is so awkward, but —

DICKON [*with his peculiar intonation of Act I*]. Not at all.

JUSTICE MERTON [*starting*]. I — I confess, sir, my youthful memory fails me. Will you be so very obliging; this — this Marchioness of R. —?

DICKON [*enjoying his discomfiture*]. Yes?

JUSTICE MERTON. The R, I presume, stands for —

DICKON. Rickby.

RAVENSBANE [*calls*]. Dickon, my pipe! [DICKON *glides away to fill* RAVENSBANE's *pipe*]

JUSTICE MERTON [*stands bewildered and horror-struck*]. Great God! — Thou inexorable Judge!

RICHARD [*to* MISTRESS MERTON, *scowling at* RAVENSBANE *and* RACHEL]. Are these court manners, in London?

MISTRESS MERTON. Don't ask *me*, Richard.

RAVENSBANE [*dejectedly to* RACHEL, *as* DICKON *is refilling his pipe*]. Alas! Mistress Rachel is cruel.

RACHEL. I? — cruel, your lordship?

RAVENSBANE. Your own white hand has written it. [*Lifting her palm*] See, these lines: Rejection! you will reject one who loves you dearly.

RACHEL. Fie, your lordship! Be not cast down at fortune-telling. Let me tell yours, may I?

RAVENSBANE [*rapturously holding his palm for her to examine*]. Ah! Permit me.

JUSTICE MERTON [*murmurs, in terrible agitation*]. Dickon! Can it be Dickon?

RACHEL. Why, Lord Ravensbane, your pulse. Really, if I am cruel, you are quite heartless. I declare I can't feel your heart beat at all.

RAVENSBANE. Ah! mistress, that is because I have just lost it.

RACHEL [*archly*]. Where?

RAVENSBANE [*faintly*]. Dickon, my pipe!

RACHEL. Alas! my lord, are you ill?

DICKON [*restoring the lighted pipe to* RAVENSBANE, *speaks aside*]. Pardon me, sweet young lady, I must confide to you that his lordship's heart is peculiarly responsive to his emotions. When he feels very ardently, it quite stops. Hence the use of his pipe.

RACHEL. Oh! Is smoking, then, necessary for his heart?

DICKON. Absolutely — to equilibrate the valvular palpitations. Without his pipe — should his lordship experience, for instance, the emotion of love — he might die.

RACHEL. You alarm me!

DICKON. But this is for you only, Mistress Rachel. We may confide in you?

RACHEL. Oh, utterly, sir.

DICKON. His lordship, you know, is so sensitive.

RAVENSBANE [*to* RACHEL]. You have given it back to me. Why did not you keep it?

RACHEL. What, my lord?

RAVENSBANE. My heart.

JUSTICE MERTON [*to* DICKON]. Permit me, one moment; I did not catch your name.

DICKON. My name? Dickonson.

JUSTICE MERTON [*with a gasp of relief*]. Ah, Dickonson! Thank you. I mistook the word.

DICKON. A compound, your worship. [*With a malignant smile*] Dickon- [*then jerking his thumb over his shoulder at* RAVENSBANE] son! [*Bowing*] Both at your service.

JUSTICE MERTON. If — if you can show pity — speak low.

DICKON. As hell, your worship?

JUSTICE MERTON. Is he — he there?

DICKON. Bessie's brat; yes; it didn't die, after all, poor suckling! Dickon weaned it. Saved it for balm of Gilead. Raised it for joyful homecoming. Prodigal's return! Twenty-first birthday! Happy son! Happy father!

JUSTICE MERTON. My — son!

DICKON. Felicitations!

JUSTICE MERTON. I will not believe it.

DICKON. Truth *is* hard fare.

JUSTICE MERTON [*faintly*]. What — what do you want?

DICKON. Only the happiness of your dear ones. [*Indicating* RACHEL *and* RAVENSBANE] The union of these young hearts and hands.

JUSTICE MERTON. What! he will dare — an illegitimate —

DICKON. Fie, fie, Gilly! Why, the brat is a lord now.

JUSTICE MERTON. Oh, the disgrace! Spare me that, Dickon.

RICHARD [*in a low voice to* RACHEL, *who is talking in a fascinated manner to* RAVENSBANE]. Are you mad?

RACHEL [*indifferently*]. What is the matter? [*Laughing, to* RAVENSBANE] Oh, your lordship is too witty!

JUSTICE MERTON [*to* DICKON]. After all, I was young then.

DICKON. Quite so.

JUSTICE MERTON. And she is innocent; she is already betrothed.

DICKON. Twiddle-twaddle! Look at her eyes now! [RACHEL *is still telling* RAVENSBANE'S *fortune; and they are manifestly absorbed in each other*] 'Tis a brilliant match; besides, her ladyship's heart is set upon it.

JUSTICE MERTON. Her ladyship —?

DICKON. The Marchioness of Rickby.

JUSTICE MERTON [*glowering*]. I had forgotten.

DICKON. Her ladyship has never forgotten. So, you see, your worship's alternatives are most simple. Alternative one: advance his lordship's suit with your niece as speedily as possible, and save all scandal. Alternative two: impede his lordship's suit, and —

JUSTICE MERTON. Don't, Dickon! don't reveal the truth; not disgrace now!

DICKON. Good; we are agreed, then?

JUSTICE MERTON. I have no choice.

DICKON [*cheerfully*]. Why, true; we ignored that, didn't we?

MISTRESS MERTON [*approaching*]. This young lord — Why, Gilead, are you ill?

JUSTICE MERTON [*with a great effort, commands himself*]. Not in the least.

MISTRESS MERTON. Rachel's deportment, my dear brother —

RACHEL. I am really at a loss. Your lordship's hand is so very peculiar.

RAVENSBANE. Ah! Peculiar.

RACHEL. This, now, is the line of life.

RAVENSBANE. Of life, yes?

RACHEL. But it begins so abruptly, and see! it breaks off and ends nowhere. And just so here with this line — the line of — of love.

RAVENSBANE. Of love. So; it breaks?

RACHEL. Yes.

RAVENSBANE. Ah, then, that must be the *heart* line.

RACHEL. I am afraid your lordship is very fickle.

MISTRESS MERTON [*horrified*]. I tell you, Gilead, they are fortune-telling!

JUSTICE MERTON. Tush! Tush!

MISTRESS MERTON. Tush? "*Tush*" to *me?* Tush!

[RICHARD, *who has been stifling his feelings at* RACHEL'S *rebuff, and has stood fidgeting at a civil distance from her, now walks up to* JUSTICE MERTON]

RICHARD. Intolerable! Do you approve of *this*, sir? Are Lord Ravensbane's credentials satisfactory?

JUSTICE MERTON. Eminently, eminently.

RICHARD. Ah! So her ladyship's letter is —

JUSTICE MERTON. Charming; charming.

RICHARD. To be sure; old friends, when they are lords, it makes such a difference.

DICKON.
　　True friends — old friends;
　　New friends — cold friends.
N'est ce pas, your worship?

JUSTICE MERTON. Indeed, Master Dickonson; indeed! [*To* RICHARD, *as* DICKON *goes toward* RAVENSBANE *and* RACHEL] What happiness to encounter the manners of the nobility!

RICHARD. If you approve them, sir, it is sufficient. This is your house. [*He turns away*]

JUSTICE MERTON. Your lordship will, I trust, make my house your home.

RAVENSBANE. My home, sir.

RACHEL [*to* DICKON, *who has spoken to her*]. Really? [*To* JUSTICE MERTON] Why, uncle, what is this Master Dickonson tells us?

JUSTICE MERTON. What! What! he has revealed —

RACHEL. Yes, indeed. Why did you never tell us?

JUSTICE MERTON. Rachel! Rachel!

MISTRESS MERTON. You are moved, brother.

RACHEL [*laughingly to* RAVENSBANE]. My uncle is doubtless astonished to find you so grown.

RAVENSBANE [*laughingly to* JUSTICE MERTON]. I am doubtless astonished, sir, to be so grown.

JUSTICE MERTON [*to* DICKON]. You have —

DICKON. Remarked, sir, that your worship had often dandled his lordship — as an infant.

JUSTICE MERTON [*smiling lugubriously*]. Quite so — as an infant merely.

RACHEL. How interesting! Then you must have seen his lordship's home in England.

JUSTICE MERTON. As you say.

RACHEL [*to* RAVENSBANE]. Do describe it to us. We are so isolated here from the grand world. Do you know, I always imagine England to be an enchanted isle, like one of the old Hesperides, teeming with fruits of solid gold.

RAVENSBANE. Ah, yes! my mother raises them.

RACHEL. Fruits of gold?

RAVENSBANE. Round like the rising sun. She calls them — ah! punkins.

MISTRESS MERTON. "Punkins!"

JUSTICE MERTON [*aside, grinding his teeth*]. Scoundrel! Scoundrel!

RACHEL [*laughing*]. Your lordship pokes fun at us.

DICKON. His lordship is an artist in words, mistress. I have noticed that in whatever country he is traveling, he tinges his vocabulary with the local idiom. His lordship means, of course, not pumpkins, but pomegranates.

RACHEL. We forgive him. But, your lordship, please be serious and describe to us your hall.

RAVENSBANE. Quite serious: the hall. Yes, yes; in the middle burns a great fire — on a black — ah! — black altar.

DICKON. A Druidical heirloom. His lordship's mother collects antiques.

RACHEL. How fascinating!

RAVENSBANE. Quite fascinating! On the walls hang pieces of iron.

DICKON. Trophies of Saxon warfare.

RAVENSBANE. And rusty horseshoes.

GENERAL MURMURS. Horseshoes!

DICKON. Presents from the German emperor. They were worn by the steeds of Charlemagne.

RAVENSBANE. Quite so; and broken cart-wheels.

DICKON. Reliques of British chariots.

RACHEL. How mediæval it must be! [*To* JUSTICE MERTON] And to think you never described it to us!

MISTRESS MERTON. True, brother; you have been singularly reticent.

JUSTICE MERTON. Permit me; it is impossible to report all one sees on one's travels.

MISTRESS MERTON. Evidently.

RACHEL. But surely your lordship's mother has other diversions besides collecting antiques. I have heard that in England ladies followed the hounds; and sometimes — [*Looking at her aunt and lowering her voice*] they even dance.

RAVENSBANE. Dance — ah, yes;

my lady mother dances about the — the altar; she swings high a hammer.

DICKON. Your lordship, your lordship! Pray, sir, check this vein of poetry. Lord Ravensbane symbolizes as a hammer and altar a golf-stick and tee — a Scottish game, which her ladyship plays on her Highland estates.

RICHARD [*to* MISTRESS MERTON]. What do you think of this?

MISTRESS MERTON [*with a scandalized look toward her brother*]. He said to me "tush."

RICHARD [*to* JUSTICE MERTON, *indicating* DICKON]. Who is this magpie?

JUSTICE MERTON [*hisses in fury*]. Satan!

RICHARD. I beg pardon!

JUSTICE MERTON. Satan, sir — makes you jealous.

RICHARD [*bows stiffly*]. Good morning. [*Walking up to* RAVENSBANE] Lord Ravensbane, I have a rustic colonial question to ask. Is it the latest fashion to smoke incessantly in ladies' parlours, or is it — mediæval?

DICKON. His lordship's health, sir, necessitates —

RICHARD. I addressed his lordship.

RAVENSBANE. In the matter of fashions, sir — [*hands his pipe to be refilled*]. My pipe, Dickon! [*While* DICKON *holds his pipe — somewhat longer than usual* — RAVENSBANE, *with his mouth open as if about to speak, relapses into a vacant stare*]

DICKON [*as he lights the pipe for* RAVENSBANE, *speaks suavely and low as if not to be overheard by him*]. Pardon me. The fact is, my young pupil is sensitive; the wound from his latest duel is not quite healed; you observe a slight lameness, an occasional absence of mind.

RACHEL. A wound — in a real duel?

RICHARD. Necessitates his smoking! A valid reason!

DICKON [*aside*]. You, mistress, know the *true* reason — his lordship's heart.

RACHEL. Believe me, sir —

RICHARD [*to* RAVENSBANE, *who is still staring vacantly into space*]. Well, well, your lordship! [RAVENSBANE *pays no attention*] You were saying —? [DICKON *returns the pipe*] in the matter of fashions, sir —?

RAVENSBANE [*regaining slowly a look of intelligence, draws himself up with affronted hauteur*]. Permit me! [*Puffs several wreaths of smoke into the air*] I am the fashions.

RICHARD [*going*]. Insufferable! [*He pauses at the door*]

MISTRESS MERTON [*to* JUSTICE MERTON]. Well — what do you think of that?

JUSTICE MERTON. Spoken like King Charles himself.

MISTRESS MERTON. Brother! brother! is there nothing wrong here?

JUSTICE MERTON. Wrong, Cynthia! Manifestly you are quite ignorant of the manners of the great.

MISTRESS MERTON. Oh, Gilead!

JUSTICE MERTON. Where are you going?

MISTRESS MERTON. To my room. [*Murmurs, as she hurries out*] Dear! dear! if it should be that again!

[DICKON *and* JUSTICE MERTON *withdraw to a corner of the room*]

RACHEL [*to* RAVENSBANE]. I — object to the smoke? Why, I think it is charming.

RICHARD [*who has returned from the door, speaks in a low, constrained voice*]. Rachel!

RACHEL. Oh! — you?

RICHARD. You take quickly to European fashions.

RACHEL. Yes? To what one in particular?

RICHARD. Two; smoking and flirtation.

RACHEL. Jealous?

RICHARD. Of an idiot? I hope not. Manners differ, however. Your confidences to his lordship have evidently not included — your relation to me.

RACHEL. Oh, our relations!

RICHARD. Of course, since you wish him to continue in ignorance —

RACHEL. Not at all. He shall know at once. Lord Ravensbane!

RAVENSBANE. Fair mistress!

RICHARD. Rachel, stop! I did not mean —

RACHEL [*to* RAVENSBANE]. My uncle did not introduce to you with sufficient elaboration this gentleman. Will you allow me to do so now?

RAVENSBANE. I adore Mistress Rachel's elaborations.

RACHEL. Lord Ravensbane, I beg to present Squire Talbot, *my betrothed*.

RAVENSBANE. Betrothed! Is it — [*noticing* RICHARD'S *frown*] is it pleasant?

RACHEL [*to* RICHARD]. Are you satisfied?

RICHARD [*trembling with feeling*]. *More* than satisfied. [*Exit*]

RAVENSBANE [*looking after him*]. Ah! Betrothed is *not* pleasant.

RACHEL. Not always.

RAVENSBANE [*anxiously*]. Mistress Rachel is not pleased?

RACHEL [*biting her lip, looks after* RICHARD]. With him.

RAVENSBANE. Mistress Rachel will smile again?

RACHEL. Soon.

RAVENSBANE [*ardent*]. Ah! if she would only smile once more! What can Lord Ravensbane do to make her smile? See! will you puff my pipe? It is very pleasant. [*Offering the pipe*]

RACHEL [*smiling*]. Shall I try? [*Takes hold of it mischievously*]

JUSTICE MERTON [*in a great voice*] Rachel!

RACHEL. Why, uncle!

JUSTICE MERTON [*from where he has been conversing in a corner with* DICKON, *approaches now and speaks suavely to* Ravensbane*]. Permit me, your lordship — Rachel, you will kindly withdraw for a few moments; I desire to confer with Lord Ravensbane concerning his mother's — her ladyship's letter; [*Obsequiously to* DICKON] — that is, if you think, sir, that your noble pupil is not too fatigued.

DICKON. Not at all; I think his lordship will listen to you with much pleasure.

RAVENSBANE [*bowing to* JUSTICE MERTON, *but looking at* RACHEL]. With much pleasure.

DICKON. And in the meantime, if Mistress Rachel will allow me, I will assist her in writing those invitations which your worship desires to send in her name.

JUSTICE MERTON. Invitations — from my niece?

DICKON. To his Excellency, the Lieutenant Governor; to your friends, the Reverend Masters at Harvard College, etc., etc.; in brief, to all your worship's select social acquaintance in the vicinity — to meet his lordship. It was so thoughtful in you to suggest it, sir, and believe me, his lordship appreciates your courtesy in arranging the reception in his honour for this afternoon.

RACHEL [*to* JUSTICE MERTON]. This afternoon! Are we really to give his lordship a reception this afternoon?

DICKON. Your uncle has already given me the list of guests; so considerate! Permit me to act as your scribe, Mistress Rachel.

RACHEL. With pleasure. [*To* JUSTICE MERTON] And will it be here, uncle?

DICKON [*looking at him narrowly*]. Your worship said *here*, I believe?

JUSTICE MERTON. Quite so, sir; quite so, quite so.

DICKON [*aside to* JUSTICE MERTON]. I advise nothing rash, Gilly; the brat has a weak heart.

RACHEL. This way, Master Dickonson, to the study.

DICKON [*as he goes with* RACHEL]. I will write and you sign?

RACHEL. Thank you.

DICKON [*aside, as he passes* RAVENSBANE]. Remember, Jack! Puff, puff!

RACHEL [*to* RAVENSBANE, *who stretches out his hand to her with a gesture of entreaty to stay*]. Your lordship is to be my guest. [*Courtesying*] Till we meet again!

DICKON [*to* RACHEL]. May I sharpen your quill?

[*Exeunt*]

RAVENSBANE [*faintly, looking after her*]. Till — we — meet — again!

JUSTICE MERTON [*low and vehement to* RAVENSBANE]. Impostor!

RAVENSBANE [*still staring at the door*]. She is gone.

JUSTICE MERTON. You at least shall not play the lord and master to my face.

RAVENSBANE. Quite — gone!

JUSTICE MERTON. I know with whom I have to deal. If I be any judge of my own flesh and blood — permit me — you shall quail before me.

RAVENSBANE [*dejectedly*]. She did not smile — [*joyously*] She smiled!

JUSTICE MERTON. Affected rogue! I know thee. I know thy feigned pauses, thy assumed vagaries. Speak; how much do you want?

RAVENSBANE. Betrothed, — he went away. That was good. And then — she did not smile: that was not good. But then — she smiled! Ah! that was good.

JUSTICE MERTON. Come back, coward, and face me.

RAVENSBANE. First, the great sun shone over the cornfields, the grass was green; the black wings rose and flew before me; then the door opened — and she looked at me.

JUSTICE MERTON. Speak, I say! What sum? What treasure do you hope to bleed from me?

RAVENSBANE [*ecstatically*]. Ah! Mistress Rachel!

JUSTICE MERTON. Her! Scoundrel, if thou dost name her again, my innocent — my sweet maid! If thou dost — thou godless spawn of temptation — mark you, I will put an end — [*reaching for a pistol that rests in a rack on the wall, — the intervening form of* DICKON *suddenly appears, pockets the pistol, and exit*].

DICKON. I beg pardon; I forgot something.

JUSTICE MERTON [*sinking into a chair*]. God is just. [*He holds his head in his hands and weeps*]

RAVENSBANE [*for the first time, since* RACHEL'S *departure, observes* MERTON]. Permit me, sir, are you ill?

JUSTICE MERTON [*recoiling*]. What art thou?

RAVENSBANE [*monotonously*]. I am Lord Ravensbane: Marquis of Oxford, Baron of Wittenberg, Elector of Worms, and —

JUSTICE MERTON. And my son! [*Covers his face again*]

RAVENSBANE [*solicitously*]. Shall I call Dickon?

JUSTICE MERTON. Yea, for thou art my son. The deed once done is never done, the past is the present.

RAVENSBANE [*walking softly toward the door, calls*]. Dickon!

JUSTICE MERTON [*starting up*]. No, do not call him. Stay, and be merciful. Tell me: I hate thee not; thou wast innocent. Tell me! — I thought thou hadst died as a babe. — Where has Dickon, our tyrant, kept thee these twenty years?

RAVENSBANE [*with gentle courtesy*]. Master Dickonson is my tutor.

JUSTICE MERTON. And why has thy mother — Ah, I know well; I deserve all. But yet, it must not be published now! I am a justice now, an honoured citizen — and my young niece — Thy mother will not demand so much; she will be considerate, she will ask some gold, of course, but she will show pity!

RAVENSBANE. My mother is the Marchioness of Rickby.

JUSTICE MERTON. Yes, yes; 'twas well planned, a clever trick. 'Twas skilful of her. But surely thy mother gave thee commands to —

RAVENSBANE. My mother gave me her blessing.

JUSTICE MERTON. Ah, 'tis well then.

Young man, my son, I too will give thee my blessing, if thou wilt but go — go instantly — go with half my fortune, go away forever, and leave my reputation unstained.

RAVENSBANE. Go away? [*Starting for the study door*] Ah, sir, with much pleasure.

JUSTICE MERTON. You will go? You will leave me my honour — and my Rachel?

RAVENSBANE. Rachel? Rachel is yours? No, no, Mistress Rachel is mine. We are ours.

JUSTICE MERTON [*pleadingly*]. Consider the disgrace.

RAVENSBANE. No, no; I have seen her eyes, they are mine; I have seen her smiles, they are mine; she is mine!

JUSTICE MERTON. Consider, one moment consider — you, an illegitimate — and she — oh, think what thou art!

RAVENSBANE [*monotonously, puffing smoke at the end*]. I am Lord Ravensbane: Marquis of Oxford, Baron of Wittenberg, Elector of Worms, and Count —

JUSTICE MERTON [*wrenching the pipe from* RAVENSBANE'S *hand and lips*]. Devil's child! Boor! Buffoon! [*Flinging the pipe away*] I will stand thy insults no longer. If thou hast no heart —

RAVENSBANE [*putting his hand to his side, staggers*]. Ah! my heart!

JUSTICE MERTON. Hypocrite! Thou canst not fool me. I am thy father.

RAVENSBANE [*faintly, stretching out his hand to him for support*]. Father!

JUSTICE MERTON. Stand away. Thou mayst break thy heart and mine and the devil's, but thou shalt not break Rachel's.

RAVENSBANE [*faintly*]. Mistress Rachel is mine — [*He staggers again, and falls, half reclining, upon a chair*].

JUSTICE MERTON. Good God! Can it be — his heart?

RAVENSBANE [*more faintly, beginning to change expression*]. Her eyes are mine; her smiles are mine. [*His eyes close*]

JUSTICE MERTON [*with agitated swiftness, feels and listens at* RAVENSBANE'S *side*]. Not a motion; not a sound! Yea, God, Thou art good! 'Tis his heart. He is — ah! he is my son. Judge Almighty, if he should die now; may I not be still a moment more and make sure. No, no, my son — he is changing. [*Calls*] Help! Help!

Rachel! Master Dickonson! Help! Richard! Cynthia! Come hither!

[*Enter* DICKON *and* RACHEL]

RACHEL. Uncle!

JUSTICE MERTON. Bring wine. Lord Ravensbane has fainted.

RACHEL. Oh! [*Turning swiftly to go*] Micah, wine.

DICKON [*detaining her*]. Stay! His pipe! Where is his lordship's pipe?

RACHEL. Oh, terrible!

[*Enter, at different doors*, MISTRESS MERTON *and* RICHARD]

MISTRESS MERTON. What's the matter?

JUSTICE MERTON [*to* RACHEL]. He threw it away. He is worse. Bring the wine.

MISTRESS MERTON. Look! How strange he appears!

RACHEL [*searching distractedly*]. The pipe! His lordship's pipe! It is lost, Master Dickonson.

DICKON [*stooping, as if searching, with his back turned, having picked up the pipe, is filling and lighting it*]. It must be found. This is a heart attack, my friends; his lordship's life depends on the nicotine. [*Deftly he places the pipe in* RACHEL'S *way*]

RACHEL. Thank God! Here it is. [*Carrying it to the prostrate form of* RAVENSBANE, *she lifts his head and is about to put the pipe in his mouth*] Shall I — shall I put it in?

RICHARD. No! not you.

RACHEL. Sir!

RICHARD. Let his tutor perform that office.

RACHEL [*lifting* LORD RAVENSBANE'S *head again*]. Here, my lord.

RICHARD *and* JUSTICE MERTON [*together*]. Rachel!

RACHEL. You, too, uncle?

DICKON. Pardon me, Mistress Rachel; give the pipe at once. Only a token of true affection can revive his lordship now.

RICHARD [*as* RACHEL *puts the pipe to* RAVENSBANE'S *lips*]. I forbid it, Rachel.

RACHEL [*watching only* RAVENSBANE]. My lord — my lord!

MISTRESS MERTON. Give him air; unbutton his coat. [RACHEL *unbuttons* RAVENSBANE'S *coat, revealing the embroidered waistcoat*] Ah, heavens! What do I see?

JUSTICE MERTON [*looks, blanches,*

and signs silence to MISTRESS MERTON]. Cynthia!

DICKON. See! He puffs — he revives. He is coming to himself.

MISTRESS MERTON [*aside to* JUSTICE MERTON, *with deep tensity*]. That waistcoat! that waistcoat! Brother, hast thou never seen it before?

JUSTICE MERTON. Never, my sister.

RACHEL [*as* RAVENSBANE *rises to his feet*]. At last!

DICKON. Look! he is restored.

RACHEL. God be thanked!

DICKON. My lord, Mistress Rachel has saved your life.

RAVENSBANE [*taking* RACHEL'S *hand*]. Mistress Rachel is mine; we are ours.

RICHARD. Dare to repeat that.

RAVENSBANE [*looking at* RACHEL]. Her eyes are mine.

RICHARD [*flinging his glove in his face*]. And that, sir, is yours. I believe such is the proper fashion in England. If your lordship's last duelling wound is sufficiently healed, perhaps you will deign a reply.

RACHEL. Richard! Your lordship!

RAVENSBANE [*stoops, picks up the glove, pockets it, bows to* RACHEL, *and steps close to* RICHARD]. Permit me! [*He blows a puff of smoke full in* RICHARD'S *face*]

ACT III

The same day. Late afternoon. The same scene as Act II.

RAVENSBANE *and* DICKON *discovered at table, on which are lying two flails.* RAVENSBANE *is dressed in a costume which, composed of silk and jewels, subtly approximates in design to that of his original grosser composition. So artfully, however, is this contrived that, to one ignorant of his origin, his dress would appear to be merely an odd personal whimsy; whereas, to one initiated, it would stamp him grotesquely as the apotheosis of scarecrows.*

DICKON *is sitting in a pedagogical attitude;* RAVENSBANE *stands near him, making a profound bow in the opposite direction.*

RAVENSBANE. Believe me, ladies, with the true sincerity of the heart.

DICKON. Inflection a little more lachrymose, please: "The *true* sincerity of the *heart*."

RAVENSBANE. Believe me, ladies, with the *true* sincerity of the *heart*.

DICKON. Prettily, prettily! Next!

RAVENSBANE [*changing his mien, as if addressing another person*]. Verily, sir, as that prince of poets, the immortal Virgil, has remarked: "Adeo in teneris consuescere multum est."

DICKON. Hm! Act up to the sentiment.

RAVENSBANE. Verily, sir, as that prince —

DICKON. No, no; *basta!* The next.

RAVENSBANE [*with another change to courtly manner*]. Trust me, your Excellency, I will inform his Majesty of your courtesy.

DICKON. His Majesty more emphatic. Remember! You must impress all of the guests this afternoon.

RAVENSBANE. *His Majesty* of your courtesy.

DICKON. Delicious! O thou exquisite flower of love! How thy natal composites have burst in bloom: The pumpkin in thee to a golden collarette; thy mop of crow's wings to these raven locks; thy broomstick to a lordly limp; thy corn-silk to these pale-tinted tassels. Verily in the gallery of scarecrows, thou art the Apollo Belvedere! But continue, Cobby dear: the retort now to the challenge.

RAVENSBANE [*with a superb air*]. The second, I believe.

DICKON. Quite so, my lord.

RAVENSBANE. Sir! The local person whom you represent has done himself the honour of submitting to me a challenge to mortal combat. Sir! Since the remotest times of my feudal ancestors, in such affairs of honour, choice of weapons has ever been the prerogative of the challenged. Sir! This right of etiquette must be observed. Nevertheless, believe me, I have no selfish desire that my superior attainments in this art should assume advantage over my challenger's ignorance. I have, therefore, chosen those combative utensils most appropriate both to his own humble origin and to local tradition. Permit me, sir, to reveal my choice. [*Pointing grandly to the table*] There are my weapons!

DICKON [*clapping his hands*]. My darling *homunculus!* Thou shouldst have acted in Beaumont and Fletcher!

RAVENSBANE. There are my weapons!

DICKON. I could watch thy histrionics till midnight. But thou art tired, poor Jacky; two hours' rehearsal is fatiguing to your lordship.

RAVENSBANE. Mistress Rachel — I may see her now?

DICKON. Romeo! Romeo! Was ever such an amorous puppet show!

RAVENSBANE. Mistress Rachel!

DICKON. Wait; let me think! Thou art wound up now, my pretty apparatus, for at least six and thirty hours. The wooden angel Gabriel that trumpets the hours on the big clock in Venice is not a more punctual manikin than thou with my speeches. Thou shouldst run, therefore, —

RAVENSBANE [*frowning darkly at* DICKON]. Stop talking; permit me! A tutor should know his place.

DICKON [*rubbing his hands*]. Nay, your lordship is beyond comparison.

RAVENSBANE [*in a terrible voice*]. She will come? I shall see her?

[*Enter* MICAH]

MICAH. Pardon, my lord.

RAVENSBANE [*turning joyfully to* MICAH]. Is it she?

MICAH. Captain Bugby, my lord, the Governor's secretary.

DICKON. Good. Squire Talbot's second. Show him in.

RAVENSBANE [*flinging despairingly into a chair*]. Ah! ah!

MICAH [*lifting the flails from the table*]. Beg pardon, sir; shall I remove —

DICKON. Drop them; go.

MICAH. But, sir —

DICKON. Go, thou slave! [*Exit* MICAH]

RAVENSBANE [*in childlike despair*]. She will not come! I shall not see her!

DICKON [*handing him a book*]. Here, my lord; read. You must be found reading.

RAVENSBANE [*flinging the book into the fireplace*]. She does not come!

DICKON. Fie, fie, Jack; thou must not be breaking thy Dickon's apron-strings with a will of thine own. Come!

RAVENSBANE. Mistress Rachel.

DICKON. Be good, boy, and thou shalt see her soon.

RAVENSBANE [*brightening*]. I shall see her?

[*Enter* CAPTAIN BUGBY]

DICKON. Your lordship was saying — Oh! Captain Bugby?

CAPTAIN BUGBY [*nervous and awed*].

Captain Bugby, sir, ah! at Lord Ravensbane's service — ah!

DICKON. I am Master Dickonson, his lordship's tutor.

CAPTAIN BUGBY. Happy, sir.

DICKON [*to* RAVENSBANE]. My lord, this gentleman waits upon you from Squire Talbot. [*To* CAPTAIN BUGBY] In regard to the challenge of this morning, I presume?

CAPTAIN BUGBY. The affair, ah! the affair of this morning, sir.

RAVENSBANE [*with his former superb air — to* CAPTAIN BUGBY]. The second, I believe?

CAPTAIN BUGBY. Quite so, my lord.

RAVENSBANE. Sir! the local person whom you represent has done himself the honour of submitting to me a challenge to mortal combat. Sir! Since the remotest times of my feudal ancestors, in such affairs of honour, choice of weapons has ever been the prerogative of the challenged. Sir! this right of etiquette must be observed.

CAPTAIN BUGBY. Indeed, yes, my lord.

DICKON. Pray do not interrupt. [*To* RAVENSBANE] Your lordship: "observed."

RAVENSBANE. — observed. Nevertheless, believe me, I have no selfish desire that my superior attainments in this art should assume advantage over my challenger's ignorance. I have, therefore, chosen those combative utensils most appropriate both to his own humble origin and to local tradition. Permit me, sir, to reveal my choice. [*Pointing to the table*] There are my weapons!

CAPTAIN BUGBY [*looking, bewildered*]. These, my lord?

RAVENSBANE. Those.

CAPTAIN BUGBY. But these are — are flails.

RAVENSBANE. Flails.

CAPTAIN BUGBY. Flails, my lord?

RAVENSBANE. There are my weapons.

CAPTAIN BUGBY. Lord Ravensbane — I — ah! express myself ill — Do I understand that your lordship and Squire Talbot —

RAVENSBANE. Exactly.

CAPTAIN BUGBY. But your lordship — flails!

RAVENSBANE. My adversary should be deft in their use. He has doubtless wielded them frequently on his barn floor.

CAPTAIN BUGBY. Ahaha! I understand now. Your lordship — ah! is a wit. Haha! Flails!

DICKON. His lordship's satire is poignant.

CAPTAIN BUGBY. Indeed, sir, so keen that I must apologize for laughing at my principal's expense. [*Soberly to* RAVENSBANE]. My lord, if you will deign to speak one moment seriously —

RAVENSBANE. Seriously?

CAPTAIN BUGBY. I will take pleasure in informing Squire Talbot — ah! as to your *real* preference for —

RAVENSBANE. For flails, sir. I have, permit me, nothing further to say. Flails are final. [*Turns away haughtily*]

CAPTAIN BUGBY. Must I really report to Squire Talbot — ah! — flails?

DICKON. Lord Ravensbane's will is inflexible.

CAPTAIN BUGBY. And his wit, sir, incomparable. I am sorry for the Squire, but 'twill be the greatest joke in years. Ah! will you tell me — is it — [*indicating* RAVENSBANE'S *smoking*] is it the latest fashion?

DICKON. Lord Ravensbane is always the latest.

CAPTAIN BUGBY. Obliged servant, sir. Aha! Such a joke as — O lord! flails! [*Exit*]

DICKON [*returning to* RAVENSBANE]. Bravo, my pumpky dear! That squelches the jealous betrothed. Now nothing remains but for you to continue to dazzle the enamoured Rachel, and so present yourself to the Justice as a pseudo-son-nephew-in-law.

RAVENSBANE. I may go to Mistress Rachel?

DICKON. She will come to you. She is reading now a poem from you, which I left on her dressing-table.

RAVENSBANE. She is reading a poem from me?

DICKON. With your pardon, my lord, I penned it for you. I am something of a poetaster. Indeed, I flatter myself that I have dictated some of the finest lines in literature.

RAVENSBANE. Dickon! She will come?

DICKON. She comes! [*Enter* RACHEL, *reading from a piece of paper*] Hush! Step aside; step aside first. Let her read it. [DICKON *draws* RAVENSBANE *back*]

RACHEL. Once more, [*reads*] "To Mistress R——, enchantress:

If faith in witchcraft be a sin,
Alas! what peril he is in
Who plights his faith and love in thee,
Sweetest maid of sorcery.

If witchcraft be a whirling brain,
A roving eye, a heart of pain,
Whose wound no thread of fate can stitch,
How hast thou conjured, cruel witch,
  With the brain, eye, heart, and total
mortal residue of thine enamoured
        JACK LANTHORNE,
          [LORD R——.*"*]

DICKON. Now to leave the turtles alone. [*Exit*]

RACHEL. "To Mistress R——, enchantress: If faith in witchcraft be —" "To Mistress R——." R! It *must* be. R—— must mean —

RAVENSBANE [*with passionate deference*]. Rachel!

RACHEL. Ah! How you surprised me, my lord.

RAVENSBANE. You are come again; you are come again.

RACHEL. Has anything happened? Tell me, my lord. Has Squire Talbot been here?

RAVENSBANE. No, Mistress Rachel; not here.

RACHEL. And you have not — Oh, my lord, I have been in such terror. But you are safe. — You have not fought?

RAVENSBANE. No, Mistress Rachel; not fought.

RACHEL. Thank God for that! But you will promise me — promise me that there shall be — no — duel!

RAVENSBANE. I promise Mistress Rachel there shall be no duel.

RACHEL. Your lordship is so good. You do not know how gratefully happy I am.

RAVENSBANE. I know I am only a thing to make Mistress Rachel happy. Ah! look at me once more. When you look at me, I live.

RACHEL. It is strange indeed, my lord, how the familiar world, the daylight, the heavens themselves have changed since your arrival.

RAVENSBANE. This is the world; this is the light; this is the heavens themselves. Mistress Rachel is looking at me.

RACHEL. For me, it is less strange perhaps. I never saw a real lord before. But you, my lord, must have seen so many, many girls in the great world.

RAVENSBANE. No, no; never.

RACHEL. No other girls before to-day, my lord!

RAVENSBANE. Before to-day? I do not know; I do not care. I was not here. To-day I was born — in your eyes. Ah! my brain whirls!

RACHEL [*smiling*]
"If witchcraft be a whirling brain,
  A roving eye, a heart of pain, —"
[*In a whisper*] My lord, do you really believe in witchcraft?

RAVENSBANE. With all my heart.

RACHEL. And approve of it?

RAVENSBANE. With all my soul.

RACHEL. So do I — that is, innocent witchcraft; not to harm anybody, you know, but just to feel all the dark mystery and the trembling excitement — the way you feel when you blow out your candle all alone in your bedroom and watch the little smoke fade away in the moonshine.

RAVENSBANE. Fade away in the moonshine!

RACHEL. Oh, but we mustn't speak of it. In a town like this, all such mysticism is considered damnable. But your lordship understands and approves? I am so glad! Have you read the "Philosophical Considerations" of Glanville, the "*Saducismus Triumphatus*", and the "Presignifications of Dreams"? What kind of witchcraft, my lord, do you believe in?

RAVENSBANE. In all yours.

RACHEL. Nay, your lordship must not take me for a real witch. I can only tell fortunes, you know — like this morning.

RAVENSBANE. I know; you told how my heart would break.

RACHEL. Oh, that's palmistry, and that isn't always certain. But the surest way to prophesy — do you know what it is?

RAVENSBANE. Tell me.

RACHEL. To count the crows. Do you know how? One for sorrow —

RAVENSBANE. Ha, yes! — Two for mirth!

RACHEL. Three for a wedding —

RAVENSBANE. Four for a birth —

RACHEL. And five for the happiest thing on earth!

RAVENSBANE. Mistress Rachel, come! Let us go and count five crows.

RACHEL [*delightedly*]. Why, my lord, how did *you* ever learn it? I got it from an old goody here in town — a real witch-wife. If you will promise not to tell a secret, I will show you. — But you must promise!

RAVENSBANE. I promise.

RACHEL. Come, then. I will show you a real piece of witchcraft that I bought from her this morning — the glass of truth. There! Behind that curtain. If you look in, you will see — But come; I will show you. [*They put their hands on the cords of the curtain*] Just pull that string, and — ah!

DICKON [*stepping out through the curtain*]. Your pipe, my lord?

RACHEL. Master Dickonson, how you frightened me!

DICKON. So excessively sorry! I was observing the portrait of your uncle. I believe you were showing his lordship —

RACHEL [*turning hurriedly away*]. Oh, nothing; nothing at all.

RAVENSBANE [*sternly to* DICKON]. Why do you come?

DICKON [*handing back* RAVENSBANE'S *pipe filled*]. Allow me. [*Aside*] 'Tis high time you came to the point, Jack; 'tis near your lordship's reception. Woo and win, boy; woo and win.

RAVENSBANE [*haughtily*]. Leave me.

DICKON. Your lordship's humble, very humble. [*Exit*]

RACHEL [*shivering*]. Oh! he is gone. My dear lord, why do you keep this man?

RAVENSBANE. I — keep this man?

RACHEL. I cannot — pardon my rudeness — I cannot endure him.

RAVENSBANE. You do not like him? Ah, then, I do not like him also. We will send him away — you and I.

RACHEL. You, my lord, of course; but I —

RAVENSBANE. You will be Dickon! You will be with me always and light my pipe. And I will live for you, and fight for you, and kill your betrothed!

RACHEL [*drawing away*]. No, no!

RAVENSBANE. Ah! but your eyes say "yes." Mistress Rachel leaves me; but Rachel in her eyes remains. Is it not so?

RACHEL. What can I say, my lord! It is true that since my eyes met yours, a new passion has entered into my soul. I have felt — your lordship will laugh at me — I have felt an inexpressible longing — but 'tis so impertinent, my lord, so absurd in me, a mere girl, and you a nobleman of power — yet I have felt it irresistibly, my dear lord, — a longing to help you. I am so sorry for

you — so sorry for you! I pity you deeply. — Forgive me; forgive me, my lord!

RAVENSBANE. It is enough.

RACHEL. Indeed, indeed, 'tis so rude of me, — 'tis so unreasonable.

RAVENSBANE. It is enough. I grow — I grow — I grow! I am a plant; you give it rain and sun. I am a flower; you give it light and dew; I am a soul, you give it love and speech. I grow. Towards you — towards you I grow!

RACHEL. My lord, I do not understand it, how so poor and mere a girl as I can have helped you. Yet I do believe it is so; for I feel it so. What can I do for you?

RAVENSBANE. Do not leave me. Be mine. Let me be yours.

RACHEL. Ah! but, my lord — do I love you?

RAVENSBANE. What is "I love you"? Is it a kiss, a sigh, an embrace? Ah! then, you do not love me. — "I love you": is it to nourish, to nestle, to lift up, to smile upon, to make greater — a worm? Ah! then, you love me.

[*Enter* RICHARD *at left back, unobserved*]

RACHEL. Do not speak so of yourself, my lord; nor exalt me so falsely.

RAVENSBANE. Be mine.

RACHEL. A great glory has descended upon this day.

RAVENSBANE. Be mine.

RACHEL. Could I but be sure that this glory is love — Oh, *then!* [*Turns toward* RAVENSBANE]

RICHARD [*stepping between them*]. It is *not* love; it is witchcraft.

RACHEL. Who are you? — Richard?

RICHARD. You have indeed forgotten me? Would to God, Rachel, I could forget you.

RAVENSBANE. Sir, permit me —

RICHARD. Silence! [*To* RACHEL] Against my will, I am a convert to your own mysticism; for nothing less than damnable illusion could so instantly wean your heart from me to — this. I do not pretend to understand it; but that it is witchcraft I am convinced; and I will save you from it.

RACHEL. Go; please go.

RAVENSBANE. Permit me, sir; you have not replied yet to flails!

RICHARD. Permit *me*, sir. [*Taking something from his coat*] My answer is — bare cob! [*Holding out a shelled corn-cob*] Thresh this, sir, for your antagonist. 'Tis the only one worthy your lordship. [*Tosses it contemptuously towards him*]

RAVENSBANE. Upon my honour, as a man —

RICHARD. As a *man* forsooth! Were you indeed a man, Lord Ravensbane, I would have accepted your weapons, and flailed you out of New England. But it is not my custom to chastise runagates from asylums, or to banter further words with a natural and a ninny.

RACHEL. Squire Talbot! Will you leave my uncle's house?

RAVENSBANE. One moment, mistress: — I did not wholly catch the import of this gentleman's speech, but I fancy I have insulted him by my reply to his challenge. One insult may perhaps be remedied by another. Sir, permit me to call *you* a ninny, and to offer you — [*Drawing his sword and offering it*] swords.

RICHARD. Thanks; I reject the offer.

RAVENSBANE [*turning away despondently*]. He rejects it. Well!

RACHEL [*to* RICHARD]. And *now* will you leave?

RICHARD. At once. But one word more. Rachel — Rachel, have you forgotten this morning and the glass of truth?

RACHEL [*coldly*]. No.

RICHARD. Call it a fancy now if you will. I scoffed at it; yes. Yet *you* believed it. I loved you truly, you said. Well, have I changed?

RACHEL. Yes.

RICHARD. Will you test me again — in the glass?

RACHEL. No. Go; leave us.

RICHARD. I will go. I have still a word with your aunt.

RAVENSBANE [*to* RICHARD]. I beg your pardon, sir. You said just now that had I been a man —

RICHARD. I say, Lord Ravensbane, that the straight fibre of a true man never warps the love of a woman. As for yourself, you have my contempt and pity. Pray to God, sir, pray to God to make you a man. [*Exit, right*]

RACHEL. Oh! it is intolerable! [*To* RAVENSBANE] My dear lord, I do believe in my heart that I love you, and if so, I will with gratitude be your wife. But, my lord, strange glamours, strange darknesses reel, and bewilder my mind. I must be alone; I must think and decide. Will you give me this tassel?

RAVENSBANE [*unfastening a silk tassel from his coat and giving it to her*]. Oh, take it.

RACHEL. If I decide that I love you, that I will be your wife — I will wear it this afternoon at the reception. Good-by. [*Exit, right*]

RAVENSBANE. Mistress Rachel! — [*Solus*] God, are you here? Dear God, I pray to you — make me to be a man! [*Exit, left*]

DICKON [*appearing in the centre of the room*]. Poor Jacky! Thou shouldst 'a' prayed to t'other one. [*He disappears. Enter, right,* RICHARD *and* MISTRESS MERTON]

MISTRESS MERTON [*pointing to the wall*]. That is the portrait.

RICHARD. Indeed! The design is very like.

MISTRESS MERTON. 'Tis more than like, Richard; 'tis the very same. Two and twenty years ago she embroidered it for him, and he would insist on wearing it for the portrait he was then sitting for.

RICHARD. That same Goody Rickby!

MISTRESS MERTON. A pretty girl! — and a wild young man was my brother. The truth comes hard to tell thee, Richard; but he was wild, Gilead was wild. He told me the babe had died. But God worketh His own righteousness. Only — he must be saved now; Rachel must be saved; we must all be saved.

RICHARD. You feel sure — very sure, Mistress Merton?

MISTRESS MERTON. Yea, that waistcoat; 'tis the very one, I know it too well. And you see it accounts for all, — this silly impostor lord; my brother's strange patronage of him; the blackmail of this Master Dickonson —

RICHARD. But who is *he?*

MISTRESS MERTON. Nay, heaven knows! Some old crony perchance of Gilead's youth; some confederate of this woman Rickby.

RICHARD. O God! — And Rachel sacrificed to these impostors; to an illegitimate — your brother would allow it!

MISTRESS MERTON. Ah! but think of his own reputation, Richard. He a justice — the family honour!

RICHARD. 'Tis enough. Well, and I must see this Goody Rickby, you think?

MISTRESS MERTON. At once — at once. My brother has invited guests for this afternoon to meet "his lordship"! Return, if possible, before they come. She dwells at the blacksmith shop — you must buy her off. Oh, gold will buy her; 'tis the gold they're after — all of them; have her recall both these persons. [*Giving a purse*] Take her that, Richard, and promise her more.

RICHARD [*proudly*]. Keep it, Mistress Merton. I have enough gold, methinks, for my future wife's honour; or if not, I will earn it. [*Exit*]

MISTRESS MERTON. Richard! Ah, the dear lad, he should have taken it.

[*Enter* MICAH]

MICAH. The minister and his wife have turned into the gate, madam.

MISTRESS MERTON. The guests! Is it so late?

MICAH. Four o'clock, madam. [*Going to the table*] Shall I remove these?

MISTRESS MERTON. Flails! Flails in the parlour? Of course, remove them.

MICAH [*at the door*]. Madam, in all my past years of service at Merton House, I never waited upon a lord till to-day. Madam, in all my future years of service at Merton House, I trust I may never wait upon a lord again.

MISTRESS MERTON. Micah, mind the knocker.

MICAH. Yes, madam. [*Exit at left back. Sounds of a brass knocker outside*]

MISTRESS MERTON. Rachel! Rachel! [*Exit, right. Enter, left,* JUSTICE MERTON *and* DICKON]

JUSTICE MERTON. So you are contented with nothing less than the sacrifice of my niece?

DICKON. Such a delightful room!

JUSTICE MERTON. Are you merciless?

DICKON. And such a living portrait of your worship! The waistcoat is so beautifully executed.

JUSTICE MERTON. If I pay him ten thousand pounds —

[*Enter* MICAH]

MICAH. Minister Dodge, your worship; and Mistress Dodge. [*Exit. Enter the* MINISTER *and his* WIFE]

JUSTICE MERTON [*stepping forward to receive them*]. Believe me, this is a great privilege. — Madam! [*Bowing*]

MINISTER DODGE [*taking his hand*]. The privilege is ours, Justice; to enter a righteous man's house is to stand, as it were, on God's threshold.

JUSTICE MERTON [*nervously*]. Amen, amen. Permit me — ah! Lord Ravensbane, my young guest of honour, will be here directly — permit me to present his lordship's tutor, Master Dickonson; The Reverend Master Dodge, Mistress Dodge.

MINISTER DODGE [*offering his hand*]. Master Dickonson, sir —

DICKON [*barely touching the minister's fingers, bows charmingly to his wife*]. Madam, of all professions in the world, your husband's most allures me.

MISTRESS DODGE. 'Tis a worthy one, sir.

DICKON. Ah! Mistress Dodge, and so arduous — especially for a minister's wife. [*He leads her to a chair*]

MISTRESS DODGE [*accepting the chair*]. Thank you.

MINISTER DODGE. Lord Ravensbane comes from abroad?

JUSTICE MERTON. From London.

MINISTER DODGE. An old friend of yours, I understand.

JUSTICE MERTON. From London, yes. Did I say from London? Quite so; from London.

[*Enter* MICAH]

MICAH. Captain Bugby, the Governor's secretary.

[*Exit. Enter* CAPTAIN BUGBY. *He walks with a slight lameness, and holds daintily in his hand a pipe, from which he puffs with dandy deliberation*]

CAPTAIN BUGBY. Justice Merton, your very humble servant.

JUSTICE MERTON. Believe me, Captain Bugby.

CAPTAIN BUGBY [*profusely*]. Ah, Master Dickonson! my dear friend Master Dickonson — this is indeed — ah! How is his lordship since — aha! but discretion! Mistress Dodge — her servant! Ah! yes, [*Indicating his pipe with a smile of satisfaction*] the latest, I assure you; the very latest from London. Ask Master Dickonson.

MINISTER DODGE [*looking at* CAPTAIN BUGBY]. These will hatch out in the springtime.

CAPTAIN BUGBY [*confidentially to* DICKON]. But really, my good friend, may not I venture to inquire how his lordship — ah! has been in health since — ah! since —

DICKON [*impressively*]. Oh! quite, quite!

[*Enter* MISTRESS MERTON; *she joins* JUSTICE MERTON *and* MINISTER DODGE]

CAPTAIN BUGBY. You know, I informed Squire Talbot of his lordship's epigrammatic retort — his retort of — shh! ha haha! Oh, that reply was a stiletto; 'twas sharper than a sword-thrust, I assure you. To have conceived it — 'twas inspiration; but to have expressed it — oh! 'twas genius. Hush! "Flails!" Oh! It sticks me now in the ribs. I shall die with concealing it.

MINISTER DODGE [*to* MISTRESS MERTON]. 'Tis true, mistress; but if there were more like your brother in the parish, the conscience of the community would be clearer.

[*Enter* MICAH]

MICAH. The Reverend Master Rand of Harvard College; the Reverend Master Todd of Harvard College.

[*Exit. Enter two elderly, straight-backed divines*]

JUSTICE MERTON [*greeting them*]. Permit me, gentlemen; this is fortunate — before your return to Cambridge.

[*He conducts them to* MISTRESS MERTON *and* MINISTER DODGE, *center. Seated left,* DICKON *is ingratiating himself with* MISTRESS DODGE; CAPTAIN BUGBY, *laughed at by both parties, is received by neither*]

CAPTAIN BUGBY [*puffing smoke toward the ceiling*]. Really, I cannot understand what keeps his Excellency, the Lieutenant Governor, so long. He has two such charming daughters, Master Dickonson —

DICKON [*to* MISTRESS DODGE]. Yes, yes; such suspicious women with their charms are an insult to the virtuous ladies of the parish.

CAPTAIN BUGBY. How, sir!

MISTRESS DODGE. And to think that she should actually shoe horses herself!

DICKON. It is too hard, dear Mistress Dodge; too hard!

MISTRESS DODGE. You are so appreciative, Master Dickonson.

CAPTAIN BUGBY [*piqued, walks another way*]. Well!

REV. MASTER RAND [*to* JUSTICE MERTON]. It would not be countenanced in the college yard, sir.

REV. MASTER TODD. A pipe! Nay, *mores inhibitae!*

JUSTICE MERTON. 'Tis most unfortunate, gentlemen; but I understand 'tis the new vogue in London.

[*Enter* MICAH]

MICAH. His Excellency, Sir Charles Reddington, Lieutenant Governor; the Mistress Reddingtons.

CAPTAIN BUGBY. At last!

MISTRESS MERTON [*aside*]. Micah.

[MICAH *goes to her. Enter* SIR CHARLES, MISTRESS REDDINGTON, *and* AMELIA REDDINGTON]

JUSTICE MERTON. Your Excellency, this is indeed a distinguished honour.

SIR CHARLES [*shaking hands*]. Fine weather, Merton. Where's your young lord?

THE TWO GIRLS [*courtesying*]. Justice Merton, Mistress Merton.

MICAH [*to* MISTRESS MERTON, *as he is going out, right*]. I will speak to them, madam.

CAPTAIN BUGBY. Oh, my dear Mistress Reddington! Charming Mistress Amelia! You are so very late, but you shall hear — hush!

MISTRESS REDDINGTON [*noticing his pipe*]. Why, what is this, Captain?

CAPTAIN BUGBY. Oh, the latest, I assure you, the very latest. Wait till you see his lordship.

AMELIA. What! isn't he here? [*Laughing*]. La, Captain! Do look at the man!

CAPTAIN BUGBY. Oh, he's coming directly. Quite the mode — what? Ah! but, ladies, you shall hear. [*He talks to them aside, where they titter*]

SIR CHARLES [*to* DICKON]. What say? Travelling for his health?

DICKON. Partially, your Excellency; but my young pupil and master is a singularly affectionate nature.

THE TWO GIRLS [*to* CAPTAIN BUGBY]. What! flails — really! [*They burst into laughter among themselves*]

DICKON. He has journeyed here to Massachusetts peculiarly to pay this visit to Justice Merton — his father's dearest friend.

SIR CHARLES. Ah! knew him abroad, eh?

DICKON. In Rome, your Excellency.

MISTRESS DODGE [*to* JUSTICE MERTON]. Why, I thought it was in London.

JUSTICE MERTON. London, true,

quite so; we made a trip together to Lisbon — ah! Rome.

DICKON. Paris, was it not, sir?

JUSTICE MERTON [*in great distress*]. Paris, Paris, very true; I am — I am — sometimes I am —

[*Enter* MICAH, *right*]

MICAH [*announces*]. Lord Ravensbane.

[*Enter right*, RAVENSBANE *with* RACHEL]

JUSTICE MERTON [*with a gasp of relief*]. Ah! his lordship is arrived.

[*Murmurs of "his lordship" and a flutter among the girls and* CAPTAIN BUGBY]

CAPTAIN BUGBY. Look! — Now!

JUSTICE MERTON. Welcome, my lord! [*To* SIR CHARLES] Permit me, your Excellency, to introduce —

RAVENSBANE. Permit me; Mistress Rachel will introduce —

RACHEL [*courtesying*]. Sir Charles, allow me to present my friend, Lord Ravensbane.

MISTRESS REDDINGTON [*aside to* AMELIA]. Her *friend* — did you hear?

SIR CHARLES. Mistress Rachel, I see you are as pretty as ever. Lord Ravensbane, your hand, sir.

RAVENSBANE. Trust me, your Excellency, I will inform his Majesty of your courtesy.

CAPTAIN BUGBY [*watching* RAVENSBANE *with chagrin*]. On my life! he's lost his limp.

RAVENSBANE [*apart to* RACHEL]. "A great glory has descended upon this day."

RACHEL [*shyly*]. My lord!

RAVENSBANE. Be sure — O mistress, be sure — that this glory is love.

SIR CHARLES [*watching the two, whispers a loud aside to* JUSTICE MERTON]. Hoho! is it congratulations for your niece?

JUSTICE MERTON. Not — not precisely.

DICKON [*aside to* JUSTICE MERTON]. Why so, Gilly?

SIR CHARLES. My daughters, Fanny and Amelia — Lord Ravensbane.

THE TWO GIRLS [*courtesying*]. Your lordship!

SIR CHARLES. Good girls, but silly.

THE TWO GIRLS. Papa!

RAVENSBANE. Believe me, ladies, with the *true* sincerity of the *heart*.

MISTRESS REDDINGTON. Isn't he perfection!

CAPTAIN BUGBY. What said I?

AMELIA [*giggling*]. I can't help thinking of flails.

MISTRESS REDDINGTON. Poor Squire Talbot! We must be nice to him now.

AMELIA. Oh, especially *now!*

RAVENSBANE [*whom* RACHEL *continues to introduce to the guests; to* MASTER RAND]. Verily, sir, as that prince of poets, the immortal Virgil, has remarked: "Adeo in teneris consuescere multum est."

DICKON. Just a word, your worship.

JUSTICE MERTON [*going with him*]. Intolerable!

REV. MASTER TODD. His lordship is evidently a university man.

REV. MASTER RAND. Evidently most accomplished.

JUSTICE MERTON [*aside to* DICKON]. A song! Why, it is beyond all bounds of custom and decorum.

DICKON. Believe me, there is no such flatterer to win the maiden heart as music.

JUSTICE MERTON. And here; in this presence! Never!

DICKON. Nevertheless, it will amuse me vastly, and you will announce it.

RAVENSBANE [*to* MINISTER DODGE]. My opinion is simple: In such matters of church government, I am inclined toward the leniency of that excellent master, the Rev. John Wise, rather than the righteous obduracy of the Rev. Cotton Mather.

MINISTER DODGE. Why, there, sir, I agree with you. [*Aside to his wife*] How extremely well informed!

MISTRESS DODGE. And so young, too!

JUSTICE MERTON [*with hesitant embarrassment, which he seeks to conceal*]. Your Excellency and friends, I have great pleasure in announcing his lordship's condescension in consenting to regale our present company — with a song.

SEVERAL VOICES [*in various degrees of amazement and curiosity*]. A song!

MISTRESS MERTON. Gilead! What is this?

JUSTICE MERTON. The selection is a German ballad — a particular favourite at the court of Prussia, where his lordship last rendered it. His tutor has made a translation which is entitled : "The Prognostication of the Crows", and I am requested to remind you that in the ancient heathen mythology of

Germany, the crow or raven, was the fateful bird of the God Woden.

CAPTAIN BUGBY. How prodigiously novel!

MINISTER DODGE [*frowning*]. Unparalleled!

SIR CHARLES. A ballad! Come now, that sounds like old England again. Let's have it. Will his lordship sing without music?

JUSTICE MERTON. Master Dickonson, hem! has been — persuaded — to accompany his lordship on the virginals.

AMELIA. How delightful!

REV. MASTER RAND [*aside to* TODD]. Shall we remain?

REV. MASTER TODD. We must.

RAVENSBANE [*to* RACHEL]. My tassel, dear mistress; you do not wear it?

RACHEL. My heart still wavers, my lord. But whilst you sing, I will decide.

RAVENSBANE. Whilst I sing? My fate, then, is waiting at the end of a song?

RACHEL. At the end of a song.

DICKON [*touches* RAVENSBANE'S *arm*]. Your lordship.

RAVENSBANE [*starting, turns to the company*]. Permit me.

[DICKON *sits, facing left, at the virginals. At first, his fingers in playing give sound only to the soft tinkling notes of that ancient instrument; but gradually, strange notes and harmonies of an aërial orchestra mingle with, and at length drown, the virginals. The final chorus is produced solely by fantastic symphonic cawings, as of countless crows, in harsh but musical accord. During the song* RICHARD *enters.* DICKON'S *music, however, does not cease but fills the intervals between the verses. To his accompaniment, amid the whispered and gradually increasing wonder, resentment, and dismay of the assembled guests,* RAVENSBANE, *with his eyes fixed upon* RACHEL, *sings*]

Baron von Rabenstod arose;
　(The golden sun was rising)
Before him flew a flock of crows:
　Sing heigh! Sing heigh! Sing heigh!
　Sing —
" Ill speed, ill speed thee, baron-wight;
　Ill speed thy palfrey pawing!
Blithe is the morn but black the night
　That hears a raven's cawing."

　　　　　[*Chorus*]

　　Caw! Caw! Caw!

MISTRESS DODGE [*whispers to her husband*]. Did you hear them?

MINISTER DODGE. Hush!

AMELIA [*sotto voce*]. What *can* it be?

CAPTAIN BUGBY. Oh, the latest, be sure.

DICKON. You note, my friends, the accompanying harmonics; they are an intrinsic part of the ballad, and may not be omitted.

RAVENSBANE [*sings*].
The baron reckèd not a pin;
　(For the golden sun was rising)
He rode to woo, he rode to win;
　Sing heigh! Sing heigh! Sing heigh!
　Sing —
He rode into his prince's hall
　Through knights and damsels flow'ry:
" Thy daughter, prince, I bid thee call;
　I claim her hand and dowry."

[*Enter* RICHARD. MISTRESS MERTON *seizes his arm nervously*]

MISTRESS MERTON [*aside*]. Well?

RICHARD. Gold will not buy her. She defies us.

SIR CHARLES [*to* CAPTAIN BUGBY]. This gentleman's playing is rather ventriloquistical.

CAPTAIN BUGBY. Quite, as it were.

REV. MASTER TODD. This smells unholy.

REV. MASTER RAND [*to* TODD]. Shall we leave?

JUSTICE MERTON [*sternly to* RICHARD, *who has attempted to talk with him aside*]. Not now.

RICHARD. Pardon me — it *must* be now.

JUSTICE MERTON. Squire Talbot —

RICHARD [*very low*]. Sir — I come from Goody Rickby.

JUSTICE MERTON. Hush! [*They go apart*]

RAVENSBANE [*sings*].
" What cock is this, with crest so high,
　That crows with such a pother?"
" Baron von Rabenstod am I;
　Methinks we know each other."
" Now welcome, welcome, dear guest of mine,
　So long why didst thou tarry?
Now, for the sake of auld lang syne,
　My daughter thou shalt marry."

JUSTICE MERTON [*to* RICHARD]. Spare me, I am helpless.

RICHARD. What! you will sacrifice her?

JUSTICE MERTON. What can I do?

RICHARD. Tell her the truth at least.

JUSTICE MERTON. Never, Richard, no, no, never that!

AMELIA [*to* BUGBY]. And he kept right on smoking!

MINISTER DODGE [*who, with* RAND *and* TODD, *has risen uneasily*]. This smacks of witchcraft.

REV. MASTER RAND. The Justice seems moved.

RAVENSBANE [*sings*].
The bride is brought, the priest as well;
(The golden sun was passing)
They stood beside the altar rail;
Sing ah! Sing ah! Sing ah! Sing—
"Woman, with this ring I thee wed."
What makes his voice so awing?
The baron by the bride is dead:
Outside the crows were cawing.

Chorus

[*Which grows tumultuous, seeming to fill the room with the invisible birds*]

Caw! Caw! Caw!

[*The guests rise in confusion.* DICKON *still plays delightedly, and the strange music continues*]

MINISTER DODGE. This is no longer godly. — Justice Merton!

RICHARD [*to* JUSTICE MERTON]. I told you, sir, that witchcraft, like murder, will out. If you want further proof, I believe I can provide it.

MINISTER DODGE. Justice Merton, sir!

RAVENSBANE [*to* RACHEL, *who holds his tassel in her hand*]. Ah! and you have my tassel!

RACHEL. See! I will wear it now. You yourself shall fasten it.

RAVENSBANE. Rachel! Mistress!

RACHEL. My dear lord!

[*As* RAVENSBANE *is placing the silken tassel on* RACHEL'S *breast to fasten it there,* RICHARD, *by the mirror, pulls the curtain back*]

RICHARD. Lovers! This is the glass of truth. Behold yourselves!

RACHEL [*looking into the glass, screams and turns her gaze fearfully upon* RAVENSBANE]. Ah! Do not look!

DICKON [*who, having turned round from the virginals, has leapt forward, now turns back again, biting his finger*]. Too late!

[*In the glass are reflected the figures of* RACHEL *and* RAVENSBANE — RACHEL *just as she herself appears, but* RAVENSBANE *in his essential form*

of a scarecrow, *in every movement reflecting* RAVENSBANE'S *motions. The thing in the glass is about to pin a wisp of corn-silk on the mirrored breast of the maiden*]

RAVENSBANE. What is there?

RACHEL [*looking again, starts away from* RAVENSBANE]. Leave me! Leave me! — Richard!

RAVENSBANE [*gazing at the glass, clings to* RACHEL *as though to protect her*]. Help her! See! It is seizing her.

RACHEL. Richard! [*She faints in* RICHARD'S *arms*]

RAVENSBANE. Fear not, mistress, I will kill the thing. [*Drawing his sword, he rushes at the glass. Within, the scarecrow, with a drawn wheel-spoke, approaches him at equal speed. They come face to face and recoil*]. Ah! ah! fear'st thou me? What art thou? Why, 'tis a glass. Thou mockest me? Look, look, mistress, it mocks me! O God, no! no! Take it away. Dear God, do not look! — It is I!

ALL [*rushing to the doors*]. Witchcraft! Witchcraft! [*As* RAVENSBANE *stands frantically confronting his abject reflection, struck in a like posture of despair, the curtain falls*]

ACT IV

The same. Night. The moon, shining in broadly at the window, discovers RAVENSBANE *alone, prostrate before the mirror. Raised on one arm to a half-sitting posture, he gazes fixedly at the vaguely seen image of the scarecrow prostrate in the glass.*

RAVENSBANE. All have left me — but not thou. Rachel has left me; her eyes have turned away from me; she is gone. And with her, the great light itself from heaven has drawn her glorious skirts, contemptuous, from me — and they are gone together. Dickon, he too has left me — but not thou. All that I loved, all that loved me, have left me. A thousand ages — a thousand ages ago, they went away; and thou and I have gazed upon each other's desertedness. Speak! and be pitiful! If thou art I, inscrutable image, if thou dost feel these pangs thine own, show then selfmercy; speak! What art thou? What am I? Why are we here? How comes it that we feel and guess and suffer? Nay, though thou answer not these doubts, yet mock them, mock them aloud, even as there, monstrous, thou counterfeitest mine actions. Speak, abject enigma! — Ah! with what vacant horror it looks out and yearns toward me. Peace to thee! Thou poor delirious mute, prisoned in glass and moonlight, peace! Thou canst not escape thy gaol, nor I break in to thee. Poor shadow, thou — [*Recoiling wildly*] Stand back, inanity! Thrust not thy mawkish face in pity toward me. Ape and idiot! Scarecrow! — to console me! Haha! — A flail and broomstick! a cob, a gourd and pumpkin, to fuse and sublimate themselves into a mage-philosopher, who puffeth metaphysics from a pipe and discourseth sweet philanthropy to tself — itself, God! Dost Thou hear? Itself! For even such am I — I whom Thou madest to love Rachel. Why, God — haha! dost Thou dwell in this thing? Is it Thou that peerest forth at me — *from* me? Why, hark then; Thou shalt listen, and answer — if Thou canst. Hark then, Spirit of life! Between the rise and setting of a sun, I have walked in this world of Thine. I have gazed upon it, I have peered within it, I have grown enamoured, enamoured of it. I have been thrilled with wonder, I have been calmed with knowledge, I have been exalted with sympathy. I have trembled with joy and passion. Power, beauty, love have ravished me. Infinity itself, like a dream, has blazed before me with the certitude of prophecy; and I have cried, "This world, the heavens, time itself, are mine to conquer," and I have thrust forth mine arm to wear Thy shield forever — and lo! for my shield Thou reachest me a mirror — and whisperest: "Know thyself! Thou art — a scarecrow: a tinking clod, a rigmarole of dust, a lump of ordure, contemptible, superfluous, inane!" Haha! Hahaha! And with such scarecrows Thou dost people a planet! O ludicrous! Monstrous! Ludicrous! At least, I thank Thee, God! at least, this breathing bathos can laugh at itself. At least this hotch-potch nobleman of stubble is enough of an epicure to turn his own gorge. Thou has vouchsafed to me, Spirit, — hahaha! — to know myself. Mine, mine is the consummation of man — even self-contempt! [*Pointing in the glass with an agony of derision*] Scarecrow! Scarecrow! Scarecrow!

THE IMAGE IN THE GLASS [*more and more faintly*]. Scarecrow! Scarecrow! Scarecrow!

[RAVENSBANE *throws himself prone upon the floor, beneath the window, sobbing. There is a pause of silence, and the moon shines brighter. — Slowly then* RAVENSBANE, *getting to his knees, looks out into the night*]

RAVENSBANE. What face are you, high up through the twinkling leaves? Why do you smile upon me with such white beneficence? Or why do you place your viewless hand upon my brow, and say, "Be comforted"? Do you not, like all the rest, turn, aghast, your eyes away from me — me, abject enormity, grovelling at your feet? Gracious being, do you not fear — despise me? To you alone am I not hateful — unredeemed? O white peace of the world, beneath your gaze the clouds glow silver, and the herded cattle, slumbering far afield, crouch — beautiful. The slough shines lustrous as a bridal veil. Beautiful face, you are Rachel's, and you have changed the world. Nothing is mean, but you have made it miraculous; nothing is loathsome, nothing ludicrous, but you have converted it to loveliness, that even this shadow of a mockery myself, cast by your light, gives me the dear assurance I am a man. Yea, more, that I too, steeped in your universal light, am beautiful. For you are Rachel, and you love me. You are Rachel in the sky, and the might of your serene loveliness has transformed me. Rachel, mistress, mother, beautiful spirit, out of my suffering you have brought forth my soul. I am saved!

THE IMAGE IN THE GLASS. A very pretty sophistry.

[*The moonlight grows dimmer, as at the passing of a cloud*]

RAVENSBANE. Ah! what voice has snatched you from me?

THE IMAGE. A most poetified pumpkin!

RAVENSBANE. Thing! dost thou speak at last? My soul abhors thee.

THE IMAGE. I *am* thy soul.

RAVENSBANE. Thou liest.

THE IMAGE. Our Daddy Dickon and our mother Rickby begot and conceived us at sunrise, in a Jack-o'lantern.

RAVENSBANE. Thou liest, torturing illusion. Thou art but a phantom in a glass.

THE IMAGE. Why, very true. So art thou. *We* are a pretty phantom in a glass.

RAVENSBANE. It is a lie. I am no longer thou. I feel it; I am a man.

THE IMAGE.
And prithee, what's a man? Man's but a mirror,
Wherein the imps and angels play charades,
Make faces, mope, and pull each other's hair —
Till crack! the sly urchin Death shivers the glass,
And the bare coffin boards show underneath.

RAVENSBANE. Yea! if it be so, thou coggery! if both of us be indeed but illusions, why, now let us end together. But if it be not so, then let *me* for evermore be free of thee. Now is the test — the glass! [*Springing to the fireplace, he seizes an iron cross-piece from the andirons*] I'll play your urchin Death and shatter it. Let see what shall survive! [*He rushes to strike the glass with the iron.* DICKON *steps out of the mirror, closing the curtain*]

DICKON. I wouldn't, really!

RAVENSBANE. Dickon! dear Dickon! is it you?

DICKON. Yes, Jacky! it's dear Dickon, and I really wouldn't.

RAVENSBANE. Wouldn't what, Dickon?

DICKON. Sweep the cobwebs off the sky with thine aspiring broomstick. When a man questions fate, 'tis bad digestion. When a scarecrow does it, 'tis bad taste.

RAVENSBANE. At last, *you* will tell me the truth, Dickon! Am I then — that thing?

DICKON. You mustn't be so sceptical. Of course you're that thing.

RAVENSBANE. Ah me despicable! Rachel, why didst thou ever look upon me?

DICKON. I fear, cobby, thou hast never studied woman's heart and hero-worship. Take thyself now. I remarked to Goody Bess, thy mother, this morning, as I was chucking her thy pate from the hay-loft, that thou wouldst make a Mark Antony or an Alexander before night.

RAVENSBANE. Thou, then, didst create me!

DICKON [*bowing*]. Appreciate the honour. Your lordship was designed for a cornfield; but I discerned nobler potentialities: the courts of Europe and Justice Merton's *salon*. In brief, your lordship's origins were pastoral like King David's.

RAVENSBANE. Cease! cease! in pity's name. You do not know the agony of being ridiculous.

DICKON. Nay, Jacky, all mortals are ridiculous. Like you, they were rummaged out of the muck; and like you they shall return to the dunghill. I advise 'em, like you, to enjoy the interim, and smoke.

RAVENSBANE. This pipe, this ludicrous pipe that I forever set to my lips and puff! Why must I, Dickon? Why?

DICKON. To avoid extinction — merely. You see, 'tis just as your fellow in there [*Pointing to the glass*] explained. You yourself are the subtlest of mirrors, polished out of pumpkin and pipe-smoke. Into this mirror the fair Mistress Rachel has projected her lovely image, and thus provided you with what men call a soul.

RAVENSBANE. Ah! then, I have a soul — the truth of me? Mistress Rachel has indeed made me a man?

DICKON. Don't flatter thyself cobby. Break thy pipe, and whiff — soul, Mistress Rachel, man, truth, and this pretty world itself, go up in the last smoke.

RAVENSBANE. No, no! not Mistress Rachel — for she is beautiful; and the images of beauty are immutable. She told me so.

DICKON. What a Platonic young lady! Nevertheless, believe me, Mistress Rachel exists for your lordship merely in your lordship's pipe-bowl.

RAVENSBANE. Wretched, niggling caricature that I am! All is lost to me — all!

DICKON. "Paradise Lost" again! Always blaming it on me. There's that gaunt fellow in England has lately wrote a parody on me when I was in the apple business.

RAVENSBANE [*falling on his knees and bowing his head*]. O God! I am so contemptible!

[*Enter, at door back,* GOODY RICKBY *her blacksmith garb is hidden under a dingy black mantle with peaked hood*]

DICKON. Good verse, too, for a parody! [*Ruminating, raises one arm rhetorically above* RAVENSBANE]

"Farewell, happy fields
Where joy forever dwells! Hail, horrors; hail,
Infernal world! and thou, profoundest Hell,
Receive thy new possessor."

GOODY RICKBY [*seizing his arm*]. Dickon!

DICKON. Hullo! You, Bess!

GOODY RICKBY. There's not a minute to lose. Justice Merton and the neighbours have ended their conference at Minister Dodge's, and are returning here.

DICKON. What! coming back in the dark? They ran away in the daylight as if the ghosts were after 'em.

GOODY RICKBY [*at the window*]. I see their lanterns down the road.

DICKON. Well, let 'em come. We're ready.

GOODY RICKBY. But thou toldst me they had discovered —

DICKON. A scarecrow in a mirror. Well? The glass is bewitched; that's all.

GOODY RICKBY. All? Witchcraft is hanging — that's all! Come, how shall the mirror help us?

DICKON. 'Tis very simple. The glass is bewitched. Mistress Rachel — mind you — shall admit it. She bought it of you.

GOODY RICKBY. Yea, of me; 'twill be me they'll hang.

DICKON. Good! then the glass is bewitched. The glass bewitches the room; for witchcraft is catching and spreads like the small-pox. *Ergo*, the distorted image of Lord Ravensbane; *ergo*, the magical accompaniments of the ballad; *ergo*, the excited fancies of all the persons in the room. *Ergo*, the glass must needs be destroyed, and the room thoroughly disinfected by the Holy Scriptures. *Ergo*, Master Dickonson himself reads the Bible aloud, the guests apologize and go home, the Justice squirms again in his merry dead past, and his fair niece is wed to the pumpkin.

RAVENSBANE. Hideous! Hideous!

GOODY RICKBY. Your grateful servant, Devil! But the mirror was bought of me — of me, the witch. Wilt thou be my hangman, Dickon?

DICKON. Wilt thou give me a kiss, Goody? When did ever thy Dickon desert thee?

GOODY RICKBY. But how, boy, wilt thou —

DICKON. Trust me, and thy son. When the Justice's niece is thy daughter-in-law, all will be safe. For the Justice will cherish his niece's family.

GOODY RICKBY. But when he knows —

DICKON. But he shall *not* know. How can he? When the glass is denounced as fraudulent, how will he, or any person, ever know that we made this fellow out of rubbish? Who, forsooth, but a poet — or a devil — *would* believe it? You mustn't credit men with our imaginations, my dear.

RAVENSBANE. Mockery! Always mockery!

GOODY RICKBY. Then thou wilt pull me through this safe?

DICKON. As I adore thee — and my own reputation.

GOODY RICKBY [*hurrying away*]. Till we meet, then, boy.

DICKON. Stay, marchioness — his lordship!

GOODY RICKBY [*turning*]. His lordship's pardon! How fares "the bottom of thy heart", my son?

DICKON. My lord — your lady mother.

RAVENSBANE. Begone, woman.

GOODY RICKBY [*courtesying, laughs shrilly*]. Your servant — my son! [*About to depart*]

RAVENSBANE. Ye lie! Both of you! Ye lie — I was born of Rachel.

DICKON. Tut, tut, Jacky; you mustn't mix up mothers and prospective wives at your age. It's fatal.

GOODY RICKBY [*excitedly*]. They're coming! [*Exit*]

DICKON [*calling after her*]. Fear not; if thou shouldst be followed, I will overtake thee.

RAVENSBANE. She is coming; Rachel is coming, and I may not look upon her!

DICKON. Eh? Why not?

RAVENSBANE. I am a monster.

DICKON. And born of her — Fie! fie!

RAVENSBANE. O God! I know not; I mock myself; I know not what to think. But this I know, I love Rachel. I love her, I love her.

DICKON. And shalt have her.

RAVENSBANE. Have her, Dickon?

DICKON. For lover and wife.

RAVENSBANE. For wife?

DICKON. For wife and all. Thou hast but to obey.

RAVENSBANE. Ah! who will do this for me?

DICKON. I!

RAVENSBANE. Dickon! Wilt make me a man — a man and worthy of her?

DICKON. Fiddlededee! I make over no masterpieces. Thy mistress shall be Cinderella, and drive to her palace with her gilded pumpkin.

RAVENSBANE. It is the end.

DICKON. What! You'll not?

RAVENSBANE. Never.

DICKON. Harkee, manikin. Hast thou learned to suffer?

RAVENSBANE [*wringing his hands*]. O God!

DICKON. *I* taught thee. Shall I teach thee further?

RAVENSBANE. Thou canst not.

DICKON. Cannot — ha! What if I should teach Rachel too?

RAVENSBANE. Rachel! — Ah! now I know thee.

DICKON [*bowing*]. Flattered.

RAVENSBANE. Devil! Thou wouldst not torment Rachel?

DICKON. Not if my lord —

RAVENSBANE. Speak! What must I do?

DICKON. *Not* speak. Be silent, my lord, and acquiesce to all I say.

RAVENSBANE. I will be silent.

DICKON. And acquiesce?

RAVENSBANE. I will be silent.

[*Enter* MINISTER DODGE, *accompanied by* SIR CHARLES REDDINGTON, CAPTAIN BUGBY, *the* REV. MASTERS RAND *and* TODD, *and followed by* JUSTICE MERTON, RICHARD, MISTRESS MERTON, *and* RACHEL. RICHARD *and* RACHEL *stand somewhat apart,* RACHEL *drawing close to* RICHARD *and hiding her face. All wear their outer wraps, and two or three hold lanterns, which, save the moon, throw the only light upon the scene. All enter solemn and silent*]

MINISTER DODGE. Lord, be Thou present with us, in this unholy spot.

SEVERAL MEN'S VOICES. Amen.

DICKON. Friends! Have you seized her? Is she made prisoner?

MINISTER DODGE. Stand from us.

DICKON. Sir, the witch! Surely you did not let her escape?

ALL. The witch!

DICKON. A dame in a peaked hood. She has but now fled the house. She called herself — Goody Rickby.

ALL. Goody Rickby!

MISTRESS MERTON. She here!

DICKON. Yea, mistress, and hath confessed all the damnable art, by which all of us have lately been so terrorized and his lordship, my poor master, so maligned and victimized.

RICHARD. Victimized!

JUSTICE MERTON. What confessed she?

MINISTER DODGE. What said she?

DICKON. This: It appeareth that for some time past, she hath cherished revengeful thoughts against our honoured host, Justice Merton.

JUSTICE MERTON. Sir! What cause — what cause —

DICKON. Inasmuch as your worship hath ever so righteously condemned her damnable faults, and threatened them punishment.

MINISTER DODGE. Yea — well?

DICKON. Thus, in revenge, she bewitched yonder mirror, and this very morning unlawfully inveigled this sweet young lady into purchasing it.

SIR CHARLES. Mistress Rachel!

MINISTER DODGE [*to* RACHEL] Didst thou purchase that glass?

RACHEL [*in a low voice*]. Yes.

MINISTER DODGE. From Goody Rickby?

RACHEL. Yes.

RICHARD. Sir — the blame was mine.

RACHEL [*clinging to him*]. O Richard!

DICKON. Pardon, my friends. The fault rests upon no one here. The witch alone is to blame. Her black art inveigled this innocent maid into purchasing the glass; her black art bewitched this room and all that it contained — even to these innocent virginals, on which I played.

MINISTER DODGE. Verily, this would seem to account — but the image; the damnable image in the glass?

DICKON. A familiar devil of hers — a sly imp, it seems, who wears to mortal eyes the shape of a scarecrow. 'Twas he, by means of whom she bedevilled this glass, by making it his *habitat*. When, therefore, she learned that honour and happiness were yours, Justice Merton, in the prospect of Lord Ravensbane as your nephew-in-law, she commanded this devil to reveal himself in the glass as my lord's own image, that thus she might wreck your family felicity.

MINISTER DODGE. Infamous!

DICKON. Indeed, sir, it was this very

evil whom but now she stole here to onsult withal, when she encountered ne, attendant here upon my poor prostrate lord, and — held by the wrath in my eye — confessed it all.

SIR CHARLES. Thunder and brimstone! Where is this accursed hag?

DICKON. Alas — gone, gone! If you had but stopped her.

MINISTER DODGE. I know her den — the blacksmith shop.

SIR CHARLES [*starting*]. Which way?

MINISTER DODGE. To the left.

SIR CHARLES. Go on, there.

MINISTER DODGE. My honoured friend, we shall return and officially destroy this fatal glass. But first, we must secure the witch. Heaven shield, with her guilt, the innocent!

THE MEN [*as they hurry out*]. Amen.

SIR CHARLES [*outside*]. Go on!

Exeunt all but RICHARD, RACHEL, JUSTICE MERTON, MISTRESS MERTON, DICKON, *and* RAVENSBANE]

DICKON [*to* JUSTICE MERTON, *who has importuned him, aside*]. And reveal thy youthful escapades to Rachel?

JUSTICE MERTON. God help me! no.

DICKON. So then, dear friends, this strange incident is happily elucidated. The pain and contumely have fallen most heavily upon my dear lord and master, but you are witnesses, even now, of his silent and Christian forgiveness of your suspicions. Bygones, therefore, be bygones. The future brightens — with orange-blossoms! Hymen and Felicity stand with us here ready to unite two amorous and bashful lovers. His lordship is reticent; yet to you alone, of all beautiful ladies, Mistress Rachel —

RAVENSBANE [*in a mighty voice*]. Silence!

DICKON. My lord would —

RAVENSBANE. Silence! Dare not to speak to her!

DICKON [*biting his lip*]. My babe is weaned.

RACHEL [*still at* RICHARD'S *side*]. Oh, my lord, if I have made you suffer —

RICHARD [*appealingly*]. Rachel!

RAVENSBANE [*approaching her, raises one arm to screen his face*]. Gracious lady! let fall your eyes; look not upon me. If I have dared remain in your presence, if I dare now speak once more to you, 'tis because I would have you know — O forgive me! — that I love you.

RICHARD. Sir! This lady has renewed her promise to be my wife.

RAVENSBANE. Your wife, or not, I love her.

RICHARD. Zounds!

RAVENSBANE. Forbear, and hear me! For one wonderful day I have gazed upon this, your world. The sun has kindled me and the moon has blessed me. A million forms — of trees, of stones, of stars, of men, of common things — have swum like motes before my eyes; but one alone was wholly beautiful. That form was Rachel: to her alone I was not ludicrous; to her I also was beautiful. Therefore, I love her. You talk to me of mothers, mistresses, lovers, and wives and sisters, and you say men love these. What is love? The sun's enkindling and the moon's quiescence; the night and day of the world — the *all* of life, the all which must include both you and me and God, of whom you dream. Well then, I love you, Rachel. What shall prevent me? Mistress, mother, wife — thou art all to me!

RICHARD. My lord, I can only reply for Mistress Rachel, that you speak like one who does not understand this world.

RAVENSBANE. O God! Sir, and do you? If so, tell me — tell me before it be too late — why, in this world, such a thing as *I* can love and talk of love. Why, in this world, a true man and woman, like you and your betrothed, can look upon this counterfeit and be deceived.

RACHEL *and* RICHARD. Counterfeit?

RAVENSBANE. Me — on me — the ignominy of the earth, the laughing-stock of the angels!

RACHEL. Why, my lord. Are you not —

RAVENSBANE. No.

JUSTICE MERTON [*to* RAVENSBANE]. Forbear! Not to her —

DICKON. My lord forgets.

RACHEL. Are you not Lord Ravensbane?

RAVENSBANE. Marquis of Oxford, Baron of Wittenberg, Elector of Worms, and Count of Cordova? No, I am *not* Lord Ravensbane. I am Lord Scarecrow! [*He bursts into laughter*]

RACHEL [*shrinking back*]. Ah me!

RAVENSBANE. A nobleman of husks, bewitched from a pumpkin.

RACHEL. The image in the glass was true?

RAVENSBANE. Yes, true. It is the

glass of truth — thank God! Thank God for you, dear.

JUSTICE MERTON. Richard! Go for the minister; this proof of witchcraft needs be known. [RICHARD *does not move*]

DICKON. My lord, this grotesque absurdity must end.

RAVENSBANE. True, Dickon! This grotesque absurdity must end. The laughter and the laughing-stock, man and the worm, possess at least one dignity in common: both must die.

DICKON [*speaking low*]. Remember! if you dare — Rachel shall suffer for it.

RAVENSBANE. You lie. She is above your power.

DICKON. Still, thou darest not —

RAVENSBANE. Fool, I dare. [*Turning to* RACHEL] Mistress, this pipe is I. This intermittent smoke holds, in its nebula, Venus, Mars, the world. If I should break it — Chaos and the dark! And this of me that now stands up will sink jumbled upon the floor — a scarecrow. See! I break it. [*He breaks the pipe in his hands, and flings the pieces at* DICKON'S *feet in defiance; then turns, agonized, to* RACHEL] Oh, Rachel, could I have been a man —!

DICKON [*picking up the pieces of pipe, turns to* RACHEL]. Mademoiselle, I felicitate you; you have outwitted the devil. [*Kissing his fingers to her, he disappears*]

MISTRESS MERTON [*seizing the* JUSTICE'S *arm in fright*]. Satan!

JUSTICE MERTON [*whispers*]. Gone!

RACHEL. Richard! Richard! support him.

RICHARD [*sustaining* RAVENSBANE, *who sways*]. He is fainting. A chair!

RACHEL [*placing a chair, helps* RICHARD *to support* RAVENSBANE *toward it*]. How pale; but yet no change.

RICHARD. His heart, perhaps.

RACHEL. Oh, Dick, if it should be some strange mistake! Look! he is noble still. My lord! my lord! the glass — [*She draws the curtain of the mirror, just opposite which* RAVENSBANE *has sunk into the chair. At her cry, he starts up faintly and gazes at his reflection, which is seen to be a normal image of himself*]

RAVENSBANE. Who is it?

RACHEL. Yourself, my lord — 'tis the glass of truth.

RAVENSBANE [*his face lighting with an exalted joy, starts to his feet, erect, before the glass*]. A man! [*He falls back into the arms of the two lovers*] Rachel! [*He dies*]

RACHEL. Richard, I am afraid. Was it a chimera, or a hero?

FINIS

THE PIPER

(*1910*)

By Josephine Preston Peabody

JOSEPHINE PRESTON PEABODY

(Mrs. L. S. Marks)

THERE is in preparation, at the present time, under the supervision of Mrs. George '. Baker, a volume of Letters and excerpts from the Diaries of Josephine Preston 'eabody. These pages should undoubtedly shed plentiful light on the sensitiveness f a poet to beauty of conception and expression; in them one will be able to detect he lyrical quality of her response rather than her dramatic reaction to situation r condition. If she mentions the theatre at all, it will probably be in the spirit f disappointment that her impress upon it was so small, the channel for poetic rama so sluggish in the American Theatre, the democratic ear so impatient over rhythm that was involved, and so unwilling to pause long over the music of the onventional form.

The death of Mrs. Marks, on December 4, 1922, removed a very gentle figure from American letters. There was no revolt in her soul; there was no iconoclasm of orm to inveigle the attention of Amy Lowell or Louis Untermeyer. She followed he gleam of the old order, even though thoroughly conscious of the new social pirit in the world. She had distinctively a literary mind, and it was this literary nind that knocked at the door of the theatre. She visioned the playhouse as all overs of Shakespeare and poetic dramatists would. It was against her taste, gainst her tendency of thinking, against her spiritual training to take a militant tand. She had within her a certain eloquence, and she gave expression to this loquence in full lines, in mystical fervor. She stood against materialism with o ringing challenge, but with a declaration of faith in something far above material-sm. One catches this note in "The Piper."

To any one with such ideals, standing before the door of the American Theatre n the nineteen-hundreds, there was a path of thorns ahead. Let us see what quipment Josephine Preston Peabody had with her at the time. Educated at Radcliffe College, she had taught two years at Wellesley; she had travelled abroad nd breathed the air of Stratford. And this love for Stratford had resulted in her vriting a small play, "Fortune and Men's Eyes", in which Mary Fytton figured, nd the five-act "Marlowe", in which she lived again the times of Greene, Lodge, Nash, Peele and Marlowe. "The Piper" is our special discussion, but let us see urther what Mrs. Marks brought to the theatre: in 1912, a one-act play, "The Vings", which introduced Cerdic and Aelfric the King; in 1913, "The Wolf of Jubbio", a three-act depiction of St. Francis of Assisi, Brother Leo and Brother 'uniper; and, in 1922, the "Portrait of Mrs. W.", a distinctively biographical olay wherein Kemble, Southey, James Wilson, Godwin, Mrs. Siddons, Mrs. Inch-ald, Mary Wollstonecraft, Mary Godwin, young Shelley and Mr. Symes are the noving figures. The only play outside the literary field was "The Chameleon", vritten in three acts (1917). When one bears in mind the initial struggle of "The 'iper" for presentation in this country, and the interesting circumstance which inally brought it to the New Theatre, one can see that a playwright, literarily constituted as Mrs. Marks was, could find small place for herself in the theatrical his tory of her time. When theatre conditions changed, so too had theatre ways an fashions.

I am privileged in quoting a letter from Professor Lionel Marks regarding th evolution of "The Piper." He writes:

The first idea of the play, "The Piper", came from the little daughter of Oti Skinner, who, on reading Browning's poem, suggested to her father that it woul make a good play. This idea appealed to Mr. Skinner, and, when he was in Bostor in the Spring of 1906, he asked Miss Peabody to consider writing such a play. H had no definite ideas about the play, but was captivated by the possibilities in th character of "The Piper." Miss Peabody was married in June of that year, an permitted the idea to develop until we were in Berlin, in 1907. At that time sh wrote the first draft between the dates of February 12 and February 22. Th first draft was rather remarkably complete, considering the length of "The Piper." She always found that her best work was done after a considerable period of prepa ration by doing the work quite rapidly. She felt always that under those condi tions the characters, once established, were in the habit of taking the bit into thei own teeth, and, as she said, all she had to do was to sit back and watch what the did. For example, she had no idea as to the ending of the scene with *Veronica* a the crossways until she came to the place where she had to end the act. I ha spoken to her of the effect on me of going into a peasant's house in the Tyrol an coming across a life-sized wooden figure of Christ crucified, painted in almost natura colors; this is a not uncommon thing in the Dolomite region. Apparently thi impressed her very strongly as the symbolization of a man coming suddenly agains his own conscience.

The play was finished during our journeys through Germany, Belgium, Franc and England. She met Mr. Skinner in London and read the play to him, and, a he expressed himself at the time, "his head hit the ceiling" when he heard it. O returning to America, in the Fall of 1907, negotiations were entered into with Mr Skinner's manager, and a contract was arranged for its production by Mr. Skinner At that time Mr. Skinner was having a very successful run with a play called, believe, "The Honor of the Family", an adaptation of one of Balzac's novels, if remember rightly. This play was so successful that the term for the contract wa over while the play was still enjoying a successful run. Mr. Skinner was unwillin to renew the contract, so that it lapsed. At that time, Beulah Dix, happening t be in the house, mentioned the Stratford competition and suggested that my wif should send in any play that she had. She wrote to enquire whether a printed pla would be acceptable, and, on receiving word that it would, she sent it. . . .

The local color in the play is correct for the most part. We went to Hamelin an got some hints from the locality. I made a considerable search through the Roya Imperial Library (I think it is called), in Berlin, for contemporary chronicles. Th names in the play are all taken from contemporary chronicles of Hamelin. Th material about the strolling players is taken largely from a book called "Fahrend Leute", which considers the whole of that subject rather extensively.

The facts thus laid forth in Professor Marks's memoranda are further emphasized in Mr. Otis Skinner's "Footlights and Spotlights", as well as in the Riverside Literature Series edition of "The Piper." It was through the efforts of the actor F. R. Benson, that the play competition was initiated, the prize to be three hundred pounds, with the guarantee of a production at the Stratford Memorial Festival dur ing the Spring of 1910. "The Piper" had been published when Mrs. Marks firs heard of the conditions. She had been discouraged in America by managers; even Mr. Winthrop Ames, among the most worthy of American producers, could not then see his way to give it a production. Various reports came that the numerou manuscripts submitted in the contest were dwindling, until finally American papers were full of the American poet who had seized the honor.

According to Miss Abbie Farwell Brown, who has written of "The Piper", Mrs. Marks hastened abroad with her two children, one of them barely eight weeks old. But King Edward died on the day of the evening set for the opening of "The Piper", and Mrs. Marks had to abide the period of national mourning, contenting herself with having her baby baptized in the Shakespeare font of the Stratford Church. The play was finally produced at the Memorial Theatre on Tuesday evening, July 26, 1910, by Mr. and Mrs. F. R. Benson and their Shakespearean Company, including Miss Marion Terry. The New Theatre, in New York, which was under the directorship of Winthrop Ames, immediately reached out for the rights which he had heretofore refused, and it was produced on January 30, 1911. In that year also it was given in London at the St. James' Theatre.

Who should play "The Piper"? That was the question as soon as the play was announced for production. Edith Wynne Matthison was the inevitable selection of Mr. Ames, for her *Everyman* was a memorable portrait, and she was besides a leading figure in the New Theatre company. There were some, notably Mr. Walter Eaton, who championed a man's playing the rôle, and Mrs. Marks herself was eager for such a solution. Announcements were made that Mr. Skinner was reconsidering the part, that Walter Hampden, having an option on the American rights, would play it. Mr. Ames decided otherwise. The consequence is that such a critic as Mr. Eaton could not see the play, as produced on the stage of the New Theatre; the illusion of the story was robbed for him by the knowledge that a woman was playing the part. To him there was a fundamental error in the play as drama — the clash of wills not between persons but between the Piper and the figure of Christ on the roadside cross, which resulted in soliloquy. Others had the same fault to find with Mrs. Marks: her eloquence was very beautiful poetry at its crucial moment, but not drama. There were still others who saw in Miss Matthison's *Piper* a vital spiritual force which compensated for whatever strength of reality a man's figure might have added to the play.

"The Piper", as Mrs. Marks conceived it, was founded on a permanent basis of vital legendary interest. We have the nursery interpretation of the story in picture books, in Jacobs' "More English Fairy Tales", and in Lang's "Red Fairy Book." We have the Browning poem. A very learned thesis might be presented on the sources of "The Pied Piper of Hamelin"; very far-fetched comparisons of the legend in different forms might be made; for instance, did Ibsen have it in mind when he drew his *Rat-Wife*, in "Little Eyolf", which might be considered the Norwegian application of the story to the psychology of individual character? But it is better, in considering the play, to remain close to the legend as Browning wrote it, and the play as Mrs. Marks reset it. Some of the zest of its universal appeal to young and old alike has been taken from the story by Mrs. Marks's treatment. She seems to have searched rather consciously for some philosophy which the *Piper*, in his person, might symbolize. Secondary stories were thus mixed with the legend — which in itself is the main thread of the play — and there are certain beautiful speeches which are not drama and which slow up the action of the piece in the reading. All credit is due to the poet's conception which makes the *Piper* pipe the children away from Hamelin; and to the ethical interpretation of gold blinding the mothers and fathers of Hamelin, who are thus separated from true happiness with their children. There was in all this an added joyousness to the play as poetry.

As Mrs. Marks conceived him, the *Piper* had a sprinkling of gray in his hair; as Browning conceived him, half yellow and red, tall and thin, sharp in features but free in smiles, he was the veritable monger.　But Miss Matthison transmuted this new *Piper* into a fine frenzy of youth; she spiritualized her whole conception, making her man attract, not lure.　There was music to her laughter, light grace to her step, boyish nonchalance to the shake of her head.　*Peter Pan* was packed somewhere into this *Piper* — a good companion for the children of Hamelin.

Judged as a reading play, Mrs. Marks has written a touching story around the cripple, *Jan*, and his foreign mother — the one mother in Hamelin fit to treasure the spirit of her child.　The *Jan* motive is the thread which shows how earnestly Mrs. Marks strove to attach her drama to some centre of Christian belief: her references to the *Lonely Man*, her joining the spiritualized *Piper* with the spirit of Christ, both suffering little children to come unto them, are tender, and were effective on the stage.

As I recall the New Theatre production, there comes to mind the first scene in the market-place, where the children trail away to the *Piper's* piping; and the last, which witnesses their return, coming from a distance with the patter of footsteps, like the rustle of falling leaves.　As an external picture it was beautiful, and I believe Miss Matthison added immeasurably to this eternal child element; I believe she made convincing the spiritual intention of Mrs. Marks.

This is emphasized, not as a dramatic criticism, based on a production seen; but so as to stress Mrs. Marks's under theme, which, coupled with eloquent poetry, is difficult to get across the stage unless it is handled in a particular way.　It is the demand for a particular way which makes the poetic drama have to do such special pleading in our theatre.　It is of interest to take "The Piper" and analyze it in comparison with the Browning legend.　One begins to see where the poet often goes into side channels not wholly conducive to dramatic effect.　There is a charm to "The Piper": it is the charm of legend; it is the charm of many moments of beautiful poetry; it is the charm of scenic opportunity.　These outweigh certain handicaps of a structural character, which are the handicaps of Mrs. Marks's other plays.　The poet's interest diminishes the dramatist's concern.

THE PIPER

A PLAY IN FOUR ACTS

By JOSEPHINE PRESTON PEABODY

To
LIONEL S. MARKS

Anno 1284

Am Dage Johannis et Pauli
War der 26 Junii
Dorch einen Piper mit allerley Farve bekledet
Gewesen CXXX kinder verledet
Binnen Hamelen geboren
To Calvarie bi den koppen verloren

[THE HAMELIN INSCRIPTION]

Tuesday Evening, July 26th, 1910

FIRST PERFORMANCE

OF

The Piper

(*The Prize Play*)

By JOSEPHINE PRESTON PEABODY

Produced by MR. and MRS. F. R. BENSON and THEIR SHAKESPEAREAN COMPANY
Including MISS MARION TERRY

CHARACTERS

Strolling Players

THE PIPER	Mr. F. R. Benson
MICHAEL-THE-SWORD-EATER	Mr. Eric Maxon
CHEAT-THE-DEVIL	Mr. Alfred Wild

Men and Women of Hamelin

JACOBUS, *the Burgomeister*	Mr. Alfred Brydone
KURT, *the Syndic*	Mr. F. Moffat Johnston
PETER, *the Cobbler*	Mr. W. W. Caithness
HANS, *the Butcher*	Mr. Harry Caine
AXEL, *the Smith*	Mr. G. F. Hannam Clarke
MARTIN, *the Watch*	Mr. John Howell
PETER, *the Sacristan*	Mr. Nigel Barry
ANSELM, *a young Priest*	Mr. Murray Carrington
OLD CLAUS, *a Miser*	Mr. F. P. Wilson
TOWN CRIER	Mr. Frank Growcott
VERONIKA, *the wife of Kurt*	Miss Marion Terry
BARBARA, *daughter of Jacobus*	Miss Violet Farebrother
WIFE OF HANS THE BUTCHER	Miss Marion Foreman
WIFE OF AXEL THE SMITH	Miss Winifred Durie
WIFE OF MARTIN THE WATCH	Miss C. MacDowell
OLD URSULA	Miss Elinor Aickin

Children

JAN	Miss Hetty Kenyon
HANSEL	Miss Kathleen Yorke
ILSE	Miss Beatrice Pither
TRUDE	Miss Joan Hastings
RUDI	Master Aubrey Summerheys

Scenery by Messrs. Joseph and Phil Harker
Music specially composed by Mr. Christopher Wilson

THE NEW THEATRE, NEW YORK

Monday Evening, January 30th, 1911

FIRST PERFORMANCE IN AMERICA

OF

The Piper

BY JOSEPHINE PRESTON PEABODY

CHARACTERS

Strolling Players

THE PIPER	Miss Edith Wynne Matthison
MICHAEL-THE-SWORD-EATER	Mr. Frank Gillmore
CHEAT-THE-DEVIL	Mr. Jacob Wendell, Jr.

Men and Women of Hamelin

JACOBUS, *the Burgomeister*	Mr. Lee Baker
KURT, *the Syndic*	Mr. Ben Johnson
PETER, *the Cobbler*	Mr. John Sutherland
HANS, *the Butcher*	Mr. William McVay
AXEL, *the Smith*	Mr. Stewart Baird
MARTIN, *the Watch*	Mr. Edwin Cushman
PETER, *the Sacristan*	Mr. William Raymond
ANSELM, *a young Priest*	Mr. Pedro deCordoba
OLD CLAUS, *a Miser*	Mr. Cecil Yapp
TOWN CRIER	Mr. Robert Hamilton
VERONIKA, *the wife of Kurt*	Miss Olive Oliver
BARBARA, *daughter of Jacobus*	Miss Dora Jesslyn
WIFE OF HANS THE BUTCHER	Miss Thais Lawton
WIFE OF AXEL THE SMITH	Miss Elsie Herndon Kearns
WIFE OF MARTIN THE WATCH	Miss Mary Doyle
OLD URSULA	Mrs. Sol Smith

Children

JAN	Master John Tansey
HANSEL	Master Emmett Hampton
ILSE	Miss Jeanette Dix
TRUDE	Miss Claribel Campbell
RUDI	Miss Dorothy Vernon

Produced by Mr. George Foster Platt
Scenery and costumes under the direction of Mr. E. Hamilton Bell

CHARACTERS

The Piper
Michael-the-Sword-Eater } *Strolling Players*
Cheat-the-Devil

Jacobus, *the Burgomeister*
Kurt, *the Syndic*
Peter, *the Cobbler*
Hans, *the Butcher*
Axel, *the Smith*
Martin, *the Watch* } *Men of Hamelin*
Peter, *the Sacristan*
Anselm, *a young priest*
Old Claus, *a miser*
Town Crier

Jan
Hansel
Ilse } *Children*
Trude
Rudi

Veronika, *the wife of Kurt*
Barbara, *daughter of Jacobus*
Wife of Hans the Butcher
Wife of Axel the Smith
Wife of Martin the Watch
Old Ursula

Burghers, nuns, priests, and children

Scene. — *Hamelin on the Weser*, 1284 A.D.

SCENES

Act I. — *The market-place in Hamelin*
Act II. { Scene I. — *Inside the 'Hollow Hill'*
Scene II. — *The Cross-ways*
Act III. — *The Cross-ways*
Act IV. — *The market-place in Hamelin*

One week is supposed to elapse between Acts I and II.
Acts II and III occupy one day.
Act IV concerns the following morning.

THE PIPER

ACT I

SCENE. — *The market-place of Hamelin.
Right, the Minster, with an open
shrine (right centre) containing a
large sculptured figure of the Christ.
Right, farther front, the house of
KURT; and other narrow house-
fronts. Left, the Rathaus, and
(down) the home of* JACOBUS. *Front,
to left and right, are cornerhouses
with projecting stories and casement
windows. At the centre rear, a narrow street leads away between houses
whose gables all but meet overhead.*

*It is late summer afternoon, with a holiday
crowd. In the open casements, front
(right and left, opposite each other),
sit* OLD URSULA *and* OLD CLAUS,
*looking on at men and things. In
the centre of the place now stands a
rude wooden Ark with a tented top:
and out of the openings (right and
left) appear the artificial heads of
animals, worn by the players inside.
One is a Bear (inhabited by* MI-
CHAEL-THE-SWORD-EATER); *one is
a large Reynard-the-Fox, later apparent as the* PIPER. *Close by is the
mediæval piece of stage-property
known as 'Hell-Mouth', i.e. a red
painted cave with a jaw-like opening,
into which a mountebank dressed in
scarlet* (CHEAT-THE-DEVIL) *is pok-
ing 'Lost Souls' with a pitchfork.*

BARBARA *loiters by the tent.* VERONIKA,
the sad young wife of KURT, *watches
from the house steps, left, keeping
her little lame boy, Jan, close beside
her.*

*Shouts of delight greet the end of the show,
— a Noah's Ark miracle-play of the
rudest; and the Children continue to
scream with joy whenever an Animal
looks out of the Ark.*

*Men and women pay scant attention either
to* JACOBUS, *when he speaks (himself
none too sober) — from his doorstep,
prompted by the frowning* KURT, —

or yet to ANSELM, *the priest, who
stands forth with lifted hands, at the
close of the miracle-play.*

ANSELM. And you, who heed the
colors of this show,
Look to your laughter! — It doth body
forth
A Judgment that may take you unaware, —
Sun-struck with mirth, like unto chattering leaves
Some wind of wrath shall scourge to
nothingness.

HANS, AXEL, AND OTHERS. Hurrah,
Hurrah!

JACOBUS. And now, good townsmen
all,
Seeing we stand delivered and secure
As once yon chosen creatures of the Ark,
For a similitude, — our famine gone,
Our plague of rats and mice, —

CROWD. Hurrah — hurrah!

JACOBUS. 'Tis meet we render
thanks more soberly —

HANS. Soberly, soberly, ay! —

JACOBUS. For our deliverance.
And now, ye wit, it will be full three days
Since we beheld — our late departed
pest. —

OLD URSULA [*putting out an ear-
trumpet*]. What does he say?

REYNARD [*from the Ark*]. — Oh, how
felicitous!

HANS' WIFE. He's only saying there
be no more rats.

JACOBUS [*with oratorical endeavor*].
Three days it is; and not one mouse, —
one mouse,
One mouse, I say! — No-o-o! Quiet
. . . as a mouse. [*Resuming*]
And now . . .

CROWD. Long live Jacobus! —

JACOBUS. You have seen
Noah and the Ark, most aptly happening by
With these same play-folk. You have
marked the Judgment.

You all have seen the lost souls sent to —
   Hell —
And, nothing more to do. —
   [KURT *prompts him*]
      Yes, yes. — And now . . .

[HANS *the Butcher steps out of his group*]

HANS.   Hath no man seen the Piper?
   — Please your worships.
OTHERS.   Ay, ay, so!
         — Ay, where is he?
            — Ho, the Piper!
JACOBUS.   Piper, my good man?
HANS.   — He that charmed the rats!
OTHERS.   Yes, yes, — that charmed
   the rats!
JACOBUS [*piously*].
         Why, no man knows. —
Which proves him such a random instru-
   ment
As Heaven doth sometimes send us, to
   our use ;
Or, as I do conceive, no man at all, —
A man of air ; or, I would say — delu-
   sion.
He'll come no more.
   REYNARD [*from the Ark*].   Eh? —
   Oh, indeed, Meaow!
JACOBUS.   'Tis clearest providence.
   The rats are gone.
The man is gone.   And there is nought
   to pay,
Save peaceful worship.   [*Pointing to the
   Minister*]
   REYNARD [*sarcastically*].   Oh, indeed,
   — Meaow!

[*Sudden chorus of derisive animal noises
   from the Ark, delighting* PEOPLE
   and CHILDREN]

KURT.   Silence, — you strollers there!
   Or I will have you
Gaoled, one and all.
PEOPLE.   No, Kurt the Syndic, no!
BARBARA [*to* JACOBUS].   No, no!
   Ah, father, bid them stay awhile
And play it all again. — Or, if not all,
Do let us see that same good youth
   again,
Who swallowed swords — between the
   Ark Preserved
And the Last Judgment!
   REYNARD.   Michael-the-Sword-Eater,
Laurels for thee!

[*The* BEAR *disappears:* MICHAEL *puts
   out his own head, and gazes fixedly
   at Barbara*]

CHILDREN.   Oh, can't we see the
   animals in the Ark?

Again?   Oh, can't we see it all again?
   ILSE.   Oh, leave out Noah! And let's
   have only Bears
And Dromedaries, and the other ones! —

      [*General confusion*]

KURT.   Silence!
JACOBUS.   Good people, — you have
   had your shows ;
And it is meet, that having held due
   feast,
Both with our market and this Miracle,
We bring our holiday to close with
   prayer
And public thanks unto Saint Willi-
   bald, —
Upon whose day the rats departed
   thence.
REYNARD [*loudly*].   Saint Willibald!
BEAR.   — Saint Willibald!
OTHER ANIMALS [*looking out*].
            { Saint Willibald!
            { Saint! Oh!
CROWD.   Saint   Willibald! — And
   what had he to do
With ridding us o' rats?
HANS.   'Twas the Piping Man
Who came and stood here in the market-
   place,
And swore to do it for one thousand
   guilders!
PETER.   Ay, and he did it, too! —
   Saint Willibald!

[*Renewed uproar round the tent*]

KURT [*to* JACOBUS].   Drive out those
   mountebanks!   'Tis ever so.
Admit them to the town and you must
   pay
Their single show with riotings a week. —
Look yonder at your daughter.

[BARBARA *lingers by the Ark-Tent, gazing
   with girlish interest at* MICHAEL,
   *who gazes at her, his bear-head in his
   hand for the moment*]

JACOBUS.   Barbara!

[*She turns back, with an angry glance at*
   KURT]

AXEL [*doggedly to them*].   By your
   leave, Masters!   I would like to
   know,
How did Saint Willibald prevail with
   the rats? —
That would I like to know.   I, who ha'
   made
Of strong wrought traps, two hundred,
   thirty-nine,
Two hundred, thirty-nine.
   REYNARD [*calling*].   And so would I!

HANS. So please your worships, may
it please the Crier,
Now we be here, — to cry the Piping
Man —
PETER. A stranger-man, gay-clad, —
in divers colors!
Because he, with said piping —
HANS — Drave away
The horde of rats!
PETER [*sagely*]. To our great benefit;
And we be all just men.
OTHERS. Ay, ay! — Amen!
WOMEN. Amen, Our Lady and the
blessed Saints!
JACOBUS. Why, faith, good souls, if
ye will have him cried,
So be it. — But the ways of Heaven are
strange!
Mark how our angel of deliverance
came, —
Or it may be, Saint Willibald himself, —
Most piedly clothed, even as the vilest
player! —
And straight ascended from us, to the
clouds!
But cry him, if you will. — Peace to
your lungs! —
He will not come.

[KURT *wrathfully consults with* JACOBUS,
then signals to Crier]

CRIER. Oyez! Oyez! Oyez!
Whereas, now three days gone, our
Plague of Rats
Was wholly driven hence, our City
cleansed,
Our peace restored after sore threat of
famine,
By a Strange Man who came not back
again,
Now, therefore, if this Man have ears to
hear,
Let him stand forth. — Oyez! Oyez!
Oyez!

[*Trumpet.* — PEOPLE *gaze up and down
the little streets.* — REYNARD *steps
out of the Ark and comes down slowly,
with a modest air.* — KURT *points
him out, threateningly, and the
Crowd bursts into derisive laughter.
— He doffs his animal head at leisure,
showing a sparkling dark-eyed face*]

ALL. The Man! the Man!
KURT AND JACOBUS. The Devil! —
'Tis —
ALL. — THE PIPER!

[*The* PIPER *regards them all with debonair
satisfaction; then reverses his head-

piece and holds it out upside-down,
with a confident smile*]

PIPER. Three days of rest, your wor-
ships, you have had.
I see no signs of famine hereabout.
The rats are gone, even to the nether-
most tail:
And I've fulfilled my bargain. Is it
granted?
[*Murmurs, then cheers of "Ay, Ay,
Piper!" from the crowd*]
Thank'ee. — My thousand guilders, an
you please.
JACOBUS. One thou — Come, come!
This was no sober bargain. —
No man in reason could —
PIPER. One thousand guilders.
KURT. One thousand rogueries!
JACOBUS [*to* PIPER]. You jest too
far.
AXEL. Lucky, if he get aught! —
Two hundred traps.
And nine, and thirty! By Saint Willi-
bald,
When was I paid?
AXEL'S WIFE. Say, now!
PIPER. . . . One thousand guilders.
PETER THE COBBLER. Give him an
hundred.
HANS THE BUTCHER. Double!
HANS' WIFE. You were fool
To make agreement with him. — Ask
Old Claus.
He has the guilders; and his house was
full
O' rats!
OLD CLAUS [*shaking his stick from the
window*]. You jade! And I that
hoard, and save,
And lay by all I have from year to year,
To build my monument when I am
gone,
A fine new tomb there, in Saint Boni-
face!
And I to pay for all your city rats!
OLD URSULA [*leaning out, opposite*].
Right, neighbor, right well said! —
Piper, hark here.
Piper, how did ye charm the rats away?
PIPER [*coming down*]. The rats were
led — by Cu-ri-os-ity.
'Tis so with many rats; and all old
women; —
Saving your health!
JACOBUS. No thought for public weal,
In this base grasping on —
PIPER. One thousand guilders.
KURT [*contemptuously*]. For piping!
PIPER. Shall I pipe them back
again?

WOMEN.

Merciful heaven ! { Good Saint Boniface !
Good Saint Willi-
bald !
Peter and Paul de-
fend us !

HANS *the Butcher.* No, no; no fera
o' that. The rats be drowned.
We saw them with our eyes.
PIPER.   Now who shall say
There is no resurrection for a mouse?
KURT. — Do you but crop this fel-
low's ear ! —
VERONIKA [*from the steps*]. Ah, Kurt !
JACOBUS [*to him, blandly*]. Deal pa-
tiently, good neighbor. All is
well.
[*To the* PIPER] Why do you name a
price so laughable,
My man? Call you to mind; you have
no claim, — No scrip to show. You
cling upon —
PIPER [*sternly*].   Your word.
JACOBUS. I would say — just —
PIPER.   Your word.
JACOBUS.   Upon —
PIPER.   Your word.
Sure, 'twas a rotten parchment !
JACOBUS.   This is a base,
Conniving miser !
PIPER [*turning proudly*].   Stand forth,
Cheat-the-Devil !
[*Up steps the* DEVIL *in red.* PEOPLE
shrink, and then come closer]
Be not afeared. He pleased you all, of
late.
He hath no sting. — So, boy ! Do off
thy head. —
[CHEAT-THE-DEVIL *doffs his red head-
dress and stands forth, a pale and
timorous youth, gentle and half-
witted*]
Michael, stand forth !

[MICHAEL *comes down, bear-head in
hand*]

BARBARA [*regarding him sadly*]. That
goodly sword-eater !
PIPER [*defiantly*]. So, Michael, so. —
These be two friends of mine.
Pay now an even third to each of us.
Or, to content your doubts, to each of
these
Do you pay here and now, five hundred
guilders.
Who gets it matters little, for us friends.
But you will pay the sum, friend. You
will pay ! —
HANS, AXEL, AND CROWD. Come,
there's an honest fellow. Ay, now,
pay !

— There's a good friend. — And would
I had the same.
— One thousand guilders?
              — No, too much.
                        — No, no.
KURT. Pay jugglers? — With a rope
apiece !
JACOBUS.   Why — so —
PIPER. They are my friends; and
they shall share with me.
'Tis time that Hamelin reckoned us for
men ;
— Hath ever dealt with us as we were
vermin.
Now have I rid you of the other sort —
Right you that score ! —
KURT.   These outcasts !
PIPER [*hotly*].   Say you so?
Michael, my man ! Which of you here
will try
With glass or fire, with him?
MICHAEL [*sullenly*]. No, no more
glass, to-day !
PIPER. Then fire and sword !
              [*They back away*]
              So ! — And there's not one man
In Hamelin, here, so honest of his word.
Stroller ! A pretty choice you leave us.
— Quit
This strolling life, or stroll into a cage !
What do you offer him? A man eats
fire —
Swords, glass, young April frogs —
CHILDREN.   Do it again !
Do it again !
PIPER.   You say to such a man, —
'Come be a monk ! A weaver !' Pretty
choice.
Here's Cheat-the-Devil, now.
PETER. But what's his name?
PIPER. He doesn't know. What
would you? Nor do I.
But for the something he has seen of life,
Making men merry, he'd know some-
thing more !
The gentlest devil ever spiked Lost
Souls
Into Hell-mouth, — for nothing-by-the-
day !
OLD URSULA [*with her ear-trumpet*].
Piper, why do you call him Cheat-the-
Devil?
PIPER. Because his deviltry is all a
cheat : —
He is no devil, — but a gentle heart !
— Friend Michael here hath played the
Devil, betimes,
Because he can so bravely breathe out
fire.
He plied the pitchfork so we yelped for
mercy, —

He reckoned not the stoutness of his
arm ! —
But Cheat-the-Devil here, — he would
not hurt
Why — Kurt the Syndic — thrusting
him in hell. [*Laughter*]

CHEAT-THE-DEVIL [*unhappily*]. No,
no — I will not hurt him !

PIPER [*soothingly to him*]. Merry,
boy !

[*To the townsfolk*] And, — if ye will have
reasons, good, — ye see, —
I want — one thousand guilders.

JACOBUS. In all surety,
Payment you'll have, my man. But —

HANS. As to's friends, —
An that yon Devil be as feat wi' his
hands
As he be slow o' tongue, why, I will take
him
For prentice. Wife, — now that would
smack o' pride !

PETER. I'll take this fellow that can
swallow fire.
He's somewhat old for me. But he can
learn
My trade. — A pretty fellow !

PIPER. And your trade ?

PETER. Peter the cobbler. —

MICHAEL. I ? What, I ? Make shoes ?
[*Proudly*] I swallow fire.

PIPER. Enough.

BARBARA [*aside, bitterly*]. I'll not believe it.

PIPER [*to* HANS]. Your trade ?

HANS. I'm Hans the Butcher.

MICHAEL. Butcher ?

CHEAT-THE-DEVIL [*unhappily*].
Butcher !
Oh, no ! I couldn't hurt them. [*Loud
laughter*]

BUTCHER'S WIFE. 'Tis a fool !

[*The* PIPER *motions to* MICHAEL *and*
CHEAT-THE-DEVIL, *who during the
following join the other player-folk,
strike their tent, pack their bundles,
and wheel off the barrows that have
served them for an Ark, leaving the
space clear before the Shrine. Exeunt
Strollers, all but* MICHAEL, *who hangs
about, still gazing at* BARBARA]

JACOBUS. Good people, we have
wasted time enow.
You see this fellow, that he has no writ —

PIPER. Why not, then ? 'Twas a
bargain. If your word
Hold only when 'tis writ —

KURT. We cannot spend
Clerkship on them that neither write nor
read.

What good would parchment do thee ?

JACOBUS. My good man —

PIPER. Who says I cannot read ? —
Who says I cannot ?

OLD CLAUS. Piper, don't tell me you
can read in books !

PIPER [*at bay*]. Books ! Where's a
book ? Shew me a book, I say !

OLD URSULA. The Holy Book !
Bring that — or he'll bewitch you.

PIPER. Oh, never fear. I charm
but fools and children ;
Now that the rats are gone. — Bring me
a Book :
A big one ! —

[*Murmurs. The* PIPER *defiant. The
crowd moves towards the Minister.
Enter* ANSELM *the priest, with a little
acolyte, — the two bearing a large
illuminated Gospelbook.* ANSELM,
eyeing the PIPER *gravely, opens the
book, which the boy supports on his
head and shoulders*]

Ho, 'tis too heavy ! Come, you cherub-
head,
Here's too much laid upon one guardian
angel !

[*Beckons another small boy, and sets the
book on their two backs*]

Well ? — well ? What now ? [*He looks
in frank bewilderment at the eager
crowd*]

CROWD. Read, read !

KURT. He cannot read.

PIPER [*to* ANSELM]. Turn — turn —
there's nothing there. ANSELM
turns pages. PIPER *looks on blankly*]
. . . Ah, turn again !
The big red Letter. — [*He takes his pipe
from his belt*]
No, the green ! The green one. So.
[*Starts to pipe, looking on the book*]

CROWD. {Sure 't is a mad-man !
{But hear him piping !
{What is he doing ?

PIPER [*puzzled at their mirth*].
What the green one says. —

[*A burst of laughter from the crowd.* JAN,
*the little lame boy on the steps, reaches
his arms out suddenly and gives a
cry of delight*]

JAN. Oh, I love the Man !

[*He goes, with his crutch, to the* PIPER,
who turns and gathers him close]

JACOBUS [*to the People*]. Leave off
this argument.

KURT. In, — to the minster.

JACOBUS. Saint Willibald !

PIPER [*in a rage*]. That Saint! —
KURT. Hence, wandering dog!
PIPER. Oho! — Well, every Saint
may have his day.
But there are dog-days coming. — Eh,
your worship?
[*To* ANSELM, *suddenly*] You, there!
You — Brother — Father — Uncle
— You!
Speak! Will you let them in, to say
their prayers
And mock me through their fingers? —
Tell these men
To settle it, among their mouldy
pockets,
Whether they keep their oath. Then
will I go.
KURT [*savagely*]. Away with you! —
ANSELM. The Piper should be heard;
Ye know it well. Render to Cæsar,
therefore,
That which is Cæsar's.
PIPER. — Give the Devil his due!
JACOBUS [*warily*]. We must take
counsel over such a sum.

[*Beckoning others, he and* KURT *go into
the Rathaus, followed by all the men.
Exit* ANSELM *with the Holy Book
into the Minster. — The children
play Mouse, to and fro, round about
the* PIPER. — *The women, some of
them, spin on the doorsteps, with little
hand distaffs, or stand about, gossip-
ing.*

The PIPER *wipes his forehead and goes
up slowly (centre) to drink from the
fountain at the foot of the Shrine. —*
MICHAEL, *like one in a dream, comes
down towards* BARBARA, *who gazes
back at him, fascinated, through her
laughter*]

BARBARA. Is it for pay you loiter,
Master Player?
Were you not paid enough?
MICHAEL. No. — One more look.
BARBARA. Here, then. — Still not
enough?
MICHAEL. No! One more smile.
BARBARA [*agitated*]. Why would you
have me smile?
MICHAEL [*passionately*]
Oh, when you smiled,
It was — it was like sunlight coming
through
Some window there, [*Pointing to the
Minster*]
— some vision of Our Lady.

[*She drops her flowers. — He picks them
up and gives them back slowly*]

BARBARA. Who are you? You are
some one in disguise.
MICHAEL [*bitterly*]. A man — that
passes for a mountebank.
BARBARA [*eagerly*]. I knew!
MICHAEL. What then?
BARBARA. Thou art of noble birth.
'Tis some disguise, this playing with the
fire!
MICHAEL. Yes. — For to-day, I lord
it with the fire.
But it hath burned me, here. [*Touch-
ing his breast*]

[*Overcome for the moment, she draws
away. — The* PIPER, *coming down,
speaks stealthily to* MICHAEL, *who is
still gazing*]

PIPER. For all our sakes!
There is bad weather breeding. — Take
to thy heels.

[BARBARA *turns back to see* MICHAEL
*withdrawing reluctantly, and throws
a rose to him with sudden gayety*]

BARBARA. Farewell to you, Sword-
Swallower! — farewell!
MICHAEL [*looking back*]. Farewell to
you, my Lady-in-the-Moon. [*Exit*]

[JAN *clings once more to the* PIPER, *while
the other children hang about. Enter*
VERONIKA *from her house. She goes
towards her boy*]

VERONIKA. Darling. —
PIPER [*drawing nearer*]. Is this your
Boy?
VERONIKA. Ay, he is mine;
My only one. He loved thy piping so.
PIPER. And I loved his.
HANS' WIFE [*stridently*]. Poor little
boy! He's lame!
PIPER. 'Tis all of us are lame! But
he, he flies.
VERONIKA. Jan, stay here if you will,
and hear the pipe,
At Church-time.
PIPER [*to him*]. Wilt thou?
JAN [*softly*]. Mother lets me stay
Here with the Lonely Man.
PIPER. The Lonely Man?

[JAN *points to the Christ in the shrine.*
VERONIKA *crosses herself. The*
PIPER *looks long at the little boy*]

VERONIKA. He always calls Him so.
PIPER. And so would I.
VERONIKA. It grieves him that the
Head is always bowed,

And stricken. But he loves more to be
here
Than yonder in the church.

PIPER. And so do I.

VERONIKA. What would you, darling, with the Lonely Man?
What do you wait to see?

JAN [*shyly*]. To see Him smile.

[*The women murmur. The* PIPER *comes
down further to speak to* VERONIKA]

PIPER. You are some foreign woman.
Are you not?
Never from Hamelin!

VERONIKA. No.

AXEL'S WIFE [*to her child*]. Then run
along.
And ask the Piper if he'll play again
The tune that charmed the rats.

ANOTHER. They might come back!

OLD URSULA [*calling from her window*].
Piper! I want the tune that charmed
the rats!
If they come back, I'll have my grandson
play it.

PIPER. I pipe but for the children.

ILSE [*dropping her doll and picking it
up*]. Oh, do pipe
Something for Fridolin!

HANSEL. Oh, pipe at me!
Now I'm a mouse! I'll eat you up!
Rr — rr! —

CHILDREN. Oh, pipe! Oh, play!
Oh, play and make us dance!
Oh, play, and make us run away from
school!

PIPER. Why, what are these?

CHILDREN [*scampering round him*].
We're mice, we're mice, we're mice! . . .
We're mice, we're mice! We'll eat up
everything!

MARTIN'S WIFE [*calling*]. 'Tis
church-time. La, what will the
neighbors say?

ILSE [*waving her doll*]. Oh, please
do play something for Fridolin!

AXEL'S WIFE. Do hear the child.
She's quite the little mother!

PIPER. A little mother? Ugh!
How horrible.
That fairy thing, that princess, — no,
that Child!
A little mother? [*To her*]
Drop the ugly thing!

MARTIN'S WIFE. Now, on my word!
and what's amiss with mothers?
Are mothers horrible?

[*The* PIPER *is struck with painful memories*]

PIPER. No, no. But — care
And want and pain and age . . . [*Turns
back to them with a bitter change of
voice*]
And penny-wealth, —
And penny-counting. — Penny prides
and fears —
Of what the neighbors say the neighbors
say! —

MARTIN'S WIFE. And were you born
without a mother, then?

ALL. Yes, you there! Ah, I told
you! He's no man.
He's of the devil.

MARTIN'S WIFE. Who was your
mother, then?

PIPER [*fiercely*]. Mine! — Nay, I do
not know. For when I saw her,
She was a thing so trodden, lost and sad,
I cannot think that she was ever young,
Save in the cherishing voice. — She
was a stroller.

[*The women draw aside furtively, two by
two, and listen unwillingly from the
doorsteps with looks of dread and
aversion, as the* PIPER *continues with
growing passion*]

She was a stroller. — And she starved
and sang;
And like the wind, she wandered, and
was cold,
Outside your lighted windows, and fled
by,
Storm-hunted, trying to outstrip the
snow,
South, south, and homeless as a broken
bird, —
Limping and hiding! — And she fled,
and laughed,
And kept me warm; and died! To
you, a Nothing;
Nothing, forever, oh, you well-housed
mothers!
As always, always for the lighted
windows
Of all the world, the Dark outside is
nothing;
And all that limps and hides there in the
dark;
Famishing, — broken, — lost!
And I have sworn
For her sake and for all, that I will have
Some justice, all so late, for wretched
men,
Out of these same smug towns that drive
us forth
After the show! — Or scheme to cage
us up
Out of the sunlight; like a squirrel's
heart

Torn out and drying in the market-
place.
My mother! Do you know what
mothers are? —
Your children! Do you know them?
Ah, not you!
There's not one here but it would follow
me,
For all your bleating!

AXEL'S WIFE. Kuno, come away!

[*The children cling to him. He smiles
down triumphantly*]

PIPER. Oho, Oho! Look you? —
You preach — I pipe!

[*Re-enter the men, with* KURT *and* JACO-
BUS, *from the Rathaus, murmuring
dubiously*]

[*The* PIPER *sets down* JAN *and stands
forth, smiling*]

JACOBUS [*smoothly*]. H'm! My good
man, we have faithfully debated
Whether your vision of so great a sum
Might be fulfilled, — as by some mir-
acle.
But no. The moneys we administer
Will not allow it; nor the common weal.
Therefore, for your late service, here
you have
Full fifteen guilders,
[*Holding forth a purse*]
and a pretty sum
Indeed, for piping!

KURT [*ominously*]. Take them!

JACOBUS. Either that,
Or, to speak truly, nothing!
[*The* PIPER *is motionless*]
Come, come. Nay, count them, if you
will.

KURT. Time goes!

PIPER. Ay. And your oath?

KURT. No more; Enough.

[*There is a sound of organ music from the
Minster*]

VERONIKA [*beseechingly*]. Ah, Kurt!

KURT [*savagely to the crowd*]. What
do ye, mewling of this fellow's
rights?
He hath none! — Wit ye well, he is a
stroller,
A wastrel, and the shadow of a man!
Ye waste the day and dally with the
law.
Such have no rights; not in their life
nor body!
We are in no wise bound. Nothing is his.
He may not carry arms; nor have
redress
For any harm that men should put on
him,

Saving to strike a shadow on the wall!
He is a Nothing, by the statute-book;
And, by the book, so let him live or die,
Like to a masterless dog!

[*The* PIPER *stands motionless with head
upraised, not looking at* KURT. *The
people, half-cowed, half-doubting,
murmur and draw back. Lights
appear in the Minster; the music
continues.* KURT *and* JACOBUS *lead
in the people.* JACOBUS *picks up
the money-purse and takes it with
him*]

VOICES [*laughing, drunkenly*]. One
thousand guilders to a "masterless dog"!

[*Others laugh too, pass by, with pity and
derision for the* PIPER, *and echoes
of* "Masterless Dog!" *Exeunt*
WOMEN *and* MEN *to the Minster.*
*Only the children are left, dancing round
the motionless figure of the* PIPER]

CHILDREN. Oh, pipe again! Oh,
pipe and make us dance!
Oh, pipe and make us run away from
school!
Oh, pipe and make believe we are the
mice!

[*He looks down at them. He looks up at
the houses. Then he signs to them,
with his finger on his lips; and begins, very softly, to pipe the Kinder-
spell. The old* CLAUS *and* URSULA
in the windows seem to doze.
*The children stop first, and look at him,
fascinated; then they laugh, drows-
ily, and creep closer, —* JAN *always
near. They crowd around him. He
pipes louder, moving backwards,
slowly with magical gestures, towards
the little by-streets and the closed
doors. The doors open, everywhere.*
*Out come the children: little ones in
nightgowns; bigger ones, with play-
things, toy animals, dolls. He pipes,
gayer and louder. They pour in,
right and left. Motion and music
fill the air. The* PIPER *lifts* JAN *to
his shoulder (dropping the little
crutch) and marches off, up the
street at the rear, piping, in the midst
of them all.*
*Last, out of the Minster come tumbling
two little acolytes in red, and after
them,* PETER *the Sacristan. He trips
over them in his amazement and terror; and they are gone after the
vanishing children before the church-
people come out.*
The old folks lean from their windows]

OLD URSULA. The bell, the bell!
the church bell! They're bewitched!

[PETER *rushes to the bell-rope and pulls it.
The bell sounds heavily. Re-enter,
from the church, the citizens by twos
and threes and scores*]

OLD URSULA. I told ye all, — I told
ye! — Devils' bargains! [*The bell*]

[KURT, JACOBUS, *and the others appear*]

KURT. Peter the Sacristan! Give
by the bell.
What means this clangor?
PETER. They're bewitched! bewitched!

[*Still pulling and shouting*]

URSULA. They're gone!
KURT. Thy wits!
OLD CLAUS. They're gone — they're
gone — they're gone!
PETER. The children!
URSULA. — With the Piper!
They're bewitched!
I told ye so.
OLD CLAUS. — I saw it with these
eyes!
He piped away the children.

[*Horror in the crowd. They bring out
lanterns and candles.* VERONIKA
holds up the forgotten crutch]

VERONIKA. Jan — my Jan!
KURT [*to her*]. Thy boy! But mine,
my three, all fair and straight. —
AXEL'S WIFE [*furiously to him*].
'Twas thy false bargain, thine; who
would not pay
The Piper. — But we pay!
PETER. Bewitched, bewitched!
The boys ran out — and I ran after
them,
And something red did trip me — 'twas
the Devil,
The Devil!
OLD URSULA. Ah, ring on, and crack
the bell:
Ye'll never have them back. — I told
ye so!

[*The bell clangs incessantly*]

CURTAIN

ACT II

SCENE I. — *Inside "the Hollow Hill."*

*A great, dim-lighted, cavernous place,
which shows signs of masonry. It
is part cavern and part cellerage of a
ruined, burned-down and forgotten
old monastery in the hills. — The
only entrance (at the centre rear), a
ramshackle wooden door, closes
against a flight of rocky steps. —
Light comes from an opening in the
roof, and from the right, where a
faggot-fire glows under an iron pot.
— The scene reaches (right and left)
into dim corners, where sleeping children lie curled up together like kittens.
By the fire sits the* PIPER, *on a tree-stump
seat, stitching at a bit of red leather.
At his feet is a row of bright-colored
small shoes, set two and two. He
looks up now and then, to recount the
children, and goes back to work, with
quizzical despair.
Left, sits a group of three forlorn* STROL-
LERS. *One nurses a lame knee; one,
evidently dumb, talks in signs to the
others; one is munching bread and
cheese out of a wallet. All have the
look of hunted and hungry men. They
speak only in whispers to each other
throughout the scene; but their hoarse
laughter breaks out now and then
over the bird-like ignorance of the
children.
A shaft of sunlight steals through the hole
in the roof.* JAN, *who lies nearest the*
PIPER, *wakes up.*

JAN. Oh! [*The* PIPER *turns*]
Oh, I thought . . . I had a dream!
PIPER [*softly*]. Ahé?
JAN. I thought . . . I dreamed . . .
somebody wanted me.
PIPER. Soho!
JAN [*earnestly*]. I thought . . . Some-
body Wanted me.
PIPER. How then?

[*With watchful tenderness*]

JAN. I thought I heard Somebody
crying.
PIPER. Pfui! — What a dream. —
Don't make me cry again.
JAN. Oh, was it you? — Oh, yes!
PIPER [*apart, tensely*]. No Michael
yet!

[JAN *begins to laugh softly, in a bewildered
way, then grows quite happy and
forgetful. While the other children
waken, he reaches for the pipe and
tries to blow upon it, to the* PIPER'S
amusement. ILSE *and* HANSEL, *the
Butcher's children, wake*]

ILSE. Oh!

HANSEL. — Oh!
PIPER. Ahé?
ILSE. I thought I had a dream.
PIPER. Again?
ILSE. . . . It was some lady, calling me.
HANSEL. Yes, and a fat man called us to come quick;
A fat man, he was crying — about me!
That same fat man I dreamt of, yesterday.
PIPER. Come, did you ever see a fat man cry,
About a little Boy?

[*The* STROLLERS *are convulsed with hoarse mirth*]

HANSEL. No, — Never.
ILSE. Never!
Oh, what a funny dream!
PIPER [*checking the* STROLLERS, *with a gesture of warning towards the door*].
Strange sights of Hamelin through these little windows.
Come here, you dreamer. Tell me what he said.
HANSEL. He only said "Come home!" But I didn't go.
I don't know where . . . Oh, what a funny dream!
ILSE. Mine was a bad dream! — *Mine* was a lovely lady
And she was by the river, staring in.
PIPER. You were the little gold-fish, none could catch.
Oh, what a funny dream! . . .
[*Apart, anxiously*]
No Michael yet.
[*Aloud*]
Come, bread and broth! Here — not all, three at a time;
'Tis simpler. Here, you kittens. Eat awhile.
So there are tears in Hamelin; — warm, wet tears;
And maybe, salt. Who knows?
RUDI. Oh, I was dreaming!

[*The* PIPER *takes* JAN *on his knee and feeds him, after ladling out a big bowl of broth from the kettle for the* CHILDREN, *and giving them bread*]

PIPER. Oh, I was dreaming, too!
CHILDREN. Oh, tell it to us!
PIPER. I dreamed . . . a Stork . . . had nested in my hat.
CHILDREN. Oh!
PIPER. And when I woke —
CHILDREN. You had —
PIPER. *One hundred children!*

CHILDREN. Oh, it came true! Oh oh; it all came true!
THE STROLLERS. Ah, ho, ho, ho!

[*The dumb one rises, stretches, and steals toward the entrance, stopping to slip a blind-patch over one eye. The* PIPER *goes to him with one stride, seizing him by the shoulder*]

PIPER [*to him, and the others, apart*]
Look you. — No Michael yet! — And he is gone
Full three days now, — three days. If he be caught,
Why then, — the little ravens shall be fed! [*Groans from the three*]
Enough that Cheat-the-Devil leaked out too; —
No foot but mine shall quit this fox-hole now!
And you, — think praise for once, you have no tongue,
And keep these magpies quiet.
[*Turns away*]
[*To himself*] Ah, that girl.
The Burgomeister's Barbara! But for her,
And moon-struck Michael with his 'one more look'!
Where is he now? — And where are we?
[*Turning back to the Children*] So, so.

[*The* STROLLERS *huddle together, with looks of renewed anxiety and wretchedness. — Their laughter at the* CHILDREN *breaks out forlornly now and then. — The* PIPER *shepherds the* CHILDREN, *but with watchful eyes and ears toward the entrance always. — His action grows more and more tense*]

RUDI [*over his broth*]. Oh, I remember now! — Before I woke . . .
Oh, what an awful dream!
ILSE. Oh, tell us, Rudi, —
Oh, scare us, — Rudi, scare us! —
RUDI [*bursting into tears*].
. . . *Lump was dead!*
Lump, Lump! — [*The* CHILDREN *wail*]
PIPER [*distracted*]. Who's Lump? —
RUDI. Our Dog!
PIPER [*shocked and pained*]
The Dog! — No, no.
Heaven save us — I forgot about the dogs!
RUDI. He Wanted me; — and I always wasn't there!
And people tied him up, — and other people

Pretended that he bit. — He never
 bites!
He Wanted me, until it broke his heart,
And he was dead!
 PIPER [*struggling with his emotion*].
 And then he went to heaven,
To chase the happy cats up all the
 trees; —
Little white cats! . . . He wears a
 golden collar . . .
And sometimes — [*Aside*] — I'd forgot
 about the dogs!
Well, dogs must suffer, so that men grow
 wise.
'Twas ever so.

[*He turns to give* JAN *a piping lesson*]

 CHILDREN. Oh, what a funny dream!

[*Suddenly he lifts his hand. They listen,
 and hear a dim sound of distant
 chanting, going by on some neighbor-
 ing road. The* PIPER *is puzzled; the*
 STROLLERS *are plainly depressed*]

JAN. What is it?
PIPER. People; passing down below,
In the dark valley.
 [*He looks at the* CHILDREN *fixedly*]
 Do you want to see them?
 CHILDREN. Don't let them find us!
 What an ugly noise. —
No, no — don't let them come!
 PIPER. Hark ye to me.
Some day I'll take you out with me to
 play;
High in the sun, — close to the water-
 fall. . . .
And we will make believe — *We'll make
 believe
We're hiding!* . . .

[*The* STROLLERS *rock with mirth*]

 CHILDREN. Yes, yes! Oh, let us
 make believe!
 STROLLERS. Oho, ho, ho! — A make-
 believe! — Ho, ho!
 PIPER. But, if you're good, — yes,
 very, very soon
I'll take you, as I promised, —
 CHILDREN. — Gypsies, oh!
 PIPER. Yes, with the gypsies. We
 shall go at night,
With just a torch — [*Watching them*]
 CHILDREN. Oh!
 PIPER. Like fire-flies! Will-o'-the
 wisps!
And make believe we're hiding, all the
 way,
Till we come out into a sunny land, —

All vines and sunlight, yes, and men that
 sing!
Far, far away — forever.
[*Gives* ILSE *a bowl to feed the other
 children*]
[JAN *pipes a measure of the Kinder-spell,
 brokenly. The* PIPER *turns*]
 So! Thou'lt be
My master, some day. Thou shalt
 pipe for me.
 JAN [*piping*]. Oh, wasn't that one
 beautiful? — Now you!
 PIPER [*taking the pipe*].
*The rainbow-bridge by day,
 — And borrow a shepherd-crook!
At night we take to the Milky Way;
 And then we follow the brook!
We'll follow the brook, whatever way
The brook shall sing, or the sun shall say,
 Or the mothering wood-dove coos!
And what do I care, what else I wear,
 If I keep my rainbow shoes!*

[*He points to the little row of bright shoes.
 The* CHILDREN *scream with joy.*
 ILSE *and* HANSEL *run back*]

 CHILDREN. Oh dear! What lovely
 shoes! Oh, which are mine?
Oh! Oh! — What lovely shoes! Oh,
 which are mine?
 PIPER. Try, till you see.
 [*Taking up a little red pair*]
 But these, — these are for Jan.

[JAN *is perched on the tree-stump, shy and
 silent with pleasure*]

 ILSE. Oh, those are best of all!
 And Jan —
 PIPER. And Jan
Is not to trudge, like you. Jan is to
 wear
Beautiful shoes, and shoes made most
 of all,
To look at!

 [*Takes up a pair of bird's wings*]

 CHILDREN [*squealing*]. Oh! Where
 did you find the wings?
Bird's wings!
 PIPER. There was some hunter in
 the woods,
Who killed more birds than he could
 carry home.
He did not want these, — though the
 starling did,
But could not use them more! And
 so, — [*Fastening one to each heel*]
 And so, —
They trim a little boy.

[*Puts them on* JAN. *He is radiant. He stretches out his legs and pats the feathers*]

CHILDREN [*trying on theirs and capering*]. O Jan! — O Jan! Oh! see my shoes!

[*The* PIPER *looks at* JAN]

PIPER. Hey day, what now?
JAN. I wish . . .
PIPER. What do you wish? Wish for it! — It shall come.

[JAN *pulls him closer and speaks shyly*]

JAN. I wish — that I could show them — to the Man,
The Lonely Man.

[*The* PIPER *looks at him and backs away; sits down helplessly and looks at him again*]

Oh, can I?
PIPER. Thou! — 'Twould make me a proud man.
JAN. Oh! it would make Him smile!

[*The* CHILDREN *dance and caper.* TRUDE *wakes up and joins them. Sound of distant chanting again*]

TRUDE. — I had a dream!
PIPER. A dream!
[*Pretending to be amazed. Reflects, a moment*]
I know! — Oh, what a funny dream!

[*The* CHILDREN *all fall a-laughing when he does. — Noise without.* CHEAT-THE-DEVIL'S *voice crying,* "Cuckoo — Cuckoo!"]

CHEAT-THE-DEVIL. Quick, quick! — I've something here.

[*The others roll away a big stone, and enter by the wooden door (rear),* CHEAT-THE-DEVIL. *He does not wear his red hood. He has a garland round his neck, and a basket on his arm*]

PIPER [*sharply to himself*]. No Michael yet! [*To* CHEAT-THE-DEVIL]
Michael! — Where's Michael?
CHEAT-THE-DEVIL. Look you, — you must wait.
We must be cunning. — There's a squirrel, mark you,
Hopped after me! He would have found us out.
I wanted him; I loved him. But I ran.
For once a squirrel falls a-talking. — Ah!

Look what I have. — Guess, guess!
[*Showing his basket to the Children*]
CHILDREN. Cakes! [*He is sad*]
Shoes!
[*He is sadder*]
Then — honey!

[*He radiantly undoes his basket, and displays a honeycomb. The* STROLLERS, *too, rush upon him*]

PIPER. Ah, Cheat-the-Devil! They would crop your ears.
Where had you this?
CHEAT-THE-DEVIL. Why, such a kind old farmer!
He'd left his bee-hives; they were all alone;
And the bees know me. So I brought this for you;
I knew They'd like it. — Oh, you're happy now!
PIPER. But Michael, — have they caught him?
CHEAT-THE-DEVIL. Oh, not they!
I heard no word of Michael; Michael's safe!
Once on the road I met a countryman,
Asked me the way. And not a word I spoke!
'Tis far the wisest. Twenty riddles he asked me.
I smiled and wagged my head. Anon cries he,
"This Fool is deaf and dumb!" — That made me angry,
But still I spoke not. — And I would not hurt him!
He was a bad man. But I liked the mule. —
Now am I safe! — Now am I home at last!
PIPER. 'St. — Met you any people on the way,
Singing?
CHEAT-THE-DEVIL. No, growling, — growling dreary psalms
All on a sunny day! Behind the hedges,
I saw them go. They go from Hamelin, now;
And I know why! —
[*The* PIPER *beckons him away from the* CHILDREN]
The mayor's Barbara
Must go to Rudersheim, to be a Nun!
PIPER. To be a Nun!
CHEAT-THE-DEVIL. A penance for them all.
She weeps; but she must go! All they, you see,
Are wroth against him. — He must give *his* child —

PIPER. A nun!

CHEAT-THE-DEVIL [*nodding*]. Forever! — She, who smiled at Michael.

Look you, she weeps! They are bad
people all; —

Nothing like these.
[*Looking at the Children*]
These are all beautiful.

PIPER. To lock her up! A maiden,
shut away

Out of the sun. To cage her there for
life,

Cut off her hair; pretend that she is
dead! —

Horrible, horrible! No, I'll not endure
it.

I'll end this murder. — He shall give
up his;

But never so! — Not so! — While I do
live

To let things out of cages! — Tell me,
quick! —

When shall it happen?

CHEAT-THE-DEVIL. Why, it falls to-
day.

I saw two herds of people going by,

To be there well aforetime, for the sight.

And she is going last of all, at noon;

All sparkling, like a Bride. — I heard
them tell.

PIPER. No, never, never! — No, it
shall not be!

Hist! —
[*Steps heard scrambling down the entrance-
way*]
[*Enter* MICHAEL *in mad haste. They
rush upon him with exultation and
relief. He shakes them off, doggedly*]
So! — You had like to have hanged
us.

MICHAEL. — What of that?

PIPER. All for a lily maiden.

MICHAEL. Ah, — thy pipe!

How will it save her? — *Save her!* —
Tune thy pipe

To compass that! — You do not know—

PIPER. I know.

Tell me no more. — I say it shall not be!

To heel, lad! No, I follow, — none
but I!

Go, — go! [MICHAEL *rushes out again*]
[*To* CHEAT-THE-DEVIL, *pointing to the
Children*]
Do you bide here and shepherd these.

CHILDREN. Where are you going? —
Take us too! — us too! —

Oh, take us with you? — Take us!

PIPER [*distracted*]. No, no, no!

You shall be kittens all. And chase
your tails,

Till I come back! — So here!

[*Catches* HANSEL *and affixes to his little
jacket a long strip of leather for a
tail; then whirls him about*]

CHILDREN. Me too! — Me too!

CHEAT-THE-DEVIL. Let me make
tails, — let me!
[*Seizing shears and leather*]

PIPER [*wildly*]. Faith, and you shall.

A master tailor! — Come, here's food
for thought.

Think all, — [*To the* STROLLERS]
And hold your tongues, there! —
If a Cat —

If a Cat have — as all men say — Nine
Lives,

And if Nine Tailors go to make a Man,

How long, then, shall it take one Man
turned Tailor

To keep a Cat in Tails, until she die?

[CHEAT-THE-DEVIL *looks subdued; the*
CHILDREN *whirl about*]

But here's no game for Jan. — Stay!
Something else. —

[*He runs to a wooden coffer, rear and takes
out a long crystal on the end of a
string, with a glance at the shaft of
sunlight from the roof. The* CHIL-
DREN *watch*]

Be quiet, now. — Chase not your tails
too far,

Till I come home again.

CHILDREN. Come home — come
home!

PIPER. And you shall see my —

CHILDREN. Something Beautiful!

Oh, oh, what is it? — Oh, and will it
play?

Will it play music?

PIPER. Yes.

[*He hangs the crystal in the sun. A Rainbow strikes the wall*]
— The best of all!

CHEAT-THE-DEVIL, JAN, CHILDREN.

Oh, oh, how beautiful, — how beautiful!

PIPER. And hear it pipe and call,
and dance, and sing.

Héjà! — And hark you all. You have
to mind —

The Rainbow!

[*He climbs out, pipe in hand. The* CHIL-
DREN *whirl about after their tails.* —
CHEAT-THE-DEVIL, *and* JAN *on his
tree-stump, open-mouthed with happiness, watch the Rainbow*]

CURTAIN

SCENE II. — *The Cross-ways: on the Long
Road to Rudersheim.*

*A wooded country: high hills at back.
The place is wild and overgrown, like
the haunted spot it is reputed to be.
In the foreground, right, a ruined
stone well appears, in a mass of weeds
and vines. Opposite, left, tall trees
and dense thickets. Where the roads
cross (to left of centre), stands a large,
neglected shrine, with a weather-worn
figure of Christ, — again the " Lonely
Man," — facing toward Hamelin. —
The stage is empty, at rise of the
curtain; but the sound of chanting
from burghers just gone by fades
slowly, on the road to Rudersheim.*

*From the hillside at the rear comes the
PIPER, wrapped in a long green
cloak, his pipe in his hand. He
looks after the procession, and back
to Hamelin. — Enter, springing from
the bushes to the right, MICHAEL,
who seizes him. Their speech goes
breathlessly.*

MICHAEL.	Quick! — tell me —
PIPER.			— Patience.
MICHAEL.	Patience? — Death and
hell!
Oh, save her — save her! Give the
children back.
PIPER.	Never.	Have you betrayed
us?
MICHAEL.		I! — betrayed?
PIPER.	So, so, lad.
MICHAEL.		But to save her —
PIPER.			There's a way, —
Trust me!	I save her, or we swing to-
gether
Merrily, in a row. — How did you see
her?
MICHAEL.	By stealth: two days
ago, at evening,
Hard by the vine-hid wall of her own
garden,
I made a warbling like a nightingale;
And she came out to hear.
PIPER.			A serenade!
Under the halter!
MICHAEL.	Hush. — A	death-black
night,
Until she came. — Oh, how to tell thee,
lad!
She came, — she came, not for the nightingale,
But even dreaming that it would be I!
PIPER.	She knew you? — We are
trapped, then.
MICHAEL.			No, not so!

She smiled on me. — Dost thou re-
member how
She smiled on me that day? Alas,
poor maid,
She took me for some noble in disguise!
And all these days, — she told me, —
she had dreamed
That I would come to save her!
PIPER.				Said she this?
MICHAEL.	All this — all this, and
more! . . .
What could lies do? — I lied to her of
thee;
I swore I knew not of thy vanishment,
Nor the lost children. But I told her
true,
I was a stroller and an outcast man
That hid there, like a famished casta-
way,
For one more word, one look, without a
hope.
Helpless to save her.
PIPER.			And she told thee then,
She goes to be a nun?
MICHAEL.			Youth to the grave!
And I — vile nothing — cannot go to
save her,
Only to look my last —
PIPER.			Who knows?
MICHAEL [*bitterly*].		Ah, thou! —
PIPER.	Poor Nightingale!
	[*Fingers his pipe, noiselessly*]
MICHAEL [*rapt with grief*].	Oh, but
the scorn of her!
PIPER.	She smiled on thee.
MICHAEL.	Until she heard the
truth: —
A juggler, — truly, — and no wandering
knight!
Oh, and she wept.		[*Wildly*]
			Let us all hang together.
PIPER.	Thanks.	Kindly spoken. —
Not this afternoon!
MICHAEL.	Thou knowest they are
given up for dead?
PIPER.	Truly.
MICHAEL.	Bewitched?
PIPER.			So are they.
MICHAEL.		Sold to the Devil?
PIPER [*pacing softly up and down, with
the restless cunning of a squirrel at
watch*]. Pfui! But who else? Of
course. This same old Devil!
This kind old Devil takes on him all we
do!
Who else is such a refuge in this world?
Who could have burned the abbey in
this place,
Where holy men did live? Why, 'twas
the Devil!
And who did guard us one secluded spot

By burying a wizard at this cross-
  ways? —
So none dare search the haunted, evil
  place!
The Devil for a landlord! — So say I!
And all we poor, we strollers, for his
  tenants;
We gypsies and we pipers in the world,
And a few hermits and sword-swallow-
  ers,
And all the cast-aways that Holy
  Church
Must put in cages — cages — to the
  end!
  [*To* MICHAEL, *who is overcome*]
Take heart! I swear, — by all the
  stars that chime!
I'll not have things in Cages!
  MICHAEL.   Barbara!
So young, — so young and beautiful!
  PIPER.   And fit
To marry with friend Michael!
  MICHAEL.   Do not mock.
  PIPER. I mock not. — (Baa — Baa
    — Barbara!)
  MICHAEL.   Ay, she laughed,
On that first day. But still she gazed.
    — I saw
Her, all the while! I swallowed —
  PIPER.   Prodigies!
A thousand swallows, and no summer
  yet!
But now, — 'tis late to ask, — why did
  you not
Swallow her father? — That had saved
  us all.
  MICHAEL. They will be coming soon.
    They will cut off
All her bright hair, — and wall her in
  forever.
  PIPER. Never. They shall not.
  MICHAEL [*dully*]. Will you give them
    back,
Now?
  PIPER. I will never give them back.
    Be sure.
  MICHAEL. And she is made an offer-
    ing for them all.
I heard it of the gossips. — They have
  sworn
Jacobus shall not keep his one ewe-lamb
While all the rest go childless.
  PIPER.   And I swear
That he shall give her up, — to none
  but thee!
  MICHAEL. You cannot do it!
  PIPER.   Have I lived like Cain,
But to make good one hour of Life and
  Sun?
And have I got this Hamelin in my
  hands,

To make it pay its thousand cruelties
With such a fool's *one-more?* . . .
              — You know right well,
'Twas not the thousand guilders that
  I wanted
For thee, or me, or any! — Ten would
  serve.
But there it ached; *there*, in the money-
  bag
That serves the town of Hamelin for
  an heart!
That stab was mortal! And I thrust it
  deep.
Life, life, I wanted; safety, — sun and
  wind! —
And but to show them how that daily
  fear
They call their faith, is made of blas-
  phemies
That would put out the Sun and Moon
  and Stars,
Early, for some last judgment!
  [*He laughs up to the tree-tops*]
                And the Lord,
Where will He get His harpers and sing-
  ing-men
And them that laugh for joy? — From
  Hamelin guilds? —
Will you imagine Kurt the Councillor
Trying to sing?

[*He looks at his pipe again; then listens
  intently*]

  MICHAEL. His lean throat freeze! —
    But she — Barbara! Barbara! —
  PIPER.   Patience. She will come,
Dressed like a bride.
  MICHAEL. Ah, do not mock me so.
  PIPER. I mock not.
  MICHAEL. She will never look at me.
  PIPER. Rather than be a nun, I
    swear she will
Look at thee twice, — and with a long,
  long look.

[*Chant approaches in the distance, coming
  from Hamelin*]

  VOICES.

      Dies irae, dies illa
      Solvet saeclum in favilla,
      Teste David cum Sibylla.

      Quantus tremor est futurus,
      Quando judex est venturus,
      Cuncta stricte discussurus!

  PIPER. Bah, how they whine! Why
    do they drag it so?
  MICHAEL [*overcome*]. Oh, can it be
    the last of all? O Saints! —

O blessed Francis, Ursula, Catherine!
Hubert — and Crispin — Pantaleone —
     Paul!
George o' the Dragon! — Michael the
     Archangel!
PIPER. Michael Sword-eater, canst
     not swallow a chant?
The well, the well! — Take care.
VOICES [*nearer*].

> *Inter oves locum praesta,*
> *Et ab hoedis me sequestra,*
> *Statuens in parte dextra.*
>
> *Confutatis maledictis,*
> *Flammis acribus addictis:*
> *Voca me cum benedictis.*

[MICHAEL *climbs down the ancient well,*
reaching his head up warily, to see.
The PIPER *waves to him debonairly, points*
to the tree-tops, left, and stands a
moment showing in his face his dis-
approval of the music. He fingers
his pipe. As the hymn draws near,
he scrambles among the bushes, left,
and disappears.
Enter slowly, chanting, the company of
burghers from Hamelin, — men to-
gether first, headed by priests; then
the women. — ANSELM *and all the*
townsfolk appear (saving VERONIKA,
the wife of KURT); JACOBUS *is*
meek; KURT *very stern. — As they*
appear, the piping of the Dance-spell
begins softly, high in air. The hymn
wavers; when the first burghers reach
the centre of the stage, it breaks down.
They look up, bewildered; then, with every
sign of consternation, struggle, and
vacant fear, they begin to dance, willy-
nilly. Their faces work; they struggle
to walk on; but it is useless. The
music whirls them irresistibly into a
rhythmic pace of $\frac{3}{4}$ time, and jogs
their words, when they try to speak,
into the same dance-measure. One by
one, — two and two they go, — round
and round like corks at first, with
every sign of struggle and protest, then
off, on the long road to Rudersheim.
Fat priests waltz together. — KURT
the fierce and JACOBUS *the sleek hug*
each other in frantic endeavor to be
released. Their words jolt insanely]

KURT, JACOBUS.
{ No, no. — No, no. — No, no. — No,
     no!
  Yes, yes. — I, yes. — Yes, yes. —
     Yes, yes!

SOME.
{ *La — crymos — a — Dies — ill —*
  Bewitched — the Devil! — bewitched
     — bewitched!
  I will not — will not — will — I will!
  No, no — but where! — Help —
     help! — To arms!
OTHERS.
{ *Suppli — canti — suppli — Oh!*
  To Hamelin — back — to Hamelin —
     stay!
  No, no! — No, no, — Away, — away!
[*They dance out, convulsively, towards*
Rudersheim. KURT *and* JACOBUS,
still whirling, cry]

JACOBUS, KURT.
{ Yes, yes! — yes, yes! — Let go —
     let go —
  No, no! — I will not — No! . . . No!
     [*Exeunt, left, dancing*]
OTHERS.
{ Keep time, keep time! Have mercy!
     — Time!
  Oh, let me — go! — Let go — let go!
  Yes, yes — Yes, yes — No, no — no
     — no!

[BARBARA *appears, pale and beautiful; —*
richly dressed in white, with flowing
locks. She is wan and exhausted. —
The dance-mania, as it seizes her,
makes her circle slowly and dazedly
with a certain pitiful silliness. The
nuns and monks accompanying her
point in horror. But they, too, dance
off with each other, willy-nilly, — like
leaves in a tempest. BARBARA *is left*
alone, still circling slowly. The
piping sounds softer. She staggers
against a tree, and keeps on waving
her hands and turning her head,
vaguely, in time.
MICHAEL *looks forth from the well; then*
climbs out and approaches her]

  MICHAEL. She is so beautiful, —
     how dare I tell her?
My heart, how beautiful! The blessed
     saint! . . .
Fear nothing, fairest Lady. — You are
     saved.
[*She looks at him unseeingly, and con-*
tinues to dance. — He holds out his
arms to stop her]
Pray you, the danger's gone. Pray
     you, take breath!
Poor, shining dove, — I would not hold
     thee here,
Against thy wish. — 'Tis Michael, the
     sword-eater.

     [*The piping ceases*]

BARBARA [*murmuring*]. Yes, yes — I must — I must — I must . . .

[*Re-enter the* PIPER *from the thickets*]

MICHAEL. Look, I will guard you like a princess, here;
Yes, like Our Lady's rose-vine.

BARBARA [*gasping*]. Ah, my heart!
[*The* PIPER *comes towards her. She sees him and holds out her arms, crying*]
Oh, he has saved me! — I am thine — thine — thine!

[*Falls into his arms half-fainting. The* PIPER *stands amazed, alarmed, chagrined*]

PIPER. Mine?

MICHAEL [*furiously*]. *Thine?* So was it? All a trap? Cock's blood!
Thine, thine! — And thou hast piped her wits away.
Thine!

PIPER [*holding her off*]. No, not mine!

BARBARA [*to him*]. Why did you steal me hence?
When did you love me? — Was it on first sight?

PIPER [*confounded*]. I, love thee?

MICHAEL. — Knave! thief! liar!

PIPER. — Give me breath.
[*Holds off* BARBARA *gently*]

BARBARA. Where are you taking me?

PIPER. I? Taking thee?

MICHAEL [*to her*]. He shall not steal thee!

BARBARA [*in a daze*]. I must follow him.

PIPER. *No!* 'Tis too much. You shall not follow me!
I'll not be followed. — Damsel, sit you down.
Here is too much! I love you not.

BARBARA [*wonderingly*]. You do not?
Why did you pipe to me?

MICHAEL. — And steal her wits,
Stealer of all the children!

BARBARA [*vaguely*]. Are they safe?

PIPER [*to* MICHAEL]. Oh, your good faith! — [*To her*]
They're safe.

BARBARA. I knew — I knew it!

PIPER. And so art thou. But never shall they go
To Hamelin more; and never shalt *thou* go
To be a nun.

BARBARA. To be a nun, — no, no!
Ah me, I'm spent.
Sir, take me with you.

MICHAEL [*still enraged, to the* PIPER]
Rid her of the spell!
Is this thy pledge?

PIPER [*distracted*]. I do but rub my wits —
To think — to think. [*To himself*]
What shall I do with her,
Now she is here? What if she stayed?
— Forever? [*To them*]
Hearken. — You, Michael, on to Rudersheim —

MICHAEL. And leave her here? No, no!

PIPER. Then take the girl.

BARBARA. To Rudersheim? No, never, never!

PIPER. Well . . .

Hearken. — There is the hermit, over the hill. [*Apart, wildly*]
But how — suppose she will not marry him?
I will not take her where the children are.
And yet —
[*An idea strikes him. To her*]
Hark, now; — hark, now, and tell me truly:
Can you spin cloth?

BARBARA [*amazed*]. I? Spin?

PIPER [*eagerly*]. Can you make shoes?

BARBARA. I — *I* make shoes! — Fellow!

PIPER. So.

MICHAEL. Art thou mad!

PIPER. With me you may not go! But you'll be safe.
Hearken: — you, Michael, go to Rudersheim;
And tell the nuns —

BARBARA. No, no! I dare not have it!
Oh, they would send and take me! No, no, no!

PIPER. Would you go back to Hamelin?

BARBARA. No — no — no!
Ah, I am spent.

[*Droops towards the* PIPER; *falters and sinks down on the bank beside the well, in a swoon. — The* PIPER *is abashed and rueful for the moment*]

MICHAEL. All this, your work!

PIPER [*looking at her closely*]. Not mine.
This is no charm. It is all youth and grief,
And weariness. And she shall follow you. —
Tell the good nuns you found her sore bewitched,

Here in this haunt of "devils"; — clean
  distraught.
No Church could so receive a dancing
  nun!
Tell them thou art an honest, piteous
  man
Desires to marry her.
MICHAEL.   Marry the Moon!
PIPER. No, no, the Moon for me! —
  She shall be yours;
And here she sleeps, until her wits be
  sound.
[*He spreads his cloak over her, gently*]
The sun's still high. 'Tis barely after-
  noon. —
[*Looks at the sunshine. A thought strikes
  him with sudden dismay*]
'Tis — no, the time is going! — On my
  life,
I had forgot Them! — And They will
  not stay
After the Rainbow fades.
  MICHAEL [*confounded*]. Art thou
  moon-mad?
  PIPER   [*madly*]. No. Stir   not!
  Keep her safe! I come anon.
But first I go. — They'll not mind
  Cheat-the-Devil!
They'll creep, to find out where the
  Rainbow went.
I know them! So would I! — They'll
  all leak out!
  MICHAEL. Stay — stay!
  PIPER. No; guard her, you! —
  Anon, anon!
  MICHAEL. But you will pipe her up
  and after you!
  PIPER [*flinging him the pipe from his
  belt*]. Do you fear this? Then
  keep it till I come.
You bide! — The Other cannot.
  MICHAEL.   Who?
  PIPER.   *The Rainbow,*
The Rainbow! —

[*He runs madly up the hillside, and away*]

CURTAIN

ACT III

SCENE. — *The same, later. BARBARA lies
  motionless,   still   sleeping. — MI-
  CHAEL, sitting on the bank opposite,
  fingers the pipe with awe and wistfulness. He blows softly upon it;
  then looks at the girl hopefully. She
  does not stir.*

[*Enter the PIPER, from the hills at back.
  He carries a pair of water-jars slung
  over his shoulders, and seems to be
  in high feather*]

PIPER [*singing.*]
*Out of your cage,
Come out of your cage
And take your soul on a pilgrimage!
Please in your shoes, an if you must! —
But out and away, before you're dust:
Scribe and Stay-at-home,
Saint and Sage,
Out of your cage,
Out of your cage! —*
[*He feigns to be terror-struck at sight of
  the pipe in MICHAEL's hands*]
Ho, help! Good Michael, Michael,
  loose the charm!
Michael,   have   mercy! I'm be-
  witched! —
  MICHAEL [*giving him the pipe*].
                            Cock's faith!
Still mocking! — Well ye know, it will
  not play
Such games for me.
  PIPER. Be soothed, — 'twas as I
  guessed   [*Unslings the jars*]
All of them hungry, — and the Rain-
  bow going; —
And Cheat-the-Devil pining in a corner.
'Twas well I went: they were for leak-
  ing out,
And then, — lopped ears for two!
  MICHAEL.   Oh, that will come.
  PIPER. Never believe it! We have
  saved her, look you;
We save them all! No prison walls
  again,
For anything so young, in Hamelin
  there.
Wake her, and see.
  MICHAEL. Ay, wake her. But for me,
Her sleep is gentler.
  PIPER [*comfortingly*].
            Nay, but wait. — Good faith,
Wait. We have broke the bars of iron
  now;
Still there are golden! — 'Tis her very
  self
Is caged within herself. Once coax her
  out,
Once set her own heart free! —
  MICHAEL.   Wake her, and see!
      [*The PIPER crosses, humming*]
  PIPER.
*Mind your eyes, tune your tongue!
Let it never be said, but sung, — sung;
'Out of your cage, out of your cage!'
Maiden, maiden, —*

[*He wakes her gently. BARBARA sits up,
  plainly bewildered; then she sees the
  PIPER, and says happily*]

  BARBARA. Oh! — you have come to
  save me. They are gone.

All this, for love of me!

PIPER [*ruefully*]. No, no — I — *No !*

BARBARA. You — you are robbers?

[*Her hands go to the pearls about her neck*]

PIPER [*indignant*]. No! Blood on
the Moon!
This is the maddest world I ever blinked
at. —
Fear nothing, maiden. I will tell you
all.
Come, sit you down; and Michael
shall keep watch
From yonder hillock, lest that any pass.
Fear nothing. None will pass: they
are too sure
The Devil hath this cross-ways! — Sit
you down.

[MICHAEL *watches, with jealous wistfulness, from the road (left rear). —
*BARBARA *half fearfully sits up, on
the bank by the well*]

BARBARA. Not love? And yet . . .
you do not want my pearls?
Then why —

PIPER. For why should all be love or
money?
Money! Oho, — that mouldy thou-
sand guilders
You think of! — But it was your
Hamelin friends
That loved the guilders, and not I.

BARBARA. Then why —
Why did you steal me hence?

PIPER. Why did yourself
Long to be stolen?

BARBARA [*shuddering*]. Ah! to be
shut up . . .
Forever, — young — alive !

PIPER. Alive and singing;
Young, — young; — and four thick
walls and no more sun,
No music, and no wandering, and no
life !
Think you, I would not steal all things
alive
Out of such doom? — How can I
breathe and laugh
While there are things in cages? —
You are free ;
And you shall never more go back again.

BARBARA. And you, who are you
then?

PIPER. How do *I* know?
Moths in the Moon ! — Ask me a thing
on reason.

BARBARA. And 'twas not . . . that
you loved me.

PIPER. Loved thee? No! —
Save but along with squirrels, and bright
fish,

And bubbling water.

BARBARA. Then where shall I go !

PIPER. Oh, little bird, — is that your
only song?
Go? Everywhere! Here be no walls,
no hedges,
No tolls, no taxes, — rats nor aldermen !
Go, say you? Round the world, and
round again ! [*Apart*]
— Ah, she was Hamelin-born.
[*He watches her*]
But there's a man, —
Sky-true, sword-strong, and brave to
look upon ;
One that would thrust his hand in
dragon's mouth
For your bright sake; one that would
face the Devil,
Would swallow fire —

BARBARA. You would?

PIPER [*desperately*]. I ? — No, not I !
Michael, — yon goodman Michael.

BARBARA [*bitterly*]. A stroller ! — oh,
nought but a wandering man.

PIPER. Well, would you have a man
take root, I ask?

BARBARA. That swallows swords. . . .

PIPER. Is he a comely man?

BARBARA. That swallows swords ! —

PIPER. What's manlier to swallow?
Did he but swallow pancakes, were that
praise?
Pancakes and sausage, like your
Hamelin yokels?
He swallows fire and swords, I say, and
more.
And yet this man hath for a whole noon-
hour
Guarded you while you slept ; — still as
a dove,
Distant and kind as shadow; giant-
strong
For his enchanted princess, — even you.

BARBARA. So you bewitched me,
then.

PIPER [*wildly*]. How do I know?

BARBARA. Where are the children?

PIPER. I'll not tell you that.
You are too much of Hamelin.

BARBARA. You bewitched them !

PIPER. Yes, so it seems. But how?
— Upon my life,
'Tis more than I know, — yes, a little
more.

[*Rapidly: half in earnest and half in
whimsy*]

Sometimes it works, and sometimes no.
There are
Some things upon my soul, I cannot do.

[*Watching her*]

BARBARA [*expectantly*]. Not even with thy pipe?

PIPER. Not even so. Some are too hard. — Yet, yet, I love to try:
And most, to try with all the hidden charms
I have, that I have never counted through.

BARBARA [*fascinated*]. Where are they?

PIPER [*touching his heart*]. Here.

BARBARA. Where are they?

PIPER. How do I know? If I knew all, why should I care to live? No, no! The game is What-Will-Happen-Next?

BARBARA. And what will happen?

PIPER [*tantalizingly*]. Ah! how do I know?
It keeps me searching. 'Tis so glad and sad
And strange to find out, What-Will-Happen-Next!
And mark you this: the strangest miracle . . . .

BARBARA. Yes! —

PIPER. Stranger than the Devil or the Judgment;
Stranger than piping, — even when *I* pipe!
Stranger than charming mice — or even men —

BARBARA [*with tense expectancy*]. What is it? What?

PIPER [*watching her*]. Why, — what may come to pass
Here in the heart. There is one very charm —

BARBARA. Oh!

PIPER. Are you brave?

BARBARA [*awe-struck*]. Oh!

PIPER [*slowly*]. Will you drink the philter?

BARBARA. 'Tis . . . some enchantment?

PIPER [*mysteriously*]. 'Tis a love philter.

BARBARA. Oh, tell me first —

PIPER. Why, sooth, the only charm In it, is Love. It is clear well-water.

BARBARA [*disappointed*]. Only well-water?

PIPER. Love is only Love. It must be philters, then?
[*He comes down smiling and beckons to* MICHAEL, *who draws near, bewildered*]
This lady thirsts For magic!

[*He ties a long green scarf that he has over his shoulder, to a water-jar, and lowers it down the old well; while* BARBARA *watches, awe-struck. He continues to sing softly*]
Mind your eyes,
Tune your tongue,
Let it never be said,
But sung, — sung! —

* * *

MICHAEL [*to* BARBARA, *timidly*]. I am glad at least, fair lady,
To think how my poor show did give you pleasure
That day — that day when —

BARBARA. Ah! that day of doom!

MICHAEL. What is your will?

BARBARA [*passionately*]. I know not; and I care not! [*Apart*]
Oh, it is true. — And he a sword-eater!

[*The* PIPER *hauls up the jar, full of water*]

PIPER. Michael, your cup.
[MICHAEL *gives him a drinking-horn from his belt. The* PIPER *fills it with water, solemnly, and turns to* BARBARA, *who is at first defiant, then fascinated*]
Maiden, your ears. So: — hearken.
Before you drink of this, is it your will
Forever to be gone from Hamelin?

BARBARA. I must, — I must.

PIPER. Your mother?

BARBARA [*piteously*].
I have no mother;
Nor any father, more. He gave me up.

PIPER. That did he! — For a round one thousand guilders!
Weep not, I say! First, loose you, heart and shoes,
From Hamelin. Put off now, the dust, the mould,
The cobble-stones, the little prying windows;
The streets that dream o' *What the Neighbors Say.*
Think you were never born there. Think some Breath
Wakened you early — early on one morning,
Deep in a Garden (but you knew not whose),
Where voices of wild waters bubbling ran,
Shaking down music from glad mountaintops, —
Where the still peaks were burning in the dawn,
Like fiery snow, — down to the listening valleys,

That do off their blue mist only to show
Some deeper blue, some haunt of violets.
No voice you heard, nothing you felt or saw,
Save in your heart, the tumult of young birds,
A nestful of wet wings and morning-cries,
Throbbing for flight! . . .
Then, — for your Soul, new wakened, felt athirst,
You turned to where that call of water led,
Laughing for truth, — all truth and star-like laughter!
Beautiful water, that will never stay,
But runs and laughs and sparkles in the heart,
And sends live laughter trickling everywhere,
And knows the thousand longings of the Earth!
And as you drank it then, so now, drink here;

[*He reaches her the horn. She has listened, motionless, like a thing bewitched, her eyes fixed and wide, as if she were sleepwalking. She drinks.* MICHAEL *stands near, also motionless. When she speaks, it is in a younger voice, shy, sweet, and full of wonder*]

And tell me, — tell me, you, — what happened then?
What do you see?
    BARBARA.   Ah! —

[*She looks before her with wide, new eyes*]

    PIPER.   Do you see — a —
    BARBARA.   . . . Michael!
    PIPER.   So! — And a good one.
And you call him? —
    BARBARA.   . . . Michael.
    PIPER.   So. — 'Tis a world of wonders, by my faith! —
What is the fairest thing you see but —
    BARBARA.   Michael.
    PIPER.   And is he comely as a man should be?
And strong? — And wears good promise in his eyes,
And keeps it with his heart and with his hands?   [*She nods like a child*]
And would you fear to go with him? —
    BARBARA.   No, no!
    PIPER.   Then reach to him that little hand of yours.

[MICHAEL, *wonder-struck, runs to the jar, pours water upon his hand, rubs it off with haste, and falls on his knees before her, taking her hand fearfully*]

    BARBARA [*timidly*].   And can he talk? —
    PIPER.   Yes, yes. — The maid's bewildered.
Fear nothing. Thou'rt so dumb, man! — Yes, yes, yes.
Only he kneels; he cannot yet believe.
Speak roundly to him. — Will you go with him?
He will be gentler to you than a father:
He would be brothers five, and dearest friend,
And sweetheart, — ay, and knight and servingman!
    BARBARA.   Yes, yes, I know he will.
And can he talk, too?
    PIPER.   Lady, you have bewitched him.
    MICHAEL.   Oh! dear Lady,
With you — with you, I dare not ope my mouth
Saving to sing, or pray!
    PIPER.   Let it be singing!
Lad, 'tis a wildered maiden, with no home
Save only thee; and she is more a child
Than yesterday.
    MICHAEL.   Oh, lordly, wondrous world! —
How is it, Sweet, you smile upon me now?
    BARBARA.   Sure I have ever smiled on thee. How not?
Art thou not Michael? — *And thou lovest me.*
And I love thee! — If I unloved thee ever,
It was some spell. —   [*Rapturously*]
         But this, — ah, *This is I !*

[MICHAEL, *on his knees, winds his arms about her*]

    PIPER [*softly*].   It is all true, — all true. Lad, do not doubt;
The golden cage is broken.
    MICHAEL.   Oh! more strange
Than morning dreams! I am like one new-born;
I am a speechless babe. — And this is she,
My Moon I cried for, — here, —
    PIPER.   It is thy bride.
    MICHAEL.   Thou wilt not fear to come with me?
    BARBARA.   With thee?
With thee! Ah, look! What have I more than thee?
And thou art mine, tall fellow! How comes it now
Right happily that I am pranked so fair!

[*She touches her fineries, her long pearl-strings, joyously*]
And all this came so near to burying;
This!
MICHAEL. And this dearer gold.
[*Kissing her hair*]
BARBARA. All, all for thee! —
[*She leans over in a playful rapture and binds her hair about him*]
Look, — I will be thy garden that we lost,
Yea, everywhere, — in every wilderness.
There shall none fright us with a flaming sword!
But I will be thy garden!

[*There is the sound of a herd-bell approaching*]

PIPER. See, — how the sunlight soon shall pour red wine
To make your marriage-feast! — And do you hear
That faery bell? — No fear! — 'Tis some white creature,
Seeking her whiter lamb. — Go; find our hermit:
And he shall bless you, — as a hermit can!
And be your pledge for shelter. There's the path. — [*To* MICHAEL]
Follow each other, close!
MICHAEL. Beyond the Sun!
PIPER. A golden afternoon, — and all is well!
[*He gives* MICHAEL *his cloak to wrap round* BARBARA. *They go, hand in hand, up into the hills. The herd-bell sounds softly. — The* PIPER *cocks his head like a squirrel, and listens with delight. He watches the two till they disappear; then comes down joyously*]
If you can only catch them while they're young!

[*The herd-bell sounds nearer. He lets down a water-jar into the well again. The nearness of the bell startles him. He becomes watchful as a wild creature. It sounds nearer and nearer. A woman's voice calls like the wind: "Jan! Jan!"* —
The PIPER, *tense and cautious, moves softly down into the shrubbery by the well*]

VERONIKA'S VOICE. Jan!
PIPER. Hist! Who dared?
VERONIKA'S VOICE. . . . Jan!
PIPER. Who dared, I say?
A woman. — 'Tis a woman!

[*Enter* VERONIKA, *on the road from Hamelin. She is very pale and worn, and drags herself along, clutching in her hand a herd-bell. She looks about her, holds up the bell and shakes it once softly, covering it with her fingers again; then she sits wearily down at the foot of the ruined shrine, and covers her face, with a sharp breath*]

VERONIKA. . . . Ah, — ah, — ah!
[*The* PIPER *watches with breathless wonder and fascination. It seems to horrify him*]

PIPER [*under breath*]. That woman!
[VERONIKA *lifts her head suddenly and sees the motion of the bushes*]

VERONIKA. He is coming! — He is here!
[*She darts towards the well. — The* PIPER *springs up*]
Oh, God of Mercy! . . . It is only you!
Where is he? — Where? — Where are you hiding him?
PIPER [*confusedly*]. Woman . . . what do you, wandering with that bell?
That herd-bell?
VERONIKA. Oh! are you man or cloud? . . . Where is my Jan?
Jan, — Jan, — the little lame one! He is mine.
He lives, I know he lives. I know — yes, yes.
[*She crouches where she is, watching him*]

PIPER. Surely he lives!
VERONIKA. — *Lives !* will you swear it? Ah, —
I will believe! But he . . . is not so strong
As all the others.
PIPER [*apart*]. Aië, how horrible!
[*To her*]
Sit you down here. You cannot go away
While you are yet so pale. Why are you thus?
[*She looks at him distractedly*]
VERONIKA. You, who have torn the hearts out of our bodies
And left the city like a place of graves, —
Why am I spent? — Ah, ah! — But he's alive!
PIPER [*fiercely*]. Alive? What else? — Why would he not be living?
VERONIKA. I do not know.
PIPER. Do you take me for the Devil?

VERONIKA. I do not know.

PIPER. Yet you were not afraid?

VERONIKA. What is there now to fear?

PIPER [*watching her*]. Where are the townsfolk?

VERONIKA. They are all gone to Rudersheim . . .

PIPER [*still watchful*]. How so?

VERONIKA. Where, for a penance, Barbara, Jacob's daughter,
Will take the veil. His one, for all of ours!
t will be over now.

PIPER. Have none returned?

VERONIKA. I know not; I am searching, since the dawn.

PIPER. To-day?

VERONIKA. And every day.

PIPER. That herd-bell, there —
Why do you bring it?

VERONIKA [*sobbing*].
Oh, he loves them so.
knew, if he but heard it, he would follow,
And if he could. Only, the ways are rough —

PIPER. No more. I know!

VERONIKA. — And he had lost his crutch.

PIPER [*like a wounded animal*]. Let be. You hurt me —

VERONIKA. You! — A man of air?

PIPER. I am no man of air.

VERONIKA. — What are you then?
Give them to me, I say. You have them hid,
Under a spell.

PIPER [*struggling with pity*]. Yes.

VERONIKA. Give them back to me.

PIPER. No.

VERONIKA. But they all . . . are living? On thy soul?

PIPER. — Wilt thou believe me?

VERONIKA. And you hold them safe?

PIPER. Safe.

VERONIKA. Shut away?

PIPER. From Hamelin; forever.

VERONIKA. And are they . . . warm?

PIPER. — Yes.

VERONIKA. Are they happy? — Oh, That cannot be! — But do they laugh, sometimes?

PIPER. Yes.

VERONIKA. — Then you'll give them back again!

PIPER. No, never.

VERONIKA [*half to herself, distraught between suspense and hope*]. I must be patient.

PIPER. Woman, they all are mine.
I hold them in my hands; they bide with me.
What's breath and blood, — what are the hearts of children,
To Hamelin, — while it heaps its money-bags?

VERONIKA. You cared not for the money.

PIPER. No? — You seem
A foreign woman, — come from very far,
That you should know.

VERONIKA. I know. I was not born
There. But you wrong them. There were yet a few
Who would have dealt with you more honestly
Than this Jacobus, or —

PIPER. Or Kurt the Syndic!
Believe it not. Those two be tongue and brain
For the whole town! I know them. And that town
Stands as the will of other towns, a score,
That make us wandering poor the things we are!
It stands for all, unto the end of time,
That turns this bright world black and the Sun cold,
With hate, and hoarding; — all-triumphant Greed
That spreads above the roots of all despair,
And misery, and rotting of the soul!
Now shall they learn — if money-bags can learn —
What turns the bright world black, and the Sun cold;
And what's that creature that they call a child! —
And what this wingèd thing men name a heart,
Never to bind, never to bid be still;
And what this hunger and this thirst to sing,
To laugh, to fight, — to hope, to be *believed?*
And what is truth? And who did make the stars?

* * * * *

I have to pay for fifty thousand hates,
Greeds, cruelties; such barbarous tortured days
A tiger would disdain; — for all my kind!
Not my one mother, not my own of kin, —
All, all, who wear the motley in the heart
Or on the body: — for all cagèd glories

And trodden wings, and sorrows laughed
    to scorn.
I, — I! — At last.
    VERONIKA.   Ah, me! How can I say :
Yet make them happier than they let
    you be?
    PIPER.   Woman, you could! — They
    know not how to be
Happy!   They turn to darkness and to
    grief
All that is made for joy.   They deal
    with men
As, far across the mountains, in the
    south,
Men trap a singing thrush, put out his
    eyes, —
And cage him up and bid him then to
    sing —
Sing before God that made him, — yes,
    to sing!

*   *   *   *   *

I *save* the children. — Yes, I save them,
    so,
Save them forever, who shall save the
    world! —
Yes, even Hamelin. —
            But for only *you*,
What do they know of Children? —
    Pfui, *their own !*
Who knows a treasure, when it is his
    own?
Do they not whine ; " *Five mouths around
    the table;*
*And a poor harvest. And now comes one
    more!*
God chastens us !" — Pfui ! —
    VERONIKA [*apart, dully*]. . . . But
    I must be patient.
    PIPER.   You know, you know, that
    not one dared, save you, —
Dared all alone, to search this devil's
    haunt.
    VERONIKA.   They would have died —
    PIPER.   But never risked their *souls !*
That knew I also.
    VERONIKA.   Ah !
    PIPER.   "Young faces", sooth,
The old ones prate of ! — Bah, what is't
    they want?
"Some one to work for me, when I am
    old ;
Some one to follow me unto my grave;
Some one — for me!" Yes, yes.   There
    is not one
Old huddler-by-the-fire would shift his
    seat
To a cold corner, if it might bring
    back
All of the Children in one shower of
    light !

    VERONIKA.   The old, ah, yes!   Bu
    not —
    PIPER.   The younger men?
Aha!   Their pride to keep the nam
    alive ;
The name, the name, the little Hameli
    name,
Tied to the trade ; — carved plain upo
    his gravestone !
Wonderful !   If your name must chai
    you, live,
To your gaol of a house, your trade yo
    hate — why then,
Best go without a name, like me ! —
    How now?
Woman, — you suffer?
    VERONIKA.   Ah, yet could I laugh
Piper, yet could I laugh, for one tru
    word, —
But not of all men.
    PIPER.   Then of whom?
    VERONIKA.   Of Kurt
    PIPER.   Bah, Kurt the Councillor
    a man to curse.
    VERONIKA.   He is my husband.
    PIPER [*shortly*].   Thine? I knew it not
Thine?   But it cannot be.   He coul
    not father
That little Jan, — that little ship
    wrecked Star.
    VERONIKA.   Oh, then you love him
    You will give him back?
    PIPER.   The son of Kurt?
    VERONIKA.   No, not *his* son ! No, no
He is all mine, all mine.   Kurt's son
    are straight,
And ruddy, like Kurt's wife of Hameli
    there,
Who died before.
    PIPER.   And you were wed . .
    VERONIKA.   So young
It is all like some dream before the sun
    rise,
That left me but that little shipwrecke
    Star.
    PIPER.   Why did you marry Kurt th
    Councillor?
    VERONIKA [*humbly*].   He wanted me
    Once I was beautiful.
    PIPER [*wonderingly*].   What, mor
    than now?
    VERONIKA.   Mock if you will.
    PIPER.   I mock you
O Woman, . . . you are very beautiful
    VERONIKA.   I meant, with my poo
    self, to buy him house
And warmth, and softness for his littl
    feet.
Oh, then I knew not, — when we sel
    our hearts,
We buy us nothing.

PIPER. Now you know.
VERONIKA. I know.
His dearest home it was, to keep my heart
Alone and beautiful, and clear and still;
And to keep all the gladness in my heart,
That bubbled from nowhere! — for him to drink; —
And to be houseless of all other things,
Even as the Lonely Man.
[*The* PIPER *starts*]
Where is the child?
PIPER. No; that I will not tell. Only thus much :
I love thy child. Trust me, — I love them, all.
They are the brightest miracle I know.
Wherever I go, I search the eyes of men
To find such clearness; — and it is not there.
Lies, greed and cruelty, and dreadful dark!
And all that makes Him sad these thousand years,
And keeps His forehead bleeding. — Ah, you know!
VERONIKA. Whom do you think on?
PIPER. Why, the Lonely Man. —
But now I have the children safe with me;
And men shall never teach them what men know ; —
Those radiant things that have no wish at all
Save for what is all-beautiful! — the Rainbow,
The Running Water, and the Moon, the Moon!
The only things worth having!
VERONIKA. — Oh, you will not
Give him to me?
PIPER. How give you yours again,
And not the others? What a life for him! [*She hides her face*]
And Kurt the Syndic, left without his sons?
Bah, do not dream of it! What would Kurt do? —
And hearken here! Should any hunt me down,
Take care. Who then could bring the children back?
VERONIKA. Jan! Jan!
PIPER. He loves me. He is happy.
VERONIKA [*passionately*]. No!
Without me? — No.
PIPER. He has not even once
Called you.
VERONIKA [*staggering*]. Ah, ah! . . .
The spell. —

PIPER [*startled*]. Nay, now; — rise up now, foreign woman.
Would you not have him cheered?
VERONIKA. — O far-off God!
PIPER [*offering her water*]. Drink here. Take heart. O Woman, they must stay!
'Tis better so. No, no, I mock thee not.
Thou foldest all about me like the Dark
That holds the stars. I would I were thy child.
VERONIKA. But I will find him. I will find him —
PIPER. No,
It must not be! Their life is bound with mine.
If I be harmed, they perish. Keep that word.
Go, go!
VERONIKA [*passionately*]. My longing will bring back my Own.
PIPER. Ah, long not so.
VERONIKA. Yes, it will bring him back!
He breathes. And I will wish him home to me,
Till my heart break!
PIPER. Hearts never break in Hamelin.
Go, then; and teach those other ones to long;
Wake up those dead!
VERONIKA. Peace. I shall draw him home.
PIPER. Not till he cries for thee.
VERONIKA. Oh, that will be
Soon, — soon.
PIPER [*gently*]. Remember, — if one word of thine
Set on the hounds to track me down and slay me,
They would be lost forever; they would die, —
They, who are in my keeping.
VERONIKA. Yea, I hear.
But he will come . . . oh, he will come to me,
Soon, — soon.

[*She goes, haltingly, and disappears along the road to Hamelin. — The* PIPER, *alone, stands spell-bound, breathing hard, and looking after her. Then he turns his head and comes down, doggedly. Again he pauses. With a sudden sharp effort he turns, and crosses with passionate appeal to the shrine, his arm uplifted towards the carven Christ as if he warded off some accusation. His speech comes in a torrent*]

PIPER.   I will not, no, I will not,
    Lonely Man !
I have them in my hand.   I have them
    all —
All — all !   And I have lived unto this day.
You understand . . .
    [*He waits as if for some reply*]
            You know what men they are
And what have they to do with such as
    these ?
Think of those old as death, in body and
    heart,
Hugging their wretched hoardings, in
    cold fear
Of moth and rust ! — While these mi-
    raculous ones,
Like golden creatures made of sunset-
    cloud,
Go out forever, — every day, fade by
With music and wild stars ! — Ah, but
    You know.
The hermit told me once, You loved
    them, too.
But I know more than he, how You must
    love them :
Their laughter, and their bubbling, sky-
    lark words
To cool Your heart.   Oh, listen, Lonely
    Man ! —

*   *   *   *   *

Oh, let me keep them !   I will bring
    them to You,
Still nights, and breathless mornings ;
    they shall touch
Your hands and feet with all their
    swarming hands,
Like showering petals warm on furrowed
    ground, —
All sweetness !   They will make Thee
    whole again,
With love.   Thou wilt look up and smile
    on us !

*   *   *   *   *

Why not ?   I know — the half — You
    will be saying.
You will be thinking of Your Mother.
    — Ah,
But she was different.   She was not as
    they.
She was more like . . . this one, the
    wife of Kurt !
Of Kurt !   No, no ; ask me not this, not
    this !
Here is some dawn of day for Hamelin,
    — now !
'Tis hearts of men You want. —
Not greed and carven tombs, not misers'
    candles ;
No offerings, more, from men that feed
    on men ;

Eternal psalms and endless cruelties ! . . .
Even from now, there may be hearts in
    Hamelin,
Once stabbed awake !
[*He pleads, defends, excuses passionately ;
    before his will gives way, as the arrow
    flies from the bow-string*]
            — *I will not give them back !*
And Jan, — for Jan, that little one, that
    dearest
To Thee and me, hark, — he is wonder-
    ful.
Ask it not of me.   Thou dost know I
    cannot !

*   *   *   *   *

Look, Lonely Man !   You shall have
    all of us
To wander the world over, where You
    stand
At all the crossways, and on lonely
    hills, —
Outside the churches, where the lost
    ones go ! —
And the wayfaring men, and thieves
    and wolves
And lonely creatures, and the ones that
    sing !
We will show all men what we hear and
    see ;
And we will make Thee lift Thy head,
    and smile.

*   *   *   *   *

No, no, I cannot give them all !   No,
    no. —
Why wilt Thou ask it ? — Let me keep
    but one.
No, no, I will not. . . . .
. . . .
. . . . . *Have Thy way. — I will !*

CURTAIN

ACT IV

SCENE. — *Hamelin market-place.*

*It is early morning ; so dark that only a
    bleak twilight glimmers in the square ;
    the little streets are dim.   Every-
    where gloom and stillness.   In the
    house of* KURT, *beside the Minster,
    there is one window-light behind a
    curtain in the second story.   At the
    casements, down right and left, sit*
    OLD CLAUS *and* OLD URSULA, *wan
    and motionless as the dead.*
*The church-bell, which likewise seems to
    have aged, croaks softly, twice.*
    PETER *the Sacristan stands by the
    bell-rope.*

OLD URSULA. No, no. They'll
never come. I told ye so.
They all are gone. There will be noth-
ing young
To follow us to the grave.
OLD CLAUS. No, no, — not one!

*The Minster-door opens, and out come
certain of the townsfolk from early
mass. They look unnaturally old
and colorless. Their steps lag drear-
ily. —* HANS *the Butcher and his
wife;* AXEL *the Smith with his wife,
and* PETER *the Cobbler, meet, on their
way to the little street, left, and greet
one another with painstaking, stricken
kindness. They speak in broken
voices]*

HANS. Well, well —
AXEL. God knows!

[The bell sounds]

HANS. Neighbor, how fare your
knees?

[AXEL *smooths his right leg and gives a
jerk of pain. They all move stiffly]*

AXEL. I'm a changed man.
HANS. Peter the Sacristan,
Give by the bell! It tolls like — Oh,
well, well!
AXEL. It does no good, it does no
good at all.
PETER. Rather, I do believe it made
the demons;
And I have given much thought —
AXEL. Over thy shoes!
PETER [*modestly*]. To demons.
AXEL'S WIFE. Let him chirp philos-
ophy!
He had no children.
PETER [*wagging his head solemnly*].
I'm an altered man.
Now were we not proceeding soberly,
Singing a godly hymn, and all in tune,
But yesterday, when we passed by —
HAN'S WIFE. Don't say it!
Don't name the curseful place.
HANS. — And my poor head,
It goes round yet; — around, around,
around,
As I were new ashore from the high seas;
Still dancing — dancing —
AXEL. Neighbor, say no more.
HANS. Even as ye heard, the farmer's
yokel found me
Clasping a tree, and praying to stand
still!
AXEL. Ay, ay, — but that is naught.
PETER. All naught beside.

HANS' WIFE. Better we had the rats
and mice again,
Though they did eat us homeless, — if
we might
All starve together! — Oh, my Hans,
my Hans!
PETER. Hope not, good souls. Rest
sure, they will not come.
AXEL'S WIFE. Who will say that?
PETER [*discreetly*]. Not I; but the
Inscription.

[He points to the Rathaus wall]

AXEL. Of our own making?
PETER. On the Rathaus wall!
At our own bidding it was made and
graved : —
How, — on that day and down this very
street,
He led them, — he, the Wonderfully-
clothed,
The Strange Man, with his piping;
[They cross themselves]
And they went, —
And never came again.
HANS' WIFE. But they may come!
PETER [*pityingly*]. Marble is final,
woman; — nay, poor soul!
When once a man be buried, and over
him
The stone doth say *Hic Jacet*, or Here
Lies,
When did that man get up? — There is
the stone.
They come no more, for piping or for
prayer;
Until the trump of the Lord Gabriel.
And if they came, 'tis not in Hamelin men
To alter any stone, so graven. — Marble
Is final. Marble has the last word,
ever. [*Groans from the burghers*]
HANS. O little Ilse! — Oh! and
Lump — poor Lump!
More than a dog could bear! — More
than a dog —
[*They all break down. The Shoemaker
consoles them*]
PETER. Bear up, sweet neighbors.
— We are all but dust.
No mice, no children. — Hem! And
now Jacobus, —
His child, not even safe with Holy
Church,
But lost and God knows where!
AXEL'S WIFE. Bewitched, — be-
witched!

[HANS *and his wife, arm in arm, turn left,
towards their house, peering ahead*]

HANS' WIFE. Kind saints! Me out
and gone to early mass,

And all this mortal church-time, there's
    a candle,
A candle burning in the casement
    there; —
Thou wasteful man!
    HANS [*huskily*]. Come, come! Do
    not be chiding.
Suppose they came and could not see
    their way.
Suppose — O wife! — I thought they'd
    love the light!
I thought —
    PETER. Ay, now! And there's
    another light
In Kurt the Syndic's house.

[*They turn and look up. Other burghers
    join the group. All walk lamely and
    look the picture of wretchedness*]

    AXEL'S WIFE. His wife, poor thing,
The priest is with her. Ay, for once,
    they say,
Kurt's bark is broken.
    OLD URSULA. There will be nothing
    young
To follow us to the grave.
    AXEL'S WIFE. They tell, she seems
Sore stricken since the day that she was
    lost,
Lost, searching on the mountain. Since
    that time,
She will be saying naught. She stares
    and smiles.
    HANS' WIFE. And reaches out her
    arms, — poor soul!
    ALL.   Poor soul!

[*Murmur in the distance. They do not
    heed it*]

    AXEL [*to the Butcher*]. That was no
    foolish thought of thine, yon candle.
I do remember now as I look back,
They always loved the lights. My
    Rudi there
Would aye be meddling with my tinder-
    box.
And once I — Oh! —   [*Choking*]
    AXEL'S WIFE [*soothingly*]. Now, now!
    thou didst not hurt him!
'Twas I! Oh, once — I shut him in
    the dark!
    AXEL. Come home . . . and light
    the candles.
    PETER.   In the day-time!
    AXEL'S WIFE. Oh, it is dark enough!
    AXEL.   Lord knows, who made
Both night and day, one of 'em needs to
    shine!
But nothing does! — Nothing is day-
    light now.

Come, wife, we'll light the candles.
            [*Exit with his wife*]
    PETER.   He's a changed man
    PETER *the Sacristan*. God help us
    what's to do?
[*Tumult approaching. Shouts o[f]
    "Jacobus" and "Barbara"*]
            Hark!
    HANS' WIFE.   Neighbors!
    HANS.   Hark! Hark

[*AXEL and his wife re-enter hastily; AXE[L]
    rushes toward the noise*]

    AXEL'S WIFE. Oh, I hear something
Can it be —
    PETER.   They're shouting.
    HANS. My lambs, — my lambs!

    [*AXEL re-enters, crestfallen*]

    AXEL. 'T is naught — but Barbara
His — his!

[*Shaking his fist at the house of JACOBUS[*]
    PETER [*calling*]. Jacobus!

[*The others are stricken with disap[-]
    pointment*]

    HANS.   Wife, — 'tis none of ours
    AXEL. Let him snore on! — Th[e]
    only man would rather
Sleep late than meet his only chil[d]
    again!
    PETER [*deprecatingly*]. No man ma[y]
    parley with the gifts of Fortune
[*Knocking on the door*] Jacobus!

[*Enter, at the rear, with a straggling crowd
    BARBARA and MICHAEL, both radi[-]
    ant and resolute. She wears the lon[g]
    green cloak over her bridal array.
    JACOBUS appears in his doorway, night[-]
    capped and fur-gowned, shrinkin[g]
    from the hostile crowd. The peopl[e]
    murmur*]

    CROWD.
⎰ Barbara! — She that was bewitched
⎱ And who's the man? Is it the Piper [?]
    No!
  No, no — some stranger. Barbara
    Barbara's home; —
  He never gave her up! — Who is th[e]
    man?
    JACOBUS. My daughter! 'Tis m[y]
    daughter, — found — restored!
Oh, heaven is with us!
    ALL [*sullenly*].   Ah!
    JACOBUS.   Child, where have yo[u]
    been?
    ALL. Ay, where, Jacobus?

            [*He is dismayed*]

JACOBUS. Who is this man? — Come hither.

BARBARA [*without approaching him, lifting her face clearly*]. Good-morning to you, father! We are wed. Michael, — shall I go hither?

[*The townsfolk are amazed*]

JACOBUS.   She is mad!
She is quite mad, — my treasure.

PETER.   Let her speak.
Maids sometimes marry, even in Hamelin.

ALL.
{ Ay, tell us!
{ Who is he? Barbara?
{ Art thou mad? — How came ye hither?

JACOBUS. Who is he?

BARBARA.   Michael.

PETER.   'Tis the Sword-Eater!
A friend o' the Piper's! — Hearken —

ALL.   She's bewitched!

HANS' WIFE. This is the girl was vowed to Holy Church,
For us and for our children that are lost!

BARBARA. Ay, and did any have a mind to me,
When I was lost? Left dancing, and distraught?

ALL. We could not. We were spell-bound. Nay, we could not.

JACOBUS [*sagely, after the others*]. We could not.

BARBARA. So! — But there was one who could.
There was one man. And this is he.
[*Turning to* MICHAEL]
                                And I,
I am no more your Barbara, — I am his.
And I will go with him, over the world.
I come to say farewell.

JACOBUS.   He hath bewitched her!

MICHAEL. Why did we ever come?
Poor darling one,
Thy too-much duty hath us in a trap!

AXEL. No, no! — Fair play!

OTHERS. Don't let them go! We have them.

PETER. Hold what ye have. Be't children, rats or mice!

[*Hubbub without, and shouts. Some of the burghers hasten out after this fresh excitement.* JACOBUS *is cowed.* BARBARA *and* MICHAEL *are startled. The shouts turn savage. The uproar grows. Shouts of* "Ay, there he is! We have him! We have him! Help — help! Hold fast! Ah! Piper! Piper! Piper!"]

How now? What all! —

[*The crowd parts to admit the* PIPER, *haled hither with shouts and pelling, by* MARTIN *the Watch and other men, all breathless. His eyes burn*]

MICHAEL [*apart*]. Save us! — They have him.

MARTIN [*gaspingly*].   Help!
Mark ye — I caught him! — Help, — and hold him fast!

PIPER. I came here, — frog!

MARTIN. Ay, he were coming on;
And after him a squirrel, hopping close!

SECOND MAN. As no man ever saw a squirrel hop —
Near any man from Hamelin! And I looked —

MARTIN. And it was he; and all we rush upon him —
And take him!

PIPER.   Loose thy claws, I tell thee! —

ALL.
{ 'Ware!
{ Mercy!
{ Let him go!

[*Their cries turn into an uproar of rage and desperation. They surge and fall back between fury and fear.* HANS *the Butcher, broken with hope, cries,* "Loose him! Let him speak!" *— The* PIPER *shakes himself free. — He sees* BARBARA *and* MICHAEL *for the first time and recoils with amazement.* BARBARA *steps towards him. — It is to be understood in the following pages, where the crowd speaks, that only a general consensus of meaning comes out of the uproar*]

BARBARA. Oh, let him go, — let be. His heart is clear,
As water from the well!

[*The* PIPER *gazes at her, open-mouthed*]

ALL.
{ She talks in her sleep!
{ The maid's bewitched!
{ Now, will ye hear?

AXEL'S WIFE. He piped and made thee dance!

PETER.   'Twas he bewitched us!

AXEL. He piped away our children and our lives!

OLD URSULA. I told ye so! — ay, ay!

OLD CLAUS. I told ye so!

BARBARA. He piped; — and all ye danced and fled away!
He piped; — and brought me back my wandering wits,

And gave me safe unto my Love again,
My Love I had forgotten. . . .
PIPER.   So!
MICHAEL [*with conviction*]. Truly said.
BARBARA [*proudly*].   Michael.
JACOBUS.   Who is he, pray?
BARBARA.   My own true love.
PETER.   Now, is that all his name!
BARBARA.   It is enough.
JACOBUS.   — She's mad.   Shall these
things be?
ALL.   { *The Children! The Children!*
{ *Where are the Children?*
{ *Piper! Piper! Piper!*
PIPER   [*sternly*].   Quiet   you.   And
hear me.
I came to bring good tidings.   In good
faith,
Of mine own will, I came. — And like a
thief
You haled me hither. —
       [*They hang upon his words*]
       . . . Your children — live.
ALL.
{ Thank God!   I knew, I knew!
{ We could not think them lost.
{ Bewitched!   Oh, but they live! —
{ Piper! — O Piper!
PETER.   They're spell-bound, — mark
me!
PIPER.   Ay, they are, — spell-bound:
Fast bound by all the hardness of your
hearts;
Caged, — *in the iron of your money-lust* —
ALL.
{ No, no, not all!   Not I!   Not mine,
not mine!
{ No, no, — it is not true.
PIPER.   Your   blasphemies, — your
cunning and your fear.
ALL.   { No, no! — What can we do?
{ News, Piper, news!
{ — The Children!
PIPER.   Now   hear   me.   You   did
make Jacobus swear
To give his child. — What recks it, how
he lose her? —
Either to Holy Church — *against her
will!* —
Or to this man, — so that he give her
up!
He swore to you.   And she hath pledged
her faith.
She is fast wed. — Jacobus shall not
have her.
He breaks all bargains; and for such
as he,
You suffer. — Will you bear it?
ALL.   No, no, no!
PIPER.   Then she who was "Proud
Barbara" doth wed

Michael-the-Sword-Eater. — The pledge
shall stand.
Shall it?
ALL.   { It stands.
{ Ay, ay!
PIPER.   Your word!
ALL.
{ We swear.   We answer for him.
{ So much for Jacobus!
AXEL.   An' if yon fellow like an
honest trade,
I'll take him! — I'll make swords!

[*Cheers.*   MICHAEL *is happy*]

ALL.   Quick, quick! — Our children.
— Piper! — Tell us all!
PIPER.   'Tis well begun. — Now have I
come to say:
There is one child I may bring back to
you, —
The first.
ALL [*in an uproar*].
{ Mine — mine!   Let it be mine!
{ Ours! — All of them!   Now!
{ *Mine — mine — mine! — mine!*
PIPER [*unmoved*].   — Oh, Hamelin to
the end!
Which of you longed the most, and dared
the most?
Which of you —

[*He searches the crowd anxiously with his
eyes*]

ALL.
{ I!   I!   I!
{ We searched the hills!
{ We prayed four days!
{ We fasted twenty hours —
{ Mine!   Mine!
{ Mine — mine — mine — mine!

PIPER.   Not yet. — They all do live
Under a spell, — deep in a hollow hill.
They sleep, and wake; and lead a
charmèd life.
But first of all, — one child shall come
again.
       [*He scans the crowd still*]
Where   is   the   wife — of   Kurt,   the
Councillor?
ALL [*savagely*].   No, mine, mine, mine!
MARTIN'S WIFE.   What, that lame
boy of hers?
PIPER.   Where is the wife of Kurt?
PETER *and* OTHERS.   — Veronika?
The foreign woman?   She is lying ill:
Sore-stricken yonder — [*Pointing to the
house*]
PIPER [*gladly*].   Bid her come, look
out!

[*The crowd moves confusedly towards* KURT'S *house. The* PIPER *too approaches, calling*]

Ho, — ho, within there!

[ANSELM, *the priest, appears in the doorway with uplifted hand, commanding silence. He is pale and stern. At sight of his face the* PIPER *falters*]

ANSELM. Silence here! — Good people,
What means this?

PIPER. I have tidings for — the wife
Of Kurt — the Councillor.

ANSELM. You are too late.

PIPER. Bid her — look out!

ANSELM [*solemnly*]. Her soul is passing, now.

[*The* PIPER *falls back stricken and speechless. — The crowd, seeing him humanly overwhelmed, grows brave*]

MARTIN'S WIFE. 'Tis he has done it!

HANS. — Nay, it is God's will.
Poor soul!

PETER [*fearfully*]. Don't anger him!
'Twas Kurt the Syndic
With his bad bargain.

AXEL. Do not cross the Piper!

MARTIN. Nay, but he's spent. He's nought to fear. — Look there.
Mark how he breathes! Upon him!
Help, help, ho! —
Thou piping knave!

OTHERS. Tie — chain him! — Kill him! — Kill him!

[*They surround him. He thrusts them off*]

PETER AND OTHERS.
{ Bind him, but do not kill him! —
{ Oh, beware!
{ What is he saying? — Peace.

PIPER [*brokenly*]. The wife of Kurt!
Off! what can you do? — Oh! I came,
I came
Here, full of peace, and with a heart of
love; —
To give — but now that one live Soul
of all
Is gone! — No, no!
— *I say she shall not die!*
She shall not!

ANSELM. Hush! — She is in the
hands of God.
She is at peace.

PIPER. No, never! Let me by!

[ANSELM *bars the threshold and steps out*]

ANSELM. Thou froward fool! —
Wouldst rend with tears again

That shriven breath? And drag her
back to sorrow?
It is the will of God.

PIPER. — And I say No!

ANSELM. Who dare dispute —

PIPER. I dare!

ANSELM. With death? — With God?

PIPER. I know His will, for once!
She shall not die.
She must come back, and live! —
Veronika!

[*He calls up to the lighted window. The people stand aghast:* ANSELM *bars the threshold*]

I come, I come! I bring your Own to
you!
Listen Veronika!

[*He feels for his pipe. It is gone. — His face shows dismay, for a moment*]
Where? — Where?

PEOPLE.
{ He's lost the pipe. — He's hiding it! —
{ He cannot pipe them back! 'tis gone
{ — 'tis gone. —
{ No, 'tis to save his life. It is for time.

PIPER [*to himself*]. — 'Tis but a
voice. What matter? —

CROWD. { Seize him —
{ Bind him!

PIPER [*to them*]. Hush!

[*Passionately he stretches his arms towards the window*]

ANSELM. Peace, for this parting
Soul!

PIPER [*with fixed eyes*]. It shall not go.
[*To the Window*]

Veronika! — Ah, listen! — wife of Kurt.
*He comes . . . he comes! Open thine
eyes a moment!*
*Blow the faint fire within thy heart. He
comes!*
Thy longing brings him; — ay, *and
mine, — and mine!*
Heed not these grave-makers, Veronika.
Live, live, and laugh once more! — *Oh!
do you hear?*
Look, how you have to waken all these
dead,
That walk about you! — Open their
dim eyes;
Sing to them with your heart, Veronika,
As I am piping, far away, outside!
Waken them, — change them! Show
them how to long,
To reach their arms as you do, for the
stars,
And fold them in. Stay but one moment, — stay,
And thine own Child shall draw thee
back again

Down here, to mother him, — mother
us all !
*Oh, do you listen? — Do not try to
answer. —*
I hear ! — I hear. . . .

[*A faint sound of piping comes from the
distance. — The* PIPER *is first watchful, then radiant. — The burghers are
awe-struck, as it sounds nearer*]

BARBARA.   Listen ! —
MICHAEL.   His very tune.

[*The* PIPER *faces front with fixed, triumphant eyes above the crowd*]

MARTIN'S WIFE. O Lord, have
mercy ! —
The Pipe is coming to him, through the
air !
ALL.   'Tis coming to the Piper ; —
we are lost. —
The Pipe is coming, coming through the
air !

[*The* PIPER, *with a sudden gesture, commands silence. He bounds away
(centre), and disappears. The people, spell-bound with terror, murmur
and pray*]

ANSELM.   *Retro me, Sathanas !*

[KURT *the Syndic appears on the threshold behind* ANSELM, *whose arm he
touches, whispering. — Their faces
are wonderstruck with hope and awe*]

HANS [*to the others, pointing*]. 'Tis
Kurt the Syndic.
AXEL.   Then she lives ! —
HANS' WIFE.   Look there !
OTHERS.   *Look, look ! The casement !*
. . .

[*The casement of the lighted window opens
wide and slowly. — Re-enter the*
PIPER *with* JAN *in his arms. The
little boy holds the Pipe, and smiles
about with tranquil happiness. The*
PIPER, *radiant with joy, lifts him
high, looking toward* VERONIKA'S
*window. — The awe-struck people
point to the open casement.*

VERONIKA'S *two white hands reach out;
then she herself appears, pale, shining
with ecstasy*]

JAN.   *'Tis Mother !*

[*The* PIPER *lifts him still before the window, gazing up. Then he springs
upon the bench (outside the lower
window) and gives* JAN *into the*

arms of VERONIKA. — KURT *and*
ANSELM *bow their heads. A hush.
— Then* JAN *looks down from the
window-seat*]

PIPER [*to him, smiling wisely*]. And
all the others?
JAN.   They were all asleep.
PIPER.   I'll waken them !

[*He takes his pipe. — An uproar of joy
among the burghers*]

AXEL, HANS, ALL.
{ Bring lights, — bring lights !
{ Oh, Piper — Oh, my lambs !
{ The children ! — The children !

[*Some rush out madly; others go into their
houses for lights; some are left on
their knees, weeping for joy.*

The PIPER *sounds a few notes; then lifts
his hand and listens, smiling. —
Uproar in the distance. — A great
barking of dogs; — shouts and
cheers; then the high, sweet voices of
the* CHILDREN.

*The piping is drowned in cries of joy.
The sun comes out, still rosy, in a
flood of light. The crowd rushes in.
Fat burghers hug each other, and
laugh and cry. They are all younger.
Their faces bloom, as by a miracle.*

The CHILDREN *pour in. Some are carried,
some run hand-in-hand. Everywhere
women embrace their own. —* KURT
has his sons. — CHEAT-THE-DEVIL
*comes, with a daisy-chain around
his neck, all smiles.*

An uproar of light and faces]

HANS.   The treasure for the Piper !
ALL.   Ay, ay, Piper !
HANS.   The thousand guilders !
PIPER.   Give them Michael there,
For all us three. I hate to carry
things ; —
Saving out one !
[*He waves his hand to* JAN *in the window.
—* VERONIKA *appears behind him,
shining with new life.* JAN *leans
out and points to the ground*]
                    Héjà ! What now? —

[*Picking up one of* JAN'S *winged shoes*]

HANS' WIFE.   Look ! Look ! —
And wings upon it ! Mercy, what a
shoe. —
Don't give it back. — The child will fly
away !
PIPER.   No, no !

[*Looking up at the window soothingly*]
      He only wanted one to show —
Jan.   To Mother! — See.

[*Showing her his other foot, joyously*]

Piper [*to him*].   And this, — wilt leave it here?
Here — with —
Jan.   The Lonely Man! Oh, make Him smile!

[*The* Piper *crosses to the Shrine, with the little shoe, and hangs it up there; then he turns towards the window, waving his hand*]

Children.   Where are you going?

    [*They run and cling*]

Piper.   Ah, the high-road now!
Children.   Oh! why?

Piper.   I have to find somebody there.
Yes, now and every day, and every-where
The wide world over. — So : good-night, good-morning,
Good-by! There's so much piping left to do, —
I must be off, and pipe.
    Children.   Oh! why?
    Piper.   I promised,
Look you! . . .
    Children.   Who is it?
    Piper.   Why, — the Lonely Man.

[*He waves them farewell, and goes. The* Children *dance and laugh and spar-kle. Through the hundred sounds of joy, there comes a far-off piping*]

THE END

MRS. BUMPSTEAD–LEIGH

(1911)

By Harry James Smith

HARRY JAMES SMITH

THE short career of Harry James Smith in the theatre has left behind the memory of a very rare spirit, even if his plays in themselves are not of the highest order. He interpreted the theatre as a merry place, one in which to be entertained by humor, to be untrammelled by problems — a sort of cardboard plaything, to be used for the passing of a few hours. His is an excellent instance of that complete separation of drama from the serious concerns of life. He wrote plays as a sort of game, perturbed only in a desire to make them popular and write them well. He evidently from the beginning had a knack for dialogue, due to a talent for fiction which he exercised before he began to write for the stage. He learned the practical technique as he ran, so to speak, willing, anxious and expectant that such managers as the Fiskes and George M. Cohan should use their deft experience to set him straight. He wrote his plays as a sort of passing mood, and, as the time went by, he was surprised if they wore well. He wrote for the acting possibility, to judge by "Mrs. Bumpstead-Leigh" and "The Tailor-Made Man", and he was grateful for the creative part the actors brought to his pieces, slight in themselves, but yet actable.

This judgment of Harry James Smith is made from the delightful sheaf of letters published soon after his death — a ruthless death, caught in an automobile accident by a passing train just at the time he was performing useful service for the Government at the outset of our entrance into the World War. Unfortunate that the plays do not measure up to the delightful personality of the man himself — a man of culture, of sensitive approach to life, of gentle humor. His was the accustomed attitude of the literary worker who so often regards the theatre as a sort of puzzle house where a one, two, three cleverness — a knack at structure, and a passably amusing plot — slim enough to be a short story, yet slimmer still when stretched over a number of acts — is sufficient. And oftentimes it is sufficient to make for the writer of such pieces a comfortable fortune, to catch hold of a public that does not care to think too deeply, likes to smile pleasantly, likes homely virtues gently lauded, and eccentric character pleasantly cartooned.

In November, 1903, we find Mr. Smith saying (he is writing from Cambridge) :

As regards the drama, I am becoming exceedingly enthusiastic. The instructor is not only a student, but also a practical actor, thoroughly acquainted with stage technique, and with all the tricks of dramatic presentation ; he *makes* you enthusiastic ; you feel as if you should like to devote your life to so noble an art, to face the obliquy and persecution of the proper world and to see what you could do in the development of a worthy national drama. Don't you think that is my mission? I am going to all the good plays I can afford (" Rush seats" do for me) and am observing the field intently. I am anxious to see considerable *melodrama*, for I believe that that is to be the source of any dramatic renaissance that may come : but as I can get no one to go with me I have as yet confined my study in that direction to " Sky Farm" and " Old Kentucky."

This was during the days he was studying for his Master's degree at Harvard, and the next year he was teaching in the English Department of Oberlin.

The creative urge in Smith made him, in 1905, desert teaching, and, except for a year with the *Atlantic Monthly*, he devoted his entire time to writing. Yet it was to his first interest — the scientific interest — that he turned when the war began, and he was engaged in work on sphagnum moss as surgical dressing, when he was killed. In the interim between 1908 and his death he wrote a novel, "Amédée's Son" (1908), another novel, "Enchanted Ground" (1910), and his plays, "Mrs. Bumpstead-Leigh" (1911), "Blackbirds" (1913), "A Tailor-Made Man" (1918) and "The Little Teacher" (1918). There were many other plays written during this time, but none of them held, though several were tried out: "Suki" and "Oh, Imogen"; and such pieces as "The Countess and Patrick", "Matilda Comes Back", "Big Jerry", "Game", "Lady Bird", and "Northward Ho."

He was a tenderfoot in the theatre, and marvelled at the make-believe of it all. Through Mr. Dean, Belasco's stage director, he went behind scenes to watch a performance. No child could have delighted more in the make-believe. It was a sport to him. His letters are full of the ambition of one anxious to do good work; his self-analysis is refreshing to read. His observation as he went about in the winter time and in the summer — he was a man of the open as well as a student by the fireside — was acute. Here, then, was a recruit who, if he had been put on the proper road in the drama field, possessed a background, an insight, a literary quality which would have gone far in the theatre. As it is, he was mowed down too young to prophesy how far he might have gone.

But it seems, from his letters, that he was caught in the conventional throes of the theatre — that he was claimed by the conservatives who measured drama by way of the box-office, and that he played the game for what it was worth — still naïvely marvelling that a thing put upon paper should be made to work so nearly like life — outward life — at all. His theatre tastes, in 1910, were peculiarly conflicting, — bored by Barrie's "What Every Woman Knows", delighted with a travelling company playing James A. Herne's "Shore Acres", thinking Fitch's "The City" hideous, intellectually intoxicated by Rostand's "Chantecler." Then, in September, 1910, thick in rehearsals of "Mrs. Bumpstead-Leigh" and marvelling at the vivacious inventiveness of Mrs. Fiske. In October, 1910, he writes: "The improvement in rehearsals during this past week almost amazes me. Everybody is working like a dray-horse to do his best. And the situations and lines still remain so amusing to us, despite our deep-furrowed familiarity with them, that over and over again the rehearsal is held up while we all shake with mirth. Mrs. Fiske's sense of humor is delicious. She is a taskmistress if there ever was one; but even when most exacting, you are only too glad to serve her." He acknowledges, in a later communication, that work of this character is an excellent schooling for him in the playmaker's craft.

These letters, which show the charm of personality in Smith, trace the evolution of all his plays, picture him eagerly on the side of light entertainment, yet in his soul always yearning for big work. I emphasize the wide mark between this desire of his and his approach of the stage. ,He is forever, in these letters, communing with something bigger than the theatre he conceives. The limitation of " Mrs. Bumpstead-Leigh" is his limited interpretation of what the theatre's purpose is. I refer to these letters, because they are so full of the man himself. Now and again, we are given those glimpses of volatile spirit that come out in the plays.

But, while the letters offer one much to think about in relation to the playwright and his relation to life, his plays appear to be a game with him, not deeply felt, not too clearly seen, too much the material for stage management, too dependent on playing to fill out the half-blown humor. There is nothing husky about "The Little Teacher", though there are husky moments suggested; there is nothing of the typical American comedy about "A Tailor-Made Man": the humor in it is probably just the little wistful humor one expects Smith to have had personally. One wishes that it could have bitten deeper into irony. "Mrs. Bumpstead-Leigh" is Mrs. Fiske, to which might be added a memory of English drama of the post-Robertson period.

I have included "Mrs. Bumpstead-Leigh" in this collection because it happens to be one of the few dramas of artificial High Comedy that I have at my disposal. It is significant that High Comedy is best suited to Mrs. Fiske's talents: the dry comedy of irony and manners no better brought out than in Langdon Mitchell's "The New York Idea." This play I have already published in the third volume of my "Representative Plays by American Dramatists" (Dutton). There is something typically American about the situation in "Mrs. Bumpstead-Leigh." No one is better suited to convey across the footlights a brittle sense of fun than Mrs. Fiske, and her artistic taste has done much to heighten plays which have been entrusted to her by young dramatists. There is no telling what would have been the fate of Edward Sheldon's "Salvation Nell", had it not been that Mrs. Fiske produced it. The same might well be said for the fate of Harry James Smith's "Mrs. Bumpstead-Leigh."

It would take only a little over-accentuation to make of this comedy a very boisterous and ridiculous farce. As I recall it rightly, Mrs. Fiske gave a reticent handling, a serious touch to the artifice of the situation underlying "Mrs. Bumpstead-Leigh." I believe that this comedy was a triumph for Mrs. Fiske in the art of frolic. And I believe such was the consummation of the dramatist's idea. There is something metallic in the personality of Mrs. Fiske. There is something metallic in the rôle of *Mrs. Bumpstead-Leigh.* There is mind quality to her acting, there is no heart quality to it. And there is a hard metallic precision to the plot of "Mrs. Bumpstead-Leigh" which suited her admirably. She is the Alexander Pope of acting, and the comedy of "Mrs. Bumpstead-Leigh" is as hard as that. Smith's play is related to "Becky Sharp", and is a cross between the acerbity of *Lady Sneerwell* and the colloquialism of "The Chorus Lady."

Smith was an introspective artist. He was only thirty-eight when he died. He was working out for himself all things pertaining to the fundamentals of art and life. He had a long road to travel because he was in that part of the theatre that cared little, in 1912, for fundamentals, and a great deal for skimming the surface. To a friend he wrote, regarding the humor in "Mrs. Bumpstead-Leigh":

By the way, I draw a distinction — do you? — between *farce* and *low comedy.* *Ma* and *Swallow* belong, if I am right, to the second. Query: are the yokels in "Midsummer Night's Dream" or in a Hardy novel *farce?* My answer is *no,* because they are thoroughly true to character, a logical type, each. Farce exists for situation, ludicrous incident. True comedy is preoccupied with the crossplays of character. *Ma* is farce when the player is encouraged to throw type-truth to the winds and (in a crisis) to let her skirts creep ridiculously up to her knees. *Swallow* is farce when his familiar, hail-fellow manner becomes slap-stick buffoonery; everything that I value in the part is then lost. Do you see that I have the idea, though I haven't thought it out adequately?

In all of his plays, therefore, it strikes me that Smith was learning his job. And two no better teachers could he have had than Mrs. Fiske and George M. Cohan's office. His plays are naïvely pleasurable conceits. But his letters convince me that once he had mastered the stage technique, Smith would have given to the theatre something more deeply seen. Mrs. Fiske once wrote him that he was one of America's greatest comedians. By that I believe she meant that his humor was carefree and unsophisticated, rather purposeless in intent, and for that reason strikingly human. Even in the reading one can detect the evanescent character of his plays. Their plots are slight; their characters mere sketches that have their existence only while playing. But reading them one can get their drama value, even though that value is not abiding from a literary point of view.

MRS. BUMPSTEAD-LEIGH

A COMEDY IN THREE ACTS

By HARRY JAMES SMITH

CAST OF CHARACTERS

Justin Rawson
Miss Rawson, *his sister*
Geoffrey Rawson, *his younger son*
Anthony Rawson, *his elder son*
Leavitt
Mrs. Leavitt
Peter Swallow
Kitson
Mrs. de Salle
Mrs. Bumpstead-Leigh (Adelaide), *her elder daughter*
Violet de Salle, Adelaide's *younger sister*
Nina

The following is a copy of the playbill of the first performance of "Mrs. Bumpstead-Leigh", at the Lyceum Theatre, New York.

Week beginning Monday Evening, April 3, 1911

HARRISON GREY FISKE

PRESENTS

MRS. FISKE

And the Manhattan Company

IN

MRS. BUMPSTEAD-LEIGH

A COMEDY IN THREE ACTS

BY

HARRY JAMES SMITH

CAST OF CHARACTERS

Justin Rawson	Charles Harbury
Miss Rawson, *his sister*	Kate Lester
Geoffrey Rawson, *his younger son*	Malcolm Duncan
Anthony Rawson, *his elder son*	Douglas J. Wood
Stephen Leavitt	Paul Scardon
Mrs. Stephen Leavitt	Veda McEvers
Peter Swallow	Henry Dixey
Kitson	Cyril Young
Mrs. de Salle	Florine Arnold
Mrs. Bumpstead-Leigh	Mrs. Fiske
Violet de Salle	Kathlene MacDonell
Nina	Helena Van Brugh

Scene: *Living room in* Rawson's *Long Island Country House*

Between Acts I and II, one hour is supposed to elapse; between Acts II and III, ten minutes.

MRS. BUMPSTEAD-LEIGH

ACT I

SCENE. — *Living room in* JUSTIN RAW-
SON'S *Long Island Country house.
Late summer after breakfast of a
sunny day. The apartment is handsomely and choicely furnished, with
a suggestion in everything of dignity
and family pride. A very wide porch
door opens upon a broad veranda,
center, and beyond the veranda is seen
an Italian garden and a glimpse of
sand dunes and ocean. Hollyhocks
look in at the low window, wide open,
Left. Between the window and the
porch door is a staircase, and close to
the staircase a door admitting to
domestic offices. Right, another door
connecting with the library; a private
telephone on the wall near this door.*

When the curtain rises ANTHONY *and*
NINA *are having an intimate little
chat,* ANTHONY *half sitting on the
edge of the table Right, and* NINA
*leaning as enticingly as she knows
how on the handle of a carpet-sweeper.*

[ANTHONY *is a good-looking, polished
fellow of twenty-seven, but perhaps
you would not trust him. Just now
he is whispering something wheedling
and pleasant in the girl's ear. She
listens with sparkling eyes, roguishly*]

NINA [*standing away with a shriek of
laughter*]. Oh, Mr. Anthony! Aren't
you an article!
ANTHONY [*demurely*]. Why, what
have I said now?
NINA [*with giggles*]. Oh, you imp!
[*Feigns to slap him*] I never knew the
beat of you for reeling off nonsense.
ANTHONY. You know very well
every word I've said is solemn truth!
[*Stepping towards her*]
NINA [*gaily*]. You expect me to be-
lieve that? —
ANTHONY [*feigning jealousy*]. Oh,
you'd believe it quick enough if Mr.
Geoffrey said it.

NINA [*archly*]. He ain't that kind.
Mr. Geoffrey's rather slow about some
things. Very different from you.
ANTHONY [*aware of his own charms*].
Now! Now!
NINA. Well, it may be a break for
me to say so, seein' as he's your own
brother, Mr. Anthony; but I never
could stomach what you might call the
farmer type! Even when they're
dressed up, seems like you can always
smell the barn on them. [KITSON *has
entered Left and after a disapproving look
at the two, begins a minute inspection
of the corners of the apartment.* NINA
resumes a pretense of work but continues]
Give me cowboys on the stage; but
don't let 'em get too close to me in real
life!
ANTHONY [*patronizingly*]. Lost something, Kitson?
KITSON [*who is a highly self-respecting
family retainer, with a mournful manner*].
No, sir. [*Resumes inspection*]
ANTHONY. You seem very busy.
Might I inquire what you're doing?
KITSON [*sadly*]. My duty, sir.
NINA [*pertly*]. Mr. Kitson always
goes the rounds like that every morning,
to see I don't leave out anything.
KITSON [*bristling*]. And good enough
reason for it, I may say!
NINA. Yes, indeed! Don't know
how you'd earn your wages if it wasn't
for that. [*Puts carpet-sweeper off Right*]

[KITSON *draws himself up for a tremendous rejoinder, but recollects himself
in the presence of* ANTHONY, *saying
only in a sad voice*]

KITSON. There *was* a time when
housemaids was taught to know their
place.
ANTHONY [*laughing*]. There was a
time, Kitson — at least I'd like to think
so — when you were rather less of a
meddlesome old nuisance than you are
now.

KITSON. You would not speak so to me, sir, in the presence of Mr. Rawson.

ANTHONY. Which reminds me, have you seen my father around anywhere?

KITSON. I saw him going towards the stables, sir, just now.

ANTHONY. Looking for Geoffrey — of course! There may be need of me out there! [*Confidentially to* NINA] See you later? [*Exit by porch*]

KITSON [*with authority*]. What's that he said to you, Nina?

NINA. What's *what* he said to me?

KITSON. — Under his breath.

NINA. What'll you give me if I tell you?

KITSON [*commandingly*]. I asked you a question.

NINA [*confidentially*]. He said: "Don't tell Kitson."

KITSON [*with swelling indignation*]. You think you're very fine and clever, don't you, young lady? You think you can put on all the smart airs you like, don't you? And why? Why? Just because you're letting Anthony make a fool of you.

NINA [*irritated*]. When anybody makes a fool of *me*, I'll run straight and tell you, Kitson!

KITSON. No need! I've got two eyes in my head. I've seen you half a dozen times together in the last three days, whispering and laughing; and I tell you now, I don't want to see it again.

NINA. Well, don't look!

KITSON. You'd ought to be ashamed of yourself, and him engaged to be married, and his young lady here in this very house!

NINA. Well, that's not *my* lookout, is it? *I* didn't bring Miss de Salle here, did I; nor her family neither, did I? And if Mr. Anthony stops now and again to exchange a word with me, in a friendly way, I for one can't see no harm in it.

KITSON [*solemnly*]. You look out for that man.

[JUSTIN'S *voice, very angry is heard outside*]

NINA. My goodness! [*Dashes up to porch door and glances out*] It's Mr. Geoffrey now! He's catchin' it for fair this time! — Me for the woods! [*Exits hastily*]

JUSTIN [*speaking off stage*]. No! No! You're wrong — I say you're entirely wrong. — It is you who choose to take my words as referring to the whole question of your attitude toward Anthony. I had no wish to bring that matter up at the present time. [*Enter* JUSTIN *and* GEOFFREY. ANTHONY *is seen following*] For once, I hoped that you would consent to listen to me quietly and reasonably without flying into a passion.

GEOFFREY [*not ruffled*]. Am I really in a passion, Dad?

[*Enter* ANTHONY *who stands by deferentially*]

JUSTIN. Without flying into a passion, I said, or assuming this air of outraged virtue which exasperates me to the last degree. [*He storms up and down the room while* GEOFFREY, *more puzzled than disturbed, watches him, arms folded*]

[JUSTIN RAWSON *is an American gentleman of somewhat advanced middle-age; dignity and consciousness of race are bespoken in his every movement.* GEOFFREY, *his younger son, is a robust, outdoor fellow of twenty-four, not at all at ease amid these repressive surroundings. His attire suggests the stock-raiser*]

ANTHONY [*stepping up with anxious countenance*]. Father, don't take it so much to heart. I am sure Geoffrey meant nothing by it!

JUSTIN [*to* ANTHONY]. No. Nothing at all! Nothing more than he always means by his jealous, suspicious, unbrotherly behavior toward you. [AN-THONY *makes a deprecatory gesture*] You are with us for a week's stay, only. I insist that Geoffrey, who has nothing to do — [GEOFFREY *makes gesture of protest*] who has nothing, I say, to do, shall exert himself toward making your visit pleasurable.

ANTHONY. But, with a few exceptions, Geoffrey has been uniformly considerate, indeed —

JUSTIN [*cutting him off*]. I do not think the less of you, Anthony, for your readiness to defend him. But you are too generous. Be so kind as to leave us.

ANTHONY. But, Father! — I really — [*He is dismissed with a gesture, and exits to the library silently.* JUSTIN *suddenly perceives* KITSON, *who has the air of having heard nothing*]

JUSTIN [*in controlled voice*]. Kitson!

KITSON. Yes, sir.

JUSTIN. You may go.

KITSON. Yes, sir. [*Exits Left*]

JUSTIN. And now, sir — now you

may tell me why you are always making occasions to slight your brother. Is it because he's three years your senior? Is it because he has devoted himself assiduously to his business and is already making a name for himself; while you have been a rolling stone, now here, now in the West, agriculturist, cowboy, sheep raiser, gentleman-farmer — anything and everything except a steady, industrious, conservative citizen! — Look at Anthony! His good habits, his manners, his respect — I might say, reverence — for his elders! Do they not make you blush for shame? [*A pause*] So for once you have nothing to say for yourself?

GEOFFREY [*mildly*]. No, nothing — except that for the life of me I can't see what I've done to make you so angry.

JUSTIN. Angry, sir, — angry! [*Jumps to his feet with outraged manner*]

GEOFFREY. You suggested that I go for a ride with Miss de Salle. I said I had rather not. That was all.

JUSTIN. It does not occur to you that you have any obligations either toward your brother or our English guests.

GEOFFREY. I should think it was Anthony's place to go with her.

JUSTIN. You are perfectly well aware that Anthony doesn't know how to ride.

GEOFFREY. I'd be glad to teach him.

JUSTIN. *You* are the *animal-man* in this family. Anthony's *career* has occupied his attention while you have been riding your precious bronchos in New Mexico.

GEOFFREY [*vehemently*]. Yes, and God knows I'd be there now if you hadn't asked me to come home. Do you think I *wanted* to leave the ranch? [*His face glows with longing and memory*] Oh! *That's real!*

JUSTIN. I wished you to come back and live like a civilized member of society.

GEOFFREY. It's no use.

JUSTIN. You are certainly right, so long as you insist on being sullen and offish and discourteous.

GEOFFREY [*earnestly*]. I give you my word, Dad, I did not mean to be discourteous. [*He is embarrassed*]

JUSTIN [*peremptorily*]. Your reason, then, for refusing to ride with Miss de Salle! She loves riding.

GEOFFREY [*much embarrassed*]. I was busy.

JUSTIN [*with an outburst*]. Busy! With your pigs, I presume. Does it mean nothing to you that Anthony has chosen for his wife —

[*Enter by porch,* MISS RAWSON, *hastily*]

MISS RAWSON. Justin! Justin! [*Indicating garden*] Mrs. Leavitt!

[MISS RAWSON, *an elderly lady of distinguished demeanor, is the image of caste-pride*]

JUSTIN [*impatiently*]. Mrs. Leavitt! Mrs. Leavitt's in New York.

MISS RAWSON. She came back last night. — Please, Brother —

JUSTIN. I beg your pardon. [*To* GEOFFREY] Be so good as to come into the study. [*Exit* GEOFFREY, *Right*] This matter's not settled yet. No! Not by any means. [*Exit* JUSTIN, *Right.* MISS RAWSON *goes up to meet* MRS. LEAVITT, *a young woman of charming, rather effusive manner, hatless, in informal morning dress*]

MISS RAWSON. It's nice to have you back again! Was it very dreadful in the city?

MRS. LEAVITT [*with a gesture of stifling*]. Absolutely indescribable! Oh, it is heavenly to be home again!

MISS RAWSON [*pressing bell*]. I was so anxious to have you return before the departure of our delightful guests. They are to stay until next week.

MRS. LEAVITT. I am wild to meet the future Mrs. Anthony.

MRS. RAWSON. You will love her. [*To* NINA *who has entered*] Nina, please tell our guests that Mrs. Leavitt is here. [*Exit* NINA *by stairs*] Yes, and her family too! Mrs. de Salle, a dignified woman, silent, keeping much to herself, yet not without a certain originality — some would call it eccentricity; — and Mrs. Bumpstead-Leigh, the older daughter, who quite answers to my ideal of an English lady, — a little formal, a little —

MRS. LEAVITT. Formal! [*Rising in dismay*] Oh, dear! What will she think of me for calling so informally! [*A gesture from* MISS RAWSON *reassures her*] Well I must confess to you privately — Miss Rawson, I ran away from home.

MISS RAWSON. Ran away?

MRS. LEAVITT [*gaily*]. Yes. A fugitive. I was having cold chills.

MISS RAWSON. What do you mean?

MRS. LEAVITT [*in lowered voice*]. You know we are planning a simple little memorial at Woodlawn for Mr. Leavitt's mother; and this morning by the first train — Oh, quite without being asked to come, I assure you, — who should turn up but this strange creature; Swallow, his name is, — representing some tombstone firm in Hoboken, New Jersey! — He appeared before the gates of Willowfields at nine A.M. and evidently intends staying until the crack of doom.

JUSTIN [*heard off Right*]. Wrong! Wrong! Radically, essentially, totally wrong!

MRS. LEAVITT [*startled*]. Goodness, what's that?

MISS RAWSON [*trying to explain*]. It's only Justin. He does not always find — Geoffrey —

MRS. LEAVITT [*consolingly*]. Yes, I know so well! Many things must be hard for both of you! Yet after all, you have much to be thankful for! *Anthony* is doing so very well.

MISS RAWSON. Anthony is a *Rawson!* — Well, Nina! [*To* NINA *who has re-entered by stairs*]

NINA. Mrs. Bumpstead-Leigh presents her compliments, Madam, and says they will be down directly. [*Exit*]

MRS. LEAVITT. Bumpstead-Leigh! what a fascinating name — it seems to mean so much! And I understand the Reverend Algernon Bumpstead-Leigh is one of those British younger sons who has entered the Church and is directly in line for Bishop's orders and the House of Lords. I read all about it last night in the Evening Chronicle.

MISS RAWSON [*horrified*]. The Evening Chronicle!

MRS. LEAVITT. Yes, didn't you know? There was fully half a column on the society page.

MISS RAWSON. Oh, no! It is too horrible! Must our personal affairs be hawked and peddled about the streets? The thought makes me ill!

MRS. LEAVITT [*disconcerted*]. Oh, but you mustn't let it trouble you so, dear Miss Rawson. There was nothing more than a hint of the engagement; the tone and all was perfectly inoffensive.

MISS RAWSON. It isn't that; oh, it isn't that! No, it's the idea of having *our family* connected in any way, shape, or manner with the vulgar, sensational press of the present day.

MRS. LEAVITT. Yes, yes, I understand.

MISS RAWSON. We must not let a

word of this wretched affair get to the de Salles. They are even more conservative than we. Why, until they knew absolutely the origin and standing of Anthony's family, they would not *think* of ratifying the engagement. It was for that reason they consented to cross the ocean with him.

MRS. LEAVITT. Oh, I see. And of course, they are satisfied.

MISS RAWSON. Yes. They are satisfied. So are we. Everything about them pleases me. The Rectory occupied by the Bumpstead-Leighs in Trumpington-on-Swell is restored from an old monastery of the early Tudor period. From attic to cellar it is filled with old oak panelling, ancient plate, ancestral portraits —

MRS. LEAVITT. Of the Bumpstead-Leighs or the de Salles?

MISS RAWSON. The de Salles are American.

MRS. LEAVITT. American!

MISS RAWSON. Yes, in origin; that is one cause for my being especially drawn to them; yet the name is Norman-French — that means something.

MRS. LEAVITT. What a fascinating blend!

MISS RAWSON. Yes, the girls were born in this country — Washington, I think — but they have always lived on the other side; educated at the most exclusive *pensions;* speaking several languages; combining, one might say, a moral heritage which is truly American with the charm and culture of the older civilization.

MRS. LEAVITT. How well you put it, Miss Rawson!

MISS RAWSON. If I do, it is only because I feel so deeply what it all means in this day and age. The typical American young woman of to-day, with her manners that are anything but manners, her bold forward speech, her smartness, her slang, — downright *illiteracy*, that is what I call it; and as for *family*, it has all but perished from the face of the earth! [*Checking her own vehemence*] Oh, I know I am quite out of date; the world has changed — I do not say gone forward — since I was a girl; but there are a few things I insist upon, and I shall continue to insist upon them as long as I can insist upon anything. *Family* heads the list!

MRS. LEAVITT. Then no wonder you welcome the de Salles.

MISS RAWSON. And for more than

ne reason. Anthony was truly impressed by the home life of the Bump-
tead-Leighs. The devotion of Mrs.
Bumpstead-Leigh to her husband is very
beautiful. And, of course, though I do
not care to insist upon the point, it does
mean something to us, that in Trump-
ngton-on-Swell Mrs. Bumpstead-Leigh
s the acknowledged social leader. So
now you can understand why we welcome the de Salles and regard the union
as one I may say peculiarly happy and
suitable.

In the course of this last speech MRS.
BUMPSTEAD-LEIGH *has descended
the stairs as far as the landing and has
stood there, unseen by the other ladies,
until the suitable moment should come
for interrupting their conversation.
She concludes that the moment has
now come and descends the remaining stairs with cordial, vivid, yet
slightly patronizing eagerness.* MRS.
BUMPSTEAD-LEIGH [ADELAIDE] *is an
exceedingly British lady still in her
early thirties. She is handsome,
polished, radiant, electrical, mental;
and there is a born domination, a
concealed aggressiveness in her demeanor which suggests that it would
not be desirable nor perhaps quite
safe to antagonize her. You recognize her instantly as a leader, a com-
mander. Gracious, affable always,
you sense the iron underneath*]

ADELAIDE [*in her most voluble British
manner*]. Oh, I do love your American
way of paying calls in the morning. It
is so deliciously informal, so *en famille!*
— or perhaps, I err in thinking so?
Surely it is not the usual, the prescribed
hour. — Yet why not? Why should
not one devote these brightest and choic-
est moments of the day to social inter-
course. I do not know a fitter use for
them. [*Greeting* MRS. LEAVITT *with a
warmth which yet does not lack condescension*] With Mrs. Leavitt, I am sure, I
need not insist upon a formal introduction. I have heard so many charming
things of you from your amiable husband, Mr. Leavitt. I am truly charmed
to make your acquaintance.
MRS. LEAVITT [*overwhelmed*]. Perfectly — delighted!
ADELAIDE [*to* MISS RAWSON]. I am
so very, very sorry to precede Mamma
and Violet. I only consented to come
down upon their express promise to
follow directly.

MISS RAWSON [*to* MRS. LEAVITT].
Violet was off for a long tramp, all by herself, before breakfast. [*To* ADELAIDE]
I do hope that she was not over-fatigued.
ADELAIDE. Oh, no — not at all, and
so very kind of you to think of it. Violet is like all our English girls, in her love
for the free, outdoor life. But your
morning sun over here — I don't know
I am sure how to account for it — seems
to radiate a peculiarly burning, exhausting heat. — I wonder, might there be
some scientific explanation for that?

[ANTHONY *has just entered from porch.
He hastily scrutinizes the group and
seems dissatisfied*]

ANTHONY. How do you do, Mrs.
Leavitt! [*Coming to her*]
MRS. LEAVITT. My dear Anthony!
How well you are looking! [*Taking
his hand effusively*] Congratulations!
Sincere congratulations! We are so
awfully glad!
ANTHONY [*to* MRS. LEAVITT *rather
absently*]. Thank you, thank you. [*To*
ADELAIDE] But where is Violet?
ADELAIDE. She will be down in a
minute.
ANTHONY [*with feigned indifference*].
Of course she knows that Mrs. Leavitt is
here?

[MRS. DE SALLE *has entered by stairs*]

ADELAIDE [*brightly*]. Mamma comes
next! — the order is climactic.
ANTHONY [*repeating this time to* MRS.
DE SALLE]. Violet has been told of
course that Mrs. Leavitt is here?
MRS. DE SALLE [*embarrassed*]. Oh,
yes, a dozen times! I'm sure she'll
come down right away.

[*The grand manner sits somehow rather
grotesquely on* MRS. DE SALLE *and
like her clothes, which are irreproach-
ably elegant, seems not altogether to be
hers by original right. Underneath
her well-groomed, well-polished im-
pressiveness you might detect an
acute, unceasing anxiety, an apprehension of well, I don't know quite
what, but something*]

ADELAIDE [*with vivid emphasis as if to
prevent the possibility of* MRS. DE SALLE
saying more]. Perhaps she was a trifle
over-tired by her tramp. Though there
is not the slightest cause for apprehension.
MRS. DE SALLE. Oh, not the slightest
cause for apprehension.

[*And we cannot fail to notice how eagerly she seizes every opportunity to echo the perfectly safe pronouncements of her daughter*]

MISS RAWSON [*rising*]. Mrs. de Salle, permit me to introduce Mrs. Leavitt.

MRS. DE SALLE [*with a shadow of* ADELAIDE'S *manner*]. Very charmed.

MRS. LEAVITT. Delighted! — How interesting that your daughter should be devoted to walking. Is she a great nature-lover?

MRS. DE SALLE. Oh no! She has always been perfectly healthy.

ADELAIDE [*seating herself with a compellingly gracious air*]. I do not know what it can precisely be about our young English girls. — Though almost invariably enjoying the best of health, they seem to lack a certain rugged, brute vigor that I find everywhere amongst your girls of America.

MISS RAWSON. Indeed!

ADELAIDE. Your American girls constantly strike me with wonder; they are so lithe, so muscular, with their great splendid hands, and feet, divinely intended, one might say, without a shadow of irreverence, for struggle with your more elemental conditions over here.

MRS. DE SALLE [*approvingly*]. Yes. Elemental!

ADELAIDE. I seem to be watching a parade of magnificent animals! Am I correctly informed, Anthony, that in certain of your institutions of learning for young women, the students meet regularly in football contests with antagonists of the opposite sex?

ANTHONY. I question it.

ADELAIDE. Ça me donne les frissons! — yet why? Only because, in imagination, I seem to see *our* girls so engaged. And the thought comes; has not the American young woman inherited many of the best traits of the Indian women — what was the scientific term for them? Papooses? — that preceded her?

MISS RAWSON [*horrified but impressed*]. Of course, there is no actual blood-relationship between them.

ADELAIDE. Surely not! Oh, surely not! And yet family, here in America, impresses us English as being such an odd, tangled sort of affair!

MISS RAWSON [*who finds her own sentiments echoed*]. No doubt!

ADELAIDE. I mean to say — One never knows to whom one may be related! As Lady Fitzhugh was remarking to me one day — Anthony, you will recall Lady Fitzhugh? —

ANTHONY. Yes, of course!

ADELAIDE. One of the most charming creatures in the world — and a Granville! — "Dearest Adelaide," she exclaimed, in that odd, emphatic manner of hers, "do all American women marry their fathers' chauffeurs, and all American men their mothers' cook?"

MISS RAWSON. Dear, dear!

ADELAIDE. "By no means always," I replied. "Sometimes they remarry them," — intending, by that little emendation, to allude to the shocking frequency of divorce in this country.

MISS RAWSON. It *is* shocking!

ADELAIDE. Lady Fitzhugh, I may add, apprehended my meaning instantly, and went on to speak, with the utmost kindness and amiability, of a sermon my husband had delivered the previous Sunday upon the sanctity of the marriage bond.

MISS RAWSON. A good subject!

ADELAIDE. "I am proud," said she "that our dear Algernon takes so sound a view of this solemn institution When he is appointed *Bishop of Highchester*, we shall expect some notable utterances on these pressing social questions."

[*From the study is heard the voice of* JUSTIN]

JUSTIN. No! No! Not a word!

ANTHONY. Oh, I hope Father is not being severe with Geoffrey.

MISS RAWSON. Your Father is the soul of Justice!

ADELAIDE. He is indeed! Mr. Rawson has quite the English sense of equity So different in that respect from our popular idea of the Yankee.

MRS. DE SALLE. Yes, so different.

ADELAIDE. When I return to Staffordshire, I promise you I shall do my best to correct those false and libellous misconceptions. You can have no idea what strange beings the Americans are thought to be, even by our upper classes !

MRS. LEAVITT. Oh, I suppose not.

ADELAIDE. I recall very well how our friend, Lord Clitheroe, asked me one day: "Is it true that the accepted Yankee method of execution is by the lynch?" I hastened to assure him that, though I had not visited the States since my girlhood, such I knew to be not the case. "The law," I said, "is held in the highest respect in the older parts of the country, near the Coast." I shall be able to speak even more emphatically after my return, for I may truly say, I have seen no lawlessness, no bloodshed, no violence of any sort whatever during my present visit here.

ANTHONY. We are fortunate in having such a devoted champion.

ADELAIDE. Ah, you are too kind. England is the home of my adoption, but I can never forget what I owe to America.

MRS. DE SALLE [*echoingly*]. No! never! [*Telephone rings*]

MRS. LEAVITT. Oh, that is Mr. Leavitt — excuse me. [*Goes to 'phone*]

MISS RAWSON [*To the* DE SALLES]. The private wire brings friends even closer.

MRS. LEAVITT [*at 'phone*]. Yes? Is that you, Stephen?

ADELAIDE [*to* MRS. DE SALLE]. Dear Mamma, I do believe we must have one between the Rectory and Lady Fitzhugh's. It would be such a convenience.

MRS. LEAVITT [*at 'phone*]. Very well, I'll come over at once. [*Returning to* MISS RAWSON] I'm so sorry, but my advice is wanted at home; so I shall have to put off meeting Miss de Salle until another time, after all.

ADELAIDE. She will be inconsolable.

MRS. DE SALLE [*echoing*]. Yes — inconsolable!

MISS RAWSON [*accompanying* MRS. LEAVITT *to porch*]. My dear, couldn't you and Stephen come over to lunch? We'll have it on the porch. There is such a lovely picnic flavor in the air today.

ANTHONY [*joining them*]. Let me second the invitation!

MRS. LEAVITT. Why, yes, it would be sweet. We'll be delighted!

[*Exeunt* MRS. LEAVITT, ANTHONY *and* MISS RAWSON, *by porch*]

MISS RAWSON [*as they go*]. Then we shall look for you about one.

[*Their voices are heard outside as they leave the porch.* MRS. DE SALLE *is following them vaguely with somewhat the air of a Guilty Thing and as if hoping to avoid being left alone with her brilliant daughter. But she has not reached the porch door before she is halted dead in her tracks by a*

peremptory command from ADELAIDE]

ADELAIDE. *MA!*

MRS. DE SALLE [*turning as if expecting a whipping*]. Yes, Della?

ADELAIDE. Where you going?

MRS. DE SALLE. Nowhere.

ADELAIDE. Come here! [MRS. DE SALLE *comes*] What the dickens has got into Violet? [*Her voice is scarcely recognizable in its raw, almost strident American homespun*]

MRS. DE SALLE [*wringing her hands*]. Oh, I'm sure I haven't an idea!

ADELAIDE. Whatever it is, it's got to be knocked out, and no delay! If Ollie don't attend to business, she'll mull everything!

MRS. DE SALLE [*weakly protesting*]. Oh I'm sure — Della —

ADELAIDE [*commandingly*]. Now look here! Are you backin' her up?

MRS. DE SALLE [*collapsing*]. Della, I don't know *what* I'm a-doin'.

ADELAIDE. Humph! The usual situation! If you'd once learned to know what you were doing, you wouldn't have played so beautifully into the hands of that cat-eyed peddlar of slanders, Lady Fitzhugh!

MRS. DE SALLE [*aghast*]. Lady Fitzhugh! I never told a thing to Lady Fitzhugh! I didn't, I didn't! [*Sits helpless*]

ADELAIDE. To be sure! Of course not! But for all that, Lady Fitzhugh managed very neatly to worm out of you that we came from Missionary Loop, Indiana, and that Dad made every cent he had out of patent medicine.

MRS. DE SALLE [*on her feet*]. I never! — I never said a word about the Sayles's Favorite Stomach Elixir, or the Sissapoola Indian Herb remedies! Nothing in the world would make me open my mouth!

ADELAIDE [*curtly*]. Rats, Ma! You know you just handed over everything she wanted to serve for all her nasty innuendoes. Oh, I can hear her ringin' 'em out now! "So they came to England to find husbands! I wonder now what can be the reason for it! — considering who they were, and all!" — Ugh. Oh, why, *why* did I ever leave you alone for five minutes?

MRS. DE SALLE [*plaintively*]. Oh, why did you — why did you?

ADELAIDE. Might have known it would mean ruin!

MRS. DE SALLE [*horrified*]. Ruin!

ADELAIDE [*crisply*]. That's what I'm facing at the present moment. [*Showing envelope*] Do you know what's in this letter I got from Algernon last night?

MRS. DE SALLE [*with a gulp of horror*]. No!

ADELAIDE. It's come to *his* ears at last. Oh, it was sure to in time with Lady Fitzhugh at the guns! He's insulted, distressed — all that a faithful husband should be — *but* — he calls on me to deny everything. "Cable reply" — that's the postscript.

MRS. DE SALLE. "Cable reply!"

ADELAIDE. So now you see just where we are, and it's a good tight place! MRS. DE SALLE [*gasping*]. Did you answer it?

ADELAIDE. I did. — One word — "Lies."

MRS. DE SALLE. But — [*Rising and sitting again*]

ADELAIDE. But nothing! I didn't say "All Lies." I said, "Lies." Half of what that gassy old windbag of a Fitzhugh says is sure to be lies, anyhow.

MRS. DE SALLE [*cheeringly*]. But now, I reckon this match of Ollie's 'll stop her mouth.

ADELAIDE. Yes! Yes! [*Bitterly*] "This match of Ollie's!" That comes well from you just at the moment when you're doing your best to smash it.

MRS. DE SALLE. Me!

ADELAIDE. Look here! Don't you see, you've got to set to and help me manage Ollie? Why didn't you *make* her come down?

MRS. DE SALLE [*whimpering*]. I got on my knees to her, Dell.

ADELAIDE. Sh! — [ANTHONY *is seen entering by porch*] Now you pack off upstairs and have Violet here in five minutes. Understand? Don't be a jellyfish! — There! [MRS. DE SALLE *exits helplessly by the stairs.* ADELAIDE *turns quickly and goes with a manner of comprehending sympathy to* ANTHONY, *once more the irreproachable, unapproachable* MRS. BUMPSTEAD-LEIGH, *and holding out her hands to him she exclaims:*] My dear boy! — Something is wrong!

ANTHONY [*sullenly*]. There's something I don't understand.

ADELAIDE. Tell me, frankly, candidly, as brother to sister — there has been no — no difference?

ANTHONY. Not a shadow.

ADELAIDE. Might it not be merely the effect of excitement — the fag, the novelty of everything?

ANTHONY. Is that a reason for avoiding me?

ADELAIDE. Of course not — and yet —

ANTHONY. Let me tell you! — Since I first observed the change in her, I have been more attentive than usual, and yet she is unresponsive, — cold!

ADELAIDE. It is only a phase, — a mere transient little phase, nothing more, Anthony dear, believe me. Of her love you are sure. — You must be patient!

ANTHONY [*with dignity*]. I have been patient! She knows that Mrs. Leavitt wished to meet her and she refused to come down. It was an affront.

ADELAIDE. Tell her frankly what you think! Perhaps you will discover the trouble — and if not, let me try. But be very tender with her! —

[*At this moment,* VIOLET DE SALLE *enters by the stairs. She is a sweet, straight-forward girl of eighteen, naturally candid and sincere. Her manner is unaffected and cultivated. She hesitates; then comes reluctantly toward* ADELAIDE]

VIOLET. You wished to see me, Adelaide?

ADELAIDE [*sweetly*]. Yes, — that is, no, not now. There *was* something I wished to ask you, but it can wait. [*Glancing at her watch*] — For I promised Geoffrey to visit his kennels. I am a bit late. [*Going*]

VIOLET [*uneasily*]. Oh, mayn't I come with you?

ADELAIDE [*with gentle authority*]. Oh, no, Violet dear! It would be most imprudent after your tiresome walk this morning. You must remain quietly indoors until after lunch. [*Her eyes smile gently upon her sister; but if you look you may see one hand kindly placed on* VIOLET'S *shoulder suddenly stiffen as it imparts a vigorous push to the unwilling girl. And with this, she exits, to porch*]

ANTHONY [*after a moment's silent regard of the girl, who does not return his gaze*]. Violet, do you know that you have caused me a great deal of pain?

VIOLET [*with timid concern*]. Oh, have I, Anthony? I'm so sorry. It hasn't been intentional. Indeed it hasn't.

ANTHONY [*sharpening*]. Do you

mean to say that your failure to appear just now was unintentional.

VIOLET [*simply*]. Yes, truly, I meant to come.

ANTHONY. Then why didn't you?

VIOLET [*faintly*]. I don't know. — I — I seemed to want to be alone.

ANTHONY [*with irony*]. You seem to want to be alone often of late. What about this solitary expedition over the dunes before breakfast?

VIOLET. I wanted to think.

ANTHONY [*positively*]. Something's the matter.

VIOLET [*frightened*]. Oh — no!

ANTHONY [*putting his arm about her endearingly, shows her to the sofa where they sit*]. Come! I've got you all to myself at last. We must talk! Sit down. Violet, you are not like yourself. Tell me, are you hiding something? Have you been naughty? Eh? Have you? Have you? [*He insists wheedlingly and ends by kissing her in rather a lavish manner*]

VIOLET [*freeing herself with a little cry*]. Oh!

ANTHONY. Why, what's wrong?

VIOLET [*faintly*]. I thought I heard someone.

ANTHONY. Well, what of it? Need we be ashamed? Isn't our love noble, divinely ordained? Moments like these, when I speak to you as to my second self, are the summits of life; delectable mountains from which, hand in hand, we look into new, untraveled lands, behold transporting visions of beauty and truth!

[*It would be quite proper and natural, of course, for VIOLET to be swept away by these choice phrases, but for some reason or other, she only replies, rather feebly*]

VIOLET. What a vocabulary you have, Anthony.

ANTHONY [*fondly*]. Only when you inspire me, darling! Without you I am mute. You are like some rare, precious wine. When I put you to my lips, a new joy, an inspiration, a feeling of exuberant vitality sweeps ᴸover me. The World does not know me, Violet! It thinks me sedate, cold, passionless, — clever too, perhaps, —

VIOLET [*faintly*]. Oh, yes, very clever, Anthony; everyone speaks of that.

ANTHONY. People say, "There is a man with a future; a man who will make his mark some day!" But, of my true self, belovèd, what does the world know? Nothing! — That is for you! — [*Warming to her*] None but you has ever stirred those slumbering fires —

VIOLET [*jumping nervously up*]. Oh, there is Adelaide!

ADELAIDE [*entering gaily*]. Have you Americans that droll old saying about a bad penny always turning up again? Well, here I am.

VIOLET [*eagerly*]. Did you see the dogs, Della? Oh, aren't they the sweetest dears?

ADELAIDE. No, I didn't see the dogs. Geoffrey met a man who wanted to buy a pig. — Really, Anthony, your brother is by way of being quite a farmer, is not he!

ANTHONY [*with veiled contempt*]. The pigs are the most recent addition to his stock, I believe.

VIOLET. Oh, they are heavenly pigs, Della! There's one old mother who took a prize at the County Fair, and she has seven of the darlingest little pink babies. Geoffrey let me pick one up.

ADELAIDE [*horrified*]. Violet!

VIOLET. Why not? It has the cutest little face, — exactly like a little wee baby. — Geoffrey promised I should take it back to Trumpington-on-Swell.

ADELAIDE [*burying her face*]. Oh! Oh!

ANTHONY [*jealously*]. Strange, I have heard nothing of all these expeditions to the kennels and the pig pens.

VIOLET [*innocently*]. I didn't suppose you'd care to come, Anthony. I'm sorry if I have displeased you.

ANTHONY [*rather grandly*]. Oh, not at all — not at all.

[VIOLET *goes thoughtfully to the window, Left, and stands there looking out*]

ADELAIDE. Since *Chantecler*, barnyards have come quite into good odour, I believe. — Oh, Anthony, I had all but forgotten! Mr. Leavitt was inquiring for you, — some little business matter, he said. I promised to tell you. He is in the library, I think.

ANTHONY [*going*]. With your permission, Violet?

[VIOLET *makes no rejoinder*]

ADELAIDE [*apart to* ANTHONY, *as he passes her*]. Did you get any clue? [ANTHONY *shakes his head*] Leave it to me. [*Exit* ANTHONY. *For a moment,* ADELAIDE *silently watches her sister;*

then with decision she abruptly challenges her, and her manner is once more that of the ambitious but untutored daughter of Indiana] Ollie, you've kicked up enough how-do-do in the last forty-eight hours to smash everything! I guess you'd better give me some explanations, young lady!

VIOLET [*mildly*]. I don't know what you mean.

ADELAIDE [*with extreme disgust*]. Stuff and nonsense, girl! Do you take me for a blind bat?

VIOLET [*innocently*]. I haven't intended to offend him.

ADELAIDE [*unspeakably contemptuous*]. And pray, is *that* your recipe for holding on to a man! If any girl but my own sister said such a fool thing, I'd consign her to the psychopathic ward and be done with it. What have you been toted around Europe for all these years, if not to learn how to play the game? You've hooked a fish — I grant you, though the credit's more mine than yours! But he ain't in the frying pan yet, by a long sight, an' don't you forget it!

VIOLET [*hurt*]. Della, please.

ADELAIDE [*throwing arms about her with affectionate manner*]. There, there, dear! I may be too blunt; but after all, it's only because I'm thinking of what's best for you. Come, let's talk it over quietly! — Ollie, I want you to *trust* me. Is that wantin' too much? What has come between us lately? I feel as if I hardly knew ye any more. Perhaps you think I don't care, but I *do*, — Violet, I do care.

VIOLET [*yielding to sudden sobs, while she leans her head on* ADELAIDE'S *bosom*]. Oh, Della, I'm so unhappy! I wish I were dead!

ADELAIDE [*with shrewd smile of triumph — as she tenderly pats her*]. Tell your old sister all about it.

VIOLET. I used to think it didn't matter; but now — just these last few days, — oh, it's been making me feel so ashamed and humiliated to be deceiving everybody like this.

ADELAIDE. Deceiving everybody? — [*Pause*] Why, what do you mean, Violet?

VIOLET [*with accusing eyes*]. You know what I mean!

ADELAIDE. Indeed I do *not*! — *Whom* have you been deceiving?

VIOLET. Anthony, Geoffrey, Miss Rawson! — *everybody!*

ADELAIDE [*hardening a little*]. Ye have! What have you been deceivin' 'em about?

VIOLET [*withdrawing into herself*]. It's no use! — I don't think I could make you see it my way.

ADELAIDE [*seemingly deeply wounded*]. Oh, Violet! What have I done to get treated like this?

VIOLET [*softening again*]. I didn't mean it that way. It's only — *you* know as well as I do, that if these people knew all about us, and who we were, they wouldn't have us here for anything in the world.

ADELAIDE. Now look me straight in the eye! — Do you honestly think yourself their inferior?

VIOLET [*thoughtfully*]. No — but that's not the point.

ADELAIDE [*bitingly*]. The point is: You think we ought to tell them all about Sayles's Favorite Stomach Elixir, and the Sissapoola Indian Herb Remedies!

VIOLET [*shuddering*]. I don't think I could, even if I thought I ought to.

ADELAIDE [*remorselessly*]. You'd like them to know how, on every bottle, was emblazoned the picture of our lamented sire — thus! — [*Raising one hand, as if in blessing, and assuming a grotesquely benignant countenance*] over the words: "Old Jim Sayles, the Sufferer's Friend." [*With a groan*] Land sakes! Isn't it expiation enough to have lived — only to have *lived* with that till I was twenty years old, without forcing me now to rake up the hideous recollections! How they used to guy me about it, even in Missionary Loop! [*Imitating a native of her native town*] "Wa'l, wa'l! So you be old Jim Sayles's gal! Say, I hear tell as how up to your hum, they gives ye Stomach Elixir on yer pancakes." — Are we accountable for what our Dad happened to be and what he happened to do? Is that *our* fault? Are we *branded?* Thank God, no! That's *done* with! We've paid the price! For everything we've gained, we've paid the price!

VIOLET [*with conviction but very simply*]. Not honestly!

ADELAIDE [*urgently, with equal conviction*]. Yes, honestly! Didn't the most expensive heraldic bureau in New York say we had a perfect right to the name de Salle? Didn't they say it could be proved definitely that somebody or other back a few hundred years was named that? — Well, there's no criminality so far, *is* there! And then we went to Washington without a friend in the world. Mother rented the house on Lafayette Circle, and you and I attended the swellest day school in the city. How I worked to lay on a little culture and style and *savoir faire* for those two awful years! You were a youngster. *You* escaped all that! —

VIOLET [*with ironic emphasis*]. Oh, I remember! It wasn't until the second year that any of the girls at Miss Westleigh's would be seen with me.

ADELAIDE. Very likely not! But before we *quit* Washington, mother had a visiting list with thirty-four *bona fide* names on it — two senator's wives, and the wife of the Secretary of the French Embassy. That's something! And through Madame Epervier we got a little foothold in Paris; and then on, and on, one step after another! I've worked like a horse for everybody! — Well, haven't I! Where would *you* be to-day, I'd like to know, if it wasn't for me? Eh? Answer me that, will you. [VIOLET *is silent*] Very likely the wife of Missionary Loop's most popular grocer. And every night about bedtime, while he'd be sittin' in front of the base burner in his stockin' feet, you'd be havin' a nice piece o' apple pie together! Perhaps you'd be Secretary of the Missionary Loop Culture Club! That *would* be something to live for, wouldn't it!

VIOLET [*distressed*]. Oh, Della! How *can* you!

ADELAIDE. Well, I'm merely reminding you of where you might have been if I hadn't put my shoulder to the wheel and set to work to *do* something, and to *get* somewhere. Ten years at hard labor, that was the sentence I imposed on myself; and now I ask you to look about you and say if I can't show results! How about Ma? Haven't I made her over into a thoroughly presentable personage? — If she'd only keep her mouth shut? — Haven't I made a match for myself that a thousand American girls with family trees and five times our money would sell their souls for? Now haven't I?

VIOLET [*admiring perforce*]. You have done handsomely, Dell.

ADELAIDE. And I haven't left one single stone unturned to do as well for you! What could you ask for better than Anthony Rawson? My land, girl, if you think all this has been child's play, you're mistaken — very much mistaken! And who have I done it for? Myself?

VIOLET [*simply*]. Della, I do honestly feel grateful to you, even when I don't seem to show it.

ADELAIDE [*indulgently*]. There, there! Say nothing more about it. And now I hope that affair is settled once and for all — Eh? — [*Pause*] Well?

VIOLET. There's something else. — Something a great deal more important.

ADELAIDE [*crisply*]. I thought so! — Now, we're getting at it! — [*With dry emphasis*] You don't love Anthony any more!

VIOLET [*startled*]. Oh, — how could you guess?

ADELAIDE. I'm a crystal-gazer, dear.

VIOLET [*simply*]. I don't know whether I ever really loved him. I used to think I did — at least *enough* — but now — Oh, I can't bear to have him *come near* me!

ADELAIDE [*curtly*]. In other words, he's not what you took him for!

VIOLET [*timidly*]. Very likely, I'm wrong about it.

ADELAIDE [*matter-of-fact*]. No, you're right about it!

VIOLET [*crushed*]. Oh, it's too dreadful!

ADELAIDE [*with positive, clear pronouncement*]. No it's not! — You've simply found out the truth; and it's bound to be hard — for a week or two! He *isn't* what you thought him. Not one man in a dozen is what a nice woman would like to think him. He's selfish, he's greedy, he's egotistical; and the more he fiddle-diddles about the beauty and sacredness of love, the more you'd better look out for him!

VIOLET [*with dismay*]. *Oh!* How can you bear to live!

ADELAIDE [*with buoyant conviction*]. Oh, I decided quite a long time ago — just as you are going to decide — that there's something — very — well — worth — living for — after all! [*Measuring each word*]

VIOLET. Yes?

ADELAIDE. To strike — the best bargain — with the world — you can! Now listen to me while I tell you something. Do you remember Pete Swallow, of Missionary Loop? [*Yes, she actually pronounces it: Swallah*]

VIOLET. Was he the man who used to show me the pictures of tombstones with urns and weeping willows on top?

ADELAIDE. I was engaged to Pete.
[*Without the slightest hesitation or sentiment, even with a perception of the humor
of the story*] I thought I loved him —
loved him in the approved, turtle-dove
way — *your* way. Well, Pete Swallow
taught me a whole lot of things. He
was a good teacher, and when I'd
studied under him long enough, I decided I could strike a better bargain elsewhere. — *I did!*

VIOLET. Oh, Della!

ADELAIDE [*matter-of-fact*]. Oh, don't
misunderstand me! I know Algernon's
stupid; I know he's petty and narrow-
minded and egotistical; but he's *exactly
the kind of a husband I happen to want,*
so I'm satisfied! Now here's *your* bargain — not a mark-down, department-
store affair, either. But a *Prize! A
blue-ribboner!* And it's your business
to *take it* and to keep a *hold* of it.

VIOLET [*on verge of collapse*]. Oh,
Della, I can't.

ADELAIDE. "Can't": *must!* [*Softening*] What you need, my dear, is just
a little scrap o' common sense! You're
asking for better bread than wheat
makes; and you won't get it in this
world. You want the moon to be always full; you want, "Hertz und
Schmertz" all the time. Well, that's
not real life! That's story-books.
[*Rising*] Turtle doves never get anywhere. They always roost on the
ridge-pole. That don't suit me; and
it wouldn't suit you very long — I know
you too well for that! So put these
silly notions out of your little head,
like the sensible girl you are, and *play
up!* That's the word for the woman
who intends to make a success of life.
Play up! Life's not such a bad game
after all! — Now look at me, and tell
me you're going to do the right thing.

VIOLET [*faintly and without conviction*].
I'll try.

ADELAIDE. Good! That's the way
I like to hear you speak! Now I must
run upstairs and dash off a line for to-
morrow's boat; and when I come down,
I shall expect to find you out in the garden, with the others, *playing up!* —
Ta-ta! [*Exit*]

[VIOLET *remains seated in pensive silence*]

GEOFFREY [*entering from porch and
not perceiving her the first instant*]. Oh,
I didn't know you were in here. [*He is
going out again as if preferring not to talk
with her, then halts*] Great Scott! You

look awfully down. Is something the
matter?

VIOLET [*with dejected simplicity*].
Yes.

GEOFFREY [*fraternally*]. What?

VIOLET. Everything.

GEOFFREY [*sitting*]. Same here!

VIOLET [*inquiringly*]. Yes? [*Sympathetically*]. Oh, I'm sorry!

GEOFFREY. You know, I've about
decided I'm kind — of a sort — of a
misfit.

VIOLET. I *know* I'm one.

GEOFFREY. I'm thinking about making a move.

VIOLET. Oh, are you? — So — so
am I.

GEOFFREY. I think it would be a lot
better for everybody concerned if I cut
out and hit the trail for New Mexico.

VIOLET [*with involuntary eagerness*].
It must be lovely on a ranch!

GEOFFREY [*with enthusiasm*]. You're
right! — it's great! It's so blamed
real! — [*Checking himself*] Not that
that means anything to *you!*

VIOLET [*with involuntary exclamation*].
Oh, but it does! — more than you think!
[*A silence which becomes dangerously full
of meaning. Finally as if rousing herself
from enthrallment* VIOLET *tries to resume
casual blithe manner*] Don't — don't
you think it would be nice outside —
with the others?

GEOFFREY [*adopting her mood, with an
effort*]. Corking! Come on!

[*They are going. Enter Right,* LEAVITT
and ANTHONY]

ANTHONY [*with veiled innuendo*]. Oh,
you were just going?

VIOLET [*with cordial manner*]. Yes,
out to the pergola. — Good-morning,
Mr. Leavitt!

LEAVITT. Good-morning! — Hello,
Jeff!

GEOFFREY. Hello!

VIOLET. Won't you come along, too?

ANTHONY. Mr. Leavitt and I were
just discussing a little business matter.

VIOLET [*to* GEOFFREY]. Come on
then, we're dismissed! [*Laughing rather
nervously, she exits with* GEOFFREY]

[ANTHONY *goes up to porch and watches*
GEOFFREY *and* VIOLET *as they disappear*]

LEAVITT [*puzzled and a little irritated*].
Well, it may not interest *you,* Anthony;
but there's the story! Take it for what
it's worth.

ANTHONY. I couldn't believe a word of it. It is preposterous, absurd, utterly impossible. [*Returns to* LEAVITT *and they sit*]

LEAVITT. I agree with you. A mere coincidence, of course; yet certainly a strange one.

ANTHONY. He was sure the name was de Salle?

LEAVITT. Yes, quite positive. It was when my wife mentioned to me that she had failed to meet Miss de Salle, after all, that this Swallow spoke up so suddenly: "De Salle, de Salle — look here, where does this de Salle come from? Washington, D. C.?" I said I believed the de Salles had once lived there.

NINA *has entered Left, with a large vase of flowers; but when she observes the men in confidential talk, she sets the vase on the piano and busies herself arranging the flowers, while eavesdropping*]

ANTHONY [*thoughtfully*]. I see — and then he went on to tell you about this Sayles family?

LEAVITT. No — not right away. Not until we were alone. Then he began talking about this Della Sayles to whom he had been engaged. It was after the death of the father — the patent medicine man — that the family moved away, and beyond the one fact that they went to Washington under the name of de Salle, he was perfectly ignorant.

ANTHONY. He did not know the younger sister's name?

LEAVITT [*searching his memory*]. He said they always called her — Ollie.

ANTHONY. Ollie! Ollie! I am sure I have heard it. [*Sternly*] Oh! But it is incredible! It cannot be true!

LEAVITT. Of course! But as a friend I thought it my duty to tell you.

ANTHONY [*absently*]. Thank you! Thank you! I suspect we owe it to ourselves — and to the de Salles — to investigate this story.

LEAVITT. You will go to Mrs. de Salle?

ANTHONY [*thoughtfully*]. No — that would be unpleasant, — unpleasant in either event.

LEAVITT. What is your plan?

ANTHONY. A simple one: bring Swallow here.

LEAVITT. Here!

ANTHONY. Confront him with the de Salles.

LEAVITT. But how would you explain things?

ANTHONY. Leave that to me. Mrs. Leavitt does not know of this?

LEAVITT. Not a word.

ANTHONY. Good. I will manage it so that no suspicions will be aroused. Yes, that's it. Bring Swallow over here to lunch.

LEAVITT. At one? But he goes by the 1 : 17.

ANTHONY. So much the better — we will not detain him! — A minute — a second, will tell the story. [NINA *withdraws*] But do not misunderstand me, Leavitt — [*Rather sternly*] I entertain no suspicions whatever. [*They go up*] I simply feel that in view of what you have told me — we owe it — to our guests — to put the story to the proof.

LEAVITT [*with guarded agreement*]. I see.

ANTHONY. Thank you for coming to me in this way. I appreciate it.

LEAVITT. I knew you would understand my motive. [*At door*] Well I will have your man for you. Goodbye!

ANTHONY. Au revoir! and thank you again! [LEAVITT *exits.* ANTHONY *stands an instant in the doorway, thinking with rather a crafty expression.* NINA *enters Left, with another vase of flowers*] What's your hurry, my dear?

NINA [*halting coquettishly*]. I'm fixing the flowers, Mr. Anthony — Aren't they pretty?

ANTHONY [*coming close*]. Yes, but not half so pretty as the face behind them.

NINA [*turning archly away*]. Oh, Mr. Anthony, you're kidding again.

ANTHONY. Why so coy? You know what I want, you little lump — This! [*Catches her and kisses her*]

NINA [*squealing softly*]. Ow!

ANTHONY [*releasing her*]. Don't you know it's very wrong to make a row when a gentleman pays you a compliment? You should always keep as quiet as a mouse. Now, once more!

NINA [*feigning to protect herself with vase of flowers*]. No, sir!

ADELAIDE [*upstairs*]. Very well, mamma! I'll not forget!

NINA [*startled but concealing her fear of having been discovered by a very professional manner*]. Yes, they are pretty, aren't they? Miss Rawson picked them herself this morning, and she has such elegant taste in flowers.

ADELAIDE [*entering. Sweetly*]. Nina, has the post come?

NINA. No madam, not yet! [AN-THONY *has turned in some confusion.* NINA *goes Right*]

ADELAIDE [*to* NINA]. Oh, thank you — [*Exit* NINA] I do not wonder you stop to admire the gladiolus, Anthony. [*She is all smiles and unsuspicion*] And Nina does so well with them!

ANTHONY. Doesn't she! But I came to see if you were not ready to join us outside.

ADELAIDE. With pleasure! — after I have skimmed the London cables. Home politics are in such a mess. The poor dear Lords seem to be hanging by a hair!

ANTHONY [*escaping*]. Well, don't let their tribulations keep you indoors too long. [*Exit*]

[*As* ANTHONY *disappears from view,* ADELAIDE *strides peremptorily to door Right, and calls in a low crisp metallic voice*]

ADELAIDE. Nina!

NINA [*re-entering nervously*]. Yes, madam!

ADELAIDE [*incisively*]. Don't lie — it's no use! He kissed you.

NINA [*confounded*]. Oh — ma'am!

ADELAIDE. How often has he done it?

NINA. Oh — ma'am!

ADELAIDE. That's all — thank you so much — [*Turning away and sitting, as if intent on a newspaper*]

NINA [*blubbering*]. Oh, ma'am! [*And that is all she can say*]

ADELAIDE [*indulgently — after a long pause*]. Why should I wish you to be discharged? You've done nothing wrong, at least, not that I know of.

NINA [*vehemently*]. Oh, no, ma'am!

ADELAIDE. And if a fascinating gentleman insists upon kissing a pretty little housemaid now and then, I don't know how she's to help herself, do you?

NINA. Indeed, madam, it would be very hard to say. [*A long pause*]

ADELAIDE [*finding banknote in her bag*]. Now, there's something for telling the truth. No one who tells the truth need be afraid of *me*. [*Pause while she seems to read paper*] After this, I may count upon you to run straight to me with any little thing you believe I

ought to know. [*Pause*] Perhaps there is some little thing I ought to know now?

NINA [*with hesitating eagerness*]. Oh, ma'am, I think — perhaps you ought to know about a little thing that happened here a few minutes ago.

ADELAIDE [*kindly*]. That is for you to decide, Nina. Nothing could be further from me than a desire to pry into matters that do not concern me.

NINA. In a way, ma'am, it does concern you.

ADELAIDE [*definitely*]. Then it's quite right I should know all about it!

NINA [*looking about shyly*]. Mr. Leavitt was here, ma'am —

ADELAIDE [*encouragingly*]. Yes?

NINA. — to tell Mr. Anthony about a man he had visiting him — a Mr. Swallow.

ADELAIDE [*concealing her consternation by a terrible fit of coughing*]. Swallow? Swallow!! Dear me, what an odd name! — But how could that possibly concern me, Nina?

NINA [*confidentially*]. There! I was sure it couldn't. And so was Mr. Anthony! At least, first he was; and then he wasn't; and then he was again; and anyway so as to make sure he told Mr. Leavitt to bring Mr. Swallow to luncheon to-day.

ADELAIDE [*after another fit of coughing, perfectly self-possessed, very gracious*]. Oh, yes, I see! How very thoughtful of him!

MRS. DE SALLE [*entering by stairs*]. Adelaide, hasn't the mail come yet?

ADELAIDE. The post, mamma? No, not yet.

MRS. DE SALLE. Oh, I do hope there's word from Marie about my hats.

[*Going Right, she espies* VIOLET *who has just entered on porch and goes out to her*]

ADELAIDE [*with a dismissing gesture to* NINA]. You have shown a very commendable spirit, my good girl —

NINA [*going, confused with pleasure*]. Oh, I'm sure, madam, it's a very great privilege. [*Exits Left*]

ADELAIDE [*going resolutely toward porch with her Yankee-est manner*]. Ma! — Violet! — Come in!

VIOLET. Why, what is it?

[*They come down anxious, apprehensive*]

ADELAIDE. You'll find out soon enough. There's a great big double-barrelled shock coming. Are you ready?

MRS. DE SALLE. Oh, Della, don't frighten me so!

ADELAIDE. Sit down! — Violet! you — sit there! [*There is a long pregnant pause.* MRS. DE SALLE *almost crouches with fear.* ADELAIDE's *eyes glitter. She crosses her arms like a general and gazes directly out toward the audience unafraid, resolute, and announces*] Pete Swallow's comin' here to lunch!

MRS. DE SALLE [*gulping with terror*]. Pete! Oh, my God!

ADELAIDE. Get a grip on yourself, Ma, and listen! Pete's over to the Leavitts' for some reason or other, and he's told Leavitt about Missionary Loop; and Anthony has invited him over here to put his story to the proof.

MRS. DE SALLE. Della, we're lost.

ADELAIDE. That's what I thought for one second, but now, well, I've changed my mind.

MRS. DE SALLE [*helpless, overwhelmed, a mortal dread*]. Oh, I want 'er know. I want 'er know.

ADELAIDE [*thinking with the speed and clear-sightedness of Napoleon*]. You're hopeless, of course. He'd recognize you; you'd lose your head; you'd begin to talk! — you've got to be sick and go to bed in a dark room!

MRS. DE SALLE [*taught to submit without protest*]. Oh, all right! All right! — But how about *you!* You was engaged to Pete!

ADELAIDE [*with smiling, metallic self-assurance*]. Yes. Ten years ago! Do you think I haven't changed since then? Do you think I'd be mistaken easily for Stella Sayles of Missionary Loop, In-diana? Watch me! if I can't knock him galley-west with my lorgnette and my English fiddle-de-dee, I miss my guess!

MRS. DE SALLE. Oh, Della, what courage!

ADELAIDE. I admit it will take some nerve, when I think of the hundreds of times I've sat in his lap. But you wait! — Violet is going to back me up. She's safe! — she was only a kid then — freckles, pigtails and the rest. With her to help me, I'll take on the contract.

VIOLET [*quietly*]. Della, I want to tell the truth.

ADELAIDE [*with a sign of irritation*]. Still twanging on that string! I thought you'd got the tune played out of you!

VIOLET. It's no use! I can't go on with Anthony any further — my mind's made up.

ADELAIDE. Well, unmake it! You're engaged to Anthony; and you're going to marry Anthony!

VIOLET [*quietly decisive*]. I won't!

MRS. DE SALLE [*with mountainous dignity*]. Violet!! Are you my daughter?

VIOLET [*quivering with defiance*]. But I tell you I won't!

MRS. DE SALLE. You'll do just as you're told! I'll have no disobedience! If you go back on us now, you'll be doing a wicked, shameful thing! Do you want to bring disgrace down on your own mother, and on your sister?

VIOLET [*desperately*]. No, no, I don't! But the truth is more important than our reputation. I can't live this way any longer — I'm stifling!

ADELAIDE [*dryly*]. Well, stifle! Stifle! 'Twon't kill ye! And when you're married, you can tell 'em all you like, for all me; but married *you shall be!* This thing has gone too far to be skwiggled out of now.

MRS. DE SALLE. Della's right!

VIOLET [*helplessly*]. Mother!

MRS. DE SALLE. Yes, *mother!* I'm your mother and I've got a right to boss you!

VIOLET [*defiantly*]. You haven't a right to sell my soul!

MRS. DE SALLE [*swelling up like a turkey*]. I forbid you to use such language to me!

VIOLET. Oh, then I'm all alone! [*Collapsing*]

MRS. DE SALLE [*with vast eloquence*]. A thousand times worse than alone, if you stand out against those who know what's for your best good. And I tell you that —

ADELAIDE [*cutting her off with decision*]. Oh, dry up, ma! I'm trying to think!

VIOLET [*frightened*]. What are you doing?

ADELAIDE. Writing.

VIOLET. Adelaide! What is it?

ADELAIDE. A telegram.

VIOLET. Who to? What about?

ADELAIDE [*matter-of-fact*]. I'm asking the Evening Chronicle to send me over the best man they've got on Long Island. I've a nice little story for them — a love story!

VIOLET [*with a cry*]. You shan't! [*Trying to seize paper*]

ADELAIDE. Sit down!

MRS. DE SALLE. Ollie! Sit down! *Do you hear me?*

ADELAIDE [*scrutinizing message*]. Yes, I'm going to have the engagement announced in the Chronicle. [*Presses bell for servant*] It will make good copy. When the reporter comes, I can even suggest headlines. [*And she seems to be reading them from an imaginary newspaper*] "English Heiress, to Wed Great-Grandson of General Anthony Rawson!" — [*To* KITSON *who enters Left*] Kitson, have this wire sent at once!

KITSON. Yes, Madam! [*Exits Right*]

VIOLET [*starting up desperately*]. No!

ADELAIDE [*checking her with authority*]. Now, Violet, you are going to do the right thing. — Violet always comes around in a crisis; only she's a proud little mustang and fights it out at every step. That's all right, I don't blame her for it. See, Violet, dear, — run along upstairs and tell Briggs to lay out my afternoon gown. There's a dear! — [*Turns to her mother as* VIOLET *exits*] Now, listen ma! [*With her handkerchief she deftly removes the bloom from* MRS. DE SALLE'S *cheeks*] You're to go and find Miss Rawson and tell her that you've had one of your sudden attacks of vertigo, and that you fear you must retire for the rest of the day. Do it nicely now. Then come upstairs and give Briggs a hand with my dressing!

MRS. DE SALLE [*faintly rebellious*]. Dell, you make me look a puffect fright!

ADELAIDE. So much the better! She'll believe you! [MRS. DE SALLE *gets to her feet obediently*] Totter a bit, can't you? Put your hand *so!* — [*Demonstrating*] Don't act so blamed healthy, Ma! — Now, what is it you're going to say? You haven't the least idea, have you! [*Encouragingly, to her*] "My dear Miss Rawson, I'm so sorry" —

MRS. DE SALLE [*repeating parrot-like*]. My dear Miss Rawson, I'm so sorry, but — [*Again at a loss*]

ADELAIDE [*encouragingly*]. "But I've just had" —

MRS. DE SALLE. But I've just had one of my *terrible* —

ADELAIDE. Oh, don't be middle class! "But I've just had one of my queer little attacks — vertigo, you know — and I fear" —

MRS. DE SALLE [*taking the cue from her and performing in her best high society manner*]. — One of my queer little attacks, vertigo, you know — and I fear

— [*And now she finishes triumphantl*] I must retire for the rest of the day!

ADELAIDE. You look as if you w glad o' the chance, — but no matter! - There! Now, trot along!

MRS. DE SALLE [*turning before exi*] I don't see why it need to be for all da Couldn't it pass off after a while?

ADELAIDE. Yes, of course — tell h that. Tell her you never know, b sometimes they do pass off; and whe the creature goes, I'll get word to yc and have you let out! That is — *if* v *win!*

MRS. DE SALLE [*hands desperate clasped*]. God help us! [*Exits*]

ADELAIDE [*collecting her various belon ings, with a hard undaunted smil*] "God help us!" indeed! [*Breaks in buoyant laughter*] Well, why not? W help ourselves! [*Is going by stairs*]

CURTAIN

ACT II

SCENE. — *Same as* ACT I. *One hour late*

MISS RAWSON *is standing just outsi porch door, scrutinizing the lunche table, which is supposed to stand c porch off Right, and speaking* KITSON, *who is invisible.*

MISS RAWSON. Yes, Kitson, th will do very well.

KITSON [*appearing*]. Thank yo madam.

MISS RAWSON. There will be on eight of us after all.

KITSON. Only eight, madam?

MISS RAWSON. Mrs. de Salle w not be down.

KITSON. Very good, madam.

MISS RAWSON [*to herself, with syr pathetic recollection*]. Dear me, ho very ill she seemed! [*Sits with impatie air*] You spoke to Mr. Geoffrey?

KITSON. Yes, madam, I told hi you desired to see him.

GEOFFREY [*entering from porc briskly*]. You wanted me, Aunt Al gail?

MISS RAWSON. Yes! Decidedl I hear that you are not expecting favor us with your presence at lunch!

GEOFFREY [*at a loss for an explan tion*]. I — why — [*Kicking the rug wi his toe*] What's the use? You kno that's not my style of thing.

MISS RAWSON [*with severity*]. Don

ge that as an excuse. It's high time
u adopted the style. Your absence
ould be a slight to the Leavitts as well
 to Anthony and the de Salles.

GEOFFREY [*with boyish awkwardness*].
ou know what a mess I make of every-
ing, Aunt Abigail! We don't go in
uch for piddy-widdy in New Mexico.

MISS RAWSON. We will put all that
ide. [*Rising*] I insist that you be
resent whether you like it or not! All
e more because of your ill-timed out-
reak this morning. [*Scrutinizing him
ith disapproval*] Make yourself pre-
ntable! [*With a gesture she refuses to
sten to him*] And do not oblige me to
nd for you when the time comes.
xit with stateliness into study]

[*s GEOFFREY starts to leave the room
VIOLET enters from stairs*]

VIOLET [*quivering with anxiety*].
eoffrey! Geoffrey! Can I speak to
ou?

GEOFFREY [*startled*]. Why, of course!

VIOLET [*hurrying to him*]. I've some-
ing — terribly important — to ask
ou!

GEOFFREY. Me!

VIOLET. Yes. There isn't anybody
se.

GEOFFREY [*fraternally*]. Why, Violet,
hat is it?

VIOLET. I — I — [*Losing her cour-
ge*] Oh, I don't know that I'd better,
fter all.

GEOFFREY [*encouragingly*]. Are you
fraid of me?

VIOLET [*shyly*]. Well — listen!
nd she takes the plunge excitedly]
uppose a girl had been telling lies to
verybody all her life, without really
nowing how mean and wrong it was,
nd suppose finally some — er — some-
ing made her see it all in a different
ay. Don't you think — [*With an
ncoherent outburst*] Oh, Geoffrey, —
ometimes it's just awfully hard to know
hat's right, isn't it? I don't know
hat to do, because it isn't just myself,
ou see. And oh, if I do what I think
 ought to, it'll make everybody so
nhappy! [*Pathetic in her helplessness*]

GEOFFREY [*earnestly*]. But you really
hink you ought to do it?

VIOLET [*gaining confidence*]. I do!
 really do! Yes, my mind's made up.
'm going to tell the truth, even if I have
o hate myself forever and ever. It'll
e better than this, anyway. Oh,
lease tell me I have the courage!

GEOFFREY [*taking her hands firmly*].
If it's something you really ought to do,
I *know* you have the courage!

VIOLET [*impulsively*]. Oh, Geoffrey!
[*Releasing her hands and running to
stairs*]. Perhaps, when I've done this
thing, you'll never speak to me again.

GEOFFREY. Can't I help you, Violet?

VIOLET [*from the stairs*]. You *have*
helped me! When the time comes, I
know I can do it.

[*Exits, GEOFFREY looks after her an instant with frank adoration, then turns
as ANTHONY enters from porch*]

ANTHONY [*with an innuendo*]. Oh,
you're here! I was looking for you.

GEOFFREY [*matter-of-fact*]. Well,
that's unusual business.

ANTHONY. Failing to find you at the
pig-pen, I tried several less likely spots:
— the kennels, the cabbage patch, and
so on, — this last of all.

GEOFFREY. Well, what can I do for
you?

ANTHONY [*with irritation*]. You can
listen to me for about one minute.
You're paying decidedly too much attention to Violet, and I don't like it.
She may, for all I know; but that's not
the point.

GEOFFREY [*quietly*]. The point is —?

ANTHONY [*brutally direct*]. The point
is: she's engaged to *me*! The point is:
— hands off!

GEOFFREY [*with self-control*]. What
do you imply by that?

ANTHONY [*cuttingly*]. Do you wish
me to specify?

GEOFFREY [*facing him directly*]. Yes,
specify!

ANTHONY [*with a look at the stairs*].
I'll specify some other time. It's
enough just now for you to understand
me!

GEOFFREY. *Understand* you!

ANTHONY. Yes, I say: understand
me! [*Very clearly and bitingly, to GEOF-
FREY who is now at the door*] Do you —
understand me?

GEOFFREY [*giving him a look of unspeakable contempt*]. Oh, yes — yes —
I understand you! [*Exit to study*]

[ANTHONY *is unpleasantly startled; but
recovers himself, with a shrug of
cynical amusement, and after an
instant's delay, touches bell for
servant*]

NINA [*entering promptly*]. Oh, you
rang, Mr. Anthony?

ANTHONY [*with a cautioning gesture*]. Come here! [NINA *comes, a little backwardly*] Don't be afraid. I'm not going to eat you.

NINA. I know — but —

ANTHONY [*reassuringly*]. That's all right. One scare a day is enough for my nerves, too. [*Coming closer, in lower voice*] Tell me, did Mrs. Bumpstead-Leigh suspect anything?

NINA [*outrageously reassuring*]. Oh, no, Mr. Anthony, not a thing!

ANTHONY [*a little insistent, a little wheedling*]. Not a thing? Are you sure?

NINA [*eyes innocently wide*]. Oh, *sure!*

[*Enter* KITSON *from Right, crosses Left, with a tray. He passes the two without seeming to observe*]

ANTHONY. Didn't she speak to you?

NINA. Yes, Mr. Anthony, but not about that.

ANTHONY. Good! [*Coming closer*] Nina, you're a very clever little girl, and — [*At this moment he becomes aware of* KITSON'S *presence and immediately alters his tone and manner to one of severest censure*] — and I hope that I shall not have to speak to you again about it. I do not want any such thing to happen again! [*By this time* KITSON *has gone out, Left, and* ANTHONY *now tweaks her ear laughingly*] You little imp, you, what makes you so irresistible, anyway!

NINA [*archly*]. Oh, I'm sure, Mr. Anthony!

ANTHONY. Listen, don't you think we might manage to be even better friends? [*He is tempted to kiss her, but an impulse of caution holds him*] We must find a place some time where there's not so much coming and going — eh? [*Chucks her chin and exits*]

[NINA *has just turned to go when* KITSON *re-enters Left with silver coffee service*]

KITSON [*not putting down his burden*]. Well, I see you're at it again!

NINA [*with an indifferent shrug*]. Humph!

KITSON [*sagaciously*]. Smear yourself with honey; you'll hear the flies buzz.

NINA [*attempting vainly to pass him*]. Oh! — what talk!

KITSON. You're a proud little baggage, ain't ye! You're a-going to have your fun, ain't ye! It wouldn't mean

nothing to you, I suppose, would it, I was to tell you — [*halting himse with a significant shake of the head*] what I *could* tell you, an' I *would*, abo Mr. Anthony!

NINA. What *could* you tell me: got to know that first.

KITSON. Tell ye? Hst! [*Very dar ly*] Did you ever hear about po Mamie Tanner?

NINA [*imitating his tone*]. No, never heard about poor *Mamie Tanne* What about her?

KITSON [*with melodramatic impre siveness*]. What *about* her? — We that's something I don't intend to te to a living soul, young lady, so long I'm in Mr. Rawson's service. Go dow on your two knees to me if you lik My lips are sealed. You'll get nothin

NINA. Pooh! I can't see why yo should be so terrible close about it.

KITSON. Ye can't, eh?

NINA [*her curiosity at last arousea*] Go on! Tell!

KITSON [*drawing himself up*]. The is such a thing as family, young lad though *you* may not happen to hav heard of it. I've been five and twen years in the service of Mr. Rawso [*And he looks it*]

NINA. Do you mean to tell me eve Mr. Rawson don't know?

KITSON [*sepulchrally*]. If Mr. Raw son was once to find out — Oh! — O! But as I've many a time said to mysel — Kitson, your lips are sealed! — L 'em bring on their king's horses. L 'em bring on their king's men. They not pry a word out o' me.

NINA [*taking a new tack*]. Oh, pshaw You're just putting on airs to scare m

KITSON [*superior to all temptation* Very well. Very well. Have it just you like. But you can't say I haven done my duty by you. Now go and fi up the sandwiches! — And, remembe you're warned. [*Exits to porch*]

[NINA *goes out Left, with a piqued expre sion as* MISS RAWSON *is seen on th porch. She stops a moment scrutinize the luncheon table*]

MISS RAWSON. Yes, that is ver good. — Have Nina put some flowe there — [*indicating*] — a vase of cosmo I should think — or single asters.

MRS. LEAVITT [*who is seen to join h outside on the porch and now enters th room in her company*]. My dear Mis Rawson, really! I don't know *what* t ay! It's simply outrageous that Ste-hen should have insisted on bringing im over — I did my best —

A group consisting of LEAVITT, AN-THONY *and* SWALLOW *now appears on the porch.* PETER SWALLOW, *the central figure, conspicuous for the pseudo-Broadway cut of his clothes, faces towards the view, and to judge by his oratorical gestures is cease-lessly talking*]

MISS RAWSON [*consolingly to* MRS. LEAVITT]. There, there! Not another word, my dear! Anthony has explained everything. He was sure we would find im entertaining.

MRS. LEAVITT. At all events, the agony will soon be over. He takes the ne-seventeen.

MISS RAWSON. But I ordered lunch or one o'clock.

MRS. LEAVITT. Good! Don't sit down till he's gone.

KITSON *is taking* SWALLOW'S *hat and stick*]

JUSTIN [*entering from study*]. Mrs. Leavitt! How do you do! [*Shaking hands*] This time you are going to see our English Violet.

MRS. LEAVITT. I can hardly wait. Mrs. Bumpstead-Leigh has simply taken me by storm. Oh, how happy you all must be.

JUSTIN. We are!

MISS RAWSON. Our guests have ar-rived, you see, Justin. [*Indicating the porch*]

MRS. LEAVITT [*pointing to* SWALLOW *with comic desperation*]. That center-piece — that monument-like affair — that's — that's — Oh, Miss Rawson, do take me somewhere!

[MISS RAWSON *laughingly takes her under her wing and the two are about to exit, Right, when* SWALLOW *turning, per-ceives* MISS RAWSON, *and intercepts with exuberant cordiality.* PETER SWALLOW *is a joint product of the unsophisticated Middle West and sophisticated East. The heartiness and simplicity of his behavior com-bine strangely with his egregious self-esteem and his uncontrollable pleasure in hearing himself talk. He thinks his clothes quite the last word in the matter of style, — and so indeed they are*]

SWALLOW [*beaming upon* MISS RAW-SON]. And this, if I be not mistaken, is the old Auntie! Your years rest lightly upon you, madam — as lightly as the snow upon a new-made grave!

MISS RAWSON. You flatter me! — Come, Lottie! [*The ladies escape*]

SWALLOW [*standing in the doorway, incapable of checking the flow of his own words*]. Nice old lady! — As I was sayin', gentlemen, a callin' like mine gives a man a very pretty eye for land-scapey effects. Take a nice artistic tombstun now — say one of these monu-ments o' the Cleopatry's Needle type: — she got to be placed in a certain par-ticular way to give the very handsomest impression. You can't set 'er in a hole in the ground, it's like she was a-hollerin' out for some commandin' eminence — [*Pauses and wheels round toward ocean view, while his hand seems to be picking out a suitable site*]

LEAVITT [*ready to introduce him*]. Excuse me, Mr. Swallow, but I should like —

SWALLOW [*utterly ignoring the other's effort*]. There! Say like that 'ere sand-hill, over yonder, — supposin' all this country to be one mighty cemetery, with the eternal sea, Old Ocean, with his thunders, beyond! — that's the site for your needle! — An' put some simple, elegant mottah on her base, like *hope*, in 9-inch, high-relief letterin'. — You catch the eye at once; and similarly you create a dignified, noble and solemn effect, — in short, a 9-inch effect!

LEAVITT [*more insistently*]. Mr. Swallow, I want to make you —

SWALLOW [*quite oblivious*]. Or take the two words, *I sleep* — that's an especially chaste, very modern senti-ment that's goin' the rounds in certain sections where we do business. But, on the other hand —

LEAVITT [*desperately*]. Excuse me, Mr. Swallow, but I want you to meet Mr. Rawson.

JUSTIN [*shaking hands with* SWALLOW]. How do you do, sir!

SWALLOW [*setting by his cigar, with a lingering look of regret and fully entering the apartment*]. It's a privilege, sir, to shake hands with so notorious and hon-orable a bulwark of American finance! Your name, sir, is a synonym for a sound and conservative commercial policy, not only in Hoboken, where we have the honor of doing the largest monument business in the State of New

Jersey, but equally throughout the length and breadth of my own native state of Indiana, the population-center of this great land of ours. To be known and favorably known, in Indiana, is therefore equivalent to being known *everywhere!* —

JUSTIN. Indeed!

ANTHONY [*with amusement*]. There's logic for you!

SWALLOW. "Hark to the voice of Indiana," whisper the Sister States. "It is the voice of the people; and the voice of the people — Vox populi, Vox Dei — is the voice of God."

JUSTIN [*with veiled irony*]. You overwhelm me, sir!

SWALLOW. Thank you; thank you, sir. You honor me too much in saying so. Yet yours, Sir, is in all truth an enviable lot. Fame, wealth, position, honors — all are yours! From a pinnacle of self-satisfied serenity you may look down upon the puny struggles of your fellow men. This beautiful and luxurious villa, sir, is in itself, an emblem and monument to your success. This handsome young financeer, your son, is, as I well see, the pride and joy of his father's heart.

ANTHONY [*to* LEAVITT]. There you have me.

SWALLOW. Nor need I ask whether the stalwart fellow I met yonder on the garden walk is also a scion of the House of Rawson: — No! for I saw the father in the son's eyes!

ANTHONY [*to* LEAVITT]. Good for Geoffrey!

SWALLOW. Congratulations, sir, upon the two of them: — a brace of Romans! [*Again shakes hands vehemently*]

JUSTIN. Thank you.

SWALLOW [*to* ANTHONY]. I make bold to postulate that your brother is your companion and rival in mounting the high ladder of plutocratic attainment.

ANTHONY. Geoffrey's interests are along quite different lines. Lately he has taken up farming.

SWALLOW [*delighted to find a new theme for his eloquence*]. A farmer! Well, God prosper the farmer, say I, and say it with all my heart and soul. Why, Agriculture, sir, is the very bone and sinew of this great Commonwealth of ours. "Stay by the farm, young man" is my counsel to the restless, city-bedazzled youth of to-day. I have lived the life of cities; I have known it

to the innermost, worm-infested core
ANTHONY. How interesting!

SWALLOW. And it ain't what i cracked up to be, my young friend; sir, not by a long sight! Temptatio spawn and fester in them busy marts traffic: —

ANTHONY. Quite true.

SWALLOW. Vice stalks abroad, a tired in the spangled witcheries Delilah. —

ANTHONY. Yes, yes.

SWALLOW [*infatuated with his o volubility*]. But in the country, f from the maddening crowd — ah, the one may breathe God's own pure a drink water, *water*, from the old oak bucket that hangs in the well, and, short, live as they was intended to liv by an all-wise, all-powerful Creato [*Stops, quite out of breath*]

JUSTIN. I am surprised, sir, you d not take up oratory as a vocation.

SWALLOW. Oratory! Ha! sa we're all like that in Indiana. W imbibe it with our mother's milk. T state resounds and echoes with it fro boreal north to sunny south; and fro Orient east to sunset west. It was th little oratorical gift of mine — my silv tongue, as friends are wont to speak it — that first pointed the way to m success in the tombstone business.

JUSTIN. Indeed!

SWALLOW. My Indiana birthright is that's landed me where I am; a I'm grateful, and deeply grateful, to t Mother State that brought me forth.

JUSTIN. You ought to be.

SWALLOW [*remembering his erran* But say — where are the petticoats?

ANTHONY [*coolly*]. Mrs. Bumpstea Leigh and Miss de Salle will be dow directly. [*Turns to* LEAVITT]

SWALLOW [*to* JUSTIN]. And the o girl?

JUSTIN [*chillingly*]. Mrs. de Salle ill. I fear you will not have the chan to see *her*.

SWALLOW [*to* JUSTIN]. Look a-her She didn't know I was a-comin', d she?

JUSTIN. By some oversight, I ne lected to inform her.

SWALLOW. That's very cleverly sai sir; but I mean it quite contrariwis and no offense taken or given. [*With manifest wink at* ANTHONY]

ANTHONY [*not returning the win* Mr. Swallow tells me he has the greate curiosity to meet Mrs. Bumpstea

,eigh, never having talked to a lady
earing a hyphenated name.

SWALLOW. True it is, though I
,ight add that I recently had the priv-
ege of fillin' a order for a hyphenated
ombstun, — four names, in all —
,hirty-six letters, includin' the hyphen,
,hich counts exactly like a letter; and
,ll to go on one line.

ANTHONY. One line! [*Amused*]

LEAVITT. Quite a problem!

SWALLOW. Not for me! I recom-
,ended one o' these here broad stuns —
road and low.

ANTHONY. Oh, yes!

SWALLOW. A block o' pink Rhode
,sland granite, polished so you could
,ount your teeth in it, and on top, a sort
,f sofa-pilluh in white marble, with a
,ery chaste fringe and tassuls at the
,orners. The whole effect was stylish,
nd up-to-date, —

ANTHONY. It sounds so!

SWALLOW. And the name, "Gwen-
,olyn Frederika Threadingwell, hyphen,
,mith" showed up most handsome,
,ardly seemin' to require the customary
,' In Memory of'" above it.

JUSTIN. I can easily understand
,hat.

SWALLOW. I may declare without
,oastin' that our company pays more
,ttention to the artistic features of its
,ortuary memorials than any other
,hroughout the length and breadth of
,his country; and in case any of you in
,his house should ever be under the sad
,ecessity — as Mr. Leavitt here is at the
,resent moment — of considerin' a
,uitable monument, even so modest a
,onument as a slab of granite so gray —
,s the hymn well says, gray being the
,heapest variety — I take pleasure in
,eavin' a few o' my professional cards.
[*Is about to hand one to* LEAVITT *but
,ecollects himself*] Oh, you've got one!
[*Passes cards to* ANTHONY *and* JUSTIN]
All inquiries receive the promptest
,ttention. Our representatives are
,leased to make calls even when there
,s no immediate prospect of doin' any
,usiness — just to size up the field, as
,ou might say.

JUSTIN. That's certainly enterprise.

SWALLOW. Enterprise! Well, that's
,what you need in the monument busi-
,ness. You never know when a good
,thing may drop your way. [*Suddenly
,recalling his errand*] But, say Leavitt —
,what time does my train go? [*Consult-
,ing watch*]

LEAVITT. One-seventeen, Mr. Swallow.

SWALLOW. Ahem! Say it don't look
like I was goin' to have time to eat with
the folks, does it?

JUSTIN. But I think there's a dining
car on the train, Mr. Swallow.

SWALLOW. Diner? Cough up a dollar for fancy victuals that ain't worth
thirty cents? Not for Swallow!

JUSTIN [*curtly*]. I will have Kitson
bring you a bite.

SWALLOW [*beaming*]. That will suit
me to a T, thank you very kindly — if
it wouldn't be much bother.

JUSTIN [*impatiently*]. Oh, no, no!
Not at all. [*Exits to porch*]

SWALLOW [*perfectly at ease as he seats
himself with crossed legs and relights
his cigar*]. Talk about your Easterners
bein' stiff! *I* never could see it.
Wherever I go throughout the length
and breadth of this great country of
ours, I find a handshake and an open
heart. I say, look for what you expect
and that's what you'll see. You kow-
tow to people and naturally they play
the top-lofty. Treat 'em like they was
equals and old friends, and old friends
they be thence and forever. [*To* AN-
THONY] Say can't you hurry up your
bunch of English swells? I came here
to look 'em over, and I don't intend to
get left.

ANTHONY. Don't worry. There's
plenty of time yet.

SWALLOW [*with patronizing heartiness*].
So you reckoned you was going to marry
a *dee* Salle, did you, young man? [*And
he laughs at the comedy of it*]

ANTHONY [*cautioningly*]. Don't
speak so loud!

SWALLOW [*naïve as a schoolboy*].
Why, ain't the rest going to get let in on
the joke?

ANTHONY. Not until I know for
certain there *is* a joke. I must see with
my own eyes.

SWALLOW. You'll see fast enough!
Just wait till she finds out who's here.
If I can't knock her galley-west with one
crook of my little finger, my name ain't
Pete Swallow.

ANTHONY. You certainly show no
lack of confidence.

SWALLOW. Why should I? I'd like
to know. You've heard the whole
story, yourself — don't it fit? Ain't it
a perfect dove-tail? Don't it make her
out to be the prettiest, smartest bunch
of lies that ever come down the pike? —

Oh, and it ain't as if she wasn't capable of it, neither, no, sir! — the little monkey — the pert little monkey! [*Becomes lost in reminiscent dreams*]

ANTHONY. You haven't told us how this Della Sayles looked.

SWALLOW [*as in a trance of memory*]. Ain't I? Fourteen hands high she was — just up to my shoulder. Neat, trim, handsome, with the smartest little foot and ankle a girl ever showed; and a waist, — well, sir it was a waist; and when I say a waist, well — there's nothing more to be said. "Della, you little puss", I used often to say to her, as she was a-settin' here, [*Indicating his lap*] of a late evenin' in front o' the old base-burner, — "Della, you little puss, where'd you ever get a waist like that? Your ma ain't got one. Your Dad's a regular rhinoceros. But *you* — well, the wasp and the butterfly are your only rivals in the waist line, my dear." And she'd laugh, and laugh, and like as not box my ears in play, and so it would go, night after night! — Oh happy days! Happy days! [*Dreams with pensive smile*]

ANTHONY. But her features, you haven't spoken of them. What were they like?

SWALLOW [*still in his trance*]. A flower garden, sir, a flower garden. The rose vying with the lily — and her eyes — blue as forget-me-nots.

ANTHONY [*half to himself*]. Mrs. Bumpstead-Leigh has blue eyes.

SWALLOW. Forget-me-nots! [*Roused from trance*] Forget-me-nots! Well, by gosh, she went and forgot *me* quick enough! She gave me the go-by, and gave it good and hard. At first I was deeply embittered; life was a howling wilderness of despair. Oh, but one gets over them things. — For a few weeks, young man, *your* loss will seem a big thing to you, very like; but then you'll begin to look about you again, and remember there's other fish in the sea. It's that thought lightens the tragedy.

ANTHONY. It's not my case we're discussing, if you please.

SWALLOW. Ahem! A little wee bit sensitive, ain't ye! Well, I don't blame ye, young feller. I was myself. I'd wince. I'd chew my lip. I'd flare up against my best friend! Oh, but if I hadn't been love-blind, I might have known all along what was booked to happen. She was an odd kid — Della Sayles — restless, finicky, with more

ideers in her head than does a woma any good. And, for stage-acting - well, I never seen Burnhart, but one out in Indianapolis I ran up against tha Guinea headliner, Dooze — Elinor Dooze: you heard of her, of course She was playing Adrienne Vancouver th night I saw her. Pooh! Pooh! Yo call that acting? Why, my little Dell could put the kibosh all over her, an never let on she was acting at all! Tha was just the trouble, ye never could tell [*Enter* KITSON *with tray of eatables f* SWALLOW] Well, I reckon her game called on her this time. It's her finish [*As he now looks over the tray critically*] Thanks. — Say, waiter, ain't you go any English mustard in the house?

KITSON. Yes, sir.

SWALLOW. Well, bring me som mustard and a cup of coffee and som loaf sugar.

KITSON [*much insulted*]. Anythin else, sir?

SWALLOW. Well, throw in a couple o toothpicks, and I'll be fixed first rate [*Exit* KITSON]

[*Enter* ADELAIDE *by stairs followed b* VIOLET]

LEAVITT. Here are the ladies now.

ADELAIDE. Ah, Mr. Leavitt — thi is delightful.

[*Never was* MRS. BUMPSTEAD-LEIGH *more unapproachably the lady of hig degree, brilliant, sure of herself dazzlingly alert and dominating and of course she carries her lorgnette embattled woman's unmatchabl weapon*]

SWALLOW [*jumping up with a bound*] Della Sayles!!

ADELAIDE [*examining this stranger wit a certain air of startled offence*]. I beg your pardon. [*Bewildered, to* ANTHONY Why, Anthony dear — what is this? I had not been informed.

ANTHONY [*wincing in spite of himself but then, with steady incisiveness*]. Permit me, Mrs. Bumpstead-Leigh, to introduce Mr. Swallow — Mr. Peter Swallow, of Indiana.

ADELAIDE [*distantly*]. Pleased, I'm sure. [*She turns to* VIOLET *as if considering the advisability of withdrawal*] Violet, dear, I fear we have come down too soon.

SWALLOW. Not at all, not at all, madam. I have only a few minutes to stay, and I was particularly anxious to get in a few words with you.

ADELAIDE. Words with *me?* [*And again she seems about to withdraw, much puzzled, you would say, and certainly somewhat offended*]

ANTHONY [*anxious to account acceptably for the intruding presence*]. Mr. Swallow is ambitious to make the acquaintance of an English lady of your position, Mrs. Bumpstead-Leigh. He will consider it a great favor on your part if you will consent to stay.

ADELAIDE [*still distantly*]. I see. Oh, charmed, I'm sure. [*Turns ignoringly away, and joins* LEAVITT *on the other side of the room*]

ANTHONY [*continuing the introductions watchfully*]. Miss de Salle; Mr. Swallow.

VIOLET [*cordially and with some manner*]. I am so pleased to meet another of Mr. Rawson's friends. But where are the rest, Anthony? — Have they deserted you?

SWALLOW. No matter about the rest, Miss. It was you and your sister I wanted to see. — The rest can go ding!

VIOLET [*puzzled*]. Dear, dear! Is that a compliment, Mr. Swallow?

SWALLOW. Take it whatever way you like, young lady. I know what I mean by it, and that's enough for now.

VIOLET. Oh, dear. You've aroused my curiosity. I must tell Adelaide about it! [*Joins* LEAVITT *and* ADELAIDE *and converses*]

[SWALLOW *returning to his meal, speaks apart to* ANTHONY]

SWALLOW [*profoundly intrigued*]. Well, I take the count!

ANTHONY [*rather brusquely*]. You went wide of the mark. That's clear!

SWALLOW [*stoutly*]. The young one stumps me. The other — well, she looks like Della Sayles, and she don't look like Della Sayles. Darn'd if I know which way she looks most. — But I ain't done yet, no, sir! [*Takes his plate to sofa, Right, and begins to eat with enjoyment*]

ADELAIDE [*to* LEAVITT]. Pray don't apologize my dear Mr. Leavitt. I wish to be familiar with every phase of your complex social problems over here. [*And they stroll up to the piano and continue a vivid conversation*]

VIOLET [*sitting on the sofa beside* MR. SWALLOW, *ingratiatingly*]. I'm going to sit down by you, Mr. Swallow. I

know we two will get along famously together.

SWALLOW [*in midst of mouthful*]. I usually manage to get along with the young ones.

VIOLET. I shudder to think how many hearts you have captured.

SWALLOW [*immensely flattered, shaking his fork at her*]. Now — now!

ANTHONY [*to* VIOLET *with irony*]. You will find Mr. Swallow a brilliant conversationalist.

SWALLOW [*pleased*]. I don't know as I can do myself justice, while I'm takin' in food; but I'll try to live up to my reputation. — Say where's that waiter with the mustard?

VIOLET. It's really too bad, Mr. Swallow, you can't stay to lunch. You would love it! And then, too, we shall have seen so very little of each other before you must go!

SWALLOW. Quite true, quite true, young lady. But it's the same way all through this life of ours. We go and come like autumn leaves before the blast; here to-day, to-morrow whither? Perhaps — as my callin' so frequently reminds me — perhaps under the sod.

VIOLET [*naïvely*]. Ah, what a beautiful sentiment! You must repeat it for my sister. — Adelaide, I have asked Mr. Swallow to repeat an exquisite thought he has just expressed.

ADELAIDE [*raising her lorgnette*]. Mr. Swallow? Oh yes, — pray let us hear it.

SWALLOW [*handing his plate to* VIOLET]. Hold this, little one! I was simply remarkin' — [*Rises and approaches* ADELAIDE] Mrs. Bumpstead-Leigh, upon the transitory nature of all life; and I said it might be compared to autumn leaves, which go and come, whence nor whither who can say?

ADELAIDE [*with a humorously rapt look*]. Who indeed! [*Graciously condescending*] Charming — charming — and so very original. Might I inquire, do you write poetry?

SWALLOW [*sitting*]. I am said to be pretty slick at turning an epitaph, but along other lines I have deserted the Muse since the age of twenty-five years. — Yet, now that we are speakin' of Po'try, Madam, my thoughts are carried backward to those more youthful days and to faces that were nigh in the long ago; and I am strangely reminded by your countenance of one who was very dear to me when I was still, as the poet Gray has it, a youth to fortune and to fame unknown.

ADELAIDE [*sympathetic, — with a wink of immense amusement at* LEAVITT]. Fancy! I am sorry if I have awakened painful memories of one gone before!

SWALLOW. "Gone before!" That's just what she ain't — leastways not to my knowledge. The go-by is what she gave me. That was in Missionary Loop, Indiana, where I resided until my twenty-seventh year. Was you ever there, might I ask?

ADELAIDE [*with a blank look*]. Washington was our home, Mr. Sparrow —

SWALLOW. Swallow, if you please, ma'am.

ADELAIDE [*utterly ignoring the correction*]. Washington was our home in the old days. I have traveled very little in this country; but my present visit teaches me how much I have missed by not knowing it better. Is this Missionary Loo an interesting town? I do not remember to have met the name in Baedecker.

VIOLET [*with great interest*]. I suppose Missionary Loo was one of your early settlers who carried the Gospel to the Indians.

SWALLOW [*rising*]. Loop, Miss, Loop. Not Loo.

ADELAIDE. Loop, my dear, Loop. — Make a note of it!

SWALLOW. Sister's got it. The town is chiefly famous, ladies, because it was the home of old Jim Sayles, proprietor of Sayles's Sissapoola Indian Herb Remedies, which are known and used up and down the length and breadth of this country. —

ADELAIDE. Indian Herb Remedies! Fancy!

VIOLET. How very romantic!

SWALLOW. Well, I don't know what mottah is graved on Old Jim's headstone in Missionary Loop; but I can tell you what it ought to 'a been: — H — O — A — X.

ADELAIDE [*in doubt*]. H — O — A — X — hoax? Have I the word aright? — Oh! I begin to understand! — Violet, my dear, did you notice the very interesting Americanism Mr. Swallow has just given us — H — O — A — X — ? I have heard of it before; a corruption I believe, of our English *Hocus Pocus*. So this Mr. Sayles of Missionary Loop made pretentions for his remedies which were not warranted by facts. Dear me! How very dreadful!

SWALLOW. Yes. Wasn't it! and here's another for you, madam. Old Jim had two daughters.

ADELAIDE. Two daughters! Fancy! And did they have Indian names also?

SWALLOW. Well, the name of the oldest, ma'am was *Della*, and to *me* she plighted her troth.

ADELAIDE [*sympathetically*]. Ah, and it is she, then, who is the painful memory, Mr. Shallow?

SWALLOW [*balked for a moment by her new mis-nomenclature but too resolute to be diverted from the scent*]. Yes — and may I venture to ask you, madam, one question outright and flat-foot?

ADELAIDE [*immensely entertained*]. Flat-foot?— Oh, why, certainly! *Flatfoot!*

SWALLOW. And you promise to answer it in the same way?

ADELAIDE. You mean flat-feet?

SWALLOW. I do.

ADELAIDE [*exchanging an amused look with* LEAVITT]. Very well. I am at your disposition.

SWALLOW [*with direct challenge*]. What was your father's business?

ADELAIDE [*blankly*]. Business — Business — Papa —?

SWALLOW. Why, didn't your Pa *have* a business, lady?

ADELAIDE. Why, no! — not in the legitimate, accepted sense of the word. Oh, it would be quite improper to refer to papa's activities as business, — I mean, of course, except in a very special understanding of the term.

SWALLOW. Well, what *was* he then?

ADELAIDE [*filially tender*]. Dear papa was a philanthropist.

SWALLOW. A what?

ADELAIDE. His life was dedicated to Humanity. His name is blessed to-day in a thousand homes. I find it hard to speak to a stranger of poor dear papa: but you see you had my promise in advance. [*And the subject is evidently closed henceforth*]

SWALLOW [*recovering himself with a great effort after this momentary knockout*]. We was speaking, you remember, about this here Sayles family; and I was about to remark that after the death of Old Jim, and the moving away of the family from Missionary Loop, it got noised about that they had changed their name to *de Salle* and was residing in the National Capital.

ADELAIDE [*incredulously*]. In *Washington?*

Swallow [*doggedly*]. The same, Madam.

Adelaide. Dear me! How very odd! If such were the case, I am at a loss to understand why we should never have known of it, — the name, as you see, being identical with ours. Violet, dear, did you ever hear of any other de Salles in Washington?

Violet. Never. But probably these people Mr. Swallow tells of had no social standing.

Adelaide. Oh, of course! I understand that perfectly. Yet I wonder the *letters* never went wrong. — Ah, but now a thought comes! Did not the family of whom you speak, Mr. Wallow, spell the prefix with the Capital D?

Swallow [*baffled*]. I dunno anything about that.

Adelaide [*giving instruction with authority*]. The name de Salle is spelled in a number of ways, though our branch of the family has invariably employed the small D — comme en français, n'est-ce pas? — le petit signe de la noblesse! — But I remember even to have seen it spelled, in an old volume of memoirs — [*And she seems to search her memory*] Annales d'une famille ancienne de la Nourmandie, par Geoffroi — yes, par Geoffroi! — as a single word thus — Capital D, E, small S, A, double L, E, — curious wasn't it! — in which case it would afford an interesting analogy, would it not, with the Scotch Mac-Donald, which, as you of course know, is capable of at least three variants.

Swallow [*flabbergasted*]. A three bagger!

Adelaide [*to Leavitt, immensely amused*]. A what? — Oh, how delicious!

Swallow [*recovering again, and supplying by loudness what he has lost in confidence*]. Well, as I said, the young lady to whom I was betrothed was named Della, and it seems to me that you are the *exact* and *identical* image of her!

Adelaide [*seeming slightly offended*]. Indeed, sir!

Violet [*merrily*]. I do believe Mr. Swallow is hinting, Adelaide, that you would be a welcome substitute!

Adelaide [*reprovingly*]. Violet, dear, you know how I dislike to have a jest made of sacred subjects! I am sure Mr. Swallow could have no idea *whatever* of exceeding the bounds of the strictest propriety in my presence.

Swallow [*with violent conviction*]. Never again, Pete! Never again! [*Rising*]

Adelaide [*as if startled*]. Never again? What does he mean? Have I made some terrible *faux pas?* Have I been *gauche?*

Swallow. Oh, that's all right, madam. It ain't often that Pete Swallow puts his foot into the wrong puddle. I will say that for myself!

Adelaide [*with concern to Leavitt*]. Oh, but I don't understand. The poor fellow seems quite disordered.

Leavitt. No cause for concern, dear Lady! It's likely nothing but indigestion.

Geoffrey [*entering hastily from porch*]. Excuse me, Mr. Swallow, but it's getting very near your train time. You'll have to hurry!

Leavitt [*to* Adelaide]. Pardon me! [*He starts quickly for the porch*] I told my man to have the machine here in good season. Has he come yet?

Geoffrey. Yes, he's at the gate.

[*Exit* Leavitt *as* Kitson *enters with* Swallow's *coat, etc.*]

Swallow. Well, I reckon it's time I was a-hikin' anyhow. — There's no bokays comin' my way, I notice.

[Kitson *helps him into automobile coat*]

Violet [*rising quickly and starting to leave the room; but she pauses for one eager tremulous word with* Geoffrey]. Nobody'll ever forgive me, but I'm going to do it! I'm going to do it! [*Exit, followed after an instant by* Geoffrey]

Adelaide. But surely you are not going without a word of good-bye, Mr. Swallow?

Swallow. [*coming to her for his valedictory*]. One word, lady, and that's all. Time and tide wait for no man! and in the end Death cuts down all! The moral is: get busy! As a detective I may be a fizzle: but as a monumentalist, I'm right on the spot — with the goods! There's my card! One of these days you might be requiring a nice, up-to-date, artistic memorial. You can't tell! You English are pretty slow getting anywhere, but you do die! Look over our prices and you'll see why America heads the civilized world in the tombstone business. Put her there! — [*And he offers his hand heartily*] — You're the genuine article, all right! The real imported variety! [*Exit*]

ADELAIDE. Dear, dear! Really imported! How very reassuring! [*To* KITSON] Kitson, kindly ascertain whether Mrs. de Salle is feeling better; and say that we are just sitting down to luncheon. [*Exit* KITSON *upstairs*. ADELAIDE *goes to porch door and waves handkerchief blithely*] Ta, ta, Mr. Tombstone — Bon voyage! [*Turns merrily to* ANTHONY] Well, dear Anthony! You provided us rare and novel entertainment. Peter Swallow, Esquire, will not soon be forgotten by your English guests, I promise you. [*Studies* SWALLOW'S *card*] This is my souvenir! Priceless! "Peter Swallow, Monumentalist."

ANTHONY. I am delighted you found him amusing.

ADELAIDE. "Amusing!" Epoch-Making!

ANTHONY. Then it's too bad he could only stay a few minutes!

ADELAIDE. Momentous minutes, my dear Anthony. Monumentalistic minutes!

MRS. DE SALLE [*entering from stairs*]. Adelaide!

ADELAIDE. Why it is the dear little mother herself. [*Hurrying to her and assisting her across the room*] How lovely that you are better! Is the naughty vertigo quite, quite gone?

MRS. DE SALLE. Oh, yes — it is quite passed away. [*Grande dame manners*]

ANTHONY. Then you will lunch with us? [*She nods*] I will tell the others. [*Exits*]

MRS. DE SALLE [*with a gasping outbreak*]. Dell! Dell! Is it over?

ADELAIDE [*with a flash of Yankee triumph*]. Licked 'em, ma!

MRS. DE SALLE [*gulping*]. Oh my God!

ADELAIDE. Yes, licked 'em! Skinned 'em alive!

MRS. DE SALLE [*sinking into chair*]. Oh, Della, it knocks the wind plumb out of me!

ADELAIDE. Sh!

[*Enter from porch* MISS RAWSON *and* MRS. LEAVITT, ANTHONY, JUSTIN, LEAVITT, *and* GEOFFREY. MISS RAWSON *comes to* MRS. DE SALLE *and seems to felicitate her*]

MRS. LEAVITT [*to* ANTHONY *as they enter*]. I simply would not come in till he had gone! Anthony, I shall never, never forgive you for permitting Stephe to bring that menagerie-escape here!

ANTHONY. Mrs. Bumpstead-Leigh was just *thanking* me for bringing him.

MRS. LEAVITT. But what must she think of him as an American type? It makes me shudder!

LEAVITT [*to* JUSTIN]. But for the train whistle he'd have talked till Doomsday.

KITSON [*appearing at porch door*] Lunch is served, madam.

MISS RAWSON [*glancing about the assemblage*]. Shall we not go out to the porch? — But where is Violet?

JUSTIN. Yes — where is she?

MISS RAWSON. We will wait just a moment, Kitson.

ANTHONY [*starting out*]. Perhaps I had better — Oh!

VIOLET [*trips in, gleefully laughing and breaks out very clearly in an excited voice*]. Oh, Mamma, did Adelaide tell you about it? It was such fun! He never suspected a single thing! I don't think anybody in all the world could have believed we really did come from *Missionary Loop, Indiana!*

MRS. DE SALLE [*paralyzed*]. Ollie!

[*All the company evince great astonishment*]

JUSTIN. Missionary Loop! What does the child mean.

ADELAIDE. Violet! What ghastly joke is this?

VIOLET [*standing with uplifted face, quivering with exaltation, resolution and terror*]. It isn't a joke — I'm in earnest — I'm telling — *the truth!*

ANTHONY. The Truth! [*Amazement suddenly gives place with him to conviction and terrible anger*]

ADELAIDE [*with a stricken laugh, making a final desperate effort to gather her forces. She comes to* VIOLET *and tries to lead her upstairs*] Violet! Come to your room! [*To* MISS RAWSON] It is all the result of excitement. It will soon pass off. All she needs is absolute quiet!

MRS. DE SALLE [*coming to them*]. Yes — absolute quiet — that's all she needs! [*Quakingly*]

VIOLET [*with the same rapt, exultant countenance*]. I've said it! I've said it! Oh!

ANTHONY [*denouncingly*]. Yes, you've said it! So you have been trapped at last! Yes, the truth has come out! [*To the assemblage, bitterly*]

Permit me to introduce the wonderful Sayles Trio — from Missionary Loop, Indiana.

[*And for the moment the three* DE SALLES *are standing in an odd huddled group, three in a row*]

JUSTIN. What does this mean?

ANTHONY [*swelling up with righteous indignation*]. Oh, do not imagine I am unprepared for this! I have been watching them. I had my reasons for bringing Swallow here! — Former sweetheart of our precious Mrs. Bumpstead-Leigh, in the days when she was still *Della Sayles* — one of the *two* daughters of Old Jim Sayles!

MISS RAWSON [*aghast*]. The patent medicine charlatan!

ANTHONY. Sissapoola Indian Herb Remedies! Favorite Stomach Elixir!

[*Recoil of horror on the part of all except* GEOFFREY *who is admiring* VIOLET'S *courage and laughing with boyish glee*]

MISS RAWSON. Oh, it cannot be true!

ANTHONY. It *is* true!

MRS. LEAVITT. Oh, it is too *terrible!*

JUSTIN. If it is the truth, it is high time we knew it!

VIOLET [*almost with ecstacy*]. It *is* the truth.

MISS RAWSON. She's actually boasting of it!

ANTHONY. And it's but a fraction of the whole shameful story! Imposters from the start! Mountebanks, Parvenues! [*And he strides up and down before the guilty trio*]

JUSTIN. Tricksters!

MISS RAWSON. Cheats!

MRS. LEAVITT. Ghastly!

LEAVITT. Infamous!

ANTHONY. Yes, you are found out at last!

MISS RAWSON. And just in time.

[MRS. DE SALLE *has quite collapsed, and is wringing her hands.* VIOLET *has winced somewhat under the invective, but stands her ground with bravely shut lips, and an unflinching smile.* ADELAIDE'S *eyes glitter and she smiles electrically, as if biding her time for the fatal counterstroke*]

ADELAIDE [*with metallic, stabbing incisiveness*]. What! are all the stones cast? Oh, pray do not spare us! The exercise should prove a good stimulant

to your appetite! [*Suavely self-contained in the midst of all this consternation*] I believe there is an afternoon train, is there not, Anthony? It will not take us long to pack.

MRS. LEAVITT [*excitedly to the* RAWSON *family*]. And till then, why should not all of you come over to Willowfields? You — er — I am crazy to show you Mr. Swallow's design for the new monument. It is the sweetest thing!

LEAVITT. Yes, do come!

ANTHONY. So kind of you to suggest it.

JUSTIN. We shall intrude upon your hospitality only until Mrs. Sayles and her daughters have departed.

MISS RAWSON [*with cutting significance*]. Do you think it would be quite safe?

ADELAIDE [*ironically*]. Why not take your ancestral plate with you, madam?

MISS RAWSON [*regaining dignity — to* KITSON]. Kitson will give these ladies every assistance in his power in their preparations for departure. We shall spend the afternoon at Willowfields. [JUSTIN *and* LEAVITT *exit, to porch.* MISS RAWSON *turns with gracious smile to* MRS. LEAVITT *and takes her arm*] Thank you with all my heart, dear Lottie. [*Flanked by* ANTHONY *and* MRS. LEAVITT *she exits without turning to look at the* DE SALLES] It makes things so much easier for us all. [*Offstage*] For when all is said and done —

GEOFFREY [*who has lingered at one side, now steps quickly to* VIOLET *who stands apart from her relatives*]. Bully! Great! May I come back bye-and-bye?

VIOLET [*dazed*]. Oh, I don't know.

[*Exit* GEOFFREY]

KITSON [*at door*]. Lunch is served, Madam.

MRS. DE SALLE [*wailing still*]. Does *He* mean to insult us, too?

ADELAIDE. No thank you, Kitson, we shall not trouble you just now. [KITSON *exits*] Come, mamma. We must not lose time. Violet, stay here and enjoy your brilliant triumph! [*And she exits by stairs*]

MRS. DE SALLE. Yes, gloat! Gloat! You wicked girl! You have betrayed the mother that begat you! — [*Wailing*] Della! Della!

ADELAIDE [*above*]. Come, mamma!

CURTAIN

ACT III

SCENE. — *Same, ten minutes later.* VIO-
LET, *abandoned by her relatives, is
seated by small table, Right. The
reaction from her moments of exaltation has come; her spirits are drooping and tears very near the surface.*
KITSON *enters with plate of lunch
dainties, which he sets down beside
her.*

KITSON [*clearing his throat to attract
attention*]. There, Miss. I took the
liberty of fetching you a mouthful of
lunch, thinking as perhaps it might brace
ye up a bit.

VIOLET [*passively*]. Thank you.
That was nice of you, Kitson. [*She
plays listlessly with food*]

KITSON. I'm glad if it's to your
taste, Miss. Very glad, I'm sure. [*But
he makes no move to go, and there is an
interval of silence. Again he clears his
throat*] Ahem!

VIOLET. Is there something else?

KITSON. Well, if I might make bold
to speak such a thing, Miss, I thought I
would like to tell you as in my humble
opinion Miss Rawson and the rest was
a bit too vi'lent just now.

VIOLET [*without interest*]. You think
so?

KITSON. No doubt it were very
wrong of you to be deceiving everybody
as you did, leading 'em to think you had
blue blood in your veins when you have
none; still, and at the same time, had
they but seen it as *I* do, they would have
esteemed it a very rare privilege to have
extended their hospitality to the offspring of Old Jim Sayles, the Sufferer's
Friend. — [*He comes to her, scrutinizes
her countenance intently*] — And now I
observe ye close to, Miss, I can trace the
resemblance quite plain.

VIOLET [*smiling faintly*]. You mean
to the portrait on the bottles of the
Elixir?

KITSON. The same, Miss, the same.
The likeness is unmistakable. I could
single you out in a thousand.

NINA [*entering by stairs and crossing
Right toward the library*]. That's right,
Mr. Kitson. You're giving Miss Violet
something to eat. She'd ought to have
a good big appetite. [*And there can be
no possible doubt as to where her sym-
pathies are placed*]

KITSON [*with lofty irony*]. Thank you
kindly for your approval, young lady.

NINA. That's all right. No charge
— And if you'd like to know the rest of
what I think about this affair, I'll tell
you that, too, some time, when I
haven't got quite so much to do. [*Exits
Right*]

KITSON. Hear, hear! [*Turning
again to* VIOLET] Ah, yes, Miss. And
this is what I was about to say. That
many and many a time, as I've poured
out me two dessert spoonfuls of that
famous specific, I've said to myself,
"Him as invented this wonderful Elixir
must a' been a wonderful man — and,
may I add, a good man, to boot." Why,
young lady, there's not a single human
ill, or ail, to my thinking, which that
stomach elixir don't give a whack to —
if only, as you might say, in passing. It
saved the life of Mrs. Kitson winter before last, when three doctors with one
voice had given her up.

VIOLET. Is that really true. How
nice!

KITSON. It was indeed, Miss. And
when she finally did go, it was with a
very different complaint to the one she
started with.

NINA [*re-entering Right with books, an
English Weekly, and a scarf*]. Well, I'm
sure Miss Violet ought to be very grateful to you, Kitson, for helping her while
away the time so nicely. Oh, drat it!
[*Her books have slipped to the floor, and
she stoops to gather them up*] But what
I say is — if that's of any interest to
you — that when young misses hardly
out of their teens take it on themselves
to run their family's private affairs —

VIOLET [*interrupting with quiet decision*]. Isn't Mrs. Bumpstead-Leigh
waiting for you, Nina?

NINA. Yes, ma'am, she is! And I
wisht I had a dozen sets of hands and
feet instead of only one so's I could be
even more use to her in this hour of
trouble.

ADELAIDE [*appearing on stairs*].
Nina!

NINA [*startled*]. Yes, Madam.

ADELAIDE. Briggs is waiting to pack
the books. — [*Descending*]

[NINA, *always impressed by* MRS. BUMP-
STEAD-LEIGH'S *superiority, exits
without a word, by stairs*]

KITSON [*to* ADELAIDE]. Is there anything I can do, Madam?

ADELAIDE. No, Kitson, thank you.
Nothing at present, I believe. [KITSON
exits. ADELAIDE *paces room in intent,*

-ivid thought, *watching* VIOLET] Well, Violet, how are you enjoying yourself? [*A silence*] I hope you're not too fatigued, dear, after your exertions! — An emotional scene like that must be very taxing to the nerves! [*A silence*] And you did carry it off brilliantly — oh, brilliantly! No one could deny that. So much *élan*, so much fervor, such an acute sense of the spectacular! Oh, if I only had a photograph of it! I would have it inscribed — let me see — "Truth Crushed to Earth shall Rise Again" — and I would have it framed — beautifully framed — in gingerbread and carraway seeds. The idea fascinates me! [*Sits*]

VIOLET. Adelaide, there's no use making fun of me. I did what I did because I had to. [*In spite of herself the tears come at last*]

ADELAIDE. That's right — Squinny! — It'll do a lot of good at this stage of the game. The question is, what's to be done next? Have you got anything to say?

[MRS. DE SALLE *enters by stairs eager to know what is going on. She is in a hasty negligee, evidently having left the family packing in the midst*]

VIOLET. No. — Only I've made up my mind about one thing.

ADELAIDE [*promptly, before* VIOLET *has a chance to say the words*]. You mean you won't go back to England again! [*And she turns to* MRS. DE SALLE] Heard the latest Ma?

MRS. DE SALLE. No. No. What's happened now? [*Hastily bringing a chair. The three members of the* DE SALLE *family now form a close group.* VIOLET *in the middle, quiveringly resolute;* ADELAIDE *at her Right, undaunted and unconquerable;* MRS. DE SALLE, *as matriarchal as possible*]

ADELAIDE. Violet will tell you. Turn up your eyes, dearie, like a Virgin Martyr; wave one arm like a semaphore, and speak!

VIOLET [*quietly decisive*]. I've made up my mind not to go back to England again.

MRS. DE SALLE [*tremendously*]. Hey? Not go back to England? — Well, well! Now I reckon you'd better just hurry up and tell me what you mean!

VIOLET. I've made up my mind, and that's all there is about it.

MRS. DE SALLE. Made up your mind, have ye? Now I'd like to know who gave ye the right to make up your mind? — Set up and answer me! [*Pause*]

ADELAIDE. What *are* you going to do?

VIOLET. I haven't decided! — earn my living, somehow.

MRS. DE SALLE [*cackling*]. Earn her living — listen! why she never done a stroke of honest work in her life. [*Pause*]

ADELAIDE [*dryly*]. Are ye going to be a trained nurse?

VIOLET [*startled*]. Well — I — I *was* thinking about it.

ADELAIDE [*as if reading headlines*]. "Young heroine, disappointed in love, devotes herself to her suffering fellow men."

VIOLET [*with sturdiness*]. I've *always* thought I'd like nursing!

MRS. DE SALLE. Ye have! — Why, you wouldn't know how to nurse a sick flea.

ADELAIDE. I suppose you'll make a specialty of handsome young parsons, afflicted with heart trouble.

VIOLET. I don't think I'll ever marry.

MRS. DE SALLE. Well, I reckon you're safe there. I certainly'd pity the man who got mashed on *you*.

ADELAIDE [*with finality*]. Violet, we sail on Saturday's boat for Southampton. That much is settled.

MRS. DE SALLE [*the faithful echo*]. Yes, that much is settled! *Do ye hear me?*

VIOLET. Well, if I go back, I go back with my real name.

MRS. DE SALLE [*mightily*]. Your real name's de Salle: and de Salle's the name you'll go back with. Yes it is: don't you dare contradict me!

VIOLET. My name is Sayles.

MRS. DE SALLE [*crushingly*]. Ollie! — Are you absolutely without any moral sense whatever?

VIOLET [*desperate*]. Oh!

MRS. DE SALLE. When I think of the plight you've brought us to, I feel I'd like to give you a good smart licking. I've a mind to do it, right here this minute, too!

ADELAIDE. Not now, Ma. We're too busy.

MRS. DE SALLE. Well, I certainly would like to learn her, for once, who is boss in this family.

ADELAIDE. Now listen to me, both of you!

MRS. DE SALLE. Yes?

ADELAIDE. If either of you let out a scrap of this fracas in Trumpington-on-Swell, I'll fry ye alive. [*She crosses her arms and her eyes fairly glitter*]

MRS. DE SALLE [*a close second*]. Yes, yes. There! Do you hear *that*, Ollie?

ADELAIDE. I'll go the limit. There isn't anything I won't do to keep this story under. Wherever I see a head, I'll strike!

MRS. DE SALLE. Yes. Yes. So will I!

ADELAIDE. No you won't. — You keep your mouth shut! That's your job!

MRS. DE SALLE. Oh, all right, Della.

ADELAIDE [*thinking with all her energy*]. I shall explain we found something a little off color with the Rawsons.

MRS. DE SALLE [*fervidly playing second*]. Yes. Yes.

ADELAIDE. They didn't quite measure up.

MRS. DE SALLE. No. No.

ADELAIDE. There was a yellow streak in the family.

MRS. DE SALLE. Yes!

ADELAIDE. No one could expect us to get mixed up with people like that.

MRS. DE SALLE. No — sir — ee!

ADELAIDE. And so, just in the nick of time, Mamma definitely put her foot down on the match.

MRS. DE SALLE [*illustrating the act, forcefully*]. Yes, I did; and good and hard, too.

VIOLET [*excitedly*]. But I tell you I won't go back! You can go along without me! I'm going to live my own life! You can explain things to suit yourselves.

ADELAIDE. Ollie, I don't care if you are nineteen years old, Ma ought to give you that lickin'.

MRS. DE SALLE [*swelling up with indignation*]. Are you a child of mine, or are you a viper? — Answer me that! Answer me, I say! Answer me!

ADELAIDE. Yes, Ma, she's a viper — and you're a whale.

MRS. DE SALLE. A whale!

ADELAIDE. Yes, a spouting whale, and I guess I'll start a menagerie.

[*Enter* NINA *by stairs*]

ADELAIDE. Well, Nina, what is it?

NINA [*excitedly incoherent*]. Briggs — ma'am — the packing —

ADELAIDE. Oh, very well, I'll be up directly. [*Rising. Exit* NINA, *Left*]

Violet, this pow-wow's not done yet When I'm ready for you, I'll send down Come along Ma. We got to vamoose. [*Starting for stairs*]

MRS. DE SALLE [*reluctantly following*]. But are ye goin' to let her set there and defy us to our faces? Well, I guess not! That's not my way of runnin' a family. — Now, Ollie, don't you dare set hand or foot out of this room till you've decided to mind your Ma. I've said it before; and I say it now for the last time: — I'll have no Disobedience!

ADELAIDE [*on stairs*]. Oh, quit it, ma, and come on. [*Exits*]

MRS. DE SALLE [*submissive*]. Yes, Dell. [*Exits by stairs.* VIOLET *sits motionless with set lips, for a moment, and is not aware of the presence of* GEOFFREY, *who enters quickly from the porch*]

GEOFFREY. Hello, there! — all by your lonesome?

VIOLET. Yes. [*The note of despondency in her voice startles him*]

GEOFFREY. Why, what's the matter?

VIOLET. Oh, Geoffrey, honestly and truly I meant to do what was right, I did!

GEOFFREY [*with vehemence and tenderness*]. You did do what was right. By gee, you did the pluckiest thing I ever saw a girl do. I didn't suppose they had it in 'em.

VIOLET. Oh, but — but I'm awfully mixed up about things. You see — Oh, don't you think — perhaps — it was rather — selfish and nasty of me, Geoffrey, just to save myself, and make the others pay the price for it?

GEOFFREY. *Save* yourself? Is that what you call it?

VIOLET. Yes! Yes! Because now I'm *free*. [*Simply, earnestly, with increasing self-confidence*] I mean, I'm just myself: — can't you see, Geoffrey? Everything else has gone. — Oh, and I *am* glad!

GEOFFREY. I'm glad, too, by jimminy. Only I don't feel as if I know you this way. There's something different about you.

VIOLET. Is there? — Well I fancy you're right. I just feel different all through and through. It seems as if I could breathe! It seems — oh, it seems as if I could fly! It does honestly. I never felt like that before.

GEOFFREY. But what's made all this change, Violet? I mean, what was it started you off?

VIOLET [*after a pause, very simply and directly*]. You.

GEOFFREY [*deeply startled*]. Me? — Oh, no! You don't mean that!

VIOLET. Yes, I do.

GEOFFREY. But how?

VIOLET. Just — by being you.

GEOFFREY. Oh, but — don't you know, Violet? I don't count. I'm a failure. [VIOLET *denies it with a cry*] What? — You don't think so?

VIOLET [*with all her soul*]. How could I?

GEOFFREY [*with wonder and rapture*]. Violet! Do you mean it? — Do you mean it? — Will this stay true? [*He takes her in his arms*]

VIOLET. Always, forever, Geoffrey, if you want me!

GEOFFREY. Want you! [*He kisses her exuberantly*]

VIOLET. I have truly belonged to you since the first day, although I didn't know it.

GEOFFREY. Violet, I feel as if I'd loved you all my life, only I never found it out until a week ago.

[*They are like a pair of kids in their happiness*]

VIOLET [*surprised*]. Oh, but I thought you didn't like me at all — at least not after the very beginning.

GEOFFREY. Did I manage to be a little nasty?

VIOLET. Yes, dear, and I respect you for it very much!

NINA [*entering by stairs, with a flounce*]. Pardon, Miss.

VIOLET. What is it, Nina.

NINA. Mrs. Bumpstead-Leigh says you're to come straight upstairs!

GEOFFREY [*to* VIOLET]. Look here. Why don't you ask her to come *here?*

VIOLET [*summoning resolution*]. I will. — Nina, you may tell my sister I prefer to see her here.

NINA [*significantly*]. Well — I'll *tell* her, Miss. [*Exits upstairs*]

VIOLET [*impulsively*]. Oh, Geoffrey, are you sure you'll not be sorry you took me? It's not too late yet to say so. You know I'm not half good enough for you. — I'm not — truly, truly, I'm not!

GEOFFREY. Oh, Violet! What nonsense! It's me that's not half good enough for *you.*

VIOLET. No, it's not! It's me.

GEOFFREY. No, it's me.

VIOLET. It isn't. Hush — listen dear, I was just going to say something quite important.

GEOFFREY. Well.

VIOLET. Oh, yes, well, this is what it was — don't you think it's a perfectly awful situation, — in a way?

GEOFFREY. No doubt about it at all. Won't the family raise — Hooray? But say, will you come out to New Mexico?

VIOLET. The ranch? I'm dying to! — But oh, Della will be furious!

GEOFFREY. Suppose she is! Remember you're free. That's what you said.

VIOLET. Yes, Geoffrey and so I am. Only I don't know whether Adelaide quite realizes it.

ADELAIDE [*entering by stairs with a flash of controlled indignation*]. Violet, I understand that you wish to have me speak to you here, rather than in the privacy of our apartment. Well, so be it.

VIOLET [*vividly, breathlessly*]. I thought you ought to know — that Geoffrey has asked me to marry him, and I have said "Yes"!

ADELAIDE [*staggered*]. What! [*To* GEOFFREY]. Is this the *Truth!*

GEOFFREY [*vigorously*]. You bet it's the truth! We're going to be married just as soon as we can get the license.

[*The two youngsters face her defiantly, expecting a terrific rejoinder; but instead there is a gasping pause, and then* ADELAIDE *breaks out with a perfect gale of laughter, incapable of restraining herself.* VIOLET *and* GEOFFREY *are finally caught up into this spasm of hilarity, though perfectly bewildered*]

ADELAIDE. Ha, ha, ha! — Oh, ho, ho! — Ha, ha! — Why! — Oh, ho! [*Sitting, still shaken with cosmic mirth*]

VIOLET [*much perplexed*]. Adelaide — What's the matter?

ADELAIDE [*gradually becoming coherent*]. Oh, nothing, nothing — why, but my dear little sister! Why, — why — did you never breathe a word of this before?

VIOLET. Because I only knew it three minutes ago.

ADELAIDE [*with sudden misgiving*]. It's absolutely settled.

GEOFFREY. Settled! — Well I should say Yes!

ADELAIDE [*coming between them with the gentle benignance of a fairy god-*

mother]. Why, I'm very, very glad! How blind I must have been not to see earlier that you two were divinely meant for each other! Both so direct, so true-hearted, so — so — I mean to say — so idealistic! But does anyone know of this?

GEOFFREY. No, you see — we — we sort of wanted to tell you first.

ADELAIDE. My dear Geoffrey! You have my very heartiest good wishes! You take from me the dearest little sister in the world. [*She touches* VIOLET's *hair tenderly*] I cannot tell you what she has been to me in the past; but I give her to you, — [*And she joins their hands*] — knowing that you, and you only, can make her truly happy! But — but I suppose the others must be told at once.

VIOLET [*with some reluctance*]. I suppose they must.

ADELAIDE. My dear children, if you are willing to leave the responsibility in my hands. I shall be glad to explain to — Anthony. I think — yes, I think I can promise that he will change his attitude.

GEOFFREY [*incredulous*]. Well, I can't say it sounds very easy.

ADELAIDE. I know it; but in any event let me try. [*To* VIOLET] Trust me, dear. If I have errred in the past, — and who has not erred, some time? — it has not been through any lack of devotion to your welfare. Now that I see things in a clearer light, I want to do my best to rectify them.

GEOFFREY [*with boyish enthusiasm*]. Say, you're the kind of pal we're looking for just now.

ADELAIDE. Well, you two go off for a little ramble together. Go and see the pigs. You won't object to that, surely, Violet, — not if this affair is only five minutes old! [*And she gently but firmly impels them toward the porch*]

VIOLET [*going*]. Come on! [*At door*] But how about the train?

ADELAIDE. Don't worry.

GEOFFREY. Say, you know, I'm beginning to believe in miracles.

ADELAIDE. *Faith* for you, brother. — *Works* for me. [GEOFFREY *and* VIOLET *exit*. ADELAIDE *turns to* KITSON *who enters Left*] Kitson, is there a newspaper reporter calling for me?

KITSON. No, ma'am.

ADELAIDE. I wired for one. Let me know when he arrives.

KITSON. Yes, ma'am, and if I might presume to speak a word, Madam, —

[*He hesitates to continue, waiting for a sign of encouragement from her; but she is self-absorbed. After a silence he clears his throat and proceeds*] I thought it might not be amiss, if I was to observe to you, that for my part, I consider it a very rare privilege to have laid eyes on the Offspring of Old Jim Sayles, the Sufferer's Friend! [*Again he waits for a response*] And I may add, madam, that in my opinion you are the very image of your lamented Pa.

ADELAIDE [*bored*]. Thanks.

KITSON. And that is why I thought it might be what they call a little crumb of comfort to you if I was to remark that, for my part, I've good reason to think it's you gets the best of the deal, in the long run.

ADELAIDE [*hardly interested, slightly irritated*]. I haven't the slightest idea what you mean by that, my good man, not the slightest.

KITSON [*approaching her with mysterious confidential manner*]. I suppose you think it's a great prize you lost, when you lost Mr. Anthony.

ADELAIDE [*with a beginning of interest*]. You mean to say you know something detrimental to Mr. Anthony?

KITSON. If ever a whited sepulchre walked on two legs —

ADELAIDE [*suddenly alert, domineering*]. You must tell me everything!

KITSON. I cannot, madam.

ADELAIDE. You must! Quickly! [*She rises*]

KITSON. These lips are sealed.

ADELAIDE [*advancing upon him*]. Kitson! The daughter of Old Jim Sayles commands you to unseal them! [*She takes the attitude of a prophetess*]

KITSON [*retreating from her. Deeply shaken*]. Eh! What's that, madam?

ADELAIDE. Speak and speak quickly! [*The weight and authority of a thousand bottles of Elixir are in her voice*]

KITSON. Er — er — er —

ADELAIDE. Do not keep me waiting!

KITSON [*stuttering with awe*]. Her name, madam, was Mamie Tanner —

ADELAIDE [*noting the name to herself*]. Mamie Tanner.

KITSON. And she lived over yonder, two miles from here, at a little place called Herring Grove.

ADELAIDE. Herring Cove. Yes! yes! — she was in service here? Be quick!

KITSON [*his mind beginning to go to pieces under her electrical domination*].

Well, no, not exactly as you might say in service, but every now and again, as the occasion might require, she would be coming here to do a bit of plain sewing or —

[*At this instant* ADELAIDE *becomes aware of the approach of* ANTHONY *who is now visible on porch, and very suavely and graciously she observes*]

ADELAIDE. Thank you, Kitson, for a most appetizing lunch. You know the art of tempting an indifferent palate.

KITSON [*perceiving, with consternation, the cause of her changed manner*]. Eh, eh, that's all right, madam, I'm sure. [*Exits with tray*]

ANTHONY [*loftily*]. My aunt requests me to give you this time-table, fearing that you might not know the exact hour at which the train leaves. It leaves, you will observe, at 3 : 55. [*He indicates the figure in the folder*]

ADELAIDE [*charmingly*]. So very kind of Miss Rawson to think of it! Everything is provided for our comfort!

ANTHONY. And if there is nothing else, — I will return at once to the family. [*And he starts to do so*]

ADELAIDE [*sweetly*]. Just one word! I thought you might be interested to learn of Violet's engagement to your brother.

ANTHONY [*recoiling*]. What!

ADELAIDE [*suavely*]. Yes, they are engaged.

ANTHONY. I do not believe it!

ADELAIDE. As you choose.

ANTHONY [*furiously*]. No! We are done with the whole pack of you! Imposters! Parvenues!

ADELAIDE [*smilingly*]. And the rest! I dimly recall the list!

ANTHONY. Ten times the list would fall short of the truth!

ADELAIDE [*blandly*]. I will multiply it by ten, mentally, and let it go at that!

ANTHONY. Then you see how fortunate you are to get away with a whole skin.

ADELAIDE. I thought you had skinned us quite effectually, just now.

ANTHONY. Well then — skin for skin! [*Going*]

ADELAIDE [*stops him with a glitter*]. So be it! Wait! One little moment, — if you please!

ANTHONY [*impatiently*]. What else?

ADELAIDE [*sweetly*]. Well, suppose — just suppose I say — a purely hypo-

thetical case — of course — but suppose I should happen to possess certain facts — oh, very slight, trivial facts, of course —

ANTHONY [*loftily*]. Are you threatening me?

ADELAIDE. Oh, my dear young man, you go too fast!

ANTHONY. *What* are your threats?

ADELAIDE. Your — private life — invites the microscope?

ANTHONY [*sternly*]. What do you mean by that?

ADELAIDE [*almost toyingly*]. There are no flaws in the perfect crystal of your character? Not even a flyspeck?

ANTHONY. Insinuations! — Give us facts!

ADELAIDE [*crisply*]. What about Nina?

ANTHONY. Nina?

ADELAIDE [*bluntly*]. Yes, Nina! Would you like it reported that this very morning, while the young lady to whom you were engaged was out of the house, you were hugging and kissing the housemaid?

ANTHONY. I deny it — flatly!

ADELAIDE [*musingly*]. I see — even though Nina might corroborate me in every detail.

ANTHONY. Witness of a servant! Oh, even in America servants may be bribed! [*Completely self-possessed*] So that is your artillery, Mrs. Bumpstead-Leigh! Well, I very much fear you will have to fire again!

ADELAIDE. Very well, since you invite the fire you shall have it. I was hoping it might not be necessary, because I do hate blood.

ANTHONY [*halting — but attempting to seem confident*]. What is it?

ADELAIDE. I will tell you a story. By the shore of a little inlet from the sea, — oh, on the other side of the world, of course — clusters a tiny group of fishermen's houses — poor — weather-beaten habitations — known in the district as — as *Herring Cove!* —

ANTHONY [*sinking to chair*]. Herring Cove!

ADELAIDE. Oh, why carry this wretched story further? [*With impassioned manner*] Is there in all the world a more contemptible figure than that of the man who sits in the ancestral pew on the Sabbath Day, smug, pious as a Pharisee, and on Monday, when no one is looking, takes advantage of the ignorance and weakness of poor innocent young girls! [*Denouncingly*] Yes, it is of you I am speaking, of you, the pride of your father, the apple of your Aunt Abigail's eye — hypocrite! Scoundrel! Betrayer of poor Mamie Tanner! [*Her emotions are now permitted to overcome her. She chokes and quivers*]

ANTHONY [*trying to hold his own, but scarcely able to speak for confusion*]. Mamie Tanner — she knew a thing or two!

ADELAIDE [*ignoring*]. The world needs more such men! The race of psalm-singers needs recruits! When I tell the story of Mamie Tanner to your father, as duty bids me to do —

ANTHONY [*stricken*]. You will not do it!

ADELAIDE [*seeming immensely moved*]. I will — poor girl — My duty! My duty!

ANTHONY [*collapsing*]. Name your terms, I accept them.

ADELAIDE [*dropping into a chair, fanning herself with the time-table*]. My goodness, if you'd only said that five minutes ago, you'd have saved me a lot of hard work! On a hot day, too! Well, the terms are very simple. [*Succinctly as a general naming terms of capitulation*] First, you will persuade your father and aunt to accept the present situation. Second, you will secure an urgent invitation for us to stay out our visit here. Third, you will have business in town that will take you off the field of operations by the afternoon express — [*She shows him the time-table with precise care*] — which, "you will observe" leaves at 3:55.

ANTHONY [*cowering*]. Impossible! Impossible! They will *never* accept you. I am certain to fail.

ADELAIDE. You fail! You, the idol! — never! Wag your head, — that settles it!

ANTHONY. You do not know them. They are adamant.

ADELAIDE. There is the telephone. Suppose you ask them to come over.

ANTHONY. It's outrageous. I shall do nothing of the sort! [*But in spite of his words he goes to the telephone*] This is nothing less than blackmail!

ADELAIDE. The happiness of one I love is at stake.

ANTHONY [*at 'phone*]. Mrs. Leavitt? This is Anthony. Would you be so kind as to ask my father and Aunt Abigail to come over for a few minutes? Yes,

thank you very much. I'll explain everything later. [*Hangs up receiver*]

ADELAIDE [*to* KITSON *who has just entered from study with card tray*]. For me, Kitson?

KITSON. For you, madam. [*Presenting card*] The gentleman from the newspaper.

ADELAIDE. Ah, yes, the *Evening Chronicle*. — Ask him to wait. [*Exit* KITSON]

ANTHONY. What's this new trick?

ADELAIDE. Trick? — Why, I don't understand you.

ANTHONY. What do you mean by having a newspaper man in this house?

ADELAIDE. My dear Anthony, you think too harshly of newspaper men. Some of them are perfectly respectable persons.

ANTHONY. You are planning something against us: that's the long and short of it.

ADELAIDE. Dear Brother, you have nothing to fear so long as you do precisely what I direct. And now I think you'd better go and meet your ancestors! — Prepare their minds as gently and tactfully as you can. And I shall be waiting here. [*Exit* ANTHONY]

[ADELAIDE *is about to seat herself at table Right for writing when* NINA *enters Left*]

NINA. Madam!

ADELAIDE. Well, Nina?

NINA [*eagerly, mysteriously*]. I couldn't tell you very well while Mrs. de Salle was around upstairs. It's something private.

ADELAIDE [*delaying her writing to listen*]. Something private, my girl?

NINA. Yes, madam, I thought perhaps it was something I'd ought to tell you.

ADELAIDE. I like your strong sense of duty, Nina; but I must ask you to make haste.

NINA. Thank you, madam. After the way you treated me this morning, I'm certainly glad if I can return the favor.

ADELAIDE. Well! Proceed!

NINA. It's something I heard, madam.

ADELAIDE. Yes, yes.

NINA. Not anything so very much in a way; only I was pretty sure it would lead on to something, you know, if anybody could follow it up.

ADELAIDE. Yes, yes, I understand perfectly. Go on — go on — Nina!

NINA. It was about Mr. Anthony!

ADELAIDE. Mr. Anthony — *more* about Mr. Anthony? — and what about Mr. Anthony — this time?

NINA. Well, Mr. Kitson was telling me there was this girl named Mamie Tanner, or something like that.

ADELAIDE. Mamie Tanner. Yes, to be sure, and what about Mamie Tanner?

NINA. Well, that's just it, ma'am.

ADELAIDE. Yes, yes. That's just it. Tell me, go on, my good girl!

NINA. I can't tell any more.

ADELAIDE [*with sudden change of manner*]. You mean to say that's all you know?

NINA. That's all I could get out of Mr. Kitson.

ADELAIDE [*almost sharply*]. All you know is there was a girl named Mamie Tanner?

NINA. He wouldn't say one single solitary word more, though I pled with him to beat the band.

ADELAIDE. You mean to tell me then that all you know is there was a girl named Mamie Tanner?

NINA [*crestfallen*]. Yes, Madam. Oh, but I'm quite positive it must have been something very — very — disreputable.

ADELAIDE. Disreputable! Oh! [*Her manner suddenly becomes tender and reproachful*] My good girl, if you think that under any circumstances whatever I could have the least wish to listen to scandal, you have made a very grave blunder indeed! I make it a rule always to believe the best of everybody.

NINA. But I thought, ma'am, you kind of suggested to me this morning I was to tell you things. And after what they said to you —

ADELAIDE [*with almost martyr patience*]. If I have been made to suffer unjustly, Nina, I try to bear it uncomplainingly, with patience and fortitude. And if my words can have any influence with you, my dear girl, remember in the future, when you are tempted to hear or to repeat any unkind thing that may be said of another, it is better, it is truer, it is more Christian, to have nothing whatever to do with it. — Wait a minute! [NINA *who is about to go, halts*] Unless, I mean to say, it is something, oh *quite* definite and explicit!

NINA. Yes, ma'am. [*Exits meekly*]

ADELAIDE [*breaking into a laugh as she begins writing*]. "The engagement is announced" —

MRS. DE SALLE [*entering perturbedly by stairs*]. Oh, Dell, Dell — what you doin' down here! and not half our duds packed!

ADELAIDE. Hush! Can't you see I'm busy!

MRS. DE SALLE. But it's less than an hour to train time.

ADELAIDE [*occupied with her writing*]. Ma, I'm at the crisis of my career. Can't twiddle about trains.

MRS. DE SALLE [*baffled and desperate*]. But we're chucked!

ADELAIDE. That's why I'm busy. Goin' to be a sequel to this story!

MRS. DE SALLE. Whatever d'ye mean, Dell?

ADELAIDE [*still writing*]. Ma, if I can only play the game right for about ten minutes more, we can go home and riddle Lady Fitzhugh's old gas balloon so full of holes it'll never go up again.

MRS. DE SALLE [*with Hoosier amazement*]. How you ever goin' to do that?

ADELAIDE. Haven't an idea; but I'm goin' to do it.

MRS. DE SALLE [*momentously*]. Dell.

ADELAIDE. Well, Ma?

MRS. DE SALLE. You ken say what ye like about your pa; but you're your pa through and through.

ADELAIDE [*rising good-humoredly and impelling her mother towards the stairs*] And now you run along upstairs, like a good little mother, and put yourself in cold storage till wanted.

MRS. DE SALLE [*faintly protesting*]. Dell, I'm all topsy-turvy!

ADELAIDE. Haven't time to set you right side up! Go on upstairs, Ma, and do exactly as you're told!

MRS. DE SALLE [*mounting stairs*]. I've never had a chanst to do anything else. [*Exits*]

[*Enter on porch* ANTHONY, JUSTIN, MISS RAWSON. ADELAIDE *stands unobtrusively at one side*]

JUSTIN [*still outside*]. No, I say. No! No! It is impossible! Outrageous! I shall never give my consent! [*They enter the room*] If Geoffrey persists in tying himself up with this disreputable patent-medicine crowd, everything is at an end between him and his family.

MISS RAWSON [*coming down Left with iron-clad dignity*]. Yes, absolutely at an end.

JUSTIN. Five generations of Rawsons turn in their graves at the very mention of such an infamous alliance.

ANTHONY. But, my dear father, at least I have a right to be heard in my brother's defense.

JUSTIN. Anthony, you are out of your head. You're mad!

MISS RAWSON [*with immense authority*]. Remember, Justin, it is Anthony! However preposterous his request he shall have a hearing. [*And she sits, forcing herself to listen to an unwelcome argument*]

JUSTIN [*espying* ADELAIDE *down Right*]. May I beg that we be left alone?

ANTHONY. I have asked Mrs. Bumpstead-Leigh to be present.

JUSTIN. This is too much! [*And he turns on* ADELAIDE *commandingly*] Madam, permit me to apprize you, for the last time, that your empire in this house is at an end.

ADELAIDE. You are very explicit, Mr. Rawson. But suppose — [*Drawing near* ANTHONY] — suppose there should be means at hand whereby I could regain it.

ANTHONY [*terrorized*]. Er — er — first of all, let me speak. Let us try to consider the situation dispassionately, reasonably.

JUSTIN. Reasonably! Reasonably! Pah!

ANTHONY. Yes. What actual injury have we received from the de Salles? Family is something, I admit —

MISS RAWSON. The Main thing!

JUSTIN. They lied to us from the start.

ADELAIDE. Ah, my dear Mr. Rawson, but that is just what we did not do. We were silent — nothing more. Would you have had me wear a label on my bosom — "Daughter of Old Jim Sayles." — Would you, I ask? Would you?

MISS RAWSON. Yes, I would! And a very good thing for everybody.

ADELAIDE. How? In what way? Tell me, what relation can be found between a past that has been put behind me forever, and a present which I have created for myself, by sheer force of will — against every possible obstacle? What, I ask, is the one great, superb, inspiring thing in your vaunted American idea? Lincoln was born in a little poor log cabin. Would you, for that reason, have turned him from your doors? [*Secretly punches* ANTHONY *into action*]

ANTHONY. Yes, yes — her argument is sound. It deserves attention.

JUSTIN. Anthony, you are too softhearted.

ANTHONY. You will not refuse to listen?

MISS RAWSON [*rising to go*]. I have listened quite long enough to the adventuress from Missionary Loop, Indiana! Words may varnish facts, they cannot alter them.

ADELAIDE [*positively*]. Well, for my part, I have no wish to alter them. I am tired, tired of tacking with every shift of the wind. I am tired of apologizing for a course of action which in my heart I am proud of. Henceforth the truth, the whole truth, and nothing but the truth! I will make my appeal to the American people. [*And she takes a step towards the study*]

JUSTIN [*amazed*]. What does the woman mean!

ADELAIDE [*facing him*]. There is a newspaper representative in this house at the present moment. He comes from the *Evening Chronicle*. I am going to tell him the whole story of the Sayles Family to date — omitting nothing! *Everything* from Missionary Loop to Trumpington-on-Swell! And the American people will judge between us! You, with your hidebound, moth-eaten conservatism —

JUSTIN [*dropping into chair*]. In the papers! The whole story!

ADELAIDE. Yes. [*Takes another step towards study*]

MISS RAWSON [*distracted*]. Stop her! Stop her!

ADELAIDE. Why should I spare your feelings? Have you spared mine? [*Takes still another step toward the fatal door*]

JUSTIN [*following her*]. Wait, madam! Wait! In heaven's name!

ADELAIDE. *I* have nothing to fear from publicity. The papers will vindicate me. [*Another step*]

MISS RAWSON [*stifling*]. In the papers! Oh!

ANTHONY [*to his Aunt*]. We must yield to her.

ADELAIDE [*at the study door with rapture*]. Henceforth I live in the Daylight! [*Reaching for the knob*]

JUSTIN. Will you turn a deaf ear to the prayers of the oldest living Rawson?

ADELAIDE [*reaching again for the knob*].

Is it likely that her prayers would move me!

MISS RAWSON [*coming to her — supplicatingly*]. Oh, listen to us! Listen to us!

ADELAIDE [*reaching again for the knob*]. Listen to *you*, Madam? [*Turns the knob*]

MISS RAWSON. Whatever we have done, don't bring this awful disgrace upon us!

JUSTIN. Won't you listen, Madam? [*Pause*]

ADELAIDE [*after an apparent struggle*]. Am I perhaps thinking too much of my own happiness? [*She crosses the room thoughtfully*] Could I ever know one moment of peace at the price of another's misery?

MISS RAWSON. We will accept your sister. Violet and Geoffrey shall have our blessing.

JUSTIN. Anything! Anything! Madam!

[ADELAIDE *turns and surveys the three, who stand in an imploring group exactly where she stood with her family, at the moment of exposure*]

ADELAIDE [*seeming to master herself. — Coming to them tenderly*]. For your sake, for yours, for Anthony's sake, for the sake of that little sister whom I love and cherish more dearly than anyone else in the world, I will yield! [*Sits with exhausted manner; but if you look closely you might detect a triumphant glitter in her eye*]

MISS RAWSON. You are very kind! [*Drops into chair by table, Right*]

ADELAIDE. Once more I consent to the shackles. I promise to hold my peace. Anthony, dear, there is a little announcement of the engagement. Kindly take it to the reporter. [ANTHONY *exits, Right.* ADELAIDE *goes up to porch door and looks out*] And now — [*She waves handkerchief*] I want you to tell Violet and Geoffrey just how you feel toward them. I sent them out to play in the barnyard, the dears. There they are! [*Calling*] Come, Violet! Hurry! — Hurry!

JUSTIN [*to* MISS RAWSON]. There's no help! We must put the best face on it.

MISS RAWSON. But I shall be a Rawson, Justin, to the last!

ADELAIDE [*to* VIOLET *who is coming with* GEOFFREY *on porch*]. Miss Rawson is waiting to give you her blessing, dear!

[*Enter* VIOLET *and* GEOFFREY]

VIOLET. Oh! it's too good to be true!

ADELAIDE [*half audibly*]. Too good to be true! Yes, it is — almost! [*Seats herself with sigh*] That was a dickens of a close call!

JUSTIN [*forcing himself to carry out the letter of his promise*]. Geoffrey, my boy, I congratulate you!

MISS RAWSON [*equally conscientious and unhappy*]. Violet, my dear, I am so very glad!

VIOLET [*radiantly*]. Oh, I can hardly believe it!

MISS RAWSON. Anthony has explained everything. We hope you will be very, very happy — in New Mexico!

ADELAIDE [*wiping her eyes*]. The dears!

[GEOFFREY *summons* VIOLET *up to door with a gesture. They stand there, amused, puzzled, happy. With a final effort of self-mastery,* MISS RAWSON *turns to* ADELAIDE. *Her manner conforms to necessity; but her voice is undisguisedly hostile*]

MISS RAWSON. *Dear* Mrs. Bumpstead-Leigh, may we not hope that *you* will remain with us another week? — Do consent!

ADELAIDE. Dear Miss Rawson, you are very kind. I do wish that it might be possible. But I scarcely know what is best.

JUSTIN [*icily, from across the room*]. Let me add my entreaties, Mrs. Bumpstead-Leigh. The house would seem quite empty without you!

ADELAIDE [*sweetly*]. I think — indeed, I am all but certain, we can manage it — at least for a day or two. But, of course, you will permit me, before giving a definite response, to consult mamma. [*She seems to be going at once*] Mamma, dear! Mamma!

[*Exchanging one last significant look with* JUSTIN, MISS RAWSON *sinks into a chair*]

CURTAIN

IT PAYS TO ADVERTISE

(1914)

By Roi Cooper Megrue and Walter Hackett

THE AMERICAN FARCE: "IT PAYS TO ADVERTISE"

THE American farce was conceived in noise and reared in perpetual motion. Its logical progression was nil, but its gusto was all important, and gave an amusing life to it which fulfilled the functions of slight entertainment. I speak of these characteristics in the past tense, for there have been decided changes in the content and structure of the farce since the day Charles Hoyt began writing his successful skits.

The slap-stick humor of the old type, where every character was a convention and every make-up a scream, was still in vogue when Hoyt began to write for the theatre. Then some one suggested to him that he give to his scenes a semblance of truth and reality. So realism joined hands with incongruity, and we began to get the modern farce, of which there have been so many excellent examples. The consuming quality that makes an American farce of the past two decades distinctive has been vitality. Take a farce idea written by some one who does not have that quality, and you will understand the value of it. Remove from the farce the active principle, and it becomes flat in plot and lacking in character. Little by little the character has become more distinct, though the action is still so rapid — what they call "pace" in the theatre — that it really does not matter if the logic of the situation is consistent, or the ethics of the case tenable.

I have selected "It Pays to Advertise" as representative of the American farce at its best and its most popular. It was written by Roi Cooper Megrue and Walter Hackett, both of whom went to their work with an understanding of their subject. Since this play was written in 1914, there have gradually come into the farce some of the elements of comedy, some of the fitness of satire. But "It Pays to Advertise" is avowedly a play constructed on the model of its period. It furnished an evening of agile fun, and to the actors it gave plenty of opportunity for team work. Its good humor is catching and its wit never-ending. Its preachment is the one skein that holds its mechanical ingenuity together: that advertising will make everything go in the world; that you can fool the public all the time by "gab." Business is played as an inconsequent game of dominoes — for the fun of being active, for the thrill of winning. Wit sees everything through; accident of situation reigns supreme. The characters become mere pawns on a board, moved deftly, swiftly, unerringly, crossed and recrossed with incidents and coincidences that fit in a network of fun; such action scintillates and does not bear too much scrutiny. The people of such a play are clothed in the semblances, the symbols of outward life. The business type, the rich man type, the foolish son type, the poster heroine, the drummer type: these all have the clear-cutness of card-board figures; they have certain familiarity of feature, a certain contemporaneousness, a certain standard pattern. They smack of the average, or of the superior from the point of view of the average. There is not a whit of depth to their make-up, not a bit of thoughtfulness to their purpose. They are just a sample of the design we have called American comedy, or American farce.

There are many who have taken such a dramaturgic knack for what it is worth, and acknowledged its cleverness, its amusing quality. It is fun while one is under the spell of it, for the humor flies off in sparks, like a sharp knife against the grindstone. The nervous quality to such plays was probably the forerunner of the nervous quality the Expressionists have attempted to measure for us in such dramas as "The Adding Machine" and "Processional." There is just a little bit of madness about the American farce, — the madness of incongruity, the tragedy of commonplaceness, the irony of such a thing being just a little true, and of such a thing being relished as entertainment.

The average farce is baffling to the thinking mind, looking for entertainment of a more consistent character. Mr. Walter Lippman went to see "It Pays to Advertise", and here is what he said about it:

The authors were not writing a satire, but a panegyric backed by all the faith of Broadway. And they are as clever as the young men in their play; they, too, have their little joke. "It Pays to Advertise" is in itself an advertisement — an advertisement of advertising, and of the big national advertisers. For in the torrent of dialogue there floats bits of fact by which the names of the noisiest business, from Wrigley's Spearmint to Boston Garters, are dinned into the ears of the audience. It is, of course, not traditional in playwriting to advertise goods from the stage, to make their trademark part of a drama. But that is what this play does. It pursues one step further the magazine policy of surrounding reading matter with publicity, and if the logic of the situation is developed we shall have Bibles with the magazine advertisements, sermons in which mention can be purchased, and school-books garnished with Campbell's Soup. It even occurs to me that I am serving the same cause in this article, for, as the press-agent says: "It's being talked about that counts; what is said doesn't matter." We are a good-natured people, and the only thing we fear is priggishness. You must laugh and not criticise or you are a highbrow. You must under no circumstances confess that blatancy and cheapness lacerate your soul, for the virtue of Broadway is to be a good Indian.

This very analysis shows that to a type of mind like Mr. Lippman's the play offered up a host of thoughts that were worth while. He came pretty near convincing himself that the authors of "It Pays to Advertise" gave us a caricature of commercialism. He recognized that the very aggressiveness of youth in the three central figures in the play was an admirable quality, even though this aggressiveness led them into what might be held as methods strictly unethical. Cognizant of our characteristics as a people, such a critic is aware that only from us could such a dramatic product be possible. And that it is at times a good product, and one not easy to build, it is only necessary to see a play — with a farce idea — handled heavily. As a matter of comparison, it is worth considerable analysis, to put "It Pays to Advertise" by the side of A. A. Milne's "The Great Broxopp" — which also deals with the power of advertising — to note wherein comes the value of speed in situations essentially quick in their interplay of spirit.

Since its very beginning, "It Pays to Advertise" has been a great success. It even now draws heavily in stock. Like "Seven Days", and "Officer 666", it has the tinge of the familiar, of the standard round of daily life. Its momentum is waiting for a stage director to twirl the mechanism, as the hand twirls the pinwheel on the Fourth of July. It has had its successful run in London, where it was taken as a sign of the American times — what sign the English critics fail to emphasize. Writing in the London *Spectator* for February 9, 1924, the reviewer said : "The play's general attitude to Life and Love is exactly like that of the old-fashioned sword-and-cloak play, only that the soldiers of fortune are not bandits at all, but respectable citizens and makers, or at any rate sellers, of soap."

The English have always commented on our excellence in such plays of rapidity, but we leave them marvelling how on earth the playwrights "get away with it." The psychology of contagion is a large part of the explanation of the American farce's success. J. T. Grein went to see "A Pair of Sixes." He wrote:

> They work with a will and like Trojans ; they rush about the stage as if panic had stricken them ; they blurt out their wild bits of dialogue as if under pneumatic pressure ; they shout, gesticulate, play tricks, gambol with the irresponsible *abandon* of an amiable lunatic asylum let loose ; they give us no time to think, to analyze, or to criticise ; somehow they laugh and will make us respond — and the result is that people on the stage and people in the house let themselves gayly go, both parties really full well aware that they are " dashed " if they know what it is all about.

The fundamental incongruity in the American farce of the period represented by "It Pays to Advertise" is reflective of the incongruity in American life. When John Howard Lawson said he wanted, with his "Processional", to reflect the rhythms of American life, its incongruities, its repressions, its melodramatic contrasts, its hypocrisies, and so on, while he had a much more self-conscious purpose and a much more determined desire to produce something with the tang of art about it, he was not so far removed from the purpose of these two authors who wrote "It Pays to Advertise." Lawson went deeper and changed oftener the angle of his surfaces. Megrue and Hackett did not go deep at all ; they did not care about slapping anything. They merely chose to have fun with — to them — an absorbing phase of business. They caught at a truth and blew it lightly into a bubble. Not a bad way of handling soap !

I do not wish to be taken quite as meaning that "It Pays to Advertise" has any of the quality of Lawson's "Processional", which, I am inclined to believe, though it falls short in its theatre adaptability, in its philosophy, in its story, is a poignant criticism of American life of a certain character — old-time melodrama raised to a new technique — I do claim that the American farce of the period of "Seven Days" and "It Pays to Advertise" had a rhythm that was equally American. And that is why I have selected the "farcical fact" by Mr. Megrue and Mr. Hackett for inclusion in this volume. That it was produced under the management of George M. Cohan only emphasizes that he too recognized in it something of the heartbeat of Broadway.

IT PAYS TO ADVERTISE

A FARCICAL FACT IN THREE ACTS

By ROI COOPER MEGRUE and WALTER HACKETT

GEORGE M. COHAN THEATRE, NEW YORK CITY

September 8th, 1914

COHAN & HARRIS

IT PAYS TO ADVERTISE

A FARCICAL FACT IN THREE ACTS BY

ROI COOPER MEGRUE and WALTER HACKETT

Staged under the direction of Sam Forrest

The characters appear in the order in which they are named

MARY GRAYSON	Ruth Shepley
JOHNSON	George Schaeffer
COMTESSE DE BEAURIEN	Louise Drew
RODNEY MARTIN	Grant Mitchell
CYRUS MARTIN	John Cope
AMBROSE PEALE	Will Deming
MARIE	Cecile Bretone
WILLIAM SMITH	Harry Driscole
DONALD McCHESNEY	W. J. Brady
MISS BURKE	Vivian Rogers
ELLERY CLARK	Kenneth Hill
GEORGE BRONSON	Sydney Seaward

SYNOPSIS OF SCENES

ACT   I. — *Library at Cyrus Martin's.*
ACT II. — *The office of The 13 Soap Company.*
ACT III. — *Same as Act I.*

THE CAST

(*In the order of their appearance*)

MARY GRAYSON
JOHNSON, *butler at the Martins'*
COMTESSE DE BEAURIEN
RODNEY MARTIN
CYRUS MARTIN
AMBROSE PEALE
MARIE, *maid at the Martins'*
WILLIAM SMITH
MISS BURKE, *clerk*
GEORGE McCHESNEY
CHARLES BRONSON
ELLERY

ACT   I. — *The library at Cyrus Martin's.*
ACT II. — *Rodney Martin's office.*
ACT III. — *Same as Act I.*

AUTHOR'S NOTE: *The advertising statistics used in the play are facts, not farce.*

IT PAYS TO ADVERTISE

ACT I

SCENE. — *The library of* CYRUS MARTIN'S *home in New York City: a very handsome room, in tapestry and dark oak. Doors up left, down left, and down right. Books, chairs, divans, as necessary. Down left is an oak typewriting table with a typewriter on it. It is obviously out of place in the room, and is evidently only a temporary arrangement. Handsome walnut furniture. Mantel set on mantel. Fire dogs and irons in fireplace. All-over carpet. Handsome busts on bookcases. Chandelier and four brackets. Curtains on windows at back. It is seven o'clock in the evening — early September.*

AT RISE: MARY GRAYSON *is seated at typewriter. She strums the keys idly and indifferently with one finger. She might hum a turkey-trot, keeping time with a one-finger accompaniment. In a moment* JOHNSON, *a typical English butler, enters from door upper left.*

JOHNSON. I beg pardon, Miss Grayson.

MARY [*whirling about eagerly*]. What is it, Johnson? Has young Mr. Martin come in yet?

JOHNSON. No, Miss.

MARY. But I told you not to interrupt me until he did.

JOHNSON. I know, Miss, but it's that Mr. Ambrose Peale again; he's called four times.

MARY. Say that Mr. Martin will be back at eight o'clock.

JOHNSON. Yes, Miss. There's a lady waiting, too, Miss, to see Mr. Martin Senior. Here's her card.

MARY. Mme. la Comtesse de Beaurien. Tell her that Mr. Martin Senior can see no one.

JOHNSON. I can't make her compre-

hend anything I say. She just sits and waits.

MARY. Oh, bring her in, then. I'll make her understand somehow, but, Johnson, don't fail to let me know the minute young Mr. Martin gets home.

JOHNSON [*going to door up left*]. Yes, Miss. [MARY *rises from typewriter, takes off her sleeve-protectors and smoothes out her skirt.* JOHNSON [*announcing*] Countess dee Beauree-en —

[*The* COUNTESS *enters from door upper left. She is a very smart-looking girl of about twenty-six or twenty-seven, typically French in manner and does not speak a word of English. He exits*]

MARY [*to* COUNTESS]. How do you do?

COUNTESS [*advancing to her*]. Mam'selle Martin?

MARY. Oh, no, I'm Miss Grayson, Mr. Martin's secretary.

COUNTESS [*blankly*]. Sec-ree-taree?

MARY. I'm sorry, but it's quite impossible for you to see Mr. Martin. He is confined to the house with a severe attack of gout. If you will write him I will see that he gets your letter. You can address him here instead of the office; while he is ill I come here every day for the mail.

COUNTESS. Pardon, mais je ne comprends pas — je ne parle pas l'anglais. Vous parlez Français peut-être?

MARY [*blankly*]. You see, Mr. Martin is ill . . .

COUNTESS. Je répète que je ne parle pas anglais. Mr. Martin est-il ici?

MARY. It's quite useless for you to talk: I don't understand French.

COUNTESS. Un moment, Mam'selle — peut-être je parle trop vite . . . [*More slowly*] Je désire parler à M. Martin àpropos des affaires. Je suis riche. Mais on peut toujours être plus

335

riche. Si je pouvais obtenir l'agence du savon Martin pour la France ça serait une belle affaire. Je donnerais cinquante mille francs pour cette agence. Répêter cela à M. Martin et je suis sûre qu'il me recevra immédiatement. Vous comprenez maintenant —

MARY. But I really don't understand French. [*Slowly and loudly*] Mr. Martin is ill — sick! He can see no one — you'll have to go — please do —

COUNTESS. Mon Dieu! Vous êtes stupide. . . . [*Sitting down in chair left of table*] J'attendrai M. Martin.

MARY. There's no use your sitting down. [*She goes to her*] Mr. Martin doesn't understand French, either.

COUNTESS. C'est bien, c'est bien, mam'selle; je ne suis pas pressée.

MARY. I don't understand. Please go — [*She waves her hands*]

COUNTESS. Ah, laissez-moi donc tranquille — vous m'embêtez.

MARY. Oh, dear!

[JOHNSON *enters*]

JOHNSON. Young Mr. Martin's come in; he'll be here directly.

MARY. Good Heavens! [*She goes over and makes a wild sweeping gesture*] Mr. Martin is out — out.

COUNTESS [*with marked accent*]. Out?

MARY [*nodding her head*]. Oui —

COUNTESS [*rapidly*]. Oui? Ah vous parlez Français? Je voudrais savoir si Mr. Martin est ici. Je voudrais lui parler tout de suite.

MARY. Heavens! She's off again; let's act it for her. Let's see — [*She points to* JOHNSON] That is Mr. Martin.

COUNTESS. Eh?

MARY. We're pretending that is Mr. Martin.

COUNTESS [*shaking her head*]. Ah, non, ça ce n'est pas M. Martin.

MARY. We're pretending — see, pretending? Now, you see — Mr. Martin is out — see?

[JOHNSON *exits and enters immediately*]

COUNTESS [*suddenly*]. Ah, Mr. Martin n'est pas ici! Je comprends.

MARY. Heavens, she understands, Johnson! Take her by the arm and lead her out. [*Crosses left*]

JOHNSON [*starting to do so as* COUNTESS *rises to go out*]. Yes, Miss.

COUNTESS. Attendez! A quelle heure M. Martin rentrera-t-il? [*She sits again*]

JOHNSON. Now what's the matter? You'd better come quietly, Miss — [*He takes her by the arm*]

COUNTESS [*shaking him off*]. A quelle heure rentrera-t-il? [*There is a blank pause. To* MARY] Maintenant — faites attention à votre tour. Regardez-moi: je suis M. Martin, vous comprenez? Moi je suis M. Martin —

MARY [*nodding*]. Mr. Martin.

COUNTESS [*going to door*]. Mr. Martin n'est pas ici; il est sorti — il est au bureau. Enfin s'il n'est pas au bureau c'est pas mon affaire. Maintenant je voudrais savoir à quelle heure rentrera-t-il?

MARY [*as* COUNTESS *goes*]. Heavens, she's going. [*She turns at door*] She's coming back.

COUNTESS [*returning to* MARY]. A quelle heure M. Martin rentrera-t-il? [*There is another pause. Suddenly the* COUNTESS *takes out her watch*]

MARY [*eagerly*]. Oh, she wants to know when he'll be in! [*She runs over and points to clock*] Eight o'clock — eight — o'clock.

COUNTESS. Oui — Oui, huit heures — je comprends. Merci bien — je m'en vais maintenant, mais je reviendrai. Au revoir.

MARY. I can understand that! Au revoir — au revoir — good night.

COUNTESS [*going*]. Merci — merci a huit heures — bonsoir — bonsoir — [*She exits*]

MARY. Don't let her in here again unless you have an interpreter.

JOHNSON. Very good, Miss. [*He exits door upper left*]

[MARY *primps, and sits at typewriter again, and idly touches the keys with one finger, maintaining an eager watch on the door. She hears someone coming and hastily and busily bangs away at the typewriter.* ROD-NEY MARTIN *enters door left. He is a young man of twenty-four with a certain quaint frank charm, in spite of his funny little mustache, English morning coat, spats and white carnation. He is by no means brainless, but simply undeveloped by reason of the kind of life he has led under appallingly frictionless conditions*]

RODNEY. Miss Grayson!

[MARY'S *previous business-air has entirely disappeared, and she assumes the fluttering airs of a timid ingenue, overdoing it for anyone except a boy madly in love with her*]

MARY. What a surprise! [RODNEY *goes and locks both doors left*] Why, Mr. Martin . . . what are you doing?

RODNEY [*coming to her and facing her over back of chair*]. I want to talk with you. Mary, will you marry me?

MARY. Why, really —

RODNEY. You love me, don't you?

MARY. I — I don't know what to say —

RODNEY. Say Yes.

MARY [*shyly*]. Yes.

RODNEY [*trying to grab her*]. You angel!

MARY [*eluding him*]. Wait!

RODNEY. We'll be married right away.

MARY. But suppose your father disapproves?

RODNEY. He won't know anything about it until we're married, and then what could he do?

MARY. He might cut you off.

RODNEY. Would you care?

MARY [*hastily*]. I? No, no, indeed. I was thinking of you, dear.

RODNEY. Don't you bother about me. We'll be married to-morrow, and then come home for the parental blessing.

MARY. Oh, I couldn't do that. It wouldn't be square. I'm his private secretary: he trusts me. To bring me here to his home and then to find I'd married his son on the sly — we couldn't do that.

RODNEY. You do make it sound rather bad. I wouldn't want us to give father the worst of it; we've always been pretty good friends, he and I. I guess I'd better tell him — in a week or so.

MARY. Why, Rodney, if you love me, we must get this awful suspense over.

RODNEY. But suppose he does object?

MARY. Even then I wouldn't give you up.

RODNEY. Mary!

MARY. You could go into business, make a big man of yourself, make me proud of you —

RODNEY. You talk just like the heroine in a play I saw last night. She wanted the hero to go to work, and he did, and then for four acts everybody suffered.

MARY. Don't you want to work?

RODNEY [*seriously*]. I should say not. Imagine going to bed every night, knowing you've got to get up in the morning and go to business.

MARY. You'd be happier, wouldn't you, if you had a job?

RODNEY. Please don't talk like father; he's preached a job at me ever since I left college. Why should I work? Father made millions out of soap and is forever complaining that he's always had his nose to the grindstone, that he's worked fourteen hours a day for thirty years, that he's never known what fun was, and it's all made him old before his time. I can't see the sense of following an example like that — I really can't. He's got enough for you, and me, and our children. Yes, and our children's grandchildren. I've explained all this to him but I can't seem to make him understand. But it's simple: why work when there's millions in the family? And why even talk of money when you and I are in love? Come, kiss me. [*He leans towards her; she moves away to left. He crosses right*]

MARY. No, you mustn't — not till you've spoken to your father.

RODNEY. You won't kiss me till I tell him?

MARY. No.

RODNEY. And you will when I do?

MARY. Yes.

RODNEY. Then I'll tell him right away. [*He goes toward door left. She crosses right*]

MARY. Oh, Rodney, you're splendid! And don't be afraid.

RODNEY. Afraid! [*Pausing*] You don't think I'd better wait till the morning?

[CYRUS MARTIN *knocks at the door violently, and says "ouch" in a loud tone*]

MARTIN [*off-stage*]. Why is this door locked? What the devil does this mean?

MARY. If you don't ask him now, I'll never marry you.

MARTIN [*off-stage*]. Open the door.

RODNEY. Coming, father, coming. [*He goes and unlocks both doors*]

MARTIN [*loudly*]. Ouch, ouch! The devil! [*He enters*] Why was that door locked?

RODNEY. Was it locked?

MARTIN. You young fool, didn't you just unlock it? [*Crosses to right*]

RODNEY [*nervously*]. So I did!

[MARY *has gone to her typewriter and now begins typing*]

MARTIN. Stop that noise! [*She does so.* RODNEY *looks at her, discouraged. She motions to him to go on. Meanwhile* MARTIN *has painfully limped to a chair down-stage by table and sinks into it. His foot gives him another twinge*] Ouch! Oh, my poor foot!

[RODNEY *hastily picks up footstool and comes with it to his father*]

RODNEY. I'm afraid your foot hurts.
MARTIN. Not at all — I just pretend that it does!
RODNEY [*fervently*]. I hoped you were better.
MARTIN. Well, I'm not. What have you got there?
RODNEY. A footstool — I thought it might make you more comfortable.
MARTIN. How much do you want?
RODNEY. Why, nothing, father.
MARTIN. Well anyhow, the answer is not a nickel —
RODNEY. You do me an injustice. I'm just sorry to see you in pain.
MARTIN. Well, you want something, that's certain.
RODNEY. Why do you say that?
MARTIN. I know you — and whatever it is, you can't have it.

[RODNEY *turns appealingly to* MARY. *She ignores him. He turns back to his father and tries to muster up his courage*]

RODNEY [*clearing his throat*]. Well, as a matter of fact, I did want —
MARTIN. Now we're getting to it.
RODNEY. I wanted to have a talk with you — an important talk —
MARTIN. Curious! That's just what I wanted with you — I've wanted it all day . . . and now we'll have it — Miss Grayson!
MARY. Yes, sir? [*Rises*]
MARTIN. Get out. [*She exits through door upper left, without noticing* RODNEY, *who stands looking after her dejectedly. As he hears the door close*] Now, what do you mean by overdrawing your allowance again?
RODNEY [*innocently*]. What it simply proves is that I was right when I told you my allowance was too small.
MARTIN [*aghast*]. What!
RODNEY. And if my allowance is too small for one, it's much too small for two.

MARTIN. For two?
RODNEY. Father has it ever occurred to you that I might marry?
MARTIN. Of course it has! You're fool enough for anything.
RODNEY. I don't consider a man a fool because he's married.
MARTIN. That's because you've never tried it.
RODNEY. I intend to try it.
MARTIN. Who is the girl?
RODNEY [*nervously*]. The girl?
MARTIN. Yes, girl — you're not going to marry an automobile or a polo pony — you're going to marry a girl, aren't you? Some blue-eyed, doll-faced, gurgling, fluttering little fool. Oh, why doesn't God give young men some sense about women?
RODNEY. I object very strongly to your speaking in that way of Miss Grayson.
MARTIN. Miss Grayson? Miss Grayson? You're not going to marry a typewriter?
RODNEY. Yes, sir.
MARTIN. Does she know it?
RODNEY. Yes, sir.
MARTIN. Of course she knows a good thing like you when she sees it!
RODNEY. I won't listen to you talk of Miss Grayson in that way.
MARTIN. You've got to listen. I won't permit any such absurd, ridiculous marriage! Thank Heaven, you had sense enough not to elope —
RODNEY. I wanted to, but she wouldn't. She insisted on your being told, so you see what an injustice —
MARTIN. Injustice? Can't you see that she wished me to know, so that if I disapproved and cut you off, she'd not be stuck with *you* on her hands.
RODNEY. Please, father — it's quite useless. [*He starts to go*]
MARTIN. No, my boy, wait a minute. Remember, I'm your friend even if I am your father. [*Rises, goes to door right to ring bell*] Don't you believe it's only your money she wants?
RODNEY. I know it isn't.
MARTIN [*pushing bell*]. I'll prove it is.
RODNEY. What are you going to do?
MARTIN. Send for Miss Grayson.
RODNEY. You shan't humiliate her.
JOHNSON [*entering from door upper left*]. Yes, sir?
MARTIN. Ask Miss Grayson to come here at once.
JOHNSON. Yes, sir. [*He exits*]

MARTIN. I'll tell that scheming secretary that if you persist in this marriage, I'll disinherit you! Then watch her throw you over.

RODNEY. Even if you are my father, you shan't insult the girl I love.

MARTIN. Poppycock! You're afraid to put her to the test: you're afraid she will chuck you.

RODNEY [*quickly*]. I am not afraid.

MARY [*entering from door upper left*]. You wanted me, Mr. Martin?

RODNEY [*going to her, she crosses to center*]. Mary!

MARTIN. Wait a minute. My precious son informs me that you and he intend to marry.

MARY [*timidly*]. Oh, sir —

MARTIN. And I wish to tell you that if he marries you, he doesn't get one penny of my money and that means he'll starve.

MARY. Then at least we can starve together. [*They hold hands*]

RODNEY. Mary!

MARTIN. Making a grand-stand play, eh? You think I'm too fond of him not to relent? Well, you're wrong. Neither of you can get nickel from me: you can both starve together.

RODNEY. We won't starve.

MARTIN. What can you do? You're not a producer — you never will be. [*Crosses to left*] You're just an idler. You couldn't earn five dollars a week, but you'll have a chance to try. You'll get out of my house to-night or I'll have you thrown out.

RODNEY. Now, father —

MARTIN. Not another word, sir, not another word! [*He kicks chair, and stamps out angrily, thru lower left door*]

RODNEY [*to* MARY]. It's getting more like that play every minute.

MARY [*half crying*]. Oh, Rodney, Rodney, what have I done? I'm so — so sorry.

RODNEY. You haven't done anything — neither of us has. Father didn't seem to give us a chance to. He did it all —

MARY. Oh, Rodney —

RODNEY. You were bully the way you stuck up for me. When you said we'd starve together, I just choked all up.

MARY [*genuinely*]. Please don't, Rodney.

RODNEY. Just because he's got a lot of money he seems to think there isn't any left, but I'll show him. I may not

have much at the start, but watch my finish.

MARY. What are you going to do?

RODNEY. I'm going to work.

MARY [*excited*]. You are — really? [*Rises*]

RODNEY. Yes, indeed — father couldn't make me do it, but you have. I'll work for you.

MARY. Oh, you are splendid. Will you get a position?

RODNEY. I should say not! Work for someone else? No, sir — I'm going in business for myself — for you. I'm going to show the stuff that's in me. Of course, we can't get married till I've made good. Will you wait?

MARY [*shyly*]. Yes, dear.

RODNEY. You're a dandy.

MARY. What business are you going in?

RODNEY. I don't know yet. I'm going upstairs to pack a suit-case and think. [*Crosses to right*] I'll be back in fifteen minutes. [*He grabs her and kisses her hastily but heartily*]

MARY. Oh, oh — please —

RODNEY. Don't mind, Mary. You'll get used to 'em. [*Exits door lower right*]

[*She goes over and raps three times on the door through which* MARTIN *left, and backs away from it. She stands there expectantly. In a moment* MARTIN *tiptoes in with no trace of a limp. She puts her fingers to her lips to indicate silence, and points off-stage right to indicate where* RODNEY *has gone.* MARTIN *tiptoes nearer, nodding his head, questioning and eager.* MARY *smilingly nods her head in reply*]

MARTIN [*in stage-whisper*]. You mean our scheme worked?

MARY [*delighted*]. Yes, yes.

MARTIN. You really have got him to go to work?

MARY. I have!

MARTIN [*gleefully*]. By George, that's great!

MARY. Isn't it!

MARTIN. You're sure he wasn't just talking?

MARY. No, he's gone upstairs to pack and go out and make a name for himself.

MARTIN. You're a wise girl. Isn't it wonderful?

MARY. And you said I couldn't do it.

MARTIN. I said I didn't think you could, but you have, and I owe you $2500. [*Crosses to chair left of table to make out check*]

MARY. Oh, there's no hurry.

MARTIN. Never put off till to-morrow the money you can get to-day.

MARY. Aren't you proud I've been so successful?

MARTIN. Proud? I'm so doggone happy I'm making this out for $5000.

MARY. Oh, Mr. Martin!

MARTIN. And it's worth $50,000 to me to have my boy really want to work, not just to do it to please me. What a difference an incentive makes! [*Hands her the check*]

MARY [*smiling at check*]. Doesn't it?

MARTIN [*crosses to left*]. Especially if it's a girl. And to think I begged and threatened Rodney for months, and then you plan this scheme, you invent my gout, you rehearse me, you come up here for six short weeks and — Bing, you get him so he's in love with you.

MARY. Or thinks he is.

MARTIN. But say, what about your marriage? [*Sits in chair left of table*]

MARY. He said he wouldn't marry me till he'd made good — if I'd just wait. [*Sits in chair right of table*]

MARTIN [*anxiously*]. Do you think perhaps he may really love you?

MARY. Of course not.

MARTIN. It's the first time he's actually wanted to marry anybody.

MARY. Oh, it's just that I've been very blue-eyed and baby-faced.

MARTIN. I guess you're right!

MARY. Of course I am. When I break our engagement he may feel sort of lonely for a while and give up women forever, but pretty soon some charming girl of his world will come along — some limousine lady, and they'll live happy ever after.

MARTIN. I sort of begin to wish this marriage were going to be on the level.

MARY. It wouldn't work out. I'm a business woman. Even if your son did love me — really love — I wouldn't marry him. Just now he's twenty-four with an India-rubber heart that is easy to stretch and easier to snap back. All boys at twenty-four are like that.

MARTIN [*reminiscently*]. I guess so. I remember when I was a young man, there was a girl . . . my heart was broken for a week — perhaps ten days. I went down to the club one night and got spifflicated — however, however —

[*Abruptly changing the subject*] What's my son going to work at?

MARY. I don't know yet.

MARTIN. Do you think he'll make good?

MARY. He will if he keeps at it. [*Rises and goes right*]

MARTIN. Well, you'll keep him at it? [*Rises and goes right*]

MARY. That wasn't our agreement. I only undertook to get him to start to work.

MARTIN. Hum.

MARY [*quickly*]. Isn't that true?

MARTIN. Quite — quite. I was just thinking we might make some new agreement to have you keep him on the job.

MARY [*rubbing her fingers as if handling money*]. I'm a business woman.

MARTIN. What strikes you as fair?

MARY. I'd rather the proposition came from you.

MARTIN. What do you say to your present salary, and at the end of the year I will personally give you a check for twenty-five per cent. of what Rodney has made.

MARY. Oh, that wouldn't interest me at all.

MARTIN. What's your proposition, then?

MARY [*promptly*]. My present salary doubled.

MARTIN. Um — that's pretty steep.

MARY. You told me what I'd done *already* was worth $50,000 to you.

MARTIN. Merely a figure of speech, my dear. Let's see, you're getting $40 a week, and . . .

MARY. $50, and I want $100.

MARTIN. Sounds like a hold-up. [*Crosses right*]

MARY. Then let's drop it. This new contract was your idea, not mine. Good-evening. [*She starts to go, gets to door, which she bangs as if she had gone. She remains however in the room*]

MARTIN. Hold on — hold on — [*He turns and sees her, and then chuckles at her joke on him. She laughs, too*] I was simply figuring. Tell you what I'll do: $75 a week and 10 per cent. of what Rodney makes.

MARY. Seventy-five a week and 10 per cent. of what he makes? All right, I'll go you.

MARTIN. Good.

MARY [*goes to desk, takes note-book*]. Will you just write me a note stating the facts and the consideration?

MARTIN. You want it in writing?
[*Crosses to table right and sits*]

MARY. Certainly, it's always safer
that way. [*He writes. As he writes*]
As soon as you see Rodney, you'll have
to discharge me.

MARTIN. I will, violently. I make a
pretty good actor under your direction.
How did you like that irate father stuff?

MARY. Great! You needn't make
the note long. Just a memorandum.

MARTIN [*holding up paper*]. How's
that?

MARY [*reading*]. I think that covers
it — if you'll sign it.

MARTIN [*confused*]. Didn't I sign it?

MARY [*smiling*]. No, and never put
off till to-morrow what you can sign to-
day.

MARTIN [*signing*]. There you are.
[*Hands* MARY *paper*]

MARY [*sits on table*]. Thanks. Now,
Mr. Martin, there's just one question
I'd like to ask.

MARTIN. Go ahead, I'll answer you
anything.

MARY. Why is it, when Rodney's
been out of college for *two* years, that
it's only the last three months you've
been so persistent about getting him to
work?

MARTIN. It's like this. You know
old John Clark?

MARY. The man you dine with so
often?

MARTIN. Yes, friends and rivals for
thirty years.

MARY. He's in Ivory Soap, isn't
he?

MARTIN [*emphatically*]. I should say
he is — one of the big men there.
We've fought all our lives over soap, but
he's never been able to lick me, and —
well, I haven't been able to lick him,
either.

MARY. Perhaps that's why you're
such good friends.

MARTIN. Perhaps it is. Anyhow, as
it's fifty-fifty in business, we've lately
narrowed the fight down to a family
matter. You know old John Clark
has a son, too: Ellery — nasty, egotistical, self-satisfied young puppy.

MARY. I know, I've talked to him.

MARTIN. Well, old Clark thinks
Ellery is the prince of all modern business, and he kept pitying me so much
about Rodney's being an idler — a rich
man's son — it got on my nerves, so
lately I made a bet with him.

MARY. A bet!

MARTIN. I bet him thirty thousand
dollars my son could make more in a
year than his son could. So I had to get
Rodney busy, and he's got to make good.
He can't be such a pin-head as he looks!
If there's anything in heredity there
must be something of me in him, and
we've got to find it — we've got to develop Rodney, dig deep, maybe blast.
If he doesn't win out —

MARY. But he will, I'm sure he will.

MARTIN. It isn't just the money. I
guess I'm a sentimental old fool, but
I'm proud. I want my boy to be Rodney Martin, not just Cyrus Martin's
son, and I want to show old Clark that
as a judge of character he's a bigger fool
than I am. If I don't get that bet —

MARY. But you're going to, I'm
sure you are.

MARTIN. By George, Miss Grayson,
if I weren't a bit old and on the shelf,
I'd marry you myself. You and I could
clean up all the loose change in America.
[RODNEY *enters right*. MARTIN, *seeing
him, changes his whole attitude. Rises*]
I don't care to discuss the matter further, Miss Grayson: consider yourself
discharged. Good evening. [*Crosses
to left*]

RODNEY. It's all right, Mary. You
can have a job in my office. [*Crosses to
center*]

MARTIN [*scornfully*]. Your office, ha!
[*Suddenly*] Oh, my foot, my poor foot!
[*He limps painfully towards door*] Your
office! It's a joke, young man!

RODNEY. Oh, you needn't laugh!
I'll show you. [*Crosses left center*]

MARTIN [*winking at* MARY]. Silence,
you young puppy. Oh, my poor foot!
[*He exits*]

MARY. Oh, Rodney! [*Sits on sofa*]

[RODNEY *goes up-stage, and passes behind
sofa so that he is at the right end of
sofa*]

RODNEY. Gout's an awful thing,
isn't it? [*Sits on sofa*]

MARY. Oh, Rodney, I'm afraid I've
spoiled everything for you — your future —

RODNEY. Nonsense, you've made
my future. Without you, I'd never
have got the idea, the big idea.

MARY. Idea for what?

RODNEY. The idea to make money
out of; that's all you need. And, just
think, I found it in this book.

MARY. What idea? What book?

RODNEY. It's a cook-book.

MARY. What on earth —?

RODNEY. Well, you see, when I was packing I stumbled across this book; it fell open at this page — fate was on the job — it was a hunch. Look!

MARY [*looking*]. But what is it?

RODNEY. It's an old family recipe for making cheap soap. It says it's the cheapest soap in the world. Cheaper even than the manufacturers make it. I'm going into the soap business.

MARY [*amazed*]. What?

RODNEY. Sure. Father did; look at the money he made. Why shouldn't I?

MARY [*rises, goes left*]. You're joking.

RODNEY. I'm in dead earnest. I'm going to buck the trust. [*Rises*]

MARY. But how can you?

RODNEY. I don't know, but I will. You see, I'll have all the popular sympathy: independent young son of soap-king fights father; don't buy from the trust.

MARY. But is that very nice to your *father*?

RODNEY. Has he been nice to me? It's great! Down with monopoly! Hurrah for the people! I've heard political speeches like that. Hurrah for the people's soap! That isn't a bad name, either. The People's Soap. [*Lays book on table*]

MARY. But you haven't any capital.

RODNEY [*dejected*]. I never thought of that.

MARY. You'd need a lot of money.

RODNEY [*bracing up*]. Well, I'll have to get it, that's all, and you'll be my secretary. Of course, till I make big money I wouldn't ordinarily have thought of taking you away from father — but as long as he discharged you — well, you work for me now. What does father pay you?

MARY. Fifty dollars a week.

RODNEY. I'll pay you a hundred and fifty.

MARY. But you haven't any money.

[JOHNSON *enters from door upper left*]

JOHNSON. Beg pardon, Mr. Rodney, but Mr. Ambrose Peale is here to see you.

MARY. For the fifth time —

RODNEY [*puzzled*]. Ambrose Peale? Oh, yes, I remember. Ask him to come in.

JOHNSON. Yes, sir. [*He exits door upper left*]

MARY. Who is he?

RODNEY. He's got something to do with the theater. When I was in Harvard two years ago I met him one night in the lobby of the theater. I haven't seen him since — it was the night we had our egg fight.

MARY. You and Mr. Peale?

RODNEY. No, no, the fellows threw eggs at the people on the stage. You see, it was a college play —

MARY. Did you throw eggs?

RODNEY. I forgot to bring any. Peale was the manager of the show and was mighty decent to me — kept me out of jail.

[PEALE *enters from door upper left*]

PEALE. Well, well, Rodney Martin, how are you? [*To* MARY] How are you, dear lady?

RODNEY. How do you do? Miss Grayson — Mr. Ambrose Peale.

PEALE. Ambrose Peale — that's me absolutely. Well, I'm still in the show business. [*To* MARY] Ever see "The Belle of Broadway"? Great show, great girls, great cast.

MARY. Oh, are you an actor?

PEALE [*scornfully*]. An actor? I should say not. I'm a press-agent.

MARY. Oh!

PEALE. But, say, be sure to catch that show; it may leave the city soon — out-of-town bookings, you know — but remember the name: "The Belle of Broadway." And now if you'll excuse me, Miss, I came to talk business with Mr. Martin.

RODNEY. Business? Surely — surely. [*Winking at* MARY] I'm a business man — now.

MARY. I'll be back in a few minutes.

RODNEY. Thank you, Miss Grayson. [*She exits door lower right*]

PEALE. Now, I'm not much on handing myself flowers across the footlights, but do you happen to remember what I did for you the night of the egg fight?

RODNEY. You fixed things with the chief of police and kept me from being expelled.

PEALE. By George, you do remember. And you said any time you could do anything for me —

RODNEY. That's still true.

PEALE. You're immense, son. Now, it's this way — have a chair. [*He sits*

RODNEY *does likewise*] Between you and me, "The Belle of Broadway" is an awful thing — business gone to pot. Something's got to be done. Some great stuff pulled off to give it a boost, and that's where you come in.

RODNEY. I?

PEALE. You've got an aeroplane, haven't you?

RODNEY. Yes, but —

PEALE. Then everything's all right. Now you abduct the leading lady, Julia Clark, to-morrow night, in your aeroplane — elope with her —

RODNEY. What?

PEALE. Sure — some stunt, too — never been done. Julia'll stand for it — she's game for any press gag —

RODNEY. But I couldn't do that.

PEALE. Certainly you can. I'm telling you Julia'll stand for it — a bird of a story — no performance. Why? You're up in the air with the leading lady. The next night standing room only to catch a look at the girl you're stuck on. I can see the headlines now : Soap King's Son Takes New Star Among the Stars — with flashlights.

RODNEY. But it's out of the question. [*Rises, takes chair to table*]

PEALE. What's the matter with it?

RODNEY. I wouldn't do it, that's all.

PEALE. Gee, that's tough !

RODNEY. I'm not backing down — anything in reason, but you see, there's someone who might object.

PEALE. A girl? [RODNEY *nods*] Her? [*Pointing to where* MARY *exited*]

RODNEY. Yes.

PEALE [*rises and puts chair back*]. I guess it's cold : girls are funny about their beaux doing a little innocent thing like eloping with some other girl.

RODNEY. Why don't you try somebody else?

PEALE. I have ! You were my last card. Well, I'm fired !

RODNEY. Fired?

PEALE. Sure, that stunt would have kept us going, but now, on the level — well, the show's so bad, people won't even go see it on a pass. We'll close Saturday and I'm out —

RODNEY. A fake story like that would really have helped?

PEALE. Helped a whole lot : given us a fresh start, and then I'd have pulled off some new stunts and saved my job.

RODNEY. Oh, nonsense. If that were true, I'd feel mighty uncomfortable at not being able to oblige you, but an obvious trumped-up lie like that can't be any good.

PEALE. It can't, eh?

RODNEY. Oh, I know it's advertising —

PEALE. You bet it's advertising. What made Anna Held? Milk baths. What made Gaby Deslys? A dago king.

RODNEY. But that kind of advertising can't be of real value. [*Sits*]

PEALE. Oh, you're one of those guys who don't believe in advertising, are you? Now, don't get me talking advertising. That's where I live, where I have my town house and country estate, my yacht and motors. That's my home. Maybe you think love is important? Piffle. Advertising, my boy, the power of suggestion, the psychology of print ; say a thing often enough and hard enough and the other chap'll not only believe you, he'll think it's his own idea, and he'll fight for it. Some old gink, a professor of psychology, showed forty Vassar girls the other day two samples of satin, one blue, one pink, same grade, same value, same artistic worth. One he described as a delicate warm old rose, the other a faded blue. He asked them to choose their favorite. Thirty-nine out of the forty picked the old rose. Why? Because they'd been told it was warm and delicate ; no faded blue for theirs ! What did it? The power of suggestion — advertising !

RODNEY [*amused*]. You seem to know something about it —

PEALE. I not only seem to, I do. You heard me tell that girl of yours a few minutes ago that "The Belle of Broadway" was the biggest hit in town. Ask her to go to the theater. Give her her choice and I'll bet you four dollars to a fried egg she picks "The Belle of Broadway." Advertising !

RODNEY. I don't believe it.

PEALE. Well, try it — and say, what makes you go to the theater yourself? I'll tell you — it's what you've read about the play or what some fellows told you.

RODNEY [*beginning to be convinced*]. Why, I suppose that's true.

PEALE. And what he tells you, some other guy has told him. Ninety-seven per cent. of the public believe what they're told, and what they're told is what the other chap's been told — and the fellow who told him read it somewhere. When you see a thing in print about something you don't really know anything about, you come pretty near believing it. And all the advertiser has to do is to tell you right and you'll fall.

RODNEY. But I never read advertisements.

PEALE. Oh, you don't, eh? I guess you do. If I say His Master's Voice, you know that advertises a phonograph. You're on to what soap "It Floats" refers to. There's a Reason — Uneeda — Quaker Oats — Phoebe Show — Children Cry For It — Sapolio — Grape Nuts — Peruna — The Road of Anthracite — Spearmint — Pierce Arrow — 57 Varieties — Kodak — White Seal — Gold Dust Twins — He Won't Be Happy Till He Gets It — Bull Durham — Pianola — Cuticura — Melachrino — Clysmic — Goodyear — Steinway — Thermos — Coca-Cola — The Watch that Made The Dollar Famous. I suppose you don't know what any of them mean?

RODNEY [amused]. Why, I know what they all mean.

PEALE. You bet you do. What kind of garters do you wear?

RODNEY. Why, let me see: Boston.

PEALE. Exactly. What do you know about 'em? Nothing. Are they any better than any other garter? You don't know — I don't know — but all my life, every magazine I've ever looked into has had a picture of a man's leg with a certain kind of garter on it — Boston — so when I go into a store to buy a pair of garters I just naturally say Boston; so do you. What do you know about Mennen's Talcum Powder? Nothing, except that it has the picture of the homeliest man in the world on the box and it's so impressed your imagination, you just mechanically order Mennen's. If I say to you, E. & W., you don't think it's a corset, do you? If I say C. B., you don't think it's a collar, and what about the well-known and justly famous B. V. D.'s? You don't read advertisement? Rot!

RODNEY. But —

PEALE. No 'but' about it: advertising's responsible for everything. When a department store advertises a seven-dollar shirt-waist for four dollars, you don't believe it's on the level, do you?

RODNEY. No, I don't.

PEALE. Neither do I, but there's a hell of a lot of women who do. When Bryan advertised the Grape Juice High-ball, do you know that its sale went up 652 gallons a day?

RODNEY. How do you know it was 652?

PEALE. I'll let you into a little secret: I don't know. I don't know a damned thing about grape juice, and as long as my health and strength keep up, I hope I never will, but if I said I'd read in a newspaper that the sale had gone up 652 gallons, you wouldn't have doubted it, would you?

RODNEY. No, I suppose I wouldn't.

PEALE. And you'd have told somebody else and he'd have believed you, too. Say, do you drink much?

RODNEY. No.

PEALE. Can you tell the difference between a vintage wine and last year's champagne? Sure, you can: it costs more. Son, the world is full of bunk. Ninety-seven per cent. of the people are sheep, and you can get 'em all by advertising.

RODNEY. You are gradually making me come to the conclusion that you believe in publicity.

PEALE. Believe in it! It's my life. What kind of eggs do you eat?

RODNEY. Why, hen's eggs, of course.

PEALE. Why "of course"? Did you ever eat a duck's egg?

RODNEY. Why, no.

PEALE. Do you know anything against the duck?

RODNEY. No.

PEALE. Exactly. When a duck lays an egg it's a damn fool and keeps quiet about it, but when a hen does, my boy — cluck-cluck all over the place! She's advertising. So you eat hen's eggs.

RODNEY. You're beginning to convince me.

PEALE. If I'm beginning to convince you, that's advertising, too. Say, are you for Roosevelt or against him?

RODNEY. I'm for him strong.

PEALE. I'm against him. I read one paper, you read another. I think he's a faker, you think he's a great man. But does either of us really know anything about him except what we've read? Have you ever met Roosevelt or talked to him or known anybody who did know him? I haven't, but the point is, whatever we may think, good or bad, we've heard a lot about him, because he's the best advertiser in the world. And that, my son, is the whole secret of it: get 'em talking about you, get 'em praisin' if you can, or get 'em ussin', but for the love of Heaven, don't let 'em be quiet. Mention your name — have 'em argue about you — boost or knock — be a hero or a villain, but don't be a dub. Why, give me the money, a little time, a few pages of advertising, and I can sell you shares in the Atlantic Ocean!

RODNEY [*excited*]. You really believe that with proper advertising you could build up a great business?

PEALE. Believe! Look around you : everything's doing it.

RODNEY. And you are out of a job.

PEALE. Unless you do the aero-elopement.

RODNEY [*rises*]. Then you're out of it. Do you want to work for me?

PEALE. Sure.

RODNEY. When can you begin?

PEALE. Now.

RODNEY. What's your salary?

PEALE. I've been getting $60, but I'm worth $75.

RODNEY. I'll give you a hundred.

PEALE. What is your business? Counterfeiting?

RODNEY. No, it's —

PEALE. Don't tell me. As long as it don't send me to state's prison or the chair, it's all right. Could have about $25 advance on my salary now?

RODNEY. Is that customary?

PEALE. It is with me.

RODNEY. Oh, all right. [*He gives him the money*]

PEALE. Just as an evidence of good faith. [*He counts money*] Well, now I'm working for you, what business are you in?

RODNEY. The soap business.

PEALE [*grinning*]. Nice clean business. With father?

RODNEY. Against him!

PEALE. Oh!

RODNEY. My father and I have had a quarrel.

PEALE. I know, I know : fathers are very unreasonable these days.

RODNEY. I'm going to fight the soap trust.

PEALE. Well, you're no piker. You've picked out a nice refined job. How long have you been at it?

RODNEY. Twenty minutes.

PEALE. How's it going?

RODNEY. Fine, since I got an idea from you.

PEALE. They grow all over me — help yourself.

RODNEY. I'm going to get a factory, advertise like the very dickens : Soap King's son fights father — and licks him, too, by George!

PEALE. Wait a minute, wait a minute, do you know why your father is the soap king?

RODNEY. I suppose because he controls all the soap business in the country except Ivory.

PEALE. Exactly, and the way he keeps control of it is by buying out all his live competitors. Now, here's a blue-ribbon champion of the world scheme. Why don't we make good and sell out to father?

RODNEY. No, I don't care to do that. I want to make good myself.

PEALE. Well, if father is forced to buy you out, isn't that enough? What do you want?

RODNEY. I've got to be a success on my own. I've got to show father, and — Miss Grayson.

PEALE [*comprehending*]. Oh! Making good with the dame, eh?

RODNEY. You see, father says I can't earn five dollars a week.

PEALE. He isn't right, is he?

RODNEY. No, sir, you'll see.

PEALE. I hope so. Pretty tough if you couldn't. Some job trying to sell soap if father's against us.

RODNEY. I suppose it is.

PEALE. I tell you : why not make such a hit with the soap, advertise it so strong, he'll just have to back you?

RODNEY. Now that's settled, we're going to lick father.

PEALE. Yes, that's settled. What do I do?

RODNEY. You write the ads that make us.

PEALE. It's my chance. Think, I'll never have to see "The Belle of Broadway" again! I'll write ads, I'll conduct a campaign that'll keep your father awake, and in three months at the most he'll be begging for a chance to back us.

RODNEY. I believe we'll do it.

PEALE. Come on, come on. Let's get busy. What's the name of the soap?

RODNEY. It hasn't been named.

PEALE. Well, what is there about it that makes it different from any other soap?

RODNEY. I don't know.

PEALE. Well, what could there be about some soap that was different from some other soap?

RODNEY. Well, let's see.

PEALE. Where did you get it from?

RODNEY. From this cook-book.

PEALE. Are you kidding me?

RODNEY. No. Half an hour ago I decided to go into business, and I happened to find this recipe for soap in a cook-book — it's the cheapest soap in the world. [*Reflecting*] That's not a bad title: the cheapest soap in the world. [*A pause. They reflect*]

PEALE. You're wrong, son. There's an awful bunch of people that buy a lot of expensive stuff, not because it's better, but because it costs more — and the poor nuts think it ought to be better — so can that cheap stuff.

RODNEY. Well, how about The Most Expensive Soap in the World?

PEALE. My boy, I could kiss you. A pupil after my own heart — fifty cents a cake.

RODNEY. A dollar, and we'll make it a warm delicate old rose.

PEALE. Each cake in a separate box with a paper rose on the lid.

RODNEY. Great.

PEALE. But what'll we call it?

RODNEY. Old Rose.

PEALE. Rotten — doesn't mean anything.

RODNEY. Let's think.

PEALE. I am thinking. I never stop.

RODNEY. The Soap that Made Pittsburg Clean.

PEALE. Too long, and no good anyway, because Pittsburg isn't clean. You need something catchy.

RODNEY. I had an idea a while ago: The People's Soap.

PEALE. Not if you're going to catch the rich boobs.

RODNEY. That's true.

PEALE. We need something that's universally appealing. What is it? What is it?

RODNEY [*looking off-stage toward where* MARY *went*]. Love.

PEALE. Slush.

RODNEY. Money.

PEALE [*suddenly*]. I've got it: Superstition — everybody's superstitious.

RODNEY. Rot! I'm not.

PEALE. I say, there's a bit of luck for us right at the start — a pin with the head toward you. [RODNEY *stoops to pick it up*] See, you were going to pick it up! Everybody is superstitious. Oh, they say they're not, just as you did, but did you ever meet a guy who, if he didn't mind walking under a ladder,

didn't hate to spill salt, or else he wanted to see the moon over his right shoulder — or he picked up pins, or carried a lucky coin, wouldn't do things on Friday? Why, the whole world's superstitious. Get something on that and you hit everybody. I've got eighty-six horseshoes home myself. I never saw a gink that would sit thirteen at table. We're all crazy. [*They pause and think. They both sit on end of table*]

RODNEY. Could we —?

PEALE. What?

RODNEY. No. [*They pause*]

PEALE. Suppose we —?

RODNEY. What?

PEAL. No — [*Pause*]

RODNEY. Wait! Wait — listen! The Thirteen Soap — Unlucky for Dirt.

PEALE [*coming over and kissing* RODNEY *on the brow*]. Son, it's all over: the old man'll be on his knees in a month.

RODNEY. We open the office Monday.

PEALE. Where's the office?

RODNEY. Let's get one.

PEALE. With furniture and everything. Say — [MARY *enters from door lower right. Seeing her*] There's the dame; ask her to go to the theater, just to prove what I say. See for yourself. [*He goes up-stage*]

RODNEY [*turning to her*]. Oh, Mary, to celebrate, let's go to the theater to-morrow night?

MARY. I'd love to.

RODNEY. What do you want to see?

MARY. I hear "The Belle of Broadway" is very good.

[PEALE *yawns and stretches out his arms complacently*]

PEALE [*to* RODNEY]. I guess I don't know about advertising, eh? [*To* MARY] My last official act is giving you a box for to-morrow night. [*He writes*]

MARY. Oh, yes, you're with that play, aren't you?

PEALE. I am. [*Handing her pass*] Er — I was.

MARY. But isn't it an imposition?

PEALE. Not on us, it isn't.

MARY. Thank you. [*Crosses to* RODNEY. *To* RODNEY] I didn't mean to bother you, but I'm so interested: I thought, regarding Mr. Peale's business, I'd like to hear —

RODNEY. It's all settled, Mary. Mr. Peale, my general manager. Mr.

Peale, my secretary. Mary, here it is: The Thirteen Soap — Unlucky for Dirt: The Most Expensive Soap in the World.

MARY [*genuinely*]. Why, that's perfectly wonderful — who thought of it? [*Looking at* PEALE]

RODNEY. I did.

MARY [*turning to him*]. You did, really? Why, you're splendid.

PEALE. Youth, brains, efficiency — that's our motto.

RODNEY. We'll make a hundred thousand dollars the first year — sure.

MARY [*reflectively*]. And ten per cent. of that is —

RODNEY. What?

MARY [*quickly*]. Oh nothing, nothing — I was just figuring.

RODNEY. We're going to make our soap famous by advertising, and then force father to back us.

MARY. That sounds bully, and at the start you won't need much capital.

RODNEY. Capital?

PEALE. With fifty thousand dollars I can make the Great American People have hysterics for the Thirteen Soap.

RODNEY. Fifty thousand dollars, and I've got only a thousand. Oh! [*Sits on chair right of desk*]

MARY. Oh! [*Sitting on sofa*]

PEALE [*sitting in arm-chair left of table*]. But can't you raise it?

RODNEY [*to* PEALE]. How?

PEALE. Don't ask me. Raising money is the only thing I never got on to —

RODNEY. Peale, you're fired.

PEALE. Well, it was a good job while it lasted.

RODNEY [*rises*]. Gimme back that $25.

PEALE [*rises, takes out money and returns it to* RODNEY]. Good-bye, old pal.

MARY [*rises, and comes down-stage between* RODNEY *and* PEALE]. But couldn't you start with less?

RODNEY. Of course we could. Couldn't we, Peale?

PEALE. Not and do it right. No use wasting money piking when you advertise. Splurge, my lad, splurge or let it remain dormant.

RODNEY. I've got a thousand in the bank; the aeroplane's worth four — it cost eight.

PEALE. Then if you're lucky it might sell for two.

RODNEY. The motors ought to bring another four. That'd be seven, isn't that something?

PEALE. Seven thousand is not to be spoken of venomously, but in advertising — well, going easy, it might last you a week.

MARY. I have a —

PEALE. Some money?

RODNEY. We couldn't take money from you.

MARY. No, I know a — a man that might put in five thousand.

RODNEY. That's twelve.

PEALE [*suddenly*]. Does your father advertise much?

RODNEY. I don't think so; does he, Mary?

MARY. Not very much: he's conservative. He doesn't believe in reckless advertising.

PEALE. Nothing sensational or exciting?

MARY. No.

PEALE. Why, he's licked now, and I'll tell you why. We can advertise just for your father's benefit alone.

RODNEY. I don't quite understand your plan?

PEALE. Why, plaster this neighborhood with Thirteen Soap advertisements. Do the same around your father's office so that every time he went out or came in he'd see Thirteen Soap. We could advertise only in the newspapers he reads. We'd send him circulars every mail. I could make a splurge just for him that would look like we were giving up $10,000 a day. Within a month he'd think that Thirteen Soap was the only soap in the world.

RODNEY. How much would it take?

PEALE. Five thousand a week.

RODNEY. And you could land him in a month.

PEALE. My boy!

RODNEY. And we've got one thousand — all cash, and eleven thousand in prospects. Go ahead.

PEALE. You mean I'm hired again?

RODNEY. Sure you are.

PEALE. Gimme back that $25.

RODNEY [*giving it back*]. Certainly.

PEALE. The best thing you ever did was to engage me.

RODNEY. Peale, we'll be rich men.

PEALE. With your money and my ideas, I'll be a millionaire.

RODNEY. Well, I hope I will, too.

MARY. Me, too.

JOHNSON [*entering from door upper left*]. Countess de Beou — ree — enn.

MARY. Oh, that dreadful woman again.

COUNTESS [*entering and coming over to* RODNEY. *To* RODNEY]. Vous êtes M. Martin?

RODNEY [*nods*]. Yes.

COUNTESS. Ah, cher M. Martin — je suis enchantée de vous voir.

PEALE. The dame's looney.

MARY. No, she's French.

PEALE. Same thing.

RODNEY. What's all this, anyhow?

MARY. She wanted to see your father, and she doesn't speak English.

RODNEY. Well, let her speak to me. Fire ahead.

PEALE. Say, can you speak French?

MARY [*surprised*]. Can you?

RODNEY. No, but I can understand it. [*Going to* COUNTESS] Fire ahead.

COUNTESS. Eh?

RODNEY. Let me see — oh, yes. Parlez.

COUNTESS. Ah, Mon Dieu — enfin, quelqu'un qui comprend Français.

RODNEY. Oui.

COUNTESS. Puis-je vous parler pour cinq minutes?

RODNEY. Oui.

COUNTESS. Merci bien.

RODNEY. Oui —

PEALE. You're immense, kid.

COUNTESS [*quickly*]. Je suis Madame la Comtesse de Beaurien. Je désire parler à M. Martin àpropos des affaires du savon. Je voudrais obtenir l'agence du Savon Martin pour la France.

RODNEY. Wait a minute — wait a minute.

MARY. What did she say?

PEALE. She's a speedy spieler all right.

RODNEY [*to* COUNTESS]. Would you mind saying that over and say it slow?

COUNTESS. Comment?

RODNEY. Oh. . . . Répétez ça s'il vous plait — pas vite.

COUNTESS. Je suis Madame la Comtesse de Beaurien. Je désire obtenir l'agence du Savon Martin pour la France. Je peux donner cinquante mille francs pour cette agence. Et enfin, voulez-vous arranger cette affaire pour moi? Je suis riche, j'ai beaucoup de recommendations — je suis bien connue à Paris.

RODNEY. Wait a minute. Wait a minute. [*To* PEALE] She wants the agency for father's soap for France and is willing to pay 50,000 francs for the concession.

PEALE. How much is that in money?

RODNEY. Ten thousand dollars.

MARY. Had I better tell your father? [*Goes to door lower left*]

RODNEY [*inspired. Crosses to* MARY]. No, no, why not keep father out of this? We'll sell her the agency for the Thirteen Soap — that'd be another $10,000 for us. Peale, she's a gift from the gods! [*Goes to* COUNTESS]

PEALE. She is. Go to it.

MARY. But how can you sell her your agency?

RODNEY. I don't know — how can I?

PEALE. A pipe. Ask her if she's superstitious?

RODNEY. Oh, if I only knew how to talk French! — Madame — êtes vous superstitious?

COUNTESS. Eh?

RODNEY. I mean — superstitieuse? [COUNTESS *looks blank*]

PEALE. She doesn't get you.

RODNEY. No.

PEALE [*he goes and takes the* COUNTESS' *parasol*]. Pardon me. . . . [*Starts to raise it. With a cry of protest:* "*Faites pas ça,*" *she stops him*] She's superstitious, all right — [*To her*] It ought to be a pipe to land you.

RODNEY. Listen: je suis le fils de Museer Martin — vous savez?

COUNTESS [*delightedly*]. Oui, oui.

RODNEY [*slowly*]. Nous manfacturons, I mean manufacturong — un nouveau savon — see? Savon Treize — [*He holds up his fingers to indicate thirteen*]

COUNTESS. Oui, oui.

PEALE [*impressed*]. It must be great to have a college education.

RODNEY. Savon Treize — pas — bon — pour — what the deuce is dirt?

MARY. I don't know.

RODNEY. Oh, yes, — sal — pas bon pour sal —

COUNTESS [*laughing*]. Savon Treize — pas bon pour sal — c'est bien — c'est bien.

PEALE [*gleefully*]. She likes it — she likes it.

RODNEY. Je start — je begin — je commence — un nouveau compagnie — le très grande compagnie de la universe — je suis le president.

PEALE. Je suis le advertising agent. [*After laugh,* JOHNSON *enters from door upper left with a letter, and exits door lower left*]

RODNEY. I'm the whole thing, see — and if we can do business with you for the French agency —

[MARIE *enters*]

COUNTESS. Mais non, mais non, mais non, monsieur, je ne comprends pas.

MARIE. I beg pardon.

MARY. What is it, Marie?

MARIE [*in French dialect*]. Where is M. Martin?

RODNEY. Marie! Another gift from Heaven.

MARIE. Mr. Smith to see your father.

RODNEY. That's a man I might get money from. [JOHNSON *enters from door lower left*] He's a great friend of the family. Used to dangle me on his knee, and all that sort of thing. [*He sees* JOHNSON] Oh, Johnson.

JOHNSON. Yes, sir?

RODNEY. Mr. Smith is downstairs — in one minute bring him up here.

JOHNSON. Yes, sir. [*He exits door upper left*]

RODNEY. Now, Marie, tell the Countess you speak French.

MARIE. Je parle Français, Madame.

COUNTESS. Mon Dieu — enfin quelqu'un qui parle Français! Je suis Madame la Comtesse de Beaurien — et je désire parler avec monsieur àpropos des affaires du Savon Treize.

MARIE [*back at her quickly*]. Ah mais oui — je comprends parfaitement. Je dirai à monsieur ce que vous avez dit. Ah je suis ravie d'avoir trouvé aux Etats Unis une compatriote avec laquelle je pourrais parler ma belle langue de France. [*They talk together violently in French, and at the end of the speech, the* COUNTESS *kisses* MARIE]

RODNEY. Mary, take them away — take them into the library. Explain to Marie about the agency — Mary can translate your slang to Marie and she can turn it into French.

MARY. I'll do my best. Come, Marie. [*Crosses to door lower right, and opens it*] Bring the Countess.

MARIE. Madame la Comtesse, je vous montrai le chemin —

COUNTESS. Bien.

[MARIE *and* COUNTESS, *chattering volubly in French, followed by* MARY, *exit door lower right*]

PEALE [*looking after them*]. Paris must be a hell of a place.

RODNEY. I'll tackle Smith for a loan of $10,000.

PEALE. Will he fall?

RODNEY [*grandly*]. My father's oldest friend. Why, the way I'll handle him, ten thousand ought to be easy.

PEALE. Good luck.

[*Enter* MR. SMITH *from door upper left*]

RODNEY. Hello, Mr. Smith. That's all, now, Mr. Peale.

PEALE. Yes, sir, I understand. [*Winking*] He takes 50,000 shares at par.

RODNEY. Quite right.

[PEALE *exits door lower right*]

SMITH. Who the deuce is that, Rod?

RODNEY. One of my staff.

SMITH [*amazed*]. One of your what?

RODNEY. Staff — I've gone into business.

SMITH [*laughing uproariously*]. You've done what?

RODNEY. I'm a business man.

SMITH. That's the funniest thing I ever heard of.

RODNEY. What's funny about it?

SMITH. You in business! [*He laughs again*]

RODNEY. And as a business man I'd like to talk to you regarding a very interesting business proposition in which I am now interested.

SMITH. Nothing doing.

RODNEY [*gulping*]. I thought I'd like to borrow ten — say a few thousand dollars.

SMITH. No.

RODNEY. Perhaps five thousand.

SMITH. If it was a new club or some tomfoolery, in a minute — but to put money into your business — it'd be just throwing it away. Why don't you get your father to back you?

RODNEY. Father and I don't agree on the value of advertising.

SMITH. Oh, that's it, and you expect me to do what your father won't?

RODNEY. Well, I thought as a friend of the family —

SMITH. You were wrong. Where is your father?

RODNEY. In there, I guess. [*Indicating door lower left*]

SMITH. I'll bet he'll think this as funny as I do. [*He exits left.* RODNEY *sinks down dejectedly into a chair.* PEALE *enters with contracts*]

PEALE. Well?

RODNEY [*rises*]. He wouldn't give me a cent.

PEALE. He wouldn't? Well, he sounds like your father's oldest friend.

RODNEY. What about the Countess?

PEALE [*proudly*]. I got her.

RODNEY. You did? $10,000?

PEALE. Fifteen thousand.

RODNEY. Holy jumping Jupiter.

PEALE. Pretty good, what?

RODNEY. Good? Why — why — I'll have to raise your salary.

PEALE. Thanks, I supposed you would.

RODNEY. Where's the money?

PEALE. Oh, we don't get it till next week.

RODNEY [*dejected*]. Oh!

PEALE. But it's all right. We're going to sign the contract with her to-night.

RODNEY. But we must have some more cash to start with.

MARY [*entering*]. The Countess wants to know how much longer she must wait?

PEALE. Coming now. Sign the contract.

RODNEY. Sure, I'll sign anything — I'll sign it twice. [*Signs*]

PEALE. You know, this has got the show business beat a mile. [*He exits door lower right*]

MARY. Oh, Rodney, did Mr. Smith lend you any money?

RODNEY. He did not.

SMITH [*re-entering*]. Oh, Rod — [*Seeing* MARY] I beg your pardon.

RODNEY. That's all right — you needn't go, Mary. Mr. Smith, this is the future Mrs. Martin.

SMITH [*crosses to* MARY]. You don't say so? Well, well, a thousand congratulations!

RODNEY. I suppose you and father had your laugh?

SMITH. No, I didn't tell him.

RODNEY. Thanks for that, anyhow.

SMITH. Of course, it sounded funny to me at first, but when I thought things over, after all, why shouldn't you be a success in business?

RODNEY [*amazed*]. What?

SMITH. You have been in everything else you've tried.

RODNEY. Yes, yes, certainly — sure.

SMITH. Of course, you haven't tried much. But as you said, I am an old friend — and I figured if you gave me your word that you'd return the money within a year — perhaps after all it would only be the act of an old friend to take a chance. That's what friends are for.

RODNEY. Why, that's simply great of you, by George!

SMITH. How much was it you wanted?

[MARY *holds up fingers of both hands*]

RODNEY [*promptly*]. Ten thousand dollars.

SMITH. But, didn't you say —?

RODNEY. Oh, I'm sure I said $10,000, — that's the very least.

SMITH. Um — well I'll mail you a check to-night.

[MARY *squeaks.* SMITH *looks sharply at her. She stops*]

RODNEY [*enthusiastically*]. I'll never forget it. I tell you, old friends do count. Thanks, thanks.

SMITH [*embarrassed*]. That's all right — don't thank me. Good-night, Miss Grayson, and I hope you'll be very happy.

MARY. Good-night.

RODNEY. Good-night. Good-night. [SMITH *exits door upper left. At door, calling after him*] Oh, Mr. Smith, have you your car with you?

SMITH [*off-stage*]. Yes.

RODNEY. Well, tell the chauffeur to drive slow and careful. [RODNEY *grabs* MARY *by her two hands and dances around excitedly*] Ten thousand — and he lent it to me. Oh, isn't it great? [*He kisses her*] Wait till I tell Peale. [*Exit door right*]

COUNTESS [*off-stage, to* RODNEY]. Oh, Monsieur, c'est une affaire magnifique. [*She enters, followed by* MARIE — *to* MARIE] Je vous remercie, Marie, de ce que vous avez fait. Ah, les Américains ce sont des gens d'affaires superbes mais les dames — oh, là, là, qu'elles se fichent au diable! [*Exits door upper left*]

MARY [*to* MARIE]. What did she say?

MARIE. She said the American men are splendid but the women were crazy and they could all go to hell. [*Exits door upper left*]

MARY. Oh! [*She goes over and knocks three times at door left*]

MARTIN [*entering*]. Well, how goes it?

MARY. Oh, Mr. Martin, he's perfectly splendid. So full of energy, hustle and ideas. He's a different man already. You were right: he only needed development.

MARTIN. Good! Good! You're not saying this to flatter an old man's vanity?

MARY. Indeed, I'm not. We won't have to blast.

MARTIN [*shrewdly*]. Would you rather take a guarantee of $2500 additional and give up that 10 per cent. of his profits?

MARY. I should say not.

MARTIN. You know, Miss Grayson, you're making me believe we'll win that $30,000 from old John Clark. [*Crosses down right*]

MARY. Oh, indeed we will: you should have just seen Rodney borrow $10,000 from Mr. Smith, without the least trouble.

MARTIN [*smiling*]. Oh, that was my money.

MARY. What?

MARTIN. When Smith told me Rodney tried to touch him — well, I thought the least I could do was to back my son, so I sent Smith to make good with him.

MARY. That was nice of you.

[RODNEY *enters from door right, with dress-suit case*]

MARTIN. Well, I owed the boy a chance, anyhow. [*Seeing* RODNEY, *turns to him, crossly*] So you're still here, are you?

RODNEY. Yes, sir, but I'm going. Come, Mary. [*Crosses to* MARY]

MARTIN. Really going into business, eh? Well, when you fail, don't come sniveling back here! You can't count on a dollar from me.

RODNEY. I won't snivel — and I don't want your money. I don't need it. Why, I'd have gone to work long ago if I'd known how easy it is to raise $10,000.

MARTIN [*grinning at* MARY]. You would, eh? Well, what soft easy-going business have you picked out?

RODNEY. The soap business.

MARTIN [*genuinely annoyed*]. What? Why, he can't make any money out of soap. [*Crosses to* MARY] That takes brains.

RODNEY. Oh, yes, I can.

MARTIN. I control all the important soap business in the country.

RODNEY. I know you do, but I am going to take it away from you.

MARTIN. What?

RODNEY. Yes, sir, I'm going to manufacture the Thirteen Soap: Unlucky for Dirt: The Most Expensive Soap in the World! I'm going to break the trust; I'm going to attack monopoly. I'm going to appeal to the American people for fair play against the soap trust. You've always wanted me to go into business. Well, I'm in, and forgive me, father, but I'm going to put you out of business. I'm going to advertise all over the world.

MARTIN. You can't fight the soap trust with advertising: we're established.

RODNEY. Yes, yes, we can: think what advertising means: the power of suggestion — the psychology of print. Why, 97 per cent. of the public believe what they're told, and what they're told is what the other chaps have been told, and the fellow who told him read it somewhere. Advertising is responsible for everything. People are sheep, and advertising is the way to make 'em follow your lead. [*He is beginning to forget the speech*] Say, what makes you go to the theater? [PEALE *enters from door right.* MARTIN *starts to speak*] Don't tell me: I'll tell you. It's what you've read of the play or what some fellows told you, and the fellow that told him, read it — in a newspaper. [*Remembering — rapidly*] And that, my boy, is the whole secret of it. You've got to be talked about — get 'em praisin' or cussin', but don't let 'em be quiet. I want to tell you; what kind of duck eggs do you eat?

MARTIN [*aghast*]. What?

[*The curtain begins to fall*]

RODNEY. Do you know anything against the duck? No, you don't, but when a duck lays an egg it's a damn fool and keeps quiet, but when a hen does — cluck, cluck, all over the place! Advertising!

[*The curtain is down*]

[*The Second curtain* — PEALE *and* RODNEY *on either side of* MARTIN, *are talking advertising, while* MARY *has her fingers to her ears*]

[*The Third curtain* — MARTIN *is protesting angrily to* MARY, *while* RODNEY *and* PEALE *are talking gleefully to each other and shaking hands*]

CURTAIN

ACT II

SCENE. — *The private office of the 13 Soap Company. A rather commonplace room, furnished comfortably but not elaborately. The walls have several posters extolling the virtues of 13 Soap — such as "Do you believe in signs?" "13 Soap is unlucky for dirt." "Be Clean. Cheap Soap for Cheap People." "13 Soap is the most expensive soap in the world, one dollar a cake." There is a particularly large stand in the upstage wall bearing the legend*

"*The average cake of soap gives you 56 washes. A cake of 13 Soap gives you only 24,*

But

What Washes!"

There is a door on the left and two more at right. At back are windows through which the audience sees the building across the street literally covered with 13 Soap posters. There is a desk, down center, with chairs, cabinets, hatrack, a water-cooler, a safe, etc., which complete the equipment of the room. Light oak office furniture. Three telephones, one on stand right, one on desk left, and one on desk center. Shades on windows. All over carpet. Four brackets.

The time is one month after the first act, about ten o'clock in the morning.

The curtain rises on an empty stage.

RODNEY'S *voice heard off-stage:*

RODNEY [*enters from door upper right*]. Forward march! [*Six sandwich-men enter door upper right, bearing boards: "13 Soap — unlucky for dirt"*] Halt! [*They stop*] Now, you understand you're all to go down to Mr. Cyrus Martin's office, 226 Broadway, and parade there all day — and to-morrow the same thing. Be in front of his house to-night at six sharp, you understand?

SANDWICH MEN. Yes, sir.

RODNEY. Then forward march! [*They exit through door left.* RODNEY *goes to his desk. Business with papers, etc.* PEALE *enters from door upper right*]

PEALE. Hello, little boss. Holy Peter Piper, you've shaved off your mustache!

RODNEY [*grinning*]. Yes, I'm just beginning to get on to myself. By George, I certainly used to look like the devil. Do you observe the clothes?

PEALE [*right center. Crosses up; removes coat, and places it left of center corner left of desk*]. Why, you are getting to be a regular business man.

RODNEY. Business is great stuff. I thought it'd bore me, but it's immense; it's the best game I ever played. What's the news with you?

PEALE. We only just got back from Buffalo this morning.

RODNEY. We?

PEALE [*sits in chair left of desk*]. Yes, your father and I. He went to the Iroquois in Buffalo. I had all the billboards in the neighborhood plastered thick — and 48-sheet stands along the streets to the Union Station. From the time the old man got in until he got out, he couldn't look anywhere without seeing 13 Soap. I even found out the number of his room and had a small balloon floating 13 Soap streamers right outside his window. I took a page in all the Buffalo papers — bribed the hat boy to keep putting circulars in his hat every time he checked it, and sent him one of our new folders every mail. They have eight mails a day in Buffalo. I came back with him on the train and when he went into the washroom last night I had the porter say "Sorry, sir, we ain't got no Thirteen Soap, but you can't hardly keep any on hand — it's such grand, grand soap." [*Rises and crosses to right*]

RODNEY. Gee, that's great. [*Crosses to left*]

PEALE. Well, what's on for to-day?

RODNEY. I've got a bully new advertising scheme. When you go into a barber shop where do you look?

PEALE. At the manicure.

RODNEY. No, no at the ceiling — we'll put ads on all the barbers' ceilings.

PEALE [*scornfully*]. Old stuff! It's been done — is that what you call a new scheme?

RODNEY. Well, that wasn't my big idea. [*Goes up-stage, sits in chair behind desk*]

PEALE [*mockingly*]. No? Well, what is your big idea?

RODNEY. Plans for our new factory.

PEALE. Plans for what? Have you gone dippy?

RODNEY. Here they are. [*He produces large blue-print*] Pretty real looking, aren't they?

PEALE. You don't mean you've actually got some nut to build us a factory?

RODNEY. No, no, they are for father.

PEALE. Oh, yes, I must admit that is some idea. [*Takes blue-print*]

RODNEY. If he ever does drop in to make a deal I thought we ought to have something to make a front, something that looks like a plant.

PEALE. *Plant* is right.

RODNEY. And by the way, if we can, let it leak out that it's the Ivory Soap people who are backing us with unlimited capital.

PEALE. The Ivory Soap people?

RODNEY. Sure, father's always hated 'em in business. His oldest friend, though, is John Clark, one of the big bugs in Ivory Soap. Clark's got a son, Ellery, that father dislikes because he's such a success in business — always held him up to me as a model son to pattern by. It'd make father wild if he thought that old Clark was going to back us; Ivory's Soap's the only bunch he's never been able to lick. [*Rises and goes down right*]

PEALE [*goes down left*]. Then that scheme ought to be good for a great rise out of father.

RODNEY. Say, by the way, I put over a corker on him this morning : I arranged for a parade of sandwich-men up and down in front of his house. I just sent another bunch to his office.

PEALE. Oh, we're bound to land him sooner or later, keeping after him the way we have.

RODNEY. Funny, though, nobody's tried to buy any soap from us yet.

PEALE. Well, it takes time to create a demand. These 200 cakes of pink castile you bought looked swell in our old rose wrappers, didn't they?

RODNEY. Say, where's Miss Grayson? Have you seen her to-day?

PEALE. No, and it's after eleven.

RODNEY. I'll bet she was here before either of us — she always is. By George, isn't she a corker?

PEALE [*indifferently*]. Oh, she's all right. [*Takes pad and pencil from pocket and sits in arm-chair left*]

RODNEY. All right !? Why, the girls you read about don't mean anything compared to Mary. She's got Juliet beat a mile. Every time I think of her I want to yell or do some darn fool thing, and every time I see her I just want to get down and kiss her shoes. I just want to walk around after her all the rest of my life and say "Are you comfortable, my love? Are you happy? If there is anything on the wide earth

you want, let me get it for you, Mary." What a wonderful name that is — just like her, simple and honest and beautiful ! Mary !

PEALE [*reflectively*]. If we could only land one hard wallop on father after that Buffalo business !

RODNEY [*indignantly*]. Didn't you hear what I said?

PEALE. Not a word.

RODNEY. I was talking about Mary.

PEALE. I know you were. That's why I didn't listen.

[MARY *enters from door upper right with Mss. case. Hangs up hat, then goes to desk, sitting back of it center*]

MARY. Good-morning.

RODNEY [*to* MARY]. Ah, you're here — now everything's all right, it's a great world.

MARY. Don't be silly ; this is a business office.

RODNEY. By George, Mary —

MARY. Miss Grayson !

RODNEY. By George, Miss Grayson, you do look simply stunning ! You're twice as pretty to-day as you were yesterday, and to-morrow you'll be —

PEALE. Hey, hey, change the record or put on a soft needle !

MARY [*to* PEALE]. Quite right — in business hours, only business. [*Takes list of assets and liabilities from case*]

RODNEY. But you are the prettiest thing —

MARY. Never mind that — you listen to me. This firm's broke.

RODNEY. That we can't be —

PEALE. It must be some mistake in the books —

MARY. Is it? I was surprised myself when I balanced our accounts this morning. I have here a statement of our assets and liabilities. We owe $22,818.09.

PEALE. What's the 9 cents for?

RODNEY. What are our assets?

MARY. $133.13.

RODNEY. That's quite a showing for a month.

MARY. Mr. McChesney, the advertising man, was here this morning, and he won't wait any longer for his money.

RODNEY. But we paid him $5,000.

MARY [*looking at statement*]. Yes, and owe him $9,400. And unless he has $2,500 of it to-day he'll put you out of business.

PEALE. That's the trouble of dealing with business men. They're so particular about being paid. Now, you take a lot of actors —

MARY. But what about McChesney?

RODNEY. Yes, what are we going to do when McChesney comes here to-day for money — cash?

PEALE. Well, we don't do any more business with him.

MARY. No, I guess we won't.

PEALE. Well, don't you worry, old son, we'll fix father somehow. Nobody can stop good advertising. Why, I met a little fellow on the train last night. He gets $50,000 a year just for writing ads. He says a good trademark is 70% of the battle, and we've got the best trademark I ever heard of.

MARY. You think we ought to keep on advertising?

PEALE. Sure, if we can get credit.

RODNEY. I suppose we might as well owe forty thousand as twenty.

PEALE. Absolutely. Half of all modern advertising success is based on a good trademark, and ours is a bird.

RODNEY. By George, that's true, we simply have got to keep going. We'll manage somehow.

MARY. I like to hear you say that.

PEALE. Now you're talking. We'll conduct the greatest campaign since George W. Advertising was a young man.

MISS BURKE [*entering with one letter from door upper right*]. Here's the morning mail. [RODNEY *takes letter, returns front of desk*, MISS BURKE *exits right*]

PEALE. Pretty heavy mail. [*Coming down left of* RODNEY]

MARY. I'll bet it's another bill. [*Coming down right of* RODNEY]

RODNEY. Hurrah! Hurrah! It's from the Countess.

MARY. What does she say?

PEALE [*grabbing letter, and looking at it*] Oh, French stuff.

RODNEY. She says she was delayed abroad, but that she's due to-day on the Imperator or Rotter or whatever you call it, this morning, and that she's coming to see us at eleven.

MARY. It's half-past eleven now. Oh, dear.

PEALE. Fear not. Remember, though a Countess, she is still a woman: give her time.

MARY. Does she say anything about the $15,000?

RODNEY. No.

PEALE. Well, I've got a hunch everything's going to be all right, or she wouldn't have written us at all.

RODNEY. Her $15,000'll keep us going for quite a while.

MISS BURKE [*entering from door upper right*]. Mr. McChesney is here to see you.

MARY. The advertising man. [*Goes to typewriter desk, and pounds on it*]

MISS BURKE. He seems very angry, too.

RODNEY. Tell him I'm out. [*Goes to chair behind desk and sits*]

McCHESNEY [*entering from door upper right*]. Thought I'd come right in instead of waiting to have her tell me you were out. [*Going to* RODNEY]

[MISS BURKE *exits*]

RODNEY [*genially*]. Why, hello, Mr. McChesney.

PEALE [*trying to shake hands*]. How are you, Mac?

McCHESNEY [*throwing him off*]. You may be in the soap business, but cut out the soft soap with me. Where's my money? Have you got it?

RODNEY. Why — er — the fact is —

McCHESNEY. That means you haven't.

RODNEY. Well, you see —

McCHESNEY. That doesn't go with me. Do you think you can put me off? You can bet your blooming liabilities you can't. I think this whole concern is bunk and I'm going after you good —

RODNEY. I don't care for that kind of loud talk. Drop it.

PEALE. Drop it.

McCHESNEY [*surprised*]. What?

PEALE. He said, drop it.

RODNEY. It's simply that I haven't had time to examine your bill in detail. This afternoon, however, I —

McCHESNEY. I've heard that before. Now, see here, Mr. Martin — your father's an honest man: he won't stand for his son not paying me my money. I'll see him now. [*He starts for door*]

RODNEY. Wait a minute, wait a minute. I'll give you a check for $2500 on account. I presume that will be satisfactory.

McCHESNEY [*taken aback*]. Why, yes — sure — but —

RODNEY. You understand, Mr. Peal, that not a cent of that fifty thousand dollars we appropriated for our October advertising campaign is to go to him.

PEALE. Absolutely.

McCHESNEY. Now, Mr. Martin, I'll admit I'm hasty tempered. I'm sorry I made a mistake, but a contract is a contract and —

RODNEY. Here's your check. Goodday.

McCHESNEY. But, Mr. Martin —

RODNEY. Show Mr. McChesney out.

PEALE [*goes to* McCHESNEY, *takes his arm and leads him to door upper right*]. Come on, Mac — this way to the elevator. [*Delighted*] Watch your step.

[MR. McCHESNEY *exits*]

RODNEY [*gleefully*]. Well, I fixed him, didn't I?

MARY [*rises and goes to* RODNEY]. No, you've only got us into more difficulty. You know, there's no money in the bank.

RODNEY. But the check won't go through the clearing-house until tomorrow morning and by then we'll have the $15,000 from the Countess.

PEALE. But where is the Countess?

MARY. I'll go telephone now to see if the Imperator's docked yet.

PEALE. I'll bet she sank in midocean!

MISS BURKE [*entering*]. Mr. Ellery Clark to see you.

RODNEY. How I hate that fellow!

PEALE. What've you ever done to him?

RODNEY. Nothing. I wish I could. That's the fellow I told you about. John Clark's pride.

PEALE. Oh, yes, the son of Ivory Soap. Let's have a peek at him?

MISS BURKE. Yes, sir. [*She exits*]

PEALE. I never saw a model son before.

MARY [*she starts down right*]. Oh, Rodney, find out how Ellery's doing in business, will you?

RODNEY. Oh, I suppose so.

[MARY *exits door lower right*]

PEALE [*crosses to arm-chair left*]. You're spoiling that girl. She used to be a good business woman. Now half the time, instead of using her brains she just sits and looks at you as if you were some marvellous antique work of art. [*Sits*]

[ELLERY *enters door upper right*]

ELLERY. Hello, Rodney, mind if I come in?

RODNEY. I'm very busy to-day, Mr. Clark.

ELLERY. Oh, I suppose you are. Must take a lot of time to get up your advertisements.

PEALE [*rises, goes to* ELLERY *and offers hand*]. You like 'em? I write 'em! My name's Peale! [*Goes back to chair left. Sits*]

ELLERY [*turning from him, bored*]. How do you do? [*Sits in arm-chair right*]

RODNEY. What is it, Mr. Clark?

ELLERY. You see, it's like this, old top. I've been having rather a time with father lately — silly old man — insisted on the absurd idea of my going into business. Beastly bore.

RODNEY. But you wanted to do that?

ELLERY. I should say not.

RODNEY. But I thought you loved work?

ELLERY. It's a preposterous idea — men of intelligence go in for the professions. I paint.

PEALE [*half aside*]. You look it!

RODNEY. I'd heard you were a model son.

ELLERY. But I don't consider it a compliment to be a success in business — think of all the blighters who are.

PEALE. Yes, the bally rotters!

ELLERY. Father keeps reminding me of your success every day — most irritating. You see, of course he's sore, because I never bothered much about business. Oh, I have tackled a thing or two. But luck was always against me. It just happened it didn't work out right. Not my fault, you understand?

PEALE. You couldn't be to blame.

ELLERY. Of course, if I ever devoted myself to business! But, after all, when you know you can do a thing you want to, why bother to do it, if it bores you?

PEALE. Yes, life is a damn nuisance.

ELLERY [*sighing*]. And father has been so offensive lately, I've decided to give a little time to business and make a success of it. I can, you know.

RODNEY. Indeed?

PEALE. Seems simple.

ELLERY. Oh, rather. I have it all figured out. For my scheme I've got to raise seventy-five hundred dollars, and I wanted to talk to you about it. This idea of mine is an automobile proposition. I really need $10,000, and I've only got $2500.

[Rodney *and* Peale *exchange looks and walk over to* Ellery, *one on each side of him*]

Rodney. Ellery, why do you want to go into the automobile business? It's dangerous — unsafe —

Peale. The risk's tremendous.

Rodney. Ellery, our families are old friends. Now, if you really want to show your father you're a money-maker, why don't you buy some shares in our company?

Ellery. I don't care much about the idea of being in the soap business — rather vulgar.

Rodney. But you don't have to be in the business.

Peale. Absolutely not.

Rodney. It's a very simple proposition. All you do is invest and then sit still and deposit your checks when we pay dividends.

Ellery. I say, that sounds a bit better.

Rodney. We're not letting the general public in — but it'd be such a joke on your father for you to make money.

Ellery. Yes, wouldn't it? [*They all laugh*] I fancy he'd be mighty glad I had sense enough to go in with you.

Rodney. Yes, wouldn't he?

Ellery. But is it a safe investment?

Rodney. Why, we'd guarantee you against loss from our assets.

Peale. Yes, from our assets.

Ellery. That sounds rather ripping. But what would I get for my twenty-five hundred?

Peale. A receipt.

Ellery. I know, I know, but what interest in the business?

Rodney. Two and one-half per cent.

Ellery. I say, is that much?

Rodney. Think what two and a half per cent in the steel trust would mean.

Peale. And more people use soap than steel.

Ellery [*wisely*]. Isn't steel dearer?

Rodney. It's quantity that counts.

Peale. Four cakes a year to every person in this country would represent an annual output of 400,000,000 cakes — and think of all the babies who'll be born next year. They'll all have to be washed.

Ellery. Very true, very true. What is the annual birth-rate?

Rodney. Let me see, let me see; do you know, Peale?

Peale. There's one born every minute.

Ellery. I fancy that's true.

Peale. You can bet it is.

Rodney. Now, what do you say, Ellery, about investing in our company?

Ellery [*after a long pause, rises and shakes hands with* Rodney]. I'll do it.

Peale. God's in His Heaven, all's right with the world! [*Crosses left*]

Rodney. Have you the money with you?

Ellery. Why, no.

Peale. Then you'll send us a check to-day?

Ellery. I don't get the money until next week.

Rodney. Why not?

Ellery. Father didn't promise it to me till next Monday.

Peale. Well, ask him for it now.

Ellery. Oh, I'm afraid I can't. He's out of town.

Rodney. We can't agree to hold the matter open until next Monday. [*Goes to chair behind desk and sits*]

Peale. No, not till way next Monday. Why don't you telephone him?

Ellery. Yes, that wouldn't be so distressing. If I can get him — I find him considerably easier to talk to on the 'phone. I can always ring off.

Peale. Come this way — it'll be quieter for you if he's noisy. [*Goes to* Ellery, *takes his arm, and leads him to door lower right*]

Mary [*enters door lower right*]. Oh, how do you do, Mr. Clark?

Ellery. Oh, how do you do? [*They shake hands*]

Peale [*pushing him out*]. Never mind the social chatter. Ellery, you don't mind my calling you Ellery — do you, Ellery? [*To her*] You see, Ellery has work to do. [*Exit* Ellery. Mary *goes to left*] If that's a model son, thank God I was born a black sheep!

Rodney [*to* Mary]. Has the Imperator docked?

Mary. Three hours ago.

Peale. Then I'll bet the Countess has been hit by a taxi! [*Drinks*]

Mary. Oh, Rodney, did you find out how well Ellery's doing?

Rodney. Oh, great! Hasn't made a cent. Wanted to borrow some money from me.

Mary. Your father'd be glad to hear that.

Peale. Oh, where is our wandering Countess? [*Crosses to left*]

MISS BURKE [*entering*]. The Countess de Boureen.

PEALE. By golly, she enters on the cue.

RODNEY. We're saved now.

MARY. Oh, I do hope so.

RODNEY. Get her right in here, quick.

[MISS BURKE *exits*]

ELLERY [*sticking his head in at door*]. How do you use this 'phone? I've never run a switchboard!

MARY. Oh, I'll come show you. [*Crosses to right*]

ELLERY. Oh, thank you. I'm not much at mechanical problems. [*He exits*]

RODNEY [*to* MARY *as she goes*]. And get his father for him; it may mean $2,500 more for us.

PEALE [*runs to door right shouting to* MARY]. Do anything: hold his hand — kiss him! [*She exits*] To RODNEY] Do you need an interpreter for the Countess?

RODNEY [*as he speaks, goes over and pulls down a shade on which is painted an advertisement in French*]. I can understand anything she says about money. You can help me count it.

PEALE. That's the grandest sensation I know. [*Crosses to left*]

MISS BURKE [*announcing*]. The Countess de Bowreen.

[COUNTESS *sweeps in.* RODNEY *delighted. Goes to her and kisses her hand*]

RODNEY. Ah, bonjour — bonjour.

COUNTESS. Bonjour — bonjour.

RODNEY [*pointing to window shade*]. Regardez.

COUNTESS. Ah, magnifique, superbe, superbe! Je suis désolée d'être si en retard, mais c'est très compliqué à la douane. [*Coming down in front of desk*]

RODNEY. Not at all. [*Going to her*]

PEALE. Not at all. [*Going to her*]

COUNTESS [*threatening*]. Vous avez reçu ma lettre?

RODNEY. Letter? Yes, I got your letter.

PEALE [*leaning forward eagerly to her*]. Oh, you little life-saver.

RODNEY [*to her*]. Mon manager, you remember?

COUNTESS. Je suis enchantée de vous revoir

[PEALE *bows very low*]

RODNEY. Kiss her hand — it's French stuff.

[PEALE *kisses her hand*]

PEALE. She looks like money — ask her — ask her.

RODNEY [*nervously*]. You have the money?

COUNTESS. Eh?

PEALE [*snapping his fingers*]. Come on, kid, say yes, say yes.

RODNEY. Vous avez argent?

COUNTESS. Oui, oui, j'ai l'argent.

PEALE. What does she say?

RODNEY. She says yes.

PEALE. Shall I kiss her?

RODNEY. Do you want to spoil everything? Don't kiss her till we get the money. The money with you?

COUNTESS. Eh?

RODNEY. Argent avec vous?

COUNTESS. Oui, j'ai l'argent ici. [*Opening bag and taking out check*]

PEALE. It's real.

COUNTESS. C'est un cheque de Morgan Harjes pour cent mille francs.

RODNEY [*looking at it*]. Draft for $20,000 in full payment for French rights of the 13 Soap.

COUNTESS. Je vous donnerai ce chèque pour vingt mille dollars, mais comme je ne vous dois que cinq mille, vous pourrez me donner votre chèque pour cinq mille. Cela finira notre affaire.

PEALE. Slip it to me, kid, slip it to me. I'm dying on my feet. [*Takes check from* RODNEY]

RODNEY. She says she'll give us the draft for $20,000, but as she only owes us $15,000, we must give her back our check for $5,000.

PEALE. That seems simple, give her the check.

RODNEY. But we haven't any money in the bank. Suppose we get her check cashed first. Then we can pay her.

PEALE. Sure, great! I'll go right over to the bank to get it certified. [COUNTESS *takes check from* PEALE *and tears it up*] What's the matter with you? What's the matter?

[COUNTESS *is smiling*]

RODNEY. She's crazy —

COUNTESS. Ah mais non, l'affaire c'est fini maintenant —

PEALE. Talk French to her.

RODNEY. Pourquoi tear it up — pourquoi — pourquoi?

COUNTESS. Gee, but you're funny!

RODNEY. She spoke English! She's a fake. [RODNEY *and* PEALE *stare at her speechless,* PEALE *pointing toward the draft*]

PEALE. The draft was phoney, too.

COUNTESS [*smiling*]. Sure it was.

PEALE. But what's the idea, kid?

COUNTESS [*sits on desk*]. You see, I was going to trim you out of your $5,000 check, but as long as you haven't any money, your check's no good, so you've busted up my whole scheme.

PEALE. But why pick on us?

COUNTESS. I didn't start out to: you wished it on yourselves. I came to trim your father. You remember, I wanted to see him, but I looked so soft you thought you'd grab me off and sell me the French agency of your Thirteen Soap. I didn't think your father could be as big a boob as you were, so I changed my plans. Do you get me?

PEALE. Yes, I get you and now I'm going to get the cops to get you. [*Starts up-stage*]

COUNTESS [*laughs. Crosses down left*]. I should burst into laughter. Why, you pikers, I'm on: you're busted. You haven't any money and you have got a phoney company.

RODNEY. Now, see here — [*Goes to her*]

COUNTESS. Preserve it. Preserve it. [*Crosses to center*] Don't forget, I've understood everything you two guys were talking about.

PEALE. Whew! [*Sits in arm-chair right*]

RODNEY. Gee! [*Goes to arm-chair left*]

COUNTESS [*to* RODNEY]. "Kiss her hand — it's French stuff." [*To* PEALE] "Ah, there, you little life-saver." [*To* RODNEY] "The money with you — argent avec vous?" Gee, your French is rotten. [*To* PEALE, *who moves away*] "Shall I kiss her?" [*A pause*] Send for the cops and I'll blow the whole thing to the papers. [*A pause*] Well, I guess we're quits. If you had any money I'd ask for a piece of change to keep me quiet, but as it is, I can't waste my time.

RODNEY [*rises*]. You're not French at all?

COUNTESS. I was educated over there — immense, wasn't I? You never tumbled at all.

PEALE [*rises*]. But why the foreign stuff?

COUNTESS. Well, I can talk good French — but my English is punk. [*Sits on desk*]

RODNEY. You won't say anything now?

COUNTESS. No, I don't hit a fellow when he's down. Anyhow, we're all in the same class. Three fakes.

PEALE. She has spilled the beans.

RODNEY. Great Scott! And Mc-Chesney has our check for $2,500.

PEALE [*to* RODNEY]. Gee! We will just have to get that $2,500 from Ellery.

RODNEY. What's happened to Ellery? Let's find him. [*They start for door right*]

PEALE. If he falls down on us —

ELLERY [*entering*]. Can I see you a moment?

RODNEY. I should say you could.

PEALE. You seem very beastly pleased, Ellery.

ELLERY. Oh, I am.

RODNEY. Then everything's all right about father?

ELLERY. Oh, yes, so to speak — in a way.

RODNEY. Ah?

PEALE [*suddenly suspicious*]. What do you mean — so to speak, in a way?

ELLERY. Well, I couldn't reach the old man on the 'phone, and that did make matters so much easier. I don't fancy talking to father on the 'phone.

PEALE. Why couldn't you reach him?

ELLERY [*smiling happily*]. Why, he's on his yacht somewhere on the Sound — he won't be home till Monday, so I can't possibly get the money for you to-day.

[RODNEY *and* PEALE *walk up-stage while the* COUNTESS *drops her handkerchief.* ELLERY *picks it up and smiles back delightedly at her.* MARY *enters from door lower right*]

MARY. Look out. McChesney's coming back here — I just saw him across the street.

PEALE. Try and keep him out.

MARY. I'll do my best. [*She exits door upper right*]

RODNEY. Ellery, you'll have to go — we've got a big job on our hands. Au revoir, Countess.

COUNTESS. Au revoir, Monsieur. [*With marked accent*] Is there no one to see me to my taxi? These American buildings are so big I am lost.

RODNEY. Ellery, you take the Countess.

ELLERY. Oh, I'd love to.

RODNEY. Madame la comtesse de Beaurien — Ellery Clark.

COUNTESS. Dee-lighted.

ELLERY. So am I.

RODNEY [*opens door lower left*]. You can go out the private entrance.

ELLERY [*going toward left*]. Oh, certainly.

COUNTESS [*as they go*]. You speak the French?

ELLERY. No, not at all.

COUNTESS. A pitee.

ELLERY. But I can speak German.

COUNTESS. Aber prachtvoll — Ich habe die Deutche sprache so furchtbar gern.

ELLERY. Ich auch —

COUNTESS. Warum laden sie mich nicht zum Biltmore zum Thee ein?

ELLERY. Mit dem grössten —

COUNTESS. Vergnuegen?

ELLERY [*relieved*]. Yes, that's the word — Vergnuegen.

PEALE. I'll bet there's a Berlitz in her family somewhere.

COUNTESS. Au revoir, Mr. Martin — [*Turning to* RODNEY] Vous êtes trop aimable. Je vous remercie beaucoup de votre politesse. Au revoir — [*Goes to* PEALE — *in undertone*] So long, kid, call me up sometime. [*And then, chattering a stream of German to* ELLERY, *they exit door left*]

RODNEY [*closes door after* COUNTESS *exits*]. Well, I've got to hand it to her. The Countess is a fake. Ellery is a flivver and McChesney's on his way here with that phoney check. [*Goes to his chair behind desk*]

PEALE. I can see Sing-Sing from here. [*Goes to chair left corner, sits quickly*]

[McCHESNEY *bursts in, followed by* MARY]

McCHESNEY. No, I won't wait. You're two swindlers. I've just come from the bank. Your check's no good.

RODNEY. No good! That's impossible.

PEALE. Absolutely.

McCHESNEY. You haven't any money in the bank.

RODNEY. It must be some mistake on the part of our cashier.

McCHESNEY. Yes it is — ask him.

RODNEY. He's at lunch.

McCHESNEY. I'm going to the sheriff now, and unless you make the check good at my office in an hour, I'm going to cancel your advertising, cover up your billboards and send you both to jail, and that goes. [*He exits*]

MARY. Can't you pay him?

RODNEY. With what?

MARY. What happened to the Countess? Didn't she give you the money?

RODNEY. No, and she nearly got us for five thousand dollars.

MARY. What?

RODNEY. She's a fake.

MARY. The swindler! And the man from the Edison Company is here to say that unless they get some money at once they'll cut off the current from all our signs, and the agent of the landlord is waiting for the rent. He seems very suspicious and wants to be paid for last month right away. What can I say to them?

[RODNEY *shakes his head*]

PEALE. I don't know.

MARY. Oh, please send for your father and give in.

RODNEY. No.

MARY. You know I want you to succeed, but there's no use fighting odds like these — you haven't any money, you're way in debt, and you mustn't be disgraced. Please send for your father. I'm sure he'll help you.

RODNEY. I wonder if I'd better? What do you think, Peale?

PEALE. I don't know.

MARY. Do telephone him right away. [*Crosses to door lower right*] Now I must try to fix the Edison man and the landlord, or they'll be in here. [*To* PEALE] What can I say to them?

PEALE. I don't know.

MARY. Oh, I'll say you're both out. [*She exits door lower right*]

PEALE. That'll be a new one.

RODNEY. Do you happen to know the sheriff?

PEALE. Not yet. I'd like to have a pull enough to get a cell with a southern exposure.

RODNEY. What are we going to do?

PEALE. I don't know.

RODNEY. What are you here for?

PEALE. I know, but I can't think.

MISS BURKE [*entering*]. Mr. Cyrus Martin to see you.

PEALE *and* RODNEY. Who?

MISS BURKE. Mr. Cyrus Martin.

RODNEY. Have him wait.

PEALE. Have him what? [*Rises and goes to* RODNEY]

RODNEY. Just a minute till I think. When I ring, show him in.

MISS BURKE. Yes, sir. [*She exits*]

PEALE. He must be here to make a deal. Our scheme worked — we've put it over, and what did it? Advertising.

RODNEY. But father's no fool. We've got to be very careful. How'll we handle it? I'm not used to putting it over on father.

PEALE. Don't forget the factory and the Ivory Soap people and the plans, and get busy. You know. [*He makes motions and brings letter-file from rack and throws contents on desk*] That rubber-stamp stuff.

RODNEY. But isn't this playing it rather low down on father?

PEALE. Oh, don't get cold feet now!

RODNEY. We really haven't anything to sell him.

PEALE. Yes, we have — a trade-mark. You know it's good, so do I. We only need your father to back us and we'll make a lot of money for him in spite of himself.

RODNEY. I guess that's true.

PEALE. Sure it is, and anyhow all's fair in love and business.

ELLERY [*coming in at private door left*]. Oh, I beg pardon, but I was so fascinated at meeting the Countess, I forgot my stick.

RODNEY. Can't see you now, Ellery. [*He goes over and pulls down two window shades on which are painted ads of 13 Soap*]

PEALE [*giving him gloves*]. No, can't ever see you again, Ellery. Here's your cane. Now, hurry, Ellery. [*He starts to lead him to door*]

ELLERY. The Countess is perfectly delightful —

RODNEY [*suddenly goes to* ELLERY]. Hold on, hold on, Ellery, can you wait in there five minutes?

ELLERY [*pausing*]. But the Countess is downstairs in a taxi.

RODNEY. Oh, she'll wait for you, and charge the taxi to Mr. Peale. He'll be right in and explain everything to you.

PEALE. Oh, yes, I'll explain.

ELLERY. I don't want to detain the Countess too long. Hate to keep a lady waiting — all that sort of thing. You know what women are. [*He exits left*]

PEALE. Now, what is it, what do you want that gink for?

RODNEY. Don't you see?

PEALE. No, I'm near-sighted.

RODNEY. He's the son of Ivory Soap Coach him with some important message from old John Clark to us about a merger, and when father begins to wabble, have Ellery come in with the message. That'll send father kerflop to the map.

PEALE [*going*]. Master! Great, great, I get you. I'll fix Ellery. This is your father's Waterloo. [*At door*] As soon as I've taught Ellery's his lesson I'll be right back. I'll tell him when we ring the bell twice, to bust in with his little recitation.

RODNEY. But don't let him get on to our game.

PEALE. He couldn't get on to anything but a weighing machine. [*He goes out left*]

[RODNEY *pushes the buzzer and then takes up the 'phone, keeping his eye on the door. In a moment* CYRUS MARTIN *enters*]

RODNEY. No, much obliged, but we can't consider it. No stock for sale — it's quite out of the question. Good-bye. [*Ringing off and then pretending to be surprised, turns and sees his father*] Why, hello, father.

MARTIN. Hello, son.

RODNEY [RODNEY *gets very busy with papers and rubber-stamp*]. Sit down, won't you? Be with you in just a minute.

MARTIN [*drily*]. Thanks.

[RODNEY *very busy again with filing papers and opening and closing drawers.* MARTIN *looks at him in astonishment*]

RODNEY. Have a cigar? [*He abstractedly passes him a box*]

MARTIN. Thanks — [*He bites off end and lights it, and as he does so,* RODNEY *again gets busy with similar business*] Surprised to see me, I suppose?

RODNEY. Not a bit. [*He starts signing a contract.* MARTIN, *who has risen, attempts to glance at it, and as he does so,* RODNEY *calmly turns it over and blots it.* MARTIN *turns away*] There, that's done! Now, father, what can I do for you?

MARTIN. Well, my boy — I just dropped in for a social call. The fact is, I've rather missed you.

RODNEY. I've missed you too, father.

MARTIN [*abruptly*]. Thought I'd have a look in and find out how things were going. [*Sits in arm-chair right*]

RODNEY. Fine — fine — everything's breezing right along. Of course, I'm always glad to see you, but right now, father I'm pretty busy, so you'll excuse me if — [*He gets busy again with rubber-stamp*]

MARTIN [*with a certain sarcasm*]. Well, if you can spare the time, I'd like a little business talk with you, Rodney.

RODNEY. Certainly, in just a minute. [*Gets busy with papers. Pushes the buzzer*]

PEALE [*entering*]. Oh, excuse me.

RODNEY. That's all right, come right in. Father, you remember Mr. Peale — Peale, my father —

PEALE. Indeed yes, I recall very well —

MARTIN [*gruffly cutting him off*]. How are you?

PEALE [*sitting in chair left*]. A bit tired — just back from Buffalo where I've been conducting a big campaign.

MARTIN. Then it is to you I should address myself?

RODNEY. Either or both of us.

MARTIN [*rises and goes to desk*]. Then both of you listen to me. You've got to cut out this nonsense you call advertising.

RODNEY. What nonsense?

PEALE [*weakly*]. Yes, what?

MARTIN. This morning there was a parade of sandwich-men in front of my house for two hours. I had to have them arrested. I got to the office to find another bunch. It annoys me.

RODNEY. I'm sorry, father.

MARTIN. You're trying to make a fool of me. I open a letter. It's a circular for 13 Soap. I open my newspaper — you have a page ad. I look out of the window — there's a billboard — I take a train, the damned porter apologizes because he's all out of 13 Soap.

RODNEY. Well, of course, all that proves how wonderful our publicity is.

MARTIN [*grimly*]. You're a grand young bluff, my son.

RODNEY. Why, father, what do you mean?

MARTIN. I'll tell you exactly what I mean: I've let you ramble on to see just how far you would go, but you've been spending a lot of money on ridiculous advertising, hoping that by annoying me I'll buy your business to get rid of you. Well, I'm not going to. Now what have you got to say to that? Eh — eh?

PEALE [*rises quickly*]. Nothing — absolutely nothing. [*Sits*]

RODNEY [*quickly*]. But I have a lot to say. We may not have a big business now, but we have got a trade-mark, the catchiest trade-mark ever invented for soap. We're a growing concern. Just because our advertising annoys you, you mustn't think it's valueless. Why, it's so good that capital is chasing us: our money is practically unlimited. Is that a fair statement, Peale?

PEALE [*dazed at* RODNEY's *bluff*]. Very fair — very fair indeed —

MARTIN. Bluff, son, bluff!

RODNEY. Not at all. And since you're so skeptical, father, I don't mind letting you see the plans for our new factory. [*Takes plans from desk*]

MARTIN. New factory?

RODNEY. Yes, father — these are the offices, this is Miss Grayson's office, this is Mr. Peale's office, and this is mine.

MARTIN. Well, aren't you going to make any soap?

RODNEY. Right here, where our capacity will be —

MARTIN. Who's putting up the money?

RODNEY [*reprovingly*]. Now, father, you cannot expect me to divulge a business secret to you, a rival manufacturer.

PEALE. Oh, why not tell him, he is your father?

RODNEY. Well, Peale, if you really think it is wise?

PEALE. Oh, yes, I think it's quite wise.

RODNEY. It's the Ivory Soap people.

MARTIN [*at once impressed and annoyed*]. The Ivory Soap people?

PEALE [*rises and goes to desk. Rubbing it in*]. Yes, the Ivory Soap people.

MARTIN. You mean John Clark?

RODNEY. Yes.

PEALE. Absolutely. [MARTIN *turns and reflectively walks up-stage.* PEALE *very obviously picks up push-button and pushes buzzer twice; it rings off left. There is a pause, and then in a moment,* ELLERY *enters*]

ELLERY. Oh, excuse me. I didn't know your father was here.

RODNEY [*very genially*]. That's all right, Ellery.

PEALE [*the same*]. Come right in.

ELLERY. How do you do, Mr. Martin?

MARTIN [*gruffly*]. How are you, Ellery?

ELLERY. Well, I really can't wait any longer. The party downstairs in the taxi — you follow me?

PEALE. Yes, Ellery, you told us that —

ELLERY. Well, good-bye, then.

RODNEY. Was that all you came in to say?

ELLERY [*remembering*]. Oh, yes, of course. If you'll keep it open until Monday I'll get the money for you then.

RODNEY. But we can't wait till Monday.

ELLERY. But Mr. Peale told me —

PEALE [*interrupting quickly*]. We'll see what we can do, but just now, Ellery, we're very much occupied. [*He has him by the arm*]

RODNEY. Oh, just a minute : you'd better give your father back the plans — say they're quite satisfactory. [*Gives plans to* PEALE]

ELLERY. What plans?

PEALE. Don't you know?

ELLERY. No.

PEALE. That's too bad. Well, good-bye, Ellery.

ELLERY. I say, I do find business very confusing. [*He exits*]

PEALE [*as he comes back*]. Ellery talks too much.

RODNEY. He is very indiscreet — if it had been anybody but father he'd have given our whole plan away.

MARTIN. What's he doing here — acting for his father?

PEALE. Absolutely.

MARTIN. You're not going to take him in — that pin-head? Why, he didn't even seem to know what he was *trying* to get at.

PEALE. No, he didn't, did he?

RODNEY. But after all, he does represent Ivory Soap.

PEALE. Great soap, Ivory! Over 99 per cent. pure. [*Sits in arm-chair left*]

MARTIN [*grunting*]. Ivory Soap? [*He walks up and down while* RODNEY *and* PEALE *exchange gleeful glances. After a considerable pause*] Well, thinking things over, why should you and I fight?

RODNEY. You began it, father.

MARTIN. Quite true, and therefore I should be the one to call it off. Now,

son, here's the idea : I'd rather have you with me than against me — the money doesn't matter much. In your way, while I don't endorse that kind of publicity, I suppose you boys think your sensational ads are good.

PEALE [*rising*]. Thank you, sir.

MARTIN. Not at all. [*To* RODNEY] And if you're going to have a backer, wouldn't I be better than the Ivory Soap people?

RODNEY. After all, blood is thicker than business. What do you suggest?

MARTIN. Suppose I buy you out — including your trademark and goodwill?

PEALE. Oh, you have our goodwill now, sir. [*Rises and bows very profusely, then sits*]

RODNEY [*reflectively*]. Buying us out might be expensive for you, father.

MARTIN. Oh, I guess it won't take all the money I've got. What's your proposition?

RODNEY. What's yours?

MARTIN. Well, I'll give you $50,000 for your business as it stands.

RODNEY. But we don't want to give up our business. I like business.

PEALE [*grandly*]. We wish to continue in our chosen profession.

MARTIN. Well, suppose you take 25% of the profits in addition?

RODNEY. It's a wonderful autumn, isn't it? These crisp cold bracing mornings.

MARTIN. Well, I hardly thought you'd grab at that. What will you take?

RODNEY [*rising quickly*]. One hundred thousand dollars cash, you assume all the contracts and obligations of this company, give us 40% of the profits, a contract for me at $20,000 a year ; for Miss Grayson at $10,000, [PEALE *coughs*] — and another for Mr. Peale at the same figure.

MARTIN. Done.   [*Shakes hands with* RODNEY]

[PEALE *and* RODNEY *exchange looks and shake hands*]

RODNEY. I congratulate you, father.

MARTIN. You needn't. Your trademark might appeal to a lot of superstitious idiots, but as a business proposition I don't think much of it. But now I'll show old John Clark he can't butt into my family affairs or get Ellery mixed up with my boy's business.

RODNEY. Yes, father, we'd much rather have you than Ellery.

PEALE. Oh, *much rather*.

MISS BURKE [*entering*]. Oh, Mr. Martin!

RODNEY. Yes?

MARTIN. Yes?

RODNEY [*going to her*]. That's for me, father. [*To* MISS BURKE] What is it?

MISS BURKE. The agent for the landlord says he's got to see you immediately.

RODNEY [*motioning her to be quiet*]. I'll be right out. [*To* MARTIN, *very nervously*] You see, father, we're thinking of taking larger offices. Come, Peale. We'll be right back, father.

PEALE. Yes, father, we'll be right back. [*They hurriedly exit*]

MARTIN [*stands there watching them proudly*. MISS GRAYSON *enters door lower right*]. Hello, Miss Grayson, it's mighty good to see you again — I —

MARY. Oh, Mr. Martin, I'm so glad Rodney finally sent for you.

MARTIN [*surprised*]. Sent for me? [*Goes in front of desk*]

MARY. Have you talked to him?

MARTIN. Oh, yes, he just went out for a minute to see the agent of the landlord —

MARY. Oh, then he told you about that? [*Goes to him*]

MARTIN [*puzzled*]. Yes, he told me — why not?

MARY. I am so glad to think he wasn't ashamed to tell you the truth.

MARTIN. Oh, Rodney always was a truthful lad.

MARY. Oh, I'm so happy you've settled with him! You have settled, haven't you? [*Goes to arm-chair right*]

MARTIN. Yes, sure.

MARY. Oh, good. Isn't it wonderful for him? [*Very sweetly*] Just think! Without you he couldn't have lasted out the day. [*Crossing down in front of desk*]

MARTIN. Couldn't have lasted out the day, ha, ha! Then our little scheme to put Rodney on his feet didn't work?

MARY. But everything's all right now. You're going to help him —

MARTIN. Everything's great now — [*Knocked off his feet, then recovering himself*] Oh, by the way, in our negotiations the one thing that Rodney didn't fully go into was the nature of the assets.

MARY. The assets! They must have made even you laugh. Why, we haven't any! [*She laughs*]

MARTIN [*trying to laugh*]. Haven't any! Ha — ha — by the way, there was a report on the Street to-day that the Ivory Soap people were going to make a deal with Rodney — build him a factory —

MARY [*innocently*]. Oh, there's nothing in that.

MARTIN. Are you sure? As I got here, I thought I saw Ellery Clark leaving.

MARY. Oh, he didn't come here on business: Ellery came to borrow some money from Rodney — isn't that funny?

MARTIN. Oh, yes, very funny — but the plans?

MARY. Rodney showed you some plans? He must have been joking!

MARTIN [*changing his whole manner*]. The young scoundrel! [*Starts to go up-stage*]

MARY. What!

MARTIN [*stops*]. Thank you, Miss Grayson, for telling me. Do you know what he tried to do to me? Hold me up for a hundred thousand dollars, make me think Ivory Soap was backing him, too — and but for you, he'd have succeeded.

MARY. What have I done?

MARTIN. You saved me a lot of money and kept me from being a fool. Thank you! Good-morning. [*Starts for door upper right*]

MARY. You mean at last he'd succeeded in getting you to back him?

MARTIN. At last! [*Coming to her, lays hat on desk*] So that was his scheme all the time, was it? He didn't go into business on the level, but just for my benefit? And you were helping him. Well, he can thank you again for having failed.

MARY. It's all my fault.

MARTIN. Yes, it is, from the start. You got up the plan of my pretending to put him out of the house —

MARY. Oh, but I tell you, you must help him.

MARTIN. Help him yourself. You've got $5,000.

MARY. But I gave it to him.

MARTIN. My son took money from you?

MARY. He didn't know — I pretended it was from a friend.

MARTIN. Well, you got him in; now you can get him out.

MARY. But your bet — you bet $30,000 with John Clark. You don't want to lose that?

MARTIN. Well, if Ellery's trying to

borrow money from Rodney it looks like
an even break — and anyhow I'd lose
the bet twice over rather than have my
son think he could make a fool of his
father.

MARY. But he is a good business
man: he'd make you proud of him.
You don't know how hard he's worked,
how fine he's been; he's simply wonderful. If he could keep on a little longer,
I know he'd succeed. If you'll just help
him, he'll make money. You'll see he
will.

MARTIN. Of course, you want him
to make money. You're thinking of
that percentage contract with me.

MARY. I'm not! I'm not!
I can't see him fail. Listen: I'll try to
give you back what you've given me —
I don't care anything about the contract. I'll tear it up now if you'll just
help him.

MARTIN. By George, I believe you
really are in love with him!

MARY [*proudly*]. Yes, I am — now.
But that doesn't matter. We've got to
save him — save his business.

MARTIN. I won't give him a nickel.
Good-bye! [*Starts to go*]

MARY. But you can't go like this:
he'll be disgraced! He's in debt.

MARTIN. Let him get out of it —
it'll do him good. I've been a sentimental fool. I've made it all too easy
for him. [*Coming down right*]

MARY. But that's your fault, too.

MARTIN. Yes it is, and I don't propose to repeat the error. He's lied to
me all the way through. We'll let him
face the truth; now we'll see what he's
made of.

[RODNEY *and* PEALE *enter*]

RODNEY [*coming in*]. Well, we're going to move. [*Goes to desk and sits*]

PEALE. Yes, nice chap, that fellow.
[*Coming down right*]

RODNEY. Well, Mary, have you
heard about our deal?

MARTIN. The deal's off.

MARY. But — [*Sits in arm-chair left*]

RODNEY [*back of desk*]. Off!

PEALE. Off! [*Goes up-stage to window*]

MARTIN. Yes, off.

RODNEY. But, why — why?

MARTIN. Because you took me for a
bigger fool than I am. My own son
can't do that to me. I've found out
now that you're broke.

MARY. Oh, Mr. Martin!

MARTIN [*stopping her*]. No! [*To*
RODNEY] And all the time you were
lying to me about the Ivory Soap people
and the factory they were going to put
up. You thought you could make an
ass of me — get the best of me, did you?
Well, you can't. I'm finished with you
and your 13 Soap. You've got a
swelled head, you're a smart alec, you're
a complete fake, you're a cheat, young
man —

RODNEY [*in utter dejection*]. I guess
you're right.

MARTIN [*with satisfaction*]. Ah!

RODNEY. I did try to be smart. I
was stuck on myself. I thought business was a cinch. But you're right. I
have been a fake. This whole thing
never seemed real — it was just fun —
like a game; but I've waked up, and
now it's serious. I tried to get the best
of you, but I'll take my licking. I don't
want any charity: I know what's coming to me and I'll take my medicine.

MARTIN [*relenting a little*]. Well,
maybe I've said a little too much —

RODNEY. No, it's all true.

MARTIN. But, see here, I don't
want you disgraced — I —

RODNEY. You told me never to come
back to you for a nickel, and I won't.
I told you, too, that I wouldn't snivel —
well, I'm not going to. Good-bye,
father —

MARTIN. Now, see here —

RODNEY. Please, father, it's up to
me and nobody else, to get out of this.
Please go. [*He holds out his hand*]

MARTIN [*gently*]. Good-bye, son.
[*He shakes his hand. He exits*]

[RODNEY *sits in chair dejected*]

PEALE [*coming down to* RODNEY].
Now, see here, little boss —

RODNEY. Peale, I'm sorry, but
you're fired.

PEALE [*coming over and putting hand
on his shoulder*]. Say, little boss, you
can't fire me. I'm just going to stick
around, whatever happens.

[MARY *touches* PEALE *on the arm and
motions him to go out. He nods
understandingly and exits upper
right.* MARY *comes to* RODNEY]

MARY. Oh, Rodney, Rodney, it was
all my fault. Your father had no idea
of the truth — I didn't understand;
I thought you sent for him to help you.
I told him about our company. I did it
all — betrayed you.

RODNEY. But you didn't mean to:
t's all right, Mary.

MARY. You forgive me?

RODNEY. Why, of course: I love
ou.

MARY. Oh, Rodney, I'm so sorry.

RODNEY [*changing completely. Rises*].
But if father thinks just because he
aced it into me I'm licked, he's wrong.
Maybe I have been a fake but, by
George, I won't be any longer. [*Goes
own right*]

MARY. You're really going on?
[*Goes down left*]

RODNEY. When I've got you, you
et I am. Say, do you really think a
ong speech from father and no money
o work with are enough to stop me?
No, sir; what father said got me for a
minute, but I'm not a quitter, and I'll
rove it. There must be something of
ather in me: I can't be such a pin-head
s I look. I'll get out of this mess the
est way I can, and then I'll shine shoes
r sell peanuts. I'll start at the bottom
nstead of finishing there. I'll make
noney — I'll —

MARY. Oh, Rodney, Rodney, now I
m proud of you! [*She kisses him un-
xpectedly and heartily*]

RODNEY [*overjoyed*]. What! That's
he first time you ever really kissed me
— all by yourself — like that. By
George, you must love me!

MARY. You bet I do. [*She kisses
im again and they clinch as* PEALE *enters
xcitedly, coming down right*]

PEALE [*entering*]. Say, I didn't mean
o interrupt!

RODNEY [*still with* MARY *in his arms*]
Nothing in the world can interrupt me
— What is it?

PEALE. A telegram. It's the first
we ever received, and — I was afraid to
open it.

MARY, *taking it, looks at it nervously*]

MARY. What awful thing can it be?
[*Goes in front of desk*]

RODNEY. Gee, I wonder what it
says? [*Crosses to her*]

PEALE. Read it. Read it. [*Crosses
to her*]

MARY [*having opened it*]. "Rodney
Martin, President 13 Soap Company,
226 Broadway" —

PEALE. Go on, we know the address —

MARY. "Ship at once, collect, 50,-
000 cakes 13 Soap. Marshall Field,
Chicago."

RODNEY. Somebody really wants to
buy some soap!

PEALE. I don't believe it.

MARY [*handing* RODNEY *the telegram*].
But here it is.

RODNEY [*reading*]. Fifty thousand
cakes — it's true.

PEALE. We've started — we've begun! We're actually going to sell some
soap.

RODNEY. The tide's turned — didn't
I tell you advertising pays? We'll
sweep the country — Europe — Asia —
Africa! Go in with father? Not for a
million dollars! [*Starts up-stage*]

PEALE. I'll wire Marshall Field right
away. [*Starts for door upper right*]

RODNEY. Go ahead.

MARY [*suddenly*]. Great Heavens!

PEALE. What is it?

RODNEY. What's happened?

MARY. That order is no good.

PEALE. What! [*Coming down right*]

RODNEY. Why? [*Coming down left*]

MARY. We can't fill it: we've never
made any soap. [*Start. Stand staring at
each other aghast*]

RODNEY. What'll we do?

PEALE. Let's think. [*They sit staring straight ahead*]

[RODNEY *sits in chair left.* MARY *sits on
table.* PEALE *sits in chair right*]

RODNEY [*slowly*]. We must get some
soap.

PEALE [*slowly*]. Yes, I thought of
that.

MARY [*slowly*]. Where can we get it?

PEALE. From a soap factory!

MARY [*slowly*]. But they all belong
to father.

RODNEY [*with dawning hope. Rises*].
But he can't know about this Marshall
Field order — maybe we could buy
some soap before he'd have a chance to
stop them selling to us?

[PEAL *and* MARY *rise*]

PEALE. Great idea — let's get busy.

MARY. How?

RODNEY. Where's the 'phone book?
[*She grabs red classified directory from
desk*] We'll call up two or three of his
branch offices. [*He has hurriedly begun
turning over pages, as* PEALE *on one side
and* MARY *on the other, help him*] Skins,
skates, shirts — where's soap?

MARY [*over his shoulder*]. Skylights,
skates, slides —

PEALE [*the same*]. Smelters, smoke-stacks, snuff.

RODNEY. Ah, here it is! Soap manufacturers — [*Skimming down page*] 276 Broad — here's one of father's factories.

PEALE. I've got one, too — 374 Schuyler.

MARY. So have I: 480 Audubon. [*They drop book and each dashes to a 'phone. As they give the number of 'phone, curtain. During two curtains, till they finish lines*]

RODNEY. 276 Broad. }
MARY. 480 Audubon. } [*Together*]
PEALE. 374 Schuyler — } and hurry, sweetie —

RODNEY [*holding wire*]. It'll have to be Old Rose.

PEALE. Castile is the cheapest.

MARY. Order small cakes.

RODNEY. Hello, is this the Martin Soap Company — we want to get some soap — pink castile — small cakes — 40 or 50,000 cakes immediate delivery — what's the price?

MARY. Hello, 480 Audubon. I want to find out if I can buy a lot of soap right away — Old Rose — castile — 50,000 cakes; we want it this afternoon.

[*Together*]

PEALE. Hello, son, I want to buy a lot of soap: 50,000 cakes — got to have some of it to-day — smallest size castile cakes you keep. If you haven't Old Rose — pink'll do. Who am I? None of your business. [*And as all three are talking together violently in their separate 'phones,*

THE CURTAIN FALLS

ACT III

SCENE. — *The scene is the same as that of* ACT I, *except that it is five o'clock in the afternoon of a day in late October.*

MARTIN *is discovered behind the desk, right. Before him is a pile of evening papers and some unopened letters. As the curtain rises he opens one, displaying to the audience on its back page a page-advertisement of 13 Soap. In a moment he turns over to others, gives an annoyed exclamation and tosses it aside. He picks up one of the letters, opens it, gives an angry grunt,* mutters disgustedly "13 Soap", an[d] throws it into the waste basket.

JOHNSON [*entering door upper left*] Miss Grayson is here to see you, sir —

MARTIN [*a bit surprised*]. Miss Grayson? Well, show her in.

JOHNSON. Very good, sir. [*He exit* MARTIN *opens another paper, again see[s] an advertisement of 13 Soap and wit[h] considerable irritation sweeps the who[le] pile off the desk as* JOHNSON *enters, fo[l] lowed by* MARY] Miss Grayson [JOHNSON *exits*]

MARY. How do you do, Mr. Martin

MARTIN. Come to get your job back I suppose?

MARY. No, sir.

MARTIN. Well, you can have it — at the old salary.

MARY. I don't want it.

MARTIN. Oh, Rodney sent you t[o] plead for him?

MARY. No, sir.

MARTIN. Then, what are you her[e] for?

MARY. To make you a business prop[osition].

MARTIN. Why doesn't Rodney mak[e] it himself?

MARY. He doesn't know I'm here.

MARTIN. That's something in hi[s] favor: can't see much use in wome[n] tying up in men's business.

JOHNSON [*entering*]. Mr. Rodne[y] Martin and Ambrose Peale.

MARTIN. Oh, the whole firm! Sen[d] 'em in, Johnson.

JOHNSON. Very good, sir. [*He exits*

[RODNEY *and* PEALE *enter*]

RODNEY. Hello, father. [*Crosses t[o] table*]

PEALE. How do you do, sir? [*Com[ing] down left*]

[MARTIN *grunts to them both*]

RODNEY [*seeing* MARY]. Mary, wha[t] on earth are you doing here?

MARY. I came to tell your fathe[r] about Marshall Field's order.

RODNEY. That's why we're here, too[.]

PEALE. Absolutely.

MARTIN. Let me tell you right now I won't back any fake company.

RODNEY. But we're not a fake an[y] longer.

PEALE. We've actually sold som[e] soap.

MARY. Fifty thousand cakes.

RODNEY. To Marshall Field.

MARTIN. Then why did you send 'em only five thousand cakes?

RODNEY. Because after we'd got that much from one of your branch factories you shut off our supply.

PEALE. And we couldn't get any more soap anywhere.

MARY [*accusingly*]. And you knew it very well. [*Crossing to right side of Mr. Martin*]

RODNEY. We've still got 45,000 cakes to deliver, if we can get 'em from you. Why let all that money get out of the family? It's a business proposition.

MARTIN. No, it isn't. Don't fool yourself: I sent that telegram.

RODNEY. What telegram?

MARTIN. The telegram from Marshall Field's ordering the 50,000 cakes.

MARY. You sent it?

MARTIN. That day at the office you were pretty game, son, and to tell the truth, I felt so sorry for you, I kind of had to do something, so I sent that wire —

RODNEY. So that success is all a bluff, too? [*Sits on sofa*]

MARY. But what did you do it for?

MARTIN. Well, I figured an order like that would stall off your creditors, and then I had fixed it with one of our factories to let you have 5,000 cakes at three cents a cake. I knew it would mean some ready cash for you from Marshall Field —

PEALE. But how did you square Marshall Field?

MARTIN. Oh, I just wired 'em I'd be responsible, and, say — [*Turning to Rodney, who rises*] you had a nerve to charge 'em sixty cents a cake — and I had to pay the bill! That shipment cost me $3,000 for $150 worth of soap. [*Peale laughs*] That isn't funny, young man.

RODNEY. No, it isn't: I thought we'd really made good, and all the time it was you behind us —

MARTIN. You see, my boy, even if you did nearly trim me, I've got a sort of sneaking fondness for you. Look here, son, why not quit? There's no market for dollar soap.

RODNEY. But how do you know?

MARTIN. I had a letter from Marshall Field a few days ago asking me what to do with the soap. They hadn't sold a cake. I told 'em to dump it in the Chicago River; it might help to clean it up.

RODNEY. But you didn't give our advertising a chance.

PEALE. We only finished a great big advertising campaign in Chicago two days ago.

RODNEY. I know the soap'll make good — with that trade-mark.

MARTIN. If your trade-mark was so marvelous, somebody besides your poor old father would have bought your soap.

PEALE. Oh, what's the use? He doesn't believe in advertising!

MARTIN. Oh, yes, I do: sound, conservative advertising, but not the crazy, sensational stuff you go in for.

MARY. Oh, you're just mad because the soap trust didn't think of 13 Soap itself.

MARTIN. Why, we wouldn't touch a fool thing like that. If you deliver the goods, your goods will advertise you — that's always been our policy.

RODNEY. I'm sorry, father, but you are old-fashioned to knock the modern way of advertising. Why, do you know, the National Biscuit Company was on the verge of failing until they hit on the title, Uneeda Biscuit?

MARY. And since then, they have had over four hundred lawsuits to protect it.

RODNEY. Their trade-mark made 'em. They value that trade-mark now at six million dollars.

PEALE. Great stuff. [*Turning to Martin*] — and Spearmint Gum just as a trade-mark is worth seven millions.

RODNEY. And the Fairbanks people count their trade-mark, The Gold Dust Twins, at $10,000,000.

MARY. Ever hear of the Gillette Safety Razor?

MARTIN. I use it myself.

MARY. Tell him about it, Rodney.

RODNEY. It costs you five dollars. Don't you know there's a mighty good safety razor for a quarter, and dozens at a dollar, but you use the Gillette because Gillette was there first; you buy his razor at a high price simply because of its trade-mark.

MARY [*with gesture*]. Advertising.

RODNEY *and* PEALE [*with gesture*]. Absolutely.

PEALE. Ivory Soap in the magazines alone used $450,000 worth of space in 1913 — and at three cents a cake wholesale, that represents 15,000,000 cakes for magazine advertising alone.

MARTIN. I don't believe it.

Peale. Yes, and a lot of other guys didn't believe that iron ships would float or that machines heavier than air would fly, or that you could talk to 'Frisco on a wire or send a message across the Atlantic without a wire. Pardon me, sir, but you want to get on to yourself.

Rodney. Yes, father, you certainly do.

Mary. And you'd better hurry up.

Martin. You've got a fine lot of theories, but what have they done for those 5,000 cakes of 13 Soap out at Marshall Field's?

Peale. Why, we haven't really spent enough money advertising.

Rodney. That's true. Every time the American Tobacco Company puts out a new cigarette they start off by appropriating $200,000 to boom it.

Peale. And I suppose they are a lot of boobs?

Rodney. And think what other firms spend! I've gone into this thing, father —

Mary. Yes, Rodney, let's show him our list.

Rodney. Sure, it's an absolutely accurate list of what some of the big advertisers spent in the thirty-one leading magazines last year. Eastman Kodak, $400,000. Postum Coffee, $125,000, Arrow Collars, $400,000, Melachrino Cigarettes, $100,000, Welch's Grape Juice, $100,000.

Peale. Grape Juice, my friend!

Mary. Uneeda Biscuit, $150,000. Spearmint Gum, $140,000.

Martin. That's enough.

Rodney. I've only just begun. Grape Nuts, $228,000.

Mary. Colgate's Dental Cream, $230,000.

Peale. Campbell's Soups, $186,000.

Mary. Kellogg's Toasted Cornflakes, $200,000.

Rodney. Quaker Oats, $367,000, and these are only a few. You can't see how it pays, but you do know that it must pay or they wouldn't do it.

Mary. Does that mean anything to you?

Peale. Yes. Does it when you realize that those thirty-one magazines have only about 10,000,000 readers?

Rodney. And that there are a hundred million people in this country. Why just to appeal to one-tenth of the population, fifty million dollars was spent in magazines last year, and each year people are getting better educated —

more people are wanting to read. I[t] won't be long before there are 25,000,00[0] people buying magazines, and you ca[n] reach all of them by advertising — g[et] a new market, a new population to dea[l] with. Think what national advertisin[g] is accomplishing! It sells automobile[s] vacuum cleaners, talking machine[s] rubber heels, kodaks, washing ma[-] chines, foods, clothes, shoes, paint[s] houses, plumbing, electric irons, fireles[s] cookers — mostly to a lot of peop[le] who'd never even hear of 'em if i[t] weren't for advertisements.

Peale. But nowadays it isn't onl[y] people who have stoves to sell or tooth[-] brushes, that are spending money o[n] publicity. Banks are advertising fo[r] money, nations for immigrants, col[-] leges for students, cities for citizen[s] and churches for congregations, an[d] you sit there thinking it doesn't pay t[o] advertise.

Mary. Six hundred and sixtee[n] million dollars were spent last year i[n] magazines and newspapers, billboard[s] and electric signs.

Rodney. Bringing education an[d] comfort and fun and luxury to th[e] people of the United States. It'[s] romance, father, the romance of print[-] ing-presses, of steel rails, of the wireles[s] of trains and competition, the romanc[e] of modern business, and it's all built o[n] advertising. Advertising is the bigges[t] thing in this country, and it's only jus[t] begun.

Martin [*after a pause*]. Why didn'[t] you boys go into the advertising busi[-] ness? You seem to know somethin[g] about that?

Peale [*fairly tearing his hair*]. Oh[,] what's the use! He's the old school — we're new blood. [*Coming to left o[f] center*]

Rodney [*with enthusiasm*]. Yout[h] has got it on old age.

Mary [*coming down between* Peal[e] *and* Rodney]. You bet it has!

Martin. When you boys ge[t] through talking and you're flat brok[e] and down and out, come around an[d] see me: I'll show you an old busines[s] that has a lot of money that isn't radica[l] and manages to keep going withou[t] wasting a fortune in fool advertising.

Rodney. Then you won't let us ge[t] any soap.

Martin. Risk my business reputa[-] tion on a silly scheme like Dollar Soap[.] I should say not!

PEALE. Oh, come on. What's the use of talking to a man whose brain is deaf? [*Exeunt door upper left, keeping in step, single-file*]

MARTIN [*rises and comes to center*]. Say when you get a new line of patter, come around. I like to hear you. Dollar Soap!

JOHNSON [*enters*]. I beg pardon, a gentleman to see you, sir. [JOHNSON *hands* MARTIN *a card on silver tray*]

MARTIN. "Mr. Charles Bronson." What does he want?

JOHNSON. He says he's from Marshall Field.

MARTIN. Oh, a kick, I suppose? Send him in.

JOHNSON. Yes, sir. [*He exits*]

[*Enter* BRONSON]

BRONSON [*inquiringly*]. Mr. Martin?

MARTIN. Yes.

BRONSON. I just arrived from Chicago. I am here in reference to the 13 Soap.

MARTIN. Be seated. Well, what about it? [*Sits in chair left of table*]

BRONSON [*sits in chair right of desk*]. While, of course, we understand that the 13 Soap is made by your son, Mr. Rodney Martin, at the same time as you wired us you would be responsible for that order, Marshall Field felt that I should first see you in the matter.

MARTIN. Humph!

BRONSON. We realize, of course, that you are backing your son —

MARTIN [*gruffly*]. Well, why shouldn't I back him?

BRONSON. Of course, of course. That is why we'd like to place our order through you.

MARTIN [*amazed*]. Place your what?

BRONSON. Through some error we received only 5,000 cakes, instead of 10,000 but that's all gone.

MARTIN. All gone? What happened to it?

BRONSON. We've sold it.

MARTIN. Sold it?

BRONSON. Yes, and we want the balance of the original order you were kind enough to throw our way, and as much more soap as we can get.

MARTIN. But only the other day I had a letter from Marshall Field saying they hadn't sold a cake.

BRONSON [*laughing*]. I know, I know. We felt at first that of course there could be no popular market for a dollar soap;

we weren't as far-sighted as you were. [MARTIN *clears his throat*] But of course, when those extraordinary advertisements appeared, so different from your usual conservative publicity, the sales began immediately! We sold the 5,000 cakes in two days.

MARTIN. And the advertising did it?

BRONSON. Of course, what else? Now we want to handle your goods exclusively in the west — with extensive immediate deliveries. Can that be arranged?

MARTIN. It ought to be. What do you offer?

BRONSON. I dare say we would contract for a quarter of a million cakes of soap.

MARTIN [*amazed*]. A quarter of a million!

BRONSON [*misunderstanding him*]. Of course we might do a little better if we could settle the matter at once.

MARTIN. I should have to consult my son first.

BRONSON [*rising*]. Oh, then perhaps I ought to go see him?

MARTIN [*rising*]. Not at all — not at all. I'll attend to it.

BRONSON. But we thought that you would have full power.

MARTIN. As a matter of courtesy I should like to talk things over with my own boy —

BRONSON. But you control the product?

MARTIN. Bronson, you can trust me to handle this thing.

BRONSON. Of course, of course. When can I see you again?

MARTIN. In half an hour.

BRONSON. Very well. I've some matters to attend to. I'll be back in half an hour. [*Going to door upper left*] It's a wonderful soap, Mr. Martin.

MARTIN [*dryly*]. Oh, wonderful.

BRONSON. See you in half an hour. [BRONSON *exits*]

MARTIN. Wonderful soap — plain pink castile. I've got to get in on this. [*He goes to 'phone*] 1313 Bryant. Hello, is this the 13 Soap Company?

JOHNSON [*enters*]. Oh, beg pardon, sir, but —

MARTIN. Just a minute. Is Mr. Rodney Martin in? No? Never mind who I am. Good-bye. Johnson, call up my son's office every ten minutes and let me know the minute he comes in. Don't tell 'em who's calling. [*Crosses to right*]

JOHNSON. Yes, sir.

MARTIN. And when Mr. Bronson comes back, be sure to have him wait for me.

JOHNSON. Yes, sir. There's a lady to see you, sir. She speaks English now.

MARTIN. She does, eh? That's unusual, isn't it?

JOHNSON. I mean, sir, when she was here two months ago she could only talk French.

MARTIN. Indeed! Well, I'm not interested in the languages she speaks. Who is she, and what does she want?

JOHNSON. She wishes to see you about the French right of the 13 Soap.

MARTIN. The what?

JOHNSON. The French rights.

MARTIN. Great Scott! Send her right in.

JOHNSON. Yes, sir. The Countess de Bowreen. [*He exits*]

COUNTESS [*enters*]. How do you do?

MARTIN [*comes down in front of table*]. How do you do?

COUNTESS. I am the Countess de Beaurien. Your son have told you of me!

MARTIN. No.

COUNTESS. I bet he have not. He is a cheat — he trick me.

MARTIN. Now, my dear lady —

COUNTESS. Attendez, you listen to me: two months ago there in that very room, I buy the French rights for the 13 Soap. I pay him 15,000 dollar and now I cannot get any soap.

MARTIN. You will have to see my son.

COUNTESS. But I have seen him, and he give me no satisfaction. If I cannot get any soap, I must have my money, one or the other, or I put him in the jail. He is a cheat. I have here ze contract. I sue him in the court.

MARTIN. My dear lady, you mustn't feel that way.

COUNTESS. Feel! Ah, mon dieu — I trick no one, I play fair, I am an honest woman. Mais je vous dis que je suis honnête, très honnête dans mes affaires. Monsieur votre fils m'a donné le contrat, et j'insiste qu'il est très malhonnête. Je n'ai pas l'habitude d'être si maltraité, monsieur, et je répète que je ferai tout mon possible d'obtenir les quinze mille dollars que me doît Monsieur votre fils, et s'il ne me les donne pas, je le poursuivrai sans cesse. Comprenez-vous, Monsieur? [*She takes the contract from him*]

MARTIN. But I don't understar French.

COUNTESS. Pardon, Monsieur, a ways I am excited I speak the Frencl But! If you love your son, you pay m back, or else he go to jail. What yo say?

MARTIN. But $15,000 is a lot money.

COUNTESS. Yes. But it is more me than it is to you. You pay me, or h go to prison. Now what you say?

[JOHNSON *enters*]

MARTIN. What is it?

JOHNSON. I beg pardon, a gentlema to see you, sir.

MARTIN [*comes to* JOHNSON]. Is Bronson?

JOHNSON. No, sir. [JOHNSON *hana him card*]

MARTIN. By George, just the man want to see! Show him right in. Hol on, hold on. Now, Duchess, if yo don't mind, just step in this room minute. [*Indicating room lower right*]

COUNTESS. No, no, I do not like tha room: I have been there before.

MARTIN. Here is a nice roon [*Points to room lower left*] You will fin it very comfortable.

COUNTESS. Very well, I wai [*Crosses to left*] But in fifteen minute if I do not get the 15,000 dollar, I go t my lawyers, and your son — poof! h is done. [*Talking in French as she exit*]

MARTIN [*to* JOHNSON]. Did you ge my son's office?

JOHNSON. Yes, sir — he hasn't com in.

MARTIN. If you reach him while Mr Peale's here don't mention Rodney' name; just call him "that party." I'll understand. [*Crosses right*]

JOHNSON. Yes, sir. [*He exits*]

[PEALE *enters door upper left*]

MARTIN. Now, see here, young man

PEALE. Now, one moment, Mr Martin. I just want to say that I an a man of few words — that this isn' advertising, it's personal. I know yo don't like me.

MARTIN. Why do you say that?

PEALE. Because I'm a pretty wis gink.

MARTIN. Well, you are a bit —

PEALE. Fresh! Well, I guess that' right, too. But that's me — I'm no your style. Here's the idea: your so has been immense to me. Great kid

nd it struck me the reason you wouldn't
ack him was because I was mixed up in
is business. So I just came to say if
hat's the situation, why I'm out, that's
ll. You go ahead with him alone.

MARTIN. You're not a partner?

PEALE. I should say not. I'm just
hired hand. He could can me any
moment, but he's not the kind of guy
who'd do that.

MARTIN. Then you haven't power to
ign, to make a deal?

PEALE. I should say not. Why, he
nd Miss Grayson do all the signing.
f I could have signed contracts, I'd
ave spent a million dollars in advertis-
ng. And believe me, you ought to back
im, because, honest, Mr. Martin, it's
great scheme — the 13 Soap, on the
evel, if it's handled right and the pub-
icity end is —

MARTIN. Now don't get started on
dvertising.

PEALE. That's right, too. Well, I
uess that's all. I wanted to tell you
ow I stood about Rodney. That's off
ny chest, so good afternoon. [*Starts to
o*]

MARTIN. Wait a minute. What did
you boys mean by trimming that poor
Countess on the French rights?

PEALE. Jumping Jupiter; has she
een here?

MARTIN. She's here now.

PEALE. What did she come to see
ou for?

MARTIN. She said she'd put Rodney
n jail for fraud unless I made good that
$15,000. I've got to pay her — can't
ee the boy disgraced.

PEALE. Say, if you'd like to save
hat $15,000, I'll fix it for you.

MARTIN. But she's got a contract.

PEALE. I'll get it for you cheap.
Pardon me, sir, but I know how to
handle dames like her.

MARTIN. Mr. Peale, I like you.
[*Slaps him on shoulder*]

PEALE. Huh!

MARTIN. Have a cigar?

[PEALE *crosses right. He takes it as*
JOHNSON *enters*]

JOHNSON. I just telephoned *that
party*, he is at his office now.

MARTIN. Good, good. Peale, I've
got to go out on an important soap deal.
[*He starts to go, then goes to* PEALE] Oh,
by George, I nearly forgot. There's
another matter I must attend to first.
Peale, you'll find the Countess in there.

Do the best you can — we'll settle the
details when I get back. Make yourself
at home.

PEALE. Sure. This cigar's great
company.

MARTIN. Good cigar, eh?

PEALE. Corker.

MARTIN. Johnson, send over half a
dozen boxes of these cigars to Mr.
Peale's house. He'll give you the
address. [*He exits left*]

PEALE. And, say, Johnson, wrap
'em up now and I'll take 'em with me.

JOHNSON. Very good, sir. [*He exits.*
PEALE *walks over to the window and looks
out at the 13 Soap signs*]

PEALE [*the telephone rings.* PEALE
*looks at it, it rings again, he goes over to
desk and raises it*]. Yes, Sweetie —
this is the garage. How long does it
take to go to Coney Island? How in
hell do I know? [*Business of changing
money and watch to different pockets.
Goes to door left, and opens it*] Countess
de Bull Run. [*He goes into some fake
French*] De juis — de joie — politesse
noblesse oblige.

COUNTESS. You ought to take up
French — your accent's immense.
Well, little sweetheart?

PEALE. Say, what are you doing in
these parts?

COUNTESS. Oh, I came to see Mr.
Martin.

PEALE. What for?

COUNTESS. What do you think?

PEALE. See here, now, if you're aim-
ing to trim the old man, I won't stand
for it.

COUNTESS. Ambrose, do me a favor.

PEALE. What is it?

COUNTESS. Don't tell old Martin
what I tried to do to you boys. He's
the kind that would put me in jail.
I'll be on the level. I did come here to
try to trim him, but I'll cut it out.
Honest, I will. Oh, Ambrose, I don't
like being a grafter. I've had to do a
lot of things I didn't want to. You
don't know how hard it is for girls like
me. I never had a show. I ran away
from home when I was a kid. I've been
pretty much up against it. Is what I've
done to other guys going to butt in and
queer me?

PEALE. Nix, nix —

COUNTESS. Give me a chance to be
on the square. It ain't easy for a girl
to fight it out all by herself when she's
all alone: no money — no friends and
you got to live — live on five a week.

You got a lot for a good time, haven't you? God, I've been lonely sometimes; you've got to be pretty smart to steer straight — but I've done it, I've done it, I've done it. [*She breaks down and sits on chair right of desk*]

PEALE [*kindly*]. Now, see here, Countess — [*He pats her on back*] — don't do that — don't, don't — [*She is sobbing a little*] Oh, quit it. [*A pause*] Keep it for some poor boob who'll fall for it.

COUNTESS [*tearfully*]. Oh, Ambrose, don't talk like that —

PEALE. Say, honest, it's foolish wasting it on me, kid.

COUNTESS [*completely changing to a radiant smile. Rises*]. Well, it's always worth trying once.

PEALE [*genially*]. Sure it is. Why, you had me winging for a minute, but when you pulled that wheeze about "I've done it", three times in succession, I knew it was phoney.

COUNTESS. But, honest, I was on the level about old Martin.

PEALE. Nix, nix, you came here to trim him for the $15,000 on the French rights.

COUNTESS. Gosh, have you seen him?

PEALE. Yes, he left me here to settle it. Where's the contract? Come on — gimme — gimme —

COUNTESS. You mean you've been on all the time?

PEALE. Sure.

COUNTESS. And you let me sit there and emote all over the place.

PEALE. Gimme — gimme —

COUNTESS. Oh, I suppose I've got to. Oh, I'm sick of soap anyhow. 13 may be a lucky hunch for you boys, but it has been a hoodoo for me.

PEALE. And now, my little hearts of lettuce, this concludes your portion of the evening's entertainment.

COUNTESS. But at that, don't give me away, will you?

PEALE. I like you, you've got brains. Most chickens are just chickens.

COUNTESS. You are 18-karat, kid.

[MARY, *followed by* RODNEY, *enters hurriedly and sees* PEALE]

RODNEY. Oh, have you seen father? Is he here?

PEALE. I'm waiting for him now.

MARY. It's most important.

PEALE. You remember the Countess? [*All bow embarrassed. Pause*]

COUNTESS. Well, I guess I'm not wanted, so I'll trot. I'll trot. [*Goes t door upper left*] So long, you 13 Soa suds. [*Exits*]

MARY. Where is father?

PEALE. Yes, what's the excitement

MARY. Just after we got to the offic there was a letter from Macy's.

RODNEY. Ordering 10,000 cakes o 13 Soap.

MARY. Now what do you think o that?

PEALE. Pinch me, I'm dreaming [*Going down right*]

RODNEY. They say our advertising wonderful and has created such a de mand they want to handle the soap i town. [*Goes around table down right*]

PEALE [*wonderingly*]. Then all th things we said to your father are reall true? [*Goes up center*]

MARY. Of course they are.

RODNEY [*protesting*]. Now, see here old man —

PEALE. Gosh! [*Coming down i front of table*]

RODNEY. You see, when I sho father this letter from Macy's he's got t admit we've won out, and supply u with soap.

MARY. Isn't it a shame that yo can't get soap from anybody but him?

RODNEY. He certainly has got th soap business tied up tight.

PEALE. Yes, if he busted, the whol world would go dirty.

MARY. Suppose he's still stubbor and won't help you? What'll you do?

RODNEY. Oh, I'll just have to plo along.

PEALE. Don't plod — gallop, son — gallop — gallop.

RODNEY. You're a great pal.

MARY [*crosses to* PEALE]. Do yo know, Mr. Peele, I'd like you awfully

PEALE. Call me Ambrose.

MARY [*coyly goes to left*]. Ambrose.

RODNEY. If we ever do come out o this, you're going to be my partner 50–50.

PEALE. Aw, shut up.

JOHNSON [*entering*]. Mr. Charle Bronson; shall I show him in?

PEALE. You have my permission — [*Crosses to left.* MARY *crosses to table right*] This isn't my house. [BRONSON *enters.* JOHNSON *exits*] This way, sir

BRONSON. Oh, I beg pardon — I expected to find Mr. Martin.

RODNEY. I am Mr. Martin.

BRONSON [*eagerly*]. Mr. Rodney Martin?

RODNEY. Yes.

BRONSON. Just the very man I wanted to see — on private business.

RODNEY. Oh, these are my partners. You can talk before them. This is Mr. Peale and Miss Grayson, may I present — Mr. —?

BRONSON. Mr. Charles Bronson, of Marshall Field.

MARY [*stunned*]. Marshall Field?

PEALE [*falls in chair right of desk*]. Marshall Field?

BRONSON. Now, about your soap —?

PEALE. We're very sorry — [*Rises and goes to* BRONSON]

MARY. We are; but a bargain is a bargain. [*Rises*]

BRONSON. Sorry? Why, your 13 Soap the last few days has had a most remarkable sale at our store.

[MARY *and* PEALE, *speechless, look at each other*]

RODNEY [*gasping*]. You mean it is really selling?

BRONSON. Rather!

MARY. It's really selling?

BRONSON. Why, you seem surprised —

MARY. Oh, no — not a bit.

RODNEY. Oh, not a bit.

PEALE. — You mean people are actually coming into the store and buying it?

BRONSON. At a dollar a cake.

[MARY *and* RODNEY *take arm-chair from left of table and place it in center of stage*]

RODNEY *and* MARY. Have a chair?

PEALE. Give me your hat! [*Takes hat and fans himself*]

MARY. It was those page advertisements in Chicago that did it.

PEALE. Absolutely.

BRONSON. Extraordinary advertisements they were, too.

RODNEY. Oh, nothing to what we will do.

BRONSON. You'll keep up your campaign?

RODNEY. Double it.

PEALE. Triple it.

BRONSON. Good, good. We foresee a tremendous sale for your goods. It's an amazing soap.

RODNEY. It's more than that —

PEALE. Absolutely.

BRONSON. Do you control the company yourself?

RODNEY. Oh, entirely.

BRONSON. Then I can deal with you.

RODNEY. With us — all of us.

BRONSON. We would be glad to contract now for 250,000 cakes. [PEALE *just flops into chair*] With deliveries to begin next week.

MARY. Our capacity just at present is limited.

RODNEY. Yes, we have so many orders on hand.

BRONSON. Naturally, but how much soap can you deliver now?

RODNEY. I don't quite know. [*To* MARY] Do you?

MARY. Not quite. [*To* PEALE] Do you?

PEALE. Not quite.

BRONSON. Well, under the circumstances, what can we do?

MARY. That's the question.

PEALE. What's the answer? [*Rises. A pause*]

RODNEY. Here's an idea: in view of our pressing orders, would you consider for the moment paying us merely for the use of our trade-mark without any soap at all?

BRONSON. Yes, I think we would.

PEALE. You would?

BRONSON. Your trade-mark is of course your biggest asset.

RODNEY. Yes, of course.

BRONSON. You would naturally give us your formula?

PEALE. Yes, if we still have that cook-book.

BRONSON. I beg pardon?

PEALE. Nothing, nothing. Have a cigar?

RODNEY. You can have the formula.

BRONSON. With a license from you to use the title, we could probably arrange to have the soap manufactured by Cyrus Martin of the soap trust.

RODNEY. Oh, you think you could —?

MARY. How much would you be willing to pay us for the trade-mark?

BRONSON. I should have to call up our Chicago office, but I think I can safely say we would be prepared to offer you at least two hundred and fifty thousand dollars.

PEALE [*gasping*]. Indeed!

BRONSON. Can I have an option at that figure?

MARY. No!

PEALE. Yes! ⎫ [*Together*]

RODNEY. Yes — ⎬

MARY [*loudly*]. No!

RODNEY. No!

PEALE. No, but I hate to say it.

BRONSON. But if you control the company, why not settle matters now?

RODNEY. Why not, Mary?

PEALE. Yes, why not, Mary?

MARY. Hadn't we better discuss the matter a little more fully first among ourselves?

BRONSON. Perhaps I could wait somewhere for a few minutes while you talk things over?

MARY [*opening door left*]. Yes, do, please — in the library.

BRONSON. I am very glad to have met you.

RODNEY. Not half as glad —

PEALE. Not half so glad —

MARY. — not half as glad as we are to have met you.

PEALE. No, not half as much!

[BRONSON *exits left lower door*]

RODNEY. Why not give him an option at a quarter of a million?

PEALE. Yes, why not? For the love of gee whiz, tell us that!

MARY. Because maybe we can get more money than that out of your father.

[JOHNSON *enters with letter, and crosses to table right*]

RODNEY. Mary, you are a wonder.

PEALE. Gosh, I wish you were going to marry me!

MARY. Johnson, oh, Johnson, you know I've always liked you —

JOHNSON. I beg pardon, Miss?

MARY. Will you do me a favor?

JOHNSON. Why, yes, Miss.

MARY. When Mr. Martin comes back, don't tell him that Rodney and Mr. Peale are here, or Bronson, either; say I'm alone.

JOHNSON. Yes, Miss, but Mr. Martin just drove up in his car, he'll be here directly —

MARY. Hurry up, then, tell him I'm here, waiting for him.

[JOHNSON *exits*]

RODNEY. But I don't understand?

PEALE. Neither do I.

MARY. I do. I've got a great idea. You two boys go into that room, [*indicating lower right*] and stay there. When I ring this buzzer twice, you call me on this 'phone — there's a switch in there — and never mind what I say. Hurry now, both of you.

RODNEY. But what's your plan?

MARY. I'm going to try to make a deal with your father.

PEALE. Well, I'll slip you something that may help you when you see father. You tell him that I've got that contract. He'll understand.

RODNEY. But I don't know what any of this is about?

PEALE. Neither do I. Come on, she's got more brains than both of us. [*They exit right*]

[MARY *settles herself in chair left of desk as* MARTIN *enters*]

MARTIN. Hello, Miss Grayson, this is a pleasant surprise. Where is Rodney?

MARY. That doesn't matter. I'm here.

MARTIN. Where's that — that Mr. —?

MARY. Mr. Peale — oh, Mr. Peale's gone back to the office — but he told me to tell you that he'd got that contract —

MARTIN. Great, great! He's a smart boy.

MARY. We are all smart — it's a smart firm. We just got a letter from Macy's for 10,000 cakes of 13 Soap, and this time you didn't send a telegram —

MARTIN. Macy's, eh? Well, well. Now, I'll be frank. I want Rodney to come in with me — and you've got to help. You started this scheme. Now finish it up.

MARY. What's changed you all of a sudden?

MARTIN. Well, Macy's, for one thing. That shows sensational advertising does pay. Those boys are right. I've been too conservative, but anyhow I've got the whip hand: Rodney can't get his soap for Macy's except from me, and if I'm going to furnish three-cent soap that he sells wholesale for sixty cents, I'm going to be in on the profits. Any young man who can do that is just bound to have me for a partner whether he wants me or not. What do you say, Miss Grayson?

MARY. I'll do all I can for Rodney.

MARTIN. You have authority to close the deal?

MARY. Absolutely.

MARTIN. Good. Now, what's your proposition? [*Sits*]

MARY. Five hundred thousand dollars cash.

MARTIN [*rising*]. What!

MARY [*calmly*]. Sit down. That isn't all: we get fifty-one per cent. of the stock, you put up a factory and give Rodney $50,000 a year. Peale, $30,000, and me $20,000.

MARTIN. As my son once observed, what a lovely autumn we're having! [*He leans back and lights a cigar. As he does so,* MARY *pushes the buzzer twice. N.B. The audience must hear this buzzer. Almost instantly the 'phone rings.* MARY *quickly takes 'phone*]

MARY. Shall I answer it?

MARTIN. Go ahead — say I'm out.

MARY [*in 'phone*]. Oh, hello — [*To* MARTIN] It's for me. Hello, Rodney — you've seen Bronson?

MARTIN [*sitting up*]. Bronson?

MARY [*in 'phone*]. He did? Why, that's a splendid offer. I hardly dared think Marshall Field would be so generous.

MARTIN [*promptly. Rises*]. I'll accept your proposition, Miss Grayson.

MARY. Wait. [*In 'phone*] Have you closed with Bronson yet?

MARTIN. What'd he say?

MARY. Oh, you haven't?

MARTIN. Good.

MARY. No, I think you'd better come right up from the office and see me before you sign anything.

MARTIN. Here, let me talk to him. [*He reaches for 'phone*]

MARY [*quickly*]. Oh, hello, hello. [*She jiggles 'phone*] Oh, dear, we've been cut off. Still, it doesn't matter; it's all settled now.

MARTIN. That's splendid, Miss Grayson. I'm mighty grateful to you.

MARY [*nervously*]. Shall we sign a memorandum now?

MARTIN. Sure — sure — just the rough details.

MARY. Sure, never put off till tomorrow what you can sign to-day.

MARTIN [*he crosses to table right, sits and makes memoranda. Writing*]. Fifty-one per cent. — Rodney — fifty thousand. And what's that young man's name again — Spiel —?

MARY. Peale.

MARTIN. That certainly is one hell of a name — thirty thousand — Grayson twenty thousand. There. [*To* MARY] You sign here.

MARY. No, you sign first. [MARTIN *grunts and signs*] Now I'll sign for Rodney. [*She does so gleefully*]

MARTIN. That's great. [*Rises and goes left*]

MARY. You don't know how great it is. [MARY *starts for door*] Now, I've a big surprise for you. Rodney's not at the office — he's in there.

MARTIN. What do you mean?

MARY. Only that I thought I'd handle you less sentimentally than he would. You see, once before I spoiled Rodney's plan. This time I thought I ought to fix it up for him. [*Opening door*] Rodney — Ambrose.

MARTIN. Say, what is all this?

[RODNEY *and* PEALE *enter*]

RODNEY. Hello, father!

MARY. Rodney, it's all settled. Your father has gone in with us. I've the contract.

RODNEY. Then we can get some soap!

MARTIN. All you want.

RODNEY. Then I don't care what the arrangement is — now that we can make good — twenty per cent. of the profits, and any old salary.

MARTIN. Twenty per cent.! Why, she buncoed me out of fifty-one per cent. and half a million down.

PEALE [*gasping*]. Half a million!

RODNEY [*to* MARY]. You did? Mary, you are a peach!

PEALE. Absolutely.

MARY [*to* MARTIN]. And by the terms of my contract with you, you now owe me ten per cent. of what Rodney has made: $50,000.

RODNEY. What contract?

PEALE. I don't get you.

MARTIN. So that's why you held me up, eh? Just to get your ten per cent. Say, young lady, I've got a lot of other money that you are overlooking.

RODNEY. Father, what do you mean?

MARTIN [*to* RODNEY]. I'll tell you what I mean. She got engaged to you to make you go to work — she only left me to keep you on the job because I promised her ten per cent. of what you earned. All the time that she's been pretending she would marry you, she's been making use of you. [*Goes to right of table to sign check*]

RODNEY. Mary, you did this to me?

PEALE. I don't believe it.

MARY [*to* MARTIN]. You owe me fifty thousand dollars — can I have the check, please?

MARTIN. Yes, if you'll quit now — get out of here for good.

MARY. Certainly.

MARTIN. I'm disappointed to think you'd treat my boy like this.

MARY. What's the difference? If I'd really loved him, you'd have objected to his marrying only a type-writer.

MARTIN. Objected! If you'd been on the level I'd have been proud to have you for my daughter. [*Handing check to* RODNEY]

RODNEY [*gleefully*]. Hurrah, Mary, it's all right!

PEALE. I don't get you.

MARTIN. What is this — a joke? [*Rises*]

RODNEY. Certainly it is: you two put up a joke on me, and Mary and I thought we'd put up one for you. Mary told me about that fool contract weeks ago.

MARTIN. You mean you're going to marry her?

RODNEY. Certainly not.

PEALE. Now see here —

MARTIN. Why aren't you going to marry her?

RODNEY. Because we were married this morning, and we thought before we told you of our marriage we'd get her percentage for a wedding present. [*Hands check to* PEALE. *He gives it to* MARY]

MARY. And it's bigger than we ever hoped for.

MARTIN. By George, you boys were right: I am an old fool. Anyhow, I'll win that bet from old John Clark.

MARY. And now for Bronson. [*Goes to door left lower*] Oh, Mr. Bronson?

MARTIN. You boys know Bronson?

MARY. Oh, yes, we had a long talk, with him, right in this room, about a proposition from Marshall Field —

[*Enter* BRONSON]

BRONSON [*crosses to* MARTIN, SR.] Mr. Martin — Mr. Peale.

RODNEY [*to* BRONSON]. Now you talk to father.

MARY. Yes, you talk to him, father.

PEALE. Yes, father, you talk to him.

BRONSON [*to* RODNEY]. But I thought I was dealing with you?

MARTIN. No, sir, with me — now what's your proposition?

BRONSON. A quarter of a million cash just for the trade-mark.

MARTIN. A quarter of a million? Why, you ought to be ashamed of yourself to try to trim these poor boys like that. You know that 13 Soap is worth half a million in Chicago alone, and you try to take advantage of these kids' ignorance. Why, it's outrageous, but you can't trim me! No, sir, we wouldn't take a million. Do you know that the Uneeda trade-mark is valued at six million, the Gold Dust Twins at ten million and our trade-mark is better than theirs! We're going to advertise all over the world. That's what advertising means: the power of suggestion — the psychology of print. All you have to do is to say a thing often enough and hard enough, and ninety-seven per cent. of the public'll fall. Say, what kind of garters do you wear? Boston! Why? Because all your life every time you opened a magazine you saw a picture of a man's leg with a certain kind of a garter on it — Boston!

CURTAIN

THE FAMOUS MRS. FAIR

(1919)

By James Forbes

JAMES FORBES

Mr. Forbes has not been a prolific playwright. Considering the number of years he has been in the theatre, the number of dramas are small that are credited to him. It may be that he has written many and discarded them — a rare action on the part of an American dramatist. His early life was devoted to newspaper work, in which he finally drifted to dramatic criticism. This led to his being associated with various amusement enterprises in the capacity of press-agent. He then became the general manager of the Henry B. Harris organization. In 1906 he definitely began his playwriting career. It can be seen from his experience in these early years that he stored away ample material out of which his "The Chorus Lady" and his "The Show Shop" could be drawn. He also took with him a vast knowledge of stage technique and the ways of production. The consequence is that, at the present moment, there is not a more astute stage-manager and producer than he.

"The Chorus Lady", "The Show Shop" and "The Famous Mrs. Fair" have been published in one volume. They are three stages in the development of Mr. Forbes. Just as between "The Chorus Lady" and "The Show Shop" there is a vast change from cleverness of outward eccentricity to a more breathing, living reproduction of a special atmosphere filled with living, breathing people who move naturally and not in melodramatic trapping; so between "The Show Shop" and "The Famous Mrs. Fair" there is a change from excellent surface values to something beneath the surface. "The Chorus Lady" was clever and fitted a clever actress to perfection: Miss Rose Stahl. "The Show Shop" dramatized the theatre in a racy manner not equalled by any other of Mr. Forbes's contemporaries. But "The Famous Mrs. Fair" — more solid still in characterization — was much more a comment on life than Mr. Forbes had ever done before. It showed Mr. Forbes influenced by the war, interested in the spiritual values following the war. It showed him dealing with a problem of family life. Because of this play, he was elected to the National Institute of Arts and Letters.

It was largely through his initiative that during the World War actors were sent abroad to entertain the soldiers, Mr. Forbes himself going over to put the plans into effect. Not only were actors brought to the camps, but the soldiers themselves were organized into stock companies for their theatres behind the trenches. What he saw "over there" opened his mind as to democratic education and the inability of the doughboy to fall back on anything but amusement to counteract homesickness. In the midst of his work with such men he measured their scanty resources, and there began to stir in him certain arguments which shaped themselves eventually into "The Famous Mrs. Fair." I heard him deliver an address on the subject of his quandaries abroad. He called it "To-day's Children." It would have made an excellent play.

Mr. Forbes is a member of The Dramatists, Inc., a producing firm of New York.

In connection with "The Famous Mrs. Fair", the student is advised to read also Lee Wilson Dodd's "The Changelings" and Lewis Beach's "The Goose Hangs High."

THE FAMOUS MRS. FAIR

A PLAY IN FOUR ACTS

By JAMES FORBES

THE PERSONS OF THE PLAY

JEFFREY FAIR

NANCY FAIR

ALAN FAIR

SYLVIA FAIR

PEGGY GIBBS

ANGELICA BRICE

E. DUDLEY GILLETTE

NORA

MRS. GILBERT WELLS

MRS. LESLIE CONVERSE

MRS. KELLETT BROWN

MRS. NORMAN WYNNE

MRS. STUART PERRIN

The Scenes of the First and Second Acts are laid at the home of JEFFREY FAIR *on Long Island, in the months of May and June; the occurrences of the succeeding acts take place in his apartments in a New York hotel during an evening in October.*

THE FAMOUS MRS. FAIR

Original cast, as first presented at the Henry Miller Theatre, New York, December 22, 1919

It is arranged in the order in which they first appear.

SYLVIA FAIR	Margalo Gillmore
ALAN FAIR	Jack Devereaux
NORA	Betty Hall
E. DUDLEY GILLETTE	Robert Strange
ANGELICA BRICE	Virginia Hammond
NANCY FAIR	Blanche Bates
JEFFREY FAIR	Henry Miller
MRS. NORMAN WYNNE	Dallas Tyler
MRS. KELLETT BROWN	Marian Lord
MRS. STUART PERRIN	Maude Allan
MRS. LESLIE CONVERSE	Alice Baxter
MRS. GILBERT WELLS	Florence Williams
PEGGY GIBBS	Kathleen Comegys

THE FAMOUS MRS. FAIR

ACT I

The living-room of JEFFREY FAIR'S *home on Long Island. The walls are panelled and painted in soft tones; at the left is a fireplace, at the right a door into a hall, and at the back three French windows opening onto a terrace, beyond which is a vista of wooded hills. The room is charmingly and luxuriously furnished, everything denoting wealth and refinement. A large table with a lamp, writing materials, photographs, books and bowls of flowers is at the right. Behind it is a chair and in front of it a couch. Between the windows are consoles and, on either side of them, small chairs. In the corner of the room is a lacquer cabinet. There are two large wing chairs, one in front of the fireplace, the other against the left wall below the fireplace. Bowls and vases of flowers are in every available place, giving a festive aspect to the room. Above the centre window is a floral piece fashioned of laurel and red, white and blue flowers, in the centre the words "Welcome Home Our Heroine", at the base red, white and blue ribbons fastened with a cockade and projecting from its upper corners are miniature flags of the United States, Great Britain and France.*

SYLVIA FAIR *is coming from the garden through the sunshine of a May morning. In a simple gingham dress with her hair hanging in a golden cloud about her shoulders, her arms filled with lilacs, she is a radiant picture of sweet, unspoiled girlhood, not at all the usual modern miss of eighteen. She runs up the steps and into the room, where she flits about arranging the flowers, humming the air of a gay little song. Her task completed, she stands looking at the result with* joyful satisfaction when the voice of ALAN FAIR *is heard outside in the hall.*

ALAN [*calling*]. Oh, Sylvia!
SYLVIA. Yes, Alan.

[ALAN FAIR, *a fine example of American youth, comes in hurriedly*]

ALAN. Hello, Sis.
SYLVIA. Hello, Alan!
ALAN. Mother not here yet?
SYLVIA. No. But she will be any moment. The boat docked an hour ago.
ALAN. Did you get in touch with Dad?
SYLVIA. Yes. Last night as soon as I received the wireless.
ALAN. Why didn't you meet mother?
SYLVIA. They won't let you on the pier without an alibi or something.
ALAN. Hello! Give me John 6780!
SYLVIA. What are you going to do?
ALAN. 'Phone Peggy. I motored her in this morning. Tire went bad. She was afraid I wouldn't be here in time.
SYLVIA. I wonder why mother didn't cable that she had changed from the French Line to the *Olympic?*
ALAN. Oh, hello! Is this 6780 John? I'd like to speak to Miss Gibbs. [*To* SYLVIA] Say, but you're going to be a big surprise to mother.
SYLVIA. Yes. Two years makes a lot of difference in a woman.
ALAN. You! You're only a kid.
SYLVIA. Why, I'm eighteen!
ALAN. Oh, hello! Is that you, Peggy? Yes, I got here in time. Boat's docked.
SYLVIA. Give Peggy my love.
ALAN. Sylvia says to give you her love. That goes double for me. Oh,

383

that's all right. I'm going to tell Sylvia. No, I won't say a word to any one else. I promise.

[SYLVIA, *astonished, goes to* ALAN *and suddenly reaches over, turns the transmitter towards herself and talks into it*]

SYLVIA. Oh, Peggy, I've been hoping you were going to be my sister-in-law.

ALAN [*greatly surprised*]. Why, how did you know?

SYLVIA [*taking the telephone from* ALAN]. Peggy, Alan wants to know how I knew. Isn't that funny? When did you say "yes"? Last night? [ALAN *is impatiently trying to take the telephone from* SYLVIA] I'm so glad. Yes, I'm awfully excited. I can hardly wait until mother gets here.

ALAN [*grabbing the telephone*]. Goodbye, darling! Don't get so fresh! What number do I want? You've cut me off! [ALAN *irritably moves receiver hook up and down.* SYLVIA, *laughing, takes the telephone from* ALAN *and puts it on the table.* ALAN *goes sulkily to the armchair*] How did you know I was in love with Peggy?

SYLVIA [*coming to him*]. Oh, you weren't running up to Connecticut every other minute since you've been demobilised to see your "buddy", even if he is as nice a one as Tom Gibbs. Why, the very first time I met Peggy, I knew.

ALAN. I didn't know it myself then. [*He sits*]

SYLVIA [*leaning over the back of the chair*]. Are you going to tell mother and daddy?

ALAN. Not right away.

SYLVIA. Afraid they won't like your marrying beneath you?

ALAN. Where do you get that stuff?

SYLVIA. Peggy *is* a stenographer, and you *are* the son of Jeffrey Fair.

ALAN. Yes, and Peggy's been self-supporting and, except what Uncle Sam paid me, *I've* never earned a nickel. Marrying beneath me! I'm marrying above me.

SYLVIA [*sitting on the arm of the chair*]. I hope they think so. Of course, mother's been helping for four years to save the world for Democracy. I suppose that's made her democratic, and daddy has no use for his ancestors. Still, it's going to be an awful shock to everyone here.

ALAN. I should worry about shocking the neighbors.

SYLVIA. Then why keep it a secret?

ALAN. Peggy thinks it might spoil the family reunion for mother if I — well, spring a new member on her.

SYLVIA. That's very thoughtful, very sweet of Peggy.

ALAN. Everything about her is sweet. I'm crazy about the whole family. They have the homiest kind of a home. You know, at night Mrs. Gibbs sewing and Mr. Gibbs reading his paper and a bowl of apples on the table.

SYLVIA. Of course, an apple at night would give me the pip, but it must be lovely.

ALAN. It would be great if you liked Tom.

SYLVIA. Oh, Alan, I don't believe I could marry a policeman.

ALAN. He's not a policeman. He's a detective and the best pal. Sylvia, you're not going to be a rotten snob about a man who fought for you, side by side with your own brother?

SYLVIA. You know I'm not a snob. I love Peggy and I like Tom. But I can't marry all the men who fought for me. I don't want to marry, anyway. All I want to do is get acquainted again with my mother.

[NORA, *a housemaid, enters*]

NORA. Mr. Alan, a gentleman to see you.

[ALAN *takes the card, looks at it*]

SYLVIA. Why, Nora, we can't see any one to-day.

NORA. That's what I told him. It's something to do with your mother.

SYLVIA [*going to* ALAN]. Who is he?

ALAN [*reading*]. "E. Dudley Gillette of the Gillette Lecture Bureau."

NORA. He says it's very important.

ALAN. Show him in.

SYLVIA. What can he want?

ALAN [*reading*]. "Business Representative for Tommy Perkins, the Flying Ace; Montague Travers, War Correspondent." Seems to specialize in war heroes.

SYLVIA. I'll bet he's selling tickets. [*She sits in the armchair*]

[NORA *shows in* E. DUDLEY GILLETTE, *a man of thirty-five, of good appearance and address, but not a gentleman. His manner is over-suave, his clothes too correct*]

GILLETTE. Good morning, Captain Fair.

ALAN. No, just plain *Mr.* Fair now.

GILLETTE [*bowing to* SYLVIA]. I hope you'll excuse this intrusion — [*to* ALAN] — but I have something here for Major Fair that was too important to entrust to a messenger, as I want her to receive it immediately on her arrival. [*He takes from his pocket an envelope and hands it to* ALAN]

ALAN. Won't you sit down?

GILLETTE. Thank you.

ALAN [*indicating the envelope*]. Something of a confidential nature?

GILLETTE. Well, no. It's an offer to make a lecture tour of the country under my management.

ALAN. A what? [*He opens the envelope*]

SYLVIA. Mother lecture? Oh, how ghastly!

ALAN [*reading the contract*]. This wouldn't interest her.

GILLETTE. Oh, I don't know. My London representative cabled that she would give my offer her consideration.

ALAN. That's my mother's way of being polite.

GILLETTE. Possibly. Still she did go to London to see my man.

ALAN. You know that mother was arriving on the *Olympic?*

GILLETTE. Yes, that's why I am here. I wanted to be the first on the ground. There will be a keen competition for her among the lecture bureaus.

ALAN. Why?

GILLETTE. The newspapers have been full of the work done overseas by Major Fair and her Unit; her decoration by the French Government, all that with her social position here —

SYLVIA [*indignantly*]. Why, I think it's perfectly awful of you or any one else to think that our mother is going around the country showing off her Croix de Guerre.

ALAN. Mother has no desire to boast of her work. There is not the slightest use leaving this. [*He replaces the contracts in the envelope, which he offers to* GILLETTE, *who rises*]

GILLETTE. Because her family wouldn't permit her to accept it?

ALAN [*snubbing him*]. My mother makes her own decisions.

GILLETTE [*very suavely*]. Then why can't I leave it for her?

ALAN [*coldly*]. No reason.

GILLETTE. Well, then —

[ALAN *looks at* GILLETTE, *then, turning away, places the envelope in the*

pocket of his coat. SYLVIA *is looking at* GILLETTE. GILLETTE *looks at her interestedly, in fact rather rudely "sizes her up."* SYLVIA *is puzzled and a little embarrassed, being utterly unaccustomed to that kind of scrutiny.* ALAN *turns.* GILLETTE *quickly assumes a suave smile*]

Thank you. Good morning.

ALAN. Good morning.

[GILLETTE *goes.* SYLVIA *rises and runs over to* ALAN]

SYLVIA [*distressed — almost in tears*]. Oh, Alan, mother wouldn't do it. Surely, when she's been home only once in four years she won't want to go away again.

ALAN [*soothingly*]. Certainly not. [*He puts his arms around* SYLVIA]

[ANGELICA BRICE, *a pretty blonde widow in the thirties, fragile, appealing, essentially feminine and charmingly gowned, appears at the door to the terrace*]

ANGY. Hello, Sylvia.

ALAN [*impatiently*]. Oh — [*He turns away in disgust.* SYLVIA *runs to* ANGY]

SYLVIA. Oh, Angy, darling. Come in.

ANGY. Oh, no. I simply wanted your mother to have this little welcome from her next-door neighbor.

SYLVIA. That's lovely of you. Come in and tell me if you think the place looks nice. [*She takes the violets, places them in a bowl on the table.* ANGY *comes into the room. She looks at the decorations*]

ANGY. Oh, it's charming! How do you do, Alan?

ALAN [*coldly*]. How do you do, Mrs. Brice.

ANGY. Oh, it's charming. [*She sits in the armchair*]

SYLVIA [*running over to her*]. I'm so glad mother came home in May. She loves the Spring flowers.

ANGY. I suppose your father's at the dock.

SYLVIA. I hope so. I had such a time getting him last night at Washington.

ANGY. Oh, darling, I could have told you he'd be here to-day. I'm so glad for you that your mother's coming home at last.

ALAN [*significantly*]. I'm so glad for father's sake. [*He looks meaningly at*

ANGY, *who, although thoroughly understanding the implication in his speech, is apparently oblivious.* SYLVIA *is wholly unaware of* ANGY's *and* ALAN's *fencing*]

ANGY. He must have missed her. Hasn't it been awfully sporting of him never to have complained?

SYLVIA. If it hadn't been for you, we'd have died of loneliness. I'll never forget how good you've been to me and daddy.

ALAN. Neither will I. You've tried your darndest to take mother's place. And even if you haven't succeeded, you've made a corking good stab at it.

ANGY [*to* ALAN, *very sweetly*]. So glad you appreciate it.

ALAN. Why, no one in this family appreciates you as I do.

SYLVIA [*delightedly runs to* ALAN]. I knew you'd like Angy when you understood her.

ALAN. Why, Sylvia, I've always understood Mrs. Brice. [*He is standing, his arm about* SYLVIA, *smiling at* ANGY, *who is furious with him, although she seems to be unruffled. The voices of* NANCY *and* JEFFREY *are heard in the hall*]

NANCY [*outside*]. Oh, children! Where are you?

SYLVIA. Mother!

ALAN. It's mother!

[*They rush into the hall calling excitedly, "Mother! Mother!" There is a babel of excited greeting.* ANGY *rises and retires to a position where she can watch unobserved the advent of* NANCY FAIR, *who appears presently, between* SYLVIA *and* ALAN, *her arms about their shoulders. In her Overseas uniform of horizon blue, Sam Browne belt, beret and ribbon of the Croix de Guerre, she is a vividly arresting figure, the personification of those American women brought into prominence during the war because of their executive ability, gay courage and unselfish devotion.* NANCY *is overjoyed at the meeting with her children. She hugs and kisses* SYLVIA *repeatedly.* ALAN *is trying to attract his mother's attention and finally taps her affectionately on the shoulder*]

ALAN. Mother, I could do with a little of that.

NANCY. Alan! Alan!

[*She turns to him and he takes her in his arms. She kisses him, puts him away from her, looks at him fondly, then embraces him again and again.* SYLVIA *has run across to* JEFFREY FAIR, *who has followed them and is watching, happily, the reunion of his family. He is fifty and represents the highest type of the American man of affairs.* ANGY, *coming forward, is seen by* JEFFREY. *He is slightly startled and visibly annoyed, but controlling himself he bows, smilingly, then tries to attract* NANCY's *attention*]

JEFFREY. Oh, Nancy! [NANCY *does not hear him. He raises his voice*] Oh, Nancy —! [NANCY *turns to him. He indicates* ANGY] This is Mrs. Brice.

[ALAN, *annoyed, moves away.* NANCY *turns to* MRS. BRICE, *smiling, and is about to go to her, when* SYLVIA *runs to* ANGY *and, taking her by the hand, brings her to* NANCY]

SYLVIA. Mother, this is Angy!

NANCY [*very cordially*]. Oh, you are Sylvia's Angy. The child's letters have been full of you. You've been so kind to my little girl.

ANGY [*very sweetly*]. Sylvia and her father have been very kind to me. I hadn't meant to intrude.

SYLVIA. Oh, Mother, Angy brought these. [*She picks up the bowl of violets, shows them to* NANCY, *who exclaims at the sight of them*]

NANCY. Oh, how sweet of you!

ANGY. I must go. Good-bye, Sylvia. [*She starts toward the door to the terrace*]

NANCY. You'll come again very soon, won't you?

ANGY. Oh, I'll be sure to! [*She smiles very sweetly at* NANCY, *turns, looks at* JEFFREY, *waves her hand airily*] Byebye, Jeffie! [*She goes*]

[*A slight pause.* NANCY *is surprised, amused —* JEFFREY *annoyed, confused*]

NANCY [*imitating* ANGY]. "Jeffie" — [*Very innocently*] Darling, have you been carrying on a little bit?

JEFFREY. Certainly not. [NANCY *laughs.* ALAN *is amused.* SYLVIA *oblivious.* JEFFREY, *embarrassed, pretends to search for something on the table*] Damn it all, you never can find a match in this house!

SYLVIA. Here they are. You never look.

[JEFFREY *goes to* SYLVIA, *who gives him a match.* NANCY *laughs. She looks about her*]

NANCY. Well, Alan, some swell dugout.

SYLVIA. Daddy, listen to mother talking slang.

ALAN. Get our decorations?

NANCY. Bless your hearts! They are lovely!

SYLVIA. *Our* decorations! *I* did it all.

NANCY. Sylvia, that placard's going it a bit strong. Your mother isn't a heroine.

SYLVIA [*expostulating*]. Aren't you a Major, and decorated, and everything?

NANCY [*with mock seriousness*]. 'N everything!

SYLVIA. Mother, when you were given the Croix de Guerre, did the General kiss you on both cheeks?

[JEFFREY *advances towards them*]

NANCY. Ask me some other time, darling; your father is listening.

JEFFREY. If he didn't, he was a poor fish!

[NANCY *blows him a kiss*]

SYLVIA. Poor daddy! When I think how you slaved in that old Quartermaster's Department, I don't see why they didn't decorate you.

JEFFREY. They don't pin any medals on you for trying to save the people's money.

NANCY [*looking about her*]. Is all this magnificence mine?

JEFFREY. Are you referring to me?

ALAN. No. She means me.

NANCY. I mean Sylvia. Gracious, child, what have you been taking to make you grow? Jeff, isn't she the prettiest daughter that ever was?

JEFFREY. Look at her father.

NANCY. Oh, you! Alan, you look simply scrumptious!

JEFFREY [*sitting in the armchair*]. What about me?

NANCY. You! You haven't pined away for me at all. I'm frightfully disappointed.

SYLVIA. Oh, Mother! Why?

NANCY. He should be pale and wan, and look at him! He's fat, positively fat!

JEFFREY [*indignantly*]. I am not fat!

SYLVIA. He's not!

NANCY [*laughing*]. Alan, we'll have to take him in hand. You know — [*illustrating*] — fifty times before breakfast.

ALAN [*laughs*]. Too late. [*He sits on the couch*]

SYLVIA. You two stop picking on my daddy. I think he's perfectly grand.

NANCY. He has me hypnotized just that same way, darling.

ALAN. Yes. Taken by and large, he's not a bad old scout.

JEFFREY. Here, son, my wife has been mingling with the flower of the youth of both hemispheres, so cut that *old*.

[NANCY *goes to* JEFFREY, *sits on the arm of his chair and hugs him*]

NANCY. None of them so nice as you.

JEFFREY. Sure?

NANCY. Well, pretty sure.

SYLVIA. Oh, Mother, you look so young!

NANCY. Nobody ever had a nicer daughter.

ALAN. They've got to go some to tie you, Mother — eh, Dad?

JEFFREY. I'll say it!

NANCY. Such compliments from my family! You're not getting me in a good humor so that you can spring something on me?

ALAN. How does it seem to be home, Mother?

NANCY. If Sylvia won't be shocked by my language, I'll confess I'm having a pippin of a time!

[JEFFREY *puts his arm around her*]

ALAN. You are going to find it awfully flat.

[NANCY *is smiling. Her expression changes. She looks at* ALAN *curiously.* SYLVIA *turns.* JEFFREY *leans forward in his chair. They also look in surprise at* ALAN]

NANCY. What do you mean?

JEFFREY [*indignantly*]. Yes, I'd like to know what he means.

SYLVIA. Alan! The idea! She didn't find it flat when she was here the last time.

ALAN. Mother was busy getting money for her Unit, and she was going back. Take it from me. I've been through it. You're going to miss the something — I don't know what it is — but life over there gets you. You know that, Mother. You'll find yourself thinking more about the people you left over there than your old friends here.

[NANCY *rises and moves toward* SYLVIA. *She is thinking. The others watch her closely. Seeing that* SYLVIA *is looking at her anxiously, she smiles and goes to her*]

NANCY. What are you worrying about, dear?

SYLVIA. You won't get bored at home, will you, Mother?

JEFFREY. Sylvia, don't pay any attention to this young kill-joy. [*He rises and advances on* ALAN] What the devil is the matter with you? [*He glares in indignation at* ALAN, *who rises and goes to the door to the terrace.* SYLVIA, *even with her mothers' arms around her, is still unconvinced*]

SYLVIA. But you won't get bored, will you?

NANCY. No. No. No. You silly little goose! [*She has taken* SYLVIA's *face in her hands, kissing her after each "No" and at the end of the speech, then, taking her over to the armchair, swings her onto the arm of the chair, where* SYLVIA *perches, all smiles again, her arm around* NANCY, *who is seated.* JEFFREY *is sitting on the couch, looking at them and smiling happily*]

JEFFREY. It's good to see you over there, Nancy. We missed you — eh, Sylvia?

SYLVIA. You missed us, didn't you, Mother?

ALAN. When she had the time to think about you. But you never had the time —

JEFFREY. Say, will you let your mother speak for herself?

ALAN. Just the same, I'm right, aren't I, Mother?

NANCY. Perhaps — in a way. But I had lots of time to be lonesome for all of you. [*She looks lovingly at* JEFFREY]

[NORA *comes in, bringing a tray*]

NANCY. Well, if it isn't Nora! I am glad to see you. [*She rises, greeting* NORA *warmly*]

NORA. It's glad I am to see you, Mrs. Fair, safe and sound out of them trenches.

[NANCY *moves toward the tray and begins to examine its contents.* JEFFREY *and* SYLVIA *join* ALAN. *They stand watching her, much amused*]

NANCY. What's this?

NORA. Luncheon's a couple of hours off and cook thought you might like a snack.

NANCY. Don't tell me it's honest-to-God American boiled coffee? And sugar! And butter! And real cream from a cow! I simply can't bear it!

NORA. It's starved you've been by them Paris chefs!

NANCY. You've said it, Nora. Give cook a kiss. How are all the others?

NORA. Oh, fine, and waiting in the kitchen to welcome you.

NANCY. I'll be there very soon.

NORA. Oh, Mrs. Fair, take no notice of William if he's kinda short with you. He's that annoyed; he didn't know you were coming. He was for having a triumphal arch over the front door.

NANCY. I won't.

[*They laugh.* NORA *goes.* NANCY *sits on the couch.* SYLVIA *brings a chair and sits beside her*]

SYLVIA. Now, Mother, tell us everything.

JEFFREY. Oh, let your mother drink her coffee. We've all the rest of our lives to hear about it.

ALAN. Oh, Mother, they won't understand. You can't talk about it.

SYLVIA. What?

JEFFREY [*guyingly*]. You've done nothing else since you've been home. [*Tenderly*] But you've always had one proud listener, son.

ALAN [*shyly*]. Dad!

NANCY. And here's another! Come over here this instant and kiss your proud mother.

ALAN. Oh, Mother!

NANCY. This instant minute.

JEFFREY. Captain Fair, the Major is talking to you.

[ALAN *snaps to a salute.* NANCY *jumps to her feet, returns it. They laugh.* ALAN *kisses* NANCY *and she sits on the couch with* ALAN *and* SYLVIA *beside her.* JEFFREY, *in the armchair, looks fondly at the group*]

ALAN. Say, we're going to have some great talks!

NANCY. We're going to fight this old war right from the beginning!

JEFFREY. Sylvia, it's going to be great to hear just what Foch should have done.

SYLVIA. You don't need to think you're going to sneak off by yourselves.

NANCY. You can trail right along, darling. Well, Alan, I suppose you can't wait to get back to Yale.

JEFFREY. He's not going back.

NANCY. What?

ALAN. I'm going in for mining.

NANCY. Going to be a horny-handed son of toil with a little lamp in your hat and everything. Now, I'm only teasing. Bless your heart, you do what you want to do. You would, anyway. [*To* SYLVIA] How are Biddy Wynne and all my girls?

SYLVIA. Oh, fine. They're coming over later.

JEFFREY [*annoyed*]. To-day?

SYLVIA. Yes. I 'phoned them last night. I knew mother's Unit would want to welcome her home.

NANCY. Quite right, dear. I'm crazy to see them.

JEFFREY [*grumbling*]. I think people might let us have you to ourselves the first day.

NANCY [*changing the subject*]. Now, Sylvia, tell me all the news, and I wouldn't mind a little gossip.

SYLVIA. The Wellington-Smiths have a new baby.

NANCY. So? Who's been divorced?

SYLVIA. Not a soul.

NANCY. What?

ALAN. Yes, this war has done that for the country. Fighting in France has given a lot of husbands a rest from battles at home.

JEFFREY. Old stuff, Alan. Possibly gave the wives a rest, too.

NANCY. Thank you, Jeffrey. Sylvia, no matter how many times you marry, always select a gentleman like your father. Who is this Angy Brice?

ALAN. Oh, Mother, just as we were all so happy!

SYLVIA. Why, I wrote to you about her.

NANCY. Yes, darling, I know your Mrs. Brice. [*Meaningly*] I want to know Jeff's Mrs. Brice.

JEFFREY [*irritably*]. She's not my Mrs. Brice.

NANCY. Why, Jeffrey, don't you want to tell me about your little playmate?

JEFFREY [*casually*]. Of course. She's a little widow who lives next door. Wasn't she here when you came over last time?

NANCY. No —

SYLVIA. Daddy, don't you remember we met her just after mother sailed?

JEFFREY [*indifferently*]. Oh, yes, I believe we did. I'd forgotten. She's a charming woman.

NANCY. Uhmm.

JEFFREY. Took a great shine to Sylvia.

NANCY. Oh, I think she likes you, too.

SYLVIA. She's devoted to us. We've seen her every day. We three had great times. Motor rides, picnics —

NANCY. Just a moment, Sylvia. Did I hear correctly? Your father on a *picnic?*

JEFFREY. Sylvia liked them.

NANCY. Oh, I hope Angy did, too. Alan, don't you like picnics?

SYLVIA. Alan! Oh, he hasn't been here.

NANCY. Where have you been? Now, Alan, 'fess up. Who is she?

[ALAN *is embarrassed, confused.* SYLVIA *enjoys it for a moment, then comes to his rescue*]

SYLVIA. Alan has been visiting his "buddy."

NANCY. Oh!

[ALAN *looks gratefully at* SYLVIA]

SYLVIA. So you see, Mother, I had to depend on Angy. I Red Crossed with her in town.

NANCY. Rather a fag, going to New York, wasn't it?

SYLVIA. Oh, daddy drove us in and out. Sometimes we dined on the way home, and when I was too tired I let Daddy and Angy dine together. They didn't mind.

NANCY [*quizzically*]. No?

SYLVIA. Wasn't it sweet of them?

NANCY. That was thoughtful. What made you tired, dear?

JEFFREY [*irritably*]. Oh, the heat and one thing and another. But let us drop Mrs. Brice.

NANCY. Oh, my dear, I couldn't. What would people say when she has been so kind to you? I am going to be very nice to her.

[NORA *enters*]

NORA. Oh, Mr. Alan, Mr. Gillette has just telephoned.

ALAN. Yes?

NORA. I told him you couldn't be disturbed and he asked me to remind you about the contract he left for Mrs. Fair. [*She takes the tray and goes.* ALAN *and* SYLVIA *exchange glances*]

NANCY. Contract? What contract?

ALAN. Oh, it's nothing you need bother about now, Mother.

SYLVIA. It can wait.

NANCY [rising]. Children, I am dying of curiosity.

ALAN. Honestly, it's of no importance.

JEFFREY. Your mother is the best judge of that. Give it to her.

ALAN [giving NANCY the envelope]. Oh, all right. [To JEFFREY] It's a contract for a lecture tour.

JEFFREY. A wha — a lecture tour! Oh, this is immense! [JEFFREY shrieks with laughter. NANCY, who has been reading the contract, goes toward him]

NANCY. Well, Mr. Jeffrey Fair, there is nothing funny about the money he offers me. Alan, what's a hundred times $300?

ALAN. $30,000.

NANCY. Help!

JEFFREY. Oh, it's a fake.

SYLVIA [rising]. Mother, you couldn't lecture. You don't know how.

NANCY. Oh, don't I, miss? I gave a little talk one night to the boys on the boat and they assured me that I was a "riot."

JEFFREY. What did you talk about?

NANCY. My experiences.

SYLVIA. Did you like doing it?

NANCY. It was rather fun. Of course, if I did it here it wouldn't be for money.

JEFFREY. But, Nancy, you're not going to do it here.

ALAN. That contract calls for a Coast-to-Coast tour.

NANCY. I've never been to California.

JEFFREY. Why, you haven't been home for more than twenty minutes. You're surely not contemplating going away again? [NANCY is silent] Nancy, what are you thinking about?

NANCY. I was just thinking that $30,000 would do a lot of reconstructing —

ALAN. She's back in France. What did I tell you?

JEFFREY [rising]. This home could do with a little "reconstructing."

NANCY [meaningly]. Oh, come now, Jeff! After what I've seen and heard to-day, you can't tell me that you really need anything.

SYLVIA. We need you, Mother, awfully. [She goes to NANCY]

NANCY [kissing her]. Well, my lamb, you are going to have me.

JEFFREY. The question is, for how long?

NANCY. It's a wise wife who keeps her husband guessing. Come along, Sylvia, and watch mother get the glad hand from the help.

[SYLVIA laughs as they leave the room with their arms about each other]

ALAN. I could choke Nora. I was going to hide that contract.

JEFFREY. Oh, this Gillette individual would have got to her sooner or later. [There is a slight pause] Alan, I don't want you to misunderstand about Mrs. Brice.

ALAN. I don't on your end of it. But she's after you, Dad.

JEFFREY. Maybe. But that'll be finished. As a matter of fact, I didn't mean to go it so strong. Lonely.

ALAN. Oh, Hell! I know, I know.

JEFFREY. Do you think there's been any talk?

ALAN. You can bet your life not where I could hear it.

JEFFREY. Alan, you're a great old son.

ALAN. You're some dad! [A pause] Say, Dad, do you mind if I say something to you?

JEFFREY. If you have some advice up your sleeve, shake it out.

ALAN. Kind of fresh, me advising you.

JEFFREY. You've seen things. You're not a kid any longer. You fought for me. It seems to me that gives you the right to speak your mind.

ALAN. You know, mother is the greatest —

[JEFFREY has started to say "greatest ever" also. He stops]

JEFFREY. If you are going to do this as a duet, let's get together.

ALAN and JEFFREY. Mother is the greatest ever.

JEFFREY. That's unanimous. Now, fire away!

ALAN. Mother made a whale of a hit in France.

JEFFREY. Yes, I know. If she wanted to she could call Pershing "Jack" and Haig "Doug."

ALAN. Not forgetting "Ferdie" Foch. [They laugh] Over here, they are going to be there strong with the palaver.

JEFFREY. Yes, I expect that.

ALAN. Mother's going to fall for it.

JEFFREY. Yes, I've discounted that, too.

ALAN. Have you discounted the effect on her when it's all over?

JEFFREY. I hadn't gotten as far as that.

ALAN. Take a running jump and arrive there.

JEFFREY. Humm.

ALAN. You've got to heel yourself for the day when mother takes a look around and says: "France never was like this."

JEFFREY. *Humm.*

ALAN. And when that cold gray morning arrives, don't be too busy to make life very damned interesting for mother.

JEFFREY. That's a pretty tall order for a man without any gold lace on his chest, but I'll do my damnedest.

ALAN. And if I see the symptoms coming, having been through it myself, I'll give you the high sign.

JEFFREY. Do. Have a cigarette?

ALAN. Thanks.

[*They go out to the terrace, stopping to light their cigarettes. They go down the steps into the garden.* NORA *appears, showing in* MRS. WYNNE]

NORA. I'll tell Mrs. Fair you're here.

MRS. WYNNE. Thank you, Nora.

[NORA *goes. From the hall, arm in arm, like three musketeers, come* MRS. BROWN, MRS. PERRIN *and* MRS. CONVERSE. *These women, including* MRS. WYNNE, *are members of the Unit which has served with* NANCY *in France. They are of contrasting types; all of them in their thirties; they wear uniforms similar to that of* NANCY. MRS. BROWN, MRS. PERRIN *and* MRS. CONVERSE *are gay, excited;* MRS. WYNNE *is rather tearful*]

MRS. BROWN. I'm so excited. I can hardly wait to see Nancy.

MRS. PERRIN. First real thrill I've had since I've been home.

MRS. CONVERSE. Soft pedal on that, Lila, when your hubby's around. [*She sits on the couch*]

MRS. BROWN. Look at Biddy! Biddy, you poor old fish, wake up; your buddy's home.

MRS. WYNNE [*tearfully*]. I can't seem to realize it.

MRS. CONVERSE. Cut out the sob stuff, darling.

[*She sits beside* MRS. PERRIN. *Their laughter is interrupted by the appearance of the remaining member of the Unit,* MRS. WELLS, *a woman of dominating personality, about fifty years of age; she also is in uniform, and carries a large and very elaborate bouquet*]

MRS. BROWN. Get Wellsie!

MRS. WELLS. Now, girls, after the salute — and for goodness' sake get some snap in it — you advance, Bridget, and present the bouquet to Major Fair.

MRS. WYNNE [*protesting*]. Why is this presentation stuff wished on me?

MRS. WELLS. Weren't you Nancy's buddy?

MRS. WYNNE [*sarcastically*]. I never handed her any bouquets.

MRS. BROWN. Now's your chance. [*She sits on the armchair*]

MRS. WYNNE [*scornfully*]. It seems such a damn silly thing to do.

MRS. CONVERSE. It is kind of sissy.

MRS. WELLS [*indignantly*]. I think it's a sweet idea.

MRS. WYNNE. How in blazes can I salute and hand her a bouquet at the same time? [*She salutes with her right hand, presenting the bouquet with her left. It is obviously awkward*]

MRS. PERRIN. I have an idea.

MRS. CONVERSE [*guyingly*]. No!

MRS. WELLS. Impossible!

MRS. WYNNE. Really!

MRS. PERRIN [*going to* MRS. BROWN]. Why couldn't you hold it at your side like a sword and draw it — see?

MRS. WYNNE [*disgusted*]. Oh! You poor simp!

MRS. CONVERSE. Oh, Lila, awful!

MRS. BROWN. Terrible!

MRS. PERRIN. Oh, if any of you had thought of it!

MRS. WELLS [*witheringly*]. Throw the old thing out the window. I don't care. [*She sits beside* MRS. CONVERSE *on the couch*]

MRS. WYNNE. I was the goat of this Unit for four years.

MRS. BROWN [*teasingly*]. Well, won't you be our little nanny for one more day?

MRS. CONVERSE [*innocently*]. What are you going to say, darling, when you give it to her?

MRS. WELLS [*casually*]. A few graceful words of welcome.

MRS. WYNNE [*furiously*]. I haven't got to make a speech?

MRS. PERRIN. Why, sweetie, you can't just shove it at her.

MRS. WYNNE. Here, Wellsie, take your pretty posies. I'm going home. [*She throws the bouquet on the couch where* MRS. WELLS *is seated, then starts to go.* MRS. PERRIN *stops her, bringing her over to* MRS. BROWN. *They expostulate with her*]

MRS. PERRIN. Why, Bridget! Nancy would be sick if you weren't here.

MRS. WYNNE. No, I tell you it's "finis."

MRS. WELLS. I seem to be the one at fault. I'll go. [*She starts to the door.* MRS. CONVERSE *stops her*]

MRS. CONVERSE. Oh, Wellsie, what's the matter with you? Behave! It's like old times, hearing you two scrap.

NANCY [*outside*]. Hurry up, Sylvia.

MRS. BROWN [*joyously*]. She's coming!

MRS. WELLS [*in great excitement*]. Fall in Wynne here. Then Brown. Converse next. [*She turns in irritation to* MRS. CONVERSE, *who has started to the door*] Converse! [MRS. CONVERSE *runs to* MRS. WELLS, *who grabs her and places her next to* MRS. BROWN] Perrin! [*She shoves* MRS. PERRIN *into place next to* MRS. CONVERSE, *then takes her own position at the end of the line. The women "dress" to a perfect formation*] Attention!

[NANCY *rushes in, followed by* SYLVIA]

NANCY. Oh, girls!

MRS. WELLS. Salute!

[*All the women snap to a salute, which is returned by* NANCY. MRS. WYNNE *takes two paces forward in military manner and salutes again.* NANCY *returns it*]

MRS. WYNNE. Major Fair, in the name of your Unit, I wish to extend — Oh, Buddy! Buddy! [*She breaks down and, rushing to* NANCY, *throws her arms about her. They embrace wildly*]

NANCY. Biddy! Biddy! My dear old Biddy! Oh, Billy Brown! And Mary Anne! Oh, Lila! and Wellsie, old girl! Oh, this is wonderful! [*She embraces them all in turn. They are laughing, crying, in hysterical joy over their reunion.* SYLVIA, *who has been watching them, is much affected*]

MRS. PERRIN [*tearfully*]. Hello, Sylvia.

SYLVIA [*tearfully*]. Hello.

MRS. CONVERSE [*tearfully*]. Oh, Sylvia! Isn't it wonderful, having mother home?

SYLVIA [*crying*]. Wonderful.

MRS. WYNNE [*suddenly seeing the bouquet on the couch*] Oh, damn it all, I forgot the bouquet! [*She picks up the bouquet and gives it to* NANCY, *who laughs*]

MRS. BROWN. Everybody cried all they're going to?

MRS. CONVERSE. Well, Nancy, spill us the news.

NANCY. What do you want to know?

MRS. PERRIN. How's Clementine?

NANCY. Splendid. Sent all of you her dearest love.

MRS. CONVERSE. Was there ever a cook like Clementine!

MRS. PERRIN. Never.

NANCY. You know that tin Lizzie she used to drive? "Ma chère Lizette." I gave her "Lizette" and four new tires. I marked it on my report "abandoned."

MRS. WELLS. What will she do with it?

NANCY. I suppose she'll move the pig out of the parlor. Oh, God love her, how I hated to say good-bye! I hope the people at the Gare du Nord wore rubbers. We wept buckets!

[*The women are seated, clustered about* NANCY. SYLVIA *stands beside her*]

MRS. CONVERSE. My, doesn't it bring it all back!

MRS. WELLS. Yes, if somebody would only drop a bomb I'd feel perfectly at home.

MRS. BROWN. Speaking of bombs — remember Coucy?

MRS. PERRIN. Oh, Billy, don't.

MRS. WYNNE [*to* NANCY]. Buddy, I'll always remember you driving that first ambulance down the road with those Jerrys overhead, shooting at you.

SYLVIA. Oh, Mother, how could you?

NANCY. Thank heaven, the Boche who followed me couldn't hit anything smaller than the Hippodrome.

MRS. BROWN. That's why they decorated your mother — for that and a few such trifles.

SYLVIA. Did they only give her one measly little Croix de Guerre for that? Why, they ought to have hung medals all over her!

NANCY. Oh, girls, I have a lovely letter from Poincare and a screed from Petain, thanking us for our four years' work with the French Army.

MRS. CONVERSE. Some Unit!

MRS. PERRIN. I'll say it was.

MRS. BROWN. Not so worse.

MRS. WELLS. We'll frame those letters and hang them in the club.

MRS. BROWN. Yes. In the smoking-room, where all the women will be sure to see it.

NANCY [*giving* SYLVIA *the bouquet*]. Oh, Sylvia, will you put these in my room? Then look in my despatch box. Here are the keys. Bring those kodaks. I had them finished at last. [*She gives the keys to* SYLVIA, *who runs out*]

NANCY. Now, girls, tell me and tell me true: How does it feel to be at home? [*There is silence*] Don't everybody shriek with joy at once!

MRS. WYNNE. Seems to me I've been home a million years.

MRS. PERRIN. After a couple of days with my kiddies, I sighed for the peace and quiet of an air raid.

MRS. BROWN. You're in luck to have them. I've been driven to card-indexing my hens!

MRS. CONVERSE. I wish you'd come over and card-index my Swede!

MRS. WELLS. I must confess that after I had kissed my old man and all the grandchildren, they looked sort of strange to me.

NANCY. Girls, this sounds awful! Possibly Alan was right. He said I would find it flat.

MRS. WYNNE. After being on the hop, skip and jump for four years, it's the very devil to sit around "Bla."

MRS. PERRIN. Have you any plans?

NANCY. I had thought of buying all the clothes in New York, seeing all the shows, playing around with my family . . .

MRS. CONVERSE. We've done all that. And then what?

NANCY. Why, eh —

MRS. PERRIN. Exactly. "Why, eh —"

MRS. BROWN. You see, Nancy, now we have time to burn and no matches.

NANCY. What are all the other war workers doing?

MRS. BROWN. Kicking about being demobilised.

NANCY. It's a burning shame that Washington couldn't have used all this organized talent.

MRS. WELLS. Oh, what could you expect from Congress?

SYLVIA [*entering*]. Here are the photographs! Oh, Mother, there are a lot of reporters here to see you.

NANCY. Where?

SYLVIA. On the front door-step.

NANCY [*rises quickly*]. Goodness, child! Run and ask your father for some of his best cigars.

[SYLVIA *runs into the garden, calling* "Daddy." *The women have risen excitedly at the news of the reporters' arrival. They are congregated about the table, examining the photographs, selecting those they think most suitable for publication.* NANCY *is adjusting her uniform*]

NANCY. My hair's a sight.

MRS. WELLS. You look lovely.

MRS. WYNNE. I'd give them these, Nancy; they're bully of you.

NANCY. I don't think I want any photographs. Jeff mightn't like it.

MRS. CONVERSE. If you don't, they are sure to dig up some horror.

NANCY. Well, give me some of the bunch.

MRS. BROWN. Nancy, where's your Croix de Who's Whoser?

NANCY. Would you wear it?

MRS. PERRIN. Certainly.

[NANCY *is pinning on the Croix de Guerre as* SYLVIA, JEFFREY *and* ALAN *appear from the terrace*]

JEFFREY. Hello.

ALL. Hello, Jeff.

JEFFREY. Which one of you girls wants a cigar?

NANCY. They're for the reporters.

JEFFREY. What reporters?

NANCY. From New York. Come on, girls.

JEFFREY. You're not going to see them?

ALAN [*whispering*]. Careful, Dad.

NANCY. Not if you don't wish it.

JEFFREY. Well, all right.

MRS. WELLS. Hurry up, dear, before he changes his mind.

[*The women surround* NANCY *and leave the room,* SYLVIA *in the lead. They are laughing and talking.* JEFFREY *stands watching them, bewildered*]

JEFFREY. My wife! Can you beat it?

ALAN. That's not your wife, Dad; that's Major Fair.

CURTAIN

ACT II

The scene is the same as that of the previous act. It is an afternoon in June.

MRS. BROWN, MRS. WELLS, MRS. CONVERSE, MRS. WYNNE *and* MRS. PERRIN *and* GILLETTE *are seated, all of them engrossed in the afternoon editions of the New York newspapers. The women, in contrast to the uniforms of the first act, are now wearing very charming afternoon gowns.*

MRS. WELLS. This reporter knows what he's talking about.

MRS. CONVERSE. Nancy's lecture sure made a hit last night.

MRS. BROWN. A hit! Listen to this: [*reading*] "Another Platform Star. Major Fair Wins an Ovation. Thrills Her Audience."

GILLETTE. I should say she did. I've managed a great many lecturers, but I have never seen so successful a first appearance.

MRS. WYNNE. Did you hear what Angy Brice said last night?

MRS. CONVERSE. No.

MRS. WYNNE [*imitating* ANGY's *manner*]. Nancy's account of our work overseas made her quite envious that she had never been one of the Thank-God-For-The-War-Women.

MRS. CONVERSE. Kitty, kitty, kitty.

MRS. BROWN. Meow! Meow!

MRS. PERRIN. Oh, Mr. Gillette, is Mrs. Fair going to sign that contract with you?

GILLETTE. I hope so. You all might help me to persuade her.

MRS. WELLS. When do you want her to go?

GILLETTE. In July.

MRS. BROWN. Isn't that too early?

GILLETTE. The coast is full of tourists then; besides, I want her to go out and get the money before the people forget that there has been a war.

MRS. WYNNE. But she's only been home a month.

MRS. PERRIN. A month! Isn't that punishment enough?

[*From the hall come* NANCY *and* SYLVIA, *both of them in pretty summer frocks.*

NANCY *has in her hand the contract offered her by* GILLETTE *and has evidently been considering it*]

NANCY. Hello, girls.

EVERYBODY. Hello, Nancy; hello, Sylvia.

NANCY. Mr. Gillette, there's a photographer outside who wants to see me.

GILLETTE. It's the man to take the photographs for that Syndicate story.

NANCY. Which one?

GILLETTE. "A Day in the Life of Major Fair." It's to show your domestic side.

NANCY. Oh, I don't know. Girls, don't you think it's rather intimate?

MRS. PERRIN. Not at all.

MRS. CONVERSE. Go on, Nancy; be a sport.

SYLVIA [*going to him*]. Mr. Gillette, what photographs are you going to take?

GILLETTE. Major Fair with her morning's mail.

NANCY. Can't you use that one at my desk that was published?

GILLETTE. That'll be fine. Then one in the garden.

NANCY [*satirically*]. Another on my knees to the cook.

GILLETTE [*enthusiastically*]. One in the kitchen would be great stuff.

SYLVIA. I had better go out and break it to Hulda.

NANCY. She'll say, "Ay ban goin' quit."

MRS. CONVERSE. Put her in the photograph and she'll stay for life.

NANCY. I hope so. She's the seventh in four weeks.

GILLETTE. We'll have the first picture in the garden. I'll go and arrange it. Come on, Sylvia.

NANCY. Don't put me among the lilies. They toil not, neither do they spin.

[GILLETTE *laughs and exits with* SYLVIA *to the garden.* MRS. WELLS *rises and goes to* NANCY, *who has joined* MRS. CONVERSE]

MRS. WELLS. Now, Nancy, you're not going to refuse this great opportunity Mr. Gillette's offering you? Think what we could do with the money.

NANCY. Reconstruction work in France?

MRS. WELLS. No. We could reconstruct some slums in this country.

MRS. WYNNE. Great idea, Wellsie!

MRS. CONVERSE. Splendid scheme!

MRS. PERRIN. It's what we ought to do.

MRS. BROWN. And right now.

MRS. WELLS. We could keep the Unit together.

MRS. BROWN [*rising*]. I'm for that.

MRS. PERRIN [*rising*]. I'm for anything that would give us all something real to do.

MRS. WYNNE. You've said it.

NANCY. I can't make up my mind. I don't believe Jeff would approve, and unless he did I wouldn't want to go.

MRS. WELLS. Wasn't he very proud of your success last night?

NANCY. If he was, he has concealed it most carefully.

MRS. BROWN. Hasn't he congratulated you?

NANCY. Not a congrat. "Kinda" took the joy out of it.

MRS. CONVERSE. Don't let that worry you, Nancy. A husband hates to admit that his wife can do anything.

MRS. WELLS. He's likely making himself a bore at the club right now, bragging about you.

NANCY. Do you think so? But if I went, what about Sylvia?

MRS. WYNNE. Why not take her with you?

NANCY. I don't believe she'd want to leave her father. And I don't know that I'd be happy thinking of Jeff here alone again.

MRS. PERRIN. Alan would be here.

NANCY. I hadn't thought of that. Well, I'll think it over.

MRS. WELLS. Think it over seriously.

[SYLVIA *appears at the door to the terrace*]

SYLVIA. Oh, Mother, Mr. Gillette's ready.

NANCY. All right. Come on, girls. How do I look?

MRS. BROWN. Fine.

MRS. WELLS. Nancy, I ought to go to market and get Gilbert's fruit for breakfast. It's Saturday and all the melons may be sold.

NANCY. Oh, Wellsie, you should worry. Give him prunes.

[*The women laugh.* NANCY *takes* MRS. WELLS *by the arm and leads her up to door,* MRS. WELLS *expostulating. They all go down the steps to the garden, talking.* NANCY *has given* SYLVIA *the contract.* SYLVIA *places it on the table and is about to follow*

the women when ALAN *appears from the hall. He is in golf clothes*]

ALAN. Oh, sis.

SYLVIA. What?

ALAN. Did you fix it with Peggy?

SYLVIA. Yes. She's coming to tea.

ALAN. That's great.

SYLVIA. Are you going to tell mother and daddy this afternoon?

ALAN. Sure.

SYLVIA. Before Peggy arrives?

ALAN. No.

SYLVIA. You should.

ALAN. Not at all. If I tell them I'm going to marry a stenographer they might be prejudiced. Once they see her they won't care what she is.

SYLVIA. I hope so.

ALAN. Oh, she'll bowl them right over as she did me.

SYLVIA. Where's Daddy?

JEFFREY [*entering*]. Right here.

SYLVIA. How was your game?

JEFFREY. Rotten! Why didn't you and your mother join us at luncheon?

SYLVIA. Mr. Gillette came and we couldn't.

ALAN [*sitting*]. Is that pest here?

SYLVIA [*indignantly*]. Dudley's not a pest. [*Smiling*] He's charming.

ALAN. Since when, "Dudley"?

SYLVIA. I can't go on calling a man I've seen almost every day for a month "Mr." Gillette. Can I, Daddy?

ALAN [*coming over to her*]. Don't let me catch you flirting with him.

SYLVIA. Why, Alan Fair, I don't know how.

JEFFREY. Alan, don't talk such damn nonsense.

SYLVIA. Thanks, Daddy.

[ALAN *returns to the armchair*]

JEFFREY. Where's your mother?

SYLVIA. In the garden, being photographed.

JEFFREY. *Again?*

ALAN. What's the idea this time?

SYLVIA. It's for a magazine article showing her domestic side.

JEFFREY. I hope the camera can find it. [*As he passes the table he sees the contract lying on it. He picks it up, sits, and begins to read it*]

[SYLVIA *goes over to* ALAN, *who is seated*]

SYLVIA. Oh! Have you seen the afternoon papers?

JEFFREY. We have.

SYLVIA. Aren't they wonderful?

[ALAN *is silent.* SYLVIA *goes to* JEFFREY] Aren't they wonderful? [JEFFREY *does not answer*] Oh, I think that you are both as mean as you can be about mother! I should think you'd be proud of her!

JEFFREY. We were.

SYLVIA. Why aren't you now? Everybody was crazy about her last night and neither of you so much as congratulated her.

ALAN. I couldn't get near her.

SYLVIA. You didn't try very hard. And, Daddy, you left us flat and went home with Angy Brice.

JEFFREY. Angy was feeling seedy.

SYLVIA. Humph! Maybe. Sometimes I think Angy doesn't like mother.

ALAN. Just finding that out?

JEFFREY. Nonsense, children; she admires her enormously.

SYLVIA. You might have waited and said something nice to mother this morning.

ALAN. We had a foursome on and she wasn't up.

JEFFREY. Oh, enough people will make a fuss over her.

SYLVIA. I don't see why you two hate the "fuss" everyone makes over mother. She can't help being celebrated and having people chase after her. You see just as much of her as I do. I don't mind, but you and Alan act so funny. [*Tearfully*] Nothing's the same as I thought it would be when mother came home. I don't know what's the matter.

JEFFREY [*going to* SYLVIA]. Why, Sylvia, Alan and I wouldn't do anything to worry you for the world, would we?

ALAN. Certainly not.

SYLVIA [*tearfully*]. Then why aren't you both nicer to mother?

JEFFREY [*taking her in his arms*]. Oh, come now; don't cry. Don't you know that your old daddy wouldn't hurt you? Pick out your spot and I'll lie down and let you walk on me. [SYLVIA *smiles*] That's better. [*He kisses her, then* SYLVIA *takes his hands and tries to pull him towards the door to the terrace*]

SYLVIA. Don't you want to come out and get in the muss?

JEFFREY. Who's out there?

SYLVIA. Bridget Wynne and the others.

JEFFREY [*dropping* SYLVIA'S *hands*]. No. I saw all of them yesterday.

SYLVIA. Now, Daddy, you're not going to be nasty about these photographs?

JEFFREY. Not a yap out of me. [*He laughs.* SYLVIA *kisses him, then runs down the steps, calling* "Oh, Mother!" NANCY *and the women who are at the right of the garden call to her.* JEFFREY *follows* SYLVIA *to the door, where he stands looking off into the garden, from which comes the sounds of laughter and conversation*] Gosh, I'd like to come into this place just once and not find that bunch of women here. A man would have more privacy in the Grand Central Depot.

ALAN. You said it. Whenever mother *is* at home this house looks like a club women's Old Home Week.

JEFFREY. Wouldn't you think, after four years together, they'd be tired of each other?

[ALAN *joins* JEFFREY *at the door*]

ALAN. And the line of flattery they hand out and mother lapping it up like a cat does cream!

JEFFREY. I know. Even a woman as levelheaded as your mother will soon believe she's the greatest thing in the world. [*He goes to the armchair and sits*]

ALAN. Why don't you take her away, out of it all?

JEFFREY. She's booked up a month ahead. Banquets, receptions, although I thought she had been given one by everybody from the Mayor down to the Conductorettes' Union.

ALAN. And they have almost worn out that Croix de Guerre passing it around from hand to hand.

JEFFREY. Yes, and what are you going to do about it?

ALAN. Why did you let her start?

JEFFREY. Who told me to keep her busy?

ALAN. I did — I did. I wasn't counting on the endurance of women. If I had hit a gait like mother's —

JEFFREY. She hasn't rested a day since she arrived.

ALAN. It's a wonder to me that she hasn't had a nervous breakdown.

JEFFREY. Son, the only thing that makes a woman have a nervous breakdown nowadays is having to stay at home. [*A noise of laughter and high-pitched gabble comes from the garden*] Listen to that cackle. What are they doing?

ALAN. They're leaving.

JEFFREY. All of them?

ALAN. No. Mrs. Wynne, the body-guard, is sticking around.

JEFFREY. What's Sylvia doing?

ALAN. Standing there, adoring mother as usual.

JEFFREY. She is the sweetest kid.

ALAN [*coming to* JEFFREY]. She is that. Doesn't even see that mother is neglecting her. Why can't she settle down and devote herself to Sylvia?

JEFFREY. She would if it weren't for those women and that damn Gillette! He'll have her signed, sealed and delivered.

ALAN. Why don't you tie a can to him?

JEFFREY. How? By forbidding him to come here? My boy, I haven't lived with your mother all these years without realizing that, if you want her to do something, tell her she can't.

ALAN. I'm "kinda" that way.

JEFFREY. Yes. It works with you, too. [*They laugh.* JEFFREY, *rising, sees* ANGY, *who has come from the left side of the garden, and is now at the top of the steps*] Hello, Angy!

ANGY. May I come in?

JEFFREY. Certainly.

ANGY. Sure I'm not intruding?

ALAN [*sarcastically*]. Oh, not at all. Won't you sit down?

ANGY. Oh, I simply wanted to see Jeff a minute —

ALAN. Might as well be comfortable while you're looking at him.

[*With elaborate politeness, he indicates the armchair.* ANGY *looks at him sharply.* ALAN *smiles sweetly.* ANGY *controls her annoyance, smiles at him and sits.* JEFFREY, *oblivious, sits on the couch on the opposite side of the room.* ALAN *wanders over back of* ANGY'S *chair, and takes up his position in the center of the room between* ANGY *and* JEFFREY]

JEFFREY. All right again?

ANGY. Oh, yes. It was very close in the clubroom last night. Then I got quite worked up over Mrs. Fair's lecture. It was so harrowing.

ALAN [*very pleasantly*]. Quite a success, though.

ANGY [*smiling sweetly at him*]. Yes, being a woman in uniform helped a lot, don't you think? I'm sure she'll be a great success on tour. She's so well advertised. You can't pick up a magazine without seeing your mother's picture under "In the Public Eye."

JEFFREY [*annoyed*]. She's not on tour yet.

ANGY [*innocently*]. She's going, isn't she?

ALAN. It isn't decided.

ANGY [*affecting great surprise*]. Why, Mr. Gillette told me the other day that it was practically settled. He was afraid that the family might interfere. I laughed at the idea. Why should you object to Mrs. Fair going away for a few months when she had left you all alone so long?

ALAN. That was kind of you to reassure him.

ANGY. Of course you could go too, Jeff.

JEFFREY. I?

ANGY [*sympathetically*]. I suppose it would get tiresome, being merely the husband of Major Fair.

JEFFREY. Yes, one can get fed up on it.

ANGY. I'd be perfectly willing to take charge of Sylvia again.

ALAN. Mother hasn't gone yet.

ANGY [*protesting*]. If she wants to, I think she should. It isn't as though Mrs. Fair were a home body like me, just content to make a man comfortable and happy. You can't expect any one so brilliant as your mother not to get bored with her home and her family. Not that I'm insinuating that she is.

ALAN. Oh, no.

JEFFREY [*tired of the discussion*]. What did you want to see me about, Angy?

ANGY. This letter, but there's no hurry. [*There is a pause;* ANGY *looks at* ALAN *and turns away, annoyed.* ALAN *smiles. Finally* ANGY, *determined to be rid of him, turns and smiles sweetly*] Oh, Alan, been to see your "buddy" lately?

ALAN [*confused*]. Why, yes.

ANGY. He must be awfully attractive to have you so devoted to him. [*Meaningly*] Sylvia says he has a very charming sister.

ALAN [*more confused*]. Yes — yes, he has.

JEFFREY [*rising*]. What's this I hear?

ALAN [*very much embarrassed*]. I think I'll go change. [*He hurriedly leaves the room.* JEFFREY *watches, amused.* ANGY *smiles to herself, pleased at having rid herself of* ALAN. JEFFREY *goes to* ANGY]

JEFFREY. Well, Angy, let me see the letter.

ANGY. The letter was only an excuse. I saw those stupid women in the garden and I knew how it bored you to have them around, so I came over to give you an excuse to get away.

JEFFREY. Good for you, Angy, but I'll stay here. They have to go home some time, if it's only to sleep. [*He goes to a chair below the fireplace, where he sits facing* ANGY, *who looks annoyed at the failure of her ruse; as* JEFFREY *turns to her she smiles sweetly*]

ANGY [*sighing*]. I'd like to be celebrated and have women like me.

JEFFREY. They do.

ANGY. They don't. All their nasty husbands do.

JEFFREY. Why aren't you as nice to the wives?

ANGY. I don't get a chance. The husbands always grab me and rush me off to a corner. The next man I marry has to build me a house that's perfectly round. I'm sick of corners. [JEFFREY *laughs*] And I'm sick of other women's husbands, too.

JEFFREY. Including me?

ANGY. I haven't had enough of your society since your wife came home to get tired of you, and as I'm not going to have any of it to-day, I may as well go home. [*She rises and starts toward the terrace.* JEFFREY *follows her*]

JEFFREY. Oh, wait, Angy, I — [*He stops, arrested by the appearance of* NANCY *and* MRS. WYNNE *entering from the terrace.* NANCY *is surprised at the sight of* ANGY, *then comes toward her.* NANCY'S *manner is polite but not cordial*]

NANCY. How do you do, Mrs. Brice? Oh, Jeff! I was so sorry we couldn't come to the club.

JEFFREY [*coldly*]. That's all right. Sylvia explained.

ANGY. Oh, Mrs. Fair, I don't know what you must have thought of me running away with Jeff last night.

NANCY. Didn't even know you did!

ANGY. I wanted to stay and tell you how splendid you were, but I was rather upset.

MRS. WYNNE [*smiling*]. Yes. Don't you hate to hang around where another woman is making the hit?

NANCY. That doesn't often happen where Mrs. Brice is. Does it, Jeff?

ANGY. Oh, really.

NANCY. You will have to excuse me.

I have to put on my hat and powder my nose. Come along, Biddy.

JEFFREY. Are you going out again, Nancy?

NANCY. Yes, dear, going over to the Club.

ANGY. Oh, then may I borrow your nice husband to help me with some stupid business things?

NANCY. If you'll be sure to return him.

ANGY. I always have, haven't I? See you later, Jeff.

JEFFREY. If I can manage it.

ANGY. Good-bye, Mrs. Wynne; give my love to dear old Wynne. Good-bye, Mrs. Fair. Hope the photographs are a success. I wish somebody wanted to take mine. It must be lovely to be notorious. [*She smiles very sweetly, then goes down the steps through the garden to the left*]

NANCY. Sweet woman!

MRS. WYNNE. She's some fast worker with the harpon. Bye-bye, Jeff. [*She goes.* NANCY *is following her, but at the door to the hall she stops, looks at* JEFFREY, *who is standing at the fireplace, then advances toward him*]

NANCY. Jeff, dear, why don't you come with us?

JEFFREY. What are you going to do?

NANCY. Mr. Gillette wants a photograph of me with my girls on the steps of the clubhouse.

JEFFREY. Absurd idea!

NANCY. Why, what's absurd about it? You and Alan were photographed in the Father and Son Tournament.

JEFFREY. That's different. I'm guyed enough by the crowd as it is. I can't pick up a magazine at the club without someone asking me if I'm looking for the Major's picture. [*He comes to her angrily*] I can't come into this house without falling over a camera, or finding some interviewer smoking my best cigars.

NANCY [*taken aback*]. I'm sorry. I don't know quite how I would explain to Mr. Gillette and the girls that you object —

JEFFREY. Don't let me embarrass you. If you want to go on making yourself and your family ridiculous, don't let me stop you. [*He starts toward the door to the terrace.* NANCY *is indignant, then controls herself*]

NANCY [*expostulating*]. Jeff!

JEFFREY [*turning*]. Yes?

NANCY. I didn't think —

JEFFREY. No. You never think about anybody but yourself.

[NANCY *stands, annoyed, hurt, speechless.* GILLETTE *enters hurriedly from the terrace*]

GILLETTE. Oh, Mrs. Fair — [*Sees* JEFFREY] I beg your pardon.

JEFFREY. Oh, that's all right. [*He goes, meeting* SYLVIA *at the foot of the steps to the garden. They talk.* GILLETTE *watches* NANCY *narrowly. There is a slight pause, then* NANCY *turns to go*]

GILLETTE. Mrs. Fair, are you going to sign that contract to-day?

NANCY. I haven't decided. I'll let you know before the day is out. I'll be right down. [*She goes,* GILLETTE *looking after her, annoyed.* JEFFREY *leaves* SYLVIA *and goes through the garden in the direction taken by* ANGY. SYLVIA *runs up steps and comes into the room.* GILLETTE *turns to her*]

GILLETTE. Aren't you coming with us?

SYLVIA. No. Miss Gibbs is coming to tea.

GILLETTE. Who's she?

SYLVIA. Alan's buddy's sister.

GILLETTE. [*thoughtfully*]. Gibbs? What's her brother's name?

SYLVIA. Tom Gibbs.

GILLETTE [*quickly*]. Tom Gibbs? What does he do?

SYLVIA. Arrests people.

GILLETTE [*startled*]. What?

SYLVIA. He's a detective. Same thing as a policeman, only he doesn't wear a uniform or stand on the corner.

GILLETTE. I know what a detective is! Are these Gibbs friends of yours?

SYLVIA. Oh, yes.

GILLETTE. That's queer. They don't belong in your set.

SYLVIA. Oh, Dudley, you mustn't be a snob. It isn't being done since the war.

GILLETTE. What does Miss Gibbs do now?

SYLVIA. She is a stenographer. Why are you so interested in her?

GILLETTE. Interested in her! With you here! [*He goes over to* SYLVIA, *who is seated in the armchair. His manner becomes subtly, almost impudently, familiar. He flatters* SYLVIA *in order to extract information from her*]

SYLVIA. You're not interested in me.

GILLETTE. I wouldn't dare tell you how much.

SYLVIA. Why not?

GILLETTE. Your mother wouldn't like it.

SYLVIA. She's not here.

GILLETTE. But she will be. Think your mother will sign that contract?

SYLVIA. I don't know. [*Girlishly, but not flirtatiously*] Why don't you tell me why you're interested in me?

GILLETTE [*leaning over the arm of chair*]. Don't tempt me, you little siren.

SYLVIA. I'm not.

GILLETTE. You're a regular little baby vamp.

SYLVIA. You mustn't. You're dreadfully bold.

GILLETTE. You like it, don't you?

SYLVIA. Uh huh. [*Giggling*] It's funny, but you shouldn't —

GILLETTE [*leaning over so that his face is very close to* SYLVIA'S]. You shouldn't be so fascinating. [SYLVIA *is a little embarrassed, but is enjoying it.* GILLETTE, *feeling that he has impressed her sufficiently, turns away and in business-like tone and manner begins to question her*] Has your mother said anything about signing the contract?

SYLVIA [*disappointed*]. I don't know. [*She rises slowly and goes to the mantel, her back toward* GILLETTE, *who is not looking at her*]

GILLETTE. Do you think your father will object?

SYLVIA [*impatiently*]. I don't know.

GILLETTE. Do you think that Alan will put his oar in to prevent your mother —

SYLVIA [*angrily*]. Oh, I don't know! [*She stamps her foot and starts to go.* GILLETTE *realizes his mistake*]

GILLETTE. Why, Sylvia, what's the matter?

SYLVIA [*flaring out*]. Oh, it's always mother, mother, mother. I'm sure Alan needn't worry about my flirt — [*She stops abruptly and turns away, confused.* GILLETTE *smiles*]

GILLETTE. About your what?

SYLVIA. Oh, nothing.

GILLETTE. Flirting with me?

SYLVIA. I didn't say it.

GILLETTE. You were going to.

SYLVIA. I won't tell you. [*Very much embarrassed, she runs away to the other side of the room.* GILLETTE *looks at her as though what she had said had given him an idea*]

GILLETTE [*slowly*]. It had never occurred to me. [SYLVIA *turns quickly*] I mean, that you would.

SYLVIA. Well, I wouldn't, Mr. Dudley Gillette, so there! [*She goes toward the door to the hall.* GILLETTE *is much amused.* NORA *shows in* PEGGY GIBBS]

SYLVIA. Oh, Peggy, dear! Nora, tell Mr. Alan that Miss Gibbs is here.

[NORA *exits.* GILLETTE *has turned and starts slightly at the sight of* PEGGY, *who is a girl of twenty-five, sincere, clear-thinking, practical, yet not lacking in feminine charm and humor. She wears a severely plain yet modish frock*]

Peggy, may I present Mr. Gillette?

GILLETTE [*bowing*]. Miss Gibbs.

PEGGY [*puzzled*]. I think we've met before.

GILLETTE [*on his guard*]. Really?

SYLVIA. Where?

PEGGY. At the War Relief Bazaar in 1914. I was a volunteer there.

SYLVIA. The one there was all the scandal about?

GILLETTE [*casually*]. I do remember something about it. But I wasn't in New York then.

PEGGY. Then I'm mistaken.

GILLETTE [*impressively*]. Yes. I'm sure if I ever had the pleasure of meeting you it would have been utterly impossible for me to forget you.

[PEGGY, *annoyed at the flattery, turns away.* SYLVIA *is pleased and smiles at* GILLETTE. NANCY *enters, wearing a hat, carrying gloves and a parasol. She is followed by* MRS. WYNNE]

NANCY. I'm ready, Mr. Gillette.

SYLVIA. Oh, Mother —

[NANCY *turns.* SYLVIA *and* PEGGY *advance to her*]

NANCY [*shaking hands*]. Oh, is this Miss Gibbs? Sylvia told me you were coming to tea. I'm so glad to meet you. I've heard of you from Sylvia and of course Alan's told me all about your wonderful brother.

PEGGY. This is a great pleasure for me. I've heard so much of you and I've been so thrilled by all the great things you've done.

NANCY. Oh, Sylvia, isn't that sweet! Oh, Biddy, isn't that charming! [*To* PEGGY] This is Mrs. Wynne, one of my Unit. I wonder if you are going to be very generous and forgive me if I run away for a few minutes? Something unexpected and important. I'll

hurry back as fast as I can, for I wan' to have a real visit with you.

PEGGY. Of course. Don't let m' interfere.

NANCY. That's very understanding o you. I won't be ten minutes. Sylvi' will take excellent care of you. [*Sh goes, followed by* MRS. WYNNE *an* GILLETTE. *They disappear through th garden,* PEGGY *watching them from th door as they go*]

SYLVIA. Well?

PEGGY. Oh, Sylvia, she's charming

SYLVIA. Have I said too much abou' her?

PEGGY. Not half enough.

[ALAN, *in immaculate flannels, come rushing in from the door to the hall*

ALAN. Peggy! [PEGGY *turns.* ALAN *goes to her quickly and puts his arm around her*] Don't look, Sylvia.

PEGGY [*expostulating*]. Oh, Alan!

[ALAN *kisses her*]

ALAN. Now, where's mother?

SYLVIA. She's gone to be photographed at the Club.

ALAN. What! That's the limit! Didn't she know Peggy was coming?

PEGGY. I've just met her and she's made her excuses and is coming right back.

ALAN. Oh!

PEGGY. You'd better "Oh." Sylvia, has he always spoken before he thinks?

SYLVIA. Always.

ALAN. Where's Dad?

SYLVIA. I'll get him. He is at Mrs. Brice's. [*She goes*]

PEGGY. Oh, Alan, I'm going to love your mother. I hope she likes me.

ALAN. You should worry.

PEGGY. That's just what I'm doing — worrying.

ALAN. Well, if anybody in my family doesn't like you, you know what they can do, don't you?

PEGGY. Yes. Make it distinctly uncomfortable for you.

ALAN. Well, anyway, I'm going to announce our engagement to-day.

PEGGY. Why, if Sylvia had told me that I wouldn't have come. She said that you simply wanted to introduce me to your father and mother.

ALAN. I didn't tell her in what capacity.

PEGGY. Please, Alan, let your

nother get to know me first. If you
hrust me at her it may prejudice her.

ALAN. Nonsense. What's more, I'm
going to tell them that we are to be mar-
ied right away.

PEGGY. We are not. I'm not going
o be rushed into marriage.

ALAN. Rushed? Why, I've known
you *eight* weeks.

PEGGY. Yes, you had me engaged
;o you before I knew what was happen-
ng to me.

ALAN. Only way to handle you. If
you get too much time to think —

PEGGY. I'm going to have a good
.ong think before I get married.

ALAN. It's cold, then. Good-bye,
darling. [*He moves away.* PEGGY *follows him*]

PEGGY. Oh, be sensible. How can
we be married?

ALAN. Why, you have a license and
a ring and a minister —

PEGGY. Yes, and money that you've
earned, not that you get from your
father.

ALAN. Don't need his money. I've
got a job.

PEGGY. What? What sort of a
job?

ALAN. That's my secret.

PEGGY. Oh, is it so bad that you're
ashamed of it?

ALAN. Bad enough to pay me thirty
dollars a week!

PEGGY. I knew that you had hypnotic charm for women. What did you
do to the man? Frighten him?

ALAN. No. He used to be my top
sergeant.

PEGGY. Oh, that explains it.

ALAN. I thought you'd be pleased.

PEGGY. Did he get himself a little
job? Oh, darling, I'm only funning.
I'm very proud of you.

ALAN. Then you'll marry me?

PEGGY. Can't we wait until —

ALAN. Look here. I postponed our
marriage to wait for a family reunion
that didn't "reune." Then I had to
wait until I got a job. Well, I have
one. Now it's up to you. If you don't
want to marry me, say so.

PEGGY. I do, Alan. You know I do.
But I want your father and mother to
approve. There is a chance they
mightn't like me.

ALAN. You're not marrying them.
Who are you marrying, darling?

PEGGY [*mischievously*]. None of your
business.

ALAN. Just for that, you sassy little
devil — [*He tries to take* PEGGY *in his
arms. She dodges and runs away.*
ALAN *catches her and swings her around
into his arms. They are laughing and
struggling, their backs to the door to the
terrace at which* JEFFREY *appears. He
stands amazed at what seems to be* ALAN's
*efforts to kiss a girl against her will. He
frowns in annoyance and starts toward
them*]

JEFFREY [*sharply*]. Alan!

ALAN [*over his shoulder*]. It's all
right, Dad. We're engaged. [PEGGY,
who has ceased to struggle at the sound of
JEFFREY's *voice, is kissed by* ALAN, *then
released. She is much embarrassed.*
ALAN *crosses to* JEFFREY, *leading* PEGGY
by the hand] Dad, this is Peggy.

JEFFREY. Peggy?

ALAN. Peggy Gibbs.

JEFFREY [*coldly*]. How do you do,
Miss Gibbs?

PEGGY. Mr. Fair.

ALAN. Well, Dad, I suppose you're
surprised.

JEFFREY [*sarcastically*]. Has the engagement just occurred?

ALAN. Oh, no; it's a month old.

JEFFREY. Really, Alan, I —

ALAN. Dad, don't be hurt because
we didn't tell you.

PEGGY. Alan didn't want to spoil
his mother's home-coming by the
announcement.

ALAN. It wasn't my idea at all: it
was Peggy's.

JEFFREY. Why should this engagement distress your mother?

ALAN. You see, Dad, Peggy is my
"buddy's" sister.

JEFFREY. Yes?

PEGGY. Oh, Alan let us be frank.
[*To* JEFFREY] It annoys him when I
say it, but I'm not of your class. I'm
a stenographer.

ALAN [*proudly*]. She's a private
secretary.

JEFFREY. What is the difference?

PEGGY. Twenty dollars a week.

JEFFREY. Thank you; I deserved
that.

ALAN. Well, Dad, are you for me or
"agin" me?

JEFFREY. That depends.

ALAN. On what?

PEGGY [*hastily*]. On me. You can't
expect your father to give a snap judgment on a person he has just met. Suppose you leave us together so that we
can have a little talk. [*She moves away*]

JEFFREY. A very good idea.

[ALAN *goes to* PEGGY]

ALAN [*whispering*]. Don't be nervous, dear. Dad's aces. [*He kisses* PEGGY, *then goes to* JEFFREY] Now, Dad, no heavy father stuff. [*He leaves them*]

JEFFREY. Won't you be seated?

PEGGY. Thank you. [*She sits on the couch.* JEFFREY *brings a chair and sits facing her*]

JEFFREY. Well, Miss Gibbs?

PEGGY. To begin with, Mr. Fair, my family and I are, socially speaking, a total loss.

JEFFREY. In what way?

PEGGY. My father is the village postman. My brother is now in the Detective Bureau, but was a policeman.

JEFFREY. I see.

PEGGY [*dryly*]. Yes, I thought you would. My mother does her own work, but the weekly washing is sent out.

JEFFREY. Very interesting, especially that bit about the laundry.

PEGGY. I graduated from High School, then went to Brown's Business College. I am now employed at forty dollars a week as a private secretary in the office of a firm of lawyers, O'Brien and Rosenweber.

JEFFREY. I know of them.

PEGGY. I am twenty-three years old, quite healthy, am supposed to have a good disposition. Oh, there is one thing more : I'm a suffragette, and while I am not militant, I do parade. I believe that is all.

JEFFREY. And you have Thursdays off? My dear Miss Gibbs, I'm not interviewing you as a prospective servant, but as a possible daughter-in-law.

PEGGY. Well, you wanted to know about me, didn't you?

JEFFREY. You suggested the interview. I appreciate that it's a very difficult one for you. It isn't exactly easy for me. Yet, if I didn't learn something of the girl my son wishes to marry, I would be failing in my duty as a father, wouldn't I?

PEGGY. Yes.

JEFFREY. Why are you so on the defensive?

PEGGY. Possibly because I'm a little afraid.

JEFFREY. Surely not of me? Unless you're marrying Alan for —

PEGGY. For money and this sort of thing? No! Not that I wouldn't like

it and enjoy it, but only if Alan earned it. And he will in time. He's made a start. He has a job.

JEFFREY. Why didn't he come to me for a position?

PEGGY. Oh, Mr. Fair, please don't help him. That would spoil all my plans.

JEFFREY [*surprised*]. How?

PEGGY. It's better for him to be entirely on his own.

JEFFREY [*puzzled*]. Why?

PEGGY. The dear boy is full of the brotherhood of man. He got that from the trenches, and if he is going to keep it, it's necessary for him to live simply for a time at least.

JEFFREY. Sounds to me like a very serious courtship.

PEGGY. Is anything more serious than marriage? I'm scared to death of it.

JEFFREY [*amused*]. Why?

PEGGY. I have to give up a great deal of my liberty and I want to be sure it's worth it. Oh, dear, life and what to do with it and Alan's problem and mine seems so much simpler on our back veranda. I suppose my family are right.

JEFFREY [*surprised*]. Doesn't your family approve of the marriage?

PEGGY. Not at all.

JEFFREY [*indignantly*]. Well, I — Don't they like my son? [*He rises*]

PEGGY [*smiling*]. I like you for that.

JEFFREY [*sputtering*]. Well, I —

PEGGY. Oh, they are devoted to Alan, but they can't see any happiness in the marriage for me. They're afraid that the two families won't harmonize.

JEFFREY. That's true; they mightn't. [*There is a slight pause*] It seems to me you love my son.

PEGGY. Very much.

JEFFREY. Then if I were Alan and you were you, I'd marry you and say damn the families.

PEGGY. Oh, Mr. Fair! [*She rises impulsively, starts as though to embrace him, catches herself and recedes a little.* JEFFREY *follows her, inviting her to embrace him. They laugh*]

JEFFREY. Now we will put Alan out of his misery. [*Calls*] Alan! Come here, young man.

[ALAN, *who has been in the hall awaiting the verdict, comes in quickly. He looks anxiously at* JEFFREY]

ALAN. Well?

JEFFREY. Son, I hope you appreciate how lucky you are.

ALAN [*joyfully*]. Dad! [*He goes quickly to* PEGGY] Excuse us. [*He kisses her*]

JEFFREY. I could do with one myself. [PEGGY *crosses to* JEFFREY *and offers her lips to him shyly. He kisses her tenderly*] Now, young man, what is this job?

ALAN. It's with the Iverson Construction Company. Time-keeper.

JEFFREY. Well, you held the interscholastic record of America for wasting time. It's up to you to keep a little.

ALAN. Dad, that's pretty awful.

JEFFREY. Peggy smiled.

ALAN. Brazen truckling to her father-in-law.

SYLVIA [*running in*]. Is it all right?

JEFFREY. If you mean Peggy, she's very much all right.

SYLVIA [*delightedly*]. Oh, wait until you know her. Now I wish mother would come.

JEFFREY. So she went to the club after all.

SYLVIA. Yes. She won't be long. [*She goes up to the door to the terrace and looks off toward the entrance to the garden*]

JEFFREY [*annoyed*]. Did she know that Peggy was coming here this afternoon?

PEGGY [*hastily*]. Oh, yes, I met Mrs. Fair and she explained.

JEFFREY. Left you here. That's most annoying.

SYLVIA. Here is mother now.

[NANCY *hurries in*]

NANCY. You see, Miss Gibbs, I haven't been long. Oh, you haven't had tea. Sylvia, dear, take mother's things and tell them to bring tea right in. [SYLVIA, *taking* NANCY'S *hat and gloves, runs out.* NANCY *goes to the telephone on the table*] I must 'phone to the Colony Club right away.

JEFFREY [*irritably*]. Can't that wait?

NANCY. It's very important.

JEFFREY [*severely*]. More important than to pay some attention to the girl your son is going to marry?

[NANCY *looks at* JEFFREY, *dazed, then slowly turns her regard upon* PEGGY, *then on* ALAN]

NANCY. Alan, how long have you been engaged?

ALAN. Since the day before you came home.

NANCY. A month ago. Why didn't you tell me?

PEGGY. I'm to blame, Mrs. Fair. I didn't want Alan to tell you because I feared it might distress you and spoil your home-coming.

NANCY. Why should it do either?

ALAN. Peggy's afraid that because she's a stenographer — you —

NANCY. What right had Miss Gibbs to judge how I would receive the news of my son's engagement?

PEGGY. I can see now that what I did might be misjudged, but really my motives —

ALAN. It isn't necessary to explain your motives.

JEFFREY. I can vouch for Peggy.

ALAN. Thank you, Dad, but no one needs to vouch for her. The fact that I am going to marry her, that Sylvia loves her, and that you approve, should be enough for mother.

[NANCY *flinches, but is so shocked by the news that she says nothing, simply looks at* ALAN. *Her eyes fill with tears, her lips quiver, and to conceal her emotion she turns away and goes to the door to the terrace*]

PEGGY. Mrs. Fair, I know what you are thinking — feeling. [NANCY *is silent.* PEGGY, *distressed, turns to* JEFFREY] It is much better that I should go.

JEFFREY. Perhaps it would be as well. Alan, take Peggy to the station. [ALAN *and* PEGGY *go.* NANCY *turns, stretches out her hand as if to stop them. Then, covering her face with her hands, she stands crying silently.* JEFFREY, *ashamed of his outburst, manlike takes refuge in irritation. He goes to the table, picks up a paper and sits, making a pretence of reading. He waits, expecting* NANCY *to speak, then breaks the silence*] You've made a nice mess of things.

NANCY [*surprised*]. I?

JEFFREY. Yes. If you hadn't been so keen on publicity, all this needn't have happened.

NANCY [*coming toward him*]. Do you suppose if I had been told why Miss Gibbs was coming here that I would have allowed a stupid photograph to interfere? Isn't Alan's engagement something that could have been told me without shocking me, bewildering me so that — Oh, you've made me seem ungracious to my boy. It was wicked, cruel of you. [*She turns away and sits on the couch, crying*]

JEFFREY. How did I know you were going to take it like this?

NANCY. What did you expect me to do?

JEFFREY. Open your arms to her as any mother should.

NANCY. How long have you known of this engagement?

JEFFREY. Not until to-day.

NANCY. And did you welcome her with outstretched arms at once?

JEFFREY. Frankly, I was surprised! But after I had had a talk with her —

NANCY. Exactly. You had an opportunity to judge of her before you gave your approval, but I am expected to give at once the son I've loved, watched over, prayed for, to a girl of whom I know nothing.

JEFFREY. I told you I vouched for her.

[NANCY, *in a rage, springs to her feet*]

NANCY. What's that to me? He's my son, too.

JEFFREY. That's jealousy talking.

NANCY. Is it strange that I should be jealous? Isn't it hard for any mother at first to give her son to another woman? If Alan had had any right feeling for me he would have told me tenderly, tactfully, that he loved someone else more than me. Instead, he let you thrust the fact at me. I don't know what I have ever done that he should have told you, even Sylvia, before me; made me feel like an outsider.

JEFFREY. Who is to blame for that? You put yourself outside your home. You can't hope to receive Alan's confidence if you are never here to get it. You can't go on neglecting your family —

NANCY [*indignantly*]. What? I give up everybody and everything belonging to me and endure privations, horrors, because I think it's my greatest duty, and then I am neglecting my family! [*Bitterly*] My family seems to have gotten along very well without me. Ever since I came home you and Alan have resented everything I've done.

JEFFREY. We don't approve of what you've been doing. [*He rises and begins to pace up and down*]

NANCY [*scornfully*]. Approve! Must

I secure the approval of my husband and my son for what I think best to do?

JEFFREY. Your desire to appear in public, for instance?

NANCY [*very calmly*]. If you had been overseas and had been urged to appear in public, would you have had to ask my approval? No. It would have been the perfectly natural thing for you to do.

JEFFREY. It's not the same thing.

NANCY. Because I'm a woman. Well, this war has settled one thing definitely. A woman's work counts for just as much as a man's and she is entitled to all the rewards it brings her. [*Her calmness maddens* JEFFREY. *He advances on her furiously*]

JEFFREY. You've done your duty by your country, but, by God, you're capitalizing it.

NANCY [*turning upon him*]. Jeffrey!

JEFFREY. Ever since you've been home you've thought of everything but your duty to your family. All you think of is your appearance at public functions, getting your name and photograph in print. Can you deny that you are eager to sign that contract so that you can make a triumphant tour of the country, telling the Great American public how you helped win the war? Well, you'll put an end to all this publicity. You'll stop all these ridiculous lectures. You'll tear up that contract. You'll give up this tour and remain where you belong.

NANCY [*very quietly*]. And why must I do all this? Why must I remain here where I belong?

JEFFREY [*emphatically*]. Because I am your husband and I forbid you to go.

[*They look at each other for an instant in silence.* JEFFREY, *feeling that he is master of the situation, walks slowly away and stands at the fireplace, his back toward* NANCY, *who smiles satirically, then goes quietly to the table. She sits, draws the contract, which is on the table, to her, and signs it. At the sound of the scratching of her pen* JEFFREY *turns quickly. He crumples the folded newspaper in his hand and throws it irritably on the chair.* NANCY *rises. They are standing facing each other in defiance as the*

CURTAIN FALLS

ACT III

The sitting-room of JEFFREY FAIR'S *apartment in a New York hotel. The decorations, furnishings and appointments are tasteful, luxurious and characteristic of a modern "smart" hotel. On the left are double doors to the private hall and a door to a bedroom; at the back is a large window and at the right a fireplace and a door to another bedroom. A console table with a mirror over it stands against the right wall below the fireplace, in front of which is a Lawson sofa. On the opposite side of the room is a writing desk, near the window a small table with a telephone, and in the center an oval table to the left of which is an armchair. There is a small chair in front of the desk, another at the window and a third at the back of the center table.*

There are no photographs, books nor flowers; in fact, there is a noticeable lack of any attempt to create a homelike atmosphere, and, although the room is brilliantly lighted, the curtains drawn and a fire in the grate, the effect is one of dreariness in contrast to the charm of the environment in the preceding acts. It is an evening in October.

As the curtain rises JEFFREY *enters from the door at the right of the room. He wears informal evening dress and carries an overcoat and a hat which he places on the sofa. Then going to the doors to the hall, he opens them, showing across the hall a door, on which he knocks. There is a slight pause and he knocks again, calling, "Sylvia." There is no response. He opens the door, looks into the room, then closing the door returns and goes to the telephone.*

JEFFREY. Give me the desk, please. [*A pause*] Is this the desk? This is Mr. Fair speaking. Are you quite sure my daughter did not leave a note for Mrs. Fair? If you find one, send it up. By the way, what is the correct time? Nine twenty-three. Thank you.

[JEFFREY *sets his watch, then takes a cigarette, lights it and sits on the couch. His attitude is one of deep dejection. There is a slight pause,* then ALAN *enters from the room at the right*]

JEFFREY [*turning to him*]. Well, son?
ALAN [*happily*]. It's all right.
JEFFREY. Made it up with your mother? [ALAN *nods*] That's fine. Did she mention Mrs. Fair, Jr.?
ALAN. Yes. She inquired very cordially for Peggy. [*He sits*]
JEFFREY. Did she accept Peggy's invitation for dinner?
ALAN. She couldn't. Her secretary reminded her that she was to be the guest of honor at some banquet or other.
JEFFREY [*satirically*]. I suppose that's why she came home.
ALAN. Why wasn't Sylvia here to meet mother?
JEFFREY. She wasn't expected until the day after to-morrow and Sylvia had made a dinner engagement that she didn't care to break.
ALAN. That's queer. I wonder if they've had a quarrel?
JEFFREY. What gave you that idea?
ALAN. Well, Peggy and I have never been able to get anything out of Sylvia as to why she remained only a month on tour with mother.
JEFFREY. I can understand just what happened. Her mother was entertained a great deal. That was part of the game of being the famous Mrs. Fair. It wasn't possible to include Sylvia in all of the functions. Naturally she was bored. So she came home.
ALAN. Considering they haven't seen each other for two months and that this is mother's first night at home, it is very selfish of Sylvia not to give up one party.
JEFFREY [*irritably*]. Sylvia's had to make her life without her mother and can't be expected to drop everything whenever she chooses to appear on the scene.
ALAN. All right, Dad, all right. You are so touchy about Sylvia.
JEFFREY. You've shown a disposition of late to criticize your sister, and I don't like it.
ALAN. Don't let us scrap about Sylvia. I'm sorry if I have seemed unkind. But you know, Dad, you are spoiling her.
JEFFREY. Oh, Hell, why not? A man's got to have some woman to spoil. Sylvia's sweet and loving to me. I was mighty glad to have her home again. It would have been a

damn sight better for me if I had never let her go away.

ALAN. Now that mother is home, I suppose you'll give up these rooms and go back to the country?

JEFFREY. She's going on another tour. [*He rises and begins to walk about the room restlessly*]

ALAN. I am disappointed. Damn Gillette.

JEFFREY. It isn't his fault.

ALAN [*surprised*]. You're not sticking up for him?

JEFFREY. He's not a bad sort when you get to know him.

ALAN. You don't like him?

JEFFREY. No. But I no longer hold him responsible for your mother going lecturing. If it hadn't been he it would have been some other manager.

ALAN. Gillette's around here a good deal, isn't he?

JEFFREY. Yes. [*Bitterly*] I wouldn't deprive Sylvia from seeing a man who knows a damn sight better what her mother's doing than I do. [*He sits behind*]

ALAN. Sylvia is around with Gillette and his crowd a lot, isn't she?

JEFFREY. Yes, he's been very kind to her. He's introduced her to his friends.

ALAN. You've met them?

JEFFREY. Casually.

ALAN. Dancing a good deal, isn't she?

JEFFREY. Everybody does. Keeps good hours, always tells me where she's going.

ALAN. Where is she to-night?

JEFFREY. I ought to know. I don't remember. [*Defiantly*] Why?

ALAN [*apologetically*]. Oh, nothing. It's getting late and I wondered if I would see her before I go home.

JEFFREY [*smiling*]. She'll come toddling in soon, bless her. I hope she's had a good time.

ALAN. By the way, what's become of Angy Brice? Sylvia never mentions her.

JEFFREY [*slightly confused*]. She hasn't seen Mrs. Brice. Don't you remember I had this place ready for Sylvia when she came home? I thought she'd find the country dull without her mother. [*Slightly embarrassed, he picks up a magazine, turns over its leaves.* ALAN *watches him narrowly as* JEFFREY *replies to his questions*]

ALAN [*casually*]. Hasn't Mrs. Brice been in town?

JEFFREY. Yes.

ALAN. Have you seen her?

JEFFREY [*carelessly*]. Occasionally.

ALAN. Odd Sylvia hasn't looked her up. They used to be such great pals.

JEFFREY. Angy's too old for Sylvia, and Sylvia's made new friends.

ALAN [*disarmed*]. When mother goes, Peggy and I must see Sylvia oftener. I'm afraid we've been rather selfish.

JEFFREY. Every newly married couple has that right. My boy, if your wife wants to associate with you, don't discourage her.

ALAN. Peggy works all day. I study all evening, so we don't have time to get bored with each other.

JEFFREY. I wish Peggy would give up her job. What the devil's the good of all my money? I can't spend it all on Sylvia.

ALAN. Well, Dad, if a wife wants to work these days, you have to let her.

JEFFREY. Yes, but sometimes I wonder in this modern scheme of things where in hell the husband belongs.

ALAN. Why don't you put up an argument about this new tour?

JEFFREY. I put up a good one once, but she went, didn't she? No, son.

ALAN [*eagerly*]. Perhaps if I talked to her —

JEFFREY [*rising*]. Don't you complicate things with her by trying to force anything for me. Let me give you a bit of advice. Never try to play God for your family. You only raise the devil.

ALAN. Very well, Dad, you know best.

JEFFREY [*ruefully*]. Son, I don't know anything any more. Don't you worry about me. So long as I have Sylvia I can stagger along. [*He crosses and gets his hat and coat*]

ALAN [*surprised*]. Are you going out?

JEFFREY. Yes.

ALAN [*rising*]. But mother?

JEFFREY. I wouldn't dream of intruding. She took great pains to tell me at dinner that she had a stack of mail waiting for her a mile high. Can I drop you at the subway?

ALAN. I'm not going home. Peggy's at the office to-night, working on an important case. I'm going to call for her. Anyway, I think I'll leave a little line for Sylvia.

JEFFREY [*pleased*]. Fine! Good night.

ALAN. Good night.

JEFFREY. Give my love to Peggy. [*He turns to leave the room, stops, hesitates, turns to* ALAN] Tell her if she wants me to-morrow night, I'd be very glad to come.

ALAN [*going to him quickly*]. Why, Dad, we always want you.

[JEFFREY *taking* ALAN's *outstretched hand, puts his arm around* ALAN's *shoulder*]

JEFFREY [*smiling*]. Good night. [*He goes*]

[ALAN *watches him. His lips quiver; there are tears in his eyes. He brushes them away and is starting towards the desk, when from the door at the left of the room* NANCY *enters. She wears a simple evening gown*]

NANCY. Oh, Alan, I'm so glad you haven't gone. I have been thinking it over and I'm not going to that boring banquet. I'm going to dine with you instead.

ALAN. That's bully of you, Mother. But it isn't necessary. You can come another night.

NANCY. No, no. I insist. I want to telephone your wife now.

ALAN. Peggy's not at home. She's at the office to-night. I'm going down to fetch her.

NANCY. I've a nice idea. I wonder if she would be too tired to drop in on the way home?

ALAN [*surprised*]. To-night?

NANCY. It's early, and — [*shyly*] — if Peggy is willing, I'd love to kiss and make up.

ALAN. Mother!

[*He goes quickly to* NANCY *and takes her in his arms. She begins to cry. He kisses her and soothes her*]

NANCY. My boy, my boy!

ALAN [*very much affected*]. There — there — Mother.

NANCY. Alan, promise me you'll never be on the "outs" with me again?

ALAN. I won't. I won't.

NANCY. It's almost made an old woman of me.

ALAN. It's been tough on me. I was wrong.

NANCY. No, no, I was to blame.

ALAN. I won't stand for that.

NANCY. Oh, my dear, it doesn't matter who was wrong, so that it's all right now.

ALAN. You bet it is, but — but —

NANCY. We won't spoil this by any post-mortems. [*She kisses him*] Did you see your father?

ALAN. Yes.

NANCY. Where is he?

ALAN. He went out.

NANCY [*disappointedly*]. Oh!

ALAN. He thought you were too busy to be disturbed.

NANCY. I sent my secretary away, but it doesn't matter.

ALAN. I must go for Peggy. She'll be on her ear.

NANCY. Don't you think you had better rescue her? Now hurry right back. Oh, Alan, I have something for her and I want you to see if you think she will like it. [*Tenderly*] I'm going to see you and Peggy very often before I go away again.

ALAN. When do you go?

NANCY. I don't know just what arrangements Mr. Gillette has made. He is coming to see me about them to-night.

ALAN. Mother, do you think you ought to go? I mean — ought to come to us instead of to that banquet?

NANCY. That's all settled. I put them on the trail of another celebrity.

[*She laughs and goes into her room.* ALAN *is smiling happily, humming a little tune, when the doors to the hall open and* SYLVIA *enters. She is completely transformed. In dress, coiffure and manner, she is the modern "cutie." Her face is rouged, her lips painted. On her head at a rakish angle is an ermine toque and wrapped about her throat is an ermine stole. She saunters over to the mirror at the right, greeting* ALAN *as she passes him*]

SYLVIA [*indifferently*]. Hello, Alan.

ALAN. Hello, Sylvia.

SYLVIA. Mother here yet?

ALAN. Yes.

SYLVIA [*"primping"*]. What about friend wife?

ALAN. It's all right. [*Indignantly*] Why weren't you here to meet mother?

SYLVIA [*carelessly*]. I had a very special date.

ALAN [*disgustedly*]. With that Gillette, I suppose.

SYLVIA. That's my affair.

ALAN. How you or any one else can —

SYLVIA [*crossly*]. Alan Fair, don't

you dare to knock Gillie. You don't like him — I do.

[*Enter* NANCY, *smiling happily. She sees* SYLVIA *and is so shocked by the change in her appearance that she stops, speechless. The little jewelry box that she is carrying falls from her hand.* SYLVIA, *quite oblivious of the effect she has made on* NANCY, *runs towards her*]

SYLVIA. Oh, hello, Mother.

[NANCY *cannot speak.* SYLVIA, *surprised, stops. There is a slight pause*]

NANCY [*inarticulately*].   Sylvia! [*Heart-brokenly*] Sylvia! Sylvia!

[*She rushes to* SYLVIA, *folds her in her arms, kissing her frantically.* SYLVIA *is happy, but rather puzzled*]

SYLVIA. I was awfully sorry not to be here. You got my note?
NANCY. No.
SYLVIA. Isn't that the limit? I gave it to the clerk myself. I'll just ask him "what's the idea." [*She turns toward the telephone, and sees a hat box on the table*] Oh, the darn thing came at last. [*She opens the box and takes out a "freakish" hat*] I was going to wear this to-night. [*She holds it up admiringly*] Isn't that a sweetie?
ALAN [*disgustedly*] Where did you get it?
SYLVIA [*going to the mirror*]. At Francine's. She makes for all the smart chorus girls. [*She puts it on, then strikes a pose*] How do I look?
ALAN. Just like a movie "cutie."
NANCY [*reprovingly*]. Alan!
SYLVIA. Oh, Mother, don't mind Alan. He's always knocking my taste in clothes. [*She is furious, and, snatching the hat off her head, throws it into the box and tosses it into a corner of the room. As she turns away,* NANCY, *who has been watching her in amazement, goes to* ALAN]
NANCY. Oh, what have you all done to her?
ALAN. It isn't our fault.
NANCY. No, it's mine. [*A slight pause*] Alan, say good night to your sister.
SYLVIA. Where's daddy?
ALAN. He's gone out. Mad?
SYLVIA [*kissing him*]. Not so you'd notice it.
ALAN. See you later, Mother. [*He goes*]

NANCY. Well, darling, glad to have your mother home again?
SYLVIA. Believe me, I am. [*She is wearing her hair in exaggerated curves over her ears.* NANCY *puts her hands on either side of* SYLVIA's *face and pushes the hair gently off her cheeks*]
NANCY. Why do you wear your hair like that?
SYLVIA. Everyone in my crowd does.
NANCY. Come and sit down. I want to know all that you've been doing.
SYLVIA. I wrote to you.
NANCY. Not so often lately.
SYLVIA [*resentfully*]. With somethin' doin' every minute I didn't have the time.
NANCY [*quickly*]. I'm not reproaching you, darling. Let's have a nice snuggly time. [*She sits in the armchair, taking* SYLVIA *on her lap. Then drawing* SYLVIA's *head down on her shoulder, puts her arms about her, kisses her.* SYLVIA *begins to cry*]
SYLVIA. My, I've missed this.
NANCY [*very much affected*]. So have I, dear. [*She takes her handkerchief and wipes* SYLVIA's *eyes and at the same time seizes the opportunity to remove a little of the rouge from* SYLVIA's *face and lips*]
NANCY. Now let's begin at the beginning.
SYLVIA. Let's skip the beginning. It was horrid.
NANCY [*surprised*]. In what way, dear?
SYLVIA. I was so lonesome.
NANCY. As soon as I knew you were to be at this hotel, instead of at home, I wired to Bridget Wynne. Didn't she look you up?
SYLVIA. Oh, all the women came once. Mrs. Wynne gave me a luncheon and a box party and asked all the girls in our set. It was a perfect lemon.
NANCY. How?
SYLVIA. For all the attention they gave to me I might as well not have been there.
NANCY. Why should they be rude to you?
SYLVIA. They didn't mean to be. I didn't know all the little intimate things they talked about. One girl's mother was doing this for her, and another one's mother was doing that — anyway, I felt like an outsider in what should have been my own crowd. When I got home I just bawled my head

off, and daddy said we wouldn't bother with any of them again, but it was pretty awful, especially as I didn't have Angy to fall back on.

NANCY. No?

SYLVIA. Daddy said you didn't like me to be intimate with her.

NANCY. I see. Haven't you seen Alan and Peggy?

SYLVIA. It's terribly dull at their flat. They are so crazy about each other that half the time they don't know you're around. [*They laugh*]

NANCY. Didn't father go about with you?

SYLVIA. Oh, yes, daddy's a darling, but he is old. Gillie's been my life-saver.

NANCY [*mystified*]. Who is Gillie?

SYLVIA. Mr. Gillette. He took me to a tea one day at a dancing place and introduced me to his friends. When he found I liked them, he said, "Sylvia, this little old town is yours. We'll take it all apart and see what makes it tick."

NANCY. That doesn't sound like Mr. Gillette.

SYLVIA. Oh, he puts on his grand manners with you. You don't know the real Gillie.

NANCY [*thoughtfully*]. No, I don't believe I do. [*A slight pause*] Who are these friends?

SYLVIA. I don't know. Just New Yorkers.

NANCY. Has your father met them?

SYLVIA. Oh, yes.

NANCY. Has he gone around with you?

SYLVIA. Not to the lively parties.

NANCY [*shocked*]. My dear, who chaperoned you?

SYLVIA. A woman pal of Gillie's.

NANCY. Is she a married woman?

SYLVIA [*giggling*]. Is she? Three times.

NANCY. How awful!

SYLVIA [*protestingly*]. She's terribly nice. You must know her. So sweet to me. Takes me motoring in the park almost every afternoon.

NANCY. Where did you meet her, dear?

SYLVIA. At a party at "The Drowsy Saint."

NANCY. Where's that?

SYLVIA. It's a new freak place in the Village.

NANCY. Who took you *there?*

SYLVIA. Gillie. He's a sweetie

lamb, and so generous. He spends money like water.

NANCY [*puzzled*]. He does?

SYLVIA. Yes, he's taken me on parties to all the cabarets, 'n' everywhere.

NANCY. Does your father know that you go to these places?

SYLVIA. Sure.

NANCY. He never objects?

SYLVIA. Why should he when you go with your own crowd; there's no harm in them, is there?

NANCY. They are not exactly the places for a girl who has been brought up as you have been. Is Mr. Gillette always your escort to these parties?

SYLVIA [*smiling*]. He's my "gentleman friend."

NANCY. He doesn't make love to you?

SYLVIA [*giggling*]. No, but I guess he'd like to.

NANCY. Darling, you mustn't say such things. It isn't nice.

SYLVIA [*sulkily*]. Why not?

NANCY. Well, nice girls don't — that's all.

SYLVIA [*resentfully*]. What else don't they do?

NANCY [*hesitatingly*]. Well, dear, they don't go to the places you have been going, and they don't use rouge, or wear hats from Francine's.

SYLVIA. All the women in my crowd do.

NANCY. Then I think you're going with the wrong crowd.

SYLVIA [*indignantly*]. How do you know? You've never seen any of them. They may not belong, but they know how to be kind.

NANCY. Sylvia, I'm sorry. I don't mean to criticize —

SYLVIA [*rising in a fury of rage*]. But you are, you are! Daddy is the only one that never finds fault with me. He's the only one that loves me really.

[NANCY, *horrified at the implication that she does not love* SYLVIA, *rises quickly, grasps her in her arms, and almost roughly places her hand over* SYLVIA's *mouth. She stands there crucified by the realization of the fact that she has apparently lost the love of her child*]

NANCY. Oh, my dear, my dear — never say that to me again. [*She pauses a moment, then very tenderly*] It isn't always kind to allow you to do just as you please.

SYLVIA [*sullenly*]. Doesn't every one else in this family do as they darn please?

NANCY [*hopelessly*]. Yes, I suppose we do.

[*There is a slight pause. SYLVIA looks defiantly at NANCY, who moves slowly across to the fireplace where she stands, her elbows resting on the mantelpiece, her face buried in her hands. The telephone bell rings sharply. SYLVIA turns quickly to answer it*]

SYLVIA. Yes. [*Turning to NANCY*] Dudley's downstairs. If you don't want to be bothered I can see him in the lounge.

NANCY. Ask him to come up.

SYLVIA. Have Mr. Gillette come right up. [*To NANCY*] Were you expecting him?

NANCY. Yes, he's coming to talk to me on business.

SYLVIA. I want to talk to him, too, but I hadn't better butt in on your party.

NANCY. It won't interfere, dear.

SYLVIA. I've a message for Gillie from the bunch.

NANCY. Can't you give it to Mr. Gillette now?

SYLVIA [*defiantly*]. Any objection to my seeing him alone?

NANCY. Why, none at all, dear; I'll let you know as soon as we have finished.

[*The buzzer at the double door sounds*]

SYLVIA. Come in. [*GILLETTE enters. He wears informal evening dress*] Oh, there you are. I thought you were going with us to dinner to-night.

[*GILLETTE, who has entered smilingly, frowns in annoyance at SYLVIA, and motions her to silence; then, smiling suavely, advances toward NANCY*]

GILLETTE. Good evening, Mrs. Fair. It's a very great pleasure to see you again.

[*NANCY acknowledges GILLETTE's greeting coldly*]

SYLVIA. Mother, when you're through with Gillie, have them page me in the lounge. I'll go down and hear a little jazz. [*She smiles sweetly at GILLETTE, who turns and smiles at her. She starts towards the door into the hall. NANCY crosses quickly to her*]

NANCY. No, Sylvia, you wait in my room, please.

[*SYLVIA turns angrily, looks at NANCY; there is a brief clash of wills, then SYLVIA goes into NANCY's room, slamming the door. NANCY sinks wearily into the chair and sits staring before her, lost in thought. GILLETTE places his hat, cane and gloves on the sofa, then approaches NANCY*]

GILLETTE [*effusively*]. Mrs. Fair, I must congratulate you on the success of your tour. It was phenomenal. I am proud to have had the privilege of presenting you to the American public. [*NANCY makes no reply. GILLETTE looks at her in surprise*] I trust that you have found it agreeable to appear under my management. [*There is no response and GILLETTE looks at her again*] I hope our association will continue. I've secured even better terms for the new tour. [*He sits*]

NANCY. I am not going on another tour.

GILLETTE [*astounded*]. You are not going on — but, Mrs. Fair, all the arrangements have been made.

NANCY. They will have to be cancelled.

GILLETTE. But you agreed to it by letter. You 'phoned me to bring these contracts to-night.

NANCY. Things have occurred that have made me change my mind.

GILLETTE. Are you dissatisfied with me?

NANCY. No. But I can't go on.

GILLETTE. You can't mean that you are going to give up all your triumphs?

NANCY [*satirically*]. "Triumphs!"

GILLETTE. Why, Mrs. Fair, I am leaving to-night for Montreal to arrange for your appearance in Canada. The people in the East haven't heard you talk of your great work.

NANCY. Mr. Gillette, there is nothing that could induce me to talk of my great work again. [*A pause*] I will be very much obliged if you will bring me an accounting to-morrow.

GILLETTE [*nervously*]. To-morrow? [*He rises quickly*]

NANCY. Yes. I think there is about fifteen thousand dollars due.

GILLETTE [*stammering*]. Why — why — I won't be able to make a settlement to-morrow. It will take the bookkeeper several days to make out a statement.

NANCY. Let me have it as soon as possible, as I am going to re-open our house in the country. And now I believe Sylvia has some message for you. I will send her in and you can say good-bye to her. [*She rises and goes to the door of her room*]

GILLETTE [*astonished*]. Good-bye?

NANCY [*turning to him*]. I think it wiser. Sylvia has been telling me of your kindness to her. I don't wish to seem ungrateful, but I would rather you did not see her again, at least for the present.

GILLETTE [*angrily*]. Are you insinuating that I am not good enough to associate with your daughter?

NANCY. I never insinuate, Mr. Gillette. If I must speak more plainly, I will, and I hope you will not resent it.

GILLETTE [*rudely*]. Well —

NANCY. Sylvia's story of her friendship with you has made me realize that you and I have rather different standards as to the sort of associates and amusements that are suitable for a girl of her age and up-bringing.

GILLETTE [*sneeringly*]. She enjoyed the associates and the amusements.

NANCY. Possibly, but I am sure that she will like much more the ones I intend to provide for her from now on. When may I expect the statement?

GILLETTE. The day after to-morrow.

NANCY. Good night, Mr. Gillette.

GILLETTE. Good night, Mrs. Fair.

[NANCY *goes into her room.* GILLETTE *walks up and down. He is deeply annoyed, worried. Enter* SYLVIA. *She runs across to him*]

SYLVIA. Oh, Gillie, the bunch said to tell you —

GILLETTE [*irritably*]. Oh, hang the bunch!

SYLVIA. Why, Dudley, what's the matter?

GILLETTE. Your mother has thrown me down. She has cancelled her tour.

SYLVIA [*surprised*]. Mother's not going away?

GILLETTE. No, and she has put me in an awful hole.

SYLVIA. How?

GILLETTE. Oh, you wouldn't understand about business. Where the devil am I going to find fifteen thousand dollars by the day after to-morrow?

SYLVIA. I'm so sorry you're so worried.

GILLETTE. I can do with a little

sympathy. She's made me feel like a yellow dog.

SYLVIA. Did mother say something unkind to you?

GILLETTE [*bitterly*]. Did she? She spoke "plainly" and "hoped I wouldn't resent it." Me doing all I could so that you wouldn't be lonely. A lot of thanks I got. Told me I wasn't good enough to associate with you. [*He laughs*] Well, if she objects to me, what's she going to say about your father and Angy Brice?

SYLVIA. Dudley! What do you mean?

GILLETTE. The minute your mother's wise, she'll get a divorce.

SYLVIA [*shocked*]. Divorce!

GILLETTE. Why, you poor kid, aren't you onto your father and Angy Brice? Everybody else in town is.

SYLVIA. Oh, I never thought my daddy would go back on me. [*Broken-hearted, she sinks into a chair, sobbing*]

GILLETTE. Your whole family has gone back on you. That selfish brother of yours has no time for anybody but his wife. Your mother leaving you alone for years at a stretch, and your father running around with Angy Brice. A lot they care about you.

SYLVIA. Nobody wants me.

[GILLETTE, *suddenly alarmed lest* SYL-VIA'S *sobs may be overheard by her mother, crosses quickly to her and quiets her*]

GILLETTE. I want you. I'm the only one that cares anything about you, and I've been ordered to say good-bye to you.

SYLVIA [*bewildered*]. Good-bye?

GILLETTE. Yes, you're going to be taken down to the country.

SYLVIA. I won't go.

GILLETTE. You'll have to go and you'll soon forget all about me.

SYLVIA. I won't.

GILLETTE. Oh, yes, you will.

SYLVIA. I won't.

GILLETTE. No? Then prove it.

SYLVIA. How?

GILLETTE. Come with me to Montreal to-night.

SYLVIA. Oh, Dudley!

GILLETTE. We'll be married as soon as we get there.

SYLVIA. I couldn't. They'd never forgive me.

GILLETTE. Sure they will. Didn't they forgive Alan? Forgive you! Why, they'll be on their knees to you, and to me, too.

SYLVIA. I don't know what to do.

GILLETTE. Oh, all right. I might have known you wouldn't come through. You pretend to care for me. It's only a bluff. Well, stay here where nobody wants you. Good-bye. [*He makes a pretense of leaving hurriedly.* SYLVIA *rises and runs to him*]

SYLVIA. Oh, Dudley, please don't go.

GILLETTE. Well, what are you going to do about it?

SYLVIA [*pathetically*]. You're sure you really want me?

GILLETTE. Of course I want you. We can't talk here. Meet me downstairs in the lounge and we will talk it over. Now you won't weaken?

[*He opens the door to the hall.* SYLVIA *crosses it to her room. He closes the door and stands for an instant, smiling in triumph as he looks at the door to* NANCY'S *room, then chuckling, goes hurriedly and gets his hat and cane from the sofa, and is starting to leave the room quickly when* NANCY *enters from her room. He stops and assumes a nonchalant attitude*]

NANCY [*surprised*]. Oh, Mr. Gillette, where is Sylvia?

GILLETTE. I've said good-bye to her. She's gone to her room. Good night, Mrs. Fair.

NANCY. Good night. [GILLETTE *bows smilingly and leaves the room, closing the door.* NANCY *stands thinking, then goes towards the door on her way to* SYLVIA'S *room. Her hand is on the knob when the telephone rings sharply, then again.* NANCY *answers it*] Hello. Put her on, please. Who? Mrs. Brice? Oh, this is *Mrs.* Fair. Yes. I'll give Mr. Fair your message. [*Enter* JEFFREY] That was Mrs. Brice on the telephone.

JEFFREY [*surprised*]. Really? Why, I saw her —

NANCY. Yes, I know. She said that you had just been there, but she wants to see you to-morrow.

JEFFREY. Oh, all right. [*He goes towards his room*] Sylvia home?

NANCY. Yes, she is in her room. Jeffrey — [*He stops*] — I hardly know how to say it. I understand about Mrs. Brice, but has it ever occurred to you that other people mightn't?

JEFFREY. What do you mean?

NANCY. The worst of these platonic friendships is, that people will talk.

JEFFREY. Have you heard any talk?

[*He places his overcoat and hat on a chair and goes toward* NANCY]

NANCY. Well, Bridget Wynne isn't a gossip, but even she wrote to me that you and Mrs. Brice were about a good deal together.

JEFFREY. Oh, she is still reporting to her senior officer. [*He sits at the right of the table.* NANCY *sits at the left of it*]

NANCY. Jeffrey, frankly, do you think it courteous to go to see Mrs. Brice a few hours after my arrival?

JEFFREY. You were busy with your own affairs as usual.

NANCY. I have some pride.

JEFFREY. I don't understand.

NANCY. I was very glad to have the excuse of letters so that I need not prolong your boredom at dinner.

JEFFREY. I wasn't bored. Sorry if you were. I thought I was very entertaining. You'll have to make allowances for me. I haven't had the advantage of mingling with the mighty minds of two continents.

NANCY. Jeffrey, I'd like you to be serious.

JEFFREY. Oh, haven't we been? I think being told by your wife that you are a bore is fairly serious. Still if there's more, let's have it. [*There is a slight pause*]

NANCY. Jeffrey, long ago we decided that if we ever came to the conclusion that our marriage had been a mistake —

JEFFREY. I haven't said so.

NANCY. Words aren't necessary. Actions sometimes —

JEFFREY. When it comes to actions, I haven't forsaken my bed and board.

NANCY. We needn't go into that.

JEFFREY. Pardon me, but that is the crux of the whole affair.

NANCY. Oh, no, Jeffrey, your attentions to Mrs. Brice are the crux of the affair.

JEFFREY. What right have you to object to anything I do?

NANCY. My right as your wife.

JEFFREY. Haven't you forfeited that right?

NANCY. How?

JEFFREY. If you prefer the public to your husband, you mustn't kick at the price you have to pay.

NANCY. Meaning that I am not to protest if you choose to make me conspicuous by your attentions to that woman? Really this is delicious. [*She laughs, rises and goes to the desk, at which she sits*]

JEFFREY. Are you paying me the compliment of being jealous of me?

NANCY. Jealous of a man who doesn't want me!

JEFFREY. Oh, Nancy, you know damn well I want you. You may not be jealous of me, but I am of you, and of everything that concerns you. I'm jealous of your career because it takes you away from me. [*He rises*] I tried to live up to our agreement. Haven't I the right to expect that you'd live up to it, too? If it was my job to provide the home, wasn't it your job to take care of it? Had you the right, be honest, Nancy, to go on this tour? You can't be married and be a free agent without making some one suffer. I'm so damned sick of my life, as I'm living it now — but there, I don't want to keep you if you want to be free. [*He turns away from* NANCY, *who rises and follows him quickly*]

NANCY. I don't want to be free. [*As* JEFFREY *turns to take her in his arms, she stops him*] Oh, wait, I want to be honest with myself and with you. I couldn't go back to my life as I lived it four years ago. It isn't that I don't want a home. While I was in France there were glorious moments and honors and flattery, but there were nights when I was so sick of the horrors, the pain, the misery, that it seemed to me if I couldn't put my head on your shoulder and cry out the loneliness of my heart against yours I couldn't go on. [JEFFREY *takes her in his arms, kisses her*] With death on every side I used to worry for fear you weren't taking care of yourself. They decorated me for bravery. They never knew what a coward I was about you. Why, on this tour the nights when I had had a great success and while people were crowding around me congratulating me, I'd see some wife tuck her hand through her husband's arm, just as I had tucked mine so many times through yours, and she would trot away home with her man and I would go to a lonely hotel room and think about you. Then is when I would realize that success meant nothing if I had to give up you. [*She breaks down and cries.* JEFFREY'S *arms are about her. He murmurs her name and kisses her*]

JEFFREY. Then, Nancy, I've got you again.

NANCY. Yes, and hang on to me. If I ever try to go away again, lock me up on bread and water.

JEFFREY. What about this supplementary tour?

NANCY [*laughing in hysterical relief*]. There "ain't going to be no tour."

JEFFREY. Fine! When did you decide that?

NANCY. To-night. But don't ask me why.

JEFFREY. I don't care a damn why, just so you're not going. [*He kisses her*]

NANCY. Bless you. The first thing we'll do will be to get out of this hole. [*She moves away from him*]

JEFFREY. I don't believe Sylvia will like the country.

NANCY. She'll like it with me. She's going to have all the fun she's missed in four years crowded into as many months. It's going to be very expensive for you, darling. [*She laughs and sits on the sofa.* JEFFREY *follows her and sits beside her*]

JEFFREY. Go as far as you like.

NANCY. She and I are going out to-morrow and buy a lot of frills. And if the exchequer runs to it I want new curtains for the living-room and then I am going to give the grandest party for my two daughters!

JEFFREY [*pleased*]. You're going to take Peggy up?

NANCY. No, I'm going to try to make her love me, that's all.

JEFFREY. She will. After that, what? Remember, Nancy, I don't want to tie you down to the home.

NANCY. If you can have a career and do your duty to the family too, can't I? I ought to be as smart as you. But you'll help me find some welfare work to keep me and my Unit out of mischief, won't you?

JEFFREY. Sure.

NANCY. That's settled. Oh, Jeff, you are a nice old thing! [*She leans back in his arms*]

JEFFREY. Nancy, you're a darling!

NANCY [*teasingly*]. And you're quite sure that I am as well suited to you as Angy Brice?

JEFFREY. Oh, forget her. I discharged all my obligations to her to-night.

NANCY. I am kind of sorry for poor Angy. [*A pause*] Obligations? What obligations? [JEFFREY *does not reply.*

NANCY *draws herself away from him; looks at him*] Has she any real claim on you? Tell me the truth. Tell me the truth.

JEFFREY. Nancy, for God's sake, be big enough to understand.

NANCY. Oh! [*She shudders away from him, rises, goes to the mantelpiece and buries her face in her hands*]

JEFFREY. It was just after you had gone on this tour. You know how we parted. You didn't write to me. I was lonely, reckless. But I've never loved her. You won't believe it, but I've never ceased loving you.

NANCY. Stop, stop! Everything you say only makes it more horrible! [*She moves away from him across the room. JEFFREY rises, moves about and finally stands looking into the fireplace. There is silence. Then NANCY goes towards the door to her room. She stops*] I will go West and establish a residence. We won't drag in Mrs. Brice. Your lawyer will make all the necessary arrangements and communicate with me. [*She turns to go*]

JEFFREY. You're going to divorce me?

NANCY [*turning to him*]. You don't think I'd go on living with you?

JEFFREY. Nancy, you're not going to hold me entirely to blame? You're not going to dodge your own responsibility?

NANCY. For what am I responsible?

JEFFREY. Surely you don't think my affair with Mrs. Brice was a greater sin against our love than your craving for a career?

NANCY. And surely you are not daring to place me in the same category as yourself?

JEFFREY. Why not? Do you think you can starve my affections, my passion, for years, without moral guilt?

NANCY. You must be mad to think such thoughts, and lost to all sense of decency to express them.

JEFFREY. I —

NANCY. I refuse to listen to anything more. All I want to know is, are you going to try to keep me against my will, or must I make a scandal to get free? [*JEFFREY is silent*] Surely you don't want to blacken the name of the woman you are going to marry?

JEFFREY. I'm not going to marry her. She knows it. I'm not in love with her, nor she with me. A sum of money will console her.

NANCY. Your bargain with her has no interest for me. You may make what use of your freedom you choose. I mean to have mine.

JEFFREY. Very well. My lawyer knows the amount of my income. You may have what you wish of it.

NANCY. I wouldn't take any of it, were it not for Sylvia.

JEFFREY. What do you mean? Sylvia?

NANCY. Do you think I would allow her to remain with you? Look what your neglect has made of her. Through your carelessness Mr. Gillette has been allowed to introduce her to a sort of life until she is no more the child I sent home to you than — Do you think when I realize that you are responsible that I would trust her to you again? Never! Never!

JEFFREY. And do you think I'm going to let you have her? She's the biggest thing in my life. I'll never let her go.

NANCY. She's the only thing in mine. If you force me to do it, I'll tell her the truth about you.

JEFFREY. So that is your threat! She is in her room, you say. Well, you tell her the truth about me and let her decide. [*He starts toward the door to the hall. NANCY stands aghast. ALAN rushes in, followed by PEGGY*]

ALAN. Dad! Mother! Where is Sylvia?

NANCY. She is in her room.

ALAN. She is not. [*To PEGGY*] I was right. It *was* Sylvia in that taxicab with Gillette. [*To JEFFREY*] They drove away just as we arrived.

PEGGY. I found this letter on Sylvia's dressing-table. [*She gives the letter to ALAN, who hands it to JEFFREY*]

ALAN. For you, Dad.

[*JEFFREY takes the letter. The others watch him apprehensively as he opens it*]

JEFFREY [*reading*]. "Dear Daddy — I —" [*He mumbles indistinctly, then, overcome by its contents, he crumples it in his hand and drops his head in misery. NANCY, who has been watching him in fear, starts toward him. She is trembling and can scarcely walk. Her hands are outstretched toward the letter*]

NANCY [*hoarsely*]. Jeff, Jeff!

[*JEFFREY looks at NANCY, then hands her the letter*]

JEFFREY. Sylvia has decided. [*He rushes to the telephone*] Hello, hello, give me Police Headquarters quickly, quickly.

[JEFFREY *is at the telephone, frantically calling Police Headquarters.* ALAN *and* PEGGY *are beside him.* NANCY, *with the letter crushed against her breast, leans for support against the table. She stares straight ahead, her face drawn with agony, as the*

CURTAIN FALLS

ACT IV

The scene is the same as that of the previous act. The room is in semi-darkness, the curtains drawn aside showing through the window, blurred by the drizzling rain, the lights of a building across the street. Two hours have elapsed.

NANCY *is standing at the window, peering into the street. Presently* PEGGY, *a wrap over her arm, enters from* NANCY'S *bedroom.* NANCY, *with a little cry, turns quickly at the sound of the closing door, then with a sigh of disappointment resumes her watching attitude.* PEGGY *goes to her and places the wrap about her shoulders.*

NANCY. Thank you, Peggy dear.

[PEGGY *switches on the light in the chandelier. The bell of the telephone on the writing-desk rings shrilly.* PEGGY *rushes to it.* NANCY *turns sharply and during the telephone conversation, to which she listens intently, moves down and stands behind* PEGGY]

PEGGY [*excitedly*]. Hello, yes. Police Headquarters. Oh, yes, Tom. Any news? — None. Oh — Gillette went to his apartment. Was Sylvia with him then? — She waited outside in the taxi. You haven't any idea where they went from there. — Your men are watching all the depots and ferries. [*She breaks down*] Oh, Tom, you've got to find her. — No. I won't. He's there with you? — Hello, Alan. Your mother? Why — [*Not knowing what to say, she turns to* NANCY, *who takes the telephone.* PEGGY *bows her head on the desk, crying*]

NANCY. Yes, dear, I'm all right. Don't worry about me, there's a good boy. Your father? He's gone out. I don't know where. — Now, Alan, dear, you mustn't give up hope. You'll find her. — That's better. — That's more like my boy. Of course you'll bring her back to me. I know you will. — That's it. Good-bye, dear. [*She puts the telephone on the table and, smiling bravely, places her hand on* PEGGY'S *head*] Don't cry, Peggy dear; they'll find her. They'll find her. [*Then, beginning to lose her self-control, she turns away to the window, her hands folded as though in prayer*] Oh, God, find her! Find her! Find her! [*She goes to the window and, leaning against it, her face pressed against the panes, breaks into long shivering sobs.* PEGGY *goes to her and, putting her arms about her, leads her to the fireplace and places her in the couch, where* NANCY *sits, holding out her hands to the blaze.* PEGGY *kneels beside her. There is a pause, then* NANCY *looks at the clock on the mantel*] It's almost twelve o'clock.

PEGGY. We'll hear some good news very soon now. [*Rising*] Wouldn't you like a cup of tea? [NANCY *shakes her head*] Not if I sent for the things and made it myself? I make very nice tea.

NANCY. I'm sure you do. But I couldn't. [*There is a pause*]

PEGGY. Oh, Mrs. Fair! I wouldn't keep on reading that letter.

NANCY. Oh, Peggy, I know it by heart. "I'm in everybody's way. Nobody wants me. Dudley does, so I'm going with him. . . . Sylvia." Oh, my baby! [*She breaks down again*]

PEGGY. Please don't cry — please!

NANCY. No, I mustn't. I mustn't. [*A slight pause*] Oh, if I could only do something!

PEGGY. There is nothing to do but wait. [*She sits on the arm of the couch, her arms around* NANCY. *Again there is a pause*]

NANCY [*wildly*]. Oh, Peggy, tell me again that they'll find her!

PEGGY. Of course they will. Now, Mrs. Fair, you mustn't. Please don't cry.

NANCY [*controlling herself*]. Why are you so good to me?

PEGGY [*very tenderly*]. Because you're Alan's mother. And because you're you.

NANCY. I don't deserve this, my dear, but I'm very grateful.

PEGGY. I've been wanting to do this ever since that day we hurt you so

cruelly. [NANCY *pulls* PEGGY'S *head
down to her and kisses her.* PEGGY *sits
beside* NANCY *and taking* NANCY'S *hand
in hers, strokes it affectionately. There
is a pause. Both of them are lost in
thought*] The one thing I can't understand is Sylvia's leaving her father.
She would never have gone if she hadn't
felt that in some way he had turned
against her. She might have left —
[*She stops abruptly*]

NANCY. You could understand her
leaving me. I'm beginning to understand that, too. I'm beginning to see
that he has more right to her than I
have.

PEGGY. Oh, I don't mean that she
doesn't love you, but the love Sylvia
had for her father was wonderful.

NANCY. He had earned it.

PEGGY. I don't think Mr. Fair
realized it, but he didn't want her to
love any one more than she did him.

NANCY. This is going to be terrible
for Jeffrey. [*A pause*] It's strange,
Peggy, how one can seem to be doing
one's duty and fail so miserably — go
so hopelessly wrong. [*A pause, then*
NANCY *looks toward the telephone*]
Queer they don't telephone. I wonder
where Jeffrey is? If they don't find
Sylvia —

PEGGY. Oh, they will, they will.

NANCY [*rising*]. Oh, what is her
father going to do without her?

PEGGY. Thank God, you're here.
At least, whatever happens, he has
you.

[NANCY *winces and turns away as the
door opens to admit* JEFFREY, *tired,
haggard. Both the women turn to
him inquiringly. He shakes his
head. Then places his hat and
coat on the chair beside the door.*
PEGGY *goes to him*]

JEFFREY. Any news?

PEGGY [*cheerfully*]. Not yet. But
there will be very soon.

JEFFREY. You all right, Nancy?

NANCY. Yes, Jeffrey.

JEFFREY. Did Alan telephone?

PEGGY. Yes, just a moment ago.

JEFFREY. No trace of them?
[PEGGY *shakes her head.* JEFFREY *moves
slowly down to the chair at the desk, where
he sits brooding.* PEGGY *sits in the arm-
chair at the table. A pause*] [*Savagely*]
Curse the day the swine came into my
house!

NANCY. Oh, Jeff, don't make me
feel my responsibility for it all any more
than I do. I can't bear it. I can't
bear it.

JEFFREY. I'm sorry, Nancy.

NANCY. That's all right, Jeff.
[NANCY *goes to the window and looks
down into the steet, shading her eyes with
her hands to cut off the light from the
chandelier. Presently she rubs the mois-
ture off the pane and peers out again.
Then she lifts the sash and leans out,
looking down into the street. Suddenly
she gives a little start*] Jeff! Here
comes a taxi!

[JEFFREY *and* PEGGY *run to the window
and look out over* NANCY'S *shoulder*]

PEGGY [*excitedly*]. Is it stopping?

NANCY. No, it's going on.

[PEGGY *and* JEFFREY *return to their
chairs;* NANCY *remains at the window. A pause, then* JEFFREY *takes
out his watch*]

PEGGY [*whispering*]. What time is
it?

JEFFREY [*whispering*]. A quarter
past twelve. [PEGGY, *sighing, sinks
back into the chair, and after a moment*
JEFFREY *turns and looks at* NANCY]
Mother, you'd better come away from
that window; there is a draught.
You'll take cold. [NANCY *does not
reply*] Nancy, you'll take cold.
[NANCY *does not answer. Another pause.
Then* JEFFREY, *rising, goes to* PEGGY,
touches her quietly on the shoulder]
Peggy, get her away from that window.
I can't stand it. I can't stand it.
[*Profoundly moved, he walks over to the
sofa and sits.* PEGGY *goes to* NANCY *and
touches her on the shoulder*]

NANCY. Yes, dear?

PEGGY. I wouldn't watch for them,
dear.

NANCY. No?

PEGGY. You know a watched kettle
never boils. [NANCY *smiles, but remains
at the window.* PEGGY *returns to the
armchair and stands behind it*] Is it
raining now, Mr. Fair?

JEFFREY. Yes.

NANCY [*quite unemotionally*]. I hope
Sylvia hadn't on thin shoes. She takes
cold so easily. At least, she used to.

[JEFFREY *buries his face in his hands.*
PEGGY'S *lips quiver. Her eyes fill
with tears. They wait*]

JEFFREY. Nancy, did Gillette owe you any money?

NANCY [*intently watching the street*]. Yes, several thousand.

JEFFREY. That's it!

NANCY [*indifferently*]. What do you mean?

JEFFREY. I found out from Tom Gibbs to-night that Gillette was the man who was mixed up in that Bazaar scandal. He has stolen your money or was going to.

NANCY. I don't understand.

JEFFREY. Don't you see you can't prosecute him now without bringing Sylvia into it? . . . Damn him!

[*It all seems of little moment to* NANCY, *and she turns again to the window. The door to the hall opens very softly and* ALAN *stands in the doorway, unseen by* JEFFREY *and* NANCY. PEGGY, *moving to sit in the chair, sees* ALAN *and goes quietly to him. He whispers to her and she darts out and across the hall into* SYLVIA'S *room. He comes in quickly, closing the door. At the sound* NANCY *and* JEFFREY *turn.* JEFFREY *springs to his feet*]

NANCY [*with a great cry*]. Alan!

ALAN. She's here!

JEFFREY. Thank God!

[NANCY *makes a rush for the door*]

ALAN [*stopping her*]. Wait, Mother. What are you going to say to her? What are you going to do?

NANCY. Oh, Alan, what would I do?

ALAN. I didn't know.

JEFFREY. Where did you find her?

ALAN. At 125th Street station. They were on their way to Montreal.

JEFFREY. Where is he?

ALAN. I've taken care of him. He's —

NANCY [*hysterically, and trying to pass* ALAN]. What does it matter where he is? All that matters is that she's here. Don't shut her outside. Alan, do you hear me? Let me go to her!

JEFFREY. Easy, Nancy, easy!

ALAN [*taking her in his arms*]. All right, Mother, all right. But be careful — treat her very gently. [*He goes*]

NANCY. Jeffrey, I'm giving up my claims to her. She's yours. So be kind to her. [SYLVIA *enters, white-faced, defiant, followed by* PEGGY *and* ALAN. NANCY *rushes toward her to embrace her.*

SYLVIA, *stretching out her hands, stops her.* NANCY, *surprised, stunned for the moment, looks toward* JEFFREY *bewilderedly*] Jeff —

[JEFFREY *looks at* SYLVIA, *who looks coldly at him*]

NANCY. Won't you sit down, dear?

SYLVIA. I can take what everybody has to say, standing.

NANCY [*very tenderly*]. Darling, don't be afraid.

SYLVIA. I'm not afraid.

NANCY. We're not going to scold you. We're not going to say anything.

SYLVIA. No? Well, I am.

JEFFREY [*sternly*]. Very well. Go on. I'm interested to hear what *you* have to say.

NANCY [*turning to him*]. Jeff, please!

JEFFREY. I'll handle this, Nancy. Alan, take Peggy into your mother's room.

SYLVIA. She needn't go. She's in on this.

PEGGY. I?

SYLVIA. You were responsible for our arrest, weren't you?

ALAN. You weren't arrested.

SYLVIA. We would have been if you hadn't been there.

PEGGY. No, no, dear. Tom would have brought you here to us.

SYLVIA. Oh, then you did arrange it all? Don't you think, for a new member of this family, you were taking a good deal on yourself to —

JEFFREY. Come, come, Sylvia; it was I who got Tom Gibbs on the wire. You should be very grateful to Peggy and her brother. God knows we are.

SYLVIA [*turning upon him*]. I'm not. What right has she — what right have any of you — to butt in on my affairs?

NANCY. Why, my dear, we all love you.

SYLVIA. You acted like it, didn't you? What have you all got against Dudley?

ALAN. Sylvia, I've told you that he was an embezzler, and that his only idea in marrying you was to use you to prevent mother prosecuting him.

SYLVIA. That's what you say. Mother, has Dudley taken any money from you?

NANCY. No.

SYLVIA. Well, Alan, mother ought to know.

ALAN. He confessed that he was short in his accounts.

SYLVIA. I didn't hear him.

ALAN. You weren't there when he was begging Gibbs to let him go.

SYLVIA. No. I was being made conspicuous, seated on a bench on the platform between two officers. Oh, I'll never forget it! [*She puts her hands to her face as though to shut out the memory. Momentarily her spirit is broken*]

NANCY [*whispering*]. Jeff, go to her now.

JEFFREY [*going to* SYLVIA]. I am sorry, dear, that all this had to happen — that you feel we've all conspired to disgrace you. But we were only trying to protect you.

SYLVIA. Protect me? If you wanted to protect me, why wait? You knew that I was going about with him.

NANCY. But, Sylvia, dear, your father didn't realize the sort of friends that Mr. Gillette had — introduced —

SYLVIA. He introduced me to the only friends he had. What do you know about them? You never met them.

JEFFREY. Sylvia, I forbid you to use that tone to your mother.

NANCY. Sylvia is right, Jeff. I judged them solely by what she told me of them.

SYLVIA. And while you were judging you passed sentence on Dudley, too, didn't you? You forbade my best friend seeing me again.

JEFFREY. Your mother had every right to do that.

SYLVIA. She had no right to make him feel that he wasn't fit to associate with me, when it was she who introduced him to me.

JEFFREY. She did not know that you were *associating* with him so intimately.

SYLVIA. No. She wasn't here, was she?

NANCY. No, Sylvia, I wasn't here.

JEFFREY. But I was. I'm to blame. I should have watched over you.

SYLVIA. But you didn't care what I was doing, where I was going, just so you were free to run around with Mrs. Brice.

[JEFFREY *flinches as though he had been struck*]

NANCY. Sylvia, how dare you talk like that to your father?

ALAN. Haven't you any respect? Haven't you any feeling? Can't you see that you are hurting father and mother cruelly?

SYLVIA. Well, haven't they hurt me?

ALAN [*indignantly*]. Hurt you! You ought to be down on your knees, thanking them for saving you from a marriage —

SYLVIA. Were you worrying about how cruelly you hurt mother when you told her about Peggy? Would you have been on your knees thanking them if they had tried to save you from marrying her?

JEFFREY. Stop, Sylvia! How can you? If it hadn't been for Peggy —

SYLVIA. I wouldn't have had to stand all this.

ALAN. You don't think it's pleasant for us, do you?

SYLVIA. There's an easy way of stopping it.

JEFFREY. How?

SYLVIA [*hysterically*]. Let me get out of here. [*She makes a rush for the door.* ALAN *stops her*]

JEFFREY. Where do you want to go?

SYLVIA [*jerking herself away from* ALAN]. Anywhere away from all of you! Why am I dragged back here, where nobody loves me, wants me? [*She throws herself in the armchair at the table, sobbing wildly*]

NANCY. Your father loves you, wants you.

SYLVIA. A lot he loves me! He loves Angy Brice.

ALAN. Who told you this damn lie?

SYLVIA [*sobbing*]. It's not a lie. Everybody has known but us that he was going to get rid of mother and marry Angy.

ALAN. Dad — my God! — this isn't true?

SYLVIA [*rising*]. It is true. Mother, aren't you going to leave Daddy?

[*There is a pause.* SYLVIA, ALAN *and* PEGGY *are waiting for the answer.* JEFFREY *stands with bowed head*]

NANCY. No.

JEFFREY [*turning, makes an effort to speak, and finally articulates*]. Nancy! [*Then, overcome, he turns away to the window*]

SYLVIA [*going to* NANCY]. Why, Dudley said — That's why I went away with him. I didn't know what would become of me when you separated. I thought my daddy had gone back on me.

[NANCY *folds her in her arms, kissing her.* JEFFREY *comes to them*]

JEFFREY. Your daddy will never go back on you, if you will only —
NANCY. Jeff, don't make conditions; we've both been wrong. We must be content with whatever Sylvia wants.

SYLVIA. I only want you all to want me.

NANCY. Oh, my dear! my dear!

PEGGY [*snivelling*]. Alan, where is Gillette?

ALAN. In an ambulance. [*He smiles and shows his clenched fist*]

THE END

THE EMPEROR JONES

(1920)

By Eugene O'Neill

EUGENE O'NEILL

THERE is no doubt that at the present moment Eugene O'Neill is the most considerable figure we have in the American Theatre. The spread of his fame has not been a local matter; he is very generally known in England, France and Germany, and his distinctive genius has received particular and careful analysis everywhere. At first flush it would seem that O'Neill had been overestimated, that undue value had been given to all of his work, whereas it is only some that warrants the distinction that has been credited to the whole. But an examination of much of the matter that has been written about him justifies us in saying that O'Neill has received his quota of criticism, has heard of his limitations quite as often as he has been praised. Yet, whatever the strictures, the fact remains that he is our most hopeful sign, combining in him a literary sense, an unusualness, a vitality of expression which are of the theatre as well as of the library, and an imagination which builds from its own particular angle.

In one sense, O'Neill is the typical Playboy of the Western World: by that, I do not mean that his spirit is volatile; on the contrary, it strikes us at times as being heavy laden. Nor do I mean that there is about O'Neill any of the imaginative lying of *Peer Gynt* or of *Christy*, for his imagination is rather steadyingly relentless; it moves, as Walter Eaton has said, speaking of "Beyond the Horizon" in comparison with Moody's "The Great Divide", inward, rather than in spirals upward toward exultation. But what I really mean is that his literary career has pretty well been determined by what he felt like doing. Though he went to Harvard to learn how to write plays, he went afterwards to the Provincetown Playhouse where he found a group willing to present whatever he had to give them, in whatever form, under whatever condition of scene or dialogue. There was no box-office lure to O'Neill, no dalliance with expediency so as to win a manager's favor. Indeed, on that score alone he was a new figure in the American Theatre.

So often has it been repeated, one might almost say that the American people knew by heart the saga of Eugene O'Neill. This may be because he is the rare example of a man in the theatre with any sort of a personal background from which literature comes. One can explain Galsworthy, and Walpole, and Swinnerton, because back of them there is an experience of a strictly class character. Even more strikingly so is the literary background of Kipling and Conrad, who have dealt with the things they have seen and believed in. O'Neill is the rare exception in the American literary life, where he has brought to his work a burning sense of the material he deals with. And even though, at the present moment, he is a little self-conscious about it — just as Dunsany became self-conscious when he had been exalted by the Little Theatre groups — his individuality stamps everything he does, and his method has vigor if not always perfect form.

A glance at the list of plays written by him would lead one to conclude that he has no conventional attitude toward form, that he bends it to his own necessity, that he will write a one-act play in many scenes, and end his play at the end of th second act if he deems that his theme does not require an additional act. He break the canons of the theatre, and it remains to be seen if he has established or justifie any new ones. For even though outwardly he seems to be restless about the cor ventional molds of the theatre, he resorts to many theatrical devices which tak away from the wholly realistic or naturalistic approach of his intellect. A clos examination of "The Emperor Jones" will reveal that, though the narrative broken eight times by a change of scene, the emotional theme is unified, continuou and not of the long-play character. For that reason one might well consider it one-act drama.

The emotional aspect of O'Neill's work has definiteness, and directs his dia logue, his situations, his characters into channels of the most impassioned poetry This we claim despite the fact that sometimes, as Von Hoffmansthal has writter the dialogue has a somewhat detached relationship. In the midst of the roughnes and coarseness and sordidness of his theme, he will rise to the heights of the mos exquisite rhythmical expression, whether of love or of social belief — but alway from the angle of the nether world of spirit. The bitterness that he sometime shows, the restlessness of vision that looks upon the world and sees very little tha is good, the youthfulness that has experienced so far only the agony of looking from limited range, sometimes forget themselves in moments of sheer dramatic exultation which are almost wholly spiritual, if not quite so. I have failed to see in O'Neill ai enemy to the theatrical conventions of old. He is melodramatic when he wants t be; "Desire Under the Elms" thunders with many moments of sheer rasping overemphasis. He is sentimental at times. But he is not cheap or tawdry for the sake of catching idle curiosity. Inasmuch as he does not see life whole, but from the bridge of the fo'castle, he can fall into stilted areas where knowledge and experienc are replaced by imitation — as, for example, the awkward artificiality of the scene with the society girl on the steamer deck in the second scene of "The Hairy Ape."

O'Neill stands as an example of how success of a widespread nature may be wrung from the most disquieting surroundings. Out of most unpropitious beginnings both he and the Provincetown Players emerge with certain well-earned glory. Just as the Neighborhood Playhouse fostered Dunsany, so this group, born on the wharf at Provincetown, Massachusetts, and hammering at theatrical conditions from their stable theatre on Macdougal Street in New York, has been a large factor in the artistic life of O'Neill. On the other hand he has had something striking to contribute. Life had hit him hard before he put pen to paper: he had fought against conventional education, so that preparatory school and Princeton were places to rebel against; he had been restless in earning a living, and had run away to sea; he had faced the agony of a future with pulmonary tuberculosis; he had served his apprenticeship on a small newspaper in New London, Connecticut — living on a bare pittance which his father, the well-known actor, James O'Neill, allowed him with the idea that he couldn't run away again on such an income. And then, through the kindly incentive of Clayton Hamilton, he went to Harvard and joined Baker's class, Workshop 47. Before that he had satisfied his taste for the theatre: he had played with his father in a tabloid version of the famous "Monte Cristo"; he had been assistant manager for Viola Allen in "The White Sister."

In the long winter that he spent in New London, communing very largely with himself, experience began shaping itself. The incentive to write began to urge him forward. He groped in form, but expression came hot and unregulated. The

Harvard course further urged him forward, and Baker may be said to have fathered him, as he has fathered so many, in the ways of technique. He emerged from Harvard by no means a perfect technician, but with an originality that won for him at college a distinction far above his fellow students. At his father's expense, in 1914, he issued his first volume of plays, "Thirst", and then went forth to find what he should find.

The young man's equipment was a striking one. He had no mistaken notions about laying siege to Broadway. He went to his job with his mind full of burning concepts of character, injustice, ugliness, superstition, vulgar blows that were nearer the brute than civilization. The under dog interested him because he had been the under dog. He had undergone bitter and rough contact with life. "The Moon of the Caribbees", "Bound East for Cardiff", "The Long Voyage Home" and "In the Zone", which were about to be written, were a vivid reflection of what was seething in his mind. It is thus, one imagines, that John Masefield — O'Neill's counterpart in experience — was urged to write "Dauber", among the most wonderful sea narratives in the field of English poetry — and it was thus he later gave us "The Widow in the Bye Street."

The early volume, "Thirst", gave measure of O'Neill's tragic approach, — tragedy that is colorful, that is sordid and terrible, as in "The Web." In most of this work, the motive of the sea entered — shipwrecks, icebergs, wireless, tramp steamer decks, the rush of water, the cruelty of the wind, and the after calm of sun and starlight. There is something fatalistic in all this, something outside of faith, of any spiritual hope; a giving over to the working of chance, a weighing down hopelessly by something superimposed from without. O'Neill has not yet passed from this phase of his social philosophy. It is a bare feather in the scales which sends the wrong brother in "Beyond the Horizon" to sea, and keeps the poet on the farm.

At this time, O'Neill unfortunately did not put himself into the rigorous path of form; had he done so he might have escaped some of the murkiness of his later plays. His dramas are always rich in background, and the story of each play has ample possibility, but the characterization is too often dimmed by the lack of proper balance in the handling of elements at the dramatist's command. This leaves many of his plays lacking in the correctness of their spiritual content. For example, there is a statement of agony in "Warnings", when the wireless operator, who is deaf, fails to catch the message which might save a sinking ship, but there is wanting the actual agony itself. Yet such limitations did not affect the dramatic strength of these first pieces. And his conceiving of the little plays which afterwards became known as the "SS. Glencairn" cycle would indicate that O'Neill did not throw out his plays from an instinct which was unprompted by artistic feeling. To see "The Moon of the Caribbees", "Bound East for Cardiff", "The Long Voyage Home" and "In the Zone" separately — or to read them so — results in striking individual effectiveness; but to follow them in quick succession leaves a more vivid impression, a stronger understanding of their binding mood.

When "Beyond the Horizon" was given to the theatre, through the initiative of a progressive manager, John D. Williams, Eugene O'Neill — without any compromises or parleying — entered as a factor in the larger theatre. His play was not to be a money-maker but a soul stirrer. When one is fresh and young, beyond the horizon there may be minarets of gold; but on a New England farm, the hills bind one and choke one and make death a welcome boon, especially if the romantic mistake in life smites with all its hideous entanglements. At that time "Beyon the Horizon" was the most distinctive tragedy America had produced.

The elements detected in the theme of this play were not alone thought out an woven into one product. They were elements in the personal outlook of Eugen O'Neill himself. "Desire Under the Elms" is perhaps a more relentless workin out of the New England motive, but with less successful effect. Where in his firs play O'Neill gave his story with a certain broad sweep, in the later drama he be comes such a bitter critic of the New England spirit, that he is not able to see aroun his subject, but is blinded by the injustice of it. In the new play, there are marvel lous moments — just as there are in "Anna Christie" — and these moments ar stark poetry down to the bone of the emotion, so to speak — love scenes with pulsing life to them. But there are also murky screens of crude thinking, and unsatisfying conclusions. "Desire Under the Elms" shows that O'Neill has not yet mastered structure. Yet through the play there runs the dominant mood that leaves on shaken by the realization of something uncommon, if not wholly great.

When "The Emperor Jones" was played, there were certain elements of humor in the text that revealed a new phase of O'Neill — one that is only occasionally flashed to the fore. For his nature is not one that begets humor. You find in him the note of Job, or the romantic darkness of The Ancient Mariner. Yet in his study of the negro character, *Jones*, ex-Pullman porter and ex-convict, there is a profoundness of study that catches the glint of the negro's native wit.

To this play "All God's Chillun Got Wings" bears the same relationship that "Desire Under the Elms" does to "Beyond the Horizon." In one the story motivates above the conditions; in the other the reverse happens. That is why there was so much discussion about the racial elements underlying "All God's Chillun Got Wings." O'Neill is reported to have said about this latter play :

The persons who have attacked my play have given the impression that I make *Jim Harris* a symbolical representative of his race and *Ella* of the white race — that by uniting them I urge intermarriage. Now *Jim* and *Ella* are special cases and represent no one but themselves. Of course, the struggle between them is primarily the result of the difference in their racial heritage. It is their characters, the gap between them and their struggle to bridge it which interests me as a dramatist, nothing else. I didn't create the gap, this cleavage — it exists. And members of both races do struggle to bridge it with love. Whether they should or not isn't in my play.

It is one thing to state a problem mathematically, it is another to clothe it in emotion, and leave it for what it is worth. O'Neill is prone thus to stand aside impersonally and watch the tumult. One can see his desire to disregard the ethnological consequences, his daring, and a certain unattached justice to his case. But as soon as he gives a realistic treatment to his subject, he must look for realistic (literal) interpretation from the public. Such social problem did not confront him in "The Emperor Jones." Here he was dealing with tribe, with folklore superstition, with inherited emotion, and he conveyed it unerringly, breaking up his story into a number of scenes, but binding them together on the stage by a continuous beating of the tomtom, and in the printed play, by the increasing growth of racial fear.

"Anna Christie" is O'Neill's most successful play, measured by the standard of the box-office and the moving-picture. It is the one he is least interested in, for the simple reason that its structure is of the order known to the theatre, and O'Neill ems to have the desire to bring to the theatre that which is not so well known, that hich is created for its own sake. He is much more interested in the expressionism "The Hairy Ape", in the articulate soul quality of his two jealous lovers in Welded", than in "Anna Christie." Yet here is the type of play the English itics said was derived from Synge.

The fact is, O'Neill leads us to believe, from what he has written, that if he has model, it is Strindberg. He writes:

We have endured too much from the banality of surfaces. Strindberg knew id suffered with our struggle years before many of us were born. He expresses by intensifying the method of his time and by foreshadowing both in content id form the methods to come. All that is enduring in what we loosely call "ex-ressionism" — all that is artistically valid and sound theatre — can be clearly aced back through Wedekind to Strindberg's "The Dream Play", "There Are rimes and Crimes", "The Spook Sonata", etc.

Every year now the name of Eugene O'Neill is heralded among the season's xpectant offerings. Where once the manager thought him an exotic figure, he to-day hailed on the Broadway which neither reared him nor molded him in its nage. He has been true to his Provincetown atmosphere, and is now one of the irectors of the Macdougal Street Theatre, where he is its chief attraction, filling s well a conspicuous place in the life of the Greenwich Village Theatre, also under ie Provincetown direction. He lives on his farm at Ridgefield, Connecticut, in ie winter; he goes to his home at Provincetown, overlooking the sea, in the sum-ier. He is a dramatist who is aloof from the life of the American Theatre, but ho means much to that life. For at present he is the one man writing for the tage, the quality of whose work is neither accidental nor imitative. He appeals irough innate forcefulness of theme and treatment. He makes no compromises. nd the significant thing is that the American Theatre has reached that stage where is eager that he should do that which he is prompted to do.

THE EMPEROR JONES

By EUGENE O'NEILL

CHARACTERS

BRUTUS JONES, *Emperor*

HENRY SMITHERS, *A Cockney Trader*

AN OLD NATIVE WOMAN

LEM, *A Native Chief*

SOLDIERS, *Adherents of Lem*

The Little Formless Fears; Jeff; The Negro Convicts; The Prison Guard; The Planters; The Auctioneer; The Slaves; The Congo Witch-Doctor; The Crocodile God.

The action of the play takes place on an island in the West Indies as yet not self determined by White Marines. The form of native government is, for the time being an Empire.

———

SCENES

THE EMPEROR JONES

SCENE ONE

The audience chamber in the palace of the Emperor — a spacious, high-ceilinged room with bare, white-washed walls. The floor is of white tiles. In the rear, to the left of center, a wide archway giving out on a portico with white pillars. The palace is evidently situated on high ground for beyond the portico nothing can be seen but a vista of distant hills, their summits crowned with thick groves of palm trees. In the right wall, center, a smaller arched doorway leading to the living quarters of the palace. The room is bare of furniture with the exception of one huge chair made of uncut wood which stands at center, its back to rear. This is very apparently the Emperor's throne. It is painted a dazzling, eye-smiting scarlet. There is a brilliant orange cushion on the seat and another smaller one is placed on the floor to serve as a footstool. Strips of matting, dyed scarlet, lead from the foot of the throne to the two entrances. is late afternoon but the sunlight still blazes yellowly beyond the portico and there is an oppressive burden of exhausting heat in the air.

the curtain rises, a native negro woman sneaks in cautiously from the entrance on the right. She is very old, dressed in cheap calico, bare-footed, a red bandana handkerchief covering all but a few stray wisps of white hair. A bundle bound in colored cloth is carried over her shoulder on the end of a stick. She hesitates beside the doorway, peering back as if in extreme dread of being discovered. Then she begins to glide noiselessly, a step at a time, toward the doorway in the rear. At this moment, SMITHERS appears beneath the portico.

ITHERS is a tall, stoop-shouldered man about forty. His bald head, perched on a long neck with an enormous Adam's apple, looks like an egg. The tropics have tanned his naturally pasty face with its small, sharp features to a sickly yellow, and native rum has painted his pointed nose to a startling red. His little, washy-blue eyes are red-rimmed and dart about him like a ferret's. His expression is one of unscrupulous meanness, cowardly and dangerous. He is dressed in a worn riding suit of dirty white drill, puttees, spurs, and wears a white cork helmet. A cartridge belt with an automatic revolver is around his waist. He carries a riding whip in his hand. He sees the woman and stops to watch her suspiciously. Then, making up his mind, he steps quickly on tiptoe into the room. The woman, looking back over her shoulder continually, does not see him until it is too late. When she does SMITHERS springs forward and grabs her firmly by the shoulder. She struggles to get away, fiercely but silently.*

SMITHERS [*tightening his grasp — roughly*]. Easy! None o' that, me birdie. You can't wriggle out, now I got me 'ooks on yer.

WOMAN [*seeing the uselessness of struggling, gives way to frantic terror, and sinks to the ground, embracing his knees supplicatingly*]. No tell him! No tell him, Mister!

SMITHERS [*with great curiosity*]. Tell 'im? [*Then scornfully*] Oh, you mean 'is bloomin' Majesty. What's the gaime, any 'ow? What are you sneakin' away for? Been stealin' a bit, I s'pose. [*He taps her bundle with his riding whip significantly*]

WOMAN [*shaking her head vehemently*]. No, me no steal.

SMITHERS. Bloody liar! But tell

431

me what's up. There's somethin' funny goin' on. I smelled it in the air first thing I got up this mornin'. You blacks are up to some devilment. This palace of 'is is like a bleedin' tomb. Where's all the 'ands? [*The woman keeps sullenly silent.* SMITHERS *raises his whip threateningly*] Ow, yer won't, won't yer? I'll show yer what's what.

WOMAN [*coweringly*]. I tell, Mister. You no hit. They go — all go. [*She makes a sweeping gesture toward the hills in the distance*]

SMITHERS. Run away — to the 'ills?

WOMAN. Yes, Mister. Him Emperor — Great Father. [*She touches her forehead to the floor with a quick mechanical jerk*] Him sleep after eat. Then they go — all go. Me old woman. Me left only. Now me go too.

SMITHERS [*his astonishment giving way to an immense, mean satisfaction*]. Ow! So that's the ticket! Well, I know bloody well wot's in the air — when they runs orf to the 'ills. The tom-tom 'll be thumping out there bloomin' soon. [*With extreme vindictiveness*] And I'm bloody glad of it, for one! Serve 'im right! Puttin' on airs, the stinkin' nigger! 'Is Majesty! Gawd blimey! I only 'opes I'm there when they takes 'im out to shoot 'im. [*Suddenly*] 'E's still 'ere all right, ain't 'e?

WOMAN. Him sleep.

SMITHERS. E's bound to find out soon as 'e wakes up. 'E's cunnin' enough to know when 'is time's come. [*He goes to the doorway on right and whistles shrilly with his fingers in his mouth. The old woman springs to her feet and runs out of the doorway, rear.* SMITHERS *goes after her, reaching for his revolver*] Stop or I'll shoot! [*Then stopping — indifferently*] Pop orf then, if yer like, yer black cow. [*He stands in the doorway, looking after her*]

[JONES *enters from the right. He is a tall, powerfully-built, full-blooded negro of middle age. His features are typically negroid, yet there is something decidedly distinctive about his face — an underlying strength of will, a hardy, self-reliant confidence in himself that inspires respect. His eyes are alive with a keen, cunning intelligence. In manner he is shrewd, suspicious, evasive. He wears a light blue uniform coat, sprayed with brass buttons, heavy gold chevrons on his shoulders, gold braid on the* collar, cuffs, etc. His pants ar bright red with a light blue strip down the side. Patent leather lace boots with brass spurs, and a be with a long-barreled, pearl-handle revolver in a holster complete his make up. Yet there is something not alto gether ridiculous about his grandeur He has a way of carrying it off]

JONES [*not seeing any one — greatl irritated and blinking sleepily — shouts*] Who dare whistle dat way in my palace Who dare wake up de Emperor? I' git de hide frayled off some o' you nig gers sho'!

SMITHERS [*showing himself — in manner half-afraid and half-defiant*]. I was me whistled to yer. [*As* JONE *frowns angrily*] I got news for yer.

JONES [*putting on his suavest manner which fails to cover up his contempt for th white man*]. Oh, it's you, Miste Smithers. [*He sits down on his throne with easy dignity*] What news you go to tell me?

SMITHERS [*coming close to enjoy his dis comfiture*]. Don't yer notice nothin funny today?

JONES [*coldly*]. Funny? No. ain't perceived nothin' of de kind!

SMITHERS. Then yer ain't so foxy a I thought yer was. Where's all you court? [*Sarcastically*] the Generals an the Cabinet Ministers and all?

JONES [*imperturbably*]. Where de mostly runs to minute I closes my eye — drinkin' rum and talkin' big down i de town. [*Sarcastically*] How com you don't know dat? Ain't you sousin with 'em most every day?

SMITHERS [*stung but pretending indif ference — with a wink*]. That's part o the day's work. I got ter — ain't I — in my business?

JONES [*contemptuously*]. Yo' busi ness!

SMITHERS [*imprudently enraged*] Gawd blimey, you was glad enough fo me ter take yer in on it when you lande here first. You didn' 'ave no 'igh an mighty airs in them days!

JONES [*his hand going to his revolve like a flash — menacingly*]. Talk polite white man! Talk polite, you heah me I'm boss heah now, is you fergettin' [*The Cockney seems about to challenge thi last statement with the facts but somethin in the other's eyes holds and cowes him*]

SMITHERS [*in a cowardly whine*]. N 'arm meant, old top.

JONES [*condescendingly*]. I accepts yo' apology. [*Lets his hand fall from his revolver*] No use'n you rakin' up ole times. What I was den is one thing. What I is now's another. You didn't let me in on yo' crooked work out o' no kind feelin's dat time. I done de dirty work fo' you — and most o' de brain work, too, fo' dat matter — and I was yu'th money to you, dat's de reason.

SMITHERS. Well, blimey, I give yer a start, didn't I — when no one else would. I wasn't afraid to 'ire you like the rest was — count of the story about your breakin' jail back in the States.

JONES. No, you didn't have no cuse to look down on me fo' dat. You been in jail you'self more'n once.

SMITHERS [*furiously*]. It's a lie! [*Then trying to pass it off by an attempt at scorn*] Garn! Who told yer that fairy tale?

JONES. Dey's some tings I ain't got to be tole. I kin see 'em in folk's eyes. [*Then after a pause — meditatively*] Yes, you sho' give me a start. And it didn't take long from dat time to git dese fool, woods' niggers right where I wanted em. [*With pride*] From stowaway to emperor in two years! Dat's goin' some!

SMITHERS [*with curiosity*]. And I bet you got yer pile o' money 'id safe some place.

JONES [*with satisfaction*]. I sho' has! And it's in a foreign bank where no isson don't ever git it out but me no matter what come. You didn't s'pose I was holdin' down dis Emperor job for de glory in it, did you? Sho'! De fuss and glory part of it, dat's only to turn de heads o' de low-flung, bush niggers dat's here. Dey wants de big circus show for deir money. I gives it to 'em an' I gits de money. [*With a grin*] De long green, dat's me every time! [*Then rebukingly*] But you ain't got no kick agin me, Smithers. I'se paid you back all you done for me many times. Ain't I pertected you and winked at all de crooked tradin' you been doin' right out in de broad day. Sho' I has — and me makin' laws to stop it at de same time! [*He chuckles*]

SMITHERS [*grinning*]. But, meanin' no 'arm, you been grabbin' right and left yourself, ain't yer? Look at the taxes you've put on 'em! Blimey! You've squeezed 'em dry!

JONES [*chuckling*]. No, dey ain't *all* dry yet. I'se still heah, ain't I?

SMITHERS [*smiling at his secret thought*]. They're dry right now, you'll find out. [*Changing the subject abruptly*] And as for me breakin' laws, you've broke 'em all yerself just as fast as yer made 'em.

JONES. Ain't I de Emperor? De laws don't go for him. [*Judicially*] You heah what I tells you, Smithers. Dere's little stealin' like you does, and dere's big stealin' like I does. For de little stealin' dey gits you in jail soon or late. For de big stealin' dey makes you Emperor and puts you in de Hall o' Fame when you croaks. [*Reminiscently*] If dey's one thing I learns in ten years on de Pullman ca's listenin' to de white quality talk, it's dat same fact. And when I gits a chance to use it I winds up Emperor in two years.

SMITHERS [*unable to repress the genuine admiration of the small fry for the large*]. Yes, yer turned the bleedin' trick, all right. Blimey, I never seen a bloke 'as 'ad the bloomin' luck you 'as.

JONES [*severely*]. Luck? What you mean — luck?

SMITHERS. I suppose you'll say as that swank about the silver bullet ain't luck — and that was what first got the fool blacks on yer side the time of the revolution, wasn't it?

JONES [*with a laugh*]. Oh, dat silver bullet! Sho' was luck! But I makes dat luck, you heah? I loads de dice! Yessuh! When dat murderin' nigger ole Lem hired to kill me takes aim ten feet away and his gun misses fire and I shoots him dead, what you heah me say?

SMITHERS. You said yer'd got a charm so's no lead bullet'd kill yer. You was so strong only a silver bullet could kill yer, you told 'em. Blimey, wasn't that swank for yer — and plain, fat-'eaded luck?

JONES [*proudly*]. I got brains and I uses 'em quick. Dat ain't luck.

SMITHERS. Yer know they wasn't 'ardly liable to get no silver bullets. And it was luck 'e didn't 'it you that time.

JONES [*laughing*]. And dere all dem fool bush niggers was kneelin' down and bumpin' deir heads on de ground like I was a miracle out o' de Bible. Oh Lawd, from dat time on I has dem all eatin' out of my hand. I cracks de whip and dey jumps through.

SMITHERS [*with a sniff*]. Yankee bluff done it.

JONES. Ain't a man's talkin' big what makes him big — long as he makes folks believe it? Sho', I talks large when I ain't got nothin' to back it up, but I ain't talkin' wild just de same. I knows I kin fool 'em — I *knows* it — and dat's backin' enough fo' my game. And ain't I got to learn deir lingo and teach some of dem English befo' I kin talk to 'em? Ain't dat wuk? You ain't never learned ary word er it, Smithers, in de ten years you been heah, dough you knows it's money in you' pocket tradin' wid 'em if you does. But you'se too shiftless to take de trouble.

SMITHERS [*flushing*]. Never mind about me. What's this I've 'eard about yer really 'avin' a silver bullet moulded for yourself?

JONES. It's playin' out my bluff. I has de silver bullet moulded and I tells 'em when de time comes I kills myself wid it. I tells 'em dat's 'cause I'm de on'y man in de world big enuff to git me. No use'n deir tryin'. And dey falls down and bumps deir heads. [*He laughs*] I does dat so's I kin take a walk in peace widout no jealous nigger gun- nin' at me from behind de trees.

SMITHERS [*astonished*]. Then you 'ad it made — 'onest?

JONES. Sho' did. Heah she be. [*He takes out his revolver, breaks it, and takes the silver bullet out of one chamber*] Five lead an' dis silver baby at de last. Don't she shine pretty? [*He holds it in his hand, looking at it admiringly, as if strangely fascinated*]

SMITHERS. Let me see. [*Reaches out his hand for it*]

JONES [*harshly*]. Keep yo' hands whar dey b'long, white man. [*He replaces it in the chamber and puts the revolver back on his hip*]

SMITHERS [*snarling*]. Gawd blimey! Think I'm a bleedin' thief, you would.

JONES. No, 'tain't dat. I knows you'se scared to steal from me. On'y I ain't 'lowin' nary body to touch dis baby. She's my rabbit's foot.

SMITHERS [*sneering*]. A bloomin' charm, wot? [*Venomously*] Well, you'll need all the bloody charms you 'as before long, s' 'elp me!

JONES [*judicially*]. Oh, I'se good for six months yit 'fore dey gits sick o' my game. Den, when I sees trouble comin', I makes my getaway.

SMITHERS. Ho! You got it all planned, ain't yer?

JONES. I ain't no fool. I knows dis Emperor's time is sho't. Dat why I

make hay when de sun shine. Was yo thinkin' I'se aimin' to hold down di job for life? No, suh! What good i gittin' money if you stays back in di raggedy country? I wants action whe I spends. And when I sees dese nigger gittin' up deir nerve to tu'n me out, an I'se got all de money in sight, I resign on de spot and beats it quick.

SMITHERS. Where to?

JONES. None o' yo' business.

SMITHERS. Not back to the blood States, I'll lay my oath.

JONES [*suspiciously*]. Why don't I [*Then with an easy laugh*] You mea 'count of dat story 'bout me breakin from jail back dere? Dat's all talk.

SMITHERS [*skeptically*]. Ho, yes!

JONES [*sharply*]. You ain't 'sinuatin I'se a liar, is you?

SMITHERS [*hastily*]. No, Gawd strik me! I was only thinkin' o' the blood lies you told the blacks 'ere about killin white men in the States.

JONES [*angered*]. How come dey'r lies?

SMITHERS. You'd 'ave been in ja if you 'ad, wouldn't yer then? [*Wit venom*] And from what I've 'eard, ain't 'ealthy for a black to kill a whit man in the States. They burns 'em i oil, don't they?

JONES [*with cool deadliness*]. Yo mean lynchin' 'd scare me? Well, tells you, Smithers, maybe I does ki one white man back dere. Maybe does. And maybe I kills another righ heah 'fore long if he don't look out.

SMITHERS [*trying to force a laugh*]. was on'y spoofin' yer. Can't yer take joke? And you was just sayin' you' never been in jail.

JONES [*in the same tone — slightl boastful*]. Maybe I goes to jail dere f gettin' in an argument wid razors ova a crap game. Maybe I gits twent years when dat colored man di Maybe I gits in 'nother argument wid d prison guard was overseer ovah us whe we're wukin' de road. Maybe he hit me wid a whip and I splits his head wi a shovel and runs away and files de chai off my leg and gits away safe. Maybe does all dat an' maybe I don't. It's story I tells you so's you knows I'se d kind of man dat if you evah repeats on word of it, I ends yo' stealin' on di yearth mighty damn quick!

SMITHERS [*terrified*]. Think I'd peac on yer? Not me! Ain't I always bee yer friend?

JONES [*suddenly relaxing*]. Sho' you as — and you better be.

SMITHERS [*recovering his composure — and with it his malice*]. And just to show 'er it his malice]. And just to show yer I'm yer friend, I'll tell yer that bit o' news I was goin' to.

JONES. Go ahead! Shoot de piece. Must be bad news from de happy way you look.

SMITHERS [*warningly*]. Maybe it's gettin' time for you to resign — with that bloomin' silver bullet, wot? [*He finishes with a mocking grin*]

JONES [*puzzled*]. What's dat you say? Talk plain.

SMITHERS. Ain't noticed any of the guards or servants about the place today, I 'aven't.

JONES [*carelessly*]. Dey're all out in de garden sleepin' under de trees. When I sleeps, dey sneaks a sleep, too, and I pretends I never suspicions it. All I got to do is to ring de bell and dey come flyin', makin' a bluff dey was wukin' all de time.

SMITHERS [*in the same mocking tone*]. Ring the bell now an' you'll bloody well see what I means.

JONES [*startled to alertness, but preserving the same careless tone*]. Sho' I rings. [*He reaches below the throne and pulls out a big, common dinner bell which is painted the same vivid scarlet as the throne. He rings this vigorously — then stops to listen. Then he goes to both doors, rings again, and looks out*]

SMITHERS [*watching him with malicious satisfaction, after a pause — mockingly*]. The bloody ship is sinkin' an' the bleedin' rats 'as slung their 'ooks.

JONES [*in a sudden fit of anger flings the bell clattering into a corner*]. Low-flung, woods' niggers! [*Then catching SMITHERS' eye on him, he controls himself and suddenly bursts into a low chuckling laugh*] Reckon I overplays my hand dis once! A man can't take de pot on a bob-tailed flush all de time. Was I bayin' I'd sit in six months mo'? Well, 'se changed my mind den. I cashes in and resigns de job of Emperor right dis minute.

SMITHERS [*with real admiration*]. Blimey, but you're a cool bird, and no mistake.

JONES. No use'n fussin'. When I knows de game's up I kisses it goodbye widout no long waits. Dey've all run off to de hills, ain't dey?

SMITHERS. Yes — every bleedin' man jack of 'em.

JONES. Den de revolution is at de post. And de Emperor better git his feet smokin' up de trail. [*He starts for the door in rear*]

SMITHERS. Goin' out to look for your 'orse? Yer won't find any. They steals the 'orses first thing. Mine was gone when I went for 'im this mornin'. That's wot first give me a suspicion of wot was up.

JONES [*alarmed for a second, scratches his head, then philosophically*]. Well, den I hoofs it. Feet, do yo' duty! [*He pulls out a gold watch and looks at it*] Three-thuty. Sundown's at six-thuty or dereabouts. [*Puts his watch back — with cool confidence*] I got plenty o' time to make it easy.

SMITHERS. Don't be so bloomin' sure of it. They'll be after you 'ot and 'eavy. Ole Lem is at the bottom o' this business an' 'e 'ates you like 'ell. 'E'd rather do for you than eat 'is dinner, 'e would!

JONES [*scornfully*]. Dat fool no-count nigger! Does you think I'se scared o' him? I stands him on his thick head more'n once befor' dis, and I does it again if he comes in my way — [*Fiercely*] And dis time I leave him a dead nigger fo' sho'!

SMITHERS. You'll 'ave to cut through the big forest — an' those blacks 'ere can sniff and follow a trail in the dark like 'ounds. You'd 'ave to 'ustle to get through that forest in twelve hours even if you knew all the bloomin' trails like a native.

JONES [*with indignant scorn*]. Look-a-heah, white man! Does you think I'se a natural bo'n fool? Give me credit fo' havin' some sense, fo' Lawd's sake! Don't you s'pose I'se looked ahead and made sho' of all de chances? I'se gone out in dat big forest, pretendin' to hunt, so many times dat I knows it high an' low like a book. I could go through on dem trails wid my eyes shut. [*With great contempt*] Think dese ig'nerent bush niggers dat ain't got brains enuff to know deir own names even can catch Brutus Jones? Huh, I s'pects not! Not on yo' life! Why, man, de white men went after me wid bloodhounds where I come from an' I jes' laughs at 'em. It's a shame to fool dese black trash around heah, dey're so easy. You watch me, man. I'll make dem look sick, I will. I'll be 'cross de plain to de edge of de forest by time dark comes. Once in de woods in de night, dey got a swell chance o' findin' dis baby! Dawn tomorrow I'll be out at de oder side and on de coast whar dat French gunboat is stayin'. She picks me up, take me to Martinique when she go dar, and dere I is safe wid a mighty big bankroll in my jeans. It's easy as rollin' off a log.

SMITHERS [*maliciously*]. But s'posin' somethin' 'appens wrong 'an they do nab yer?

JONES [*decisively*]. Dey don't — dat's de answer.

SMITHERS. But, just for argyment's sake — what'd you do?

JONES [*frowning*]. I'se got five lead bullets in dis gun good enuff fo' common bush niggers — and after dat I got de silver bullet left to cheat 'em out o' gittin' me.

SMITHERS [*jeeringly*]. Ho, I was fergettin' that silver bullet. You'll bump yourself orf in style, won't yer? Blimey!

JONES [*gloomily*]. You kin bet yo' whole roll on one thing, white man. Dis baby plays out his string to de end and when he quits, he quits wid a bang de way he ought. Silver bullet ain't none too good for him when he go, dat's a fac'! [*Then shaking off his nervousness — with a confident laugh*] Sho'! What is I talkin' about? Ain't come to dat yit and I never will — not wid trash niggers like dese yere. [*Boastfully*] Silver bullet bring me luck anyway. I kin outguess, outrun, outfight, an' outplay de whole lot o' dem all ovah de board any time o' de day er night! You watch me! [*From the distant hills comes the faint, steady thump of a tom-tom, low and vibrating. It starts at a rate exactly corresponding to normal pulse beat — 72 to the minute — and continues at a gradually accelerating rate from this point uninterruptedly to the very end of the play. JONES starts at the sound. A strange look of apprehension creeps into his face for a moment as he listens. Then he asks, with an attempt to regain his most casual manner*] What's dat drum beatin' fo'?

SMITHERS [*with a mean grin*]. For you. That means the bleedin' ceremony 'as started. I've 'eard it before and I knows.

JONES. Cer'mony? What cer'mony?

SMITHERS. The blacks is 'oldin' a bloody meetin', 'avin' a war dance, gettin' their courage worked up b'fore they starts after you.

JONES. Let dem! Dey'll sho' need it!

SMITHERS. And they're there 'oldin' their 'eathen religious service — makin no end of devil spells and charms to 'el 'em against your silver bullet. [*H guffaws loudly*] Blimey, but they'r balmy as 'ell!

JONES [*a tiny bit awed and shaken i spite of himself*]. Huh! Takes more' dat to scare dis chicken!

SMITHERS [*scenting the other's feelin — maliciously*]. Ter-night when it' pitch black in the forest, they'll 'av their pet devils and ghosts 'oundin' afte you. You'll find yer bloody 'air'll b standin' on end before termorrov mornin'. [*Seriously*] It's a bleedin queer place, that stinkin' forest, eve in daylight. Yer don't know wha might 'appen in there, it's that rotte still. Always sends the cold shiver down my back minute I gits in it.

JONES [*with a contemptuous sniff*]. ain't no chicken-liver like you is. Tree an' me, we'se friends, and dar's a ful moon comin' bring me light. And le dem po' niggers make all de fool spell dey'se a min' to. Does yo' s'pect I's silly enuff to b'lieve in ghosts an' ha'nts an' all dat ole woman's talk? G'long white man! You ain't talkin' to me. [*With a chuckle*] Doesn't you know dey's got to do wid a man was member in good standin' o' de Baptist Church? Sho' I was dat when I was porter on de Pullmans, befo' I gits into my little trouble. Let dem try deir heathen tricks. De Baptist Church done perfect me and land dem all in hell. [*Then with more confident satisfaction*] And I'se got little silver bullet o' my own, don't forgit!

SMITHERS. Ho! You 'aven't give much 'eed to your Baptist Church since you been down 'ere. I've 'eard myself you 'ad turned yer coat an' was takin' up with their blarsted witch-doctors, or whatever the 'ell yer calls the swine.

JONES [*vehemently*]. I pretends to! Sho' I pretends! Dat's part o' my game from de fust. If I finds out dem niggers believes dat black is white, den I yells it out louder 'n deir loudest. It don't git me nothin' to do missionary work for de Baptist Church. I'se after de coin, an' I lays my Jesus on de shelf for de time bein'. [*Stops abruptly to look at his watch — alertly*] But I ain't got de time to waste no more fool talk wid you. I'se gwine away from heah dis secon'. [*He reaches in under the throne and pulls out an expensive Panama hat with a bright* multi-colored band and sets it jauntily on is head] So long, white man! [*With a grin*] See you in jail sometime, maybe!

SMITHERS. Not me, you won't. Well, I wouldn't be in yer bloody boots or no bloomin' money, but 'ere's wishin' yer luck just the same.

JONES [*contemptuously*]. You're de frightenedest man evah I see! I tells you I'se safe's 'f I was in New York City. It takes dem niggers from now to dark to git up de nerve to start somethin'. By dat time, I'se got a head start dey never kotch up wid.

SMITHERS [*maliciously*]. Give my regards to any ghosts yer meets up with.

JONES [*grinning*]. If dat ghost got money, I'll tell him never ha'nt you less'n he wants to lose it.

SMITHERS [*flattered*]. Garn! [*Then curiously*] Ain't yer takin' no luggage with yer?

JONES. I travels light when I wants to move fast. And I got tinned grub buried on de edge o' de forest [*Boastfully*] Now say dat I don't look ahead an' use my brains! [*With a wide, liberal gesture*] I will all dat's left in de palace to you — and you better grab all you kin sneak away wid befo' dey gits here.

SMITHERS [*gratefully*]. Righto — and thanks ter yer. [*As* JONES *walks toward the door in rear — cautioningly*] Say! Look 'ere, you ain't goin' out that way, are yer?

JONES. Does you think I'd slink out de back door like a common nigger? I'se Emperor yit, ain't I? And de Emperor Jones leaves de way he comes, and dat black trash don't dare stop him — not yit, leastways. [*He stops for a moment in the doorway, listening to the far-off but insistent beat of the tom-tom*] Listen to dat roll-call, will you? Must be mighty big drum carry dat far. [*Then with a laugh*] Well, if dey ain't no whole brass band to see me off, I sho' got de drum part of it. So long, white man. [*He puts his hands in his pockets and with studied carelessness, whistling a tune, he saunters out of the doorway and off to the left*]

SMITHERS [*looks after him with a puzzled admiration*]. 'E's got 'is bloomin' nerve with 'im, s'elp me! [*Then angrily*] Ho — the bleedin' nigger — puttin' on 'is bloody airs! I 'opes they nab 'im an' gives 'im what's what!

CURTAIN

SCENE TWO

The end of the plain where the Great Forest begins. The foreground is sandy, level ground dotted by a few stones and clumps of stunted bushes cowering close against the earth to escape the buffeting of the trade wind. In the rear the forest is a wall of darkness dividing the world. Only when the eye becomes accustomed to the gloom can the outlines of separate trunks of the nearest trees be made out, enormous pillars of deeper blackness. A somber monotone of wind lost in the leaves moans in the air. Yet this sound serves but to intensify the impression of the forest's relentless immobility, to form a background throwing into relief its brooding, implacable silence.

[JONES *enters from the left, walking rapidly. He stops as he nears the edge of the forest, looks around him quickly, peering into the dark as if searching for some familiar landmark. Then, apparently satisfied that he is where he ought to be, he throws himself on the ground, dog-tired*]

JONES. Well, heah I is. In de nick o' time, too! Little mo' an' it'd be blacker'n de ace of spades heahabouts. [*He pulls a bandana handkerchief from his hip pocket and mops off his perspiring face*] Sho'! Gimme air! I'se tuckered out sho' 'nuff. Dat soft Emperor job ain't no trainin' fo' a long hike ovah dat plain in de brilin' sun. [*Then with a chuckle*] Cheer up, nigger, de worst is yet to come. [*He lifts his head and stares at the forest. His chuckle peters out abruptly. In a tone of awe*] My goodness, look at dem woods, will you? Dat no-count Smithers said dey'd be black an' he sho' called de turn. [*Turning away from them quickly and looking down at his feet, he snatches at a chance to change the subject — solicitously*] Feet, you is holdin' up yo' end fine an' I sutinly hopes you ain't blisterin' none. It's time you git a rest. [*He takes off his shoes, his eyes studiously avoiding the forest. He feels of the soles of his feet gingerly*] You is still in de pink — on'y a little mite feverish. Cool yo'selfs. Remember you done got a long journey yit befo' you. [*He sits in a weary attitude, listening to the rhythmic beating of the tom-tom. He grumbles in a loud tone to cover up a growing uneasiness*] Bush niggers! Wonder dey wouldn't git sick o' beatin' dat drum. Sound louder, seem like. I wonder if dey's startin' after me? [*He scrambles to his feet, looking back across the plain*] Couldn't see dem now, nohow, if dey was hundred feet away. [*Then shaking himself like a wet dog to get rid of these depressing thoughts*] Sho', dey's miles an' miles behind. What you gettin' fidgetty about? [*But he sits down and begins to lace up his shoes in great haste, all the time muttering reassuringly*] You know what? Yo' belly is empty, dat's what's de matter wid you. Come time to eat! Wid nothin' but wind on yo' stumach, o' course you feels jiggedy. Well, we eats right heah an' now soon's I gits dese pesky shoes laced up. [*He finishes lacing up his shoes*] Dere! Now le's see! [*Gets on his hands and knees and searches the ground around him with his eyes*] White stone, white stone, where is you? [*He sees the first white stone and crawls to it — with satisfaction*] Heah you is! I knowed dis was de right place. Box of grub, come to me. [*He turns over the stone and feels in under it — in a tone of dismay*] Ain't heah! Gorry, is I in de right place or isn't I? Dere's 'nother stone. Guess dat's it. [*He scrambles to the next stone and turns it over*] Ain't heah, neither! Grub, whar is you? Ain't heah. Gorry, has I got to go hungry into dem woods — all de night? [*While he is talking he scrambles from one stone to another, turning them over in frantic haste. Finally, he jumps to his feet excitedly*] Is I lost de place? Must have! But how dat happen when I was followin' de trail across de plain in broad daylight? [*Almost plaintively*] I'se hungry, I is! I gotta git my feed. Whar's my strength gonna come from if I doesn't? Gorry, I gotta find dat grub high an' low somehow! Why it come dark so quick like dat? Can't see nothin'. [*He scratches a match on his trousers and peers about him. The rate of the beat of the far-off tom-tom increases perceptibly as he does so. He mutters in a bewildered voice*] How come all dese white stones come heah when I only remembers one? [*Suddenly, with a frightened gasp, he flings the match on the ground and stamps on it*] Nigger, you gone crazy mad? Is you lightin' matches to show dem whar you is? Fo' Lawd's sake, use yo' haid. Gorry,

I'se got to be careful! [*He stares at the plain behind him apprehensively, his hand on his revolver*] But how come all dese white stones? And whar's dat tin box o' grub I hid all wrapped up in oil cloth? [*While his back is turned, the LITTLE FORMLESS FEARS crept out from the deeper blackness of the forest. They are black, shapeless, only their glittering little eyes can be seen. If they have any describable form at all it is that of a grub-worm about the size of a creeping child. They move noiselessly, but with deliberate painful effort, striving to raise themselves on end, failing and sinking prone again. JONES turns about to face the forest. He stares up at the tops of the trees, seeking vainly to discover his whereabouts by their conformation*] Can't tell nothin' from dem trees! Gorry, nothin' 'round heah looks like I evah seed it befo'. I'se done lost de place sho' 'nuff! [*With mournful foreboding*] It's mighty queer! It's mighty queer! [*With sudden forced defiance — in an angry tone*] Woods, is you tryin' to put somethin' ovah on me? [*From the formless creatures on the ground in front of him comes a tiny gale of low mocking laughter, like a rustling of leaves. They squirm upward toward him in twisted attitudes. JONES looks down, leaps backward with a yell of terror, yanking out his revolver as he does so — in a quavering voice*] What's dat? Who's dar? What is you? Git away from me befo' I shoots you up! You don't? — [*He fires. There is a flash, a loud report, then silence broken only by the far-off, quickened throb of the tom-tom. The formless creatures have scurried back into the forest. JONES remains fixed in his position, listening intently. The sound of the shot, the reassuring feel of the revolver in his hand, have somewhat restored his shaken nerve. He addresses himself with renewed confidence*] Dey're gone. Dat shot fix 'em. Dey was only little animals — little wild pigs, I reckon. Dey've maybe rooted out yo' grub an' eat it. Sho', you fool nigger, what you think dey is — ha'nts? [*Excitedly*] Gorry, you give de game away when you fire dat shot. Dem niggers heah dat fo' su'tin! Time you beat it in de woods widout no long waits. [*He starts for the forest — hesitates before the plunge — then urging himself in with manful resolution*] Git in, nigger! What you skeered at? Ain't nothin' dere but de trees! Git in! [*He plunges boldly into the forest*]

SCENE THREE

*n the forest. The moon has just risen. Its
beams, drifting through the canopy of
leaves, make a barely perceptible, suffused, eerie glow. A dense low wall
of underbrush and creepers is in the
nearer foreground, fencing in a small
triangular clearing. Beyond this is
the massed blackness of the forest like
an encompassing barrier. A path is
dimly discerned leading down to the
clearing from left, rear, and winding
away from it again toward the right.
As the scene opens nothing can be distinctly made out. Except for the
beating of the tom-tom, which is a
trifle louder and quicker than at the
close of the previous scene, there is
silence, broken every few seconds by
a queer, clicking sound. Then gradually the figure of the negro, JEFF,
can be discerned crouching on his
haunches at the rear of the triangle.
He is middle-aged, thin, brown in
color, is dressed in a Pullman porter's
uniform and cap. He is throwing a
pair of dice on the ground before him,
picking them up, shaking them, casting them out with the regular, rigid,
mechanical movements of an autom-
aton. The heavy, plodding footsteps of someone approaching along
the trail from the left are heard and
JONES' voice, pitched on a slightly
higher key and strained in a cheery
effort to overcome its own tremors.*

JONES. De moon's rizen. Does you
heah dat, nigger? You gits more light
'rom dis out. No mo' buttin' yo' fool
head agin de trunks an' scratchin' de
hide off yo' legs in de bushes. Now you
ees whar yo'se gwine. So cheer up!
From now on you has a snap. [*He steps
'ust to the rear of the triangular clearing
and mops off his face on his sleeve. He
has lost his Panama hat. His face is
scratched, his brilliant uniform shows
several large rents*] What time's it
gittin' to be, I wonder? I dassent
light no match to find out. Phoo'.
It's wa'm an' dat's a fac'! [*Wearily*]
How long I been makin' tracks in dese
woods? Must be hours an' hours.
Seems like fo'evah! Yit can't be, when
de moon's jes' riz. Dis am a long night
fo' yo', yo' Majesty! [*With a mournful
chuckle*] Majesty! Der ain't much
majesty 'bout dis baby now. [*With
attempted cheerfulness*] Never min'.

It's all part o' de game. Dis night come
to an end like everything else. And
when you gits dar safe and has dat bankroll in yo' hands you laughs at all dis.
[*He starts to whistle but checks himself
abruptly*] What yo' whistlin' for, you
po' dope! Want all de worl' to heah
you? [*He stops talking to listen*] Heah
dat ole drum! Sho' gits nearer from de
sound. Dey's packin' it along wid 'em.
Time fo' me to move. [*He takes a step
forward, then stops — worriedly*] What's
dat odder queer clicketty sound I heah?
Dere it is! Sound close! Sound like
— sound like — Fo' God sake, sound
like some nigger was shootin' crap!
[*Frightenedly*] I better beat it quick
when I gits dem notions. [*He walks
quickly into the clear space — then
stands transfixed as he sees* JEFF — *in a
terrified gasp*] Who dar? Who dat?
Is dat you, Jeff? [*Starting toward the
other, forgetful for a moment of his surroundings and really believing it is a living
man that he sees — in a tone of happy
relief*] Jeff! I'se sho' mighty glad to
see you! Dey tol' me you done died
from dat razor cut I gives you. [*Stopping suddenly, bewilderedly*] But how
you come to be heah, nigger? [*He stares
fascinatedly at the other who continues
his mechanical play with the dice.* JONES'
eyes begin to roll wildly. He stutters]
Ain't you gwine — look up — can't you
speak to me? Is you — is you — a
ha'nt? [*He jerks out his revolver in a
frenzy of terrified rage*] Nigger, I kills
you dead once. Has I got to kill you
ag'in? You take it den. [*He fires.
When the smoke clears away* JEFF *has disappeared.* JONES *stands trembling —
then with a certain reassurance*] He's
gone, anyway. Ha'nt or not ha'nt, dat
shot fix him. [*The beat of the far-off tom-
tom is perceptibly louder and more rapid.*
JONES *becomes conscious of it — with a
start, looking back over his shoulder*]
Dey's gittin' near! Dey'se comin' fast!
And heah I is shootin' shots to let 'em
know jes' whar I is! Oh, Gorry, I'se
got to run. [*Forgetting the path he
plunges wildly into the underbrush in the
rear and disappears in the shadow*]

SCENE FOUR

*In the forest. A wide dirt road runs diag-
onally from right, front, to left, rear.
Rising sheer on both sides the forest
walls it in. The moon is now up.*

Under its light the road glimmers ghastly and unreal. It is as if the forest had stood aside momentarily to let the road pass through and accomplish its veiled purpose. This done, the forest will fold in upon itself again and the road will be no more. JONES *stumbles in from the forest on the right. His uniform is ragged and torn. He looks about him with numbed surprise when he sees the road, his eyes blinking in the bright moonlight. He flops down exhaustedly and pants heavily for a while. Then with sudden anger.*

JONES. I'm meltin' wid heat! Runnin' an' runnin' an' runnin'! Damn dis heah coat! Like a strait jacket! [*He tears off his coat and flings it away from him, revealing himself stripped to the waist*] Dere! Dat's better! Now I kin breathe! [*Looking down at his feet, the spurs catch his eye*] And to hell wid dese high-fangled spurs. Dey're what's been a-trippin' me up an' breakin' my neck. [*He unstraps them and flings them away disgustedly*] Dere! I gits rid o' dem frippety Emperor trappin's an' I travels lighter. Lawd! I'se tired! [*After a pause, listening to the insistent beat of the tom-tom in the distance*] I must a' put some distance between myself an' dem — runnin' like dat — and yit — dat damn drum sounds jes' de same — nearer, even. Well, I guess I a'most holds my lead anyhow. Dey won't never catch up. [*With a sigh*] If on'y my fool legs stands up. Oh, I'se sorry I evah went in for dis. Dat Emperor job is sho' hard to shake. [*He looks around him suspiciously*] How'd dis road evah git heah? Good level road, too. I never remembers seein' it befo'. [*Shaking his head apprehensively*] Dese woods is sho' full o' de queerest things at night. [*With a sudden terror*] Lawd God, don't let me see no more o' dem ha'nts! Dey gits my goat! [*Then trying to talk himself into confidence*] Ha'nts! You fool nigger, dey ain't no such things! Don't de Baptist parson tell you dat many time? Is you civilized, or is you like dese ig-n'rent black niggers heah? Sho'! Dat was all in yo' own head. Wasn't nothin' dere. Wasn't no Jeff! Know what? You jus' get seein' dem things 'cause yo' belly's empty and you's sick wid hunger inside. Hunger 'fects yo' head and yo' eyes. Any fool know dat.

[*Then pleading fervently*] But bless God, I don't come across no more o' dem, whatever dey is! [*Then cautiously*] Rest! Don't talk! Rest! You needs it. Den you gits on yo' way again. [*Looking at the moon*] Night's half gone a'most. You hits de coast in de mawning! Den you'se all safe. [*From the right forward a small gang of negroes enter. They are dressed in striped convict suits, their heads are shaven, one leg drags limpingly, shackled to a heavy ball and chain. Some carry picks, the others shovels. They are followed by a white man dressed in the uniform of a prison guard. A Winchester rifle is slung across his shoulders and he carries a heavy whip. At a signal from the* GUARD *they stop on the road opposite where* JONES *is sitting.* JONES, *who has been staring up at the sky, unmindful of their noiseless approach, suddenly looks down and sees them. His eyes pop out, he tries to get to his feet and fly, but sinks back, too numbed by fright to move. His voice catches in a choking prayer*] Lawd Jesus! [*The* PRISON GUARD *cracks his whip — noiselessly — and at that signal all the convicts start to work on the road. They swing their picks, they shovel, but not a sound comes from their labor. Their movements, like those of* JEFF *in the preceding scene, are those of automatons, — rigid, slow, and mechanical. The* PRISON GUARD *points sternly at* JONES *with his whip, motions him to take his place among the other shovellers.* JONES *gets to his feet in a hypnotized stupor. He mumbles subserviently*] Yes, suh! Yes, suh! I'se comin'. [*As he shuffles, dragging one foot, over to his place, he curses under his breath with rage and hatred*] God damn yo' soul, I gits even wid you yit, sometime. [*As if there were a shovel in his hands he goes through weary, mechanical gestures of digging up dirt, and throwing it to the roadside. Suddenly the* GUARD *approaches him angrily, threateningly. He raises his whip and lashes* JONES *viciously across the shoulders with it.* JONES *winces with pain and cowers abjectly. The* GUARD *turns his back on him and walks away contemptuously. Instantly* JONES *straightens up. With arms upraised as if his shovel were a club in his hands he springs murderously at the unsuspecting* GUARD. *In the act of crashing down his shovel on the white man's skull,* JONES *suddenly becomes aware that his hands are empty. He cries despairingly*] Whar's my shovel? Gimme my shovel 'till I splits his damn head! [*Appealing to his fellow convicts*] Gimme a shovel, one o' you, fo' God's sake! [*They stand fixed in motionless attitudes, their eyes on the ground. The* GUARD *seems to wait expectantly, his back turned to the attacker.* JONES *bellows with baffled, terrified rage, tugging frantically at his revolver*] I kills you, you white debil, if it's de last thing I evah does! Ghost or debil, I kill you agin! [*He frees the revolver and fires point blank at the* GUARD'S *back. Instantly the walls of the forest close in from both sides, the road and the figures of the convict gang are blotted out in an enshrouding darkness. The only sounds are a crashing in the underbrush as* JONES *leaps away in mad flight and the throbbing of the tom-tom, still far distant, but increased in volume of sound and rapidity of beat*]

SCENE FIVE

A large circular clearing, enclosed by the serried ranks of gigantic trunks of tall trees whose tops are lost to view. In the center is a big dead stump worn by time into a curious resemblance to an auction block. The moon floods the clearing with a clear light. JONES *forces his way in through the forest on the left. He looks wildly about the clearing with hunted, fearful glances. His pants are in tatters, his shoes cut and misshapen, flapping about his feet. He slinks cautiously to the stump in the center and sits down in a tense position, ready for instant flight. Then he holds his head in his hands and rocks back and forth, moaning to himself miserably.*

JONES. Oh Lawd, Lawd! Oh Lawd, Lawd! [*Suddenly he throws himself on his knees and raises his clasped hands to the sky — in a voice of agonized pleading*] Lawd Jesus, heah my prayer! I'se a po' sinner, a po' sinner! I knows I done wrong, I knows it! When I cotches Jeff cheatin' wid loaded dice my anger overcomes me and I kills him dead! Lawd, I done wrong! When dat guard hits me wid de whip, my anger overcomes me, and I kills him dead. Lawd, I done wrong! And down heah whar dese fool bush niggers raises me up to the seat o' de mighty, I steals all I could grab. Lawd, I done wrong! I knows it! I'se sorry! Forgive me, Lawd!

Forgive dis po' sinner! [*Then beseeching terrifiedly*] And keep dem away, Lawd! Keep dem away from me! And stop dat drum soundin' in my ears! Dat begin to sound ha'nted, too. [*He gets to his feet, evidently slightly reassured by his prayer — with attempted confidence*] De Lawd'll preserve me from dem ha'nts after dis. [*Sits down on the stump again*] I ain't skeered o' real men. Let dem come. But dem odders — [*He shudders — then looks down at his feet, working his toes inside the shoes — with a groan*] Oh, my po' feet! Dem shoes ain't no use no more 'ceptin' to hurt. I'se better off widout dem. [*He unlaces them and pulls them off — holds the wrecks of the shoes in his hands and regards them mournfully*] You was real, A-one patin' leather, too. Look at you now. Emperor, you'se gittin' mighty low! [*He sighs dejectedly and remains with bowed shoulders, staring down at the shoes in his hands as if reluctant to throw them away. While his attention is thus occupied, a crowd of figures silently enter the clearing from all sides. All are dressed in Southern costumes of the period of the fifties of the last century. There are middle-aged men who are evidently well-to-do planters. There is one spruce, authoritative individual — the* AUCTIONEER. *There are a crowd of curious spectators, chiefly young belles and dandies who have come to the slave-market for diversion. All exchange courtly greetings in dumb show and chat silently together. There is something stiff, rigid, unreal, marionettish about their movements. They group themselves about the stump. Finally a batch of slaves are led in from the left by an attendant — three men of different ages, two women, one with a baby in her arms, nursing. They are placed to the left of the stump, beside* JONES.

The white planters look them over appraisingly as if they were cattle, and exchange judgments on each. The dandies point with their fingers and make witty remarks. The belles titter bewitchingly. All this in silence save for the ominous throb of the tom-tom. The AUCTIONEER *holds up his hand, taking his place at the stump. The groups strain forward attentively. He touches* JONES *on the shoulder peremptorily, motioning for him to stand on the stump — the auction block.*

JONES *looks up, sees the figures on all sides, looks wildly for some opening to escape, sees none, screams and leaps madly to the top of the stump to get as far away from them as possible. He stands there, cowering, paralyzed with horror. The* AUCTIONEER *begins his silent spiel. He points to* JONES, *appeals to the planters to see for themselves. Here is a good field hand, sound in wind and limb as they can see. Very strong still in spite of his being middle-aged. Look at that back. Look at those shoulders. Look at the muscles in his arms and his sturdy legs. Capable of any amount of hard labor. Moreover, of a good disposition, intelligent and tractable. Will any gentleman start the bidding? The* PLANTERS *raise their fingers, make their bids. They are apparently all eager to possess* JONES. *The bidding is lively, the crowd interested. While this has been going on,* JONES *has been seized by the courage of desperation. He dares to look down and around him. Over his face abject terror gives way to mystification, to gradual realization — stutteringly*] What's you all doin', white folks? What's all dis? What you all lookin' at me fo'? What you doin' wid me, anyhow? [*Suddenly convulsed with raging hatred and fear*] Is dis a auction? Is you sellin' me like dey uster befo' de war? [*Jerking out his revolver just as the* AUCTIONEER *knocks him down to one of the planters — glaring from him to the purchaser*] And *you* sells me? And *you* buys me? I shows you I'se a free nigger, damn yo' souls! [*He fires at the* AUCTIONEER *and at the* PLANTER *with such rapidity that the two shots are almost simultaneous. As if this were a signal the walls of the forest fold in. Only blackness remains and silence broken by* JONES *as he rushes off, crying with fear — and by the quickened, ever louder beat of the tom-tom*]

SCENE SIX

A cleared space in the forest. The limbs of the trees meet over it forming a low ceiling about five feet from the ground. The interlocked ropes of creepers reaching upward to entwine the tree trunks gives an arched appearance to the sides. The space thus enclosed is like the dark, noisome hold of some ancient vessel. The moonlight is almost completely shut out and only a vague wan light filters through. There is the noise of some one approaching from the left, stumbling and crawling through the undergrowth. JONES' *voice is heard between chattering moans.*

JONES. Oh, Lawd, what I gwine do now? Ain't got no bullet left on'y de silver one. If mo' o' dem ha'nts come after me, how I gwine skeer dem away? Oh, Lawd, on'y de silver one left — an' I gotta save dat fo' luck. If I shoots dat one I'm a goner sho'! Lawd, it's black heah! Whar's de moon? Oh, Lawd, don't dis night evah come to an end! [*By the sounds, he is feeling his way cautiously forward*] Dere! Dis feels like a clear space. I gotta lie down an' rest. I don't care if dem niggers does cotch me. I gotta rest. [*He is well forward now where his figure can be dimly made out. His pants have been so torn away that what is left of them is no better than a breech cloth. He flings himself full length, face downward on the ground, panting with exhaustion. Gradually it seems to grow lighter in the enclosed space and two rows of seated figures can be seen behind* JONES. *They are sitting in crumpled, despairing attitudes, hunched, facing one another with their backs touching the forest walls as if they were shackled to them. All are negroes, naked save for loin cloths. At first they are silent and motionless. Then they begin to sway slowly forward toward each and back again in unison, as if they were laxly letting themselves follow the long roll of a ship at sea. At the same time, a low, melancholy murmur rises among them, increasing gradually by rhythmic degrees which seem to be directed and controlled by the throb of the tom-tom in the distance, to a long, tremulous wail of despair that reaches a certain pitch, unbearably acute, then falls by slow gradations of tone into silence and is taken up again.* JONES *starts, looks up, sees the figures, and throws himself down again to shut out the sight. A shudder of terror shakes his whole body as the wail rises up about him again. But the next time, his voice, as if under some uncanny compulsion, starts with the others. As their chorus lifts he rises to a sitting posture similar to the others, swaying back and forth. His voice reaches the highest pitch of sorrow, of desolation. The light fades out, the other voices cease, and only darkness is left.* JONES *can be heard scrambling to his feet and running off, his voice sinking down the scale and receding as he moves farther and farther away in the* forest. *The tom-tom beats louder, quicker, with a more insistent, triumphant pulsation*]

SCENE SEVEN

The foot of a gigantic tree by the edge of a great river. A rough structure of boulders, like an altar, is by the tree. The raised river bank is in the nearer background. Beyond this the surface of the river spreads out, brilliant and unruffled in the moonlight, blotted out and merged into a veil of bluish mist in the distance. JONES' *voice is heard from the left rising and falling in the long, despairing wail of the chained slaves, to the rhythmic beat of the tom-tom. As his voice sinks into silence, he enters the open space. The expression of his face is fixed and stony, his eyes have an obsessed glare, he moves with a strange deliberation like a sleep-walker or one in a trance. He looks around at the tree, the rough stone altar, the moonlit surface of the river beyond, and passes his hand over his head with a vague gesture of puzzled bewilderment. Then, as if in obedience to some obscure impulse, he sinks into a kneeling, devotional posture before the altar. Then he seems to come to himself partly, to have an uncertain realization of what he is doing, for he straightens up and stares about him horrifiedly — in an incoherent mumble.*

JONES. What — what is I doin'? What is — dis place? Seems like seems like I know dat tree — an' dem stones — an' de river. I remember — seems like I been heah befo'. [*Tremblingly*] Oh, Gorry, I'se skeered in dis place! I'se skeered. Oh, Lawd, pertect dis sinner! [*Crawling away from the altar, he cowers close to the ground, his face hidden, his shoulders heaving with sobs of hysterical fright. From behind the trunk of the tree, as if he had sprung out of it, the figure of the* CONGO WITCH-DOCTOR *appears. He is wizened and old, naked except for the fur of some small animal tied about his waist, its bushy tail hanging down in front. His body is stained all over a bright red. Antelope horns are on each side of his head, branching upward. In one hand he carries a bone rattle, in the other a charm stick with a bunch of white cockatoo feathers tied to the end. A great number of glass beads and bone ornaments are about his neck, ears, wrists, and ankles. He struts noiselessly with a queer prancing step to a position in the clear ground between* JONES *and the altar. Then with a preliminary, summoning stamp of his foot on the earth, he begins to dance and to chant. As if in response to his summons the beating of the tom-tom grows to a fierce, exultant boom whose throbs seem to fill the air with vibrating rhythm.* JONES *looks up, starts to spring to his feet, reaches a half-kneeling, half-squatting position and remains rigidly fixed there, paralyzed with awed fascination by this new apparition. The* WITCH-DOCTOR, *sways, stamping with his foot, his bone rattle clicking the time. His voice rises and falls in a weird, monotonous croon, without articulate word divisions. Gradually his dance becomes clearly one of a narrative in pantomime, his croon is an incantation, a charm to allay the fierceness of some implacable deity demanding sacrifice. He flees, he is pursued by devils, he hides, he flees again. Ever wilder and wilder becomes his flight, nearer and nearer draws the pursuing evil, more and more the spirit of terror gains possession of him. His croon, rising to intensity, is punctuated by shrill cries.* JONES *has become completely hypnotized. His voice joins in the incantation, in the cries, he beats time with his hands and sways his body to and fro from the waist. The whole spirit and meaning of the dance has entered into him, has become his spirit. Finally the theme of the pantomime halts on a howl of despair, and is taken up again in a note of savage hope. There is a salvation. The forces of evil demand sacrifice. They must be appeased. The* WITCH-DOCTOR *points with his wand to the sacred tree, to the river beyond, to the altar, and finally to* JONES *with a ferocious command.* JONES *seems to sense the meaning of this. It is he who must offer himself for sacrifice. He beats his forehead abjectly to the ground, moaning hysterically*] Mercy, Oh Lawd! Mercy! Mercy on dis po' sinner.

[*The* WITCH-DOCTOR *springs to the river bank. He stretches out his arms and calls to some God within its depths. Then he starts backward slowly, his arms remaining out. A huge head of a crocodile appears over the bank and its eyes, glittering greenly, fasten upon* JONES. . . . *He stares into them fascinatedly. The* WITCH-DOCTOR *prances up to him, touches him with his wand, motions with hideous command toward the waiting monster.* JONES *squirms on his belly nearer and nearer, moaning continually*]

JONES. Mercy, Lawd! Mercy! [*The crocodile heaves more of his enormous hulk onto the land.* JONES *squirms toward him. The* WITCH-DOCTOR'S *voice shrills out in furious exultation, the tom-tom beats madly.* JONES *cries out in a fierce, exhausted spasm of anguished pleading*] Lawd, save me! Lawd Jesus, heah my prayer! [*Immediately, in answer to his prayer, comes the thought of the one bullet left him. He snatches at his hip, shouting defiantly*] De silver bullet! You don't git me yit! [*He fires at the green eyes in front of him. The head of the crocodile sinks back behind the river bank, the* WITCH-DOCTOR *springs behind the sacred tree and disappears.* JONES *lies with his face to the ground, his arms outstretched, whimpering with fear as the throb of the tom-tom fills the silence about him with a somber pulsation, a baffled but revengeful power*]

SCENE EIGHT

Dawn. Same as Scene Two, the dividing line of forest and plain. The nearest tree trunks are dimly revealed but the forest behind them is still a mass of glooming shadow. The tom-tom seems on the very spot, so loud and continuously vibrating are its beats. LEM *enters from the left, followed by a small squad of his soldiers, and by the Cockney trader,* SMITHERS. LEM *is a heavy-set, ape-faced old savage of the extreme African type, dressed only in a loin cloth. A revolver and cartridge belt are about his waist. His soldiers are in different degrees of rag-concealed nakedness. All wear broad palm-leaf hats. Each one carries a rifle.* SMITHERS *is the same as in Scene One. One of the soldiers, evidently a tracker, is peering about keenly on the ground. He points to the spot where* JONES *entered the forest.* LEM *and* SMITHERS *come to look.*

SMITHERS [*after a glance, turns away in disgust*]. That's where 'e went in

right enough. Much good it'll do yer. 'E's miles orf by this an' safe to the Coast, damn 's 'ide! I tole yer yer'd lose 'im, didn't I? — wastin' the 'ole bloomin' night beatin' yer bloody drum and castin' yer silly spells! Gawd blimey, wot a pack!

LEM [*gutturally*]. We cotch him.

[*He makes a motion to his soldiers who squat down on their haunches in a semi-circle*]

SMITHERS [*exasperatedly*]. Well, ain't yer goin' in an' 'unt 'im in the woods? What the 'ell's the good of waitin'?

LEM [*imperturbably — squatting down himself*]. We cotch him.

SMITHERS [*turning away from him contemptuously*]. Aw! Garn! 'E's a better man than the lot o' you put together. I 'ates the sight o' 'im but I'll say that for 'im.

[*A sound comes from the forest. The soldiers jump to their feet, cocking their rifles alertly.* LEM *remains sitting with an imperturbable expression, but listening intently. He makes a quick signal with his hand. His followers creep quickly into the forest, scattering so that each enters at a different spot*]

SMITHERS. You ain't thinkin' that would be 'im, I 'ope?

LEM [*calmly*]. We cotch him.

SMITHERS. Blarsted fat 'eads! [*Then after a second's thought — wonderingly*] Still an' all, it might 'appen. If 'e lost 'is bloody way in these stinkin' woods 'e'd likely turn in a circle without 'is knowin' it.

LEM [*peremptorily*]. Sssh! [*The reports of several rifles sound from the forest, followed a second later by savage, exultant yells. The beating of the tom-tom abruptly ceases.* LEM *looks up at the white man with a grin of satisfaction*] We cotch him. Him dead.

SMITHERS [*with a snarl*]. 'Ow d'yer know it's 'im an' 'ow d'yer know 'e's dead?

LEM. My mens dey got um silver bullets. Lead bullet no kill him. He got um strong charm. I cook um money, make um silver bullet, make um strong charm, too.

SMITHERS [*light breaking upon him*]. So that's wot you was up to all night, wot? You was scared to put after 'im till you'd moulded silver bullets, eh?

LEM [*simply stating a fact*]. Yes. Him got strong charm. Lead no good.

SMITHERS [*slapping his thigh and guffawing*]. Haw-haw! If yer don't beat all 'ell! [*Then recovering himself — scornfully*] I'll bet yer it ain't 'im they shot at all, yer bleedin' looney!

LEM [*calmly*]. Dey come bring him now.

[*The soldiers come out of the forest, carrying* JONES' *limp body. He is dead. They carry him to* LEM, *who examines his body with great satisfaction.* SMITHERS *leans over his shoulder — in a tone of frightened awe*]

SMITHERS. Well, they did for yer right enough, Jonsey, me lad! Dead as a 'erring! [*Mockingly*] Where's yer 'igh an' mighty airs now, yer bloomin' Majesty? [*Then with a grin*] Silver bullets! Gawd blimey, but yer died in the 'eighth o' style, any'ow!

CURTAIN

NICE PEOPLE

(1921)

BY RACHEL CROTHERS

NICE PEOPLE

By RACHEL CROTHERS

RACHEL CROTHERS

MISS RACHEL CROTHERS has been writing for the theatre for many years. She started with an individual vein, and her headway at first was slow. Her point of view, during the days of "The Three of Us" and "A Man's World", was strictly feministic. She was interesting because she was, for her time, a little unconventional. Having had experience as a teacher in the Nelson Wheatcroft School of Acting, she at times used to appear in her own plays. For instance, when "He and She" (called afterwards "The Herfords") was on the road, she assumed the leading part. Her treatment in this play is interesting to contrast with James Forbes's "The Famous Mrs. Fair."

Most of her later plays show Miss Crothers to be writing for the time only. Her dramas are soon dated. The problems that she discusses so lightly are problems contrived for the stage, not for too close scrutiny. They suggest that something's the matter with the world: the world at that immediate hour, A.D. Such a play as "Young Wisdom" is now the oldest kind of wisdom to the younger generation that looks on 1914 — the date of the writing of this play — as "before the War" and antediluvian. The social life depicted in "Nice People" is slightly passé. The dialogue is dotted with lines that epitomize the evils of young life, and the better freedom of it in contrast with the bottled-up, suppressed existence of the younger generation of the past. But there is not the irony which, had Miss Crothers bitten deeper into her theme, would have resulted in a more poignant comedy. As it is, "Nice People" is clever where it could have been true.

Miss Crothers's latest play, "Expressing Willie", is a clever and sophisticated study of a weak-minded individual who is persuaded by a fast set that he has unexpressed depths in him. The tragedy of insufficiency is treated by Miss Crothers lightly, expertly, entertainingly. But, like "Nice People", it is artificially constructed: the material is not felt.

Miss Crothers knows her theatre sufficiently to realize how far sentiment will carry a play. I enjoy the quickness of her comedy, which gives it the semblance of life. Her sketches of society evils are amusing, though I doubt how far they are amusing outside the sophisticated communities that are so good-natured about everything that they don't know they are being slapped, even mildly. But I resent a certain defection in Miss Crothers: which makes such a rift between the plays of the period of "The Three of Us" and "A Man's World", and of "Nice People" and "Expressing Willie." It would seem that the theatre which nurtured Mr. Fitch and Mr. Thomas, and of which she is a part, has made her a little timid in her mental attitude. But that very theatre sharpened her technique, even if it diluted her ideas, and Miss Crothers' plays to-day are better articulated than they were in those early days.

Yet I recall Bronson Howard's joy when he found the independence of a woman playwright revealed in "The Three of Us" — the first of a series of plays in which Miss Crothers went forth to champion her sex, to decry the double standard of morality by which men and women were judged. That shock she gave to a conservative world then is a very mild shock now, with a generation that considers Ibsen's "A Doll's House" old-fashioned. That clarion note seems with the years to have diminished to a feeble tremor, drowned by the jazz of a new age, outside which Miss Crothers stands as commentator — and a deft commentator at that.

NICE PEOPLE

A PLAY IN THREE ACTS

———

By RACHEL CROTHERS

THE CAST

As first presented in New York at the Klaw Theater, March 3d, 1921

HALLIE LIVINGSTON	Tallulah Bankhead
EILEEN BAXTER-JONES	Katharine Cornell
TREVOR LEEDS	Edwin Hensley
THEODORA GLOUCESTER	Francine Larrimore
OLIVER COMSTOCK	Guy Milham
SCOTTY WILBUR	Hugh Huntley
MARGARET RAINSFORD	Merle Madden
HUBERT GLOUCESTER	Frederick Perry
BILLY WADE	Robert Ames
MR. HEYFER	David M. Murray

NICE PEOPLE

ACT I

SCENE. — *The Gloucester Apartment in Park Avenue, New York City.*

TIME. — *Eleven-thirty — an evening in May.*

The walls of the room are hung in very old silk of a soft greenish gray in tone. At back is a fireplace set in a jog which comes about two feet into the room. To the left of this jog is a single door opening into hall. In the left wall are two long windows hung with velvet curtains which melt into the walls in color. At right are double doors standing open and showing a grand piano in the room beyond. Over the mantelpiece hangs a large picture of three nude figures of girls running, with cloud-like draperies which also have the tone of the walls. The furniture is upholstered in an old brocade of ashes of roses which makes a charming background for the delicate orchid tints of HAL-LIE'S gown — the rose velvet of EILEEN'S and the white transparent tissue of TEDDY'S.

EILEEN, HALLIE *and* TREVOR *are in the room, singing gaily and carelessly to the music which* OLIVER *is playing in the room beyond.*

EILEEN BAXTER-JONES — *about twenty-one, is dark and piquant, frankly impertinent and very wholesomely lovable. She is sitting on the low seat at center with her back to the audience and her legs crossed unconcernedly — smoking a cigarette.*

HALLIE LIVINGSTON — *perhaps twenty-three, beautiful in a brilliantly blonde way, half reclining on the couch, is sipping her Scotch with a slow and self-centered enjoyment, indicative of her general psychology. The girls are exquisite in their youth and freshness, finely bred animals of care, health and money — dressed with daring emphasis of the prevailing*
fashion, startling in their delicate nakedness and sensuous charm.

TREVOR LEEDS *is tall and amazingly thin. He goes in for a great deal of manner and rather an English accent. As the music stops he crosses to the sofa to look at* HALLIE *critically and condescendingly.*

TREVOR LEEDS. You look like an orchid, Hallie, absolutely.

HALLIE. You say it as though you'd made a great discovery. That's what I'm supposed to look like — darling.

EILEEN. You're slow getting that, Trevor. [*Calling*] Did you say we were going some place to dance, Teddy?

TEDDY [*calling back from room at right*]. Yes. Don't you want to?

EILEEN. *Crazy* about it.

TEDDY. I thought we'd wait just a few more minutes for Scotty.

TREVOR [*filling his glass again*]. Well, why the devil doesn't he come? He's got a nerve.

HALLIE. But there's no other man in the world for Teddy. Of course, she'll make us wait for him.

TEDDY [*coming in from the right with a glass in her hand*]. Have another one, Oliver.

OLIVER [*following* TEDDY *in*]. Thanks.

TEDDY. Eileen?

EILEEN. No, thanks. I know when I've had enough.

OLIVER [*as he pours another drink for himself*]. You mean you *think* you do. You're never so enticing as when you have a nice little bun, Eileen.

[THEODORA *is twenty — slender and vibrating, pretty, intelligent and high keyed, alertly and intensely interested in herself and the art of extracting from life all which she considers her due. She has a very radiant charm and vivid responsiveness.*

There is about them all the carelessness and indifference of very intimate friendship and a keen alertness to each other's foibles and idiosyncrasies]

TEDDY. What time is it, Trevor?

TREVOR [*looking at his watch*]. Ten forty-seven, to be exact.

EILEEN. Time Scotty was turning up, I should say, if he is ever going to.

TEDDY. I'm not at all sure that he will. I know of nothing in life so certain as the uncertainty of Scotty Wilbur.

HALLIE. How you can allow him to be so rude to you, Teddy, is absolutely beyond my comprehension.

TEDDY. There are so many things beyond your comprehension Hallie, dearest. Scotty isn't rude to me in the least. On the contrary, he's perfect.

HALLIE. Not according to my ideas of taste and sensibilities. I call it horribly rude to phone you at the last minute he couldn't come to dinner.

EILEEN. Sweetly adding he forgot he was booked for some place else.

OLIVER. At least he might have had the decency to lie a little.

TEDDY. But it was adorable of him *not* to lie. How can he help it if he forgot? I think it was wonderful of him to go there when he wanted to be here. Rena Maxwell actually needed him. Rena is so intellectual her dinners are stupid. The repartee sounds like the encyclopædia. And there's nothing to drink there now — not a drop. She's taken Prohibition seriously. [*Finishing her drink*]

EILEEN. She's taken it as an *excuse* you mean. She always was too stingy to give a fellow a real drink.

TEDDY. Rena believes in drinking only with thine eyes.

TREVOR. Yes — Rena's a fish. [*Singing a snatch of "Drink to me only with thine eyes" — off key on the last note. They all scream at him to stop*]

HALLIE. It's so awfully middle class to make one's education as evident as she makes hers. Isn't it?

EILEEN. Is that why you conceal yours so carefully?

HALLIE. I was beautifully educated in Paris, of course.

TEDDY. But not in much of anything else.

HALLIE. Mother was clever enough to have me taught just enough to appreciate everything in the world — but not to go far enough to be — you know.

They said I might have been a grea[t] musician, but that would have been to[o] stupid.

[OLIVER *lights* TEDDY'S *cigarette*]

TREVOR. Of course appreciation i[s] our vocation — appreciation of othe[r] people's work. I could open a shop an[d] go in for interior decoration. Lor[d] knows I know far more about it tha[n] most of the dubs who are in it. But i[t] reduces it all to such a beastly commer[-]cial basis immediately.

EILEEN. I don't know — sometime[s] I think I'd like to be able to do som[e] one thing awfully well. To dance, fo[r] instance, I'd like to dance on the stage[.]

HALLIE. Horrors!

EILEEN. I would, really.

TEDDY. Why don't you?

EILEEN. They wouldn't let me.

TEDDY [*going to the fire*]. Piffle! D[o] it anyway. What are you afraid of[?] I think the most vulgar second rat[e] thing in the world is to be afraid. Any[-]thing can be made chic and frightfull[y] individual — if one just does, you know[.]

TREVOR. Of course, if one has th[e] individuality to get away with it.

OLIVER. Ted, I think you come a[s] near getting away with anything yo[u] want to do as anybody I know.

HALLIE. I do, too. If I did half th[e] things you do, Ted, I'd be horribl[y] talked about.

TEDDY. Well, of course, becaus[e] you're always trying to hide thing[s.] Do everything right before everybody'[s] eyes — and dare them to talk. [*The laugh. The phone rings*] There'[s] Scotty now. Take it Trevor. If he'[s] downstairs tell him to come up and hav[e] a drink before we go.

TREVOR [*taking the receiver and imi[-] tating* TEDDY'S *voice*]. Hello! Oh [*Drawing away*] You'd better come Ted. He's yelling for you. Wher[e] the devil are you Scotty? [*Speakin[g] in the phone again*]

HALLIE [*as* TEDDY *goes to the phone*] Tell him to meet us some place. Wh[y] should we wait?

TEDDY [*taking the receiver*]. Wher[e] are you? Well, hurry. Yes — we wil[l] if you're here in five minutes. Ten's th[e] limit. Is it a very dry party? Thi[s] isn't. Hurry, or there won't be any[-]thing left. [*Putting up the receiver*]

EILEEN. Is he headed this way a[t] last?

TEDDY. Well — let's go. You mus[t]

e having a rotten time here. [*She
throws her cigarette into the fire*]

HALLIE. Oh, we don't mind waiting,
but it's so killing to see *you* holding your
breath till he gets here. Of course,
everybody's chasing Scotty more or less.
Ethel Montague certainly is at it hard.
She's the one who says Scotty wants to
marry you for your money, Ted. Silly
of her to say that, isn't it?

TEDDY. I notice when you have
anything particularly disagreeable to
say to me, Hallie, you pretend somebody
else said it.

EILEEN. Hallie, you're always nasty
when you've had too long a drink.

TEDDY. Yes, but it's the only time
she's honest. Give her another one,
Oliver. What's biting you? Go on —
get it out of your system.

HALLIE. Heavens — don't take it
seriously. You must be used to that by
this time. Any girl who has as much
money as you have, Teddy, must expect
somebody to say that every man who
looks at her wants her money.

TEDDY. I don't know that I have so
much more than you have, for instance.

HALLIE [*getting up from the sofa a little
unsteadily and going to* TEDDY]. But you
look as though you had, honey. You
have so many cars and things, you know.
Three of your own, isn't it? And your
pearls are *marvelous* — simply *marvelous*.
No wonder Scotty wants you. [*She
walks slowly and a trifle insolently into
the room at right, and sits at the piano.
She plays softly. A pause —* TREVOR
goes after her. OLIVER *goes to* TEDDY,
about to speak, but follows TREVOR *out*]

EILEEN [*going to* TEDDY]. To put it
delicately, Hallie is tight.

TEDDY [*looking after* HALLIE]. Oh
no — she isn't. What did she mean?

EILEEN. Yes, she is, too. She's
getting entirely too fond of booze lately
and it's disgusting — absolutely disgusting.

TEDDY. *What did she mean?* Do
people say Scotty only wants to marry
me for my money?

EILEEN. You know she's mad about
him herself, and she's always been
jealous of you. I like Hallie but she is
a damn cat, and she can't help scratching *you.*

TEDDY. Scotty doesn't care anything
more about money than anybody does.
And he *does* care for me.

EILEEN. Of course. That's why
Hallie is so vicious.

HALLIE [*coming back into the room*].
Hasn't Scotty come yet? If I don't
dance soon I shall expire.

TEDDY. Come on, Hallie, be a sport.
Pretend you like me — for the sake of
the party.

HALLIE. I like your gown.

TEDDY. Can you dance in that one?

HALLIE. Of course. Just throw it
over my arm. [*Throwing the sash train
over her arm and going up to the fire*]

TEDDY. Oh, I didn't mean that.
The back — where's a man going to put
his hand?

HALLIE. Where he always does, of
course. What's the matter with my
back? [*Turning her back to the girls*]

TEDDY. Nothing at all. It's doing
very well this evening — so far as I can
see.

EILEEN. That's the most economical
kind of costume going — because you
can wash your back — but when a man
puts his old wet hand on this velvet — I
nearly die. It simply ruins it.

HALLIE. Did you see Rena Maxwell's gown last night? [*Throwing herself into the armchair near the fireplace*]

EILEEN. I don't see why Rena
doesn't stay at home altogether.

HALLIE. I don't either. Nobody
dances with her. Scotty was stuck with
her last night and nobody would cut in.
He whistled and made signs till he was
black in the face and had to go through
the whole dance with her.

TEDDY. Of course, no man wants
to dance with her if she will wear corsets.

EILEEN. Old Ironsides — they call her.

TEDDY. Rena doesn't go in for much
personal contact when she dances.

HALLIE. No — this is the way she
stands. [*Rising, and standing very
straight in an old-fashioned way*] You
know if her head were only turned
around the other way she wouldn't have
such a bad figure. [*Slumping to show
how* RENA *ought to stand*] Oh, I'm
dying to dance with Scotty. Don't
you think he's the best dancer in town,
Teddy?

TEDDY. He thinks *I* am — so of
course I like dancing with him.

HALLIE. I adore the way he holds
me. Just as though he were going
to crush me.

TEDDY. But he never *does*.

HALLIE. Not while we're dancing.
I adore a man who is absolutely mad
about me and yet who controls himself
in that perfectly marvelous way.

TEDDY. Oh, I don't know. I'm not so keen about so much self-control.

HALLIE. Oh, I am. I think it's much more subtle.

EILEEN. Well, I must say I like sort of a frank flash of pash — once in a while — so you know where you're at. Elemental stuff, you know.

TEDDY [*giggling at* EILEEN]. You like being in danger sometimes.

HALLIE. Oh, I hate horribly obvious emotion. It doesn't interest me in the least.

EILEEN. You're trying to make us think you're subtly and insidiously wicked, Hallie.

TEDDY. Like Trevor. Psychologically he's a devil — but *physiologically* he's as tame as your grandmother. Eileen, did Trevor ever kiss you?

EILEEN. Don't remember.

HALLIE. Well — *really!* I don't *tell.*

TEDDY. That's just it. There'd be nothing *to* tell if he ever did.

HALLIE. Your pearls *are* large — aren't they?

TEDDY. They're just the way I want them.

HALLIE. Someone was saying the other day they're just like Mrs. Allister's, and wondered if your father got them both at the same time.

TEDDY [*after a pause*]. I have to hand it to you, Hallie. You can say the rottenest things in the sweetest way of anybody I know.

TREVOR [*coming back into the room*]. Hasn't Scotty come yet?

HALLIE. Oh no, we're still waiting. [*Going back into the other room to play again*]

TEDDY. We'll only give him three minutes longer.

TREVOR [*beginning to dance with* EILEEN]. You don't mind so long as you have me, do you, love?

EILEEN. I don't mind anything as long as I'm in your arms. We've just been saying how dangerous you are, Trevor.

TREVOR. I might fool you some of these days.

EILEEN [*bending back as she flings herself against him*]. Well, why don't you? [*They dance out of the room*]

OLIVER [*coming back*]. Don't you want to go without Scotty?

TEDDY. Of course. [*She holds out her arms to him and they dance*]

OLIVER. No, you don't. You care an awful lot — don't you? [*She shakes her head*] Yes, you do. He'll never love you as much as I do. I've always been crazy about you, Teddy. You did care a little, didn't you? Don't you any more?

TEDDY. Yes, I do. Of course I do. You're a dear.

OLIVER. Oh, I know — pal stuff. I don't want that.

TEDDY. But I'm awfully fond of you — really, dear, I am.

OLIVER. Then kiss me.

TEDDY. No.

OLIVER. Please.

TEDDY. No.

OLIVER. Not even a sisterly one? [TEDDY *kisses his cheek. He stops dancing and kisses her lips*]

TEDDY. Don't, please. No, I don't like it. Go on. You do dance divinely old man. You're the only man I can dance with.

OLIVER. Will you give the others the slip after awhile and go some place else to dance with me?

TEDDY. I'll — se-see.

OLIVER. Promise.

TEDDY. I'll ——

SCOTTY. Hello! [SCOTTY WILBUR *dashes in from the hall, excited and smiling — with irresponsible and irresistible charm*]

TEDDY. Hello, Scotty! [*She stops dancing quickly and goes to* SCOTTY *eagerly*]

SCOTTY. Terribly sorry, Teddy. I beat it as soon as I could. Wasn't it the limit? Don't know how I ever did such a thing. But I knew you'd understand. You always do.

TEDDY [*beaming at* SCOTTY]. We're going some place to dance. Get them started, Oliver, will you?

OLIVER. Hello, Scotty. [OLIVER *looking not too graciously at* SCOTTY, *goes into the room at right*]

SCOTTY. You're a peach not to care. [*She lets him take her in his arms and kiss her*] You're the ——

TEDDY [*drawing away*]. Careful!

SCOTTY. Who's here?

TEDDY. Eileen and Hallie. Let's get off. Was the dinner awful?

SCOTTY. Not so bad. Only, of course, I wanted to be *here.*

TEDDY. It really doesn't make the slightest difference to you where you are, Scotty, does it? So long as the food is good.

SCOTTY. It wouldn't if you were along.

TEDDY. Every girl you know thinks you mean that.

SCOTTY. And you *know* I do.

TEDDY. I know you *don't*. That's why we — That's why it's all right with us.

SCOTTY. It is all right, isn't it?

TEDDY. Come on — let's dance. You're the only man I can dance with.

SCOTTY. I adore you. [*They dance — pressing their cheeks together*]

MARGARET RAINSFORD *enters from the hall. She is extremely distinguished, a little tired, a little pale, with a critical intelligence in her face, which makes her a trifle cold, but a frank simplicity of manner which is very appealing. She is wearing a black evening gown — at once modish but conservative, with an air of exclusiveness which lifts it beyond mere smartness*]

TEDDY [*as they stop dancing*]. Aunt Margaret, this is Scotty Wilbur. My aunt, Mrs. Rainsford.

SCOTTY [*going to* MARGARET *as she extends her hand*]. How do you do?

MARGARET. How do you do? Are you Arthur Wilbur's son — the Philadelphia Wilburs?

SCOTTY. No. I'm afraid not. We aren't anything in particular — just New York.

[MARGARET *laughs agreeably and* SCOTTY *laughs with her*]

MARGARET. You see, I've been away a long time and I keep trying to catch hold of threads I used to know. Rather foolish, I suppose.

SCOTTY. Rather hopeless, I expect. Threads break awfully fast — don't they — and awfully short.

MARGARET. They seem to. [*Smiling tolerantly as she crosses to sit on the sofa*]

TEDDY. Aunt Margaret was my mother's sister, you know, Scotty.

SCOTTY. Oh, really?

MARGARET. Did you know my sister?

SCOTTY. No — no, I didn't. I — no — I didn't.

TEDDY. Oh no — I've only known Scotty long enough to still like him. How long is it, Scotty? Oh, Dad, may we take your car? [*As* HUBERT GLOUCESTER *enters from the hall*] You aren't going to use it tonight, are you?

SCOTTY. I've got mine here.

TEDDY. But yours is open. We don't want that. May we, Dad?

HUBERT. Certainly.

TEDDY. You're an angel. Phone for yours and mine both, will you? There's a dear. And tell them to hurry. Your man's awfully slow, Dad. I wouldn't have him.

HUBERT. I didn't engage him to keep up with you, you know. [*He goes to the phone good naturedly*]

[GLOUCESTER *is fifty, of medium height, slightly inclined to portliness. His hair, which grows with an attractive wave, is white, heightening the very young color and general brightness of his face. He has a tolerant air of well being and is entirely satisfied with life in general*]

SCOTTY [*to* MARGARET]. Aren't you coming with us?

MARGARET. Do you need me? Haven't you a chaperon?

TEDDY. Heavens, Aunt Margaret! We're not babies.

MARGARET. You don't mean to say you're going without one?

TEDDY. Why, I haven't been any place with a chaperon for a million years.

MARGARET. You're twenty, I believe.

TEDDY. I believe I am — something like that.

MARGARET. You surely don't consider that old enough to go about alone?

TEDDY. We won't be alone. We'll all be together. Everybody does it. It would be too foolish to have — Why, I'd feel as if I had a nurse.

[*The four other young people come in from the room at right greeting* MR. GLOUCESTER *carelessly without stopping their conversation*]

OLIVER. I'll bet you anything you like she stands up better than any car going. [*Heard above the others as they all talk at once*]

TREVOR. I don't agree with you. I'll put my car up against anything.

OLIVER. You're hipped on that little wagon of yours, Trevor.

SCOTTY. It hasn't got a look-in with a real car. [*Going to the table at right to pour out a drink*]

HALLIE [*stopping by* SCOTTY *as she comes back into the room*]. Oh, hello, Scotty. Did you condescend to come, after all?

SCOTTY. I broke my neck to get here.

HALLIE. I wouldn't forgive you if I were Teddy. Don't ever break a date with me. [*Moving close to him as she lowers her voice*]

SCOTTY. I never did — did I?

HALLIE. Do you want to come to dinner tomorrow night?

SCOTTY. Love to.

HALLIE. Nobody else — just me. Like it?

SCOTTY. Crazy about it. If I haven't anything on.

HALLIE. Break it. I want to talk to you. We haven't had a real talk for such a —

TEDDY [*having watched* HALLIE *and* SCOTTIE]. Let's go. Did you get the cars, Dad?

HUBERT. They'll be here in a very few minutes. Won't you young men have something more before you go? In the dining-room. Help yourself.

THE MEN [*indefinitely through the other voices*]. Thanks. [*They slowly move toward hall door, all talking at once.* MARGARET *sits on the couch watching them.* HUBERT *goes to stand before the fire*]

TREVOR [*holding* TEDDY *back as the others go into the hall*]. Will you dance with me first?

TEDDY. Of course. You're the only man I can dance with. Oh, Dad, let me have your key. I can't find mine.

HUBERT [*slipping a key off the ring*]. That's about the third one I've given you this week, young lady. Mind you give that back.

TEDDY. Thanks a lot. Good night, Aunt Margaret. Good night, Dad. Oh, Lordy, I forgot. [*Coming back to her father*] I haven't a cent and this is my party.

HUBERT. I don't think I can do much for you.

TEDDY [*counting as her father unfolds some bills*]. Twenty — forty. Oh, come on, Dad, you must have some more. Try again. [*He takes out more bills*] Forty — eighty. That all?

HUBERT. Absolutely.

TEDDY. For this relief much thanks. If anybody telephones — tell them I'll be home early — in the morning. Good-night. [*Teddy flutters out through the hall.* HUBERT *lights a cigarette*]

MARGARET [*after a pause*]. The guests didn't even say goodnight. It isn't done, I suppose.

HUBERT [*with an amused chuckle*]. Nothing's done that's too much trouble — you can count on that.

MARGARET. You think bad manners are amusing then?

HUBERT. Not especially — no — just prevalent.

MARGARET. It's appalling — simply appalling.

HUBERT. What?

MARGARET. All of it — everything.

HUBERT. Oh, you take it too seriously entirely, Margaret.

MARGARET. You mean, you think it's all right — all of it.

HUBERT [*smoking comfortably with his back to the fire*]. It's the way things are. The manners of yesterday have nothing to do with the case. This is today.

MARGARET. If my sister could see her daughter now! I only hope she can't.

HUBERT. Bosh! If Lucille had lived she would have come right along with the tide.

MARGARET. No!

HUBERT. Yes!

MARGARET. Never!

HUBERT. Yes! She was too much a woman of the world not to.

MARGARET. A woman of the world yes — but a gentlewoman.

HUBERT. See here, Margaret, do you mean you think I'm not keeping Teddy up to what Lucille would have made her?

MARGARET. Well, do you think you are?

HUBERT. Why — these are the nicest kind of young people. Smart families — every one of them.

MARGARET. That's just it. That's what makes it so horrible. If they were common little upstarts and parvenues it would be easy to understand. But nice people! What are their parents thinking of? Can't they see what it's going to do to the future generations?

HUBERT. There never was a generation that grew up that didn't think the next one coming on was going to the dogs. They're freer — yes — because they *are* younger. But, by Jove, I actually believe they are safer than the bottled up age I went through — when we had to sneak about all the deviltry we got into. They're perfectly open and above-board about it. You'll have to admit that. And they're going to work out their own salvation in their own way — and come out all right.

MARGARET. There's something far more serious in it than merely the difference between two generations.

HUBERT. Oh, you exaggerate. Frankly I think you're awfully priggish. If you measure everything from your own conservative ideas of good form, of course, these youngsters seem a little raw. But this is their day —

MARGARET. Oh — *their day!* I'm not talking about superficial fashions and manners. The vital things of character don't belong to anybody's day — they're eternal and fundamental and I see Lucille's daughter without them.

HUBERT [*after a slight pause of surprise*]. That's rather plain talk.

MARGARET. I mean to be plain. Why not? I know what I am feeling now — she would feel. I know that what I find in her house since I have come back would have —

HUBERT. And what have you found? I'm able to do more for Teddy than I did for Lucille. That's the only bad thing about it — that she isn't here to have it.

MARGARET. She would have hated it. She wouldn't have let you give that child eighty dollars to throw away in an evening.

HUBERT. Eighty dollars! That won't get them more than a sandwich or two apiece.

MARGARET. She wouldn't have let her go about half naked and wearing pearls that no young girl should ever wear.

HUBERT. Nonsense! You're old-fashioned and entirely too damned — something. What in the name of heaven is the matter with Teddy? What's the matter with her? She's a charming girl and a great success and her friends are as nice as anybody in New York.

MARGARET. The emptiness — the soul-lessness of it all!

HUBERT. What?

MARGARET. I've been here three days and I haven't heard her, nor any of her friends, say a single word or express a thought about anything on earth but their clothes and their motors and themselves. They all talk alike, think alike, dress alike, sound alike. And the drinking! Your house is a bar. It pours out — at all hours.

HUBERT. That's Prohibition. It only amuses them to have it about when they can't get it other places.

MARGARET. Is that all you can see in it?

HUBERT. That's all there is in it.

MARGARET. And the smoking! Those delicate young girls are as dependent upon their cigarettes to quiet their nerves as any — Oh, it's too terrible.

HUBERT. I have rowed with Ted about the cigarettes. That is bad, I admit, but what are you going to do? It's not her fault, they all do it.

MARGARET. Who are these boys who are making love to her — running about with her alone? Are you willing for her to marry them?

HUBERT. I don't know that she wants to.

MARGARET. Do you never advise her?

HUBERT. I'm doing all I can to make her happy. She's a nice girl and she's perfectly capable of taking care of herself.

MARGARET. She isn't! She isn't! She's only a child. She's surrounded by everything that can hurt her and nothing that can help her. It's all chaos and waste and degeneracy. And my boy — lying out there in France! And this is all it was for! He went so gladly. He gave himself for something greater than himself — to save civilization. Oh, the farce of it! The hideous, horrible useless sacrifice! [*She leans back on the pillows — shaken with sobs*]

HUBERT. Don't think I don't know how you feel. Of course you're cut up. But Margaret — if you'll allow me to say so — you're allowing your own personal sorrow to color everything. You're letting it make you bitter and — well, I don't see what all this has to do with Teddy.

MARGARET. It has everything to do with her. She's the most poignant part of it all. I came back so eager to see her because she meant part of Lucille. I was so thankful she was alive even if John — [*Her voice breaks*]

HUBERT. Margaret! [*Putting a hand on her shoulder kindly*]

MARGARET. I said, I'll try to put my own grief aside. I'll try to mean something to her — something of what she's lost in her mother. I could scarcely wait to get here. She was going to be so wonderful — and —

HUBERT. Well?

MARGARET. And instead of that —

HUBERT. Well — what?

MARGARET. Oh, my God, Hubert,

she's been killed and thrown away just as absolutely as John was. She's the very essence of this thing that's in the air. Why have you let it kill Theodora?

HUBERT [*moving away and strongly resisting her argument*]. I don't admit what you say — I don't admit that she's doing or having anything that isn't the custom of any nice girl with —

[TEDDY *throws the hall door open and comes in quickly followed by* SCOTT. *She hesitates a moment, a little surprised at finding* MARGARET *and her father still in the room. There is a pause*]

TEDDY. Are you two still up?

HUBERT. I thought you'd gone to dance.

TEDDY. We changed our minds. We're going some place else.

HUBERT. Where?

TEDDY. Why — some place — further up — out. Everything's so frightfully crowded, you know, it's really no fun.

HUBERT. What place? Where are you going?

TEDDY. A place Oliver knows. Where is it, Scotty?

SCOTTY. I'm not dead sure. I've been there. Awfully nice. But Oliver'll have to direct us. We're all going together, you know.

HUBERT [*looking at his watch*]. Everything closes at one. You wouldn't more than have time to get there till you would have to come back.

TEDDY. It will be fun to drive up anyway. I'm going to get a heavier coat. That's what I came back for.

HUBERT. I don't want you to go.

TEDDY. What?

HUBERT. I don't want you to go.

TEDDY [*in amazed amusement*]. Why Dad! What do you mean?

HUBERT. Just that. It's too late. You've done enough tonight.

TEDDY. You're frightfully amusing. Why this sudden sternness? Of course, I'm going. The others are waiting.

HUBERT. You can't go.

TEDDY. Why, Father —

HUBERT. Say goodnight to Mr. Wilbur.

TEDDY. Really, you're funny. I'll do nothing of the kind. I'm not going to disappoint those people. [*She starts to the door*]

HUBERT. You'll not go.

TEDDY. You can't speak that way t me. I'm not a baby.

HUBERT. I'm sorry but —

TEDDY. I'm sorry, too — but I' going.

HUBERT. You're not.

TEDDY. You're extremely disagre able. You can't make me break positive engagement and treat people -

HUBERT. We won't say anythin more about that. You're not goin That will do.

TEDDY [*after a pause she goes quickly the table, tears a small piece of pape writes on it, folds it*]. Scotty, there the telephone number I promised yo Goodnight, Scott. Please apologize t the others for me and tell them ho extremely sorry I am that such a ridic lously embarrassing thing has happene Goodnight.

SCOTTY [*a little embarrassed, but sti smiling*]. Goodnight. Goodnigh Goodnight. [*He goes out*]

TEDDY. What on earth do you mea Dad? How dare you treat me lik that? [*She faces her father with a bla of anger*]

HUBERT. You shouldn't have mad it necessary. If you don't know by th time that a young girl can't be motorin out to dance halls at this time of nigh it's high time you did.

TEDDY. You've never questioned m good taste before about where I go an what I do. Why this sudden —

HUBERT. I hope you've never don anything before that needed questior ing.

TEDDY. Do you think we've neve done this before? We do it all the tim and then we come downtown and hav breakfast at Childs — and it's a lot c fun and I intend to keep on doing it — or anything else I want to do. I sup pose I can thank you, Aunt Margaret for this sudden interest in my affairs

HUBERT. Teddy!

TEDDY. I've never been so humi iated in my life.

HUBERT. Teddy!

TEDDY. Father's always had th decency and common sense to believ that whatever I did was all right. Thi is absolutely the first time he's eve behaved in this absurd manner and know you put it into his head.

HUBERT. Be careful.

TEDDY. Well — isn't it true?

HUBERT. I — I simply didn't knov you were doing such things. It isn'

ecessary. There are plenty of other
things to do for amusement.

TEDDY. I think I must be the judge
of what I find amusing. I like this.

HUBERT. Then your judgment is not
to be trusted.

TEDDY. Trusted? I don't know
what yours is, father. You do a great
many things that I don't like. Mrs.
llister, for instance, is far from what I
call good taste and yet you seem to find
her extremely amusing.

HUBERT [*helplessly and much embarrassed*]. A — go to bed.

TEDDY. I don't want to go to bed.

HUBERT. Well, you ought to want
to.

TEDDY. Are you going to decide
when I go to bed, too? You'd better
put me on a leash, father. It would be
much easier for you.

HUBERT. You don't treat me with
any respect.

TEDDY. I didn't know you wanted
me to.

HUBERT. You — [*Trying to be dignified and stern, he goes helplessly out of
the room through the hall door.* TEDDY
turns to MARGARET. *A pause as they
look steadily at each other*]

MARGARET [*rising*]. Oh, my dear
girl — understand this. It all happened
because I'm interested in you — because
I love you very much.

TEDDY. Please don't let your interest
make father lose his head and behave
like this again.

MARGARET. Don't, Theodora!
You're so young, dear. I'm saying
things your mother would say to you if
she were here.

TEDDY. Just what's wrong with
what we were going to do tonight?
Just what's wrong, pray? Don't you
think we're to be trusted? Don't
you think we're decent enough to behave
without being watched every minute?

MARGARET. I think you're young
and impetuous and human and that
you're getting your pleasure in the very
same way that the fastest, commonest
sort of people get it, and it all leads to a
looseness and laxness that can't possibly
have anything but harm in it.

TEDDY. I don't agree with you at all.
I believe in freedom. I think it makes
us strong and independent. Nothing is
so dangerous as narrow, evil-mindedness
— and nothing is as safe as frankness.

MARGARET. That's the song the
world is riding to the devil on just now.

That's what we're fooling ourselves
with.

TEDDY. If you're going to judge me
and what I do by yourself and what you
think is right, I dare say everything I do
and say and think is wrong. But I
don't — Oh, we aren't getting anywhere. Let's drop it and say good
night. [*She starts toward the door*]

MARGARET. Theodora — wait,
please. You surely know it's very hard
to say these disagreeable things to you.

TEDDY. Then why on earth do you
do it?

MARGARET. Because you're in danger — because I want to help you.

TEDDY. What a joke!

MARGARET. The very dress you have
on is indecent. Positively indecent.
These boys — the promiscuous love
making I see going on here all the time
— the familiarity — the freedom as you
call it — the kissing — it's all wrong —
as wrong as it can be.

TEDDY. Kissing? How silly!
There are kisses and kisses. Kissing
doesn't mean any more now than shaking hands did — when you were a girl.

MARGARET. Don't you know that
you're wasting the most precious years
of your life without doing one ounce of
good to anybody — or thinking one
thought of anything but yourself and
your body? Don't you know you are
spending too much money — wasting it
here and there, when there never was a
time that greater good could be done
with it? Don't you know you're being
horribly criticized for it? [*She comes
close to* TEDDY]

TEDDY. You've said quite enough,
Aunt Margaret.

MARGARET. I've hurt you and I only
want to help you.

TEDDY. But I don't consider I need
your help. Goodnight.

MARGARET. My dear little girl —
try to see that I'm only — Won't you
kiss me goodnight? [TEDDY *doesn't
move.* MARGARET *goes to the hall door*]
You will see when you aren't angry.
Goodnight, dear. [*She goes out*]

[*Slow tears come into* TEDDY'S *eyes. She
fights them away — and goes to the
telephone, taking the receiver*]

TEDDY. Hello. Is there a young
man down there? Ask him to come to
the telephone. Hello — Scotty — I'll
change my dress and be down in fifteen
minutes. Telephone the others and ask

them to wait for us. I know a peach of a place to go for breakfast. What? Yes, of course he nearly choked. Stuff! I hope you don't think I'm afraid of Dad. He was only showing off before Aunt Margaret — trying to make a noise like a father. [*She puts up the receiver*]

THE CURTAIN FALLS

ACT II

SCENE I — TIME. *Seven o'clock the following evening.*

PLACE. — *The Gloucester cottage in Westchester.*

The room shows that the house is old and simple and that it has been done over with modern taste and comfort.

The upper left half of the room is an alcove with two windows in it and a slanting ceiling. At center of the left side of the room is a fireplace and simple wooden mantel. At lower left is a jog and in this a single door leading into the dining room.

At right are three small windows placed close together and in the middle of the right half of back wall is the outside door leading into the garden.

Before the windows at right is a long narrow wooden seat with a spindle back and arms and an upholstered cushion. In front of this seat is a medium sized round table — with small quaint chairs about it.

Before the fireplace is a large wing-chair and in the alcove a smaller table.

The furniture and chintz curtains have an air of having been picked up by someone who loved them, but of being now neglected and long out of use. Some of the pieces are covered with dustcovers of muslin.

At curtain the room is empty and only a faint light comes in from the windows:

After a moment TEDDY *and* SCOTT *appear at the window in the alcove.* SCOTT *tries to raise the window.*

SCOTTY. The window's locked. What do I do now?

TEDDY. Break it. Break the pane near the catch. Let me do it. It's one of those little funny ones. Take my slipper off. [SCOTTY *takes one of* TEDDY'S *slippers off and she breaks a*

pane of glass with it, puts her hand in slips the catch and pushes the window up] Pretty spiffy! Now give me a boost. [SCOTTY *helps her, and she climbs in at the window*] Come on. Don' stand on ceremony. [SCOTTY *climbs in* TEDDY *hops down stage on one foot and puts her slipper on*]

SCOTTY. Oh, is it all done up in moth balls? [*Seeing the coverings on the furniture as he goes towards the other windows*]

TEDDY. Dad and I only use it for week-ends once in a while. It's really a peachy little place. It was mother's. She loved it. Take the covers off the table and those two chairs. Now where's the key? I know. Here [*Getting the key which hangs at side of door and unlocking the door*] Pull! It sticks! [*They get the door open*] Oh isn't it pretty out there! It's going to be divine going home. Those little cross roads are too heavenly in the moonlight.

SCOTTY. This is immense!

TEDDY. Get the coffee. [*He gets the Thermos bottle and packages of sandwiches from the doorstep outside.* SCOTTY *whistles.* TEDDY *sings*] See if you can start a fire.

SCOTTY [*going to the fireplace*]. There's just a speck of stuff here.

TEDDY. The wood house is straight through the dining room beyond the kitchen. [*Pointing to door at left*] Keep going till you bump your head against a funny little door.

SCOTTY [*as he goes out*]. If I fall dead come and get me.

TEDDY [*calling after him as she unscrews the two cups which are on the top of the Thermos bottle — takes out the cork, opens the sandwiches — looks at her watch*]. It's just a little after seven now. The others are all dressing for dinner and wondering where we are and cussing us out for giving them the slip. And father is pacing up and down foaming at the mouth. Oh fine! [*As* SCOTTY *comes back with an arm full of wood*] Put some on.

SCOTTY [*beginning to build the fire*]. Will he raise the devil?

TEDDY. I hope so. It will do him good. This will show him the stern parent idea is extinct.

SCOTTY. He's pretty fine you know.

TEDDY. Dad's really a peach. I was awfully disappointed in him — kicking up such a row last night. I thought I had him too well trained for that. Shut the door. It's not exactly balmy in here, is it?

SCOTTY [*closing the door*]. It's always balmy for me where you are, sweetie.

TEDDY. It's always tropical for me where you are, precious.

SCOTTY. Angel! [*He starts to kiss her*]

TEDDY. Let's eat. Um! I never was so hungry in my life. [*They sit in the two chairs above the table at right*] Oh, the coffee's boiling hot.

SCOTTY [*as he takes a sip*]. Gosh!

TEDDY. What?

SCOTTY. I forgot. I had a date with Hallie tonight.

TEDDY. Oh, I thought it was something important.

SCOTTY. Promised I'd go to dinner with her.

TEDDY. Well, you've escaped that. She won't do a thing to me for keeping you out all night. I'll bet she's telephoned Dad every fifteen minutes all day just to keep him stirred up. By *this* time I bet she's got him thinking we've been out *two* nights.

SCOTTY. You can't expect him to be exactly calm about it, you know, old girl. This is going some even for you.

TEDDY. Well, I want to make an impression — so he won't misbehave again. We can get back by ten. That will be a very *chaste* hour to stroll in and say we had a *sweet* quiet day in the country.

SCOTTY. Having left home last night about midnight —

TEDDY. Danced all night at three different joints —

SCOTTY. Four!

TEDDY. Had breakfast at a very queer roadhouse and then with a few deft lies gave the others the slip —

SCOTTY. Motored with me all day — and here we are.

TEDDY. Alone at last with night coming on apace. Don't you love it? I'm crazy about it.

SCOTTY. You're a peach. I adore you. See here, honey, there couldn't be a better time and place to tell me you'll marry me. [*Lighting their cigarettes*]

TEDDY. Why do you want to marry me, Scott?

SCOTTY. I like that!

TEDDY. I mean — how do you know you do?

SCOTTY. How do I know anything?

TEDDY. But you've been in love with so many girls.

SCOTTY. But I never wanted to marry so many.

TEDDY. Am I the *great* passion of your life?

SCOTTY. You are! [*He starts to kiss her. The door blows open*]

TEDDY. Oh, shut it tight! Heavens, is it raining?

SCOTTY. Don't think so. [*He closes the door with a bang*] Are you cold, dear?

TEDDY. N-o, but I'm not exactly roasting.

SCOTTY. This will make you all right. [*Taking a flask from his pocket*]

TEDDY. Goodness, is there any left?

SCOTTY [*pouring some whiskey into the cups*]. I got it refilled at the last place. [*Giving her a cup*]

TEDDY. Yes, *you* got refilled in the last place. [*Taking a sip*] Oh, I hate it this way — without water.

SCOTTY. But there isn't any water — so don't be so fastidious. Drink it all, dearest. You must. I wouldn't have you take cold for anything. Come and sit over here by the fire. [*Drawing the armchair out*]

TEDDY. We must go in a minute. Aren't there any candles there to light?

SCOTTY. What's the use? I love it this way. [*She sits in the chair. He sits on the arm*] I adore being really alone with you, sweetheart — way off like this. It makes me feel you really do care. Tell me how much. [*Putting his head against hers*]

TEDDY. I don't know.

SCOTTY. Ah, don't say that, Ted. You make me miserable. Tell me this — has there ever been anybody you cared for *more?* Be honest.

TEDDY. No. Unless, perhaps — Oh no there really wasn't.

SCOTTY. Was Oliver *the* one? [*Drinking from the flask*]

TEDDY. Dear old Ollie! I always *will* love him.

SCOTTY. *Don't!*

TEDDY. Not *this* way — silly. He's just a perfectly adorable old darling.

SCOTTY. Yes, with money to burn and I haven't a cent. That's why I'm jealous of him.

TEDDY. Don't be stupid! Dad's got enough. I'm glad you *haven't* any, Scott, so if I do marry you I'll know it's for yourself alone, see?

SCOTTY. Don't say *if*. You aren't just flirting with me, are you, Ted?

TEDDY. Of course not. I'm making up my mind.

SCOTTY. Well, how's your mind getting along? Where are we now?

TEDDY. I'll tell you *one* thing — pos-i-tively — I feel very much more as if I *might* marry you than I ever did anybody else.

SCOTTY. That's wonderful! [*He takes another drink*]

TEDDY. I thought you'd appreciate it. I believe, Scotty, I like you because you haven't any character.

SCOTTY. Thanks.

TEDDY. You're so nice and *drifty*. See that queer light in the fire. Pretty! Isn't it weird and sweet — shut up here with the whole world outside? I *want* to believe in love. It *ought* to be the most wonderful thing in the world.

SCOTTY. It is. [*Putting his arm about her and speaking with his lips on her cheek*] I'm mad about you. I don't give a rap about anybody else in the world.

TEDDY. Not even Hallie?

SCOTTY. Hallie — stuff!

TEDDY. She's mad about *you*.

SCOTTY. *Are* you jealous of Hallie, sweetheart?

TEDDY. Not a bit. I think she's a pill!

SCOTTY. Kiss me! [*He snatches her in his arms and kisses her lips*] Dearest! Take your hat off!

[*There is a faint flash of lightning*]

TEDDY. No!

SCOTTY. Please! I want to see your wonderful hair. Let me! [*He takes her hat off and kisses her hair, then her lips*] I adore you, Ted, have you ever kissed anybody that way before? [*She doesn't answer*] You *have*. Who?

TEDDY. I can't always help — *how* people kiss me!

SCOTTY. But have *you* kissed — too?

TEDDY. Um — I don't remember!

SCOTTY. Kiss me, with all your heart now, dear. Please. [*She leans slowly towards him and kisses his lips. He stands up and lifts her in his arms*]

TEDDY. Do you know what would make us know that we loved each other?

SCOTTY. What?

[*A sudden downpour of rain begins with thunder, lightning and wind*]

TEDDY. If we hadn't any money at all, just ourselves, then we'd know.

SCOTTY [*holding her*]. Couldn't be done.

TEDDY. But what if I *hadn't* any money?

SCOTTY. But you *have*. Thank God, there's nothing like that with us.

TEDDY [*looking at him keenly and drawing away from him a little, realizing that he has had too much to drink*]. Scott — does it really mean an awful lot to you — my money?

[*The storm grows more violent*]

SCOTTY. Kiss me. What does anything else mean?

TEDDY [*holding him off*]. What if you knew this minute I didn't have a cent? What would you do?

SCOTTY. Don't say disagreeable things. We're happy.

TEDDY. Would you want to marry me then?

SCOTTY. What's the use talking moonshine? We know each other too well. I couldn't marry anybody on earth without money.

TEDDY. *Is* money the most important thing in the world to you, Scott?

SCOTTY. Kiss me.

TEDDY. No! No! No! You don't love me. This is horrible. I want to go. [*Getting away from him*] Listen. It *is* raining. [*A slow flash of lightning lights the room and the heavy rain and wind are heard*]

SCOTTY. Nothing but a little Spring shower. We have to wait till it's over. Come and sit down again.

TEDDY. No, I don't want to. [*Moving away from him*]

SCOTTY. Why not? I want to tell you how much I love you. Kiss me!

TEDDY. No!

SCOTTY. You've got to.

TEDDY. I won't. Let me go. Scott — *don't*.

[*He draws her onto the seat at right. She gets to her feet and pushes him so he falls on the bench*]

SCOTTY. Oh, this feels good! Come here, dearie. Where are you? Come here and sit beside me. Look! See? Here's a nice little place for you right here.

[*Another flash shows* TEDDY *standing in the middle of the room, horror stricken* — SCOTTY *lying full length on the bench*]

TEDDY. Scotty, get up. We must go! I *hate* this! You're not going to sleep. [*There is a peal of thunder. The storm increases. She goes to the fireplace*] Oh, aren't there any candles here? *She looks on the table in the alcove, and closes the window. After a moment a man opens the outer door. A flash of lightning shows him to be young and strong. He wears a rain-soaked top coat and cap and carries an electric lantern*]

BILLY. Oh, I hope I didn't frighten you. [*Coming in and closing the door*] I guess you didn't hear me knock so I thought I'd take a chance and walk in.

TEDDY. Where did you come from? [*They shout above the noise of the storm*]

BILLY. Up in the country further. I'm trying to get back to town. Never dreamed this storm was coming. She's a bird. Regular cloud burst. [*Lifting his lantern to see* TEDDY *better*]

TEDDY. How long is it going to last?

BILLY. Don't know. Looks like an all nighter. These country roads are going to be in a sweet mess for a car. I skidded at the top of this hill out there till I thought I was going to glory. [*Another flash of lightning*] Awful — isn't it? [*He turns his flashlight on* SCOTTY *and then back on* TEDDY]

TEDDY [*embarrassed as* BILLY *sees* SCOTT]. Yes — we — just came in for a few minutes ourselves and got caught — got caught in the *rain* — I mean. This is my house.

BILLY. Oh, I see. You're not living here?

TEDDY. I've got to get to New York. I've *got* to. Do you think my car can make it?

BILLY. I'm afraid nothing could do it in this. It's terrific — absolutely terrific. I'm sorry. It's a shame. I wish I could get you back. Can't I make that fire a little better for you? [*He puts his lantern on the mantel shelf and builds up the fire. The lantern and the fire throw a circle of light over them*] You're lucky you made this house. At least it's better than lying in the ditch. [*He glances at* SCOTTY]

TEDDY. I'm going on the minute it stops a little.

BILLY. She's not going to do that in a hurry. Gee, I'm pretty well soaked. Do you mind if I try to dry out a little?

TEDDY. If you can get anything dry tonight, you're welcome. [*She goes to the armchair.* Billy *takes off his top coat and puts it over a chair in the alcove*]

BILLY. Thanks. It was a great piece of luck for me that you were here, I can tell you. [SCOTTY *groans in his sleep.* BILLY *looks inquisitively at him*]

TEDDY. He doesn't feel very well.

BILLY. Is he ill? Could I do anything?

TEDDY. No — no. He's only dead for sleep. We've been motoring all day.

BILLY. I know. It gets you that way. [*A pause*] Are you warm enough?

TEDDY. Oh yes — yes. It's all very delightful.

BILLY. It is for me. I must say this is the last thing I ever expected to happen.

TEDDY. I can't say I exactly planned and schemed for the situation myself.

BILLY. Do you mind my pipe?

TEDDY. Not if you give me one, too.

BILLY. I'm afraid Luckies are the best I can offer you. [*He begins to look at her with keen amusement and interest*]

TEDDY. They're all right — if you just have enough of them. [*He lights her cigarette. There is another crash of thunder*] Oh, why did this have to happen!

BILLY. The storm? [*He stands with his back to the fire*]

TEDDY. It's put everything on the blink for me.

BILLY. I s'pose there never was a storm that didn't spill the beans for somebody. But nothing ever seems half as bad in the morning.

TEDDY. This is once when everything's going to seem much worse in the morning. [*Sitting in the armchair*]

BILLY. But you can make yourself pretty comfortable here for the night.

TEDDY. Oh, yes. I never was more comfortable in my life. Well, it's a delightful evening for a long chat by the fire. I must say I'm glad *you* dropped in. The other member of the party doesn't seem to be adding much to the gayety of nations.

BILLY. I'm glad to be a better talker than the other fellow for once.

TEDDY. It certainly is the chance of your life to sparkle. [BILLY *laughs*] Go on — I was never so much in need of entertainment.

BILLY. Well, here's a bright gem. Do you dwell in New York?

TEDDY. Yes. Don't you?

BILLY. Y—e—s. I s'pose I do.

TEDDY. Don't you know whether you do or not?

BILLY. I hardly know whether I'm on earth or not.

TEDDY. What?

BILLY. When you hit the great city for the first time you don't know whether you're living in it or just having a pipe dream.

TEDDY. The first time in your whole life?

BILLY. Yep!

TEDDY. You don't look it.

BILLY. I s'pose you think I ought to have a ring in my nose.

TEDDY. Go on — sparkle some more.

BILLY. I'm afraid I'm running down.

TEDDY. Oh, don't. If you'll choose a topic of conversation, I'll do my best to keep up.

BILLY. I know a good one.

TEDDY. All right. Fire away.

BILLY. *You.* Who are you? What are you? What do you do with yourself — and what do you like best?

TEDDY. I said a conversation, not a catechism.

BILLY. That's the best I can do.

TEDDY. Well — who am I? Anonymous. What am I? Just an ordinary girl. What do I do? Amuse myself as much as possible. A —

BILLY. What do you like best?

TEDDY. To have my own way about everything in the world. Now you. You must be the "dook" in disguise at least.

BILLY. No — nothing so dressy. I'm an everyday guy — not so long out of the army — who fell into an awfully soft snap in New York.

TEDDY. What sort of a snap?

BILLY. A job somebody got for me through pull — with so much salary to it, it makes me dizzy.

TEDDY. Rather a spiffy dizziness, I should say.

BILLY. Yes, it is. I've been pretty lucky. I've fallen in with some awfully nice people and I don't mind telling you I don't know whether I'm coming or going.

TEDDY. I advise you to keep going.

BILLY. You either have to do that or get out. If you stop in the middle, you drown. [SCOTTY *groans. They both look at him*]

TEDDY. No — I don't think he's going to contradict you. Go on. Oh, yes — how do you like New York? Was it all as wonderful as you thought it would be?

BILLY. Much more wonderful and much more rotten.

TEDDY. What do you like best about it?

BILLY. The excitement, I s'pose.

TEDDY. What do you hate most?

BILLY. Oh, it would take a week to tell that.

TEDDY. Well, I think we'll be here a week.

BILLY. I hope so. [*Bowing low to her*]

TEDDY. You say you've met some awfully nice people.

BILLY. I'm just coming from a house party now — on up further.

TEDDY. Any attractive girls there?

BILLY. Oh yes. One beauty, one stunner and one peach.

TEDDY. I s'pose you gobbled up the peach.

BILLY. No — the bloom on her cheek kept me guessing.

TEDDY. That's the cleverest thing a cheek can do.

BILLY. Oh, I don't know.

TEDDY. There's nothing so dull as being *sure.* Don't you like something left to the imagination?

BILLY. I *do.* But Lordie! There's precious little a girl leaves to the imagination now.

TEDDY. That sounds as though you'd been shocked.

BILLY. Shocked? I've been stunned. I knew the pace was pretty swift but — Wow!

TEDDY. Can't you keep up with it?

BILLY. I'm coming right along. But it knocks the wind out of me sometimes.

TEDDY. If you don't like it — why don't you get out?

BILLY. Oh, I don't want to go back to the same old thing. I was born on a farm so big you could lose one of these dinky little fellows around here in the fence corners. I wanted to be in New York and see life, and it's got me all right. I'm doing just what everybody else is.

TEDDY. You'll get over your provincial ideas. Freedom and frankness and beauty are so easily misunderstood by the outsider.

BILLY. I'm allowing for all I don't understand, but there's one thing I'm dead sure of.

TEDDY. What?

BILLY. They're making a circus out of some things. The casual way they

et engaged and unengaged — for in-
tance — makes my hair stand on end.
What do they think it is — anyway?
A game of tag?

TEDDY. Well — why not? What
else can it be?

BILLY. The chasing's fun enough,
but why get caught till you're sure you
want to stay caught forever — till the
whole game's over?

TEDDY. How can anybody be sure
of that?

BILLY. They could be a darn sight
more sure if they went at it as if it were a
little something more than a try-out.
What on earth do they think being
married means?

TEDDY. And what on earth do you
think it means?

BILLY. Oh — just the most important thing in the world — where everything starts, and where great things
come from — if it's right — and where
the worst things come from if it's wrong.
What do you think it all means?

TEDDY. Nobody ever finds what he
wants, anyway. And I think it's
better to keep our dreams shut up tight
and never let 'em out — so we won't be
disappointed. [*She speaks with great
wistfulness and honesty for the first time*]

BILLY. I don't. I think it's better
to let 'em out and make 'em come
through.

TEDDY. Can't be done.

BILLY. Oh, yes it can.

TEDDY. How?

BILLY. By wishing and wishing —
and never taking anything but the best
wish.

TEDDY. I — I wish —

BILLY. What? [*There is a long
flash of lightning*]

TEDDY [*rising*]. Nothing. I wish
the storm would stop.

BILLY. I wish I could stop it for you.
Let's see how it looks. [*Opening the
door and shutting it quickly*] It's getting
worse. You might as well try to swim
across the ocean as get to town in this.

TEDDY. Well, I can't help it — and
that's all there is to it. [*Pause*] You
must wonder why I'm here. It isn't
very easy to explain.

BILLY. Don't try. Why should you?

TEDDY. I came out — because somebody told me not to. And you see, I'm
having the time of my life.

BILLY. Well — a — a — a —

TEDDY. Exactly. Nobody will ever
quite understand, but I hope *you* do.

BILLY. I understand it's tough luck
and I wish to heaven I could get you
back — but it can't be done. This is
your house. You go up stairs and make
yourself as comfortable as you can.
It's the best thing to do — for a fact.
I'll sit here — in this chair by the fire —
and everything'll be all right. You'll
have to be game. And you *will* be.

TEDDY. I'm game all right.

BILLY. That's right. You take the
light. [*They go to the little door at left*]
I'll get you back in town in the morning
— at daylight.

TEDDY. Oh no — please — please
don't wait. I don't want you to — no,
please. I'll get back all right. I'd
rather you'd go before. I'd rather
you'd be gone when I come down in the
morning. It would be easier.

BILLY. Then I'll never see you again.
But I'll never forget you. My name's
Wade — Billy Wade. Do you want to
tell me yours?

TEDDY. I'd rather not.

BILLY. And don't be afraid of anything tonight — will you?

TEDDY. Of course not — with you
here. You've helped me through an
awfully hard place — and you're splendid to understand.

BILLY. Why shouldn't I understand? You were held up by the storm
and so was I. Why should I misunderstand you any more than you did me?
You didn't seem to think I was a highway robber or anything when I banged
through that door.

TEDDY. Perhaps you are. Good-
night.

BILLY. Goodbye.

TEDDY. Goodbye. A — goodbye.

[*Exits.* BILLY *watches her off, closes the
door, puts some wood on the fire,
takes a blanket with which the table
in the alcove is covered, starts to sit
and wrap himself in it, remembers*
SCOTTY — *goes to him and puts*
SCOTTY'S *coat over him, goes back to
the armchair, wraps himself in the
blanket and prepares to sleep for
the night. The storm rages all
through this scene. The curtain is
lowered to denote the passing of the
night*]

SCENE II. — *Daylight comes in at the
windows. Both boys are still asleep.
After a moment* BILLY *rouses himself
— surprised to find the blanket en-*

tirely across his chest. Standing up he shakes his stiff legs, smooths his hair, and after listening at the door left, goes over to look at SCOTTY. *After a long look of curiosity, amusement and disgust he gets his hat and coat, throws the outer door open letting in a bright stream of light — and listening again, goes reluctantly out. The morning is fresh, the sun gradually comes in.*

After a moment MR. HEYFER *passes the windows at back, comes to the door and seeing it is open enters quickly and pugnaciously.* MR. HEYFER *is seventy, the typical product of a long life of hard work and nothing but work. Looking about he discovers* SCOTTY.

HEYFER [*shouting at* SCOTTY]. Hey there, what you doin' in this house? Hey! Who are ye? [*Going to* SCOTTY *and shaking him*]

SCOTTY [*very sleepy*]. What? What's the matter? What? [*Half seeing* HEYFER]

HEYFER. I say, what you doin' on this property? How'd you get in? There's a heavy fine fer trespassin'. Don't ye know that?

SCOTTY [*getting up*]. Who are you?

HEYFER. None of yer business who I am. Git out o' this house.

SCOTTY. I will not.

HEYFER. Well, I guess ye will. I got stric' orders not to let nobody in — never — fer nothin'.

SCOTTY. Hold on till you know what you're talking about.

HEYFER. Don't give me no back talk or I'll — [TEDDY *comes in from the left, carrying her hat and coat*] Who a'r ye?

TEDDY. Who are *you*?

HEYFER. This is private property.

TEDDY. Oh, you're old Mr. Heyfer.

HEYFER. Lord — air you Miss Gloucester? Where in the name o' goshum did you come from this time o' day? [*Slowly taking off his hat*]

TEDDY. We were driving by last night and got caught in the storm and came in here.

HEYFER. You don't say. Is he yer husband? [*Looking at* SCOTTY]

TEDDY. He is not.

SCOTTY. Lucky we got here, wasn't it?

HEYFER. Was ye here all night?

TEDDY. We were.

HEYFER. Both of ye?

SCOTTY. Certainly we were. Wha did you expect us to do, stay out in th rain all night?

HEYFER [*staring in open-mouthe amazement from one to the other*]. I d know but what that might have bee better.

SCOTTY. I'm afraid I don't agre with your point of view. Quite shower, wasn't it? But a very delight ful morning, isn't it? [*Swaggering u to the open door*]

HEYFER. How'd ye git in?

TEDDY. We busted in. Men things, will you, please, and shut then up again. We're going on now. [*Put ting on her hat*]

HEYFER. It certainly is peculia actions. Does your pa know you're ou here?

TEDDY. No, and I don't see anything peculiar about coming into my ow house.

HEYFER. Well, that's as may be I'd' know as I jest quite understand [*He goes out dubiously*]

SCOTTY [*going to* TEDDY]. I'm to horribly sorry. I wouldn't have ha this happen for anything.

TEDDY. That's all right. It's no your fault.

SCOTTY. Don't mind it, dear. Wha difference can it make after all?

TEDDY [*starting to put on her coat*] None, *whatsoever*. Let's get home a fast as we can.

SCOTTY. But, Ted, it's going to b all right. You don't blame me, do you [*Going to her and taking her coat*]

TEDDY. Not the least little bit.

SCOTTY. It might have happened to anybody. Lots of people are caught i storms.

TEDDY. We certainly were *caught*.

SCOTTY. I'll do anything on earth to make it right.

TEDDY. There isn't anything you can do, to change it one way or the other. Get your coat and let's go.

MARGARET [*calling from outside*]. Theodora!

TEDDY. Aunt Margaret!

MARGARET. Theodora — are you there? [MARGARET *rushes in. She and* TEDDY *start to each other as* HUBERT *follows* MARGARET *in. There is a pause* HUBERT *and* TEDDY *look steadily at each other*]

TEDDY. Now, father, I've done nothing on earth I'm ashamed of in the slightest degree.

SCOTTY. Mr. Gloucester —

HUBERT. Were you here all night? [*Ignoring* SCOTTY]

TEDDY. Yes, we were. And I've done nothing that I'm ashamed of, I tell you.

MARGARET. You believe her, Hubert?

HUBERT. Believe her? Why should I?

SCOTTY. Mr. Gloucester, this thing isn't at all the way it looks.

HUBERT. Damn you! You —

TEDDY. Oh, don't, please. Do you believe I've done a rotten, low down thing, or don't you?

HUBERT. My God! How do I know?

MARGARET. Hubert!

SCOTTY. Mr. Gloucester, you must —

HUBERT. If you haven't, why are you here?

TEDDY. If you don't know that I'm not lying I don't care what you think.

MARGARET. Theodora, *explain* it all to him. Hubert, listen —

HUBERT. What is there to listen to? What is there to explain?

TEDDY. Nothing. I wouldn't try to explain for anything on earth.

SCOTTY. You've got to listen, Mr. Gloucester. The others were with us that first night and Ted and I motored all day yesterday, and came here last evening just to have a look at the place — and expected to be back in town by ten o'clock. The storm was terrific and we had to stay. We simply *had* to.

HUBERT. That's a *fine* story! By God, it's just as bad to throw your reputation away as it is to — to —

MARGARET. Hubert!

HUBERT. It *is*. What in the name of heaven do you mean — acting like the commonest, lowest kind of a thing? Does nothing mean anything to you but this brazen, disreputable, loose — Where do you get it? Where does it come from? What have you done with your bringing up? How do you expect me to believe — *anything* but the — My God! What am I to believe?

MARGARET. That she's your daughter. That all the other things you've let her do — have done this. That she needs your help now as she never needed it before. [*To* TEDDY] Theodora, you are going to *marry* this boy, aren't you?

SCOTTY. Of course, she is. We're engaged.

TEDDY. Oh no, we're not.

HUBERT. What? What do you say?

TEDDY. I'm not engaged to him.

SCOTTY. Ted!

MARGARET. But didn't you expect to be?

TEDDY. Perhaps. Probably. I don't know. I was considering.

HUBERT. Oh, you were! There'll be no more of that. You'll announce your engagement at once.

TEDDY. Why should I? What good will that do? How can that change anything?

HUBERT. At least there'd be some faint hope of persuading people that you haven't quite gone to the dogs — that you wouldn't have been quite so wild as to go off with him, if you weren't going to marry him. It's a very little thing, but at least, it's the only thing we can do.

SCOTTY. Ted — listen! Come and marry me now — quick. We'll go on to another town and telephone back to your father that we've eloped.

TEDDY. What?

MARGARET. That's a very good idea — Theodora, really it is. The best possible thing you can do.

HUBERT. Yes, it is. Do it! Do it — and get at it quick.

TEDDY. I don't want to.

HUBERT. What?

TEDDY. I don't want to.

HUBERT. It isn't a question of what you want — but a question of saving yourself.

TEDDY. Saving myself from what? I can take care of myself.

HUBERT. So you thought. And this is what you got yourself into. You need *me* now. Why do you refuse to do the one thing there is to do? Why do you refuse to do this for my sake?

TEDDY. I'd do a good deal for your sake, Dad, but I can't marry somebody I don't want to — for your sake.

HUBERT. And why don't you want to marry him?

TEDDY. Because I don't love him like that.

HUBERT. You probably love him as much as you're capable of loving anybody.

TEDDY. You must let me be the judge of that. I can't marry you, Scotty. I know now. I'm sorry.

[SCOTTY *turns away*]

MARGARET. Be careful, dear, don't

make another mistake with this serious thing.

TEDDY [*almost breaking at* MARGARET'S *tenderness, but controlling herself*]. I'm trying not to. [*To her father*] Why do you ask me to marry him when I tell you I don't want to? *I don't love him that way*, I tell you. What has anything else got to do with it? How can you be so stupid and old-fashioned and afraid? Of course, I've done a perfectly idiotic thing and I'm just as sorry as I can be. But what has that got to do with the rest of my life? What if people do talk and tell a few lies about me? I'm not going to sneak and do a trumped up thing as though I were guilty. If you can't take me home now, Dad, and hold up your head and say — "This is my daughter. I trust her and know she hasn't done anything wrong" — then I never want to go home *at all*.

HUBERT. And if you don't obey me — if you don't marry this boy — I don't *want* you to come home.

MARGARET. Hubert!

HUBERT. Are you going to do it?

TEDDY. No!

[HUBERT *goes out quickly*]

MARGARET. Teddy!

TEDDY. No!

SCOTTY. Ted!

TEDDY. No!

[*The curtain falls and remains down a moment to denote a lapse of thirty-two hours*]

SCENE III. — *Twelve o'clock the following morning.*

[MARGARET *comes in from the left wearing the simple black gown of scene II, without her coat and hat. She goes into the alcove where she examines and sorts several pairs of curtains which are on the table*]

HEYFER [*coming in through the outer door which is open*]. Good mornin'. [*He carries a basket covered with a towel*]

MARGARET. Good morning.

HEYFER. Yere's yer dinner. Do ye want yer supper brought over, too?

MARGARET. Yes — I think so. I'm not sure yet. And isn't there a woman near here who would like to come in and clean up a little and wash those dishes?

HEYFER. I ain't heard o' none wantin' to do anything like that fer some time. How long do ye calk'late stayin'?

MARGARET. I don't know exactly. Does it matter?

HEYFER. Wall no — in one way it don't, but the folks round here keep askin' *me*, an' they think it's kinda funny I don't know.

MARGARET. I'm sorry not to be able to keep them informed.

HEYFER. I s'pose ye think it ain't none o' their business but some things is enough to make even the dead say a little somethin'.

MARGARET. And may *I* say a little something?

HEYFER. Certainly.

MARGARET. This whole place must be cleaned — inside and out. Get a strong *young* man at it right away.

HEYFER. I guess I'm about the youngest round here, an' I'm pretty busy. I guess maybe sometime durin' the summer I might git 'round to doin' a little somethin' fer ye.

MARGARET. Where are they all? There used to be plenty of people about here to do things.

HEYFER. They're all ridin' round in their Ford autimobiles. We live in a infernal age. Why, my granddaughter Mamie ain't worth the powder to blow her up — runnin' into them ungodly movie shows every night of her life — gittin' home long after ten o'clock — first with one feller an' then with another, till nobody ain't got no notion, nohow, which one she's goin' ter marry — if any. The ungodly lawlessness that young folks is growin' up with now'days is a disgrace to their day an' generation. [MARGARET *laughs*] You think it's funny?

MARGARET. Oh no — I just seem to have heard it all some place before.

HEYFER. Somethin' had ought to be done about it. Somethin' had ought. We're bringin' up a reckless daredevil good for nothin' —

TEDDY [*coming in from outside, wearing old khaki riding clothes and a brown sweater*]. It's perfectly glorious outside! Why don't you go out and run around a little, Aunt Margaret? It would make you feel like a rearing charger. Little spring things are coming up all over, and Oh, Mr. Heyfer, a little rabbit that looked just like you, sat on the wall and said "Git off this property! Who the hell are you?"

HEYFER [*suddenly seeing* TEDDY'S *riding trousers*]. Law! You ben out ridin' already this mornin'? What on?

TEDDY. No — I ben waitin'. This is my waiting costume. Don't you like it? Best I could find in my wardrobe.

HEYFER. I can't say thet I do. I ben kind o' broke in to seein' 'em on a hoss — but not walkin' round on the carpet.

TEDDY. Oh, I'm sorry. I was afraid I'd look too much like the idle rich if I stayed much longer in the other one.

HEYFER. Well — as Ma says — there ain't no use tryin' ter understand city ways. There ain't nothin' to hitch to nor git hold on one way nor t'other — nohow. [*He goes out left leaving the door open*]

TEDDY. Inspiring creature! Oh — what *is* Dad going to do? He's had a day and a night to change. I don't believe he ever *is* going to. [*She stamps about restlessly and nervously*]

MARGARET. Are *you?*

TEDDY. Never. Isn't it a joke? Just because I'm a girl! Scotty's strutting about in town, of course, as usual — while I'm waiting here for my father to forgive me. Isn't it priceless? A girl can be alone all day with a man and nobody says a word — but *one night* in the most innocent accident, and she's damned. Lord, the things I could tell that have happened in the *day time! [Going to* MARGARET *and putting out her hand*] Aunt Margaret, I give you good on this. You haven't once said I told you so. I know I've done a damn fool thing and I know I deserve all that's coming to me — but I think you know what it means to me for you to stick by me. [*Turning away quickly to hide her tears*]

MARGARET [*holding on to* TEDDY'S *hand*]. Teddy, I want to ask you one question.

TEDDY. Yes?

MARGARET. Are you sure you aren't coquetting with Scotty Wilbur now? Are you sure you don't intend to marry him after you've kept him dangling a little longer and made your father suffer a little more? Um?

TEDDY. No. I give you my word I'm not. If I loved Scotty, I'd marry him like a shot. But I don't. Of course that's a pretty weak argument — coming from me. I admit I don't know much about the divine passion but I know it hasn't hit me yet — and I'll never marry anybody till it does.

MARGARET. But the pity of it is you'll play with it so much you won't know it when it comes.

TEDDY. Oh yes, I will. I saw a boy once who was so sure *he'd* know that if he had said he loved me I would have *known* he did. I would have known he would have taken care of me all my life and that it was only up to me to be worth it.

MARGARET. Who was he?

TEDDY. You wouldn't know — he was just — oh just — *different.*

HEYFER [*coming back with his basket empty*]. Ma says there ain't much ter do to yer dinner but to put it on the stove an' take it off again, when it's hot through, but she 'lowed she didn't know as you could even do that. [*He goes to the outer door,* TEDDY *follows imitating his walk*] If you belonged to me I know what I'd do to you. [*He goes out and to the left, passing the window*]

TEDDY. If you belonged to me I'd have your hair bobbed. Oh why doesn't Dad make a move one way or the other?

MARGARET. Well, if you won't give in and your father won't, the only thing I can think of for you to do is to share my little income with me and live in an economy you never even heard of.

TEDDY. Oh, you're awfully good, Aunt Margaret. But I couldn't do that. I couldn't.

MARGARET. Then what are you going to do?

EILEEN [*rushing in from outside followed by* OLIVER]. Ted!

TEDDY. Oh — Eileen! [EILEEN *throws her arms about* TEDDY] Hello, Oliver. [*Putting out her hand to him as she still holds* EILEEN]

OLIVER. Hello, Teddy! [*Going to shake hands with* MARGARET]

TEDDY [*to* OLIVER]. Well, you look like a funeral! Let's hear the worst. Everybody's very *busy* I s'pose. I haven't got a rag of character left to my back by this time. Have I? Don't look so stunned, Eileen. What's the news? Let's have it.

EILEEN. It's beastly! A beastly rotten shame the whole darn thing! [*Going to shake hands with* MARGARET]

MARGARET. Have you seen Mr. Gloucester?

EILEEN. No. I tried to but he wouldn't let me.

OLIVER. So did I. He won't see any of us. Scotty has told us the whole business, Ted.

EILEEN. We might have kept it quiet if it hadn't been for Hallie. Mrs. Rainsford, did she phone you that Teddy had said she and Scott might motor out here?

MARGARET. Yes — but she didn't do it till two o'clock that night.

TEDDY. She waited till then so if we were here, Dad couldn't get here till morning. Nicely planned — wasn't it? Well — what are people saying?

EILEEN. *Well*, I went out to tea yesterday and to dinner — and a dance afterwards, and by the time I got home the story was — you'd done this several times before. They say that's what you keep this place for.

MARGARET. Oh, how can they be so cruel?

OLIVER. Don't, Eileen. What difference does it make what they say?

TEDDY. Oh, don't be delicate. I love the details. I s'pose Dad's hearing it all, too.

EILEEN. Mrs. Allister's rubbing it in. She's not missing this chance of getting back at you for all the snubs you've given *her*.

TEDDY. Mrs. Allister must be really and truly deeply shocked. She is such a pure and holy lily herself.

OLIVER. What are you going to do, Ted? You've got to do something.

EILEEN. You can't stay here.

TEDDY. Oh yes, I can — till I rot. Dad's got to give in. He's got to. He's wrong — just as wrong as he can be.

SCOTTY [*coming in quickly*]. Hello! [*They all turn*]

TEDDY [*after a pause*]. Hello!

SCOTTY. May I see you alone, Teddy?

EILEEN. Of course.

MARGARET. Come into the dining room. Or would you rather go outside?

EILEEN. It doesn't matter. [*She and* OLIVER *follow* MARGARET *out left, closing the door*]

SCOTTY [*when he and* TEDDY *are alone*]. I've been with your father most of the time trying to get him to come and take you home without any question of marrying me one way or the other.

TEDDY. Thanks, old man.

SCOTTY. But I haven't made the slightest dent in him. I've never seen any one so angry in all my life. He's like a raging bull. Horribly cut up, too, Ted — gone to pieces. I'm sorry for him — I actually am.

TEDDY. So am I. But his way i[s] not the way out.

SCOTTY. It's the only one unde[r] heaven I see. He'll never give in, bu[t] if *you* do he's going to be awfully won[-]derful and generous to you, Ted. I[f] you don't — he's going to — H[e] threatened — you know.

TEDDY. Threatened?

SCOTTY. Money and stuff.

TEDDY. Cutting me off? [*He nods She laughs and walks away*] Oh, that[']s divine! That's the last touch. You g[o] straight back to him and tell him I don['t] care whether I ever have a cent of hi[s] money or not.

SCOTTY [*following her*]. Oh, Ted don't. Don't lose your head! Yo[u] can't live without your father. Now see here, tell him you'll marry me — announce the engagement and brea[k] it afterwards. I give you my word Teddy, I won't try to make you stick — if you don't want to.

TEDDY. You're a brick, boy — you are. But don't you see I can't do tha[t] sort of stuff? It's getting awfully awfully serious with me. I meant wha[t] I said to Dad with everything in me, an[d] if I go back on it — I go back on myself It doesn't hurt *you* a bit — or you[r] reputation — or anything about you I never promised to marry you. If [I] had, I'd come through. You know that — don't you? And I'm sorry Scotty, I don't love you that way — but I don't.

SCOTTY. I'm so sorry about th[e] whole rotten business I could kill my self.

TEDDY [*taking his hand*]. Don['t] worry! It'll all come out in the wash If we loved each other well enough w[e] could snap our fingers and tell the whol[e] lot to go sit on a tack. But we don['t] care — like that, do we?

SCOTTY [*evading her eyes*]. Why I — you — *I* do.

TEDDY. Don't try to make a brave speech.

SCOTTY. If I only had money, Ted.

TEDDY. Yes, I know, I know. It'[s] quite all right.

SCOTTY. But Ted dear — what are you going to do?

HALLIE [*coming in from the outer door followed by* TREVOR]. Oh, Teddy, dearest! [*Her sympathy a little too extravagant*]

TREVOR. Hello!

TEDDY. Hello, Trevor. Did you

come to see the show, too? Tell the others to come back, Scotty.

TREVOR [*taking her hand in both of his*]. This is rotten luck, old girl, isn't it? But we're all in it, you know. We're all red devils by this time.

HALLIE [*sitting in a chair by the right table*]. Oh yes — we're all in. Eileen and I, too. And I'm taking all on my shoulders I possibly can and telling everybody it was just the merest chance that we didn't *all* come out here.

EILEEN [*coming back from the dining room*]. Hello, hello!

OTHERS. Oh, hello! [*Following EILEEN in*]

EILEEN. I say we stop talking and go back to town and let Ted alone.

TEDDY. Oh no, don't. I think it's charming of you to come out and bring me the latest bulletins. Have you any choice tid bits, Trevor?

TREVOR. Plenty. The things I've heard about myself since this thing began would fill a book. I wonder I'm not kicked out of every club in town.

TEDDY. You devil! The girls will chase you more than ever.

TREVOR. And as for Ollie — well — they haven't done a thing to him. No girl's safe with you after dark, old man, but Scotty — oh, I *say!* [*They all laugh*]

OLIVER. Oh, shut up, Trevor. Drop it.

TEDDY. No — don't. Come on and tell us what they said about Scotty.

TREVOR. Scotty has a wife and child or two in every town in the state. [*They laugh again*]

TEDDY. I'm so relieved. I was afraid they had said *I* led Scotty into temptation. As a matter of fact I did, of course.

HALLIE. But the worst thing they say about Scotty is that he only wants Ted's money — and compromised her so she'd have to marry him. That's what *I* resent more than anything. That's what I get perfectly purple in the face about, Teddy dear.

TEDDY. Yes, dearest, you still look a little pink.

OLIVER. You know one man who wants to marry you on any terms at any time — the sooner the better. You know that, Ted.

HALLIE. Gracious! Are you offering yourself publicly, Ollie? How touching!

OLIVER. Why not? I've done it

often enough in private. Everybody knows that. If I could marry you this minute, Ted, it would be the greatest thing that could happen to me.

TEDDY. Oliver, you're the most adorable thing that ever lived.

TREVOR. Adorable — *but* — Ollie.

OLIVER. Oh, this isn't a joke, you know.

TREVOR. I'm not so emotional as Ollie, Ted — but I'm absolutely at your service. Will you take me?

HALLIE. Another great moment in a great man's life.

SCOTTY. I don't see anything so damned funny about it.

OLIVER. I don't either. It's up to us to kill this stuff and carry Ted through. If we can't we're no good.

EILEEN. That's what I say.

TREVOR. Now I've been *thinking.* Couldn't we start something like this — that you stayed all night at a neighbor's house and had just come over here in the morning when your father arrived, Ted?

TEDDY. Yes, I think that would be very convincing. Say I came out to spend the night with old Mr. Heyfer. He's attractive enough to account for *anything.*

OLIVER. Ted, you're a scream. Thank God you've got a sense of humor. About the best thing we can do is to treat it as a huge joke.

TREVOR. It is a rummy little joke. Isn't it, Scott?

HALLIE. Let's make it as absurd as possible. Scotty can describe the storm out here and when the people say "How *funny* — it didn't rain a drop in town" — he can make the storm worse and worse. Can't you, Scott? *Was* there *really* a storm?

SCOTTY. Oh no. It was a beautiful night. We stayed to see the moon come up.

TEDDY. All the fish stories you can possibly dig up won't be half as fishy as the truth. Scott and I weren't alone here that night. [*They all look at her quickly*]

OTHERS. What?

TEDDY. I haven't even told Aunt Margaret this part of it. It's too much to expect even her generosity to believe. Scotty did have a drink or two and went to sleep — over there — and the storm raged — and the door opened — and a young man walked in — out of the nowhere into the here — and we sat by the fire and talked — and talked — and talked. [*They laugh*] You see — nobody *could* believe it.

EILEEN. And what was Scotty doing all this time?

TEDDY. Scotty was sleeping. [TEDDY *has been sitting in a small chair at center with her back to the audience*]

TREVOR. Oh! That was very careless of you, Scotty.

TEDDY [*rising and going up to lean on the open door. The strong sunlight falls over her. A new note, tender and wistful, comes into her voice. They watch her, puzzled and interested but believing she is only joking*]. This strange young man said he lived in New York and thought some of the nice people he had met did rather asinine things. And then he said the storm was going to last all night and that I'd better go to bed. And I said I thought I would. So I took the young man's light and opened that door, and he said there was nothing to be afraid of — that he would take care of me — that his name was Billy Wade and that he would never see me again, but he would never forget me, and then he said goodbye and I went upstairs, and when I came down in the morning — the door was open and the young man was gone — and — [*She stops suddenly — after a slight pause* BILLY WADE *comes into sight in the doorway*] Oh — how do you do?

BILLY. Good morning.

TEDDY. I — I — I — I was just talking about you. [*To the others*] This is the strange young man.

BILLY [*coming into the room*]. I came back to see if by any chance you were still here. I was afraid you had some difficulty getting away. I hoped you had got back to town all right — and yet I hoped by some fluke I'd find you here. That's the only excuse I have for coming back. [TEDDY *and* BILLY *laugh*]

TEDDY. I think that's excuse enough — to come back to find a really old friend like me. But they don't believe the story I was telling them — how you blew in.

BILLY. Don't they? I can scarcely believe it myself. [*Looking at the others for the first time*]

TEDDY. If he knows which one is Scotty — will you believe it? [*Appealing to all of them*]

OLIVER. Try it.

TEDDY [*to* BILLY]. Which is the one who was asleep on the sofa that night?

BILLY [*nodding at* SCOTTY]. This one of course.

TREVOR. How do you do it, Ted?

TEDDY. You never saw *him* — did you, Scott?

SCOTTY. What in the world are you trying to do, Ted?

TEDDY. Mr. Wade — this is Mr. Wilbur.

BILLY. How do you do?

SCOTTY. How do you do?

HALLIE. How very amusing you are, Ted. You always have something up your sleeve. What *is* this?

TEDDY. They don't believe you were here at all. Can't you say something to convince them?

BILLY. Nothing but just the truth.

TEDDY. But that's the last thing in the world they can possibly believe.

BILLY. The whole thing was sort of funny, wasn't it?

TREVOR. Quite funny. But we don't see the point yet.

TEDDY. I *am* telling the truth. I'm not fooling — really. You believe me, don't you?

HALLIE. It's a priceless story. You're as clever as the deuce. And we've actually *seen* the strange young man with our own eyes. And what shall we say when people say "But *would* she have been alone all night with Scott Wilbur if the strange young man *hadn't* fallen from the skies?"

TEDDY. How *dare* you say that to me, Hallie! How dare you! I've been the biggest fool in the world, I know, and I've walked right into a beautiful mess with my eyes wide open. I don't want anybody to be sorry for me. It's absolutely my own fault. But I do expect *you* Eileen, and you Ollie, not to think I'm telling a ridiculous lie and trying to put something over on you.

EILEEN. But we don't understand.

TEDDY. What if you *don't* understand? What difference does that make? And what difference does it make how it all looks? I've asked you to believe me — in spite of everything. A perfect stranger came in when things looked just as rotten as they possibly could — but he was big enough and kind enough to — to — trust me. And now he sees that you don't. You can go back to town and say I've told the most impossible lie. You can also say I'm not going to marry Scotty, and nobody knows *what* I'm going to do next, and I don't give a damn what *any* of you think. [TEDDY *breaks for the first time and hurries out. There is a pause*]

BILLY [*looking slowly from one to the other*]. Do you mean you really don't believe I was here that night? [*Each one looks away without answering*] I told you I was. I sat here in that chair — till morning — while she was upstairs and he was asleep — there. If it makes any great difference, one way or the other whether I was here or not, I'll do anything on earth to prove it.

TREVOR [*with a steady insolent look at* BILLY]. But there isn't anything you can do to prove it, old man. You just ask us to take your word for it — and that's all there is to it.

BILLY. And you do take my word — of course? [*Looking from* TREVOR *to* OLIVER]

OLIVER. We take Miss Gloucester's word. It isn't necessary to discuss it further.

BILLY. Yes — I see you believe everything she says. You're her friends and know her well. You couldn't possibly be rotten enough to doubt her in any way. She's lucky to have you to stand by and fight for her. I think I'll wait around — in case she needs somebody who *knows* she isn't lying. [*Controlling his blazing anger he goes outside quickly*]

TREVOR. Charming person! Wonder where Ted dug him up?

HALLIE. Somebody who lives round here and Ted's making it worth while for him to —

EILEEN. *Hallie* — how *can* you!

HALLIE. Now don't take that tone with me. I'm just as sorry as *you* are that Ted told such a cock and bull story, but I'm not going to be fool enough to pretend to believe it. Why in the name of Heaven couldn't she have told Scott — if it's true?

OLIVER. It *is* true. But don't tell anybody else — for God's sake. Let's shut up about the whole infernal business.

EILEEN. I'd believe Ted Gloucester above everybody else on earth. But it would be the *worst possible* thing we could do for her — to try and make anybody else believe this story — and you've all got to promise that you'll never breathe it to a living soul. [*She looks at the two men. They nod seriously to her*] Hallie?

HALLIE. I scarcely think you have to say that to *me*.

EILEEN. And I'm going to make Ted swear she'll never tell it again. [*She goes out into the dining room, closing the door*]

OLIVER [*after a long look at* HALLIE]. That's a dead serious thing we've sworn to.

HALLIE. Yes — not to tell anybody there were two men here instead of one. You look so tragic, Ollie. [*She laughs*]

OLIVER. Ted's up against it. We all think we can get away with anything. This is one time we didn't. [*He goes out.* TREVOR *goes with him.* SCOTTY *starts to follow them*]

HALLIE. Scott, don't go. [*He stops, going slowly back to her. She is still in the chair*] Isn't it awful? I'm so sorry for Ted.

SCOTTY. It's the rottenest deal a girl ever got.

HALLIE. And isn't it marvelous the way she takes it? I'm so sensitive — if it had happened to me it would have killed me. You've been marvelous about the whole thing, Scott. I'm awfully sorry for *you* — too.

SCOTTY. You needn't be.

HALLIE. But I am. You've done everything under the shining heaven you can be expected to do. Don't sacrifice yourself, old dear.

SCOTTY. Sacrifice myself?

HALLIE. What's this tale Mrs. Allister's telling about her father cutting Ted off if she doesn't marry you?

SCOTTY. That damned Allister woman ought to have her throat cut.

HALLIE. Oh, it's *true* then? You wouldn't be fool enough to be caught like *that?* You don't have to be quixotic about it. Ted's no ingenue. She knew what she was doing all right.

SCOTTY. She was only in a dare devil mood. She didn't mean any more harm than a baby.

HALLIE. *Didn't* she? You are wonderful about it, dear. I'm crazy about the way you're taking it. So awfully generous. She's such a ninny not to grab you — now that she's got you.

SCOTTY. Grab me nothing! She doesn't want me.

HALLIE. Oh — I can't believe that.

SCOTTY. It's so, all right.

HALLIE. Poor boy! I can't bear to see you unhappy. I wish there was something I could do to buck you up. When you're lonely come and play with me. I understand you so well.

SCOTTY. Do you, Hallie? [*Looking at her and moving a little closer to her*]

HALLIE. All you need is money to make you perfect. I think it would be *awful* to have your *personality* hurt by anything so disgusting as no money.

SCOTTY. But I'll never make any.

HALLIE. Oh, cheer up! God knows the men a girl *can* love are scarce enough. You ought to have a very large income settled on you for merely being one of *those*. And Ted hasn't *all* the money there is in the world, you know. [*Using her lip stick as enticingly as possible*] Are my lips all right?

SCOTTY. Perfect!

HALLIE. Are they really! [*Rising and putting her hands on his shoulders*]

EILEEN [*coming in quickly and stopping as she sees what HALLIE is doing*]. Well — I don't think this is a particularly good time for that sort of thing.

HALLIE. It's a good time for you to mind your own business.

EILEEN. This is my business. Ted's come to her senses and is going to do the only sane thing there is to do. She's going to — [TEDDY *comes in. There is a pause as they turn to her*]

TEDDY. May I speak to Scotty alone — please?

HALLIE. Of course, dear — of course. And Ted, don't go to pieces again. You must be awfully brave. I hope it isn't *too* late to save yourself. I suppose the only thing you can do is to live it down — the way most people do. And you can count on me to do everything in my power to help you.

TEDDY. But, I don't intend to lie down and die.

HALLIE. No matter how ghastly people are to you or how many drop you and cut you completely you just mustn't mind. You *must* be brave.

TEDDY. The cutting and dropping will be all on *my* side.

HALLIE. Oh — very well — if you don't want any help —. Goodbye, Scott. See you very soon, old man. [*She goes out with insolent bravado*]

TEDDY. I'm not going to be insulted the rest of my life for this.

EILEEN. That's right. Ted. Hold your head so high no one can touch you. Shall I tell the others what you're going to do?

TEDDY. Yes — please.

EILEEN. And I won't let them come back to speak to you now. Buck up, Ted. I'll settle Hallie. [EILEEN *goes out*]

TEDDY. Scott — I've got myself

where people won't believe me an where my friends can't help me. you still want me, I'll marry you.

SCOTTY. Ted!

TEDDY. Go in town and tell Dad I' marry you — that we'll *blaze* and hav the most gorgeous wedding anybod ever had.

SCOTTY. Now you're yourself agair I adore you.

TEDDY. Oh no, you don't.

SCOTTY. I do.

TEDDY. Let's be honest. It's jolly good thing for us both — and we' probably get on as well as most peopl do who pretend to be in love.

SCOTTY. But I *do* love you, Ted.

TEDDY. Yes — with all my acces sories. Now let's play fair and ru straight and make the best of it.

SCOTTY. Dear old girl, I'll try t make you happy.

TEDDY. Well, everybody's going t *think* I'm happy. I can promise yo that, and if we don't make a go of i we'll get our divorce right off the bat.

SCOTTY. Oh, Ted, don't go into i that way.

TEDDY. Why not? Lord knows it' better to go into it *prepared* to have divorce than to suddenly be hit in th head with it later.

SCOTTY. I can't bear to have yo take it this way.

TEDDY. I'm only being sensible I'll make a settlement on you now Scott, and the whole transaction wil be very neat.

SCOTTY. That's horrible.

TEDDY. Slush! I'm only calling things by their own names. Wha right have we to expect anything else We've set our own tune. Now we'l have to dance to it, and for Heaven' sake let's dance well.

SCOTTY. But —

BILLY [*coming into the outer door*]. Pardon me. I don't want to butt in, but I would like to talk to you a minute before I go back — if I may.

TEDDY. Of course you may.

SCOTTY. But Ted, you must hurry back to town now.

TEDDY. I have to change. You must hurry in yourself.

BILLY. I'll take you in.

TEDDY. Oh — can you? Go on then, Scott — and Aunt Margaret and I will come with Mr. Wade.

SCOTTY. Not at all. I can't let anybody else take you.

BILLY. Oh, I think you can trust me to get Miss Gloucester in safely.

SCOTTY. I'll take her in myself.

BILLY [*to* TEDDY]. Do you want me to go — or shall I wait to take you in?

TEDDY. I want you to wait.

BILLY [*looking at* SCOTTY]. I'll wait.

SCOTTY [*looking at* TEDDY]. How soon will you get her in?

BILLY. Just as soon as Miss Gloucester *wants* to go.

SCOTTY [*starting to the door and stopping to speak to* BILLY]. You seem to be rather interested in the situation.

BILLY. You can't blame me for that, can you?

SCOTTY. But you must realize that it doesn't matter in the least whether you were here or not the other night. [*He goes out*]

BILLY. It matters a good deal to *me*. I suppose you're disgusted with me for coming back. I suppose I made everything a thousand times worse than if I'd stayed away. I'm sorry.

TEDDY. Nothing could make it any worse. I gummed it up as much as I possibly could.

BILLY. I was a fool not to have stayed right through — with you — to have told it all myself to everybody.

TEDDY. I didn't want you to. And it wouldn't have done any good. As Hallie says people will say, "Would she have been alone all night with Scott, if the strange man *hadn't* fallen from the skies?" You see it's a hopeless mess — any way you look at it. And I was stupid to have said anything about you. But it seems a pity not to be able to tell the most beautiful thing that ever happened to me.

BILLY. They're blockheads.

TEDDY. Oh no. They're just my friends. Why should I expect anybody to believe me?

BILLY. I'd believe anything you told me.

TEDDY [*looking at him deeply with a sudden tenseness*]. But you don't know me.

BILLY. Oh, yes I do. I know you better than I ever knew *anybody*. I've thought about you every minute since I saw you and I came back just to find you.

TEDDY. And you found me in a worse fix than when you went away, but I've taken the only way out there is. I'm going to marry Mr. Wilbur — and I won't lose my father's money — and I'm not going under.

BILLY. Marry him? Are you only doing it because — of this thing that happened?

TEDDY. He's marrying me for my money and I'm marrying him to save my reputation.

BILLY. That's *hell*.

TEDDY. Is it? It's often done, you know.

BILLY. You don't have to do that.

TEDDY. My father has a right to force me into it, I suppose.

BILLY. He has *not*.

TEDDY. What did *you* think when you found me here alone with a man?

BILLY. I knew when I saw your eyes that you didn't have anything to hide.

TEDDY. But you think I did a deadly common stupid thing coming out here just to be reckless — by way of amusing myself?

BILLY. Yes — I do. But why in the name of Christopher should that put a crimp in your whole life and make you do a much worse thing now — marry a man you don't love?

TEDDY. It's the only way out.

BILLY. No, it's not. You're in bad — but you could come out big.

TEDDY. How?

BILLY. By turning this into something big.

TEDDY. It's easy enough for you to talk. You're a man. Men can do anything.

BILLY. If they *will*. So can a girl!

TEDDY [*going to sit in the chair above the table*]. Oh no — one dose of a thing like this for a girl — and she's done for if she hasn't any money.

BILLY [*sitting near her at the table*]. Listen. How much money do you need to live?

TEDDY. I don't know. I don't know. Dad gives me twenty-four thousand a year and then pays all my debts. I have three thousand a year of my very own from my mother and this little place — so that doesn't leave much if I throw Dad over? Does it?

BILLY. Well, I've just thrown up a job of ten thousand a year which seemed like a million to me.

TEDDY. Given it up?

BILLY. Yes. I got just what was coming to me. I knew it was crooked when I went into it. I knew the man stole from the Government, and called it big business, but I fell for it — and I stuck because of what it could do for me — but it was eating into me all the time good and hard. And do you know what happened to me? After I saw you the other night I hated it so — I went back and chucked it. I haven't got a job and it won't be so easy to get another one — but I can look myself in the face — and I'm free. And I don't see why you can't do the same.

TEDDY. You don't know what you're talking about.

BILLY. The whole point is this. Do you *want* what you're going back to or don't you?

TEDDY. It doesn't matter whether I want it or not. It's what I've got to take.

BILLY. Do you hate it?

TEDDY. That doesn't matter either.

BILLY. Are you going to let it get you — so you'll be just like the rest of them?

TEDDY. I am just like them. I'm one of them. What else can I be? I thought for a few minutes that I could defy it and run away from it. I thought I'd give my *soul* not to have to go back. It all seemed so horrible. I thought I never could *face* it and bluff and fight and pretend that I didn't care.

BILLY. You do care! You *do* hate it!

TEDDY. I don't dare to let myself hate it — or I never can come through. I don't dare *think* what I'm going to do — but I know — oh I know. [*She puts her head on her arms on the table with a sob*]

BILLY. Then why in the name of God do you do it? How can you — you — do anything you're ashamed of?

TEDDY [*rising suddenly and going to the outer door*]. But I can't live without my father.

BILLY [*following her*]. With this little place? What's the reason you can't? You can take care of yourself. I'll help you. That's where I belong — outdoors. I could make this little farm *sit up* — if you'd help me.

TEDDY. How could I help?

BILLY. Work — with your own hands.

TEDDY. I can't. I don't know how.

BILLY. Learn. I'll help you. I'll go halves. I'll put what I've got into it.

TEDDY. If I try — with *all I've got* — if I work — do you think I can take care of myself?

BILLY. I *know* you can.

TEDDY. How wonderful of you to believe in me! I don't see how you can.

BILLY. I do. Believe in yourself.

TEDDY. But it's all so strange. I've never done anything like this in my life.

BILLY. Don't be afraid. You're stronger now than you ever were.

TEDDY. No, I'm not. I'm awfully weak. I may fail.

BILLY. You can't. You've got hold of something to fight for.

TEDDY. Oh — I'm afraid I'm doing something wild again.

BILLY. No, you're not.

TEDDY. I'll fall down.

BILLY. No, you won't. Pull yourself up. Pull yourself up high.

TEDDY. I'll try. I'll try.

BILLY. No — you're going to *do* it.

TEDDY. I will — *I will!!*

THE CURTAIN FALLS

ACT III

SCENE. — *Outside of the Gloucester cottage. Afternoon — Three Months Later.*

The lawn before the cottage. The small white frame house is seen at left. The single door opens on to the lawn. The house is a story and a half high with small windows and solid wooden shutters, faded to a soft green. The ground slopes up at back to an old stone wall. Three stone steps, at center back, lead to the road. At right the lawn extends off stage where a group of trees is seen. A rustic table, two rustic armchairs are at left center and a garden bench at right. The scene is simple in the extreme — full of quiet brightness.

EILEEN, *wearing sport clothes, is selecting a golf club from her bag. She draws an iron out and practices a stroke.* MARGARET *sits below the table sewing.*

EILEEN. I'm off my feed entirely. Playing a wretched game lately.

MARGARET. It always sort of comes and goes, doesn't it?

EILEEN. Yes — especially goes.

MARGARET. Is anybody coming out to play with you?

EILEEN. Teddy says Trevor and Ollie are coming. Mrs. Rainsford, Ted never speaks of her father to me. Would you think me awfully imper-

inent if I asked if she ever hears from
.im?

MARGARET. She never has — not a
vord. It's been three months now.

EILEEN. Awful, isn't it?

MARGARET. Yes — and yet it has
nade Theodora.

EILEEN. But the future, Mrs. Rains-
ord! It will be horrible if they never
nake up.

MARGARET. I used to think so —
ut — [*She shakes her head*]

EILEEN. You don't mean you'd like
er to marry Billy?

MARGARET. Why not?

EILEEN. Oh! I think perhaps I
ught to say this to you. You know we
promised never to tell anybody that
3illy was here that night. We knew it
vould do Teddy more harm than good.
But Hallie *has* told — and it's started
everybody's tongue off again.

MARGARET. Oh! Why did she do it?

EILEEN. She did it to stir Mr.
Gloucester up and widen the breach
between him and Teddy. She's afraid
Scotty may get Ted with her father's
money — after all.

MARGARET. It's hideous!

EILEEN. Isn't there something you
can do to make Ted go to her father?
I've heard that Mr. Gloucester is
beginning to melt. Can't you do something?

MARGARET. I don't know that I
want to.

EILEEN. Don't you want them to be
reconciled? [MARGARET *thinking, does
not answer*] When the boys come,
tell them to give me a shout. [*She
goes into the cottage.* MARGARET *goes
on sewing. After a moment* HUBERT
GLOUCESTER *comes in from the right*]

MARGARET. Hubert!

HUBERT. Where's Theodora?

MARGARET [*rising*]. Out — somewhere about. [*Going to him and giving
him both her hands*]

HUBERT. Margaret — if you've let
something go on out here and haven't
told me, I'll never forgive you — never.

MARGARET. What? [*Drawing away
from him*]

HUBERT. If you've let Ted get
mixed up in another affair and haven't
warned me —

MARGARET. What do you mean?

HUBERT. Why haven't you told me?
Why haven't you kept me informed
about everything she was doing?

MARGARET. Why should I have told

you anything about Theodora? Didn't
you give her up when she needed you
most?

HUBERT. What *is* this thing out
here? What's going on?

MARGARET. You'll have to tell me
what you mean.

HUBERT. The story is all over town
that another boy was here with her that
night while Scotty was drunk and
asleep — that *this* boy was the reason
she so suddenly refused to marry Scotty
— that he gave up a ten thousand dollar
job in New York to come here and work
for her — that he wants her money —
and is making love to her. Is it true?
Is it true?

MARGARET. No — well — yes —
some of it.

HUBERT. How much?

MARGARET. Some of the bare facts.
The boy was here — yes — Billy Wade.
He came in out of the storm that night
— and stayed with her — and kept her
from being terrified.

HUBERT. And he *did* come back?

MARGARET. Yes — but not because
he wants her money.

HUBERT. But he *did* give up his job?

MARGARET. Yes. But —

HUBERT. But not because he wants
her money! Good heavens, Margaret,
have you been taken in like that? Why,
the fellow's a bounder — an adventurer.

MARGARET. Hubert!

HUBERT. How could you be so
gullible? I let Ted stay here with you
because I thought it would be the best
thing on earth for her. And now *this*
thing bumps me in the head.

MARGARET. But it isn't true.

HUBERT. Oh, yes it is. Eileen tells
me they had all sworn to keep still —
never to tell it — but it seems Hallie
wants Scott Wilbur and is still afraid
Ted will marry him — so she's broken
her word and told the whole thing to stir
up another scandal.

MARGARET. Oh yes, it's *very* plain.
Of course Hallie told it — and it's all
distorted and twisted.

HUBERT. They say they were *all*
drinking that night — and there's no
telling *what* happened to make Ted give
Scotty up.

MARGARET. Hubert! Hubert! You
don't believe such stuff.

HUBERT [*sitting on the bench at right*].
Oh, I'm in despair, Margaret — I don't
know what to think or what to do.

MARGARET. Teddy certainly has

paid for that one foolish headstrong thing. Now they're making something ugly out of her really good and beautiful friendship with this boy.

HUBERT. You've been taken in, Margaret.

MARGARET. Oh no. I haven't. I happen to know the truth. I suppose it does sound like a fairy story if you hear it with sordid ears that can't believe in anything unselfish and disinterested.

HUBERT [*rising*]. God! And you let Teddy be fooled too. Is this fellow making love to her?

MARGARET. You'll have to ask her that.

HUBERT. You've made a hero of him evidently. Who is he? What is he?

MARGARET. You'll have to judge for yourself.

HUBERT. Is she going to marry him?

MARGARET. I don't know. Hubert, I've been absolutely quiet in this whole thing — merely watching Theodora work out her own salvation — but I won't be now. If you try to kill the good that is beginning to come to her — I'll fight for her, and I'll fight you.

HUBERT. Do you promise you won't tell her I'm here? Not say one *word* of all this till I see her?

MARGARET. Yes — I promise that.

HUBERT. Where am I likely to find her?

MARGARET. I actually don't know. Perhaps in the lower garden.

[HUBERT *goes up the steps and off along the road to left. After a pause* MARGARET *sits and takes her sewing.* BILLY *whistling comes swinging along the road from the right. He wears blue overalls and carries a scythe*]

BILLY [*stopping by the steps to examine the handle*]. You can see through to the other side of the brook now. About two more days and I'll have all this side cleared.

MARGARET. Splendid!

BILLY. Has Ted come in yet?

MARGARET. Not yet.

BILLY. I struck another berry patch all choked up. Find something new on this little place every day. Gosh — it's fun.

TEDDY [*coming in through the trees at right*]. Billy, the black hen has twenty-seven chickens and one duck.

BILLY. Ye gods! The first scandal on the farm.

[TEDDY *is wearing blue overalls and large straw hat. She carries an old market basket with some working tools in it*]

MARGARET. I speak for the duck. You must let me have *something*.

TEDDY. Well — we'll see what kind of a disposition he has. If he's a grouch you can roast him. What's the matter? [*As* MARGARET *wipes her eyes*] You have been crying?

MARGARET. No — of course not.

TEDDY. No tears around here, young woman, or you'll have to pay a fine. [*Goes to* MARGARET *and kisses her*] You blessed thing!

MARGARET [*going to the door of the cottage and turning*]. Oh, my dear children —

BILLY [*going to her*]. Is anything the matter?

MARGARET. I'm so afraid for you somehow.

BILLY. Why?

MARGARET [*putting a hand on his shoulder*]. Be strong and *sure*, won't you?

BILLY [*putting a hand over hers*]. What about?

MARGARET. About everything. [*Goes in*]

[BILLY *stands looking after her*]

TEDDY. Aunt Margaret's got the gloom. This is Saturday afternoon, you ought to have on your Sunday clothes.

BILLY [*throwing himself down on the grass*]. Well — have you done everything today you thought you were going to do when you went to sleep last night?

TEDDY [*beginning to wind the string which is dangling from her pocket*]. Just about. I got a new chicken coop made — a tiny weeny one for the debutantes.

BILLY. They're having a big season, aren't they?

TEDDY. And I got two roosters to stop fighting.

BILLY. How?

TEDDY. Sat on one of them and fought the other one myself. [BILLY *turns over on the grass and laughs*] And I moved the pigs over into their new quarters and began painting the old ones.

BILLY. Painting the old pigs?

TEDDY. Their *quarters*.

BILLY. Their hind quarters?

TEDDY. You know I'm not going in for snappy dialogue. I'm working.

BILLY. I'm not — go on.

TEDDY. And I got up on the kitchen roof to see if I could find that leak and coming down I got that place in the stairs mended. I got every blooming weed out of the garden. Then I had to go and show Heyfer how to dig that ditch. He wasn't doing it *my* way at all.

BILLY. I'm sorry I missed that conversation.

TEDDY. Then I had to get a board nailed on.

BILLY. Good.

TEDDY. And then I got that. [*Sitting beside* BILLY *and showing him her thumb which is tied up in a rag*]

BILLY. Bad! But you've still got both arms and legs. I think you've pulled through remarkably well — so far — considering the enterprises you've had your hands in — to say nothing of your feet. Where's the other one? Oh, yes. [*Looking for the foot she is sitting on. They both laugh and lean toward each other impulsively*]

BILLY. You've got two more freckles on your nose.

TEDDY. You've got a button off your shirt. I'll sew it on for you. Wasn't I pretty magnificent to darn those socks for you last night?

BILLY. Oh! [*Looking at his feet*] I've been wondering all day what was the matter with my feet.

TEDDY. I thought it would be a good idea to do it *once* so I'd never be requested to do it again. [*They laugh again like children*]

BILLY. Is anybody coming out for tea?

TEDDY. I hope so. Why?

BILLY. It amuses 'em to come out and see the flowers bloom, but they haven't the dimmest idea what you've gone through to make them.

TEDDY. That doesn't matter. It's been the most beautiful summer of my whole life.

BILLY. Would you want another one just like it?

TEDDY. Of course if it were necessary, but it won't be. Each summer is going to be easier and better.

BILLY. This little farm is just a spring board to jump from — to something else. I'm not afraid of money, Ted. Good work'll always make it. But gosh — aren't you sick of measuring everything with money? I want to do some things that are worth doing whether they ever make a damn cent or not, and some things that are worth losing money on — just because you want to try. And some that are worth spending all you can get on — just because they ought to be done.

TEDDY. Of course — things for other people, Billy.

BILLY. Yes.

TEDDY. I never used to think of that at all — but oh — I've found out so much, since I've known you, Billy.

BILLY. Me, too — since I've known you. I've got some great schemes to tell you about. I'm awfully ambitious, Ted. But I'll have to work like the devil to make the money first to tackle the big things.

TEDDY. I'll help.

BILLY. But there are things ahead we've got to look square in the face. Winter's coming and it will be harder than the summer — lonelier for you. Not so many friends coming out — and you'll be bored.

TEDDY. Will you be bored?

BILLY. It doesn't matter about me.

TEDDY. And how about you *and* me?

BILLY. That's it. That's the thing I've got to face. How can there be any you *and* me?

TEDDY. How can there be anything else? Aren't we going to be together forever?

BILLY. Are we?

TEDDY. I can't imagine anything else — unless the world comes to an end, and then we'd go on together anyway.

BILLY. Do you mean you could — marry me?

TEDDY. Why, I've always taken that for granted since — well — since — I can't tell when it began — any more than I can think of it ending. [BILLY *puts his face down in the grass before her, grasping her hands*] Billy — look at me. Look at me. [*She lifts his head and holds it in her arms*] Isn't that the way you've always thought it was?

BILLY. I didn't dare. Oh, Teddy, I don't know whether you realize it yet — what it would really mean to give up all you've had — forever. To begin all over again — at the very bottom. What if you find you just can't get on without it? You'd hate me then.

TEDDY. Why do you think about what I've had? It's what we'll do that matters. And we'll never stop doing. The end is in *us* — not in anything else. We may be two great birds in the air — you and I, we may see things no one has ever seen before. It's in us the magic is.

BILLY. It's in you. If you love me I'm not afraid of anything. [*He kisses her lips in a long kiss. A whistle is heard. He springs up*] Someone's coming.

TEDDY. I thought you said you weren't afraid of anything.

BILLY. I'm not. [*He tries to catch her. She runs to the door and goes in*]

OLIVER [*coming in from the right followed by* TREVOR]. Hello, there! You look as though somebody had given you a gold mine.

BILLY. Somebody has. Hello!

TREVOR. How are you? [*Correct and condescending in his golf clothes*]

OLIVER. Where's Ted? Aren't we going to have some golf?

BILLY. Eileen is. I don't know about Ted. I'll tell her you're here.

OLIVER. Eileen here?

BILLY. Yes, she came out yesterday.

EILEEN [*coming from the house*]. Hello — hello. It's a wonder you wouldn't get here sooner.

OLIVER. Hello, Eileen.

TREVOR. Greetings.

EILEEN. Aren't you going to play, Billy?

BILLY. I'm afraid I can't, thanks. Me for the tub. [*Starting to the house*]

TREVOR. I say, old man — have you heard the rumor that Gloucester is coming out to snatch Teddy out of this? Kill the fatted calf in a blaze of glory and all that sort of thing?

BILLY [*looking from one to the other*]. No — I haven't.

TREVOR. I thought you'd be awfully glad to know it. It would let you out of a nasty situation.

BILLY. What?

TREVOR. You don't relish the story, I'm sure, that you're after Ted's money, and if you gracefully retire, that will kill it pretty quickly.

BILLY [*after a pause*]. I thought Ted's money was a thing of the past — out of the running entirely.

TREVOR. Oh, *did* you? I wouldn't have supposed you were so unsophisticated. That's just a little temporary chastisement on father's part of course. Ted Gloucester's going to be one of the richest girls in the country some day. That's why I say I know you'll be glad to clear out — so you won't be accused

of making a grandstand play for her money under rather disagreeable circumstances.

BILLY. What circumstances, for instance?

TREVOR. Such as chucking your job — rushing out here to Ted and persuading her to stay out here — after she's just decided to marry Wilbur.

BILLY. Oh yes. I have been a nut. Of course that's what you think I'm doing. All of you I suppose.

TREVOR. We're merely checking up the details as other people see them.

BILLY. Yes, circumstantial evidence.

TREVOR. We're only telling you that now is the psychological time for you to step out — as it's in the air that father's going to make a move.

OLIVER. We merely mean that we know you wouldn't want to stand in Ted's way if this *is* going to happen.

BILLY. Oh yes. I see it all very clearly from your standpoint.

TREVOR. There isn't much of any other standpoint to see it from — is there?

BILLY. None — except mine — which cuts no ice whatsoever with you — but a good deal with me. You couldn't possibly get it through you that Ted Gloucester means a damned sight more to me without her money than she does with it. Could you? That would be a little too much to expect *you* to believe.

TREVOR. Right you are — a little too much.

BILLY. In other words, you think I'm a skunk.

TREVOR. Oh no — just human.

BILLY. Damn your filthy, low-down — [*Starting at* TREVOR]

EILEEN. Please!

OLIVER [*after a pause*]. Well — that's the way things look, Wade. And it's easy enough for you to show that there's nothing in it.

TREVOR. Perfectly easy — by merely retiring. [EILEEN *motions for* OLIVER *and* TREVOR *to leave her alone with* BILLY. OLIVER *goes out at right*] A magnificent opportunity to prove that you believe the moon is made of green cheese. But don't expect other people to believe it, dear boy. [TREVOR *goes out after* OLIVER]

BILLY. Do you think what they do?

EILEEN. No — I don't. But the case is too strong against you to convince them.

BILLY. Damn their souls.

EILEEN. No use damning them, Billy. They're only saying what other people think.

BILLY. Ted knows. Nothing else matters.

EILEEN. But something else does matter.

BILLY. Well?

EILEEN. Ted's going to get so tired and sick of this when the novelty wears off, she'll die. She couldn't any more live without what she used to have than she could fly.

BILLY. How do you know what she can live without?

EILEEN. I know her like a book. And I like you too well, Billy Wade, to see her make a fool of you.

BILLY. Don't worry about me.

EILEEN. It's the new thing that gets her and interests her. She likes new excitement. That's why she's been so amazing about all she's done out here. It was a novelty and *you* were new to her, Billy. Something she'd never come in contact with before, and she's flirted with you from a new standpoint altogether.

BILLY. Why are you telling me this, Eileen? You say you're her best friend.

EILEEN. I am — and I'm saying it because I honestly think if she married you it would be the worst possible thing that could happen to you both. You don't realize you're only a new experience to her.

BILLY. I can take care of myself, I think.

EILEEN. I've seen a good many other people who thought that too. Poor old Ollie hasn't given up hope yet.

BILLY. Oliver Comstock?

EILEEN. Of course. You don't think you're going to fare any better than he has — with all his charm and all his money, do you? It's because I like you, Billy, I'm saying this. And by Jove, I know you're too decent to hang on to her and try to keep her from going back to all the wonderful things that are waiting for her.

TEDDY. Hello boys — hello, everybody! [*Coming from the house, she carries a tray with glasses, spoons and paper napkins. BILLY hurries past her and out below the house*]

TREVOR. What ho? [*Coming back*]

TEDDY. What ho, yourself.

OLIVER [*following* TREVOR *in*]. Hello, Ted.

TEDDY. Oh, Ollie, you must come and see my chickens. They know me now, every one of them.

OLIVER. Oh, come!

TEDDY. They do. They run like mad when I open the gate.

OLIVER. They'd be damn fools if they didn't.

TEDDY. That's the most impassioned thing you've said to me in ages. Keep it up. I've got eight hundred and eighty-eight. What do you think of that?

OLIVER. I think it's a big whopper!

[MARGARET *enters from the house with a pitcher of iced tea and a basket of gingerbread*]

EILEEN. Oh, see Mrs. Rainsford. She looks good enough to eat. I'm starving.

OLIVER. How are you, Mrs. Rainsford?

MARGARET. Hello, Oliver. Are you thirsty?

OLIVER. All the way down.

TREVOR. Hello, Mrs. Rainsford. What's in the pitcher? It has a nice color.

TEDDY [*pouring the tea*]. Iced tea. Nothing stronger on the place — unless you'd like a glass of hot milk.

TREVOR. No hot milk, thank you!

OLIVER [*taking a bite of gingerbread*]. Lordy, this gingerbread's good!

MARGARET. Give Eileen some. It's Theodora's first attempt.

TREVOR [*choking*]. My God! Why didn't you say so before?

OLIVER. Ted, I brought you some cocktails. Right here. [*Getting a bottle from his golf bag*]

TEDDY. I'd rather you didn't — really. I don't like it.

EILEEN. Well, I do. Give me one, Oliver.

[EILEEN *and* TREVOR *sit on the bench.* MRS. RAINSFORD *sits below the table and takes up her sewing*]

OLIVER. You mean you don't want me to open it, Ted?

TEDDY. Yes, please. I hate it.

TREVOR. Hate what?

TEDDY. Thinking you have to have a drink on all occasions.

TREVOR. It's the pleasantest thought I have.

TEDDY. I have a very good reason for despising it.

OLIVER. That's all right, Ted. I'm sorry.

TREVOR. Do you mean to say I don't get any?

OLIVER [*putting the bottle back in the bag*]. I guess you can wait. [*He goes to sit on the stone steps*]

TREVOR. The country certainly does peculiar things to people. Awfully upsetting — don't you think, Mrs. Rainsford?

MARGARET. Yes, it certainly upsets some things and sets *up* others. All the important things get more important and the worthless ones more and more worthless. Don't they?

TREVOR. I have a horrible suspicion from the gleam in your eye that you think I come under the head of more and more worthless.

TEDDY. You come under the head of nothing at all, Trevor.

OLIVER. What are you going to do this winter, Ted?

TEDDY. Stay right here. [*Moving about as she gives them more gingerbread*]

OLIVER. That's impossible.

TEDDY. The joke of it is you're all sorry for me and I'm having the time of my life. I've discovered that too much money cheats people out of half the thrilling things in the world.

EILEEN. You sound like — Who was it said "It's easier for something to go through a camel than for something or other to — something?"

TREVOR. You mean it's easier for a camel than for a rich man to cross the desert without a drink.

TEDDY. I had my first lesson in milking this morning. Trevor, what would you do if you had to milk a cow?

TREVOR. I should ask the beast to excuse me.

TEDDY. She probably would, too.

OLIVER. You never looked so well in your life, Teddy.

TEDDY. Of course — I'm husky. No more smokes — no more nerves. I sleep all night and am interested all day. It's great to feel this way. Trevor, even you would get to like it. You'd wake up feeling like an ox instead of a shoestring.

TREVOR. I don't know that I'm so keen about the ox effect.

OLIVER [*to* TEDDY]. Well it's a miracle, nothing less, what you've done.

TEDDY. Any of you could do it if you had to.

MARGARET. Of course. You have more energy and daring and cleverness and intelligence for your age than any set of people in the world.

TREVOR. Mrs. Rainsford, I suspect you.

MARGARET. It's true — in spite of appearances. You have it all and you're throwing most of it away.

TREVOR. Am I included in this?

MARGARET. You haven't the faintest idea of your own importance.

TEDDY. You're not included in *that*, Trevor.

MARGARET. You're an institution — envied and imitated — dreamed of and read about. In every city, in every little town, all the way down, there's a set of you — and you *might* be an absolutely dynamic power for good. [*Smiling at them tolerantly she goes slowly across the lawn to the right*]

OLIVER. Might be? What are we?

MARGARET. An equally great one for harm. You don't mind my saying so — quite honestly — do you? [*She goes out*]

TREVOR. Neat little parting shot.

TEDDY. What do *you* think we are — "quite honestly"?

TREVOR. I think *I'm* a very charming person with a great many friends almost as charming as I am.

TEDDY. Trevor, I love you very much but I can't quite keep up with the way you love yourself. Come and see the chickens — they'll appreciate you.

TREVOR. I know a great many who do.

EILEEN. Don't look at *me*.

[TEDDY *starts off with* EILEEN *and* TREVOR]

OLIVER [*calling her back*]. Ted — I'm awfully unhappy about you.

TEDDY. Why, Ollie?

OLIVER. You're just fooling yourself thinking you can go on like this. What on earth have you got to look forward to? What are you going to do when it settles down to beastly monotony?

TEDDY. Why, I never was so happy in my life.

OLIVER. But the future, Ted. Have you thought of it?

TEDDY. No — the present's more than I can take care of.

OLIVER. I could make you awfully happy.

TEDDY. Oh, Ollie. You say it so well — but you've said it so often.

OLIVER. I love you. I'd be so good to you.

TEDDY. Don't, Oliver — please. I used to adore having people propose to me. But I've had enough of that to last me the rest of my life. [BILLY *enters from the house. He and* OLIVER *look at each other tensely.* OLIVER *goes out slowly at right*] Billy, I've been thinking. I want money now more than ever did in my life.

BILLY. What?

TEDDY. I want it for you. Dad's got an awful lot. — Now is when you ought to have it so you can go on with your dreams and schemes.

BILLY. My schemes can take care of themselves.

TEDDY. No, they can't. And do you know what I'm going to do? I'm going to Dad, and tell him my pride's all gone. I'm going to tell him how wonderful you are.

BILLY. You'll do nothing of the sort.

TEDDY. He'll be so proud of you. So glad to have me marry anybody so splendid. I'm going to him tomorrow.

BILLY. Not to tell him anything about me.

TEDDY. Of course I will.

BILLY. They think I want your money. They couldn't think anything else.

TEDDY. Who does? No, they don't. Why shouldn't you want it? It's mine. It will be yours.

BILLY. It won't.

TEDDY. I want you to have what everybody else has. I want you to have all that Oliver has. I want everybody to respect you and feel your power.

BILLY. You want it yourself — you mean.

TEDDY. But for you.

BILLY. Of course you're tired of this. Why shouldn't you be? It's pretty dull — and pretty grubby.

TEDDY. Billy, don't be nasty.

BILLY. I've been up in the clouds all right. I don't blame you a bit, Ted. It couldn't have turned out any other way.

TEDDY. What are you talking about?

BILLY. I was even stupid enough to actually think perhaps you'd be willing to give up the whole blooming business — after a while. I'm awfully glad you've said this now. Of course, you want your money. Why shouldn't you? Don't think I'm hanging around

your feet. You're just as free as the first minute I saw you. Nothing that's happened out here is going to keep you from what you want — not for a second.

TEDDY. From what I *want?*

BILLY. You want everything you've given up, don't you?

TEDDY. Yes. Why not? What's wrong with that?

BILLY. I was a bloomin' idiot to think I meant any more to you than any of the others.

TEDDY. Than any of the others? Do you think I've ever — anybody has ever meant what you do to me?

BILLY. I was a novelty, I suppose. Something different that happened along at a convenient time.

TEDDY. Billy! I hate you!

BILLY. Isn't it true?

TEDDY. Are you saying this because of Oliver?

BILLY. He's only one of a good many, isn't he?

TEDDY. Oh!

BILLY. They've always been throwing it into me that I was only something new — and I wouldn't believe it. But what you've just said to me now — yourself — has opened my eyes. Fool? I should say I have been.

TEDDY. Somebody's kindly told you how many times I'm supposed to have been in love. I've done a very great many things which were pretty silly and which you would hate if you knew. I didn't think it was necessary to review my whole life to you. I certainly didn't expect you to do that for me. But I thought you did understand the new part of me — and that nothing on earth could shake your faith in me — or make you doubt what I've given to you.

BILLY. You'll want the old excitement so much you can't live without it.

TEDDY. Are you asking me to give up everything — *all my friends, forever?*

BILLY. I'm not asking you to give up *anything.*

TEDDY. I — can't make myself over — entirely. I can't change all my old habits and feelings and point of view. I can't. I'm just like my friends. I'm one of them. After all, how can you expect me to change? [*Taking up a cigarette, and throwing it down*]

BILLY. My God, I'm not asking you to change. I love you — but I know now I can't take the place of all you've had. And you want it, Ted. You want it.

TEDDY. Of course I do — and I want it for *you*. Why shouldn't you come into my world and be somebody in it?

BILLY. Because I despise it. But I want you to be happy, Ted — and to have what you want — and what you think is worth while in the whole game. And I'm going to clear out so you'll get it quick. [*He goes into the house.* TEDDY *stands alone a moment*]

MARGARET [*coming in from the right*]. Has your father — Has anything happened, Teddy?

TEDDY [*goes slowly to* MARGARET *who puts her arms about her*]. Billy says he won't have my money and he won't marry me.

MARGARET. How much do you love him?

TEDDY. More than I ever thought anybody could love anything.

MARGARET [*a very happy and knowing look coming into her face*]. Billy's a big person. It would take a big person to hold him and to live up to his ideals.

TEDDY [*moving back in amazement*]. Don't you think I could?

MARGARET. You're just a little spoiled girl, dear, who's had her own way all her life, and expected every man she took the trouble to flirt with to be her slave. Billy isn't anybody's slave, you know. If you've burned your fingers on him I'm sorry. Has he found you out? Is it all over?

TEDDY. It certainly is so far as I'm concerned. If he's so darn big, I don't want him stooping to me. I may be very small potatoes to some people, but there are people who think I'm rather worth while. If you and Billy are living on such a lofty plane that you can't commune with me I think I'll clear out and go where — [*She sees* HUBERT *who comes from left along the road and down the steps*] Oh, Daddy — Daddy, dear. [*After a moment she goes to him with a sob, putting her arms about his neck.* MARGARET *turns away to hide her own tears*]

HUBERT [*scarcely able to speak*]. There's never been a day or an hour that I haven't wanted you back.

TEDDY. There's never been a day or an hour when I haven't wanted you.

HUBERT. Why didn't you come, dear?

TEDDY. How could I? I've waited for you to come and tell me you trusted me.

HUBERT. My little girl! I'll mak[e] it up to you.

TEDDY [*putting her arms about h[er] neck again*]. Oh, Daddy, I'm glad yo[u] came. Take me home.

[MARGARET *turns to them again*]

HUBERT. Margaret, she wants to g[o] home.

TEDDY. Do you want me?

HUBERT. Ted! [*Taking her in h[is] arms*] We'll shut up the house an[d] leave it. Let's get off.

TEDDY. Oh — not just this minut[e].

HUBERT. Well — why not? I ha[ve] the place. I'm going to sell it. I wan[t] all association with it wiped out.

TEDDY. It's mine, Daddy. Yo[u] can't do that.

HUBERT. Why can't I?

TEDDY. I love it. I've been mor[e] happy here than I ever —

HUBERT. Tut! I'm going to mak[e] you happier than you ever have bee[n] in your whole life.

TEDDY. How?

HUBERT. By giving you everythin[g] you want.

TEDDY. I'm afraid you can't do tha[t]

HUBERT. What? What is there yo[u] want that I can't give you?

[TEDDY *moves away.* HUBERT *looks [at]* MARGARET]

MARGARET [*coming forward*]. Teddy['s] had a great disappointment.

TEDDY. Oh, don't tell father that[.]

HUBERT. Now don't keep thing[s] from me.

MARGARET. He'll have to know[,] dear. Everybody will know it.

HUBERT. What?

MARGARET. Billy Wade — who ha[s] been so splendid this summer — well — Teddy and he — thought they were i[n] love with each other.

TEDDY. Oh, I'll tell it. He — h[e] — Billy and I — We — He — That['s] all there is to it.

MARGARET. I think you'd better ge[t] her away at once. Billy's changed hi[s] mind. He doesn't want to marry her.

HUBERT [*not believing his ears*]. Wha[t] do you say?

TEDDY. Pretty hard for you to ge[t] that — isn't it, Dad?

HUBERT. He must be insane. Bu[t] it's a blessing of course — the bes[t] possible way out of any complicatio[n]

ou may have got yourself into. What
o you want to do, Ted? And we'll do
. Go round the world?

TEDDY [*sitting on the bench*]. No,
hank you.

HUBERT. Go to London to live?

TEDDY. No, thank you.

HUBERT. What do you suggest,
Margaret? Build a house in town of
ur own?

TEDDY. *No!*

HUBERT. Want a yacht and cruise?

TEDDY. Oh, you always want to
uy something, Dad.

HUBERT. Well, I don't know many
hings that can't be bought.

TEDDY. I know one — and it's the
nly thing I want.

HUBERT. Now see here, Teddy, if
ou want this fellow — I'll buy *him*
or you.

TEDDY. I'd like to see you try.
Vhy do you want to dispose of me?
et me do it myself. First of all, I
ant to be left alone — to think. Men
ren't everything on earth. I don't
ant to leave my chickens. I love
hem.

HUBERT [*frankly puzzled and helpless
ut doing the best he can*]. Well, you
on't intend spending the rest of your
fe sitting here with the chickens, do
ou?

TEDDY. I may. I don't know at all.
Regardless of you — or any other man
the world, I'm going to take care of
nyself.

MARGARET. You must expect her to
eel this way, Hubert. As I told you
he's had a great disappointment.
Billy Wade is a very impressive person.
ou can't blame her for falling head over
eels in love with him. If I were her
ge I'd do the same thing.

HUBERT. Well, let's have a look at
he paragon. At least I'd like to pay
im back for his work out here.

TEDDY. And I'd like to see you try
hat.

HUBERT. Get him. Get him.
Vhere is he?

MARGARET. I'll see if he *will* see
ou. [*She goes into the house*]

HUBERT. My dear child, I want to
elp you forget all this and make you
appy.

TEDDY. That's what several people
ave said this afternoon. But I seem
o have my own ideas of being happy.
Do you want me to go back to the same
hings that made me the selfish, extrav-

agant, absolutely useless thing that I
was?

HUBERT. Don't put it on too thick,
Ted. After all you were one of the
most successful girls in New York.

TEDDY. Yes of course. All those
things helped to make me a success —
to say nothing of what you did for me.
Don't think I don't want all you can do
for me now. One side of me wants it
awfully.

HUBERT. And you're going to have
it.

TEDDY. But there's something in
the world that you and I have never had
at all. I've found out there are some
things that are worth suffering for and
some that —

MARGARET [*coming out of the house
with* BILLY]. Billy, this is Mr. Gloucester.

BILLY [*coming forward*]. How do you
do?

HUBERT [*after a steady look at* BILLY].
It seems my daughter is under very
heavy obligations to you for what you've
done here this summer. I'd like to express my appreciation in a practical
way. It will be quite possible to put
you into something good in New York.

BILLY. Thank you. I don't care
for it.

TEDDY. Um!

HUBERT. I understand you gave up
something pretty fair once before in
New York. What was that?

BILLY. I was with Alfred Tate.

HUBERT. Indeed! I've had a good
many deals with Tate. And why did
you give it up, may I ask?

BILLY. If you insist, because the
business is crooked.

HUBERT. Um! And you gave it
up to make a living on this scrubby little
place instead?

BILLY. It's a pretty poverty-stricken
living out here.

HUBERT. And yet you persuaded my
daughter it was a good thing for her.

BILLY. And it was, wasn't it?
Better than the other thing that was
offered her just then?

HUBERT. And you've had the audac-
ity to speak of marriage to her — and
now you've decided you don't want
her? Have you the faintest idea of the
insufferable impertinence of that?

BILLY. Theodora has decided she
wants her money and I can't marry her
if she has it.

HUBERT. *What?!!!*

TEDDY [*rising and going to* BILLY]. Billy — when you thought I didn't have any money you loved me, and I know you love me now. It's the money, Dad. He won't take me with it, so I give it up — absolutely — everything you could possibly give me.

HUBERT. Steady, Ted. You're talking very big.

TEDDY. Billy, I'm just the way I was an hour ago — and I love you better than anything in the world. Will you marry me?

HUBERT. *My God!*

BILLY. Ted!

MARGARET. You ask him, too —

Hubert. Do all you can to hold him.

HUBERT. Is there anything I coul do — to induce you to accept me as father-in-law?

TEDDY. You leave me alone wit him a minute, Dad, and I'll see what can do for you. [HUBERT *goes out right after* MARGARET] Billy — will yo marry me?

BILLY. Ted — I know you've flirte an awful lot but you're the only girl i my life — and if you're fooling me, I' kill you.

TEDDY [*putting her arms around h neck*]. Go on, dear — I love that!

THE CURTAIN FALLS

THE DETOUR

(1921)

By Owen Davis

OWEN DAVIS

Mr. Owen Davis wrote a play which he called "Icebound." It was produced
n New York on February 10, 1923, and ran for several months. It was not a suc-
ess in the box-office sense, but it won for Mr. Davis an added literary worth. It
as awarded the Pulitzer prize of $1,000, and, because of it and of his previous
lay, "The Detour", he was elected a member of the National Institute of Arts
nd Letters.

These two plays of Mr. Davis mark a type that is entirely separate from his other
ork in the theatre. As a dramatist he has probably written more plays of varied
haracter than any one of his contemporaries. And living close to the theatre, he
as attained for himself a certain surety of technique which makes his architectural
rasp of what constitutes a play very complete. This precise way of doing things
 probably the most emphatic fault in both of these plays which are, to the present
ditor's way of thinking, very notable contributions to native dramaturgy. "Ice-
ound" has about it much of the bitterness of close observation and personal
xperience; the use of those ugly circumstances which constitute the life of the
ordan family, and which are so heavily laid on, seems to suggest not so much the
fe of the matter as the technique of the dramatist. And the skill of the theatre
 Mr. Davis has, both in "Icebound" and "The Detour", made him at times
anipulate the plot slightly, resort to tricks that had heretofore been "worked"
n the stage, and he knew would work again with audiences.

But, in both plays, Mr. Davis has dug deep into native material. He seems a
ttle proud of this. In his foreword to "Icebound" he writes:

Here I have at least tried to draw a true picture of these people, and I am of
eir blood, born of generations of northern Maine, small-town folk, and brought up
nong them. In my memory of them is little of the "Rube" caricature of the con-
entional theatre; they are neither buffoons nor sentimentalists, and at least neither
eir faults nor their virtues are borrowed from the melting-pot but are the direct
sult of their own heritage and environment.

I have selected "The Detour" for this volume rather than "Icebound", for I
elieve it was the incentive for the other, the overflow of interest in a narrow, close
fe, and its effect on character. Mr. Davis wrote these plays because he wanted
, not because he thought they were for the theatre he had been accustomed to
 his earlier days. I am inclined to believe that, even though they interested him,
ey showed him that their appeal was a limited one — a literary one, which is
ot the way of the masses. The man who writes thus is for the special theatre,
e special audience, not for the theatre in which, I believe, Mr. Davis is essentially
terested. He even now is member of a conventional producing group calling
emselves The Dramatists, Inc., and that shows he is not intent on thrusting him-
lf into another atmosphere — a revolutionary atmosphere. His associates all are
en of the theatre "as it is."

491

Yet "The Detour" and "Icebound" are of the American theatre we hope wi
be. That does not necessarily mean that we want all our plays of a uniform dra
ness; rather any time the active criticism of O'Neill in "Desire Under the Elms
than a series of plays like "Icebound." But Davis, in both his plays, has com
mented deeply on life; sometimes he has photographed too cruelly — his humo
is not so real as his characterization. At times, in both plays, he has not quite bee
able to escape the theatre: his moral sentiments somehow seem to be maxims se
with precision; his comic reliefs are calculated. They are not, as in "The Show
Off", part of something that rises out of the people themselves. But "The Detour
and "Icebound", despite their minor structural defects, are worthy treatments o
American local conditions.

"The Detour" needs no justification for its appearance in print. It is one o
those studies in realism which — whether seen or read — impresses by reason o
its tremendous effectiveness. As such, it should be regarded as an encouraging, a
all too rare sign of the deepening of native dramaturgic art in the American Theatr

The dramatic critic was right who declared that, had "The Detour" been pro
duced as the work of an unknown author, it would have been hailed as the puttin
forth, the flowering of a rare native plant, from which much might be expected i
the future. I see no reason why this should not apply just as well to a dramatis
who, like Mr. Davis, has been brought up, dramatically, in the glare of melodrama
and who has — after learning the tricks of his trade — broken from the type o
play expected of him, only to give us something bigger, something more profound
more nearly what might be designated as an American *genre* drama. All the mor
reason, it seems, for us to rejoice that gold has turned up — as precursor, we hope
of a rich vein to follow.

Sincerity is at the basis of any worthy play, whether of realism or of the imagina
tion. Otherwise, painting things as they are degenerates into mere photograph
and usually attracts by reason of two cardinal excellences or faults, according to
your point of view: curiosity and vulgar attractiveness. Naturalism is a cancerou
growth on the face of art; realism is the arrangement of life as we know it, risin
out of human relationship. The one is bald fact, the other truth artistically cla
because of a burning faith in life's continuity.

This burning faith enriches the whole story of "The Detour"; and continuity
marks the merit of its structure. Mr. Davis has seen clearly, has sensed fully —
noting the myriad facets shaped from the materials of the humblest life — shades
of character and various motives inherent in locality and tradition. His play ha
the tang of the soil about it; it exudes a flavor born of struggle against environment
It does not strain after contrast of fitness with unfitness, with a certain cruel form
lessness which marks Eugene O'Neill's "Beyond the Horizon." It does not
attempt to compress folk-legend with reality as Alice Brown does in her passionles
"Children of Earth." It does not strive for miniature interest, so strikingly con
centrated in Susan Glaspell's "Trifles." "The Detour" — if there is anything
conscious at all about its structure — systematically discards the machinery o
theatricalism and is starkly simple. But, like all simple things in life, it is able to
carry with it, rising out of character and situation, real racy humor and problems
common to all — not alone to those whose vision is closed in by the boundaries o
farm life.

The burning glass of drama has persistently narrowed the canvas of the theatre
these many years. Yet dramatists in America have been loath to give up manipu-

tion of action for the sake of *genre* work and genuine creativeness. James A. Herne, our early realist in the modern America Theatre, rose far above the rural drama with which he is mistakenly identified; he possessed a profound sympathy for character and could draw from narrow, yet rich circumstance, homely truth — in its fundamentals not so unlike universal truth. Amidst the melodrama f "Shore Acres" he wrote such palpitant scenes as that of *Nathaniel Berry* and his brother discussing the sale of the farm. He wrote an entire play, "Margaret Fleming," daring for its day, an intensive domestic tragedy. "The Detour", in its treatment, is of the same caliber — with the technique of life itself.

I recall once — in the olden days when an eighteen-hour flier-train service between New York and Chicago was a novelty — riding in the cab of an engine thus destined to eat up space on a cold February afternoon, just as the shadows of twilight were beginning to turn the Hudson River into a sheet of cold white steel. There were streaks of color in the wintry sky and a streak of red glow from the intense furnace of our cab, as the train sped on at sixty miles an hour. At a curve, the fireman crept to the cab door of the engine and swung out on the step, clinging to a side rail. Against the cold swish of wind he let fly a bundle of papers in the direction of a shanty, far down a bankside and into a hollow. I leaned out of the window in time to see a bent old woman open the door of her shack and make for those papers. The fireman yelled to me an explanation — above the roar of the steam, the shrill blast of the whistle, the rumble of wheels over the ribbons of rail — I bring her the news from New York once a week."

Here, in this action, was material for melodrama and realism. Mr. Davis, by evidence of "The Detour", could handle both treatments. In art, the difference in the technique would be the difference between a poster that arrests the eye, and Rembrandt's "Old Woman Paring Her Nails" that challenges the creative instinct in us. In one mood, the thrill of the ride, the danger of the fireman's precarious position would have appealed to Mr. Davis, as an unconscious act of daily heroism; in another mood he would have wondered at the life of the woman in the shack — tried to square with her bowed figure the forces shaping her destiny, as Maeterlinck said of the old man seated silent in his armchair. There is no question as to which is the profounder drama.

One day, at Northport, Long Island, Mr. Davis sat in his car, overlooking a farm, with its lonely house in the distance. There were evidences around it, even in its typical isolation, of a woman's hand. The creative mind is always eager for such sign-posts of life on which to fasten its tentacles. Mayhap a detour made his chauffeur skirt around the farm, thus denying it contact with the life of the open road. From such simple beginnings, "The Detour" was evolved.

Mr. Davis has always claimed and asked that a critic judge each separate work of his on its own merits. He is justified in this request. We do judge the present play as a supreme picture of farm life, of mother love and wifely rebellion, where the tragedy is twofold — in the woman's yearning and stirring for self-expression through her daughter; and in the daughter's inadequacy through the inheritance of her father's stodginess and the confining claim of the soil upon her. In most of its dimensions the play holds measure. I do not claim flawlessness for it; I do claim for it bigness of intent.

Mr. Davis's previous inroads into the realm of melodrama do not have to be known for any appreciation of "The Detour." There is no special reason for recalling those days when he wrote from ten to twelve such pieces a year — their names

are as bloodcurdling as those which came from the pen of David Belasco when he w
writing for mining towns out in California — except to state that he must ha
perfected his technical expertness in such a hard school.   It is a glowing tribute
Mr. Davis's essential worth that he can now give us "The Detour" — so calm,
progressively fatalistic, so quiet in its outbursts — after association with a methe
that often deadens sensitiveness to character.

But we are all conscious — we who go continually to the theatre or read mar
plays — that there is another step to take beyond realism.   I find Mr. Davis ready
take it.   Amidst the atmosphere of realism, with which our stage has been drenche
there has been felt the need of a more palpitant spirit, akin to mysticism, yet mo
attached to earthly attainment.   The mother, in "The Detour", shows glints
this spirit — the unquenchable determination to outwit environment, rise high
than circumstance.   It is a step thoroughly in consonance with the Americ
character.   Given the ability to write such realistic scenes as are here depicted, a
the desire to infuse into the materials of character an aspiration which overcom
adversity, and a play greater and wider in its stage appeal than "The Detou
could be written.   But one must have evidences of such a play as the present or
before one can hope for the other.

I am confident that "The Detour" represents thus far one of our high attai
ments in American realism for the stage.   It is worthy to be read widely ; as
representative of native *genre* work it is worthy of consideration abroad.   It is
play that any repertory theatre should welcome.   Such sheer realism requir
sheer acting, and invites and challenges the best in players.   It is rarely that
American playwright penetrates so deeply into American life.   That is why
greet "The Detour" heartily as "the real thing" in the theatre.

THE DETOUR

By OWEN DAVIS

"The Detour" was originally produced in New York August 23, 1921, with th
following cast:

STEPHEN HARDY	Augustin Duncan
HELEN, *his wife*	Effie Shannon
KATE, *their daughter*	Angela McCahill
TOM LANE	Willard Robertso
DANA LAMONT	Harry Andrews
DORA LAMONT	Eva Condon
BEN GLENNY	Claude Cooper
WEINSTEIN	James R. Waters
JAKE	Chester Herman

ACT I. — *Mrs. Hardy's kitchen.*
ACT II. — *The veranda, that afternoon.*
ACT III. — *The kitchen, a little later.*

TIME. *The present*
THE PLACE. *Near Northport, L. I.*

THE DETOUR

ACT I

SCENE. — *Kitchen of* STEPHEN HARDY'S *farmhouse on the road to Northport (Long Island), a simple, homelike room quite without any of the conveniences of modern invention, and equally without any studied air of grimness. The room should be as unpretentious as the play and as far away from symbolism, — just the plain home of plain people. Door back left to yard; a rather wide window back right looks out upon side veranda. Door to hall at left. Cook stove right. Sink above stove. This kitchen, out of respect for the "parlor", is used as the family living room, and the small dining table at right is now covered with a dull red cloth. Door to a "pantry" at right below stove; when this door is open it is possible to see the usual flour barrel, sugar bucket, etc. Near the window at back is a cheap easel on which is a conventional water color; on a stand by the easel are a few odds and ends of an artist's paraphernalia. There is a shelf above the stove, and among the articles on this shelf is a rather hideous old jug in which is a bunch of artificial flowers.*

It is early afternoon of a July day. At right center, seated by the table, is KATE HARDY, *a girl of eighteen;* HELEN HARDY, *her mother, is in the doorway looking out.*

HELEN. All right! [*She crosses down to shelf above the stove and taking the jug in which are the artificial flowers, she crosses to the table at right center*]

KATE. Somehow it always frightens me!

HELEN. It needn't! What's here is ours. [*She removes the artificial flowers and turns the jug upside down. The jug is about one third full of money, old bills, one or two gold pieces, and silver. Kate takes five dollar bills from her little pocketbook and adds them to the pile*]

KATE. It's the last of my school-teaching money until September.

HELEN. You'll get your pay for clerking in the drug store in another week. [*She sits by table*] How much did you put in just now?

KATE. Five dollars.

HELEN. Where's the rest of it?

KATE [*hesitates*]. I — I was going to buy some goods for a dress; we could make it ourselves, of course. Just a little organdy or something.

HELEN. You can get along, I guess, without it.

KATE [*wistfully*]. I'm ashamed to go to the pictures Saturday nights; I haven't a thing!

HELEN [*firmly*]. Your blue dress will do well enough, put it all in.

KATE [*reluctant*]. Yes, mother. [*She takes a few more bills from her pocketbook and adds them to the pile*]

HELEN. I'm going to count it.

KATE. You'll wear it all out before it's any good to us!

HELEN [*almost gaily. Starting to count money*]. I'm like a miser I saw once in an opera, — I think it was "The Chimes of Normandy." *He* took me to the theatre in New York three or four times the first year we were married. You count the silver.

KATE [*piling up the coins*]. Some of the summer people from here, and even as far down as Shoreham, drive their automobiles up to New York almost every day!

HELEN [*counting bills*]. I know.

KATE. And I've never been there!

HELEN. You will!

KATE. I never used to believe it, but we've saved a lot.

HELEN [*looking over at her*]. How much?

KATE. Sixty dollars and fifty cents, counting the gold pieces.

HELEN. I've got six hundred and forty; let's see — that's six hundred and forty and sixty dollars and fifty cents —?

KATE [*promptly*]. Seven hundred dollars and fifty cents.

HELEN. You're quick at figures!

KATE [*laughs*]. You're not!

HELEN. I get it mixed with receipts for gingerbread and when to give the calf that medicine your father left for it. [*She starts to put the money back into the jar*] Seven hundred dollars and fifty cents! Just my chicken and egg money and little odds and ends, and your pay for school teaching and for clerking at Nepper's, summers! It's almost like the loaves and fishes in the Bible!

KATE. If you'd only let me go with that!

HELEN. No, not till we get a thousand.

KATE [*sadly*]. Three hundred dollars more!

HELEN. All but fifty cents.

KATE [*impatiently*]. What's fifty cents?

HELEN. If you'd remember how we've had to scrimp for every penny, you wouldn't ask that.

KATE. How could I help remembering! Sometimes I hate that money! It's all the good times I've never had, and all the things I've done without!

HELEN. You'll thank me for it some time.

KATE. Oh, yes! Only couldn't I just take this seven hundred and make it do?

HELEN. No, I always said a thousand. It would be so awful if you had to come back! Two years it might take you, and *he* won't want *you* to go; he wouldn't send you anything; good teachers cost money, and painting things, and a studio! We've got to get a thousand; we can save it in another year.

KATE. We never have saved that much.

HELEN. All the more reason why we should this time.

KATE. A year — [*She sighs*] It's so long to wait.

HELEN. I been here twenty.

KATE. But not knowing that pretty soon you were going! It was your home; you knew you were going to live here always.

HELEN. I've told you times enough about that, how hard it was for me 1 settle down.

KATE. But, mother! *I'm* young!

HELEN. So was I, once, and as fa as that goes, I've still got my teeth! guess you can stand it another year.

KATE. You wouldn't go away fro here if you could!

HELEN. Yes, I would — quicl Lookin' back, it seems like I was craz I didn't go!

KATE [*shocked*]. From father?

HELEN [*bitterly*]. From this! [*S looks about the room bitterly*] It ain enough! Life ought to be bigger tha — than this kitchen! It ought to b brighter than I been able to keep tho old pots and pans! I knew that, when was your age, but somehow I forgot for a while. I'd always meant to g away and go to New York, or som where's where bein' born an' bein' dea wasn't the only things that ever hap pened. I'd made my mind up to g I'd saved for it harder even than we'v been savin'; one more term of wint school teachin' an' I figured I'd ha enough.

KATE. But you didn't go!

HELEN. No, I took my money an bought my weddin' things. It wa awful lonesome around here winter and your father's got a way of getti what he wants.

KATE. Mother! You're not sorr

HELEN. I tell you it ain't enoug [*She looks out the window at the vista truck gardens then half-turns toward KAT* At first, when we were married, thought it was. Then it got to be ju drudgery, just work, nothing els every other part of me just shriveled u [*She walks slowly down to table*] Whe I was a girl I used to watch marri folks and I thought it was like that, b somehow I got to loving him before knew it. I didn't have any talent lik you have; I just had the hunger to things.

KATE. But if we're wrong? If haven't really a talent?

HELEN. No, there's more justi than that in the world. You've g what I didn't have.

KATE. We can't be sure.

HELEN. You'll be a great artist!

KATE. Mother!

HELEN. You will! I've known ever since I got you that first box water colors when you were a lit girl. You're more like his people

oks, but the rest of you is *me!* The
hing I wanted to do you're going to
o!

KATE. Yes, mother!

HELEN. As soon as I saw you fav-
red me in spirit, only you had the talent
didn't have, I knew just what we had
o do, and I started over again saving
or it. Your life isn't going to be like
his, not even with a good man like your
ather!

KATE. He *is* good, but he's hard.

HELEN. He's had to be, to live!

KATE. But he never thinks of any-
hing but land, then more and more!

HELEN. There's no money in garden
ruck unless you have a lot of land.

KATE. But he keeps us so poor,
uying it, and he's always so worried
bout the taxes and the mortgages —
nd before he's paid for the last piece
e's always buying another.

HELEN. He loves it! Just land!

KATE. It's merciless, the way he
nakes you work, and the way he works
imself!

HELEN. It's being a slave just to
things, just cooking and cleaning and
ligging and planting! You sha'n't be
hat! [*She picks up the jug and puts the
artificial flowers back in it*]

KATE. I'm always worried about
that money; supposing something happened to it?

HELEN. Nobody'd look in here.
[*She crosses to shelf and puts the jug
away*]

KATE. They might!

HELEN. No, it's safe; it's been
over ten years I've been saving up and
no one but us two knows about it.
Your father don't notice things much.

KATE. Only if it's good growing
weather, or if it isn't! Or if it's an
acre of land he could buy! Mother!
Was he always like that?

HELEN. I guess so, only I didn't
know it! [*She sighs and crosses and
stands in the open door*] I guess folks
don't change much. [*She stands for a
moment looking out*] He's comin',
they've finished pickin' the string beans;
weren't many of 'em, I guess. [*She
sighs again*] No, folks don't change
much; he's heavier than he was, and
he don't hardly ever smile. He used to,
he had a real nice smile. [*She crosses
slowly back to* KATE] Farmin's pretty
hard on a man.

KATE. And on a woman too.

HELEN. Yes.

[STEVE HARDY *enters, a tall, strong
farmer of forty-five, dressed for his
work in the fields*]

STEVE. We got the beans all picked.
[*He crosses and draws a dipper of water
from the sink*] I'm goin' to make up
the truck load with the summer cabbages — what there is of them. [*He
drinks heartily*] It's hot out there?

KATE. I picked beans for an hour;
then mother made me stop.

STEVE. Your mother's spoiled you,
but that's all right. I don't want you
working in the fields.

HELEN. I won't have it — you both
know that; that's why I called her in!
I don't want her to neglect her painting.

STEVE [*pleasantly enough*]. I guess the
world would get along without her
painting, all right. You're going to
work at Nepper's to-morrow, ain't you?

KATE. Yes, I promised to go down
this afternoon to learn the stock! It
doesn't seem as though I *could* begin
that all over again!

STEVE. How much is he giving you
this year?

KATE. Fourteen dollars a week.

STEVE. That's a lot for just standing
behind a counter and waiting on folks,
and it's cash every Saturday night.
I'd feel rich if I had it after I pay my
help and put aside for my taxes and
interest.

HELEN. That's because we're land
poor, the same as we've always been.

STEVE [*angrily*]. It's because I
haven't land enough to make truck
farming a business like it ought to be,
so as I could have help and teams and
tools and do things right, and make
money! I need twice the land I've got,
and I'm going to have it. [*He turns on
the water at the sink and holds his hand
under it; for the first time it is seen that
he has hurt his hand slightly and that
there is blood on it*]

HELEN. Your hand's cut!

STEVE. That's what I came in for, to
tie it up. I sprayed the cabbages only
Tuesday and I don't want to get the
poison in it.

HELEN. Let's see. [*She takes his
hand and looks at it*]

STEVE. Knife slipped. I wouldn't
notice it only for the poison.

HELEN. I'll fix it before you touch
the cabbages; clean it good, I'll get a
rag. [*He holds it under the water as she
selects a bit of cloth from the table drawer*]

STEVE. Tom Lane's opening his garage to-day.

KATE. I know.

STEVE. No fool like a young fool!

HELEN [*crosses with her improvised bandage*]. Here! [*He holds out his hand and she deftly binds it up*] I never saw so many cars as there are this year, and the summer business has hardly started. I shouldn't wonder if Tom made money.

STEVE. A man's a farmer or he ain't!

HELEN. There's money in other things besides truck farming.

STEVE. The twenty acres this side of his house is the best truck land on the north shore, if a man had it that knew how to lay it out.

HELEN [*finishes bandage*]. There!

STEVE. I must get them started at the cabbages. [*He turns and stops in front of the easel. The picture on the easel is facing the window and he sees only the back of it*] What's that?

HELEN. Kate's painting. I made her bring it down; I wanted you to look at it.

KATE [*nervously*]. No, mother!

STEVE. What do you want me to look at it for?

HELEN. She's your daughter, too; it don't seem right your not knowing what she's doing.

STEVE. She paints good enough. I always thought. What of it?

HELEN. She's an artist! I mean a real artist! Two or three years' teachin' in New York will make her as good as any of 'em.

[*He laughs a rather coarse and jarring laugh*]

KATE [*hurt*]. You see, mother!

HELEN. It's your father that don't see, but he's got to; everybody has! I want you to look at this painting right now! [*She faces him angrily*]

STEVE. What do I know about pictures?

HELEN. You've got eyes! [*She crosses to painting*] It's just a painting she's made sitting in her window. It's just what you see every day of your life. Look! [*She turns the painting to face him and the audience. A simple water color of a rural landscape*]

STEVE. I see!

KATE [*fearful*]. I don't think father cares about —

[STEVE *bends forward and takes the painting from* HELEN. KATE *stops*]

HELEN [*greatly pleased*]. He do He likes it!

KATE [*proudly*]. Father!

HELEN. You see something in don't you, Stephen?

STEVE. I see Tom Jones' twenty-a field in it. Look how it lies to the s there, sloping just enough! I'm goi to have that land. I've got to!

HELEN [*anxiously*]. But the pictur

STEVE. Here! Take it! [*He dro it on table*] All Tom can think of is new garage. He'd sell, I know would! [*He crosses to door, stops a turns*] Kate!

KATE [*quite crushed*]. Yes, father.

STEVE. I've got to ask you to he me out with the money you earn fro Nepper this summer!

HELEN [*alarmed*]. Stephen!

STEVE. She had her school mone I never touched it. It ain't a thing want to do, but I've got to! [*He tur to* KATE] You give your mother te dollars every Saturday. I'll be e pectin' it. [*He exits*]

KATE [*takes up picture*]. He didr care about my painting — all he cou see was the land!

HELEN [*sadly*]. He'll take yo money! Now we can't do it in a yea

KATE [*angrily*]. It isn't fair. Wh right has he to make me —

HELEN [*interrupts her*]. Hush, dea I'm going to find a way!

KATE. You can't!

HELEN. I don't know. . . .

[TOM LANE, *a young fellow of abo twenty-five, comes to the open doo* TOM *is in working clothes, a health sturdy young animal*]

TOM. Can I come in, Mrs. Hardy?

HELEN. Of course you can, Tom.

[*As he enters*]

KATE [*smiles at him*]. How's th new garage?

TOM. Great! My stock's in — more'n a thousand dollars' worth, an five hundred gallons of gas.

KATE. So you've really started!

TOM [*proudly*]. My sign's out; look good if I did paint it myself. [*He grin cheerfully at* KATE] I don't pretend t be an artist.

HELEN [*proudly*]. Artists don't pain signs!

TOM. I got my first job, too, fixin a car for a man named Lamont, Dan Lamont. [KATE *looks up at the mentio of the name, then looks closely at her painting*] He's taken the Curtis bungalow for the summer.

HELEN [*busy about kitchen*]. His wife's been here twice for eggs and butter, — she's a nice woman; she made me show her all over the house yesterday. I never saw anybody make such a fuss as she did over mother's old curly maple bed and dresser.

TOM. Why?

HELEN. She liked it, but she don't know a thing about furniture. When I took the covers off the red plush set in the parlor she hardly so much as looked at it!

TOM. Well, they've got money, and they're going to be good customers of mine. His car's in my place now.

KATE. I think it's better than farming.

TOM. I know it is. I'm worried about the roads being so bad just below; that's going to hurt. Some folks will go up the Middle Island Road, and I'll lose them, but I'm bound to make good money.

HELEN. That Mrs. Lamont is coming for a dozen more eggs to-day. She's expecting company. [*She takes a basket from shelf*] I'll get them for her.

KATE. I'll do it.

HELEN. No, show Tom your painting. You've been out enough in the hot sun. [*She exits*]

TOM. She's good to you!

KATE. Mother's wonderful!

TOM. She takes care of you just like you were some — some sort of a treasure!

KATE [*laughingly*]. I know!

TOM. Too good for rough things — too good for rough people — and she thinks I'm one of 'em — and I guess I am.

KATE. My painting's finished.

TOM. Is it? Let's look. [*Crosses and looks*]

KATE [*anxiously*]. I tried so hard, and now I don't know.

TOM. Don't know what?

KATE. If it's really good.

TOM [*after a long look*]. It's great!

KATE. Don't say so if you don't mean it!

TOM. It's great! [*He points with his finger*] That's the fence between your place and mine, and that's my twenty-acre lot! Any fool knows that's a good picture!

KATE. I think it's good. I'm almost sure of it! I've worked so hard, Tom, without anybody much to help me — sometimes I'm not sure, and that's awful — it would break mother's heart, and mine, of course!

TOM. It's a nice way to spend your time, when you ain't workin'. Doing anything to-night? I might come over.

KATE. The movie theater's opening to-night for the summer. I sort of thought I might walk down there with — with one of the girls.

[HELEN *re-enters at back with a dozen eggs in her basket*]

TOM [*very reluctant*]. I — I'll take you, if you want to go.

KATE. Don't you?

TOM. They bother me, movin' pictures, all about other folks' wives and murders and poor girls gettin' married to rich men, an' young fellers makin' a million dollars in a couple of days, when everybody knows they can't. It wastes your time, and I don't know as it's right, puttin' ideas into peoples' heads.

HELEN. What would you put there?

TOM. It's hard enough to keep on your job without thinking about things.

KATE. But you can't just work!

TOM. Why?

KATE. I think the pictures are fun, and they're a change from reading.

TOM. Book reading? Books are just as bad! Seems like every liar took to writin' books! I gave 'em all up but one.

KATE. What one?

HELEN [*dryly*]. His account book.

TOM [*grins at her*]. That's right.

HELEN. Maybe it ain't right, but it's *true*.

TOM. Laugh, all you please, and of course I know you're laughing. I ain't mean, anyhow, I ain't dog mean — but what I want is money. When I get enough of that I guess folks will forgive me if I don't know Charlie Chaplin from Douglas Fairbanks, an' even if I ain't a fancy dancer. [*He steps toward door*]

HELEN. There's more folks know how to save money than there is that know how to spend it.

TOM. By the time a feller learns enough to save it he's got too much sense to spend it. I'm going back to the garage and sit and wait for trade. That's got the pictures beat, I guess! [*He crosses stage.* KATE *looks after him a little wistfully*]

KATE. Good-by, Tom.

TOM. See you later. [*He exits*]

KATE. It's funny — in some ways he is so like father, and living right next door to us.

HELEN. Maybe it's catchin'. [*She crosses to* KATE *and putting her hand on* KATE'S *shoulder she looks down at her gravely*] Kate?

KATE. Yes, mother.

HELEN. He's been around a lot lately!

KATE. Yes.

HELEN. You're not thinkin' of him? [KATE *drops her eyes.* HELEN *looks frightened*] Kate! If you was to do that, what's the good of all we've done?

KATE. Oh, I wouldn't. Not — not the way you mean — only — only I think he likes me — and — and — [*She stops*]

HELEN. And he's the best you know.

KATE. Yes, he's that.

HELEN. But not the best you're going to know! We think that thousand dollars it will take us most ten years to save is a lot of money?

KATE. I should say so!

HELEN. In New York it isn't anything!

KATE [*worried*]. But —

HELEN. Don't be silly! You've got a talent! They'll make room for you!

KATE. I hope so.

HELEN. They will — if you work hard — and you must! If you was to fail, I'd feel somehow as if all my life had been just wasted!

KATE [*earnestly*]. I'll work.

HELEN [*tenderly*]. I know you will.

KATE [*touched*]. You're the one who ought to go, mother!

HELEN. I'm going, the very best way — the part of me that's in you is going — what I was once — what I wanted to be — I gave all that to you. When they all come crowding around you some day, saying you're a great artist, men and women, different from the kind we know, you'll be proud, but you won't be so proud as I'll be!

[DANA LAMONT, *a New York artist, comes to the door.* LAMONT, *although an artist, is not at all of the "artistic type", he is just a cultivated, well-mannered man of middle age*]

DANA. I beg your pardon, but I was to meet my wife here, Mrs. Lamont.

HELEN. She was coming for some eggs, but I haven't seen her. Come in and wait, won't you?

DANA [*enters*]. Thank you. She asked me to meet her here.

HELEN. This is my daughter, Mr Lamont.

DANA. Good morning, Miss — Hardy — isn't it?

KATE. Yes, sir.

HELEN. Won't you sit down? [*Offers chair*]

DANA. Thanks — no — I am going to leave a message for my wife, if you don't mind. Please say that I have walked on to the new garage to see what is being done about my car. If the man here can't fix it, I shall have to arrange to have it towed to Huntington.

HELEN. Tom Lane will fix it!

DANA. Really — is he a good mechanic?

HELEN. He's a good business man.

KATE. He's a good mechanic, too, mother!

HELEN. I guess so; anyhow he won't let it go to Huntington.

DANA. Would you mind asking Mrs. Lamont to walk along and meet me on the road?

HELEN. I'll tell her if she comes.

DANA. She'll come! Thank you very much. [*He turns to doorway*] I envy you the view from your front windows, Mrs. Hardy; it's quite unusual.

HELEN. That depends on how long you've been looking at it.

DANA. I think I could enjoy looking at it forever.

HELEN. I haven't tried that yet, but I was born right on the other side of the road.

DANA. And you are tired of it, of course. Just as my eyes have grown tired of bricks and mortar, of curbstones and asphalt! Beauty, after all, is in contrasts.

HELEN. We don't raise 'em around here.

DANA. You have managed to keep a twinkle in your eyes, in spite of monotony — so you're all right! Good afternoon! Good afternoon, Miss Hardy.

[KATE *bows shyly and he exits*]

HELEN [*looking after him*]. That's what I meant, a gentleman! That's the kind of men you're going to know!

KATE. Dana Lamont! Don't you know who he is? Wait! [*She selects a magazine from the small table and turns the pages until she finds the page, then*

rosses to HELEN] Look! I knew as
oon as Tom spoke his name.

HELEN [*awed*]. He painted that!
*She looks at the reproduction in the maga-
ine with something almost like reverence*]
)ana Lamont! Kate! Why didn't
'ou show him the picture! [*She points
o* KATE's *picture*]

KATE. Mother! I wouldn't have
lared!

HELEN [*firmly*]. I wish I'd known!

KATE. Mother!

HELEN. That's the way to learn,
rom the real big ones; from folks that
<now!

KATE. But I wouldn't have any
'ight to bother a man like Dana La-
nont!

HELEN. Why! I showed his wife
1ow to bake corn bread yesterday.

KATE. That's different.

HELEN. It ain't! I know how to
bake and he knows how to paint. Folks
that *know* ain't mean; it's only fools.

[DORA LAMONT *comes to door.* DORA
*is a pretty and beautifully dressed
woman with a frank, jolly nature,
quite unaffected and kindly*]

DORA. Was that my husband I saw
disappearing down the road?

HELEN. Yes, it was. Come in,
Mrs. Lamont. [DORA *enters*] This is
my daughter.

DORA. How do you do!

KATE [*shyly*]. I'm pleased to meet
you.

HELEN [*shows magazine*]. We were
just looking at this.

DORA [*looks*]. "The Harvest." Isn't
it lovely!

HELEN [*gravely*]. Yes — lovely!
[*She puts magazine on table*] She paints
too! [*She looks proudly at* KATE]

DORA. Really — that's splendid!

KATE. Please, mother!

HELEN [*gets basket*]. Here's your eggs
— Mr. Lamont said he was going to the
garage and you was to meet him on the
road.

DORA. Thank you, but these are
only eggs — where is my butter?

HELEN. You got a pound yesterday!

DORA. But I want it every day!

HELEN. Oh — well, butter won't
hurt you! Get a pound of butter from
the spring house, Kate.

KATE. Yes, mother. [*She crosses
and gets a plate*] I won't be a minute.
[*She exits*]

DORA. She's pretty!

HELEN. She's more than that — I
want to show you something — that's
why I sent her. [*She crosses and turns*
KATE's *painting*] Look!

[DORA *looks*]

DORA. Why, it's really very nice!

HELEN. Yes.

DORA. You must be proud of her!

HELEN. Yes.

DORA [*looking at picture*]. What a
lovely country it is about here. The
slope of that hill side is exquisite!

HELEN. That's what my husband
says, but he was thinking of the drain-
age.

DORA [*laughs*]. That's like a husband; not mine, of course, but artists
are different.

HELEN. Yes — you think it's good,
that picture; I mean, really good?

DORA. I am sure it is!

HELEN [*anxiously*]. Not for a girl,
I don't mean — I mean for anybody —
for an artist?

DORA [*hesitates*]. Why —

HELEN. She's going to New York
to study, we've been planning it all her
life. All the help she's had was a
Miss Crosby at Northport. You think
she's got talent — I mean real talent?

DORA. My husband says no one has
a right to say that unless it's really so,
and of course I'm not a judge.

HELEN. He is.

DORA. Yes.

HELEN. Would he look at it if you
was to ask him?

DORA. Of course he would.

HELEN. And tell her where to go
when she gets to New York, — who the
best teachers are?

DORA. I am sure he would; I'll
bring him here myself.

HELEN. It's awful to ask favors, but
you do sometimes, for people you love
enough!

DORA. Of course you do, and it isn't
a favor. My husband says one proof
of a real artist is his willingness to help
another.

HELEN. I knew that.

DORA [*laughs*]. You know a lot,
don't you?

HELEN. Yes and no — mostly no.

[KATE *enters with* BEN GLENNY, *a tall,
lank, serious-looking fellow who is in
his shirt sleeves. In one hand he
has a hammer and in the other a
pine board on which, in black letters,*

is *painted the word* DETOUR. KATE *comes forward with the plate of butter in her hand,* BEN GLENNY *stops in the doorway*]

KATE. Here's Mr. Glenny, he wants to borrow a nail.

BEN. Got to put this up. [*Holds up the sign*] Going to close the road and send folks around Smithtown way. I thought I had nails with me, but I ain't.

KATE [*at drawer of table*]. This big enough? [*She holds up nail*]

BEN. About right.

KATE. Here. [*She brings him four or five nails*] Sure they're enough?

BEN. Plenty, thanks; the men are closing the road now and I ought to get this up quick.

[*He exits.* HELEN *rolls the butter up in a clean cloth and puts it in the basket with the eggs*]

HELEN. The road's pretty bad; it's a good thing they're fixing it. Detour, that's a new word; seems we're borrowing lots of things from France. It ain't a bad word — Detour — only I don't know as I get the meaning of it exactly.

KATE. It means a turning.

DORA. Another way around, to get to the same place.

HELEN. Oh, well, so long as a person gets where they want to go, I guess a detour don't matter much.

DORA [*lightly*]. Unless it takes you where you don't want to go. [*She takes out her pocketbook*] How much do I owe you?

HELEN. Sixty cents for the butter, and eighty-five for the eggs, a dollar and — and —

KATE. Forty-five.

HELEN [*to* KATE]. When you go I'll get a slate.

[DORA *puts the money on the table*]

DORA. And thank you very much! Oh! I knew I was forgetting something. I was in Huntington yesterday and I spoke to a dealer there — a rather dreadful person named Weinstein — about that wonderful old curly maple of yours.

HELEN. What about it?

DORA. All about it. He is going to drive over here very soon.

HELEN. What for?

DORA. To buy it, of course.

HELEN. Buy it? It's a real good

bed, and the bureau's all right if you're patient when the drawers stick. I wouldn't be able to get along without 'em.

DORA. Oh — I thought you would be glad of the chance of disposing of them.

HELEN. No, I guess not. They were mother's, you see. I don't think I'd like other folks having them.

DORA. Just tell him so then. I thought you cared more for your parlor furniture.

HELEN. I do; nobody can help liking fine things like my parlor set better than old truck, but being mother's makes a difference.

DORA. Of course it does. [*She crosses to door*]

HELEN. And you won't forget about bringing your husband to look at the painting?

KATE [*afraid*]. Oh, no!

DORA. I'll bring him in the very first time we pass this way. [*She exits*]

HELEN [*follows her to door*]. I'll be a lot obliged.

DORA [*outside*]. Not a bit, good afternoon.

HELEN [*in doorway*]. Good afternoon. [*She goes to shelf and drops the money in the old jar, then crosses to where* KATE *stands looking down at her painting.* HELEN *puts her arm about her and they stand together looking at it*]

KATE. It frightens me to have him see it!

HELEN. Because he knows?

KATE. Yes.

HELEN. That's why I want him to.

KATE. He may just see the faults, not all it's meant to us!

HELEN. It's all there! Sometimes it seems like a part of it was mine.

KATE. Of course it is!

HELEN. The hope that was in me, the wanting to see something different to do something bigger!

KATE [*anxiously*]. How can he see all that?

HELEN. It's there! *I* see it!

[TOM LANE *enters at back, he is angry and shocked. He shuts door behind him*]

TOM. It's a joke on me, at least if you can call it a joke! They've closed the road!

HELEN. So Ben Glenny was sayin'.

TOM. A detour out toward Smithtown.

HELEN. Yes.

TOM. And blocked at the other end five miles up!

HELEN. The road needed it bad enough; it's sort of a bother, but why should you —

KATE [*breaks in*]. Tom! Your garage! [*She is dismayed*]

TOM. Yes — they got me shut up like I had the smallpox!

HELEN [*shocked*]. I'm stupid! I didn't think!

TOM. I guess I'm the stupid one! Anybody that buys gas of me now would have to come for it in an airship.

HELEN. I'm sorry.

KATE. It's a shame!

TOM [*bitterly*]. I didn't plant much more than half a crop, countin' on this garage! Thought I was too smart to be a farmer!

KATE. It wasn't your fault! It was a good idea!

TOM. That's it — damn ideas! [*He crosses up and looks out window*]

HELEN. Swearin' won't help!

KATE. Don't, mother.

HELEN. It's hard; nobody can deny that, Tom, especially when you was countin' on it so much. [*She crosses toward hall door at left*] Don't go down to the Port without seeing me, Kate; I've got a couple of errands. [*She exits. KATE crosses up to TOM who stands with back toward her*]

KATE. You'd put more money into it than you could afford?

TOM [*without turning*]. Yes.

KATE. What will you do?

TOM. What can I do? [*He turns on her*] All the cash I had, and I owe most a thousand that's past due. I tried to save money by doin' the concrete work myself, and I lost a month; my stock's been here five weeks and I had it on thirty-day notes. They've been waitin' for me to open; nobody's going to wait now!

KATE. You'll find a way out of it!

TOM. No, I'm licked!

KATE. I know better!

TOM. Oh, I'm no milksop, but I *can* be licked. I was half licked even before this, by you!

KATE. How silly!

TOM. I was — I wasn't gettin' anywhere with you, you and your mother planning something together all the time — figuring on something that I didn't know about, that I don't suppose I'd have known about if you'd told me!

KATE. Just what we've always been planning — that I should go away!

TOM. I wasn't going to let you go! Now I can't help myself!

KATE. I hate to say it, but you couldn't have helped it, anyway.

[*There is a knock on the outside door*]

TOM. You don't mean that.

[*The knock is repeated*]

KATE. There's some one at the door!

TOM. You don't mean that.

[KATE *turns and crosses and opens door. WEINSTEIN, a Jew, a trader in furniture, is in the doorway. He is an elderly, benevolent fellow, not at all grotesque but with much of the inherited instinct of the buyer. He is bland and smiling and extremely gentle in his manner; he speaks with a trace of dialect*]

WEINSTEIN. Mrs. Hardy, she lif here?

KATE. Yes.

WEINSTEIN. I am Weinstein. I haf a store by Huntington. There is some curly maple furniture; I come to see it.

KATE. Grandmother's curly maple! Mrs. Lamont sent you!

WEINSTEIN. She said you haf some old furniture; maybe it ain't so good but I buy effery thing.

KATE. I am almost sure mother won't sell it.

WEINSTEIN. Maybe I gif you something pretty good!

KATE. Oh, I'll ask her, but I don't think it's any use. Come in.

[WEINSTEIN *enters, smiling and friendly, bowing politely to* TOM, *who is still in a bad temper*]

WEINSTEIN. Thank you. Good day, sir.

KATE [*who has crossed to door at left and calls*]. Mother! Mother!

HELEN [*out left*]. Yes.

KATE. Come here a minute.

HELEN [*outside*]. All right.

[WEINSTEIN *has been looking at the furniture with the quick eye of an expert. He puts his hand on the back of a small mahogany rocking chair*]

WEINSTEIN. That's nice.

KATE. That was Grandma's too.

WEINSTEIN. I buy effery thing.

[HELEN *enters*]

HELEN. What is it?

WEINSTEIN [*bowing*]. Good day, lady!

KATE. It's the man Mrs. Lamont spoke about; he wants to look at Grandma's furniture.

WEINSTEIN. Curly maple bed it was, and a dresser.

HELEN. It's all a mistake. I'm sorry you came so far. I don't want to sell it.

KATE. I told him that.

WEINSTEIN. I might look at it?

HELEN. I don't see what good that would do, but I don't mind if you want to.

WEINSTEIN. If it's good curly maple I like to buy it; if I can't buy it, I like to look at it anyhow.

HELEN. Well, you can't buy it, and I don't know how good it is, I sort of value it for the sentiment.

WEINSTEIN. I buy effery thing! Maybe we look at it now?

HELEN. Lookin' at it won't hurt it; it's right upstairs.

[*Exit to hall,* HELEN *and* WEINSTEIN. TOM *crosses down to* KATE]

TOM. You said I couldn't have helped your going away, even if I'd made good money, like I thought I would?

KATE. No. I am going to New York.

TOM. When?

KATE. When I can. Not for a long time, but I'm going!

TOM. This summer?

KATE. Not till we can get the money. I don't know when, but it doesn't matter how long it is — I'm going!

TOM. Do you want to go?

KATE. Of course I do.

TOM. I don't know — you don't tell me much — but if it wasn't for *her* you wouldn't go.

KATE. If it wasn't for her, I wouldn't be here at all!

TOM. *She* wants you to go!

KATE. Because she knows what living in a place like this all your life is like!

TOM. How does she? She knows what it was like for her; she don't know what it will be like for you!

KATE. It's the same thing.

TOM. She's stronger than you, she likes fighting better! You'd be happy here, or anywhere; if you'd let yourself care about some one — about me!

KATE. I can't, Tom! No! [*She steps away from him nervously, he follows*]

TOM. You could!

KATE [*desperately*]. No — No — I don't even want to!

TOM. I'm in trouble, I'm going to lose a lot of money — maybe all I've got — if it wasn't for that I wouldn't let you go — I'd keep you — in spite of *her!*

KATE. Don't, Tom! Mother'll hear you! [*She steps away from him as* HELEN *and* WEINSTEIN *enter*]

HELEN [*as she enters*]. I don't care! Somehow it wouldn't seem right!

WEINSTEIN. It's a good offer!

HELEN. Oh, yes, but I couldn't! That set was mother's wedding present! It's fifty years old! It seems as if it was one of the first things I can remember! Mostly when I think of her, it's the way she looked lying there so long.

WEINSTEIN. Vell, I gif you a new bed for it that nobody effer died on.

HELEN. No.

WEINSTEIN. And maybe a hundred dollars!

HELEN. I couldn't.

WEINSTEIN. Even a hundred and fifty!

HELEN. No, I won't. I don't care what you offer! I wouldn't sell it for — [*She stops and turns on him suddenly*] You wouldn't give me three hundred dollars for it, would you!

WEINSTEIN [*steps back in alarm*]. Three hundred dollars!

HELEN. I'm glad of it! I'd been sorry, I know.

WEINSTEIN. A hundred and seventy-fife.

HELEN. No.

WEINSTEIN. Vell, it's too bad. [*He crosses but stops in the door and turns*] Effen two hundred?

HELEN. No.

WEINSTEIN. Vell — [*He hesitates*] Good-by!

HELEN. Good-by. [*He exits, shutting the outside door*] That shows you what a person will do for money! I'd have been ashamed always!

TOM [*faces her angrily*]. Kate was tellin' me that she's going to New York as soon as she can.

HELEN. Yes, she is.

TOM [*bitterly*]. And I was tellin' her that if it wasn't for you she wouldn't ever go.

HELEN. Maybe, but you see there *is* me!

TOM. And there's *me!* She can't go till she gets the money, and money's scarce around here!

HELEN. Yes.

TOM. Maybe I'll have something to say before that time comes!

HELEN. Say it now?

TOM. I can't! You know that!

HELEN. Now's the time! You want to go, don't you, Kate?

KATE. I told him I did.

TOM. I got a year anyhow! I won't let her go!

[*There is a knock on door*]

HELEN. Wait a minute. [*She crosses and opens door.* WEINSTEIN *is in doorway with* JAKE, *his helper, who has several old quilts in his arms.* HELEN *looks at him coldly*] What do you want now?

WEINSTEIN. The curly maple.

HELEN. I thought you didn't want to pay me three hundred dollars for it?

WEINSTEIN. I don't, but I got to. Come in, Jake. [*He enters*]

JAKE. All right, popper. [JAKE *enters — a Jewish boy with a comic likeness to* WEINSTEIN]

HELEN [*looking at* TOM]. You've got a year anyway, you said, Tom!

WEINSTEIN [*counting money from pocketbook on table*]. Three hundred dollars!

KATE. You're not going to sell it!

HELEN. Yes — I am! I'll move your bed into my room. There's that old cot you can sleep on to-night — You're going to New York to-morrow!

KATE. To-morrow!

[HELEN *turns to* WEINSTEIN]

HELEN. Where's the money! [*She takes it from* WEINSTEIN *and counts*] Yes. [*She turns to* KATE] Take him upstairs.

KATE. Without father's knowing?

HELEN. The bed and the dresser! Go along!

KATE. Yes, mother. [*She crosses to door at left.* WEINSTEIN *follows*]

WEINSTEIN. Come along, Jakie.

JAKE. Yes, Popper!

[JAKE, KATE, WEINSTEIN *exit door left*]

TOM [*to* HELEN]. You know I was right! You knew I could stop her if I only had a chance! That's why you took that money!

HELEN. No, I didn't know it. I don't think you could.

TOM. But you weren't sure.

HELEN. No!

TOM. How do you know she'll be happier there than she'd be here with me?

HELEN. I don't know much about *there*, Tom. But I know a lot about *here*, so she's going!

TOM. Nobody's got a right to spoil another person's life!

HELEN. That's why I ain't going to let anybody spoil hers! You say you could stop her going if you had another year. Perhaps you could — you live next door, you see her every day and there's hardly anybody else — and you're young, and she's young! Don't I know! Haven't I been through it all! Youth's all she's got that's fine, and you want to take it for yourself! You want to make her stay here and do ugly things, dirty things with her hands, all day long — and I want her to go where she can be big, and free — and use her hands just to make things that's beautiful.

[STEPHEN HARDY *enters from outside*]

STEVE. Hardly enough cabbages to pay for pulling. I scarcely made up a truck load between 'em and the beans.

TOM. You saw what they've done to the road, didn't you?

STEVE. Yes — I guess it won't help you much with your new garage business. I never did believe in it; a man's a farmer or he ain't!

TOM. It's deeper than that. A man's a fool or he ain't. I guess it's easy enough to tell about me!

[WEINSTEIN'S *voice is heard out left*]

WEINSTEIN [*outside*]. Easy now! Hold your end vay up! [*At the sound* STEVE *turns and looks at door in amazement.* WEINSTEIN'S *voice goes on*] Hold your end vay up, Jakey!

JAKEY [*outside*]. All right, Popper.

STEVE. Who's that?

HELEN. It's the man from Huntington; he buys furniture. I sold him a couple of things.

[KATE *enters and holds the door open. She is followed by* WEINSTEIN *and* JAKE, *who carry the headboard of a wooden bed covered by one of their old quilts*]

KATE. Be careful of the door!

WEINSTEIN. Careful, Jakie!

JAKE. All right, Popper.

[*As they start to cross the stage,* STEPHEN *steps forward and speaks*]

STEVE. What you got there?

WEINSTEIN. Vot? [*He is carrying his end of the bed in such a way as to practically place himself behind the bed so that he can't see* STEPHEN]

STEVE [*repeats sternly*]. What you got there?

WEINSTEIN. Vot? [*He lowers his end suddenly*]

JAKE. Look out, Popper! [*He catches it*]

WEINSTEIN [*sees* STEPHEN]. Excuse me. I didn't see you!

STEVE [*to* HELEN]. What'd you sell this man?

HELEN. The bed and the dresser from our room.

STEVE. Have you gone crazy!

HELEN. No.

STEVE [*to* WEINSTEIN]. Take it upstairs again.

WEINSTEIN. I bought them of the lady!

STEVE. You'll get your money back; do as I tell you.

WEINSTEIN. But —

HELEN. I sold 'em to him, Stephen!

STEVE. Put it back! This is my house!

HELEN. 'Twas mother's and she gave it to me, and I've sold it!

STEVE [*to* WEINSTEIN]. I wouldn't advise you to make any trouble here, not with me! I tell you to take that thing upstairs!

WEINSTEIN. It was a fair bargain.

STEVE [*bitterly*]. Fair! What does your kind know about fairness? You come here when you see there's no man around and start to strip my house, leave me without a bed to sleep in! We've had talk enough. [*He steps forward angrily*] You'd better put it back!

HELEN. I'm going to move Kate's bed in our room; and he's a fool if he puts it back, because it's his and I'm going to keep what I got.

STEVE. I suppose you *want* to be robbed! That set's worth money! Nevin's wife sold an old bed and dresser no better'n that a while ago for almost a hundred dollars.

HELEN. I know, she was always flighty. [*She holds up her roll of bills*] I sold mine for three hundred.

STEVE [*in awe*]. Three — hundred!

HELEN. Dollars!

STEVE. Three hundred!

WEINSTEIN [*looking at him anxiously*]. Vell?

HELEN. Go on. [*She nods toward the door.* JAKE *and* WEINSTEIN *exit with the bed*]

CURTAIN

ACT II

The HARDY'S *side porch a few hours later. The porch, which is not raised above the stage level, takes up the greater part of the stage. Over this porch is a pagoda-like roof above which the second-story windows of the house are shown. A door and a window at right of the door open onto the kitchen. On the porch are two chairs, a small table, and a bench. At left of porch a fence makes a turning, as though here was a sharp curve in the highway; a tree is near by, and just inside of this fence and on this tree the detour sign. A gate just above this opens into the back yard. In this scene everything must be sacrificed to the acting space which is the porch itself.*

At rise of curtain, STEPHEN HARDY, *a pipe in his mouth, sits alone on the porch, he is thoughtful and silent, he just sits slowly puffing at his pipe. In a moment* TOM LANE *enters in the road at back, walking slowly. He enters the yard through the gate and steps onto porch.* STEVE *glances at him without moving.*

STEVE. Oh.

[TOM *sits, takes out his pipe and fills it but makes no answer and hunts in his pocket for a match*]

TOM. Light?

[STEVE *throws him a box of matches,* TOM *lights his pipe and tosses them back; both smoke in silence*]

STEVE. Ought to cut that field of yours down by this fence — it'll spoil on you.

TOM. Yes. [*For a moment they puff away*] Steve — I'm in a hell of a mess!

STEVE. Yes?

TOM. Yes!

STEVE. Talkin' won't help it. [*There is a pause*] You don't half farm your place lately; seems like you had something better to do. Maybe you got too much land. I don't know but I'd like to own that twenty acres of yours — join' onto mine.

TOM. You can.

STEVE. You mean that?

TOM. Yes, you've always thought you could do more'n I could with it.

STEVE. I'd lay it out different. I've had my eye on it ever since I was a boy.

TOM. I always thought you had. Well . . . if I've got to sell, I'd rather it would be yours than anybody's.

STEVE. All that bothers me is cash.

TOM [*alarmed*]. I need cash bad.

STEVE. What's the twenty acres worth?

TOM. Six thousand.

STEVE. Five's enough, two-fifty an acre.

TOM. It's time more'n it's price with me. You want that land?

STEVE [*earnestly*]. Yes — I do!

TOM. You can have it for five thousand.

STEVE. It's the cash bothers me!

TOM. I telephoned the jobber to New York just now an' I asked him for an extension on my note; he wouldn't do anything. I offered him his stock back and he laughed at me! He's going to get out an attachment, if he ain't already.

STEVE. That's bad!

TOM. What's the most cash you could raise for me to-day?

STEVE. Five hundred.

TOM. It wouldn't help! [*He sits back and draws on his pipe*] My pipe's out!

STEVE [*tosses him box of matches*]. Here! [TOM *relights pipe*] I'd pay another five hundred in four weeks; my potatoes will fetch that.

TOM. It's to-day I want it. I'll sell you my twenty acres for five thousand — that's fifteen hundred cash above what it's mortgaged for, and you can let the mortgage stand.

STEVE. Five hundred is every cent I've got in the bank, an' I was figuring that for something else.

TOM. Then we can't trade.

[*For a moment they both smoke in silence*]

STEVE. Gimme back my matches! [TOM *tosses them to him and he puts them in his pocket*] Gimme two days to raise this money?

TOM. Two hours.

STEVE. I'll try! [*He rises from his chair*] I only got one chance; wait till I telephone.

[*He exits into kitchen,* TOM *sits in thought.* HELEN's *face is seen for a moment as she glances out of window from the kitchen. A moment later she comes to the open doorway; she has evidently been baking, as her arms are covered with flour, and as she speaks to* TOM, *she wipes them on her apron*]

HELEN. What's *he* calling Ben Glenny for on the telephone?

TOM. He didn't say.

[HELEN *opens the screen door and steps out on porch*]

HELEN. Nothin's upsets me more'n his law business with Ben Glenny! Ben's all right as a man, but a body can't seem to think of him like he was human. To me he always seems sort of a walking calamity!

TOM. Ben ain't got no law business! He never was admitted to the bar!

HELEN. He's County Clerk, Notary Public and most everything, especially Tax Collector. Last time he was here I told him as long as he *was* Tax Collector I didn't know but what it would be more convenient if I was to arrange to board him.

TOM. That's like the sort of things you're always sayin'! Things you don't mean, and you know folks know you don't mean. You say 'em just because they seem kind of funny to you.

HELEN. I s'pose so —

TOM. It's sort of an aggravatin' habit.

HELEN. So *he's* told me, often!

TOM. Excuse me for speakin' of it.

HELEN. Oh, I don't mind! It's just my way of being impolite, like you smokin' your pipe on my porch without askin' me if you could.

TOM. Oh! [*He knocks the ashes out of his pipe hastily and drops it in his pocket*]

HELEN. You didn't have to stop. I ain't goin' to.

TOM. I guess you couldn't.

HELEN. I guess not — I get so tired of sayin' nothin' but just exactly what's so, and listen to folks that don't ever mean the least mite more'n they say, or the least mite less! What's the use of your imagination!

TOM. Mine? I ain't got any, have I?

HELEN. Oh, I guess so — but it's like a muscle; it gets awful puny if you don't use it.

TOM. I'd rather have one real dollar than dream I was a millionaire!

HELEN. I s'pose so — I'd rather have one real dream than *be* a millionaire!

TOM. Well, it's all right so long as we're both satisfied. Where's Kate?

HELEN. At the Port, buying some things.

TOM. Did you mean what you said a while ago — that she was goin' to New York to-morrow?

HELEN. No.

TOM. Just another dream?

HELEN. She's goin' to-night.

TOM. To-night! When did you settle on that?

HELEN. Just a minute ago — [*She looks at him*] I happened to think of something that frightened me.

TOM. If I was her father I wouldn't let her go.

HELEN. I believe you; you're a lot like Steve —

TOM. I hope so, Steve Hardy's a sensible man, and an honest man!

HELEN. And a good man. Never was wild in his life, an' he's truthful, and he never drank or gambled.

TOM. I know.

HELEN. And you never did.

TOM. Never wanted to.

HELEN. That's a comfort.

TOM. A lot of good it does me! You don't want her to marry me.

HELEN. No.

TOM. Why?

HELEN. Oh, I guess it's because she's got too much of what I used to be in her.

TOM. If I'm like him, and she's like you, why can't we be married same as you was?

HELEN. I said she was like what I *used* to be.

TOM. If you ask me I'd say it's *him* she takes after. [HELEN *laughs*] She does! She's slower thinkin', like him, and more set, more contented. She's quieter than you, and she ain't so smart.

HELEN. You flatter me!

TOM [*seriously*]. That ain't how I meant it. She's just what I like; that's why I don't want her to go. I want to marry her; I been figurin' on it two years.

HELEN. That's longer than you've been planning your garage!

TOM. Yes, I been so busy buildin' the garage I ain't seen much of her.

HELEN. But it wouldn't have done to neglect the garage.

TOM. No.

HELEN. There's something in the Bible about trying to serve two masters. [STEVE *enters from kitchen and sits*] What did you want of Ben Glenny?

STEVE. Money!

HELEN. You've got more imagination than I gave you credit for.

STEVE. He's goin' to drive around pretty soon.

HELEN [*alarmed*]. You ain't tryin' to raise more money on this place?

STEVE. I'm tryin' to.

[*She looks at him and sighs at the hopelessness of it as* KATE *comes rapidly along the road and enters gaily through the gate. She has with her a long cardboard box, a hat box and several small packages. As she turns a corner of the house and sees them, she stops for a moment startled*]

KATE. Oh!

STEVE. Been down to the Port?

KATE. Yes.

STEVE. To Neppers?

KATE [*evasively*]. I was there for a minute — yes.

STEVE. It didn't take you long to learn the stock.

KATE. I — I —

STEVE [*rises, sternly*]. What is it? You're hidin' something'!

KATE [*desperately*]. Mother! Doesn't he know?

HELEN. It's all right, dear! [*She puts her hand on* KATE's *shoulder and turns to* STEVE] She ain't going to work for Nepper this year, Stephen; she's going to New York.

STEVE. No.

HELEN. She's going to study art.

STEVE. That's nonsense!

HELEN. We don't think so!

STEVE. Think! That's the trouble with yer, both of yer; you don't think!

HELEN. Maybe not, but we feel a lot.

STEVE. Study *art!*

HELEN. Yes.

STEVE. I won't have it!

HELEN. I made my mind up to it, whether I think or I don't, over ten years ago. It's just as much a part of my life — what I've planned she's goin' to do and be — as the work I do is, or this old dress that I've worn and worn and worn until I wouldn't know myself in any other. I couldn't any more live without the hope of what's coming to her than I could live without drink or food.

STEVE. She's my child as much as she's yours!

HELEN. No, not quite so much. She's your daughter, but I guess I did a little more for her than you did.

STEVE. When was you plannin' for her to go?

HELEN. To-night!

KATE [*startled*]. To-night, mother?

HELEN. Yes. Mary Barton's going up on the six o'clock train. She was here just after you left. She is going visitin' her sister way up town in New York, an' she said she could keep you over night just as well as not.

STEVE. What would she do to-morrow?

HELEN. That Mr. Lamont, an artist, that's taken the bungalow for the summer, is goin' to tell us the names of the best teachers — his wife promised — and the Y. W. C. A. folks in New York will help her find a place to board.

STEVE. How long before she comes back?

HELEN [*bitterly*]. Here!

STEVE. Yes.

HELEN. That's for her to say — I been workin' a long time; she's got to do the rest.

STEVE. What's the sense of it, I can't see. Can you, Tom?

TOM. There ain't any.

STEVE. There! You heard that?

HELEN [*wearily*]. I wasn't listenin'!

TOM. I guess she heard me right enough, only I guess she thinks it ain't any of my business.

STEVE. It could be easy enough; I always thought 't would be! I thought, seein' you two together so much, that sooner or later you'd ask her to marry you.

TOM. I did.

HELEN. And she said no.

STEVE [*angrily*]. She did.

TOM [*spitefully*]. She didn't — she wouldn't say yes, but she never really said no, so as a fellar would know she meant it! The *no* come from somewhere's else!

STEVE. What do you mean?

TOM. From her! [*He looks at* HELEN *bitterly*]

STEVE. Hold on. Let's get the rights of this!

HELEN. That's easy. Do you s'pose I'd try to make her do anything she didn't want to do?

TOM. Yes, I do.

STEVE. She can't! I guess I figure in this!

HELEN. I wouldn't! Kate!

KATE. Yes, mother!

HELEN. You've heard them — I want you to tell your father the truth!

TOM. One way or the other. You know what I want you to say. I may be in hard luck now, but I won't be always. I'm a man that means to get ahead!

STEVE. And he will! I know Tom. I want you to answer him, Kate!

HELEN. And so do I! He offers you one thing — I guess you know what it is — all's you've got to do is to open your eyes and look around you.

STEVE. What are you offerin' her that's so much better? Just what is it?

HELEN. It's hard to say — just in words, but I think she knows.

STEVE. Well, I don't know!

HELEN. Tom here said a while ago I was always dreaming — that's so I guess — [*She turns to* KATE *with a sudden overflow of great tenderness*] And that's what I'm offerin' you, my dear! One of my dreams — come true.

KATE. And I'm going to take it, mother, and make it true.

HELEN. I knew you was. [*She puts one hand on* KATE's *shoulder and faces them*] There are times when I've got courage enough to laugh even at a man! [*She turns to* KATE] Now you run upstairs. There's lots for you to do if you're goin' to-night.

KATE. But father?

HELEN. I've tried hard to be a good wife to him, I guess he knows that. I hope he doesn't think that because I never made a real fight before that I ain't got the spirit to make one now. You run along — I'll tend to everything.

KATE. Yes, mother. [*She exits*]

STEVE. You talk big. Where's the money comin' from? Three hundred dollars won't last forever!

HELEN. We got a little more.

STEVE. How much?

HELEN. Just a little we saved up.

STEVE. Seems like I was the only one around 'this place that couldn't save nothin'. Seems like what happened to a girl like that was more im-

portant than what happened to me!
We'll talk about this again after I see
Ben Glenny, but I don't want you to
think I'm going to stand for any nonsense. [*He exits at left around the house*]

Tom [*with rather malicious pleasure*].
He's mad!

Helen. He'll get over it.

Tom [*doubtfully*]. I don't know!

Helen. You've never been married.
If you had you'd know there ain't anything else for married folks to do.

Tom. I don't blame him none for
bein' mad!

Helen. It's natural. He thinks he
ought to be let to say what Kate does
with her life.

Tom. Of course.

Helen. Because it's right that every
man should be the master, and decide
things that really matter. Women
ought to just cook, and clean, and sew,
and maybe chop a little wood, and have
the babies.

Tom. That's how God meant it to be.

Helen. And if a woman sometimes
gets to thinkin' it ain't quite fair, if she
sets herself to sort of change things a
little, she's flyin' in the face of Providence!

Tom. I look at it like this — a fellar
ought not to be hard on a woman if she
kinder fusses once in a while.

Helen. So long as she ain't let to
do anything?

Tom. That's it!

Helen. That idea ain't original,
is it?

Tom [*suspiciously*]. Whatter you
mean?

Helen. You borrowed it!

Tom. Who from?

Helen. Adam! [*She exits to house
and through the window she is seen for a
moment at her kitchen work.* Tom *turns
sulkily and crosses left as* Dora Lamont
crosses in from left on the road]

Dora. Oh, Mr. Tom! I was on
my way to see you!

[Tom *crosses to her and they stand with
the fence between them*]

Tom. There ain't much use my
hangin' around my place with the road
blocked. [*He points angrily at the detour
sign on the tree*] This is as far as anybody can go.

Dora. That's what I wanted to talk
to you about. They have put this
barricade up, but the workmen aren't
here yet.

Tom. They've been here and gon[e]
Nobody's goin' to do any hurryin' abo[ut]
this job, you know; it's the taxpayer[s']
money.

Dora. My husband wants you t[o]
let our car out of your garage and brin[g]
it up to the bungalow right away.

Tom. Oh!

Dora. You could lift that barr[i-]
cade away, couldn't you?

Tom. Yes, I could.

Dora. Well? What is it?

Tom. Nothin', only you see you[r]
car was all I had, the only one — I sor[t]
of hate to part with it.

Dora [*smiling*]. That's about th[e]
way we feel about it.

Tom. I know. I'll bring it up.

Dora. I'm sorry, but after all yo[u]
have that great big farm!

Tom. Oh, I'm all right.

Dora. That's good. We'll expec[t]
the car some time to-day.

Tom. You'll get it.

[Dora *exits at left the same way she cam[e]*
Tom *stands for a moment in gloom[y]
thought as* Kate *enters to the porc[h]
from the kitchen.* Kate *has put o[n]
her pretty new dress — quite moder[n]
in cut — and with it she has put on [a]
new air of coquetry as though she ha[d]
suddenly blossomed into womanhoo[d]
and rejoiced in its power*]

Kate. Hello, Tom!

Tom. Kate! [*He steps toward he[r]
quite overwhelmed*] Kate! What yo[u]
been doin' to yourself?

Kate. Oh, just trying on my ne[w]
dress.

Tom. Yes — yes — I see! [*He turn[s]
away as if to go*]

Kate. Tom? [*He takes another ste[p]
and she speaks louder*] Tom!

Tom. Well? [*He stops but he doesn'[t]
turn*]

Kate. Turn around here, Tom
Lane! [*He turns slowly and faces her*]
Aren't you going to tell me how yo[u]
like it?

Tom. About as much as the fella[r]
likes to hear the Judge say, "And may
God have mercy on your soul."

Kate [*hurt*]. You're spoiling everything!

Tom [*sadly*]. Something is, righ[t]
enough.

Kate. The only decent dress I eve[r]
had.

Tom. I didn't say it was pretty —

didn't say how I thought you looked in
t — I didn't dare to.

KATE. Why not?

TOM. I ain't an artist — artists like
hings that are pretty just because they
re pretty — I don't care nothin' about
em unless they're *mine!*

KATE [*archly*]. Meaning the dress?

TOM. You know well enough what I
nean!

KATE. Yes, I know. I'm sorry,
Tom! I don't want to go away — with
ou hating me! You're mad with me
now, and I know how hard it is for you
o forgive anybody that makes you mad
— but, Tom — you're not going to be
angry with me always.

TOM. A lot you'd care! How much
will you think about this place, or anybody here, once you get out of it!

KATE [*shocked*]. Why! There's father
— and mother!

TOM [*darkly*]. I know, plenty of girls
get to be ashamed of their folks!

KATE. I wouldn't, and of course I
couldn't help thinking about you sometimes. Tom, remembering things —
we've been such good friends.

TOM. It don't take long to lose a
friend.

KATE. You're blaming me because
I'm going!

TOM [*bitterly*]. No! I'm blaming
her!

KATE. You mustn't! All that's
good I've ever had she gave me.

TOM. Maybe it won't be so good as
you two think it will.

KATE [*frightened*]. You think I'm
going to fail.

TOM. All I'm thinkin' about is if
you'd stayed here we'd have been happy.

KATE. Not unless — unless I'd —
I'd cared.

TOM. *She* wouldn't let you care!

KATE. You just won't *try* to understand! This is something mother's
planned for me all my life. I can't
help doing it.

TOM. Your mother gets ideas!

KATE. She used to sit by my bed, in
the dark, and talk about it when I was
a little girl. Daytimes she'd take me
walking with her and point out the
pretty places in the woods, and the colors in the sky, and show me how different they were, and how wonderful.
How could I help getting so I wanted to
paint them? How can I help wanting
to go where some one can teach me to
be what she's so hungry for me to be?

TOM. I guess you couldn't, not unless it was like you said. Unless you
cared about somebody else more'n you
do about her.

KATE. And I don't! If I did, I'd
hate myself!

TOM. It's all right! I ain't goin'
to take no advantage, I ain't goin' to
try to keep you — but I could!

KATE. No!

TOM. Oh, yes, I could! Your
father'd stop your goin', quick enough,
if I was to tell him a few things.

KATE. I don't know what you're
talking about!

TOM. I guess he'd say if you was in
love with me you couldn't go, and if
you weren't in love with me — and if he
knew about your lettin' me kiss you
four or five times, like I did last winter,
and your puttin' your arms around my
neck — then I guess he'd say he
wouldn't trust you out of his sight.

KATE. You'd tell him that — when
you begged me so — when I was so
lonesome!

TOM. I don't say I'll tell him, but it's
a satisfaction knowin' I could stop this
thing if I wasn't so sort of sentimental.

KATE [*angrily*]. I'd go now, no
matter what you told him! If he said
I couldn't go, I'd run away!

TOM [*thoughtfully*]. You've got spirit
in you once in a while like your mother's.
I wonder if maybe you don't favor her
more'n I figured you did!

[BEN GLENNY *is seen to enter at left on
the road. He looks off right, back of
house, as if he saw* STEPHEN *there,
and calls*]

BEN. Hello, Steve!

[STEPHEN *answers from right, back of
house*]

STEVE. I been waitin' for you!

KATE. They'll be here in a minute.
Come in with me, Tom; I want to
talk to you.

TOM. You needn't worry, I ain't
going to tell on you!

KATE. It isn't that, but I won't see
you again, and I don't want to have to
remember you like this!

TOM. No, you'll give me one kiss, I
suppose, and you'll think it's damned
funny if I don't think anything you
want to do is right.

KATE. I'm going in, you can suit
yourself! [*She exits, to kitchen; after*

a second's sulky hesitation he follows. STEVE *has joined* BEN GLENNY *at gate and they cross downstage together*]

STEVE. Well?

BEN. I saw both of them.

STEVE. Sit down. [*They sit*]

BEN. It's hot walkin'. [*He wipes the perspiration from his face with a cotton handkerchief*]

STEVE. Saw both of 'em?

BEN. Yes.

STEVE. Already? That looks bad; funny how much quicker a man says no than he'll say yes!

BEN. Both of 'em says your farm won't stand any more borrowin' on. Billings said you had so many mortgages on it now he didn't see where you found any room to raise crops. He was sort of jokin'.

STEVE. He's a fool!

BEN. Allers was.

STEVE. But he's got the money and I haven't!

BEN. And he keeps what he's got, and you don't.

STEVE. I ain't throwed away a dollar in twenty years, not so much as fifteen cents for a movin' picture!

BEN. You're land hungry!

STEVE. I've *got* to get more land! I'm bound to do it! I've got to get fifteen hundred dollars.

BEN. I wish you'd get the three hundred and seven you owe for taxes. I'm way back in my collectin'.

✗STEVE. I got it in the bank. But I was figurin' to use it to buy Tom Lane's twenty acres, if I could raise the balance.

BEN. And you need a thousand?

STEVE. Yes. It's a chance I won't get again. If Tom's sold up for what he owes, the land's gone for good, an' if he pulls through an' makes money with his garage, he wouldn't want to sell.

BEN. They was some talk about Tom Lane an' your girl Kate's runnin' around together. That'd be one way of gettin' that land in your family.

STEVE. I stopped dependin' on a woman the day I was weaned.

BEN. Well, I can't do nothin' fer yer. [*He rises*] I tried.

STEVE. You ain't got money enough to lend it to me yourself?

BEN. No, I ain't! Bein' a tax collector, an' process server an' county clerk has sort of made me lose confidence in home folks. I don't pretend to know more'n anybody else, but I'm savin' up all my money an' buyin' oil stocks. [*He starts left*] Sorry I couldn' do nothin' for you, Steve.

STEVE. I didn't have much faith in your gettin' it, but 'twas my only chance.

BEN. Well if you'd got it I s'pose 'twould have been all the harder for me to get your taxes out of yer.

STEVE. Maybe — but I'd of had the land.

BEN. Well — good day. It's some hot.

STEVE. An' we need rain — good day, Ben.

[BEN *exits out gate and along the road at left.* STEVE *sits in deep thought* HELEN *comes to window and looks out, then crosses to door and standing back of the screen door, she speaks*]

HELEN. I heard Ben Glenny's voice.

STEVE. Yes.

HELEN. You didn't get the money you wanted out of him?

STEVE. No.

HELEN. I am sorry if you're disappointed.

STEVE. Come out a minute, I want to talk to yer.

[HELEN *opens the screen door and steps out on porch*]

HELEN. Kate an' Tom Lane are in the parlor. She ought to be packin' her trunk; you'll have to take it to the station.

STEVE. You get three hundred dollars for that old truck of your mother's?

HELEN. Yes.

STEVE. And I've got five hundred in the bank. I'm going to ask Tom if he'll take eight hundred and my note for the balance.

HELEN. You're goin' to give Tom Lane my three hundred dollars?

STEVE. If he'll take it.

HELEN. No.

STEVE. He's *got* to take it! He would, I know, if we was to get Kate to ask him.

HELEN. You don't mean that!

STEVE. Yes.

HELEN. You'd do a thing like that just for more land?

STEVE. For *that* land!

HELEN. I've been a slave to land ever since I married you; I'm tired of it!

STEVE. You ain't been any more of a slave than I've been! You're a good worker, but you ain't worked like I do!

There ain't a foot of this land here I ain't watered with my sweat!

HELEN. And you want more, and it's all you do want! More work for you and for me, more taxes and mortgages hangin' over us.

STEVE. I want a *farm!* I'm bound to get it! I'm no damned Japanese! I tell you this is my chance!

HELEN. It's Kate's chance too, Steve. You're forgettin' that! You wouldn't take her chance away from her?

STEVE. Yes — I would. I'm goin' to!

HELEN. I won't let you — that's all — I just won't! [*He rises without a word and crosses into the house. She looks distressed and anxious. In a moment he returns, in his hand the jug in which is the money and the dusty bunch of artificial flowers. As she sees this in his hand, she steps back almost in terror*] Stephen!

STEVE. There's money here. I always knew you kept somethin' in here, but it was no business of mine! That three hundred dollars is here?

HELEN [*nervously*]. Yes.

STEVE. There's more, too; it's heavy! [*He shakes the jar and the sound of the silver is heard*]

HELEN. All that's there is mine and Kate's.

STEVE. How much?

HELEN. You said just now that what I kept in there wasn't any business of yours, and it ain't!

STEVE. How much?

HELEN. If I've got any rights at all! If you've got any bit of feelin' left for me, or for what I ask of you, I want you to put that down!

[*By way of answer, he throws the artificial flowers contemptuously aside, and turning the jug up he pours the contents out on the table*]

STEVE [*as he sees*]. By God!

HELEN. It's just like you struck me in the face. [*She drops into chair, hiding her eyes with her fingers. He counts the money eagerly and with growing joy and excitement*]

STEVE. Over a thousand dollars!

HELEN. More'n ten years I done without — I made *her* do without! Many a time I took her teachin' money when she wanted a pretty dress, an' I cried myself to sleep that night — but I took it!

STEVE. With my five hundred it'll be enough! Tom's in the parlor, you say? [*He crosses to door of kitchen and calls*] Tom! Tom! I want you! [*As he turns back,* HELEN *springs between him and the table*]

HELEN. Don't shame me before them, Steve, don't.

STEVE [*sternly*]. I want you not to make a fuss now, Helen.

HELEN. I tried to be a good wife to you all these hard, hard years. Once before I had money — I'd saved it, just like I saved this — 'twas like a key — a key to the door that was shuttin' me out from life — and I gave it up, for you — because you made me love you — when I didn't want to. Now, when I ain't got anything but that, too — don't make me hate you!

[TOM *and* KATE *enter from the kitchen.* KATE *looks at her father and mother with dismay*]

KATE. What is it?

STEVE. I'll take that offer of yours, Tom. We'll get Ben Glenny to draw up a bill of sale. Fifteen hundred cash and a mortgage for the balance!

HELEN [*to* KATE]. It's your money! He's takin' it.

KATE. Father!

HELEN. You'll waste your time beggin' him! He's a hard man!

TOM [*to* STEVE]. You're goin' to buy my land?

STEVE. Yes.

HELEN [*turns desperately to* TOM]. Tom! You won't take it; tell him you won't take it, knowin' what it means to me an' Kate!

KATE. Of course he won't take it, mother!

STEVE. Why won't he? He needs it, don't he? Course he'll take it, won't you, Tom?

KATE [*proudly*]. He won't!

TOM. I want the money and he wants the land. I don't see no reason why I shouldn't take it.

KATE [*scornfully*]. After the way you were just talking to me in there? [*She points to house*]

TOM. Buyin' land, or sellin' it is a matter of business.

HELEN [*to* KATE]. We might have known he would!

STEVE. I'll telephone fer Ben Glenny! [*He steps towards table, putting out his hand for the money*]

HELEN [*steps in front of him*]. You're a thief, Steve Hardy!

STEVE. Helen! [*He draws back, horrified*]

HELEN. Just a thief! A common thief! Ain't you robbed me always — of my youth — of my life — of my looks — I ain't forty — and look at me — look what you've done to me! You thief — and now it's her!

STEVE. Nobody ever called me a name like that! Nobody ever dared!

HELEN. Why should I be afraid? What more could you do to me!

STEVE. You can't call me a thief! This is *my* house; what's in it is mine, all of it!

HELEN. My mother's furniture wasn't yours!

STEVE. It's been part of the furnishin' of my house for twenty years. Of course it's mine! So's the rest of this money!

HELEN. The savings out of her salary, teachin' school and tendin' store!

STEVE. She's my daughter, and she ain't of age!

HELEN. And ten years of savin' dime by dime out of my egg and chicken money!

STEVE. That's the thanks I get fer lettin' you call 'em yours — the hens was mine!

HELEN. Everything is yours!

STEVE. Of course it is!

HELEN. And I get my keep! I haven't had a dress in two years, and then one I made myself. I get my food, but I have to cook it first. Where else would you get a cook who'd work like I work and only get her keep! They ain't but one way to get a girl as cheap as that, and that's to marry her!

KATE. Like Tom Lane wanted to marry me!

HELEN. The summer folks here pay a cook seventy-five dollars a month who'd be too proud to do the work I do! That Mrs. Lamont paid an agent ten dollars just for *gettin'* her a cook! That shows how smart you are, Steve Hardy; alls you paid was one dollar for a weddin' license!

STEVE [*putting money back into jar*]. You're callin' pretty hard names, wife, and I ain't a patient man!

HELEN. I've been a patient woman, but I can't be any more! Kate! [*She throws her arms about her*] I don't seem like I could stand it!

KATE [*clinging to her*]. Don't mother! Don't! You break my heart

STEVE. What's all the fuss about Why not let her stay here, same as a the other girls, an' marry a decent ma like Tom?

HELEN. Another wife — to anothe man like you!

STEVE. Better maybe than sendin a young girl like she is out alone to mi with strangers in a place like New Yor} City.

HELEN. Why is it? Why? How *could* it be?

STEVE. How do you know wha would become of her?

HELEN. How could I know? only know what would become of he here!

STEVE. You never thought abou the other thing, did you! About whe she might meet, alone there — abou what she might get to be.

HELEN. She might get to be a grea artist, like I've prayed she would.

STEVE. And she might get to be : woman of the streets!

HELEN. And if she did would she sell herself as cheap as I did! Woulc she fall any lower than I am? She'c have had her chance; win or lose, she'c have had it, she'd have had some hours anyway, somethin' to remember!

STEVE [*shocked*]. You mean ther that like *that* she'd be better off than you've been here with me!

HELEN. Yes!

STEVE. All right! My house is no place for you, not if you feel like that [*He holds the jug out to her*] You claim this money.

HELEN. I do! I'll keep on claimin' it!

STEVE. Take it, then, but remember this — if you do take it, and if she goes against my will — you go with her!

KATE. Father!

STEVE [*to* HELEN]. You go, and you don't come back.

HELEN. Wait — we got to understand each other! You're turnin' me out!

STEVE. You always claimed to be smarter than I was. I guess you got my meanin'!

HELEN. Oh, yes, I got that long ago — that everything must be for you, an' nothin' for me! The only thing you ever gave me was your name, I bought that from you when I was young. I paid you for it with all I had — now I

n't young, any more, an' you're sick
' your bargain — you want to call it
t. I wish to God you could — I'd
ve you back your name if you'd give
e back what I paid for it!

STEVE. Just words! That's all!
ou heard mine! If she goes — you go!

KATE. You don't mean it, father!
ou *can't!*

STEVE [*to* HELEN]. I'm going to let
ou choose!

HELEN. All right! There's a train
t seven! [*She puts her arm about* KATE
nd they turn and exit to the kitchen]

CURTAIN

ACT III

CENE. — HARDY'S *kitchen* [*same as Act I*]
about an hour later.

TEPHEN, *his pipe in his mouth, sits
moodily by stove.* TOM LANE, *also
with a pipe, stands in open doorway
to the hall, shamelessly listening.*

TOM. Wait a minute! [*He bends
agerly out into hall,* STEPHEN *rises from
is chair and stands looking at door. In
moment* TOM *turns back into room*]
Jo, they're movin' around all right, but
hey ain't comin' down.

STEPHEN. Oh! [*He drops back into
hair*]

TOM [*contemptuously*]. And you're
oing to let 'em go!

STEPHEN. I ain't goin' to stop 'em.

TOM. You could — if you was to
how a little spirit!

STEPHEN. It's for them to say;
nly if they go they can't come back —
ot ever!

TOM. As far as that goes, maybe
hey'd never want to. [*He hears a sound*]
Vait! They're movin' again! [*He
uts his head out into hall.* STEVE *looks
t him but does not again get up. In a
noment* TOM *turns back*] What do you
'pose I heard 'em doin'?

STEVE. Cryin'?

TOM. Singin'!

STEVE. No!

TOM. Yes! And not hymns —
unes! I guess you can take a rest
rom feelin' like you was Simon Legree
eatin' Uncle Tom to death! Looks to
ne like they was glad they was goin'!

STEVE [*sternly*]. Then it's best they
vent!

TOM. It's a serious thing when a
man's wife leaves him!

STEVE. Yes.

TOM. It's *awful* when she takes a
thousand dollars with her!

STEVE. Yes. [*He smokes in silence.*
TOM *sits moodily in chair*]

TOM. If they was mine they wouldn't
go!

STEVE [*coldly*]. Well — they ain't.

TOM [*a little resentful*]. I got to give
you credit for one thing; everything you
say is always true, even if it ain't very
interestin'.

STEVE [*thoughtfully*]. It takes a lot
of patience to get along with any woman.

TOM. Seems so.

STEVE. She had her faults.

TOM. I know it.

STEVE. In most ways she's been a
good wife to me.

TOM. She'd ought to be.

STEVE. I ain't defendin' her.

TOM. She was the kind I couldn't 'a
got along with.

STEVE. Why couldn't you? You
wanted to marry Kate!

TOM. She ain't like her mother, she's
the "spit and image" of you.

STEVE. Kate?

TOM [*losing confidence*]. Leastways
I always thought so.

STEVE. If you don't know no more
about an automobile than you do about
a woman, I guess it's just as well they
closed the road. [*He turns disgusted*]

TOM. Hark! [*He rises suddenly*]
Some one's on the stairs! [*He crosses
and looks out to hall, then turns in great
excitement*] Yes! Now we'll know!

STEVE. What will we know?

TOM. If they're really goin'! I bet
they ain't.

STEVE. Humph!

[TOM *sits; in a moment* KATE *and* HELEN
*enter. Between them they carry a
trunk, and* HELEN *has an old cardboard box under one arm. They
pay not the slightest attention to the
men but put the trunk down left of
center two or three feet away from
where* STEVE *is sitting*]

HELEN. Now we'll get the trays.

KATE [*without glancing at* TOM *or*
STEVE, *who sit stolidly smoking their
pipes*]. It's too bad they're no men in
the house to help us.

HELEN [*sniffs scornfully*]. You don't
smell anything peculiar, do you?

KATE [*doubtfully*]. I don't know!

HELEN. I s'pose it was that awful imagination of mine; of *course* nobody would smoke in my kitchen!

[HELEN *and* KATE *exit to hall*]

TOM. They *are* goin'!

STEVE. After this I ain't *never* comin' in here without I smoke!

TOM. Yes, sir! They're goin'!

STEVE. What time is it?

TOM. You asked me that twice already! What do you care; you never do nothin'!

STEVE [*wistfully*]. We used to eat at six.

TOM. Well, it's about that now. Who's going to get your meals for you?

STEVE. It don't take no brains to cook! I can run a house as good as a woman. I ain't going to have no hired girl; I'll do for myself!

TOM. Anybody can; it's nothin' to make a fuss about.

STEVE [*anxiously*]. I don't s'pose she'll take her cook book?

TOM. What if she does? All you need is a little common sense and a good appetite.

STEVE. You said 'twas six, didn't yer?

TOM. There's a clock right in front of yer!

[*They sit back puffing at pipes.* HELEN *and* KATE *enter; in their hands they carry the two trays of the trunk*]

HELEN. Wait, I'll open it. [*She puts the tray on the floor and opens trunk.* KATE *puts her tray in.* HELEN *sniffs at the tobacco smoke and crosses and opens the window directly back of* TOM's *chair, then goes and opens door; a strong wind outside blows the window curtains and the draft annoys both* TOM *and* STEVE]

KATE [*takes a deep breath*]. Ah! That's better!

HELEN [*pleasantly*]. It'll air the room.

KATE [*with a cold look at* TOM]. I noticed something disagreeable in here.

[*This, and the cold air blowing on their backs, is too much for* TOM *and* STEVE, *who rise sheepishly and exit to the porch and out of sight.* HELEN *looks after them and laughs*]

HELEN. I do declare it's funny. I guess I'm feelin' sort of flighty or I wouldn't act so silly. I ought to be ashamed, makin' 'em uncomfortable on purpose!

KATE. I guess they deserve to ▋ more uncomfortable than anything w▋ say could make them.

HELEN. We'd better hurry; we'▋ got lots to do.

KATE. I left that other new dress ▋ mine on a chair in your room; you'▋ better try it on.

HELEN. I wouldn't dare to wear i▋ It's cut so young!

KATE. You can't go to New Yor▋ in that old thing! After this, I'm goin▋ to see that you have everything I hav▋ and I'm going to have all I can get.

HELEN. We'll have to be awf▋ careful! I don't know as a thousan▋ will be enough!

KATE. Your going makes all th▋ difference. I am not afraid any mor▋

HELEN. Why should we be?

KATE. I'll be making plenty ▋ money long before we need it.

HELEN. I'm as sure of it as I am ▋ livin'!

KATE. Mother! Just think! We'▋ really going!

HELEN. I don't dare think. I jus▋ keep on doin' things!

KATE. Who's afraid now?

HELEN. It don't seem real at all▋ I guess thinkin' about it so many year▋ kinder makes it all seem like a story i▋ a book — like it was about somebod▋ else.

KATE. Well, it isn't.

HELEN. I know it, because ever▋ once in a while I get a kind of a sinkin▋ here. [*She puts her hand for a momen▋ on her stomach*] Like a person doe▋ when they go down fast in an elevator▋

KATE. You don't think I am going t▋ fail?

HELEN. I know you've got the tal▋ ent; that's all that matters. God gav▋ it to you; He'll help us.

KATE. And you're not worryin▋ about — about father?

HELEN. Why should I? He ain'▋ worryin' much about me.

KATE. No, neither's Tom Lan▋ worrying! They don't know how!

HELEN. Some day, when I ge▋ settled down to think again, it's goin▋ to hurt — your father's turnin' me ou▋ like he did, forgettin' in a minute a▋ I'd been to him for half a lifetime — bu▋ right now about all I've got room for i▋ my head is we're goin'!

KATE. And you're going to wear tha▋ new red dress!

HELEN. I don't know but I'd abou▋

as well be hung for a sheep as a lamb! [*She takes a bulky roll of bills from her apron pocket*] Here, dear, the silver's in a bag in the top tray of the trunk; here's the rest of it.

KATE. Why should I take it?

HELEN. It's your money. I'm just going with you.

KATE. But —

HELEN. That's the way I want it!

KATE [*takes money*]. I don't see what difference it makes; what's mine is yours.

HELEN. Two people so much alike as we are, just living together, can't help being happy. [*She puts the cardboard box she has been holding on her arm on the table and opens it. KATE looks up from packing the top tray of her trunk and sees her mother sorting over the contents of the box*]

KATE. What's that?

HELEN. Just rubbish, things I've had ever since I was a girl. I s'pose I'd better burn it. [*She is looking through old letters, a few dance cards, a photograph or two*] Goodness! What truck folks keep! [*She comes across a faded old photograph and after glancing at it, stands looking at it intently*]

KATE. Let's see what you're looking at. [*She crosses and looks at the photograph at first with simple curiosity, then with amazed recognition*] Oh, mother! [*She laughs*]

HELEN [*indignant*]. I don't see anything to laugh at!

KATE. But to think of father — young!

HELEN. Well, he *was!*

KATE. Of course, he must have been! I should think he would have *hated* it!

HELEN. He was young as anybody once!

KATE [*looking at photo*]. He was about Tom's age, wasn't he?

HELEN. He was better lookin'.

KATE [*doubtfully*]. Do you think so?

HELEN. I know it! [*She puts the photograph aside*] I won't burn it! I ought to, but I won't! [*She starts to sort over the other things*]

KATE. It's no use! I can't think of him as young! Did he — [*She giggles*] — Did he use to make love to you?

HELEN. It might be a good thing if you minded your own business.

KATE. Wrote you love letters and everything?

HELEN. Of course he did!

KATE. I'll bet they're all there!

HELEN. He didn't write many.

KATE. I'll bet he didn't.

HELEN. They're here somewhere — ah! [*As she finds a pitifully thin package bound up with a faded ribbon*]

KATE. Is that all?

HELEN [*defencelessly*]. He wasn't any much!

KATE [*puts out her hand*]. I want to read them!

HELEN [*draws away*]. Well, you can't! [*She opens one of the letters and looks at it*] "January tenth, nineteen hundred." That's a long time ago!

KATE. You can't make me believe it's a love letter!

HELEN. Well, it is! "My dear Helen!" [*She reads*] I can remember how happy I was the day I got this. Just as if it was yesterday! [*She reads*] "I got to New York all right, about six o'clock and went to the Bartholdi Hotel and got a room. It was most eight before I got through supper, so I went right to bed."

KATE. Go on!

HELEN. That's all; he didn't write long letters.

KATE. Let's see how he ended it!

HELEN [*reads*]. "Yours truly, Stephen Hardy."

KATE [*laughs*]. He *would.*

HELEN. That was just before we was married! [*She opens another one*] Oh, yes! [*As she looks at it*] This was the year you was born — I was waitin' for you, an' he went to New York to raise the first mortgage we ever had on the farm.

KATE. Regular pleasure trip for *him!*

HELEN [*looking at letter*]. It's funny, my forgettin' so much! I *was* happy sometimes! Look where I cried right on that letter! [*She points to stain on the old paper*] "My dear Wife." [*She reads*] "I don't like it here, and I wish I was back with you!" [*She sighs*] "The food here don't agree with me, and eating costs so much you've either got to starve, or eat and suffer! I've been thinking about you a lot, and about the hard time that's coming to you — You're a brave girl and a good wife — I know you're going to be a good mother! — if the calf won't eat, you'll have to give him a little warm milk morning and night. Remember you've got to take good care of yourself until the baby comes. The rubbage from the garden will do for the pigs 'til I get home. Your loving husband — Steve!" [*She sits in the chair and for a moment hides her face in her hands*]

KATE. Don't, mother! [*She puts her hand tenderly on* HELEN's *shoulders*]

HELEN. If he wanted me, I'd stay, just so long as he'd let you go!

KATE. He didn't want you, and he wouldn't let me go, not if he could help it!

HELEN. I wonder, while God was doin' it, he didn't fix it so's we'd be always young!

KATE. Maybe because he meant for us to take all the happiness we could while we could get it, and if we let it slip away from us, nobody but ourselves would be to blame.

HELEN. Maybe — that's why I don't know as I deserve another chance.

[TOM LANE *looks slyly in at the window.* KATE *sees him out of the corner of her eye and stoops close to her mother's ear and speaks low*]

KATE. They're looking at us through the window!

[HELEN *straightens up with dignity and puts the letters back into the box and crosses and drops the box into the top tray of the trunk; then, her head thrown proudly back, she exits to the hall, followed by* KATE. TOM *looks in window again and speaks over his shoulder*]

TOM. They're goin'! [*He and* STEVE *pass the window and enter*] I couldn't hear what they was sayin'!

STEVE. 'Twas none of your business.

TOM. I wouldn't listen! Anyhow, they talked awful low.

[STEVE *crosses to the kitchen clock and after looking at it earnestly, he takes it down from the shelf and shakes it*]

STEVE. Seems later than 'tis! I'm goin' to get supper. [*He crosses to cupboard*]

TOM. I suppose you've got to get used to doin' it.

STEVE. Any fool can do it! [*He looks over the shelves of the cupboard*] There's plenty here, wasteful plenty!

TOM. Whatter you goin' to get?

STEVE. W-w-e-l-l? [*He takes down a package of prepared buckwheat flour*] I don't know but what I'll make flapjack.

TOM [*doubtfully*]. If I was you I'd boil an egg!

STEVE [*reading directions*]. Simpl' enough! Anybody can make a flap jack. [*He gets frying pan and puts it on the stove*]

TOM. I guess so, I never tried.

STEVE. There's directions. [*He reads what is on package*] I see! [*He pours some flour directly into the frying pan*] I'll make plenty and you can stay an' eat. [*He draws a dipper of water and pours it into the flour in the pan and stirs it with a spoon.* TOM *looks at the resulting mess doubtfully*]

TOM. No! No! I guess I'll eat at home!

STEVE [*angrily*]. What's the matter with it?

TOM. I don't know. [*He bends over it curiously*] It looks indecent.

STEVE. It'll be all right!

TOM. I wasn't hungry even *before* I looked at that! [*He crosses toward door*] I'll see if they've started workin' on the road.

STEVE. I'll be out after a while.

TOM. Not if you eat them flapjacks! [*He exits.* STEVE *bends anxiously over his cooking as* KATE *enters with some clothes on her arm and stops in surprise*]

KATE. Father!

STEVE. Well!

[KATE *crosses over and looks into the frying pan*]

KATE [*in horror*]. What's that?

STEVE. A flapjack. It ain't quite boiled.

KATE. If you eat anything like that while we're away, mother will have to hurry right home and nurse you!

STEVE. If she goes she can't come back; I told her that.

KATE. But you didn't really mean it?

STEVE. Yes — she knows I meant it, and she'll go for good; she was always proud! I got some pride myself and I ain't likely to forget what she said — about bein' unhappy here always. I ain't likely to forget.

KATE. She'd have been happy if you'd been a little kinder to her. If you'd showed her a little plainer that you loved her.

STEVE. It was her business to know it.

KATE. I don't see how she could.

STEVE. A man can't be talkin' about love all the time! It's just like religion — every day ain't Sunday! [*He looks at the mess in the frying pan desperately*] How long has this damned thing to boil!

KATE. Father! Ha! ha! ha! I never saw anything so funny in all my life! Ha! ha! ha!

She runs out, laughing wildly. STEVE *considers his mess gravely then picks up the package and adds more flour, finally emptying the whole package into it. As he bends over the stove,* HELEN *enters. She has on a smart dark red dress and has arranged her hair to give a new look almost of girlishness. She sees him at the stove and crosses firmly and pushes him away and looks at the mess*]

STEVE [*defensively*]. It would have been all right in another minute.

HELEN. I fed the pigs *once* to-day!

STEVE. I was going to eat it.

HELEN. Go away! [*She picks up the frying pan and throws the contents in a garbage pail*] I'll fix you something!

STEVE [*stiffly*]. I won't trouble you.

HELEN. Some eggs; that's quick. [*She starts to prepare some scrambled eggs. He looks at her furiously*] What is it? What are you lookin' at me for?

STEVE. You look — different — sort of!

HELEN. Oh, this dress; it's Kate's. She made me put it on.

STEVE. It's — sort of — er — red!

HELEN. Yes. I think it's nice.

STEVE. I don't know as I like it so well as the red one you had.

HELEN. I haven't had a red one for twenty years.

STEVE. That's the one I meant. [*He crosses and sits at table*]

HELEN [*at* STEVE]. You'll die if you was to try to look after yourself! I guess you can get a girl to come in for about seven dollars a week.

STEVE [*in horror*]. Seven dollars a week!

HELEN. About. [*She cuts him some bread*]

STEVE. A man would have a right to divorce a woman that's actin' like you're doin'!

HELEN. Then you could *marry* a girl and save money! That Mrs. Lamont will be around for her eggs. I put 'em in this basket. [*She shows basket on table*] Eighty-five cents is a fair price. [*She crosses and puts food on his table*] There! Eat!

STEVE [*looks up at her*]. Was it twenty years since you had that red dress?

HELEN. I made it before we was married. How'd you come to remember it?

STEVE. I don't know — seems like you'd always had it.

HELEN. Before it wore out that's how it seemed to me.

STEVE. Somehow I sort of see you in it — I mean when you ain't really around — and I'm sort of seein' you, in my mind like. You were a good-lookin' girl, a mighty good-lookin' girl. [*He looks up at her; she is quite softened*] You ain't changed much. [*She half turns away, confused by his compliment*] I mean you ain't changed so much as I thought you had!

HELEN [*angrily*]. Eat your supper!

STEVE. Yes. [*He draws his place to him and starts to butter his bread*] It's past my time; I hate my vittals late! Twenty years — I remember the first time ever I saw that red dress.

HELEN. Huh!

STEVE. You was in the kitchen at your house, an' I came to take yer to a dance down to the Port.

HELEN. It was New Year's night. It had been snowin', and it was so lovely in the moonlight. You pulled me all the way on your sled, down to the Port! [*She drops into the chair opposite him, and bends eagerly across the table*] It was a big party, the only big one I ever went to, before or since. It was the first time I'd ever waltzed, I mean before folks, with a *man*. I remember how it scared me, it seemed so bold!

STEVE. There's dances now that's worse than waltzing! You'll see 'em in New York.

HELEN. My goodness! [*She rises hastily*] I almost forgot New York.

STEVE [*slowly*]. Helen! I want you not to go!

HELEN. Talkin' about — about that old red dress of mine has made us sort of sentimental. I guess you don't mean that, Steve!

STEVE. I do. You didn't act right, Helen, but I'll try and forget it.

HELEN. And you'll let Kate take the money and go, like I always planned she should!

STEVE. She'll be all right here.

HELEN. She's going, Steve! That's settled! As for me, it's for you to say.

STEVE [*angrily*]. I say she ain't goin'!

HELEN [*coldly*]. Yes, she is, and so am I. You'd better eat your supper.

STEVE. I won't! [*He pushes his chair away and rises angrily*] I can't! To hell with it!

[*He exits to the outside, slamming the door. HELEN looks after him for a moment tearfully; then her pride asserts itself and she crosses grimly to the trunk. Taking her box of treasured letters and photographs, she goes to the stove, and lifting up one of the lids she dumps the whole mass into the fire. Then, thinking of his photograph, she crosses and gets it from the table and returns firmly and throws it into the flames, and crosses out to hall. BEN GLENNY comes to outside door and knocks. There is no answer and he knocks again. KATE enters from hall and crosses to trunk with a bunch of keys in her hand. She hears the knock*]

KATE. Come in! [*The door opens and BEN enters*] Oh! It's you, Mr. Glenny! [*She puts things in trunk and clears away the dishes on the table, putting the bread away and throwing the egg out*]

BEN. I was lookin' for Tom Lane.

KATE [*coldly*]. He doesn't live here!

BEN. He's here a lot, and I've got to find him.

KATE. He's probably at his garage.

BEN. No, he ain't. [*KATE crosses to the easel and takes her painting and puts it on table. BEN sees it*] What's that?

KATE. My painting.

BEN [*looks at it*]. It's nice.

KATE. Thank you.

BEN. It's as good as some photographs.

[*KATE starts to cover the painting with stout paper*]

KATE. You flatter me. I am going to take this to New York with me. Mother and I are going in about half an hour.

BEN. What are you going to take it to New York for?

KATE. To sell it! [*He grins*] Don't you believe I can?

BEN. Yes, I do! Ain't they the darndest fools! [*He crosses to door*] If Tom comes, tell him I've got to see him.

[*He exits to outdoors. KATE, who i covering her painting with paper stops and looks about for somethin to fasten it with. She crosses to hal door, and raising her voice, calls t her mother*]

KATE. Mother! Mother! Where' some string?

HELEN [*upstairs*]. Up here!

KATE. I'm coming!

[*She runs out. STEVE wanders in from outdoors and stops in front of the clock and scowls at it, then crosse to the cupboard and butters the en of the half loaf of bread, and cuts a slice. And he is about to bite int it, there is a knock on the door. He pauses, with his mouth open, and looks angrily toward door as the knock is repeated. He puts his bread down with a patient sigh and crosses and opens door. DANA and DORA LAMONT are discovered, as they stand in the doorway*]

DORA. We want to speak to Mrs. Hardy. I am Mrs. Lamont.

STEVE. She left the eggs, they're in this basket. [*He crosses and gets basket from table*] She said you'd be over for 'em in the mornin'; it will be ninety cents.

DORA. Ninety? Why I have only been paying your wife eighty-five!

STEVE. Eggs is up.

DORA. Give him ninety cents, please, Dana. [*She takes the basket from STEVE as DANA hunts in his pocket, then draws out a roll of bills*]

DANA. I've nothing less than a dollar. [*He holds out a dollar bill*] You can collect next time or you may owe me ten cents.

STEVE [*takes the dollar*]. Looks like it would be fairer if I was to owe you ten cents.

DORA. No. [*She hunts in her bag and finds the change*] Give him back the dollar; here is the right change.

STEVE. Just as you say. [*He returns the dollar to DANA and takes the change; counting it carefully, he drops it in his pocket*] My wife's upstairs if you want to see her, but she an' my daughter are going to New York in just a few minutes.

DORA. They wanted Mr. Lamont to look at a painting.

STEVE. Oh? [*He turns to DANA*] You're an artist?

DANA. Yes.

STEVE. I'm glad you're here. I got a reason for wantin' you to look at Kate's picture! I guess this is it. [*He crosses to table and removes the wrapping-paper and turns the picture over*] Yes — there it is.

DANA. Yes. [*He crosses and stands looking down at the painting*]

DORA [*with him*]. The mother is so ambitious for her, Dana. I want you to like it, if you can!

There is a pause, during which DANA looks at the painting. KATE enters behind them, unnoticed, and stands in the door, looking on anxiously]

STEVE. Well?

DANA [*gravely, to* STEVE]. You said you had a reason for wanting me to see this. What was your reason?

STEVE. I guess no man knows less about art, and such as that, than me; but it happens to be a bit of land around here she painted, and I know land.

DANA. Your opinion should be of as much value, then, as my own — what do you think of this yourself?

STEVE [*slowly*]. Somehow, it seems to me it don't look like it ought — not just like — I don't know — it's Tom Lane's twenty acres all right — but it don't look just like it was alive, somehow, does it?

DANA [*gravely*]. No.

STEVE. It's grass, but it ain't growing grass; there's the spring wheat, but you can't somehow think of its ever ripening — like wheat does.

DANA. No.

STEVE. Do you mean she can't paint?

DANA. I am afraid —

[KATE *gives a moan of anguish, and* DORA *turns and sees her*]

DORA [*sharply*]. Dana!

[*The two men look around, and see her; there is a pause.* KATE *comes forward, trembling, looking from one to another. They all are distressed and uneasy*]

STEVE. I — I was speakin' to this gentleman here about your picture. He was sayin' it was pretty good, real good he seemed to think it was, for — for a girl that hadn't had much teachin' — I — I got to see if my stock's all fixed for the night. [*He crosses toward door*] He liked that picture real well; he'll tell you so himself, if you ask him.

[*He exits.* KATE *comes slowly down and looks at her painting*]

DORA. My husband will tell you how very nice —

KATE. Please! [*She puts out her hand sharply, and* DORA *stops.* KATE *bends over picture*] It doesn't look — alive — he said — that's grass, but it doesn't seem to grow! I wonder! — [*She looks at* DANA] Was he right? I want to know the truth. Can't I paint?

DANA. That might mean so many things.

KATE. No, there's only one thing it can mean! Have I a talent, a real talent, like my mother's always told me?

DANA. I am sorry, I am afraid you haven't.

KATE. If I worked hard — and I would — if I had good teachers, couldn't they teach me to be an artist?

DANA. That is something that can't be taught; one *is* or isn't.

KATE. And I'm — I'm — not?

DANA. I see nothing here but the conventional schoolgirl water color. Your color and drawing you could improve, but there is nothing here to justify the effort.

KATE. No talent? Nothing?

DANA. I am sorry!

KATE. You have been honest — you are a man who knows.

DANA. It hasn't been an easy thing to say.

KATE. I — I don't just seem to know what to do.

DORA. My poor child! [*She comes forward with ready sympathy*]

KATE. No! [*She draws away*] I had to *know!* You see, it means so much to us, to mother and me, we've planned so long! I — [*She breaks down and turns and almost runs outdoors*]

DORA [*to* DANA]. You brute! You could have lied to her.

DANA. About anything else.

DORA. There're other things in the world besides your paints and brushes!

DANA. For girls like her. I'll take the eggs. [*He takes the basket*] Poor kid!

DORA. You are absolutely heartless!

DANA. New York is full of them, breaking their hearts, — painters, musicians, writers, men and women who want to create something and who can't. Wanting to do it doesn't help much; even trying doesn't — when it isn't there! We'll get the butter in the morning.

[*They exit together to the outside. In a moment* STEVE, TOM *and* BEN GLENNY *pass the window and enter through the same door*]

BEN. I know it's hard, Tom, an' it's a thing I ain't even got used to really relish doin', but it's part of my job!

STEVE. Seems like they might have given the boy a chance.

BEN. Eight hundred dollars is a lot of money!

TOM. I can't pay it, not now; mebby I could if they'd give me time.

BEN. The writ of attachment don't say nothin' about givin' any time! I'll have to ask you fer the keys to your garage, Tom. I take formal possession accordin' to the law. Here's ther writ. [*He shows paper*]

TOM. It's the damned detour that done it! If they hadn't known about that, they'd have waited till cash was comin' in!

BEN. An' the aggravatin' part of it is they ain't goin' to be no detour!

TOM. What?

BEN. I just got word the road's open again; they decided not to fix it till next fall. Seems the summer folks have been objectin'!

TOM. The road's open!

BEN. Yes.

TOM. And you're attachin' my garage!

BEN. Less you can pay me eight hundred dollars.

TOM. Damned if I ain't disgusted! Talk about luck! Lost my garage! Lost everything! Just by a day!

[HELEN *enters with her hat on and a small old-fashioned traveling bag in her hand*]

HELEN. Where is Kate! It's time we started!

STEVE. I ain't seen her!

HELEN. Somebody's got to get that trunk to the station. Is your car here, Mr. Glenny?

BEN. Sure, I'll fetch it down.

STEVE [*coldly to* HELEN]. So you're goin'?

HELEN. Yes — you an' Tom carry the trunk out, an' put it in Mr. Glenny's car. Hurry up.

STEVE. I don't know as —

HELEN [*locks trunk*]. Well, I do It's the last favor I'm ever goin' t ask of either one of you, an' I guess won't hurt you none!

STEVE. No, I don't know as it woul hurt us none. Come on, Tom!

[STEVE *and* TOM *pick up trunk*]

HELEN. Put it right in the car. I get a check for it at the station. [KAT *enters from outside*] Oh! There yo are, Kate, Mr. Glenny's goin' to tak us down. Hurry and get your hat.

BEN. Wait a minute, Tom. I go to ask you for them keys.

TOM. Oh, yes. [*He and* STEVE s *the trunk down and* TOM *takes out a bunc of keys and starts to take one key off*]

STEVE. It's pretty hard on Tom!

HELEN. What is?

STEVE. Ben Glenny's got an attach ment on his place; he's takin' posses sion.

HELEN. Oh, I'm sorry!

TOM. An' ther road's open! I'd 'a made big money; now I'm done for?

HELEN. Can't somethin' be don about it?

BEN. Not without I'm paid eigh hundred dollars.

KATE. I'll pay it.

HELEN. What are you talkin' about?

KATE. You said it was my money [*She shows the roll of bills*] I'm going to pay it.

HELEN. You can't!

KATE. I'm going to! That's all [*She starts to count money*]

HELEN. But that only leaves us two hundred dollars!

KATE. You can have that! I don't want it! Here's the eight hundred, Mr. Glenny!

[BEN *takes the money and starts to count it*]

HELEN. But how can we live till you get so's you can sell your paintings!

KATE. Sell my paintings! Ha! ha! ha! Sell my grass that doesn't grow, and my wheat that will never ripen! Mr. Glenny here said they were all fools in New York. They'd have to be to buy any picture I ever painted!

HELEN. Do you know what you're sayin'?

KATE. Mr. Lamont was here! Father made him look at that! [*She points to the painting on table*] At that awful, awful thing!

HELEN. He saw it?

KATE. And he said it was *bad!* He said it was hopeless. No talent! Nothing! Never — never in all my life will I paint again! Never! Never!

TOM [*sincerely touched*]. He told you that! The damned brute! He hurt you like that! Oh, my poor little girl — I'm sorry! [*He holds out his arms to her, and she runs into them, clinging to him*]

KATE. Be good to me, Tom! Comfort me! Help me!

TOM [*pets her*]. There — there — don't you cry!

HELEN. Said you couldn't paint! It ain't so! It ain't! It can't be! We won't give up!

STEVE [*turns on her sternly*]. Hush! Can't you see she's feelin' bad!

TOM [*arms about* KATE]. You'd ought to be ashamed! Makin' more trouble at a time like this?

KATE. You mustn't speak like that, Tom. [*She turns severely to* HELEN] But he's right, mother! It's all your fault! I never would have thought of painting if it hadn't been for you!

TOM. I guess the less we say about it the better, so long as it turned out all right.

STEVE. That's what I say! Let bygones be bygones!

HELEN. I won't believe it! I can't. You ain't going to give that money to Tom Lane; the money I've slaved for all these years! I won't let you do it! We won't give up, we'll keep on tryin'!

KATE. I won't. I couldn't.

HELEN. I say he can't have it.

TOM. All right. I won't be under any favors to yer, if you feel that way about it! Give her back the money, Ben!

BEN. Just as you say. [*He hands the money to* KATE] Settle it among yerselves.

TOM. Now she's got it, an' I tell yer somethin' yer can't stop, Mrs. Hardy? Supposin' she was to give all that money to her own father, an' supposin' he was to give it to me as a payment on my twenty acres!

STEVE. *Now* you're talkin'!

KATE [*giving him money*]. That's just what I'll do.

HELEN. And he'll have more land to pay taxes and interest on all our lives, and you'll have your garage — and you'll have *her*, my daughter!

TOM. Everybody will have what they've allers wanted; nobody will lose

nothin' at all, unless maybe it's *you*, and all you'll lose is just a dream.

HELEN. That's all. [*She sits heavily by table*]

STEVE [*to* BEN]. Here's yer eight hundred. You can fix that bill of sale the first thing in the mornin'.

BEN [*writes receipt*]. Just so long as everybody's satisfied. Here! [*He hands receipt to* TOM]

TOM. All right. Have them papers ready early.

[*He and* KATE *walk to door with* BEN]

BEN. About ten.

TOM. Kate an' her father'll bring 'em down, I figgur on bein' busy with my garage.

[KATE, TOM *and* BEN *exit*]

STEVE. I hope this'll be a warnin' to yer, Helen. You might have made a lot of trouble, if it hadn't been for me and Tom!

[BEN *comes to door, in his hand the board on which is painted* Detour]

BEN [*holds up board*]. Here's the end of this. I pulled it down.

HELEN. And everything is just the same as it was before?

BEN. That's right.

HELEN. Just the same as it always will be!

BEN. You bet; good evenin'.

[*He exits*]

HELEN [*very low*]. God — help — me!

STEVE [*looks at clock*]. I bet that clock's slow!

HELEN. Slow? [*She looks up at the clock*] I guess not; mebby you're hungry.

STEVE. It's later'n I like waiting.

HELEN [*rises*]. I'll fix you a good hot supper.

[*As she crosses, he steps in front of her, holding out the ninety cents he takes from his pocket*]

STEVE. Here.

HELEN. What?

STEVE. That Mrs. Lamont left it; it's your egg money.

HELEN. I thought the hens was yours.

STEVE. After this, I want you should have ther egg money for yourself.

HELEN. The trouble is that after this I won't have no use for money, Steve.

STEVE. I'll put it here. [*He puts it on table*] I'd feel better if you took it; it's only ninety cents!

HELEN. Ninety cents for a dozen eggs! I told you to say eighty-five!

STEVE. I know, an' I tried to say it, only somehow it came out ninety.

HELEN. Mebby *you* was the one that should have gone to New York. [*She crosses to* STEVE *and starts to work*] Ham and eggs is best, I guess. I suppose she'll want Tom to stay.

STEVE. That looks like it, don't it? [*He points out window to where* TOM *and* KATE *stand in the glow of the summer sunset.* TOM'S *arm is about* KATE, *her head is on his shoulders*] See how happy they are!

HELEN. Yes — I know — right now.

STEVE. They look nice, don't they? And in a year or so maybe there'll be a baby. [*She turns at this, startled*] Yes — of course there'll be a baby, — a girl, I hope; girls are easier managed. Yes, I hope it's a girl; girls stay at home.

HELEN. Yes, girls stay at home!

STEVE. I sort to like to think about it, don't you? [*He drops into chair*]

HELEN [*thoughtfully*]. A girl!

STEVE. You're a good woman, Helen. I sort of hope she favors you.

HELEN. Another girl! Life sort of keeps goin' on forever, don't it? [*She crosses to table*] Steve?

STEVE. Yes?

HELEN. I guess I might as well keep the egg money. [*She draws the empty jug in which she had so long kept her treasure to her and slowly picks up the coins*]

STEVE [*amused*]. Goin' to start saving up again?

HELEN. I might. [*She drops the first coin into the empty jug. It falls with a clatter against the china bottom*]

STEVE. What for?

HELEN. Oh — it might come in handy — some day. [*She drops the others*]

STEVE. What for?

HELEN. Oh — I don't know.

STEVE. I do! [*He looks at her with a broad grin*] I bet I do! For her! For the baby that ain't even born yet. Ha Ha, ha, ha, ah ha!

[*But his loud, coarse laughter does not hurt her. She is standing, her face glorified, looking out into the future, her heart swelling with eternal hope*]

THE END

DULCY

(1921)

By George S. Kaufman

AND

Marc Connelly

DRAMATIZING THE BROMIDE: "DULCY"

THE American Drama of the past has had but few instances of plays that commented on life. In their attempt at amusement, they have deserted comment entirely, and clung desperately to external situation. They have clung to sentiments that have borne the trademark of generations of "theatre" about them, and they have offered us panaceas in the way of "happy endings." Their one virtue has been that they have been good-natured; their one claim to the theatre has been that emotionally they have afforded actors outlets for their various abilities. Such drama has only been a variation of a set formula — the one-, two-, three-act variation of the triangle from its three corners.

The immediate revolution that is taking place in the theatre is changing this. Satirizing ourselves is becoming a fashion of which not enough good can be said. The audience has not yet accustomed itself to this shift of things; the good-natured laugh is becoming just a little nervous. And the nervousness is excellent. It shows the beginning of a sense of values. As I have pointed out in the comments on "It Pays to Advertise", the cartoon showed itself some years ago; and the racy burlesque of Weber and Fields was the rage for a time. The cartoon has done much for drama and hasn't received its full credit. Mr. Dooley and George Ade also helped things along toward a more subtle view of ourselves. And then, in the "column", writers began saying things about the public which were enjoyed because they were in the "column", but for which writers would have been stoned had they said them from any other position. Tom Nast and John McCutcheon had the insight and the real sense of cartoon values which Charles Klein did not possess when he wrote "The Lion and the Mouse."

"Dulcy" came out of the newspaper "column" sense. In fact, now as I read her and watch her growth in F. P. A.'s "Conning Tower", I can see her irresistible claim upon the theatre as a new and novel type. If space allowed, I would extract from the files of the New York *Tribune* every bit of the Dulcinea "fun" which grew by what it fed on — Mr. Adams's fertile imagination, his excellent irony, and the assistance of his friends who added to the literature of the Bromidic in daily glee.

For those who would like to search the files, let us say that Dulcinea came to birth in the issue of June 4, 1914. She met George S. Kaufman a month after. There is only one way of fully knowing *Dulcy* of the play; study every bit of the fluffy stuff of Dulcinea in the *Tribune*. The psychology is distinct, the formula is catching. You begin to hear *Dulcy* at every moment of the day in everybody's conversation. You begin to see that it is not only *Dulcy* who has Bromideas and Bromideals. You get so saturated with *Dulcy* in all her fluffy contacts that you feel as though you would like to write a play about her yourself. And you can see her acted. Knowing something of the technique of Miss Lynn Fontanne as an actress, you begin to realize that she was the only one to play *Dulcy* on the stage. Really,

George S. Kaufman and Marc Connelly, who wrote the play together, ow*
much more than a bow to Franklin P. Adams. The bromidic Dulcinea is much
more of a contribution than "Our Samuel Pepys." She was a stroke of genius, a bit
of irony for which Mr. Adams would have been disliked had he thrust the type into
our "national face." The mask is a protection only the comedian values. Al
Jolson can say anything he wants to when his face is blacked; but let him say the
same things without his mask and audiences would leave the theatre. Dulcinea,
in the "Conning Tower" was — Dulcinea, a thing to be laughed at because she
was "column stuff."

Kaufman and Connelly saw the drama value of this creation, and they put it
to excellent advantage. It set them on the road toward something satiric that
might be used as healthfully as Gilbert used it in his opera librettos. They resorted
to satire in the lightest species of comedy, bordering on farce. They created *Dulcy*
out of Dulcinea and gave us a merry entertainment with something to bite into.

I dislike repeating some of another anthologist's thunder. But, if one goes to
the same source, one can't help but see the same thing. It is necessary for the
understanding of the ground structure on which *Dulcy* rose, to give excerpts from
"The Conning Tower." Here then are the notes I find in "The Conning Tower",
— only a few to set the rhythm, to give the cast of mind.

June 4, 1914. Probably Fanning Only Makes Her Warmer

"How are Don Juan's dates for this week? I'd like to take him to Dulcinea's
Del Tabasco's for tea smafternoon and let her spring 'You know, hot tea is really
more cooling than iced tea in warm weather' on him."

June 5, 1914. It Isn't the Place, though, It's the People

"Sir: Tell Don Juan I can produce one upon a day's notice guaranteed to say:
'I want to go somewheres where it's quiet, *this* summer.'"

Oh, It's a Fine Town to Visit but no Place to Live In

"Sir: Dulcinea tells me she knows Don Juan, and that he told her New York,
for a man, is really as comfortable a place as any to spend the summer."

June 8, 1914. Dulcinea and the Bromidian Touch

M. L. E. "Each Spring she says: 'I like to do Coney Island just once every
summer, and that's enough.'"

Sartor. "Perhaps she 'lives in Europe, but only exists in America.'"

Helen. "I know her. She 'doesn't care for money for its own sake — only
for what it will buy.'"

R. C. M. "'You don't need to care much what kind of people are there, Dulcinea,
if you have your own crowd.'"

"We feel certain that Dulcinea doesn't care much about what kind of room she
gets at that summer resort. 'One is never in one's room except to sleep, you
know.'"

June 11, 1914. Dulcinea and the Bromidian Touch

T. S. W. "'Bet she hasn't ridden horseback for years, but used to ride bareback
when she was a girl.'"

G. B. H. "'If there's swimming at Dulcinea's summer resort, she'll find that the water's cold, but it's fine after you get in.'"

Don Juan. "'She doesn't care a hang about dancing unless there's a good floor and good music?'"

H. & C. "Dulcinea says that at that summer resort 'all the nice men are married.'"

So the badinage flowed in the "Conning Tower" — bits from Bromidlewild that made one eager for the morning paper. The acme of the type of mind was in the following letter coming from Dulcinea:

"Last night was one of those nights in the country that makes you feel so sad, you don't know why. So I went up to my room and read some poetry. Don't you just *love* Poe? His poems are so musical, especially 'The Bells', and 'The Raven' is a wonderful thing. He must have been awfully distressed to have written that. It might seem funny to you, but I've always thought he had his own life in mind when he wrote and that it is symbolic of his passion for drink and the remorse that followed. Then again there's Browning, — so entirely different, but so true to life."

When G. S. K. met Dulcinea and told her he was going to England, she asked him to "give her regards to the King." I think that finished Kaufman. The play, "Dulcy", was the result.

It was produced in New York, at the Frazee Theatre, August 13, 1921. It instantly caught the popular fancy.

"Dulcy is the queen of platitude," wrote Francis Hackett, in *The New Republic*, ". . . the girl with the humanoid mind. That was a pungent element in one's pleasure, the lick of garlic, but Messrs. Kaufman and Connelly very wisely converted *Dulcy* from the world's most perfect exponent of familiar quotation, the Bartlett of Suburbia, to a kind of *Mrs. Malaprop* whose 'I always think' went in with some enormous fatuity in action. In their management of this fatuity, connected for the most part with her efforts to cultivate her husband's prospects, the authors happily though barely avoided the pitfall of satire, and landed *Dulcy* into the exquisitely narrow but fully delightful rôle of comedy."

I am inclined to believe Mr. Kaufman's declaration that it took but five weeks to evolve "Dulcy" is only another tribute to the completeness with which the "Conning Tower" made notes for her character. The habit of quick writing is also a journalistic feat. And both Mr. Kaufman and Mr. Connelly are journalists; a whole line of newspapers gave them a wide experience which has stretched from the "colyumnist" repartee to dramatic criticism.

For other data concerning these two dramatists, see Bibliography.

DULCY

A COMEDY IN THREE ACTS

By GEORGE S. KAUFMAN
AND MARC CONNELLY

CHARACTERS

Produced by George C. Tyler and H. H. Frazee, at the Cort Theatre, Chicago, February 20, 1921, with the following cast:

DULCINEA . . . . Lynn Fontanne
GORDON SMITH, *her husband* . . . . John Westley
WILLIAM PARKER, *her brother* . . . . Gregory Kelly
C. ROGER FORBES . . . . Walter Clark
MRS. FORBES . . . . Constance Pelissier
ANGELA FORBES . . . . Norma Lee
SCHUYLER VAN DYCK . . . . Gilbert Douglas
TOM STERRETT, *advertising engineer* . . . . Elliott Nugent
VINCENT LEACH, *scenarist* . . . . Howard Lindsay
BLAIR PATTERSON . . . . George Alison
HENRY . . . . Harry Lillford

Produced at the Frazee Theatre, New York, August 13, 1921, with the same cast.

DULCY

ACT I

The scene is the living-room in the suburban home of DULCINEA *and her husband — in Westchester County, within commuting distance of New York. It is a room that is splashing rather than merely striking. The furniture, for no particular reason, is old Italian, but most of it is hidden beneath beautiful and variously colored batiks and drapes. Over the divan, for example, is a golden brocade, and on it three blue pillows. Across the grand piano is a red drape, and on it a blue book. The window curtains are also of blue; there are two or three striking lamps in the background, and the tinted walls are covered here and there by a couple of good-looking tapestries. There are no pictures, for* DULCINEA *is nothing if not modern. On a platform at the rear, where the stairs begin to ascend, stands a great blue urn, filled with hydrangeas. On a cabinet at one side is an iridescent bowl containing tea roses; at each side of the cabinet stands a floor candlestick of Italian design. In a word, the room is* DULCY. *If there were a telephone* DULCY *would have it covered with a cute little doll — but this is a play without a telephone.*

In addition to the stairs there are three means of exit — at the rear are French windows which open onto the lawn and DULCY'S *cherished garden; at the right is a door that leads to the interior of the house, and at the left another that leads to the hallway and the outer door.*

The time is five o'clock on a Friday afternoon in late summer. The French windows are closed, subduing somewhat the light in the room. The rising curtain reveals WILLIAM PARKER, DULCY'S *brother, stretched out in an easy chair, reading a magazine. After a moment* HENRY, *the buttler, enters. He goes up to the windows, opens them, and comes back to* BILL.

HENRY. Mr. Smith has just come in, sir.

BILL [*after a pause, not looking up from his magazine*]. Yeh?

HENRY. Yes, sir.

BILL. My sister with him?

HENRY. Oh, no, sir! Mrs. Smith is at her Friday afternoon club, over at Mrs. Kennedy's. [HENRY *picks up a magazine from the floor and puts it on the table*]

BILL [*getting to his feet*]. What time's dinner?

HENRY [*hesitates*]. Seven-fifty, sir.

BILL. Seven-*fifty?* My God!

HENRY. Yes, sir.

BILL. Oh — James!

HENRY. Henry, sir.

BILL. Henry?

HENRY. Yes, sir.

BILL. Henry. [*He pauses*] Who else is coming to this — week-end? I mean, besides Mr. Forbes, and — ah — his wife and daughter?

HENRY. I'm not certain, sir. I've rooms ready for a number, sir.

BILL. M'm. Well — [*Enter* GORDON SMITH, DULCINEA'S *husband. He is an alert young business man, with worry just beginning to set on his shoulders*]

GORDON [*as he enters*]. Good evening, Bill. You're early.

HENRY [*turning away from* BILL]. Yes, sir.

BILL. Hello, Gordon.

[BILL *lights a cigarette.* HENRY *goes out;* GORDON'S *eyes follow him*]

GORDON [*looks around, yawns, stretches*]. Been here long?

BILL. Oh, not so very. It was sort of dull in town, so I thought I'd come out early.

GORDON. Of course — glad you did. [*He takes another moment to stretch, then drops onto the sofa*] Tired to-night.

BILL [*observing a folded newspaper in* GORDON'S *pocket*]. What's that — the *Sun?*

GORDON. No — *Post.* [*He hands him the paper —* BILL *drops into a chair with it. There is a considerable pause while* BILL *reads and* GORDON *indulges in another yawn*] Dulcy not home yet, huh?

BILL [*reading the paper at the same time*]. No. She's — across the street — some place. Mrs. Kennedy's, I think.

GORDON. Oh, yes. It's a — Friday afternoon thingmajig.

BILL [*still with the paper*]. M'm..

GORDON [*another pause; musters up some energy*]. Well! How's business?

BILL [*puts down the paper and looks at him*]. What?

GORDON. I say, how's business?

BILL [*as though announcing a death*]. Haven't you heard?

GORDON [*a bit cheerily*]. Oh, I don't know — I have an idea it may be picking up presently.

BILL [*tapping the newspaper*]. You've been reading Mr. Schwab. [*He quotes*] "Steel Man Sees Era of Prosperity."

GORDON. Well — I think he's right at that.

BILL. Yes. [*A pause*] Rockefeller expects to break even this year, too.

GORDON. Just the same, I look for an improvement. [*Earnestly*] Bill, if it could just be arranged that all the outstanding accounts could be absorbed by the banks, and then turn those into accounts payable —

BILL [*interrupting*]. I know. You mean — things would be better if we weren't all broke.

GORDON. That's one of the things that holds us back — pessimism.

BILL. How's the artificial jewelry business? If any?

GORDON. Well, it's — looking up a bit.

BILL. Anything new on Forbes' merger?

GORDON. It's coming along. It's practically settled, I think, that I'm to go in with him.

BILL. That's great. I hadn't said anything, but I rather felt that you were up against it, when I saw you last week.

GORDON. Thanks, old man. I — was, a bit.

BILL. You'll be all right if this deal goes through?

GORDON. I think so. It will end this fighting among us smaller men.

BILL. How many of you are going into this pool?

GORDON. About half the trade. I'm to get sixteen and two-thirds per cent of the stock of the combine.

BILL. Just for the factory?

GORDON [*unwillingly*]. Well, the plant *and* the pearl formula.

BILL. Oh, I see.

GORDON [*justifying himself*]. Of course, that means a cash payment when the papers are signed, and that will just about see me through.

BILL. You think that's enough — sixteen and two-thirds? Those pearls of yours are pretty good, you know, even if they *are* imitations.

GORDON. I know — but I'm up against it. I've got to take what he gives me, or have that crowd to fight. Forbes is a tough customer.

BILL. That's hard luck.

GORDON [*doubtfully*]. Of course, I *may* be able to do something with him over the week-end.

BILL. Huh?

GORDON. He's coming out here, you know.

BILL. So I understand.

GORDON [*looks at his watch*]. They're driving up from town.

BILL. Uh-huh. [*Thoughtfully*] Bringing his wife and — daughter, too, isn't he?

GORDON. Yes. They're going to stay over Sunday.

BILL. I didn't know you knew them that well.

GORDON. Well, I don't — except Forbes — in a business way. [*He pauses*] I wasn't keen for it.

BILL. Well, then —

GORDON [*rises*]. Well, Dulcy thought it would be nice to have them out here, and — well —

BILL [*as* GORDON *pauses*]. Yes, I know. [*There is a pause*] Does he play Russian bank?

[HENRY *enters with the afternoon papers, which he puts on the table.* GORDON *watches him narrowly, and believes that he detects* HENRY *looking furtively at him.* HENRY *departs again*]

GORDON [*paying no attention to* BILL'S *question*]. Did you notice that?

BILL. What?

GORDON. The way he looked at me.

BILL [*lightly*]. Henry?

GORDON. Didn't Dulcy tell you?

BILL. She's over at Mrs. Kennedy's.

GORDON. Well — he's an escaped convict!

BILL [*with a start*]. He's — what?

GORDON. No — I don't think that's just what I mean. It's a — suspended sentence. Dulcy got him off by — *you* know. Promised to take care of him, and give him work, and —

BILL. What's his line?

GORDON. He's a — butler.

BILL. I mean, what *was* his line?

GORDON. Oh! He — wrote a little check or something.

BILL. And the judge turned him over to Dulcy?

GORDON. After she made about twenty trips to town, and exhausted the judge, and used up a hundred dollars' worth of my lawyer, and —

BILL. She does things right.

GORDON. Oh, well, I suppose it's all right. After all, there *was* some doubt about him. Dulcy went to see his wife and family, and — she felt pretty badly over it — [*Door bell rings*]

GORDON. Here they are!

BILL. The Forbeses?

GORDON. Yes.

BILL. Better send them over to Mrs. Kennedy's, so that Dulcy can receive them.

GORDON. Darn it! — the man coming *here*, with a business deal on. I don't like it! [*Enter* HENRY] It looks too much as if I were trying to —

BILL. Oh, I don't know. [HENRY *crosses and goes out at the other side.* BILL *watches him off*] Are you always sure he's coming back?

GORDON. I don't like mixing business with social affairs.

BILL [*solemnly*]. Why don't you make Dulcy lay off?

GORDON. Why don't I? How *can* I?

BILL [*after considering it*]. I never thought of that.

[*Enter* HENRY]

HENRY. It's a Mr. —

[*Enter* TOM STERRETT, *a very much-alive young man. He is the kind of youth who pulls weights in his bedroom every morning, and who feels that a vigorous good health is the first aid toward business success. His business is advertising. He could tell you hundreds of interesting facts about type psychology, direct sales drives and national conferences; and would, if you gave him half a chance. He believes in Presence and knows he has it*]

STERRETT [*brushing past* HENRY *with an Open, Sesame! smile*]. I beg your pardon! I'm Mr. Sterrett!

BILL [*first looking at* GORDON *to see if he knows him; sees he does not*]. That's fine.

GORDON. You're looking for — Smiths? [HENRY *departs at this point*]

STERRETT. Yes, sir. I'm expected to meet Mr. Forbes here. Your man says —

GORDON [*a bit more cordial*]. Oh! Mr. Forbes hasn't arrived yet — I'm expecting him very soon. [*Extending his hand*] I am Mr. Smith.

STERRETT [*inflicting a brisk handshake*]. Smith Pearls?

GORDON. Ah — yes.

STERRETT. I follow your campaigns. Your advertising.

GORDON. This is Mr. Parker, my brother-in-law.

STERRETT. How are you, sir! [*Shaking his hand vigorously*] Didn't I meet you at the A. C. A. Convention? — in Detroit last summer? [*Renewing the hand-shake with the explanation*] Advertising Clubs of America?

BILL [*returning the shake with interest*]. I'm afraid not.

STERRETT [*very quickly*]. Sorry, my mistake.

BILL [*adopting* STERRETT'S *snappy style*]. It's all right! Have a cigarette! [*He whips out his case; clicks his heels with military precision*]

STERRETT [*accepting one and glancing at it*] Ah! C & G! Thanks! [*Pulls forward a chair, sits, and lights his cigarette*]

GORDON [*knowingly saying the unnecessary*]. Won't you — wait?

STERRETT. Surely! Mr. Forbes left word at his office for me to meet him here. It's about some contracts that have to be —

GORDON [*somewhat more cordially*]. Oh, I see. You're in the Forbes organization?

STERRETT [*with a trace of reproof*]. Oh, no! I handle Mr. Forbes' advertising. S. S. Q. & L. Agency.

BILL [*airily*]. Oh, the S. S. U. & L. !

STERRETT [*correcting him*]. S. S. Q. & L. Simpson, Simpson, Querrida and Lawford.

BILL [*taking a moment to digest it*]. That's fine.

STERRETT [*hitching his chair towards* SMITH]. Have you followed our Forbes copy, Mr. Smith?

GORDON. Well — to a degree — yes.

STERRETT [*a bit disappointed in* GORDON; *turns to* BILL]. You're interested in advertising, Mr. Parker?

BILL. I buy the *Saturday Evening Post.*

STERRETT [*missing it by sixty feet*]. But speaking generally of the other media —

BILL. I'm afraid I don't know much about advertising. In fact, I've never *been* in Detroit.

STERRETT [*answering without thinking*]. Well, that's too bad. [*Realizing he hasn't understood*] Huh? [*Thinking he understands*] Oh, yes — great town! Town that's made itself through advertising! [*He consults watch*] What time do you expect — ah — Mr. —

GORDON. Mr. Forbes and his family will be here presently.

STERRETT. Oh, is Mr. Forbes' family coming?

GORDON. Yes, they're going to spend the week-end.

STERRETT. Mr. and Mrs. Forbes?

GORDON. Yes.

STERRETT. And Miss Forbes?

GORDON. Yes.

BILL. Are you a friend of the — family's?

STERRETT. Oh, yes! [*A pause*] Yes, indeed!

BILL [*giving* GORDON *a significant look*]. H'm.

STERRETT. What was that?

BILL. I didn't say anything.

STERRETT. Oh, beg pardon, I'm sure.

GORDON. Well — ah — [*He is saying what seems to be expected of him*] You must stay for dinner, Mr. Sterrett.

STERRETT. Many thanks. If I won't be —

GORDON [*a bit curtly*]. That's splendid.

BILL. Yes — that's fine. We generally need one more for Dulcy's parlor games, don't we?

STERRETT. Now, I want to be sure I'm not intruding.

GORDON. Not at all. We're only too glad to have you.

[DULCINEA *enters through the French window. She is dressed in a gown that is just a bit too much for an afternoon gathering; she carries an armful of flowers, and she is in her customary bubbling good humor*]

DULCY. Hello, everybody!

BILL. Hello, Dulcy.

DULCY. M'm! It's nice and cool in here, isn't it? You know, if there is any breeze going at all, we get it in this room. [*She has a way of speaking an age-old platitude as though it were a wise and original thought — a little thing casually tossed off in the course of conversation*] Don't we, Gordon, darling? [*She kisses him*] Did you have a good day at the office? Send for Henry to fix these, will you? [*She indicates the flowers*] Aren't they pretty? — right out of my own garden. [BILL *comes down to her*] Hello, Willie. [*Kisses him*] Whom have you been doing? Eh? [*She laughs loudly at her own joke*]

GORDON. Dulcy, this is Mr. Sterrett. My wife.

DULCY. Oh, how do you do? [*Shaking hands somewhat appraisingly*]

STERRETT [*with great assurance*]. How do *you* do!

DULCY [*trying to estimate* STERRETT'S *position in the scheme of things*]. Have you been over the grounds? Gordon, you must show Mr. Sterrett over the grounds.

GORDON. Mr. Sterrett is a friend of the Forbeses.

DULCY [*as this explains* STERRETT *to her*]. Oh, the Forbeses — really! Oh, that *is* nice! [*Then with a bit of panic*] Have they come? Where are they? Why didn't you tell me! [*She rushes up toward the staircase, then toward the windows*] Upstairs or in the garden or where —

BILL [*holding up his hand*]. Now — wait.

DULCY [*coming to* BILL]. But what are they going to think? My not being here — how rude — why, if they —

BILL. Now, wait — wait! [*She finally pauses*] The Forbeses are not here.

DULCY. Well, why didn't you tell me so in the first place? After all, Willie, I'm not a mind reader.

GORDON. Mr. Sterrett has come to see Mr. Forbes on a matter of business.

BILL. And since he is also a friend of *Miss* Forbes —

GORDON. I've invited him to stay for dinner.

DULCY [*none too pleased, particularly about* STERRETT'S *being a friend of* ANGELA'S]. Oh! So, you're a friend of Angela's — that's lovely! Yes, you *must* stay! [HENRY *enters and stands awaiting instructions*] Just take pot luck with us, Mr. Sterrett. I always say that anyone can drop in — I think that's the nicest kind of a household, don't you? [*This one is No. 213, Series L, but* DULCY *utters it as though no one had ever thought of such a thing before*]

STERRETT. Why, yes. You know, I have a dear old aunt —

DULCY [*not waiting to hear*]. Oh, Henry, get some vases for these flowers — then I'll arrange them. I think arranging flowers is quite a knack, don't you, Mr. Sterrett? Some people can do it, and others can't, you know . . . it's just like an ear for music. Either you have it, or you haven't it, and there you are!

BILL. Mr. Sterrett is in the advertising business — not the music business.

STERRETT. Oh, but what she says is very true — very true, indeed. But as I was saying — this dear old aunt of mine — I — ah — she — [DULCY *is giving the flowers to* HENRY *and pays no attention.* STERRETT *fails to make an audience either of* SMITH *or* BILL] I — ah — suppose I wait in the next room for Mr. Forbes?

DULCY. Of course. Henry, show Mr. Sterrett into the library. There are some lovely books there. My books are my best friends, Mr. Sterrett.

STERRETT. Thank you. [*He departs — and glad of the opportunity*]

DULCY. Henry, fix up the little green room for to-night. Fix it nicely.

HENRY. Yes, ma'am. [*He follows* STERRETT *off*]

GORDON. He's not going to stay to-night!

DULCY [*has picked up an evening paper, and is already absorbed in it*]. No, darling, but someone else is.

BILL. Still another?

DULCY [*with the paper*]. Oh, what do you think? Mrs. Harper was acquitted! I always say, if a woman is good looking, no jury on earth will convict her.

GORDON. Dulcy, never mind that. Who else is coming?

DULCY [*immersed in paper*]. "A demonstration that lasted fifteen minutes greeted the acquittal of Mrs. —"

GORDON. Dulcy!

DULCY [*slowly, as she scans the article*]. I just want to see what she wore.

GORDON. Dulcy, listen to me!

DULCY. Well, dear?

GORDON. Who else is coming?

DULCY [*putting paper down*]. You'll never guess.

GORDON [*tiredly*]. I'm sure I've no idea, Dulcy.

DULCY [*going to him*]. Schuyler Van Dyck!

BILL. Schuyler Van Dyck!

DULCY. One of *the* Van Dycks, and he's worth millions!

GORDON. Schuyler Van Dyck's coming *here!*

DULCY. Yes — isn't it wonderful! He's a marvelous man, and you ought to hear him play the piano. You'd never think he was a Van Dyck — he's so democratic.

BILL. Where the devil did you meet *him?*

DULCY. Oh, several places, and this afternoon he was at Mrs. Kennedy's and played for us. He had a lot of invitations, and he accepted mine. [DULCY *returns to the table and replaces the newspaper neatly, then gives the sofa cushions a touch.* GORDON *follows her, speaking as he goes*]

GORDON. But, my dear, having this man here with Forbes — how do we know it's going to —

DULCY. Oh, but it will — Mr. Van Dyck's a business man too, darling. He owns all kinds of things — railroads — railroads — I think — some of them are. He'll help entertain Mr. Forbes with them.

GORDON. But Forbes isn't the kind of man that wants to be entertained. That's just it!

DULCY. Darling, leave Mr. Forbes to me. [*Puts arm around him*] I've got a *real* surprise for you!

GORDON. Another one?

DULCY. A wonderful one! Just for you!

BILL. One thing that Dulcy never learned is the difference between a surprise and a shock. [HENRY *returns with a bowl and a vase of flowers*]

DULCY. You shut up, Willie.

GORDON. But what is it? Has it got to do with Forbes?

DULCY. Yes, darling, and it's something that's going to help you a great deal with Mr. Forbes. [BILL *goes solemnly to* GORDON *and shakes his hand*]

BILL. Sometimes I think our family must have adopted Dulcy. [*He makes a melancholy exit*]

DULCY. Oh, Henry! There'll be two more for dinner.

HENRY. Yes, ma'am.

DULCY. That makes — nine, doesn't it?

HENRY. Yes, ma'am. [HENRY *goes upstairs*]

DULCY. I love a big table, don't you, Gordon? There's something so hospitable about it. [*She is looking around for the spots at which to place the flowers*]

GORDON. Nine? Then there's still another coming — besides Van Dyck?

DULCY [*with the air of someone revealing a great secret*]. Yes!

GORDON. What are you trying to do — solve the housing problem?

DULCY [*picking up vase of flowers*]. Just wait, darling! You'll be so excited! [*Breaking the big news over* SMITH'S *shoulder*] Vincent — is coming!

GORDON [*at sea*]. Vincent?

DULCY. Yes. Isn't it *wonderful?* [*Puts the vase on the piano*] That looks pretty, doesn't it?

GORDON [*trying to recall*]. Vincent — Vincent — who the devil is Vincent?

DULCY [*indicating the bowl*]. Or do you think this one ought to go over there and that one here?

GORDON [*annoyed*]. I don't know. Who is this man?

DULCY. Well, you don't need to get angry at me, darling, just because I want to make the place look nice.

GORDON. I'm not angry — but —

DULCY. I'm doing it for you, darling. You know, with Mr. Forbes coming —

GORDON. I know, but — tell me about this man —

DULCY. *Vincent Leach?* Don't you remember? You and I met him at Mrs. Peabody's last week — you know, the big scenario writer.

GORDON [*faintly recalling*]. Oh, yes. Is *he* coming here?

DULCY. Yes! Isn't it wonderful? [*Picks up the bowl from the table and starts toward piano with it*]

GORDON. But look here now — Dulcy, will you leave those flowers alone, and come here and talk to me?

DULCY. Just a minute, darling. [*She replaces the vase on the piano with the*

bowl, *then takes the vase back and puts* ? *on the table*] A time and a place fo everything. There! [*She seats hersel on his lap*]

GORDON. But, dear, why do yo want to mix this man Leach up with Forbes? Van Dyck may be all right but —

DULCY. Ah! That's the secret!

GORDON. But I don't like — secrets This isn't a — game.

DULCY. Promise you won't tell Cross your heart!

GORDON. Yes, yes.

DULCY. Well, then — Vincent and Angela — [*she kisses him*] — like each other.

GORDON. You mean — Forbes' daughter?

DULCY [*nodding*]. Isn't it wonderful? So I invited them both here so they'll have the whole week-end together. And at the same time he can meet her parents. You never can tell what will happen.

GORDON. But, Dulcy, dear, you don't know Angela so well, and — this man Leach — what do you know about him?

DULCY. I know all about him. He's a big scenario writer, and just the man for Angie. He's — he's so practical, and she's a dreamer. Opposites should marry — you know that, darling.

GORDON. But, Dulcy, now —

DULCY. And what else do you think? I'm going to get him to help me with some of *my* scenarios while he's here.

GORDON. But why, dear —?

DULCY. To make them better.

GORDON. No, no — I mean — why are you trying to match this fellow Leach with Angela? What do *you* care about it?

DULCY. Don't you see?

GORDON. No.

DULCY. Can't you guess?

GORDON. No.

DULCY. Well, if Angie *likes* Mr. Leach, and marries him —

GORDON. Yes?

DULCY. And *I* fix it —

GORDON. Well?

DULCY. Well — I'm your wife — [GORDON *springs up in alarm, dropping* DULCY *off his lap*]

GORDON. Now, Dulcy dear —

DULCY. That will make Mr. Forbes so grateful that he'll have to give you more than sixteen and two-thirds of the percentage.

GORDON. Good heavens, Dulcy! Now —

DULCY [*ecstatically*]. I figured it all out myself!

GORDON. But, now wait! [*He paces the floor*]

DULCY. Gordon, darling — don't be upset about it. I know they ought to marry — I just know it. It's a woman's intuition. [*A pause*] Just as I knew I ought to marry you, dear. [GORDON *stops*] It was because I loved you, darling, and wanted to help you, and — and —

GORDON [*going to her and embracing her*]. Yes, and you do help me.

DULCY. Well, then —

GORDON [*tenderly*]. And you're not sorry that you married me, instead of Arthur, with all those millions?

DULCY. You're going to have millions, too, dear — at least thousands. And I loved you — not Arthur. [*She buries her head on his shoulder*]

GORDON. Dulcy, dear. [*He kisses her neck*]

DULCY. And I'd love you if you didn't have a cent, and — and stand by you, and help you. You do want me to help you, don't you?

GORDON [*reluctantly*]. Why — I — ah — yes — ah —

DULCY. Well, then, let me!

GORDON. But you don't understand, dear. Try to see my position.

DULCY. But I do see it. You need Mr. Forbes' help and I'm going to get it for you.

GORDON. I need it in a business way. And as it's only in a business way, I feel that I ought to handle it alone — in office hours. Don't you see?

DULCY [*turning away on the verge of tears*]. I feel almost as if I were being — exiled.

GORDON [*embracing her*]. Well, you mustn't — you aren't being exiled. Just realize that in this particular affair you're my silent partner, and a very important one, too. Don't you know, dear, if it weren't for you I couldn't go to town day after day and fight! There! — you're really helping me all the time, by just being *you*. [*He steps back from her*] Furthermore, don't you remember that you promised me that you'd let me manage my own business matters?

DULCY. When?

GORDON. Three months ago? When we came back from our honeymoon?

DULCY. Why, I never did.

GORDON. The time that you practically discharged my secretary?

DULCY [*remembering*]. Oh!

GORDON. You thought Shepherd was dishonest simply because he wore a heavy black moustache.

DULCY. Oh, Gordon, darling, I know I've done some silly things, but when I married you, dearest, I did promise to stand beside you all my life and love you and help you, and that's what I think I ought to do now. That's why I'm doing it.

GORDON. But, Dulcy —

DULCY. Well, Mr. Forbes *is* taking advantage of you and I'm not going to let him — that's all!

GORDON [*desperately*]. But that isn't the point! In the position that I am I have to go ahead with it. I wouldn't want anything to happen. [*Pleading affectionately*] Don't you see, dear, if I'm not in that merger, I'll lose — everything!

DULCY. But only sixteen and two-thirds per cent — it's such a funny number, too. I don't see why you couldn't get a nice even number — like twenty-five. [*She pauses*] Or fifty! But sixteen and two-thirds — they could never divide it.

[BILL *returns*]

BILL. Well, has she fixed it?

DULCY. We've been all through it quietly, Willie, and it's settled.

GORDON. Now, Dulcy, you must listen —

DULCY. Now — now — not another word. Just let — let — sleeping dogs lie and everything is bound to come out all right. It always does. [*She looks toward the window*] Oh, here's Mr. Van Dyck! [*Rushing to the window*] Come right in this way, Mr. Van Dyck! That's right — here you are! [SCHUYLER VAN DYCK *enters through the French window. He is aristocratic in bearing and well dressed. He has a bag of golf-clubs over his shoulder and is carrying a suitcase*] Well, you found the way, didn't you — you're like me — you've got a bump of location! Henry will take your things — where's Henry? — Willie, send for Henry! My, this is lovely! [BILL *pulls the bell cord*] So glad to see you in our own little nest, Mr. Van Dyck. [VAN DYCK *has put his suitcase and golfbag down. DULCINEA leads him down to* GORDON] This is my husband, Mr. Van Dyck. Mr. Van Dyck, Gordon, that I've been telling you so much about. [*As an afterthought*] And my brother, Willie. [HENRY *comes downstairs*]

VAN DYCK [*as he shakes* SMITH'S *hand*]. Mr. Smith, how do you do, sir?

GORDON. I'm very pleased to know you, Mr. Van Dyck.

DULCY. Henry, take Mr. Van Dyck's things. So glad you brought your golf clubs. We'll see that you use them. [BILL *has circled down to* VAN DYCK *and offers his hand*]

BILL [*quietly*]. My name is Parker.

VAN DYCK. I'm delighted, Mr. Parker. [BILL *retires again*] I'm very much afraid that I'm intruding.

GORDON. Why, not at all!

DULCY. Intruding! I should say not! [HENRY *has picked up the bags and is awaiting* VAN DYCK *on the stairs*]

VAN DYCK. Mrs. Smith was so — so very gracious as to ask me to be your guest. May I — accept with a proviso?

GORDON. Why, certainly.

VAN DYCK. It is barely possible that some business matters will call me back to town. In that event — [*He smiles his rare smile*] I hope you will pardon me.

DULCY. Of course! We all understand business here — don't we, Gordon, darling? Business before pleasure!

VAN DYCK. You're very good.

DULCY. Henry, show Mr. Van Dyck to his room. Henry will show you, Mr. Van Dyck. [*It is not in her nature to say a thing* ONCE]

VAN DYCK. Thank you — if I may. I shall rejoin you presently.

DULCY [*calling to him as he goes upstairs*]. Dinner at eight-twenty!

BILL. Eight-twenty? Have you been reading *Vanity Fair* again?

DULCY. Everybody dines at eight-twenty, Willie. It's continental. [DULCY *turns to her husband*] Well, how do you like Mr. Van Dyck? Nice, isn't he?

GORDON. He's all right, I guess.

DULCY. Wait till you hear him play the piano. A lovely touch, and so soulful.

BILL. Don't forget to ask him to play.

[HENRY *comes down the steps*]

DULCY [*going to* BILL *and sitting beside him*]. Dear, no — right after dinner. We're going to have a nice musical evening. Music after eating helps digestion. All the new doctors say so. [HENRY *departs again.* BILL *looks after him uncomfortably*]

BILL. Dulcy!

DULCY. Well, Willie?

BILL. When you took this butler out of Sing Sing —

DULCY [*rising*]. Sing Sing? He wasn't in Sing Sing!

BILL. You didn't go way out to Leavenworth, did you?

DULCY. Now, I know just what you're going to say, but it isn't true. Just because Henry made one false step doesn't mean he's going to make another. If you ask me, I think there's enough sorrow in the world without trying to make things worse. Every cloud has a silver lining, and — so has Henry.

BILL. Yes. The question is, how did he get it?

DULCY. It doesn't matter in the least — he's all right now. He promised me. Besides, he has to report to the probation officer every week, and tell him everything he does.

BILL. Oh, he *has* to tell him everything?

DULCY. Every week.

BILL. You don't think he has any — secrets?

DULCY. You must be more tolerant, Willie. You know, there's so much good in the best of us — and so much bad in the worst of us — well, it ill behooves the best of us — [*She flounders, but is saved by the door bell*]

GORDON. Here are the Forbeses!

DULCY. Wait, Gordon — let that poor Henry answer! The trouble with the world, Willie, is that it doesn't give the under-dog a chance! Live and let live — is my motto. [HENRY *returns to answer the bell*]

BILL. I surrender. [*A pause*] Oh, Dulcy! [HENRY *goes out at the other side*] Why don't you raise his salary?

DULCY. I have!

GORDON. Now remember, Dulcy, just leave Forbes to me — and — don't forget this is a very important business matter —

DULCY. Now, don't worry, darling. Worrying is the very worst thing you can do — everybody says so. I was reading where Dr. Crane said it in the *Globe* the other day — by worrying you can catch things.

[HENRY *opens the door. The voices of the* FORBESES *are heard; they enter.* First, MR. FORBES — *then* MRS. FORBES — *then* ANGELA. *The greetings are ad lib.* DULCY *shakes hands with each, passing them to* GORDON, *who does likewise*]

DULCY. Well, here is Mr. Forbes now, and Mrs. Forbes! How charming you look! Green's your color! [*She turns to* GORDON *to tell him about it*] Green's her color, darling! And Angela!! You've come to see me at last! My, such red cheeks! Just like two ripe apples! [FORBES *is already deep in business talk with* SMITH, *but* DULCY *turns to him blithely*] Mr. Forbes — [FORBES *turns to her*] Did you have a nice ride out from the city? Awfully pretty, isn't it — Westchester? [FORBES *agrees with a nod — is about to turn back to* SMITH] Did you come out the short way or the long way?

FORBES [*it is already evident that* DULCY *is going to be just the person for him*]. Ah — what was that?

DULCY. Did you come out the short way or the long way?

FORBES. Ah — let me see. [*A pause*] Do *you* know, Eleanor?

MRS. FORBES [*his second wife; a very feminine person of about thirty-five; good looking and a bit flighty*]. What, dear?

FORBES. Mrs. Smith was just asking if —

DULCY. Did you come out the short way or the long way?

MRS. FORBES. Which is the way through Hartsdale?

DULCY. Oh, that's the short way — you should have come the long way. No, I think that *is* the long way, isn't it? Hartsdale? — Yes. No —

GORDON [*diplomatically*]. Well, it doesn't really matter.

DULCY. No, no — both ways are awfully pretty. [*She has said this to* MRS. FORBES, *and* FORBES *and* SMITH *have turned immediately to each other to renew their conversation. They haven't a chance*] Though I don't suppose *you* got much chance to look at the scenery, did you, Mr. Forbes — driving the car? Don't you think driving is awfully hard work, Mr. Forbes?

FORBES. Why, no, I rather like it.

DULCY. Like it? Really! Oh! Well, it wouldn't do if all our tastes were alike, would it? [*Turns away just as* HENRY *enters*] Henry, take the things

right up — you know the rooms. [DULCY *turns to* MRS. FORBES] Mrs. Forbes, you and your husband are to have the shell-pink suite. It looks just like a bridal suite. [MRS. FORBES *giggles and* DULCY *laughs with her*] The bridal suite! Oh, Mr. Forbes — [*She goes to him*] Mr. Forbes — you and your wife are going to have the bridal suite! [FORBES *tries to understand the joke, but without success*] And, Angie — Oh, there you are! I forgot you and Willie were old friends. Naughty, naughty! [HENRY *is on the stairs with the bags*] Well, how is little Angie! My, what a pretty necklace! It's new, isn't it? Pearls, too! [*This registers with* HENRY]

ANGELA. Father gave it to me for my birthday.

DULCY. Your father. Really — wasn't that sweet of him? [*To* FORBES] Your own manufacture?

FORBES. Oh, no!

DULCY. Real pearls! Angela, fancy your having a string of real pearls! Isn't that wonderful! [*Remembers* HENRY'S *presence*] Take the bags right up, Henry.

BILL. Yes, Henry. [HENRY *goes*]

DULCY. Angie is going to have the cutest little room of all! Just wait till you see it!

ANGELA. Oh, thank you. [VAN DYCK *comes downstairs*]

DULCY [*turning* ANGELA *away as if for a confidence*]. And wait till you see what else I've got for you! You'll be surprised, and — oh, here's Mr. Van Dyck! [*In her element*] Mrs. Forbes, Mr. Van Dyck!

MRS. FORBES. How do you do?

DULCY. And Miss Forbes —

VAN DYCK [*bowing*]. Miss Forbes! [ANGELA *bows*]

DULCY. And Mr. Forbes — Mr. Schuyler Van Dyck of New York.

VAN DYCK. C. Roger Forbes?

FORBES. I'm certainly glad to know you, Mr. Van Dyck. I believe I know something of your interests. In fact, I just missed meeting you at the International Metals conference last week.

VAN DYCK. Yes? Well, I hope we can have a little chance to talk down here. I'm very much interested in jewelry.

DULCY [*with a triumphant look at her husband*]. You see, Gordon?

FORBES [*aware that something is going on*]. What's that?

GORDON. Oh, it was just — ah — that is, Mrs. Smith thought — [HENRY *comes downstairs*]

DULCY. Oh, we're all forgetting Mr. — What's-his-name — in the library — a gentleman to see you, Mr. Forbes, on business. Henry, tell the gentleman in the library to come in.

[HENRY *departs again*]

GORDON. It's your advertising man.

FORBES. Oh, yes — Sterrett. [ANGELA *turns sharply at the mention of the name*] I took the liberty of leaving word for him to come here — I had to get away early.

GORDON. Why, certainly.

DULCY. And so that you'll have lots of time to talk business, I've invited him to stay for dinner. [*She looks proudly toward her husband as though asking approbation for this remark.* GORDON *is pleased with her for the first time*]

ANGELA. Oh! Mr. Sterrett is going to stay for dinner?

DULCY. Yes — because he's a friend of *yours*, Angie, dear. [*Quickly*] *And* because of the business, of course. Well, what do you girls say? Shall we leave the men to talk business? Wouldn't you like to see your rooms? You haven't been over the house at all, you know.

MRS. FORBES. Why, we'd love to.

DULCY. Gordon, darling, you must show Mr. Forbes and the others over the grounds. [*She is shepherding* MRS. F. *and* ANGELA *toward the stairs*] You get a beautiful view from the lawn, Mr. Forbes. And don't forget to show him the garden, darling — all our vegetables are out of our own garden, Mr. Forbes. Then later *you* must see the garden, Mrs. Forbes — and Angie. You know, there's nothing like country life, is there? Out next to Nature, you know. We're just gypsies — regular gypsies. New York is a wonderful place to visit, but I wouldn't like to live there. [*They go up the stairs*]

BILL [*breaking the spell*]. All in favor of the garden, say "Aye."

GORDON. Smoke?

FORBES. Thanks. [*He selects a cigar*]

VAN DYCK. Thank you. [*Takes a cigarette.* FORBES, *after a glance around the room, heads for a stiff chair*]

GORDON [*indicating an easy chair*]. Oh, sit here, Mr. Forbes!

FORBES. Thanks — I prefer a stiff chair — my back, you know. [STERRETT *returns*]

STERRETT. Ah! Good afternoon, Chief!

FORBES. Hello, Sterrett. Too bad to make you come way out here, but —

STERRETT. Not at all — not at all! Particularly, as Mr. Smith has insisted on my staying to dinner. Has Angela come?

FORBES [*patting him on back*]. Oh, yes, she's come. You've met Mr. Parker?

STERRETT. Oh, yes.

FORBES. And Mr. Schuyler Van Dyck?

STERRETT. Mr. Schuyler Van Dyck?

VAN DYCK [*shaking his hand*]. Mr. Sterrett.

STERRETT. I've heard of you, Mr. Van Dyck.

VAN DYCK. Yes?

STERRETT [*crisply*]. Yes, sir. They tell me you have advertising interests, on the q. t.

VAN DYCK. Well, it's — it's possible, yes.

STERRETT. I'm an advertising man myself.

VAN DYCK. Really?

BILL [*helping along*]. S. S. Q. & L. Agency.

STERRETT. Yes, I personally handle all of Mr. Forbes' business.

VAN DYCK. That so?

STERRETT. Yes, sir. I've made the nation Forbes-conscious.

BILL. Forbes — what?

STERRET. Forbes-conscious. I have made Forbes Jewelry Products a part of the country's buying habit.

FORBES. It's wonderful — wonderful what the younger generation is doing in a business way.

GORDON. It certainly is.

FORBES. Why, when I was breaking into business, sir, do you think that a young man like that would have been entrusted with the handling of such important matters?

GORDON. No, sir.

FORBES. No, sir — he would not! Would he, Mr. Parker?

BILL [*with a look at* STERRETT]. No, sir, he would not!

FORBES. But to-day, not only is he entrusted with them, but he is actually given the preference over an older man. I find myself doing it.

STERRETT. Oh, I don't know, Chief.

I'm no unusual specimen — that is, so far as my youth is concerned. Mozart was composing at fifteen; William Cullen Bryant wrote *Thanatopsis* when he was nineteen; Homer did part of the *Iliad* —

BILL [*rising*]. Suppose we *all* go out and look at the garden?

GORDON. Yes, that's a good idea.

FORBES. If you don't mind, I'll put my car in your garage.

GORDON. Certainly.

FORBES. That is, if there's room.

GORDON. Oh, plenty. Our car isn't here at present. It's being repaired.

BILL [*to* VAN DYCK]. You must find it rather a relief to get away from business occasionally.

VAN DYCK. Yes, just to relax. It's very wonderful.

FORBES [*turning back to* VAN DYCK]. I imagine you've been kept pretty well tied down lately. [*All except* STERRETT *have strolled up to the window*]

VAN DYCK. Well, yes — to a degree. Of course, I have things pretty well systematized.

FORBES. Of course.

GORDON. Now, right here at the left is where the garden begins. You can see for yourself —

[*They go out through the windows —* SMITH, FORBES, VAN DYCK *and* BILL. STERRETT, *somewhat puzzled at losing his audience, decides to go along.* ANGELA *comes down the stairway*]

ANGELA [*very impersonally*]. Oh, hello, Tom!

STERRETT. Angela! I'm here, you see!

ANGELA [*selecting a magazine*]. Yes, I see.

STERRETT. Well, aren't you glad to see me?

ANGELA. You came to see father, didn't you?

STERRETT. Why, no — that is — yes — but —

ANGELA. Have you seen him?

STERRETT. Yes, but — that was business and —

ANGELA. I know — it's always business with you men. You're all alike.

STERRETT. You talk as though you'd examined the whole city.

ANGELA. Well, I did know another man who was just like you.

STERRETT. Who is he?

ANGELA [*looking up from the magazine for first time*]. Oh, don't be silly. I shouldn't tell you even if you weren't so rude. I simply say you are all alike. Your idea of romance is to sit in the moonlight and talk about the income tax.

STERRETT [*sitting beside her*]. Now, look here, Angela — you know I'm crazy about you, and I've told you what I'll do for you. I'll devote my entire life to you.

ANGELA. And give up business?

STERRETT [*swallows*]. Well, you wouldn't want me to give it up, would you? Right at the beginning of my career! Why, when your father signs these new contracts —

ANGELA [*throwing the magazine down beside her and rising*]. Contracts! Bother the contracts! It's always contracts!

STERRETT. But they mean our future.

ANGELA. *Our* future? I didn't know that *we* were going to have any!

STERRETT. Well, we are! You just watch me! I've always got what I was after in business, and —

ANGELA. Well, I'm not — business!

STERRETT. I — I didn't mean just that, Angela.

ANGELA. Oh, sometimes I feel that I don't ever want to talk to another business man in my life!

STERRETT. I notice that you don't mind talking to a moving picture man, though!

ANGELA [*wheeling*]. What do you mean by that?

STERRETT. I saw you with that bird Leach at the Biltmore yesterday.

ANGELA. Well, what of it? Mr. Leach is a very charming man.

STERRETT. He's got a swelled head!

ANGELA. He's entitled to one.

STERRETT. Look here — has he been making love to you?

ANGELA. Well, at least he hasn't been talking business.

STERRETT. Now look here, Angela —

ANGELA. Oh, Tom, don't be silly! If I didn't know any more about girls than you do, I'd go some place and learn! That other man talked business, too, and that's why I — what does a girl care about business, and things like that? She wants something else in her life — that's what makes her a girl! She wants romance — and a thrill — and something real — and she wants a man to be like all the heroes she ever read about — if she cares about him at all! It may be foolish and all that, but that's what she wants and she's bound to have it! She wants someone to tell her how wonderful she is — whether she is or not — to sweep her off her feet and — carry her away — and — [*One look at* STERRETT'S *face tells her that all this has been wasted*] Oh, I'm going out into the garden! [*She flounces through French window.* STERRETT *follows*]

STERRETT. Now look here, Angela! I didn't mean — [*Enter* FORBES *and* SMITH. FORBES *looks back after* ANGELA *and* STERRETT]

FORBES. Smart chap, Sterrett.

GORDON. Yes, he — seems to be.

FORBES. Wide-awake! That's what I like about him.

GORDON [*eager to agree*]. Yes, wide-awake chaps certainly have an advantage.

FORBES [*bluffly*]. Now, that's the kind of a man I'd like for a son-in-law.

GORDON [*mindful of* DULCY'S *plans*]. Son-in-law?

FORBES. Yes. Good business head. No foolishness, like most young people. Substantial — that's what I mean. Lord knows, Smith, I'm just as tolerant as anybody, and a little bit more so, but if there is one thing I can't stand it's this frivol-headed, gad-about way of doing things they've got now-a-days.

GORDON. Oh, absolutely. Yes, indeed.

FORBES. Damn it — they — they play with life — they don't work. And it's not just the young people that have notions. The worst of it is that — oh, well, what's the use! [*He pauses*] That reminds me. I must apologize for not answering that letter of yours. My wife comes into my office occasionally and uses my stenographer — the one that writes English. [*He tries to appear half-joking*] All day yesterday. She likes to write little stories and movie scenarios. Of course she never sells them.

GORDON. Well — ah — probably she's just — seeking self-expression.

FORBES. Yes, I suppose so. She's quite young — Angela's step-mother, you know.

[DULCY *and* MRS. FORBES *come downstairs*]

DULCY. Come right down, Mrs. Forbes. Well, here we are! No more business now! It's time to play! [*To* FORBES] You know one thing poor Gordon has never learned is how to play! He takes everything so seriously. Now, what I like to do is cut loose once in a while — just be children again. Don't you, Mrs. Forbes?

MRS. FORBES. Yes, indeed — away from everything.

DULCY. Gordon, darling — why don't you take Mrs. Forbes for a stroll out in the garden before dinner — she hasn't seen it yet. [GORDON *realizes this would leave* DULCY *with* FORBES] Wouldn't you like to see it, Mrs. Forbes?

MRS. FORBES. Indeed, yes.

DULCY. Gordon!

GORDON [*turning to* MRS. FORBES]. Why, of course.

MRS. FORBES. It's awfully good of you. You have a beautiful place here. There are some lovely places in Westchester, aren't there? [MRS. FORBES *and* GORDON *go through the window,* GORDON *looking back nervously at the possibilities he is leaving*]

DULCY. I've got the most wonderful day planned out for you to-morrow, Mr. Forbes! You're going to play and play and play!

FORBES [*alarmed*]. Me! Thank you very much — but you know I —

DULCY. Oh, but you play golf, don't you?

FORBES. Well — ah — thank you. It's been so long since —

DULCY [*pursuing him*]. You'll love our links — they're wonderful!

FORBES. Yes, but I've been having a lot of trouble with my back lately and —

DULCY. Oh, really! That's too bad! What you need is exercise. It would be the finest thing in the world for you. Now, you play nine holes of golf with Mr. Van Dyck first thing in the morning.

FORBES. But, really, Mrs. Smith —

DULCY [*indulgently*]. You remind me so much of Gordon — that poor darling. All men are children. You know *he* gets hardly any exercise at all — he works so hard, the poor boy. I don't suppose he's told you, Mr. Forbes, but he's really got a lot of things on hand.

FORBES. Why, no —

DULCY. You might just as well know — it isn't only the pearl business. He has lots of other interests, too.

FORBES. What's that?

DULCY. It's really asking too much of him to make him give up all these other things to come into the jewelry combination — that is, unless it were made worth his while. [DULCY *effects her master stroke*] Of course, if he just got sixteen and two-thirds per cent, he couldn't afford to give up all his time to it — no! [VAN DYCK *and* BILL *come strolling through the window*] He'd have to look after his other things, too, and you'd be the loser.

FORBES. Why, I didn't know he had any other — [*Door bell rings*]

DULCY. Oh, there's Mr. Leach now! [*Calling*] Gordon! Gordon, bring Angela in! [*She sees* VAN DYCK] Are you having a nice time, Mr. Van Dyck? We want everybody to have a nice time. [GORDON *and* MRS. FORBES *return.* HENRY *enters to answer the door bell*]

VAN DYCK. Oh, delightful!

DULCY. You're to play eighteen holes of golf with Mr. Forbes the first thing in the morning. [FORBES *is delighted*]

VAN DYCK. That will be splendid!

GORDON. Now — now, *I* have a suggestion.

DULCY. Well, what is it?

GORDON. Suppose that to-morrow we just let everybody go the way they want to, and — [*Enter* HENRY, *followed by* VINCENT LEACH. DULCY *swings down to greet him*]

DULCY [*with great enthusiasm*]. Oh, here he is!

LEACH. Mrs. Smith, dear lady — [VINCENT LEACH *is young, very languid, a bit effeminate*]

DULCY. Ladies and gentlemen, this is Mr. Vincent Leach, the great scenario writer! [FORBES *looks up, puzzled and annoyed.* BILL *is merely puzzled.* VAN DYCK *is politely interested.* GORDON *is all but crazy with apprehension.* MRS. FORBES *is quite in her element.* DULCY *passes* LEACH *over towards* MRS. FORBES] Mrs. Forbes, Angela's stepmother!

LEACH [*enthusiastically*]. Oh, how do you do!

DULCY. And *Mr.* Forbes, her real father! [FORBES *rises slowly — his dislike has been immediate and intense.* LEACH *does all the bowing*] And Mr. Van Dyck! [*They bow*] You've met Gordon, haven't you? [LEACH *shakes* GORDON's *hand*] And my brother, Willie.

BILL. Parker — William.

DULCY [ANGELA *and* STERRETT *appear in the windows*]. Oh, here she is! Well — [*She leads* ANGELA *down to* LEACH]

ANGELA. Why, Mr. Leach!

LEACH. *Miss* Forbes!

STERRETT [*with cold emphasis*]. How do you do, Leach?

LEACH. Oh, how are you?

DULCY. Didn't I tell you I'd have a surprise for you?

FORBES [*to* ANGELA, *as she stands with her hand still in* LEACH's, *to* STERRETT's *great annoyance*]. Oh, then you've met Mr. Leach before?

ANGELA. Oh, yes!

DULCY. Why, didn't you know about it? Mr. Leach showed us through his studio the other day. He almost kidnapped your Angela, and made a motion picture star out of her.

FORBES [*not quite succeeding in being pleasant about it*]. Oh, is that so?

DULCY. We saw his new picture being taken. Oh, tell us about it, Mr. Leach! [*Whispering loudly to everyone*] Mr. Leach is a scenario writer — a scenario writer.

LEACH [*correcting her*]. If you will pardon me, not scenario writer — scenarist — really.

BILL [*in mock comprehension*]. Oh, scenarist!

LEACH. It's the more modern term. The scenarist of to-day is quite different from the scenario writer of yesterday.

DULCY [*in her element*]. Mr. Leach says the motion picture business is still in its infancy.

LEACH. The surface has hardly been scratched. The possibilities are enormous, and the demand for new people — new writers — [*He turns to* MRS. FORBES] Oh! Mrs. Smith tells me that *you* are writing for the films, my dear Mrs. Forbes!

MRS. FORBES. Well, I'm — trying to —

LEACH. Well, you go on writing — don't give up — don't let anyone discourage you. [FORBES *turns away with a mild attack of apoplexy*] That was my experience. I just kept on and on until — well, you see.

BILL. What?

DULCY [*in a quick aside*]. You shut up, Willie!

LEACH [*to* MRS. FORBES]. Yes, you just keep on writing. [*Then generously taking them all in*] All of you — and go and see the pictures. See them and see them and see them. [*To* MRS.

FORBES *and* VAN DYCK] Study them! [*To* MR. FORBES] Learn how they're made! Now in my last picture, *The Sacred Love* — you've all seen that, I take it?

DULCY. Oh, yes — a wonderful picture!

MRS. FORBES. Yes!

ANGELA. I saw it twice. Once with you, Tom.

STERRETT. Was *that* his picture?

LEACH. There were some points in that — did you see it, Mr. Forbes?

FORBES [*wild within*]. No, I — I don't believe I did.

LEACH. Really! You must come to one of our trade showings at the Hotel Astor —

FORBES. What?

LEACH. Just a moment. [*Consults note-book*] At the Hotel Astor, next Tuesday, at 3:30. Of course, it's — it's only a little thing. We're going to do some big things later. The possibilities —

BILL [*ever helpful*]. Are enormous.

LEACH [*falling for it*]. Oh, *very* big . . . you'd be surprised! Yes, we're going to do some of Shakespeare's things next.

DULCY. Shakespeare's? Well — [*Her arms are around her husband's shoulders and she shakes him to pick up the cue*]

GORDON [*coming to*]. Really!

LEACH. Yes, I'm at work on his continuity now. I was telling my director yesterday — I said, you know, Shakespeare had a tremendous feeling for plot. Of course, the dialogue is stilted for modern audiences — but then, you don't have to listen to that in the pictures. But he's still the master.

DULCY. He's going to organize his own company next.

BILL. Who — Shakespeare?

DULCY. No, Willie! Mr. Leach.

LEACH. Yes — the Vincent Leach Productions, Inc. The stock will be placed on the open market very soon.

DULCY. Mr. Van Dyck can tell you how to do it! He owns lots of moving picture companies — don't you, Mr. Van Dyck?

LEACH. Is that so?

VAN DYCK [*modestly, as always*]. Well, I'm interested — in a small way.

LEACH. I'd enjoy talking to you about it later. [*To* MR. FORBES] And how about you, Mr. Forbes? Didn't

I hear that *you* were interested in pictures?

FORBES [*turning away and smothering the line*]. I don't care a damn about pictures.

LEACH [*not believing his ears*]. What's that?

FORBES. I said, I make jewelry.

LEACH. Well, of course, that's very necessary too, in its way. [FORBES' *mouth opens* — GORDON *rises hurriedly*]

GORDON. Dulcy!

DULCY. Ah — let's play a rubber of bridge before dinner! It's so nice and soothing. [*Patting* LEACH *for fear he has been offended*] Let me see — [*To* MR. FORBES] Mr. Forbes, you play bridge, don't you?

FORBES. No, I'm afraid not.

DULCY. Oh, yes, you do — you're just modest. Mr. Forbes — [*She is picking the card players out with cool intent*] And Mr. Sterrett — and Gordon — And I'll make the fourth. Mr. Leach. [*He is absorbed in* ANGELA] Mr. Leach. [*He turns*] Why don't you and Angela go out on the lawn and see the view?

GORDON. Dulcy, dear —

DULCY. Where the Japanese garden is going to be?

ANGELA [*giving* LEACH *her hand*]. Come on, Vincent.

LEACH [*putting her arm through his*]. Yes, I'd love to see you framed against the glowing splendor of a twilit garden.

[ANGELA *and* LEACH *go out through the window*]

BILL. My golly, the man even makes love in subtitles!

FORBES. I'll see if my car is still in the garage. I'll come back — I think. [*He goes out through the window*]

GORDON [*to* DULCY]. Now, now, you see — [*He goes out quickly after* FORBES]

BILL [*up in the windows*]. You know, this is probably going to be the first week-end party on record that ended on Friday night. [*He departs, lugubriously*]

STERRETT. I think I'll go back to my book.

DULCY [*somewhat weakly*]. We'll be starting the game in a minute, Mr. Sterrett. [STERRETT *disappears*] Well, I'll get the bridge things. [*She turns in the doorway* — *only* MRS. FORBES *and* VAN DYCK *are left on the stage*] Two's company and three's a crowd! [*She goes*]

Mrs. Forbes [*rising with a self-conscious laugh*]. I must go and dress for dinner.

Van Dyck. Oh, please don't go — I've been wanting to have a chat with you. I've been hearing all about you this afternoon.

Mrs. Forbes. All about me? From whom?

Van Dyck. Mrs. Smith.

Mrs. Forbes. Oh!

Van Dyck. So you see, I was prepared to be interested — even before I met you.

Mrs. Forbes [*sitting*]. And now the disappointment?

Van Dyck [*sitting beside her*]. Oh, far from it. I find you even more interesting than I had anticipated. You have depths.

Mrs. Forbes. Are you going to — fathom them?

Van Dyck. If I may.

Mrs. Forbes. And how are you going about it? [Forbes *is seen strolling behind the windows at back*].

Van Dyck. That's *my* secret. But tell me, first — you've been married just a short time?

Mrs. Forbes. Not so short — four years. Why? [Forbes *comes down into window; sees and hears*]

Van Dyck. Mrs. Smith tells me that you are becoming quite a novelist.

Mrs. Forbes. Oh, but I'm not yet. I only —

Forbes. Is that you, Eleanor? [Van Dyck *rises*]

Mrs. Forbes. Yes, dear.

Forbes. Oh!

Van Dyck. I shall see you later, I hope.

Mrs. Forbes. I hope.

Van Dyck [*attempting to relieve the tension*]. I suppose you get a good many ideas for your writings from your husband? [*The tension is not relieved.* Van Dyck *departs through windows*]

Forbes [*looking from* Van Dyck *to his wife*]. Well!

Mrs. Forbes [*rises*]. Well?

Forbes. What did *that* mean?

Mrs. Forbes. Why, nothing!

Forbes. Isn't it enough to have Angela go prancing off with that — brainless — conceited — motion picture jack-ass?

Mrs. Forbes. Mr. Leach, do you mean? Why, he's a charming man, and very successful.

Forbes. Bah! And on top of it, I come in here and find you — spooning with Van Dyck.

Mrs. Forbes. Why, Charlie — how can you say such a thing!

Forbes. My God, didn't I see it!

Mrs. Forbes. But, Charlie, dear —

Forbes. I tell you this whole place is going to drive me crazy! I didn't want to come here anyhow! I had a backache, and I wanted to stay home and rest.

Mrs. Forbes. But you couldn't refuse —

Forbes. And instead of that I've got to get up at some ungodly hour in the morning and go out and play golf. If there is one thing I hate more than anything else in this world, it's golf — unless it's bridge or moving pictures!

Mrs. Forbes. Now, Charlie, dear — when you're here as a guest —

Forbes. If I could think of a good excuse, I'd go back to town to-night with Sterrett, and take Angela and you with me.

Mrs. Forbes [*alarmed*]. But, Charlie, you can't do that when —

Forbes. Don't you suppose I see that woman's plan to throw Angela and that — that film thing together!

Mrs. Forbes. But I tell you he's a most charming man.

Forbes. And I tell you, if it weren't for Smith and our business relations I would go back to-night!

Mrs. Forbes. But, Charlie — you can't be so rude!

[*Enter* Gordon]

Forbes. Sh! That reminds me — Oh, Smith!

Gordon. Yes, sir.

Forbes. Mr. Smith, Mrs. Smith has been telling me something of your other business activities.

Gordon. Other business activities? Why —

Forbes. And it came as something of a revelation to me.

Gordon. But Mrs. Smith couldn't have meant — [Van Dyck *returns and joins* Mrs. Forbes]

Forbes. As you may have been aware, my agreement to admit you on a sixteen and two-thirds basis was founded on the expectation that you would give all your time to the new enterprise.

Gordon. Yes, of course, Mr. Forbes.

Forbes. In the circumstances your business and your services would hardly be worth that amount to me.

GORDON. But, my dear Mr. Forbes — you — you don't understand. Mrs. Smith — [*Enter* DULCY, *bubbling over*]

DULCY. Oh here are the bridge players! Come right in, Mr. Sterrett. [*Enter* STERRETT *and* HENRY, *carrying the card table*] Henry, put the table right here. You know, I hope you men don't mind playing with me — I'm not very good. I always say I don't really play bridge, I play *at* it. But I do love it, and after all, that's what counts, isn't it?

FORBES [*worn out*]. Yes.

DULCY. That's right, Henry, put the chairs around. Now, I think Mr. Sterrett will sit there. [*Indicating chair opposite her*] I shall sit here. Let's see — that makes you my partner, Mr. Sterrett. You don't mind, do you?

STERRETT [*beyond minding anything*]. Not at all. [STERRETT *takes one final look out the windows after* ANGELA]

DULCY [*to* FORBES]. He *had* to say that. You know I'm an awfully unlucky player — I never have a finesse go right. Well, unlucky at cards — lucky at love — [*Turning to* GORDON] Lucky at love, Gordie, darling. You're here, of course. [GORDON *is evidently worrying about what* DULCY *could have said to* FORBES. FORBES *keeps turning uneasily for a sight of his wife and* VAN DYCK. DULCY *starts to deal*] Now look at me — I'm dealing when I ought to be shuffling! [*She gathers up the cards and shuffles awkwardly*] Come along, Mr. Sterrett! We're going to beat them! Bring that chair. [STERRETT *starts to follow her directions. Three more miserable men have never been seen*] Is everybody happy? [*The curtain starts slowly down*] Somebody tell me — which is higher — a heart or a spade? I never can remember. And do you discard from strength or weakness, Mr. Sterrett? Of course it doesn't matter — [*She continues her chatter, as*

THE CURTAIN FALLS

ACT II

The scene is the same as Act I; the time is immediately after dinner, on the same day. Although it is evening, the French windows at the rear still stand open. The stage is in semi-darkness — only one or two of the lamps are lighted — but a shaft of moonlight shoots through the windows. The dining room, at the left, is brilliantly lighted, and the chatter of many people, with the clink of glasses and the occasional scrape of a chair, can be distinctly heard. For an appreciable period after the rise of the curtain only the sound of this merry gathering can be heard. Over the others the voice of VINCENT LEACH *rings out clearly* — "I said to Mr. Breitenstein, 'Don't you worry about those German films.'" *Then the babble drowns his further remarks.*

DULCY, *resplendent in a golden evening dress, presently enters, peering back as though expecting someone to follow her. She beckons excitedly to someone in the other room, and* MRS. FORBES *enters.*

DULCY [*in excited tones*]. Isn't he wonderful?

MRS. FORBES [*also flushed with excitement*]. Who?

DULCY. Vincent Leach! [*Banteringly*] Ah, you thought I meant Mr. Van Dyck, didn't you? Ah, ha!

MRS. FORBES [*confused*]. Why — I didn't know —

DULCY. Now, now! It doesn't take a brick wall to fall on *me*. But seriously, he's mad about her!

MRS. FORBES [*with just a touch of apprehension*]. Do you really think so?

DULCY. And she hasn't taken her eyes off him since he arrived! I tell you, they're in love!

MRS. FORBES [*looking off*]. There *is* — something about him. The only thing is —

DULCY. I wouldn't be surprised if they became engaged — right here in my house. Wouldn't that be nice, after my bringing them together?

MRS. FORBES. But you're sure it's all right — positive that Mr. Leach is —

DULCY. Of course, I am — he's just the man for Angela. Ssh! Here's Mr. Sterrett! [*The two women draw up against the wall as* STERRETT *enters. His hands are deep in his pockets, and he is sore. He looks back as he enters, then starts across the room. A few steps further he looks back again, as* ANGELA'S *laugh is heard. He stalks out the windows.* DULCY *titters*] He's mad! Let's see what happened! [ANGELA *comes running on. She is happily excited, being pursued.* LEACH *follows her, capturing her at the piano, and holding her with her back toward him, giving* MRS. FORBES *and* DULCY *a chance to escape into the dining room unseen*]

LEACH. Now I've got you!

ANGELA. And what are you going to do with me?

LEACH [*turning her around*]. I'm going to tell you — how wonderful you are.

ANGELA [*liking it*]. Oh, my!

LEACH. You are! You're like a beautiful warm dawn — just your magic presence — [VAN DYCK *and* MRS. FORBES *stroll on together*]

ANGELA [*stopping* LEACH]. Ssh!

VAN DYCK. But surely if one has a talent it should be developed.

ANGELA. Shall we sit down? [LEACH *makes a gesture towards the chairs by the piano*] Oh, not there — here. [*She bounces over to the stairs and sits behind the hydrangeas.* LEACH *takes his place beside her*]

MRS. FORBES [*convinced by now she is a potential George Sand*]. But I'm afraid I'm just a dabbler and always will be.

VAN DYCK [*sitting beside her*]. Ah, but I'm sure you're wrong! You must be wrong.

[*Enter* FORBES *and* GORDON. *All of the men, except* STERRETT, *are in evening clothes*]

FORBES. Well, as a straight business proposition I must say — [*He sees his wife with* VAN DYCK, *and stops short*] Huh! [VAN DYCK *gets up from the easy chair*]

VAN DYCK. Sit here, Mr. Forbes.

FORBES. No, thank you. I prefer a stiff chair.

GORDON. Here you are, Mr. Forbes.

[*Enter* BILL]

BILL. Everybody ready for a nice musical evening?

[STERRETT, *still sulking, comes in silently through the French windows.* DULCY *enters at the same time, and immediately takes characteristic charge of the situation*]

DULCY. Well, this is going to be jolly, isn't it? Let's have a little light on the subject. [*She switches on the lights*] Let me see — Yes, everybody's here. [MRS. FORBES, *anxious to relieve the tension maintained by her husband, leaves* VAN DYCK *and follows* DULCY. DULCY *puts her arm around*

her] I love a big house and lots of company. If only it were a winter night, we could gather around the fireplace and tell ghost stories. [FORBES *has made up his mind to sit and has headed for the stiff chair.* DULCY *seizes him*] Oh, no, Mr. Forbes — you must take the easy chair — that's for you — yes. [*She pulls him across to it*]

FORBES [*cursing the conventions of chivalry*]. But I really would rather — that is —

DULCY. Now, not a word — I know you're polite and want to leave it for me, but I insist on your having it. [GORDON *tries to head her off but his efforts are unavailing.* DULCY *forces* MR. FORBES *into the chair*] I wouldn't dream of anyone else's having it but you. Now sit right in it — that's right — way back! It's awfully comfortable — just the thing after eating. [MRS. FORBES *has seated herself;* VAN DYCK *is entertaining her*] It'll rest you for to-morrow — for your horseback riding.

FORBES [*in great alarm*]. Horseback!

DULCY. Yes, didn't you hear us talking about it? In the afternoon. We're making up a party to go to the Sound and you're in it. [*Enter* HENRY *with coffee, on a tea wagon. He pushes it across to* DULCY] Well, who's for coffee? Coffee — coffee! [BILL *has wandered over to the piano and has seated himself.* DULCY *pours*] It's a lovely ride to the Sound. You'll go, won't you, Mr. Van Dyck?

VAN DYCK [*with* MRS. FORBES] What's that? Oh, yes — yes, indeed.

DULCY [*whispering*]. You and Mrs. Forbes can go together. [FORBES *turns around to locate his wife and daughter*] I'll ride with *Mr.* Forbes. Here you are, Henry. [HENRY *serves*]

GORDON [*to* FORBES]. Now this was what I wanted to show you. These are our Number Three's; we are turning these out at an extremely low price, and the German formula can't touch them. Just examine these. [FORBES *puts on glasses and does so.* HENRY *returns for two more coffees; he offers one to* FORBES, *who refuses*]

DULCY. We're going to have a lovely day for it to-morrow. Did you see that sunset? Angela, you and Mr. Leach are to go along, too. And Mr. Sterrett — where is that Mr. Sterrett?

STERRETT [*behind her*]. I'm here.

DULCY. Oh! There you are! I'd almost forgotten you.

STERRETT [*submerged in gloom*]. That's all right.

DULCY. It's too bad you can't stay over, Mr. Sterrett. I'm sure you'd enjoy it. [HENRY *serves* ANGELA *and* LEACH, *who both accept. His offers to* BILL *and* STERRETT *are refused*] You know, the paper says rain for to-morrow, but it's always wrong. I have the worst luck with the weather whenever I go any place. When I take my umbrella it never rains, and if I don't take it — [BILL *has started on a solo of "Chop Sticks" as an anodyne*] Come away from the piano, Willie. . . . Mr. Van Dyck is going to play us something — aren't you, Mr. Van Dyck?

VAN DYCK. Why — ah — a little later. [BILL *starts another one-finger solo*]

GORDON. If you'll examine those you'll see that they are the same grain and luster as the Hammond Number Six.

DULCY. Oh, do stop, Willie!

FORBES. Mmm. [*A pause*] Angela! [*There is no answer*] Angela! !

ANGELA [*coming to*]. Yes, father.

FORBES. Just let me see those pearls of yours for a minute, will you?

ANGELA. Yes, father. [ANGELA *and* LEACH *rise.* LEACH *reaches as if to remove the pearls, but* ANGELA *hands him her coffee instead and removes the pearls herself.* HENRY *steps up to* ANGELA *to relieve her of the pearls. She gives them to him.* BILL *strikes a bass note three or four times in warning, rising as he does so.* DULCY *and* GORDON *rise, their eyes on* HENRY. HENRY *gives the pearls to* FORBES; DULCY *gives a huge sigh of relief.* ANGELA *and* LEACH *resume their seat on the bench again.* BILL *sits again at piano. Quiet is restored*]

DULCY. Are you ready now, Mr. Van Dyck — it's your turn!

VAN DYCK. Oh, really, I — I don't think that I should play. Mr. Forbes and your husband would much prefer to discuss jewelry, I'm sure.

DULCY. Oh, no, they wouldn't! Would you, Mr. Forbes? [*He is studying the necklace*] Mr. Forbes!

FORBES [*looking up*]. Huh?

DULCY. Wouldn't you like to hear Mr. Van Dyck play the piano?

FORBES. Oh, yes — yes.

DULCY. You see — and I know Mrs. Forbes wants you to play — don't you, dear?

MRS. FORBES. Oh, yes.

DULCY. And *I* do! And Willie — [*Another solo of* BILL's *is obtruding*] Get away from the piano, Willie — and Mr. Sterrett. Now, Mr. Van Dyck —

VAN DYCK. Well, if you insist. [VAN DYCK *seats himself and starts to play. The selection is the Chopin Prelude, Op. 28, No. 4*]

DULCY [*seated*]. What was that little thing you played at Mrs. Kennedy's this afternoon? [*She listens.* GORDON *and* FORBES *are discussing jewelry in low tones*] No — that wasn't it. It's lovely, though. Carries me right away [GORDON *and* FORBES *become audible.* Quiet everybody — quiet! [*After a look at her they lower their tones, but not enough to satisfy* DULCY] Ssh! [*She rattles some noisy bracelets.* FORBES *turns and looks at her.* DULCY *giggles at him*] Oh, Mr. Forbes! I thought it was my husband. [DULCY's *wandering eyes light upon a box of candy, the wrapping still on it. She makes a weak attempt to turn her eyes away from it and then picks it up and tears off its paper noisily, whispering across to* MRS. FORBES] Candy that Mr. Leach brought! Yes — wasn't it nice of him? [*She removes cover and ribbon, opens box and offers some to* MRS. FORBES *and* STERRETT *in hoarse whisper*] Take some! [*They signal refusal. She reaches it towards* FORBES] Want some candy, Mr. Forbes? [FORBES *looks around, but does not understand.* DULCY *creeps across to him*] Some candy? Sherry's! Delicious! Molasses! [*She is heavily sibilant.* FORBES, *unable to hear, leans toward her. She reaches the box further toward him. After seeing the candy he refuses*]

FORBES. No, no, thank you. [*Returns to his chair.* GORDON *coughs and is hushed.* DULCY *takes a piece of candy from the box and tastes it; does not like it, looks about to make sure no one is observing — replaces it.* BILL *rises, comes down and selects two pieces*]

DULCY. Ssh!

BILL [*whispering*]. What?

DULCY. Ssh! [*The music suddenly stops.* DULCY *drops candy and applauds*]

BILL. Ssh! [*The music begins again*]

DULCY [*in a whisper to* MRS. FORBES]. I thought he had finished. [VAN DYCK *strikes the remaining chords.* DULCY *rises*] Lovely! ! [*Long drawn out*]

MRS. FORBES. It was adorable!

ANGELA. I loved it.

LEACH. It was—beautiful. It made
me think of Araby and the moon-soaked
desert. [*He loses himself in the desert
for a second*] Did you see *The Virgin of
Stamboul?*

BILL [*promptly*]. No.

DULCY. No — I don't believe I did,
either.

LEACH. That's too bad. You know,
some of *my* new picture is being laid
in the desert, and that would be wonderful music for it.

DULCY [*getting an inspiration*]. Oh!

BILL. What's the matter?

DULCY. I have an idea. [BILL *moves
toward the door*] Why not have Mr.
Leach tell us the story of his new picture,
while Mr. Van Dyck plays the music for
us?

GORDON [*springing up*]. But — but,
Dulcy —

DULCY. It'll be just like a moving-
picture theatre!

LEACH [*with fake modesty*]. Oh, but
really — I don't think that I should —
of course, it *would* be interesting.

ANGELA. Oh, please tell it, Vincent!
[*She gives a look at* STERRETT]

STERRETT. Yes, do! [*Turns away*]

MRS. FORBES. I'd love to hear it,
and so would my husband. [*She
throws her husband a look*]

DULCY. Well, now you can't refuse.

LEACH [*with no thought of refusing*].
Since you demand it.

DULCY. Oh, good! Now everybody
take their places! Mr. Van Dyck,
you go back to the piano! [*They all
take seats*] Mr. Leach, you tell him
what kind of music you want! [BILL
stands motionless and noiseless] Be
quiet, Willie. Now, I'll sit here.

BILL. Mr. Leach. [*A pause*] How
many reels is this picture?

LEACH. There are eight! [BILL
sinks into his chair] It's an extra-
super-feature, not released on the regular program!

BILL. How long does each reel
take?

LEACH. Oh, about fifteen minutes.

FORBES [*looks up*]. Two hours?

BILL. To tell it?

LEACH. Oh, no, to show it. I can
give you what *we* call an outline in
half an hour — well, three-quarters at
the most.

BILL. That's much better — three-
quarters. That's fine!

DULCY. Now keep quiet, Willie, or

he won't tell it. What's the name of
the picture, Mr. Leach?

GORDON [*striking match*]. We can
have a smoke, anyhow.

FORBES. Thanks.

LEACH [*with a winning smile*]. Of
course, I must have absolute silence.
[FORBES *looks at him*]

DULCY. Of course. Tell us the
name of it. [GORDON *lights his own,
and, as* FORBES *is about to turn for his
light*, LEACH *protests amiably*]

LEACH. I shall have to concentrate,
and if there are any distractions —

DULCY [*hastily*]. There won't be
any — tell us the name of it.

BILL. Ask him what it's called.

DULCY. Shut up, Willie!

LEACH [*waiting a moment until everyone
is quiet*]. The name of the picture —

DULCY [*lifting an arm, and thus rattling
her bracelets*]. Quiet, everybody!

LEACH. Is — *Sin*. [*This to the men*]
Sin. [*To the women*]

DULCY [*doing her bit*]. *Sin*. [VAN
DYCK *starts the Rachmaninoff Prelude.*
LEACH *steps up and stops him*]

LEACH. Not yet. And when I'm
ready, just a soft accompaniment.
[*Starting with enthusiasm*] This is really
something quite new in films. I am
going to show Sin — throughout the
ages.

DULCY [*with anticipation*]. Well!

LEACH. In the beginning the picture
is symbolic. I open with a quotation
from Hawthorne — [*For the men's
benefit*] Nathaniel Hawthorne.

BILL [*raising his hand*]. Who's the
director and the cameraman?

DULCY. Willie!

LEACH [*squelching him*]. The director
is Frank Heming Stratton.

BILL. Oh! [BILL *prepares for as
comfortable a nap as possible*]

LEACH. It begins — with the setting out — of Noah's Ark. [LEACH *signals* VAN DYCK, *who starts "Sailing,
Sailing."* LEACH *considers the music for
a second, decides it will do, and continues*]
We see Noah, a man of advanced years.
His wife, his sons, the animals — of
each of its kind two. We see the Ark
setting out upon its journey — we see
the waters rise and rise and rise. For
forty days it rains. [VAN DYCK *changes
to "Rustle of Spring"*] Civilization is
all but wiped out — it is kept alive —
and SIN is kept alive — only in the Ark.
[*At "Sin"* VAN DYCK *changes to "Kiss
Me Again"*]

DULCY [*in hoarse whisper to* MRS. FORBES]. "Kiss me again."

LEACH. Then comes a calm — [VAN DYCK *changes to* "*Morning Mood*" (*Grieg*)] The dove is sent forth — it returns, unable to find a lighting place. [*Suiting action to the word,* FORBES *strikes a noisy match and lights his cigar, unmindful of* LEACH'*s glare*] And then a second dove — and *it* returns — and then a third — and it does not return — for somewhere in the great beyond it had found LAND. [*A quick signal to* VAN DYCK] LAND! [VAN DYCK *goes loudly into* "*My Country 'Tis of Thee.*" DULCY *automatically rises, ever patriotic.* LEACH *is about to begin again, looks at her surprised.* DULCY *giggles her apology, then sits.* LEACH *continues as the curtain slowly falls*] Many years pass — we are now at King Solomon's Court — his wives are bathing in the fountain — [*The curtain remains down for a few seconds to indicate the passing of thirty minutes. As the curtain rises,* LEACH*, somewhat dishevelled, is still talking.* BILL *is asleep in his chair,* STERRETT *asleep in his chair.* GORDON *has fallen asleep in a sitting posture as though he had attempted to be a perfect host but failed.* FORBES *is the one man wide-awake. He is chewing the stump of a cigar viciously, breathing heavily and seems to be wondering how many seconds he can stand it before he commits murder.* VAN DYCK*, at the piano, looks exhausted, and by this time is contributing only an occasional chord.* MRS. FORBES*,* ANGELA *and* DULCY *are still* "*eating it up*"]

LEACH [*talking as the curtain rises*]. Frances rushes to the edge of the cliff, and, looking over, sees an inert, lifeless form. The "Weasel" is dead. [LEACH *pantomimes his excuses hurriedly and takes a drink from a glass of water on the piano.* HENRY *enters to clear away the coffee cups*]

DULCY. Not yet, Henry! How many times — [HENRY *departs with a shrug*] Yes, Mr. Leach, the Weasel is dead —

LEACH [*picking up the story*]. And then — then the Zeppelin and Jack's automobile go into the final stretch neck and neck. On — on they speed! We get another close-up of Jack in the driver's seat! We see his face — tense — and putting into the car everything that he has, he forges — slowly — slowly ahead! Then more and more! The goal is nearer and nearer! Back

in New York, Charley is seen leavin[g] the Chinese Restaurant! On the corne[r] he meets Fanny, who throws the money in his face. [*For emphasis he touche[s]* FORBES' *arm.* FORBES *jumps*] The[n] flash back to Jack — nearer and neare[r] — HE WINS. [BILL *is rudely awakene[d] and springs up*]

BILL. What?

LEACH [*explaining*]. He wins! [BILL *returns to his chair and nap wit[h] the manner of a man annoyed at being called too early.* VAN DYCK *strikes [a] chord*] Gradually he stops. The Zep[-] pelin makes a landing. Coralie get[s] out of the dirigible and rushes to Jac[k] to forgive him. Just as he takes he[r] in his arms, her father arrives with th[e] afternoon paper, which makes every[-] thing clear and vindicates Albert[.] Then the father clasps Jack's hand an[d] apologizes to him for having though[t] him the thief. And, to keep the sym[-] bolism to the end, just as Jack kisse[s] Coralie there in Chicago, Marc Anton[y] is shown kissing Cleopatra in Ancien[t] Egypt and George Washington kissin[g] Martha Washington at Mt. Vernon[.] And so, at the end of the Dream Trai[l,] we fade into a long shot of Jack and Coralie, once more in their South Sea[s] bungalow, with the faithful old Toot[a] Heva waiting to greet them in the sun[-] set — and fade out. [VAN DYCK *fin[-] ishes with a loud chord. The women rise.* LEACH *rushes to them, his hands out[-] stretched, anticipating their congratula[-] tions. The women take his hands, chat[-] tering.* VAN DYCK *gets up, raising hi[s] arms and exercising his fingers.* BILL *awakes and rises, but finds his foo[t] asleep. He gradually wakes himself up by some shakes and half-exercises, and awakens* GORDON*, who also has to ex[-] ercise and stretch his legs and arms.* STERRETT *likewise awakes.* FORBES *has risen and holds his back.* HENRY *en[-] ters, clears the cups and saucers, and goes again*]

DULCY [*when the excitement has died down a little*]. Oh, that was the most wonderful picture I ever saw! [*The women echo this*] I mean heard! Eight marvelous reels!

BILL. What a picture! My God, what a picture! [*He slips away*]

FORBES [*through his teeth*]. And now, Eleanor, they might enjoy hearing one of *your* scenarios. In fact, I'm going upstairs and get one!

MRS. FORBES. Charlie — you —

ou're not really going to get one of
mine!

FORBES. So help me God! [*He
starts up;* DULCY *stops him at the foot of
the staircase*]

DULCY. Mr. Forbes, wouldn't you
like to play a game of billiards?

GORDON. Ah! Now, that's fine!

FORBES. Why, yes, I'm very, very
fond of billiards!

DULCY. There, you see, Gordon,
darling!

FORBES. I didn't know you had a
billiard table.

DULCY. Why, yes, a wonderful one!

GORDON [*indicating the door*]. Downstairs.

VAN DYCK. That sounds interesting.
May I look on?

[GORDON *has gone to* DULCY *and squeezed
her hand in appreciation*]

GORDON [*at door*]. This way, Mr.
Forbes.

FORBES. Good God, why didn't you
mention billiards earlier! [VAN DYCK,
GORDON, *and* FORBES *depart*]

DULCY [*to* MRS. FORBES]. I think it's
good for the men to get off by themselves
once in a while — they seem to like it.
Besides, I wanted to talk to you. Angela dear, why don't you and Mr. Leach
go out for a stroll in the moonlight?
It's a wonderful night, in the moonlight.

ANGELA. Yes, let's!

LEACH. The moonlight! I would
adore it!

MRS. FORBES. You'd better put on
a wrap, Angela.

ANGELA. Oh, mother, it isn't cold.
[ANGELA *and* LEACH *stroll off, arm in
arm*]

STERRETT [*taking the pretty rough hint*].
I guess I'll watch the billiard game.
[*He goes. The two women sit down.*
DULCY *takes the box of candy from the
piano and puts it on a stool between them.
They eat and talk*]

DULCY. Isn't everything going beautifully?

MRS. FORBES. Ah — yes.

DULCY. I think Mr. Forbes is beginning to like Vincent, too.

MRS. FORBES. Do you?

DULCY. Don't you? Didn't you
see his face — so tense and excited while
Mr. Leach was telling his story?
Wasn't it nice, with Mr. Van Dyck
playing the piano?

MRS. FORBES. He plays awfully
well.

DULCY. Has he said anything to
you?

MRS. FORBES. Who?

DULCY. Mr. Van Dyck, of course.
Anybody can see he's attracted to you
— he's an awfully nice man, and he's
one of *the* Van Dycks of Newport — if
you ever want to go there.

MRS. FORBES. Oh, *is* he?

DULCY. Yes, I could fix it for you.

[GORDON *and* FORBES *return. They
have removed their coats*]

GORDON. Dulcy, dear, where did
you put those billiard balls?

DULCY. The what? [VAN DYCK
comes back]

FORBES. The — billiard balls! It's
— a little difficult to play billiards without them.

DULCY. Oh, the billiard balls!

GORDON. Yes.

DULCY. Did you look in the pockets?

GORDON [*sadly*]. There are no pockets on a billiard table.

FORBES [*willing to let the whole world
go hang*]. What's the difference —
what's the difference?

DULCY. Maybe I did put them some
place — now, wait — I wonder if I
could have — no — I put the curtains
there. [*A pause*] I'll come right away
and look for them. I think I know
where they are. Gordie, you and Mr.
Forbes come with me. [VAN DYCK
starts to improvise on the piano] That's
right, Mr. Van Dyck — you keep *Mrs.*
Forbes company. [*To* FORBES] I'm
awfully sorry about those balls. You
know, sometimes I think I'd lose my
head if it wasn't fastened on. [*She
goes, carrying* FORBES *and her husband
with her*]

MRS. FORBES. We can go along and
watch them play, if you like.

VAN DYCK [*still playing*]. Do you
want to?

MRS. FORBES. Not particularly.

VAN DYCK. Then let's don't.

MRS. FORBES [*listening to the music*].
That's pretty.

VAN DYCK. I would much rather
talk to you.

MRS. FORBES. A clever man can
do both.

VAN DYCK. But I'm not clever.

MRS. FORBES. You're at least modest.

VAN DYCK [*playing all through this
speech*]. No — I'm not even that. The
downright truth is — I'm embarrassed

by opportunities. Here I have a moment alone with you — you're perfectly willing to be entertained. If I could play at all well — which I can't — I should dash off something brilliant — now. And if I could talk well, which I can't, I should simply scintillate — for you. But, you see — I'm just mediocre. [*A pause. He continues to play*] Perhaps I wouldn't be quite so annoyed with myself if it weren't for you.

MRS. FORBES. But you're doing splendidly. You have a most respectful audience.

VAN DYCK [*stopping playing abruptly*]. Oh, please, not that! You know you're — charming.

MRS. FORBES. And just what is — a charming woman?

VAN DYCK. A charming woman? She's the one I never met until she's married someone else.

MRS. FORBES. You're incorrigible. Play something more.

VAN DYCK. Oh, no. [*He rises*] I don't feel like playing. What do you say to a stroll?

MRS. FORBES. I'd like it. I've not been out since dinner.

VAN DYCK. It's pleasant here, isn't it?

MRS. FORBES. Yes, isn't it?

VAN DYCK. I have a little place like this in the East — in Abyssinia. The moonlight comes down through the trees — have you ever been in Africa?

MRS. FORBES. No. [*They start out through the windows*]

VAN DYCK. You should go to Africa. I have some diamond interests —

[*They stroll out. HENRY enters, takes a glance around the room, and arranges the cushions on the divan. As he is replacing the one on the end his eyes fall upon something in the easy chair. He picks up ANGELA's necklace, which FORBES had dropped, thinking he was putting it in his pocket. HENRY, in a matter-of-fact way, puts it in his own pocket and goes up the stairs. ANGELA and LEACH enter through the windows. ANGELA is considerably excited*]

ANGELA. It *was* cool, wasn't it?

LEACH. Was it?

ANGELA. Weren't you?

LEACH. No — I was — afire — afire with love for you, Angela.

ANGELA. Why, what are you saying?

LEACH. Oh, those deep burning eyes! The mystery of your hair, Angela, you're wonderful! I love you! Almost from the first moment I saw you, I've loved you — wanted you — longed for you! Why, I patterned my newest heroine just after you! To be with you is to breathe the perfume of exaltation! Angela!

ANGELA [*breathlessly*]. Vincent!

LEACH. I am offering you myself — everything that I am — Oh, it's true that I've knocked about some — [*Modestly*] A good many girls have loved me, but I have never loved any but you, dearest. [*He kneels*] Say that you love me — a little — even though that love is now no greater than the glow of a single firefly in the fading day!

ANGELA [*rising*]. Oh, Vincent — my genius!

LEACH. My sweetheart! [*He kisses her and then holds her off, looking at her*] My wonder girl! Will you marry me [ANGELA's *head drops in assent*] And the day? [*Embracing her again*] Love cries for its own!

ANGELA. Whenever you say — Vincent.

LEACH [*getting an idea*]. Why not — ah — but you wouldn't!

ANGELA. What?

LEACH. Why not now — to-day — to-night?

ANGELA. To-night?

LEACH. Yes — why not — elope!

ANGELA [*pleased*]. Elope! [*Sober*] Oh, but mother and father —

LEACH. I am thinking of them. Your father would not understand.

ANGELA. Don't you think so?

LEACH. No! He doesn't know how our hearts cry for each other!

ANGELA. But he might never —

LEACH. Darling, since the beginning of Time hearts have been broken because they were not brave. And think how romantic it would be — you and I stealing away in the night — just we two — together. [*He draws her to him, they embrace again*]

ANGELA. Oh, Vincent!

LEACH. Angela, dear!

ANGELA. And we'd not tell anybody? [*Withdrawing a bit from him*] Oh, Vincent, I'd have to! Mother and —

LEACH [*quickly*]. But not your father!

ANGELA [*hesitant*]. No, I shan't tell father. But, mother — and Mrs. Smith. We'll need her.

LEACH. Just think of it, Angela — you and I eloping! [*They embrace again*] Won't the world be surprised!

[*Enter* DULCY]

DULCY. Oh, excuse me. [*They break — embarrassed*] I haven't interrupted anything, have I? [*Hoping to God she has*]

LEACH. Why — no.

ANGELA [*speaking simultaneously with* LEACH]. Why — yes.

DULCY. Can I guess it? [ANGELA *nods, too full to speak*] Angela, oh, Angela — [*She goes to her, embracing her*] Oh, if this isn't the most wonderful thing I've ever heard! It's — it's — it's — it's — wonderful, that's all I can say! I'm so happy I could cry! Good news affects me that way. [*She turns and takes* VINCENT's *hand, which he has been holding out expectantly*] Vincent! I may call you Vincent now, mayn't I?

LEACH. Of course!

ANGELA. Mrs. Smith — we're going to need your help.

DULCY. Yes, darling, of course.

ANGELA. Now, it's a secret, and you must promise that you won't tell anyone.

DULCY. Why, no — I wouldn't tell a soul.

ANGELA [*after an assenting signal from* LEACH]. Well — Vincent and I — are going to elope.

DULCY. E-elope?

ANGELA. To-night.

DULCY. T-t-to-night? You mean — run away and get married? [ANGELA *nods her head*] Why — why — why — why — that's wonderful — [*She grows incoherent*] — that's just marvelous! I never heard of anything like that! It's — it's — why, it's —

ANGELA. Now, remember — you're not to tell a soul!

DULCY. Oh, no, I wouldn't tell anybody, no — How soon are you going?

ANGELA. Just as soon as we can — aren't we, Vincent?

LEACH. Yes! If we can get away.

ANGELA. We want you to help us!

DULCY. Of course. You — you — you — should tell your mother. She'll be crazy to know about it.

ANGELA. Oh, yes.

DULCY [*indicates windows*]. I guess she must have gone out there. My, I'm

so excited I don't know what to do next! I just feel like jumping up and down! [*Enter* BILL. DULCY *rushes to him*] Willie, what do you think! [LEACH *and* ANGELA *try to stop her, but she's too fast for them*] Vincent and Angela are going to elope!

ANGELA. Oh! And you promised —

LEACH. Now you've —

DULCY. Well, it — it just came out before I could help it. But — but Willie won't tell anybody. You won't tell anybody, will you, Willie?

BILL [*slowly to* ANGELA]. You're going to elope? With Mr. Leach?

ANGELA [*not quite meeting his eye*]. Yes. [BILL *looks from* ANGELA *to* DULCY, *then back*]

BILL. I won't tell a soul.

DULCY [*vindicated*]. See?

ANGELA. Thank you.

BILL. Where are you going to elope to?

ANGELA. Why — where were we, Vincent?

LEACH. I hadn't thought about it just yet.

DULCY. There are lots of places —

BILL [*after a glance at* DULCY]. How about a marriage license?

ANGELA. Why, I don't know — Vincent? [*She turns to him*]

LEACH [*weakly*]. Well, I thought we might find some place —

BILL. Going to take your father's car?

ANGELA [*who had not thought about it before*]. Yes!

DULCY. You could have had mine — but I broke it.

BILL [*to* DULCY]. I suppose this was your idea.

DULCY. Well, I helped.

BILL. Yes, I could tell. [*Again to* ANGELA] Well, after you get this license and find a minister —

DULCY. Willie, you could help them some way, couldn't you? You know where to get a license and everything.

LEACH. Do you?

BILL [*a pause*]. Why — yes.

DULCY. See, that's why I told him!

BILL. I live in — Bronxville, and I know the borough clerk. We could go to his house and get a license.

DULCY. Oh, that would be lovely!

ANGELA [*weakly*]. Yes.

LEACH [*dubiously*]. Yes.

BILL. Yes. Then I could drive you wherever you wanted to go, and bring the car back — that is, if Mr. Leach wants it brought back.

DULCY. You see! Everything is working out splendidly! Now I'll tell you what we'll do! We'll — ah — we'll — ah — what do you suggest, Willie?

BILL. Is everything ready?

ANGELA. We just have to get our bags.

DULCY. They just have to get their bags. Vincent, now you go out and find Mrs. Forbes and tell her; then we'll all meet in the garage in ten minutes. I'll go up and get Angela's things for her. [*She starts up, then turns to consider*] Now let me see —

[*Enter* STERRETT]

STERRETT [*coming forward with attempted carelessness*]. Oh, hello!

DULCY [*weakly*]. Hello.

ANGELA [*also weakly*]. Hello, Tom. [*An awkward pause.* STERRETT *sees that there's something in the wind and that he's not part of it*]

DULCY [*coming to the rescue*]. There's nothing the matter.

STERRETT. Oh — excuse me! [*He turns on his heel and goes*]

ANGELA. You don't think he suspected?

DULCY. Of course not. I told him there was nothing the matter. Now let's see — Vincent — you go out and find Mrs. Forbes, and then go to the garage and wait for us there. Now, quick, quick! Go right through the tomatoes!

LEACH [*with his eye on* BILL]. Yes, but you know, I can drive a car, too, for that matter.

DULCY. Hurry up! The less speed the more haste, or something! •

LEACH. All right. [*To* ANGELA] My dream woman! [*He is gone*]

DULCY. Oh — well, now that's settled. I'll go up and get the things, and we'll all meet in the garage in ten minutes!

ANGELA. I'll go with you!

DULCY. No, I'll bring everything out to the garage. If anybody sees me they won't suspect. You know, I'm so excited! Now you two hurry right out! Vincent will meet you there! My, it's — it's just like times of old when knights were bold! [*She gallops up the stairs.* ANGELA *looks uncertainly at* BILL, *starts out quickly, then pauses —*

to face whatever he may have to say. BILL *turns and speaks quietly*]

BILL. All ready for the elopement?

ANGELA. I think — I think you're just horrid.

BILL. Speaking to me?

ANGELA. You know very well I am.

BILL. But of course you don't mean it. I'm really being very good to you — helping you out in this way.

ANGELA. Well — well — you don't have to be so happy about it. After all we — we *are* old friends!

BILL. But that's why I'm glad. You're glad, aren't you?

ANGELA. That has nothing to do with it! [*A pause*] Of course I am! [*Another pause*] You're just — just impossible!

BILL. Angela, you told me once that I would never change. You were right — I never *have* changed.

ANGELA [*almost in tears*]. Oh, I don't care whether you have or not! I think you're positively hopeless! [*She flounces out through the French windows.* BILL, *left alone, looks after her a moment, then starts out, but seeing someone coming downstairs, he pauses at the window. It is* HENRY *on the stairs. He wears a sack coat and is carrying a derby. He seems hurried and nervous. As he turns to go,* BILL *touches him on the shoulder.* HENRY *starts*]

BILL. Hello, Henry!

HENRY [*collecting himself*]. Yes, sir.

BILL. What seems to be the trouble?

HENRY [*nervous*]. Trouble, sir?

BILL. Yes.

HENRY. Oh, no trouble, sir. Have you the time, sir?

[BILL *takes out watch, somewhat absent-mindedly holding it too closely to* HENRY — *then, realizing this mistake, turns away to consult it*]

BILL. Sixteen minutes after ten.

HENRY. Thank you, sir. Excuse me, sir.

[*He hurries out.* BILL *stands a moment, undecided whether to investigate* HENRY, *then turns and goes out through windows. Enter* GORDON *and* FORBES]

GORDON. I'm — I'm sorry, but Dulcy — my wife — must have had the table moved for some reason, and then didn't get it quite level when it was put back.

FORBES. Oh, that's all right —

at's all right. In fact, it was rather
ovel — playing billiards up and down
ll.

GORDON. Probably I can have it
xed before you go home, and then —

FORBES. Doesn't matter, I assure
ou. I — ah — I — don't care very
uch for billiards, anyhow.

GORDON [*growing desperate*]. Some
ther time, then. Maybe you'd like to
- to look at some new golf clubs I just
t?

FORBES. What?

MRS. FORBES *comes through the windows. She is in a state of suppressed
excitement, which becomes more suppressed when she finds her husband
present*]

MRS. FORBES. Oh, hello, dear!

FORBES [*sourly*]. Hello.

MRS. FORBES [*fencing*]. Who won
ne billiard game?

FORBES [*violently*]. Mrs. Smith!

MRS. FORBES. Have you — seen
nybody?

FORBES. Have I *what?*

GORDON [*anxious to get away*]. Sup-
ose I — go and lay out those golf clubs
while, and — then you can come —
ter.

FORBES [*almost viciously*]. Yes —
uppose you do.

GORDON. Yes, yes. All right — all
ght. [*He wipes his forehead nervously
* he goes out*]

MRS. FORBES [*casting apprehensive
ances up the stairs and out the windows*].
What's the matter, dear?

FORBES. What's the matter? Why
- why — good Heavens, the — the —

MRS. FORBES [*half fearful that he has
arned about the elopement*]. Nothing
as happened, has it?

FORBES. Happened? I should say
has!

MRS. FORBES [*alarmed*]. What?

FORBES. I go in here to play a game
f — [*viciously*] — billiards. I think fi-
ally that I'm going to get ten minutes
f pleasure out of this week-end, and —
nd — what do I find?

MRS. FORBES [*sweetly*]. Well?

FORBES [*yelling*]. What's the dif-
erence? [*A pause*] You don't give a
arn — you just go ahead carrying on
ith that fellow Van Dyck.

MRS. FORBES. But, sweetheart —

FORBES. Oh, I saw the way that
oman fixed it up for you! And
ngela — where's Angela?

MRS. FORBES [*nervously*]. I don't
know, dear. [*DULCY, carrying two suit-
cases, comes tiptoeing down the stairs.*
MRS. FORBES *sees her and* DULCY *wig-
wags to her to be quiet.* FORBES *is well
down stage, with his back to* DULCY]

FORBES. Out gallivanting with that
moving picture nincompoop, I suppose.
More of that woman's work!

MRS. FORBES. Mr. Leach — do you
mean?

FORBES. Yes, Mr. Leach I mean!
[DULCY *has reached the windows;* MRS.
FORBES *is signaling to her*] Just imagine
having a fellow like that in the family —
telling you — outlines. And the idea
of you standing idly by while he and
Angela — [*He sees* MRS. FORBES' *signals*] What the devil's the matter with
you? [DULCY *slips through the windows*]

MRS. FORBES. Why, nothing, dear.

FORBES. Then stand still! And listen to me. If I find this Leach person
actually making love to Angela, why,
I'm — I'm going to raise hell, that's
all. It's been nothing but a series of
aggravations — annoyances — ever since
I came into this house. Eleanor, I can
truthfully say that in all my fifty-three
years I have never spent an unhappier
evening.

MRS. FORBES. Oh, Charlie!

FORBES. But I am not going to
spend another! I am not going to stay
here and ride golf and play horse-back!

MRS. FORBES. What are you going
to do?

FORBES. I am going — home!

MRS. FORBES. Charlie!

FORBES. I'm going upstairs and
pack! I promised Sterrett I'd drive
him in to-night, and I'm not coming
back! There's another thing! The
way they're treating Sterrett! [*Starting up the stairs*] Good *night!*

MRS. FORBES. Charlie — you can't
do that!

FORBES. Maybe I can't, but I'm
going to! You can stay here with Van
Dyck and watch Angela carrying on
with that Leach person if you want to.
BUT — mark my words — if anything
comes out of this — if Angela and that
fool *are* infatuated with each other, and
try to do anything silly — I don't ever
want to see *you* or *her* again! That —
is all! [*He storms up the stairs.* MRS.
FORBES *looks after him a minute.* DULCY
*enters through the windows and romps over
to* MRS. FORBES]

DULCY [*gleefully*]. Well, they're gone!

MRS. FORBES. Oh, I'm scared! Can't you call them back?

DULCY. Huh? Why, it's lovely!

MRS. FORBES. No — no! I've got to tell him! If I don't he'll — he'll never let me come back to him! He means it — I know him!

DULCY. Vincent and Angela have eloped and everything's fine!

MRS. FORBES. Fine? But — but — oh, it was all *your* doing! That and — Mr. Van Dyck, and — everything! Charles would never have talked to me like that if it hadn't been for you. [*Sobbing*] He never talked to me like that before.

DULCY. Why, Mrs. Forbes, dear, you're tired.

MRS. FORBES. No, I'm not! I'm just mad, that's all — mad at you! It's all your fault! If my husband ever knows that — that I knew they were eloping, and didn't stop it, why, he'll — he'll — oh, I don't know what he'll do! [*She breaks down, sobbing*]

DULCY [*wanting to pat her and not quite daring to*]. There, there, dear. Why, he won't do anything. He'll be the first to congratulate —

[*Enter* GORDON]

GORDON [*coming toward them*]. Good Heavens, what's all this about? What's the matter?

DULCY. It's nothing at all, darling. Just — just — [FORBES *comes down the stairs. He is wearing a duster and carrying his hat and suitcase*]

GORDON. Why, Mr. Forbes!

MRS. FORBES. Charlie!

FORBES [*still boiling within*]. Mr. Smith — I — I am returning to New York — important business. My — ah — wife and my daughter will remain here, I *believe*. I don't *know* anything about them.

GORDON. But, Mr. Forbes, I don't understand.

FORBES. So far as our little deal is concerned, I — I haven't made up my mind yet whether to go ahead with it or not.

GORDON. My dear sir —

MRS. FORBES. Oh, Charlie — Charlie — I want to tell you something! [*She starts towards him, but* DULCY *stops her*]

DULCY. Now, Mr. Forbes, you don't really mean what you are saying. When in anger, you should always count ten.

GORDON [*sternly*]. What is this a[ll] about? [*Everybody starts to tell him [at] once and all are talking as* VAN DYC[K] *enters through the windows*]

VAN DYCK. I've got it! [*Seats him[-]self at piano*] I just thought of it!

DULCY. Ah — ah — huh?

VAN DYCK. You know, that littl[e] thing I couldn't remember. It was little Sicilian love song — It went lik[e] this. [*He launches into a pretty littl[e] thing*]

FORBES [*after a few bars have bee[n] played, in great indignation*]. Oh! [*He stalks out through windows*]

GORDON. Mr. Forbes — Mr. Forbes [*He follows him out*]

MRS. FORBES. Charlie — Charlie [*She follows*]

DULCY. Oh, Mr. Van Dyck!

VAN DYCK. Do tell me, what's th[e] trouble? Is Mrs. Forbes —

DULCY [*shaking her head*]. It's — it's Mr. Forbes.

VAN DYCK. Mr. Forbes?

DULCY. He just got angry — fo[r] no reason at all, and now he's going back home in his car. . . . [*She re[-]members that the car is gone*] He thinks —

VAN DYCK. Dear me!

DULCY. But the worst of it is — he's awfully angry at Gordon, and — he won't go ahead with the busines[s] thing.

VAN DYCK. Business thing? I[s] that the — now, I don't want to seem[m] inquisitive, but is that the jewelr[y] merger I've heard discussed?

DULCY. Yes. Didn't you know[?] Well, Mr. Forbes was getting up one and he was going to give my Gordie[e] some of it. [*Her mood changes*] I hope it *is* all off — only sixteen and two-third[s] per cent.

VAN DYCK. Just a minute. As [I] understand, it was a combination whic[h] would have taken in about fifty per cen[t] of the jewelry trade.

DULCY [*approaching tears*]. Yes, [I] think so.

VAN DYCK. And now Mr. Forbes is leaving your husband out of it? I[s] that right?

DULCY. Yes. [VAN DYCK *consider[s] very seriously*] Why? Oh, dear, maybe[e] I shouldn't have told you. [VA[N] DYCK *in deep thought*] Oh, oh, I wish[h] I hadn't told you. [VAN DYCK *wheel[s] with decision*]

VAN DYCK. Mrs. Smith!

DULCY. Well?

VAN DYCK. Mrs. Smith, I like your usband very much.

DULCY [*greatly pleased*]. Oh, do you?

VAN DYCK. Would he be willing to et up his own merger, one bigger than Mr. Forbes ever dreamt of?

DULCY. Why — what do you mean?

VAN DYCK. Why doesn't he beat Mr. Forbes at his own game?

DULCY. Why — why — I never hought of that. But Mr. Forbes has ll the money — and — and Gordie asn't any.

VAN DYCK. That's it exactly! Now, 've always wanted to take a little flier n the jewelry business. Suppose I inanced Mr. Smith — suppose he and set out to beat Mr. Forbes together? How would that be?

DULCY [*incoherent*]. Be? Be? Why, t would be incredible — unbelievable! [*Tearfully*] You — do you really mean it?

VAN DYCK. I do. I'll put up my check the moment your husband says he word.

DULCY [*crying with joy*]. Oh, Mr. Van Dyck, you've — you've made me he proudest woman in all the world! You let me break the news to him, won't you?

VAN DYCK. Why — of course, if ou wish it.

DULCY. And to think I introduced you to him! Now, what will he think of me! [*Excited voices are heard off*]

VAN DYCK. It's Mr. Forbes again!

DULCY. Is it?

VAN DYCK [*at the door*]. Perhaps I'd better go. My golf things are fearfully rumpled. Will I find your man Henry through here?

DULCY [*her mind on other matters*]. He's around somewhere. [VAN DYCK *goes.* DULCY *is almost hysterical with happiness. The voices outside become definite*]

MRS. FORBES. But, Charlie dear, calm down a little, and don't fly off the handle!

FORBES. Handle! Handle, madam! Do you realize what has happened? [*He enters during this speech, wearing his coat and hat, and still carrying the suitcase. Stops short at sight of* DULCY; *then walks to her with terrible calm*] Mrs. Smith. [*He pauses*] Mrs. Smith, upon going to your garage, I first discovered that my car was gone.

DULCY. Oh, but that's nothing — [GORDON *appears in the windows*]

FORBES. Just a moment, please! My wife thereupon informed me that you had told her that my daughter and Mr. Leach — have eloped! [*He is throwing a terrific emphasis on every word*]

GORDON. What!

FORBES. Is — this — true?

DULCY [*quaking, but trying to be gay about it*]. Yes — yes! You see —

MRS. FORBES. It wasn't my fault, Charlie — honestly!

[FORBES *silences her with a gesture, his eyes not leaving* DULCY]

FORBES. Mrs. Smith — [*Turning*] and Mr. Smith. I am measuring my words very carefully. Since — my car — is gone — and the last train — is gone, it seems that I shall be compelled to remain in this house — over night. [*He pauses — his eyes find* DULCY] I shall — endeavor not to commit a murder.

GORDON. My dear Mr. Forbes, I'm sure this can be fixed up in some way.

DULCY. Yes. Of course it can. [*The old* DULCY *for a second*] You know, an angry word spoken in haste —

FORBES. Please! [*He turns to* GORDON] Mr. Smith, in the circumstances I don't see how we can possibly get on in business together. I don't like your methods!

GORDON. But, Mr. Forbes —

FORBES. I shall not call the matter off entirely, but any arrangement which we might eventually make would necessarily differ from our tentative discussions as to percentage. [GORDON *starts to speak*] I'm sorry, but that's my decision!

[STERRETT *comes running on through the windows*]

STERRETT. Mr. Forbes, Mr. Forbes — [*He comes between* FORBES *and* GORDON]

FORBES [*snapping at him*]. Well, what now?

STERRETT. *Your car is not in the garage!*

FORBES. You don't say so!

STERRETT. Leach and Angela were acting awfully funny! If you ask me, I think they've eloped in it!

FORBES. I was not aware that I *had* asked *you!*

STERRETT. But — how am *I* going to get back to town tonight?

FORBES. *You — might — try — skipping!* [STERRETT *tries to pass this off as a laugh, but a look from* FORBES *squelches him. He arranges an exit for himself*]

STERRETT. Ah — well — I'll see if I can find them. [*He goes — somewhat precipitately*]

FORBES [*to* GORDON]. I repeat — the percentage would have to be adjusted. And now I wish you good night! [*He makes for the stairs*]

MRS. FORBES. Oh, Charlie, mayn't I come with you?

FORBES. It is a matter of utter indifference to me *where* you go!

MRS. FORBES. Oh, but, Charlie, it wasn't my fault — really it wasn't! I didn't know anything about it until after they eloped! [MRS. FORBES *follows her husband upstairs*]

DULCY [*gleefully*]. Gordie!

GORDON [*turning and looking at her*]. My God, are you smiling?

DULCY. I've got the most wonderful news for you!

GORDON [*his anger rising*]. Is it a surprise? [*A pause*] Dulcy — Dulcy, how could you?

DULCY. How could I what?

GORDON. You've ruined me — that's all. Ruined me. Dulcy, I'm afraid we don't hit it off very well — you and I. This thing is too big. Say what we may, it's come between us.

DULCY. Oh, no, it hasn't, darling. Wait till you hear.

GORDON. Hear? Hear what?

DULCY [*rising and approaching him*]. How would you like — to have Schuyler Van Dyck for a partner?

GORDON. A — partner? [*Going mad*] More golf?

DULCY. Business.

GORDON. Huh?

DULCY [*with great excitement*]. How would you like to go in business with him, and have Taylor and Robbins and Spelvin and all those other people with you, and leave Mr. Forbes out of it? Get up — a — a — bigger merger than Mr. Forbes ever thought about, because — because you'd have all the money you wanted! Mr. Van Dyck said so!

GORDON [*dazed*]. He — says so?

DULCY. Yes! Think of that!

GORDON. Here! Wait a minute! You've — you've been talking to Van Dyck?

DULCY. Yes — just now!

GORDON. And he said that he'd finance a combination to beat Forbes and his crowd — with me at the head of it?

DULCY. He's just waiting for yo to say the word, darling!

GORDON. I — I — I — can't believ it.

DULCY [*caressing him as if to resto his senses*]. But it's true — it *is*, dea

GORDON. Why, it's — it's too goo to be true. I — I could be rid of Forb and put the business in for what it worth. I — I could —

DULCY [*excited*]. Yes — oh, Gordo

GORDON. I — I can really do b things! Why — [FORBES *comes dow stairs*]

FORBES. Excuse me. [DULCY *an* GORDON *break.* FORBES *is the pathet sight of a strong man reduced to tear* I am sorry — to be compelled to mak — another statement. I merely wis to announce — on top of everythin else — that my daughter's pearl necl lace has disappeared.

DULCY. Disappeared?

GORDON. What's that?

FORBES. In view of the fact that took place in this house, I thought yo might have a sentimental interest. put it in my pocket not three-quarte of an hour ago, and now —

[*Enter* VAN DYCK, *speaking as he com in*]

VAN DYCK. I'm sorry, but I've bee all over the house and I can't fin Henry any place. [VAN DYCK *sense that he faces a situation of some sort*] H must have gone out. [GORDON *an* DULCY *exchange terrible looks.* DULC *is the first to recover*]

DULCY. Henry!

GORDON. Well, I'll be —

FORBES. What's that? Who' Henry? What's he got to do with it

VAN DYCK. I'll look again, but I'r certain he's not here. [*He is about t start out*]

GORDON [*stopping him*]. Before yo go, Mr. Van Dyck — [VAN DYCK *halt* And just a second, Mr. Forbes — [*Stopping* FORBES] We'll straighten ou about the necklace later. Mr. Va Dyck, I understand that you have of fered to back me with unlimited capita in an independent jewelry merger [DULCY *sits, enjoying the situation*]

FORBES. What?

GORDON. Am I correct?

VAN DYCK. You are! Mrs. Smit has interested me very much in thi matter. I'll put up the necessary capi

l, provided, of course, we can agree on
ie details.

GORDON [*willing to agree to anything*].
h, there'll be no difficulty about that.
With dignity] I accept your offer.
Ir. Forbes, you said a minute ago that
ou were not certain whether or not our
eal was off. Well, I've decided! It
off! I am going to line up with Van
)yck and fight you — fight you till one
f us is forced to the wall. But be-
re I do it, I'm going to tell you *why*
'm fighting you! I'm fighting you
ecause you tried to take advantage of
e!

FORBES. Advantage?

GORDON. Yes, advantage! By of-
ering me less than you knew my busi-
ess was worth! You knew I was in a
ole, and now you're going to get just
hat you deserve! You're going to get
first rate licking!

DULCY. Oh, Gordie!

VAN DYCK [*anxious to get away*]. I —
'll see if I can *find* Henry, but I'm afraid
.e's gone. [*He slips out*]

FORBES. All right. Make your fine
peeches, but when you talk about fight-
ng, don't forget that I can fight, too.
.nd before you win, you're going to
.now that you've been in a *real fight!*
temember that! [*He goes upstairs*]

DULCY [*rising and going to* GORDON].
Gordie, darling, you were wonderful!
Embraces him] But the necklace!
)o you think Henry —

GORDON [*impatiently*]. What's the
lifference whether he did or not? I feel
ike a new man.

DULCY. Gordie, you see — I *was* of
ome use after all.

GORDON. Use! You were wonder-
ul! [*Taking her in his arms*] The best
— the finest little wife in the world.
He kisses her] I'm going to beat
Forbes, dear — I'm going to succeed —
.nd I'll owe it all to you.

DULCY. Wasn't it lucky, my finding
Mr. Van Dyck?

GORDON. Lucky! It was an inspiration!

DULCY. And I *am* a real helpmate?

GORDON. My darling! [*She is again
in his arms*]

DULCY. My Gordie! [*The door bell
rings*] That's the door bell. You'll
have to answer it, darling, since Henry
isn't here.

GORDON. One of the neighbors, probably. [*He goes out, leaving the door open*]

DULCY. Oh, Henry! [*Voices are
heard off stage*]

PATTERSON. Is this Mr. Smith's
house?

GORDON. I am Mr. Smith.

PATTERSON. Can I speak to you a
moment on a rather important matter?

GORDON. Won't you step in? [*Enter* BLAIR PATTERSON. *A man somewhat
under middle-age, well groomed, and with
quite an air of authority. He makes a
good impression.* GORDON *follows him
on, closing the door*] Ah — my wife.

PATTERSON. How do you do, Mrs.
Smith? I must apologize for calling at
this hour. My name is Patterson —
Blair Patterson.

GORDON. The attorney!

PATTERSON. Yes, I was referred to
you by Mrs. Kennedy.

DULCY. Oh, across the street?

PATTERSON. Ah — yes. She said you
had — guests. I just wondered if —
among them — there is a Mr. — Morgan? Can you tell me?

GORDON. Morgan? Why, no.

DULCY. No.

PATTERSON. Well — is there a Mr.
Ford?

GORDON. No. He's not here either.

PATTERSON. Mr. — Vanderbilt?

GORDON [*somewhat flattered*]. Vanderbilt? No.

PATTERSON. Mr. — Astor?

GORDON [*more flattered and somewhat
surprised*]. No. I don't understand.

PATTERSON. H'm. Well, let me ask
you — is one of your guests — tall, good-
looking, plays the piano, interested in
various — ah — investments —?

DULCY [*proudly*]. Oh, you mean
Schuyler Van Dyck?

PATTERSON [*thoughtfully*]. Schuyler
— Van Dyck.

DULCY. He's here.

PATTERSON [*slowly*]. Yes, I think I
do mean Schuyler Van Dyck. I'm his
cousin. [GORDON *and* DULCY *are cordiality itself*] I — I've come for him.

DULCY. Come for him?

PATTERSON. Yes. His real name is
Patterson — Horace Patterson. He
has an hallucination that he's a millionaire. Goes round forming big companies — But I assure you he's perfectly
harmless. [*He taps his head significantly as*

THE CURTAIN FALLS

ACT III

The scene is the same; the time is the following morning. The windows are open and bright morning sunlight is pouring into the room.

The curtain rises on a bare stage and after a second FORBES comes downstairs. He is utterly broken. After throwing a hard look toward the easy chair he sits stiff and upright in the side chair, groaning as he sits. He takes out his cigar case; it is empty; with a growl he rises and looks in humidor on table. There is nothing there. He sits again in the same chair.

STERRETT *comes tripping down the stairs.*

STERRETT [*blithely*]. Good morning, Chief!

FORBES. Got anything to smoke?

STERRETT. Oh, sure. [STERRETT *hauls out his cigarette case and opens it*]

FORBES. I meant a cigar.

STERRETT. Oh — just a minute. [*He goes for humidor*]

FORBES. There's none there. None any place. Mrs. Smith probably discovered that I *like* cigars.

STERRETT. Haven't you any in your room?

FORBES. Yes, but — ah — I don't want to disturb Mrs. Forbes.

STERRETT. Oh, I thought you had separate rooms.

FORBES [*viciously*]. No. We have the bridal suite.

STERRETT. Well, Mrs. Forbes must be up by this time. Why don't you go up and —

FORBES [*rising*]. Sterrett.

STERRETT. Yes, Chief.

FORBES. I don't want this to go any further — but I did not sleep in the bridal suite last night. I — took a walk until rather late and when I returned everyone had gone to bed. I didn't know just which rooms were unoccupied, so I slept on a couch in the hall.

STERRETT. All night?

FORBES. Now and then. I tiptoed into my room about four o'clock this morning to get this — [*Indicating his business suit*] Did you ever try to get a suit of clothes out of a closet in the dark, without making any noise?

STERRETT. Why, no.

FORBES [*putting hand to his head*]. Oh, dear.

STERRETT. You're not ill, Chief?

FORBES [*sitting*]. I wouldn't be surprised. It would be too much to expect to get out of this with just a *mental* breakdown and a celluloid son-in-law.

STERRETT. Nothing new on — th necklace, I suppose?

FORBES. Oh, yes. It was brough back and I'm wearing it.

STERRETT. You're what?

FORBES. Don't you see it? [STER RETT *makes a weak attempt at a laugh*]

STERRETT. Oh, Chief — Chief — you certainly have a sense of humor.

FORBES [*grimly*]. Yes, and at thi time of the morning I'm at my best.

STERRETT. But — ah — I meant th police.

FORBES. Huh?

STERRETT. The police were sent for weren't they?

FORBES. Probably. I asked Mrs Smith *not* to send for them, so I suppos she did.

STERRETT. Well, if I were you, I'c put them right on it.

FORBES. It may seem impossible t *you*, Sterrett, but there are times wher it does *not* pay to advertise. You may recall that my daughter eloped las night.

STERRETT. It has been a very painful experience for me, Chief.

FORBES. Well, damn it, you don't think it's been any diversion for me?

STERRETT [*hastily*]. Oh, of course not. [*Trying to say something comforting*] As her father I can keenly appreciate how you're going to suffer.

FORBES [*giving him a look*]. Thank you. The reason I don't want the police sent for is that I'm not anxious to have my daughter's elopement become public.

STERRETT. Oh!

FORBES. I can see the newspaper headlines now. "Daughter of C. Rogers Forbes Elopes With Nut." [*A pause*] I'm going to have it annulled — quietly.

STERRETT [*an idea dawning*]. Maybe they didn't get married!

FORBES. What?

STERRETT. Maybe they're not married yet! They couldn't get a license last night! I'll telephone —

FORBES. They made special arrangements to get a license. Mrs. Smith's brother saw to that. H'm. I rather like him. I wondered what *he'd* do.

STERRETT. I never trusted him.

FORBES. And on top of everything else, the third member of the family gets the Van Dyck money behind him and practically tells me to go to hell.

STERRETT. Certainly is an unlucky house. What time are we going back to town? [GORDON *comes downstairs*]

FORBES. Just as soon as possible.

GORDON [*who hasn't slept either. Meekly*]. Good morning.

STERRETT [*right back of him*]. Good morning.

FORBES [*after hesitating*]. Good morning. [*Looks away*]

GORDON. Breakfast will be ready in a minute, if the cook is still here. [GORDON *goes out,* FORBES *not noticing that he has left the room.* MRS. FORBES *comes downstairs*]

FORBES. Mr. Smith — [*Rises*] After taking into consideration everything that has happened here since my arrival — [FORBES *turns at this point and notices* GORDON *is not in the room, but sees* MRS. FORBES]

MRS. FORBES [*to* FORBES]. Good morning — [*Finishing it to* STERRETT] Mr. Sterrett.

STERRETT. Good morning, Mrs. Forbes.

MRS. FORBES. Aren't you — going to speak to me — Charlie?

FORBES. I'm speaking to no one. [GORDON *returns*] I will take up our affairs when I get back to the city — if I ever do. [*He sees* GORDON] Mr. Smith, I was about to say, when you walked away a minute ago — [DULCY *comes downstairs. She is wearing bright sport clothes and is ready for a busy day, but is somewhat subdued*]

DULCY. Good morning, everybody. All ready for breakfast? It's a lovely day, isn't it? Has anyone been out? The sun is shining; it's just good to be alive. How do you feel this morning, Mrs. Forbes?

MRS. FORBES. I'm rather depressed.

DULCY. Depressed? Well, you mustn't be. I have some wonderful news for you. It's a surprise. Who do you think will be here inside an hour?

FORBES. A couple dozen reporters, I suppose.

DULCY [*almost singing it*]. A bridal party.

FORBES. So they *are* married!

DULCY. Yes. Willie phoned me just now. He said they had trouble getting in touch with the license clerk. I sup-

pose all those people are like policemen — when you want one you never can find one. Anyway, they got him up at last and they were married at midnight.

FORBES. By a Justice of the Peace?

DULCY. No, indeed. By Dr. Carmichael — he's one of the finest ministers in Westchester. Willie knows him awfully well, so I suppose he did it as a special favor. Wasn't it nice of him?

FORBES. Yes, I appreciate it.

DULCY. So now you have a genius in the family, Mr. Forbes.

FORBES. Is he returning the car?

DULCY. Oh, of course — they'll be here any minute now — the happy couple.

FORBES. You can give *them* — the bridal suite.

DULCY. But where will you sleep?

FORBES. I shall be returning to town as soon as the car arrives. [*To* GORDON] Mr. Smith, I hope we can have a little talk before I go.

GORDON [*meekly*]. Just as you say, Mr. Forbes.

DULCY. Now, now, no business before breakfast. Come along — let's all go in before the grape fruit gets cold. [*She returns to* FORBES *and takes his arm*] Mr. Forbes. You come in with me.

FORBES [*disengaging himself*]. No, thank you. I'm afraid I must be excused. I'm not very hungry this morning. [*He goes up into windows*]

DULCY [*feeling the rebuff*]. Mr. Sterrett, you'll eat some breakfast, won't you?

STERRETT [*always willing*]. Why, surely.

MRS. FORBES [*stepping toward her husband*]. There isn't — anything — the matter, is there, Charlie?

FORBES. The matter? Oh, no! I'm just too happy to eat. [*He stamps through the windows*]

DULCY. Gordon, darling, you must eat some breakfast. Come along.

GORDON. Dulcy, will you go ahead and leave me alone?

DULCY [*persistent*]. Mrs. Forbes, you'll have some breakfast? [MRS. FORBES *nods*] Ah! [*Victorious*] You know, I'm never myself until I've had a cup of coffee in the morning. [STERRETT *opens the door for them*] Of course, we're all depressed now, but maybe after breakfast I'll think of something to cheer us up. [*All but* GORDON *depart;* BLAIR PATTERSON *comes downstairs*]

PATTERSON. Good morning, Mr. Smith.

GORDON. Oh, good morning, Mr. Patterson. *You* — slept well, I trust.

PATTERSON. Thank you — yes. [*Earnestly*] I'm very sorry to have caused you this trouble.

GORDON [*dejectedly*]. Oh, that's all right. Ready for breakfast?

PATTERSON. Thank you. I'll take Mr. Patterson home with me just as soon as he can get his things together.

GORDON. There's no hurry — any more. Have you — told him?

PATTERSON. No, he hasn't seen me yet. I'll not have any difficulty; it's happened before.

GORDON. He's — a cousin, I believe you said?

PATTERSON. A distant cousin — it's really too bad. Brilliant chap — agreeable — obliging —

GORDON. He certainly is.

PATTERSON. Quite all right. Lives on Long Island with his mother and sister. Just this one hallucination.

GORDON. That's all he has?

PATTERSON. Oh, yes. Now and then he wanders off alone like this, but happily he never causes any real trouble.

GORDON. He doesn't, eh? That's fine.

PATTERSON. It's a little hard on *me* — being compelled to round him up at intervals. I have to divide my activities as a lawyer with those of a truant officer.

GORDON. Yes, it must be hard on you.

PATTERSON [*looking about and approaching* GORDON]. Ah — if I might ask a small favor?

GORDON. Certainly.

PATTERSON. I hope none of your guests has learned about my cousin's — weakness?

GORDON. I don't think so. [*With a look toward the windows*] I hope not.

PATTERSON. If I may suggest it, it might be better to wait until I've taken him home, in case you wish to explain to anyone. It will save embarrassment.

[VAN DYCK *comes downstairs*]

GORDON. I won't say anything.

PATTERSON. Thank you.

VAN DYCK [*noticing* GORDON *only*]. Good morning.

GORDON. Good morning. [*He indicates* PATTERSON] Here's a — friend of yours.

[*Exit* GORDON *through windows*]

PATTERSON [*turning*]. Hello, Horace

VAN DYCK. Blair! Why, what in the world are you doing here?

PATTERSON. Oh, just dropped in to say hello.

VAN DYCK. You can't fool me. You've come to make me leave — that's what you've done.

PATTERSON. Oh, no — that is — unless you really want to.

VAN DYCK [*aggrieved*]. It's very — embarrassing.

PATTERSON [*annoyed*]. Well, if it's embarrassing for you, what do you think it is for me? I've a law practice to attend to. I'm getting a little tired of — these — excursions.

VAN DYCK. Well, I wish you'd leave me alone. At least half a dozen times during the past few years you've interrupted me in business negotiations that were exceedingly interesting.

PATTERSON [*suddenly suspicious*]. Have you been — putting through — something — here?

VAN DYCK. Well, yes — I've been representing my Van Dyck interests. We had all sorts of wonderful things planned. My share alone would have been eight and a half millions. Besides, we were going to play golf.

PATTERSON. Horace, haven't I told you repeatedly that I represent the Van Dyck interests? Now, you must let me handle it. You come back to town with me and we'll talk it over.

VAN DYCK [*protesting*]. But I can't leave *now*. If I do —

PATTERSON. I'm sorry, Horace, but you know our agreement. Unless you do as I say, I'll never go through with that two hundred million dollar aeroplane company of ours.

VAN DYCK [*appeased and smiling*]. Oh, all right.

[*Enter* DULCY. *Coming face to face with* VAN DYCK, *she is startled and uncertain as to how to greet him*]

DULCY. Oh, good morning. [*Timorously*] How do you — feel this morning?

VAN DYCK. Very melancholy. [DULCY *sidles away from him*] I'm afraid I must go back to town.

DULCY. Ah —! [*The height of sympathy*]

VAN DYCK. You don't know how I wish I could stay.

DULCY. Ah . . .! Well, that's too
bad. Still, it's all for the best. You —
you must have some breakfast first.

VAN DYCK. Oh, thank you.

DULCY [*in a whisper to* PATTERSON].
He can eat breakfast, can't he? [GOR-
DON *comes back*]

PATTERSON. Oh, yes.

VAN DYCK. I hope we're not the last.

DULCY. Oh, that's all right. The
last shall be first and — everything.
[VAN DYCK *goes. To* PATTERSON] I
had some soft boiled eggs prepared for
him, and some soft milk toast — all very
soft, you know. Is that all right?
[PATTERSON, *with a nod, goes in for breakfast.* DULCY *is about to follow*]

GORDON [*sharply*]. Dulcy!

DULCY [*turning nervously*]. Yes —
dear.

GORDON [*very seriously*]. Dulcy, come
here, please.

DULCY [*prattling on to cover her nervousness*]. I — I was just seeing about
Mr. Van Dyck's breakfast — Mr. —
Mr. Patterson's — I mean. He's — he's
all right, really. I mean, of course, he
isn't — *exactly* all right, but he's — he's
all right for — for what he is — and —
I mean — everything *could* be much
worse — couldn't it, darling? [*She finishes rather weakly, going to* GORDON]

GORDON. Dulcy — do you realize —
exactly what has happened?

DULCY. Well, I — I don't know — I
think so. Oh, Gordie, I didn't mean
to —

GORDON [*simply and kindly*]. You
must listen quietly, dear, until I finish.

DULCY [*momentarily subdued*]. Yes,
darling.

GORDON. The time has come when
— I must speak — frankly. [*A pause*]
Do you know what Mr. Forbes is going
to say to me when he learns who Van
Dyck really is? [DULCY *shakes her
head; she cannot speak at the moment*]
He is going to tell me that my factory
and my services are of no use to him.
Mr. Forbes thinks — that he has been
made a fool of, and — he's right. Our
future success — depended entirely on
him.

DULCY. But — but — we haven't
really done anything to him. Just because we — we asked for more.

GORDON. It wasn't — our asking for
more.

DULCY. Oh, you mean the elopement? [*She considers*] He doesn't like
pictures.

GORDON. That was the crowning
mistake.

DULCY. It was me again. It was
me as usual. Oh, dear — how will it
all end! [*She sinks onto the sofa*]

GORDON [*slowly*]. Forbes will probably force me out of business. Then
I'll have to start in all over again without — [*He glances around the room*]
Without — this.

DULCY [*forcing herself to say it*]. And
without me?

GORDON [*dispassionately*]. Dulcy, I
love you. I shall always love you. I
don't know whether it's because you
have the soul of a child, or in spite of the
fact that you act like one. [*He turns
away*] I don't know what the future is
going to do to us. You mean well, but
you just don't stop to think.

DULCY. I guess I don't think — I
just think I think. [*Rising and speaking
bravely*] I'll let you go, darling — if you
want me to. I'm just — all wrong. I'm
— a false note. I always wondered how
I'd be able to make a man like you care
for me — it seems so absurd for a man
like you ever to love — a false note.
And now — we're finding out — he can't.

GORDON [*carried away for a second*].
Dulcy, we can't end everything like
this! You're not a false note — you're
a melody — a whole tune. [*A pause.
He reverts to his previous mood*] But I
don't know what to do.

DULCY [*sadly*]. I don't think I can
reform.

GORDON. No — I suppose not.

DULCY [*a bit hopefully*]. I could make
out a kind of budget of things not to do
— you know, like the one we did for the
household expenses.

GORDON. I'm afraid — that wouldn't
do much good.

DULCY [*realizing that it's old stuff but
hopefully trying it anyhow*]. I could
make another promise. One that would
take in everything.

GORDON. Oh, I know you'd try to
keep it, but —

DULCY [*with tears in her voice*]. Oh,
but I *would* keep this one! Dearest, if
you'll let me, I'll promise that I'll never
interfere with your business affairs
again.

GORDON. But you practically promised that once, and —

DULCY. I mean in any way whatever! Inviting people to parties, and
everything! I'll — I'll revolutionize
myself.

GORDON [*turning sharply*]. Dulcy, I don't want you to change yourself a bit. I love you just as you are. [*With desperate earnestness*] I simply want you to let me handle my own affairs. Promise me that you won't even suggest helping me in business.

DULCY [*hysterically*]. All right, I'll promise! And I'll keep it! I will!

GORDON [*embracing her*]. I'm sure you will!

DULCY. I will, I will! And further-more, I'll do everything in my power to repair the damage I've done.

GORDON [*thoroughly frightened*]. Repair it?

DULCY. Yes — about Mr. Forbes. I'll go to him and tell him how sorry I am, and see if there isn't something I can do — [FORBES *comes striding in through the windows*]

FORBES. I beg your pardon, but it is extremely necessary that I get back to town immediately. Can I get a car anywhere in the village?

GORDON. Oh, but, surely — you're not going before we have our little talk?

FORBES. I regret that I must.

GORDON [*evidently conspiring to keep him there*]. But — I'm afraid you can't get in — this morning. There are no cars to be had out there — so, if you'll just make yourself comfortable —

DULCY [*spilling the beans*]. Oh, yes, he can get a car, darling — [*Starting off*] He can get one right away. I'll phone Kelly. Kelly always has a car.

GORDON [*following her*]. But, Dulcy —

FORBES. Thank you very much, Mrs. Smith.

GORDON. But, Dulcy — Duley — [*Turning back to* FORBES *hastily*] I'll be back. Dulcy! [*He races out after her.* FORBES *takes a turn around the room, automatically reaching for his cigar case, which he opens and finds empty*]

[*Enter* BLAIR PATTERSON]

FORBES. Why, Mr. Patterson —

PATTERSON. Oh, it's — ah —

FORBES. Forbes. C. Roger Forbes.

PATTERSON. Oh, of course. [*He shakes his hand*]

FORBES [*puzzled and suspicious*]. I — ah — I didn't know you were a friend of Mr. Smith's?

PATTERSON. Well — ah — no — that is, yes — I —

FORBES. H'm. Came down — this morning, did you?

PATTERSON. Ah — yes, yes. Just — got in. Beautiful country.

FORBES. Isn't it? [*A pause*] The Van Dyck interests seem to keep you quite busy.

PATTERSON. Ah — yes, yes.

FORBES. I was just — wondering what had brought you, and —

PATTERSON [*in a corner*]. Yes.

FORBES. H'm. [*Lightly*] Must be something pretty important — for him to send for *you* at — this hour?

PATTERSON. Well, ah — just a little matter of business, which he thought — advisable — [*He finishes with a cough*]

FORBES. I see. What I was about to say was — of course, I don't know just what Mr. Van Dyck is thinking of going into, but — ah — if I had a client who was — thinking of *going* into it, why, I'd look into it pretty thoroughly myself. Now I can give you a good deal of facts about —

[*Enter* STERRETT *and* VAN DYCK]

STERRETT [*as they enter*]. Well, that's certainly very interesting to me.

VAN DYCK. Yes, I — I hoped that it would be.

STERRETT. Well, Mr. Forbes, if you want *me* to handle your advertising after this you'll have to bring it to a different office.

PATTERSON [*suddenly suspicious*]. What was that?

STERRETT. I've just fixed up a little deal with Mr. Van Dyck. I'm to head his new advertising agency!

FORBES. You don't say so?

PATTERSON [*with a side glance at* VAN DYCK]. Well!

FORBES. That's splendid! Anyone who can join hands with Mr. Van Dyck is a very fortunate person.

PATTERSON. Ah — would you care to finish you packing, Mr. Van Dyck?

VAN DYCK. All right, Blair. In a minute.

PATTERSON [*going up to the staircase*]. Well, whenever you're ready — Schuy-ler. [*This informality of address registers strongly with* FORBES]

FORBES. Ah — now that we've met, Mr. Van Dyck, I hope we can see something of each other in town.

VAN DYCK. I trust so. As a matter of fact, there are several things I would be interested in going over with you.

FORBES [*eagerly*]. That so? What are they?

PATTERSON [*warningly*]. Ah — don't forget — Schuyler — your packing —

VAN DYCK [*airly*]. Oh, that's all right, Blair.

FORBES. You were saying, Mr. Van Dyck —

VAN DYCK. Well, it just occurred to me that we might have interests which — ah —

FORBES. Yes?

VAN DYCK. Which we might pool to advantage.

FORBES. Indeed, yes. Something of that kind has been in my mind for a long time. Of course I hesitated to suggest it to *you*.

PATTERSON. Don't you think that we'd better be —

STERRETT. Now, there's something I'd like to ask you, Mr. Van Dyck — and I hope you won't mind my — presuming. Ah — do you — that is, what is your attitude — just at present — on the market? Do you look for further declines, or — [*He pauses*]

VAN DYCK [*importantly*]. No, sir.

FORBES. Ah!

STERRETT. That's very interesting.

VAN DYCK. As a matter of fact, I look for a sharp rise throughout the list.

FORBES. Indeed?

STERRETT. What do you base that on, Mr. Van Dyck? [*Quickly*] If I may ask?

PATTERSON. I hardly think you have time to go into that now, Schuyler —

VAN DYCK. It'll just take a second. [*Pompously*] The reason that I look for a rising market, Mr. Forbes — is —

FORBES. Yes?

VAN DYCK. Is that a war with Spain is now inevitable!

FORBES. A war with — Spain?

VAN DYCK. Exactly.

PATTERSON. Schuyler!

STERRETT. A war between — Spain and — this country?

VAN DYCK. Oh, no! That's it, exactly. Spain and — Abyssinia!

FORBES. What's that?

STERRETT. But I don't —

PATTERSON [*reaching across* STERRETT *and leading* VAN DYCK *away*]. Come, come. I really must get back to town, Mr. Van Dyck. There's a train that goes almost immediately. [*To* VAN DYCK, *confidentially*] It's a matter of two hundred millions. [STERRETT *and* FORBES *exchange a glance*] Sorry to take Mr. Van Dyck away from you, Mr.

Forbes — Mr. Sterrett — but you know how it is. We'll see you presently.

FORBES. Certainly.

PATTERSON. Come along, Schuyler. [*He starts up with* VAN DYCK]

STERRETT [*following*]. Mr. Patterson, you don't mind if I go up — along with Mr. Van Dyck, do you?

VAN DYCK [*turning back to him*]. Come right along, Mr. Sterrett. I haven't finished with you yet. [PATTERSON *is now on the stairs. The other two work their way up the stairs as they speak*]

STERRETT. No, I didn't think you had. Now, if that April 1st date is O.K. with you —

VAN DYCK. Yes, and I'll tell you what else you can do for me. I have some copper interests out in Montana — [VAN DYCK, STERRETT *and* PATTERSON *go up the stairs*. FORBES *follows up to the foot of the stairs, looking after them*]

[*Enter* MRS. FORBES]

MRS. FORBES. Oh — Charlie —

FORBES. Oh, it's you.

MRS. FORBES [*approaching*]. Charlie, it wasn't my fault — Angela, I mean. [FORBES *listens in stony silence*] Honestly it wasn't, Charlie. [*She makes up her mind to stretch the truth just a little*] I didn't know anything about it until after they'd eloped. Really I didn't!

FORBES. Well, I — I've no wish to be unjust, Eleanor.

MRS. FORBES. Then you'll — forgive me?

FORBES. You — you're telling me the truth? You didn't know anything about the elopement until —

MRS. FORBES. Until after Mrs. Smith told me.

FORBES. That woman!

MRS. FORBES. Then you will — take me back? [FORBES *looks at her, pinches her cheeks, then embraces her awkwardly*]

FORBES. Eleanor, dear — my little widgie!

MRS. FORBES [*sinking into his embrace*]. Oh, Charlie, I'm so happy!

FORBES. My dear, this has been a most unfortunate visit.

MRS. FORBES. Yes, dearest.

FORBES. But it has done — one thing for me. I didn't know until I saw you with Mr. Van Dyck how much I really cared for you.

MRS. FORBES. Oh, Charlie — do you honestly? Say it again!

FORBES. I was actually — jealous.

MRS. FORBES [*embracing him*]. Charlie — how wonderful! I'll never talk to Mr. Van Dyck again, and I'll even give up the Smiths if you insist.

FORBES [*quickly*]. Oh, no, no, no. You must stay friendly with the Smiths no matter what happens. Smith's factory equipment couldn't be duplicated right now for any amount. I've got to have it.

MRS. FORBES. But, Charlie —

FORBES. Now don't go and tell him.

MRS. FORBES. Oh, I wouldn't.

FORBES. I just wanted to be sure.

[*Enter* DULCY]

DULCY. Oh, Mr. Forbes, they haven't any automobiles — just now. They said — maybe they'd have one later.

FORBES. To-morrow, perhaps?

DULCY. Oh, Mr. Forbes — I'm sorry — [*She pauses a second*] Sorry about — the elopement, I mean — [*There is no response from* FORBES] And everything.

FORBES [*annoyed*]. It's quite all right, Mrs. Smith — quite all right.

DULCY. And I'm sorry about the business deal, too. But it's going to come out all right.

FORBES. What's that?

DULCY. I say the business deal between you and Gordie is going to come out all right.

FORBES. Oh, is it?

DULCY. Yes. Gordie will go in with you after all. Because Mr. Van Dyck isn't Mr. Van Dyck at all.

MRS. FORBES. What?

FORBES. What's that?

DULCY. No — he has something wrong up here. [*She taps her head*] He only *thinks* he's a millionaire.

MRS. FORBES. Good heavens!

FORBES [*keeping calm*]. Oh — so Mr. Van Dyck is — not Mr. Van Dyck!

DULCY. No.

FORBES. I see.

DULCY [*after a pause*]. So everything's all right now, isn't it?

FORBES. Oh, yes. Splendid!

DULCY. And it's all right between you and Mrs. Forbes, too? [MRS. FORBES *smilingly puts her arm around him. He smiles at her.* DULCY *gurgles with joy*] Ah —! H'm —! It was sweet of you to forgive her for helping with the elopement.

MRS. FORBES [*drawing back with an involuntary exclamation*]. Oh!

FORBES. For — helping with the elopement! [*To his wife*] Then you — *did* know about it? You *helped!* [*He turns to* DULCY, *who has crept a few steps away, as if to escape*] Did she? [*Enter* GORDON. DULCY *sees escape is hopeless*]

DULCY. I — I —

FORBES [*to* MRS. FORBES]. And you told me you didn't!

MRS. FORBES [*sobbing*]. Oh, Charlie, Charlie — I didn't very much! And I was sorry I did, right away. [*She tries to embrace him; he puts her off*]

FORBES. I don't care to hear anything about it!

MRS. FORBES. Oh, but, Charlie —

DULCY. Ah! Ah! [*She crosses to her*] There! there!

MRS. FORBES. I feel faint.

DULCY. She feels faint! Come out into the garden and get some fresh air. [*Leading her into the windows and out*] Breathe deeply, dear. Ten times. One — two — three — [*They are out of sight and hearing*]

GORDON. I'm sorry. Sorrier than I can tell you — about all of it.

FORBES [*after a pause*]. Oh, Mr. Smith — I've just been hearing something from Mrs. Smith about Mr. Van Dyck.

GORDON [*scared*]. You — have?

FORBES. Yes.

GORDON [*he grits his teeth*]. Well, then of course you know that —

FORBES. Yes, I know. [*A pause*] But it won't work, Mr. Smith.

GORDON. What's that?

FORBES. I'll admit that Mrs. Smith is a clever woman — a very clever woman. [GORDON *looks at him wonderingly*] But it won't work. [*A pause*] Van Dyck *not* Van Dyck. Hah! [GORDON *laughs nervously*] I might have believed it — if I hadn't happened to meet Blair Patterson down here. No, Mr. Smith! I know Patterson, and I know that he represents the Van Dyck interests. A man like Patterson doesn't suddenly pop up in Westchester to talk business with a man with hallucinations!

GORDON [*not knowing just what to do*]. Oh! Well, of course you know —

FORBES. You bet I do! I saw it all! You began to be sorry you'd told me about the Van Dyck merger, and wanted to throw me off the trail — eh? Well, you can't do it. I know what's in the wind, and I'm going to hold you to your agreement.

GORDON. Agreement?

FORBES. Well, it was a verbal agreement. As a gentleman you agreed to come in with me and take sixteen and two thirds per cent, and you've got to do it.

GORDON [*having difficulty in not betraying himself*]. But, Mr. Forbes —

FORBES. You've not signed anything with Van Dyck yet and it was just as good as settled with me. Now, if you don't — [ANGELA *bursts through the windows — still in her evening dress.* MRS. FORBES *and* DULCY *follow her*]

ANGELA. Father!

DULCY. Well, here she is!

FORBES. Angela!

MRS. FORBES [*quaveringly, her hands on* ANGELA'S *arms*]. Angela, oh, Angela?

ANGELA. Oh, mother — father!

DULCY [*expectantly, as though awaiting a speech of forgiveness from* FORBES]. Well —?

FORBES [*as all eyes go towards him — a short pause*]. Are you — married?

ANGELA. Yes, father.

MRS. FORBES. Oh, she's married! [*She takes* ANGELA *into her arms*]

DULCY. She's married!

FORBES. Well — where is your husband? [ANGELA *looks up at him, then buries her face in her mother's shoulder*] Answer me, Angela!

[*Enter* BILL. *He still wears his dinner clothes*]

BILL [*quietly*]. Good morning, everybody.

GORDON [*casually*]. Hello, Bill.

DULCY [*carelessly*]. Oh, hello, Willie.

FORBES. Where is Leach?

ANGELA [*with a half smile*]. I don't know, father.

FORBES. You — don't know? [*To* BILL] Well, perhaps you can tell us!

BILL [*shaking his head*]. I'm sorry.

FORBES. Didn't you help to arrange this wedding?

BILL. Why — yes.

FORBES. Well, don't you know where the groom is?

BILL. Sure — I'm the groom.

FORBES [*staggering*]. You're — wh-wh-what's that?

DULCY. Gr-gr-groom — Willie!

GORDON. What?

MRS. FORBES. Why — why — Angela — [*They all come together — there*

is a burst of excitement. MRS. FORBES *embraces* ANGELA *again,* DULCY *embraces* WILLIE. FORBES *and* GORDON *exchange looks. Slowly the excitement dies down*]

DULCY. Well — well, tell us about it! Good heavens! Willie! Just think!

ANGELA [*breaking from her mother's embrace*]. It was just the most romantic thing that ever happened in the world! William — William just kidnapped me, that's all! Oh, William! [*She goes into his arms.* DULCY *laughs ecstatically*]

FORBES [*to* BILL]. Are you a — genius?

BILL. I should say not. [*They shake hands*]

DULCY [*to* FORBES]. He's a broker! Isn't it wonderful?

MRS. FORBES. Oh, Charlie!

GORDON. Well, what about Leach — where is he?

BILL. I don't know.

DULCY. Don't know?

BILL. We started from here together all right last night — but — ah — down the road a piece I suddenly thought my tail-light was out. Mr. Leach was kind enough to get out and see that everything was all right; suddenly the darned thing started. I tossed his suit-case out to him — I don't think you'll ever see him again.

FORBES [*after a laugh — slapping* BILL'S *back*]. You're pretty damn clever.

DULCY. I introduced them!

FORBES [*to* DULCY]. Oh, so this was what you were working for, underneath that Leach business?

DULCY [*suddenly seeing a chance to claim the credit*]. Yes. [*She meets* BILL'S *eye*] And no — [*She evades the issue*] You don't understand woman very well, Mr. Forbes.

[*Enter* HENRY *with the morning papers*]

GORDON [*taken off his feet*]. Henry!

HENRY [*as though it were all part of his duties*]. Good morning, sir.

DULCY [*to* GORDON]. Aren't you glad he's back?

GORDON. But — but — what's this mean?

DULCY. Oh, I forgot to tell you. Henry had to go to town last night — [*She lowers her voice*] You know — to report to the Probation Officer. Every week.

GORDON. But — but — the necklace?

FORBES. Yes, the necklace.

DULCY. Oh, I forgot to tell you that, too. Henry found it last night and took it for safe-keeping. He gave it to me back this morning.

GORDON. He did?

HENRY. Yes, sir, I found it lying about, so I thought I'd better take charge of it, with so many people in the house. [*He departs*]

DULCY [*takes her place between* BILL *and* ANGELA, *an arm around each*]. It's upstairs for you, Angie, dear. Think of Angie being a married woman, and Willie a married man! Now, Mr. Forbes, you know sixteen and two-thirds per cent isn't very much — for a relation, a brother-in-law.

FORBES. Well, I wasn't very generous about that deal of ours, or very just. Smith —

GORDON. Yes, sir.

FORBES. What do you say to coming in with me for twenty per cent?

DULCY. Twenty!

FORBES [*anticipating further objections*]. Well, then, twenty-five.

DULCY. Twenty-five!

GORDON. Dulcinea, that satisfies *me!*

DULCY. Does it? Well, if it satisfies Gordon — [*She turns to him*] I didn't mean to interfere, dear. I never will again. You can rely on me. A burnt child dreads the fire. Once bitten — [GORDON *is embracing her and stops her with a kiss, as*

THE CURTAIN FALLS

THE ADDING MACHINE
(1923)
By Elmer L. Rice

ELMER L. RICE

To any one who wishes to know fully how the new dramatists have broken with the past, both in content and form, "The Adding Machine" will be an excellent approach. For that it is representative of the new technique is apparent to the reader who has just read before it a drama of the old technique — say, for example, Augustus Thomas's "The Witching Hour." The inclusion of this interesting play by Mr. Rice necessitates some limited discussion of "expressionism" which it attempts to illustrate in its numberless scenes of changing and progressive significance.

It is still a question with many as to whether "expressionism" is as new as it claims to be; whether it is not as much at fault as the old realism against which it rebels, by using just as many distracting objects for externalizing its meaning — even more distracting, since they are often so grotesque, so morbid, so overaccentuated in their intensity. The same objections were hurled at the progressive stage designers, who, raising the cry of simplicity, essential mood, broke from the picture-frame set with its Academy background, with its cluttered realistic details represented, and became suggestive. Did they not, in the end, demand as much, detract as much by their appeal to the eye with the unfamiliar, as the realism they decried?

But the arguments could not stop the onward tendency of the new practitioners in art and drama. The artists' philosophy is giving us a new physical theatre with widened possibility for spiritual content. The dramatists are creating for us interesting plays under the Freudian influence, but their technique, lacking precision, offering looseness of locality, is so far merely an experiment in content with a form that is dangerous to use because it is so haphazardly at the mercy of murky imagination. Spiritual violences, as they are practised in "expressionism", are just as lurid as the melodramatic ones. And I do not believe that in the use of unseen effectiveness, any play of the "newest" school has given us any more definite shudder than Maeterlinck did in "The Blind", "The Intruder" or "Interior", — any more definite feeling of inner content.

Nevertheless, there is a rhythm to the new technique which one must consider, acknowledging its stage effectiveness, even if doubting its ultimate permanent conquest of more classic form. The statement of the philosophy underlying "expressionism" came to the American playwright through the enthusiasms of the scenic artists who went abroad and imbibed the experimental theories of the German theatres and studios. I think that, because of our interest in the novelty of certain imaginative daring, we have overaccentuated the word "expressionism", and gained for the play thus hailed a contumely commensurate with the dislike many have for the symbolic drama. For, given a Freudian slant, "expressionism" has much of the symbolical about it: certainly "The Adding Machine" has. And recalling Toller's "Masse Mensch", Lenormand's "Failures", J. H. Lawson's "Processional", and countless other plays of similar character, it can be said for the new form only that one is able to drop into its isolated scene arrangement any variation of real and grotesque meaning one wishes. The dramatist may start with a theme that could easily be worked into a drama of the conventional mold; instead of which he throws the conventional shape aside, throws off the outward reality, and writes a number of scenes which are psychopathic footnotes, certain minute probings of inner depths and notations of the inhibited vapors that are hid beneath the surface.

We in America are forever trying to explain new forms; we are much more concerned with noting the characteristics of "expressionism" than are the German exponents of the same. If Barrett Clark's report from these Germans is a reflection of their general belief, such dramatists as Georg Kaiser, Walter Hasenclever and Ernst Toller are not worried about the meaning. I shall leave the defining of the term, by merely quoting a few characteristic explanations of it.

Writes Kenneth Macgowan : "Since expressionism itself is an attempt to escape from representing nature in the terms of its effect on the artist, and instead to present the emotion of the artist in terms of either nature or abstract form, its drama is at utter odds with realism."

In his book on "The Primer of Modern Art", Sheldon Cheney writes : " I consider expressionism to be that movement in art which transfers the emphasis from technical display and imitated surface aspects of nature to creative form; from descriptive and representative truth to intensified emotional expressiveness; from objective to subjective and abstract formal qualities."

In his excellent review of "The Adding Machine", Professor Ludwig Lewisohn is more direct. He writes in the *Nation*, April 4, 1923 :

Expressionism has two chief aims : to fling the inner life of the dramatic figures immediately upon the stage; to synthesize, instead of describing, their world and their universe into symbolic visions that shall sum up whole histories, moralities, cosmogonies in a brief minute and a fleeting scene. If this form of art is to be effective and beautiful, it must be very sensitive and very severe at once. Beneath it must be fundamental brainwork, thinking as resilient as steel and as clean-cut as agate. The symbolic masses must glow with a clear irradiation from within. Otherwise all is murky and muddled. You can describe fragmentarily and produce fragments of truth. Realism does not commit you to any whole. In expressionism the antecedent intellectual grasp of your entire material must be form, definite, complete. Everything must be thought out and thought through. This is what, despite moments of the highest brilliancy and glow, Mr. Eugene O'Neill did not do in "The Hairy Ape." This is what, in a harder, drier, less poetical vein, Mr. Elmer Rice has actually succeeded in doing in "The Adding Machine."

The American public seems to have taken to such a form as this. I do not believe that the popularity of Molnar's "Liliom" or of the Kaufman and Connelly "Beggar on Horseback" was due to the bitter irony underlying them; nor do I believe "R. U. R." or "The Insect Comedy" drew because in form they were understood. The novelty, the unusualness of the stage set — far from the intent of the scenic artist, who was after mood rather than curious appeal — and the quick rhythm of the isolated scenes, which gave change of interest if not always continuity of thought, appealed to them. Mr. Lawson, when he constructed "Processional", tried to catch this nervous tension of the American people. He wrote about the play's mood :

I have tried to approach the procession of American life from the point of view of a strictly native idiom. During the past five years the theatre has opened many new doors. New York has discovered Europe. And the native play has plowed fresh fields. But this has been only a beginning, rich in expectation but poor in achievement. The American playwright must create his own structure and his own language. He cannot borrow expressionism from Germany any more than he can shut himself up in one of Pinero's drawing-rooms. He must find the rhythm of his own age. In a sense, perhaps, this is a jazz rhythm. At least jazz gives a superficial impression of the mechanistic unrest of the period. But the inner meaning of jazz is as hard to find as the inner meaning of a locomotive or a political campaign. It seems to me that any play worth its salt must find inner human values in this pulse of the times.

This is written by a very young recruit of the theatre, who knows little about theatre values, and has experimented less with them. "Processional" is a mixture of ill-digested motives against a background thoroughly "expressionistic" of American life and condition. Types and symbols are moved across the stage, but they are the types we have had before in the conventional drama, and they are the symbols which would be more distinct and effective in more permanent mold, and if not jazzed into indistinctness. I mention this play because it goes even farther than Mr. Rice's "The Adding Machine" in trying, through bitter irony, to show the ugliness of the machine life we live, where we are not capable of dealing with the forces we meet, whether capitalism be a man or an abstract force, but are thrown back, generation upon generation, on recurrent mediocrity.

Mr. Rice, some years ago, as clerk in a law firm, began writing plays. The first he produced created a sensation. It was "On Trial." It used, in a clever way, a technical stunt, which he had watched in the moving-picture technique, and now applied to the theatre. Such critics as Clayton Hamilton regarded it as a remarkable defiance of stated classic mandates about stage structure. For a number of years Mr. Rice has followed in more or less conservative lines, writing such plays as "The Home of the Free", "The Iron Cross" and "It is the Law." Then, in the early Spring of 1923, came "The Adding Machine", under the successful direction of The Theatre Guild. A very few days after its production, Mr. Rice wrote to the dramatic editor of the New York *Times* a letter which is worth reproducing:

In reading the reviews of "The Adding Machine", I found that the critics likened it to "Liliom", "From Morn to Midnight", "R. U. R.", "Reigen", "The Awakening of Spring", "The World We Live In", "Masse Mensch", "The Hairy Ape", "Main Street", "Roger Bloomer", and (upon my word of honor!) "Mrs. Caudle's Curtain Lectures."

This puzzled me a little at first, for, despite my acquaintance with all the works mentioned (except "Reigen" and "Masse Mensch"), I could not detect that they had anything in common with each other or with "The Adding Machine." Of course there is a graveyard scene in "The Awakening of Spring" and a heaven scene in "Liliom", but there is also a graveyard scene in "Hamlet", a heaven scene in "Faust", a nagging wife in "The Taming of the Shrew", a murder in "Electra", and so on.

I became convinced, therefore, that what the reviewers sensed was something that went deeper than a mere surface similarity of incident or locale. And upon reflection it struck me that what all these works have in common (except, of course, the amiable papers of Douglas Jerrold) is perhaps a method of attack. That is to say, they all attempt to go beyond mere representation and to arrive at interpretation. In each of them there is an element that can be called, I think, metaphysical. The author attempts not so much to depict events faithfully as to convey to the spectator what seems to him their inner significance. To achieve this end the dramatist often finds it expedient to depart entirely from objective reality and to employ symbols, condensations and a dozen devices which, to the conservative, must seem arbitrarily fantastic.

This, I suppose, is what is meant by expressionism. But I am inclined to agree with Philip Moeller that such a term is little more than a convenient label. It would be a great mistake, I think, to permit it to harden into a rigid formula, or to attempt to build a "new school" of playwriting upon it.

This leads me to say that I should like to dispel the notion that "The Adding Machine" is a "stunt" play. I did not set out with the intention of doing something startling or daring. With "On Trial" it was another matter. There I began with what I recognized as a striking technical device, and I set about to exploit it as effectively as I could. My interest in the story and characters was entirely secondary; it was the trick that amused me.

In "The Adding Machine", however, form and content are indissolubly wedded. It may very well be that the same story could have been developed just as effectively in another medium, or that another story would have been better suited to the device. That is not the point. The point is that I wrote the play just as I conceived it, without thought of theories of technique; in fact, without rationalizing about it at all.

As proof of this I may add that from the moment I first conceived the play until the moment the manuscript was completed exactly seventeen days elapsed. . . .

This is an interesting confession and explanation. It shows that a supposed dramatic form is nothing more than a clever device for gaining certain dramatic effects — effects just as pronouncedly theatrical as the introduction of the supernatural in Dante or Goethe or Shakespeare and without as much spiritual symbol on the surface. Only these effects are not for themselves alone, but a commentary on action which is not shown, and a measure of thoughts that are not expressed. The same design is used by Mr. Rice in a play which is on the eve of production, and which he calls "The Subway" — the suppressed surging of a physical vitality — a girl caught in the maelstrom of our systematized commercialism, and who is crushed in the end by the subway, brought there through her inability to understand various surgings within her or to rise above her commonplace inadequacy. Mr. Rice has an ironical social philosophy; he believes as firmly in the principal of devolution as of evolution. He sees cycles of inferiority as well as of superiority. And he is unsparing in his indication of the negative trend.

He confesses, in his letter to the *Times*, that the content easily took the form in which we have "The Adding Machine." There is a certain looseness to this form which allows of haste. Perhaps it was this very haste which made "The Adding Machine" waver in its integrity of story, a fault which the English critics detected in the play when it was presented in London by the Stage Society, during the winter of 1924. They saw in it a bold presentation, with "thought sequences" which "wander like arabesques", a "skilful and beautiful piece of writing," especially in the "intense tragedy of *Zero's* conviction." Then, says one critic, "the focus of the play changes; the motive, so clear and simple, is altered, becomes blurred."

Forgetting, however, the medium, the technique, and judged as a pure piece of theatre, "The Adding Machine" has a powerful significance both for the reader and observer. It is the best example of the expressionistic genre so far to be had in America. Behind it is that same definiteness of social philosophy one feels is behind "R. U. R." And if at times it fails to hold firmly, that is the limitation, I fear, of its form, the limitation of its content — or rather the difficulty of making visible its content in full meaning. Its seriousness is often overclouded by its novel strangeness.

Although, with Dorothy Parker, Mr. Rice can construct such an excellent middle-class tragic comedy as "Close Harmony" in the old form — though there are intimations here in the way he handles the psychology of Main Street thought, of suburban commonplaceness, that expressions are surging to come forth in places which closeness of technique will not allow — he appears, at the present moment, to be an uncompromising enemy of the old dramatic technique.   In fact, he borders on the line where in the theatre dramatists are about to give us the important words in a sentence rather than the sentence itself : half gaspings, as curious and as peculiar to handle as the iterations one found in the early plays of Maeterlinck.

It is because of the uncertainty of the form at the present stage of the revolution, that I cannot take "expressionism" as anything more than a dramatic groping for something which may be, in the distant future, far different from what the reformers intended.   They are merely, right now, putting into the picture-frame theatre a technique of art, strange in accomplishment and challenging in its philosophy, not unlike those canvasses the advanced painters are hanging in the studios.   They are gropings.   But the interesting thing about "The Adding Machine", as there is about "R. U. R." and "Liliom", is that its dramatic effectiveness is there, and its conception is backed by an intensely interesting, conscious analysis of character. I doubt whether the form of "The Adding Machine" carried it all.   But it was in the mind of the dramatist.   There are not many American dramatists who have so much in mind when they write plays.

THE ADDING MACHINE

A PLAY IN SEVEN SCENES

By ELMER L. RICE

The cast of the Theatre Guild Production as originally
presented at the Garrick Theatre, March 19th, 1923

THE ADDING MACHINE

A PLAY IN SEVEN SCENES

BY ELMER L. RICE

Production directed by PHILIP MOELLER
Settings and Costumes by LEE SIMONSON
Incidental Music by DEEMS TAYLOR

CHARACTERS (in order of appearance)

MR. ZERO	Dudley Digges
MRS. ZERO	Helen Westley
DAISY DIANA DOROTHEA DEVORE	Margaret Wycherly
THE BOSS	Irving Dillon
MR. ONE	Harry McKenna
MRS. ONE	Marcia Harris
MR. TWO	Paul Hayes
MRS. TWO	Theresa Stewart
MR. THREE	Gerald Lundegard
MRS. THREE	Georgiana Wilson
MR. FOUR	George Stehli
MRS. FOUR	Edith Burnett
MR. FIVE	William W. Griffith
MRS. FIVE	Ruby Craven
MR. SIX	Daniel Hamilton
MRS. SIX	Louise Sydmeth
POLICEMAN	Irving Dillon
JUDY O'GRADY	Elise Bartlett
YOUNG MAN	Gerald Lundegard
SHRDLU	Edward G. Robinson
A HEAD	Daniel Hamilton
LIEUTENANT CHARLES	Louis Calvert
JOE	William W. Griffith

SCENE 1	A bedroom		SCENE 4	A place of justice
SCENE 2	An office		SCENE 5	A graveyard
SCENE 3	A living-room		SCENE 6	A pleasant place

SCENE 7   Another office

Stage Manager, Lewis Barrington

THE ADDING MACHINE

SCENE ONE

SCENE. — *A bedroom.*

A small room containing an "installment plan" bed, dresser, and chairs. An ugly electric light fixture over the bed with a single glaring naked lamp. One small window with the shade drawn. The walls are papered with sheets of foolscap covered with columns of figures.

MR. ZERO *is lying in the bed, facing the audience, his head and shoulders visible. He is thin, sallow, undersized, and partially bald.* MRS. ZERO *is standing before the dresser arranging her hair for the night. She is forty-five, sharp-featured, gray streaks in her hair. She is shapeless in her long-sleeved cotton nightgown. She is wearing her shoes, over which sag her ungartered stockings.*

MRS. ZERO [*as she takes down her hair*]. I'm gettin' sick o' them Westerns. All them cowboys ridin' around an' foolin' with them ropes. I don't care nothin' about that. I'm sick of 'em. I don't see why they don't have more of them stories like "For Love's Sweet Sake." I like them sweet little love stories. They're nice an' wholesome. Mrs. Twelve was sayin' to me only yesterday, "Mrs. Zero," says she, "what I like is one of them wholesome stories, with just a sweet, simple little love story." "You're right, Mrs. Twelve," I says. "That's what I like, too." They're showin' too many Westerns at the Rosebud. I'm gettin' sick of them. I think we'll start goin' to the Peter Stuyvesant. They got a good bill there Wednesday night. There's a Chubby Delano comedy called "Sea-Sick." Mrs. Twelve was tellin' me about it. She says it's a scream. They're havin' a picnic in the country and they sit Chubby next to an old maid with a great big mouth. So he gets sore an' when she ain't lookin' he goes and catches a frog and drops it in her clam chowder. An' when she goes to eat the chowder the frog jumps out of it an' right into her mouth. Talk about laugh! Mrs. Twelve was tellin' me she laughed so she nearly passed out. He sure can pull some funny ones. An' they got that big Grace Darling feature, "A Mother's Tears." She's sweet. But I don't like her clothes. There's no style to them. Mrs. Nine was tellin' me she read in *Pictureland* that she ain't livin' with her husband. He's her second, too. I don't know whether they're divorced or just separated. You wouldn't think it to see her on the screen. She looks so sweet and innocent. Maybe it ain't true. You can't believe all you read. They say some Pittsburgh millionaire is crazy about her and that's why she ain't livin' with her husband. Mrs. Seven was tellin' me her brother-in-law has a friend that used to go to school with Grace Darling. He says her name ain't Grace Darling at all. Her right name is Elizabeth Dugan, he says, an' all them stories about her gettin' five thousand a week is the bunk, he says. She's sweet, though. Mrs. Eight was tellin' me that "A Mother's Tears" is the best picture she ever made. "Don't miss it, Mrs. Zero," she says. "It's sweet," she says. "Just sweet and wholesome. Cry!" she says, "I nearly cried my eyes out." There's one part in it where this big bum of an Englishman — he's a married man, too — an' she's this little simple country girl. An' she nearly falls for him, too. But she's sittin' out in the garden, one day, and she looks up and there's her mother lookin' at her, right out of the clouds. So that night she locks the door of her room. An' sure enough, when everybody's in bed, along comes this big bum of an Englishman an' when she won't let him in what does he do but go an' kick open the door. "Don't miss it, Mrs. Zero," Mrs. Eight was tellin' me. It's at the Peter Stuyvesant Wednesday night, so don't be tellin' me you want to go to the Rosebud. The Eights seen it downtown at the Strand. They go downtown all the time. Just like us — nit! I guess by the time it gets to the Peter Stuyvesant all that part about kickin' in the door will be cut out. Just like they cut out that big cabaret scene in "The Price of Virtue." They sure are pullin' some rough stuff in the pictures nowadays. "It's no place for a young girl," I was tellin' Mrs. Eleven, only the other day. An' by the time they get uptown half of it is cut out. But you wouldn't go downtown — not if wild horses was to drag you. You can wait till they come uptown! Well, I don't want to wait, see? I want to see 'em when everybody else is seein' them an' not a month later. Now don't go tellin' me you ain't got the price. You could dig up the price all right, all right, if you wanted to. I notice you always got the price to go to the ball game. But when it comes to me havin' a good time then it's always: "I ain't got the price, I gotta start savin'." A fat lot you'll ever save! I got all I can do now makin' both ends meet an' you talkin' about savin'. [*She seats herself on a chair and begins removing her shoes and stockings*] An' don't go pullin' that stuff about bein' tired. "I been workin' hard all day. Twice a day in the subway's enough for me." Tired! Where do you get that tired stuff, anyhow? What about me? Where do I come in? Scrubbin' floors an' cookin' your meals an' washin' your dirty clothes. An' you sittin' on a chair all day, just addin' figgers an' waitin' for five-thirty. There's no five-thirty for me. I don't wait for no whistle. I don't get no vacations neither. And what's more I don't get no pay envelope every Saturday night neither. I'd like to know where you'd be without me. An' what have I got to show for it? — slavin' my life away to give you a home. What's in it for me, I'd like to know? But it's my own fault, I guess. I was a fool for marryin' you. If I'd 'a' had any sense, I'd 'a' known what you were from the start. I wish I had it to do

over again, I hope to tell you. You was goin' to do wonders, you was! You wasn't goin' to be a bookkeeper long — oh, no, not you. Wait till you got started — you was goin' to show 'em. There wasn't no job in the store that was too big for you. Well, I've been waitin' — waitin' for you to get started — see? It's been a good long wait, too. Twenty-five years! An' I ain't seen nothin' happen. Twenty-five years in the same job. Twenty-five years to-morrow! You're proud of it, ain't you? Twenty-five years in the same job an' never missed a day! That's somethin' to be proud of, ain't it? Sittin' for twenty-five years on the same chair, addin' up figures. What about bein' store-manager? I guess you forgot about that, didn't you? An' me at home here lookin' at the same four walls an' workin' my fingers to the bone to make both ends meet. Seven years since you got a raise! An' if you don't get one to-morrow, I'll bet a nickel you won't have the guts to go an' ask for one. I didn't pick much when I picked you, I'll tell the world. You ain't much to be proud of. [*She rises, goes to the window, and raises the shade. A few lighted windows are visible on the other side of the closed court. Looking out for a moment*] She ain't walkin' around to-night, you can bet your sweet life on that. An' she won't be walkin' around any more nights, neither. Not in this house, anyhow. [*She turns away from the window*] The dirty bum! The idea of her comin' to live in a house with respectable people. They should 'a' gave her six years, not six months. If I was the judge I'd of gave her life. A bum like that. [*She approaches the bed and stands there a moment*] I guess you're sorry she's gone. I guess you'd like to sit home every night an' watch her goin's-on. You're somethin' to be proud of, you are! [*She stands on the bed and turns out the light. . . . A thin stream of moonlight filters in from the court. The two figures are dimly visible.* MRS. ZERO *gets into bed*] You'd better not start nothin' with women, if you know what's good for you. I've put up with a lot, but I won't put up with that. I've been slavin' away for twenty-five years, makin' a home for you an' nothin' to show for it. If you was any kind of a man you'd have a decent job by now an' I'd be gettin' some comfort out of life — instead of bein' just a slave, washin' pots an' standin' over the hot stove. I've stood it for twenty-five years an' I guess I'll have to stand it twenty-five more. But don't you go startin' nothin' with women — [*She goes on talking as*

THE CURTAIN FALLS

SCENE TWO

SCENE. — *An office in a department store. Wood and glass partitions. In the middle of the room, two tall desks back to back. At one desk on a high stool is ZERO. Opposite him at the other desk, also on a high stool, is* DAISY DIANA DOROTHEA DEVORE, *a plain, middle-aged woman. Both wear green eye shades and paper sleeve protectors. A pendent electric lamp throws light upon both desks.* DAISY *reads aloud figures from a pile of slips which lie before her. As she reads the figures,* ZERO *enters them upon a large square sheet of ruled paper which lies before him.*

DAISY [*reading aloud*]. Three ninety-eight. Forty-two cents. A dollar fifty. A dollar fifty. A dollar twenty-five. Two dollars. Thirty-nine cents. Twenty-seven fifty.

ZERO [*petulantly*]. Speed it up a little, cancha?

DAISY. What's the rush? To-morrer's another day.

ZERO. Aw, you make me sick.

DAISY. An' you make me sicker.

ZERO. Go on. Go on. We're losin' time.

DAISY. Then quit bein' so bossy. [*She reads*] Three dollars. Two sixty-nine. Eighty-one fifty. Forty dollars. Eight seventy-five. Who do you think you are, anyhow?

ZERO. Never mind who I think I am. You tend to your work.

DAISY. Aw, don't be givin' me so many orders. Sixty cents. Twenty-four cents. Seventy-five cents. A dollar fifty. Two fifty. One fifty. One fifty. Two fifty. I don't have to take it from you and what's more I won't.

ZERO. Aw, quit talkin'.

DAISY. I'll talk all I want. Three dollars. Fifty cents. Fifty cents. Seven dollars. Fifty cents. Two fifty. Three fifty. Fifty cents. One fifty. Fifty cents. [*She goes bending over the*

slips and transferring them from one pile to another. ZERO *bends over his desk, busily entering the figures*]

ZERO [*without looking up*]. You make me sick. Always shootin' off your face about somethin'. Talk, talk, talk. Just like all the other women. Women make me sick.

DAISY [*busily fingering the slips*]. Who do you think you are, anyhow? Bossin' me around. I don't have to take it from you, and what's more I won't. [*They both attend closely to their work, neither looking up*]

ZERO. Women make me sick. They're all alike. The judge gave her six months. I wonder what they do in the work-house. Peel potatoes. I'll bet she's sore at me. Maybe she'll try to kill me when she gets out. I better be careful. Hello, Girl Slays Betrayer. Jealous Wife Slays Rival. You can't tell what a woman's liable to do. I better be careful.

DAISY. I'm gettin' sick of it. Always pickin' on me about somethin'. Never a decent word out of you. Not even the time o' day.

ZERO. I guess she wouldn't have the nerve at that. Maybe she don't even know it's me. They didn't even put my name in the paper, the big bums. Maybe she's been in the work-house before. A bum like that. She didn't have nothin' on that one time — nothin' but a shirt. [*He glances up quickly, then bends over again*] You make me sick. I'm sick of lookin' at your face.

DAISY. Gee, ain't that whistle ever goin' to blow? You didn't used to be like that. Not even good mornin' or good evenin'. I ain't done nothin' to you. It's the young girls. Goin' around without corsets.

ZERO. Your face is gettin' all yeller. Why don't you put some paint on it? She was puttin' on paint that time. On her cheeks and on her lips. And that blue stuff on her eyes. Just sittin' there in a shimmy puttin' on the paint. An' walkin' around the room with her legs all bare.

DAISY. I wish I was dead.

ZERO. I was a goddam fool to let the wife get on to me. She oughta get six months at that. The dirty bum. Livin' in a house with respectable people. She'd be livin' there yet, if the wife hadn't o' got on to me. Damn her!

DAISY. I wish I was dead.

ZERO. Maybe another one'll move

in. Gee, that would be great. But the wife's got her eye on me now.

Daisy. I'm scared to do it, though.

Zero. You oughta move into that room. It's cheaper than where you're livin' now. I better tell you about it. I don't mean to be always pickin' on you.

Daisy. Gas. The smell of it makes me sick. [Zero *looks up and clears his throat*]

Daisy [*looking up, startled*]. Whadja say?

Zero. I didn't say nothin'.

Daisy. I thought you did.

Zero. You thought wrong. [*They bend over their work again*]

Daisy. A dollar sixty. A dollar fifty. Two ninety. One sixty-two.

Zero. Why the hell should I tell you? Fat chance of you forgettin' to pull down the shade!

Daisy. If I asked for carbolic they might get on to me.

Zero. Your hair's gettin' gray. You don't wear them shirt waists any more with the low collars. When you'd bend down to pick somethin' up —

Daisy. I wish I knew what to ask for. Girl Takes Mercury After All-Night Party. Woman In Ten-Story Death Leap.

Zero. I wonder where'll she go when she gets out. Gee, I'd like to make a date with her. Why didn't I go over there the night my wife went to Brooklyn? She never woulda found out.

Daisy. I seen Pauline Frederick do it once. Where could I get a pistol though?

Zero. I guess I didn't have the nerve.

Daisy. I'll bet you'd be sorry then that you been so mean to me. How do I know, though? Maybe you wouldn't.

Zero. Nerve! I got as much nerve as anybody. I'm on the level, that's all. I'm a married man and I'm on the level.

Daisy. Anyhow, why ain't I got a right to live? I'm as good as anybody else. I'm too refined, I guess. That's the whole trouble.

Zero. The time the wife had pneumonia I thought she was goin' to pass out. But she didn't. The doctor's bill was eighty-seven dollars. [*Looking up*] Hey, wait a minute! Didn't you say eighty-seven dollars?

Daisy [*looking up*]. What?

Zero. Was the last you said eighty-seven dollars?

Daisy [*consulting the slip*]. Forty-two fifty.

Zero. Well, I made a mistake. Wait a minute. [*He busies himself with an eraser*] All right. Shoot.

Daisy. Six dollars. Three fifteen. Two twenty-five. Sixty-five cents. A dollar twenty. You talk to me as if I was dirt.

Zero. I wonder if I could kill the wife without anybody findin' out. In bed some night. With a pillow.

Daisy. I used to think you was stuck on me.

Zero. I'd get found out, though. They always have ways.

Daisy. We used to be so nice and friendly together when I first came here. You used to talk to me then.

Zero. Maybe she'll die soon. I noticed she was coughin' this mornin'.

Daisy. You used to tell me all kinds o' things. You were goin' to show them all. Just the same, you're still sittin' here.

Zero. Then I could do what I damn please. Oh, boy!

Daisy. Maybe it ain't all your fault neither. Maybe if you'd had the right kind o' wife — somebody with a lot of common-sense, somebody refined — me!

Zero. At that, I guess I'd get tired of bummin' around. A feller wants some place to hang his hat.

Daisy. I wish she would die.

Zero. And when you start goin' with women you're liable to get into trouble. And lose your job maybe.

Daisy. Maybe you'd marry me.

Zero. Gee, I wish I'd gone over there that night.

Daisy. Then I could quit workin'.

Zero. Lots o' women would be glad to get me.

Daisy. You could look a long time before you'd find a sensible, refined girl like me.

Zero. Yes, sir, they could look a long time before they'd find a steady meal-ticket like me.

Daisy. I guess I'd be too old to have any kids. They say it ain't safe after thirty-five.

Zero. Maybe I'd marry you. You might be all right, at that.

Daisy. I wonder — if you don't want kids — whether — if there's any way —

Zero [*looking up*]. Hey! Hey! Can't you slow up? What do you think I am — a machine?

DAISY [*looking up*]. Say, what do you want, anyhow? First it's too slow an' then it's too fast. I guess you don't know what you want.

ZERO. Well, never mind about that. Just you slow up.

DAISY. I'm gettin' sick o' this. I'm goin' to ask to be transferred.

ZERO. Go ahead. You can't make me mad.

DAISY. Aw, keep quiet. [*She reads*] Two forty-five. A dollar twenty. A dollar fifty. Ninety cents. Sixty-three cents.

ZERO. Marry you! I guess not! You'd be as bad as the one I got.

DAISY. You wouldn't care if I did ask. I got a good mind to ask.

ZERO. I was a fool to get married.

DAISY. Then I'd never see you at all.

ZERO. What chance has a guy got with a woman tied around his neck?

DAISY. That time at the store picnic — the year your wife couldn't come — you were nice to me then.

ZERO. Twenty-five years holdin' down the same job!

DAISY. We were together all day — just sittin' around under the trees.

ZERO. I wonder if the boss remembers about it bein' twenty-five years.

DAISY. And comin' home that night — you sat next to me in the big delivery wagon.

ZERO. I got a hunch there's a big raise comin' to me.

DAISY. I wonder what it feels like to be really kissed. Men — dirty pigs! They want the bold ones.

ZERO. If he don't come across I'm goin' right up to the front office and tell him where he gets off.

DAISY. I wish I was dead.

ZERO. "Boss," I'll say, "I want to have a talk with you." "Sure," he'll say, "sit down. Have a Corona Corona." "No," I'll say, "I don't smoke." "How's that?" he'll say. "Well, boss," I'll say, "it's this way. Every time I feel like smokin' I just take a nickel and put it in the old sock. A penny saved is a penny earned, that's the way I look at it." "Damn sensible," he'll say. "You got a wise head on you, Zero."

DAISY. I can't stand the smell of gas. It makes me sick. You coulda kissed me if you wanted to.

ZERO. "Boss," I'll say, "I ain't quite satisfied. I been on the job twenty-five years now and if I'm gonna stay I gotta see a future ahead of me." "Zero," he'll say, "I'm glad you came in. I've had my eye on you, Zero. Nothin' gets by me." "Oh, I know that, boss," I'll say. That'll hand him a good laugh, that will. "You're a valuable man, Zero," he'll say, "and I want you right up here with me in the front office. You're done addin' figgers. Monday mornin' you move up here."

DAISY. Them kisses in the movies — them long ones — right on the mouth

ZERO. I'll keep a-goin' right on up after that. I'll show some of them birds where they get off.

DAISY. That one the other night — "The Devil's Alibi" — he put his arms around her — and her head fell back and her eyes closed — like she was in a daze.

ZERO. Just give me about two years and I'll show them birds where they get off.

DAISY. I guess that's what it's like — a kinda daze — when I see them like that, I just seem to forget everything.

ZERO. Then me for a place in Jersey. And maybe a little Buick. No tin Lizzie for mine. Wait till I get started — I'll show 'em.

DAISY. I can see it now when I kinda half-close my eyes. The way her head fell back. And his mouth pressed right up against hers. Oh, Gawd! it must be grand! [*There is a sudden shrill blast from a steam whistle*]

DAISY AND ZERO [*together*]. The whistle! [*With great agility they get off their stools, remove their eye shades and sleeve protectors and put them on the desk. Then each produces from behind the desk a hat —* ZERO, *a dusty derby,* DAISY, *a frowsy straw. . . .* DAISY *puts on her hat and turns toward* ZERO *as though she were about to speak to him. But he is busy cleaning his pen and pays no attention to her. She sighs and goes toward the door at the left*]

ZERO [*looking up*]. G'night, Miss Devore. [*But she does not hear him and exits.* ZERO *takes up his hat and goes left. The door at the right opens and the* Boss *enters — middle-aged, stoutish, bald, well-dressed*]

THE BOSS [*calling*]. Oh — er — Mister — er — [ZERO *turns in surprise, sees who it is and trembles nervously*]

ZERO [*obsequiously*]. Yes, sir. Do you want me, sir?

BOSS. Yes. Just come here a moment, will you?

ZERO. Yes, sir. Right away, sir. [*He fumbles his hat, picks it up, stumbles, recovers himself, and approaches the* Boss, *every fibre quivering*]

Boss. Mister — er — er —

ZERO. Zero.

Boss. Yes, Mr. Zero. I wanted to have a little talk with you.

ZERO [*with a nervous grin*]. Yes, sir, I been kinda expectin' it.

Boss [*staring at him*]. Oh, have you?

ZERO. Yes, sir.

Boss. How long have you been with us, Mister — er — Mister —

ZERO. Zero.

Boss. Yes, Mister Zero.

ZERO. Twenty-five years to-day.

Boss. Twenty-five years! That's a long time.

ZERO. Never missed a day.

Boss. And you've been doing the same work all the time?

ZERO. Yes, sir. Right here at this desk.

Boss. Then, in that case, a change probably won't be unwelcome to you.

ZERO. No, sir, it won't. And that's the truth.

Boss. We've been planning a change in this department for some time.

ZERO. I kinda thought you had your eye on me.

Boss. You were right. The fact is that my efficiency experts have recommended the installation of adding machines.

ZERO [*staring at him*]. Addin' machines?

Boss. Yes, you've probably seen them. A mechanical device that adds automatically.

ZERO. Sure. I've seen them. Keys — and a handle that you pull. [*He goes through the motions in the air*]

Boss. That's it. They do the work in half the time and a high-school girl can operate them. Now, of course, I'm sorry to lose an old and faithful employee —

ZERO. Excuse me, but would you mind sayin' that again?

Boss. I say I'm sorry to lose an employee who's been with me for so many years — [*Soft music is heard — the sound of the mechanical player of a distant merry-go-round. The part of the floor upon which the desk and stools are standing begins to revolve very slowly*]

But, of course, in an organization like this, efficiency must be the first consideration — [*The music becomes gradually louder and the revolutions more rapid*]

You will draw your salary for the full month. And I'll direct my secretary to give you a letter of recommendation —

ZERO. Wait a minute, boss. Let me get this right. You mean I'm canned?

Boss [*barely making himself heard above the increasing volume of sound*]. I'm sorry — no other alternative — greatly regret — old employee — efficiency — economy — business — *business* — BUSINESS — [*His voice is drowned by the music. The platform is revolving rapidly now.* ZERO *and the* Boss *face each other. They are entirely motionless save for the* Boss's *jaws, which open and close incessantly. But the words are inaudible. The music swells and swells. To it is added every off-stage effect of the theatre: the wind, the waves, the galloping horses, the locomotive whistle, the sleigh bells, the automobile siren, the glass-crash. New Year's Eve, Election Night, Armistice Day, and the Mardi-Gras. The noise is deafening, maddening, unendurable. Suddenly it culminates in a terrific peal of thunder. For an instant there is a flash of red and then everything is plunged into blackness*]

CURTAIN

SCENE THREE

SCENE. — *The* ZERO *dining room. Entrance door at right. Doors to kitchen and bedroom at left. The walls, as in the first scene, are papered with foolscap sheets covered with columns of figures. In the middle of the room, upstage, a table set for two. Along each side wall, seven chairs are ranged in symmetrical rows.*

At the rise of the curtain MRS. ZERO·*is seen seated at the table looking alternately at the entrance door and a clock on the wall. She wears a bungalow apron over her best dress.*

After a few moments, the entrance door *opens and* ZERO *enters. He hangs his hat on a rack behind the door and coming over to the table seats himself at the vacant place. His movements throughout are quiet and abstracted.*

MRS. ZERO [*breaking the silence*]. Well, it was nice of you to come home. You're only an hour late and that ain't very much. The supper don't get very cold in an hour. An' of course the part about our havin' a lot of company to-night don't matter. [*They begin to eat*] Ain't you even got sense enough to come home on time? Didn't I tell you we're goin' to have a lot o' company to-night? Didn't you know the Ones are comin'? An' the Twos? An' the Threes? An' the Fours? An' the Fives? And the Sixes? Didn't I tell you to be home on time? I might as well talk to a stone wall. [*They eat for a few moments in silence*] I guess you musta had some important business to attend to. Like watchin' the score-board. Or was two kids havin' a fight an' you was the referee? You sure do have a lot of business to attend to. It's a wonder you have time to come home at all. You gotta tough life, you have. Walk in, hang up your hat, an' put on the nose-bag. An' me in the hot kitchen all day, cookin' your supper an' waitin' for you to get good an' ready to come home! [*Again they eat in silence*] Maybe the boss kept you late to-night. Tellin' you what a big noise you are and how the store couldn't 'a' got along if you hadn't been pushin' a pen for twenty-five years. Where's the gold medal he pinned on you? Did some blind old lady take it away from you or did you leave it on the seat of the boss's limousine when he brought you home? [*Again a few moments of silence*] I'll bet he gave you a big raise, didn't he? Promoted you from the third floor to the fourth, maybe. Raise? A fat chance you got o' gettin' a raise. All they gotta do is put an ad in the paper. There's ten thousand like you layin' around the streets. You'll be holdin' down the same job at the end of another twenty-five years — if you ain't forgot how to add by that time. [*A noise is heard off-stage, a sharp clicking such as is made by the operation of the keys and levers of an adding machine. Zero raises his head for a moment, but lowers it almost instantly*] There's the door-bell. The company's here already. And we ain't hardly finished supper. [*She rises*] But I'm goin' to clear off the table whether you're finished or not. If you want your supper, you got a right to be home on time. Not standin' around lookin' at score-boards. [*As she piles up the dishes, Zero rises and goes toward the entrance door*] Wait a minute! Don't open the door yet. Do you want

the company to see all the mess? An' go an' put on a clean collar. You got red ink all over it. [*Zero goes toward bedroom door*] I should think after pushing a pen for twenty-five years, you'd learn how to do it without gettin' ink on your collar. [*Zero exits to bedroom. Mrs. Zero takes dishes to kitchen talking as she goes*] I guess I can stay up all night now washin' dishes. You should worry! That's what a man's got a wife for, ain't it. Don't he buy her clothes an' let her eat with him at the same table? An' all she's gotta do is cook the meals an' do the washin' an' scrub the floor, an' wash the dishes, when the company goes. But, believe me, you're goin' to sling a mean dish-towel when the company goes to-night! [*While she is talking Zero enters from bedroom. He wears a clean collar and is cramming the soiled one furtively into his pocket. Mrs. Zero enters from kitchen. She has removed her apron and carries a table cover which she spreads hastily over the table. The clicking noise is heard again*] There's the bell again. Open the door, cancha? [*Zero goes to the entrance door and opens it. Six men and six women file into the room in a double column. The men are all shapes and sizes, but their dress is identical with that of Zero in every detail. Each, however, wears a wig of a different color. The women are all dressed alike, too, except that the dress of each is of a different color. Mrs. Zero, taking the first woman's hand*] How de do, Mrs. One.

MRS. ONE. How de do, Mrs. Zero.

[MRS. ZERO *repeats this formula with each woman in turn. Zero does the same with the men except that he is silent throughout. The files now separate, each man taking a chair from the right wall and each woman one from the left wall. Each sex forms a circle with the chairs very close together. The men — all except Zero — smoke cigars. The women munch chocolates*]

SIX. Some rain we're havin'.
FIVE. Never saw the like of it.
FOUR. Worst in fourteen years, paper says.
THREE. Y'can't always go by the papers.
TWO. No, that's right, too.
ONE. We're liable to forget from year to year.

SIX. Yeh, come t' think, last year was pretty bad, too.

FIVE. An' how about two years ago?

FOUR. Still this year's pretty bad.

THREE. Yeh, no gettin' away from that.

TWO. Might be a whole lot worse.

ONE. Yeh, it's all the way you look at it. Some rain, though.

MRS. SIX. I like them little organdie dresses.

MRS. FIVE. Yeh, with a little lace trimmin' on the sleeves.

MRS. FOUR. Well, I like 'em plain myself.

MRS. THREE. Yeh, what I always say is the plainer the more refined.

MRS. TWO. Well, I don't think a little lace does any harm.

MRS. ONE. No, it kinda dresses it up.

MRS. ZERO. Well, I always say it's all a matter of taste.

MRS. SIX. I saw you at the Rosebud Movie Thursday night, Mr. One.

ONE. Pretty punk show, I'll say.

TWO. They're gettin' worse all the time.

MRS. SIX. But who was the charming lady, Mr. One?

ONE. Now don't you go makin' trouble for me. That was my sister.

MRS. FIVE. Oho! That's what they all say.

MRS. FOUR. Never mind! I'll bet Mrs. One knows what's what, all right.

MRS. ONE. Oh, well, he can do what he likes — 'slong as he behaves himself.

THREE. You're in luck at that, One. Fat chance I got of gettin' away from the frau even with my sister.

MRS. THREE. You oughta be glad you got a good wife to look after you.

THE OTHER WOMEN [*in unison*]. That's right, Mrs. Three.

FIVE. I guess I know who wears the pants in your house, Three.

MRS. ZERO. Never mind. I saw them holding' hands at the movie the other night.

THREE. She musta been tryin' to get some money away from me.

MRS. THREE. Swell chance anybody'd have of gettin' any money away from you. [*General laughter*]

FOUR. They sure are a loving couple.

MRS. TWO. Well, I think we oughta change the subject.

MRS. ONE. Yes, let's change the subject.

SIX [*sotto voce*]. Did you hear the one about the travellin' salesman?

FIVE. It seems this guy was in a sleeper.

FOUR. Goin' from Albany to San Diego.

THREE. And in the next berth was an old maid.

TWO. With a wooden leg.

ONE. Well, along about midnight — [*They all put their heads together and whisper*]

MRS. SIX [*sotto voce*]. Did you hear about the Sevens?

MRS. FIVE. They're gettin' a divorce.

MRS. FOUR. It's the second time for him.

MRS. THREE. They're two of a kind, if you ask me.

MRS. TWO. One's as bad as the other.

MRS. ONE. Worse.

MRS. ZERO. They say that she — [*They all put their heads together and whisper*]

SIX. I think this woman suffrage is the bunk.

FIVE. It sure is! Politics is a man's business.

FOUR. Woman's place is in the home.

THREE. That's it! Lookin' after the kids, 'stead of hangin' around the streets.

TWO. You hit the nail on the head that time.

ONE. The trouble is they don't know what they want.

MRS. SIX. Men sure get me tired.

MRS. FIVE. They sure are a lazy lot.

MRS. FOUR. And dirty.

MRS. THREE. Always grumblin' about somethin'.

MRS. TWO. When they're not lyin'!

MRS. ONE. Or messin' up the house.

MRS. ZERO. Well, believe me, I tell mine where he gets off.

SIX. Business conditions are sure bad.

FIVE. Never been worse.

FOUR. I don't know what we're comin' to.

THREE. I look for a big smash-up in about three months.

TWO. Wouldn't surprise me a bit.

ONE. We're sure headin' for trouble.

MRS. SIX. My aunt has gall-stones.

MRS. FIVE. My husband has bunions.

MRS. FOUR. My sister expects next month.

MRS. THREE. My cousin's husband has erysipelas.

MRS. TWO. My niece has St. Vitus's dance.

MRS. ONE. My boy has fits.

MRS. ZERO. I never felt better in my life. Knock wood!

SIX. Too damn much agitation, that's at the bottom of it.

FIVE. That's it! too damn many strikes.

FOUR. Foreign agitators, that's what it is.

THREE. They ought be run outa the country.

TWO. What the hell do they want, anyhow?

ONE. They don't know what they want, if you ask me.

SIX. America for the Americans is what I say!

ALL [*in unison*]. That's it! Damn foreigners! Damn dagoes! Damn Catholics! Damn sheenies! Damn niggers! Jail 'em! shoot 'em! hang 'em! lynch 'em! burn 'em! [*They all rise*]

ALL [*sing in unison*].
  "My country 'tis of thee,
    Sweet land of liberty!"

MRS. FOUR. Why so pensive, Mr. Zero?

ZERO [*speaking for the first time*]. I'm thinkin'.

MRS. FOUR. Well, be careful not to sprain your mind. [*Laughter*]

MRS. ZERO. Look at the poor men all by themselves. We ain't very sociable.

ONE. Looks like we're neglectin' the ladies.

[*The women cross the room and join the men, all chattering loudly. The door-bell rings*]

MRS. ZERO. Sh! The door-bell! [*The volume of sound slowly diminishes. Again the door-bell*]

ZERO [*quietly*]. I'll go. It's for me. [*They watch curiously as ZERO goes to the door and opens it, admitting a policeman. There is a murmur of surprise and excitement*]

POLICEMAN. I'm lookin' for Mr. Zero. [*They all point to ZERO*]

ZERO. I've been expectin' you.

POLICEMAN. Come along!

ZERO. Just a minute. [*He puts his hand in his pocket*]

POLICEMAN. What's he tryin' to pull? [*He draws a revolver*] I got you covered.

ZERO. Sure, that's all right. I just wanted to give you somethin'. [*He takes the collar from his pocket and gives it to the policeman*]

POLICEMAN [*suspiciously*]. What's that?

ZERO. The collar I wore.

POLICEMAN. What do I want it for?

ZERO. It's got blood-stains on it.

POLICEMAN [*pocketing it*]. All right, come along!

ZERO [*turning to MRS. ZERO*]. I gotta go with him. You'll have to dry the dishes yourself.

MRS. ZERO [*rushing forward*]. What are they takin' you for?

ZERO [*calmly*]. I killed the boss this afternoon. [*Quick Curtain as the policeman takes him off*]

SCENE FOUR

SCENE. — *A court of justice. Three bare white walls without door or windows except for a single door in the right wall. At the right is a jury-box in which are seated* MESSRS. ONE, TWO, THREE, FOUR, FIVE, *and* SIX *and their respective wives. On either side of the jury box stands a uniformed* OFFICER. *Opposite the jury box is a long, bare oak table piled high with law books. Behind the books* ZERO *is seated, his face buried in his hands. There is no other furniture in the room. A moment after the rise of the curtain, one of the officers rises and going around the table, taps* ZERO *on the shoulder.* ZERO *rises and accompanies the* OFFICER. *The* OFFICER *escorts him to the great empty space in the middle of the court room, facing the jury. He motions to* ZERO *to stop, then points to the jury and resumes his place beside the jury-box.* ZERO *stands there looking at the jury, bewildered and half afraid. The* JURORS *give no sign of having seen him. Throughout they sit with folded arms, staring stolidly before them.*

ZERO [*beginning to speak; haltingly*]. Sure I killed him. I ain't sayin' I didn't, am I? Sure I killed him. Them lawyers! They give me a good stiff pain, that's what they give me.

Half the time I don't know what the hell they're talkin' about. Objection sustained. Objection over-ruled. What's the big idea, anyhow? You ain't heard me do any objectin', have you? Sure not! What's the idea of objectin'? You got a right to know. What I say is if one bird kills another bird, why you got a right to call him for it. That's what I say. I know all about that. I been on the jury, too. Them lawyers! Don't let 'em fill you full of bunk. All that bull about it bein' red ink on the bill-file. Red ink nothin'! It was blood, see? I want you to get that right. I killed him, see? Right through the heart with the bill-file, see? I want you to get that right — all of you. One, two, three, four, five, six, seven, eight, nine, ten, eleven, twelve. Twelve of you. Six and six. That makes twelve. I figgered it up often enough. Six and six makes twelve. And five is seventeen. And eight is twenty-five. And three is twenty-eight. Eight and carry two. Aw, cut it out! Them damn figgers! I can't forget 'em. Twenty-five years, see? Eight hours a day, exceptin' Sundays. And July and August half-day Saturday. One week's vacation with pay. And another week without pay if you want it. Who the hell wants it? Layin' around the house listenin' to the wife tellin' you where you get off. Nix! An' legal holidays. I nearly forgot them. New Year's, Washington's Birthday, Decoration Day, Fourth o' July, Labor Day, Election Day, Thanksgivin', Christmas. Good Friday if you want it. An' if you're a Jew, Young Kipper an' the other one — I forget what they call it. The dirty sheenies — always gettin' two to the other bird's one. An' when a holiday comes on Sunday, you get Monday off. So that's fair enough. But when the Fourth o' July comes on Saturday, why you're out o' luck on account of Saturday bein' a half-day anyhow. Get me? Twenty-five years — I'll tell you somethin' funny. Decoration Day an' the Fourth o' July are always on the same day o' the week. Twenty-five years. Never missed a day, and never more'n five minutes late. Look at my time card if you don't believe me. Eight twenty-seven, eight thirty, eight twenty-nine, eight twenty-seven, eight thirty-two. Eight an' thirty-two's forty an' — Goddam them figgers! I can't forget 'em. They're funny things, them figgers. They look like people sometimes. The eights, see? Two dots for the eyes and a dot for the nose. An' a line. That's the mouth, see? An' there's others remind you of other things — but I can't talk about them, on account of there bein' ladies here. Sure I killed him. Why didn't he shut up? If he'd only shut up! Instead o' talkin' an' talkin' about how sorry he was an' what a good guy I was an' this an' that. I felt like sayin' to him: "For Christ's sake, shut up!" But I didn't have the nerve, see? I didn't have the nerve to say that to the boss. An' he went on talkin', sayin' how sorry he was, see? He was standin' right close to me. An' his coat only had two buttons on it. Two an' two makes four an' — aw, can it! An' there was the bill-file on the desk. Right where I could touch it. It ain't right to kill a guy. I know that. When I read all about him in the paper an' about his three kids I felt like a cheap skate, I tell you. They had the kids' pictures in the paper, right next to mine. An' his wife, too. Gee, it must be swell to have a wife like that. Some guys sure is lucky. An' he left fifty thousand dollars just for a rest-room for the girls in the store. He was a good guy, at that. Fifty thousand. That's more'n twice as much as I'd have if I saved every nickel I ever made. Let's see. Twenty-five an' twenty-five an' twenty-five an' — aw, cut it out! An' the ads had a big, black border around 'em; an' all it said was that the store would be closed for three days on account of the boss bein' dead. That nearly handed me a laugh, that did. All them floor-walkers an' buyers an' high-muck-a-mucks havin' me to thank for gettin' three days off. I hadn't oughta killed him. I ain't sayin' nothin' about that. But I thought he was goin' to give me a raise, see? On account of bein' there twenty-five years. He never talked to me before, see? Except one mornin' we happened to come in the store together and I held the door open for him and he said "Thanks." Just like that, see? "Thanks!" That was the only time he ever talked to me. An' when I seen him comin' up to my desk, I didn't know where I got off. A big guy like that comin' up to my desk. I felt like I was chokin' like and all of a sudden I got a kind o' bad taste in my mouth like when you get up in the mornin'. I didn't have no right to kill him. The district attorney is right about that. He read the law to you, right out o' the book. Killin' a bird — that's wrong. But there was that girl, see? Six months they gave her. It was a dirty trick tellin' the cops on her like that. I shouldn't 'a' done that. But what was I gonna do? The wife wouldn't let up on me. I hadda do it. She used to walk around the room, just in her undershirt, see? Nothin' else on. Just her undershirt. An' they gave her six months. That's the last I'll ever see of her. Them birds — how do they get away with it? Just grabbin' women, the way you see 'em do in the pictures. I've seen lots I'd like to grab like that, but I ain't got the nerve — in the subway an' on the street an' in the store buyin' things. Pretty soft for them shoe-salesmen, I'll say, lookin' at women's legs all day. Them lawyers! They give me a pain, I tell you — a pain! Sayin' the same thing over an' over again. I never said I didn't kill him. But that ain't the same as bein' a regular murderer. What good did it do me to kill him? I didn't make nothin' out of it. Answer yes or no! Yes or no, me elbow! There's some things you can't answer yes or no. Give me the once-over, you guys. Do I look like a murderer? Do I? I never did no harm to nobody. Ask the wife. She'll tell you. Ask anybody. I never got into trouble. You wouldn't count that one time at the Polo Grounds. That was just fun like. Everybody was yellin', "Kill the empire! Kill the empire!" An' before I knew what I was doin' I fired the pop bottle. It was on account of everybody yellin' like that. Just in fun like, see? The yeller dog! Callin' that one a strike — a mile away from the plate. Anyhow, the bottle didn't hit him. An' when I seen the cop comin' up the aisle, I beat it. That didn't hurt nobody. It was just in fun like, see? An' that time in the subway. I was readin' about a lynchin', see? Down in Georgia. They took the nigger an' they tied him to a tree. An' they poured kerosene on him and lit a big fire under him. The dirty nigger! Boy, I'd of liked to been there, with a gat in each hand, pumpin' him full of lead. I was readin' about it in the subway, see? Right at Times Square where the big crowd gets on. An' all of a sudden this big nigger steps right on my

foot. It was lucky for him I didn't have a gun on me. I'd of killed him sure, I guess. I guess he couldn't help it all right on account of the crowd, but a nigger's got no right to step on a white man's foot. I told him where he got off all right. The dirty nigger. But that didn't hurt nobody, either. I'm a pretty steady guy, you gotta admit that. Twenty-five years in one job an' I never missed a day. Fifty-two weeks in a year. Fifty-two an' fifty-two an' fifty-two an' — They didn't have t' look for me, did they? I didn't try to run away, did I? Where was I goin' to run to! I wasn't thinkin' about it at all, see? I'll tell you what I was thinkin' about — how I was goin' to break it to the wife about bein' canned. He canned me after twenty-five years, see? Did the lawyers tell you about that? I forget. All that talk gives me a headache. Objection sustained. Objection overruled. Answer yes or no. It gives me a headache. And I can't get the figgers outta my head, neither. But that's what I was thinkin' about — how I was goin' t' break it to the wife about bein' canned. An' what Miss Devore would think when she heard about me killin' him. I bet she never thought I had the nerve to do it. I'd of married her if the wife had passed out. I'd be holdin' down my job yet, if he hadn't o' canned me. But he kept talkin' an' talkin'. An' there was the bill-file right where I could reach it. Do you get me? I'm just a regular guy like anybody else. Like you birds, now. [*For the first time the* JURORS *relax, looking indignantly at each other and whispering*] Suppose you was me, now. Maybe you'd 'a' done the same thing. That's the way you oughta look at it, see? Suppose you was me —

THE JURORS [*rising as one and shouting in unison*]. GUILTY! [ZERO *falls back, stunned for a moment by their vociferousness. The* JURORS *right-face in their places and file quickly out of the jury-box and toward the door in a double column*]

ZERO [*recovering speech as the* JURORS *pass out at the door*]. Wait a minute. Jest a minute. You don't get me right. Jest give me a chance an' I'll tell you how it was. I'm all mixed up, see? On account of them lawyers. And the figgers in my head. But I'm goin' to tell you how it was. I was there twenty-five years, see? An' they gave her six months, see? [*He goes on haranguing the empty jury-box as the curtain falls*]

SCENE FIVE

SCENE. — *A grave-yard in full moonlight. It is a second-rate grave-yard — no elaborate tombstones or monuments — just simple headstones and here and there a cross. At the back is an iron fence with a gate in the middle. At first no one is visible, but there are occasional sounds throughout: the hooting of an owl, the whistle of a distant whippoorwill, the croaking of a bull-frog, and the yowling of a serenading cat. After a few moments two figures appear outside the gate — a man and a woman. She pushes the gate and it opens with a rusty creak. The couple enter. They are now fully visible in the moonlight —* JUDY O'GRADY *and a* YOUNG MAN.

JUDY [*advancing*]. Come on, this is the place.

YOUNG MAN [*hanging back*]. This! Why this here is a cemetery.

JUDY. Aw, quit yer kiddin'!

YOUNG MAN. You don't mean to say —

JUDY. What's the matter with this place?

YOUNG MAN. A cemetery!

JUDY. Sure. What of it?

YOUNG MAN. You must be crazy.

JUDY. This place is all right, I tell you. I been here lots o' times.

YOUNG MAN. Nix on this place for me!

JUDY. Ain't this place as good as another? Whaddya afraid of? They're all dead ones here! They don't bother you. [*With sudden interest*] Oh, look, here's a new one.

YOUNG MAN. Come on out of here.

JUDY. Wait a minute. Let's see what it says. [*She kneels on a grave in the foreground and putting her face close to headstone spells out the inscription*] Z-E-R-O. Z-e-r-o. Zero! Say, that's the guy —

YOUNG MAN. Zero? He's the guy killed his boss, ain't he?

JUDY. Yeh, that's him, all right. But what I'm thinkin' of is that I went to the hoose-gow on account of him.

YOUNG MAN. What for?

JUDY. You know, same old stuff. Tenement House Law. [*Mincingly*] Section blaa-blaa of the Penal Code. Third offense. Six months.

YOUNG MAN. And this bird —

JUDY [*contemptuously*]. Him? He was mama's white-haired boy. We lived in the same house. Across the airshaft, see? I used to see him lookin' in my window. I guess his wife musta seen him, too. Anyhow, they went and turned the bulls on me. And now I'm out and he's in. [*Suddenly*] Say — say — [*She bursts into a peal of laughter*]

YOUNG MAN [*nervously*]. What's so funny?

JUDY [*rocking with laughter*]. Say, wouldn't it be funny — if — if — [*She explodes again*] That would be a good joke on him, all right. He can't do nothin' about it now, can he?

YOUNG MAN. Come on out of here. I don't like this place.

JUDY. Aw, you're a bum sport. What do you want to spoil my joke for? [*A cat yammers mellifluously*]

YOUNG MAN [*half hysterically*]. What's that?

JUDY. It's only the cats. They seem to like it here all right. But come on if you're afraid. [*They go toward the gate. As they go out*] You nervous men sure are the limit. [*They go out through the gate. As they disappear* ZERO'S *grave opens suddenly and his head appears*]

ZERO [*looking about*]. That's funny! I thought I heard her talkin' and laughin'. But I don't see nobody. Anyhow, what would she be doin' here? I guess I must 'a' been dreamin'. But how could I be dreamin' when I ain't been asleep? [*He looks about again*] Well, no use goin' back. I can't sleep, anyhow. I might as well walk around a little. [*He rises out of the ground, very rigidly. He wears a full-dress suit of very antiquated cut and his hands are folded stiffly across his breast. Walking woodenly*] Gee! I'm stiff! [*He slowly walks a few steps, then stops*] Gee, it's lonesome here! [*He shivers and walks on aimlessly*] I should 'a' stayed where I was. But I thought I heard her laughin'. [*A loud sneeze is heard.* ZERO *stands motionless, quaking with terror. The sneeze is repeated. Hoarsely*] What's that?

A MILD VOICE. It's all right. Nothing to be afraid of. [*From behind a headstone* SHRDLU *appears. He is dressed in a shabby and ill-fitting cutaway. He wears silver-rimmed spectacles and is smoking a cigarette*]

SHRDLU. I hope I didn't frighten you.

ZERO [*still badly shaken*]. No-o. It's all right. You see, I wasn't expectin' to see anybody.

SHRDLU. You're a newcomer, aren't you?

ZERO. Yeh, this is my first night. I couldn't seem to get to sleep.

SHRDLU. I can't sleep, either. Suppose we keep each other company, shall we?

ZERO [*eagerly*]. Yeh, that would be great. I been feelin' awful lonesome.

SHRDLU [*nodding*]. I know. Let's make ourselves comfortable. [*He seats himself easily on a grave.* ZERO *tries to follow his example but he is stiff in every joint and groans with pain*]

ZERO. I'm kinda stiff.

SHRDLU. You mustn't mind the stiffness. It wears off in a few days. [*He seats himself on the grave beside* ZERO *and produces a package of cigarettes*] Will you have a Camel?

ZERO. No, I don't smoke.

SHRDLU. I find it helps keep the mosquitoes away. [*He lights a cigarette. Suddenly taking the cigarette out of his mouth*] Do you mind if I smoke, Mr. — Mr. —?

ZERO. No, go right ahead.

SHRDLU [*replacing the cigarette*]. Thank you. I didn't catch your name. [ZERO *does not reply*]

SHRDLU [*mildly*]. I say I didn't catch your name.

ZERO. I heard you the first time. [*Hesitantly*] I'm scared if I tell you who I am and what I done, you'll be off me.

SHRDLU [*sadly*]. No matter what your sins may be, they are as snow compared to mine.

ZERO. You got another guess comin'. [*He pauses dramatically*] My name's Zero. I'm a murderer.

SHRDLU [*nodding calmly*]. Oh, yes, I remember reading about you, Mr. Zero.

ZERO [*a little piqued*]. And you still think you're worse than me?

SHRDLU [*throwing away his cigarette*]. Oh, a thousand times worse, Mr. Zero — a million times worse.

ZERO. What did you do?

SHRDLU. I, too, am a murderer.

ZERO [*looking at him in amazement*]. Go on! You're kiddin' me!

SHRDLU. Every word I speak is the truth, Mr. Zero. I am the foulest, the most sinful of murderers! You only murdered your employer, Mr. Zero. But I — I murdered my mother. [*He covers his face with his hands and sobs*]

ZERO [*horrified*]. The hell yer say!

SHRDLU [*sobbing*]. Yes, my mother! — my beloved mother!

ZERO [*suddenly*]. Say, you don't mean to say you're Mr. —

SHRDLU [*nodding*]. Yes. [*He wipes his eyes, still quivering with emotion*]

ZERO. I remember readin' about you in the papers.

SHRDLU. Yes, my guilt has been proclaimed to all the world. But that would be a trifle if only I could wash the stain of sin from my soul.

ZERO. I never heard of a guy killin' his mother before. What did you do it for?

SHRDLU. Because I have a sinful heart — there is no other reason.

ZERO. Did she always treat you square and all like that?

SHRDLU. She was a saint — a saint, I tell you. She cared for me and watched over me as only a mother can.

ZERO. You mean to say you didn't have a scrap or nothin'?

SHRDLU. Never a harsh or an unkind word. Nothing except loving care and good advice. From my infancy she devoted herself to guiding me on the right path. She taught me to be thrifty, to be devout, to be unselfish, to shun evil companions and to shut my ears to all the temptations of the flesh — in short, to become a virtuous, respectable, and God-fearing man. [*He groans*] But it was a hopeless task. At fourteen I began to show evidence of my sinful nature.

ZERO [*breathlessly*]. You didn't kill anybody else, did you?

SHRDLU. No, thank God, there is only one murder on my soul. But I ran away from home.

ZERO. You did!

SHRDLU. Yes. A companion lent me a profane book — the only profane book I have ever read, I'm thankful to say. It was called "Treasure Island." Have you ever read it?

ZERO. No, I never was much on readin' books.

SHRDLU. It is a wicked book — a lurid tale of adventure. But it kindled in my sinful heart a desire to go to sea. And so I ran away from home.

ZERO. What did you do — get a job as a sailor?

SHRDLU. I never saw the sea — not to the day of my death. Luckily, my mother's loving intuition warned her of my intention and I was sent back home. She welcomed me with open arms. Not an angry word, not a look of reproach. But I could read the mute suffering in her eyes as we prayed together all through the night.

ZERO [*sympathetically*]. Gee, that must 'a' been tough. Gee, the mosquitoes are bad, ain't they? [*He tries awkwardly to slap at them with his stiff hands*]

SHRDLU [*absorbed in his narrative*]. I thought that experience had cured me of evil and I began to think about a career. I wanted to go in foreign missions at first, but we couldn't bear the thought of the separation. So we finally decided that I should become a proofreader.

ZERO. Say, slip me one o' them Camels, will you? I'm gettin' all bit up.

SHRDLU. Certainly. [*He hands ZERO cigarettes and matches*]

ZERO [*lighting up*]. Go ahead. I'm listenin'.

SHRDLU. By the time I was twenty I had a good job reading proof for a firm that printed catalogues. After a year they promoted me and let me specialize in shoe catalogues.

ZERO. Yeh? That must 'a' been a good job.

SHRDLU. It was a very good job. I was on the shoe catalogues for thirteen years. I'd been on them yet, if I hadn't — [*He chokes back a sob*]

ZERO. They oughta put a shot o' citronella in that embalmin'-fluid.

SHRDLU [*he sighs*]. We were so happy together. I had my steady job. And Sundays we would go to morning, afternoon, and evening service. It was an honest and moral mode of life.

ZERO. It sure was.

SHRDLU. Then came that fatal Sunday. Dr. Amaranth, our minister, was having dinner with us — one of the few pure spirits on earth. When he had finished saying grace, we had our soup. Everything was going along as usual — we were eating our soup and discussing the sermon, just like every other Sunday I could remember. Then came the leg of lamb — [*He breaks off, then resumes in a choking voice*] I see the whole scene before me so plainly — it never leaves me — Dr. Amaranth at my right, my mother at my left, the leg of lamb on the table in front of me and the cuckoo clock on the little shelf between the windows. [*He stops and wipes his eyes*]

ZERO. Yeh, but what happened?

SHRDLU. Well, as I started to carve the lamb — Did you ever carve a leg of lamb?

ZERO. No, corned beef was our speed.

SHRDLU. It's very difficult on account of the bone. And when there's gravy in the dish there's danger of spilling it. So Mother always used to hold the dish for me. She leaned forward, just as she always did, and I could see the gold locket around her neck. It had my picture in it and one of my baby curls. Well, I raised my knife to carve the leg of lamb — and instead I cut my mother's throat! [*He sobs*]

ZERO. You must 'a' been crazy!

SHRDLU [*raising his head, vehemently*]. No! Don't try to justify me, I wasn't crazy. They tried to prove at the trial that I was crazy. But Dr. Amaranth saw the truth! He saw it from the first! He knew that it was my sinful nature — and he told me what was in store for me.

ZERO [*trying to be comforting*]. Well, your troubles are over now.

SHRDLU [*his voice rising*]. Over! Do you think this is the end?

ZERO. Sure. What more can they do to us?

SHRDLU [*his tones growing shriller and shriller*]. Do you think there can ever be any peace for such as we are — murderers, sinners? Don't you know what awaits us — flames, eternal flames!

ZERO [*nervously*]. Keep your shirt on, Buddy — they wouldn't do that to us.

SHRDLU. There's no escape — no escape for us, I tell you. We're doomed! We're doomed to suffer unspeakable torments through all eternity. [*His voice rises higher and higher. A grave opens suddenly and a head appears*]

THE HEAD. Hey, you birds! Can't you shut up and let a guy sleep? [*ZERO scrambles painfully to his feet*]

ZERO [*to* SHRDLU]. Hey, put on the soft pedal.

SHRDLU [*too wrought up to attend*]. It won't be long now! We'll receive our summons soon.

THE HEAD. Are you goin' to beat it or not? [*He calls into the grave*] Hey, Bill, lend me your head a minute. [*A moment later his arm appears holding a skull*]

ZERO [*warningly*]. Look out! [*He seizes* SHRDLU *and drags him away just as* THE HEAD *throws the skull*]

THE HEAD [*disgustedly*]. Missed 'em. Damn old tabby cats! I'll get 'em next time. [*A prodigious yawn*] Hohum! Me for the worms! [THE HEAD *disappears as the curtain falls*]

SCENE SIX

SCENE. — *A pleasant place. A scene of pastoral loveliness. A meadow dotted with fine old trees and carpeted with rich grass and field flowers. In the background are seen a number of tents fashioned of gay-striped silks and beyond gleams a meandering river. Clear air and a fleckless sky. Sweet distant music throughout.*

At the rise of the curtain, SHRDLU *is seen, seated under a tree in the foreground in an attitude of deep dejection. His knees are drawn up and his head is buried in his arms. He is dressed as in the preceding scene.*

A few minutes later, ZERO *enters at right. He walks slowly and looks about him with an air of half-suspicious curiosity. He, too, is dressed as in the preceding scene. Suddenly he sees* SHRDLU *seated under the tree. He stands still and looks at him half fearfully. Then, seeing something familiar in him, goes closer.* SHRDLU *is unaware of his presence. At last* ZERO *recognizes him and grins in pleased surprise*]

ZERO. Well, if it ain't —! [*He claps* SHRDLU *on the shoulder*] Hello, Buddy!

[SHRDLU *looks up slowly, then recognizing* ZERO, *he rises gravely and extends his hand courteously*]

SHRDLU. How do you do, Mr. Zero? I'm very glad to see you again.

ZERO. Same here. I wasn't expectin' to see you, either. [*Looking about*] This is a kinda nice place. I wouldn't mind restin' here a while.

SHRDLU. You may if you wish.

ZERO. I'm kinda tired. I ain't used to bein' outdoors. I ain't walked so much in years.

SHRDLU. Sit down here, under the tree.

ZERO. Do they let you sit on the grass?

SHRDLU. Oh, yes.

ZERO [*seating himself*]. Boy, this feels good. I'll tell the world my feet are sore. I ain't used to so much walkin'. Say, I wonder would it be all right if I took my shoes off; my feet are tired.

SHRDLU. Yes. Some of the people here go barefoot.

ZERO. Yeh? They sure must be nuts. But I'm goin' t' leave 'em off for a while. So long as it's all right. The grass feels nice and cool. [*He stretches out comfortably*] Say, this is the life of Riley all right, all right. This sure is a nice place. What do they call this place, anyhow?

SHRDLU. The Elysian Fields.

ZERO. The which?

SHRDLU. The Elysian Fields.

ZERO [*dubiously*]. Oh! Well, it's a nice place, all right.

SHRDLU. They say that this is the most desirable of all places. Only the most favoured remain here.

ZERO. Yeh? Well, that let's me out, I guess. [*Suddenly*] But what are you doin' here? I thought you'd be burned by now.

SHRDLU [*sadly*]. Mr. Zero, I am the most unhappy of men.

ZERO [*in mild astonishment*]. Why, because you ain't bein' roasted alive?

SHRDLU [*nodding*]. Nothing is turning out as I expected. I saw everything so clearly — the flames, the tortures, an eternity of suffering as the just punishment for my unspeakable crime. And it has all turned out so differently.

ZERO. Well, that's pretty soft for you, ain't it?

SHRDLU [*wailing*]. No, no, no! It's right and just that I should be punished. I could have endured it stoically. All through those endless ages of indescribable torment I should have exulted in the magnificence of divine justice. But this — this is maddening! What becomes of justice? What becomes of morality? What becomes of right and wrong? It's maddening — simply maddening! Oh, if Dr. Amaranth were only here to advise me! [*He buries his face and groans*]

ZERO [*trying to puzzle it out*]. You mean to say they ain't called you for cuttin' your mother's throat?

SHRDLU. No! It's terrible — terrible! I was prepared for anything — anything but this.

ZERO. Well, what did they say to you?

SHRDLU [*looking up*]. Only that I was to come here and remain until I understood.

ZERO. I don't get it. What do they want you to understand?

SHRDLU [*despairingly*]. I don't know — I don't know! If I only had an inkling of what they meant — [*Interrupting him*] Just listen quietly for a moment; do you hear anything? [*They are both silent, straining their ears*]

ZERO [*at length*]. Nope.

SHRDLU. You don't hear any music? Do you?

ZERO. Music? No, I don't hear nothin'.

SHRDLU. The people here say that the music never stops.

ZERO. They're kiddin' you.

SHRDLU. Do you think so?

ZERO. Sure thing. There ain't a sound.

SHRDLU. Perhaps. They're capable of anything. But I haven't told you of the bitterest of my disappointments.

ZERO. Well, spill it. I'm gettin' used to hearin' bad news.

SHRDLU. When I came to this place, my first thought was to find my dear mother. I wanted to ask her forgiveness. And I wanted her to help me to understand.

ZERO. An' she couldn't do it?

SHRDLU [*with a deep groan*]. She's not here! Mr. Zero! Here where only the most favoured dwell, that wisest and purest of spirits is nowhere to be found. I don't understand it.

A WOMAN'S VOICE [*in the distance*]. Mr. Zero! Oh, Mr. Zero! [ZERO *raises his head and listens attentively*]

SHRDLU [*going on, unheedingly*]. If you were to see some of the people here — the things they do —

ZERO [*interrupting*]. Wait a minute, will you? I think somebody's callin' me.

THE VOICE [*somewhat nearer*]. Mr. Ze-ro! Oh! Mr. Ze-ro!

ZERO. Who the hell's that now? I wonder if the wife's on my trail already. That would be swell, wouldn't it? An' I figured on her bein' good for another twenty years, anyhow.

THE VOICE [*nearer*]. Mr. Ze-ro! Yoo-hoo!

ZERO. No. That ain't her voice. [*Calling, savagely*] Yoo-hoo. [*To* SHRDLU] Ain't that always the way? Just when a guy is takin' life easy an' havin' a good time! [*He rises and looks off left*] Here she comes, whoever she is. [*In sudden amazement*] Well, I'll be —! Well, what do you know about that! [*He stands looking in wonderment, as* DAISY DIANA DOROTHEA DEVORE *enters. She wears a much-beruffled white muslin dress which is a size too small and fifteen years too youthful for her. She is red-faced and breathless*]

DAISY [*panting*]. Oh! I thought I'd never catch up to you. I've been followin' you for days — callin' an' callin'. Didn't you hear me?

ZERO. Not till just now. You look kinda winded.

DAISY. I sure am. I can't hardly catch my breath.

ZERO. Well, sit down an' take a load off your feet. [*He leads her to the tree.* DAISY *sees* SHRDLU *for the first time and shrinks back a little*] It's all right, he's a friend of mine. [*To* SHRDLU] Buddy, I want you to meet my friend, Miss Devore.

SHRDLU [*rising and extending his hand courteously*]. How do you do, Miss Devore?

DAISY [*self-consciously*]. How do!

ZERO [*to* DAISY]. He's a friend of mine. [*To* SHRDLU] I guess you don't mind if she sits here a while an' cools off, do you?

SHRDLU. No, no, certainly not. [*They all seat themselves under the tree.* ZERO *and* DAISY *are a little self-conscious.* SHRDLU *gradually becomes absorbed in his own thoughts*]

ZERO. I was just takin' a rest myself. I took my shoes off on account of my feet bein' so sore.

DAISY. Yeh, I'm kinda tired, too. [*Looking about*] Say, ain't it pretty here, though?

ZERO. Yeh, it is at that.

DAISY. What do they call this place?

ZERO. Why — er — let's see. He was tellin' me just a minute ago. The — er — I don't know. Some kind o' fields. I forget now. [*To* SHRDLU] Say, Buddy, what do they call this place again? [SHRDLU, *absorbed in his thoughts, does not hear him. To* DAISY] He don't hear me. He's thinkin' again.

Daisy [*sotto voce*]. What's the matter with him?

Zero. Why, he's the guy that murdered his mother — remember?

Daisy [*interested*]. Oh, yeh! Is that him?

Zero. Yeh. An' he had it all figgered out how they was goin' t' roast him or somethin'. And now they ain't goin' to do nothin' to him an' it's kinda got his goat.

Daisy [*sympathetically*]. Poor feller!

Zero. Yeh. He takes it kinda hard.

Daisy. He looks like a nice young feller.

Zero. Well, you sure are good for sore eyes. I never expected to see you here.

Daisy. I thought maybe you'd be kinda surprised.

Zero. Surprised is right. I thought you was alive an' kickin'. When did you pass out?

Daisy. Oh, right after you did — a coupla days.

Zero [*interested*]. Yeh? What happened? Get hit by a truck or somethin'?

Daisy. No. [*Hesitantly*] You see — it's this way. I blew out the gas.

Zero [*astonished*]. Go on! What was the big idea?

Daisy [*falteringly*]. Oh, I don't know. You see, I lost my job.

Zero. I'll bet you're sorry you did it now, ain't you?

Daisy [*with conviction*]. No, I ain't sorry. Not a bit. [*Then hesitantly*] Say, Mr. Zero, I been thinkin' — [*She stops*]

Zero. What?

Daisy [*plucking up courage*]. I been thinkin' it would be kinda nice — if you an' me — if we could kinda talk things over.

Zero. Yeh. Sure. What do you want to talk about?

Daisy. Well — I don't know — but you and me — we ain't it really ever talked things over, have we?

Zero. No, that's right, we ain't. Well, let's go to it.

Daisy. I was thinkin' if we could be alone — just the two of us, see?

Zero. Oh, yeh! Yeh, I get you. [*He turns to* Shrdlu *and coughs loudly.* Shrdlu *does not stir*]

Zero [*to* Daisy]. He's dead to the world. [*He turns to* Shrdlu] Say, Buddy! [*No answer*] Say, Buddy!

Shrdlu [*looking up with a start*]. Were you speaking to me?

Zero. Yeh. How'd you guess it? I was thinkin' that maybe you'd like to walk around a little and look for your mother.

Shrdlu [*shaking his head*]. It's no use. I've looked everywhere. [*He relapses into thought again*]

Zero. Maybe over there they might know.

Shrdlu. No, no! I've searched everywhere. She's not here. [Zero *and* Daisy *look at each other in despair*]

Zero. Listen, old shirt, my friend here and me — see? — we used to work in the same store. An' we got some things to talk over — business, see? — kinda confidential. So if it ain't askin' too much —

Shrdlu [*springing to his feet*]. Why, certainly! Excuse me! [*He bows politely to* Daisy *and walks off.* Daisy *and* Zero *watch him until he has disappeared*]

Zero [*with a forced laugh*]. He's a good guy at that. [*Now that they are alone, both are very self-conscious, and for a time they sit in silence*]

Daisy [*breaking the silence*]. It sure is pretty here, ain't it?

Zero. Sure is.

Daisy. Look at the flowers! Ain't they just perfect! Why, you'd think they was artificial, wouldn't you?

Zero. Yeh, you would.

Daisy. And the smell of them. Like perfume.

Zero. Yeh.

Daisy. I'm crazy about the country, ain't you?

Zero. Yeh. It's nice for a change.

Daisy. Them store picnics — remember?

Zero. You bet. They sure was fun.

Daisy. One time — I guess you don't remember — the two of us — me and you — we sat down on the grass together under a tree — just like we're doin' now.

Zero. Sure I remember.

Daisy. Go on! I'll bet you don't.

Zero. I'll bet I do. It was the year the wife didn't go.

Daisy [*her face brightening*]. That's right! I didn't think you'd remember.

Zero. An' comin' home we sat together in the truck.

Daisy [*eagerly, rather shamefacedly*]. Yeh! There's somethin' I've always wanted to ask you.

Zero. Well, why didn't you?

Daisy. I don't know. It didn't seem refined. But I'm goin' to ask you now, anyhow.

Zero. Go ahead. Shoot.

Daisy [*falteringly*]. Well — while we was comin' home — you put your arm up on the bench behind me — and I could feel your knee kinda pressin' against mine. [*She stops*]

Zero [*becoming more and more interested*]. Yeh — well — what about it?

Daisy. What I wanted to ask you was — was it just kinda accidental?

Zero [*with a laugh*]. Sure it was accidental. Accidental on purpose.

Daisy [*eagerly*]. Do you mean it?

Zero. Sure I mean it. You mean to say you didn't know it?

Daisy. No. I've been wantin' to ask you —

Zero. Then why did you get sore at me?

Daisy. Sore? I wasn't sore! When was I sore?

Zero. That night. Sure you was sore. If you wasn't sore why did you move away?

Daisy. Just to see if you meant it. I thought if you meant it you'd move up closer. An' then when you took your arm away I was sure you didn't mean it.

Zero. An' I thought all the time you was sore That's why I took my arm away. I thought if I moved up you'd holler and then I'd be in a jam, like you read in the paper all the time about guys gettin' pulled in for annoyin' women.

Daisy. An' I was wishin' you'd put your arm around me — just sittin' there wishin' all the way home.

Zero. What do you know about that? That sure is hard luck, that is. If I'd 'a' only knew! You know what I felt like doin' — only I didn't have the nerve?

Daisy. What?

Zero. I felt like kissin' you.

Daisy [*fervently*]. I wanted you to.

Zero [*astonished*]. You would 'a' let me?

Daisy. I wanted you to! I wanted you to! Oh, why didn't you — why didn't you?

Zero. I didn't have the nerve. I sure was a dumb-bell.

Daisy. I would 'a' let you all you wanted to. I wouldn't 'a' cared. I know it would 'a' been wrong but I wouldn't 'a' cared. I wasn't thinkin' about right an' wrong at all. I didn't

care — see? I just wanted you to kiss me.

Zero [*feelingly*]. If I'd only knew. I wanted to do it, I swear I did. But I didn't think you cared nothin' about me.

Daisy [*passionately*]. I never cared nothin' about nobody else.

Zero. Do you mean it — on the level? You ain't kiddin' me, are you?

Daisy. No, I ain't kiddin'. I mean it. I'm tellin' you the truth. I ain't never had the nerve to tell you before — but now I don't care. It don't make no difference now. I mean it — every word of it.

Zero [*dejectedly*]. If I'd only knew it.

Daisy. Listen to me. There's somethin' else I want to tell you. I may as well tell you everything now. It don't make no difference now. About my blowin' out the gas — see? Do you know why I done it?

Zero. Yeh, you told me — on account o' bein' canned.

Daisy. I just told you that. That ain't the real reason. The real reason is on account o' you.

Zero. You mean to say on account o' me passin' out —?

Daisy. Yeh. That's it. I didn't want to go on livin'. What for? What did I want to go on livin' for? I didn't have nothin' to live for with you gone. I often thought of doin' it before. But I never had the nerve. An' anyhow I didn't want to leave you.

Zero. An' me bawlin' you out, about readin' too fast an' readin' too slow.

Daisy [*reproachfully*]. Why did you do it?

Zero. I don't know, I swear I don't. I was always stuck on you. An' while I'd be addin' them figgers, I'd be thinkin' how if the wife died, you an' me could get married.

Daisy. I used to think o' that, too.

Zero. An' then before I knew it, I was bawlin' you out.

Daisy. Them was the times I'd think o' blowin' out the gas. But I never did till you was gone. There wasn't nothin' to live for then. But it wasn't so easy to do, anyhow. I never could stand the smell o' gas. An all the while I was gettin' ready, you know, stuffin' up all the cracks, the way you read about in the paper — I was thinkin' of you and hopin' that maybe I'd meet you again. An' I made up my mind if I ever did see you, I'd tell you.

ZERO [*taking her hand*]. I'm sure glad you did. I'm sure glad. [*Ruefully*] But it don't do much good now, does it?

DAISY. No, I guess it don't. [*Summoning courage*] But there's one thing I'm goin' to ask you.

ZERO. What's that?

DAISY [*in a low voice*]. I want you to kiss me.

ZERO. You bet I will! [*He leans over and kisses her cheek*]

DAISY. Not like that. I don't mean like that. I mean really kiss me. On the mouth. I ain't never been kissed like that. [ZERO *puts his arms about her and presses his lips to hers. A long embrace. At last they separate and sit side by side in silence*]

DAISY [*putting her hands to her cheeks*]. So that's what it's like. I didn't know it could be like that. I didn't know anythin' could be like that.

ZERO [*fondling her hand*]. Your cheeks are red. They're all red. And your eyes are shinin'. I never seen your eyes shinin' like that before.

DAISY [*holding up her hand*]. Listen — do you hear it? Do you hear the music?

ZERO. No, I don't hear nothin'!

DAISY. Yeh — music. Listen an' you'll hear it. [*They are both silent for a moment*]

ZERO [*excitedly*]. Yeh! I hear it! He said there was music, but I didn't hear it till just now.

DAISY. Ain't it grand?

ZERO. Swell! Say, do you know what?

DAISY. What?

ZERO. It makes me feel like dancin'.

DAISY. Yeh? Me, too.

ZERO [*springing to his feet*]. Come on! Let's dance! [*He seizes her hands and tries to pull her up*]

DAISY [*resisting laughingly*]. I can't dance. I ain't danced in twenty years.

ZERO. That's nothin'. I ain't, neither. Come on! I feel just like a kid! [*He pulls her to her feet and seizes her about the waist*]

DAISY. Wait a minute! Wait till I fix my skirt. [*She turns back her skirts and pins them above the ankles.* ZERO *seizes her about the waist. They dance clumsily but with gay abandon.* DAISY'S *hair becomes loosened and tumbles over her shoulders. She lends herself more and more to the spirit of the dance. But* ZERO *soon begins to tire and dances with less and less zest*]

ZERO [*stopping at last, panting for breath*]. Wait a minute! I'm all winded. [*He releases* DAISY, *but before he can turn away, she throws her arms about him and presses her lips to his*]

ZERO [*freeing himself*]. Wait a minute! Let me get my wind! [*He limps to the tree and seats himself under it, gasping for breath.* DAISY *looks after him, her spirits rather dampened*]

ZERO. Whew! I sure am winded! I ain't used to dancin'. [*He takes off his collar and tie and opens the neckband of his shirt.* DAISY *sits under the tree near him, looking at him longingly. But he is busy catching his breath*] Gee, my heart's goin' a mile a minute.

DAISY. Why don't you lay down an' rest? You could put your head on my lap.

ZERO. That ain't a bad idea. [*He stretches out, his head in* DAISY'S *lap*]

DAISY [*fondling his hair*]. It was swell, wasn't it?

ZERO. Yeh. But you gotta be used to it.

DAISY. Just imagine if we could stay here all the time — you an' me together — wouldn't it be swell?

ZERO. Yeh. But there ain't a chance.

DAISY. Won't they let us stay?

ZERO. No. This place is only for the good ones.

DAISY. Well, we ain't so bad, are we?

ZERO. Go on! Me a murderer an' you committin' suicide. Anyway, they wouldn't stand for this — the way we been goin' on.

DAISY. I don't see why.

ZERO. You don't! You know it ain't right. Ain't I got a wife?

DAISY. Not any more you ain't. When you're dead that ends it. Don't they always say "until death do us part?"

ZERO. Well, maybe you're right about that but they wouldn't stand for us here.

DAISY. It would be swell — the two of us together — we could make up for all them years.

ZERO. Yeh, I wish we could.

DAISY. We sure were fools. But I don't care. I've got you now. [*She kisses his forehead and cheeks and mouth*]

ZERO. I'm sure crazy about you. I never saw you lookin' so pretty before, with your cheeks all red. An' your hair hangin' down. You got swell hair. [*He fondles and kisses her hair*]

DAISY [*ecstatically*]. We got each other now, ain't we?

ZERO. Yeh. I'm crazy about you. Daisy! That's a pretty name. It's a flower, ain't it? Well — that's what you are — just a flower.

DAISY [*happily*]. We can always be together now, can't we?

ZERO. As long as they'll let us. I sure am crazy about you. [*Suddenly he sits upright*] Watch your step!

DAISY [*alarmed*]. What's the matter?

ZERO [*nervously*]. He's comin' back.

DAISY. Oh, is that all? Well, what about it?

ZERO. You don't want him to see us layin' around like this, do you?

DAISY. I don't care if he does.

ZERO. Well, you oughta care. You don't want him to think you ain't a refined girl, do you? He's an awful moral bird, he is.

DAISY. I don't care nothin' about him. I don't care nothin' about anybody but you.

ZERO. Sure, I know. But we don't want people talkin' about us. You better fix your hair an' pull down your skirts. [DAISY *complies rather sadly. They are both silent as* SHRDLU *enters*]

ZERO [*with feigned nonchalance*]. Well, you got back all right, didn't you?

SHRDLU. I hope I haven't returned too soon.

ZERO. No, that's all right. We were just havin' a little talk. You know — about business an' things.

DAISY [*boldly*]. We were wishin' we could stay here all the time.

SHRDLU. You may if you like.

ZERO AND DAISY [*in astonishment*]. What!

SHRDLU. Yes. Any one who likes may remain —

ZERO. But I thought you were tellin' me —

SHRDLU. Just as I told you, only the most favored do remain. But any one may.

ZERO. I don't get it. There's a catch in it somewheres.

DAISY. It don't matter as long as we can stay.

ZERO [*to* SHRDLU]. We were thinkin' about gettin' married, see?

SHRDLU. You may or not, just as you like.

ZERO. You don't mean to say we could stay if we didn't, do you?

SHRDLU. Yes. They don't care.

ZERO. An' there's some here that ain't married?

SHRDLU. Yes.

ZERO [*to* DAISY]. I don't know about this place, at that. They must be kind of a mixed crowd.

DAISY. It don't matter, so long as we got each other.

ZERO. Yeh, I know, but you don't want to mix with people that ain't respectable.

DAISY [*to* SHRDLU]. Can we get married right away? I guess there must be a lot of ministers here, ain't there?

SHRDLU. Not as many as I had hoped to find. The two who seem most beloved are Dean Swift and the Abbé Rabelais. They are both much admired for some indecent tales which they have written.

ZERO [*shocked*]. What! Ministers writin' smutty stories! Say, what kind of a dump is this, anyway?

SHRDLU [*despairingly*]. I don't know, Mr. Zero. All these people here are so strange, so unlike the good people I've known. They seem to think of nothing but enjoyment or of wasting their time in profitless occupations. Some paint pictures from morning until night, or carve blocks of stone. Others write songs or put words together, day in and day out. Still others do nothing but lie under the trees and look at the sky. There are men who spend all their time reading books and women who think only of adorning themselves. And forever they are telling stories and laughing and singing and drinking and dancing. There are drunkards, thieves, vagabonds, blasphemers, adulterers. There is one —

ZERO. That's enough. I heard enough. [*He seats himself and begins putting on his shoes*]

DAISY [*anxiously*]. What are you goin' to do?

ZERO. I'm goin' to beat it, that's what I'm goin' to do.

DAISY. You said you liked it here.

ZERO [*looking at her in amazement*]. Liked it! Say, you don't mean to say you want to stay here, do you, with a lot of rummies an' loafers an' bums?

DAISY. We don't have to bother with them. We can just sit here together an' look at the flowers an' listen to the music.

SHRDLU [*eagerly*]. Music! Did you hear music?

DAISY. Sure. Don't you hear it?

SHRDLU. No, they say it never stops. But I've never heard it.

ZERO [*listening*]. I thought I heard it before but I don't hear nothin' now. I guess I must 'a' been dreamin'. [*Looking about*] What's the quickest way out of this place?

DAISY [*pleadingly*]. Won't you stay just a little longer?

ZERO. Didn't yer hear me say I'm goin'? Good-bye, Miss Devore. I'm goin' to beat it. [*He limps off at the right.* DAISY *follows him slowly*]

DAISY [*to* SHRDLU]. I won't ever see him again.

SHRDLU. Are you goin' to stay here?

DAISY. It don't make no difference now. Without him I might as well be alive. [*She goes off right.* SHRDLU *watches her a moment, then sighs and seating himself under the tree, buries his head on his arm*]

CURTAIN FALLS

SCENE SEVEN

SCENE. — *Before the curtain rises the clicking of an adding machine is heard. The curtain rises upon an office similar in appearance to that in Scene Two except that there is a door in the back wall through which can be seen a glimpse of the corridor outside. In the middle of the room* ZERO *is seated completely absorbed in the operation of an adding machine. He presses the keys and pulls the lever with mechanical precision. He still wears his full-dress suit but he has added to it sleeve protectors and a green eye shade. A strip of white paper-tape flows steadily from the machine as* ZERO *operates. The room is filled with this tape — streamers, festoons, billows of it everywhere. It covers the floor and the furniture, it climbs the walls and chokes the doorways. A few moments later,* LIEUTENANT CHARLES *and* JOE *enter at the left.* LIEUTENANT CHARLES *is middle-aged and inclined to corpulence. He has an air of world-weariness. He is barefooted, wears a Panama hat, and is dressed in bright red tights which are a very bad fit — too tight in some places, badly wrinkled in others.* JOE *is a youth with a smutty face dressed in dirty blue overalls.*

CHARLES [*after contemplating* ZERO *for a few moments*]. All right, Zero, cease firing.

ZERO [*looking up, surprised*]. Whaddja say?

CHARLES. I said stop punching that machine.

ZERO [*bewildered*]. Stop? [*He goes on working mechanically*]

CHARLES [*impatiently*]. Yes. Can't you stop? Here, Joe, give me a hand. He can't stop. [JOE *and* CHARLES *each take one of* ZERO's *arms and with enormous effort detach him from the machine. He resists passively — mere inertia. Finally they succeed and swing him around on his stool.* CHARLES *and* JOE *mop their foreheads*]

ZERO [*querulously*]. What's the idea? Can't you lemme alone?

CHARLES [*ignoring the question*]. How long have you been here?

ZERO. Jes' twenty-five years. Three hundred months, nine-one hundred and thirty-one days, one hundred thirty-six thousand —

CHARLES [*impatiently*]. That'll do! That'll do!

ZERO [*proudly*]. I ain't missed a day, not an hour, not a minute. Look at all I got done. [*He points to the maze of paper*]

CHARLES. It's time to quit.

ZERO. Quit? Whaddye mean quit? I ain't goin' to quit!

CHARLES. You've got to.

ZERO. What for? What do I have to quit for?

CHARLES. It's time for you to go back.

ZERO. Go back where? Whaddya talkin' about?

CHARLES. Back to earth, you dub. Where do you think?

ZERO. Aw, go on, Cap, who are you kiddin'?

CHARLES. I'm not kidding anybody. And don't call me Cap. I'm a lieutenant.

ZERO. All right, Lieutenant, all right. But what's this you're tryin' to tell me about goin' back?

CHARLES. Your time's up, I'm telling you. You must be pretty thick. How many times do you want to be told a thing?

ZERO. This is the first time I heard about goin' back. Nobody ever said nothin' to me about it before.

CHARLES. You didn't think you were going to stay here forever, did you?

ZERO. Sure. Why not? I did my bit, didn't I? Forty-five years of it. Twenty-five years in the store. Then the boss canned me and I knocked him cold. I guess you ain't heard about that —

CHARLES [*interrupting*]. I know all about that. But what's that got to do with it?

ZERO. Well, I done my bit, didn't I? That oughta let me out.

CHARLES [*jeeringly*]. So you think you're all through, do you?

ZERO. Sure, I do. I did the best I could while I was there and then I passed out. And now I'm sittin' pretty here.

CHARLES. You've got a fine idea of the way they run things, you have. Do you think they're going to all of the trouble of making a soul just to use it once?

ZERO. Once is often enough, it seems to me.

CHARLES. It seems to you, does it? Well, who are you? And what do you know about it? Why, man, they use a soul over and over again — over and over until it's worn out.

ZERO. Nobody ever told me.

CHARLES. So you thought you were all through, did you? Well, that's a hot one, that is.

ZERO [*sullenly*]. How was I to know?

CHARLES. Use your brains! Where would we put them all! We're crowded enough as it is. Why, this place is nothing but a kind of repair and service station — a sort of cosmic laundry, you might say. We get the souls in here by the bushelful. Then we get busy and clean them up. And you ought to see some of them. The muck and the slime. Phoo! And as full of holes as a flour-sifter. But we fix them up. We disinfect them and give them a kerosene rub and mend the holes and back they go — practically as good as new.

ZERO. You mean to say I've been here before — before the last time, I mean?

CHARLES. Been here before! Why, you poor boob — you've been here thousands of times — fifty thousand, at least.

ZERO [*suspiciously*]. How is it I don't remember nothin' about it?

CHARLES. Well — that's partly because you're stupid. But it's mostly because that's the way they fix it. [*Musingly*] They're funny that way —

every now and then they'll do something white like that — when you'd least expect it. I guess economy's at the bottom of it, though. They figure that the souls would get worn out quicker if they remembered.

ZERO. And don't any of 'em remember?

CHARLES. Oh, some do. You see there's different types : there's the type that gets a little better each time it goes back — we just give them a wash and send them right through. Then there's another type — the type that gets a little worse each time. That's where you belong!

ZERO [*offended*]. Me? You mean to say I'm gettin' worse all the time?

CHARLES [*nodding*]. Yes. A little worse each time.

ZERO. Well — what was I when I started? Somethin' big? — A king or somethin'?

CHARLES [*laughing derisively*]. A king! That's a good one! I'll tell you what you were the first time — if you want to know so much — a monkey.

ZERO [*shocked and offended*]. A monkey!

CHARLES [*nodding*]. Yes, sir — just a hairy, chattering, long-tailed monkey.

ZERO. That musta been a long time ago.

CHARLES. Oh, not so long. A million years or so. Seems like yesterday to me.

ZERO. Then look here, whaddya mean by sayin' I'm gettin' worse all the time?

CHARLES. Just what I said. You weren't so bad as a monkey. Of course, you did just what all the other monkeys did, but still it kept you out in the open air. And you weren't women-shy — there was one little red-headed monkey — Well, never mind. Yes, sir, you weren't so bad then. But even in those days there must have been some bigger and brainier monkey that you kow-towed to. The mark of the slave was on you from the start.

ZERO [*sullenly*]. You ain't very particular about what you call people, are you?

CHARLES. You wanted the truth, didn't you? If there ever was a soul in the world that was labelled slave it's yours. Why, all the bosses and kings that there ever were have left their trade-marks on your backside.

ZERO. It ain't fair, if you ask me.

CHARLES [*shrugging his shoulders*]. Don't tell me about it. I don't make the rules. All I know is you've been getting worse — worse each time. Why, even six thousand years ago you weren't so bad. That was the time you were hauling stones for one of those big pyramids in a place they call Africa. Ever hear of the pyramids?

ZERO. Them big pointy things?

CHARLES [*nodding*]. That's it.

ZERO. I seen a picture of them in the movies.

CHARLES. Well, you helped build them. It was a long step down from the happy days in the jungle, but it was a good job — even though you didn't know what you were doing and your back was striped by the foreman's whip. But you've been going down, down. Two thousand years ago you were a Roman galley-slave. You were on one of the triremes that knocked the Carthaginian fleet for a goal. Again the whip. But you had muscles then — chest muscles, back muscles, biceps. [*He feels* ZERO's *arm gingerly and turns away in disgust*] Phoo! A bunch of mush! [*He notices that* JOE *has fallen asleep. Walking over, he kicks him in the shin*] Wake up, you mutt! Where do you think you are! [*He turns to* ZERO *again*] And then another thousand years and you were a serf — a lump of clay digging up other lumps of clay. You wore an iron collar then — white ones hadn't been invented yet. Another long step down. But where you dug, potatoes grew and that helped fatten the pigs. Which was something. And now — well, I don't want to rub it in —

ZERO. Rub it in is right! Seems to me I got a pretty healthy kick comin'. I ain't had a square deal! Hard work! That's all I've ever had!

CHARLES [*callously*]. What else were you ever good for?

ZERO. Well, that ain't the point. The point is I'm through! I had enough! Let 'em find somebody else to do the dirty work. I'm sick of bein' the goat! I quit right here and now! [*He glares about defiantly. There is a thunder-clap and a bright flash of lightning. Screaming*] Ooh! What's that? [*He clings to* CHARLES]

CHARLES. It's all right. Nobody's going to hurt you. It's just their way of telling you that they don't like you to talk that way. Pull yourself together

and calm down. You can't change the rules — nobody can — they've got it all fixed. It's a rotten system — but what are you going to do about it?

ZERO. Why can't they stop pickin' on me? I'm satisfied here — doin' my day's work. I don't want to go back.

CHARLES. You've got to, I tell you. There's no way out of it.

ZERO. What chance have I got — at my age? Who'll give me a job?

CHARLES. You big boob, you don't think you're going back the way you are, do you?

ZERO. Sure, how then?

CHARLES. Why, you've got to start all over.

ZERO. All over?

CHARLES [*nodding*]. You'll be a baby again — a bald, red-faced little animal, and then you'll go through it all again. There'll be millions of others like you — all with their mouths open, squalling for food. And then when you get a little older you'll begin to learn things — and you'll learn all the wrong things and learn them all in the wrong way. You'll eat the wrong food and wear the wrong clothes and you'll live in swarming dens where's there's no light and no air! You'll learn to be a liar and a bully and a braggart and a coward and a sneak. You'll learn to fear the sunlight and to hate beauty. By that time you'll be ready for school. There they'll tell you the truth about a great many things that you don't give a damn about and they'll tell you lies about all the things you ought to know — and about all the things you want to know they'll tell you nothing at all. When you get through you'll be equipped for your life-work. You'll be ready to take a job.

ZERO [*eagerly*]. What'll my job be? Another adding machine?

CHARLES. Yes. But not one of these antiquated adding machines. It will be a superb, super-hyper-adding machine, as far from this old piece of junk as you are from God. It will be something to make you sit up and take notice, that adding machine. It will be an adding machine which will be installed in a coal mine and which will record the individual output of each miner. As each miner down in the lower galleries takes up a shovelful of coal, the impact of his shovel will automatically set in motion a graphite pencil in your gallery. The pencil will make a mark in white upon a blackened, sensitized drum. Then your work comes in. With the great toe of your right foot you release a lever which focuses a violet ray on the drum. The ray playing upon and through the white mark, falls upon a selenium cell which in turn sets the keys of the adding apparatus in motion. In this way the individual output of each miner is recorded without any human effort except the slight pressure of the great toe of your right foot.

ZERO [*in breathless, round-eyed wonder*]. Say, that'll be some machine, won't it?

CHARLES. Some machine is right. It will be the culmination of human effort — the final triumph of the evolutionary process. For millions of years the nebulous gases swirled in space. For more millions of years the gases cooled and then through inconceivable ages they hardened into rocks. And then came life. Floating green things on the waters that covered the earth. More millions of years and a step upward — an animate organism in the ancient slime. And so on — step by step, down through the ages — a gain here, a gain there — the mollusc, the fish, the reptile, then mammal, man! And all so that you might sit in the gallery of a coal mine and operate the super-hyper-adding machine with the great toe of your right foot!

ZERO. Well, then — I ain't so bad, after all.

CHARLES. You're a failure, Zero, a failure. A waste product. A slave to a contraption of steel and iron. The animal's instincts, but not his strength and skill. The animal's appetites, but not his unashamed indulgence of them. True, you move and eat and digest and excrete and reproduce. But any microscopic organism can do as much. Well — time's up! Back you go — back to your sunless groove — the raw material of slums and wars — the ready prey of the first jingo or demagogue or political adventurer who takes the trouble to play upon your ignorance and credulity and provincialism. You poor, spineless, brainless boob — I'm sorry for you!

ZERO [*falling to his knees*]. Then keep me here! Don't send me back! Let me stay!

CHARLES. Get up. Didn't I tell you I can't do anything for you? Come on, time's up!

ZERO. I can't! I can't! I'm afraid to go through it all again.

CHARLES. You've got to, I tell you. Come on, now!

ZERO. What did you tell me so much for? Couldn't you just let me go, thinkin' everythin' was goin' to be all right?

CHARLES. You wanted to know, didn't you?

ZERO. How did I know what you were goin' to tell me? Now I can't stop thinkin' about it! I can't stop thinkin'! I'll be thinkin' about it all the time.

CHARLES. All right! I'll do the best I can for you. I'll send a girl with you to keep you company.

ZERO. A girl? What for? What good will a girl do me?

CHARLES. She'll help make you forget.

ZERO [*eagerly*]. She will? Where is she?

CHARLES. Wait a minute, I'll call her. [*He calls in a loud voice*] Oh! Hope! Yoo-hoo! [*He turns his head aside and says in the manner of a ventriloquist imitating a distant feminine voice*] Ye-es. [*Then in his own voice*] Come here, will you? There's a fellow who wants you to take him back. [*Ventriloquously again*] All right. I'll be right over, Charlie dear. [*He turns to* ZERO] Kind of familiar, isn't she? Charlie dear!

ZERO. What did you say her name is?

CHARLES. Hope. H-o-p-e.

ZERO. Is she good-lookin'?

CHARLES. Is she good-looking! Oh, boy, wait until you see her! She's a blonde with big blue eyes and red lips and little white teeth and —

ZERO. Say, that listens good to me. Will she be long?

CHARLES. She'll be here right away. There she is now! Do you see her?

ZERO. No. Where?

CHARLES. Out in the corridor. No, not there. Over farther. To the right. Don't you see her blue dress? And the sunlight on her hair?

ZERO. Oh, sure! Now I see her! What's the matter with me, anyhow? Say, she's some jane! Oh, you baby vamp!

CHARLES. She'll make you forget your troubles.

ZERO. What troubles are you talkin' about?

CHARLES. Nothing. Go on. Don't keep her waiting.

ZERO. You bet I won't! Oh, Hope! Wait for me! I'll be right with you! I'm on my way! [*He stumbles out eagerly.* JOE *bursts into uproarious laughter*]

CHARLES [*eyeing him in surprise and anger*]. What in hell's the matter with you?

JOE [*shaking with laughter*]. Did you get that? He thinks he saw somebody and he's following her! [*He rocks with laughter*]

CHARLES [*punching him in the jaw*]. Shut your face!

JOE [*nursing his jaw*]. What's the idea? Can't I even laugh when I see something funny?

CHARLES. Funny! You keep your mouth shut or I'll show you something funny. Go on, hustle out of here and get something to clean up this mess with. There's another fellow moving in. Hurry now. [*He makes a threatening gesture.* JOE *exits hastily.* CHARLES *goes to chair and seats himself. He looks weary and dispirited. Shaking his head*] Hell, I'll tell the world this is a lousy job! [*He takes a flask from his pocket, uncorks it, and slowly drains it*]

CURTAIN

Historic play

607
383
24

THE SHOW-OFF

(1924)

By George Kelly

GEORGE KELLY

"THE SHOW-OFF" had its first performance in New York on February 5, 1924. It was unanimously acclaimed by the metropolitan critics as being a comedy of unusual freshness of character conception and of unerring handling of dialogue. One spoke of "the living idiom of its life and time"; another said it was "beautifully observed"; while still another spoke of its "luminous veracity." This response would indicate that "The Show-Off" had a deeper understanding than the mere surface of the play would indicate.

When it was given in London, at the Olympic, October 22, 1924, the astute J. T. Grein wrote as follows:

> Strange to say, very soon the play — story of a gas-bag who lets off hot air in an illuminating ray of financial 'cuteness — began to amuse me, and so did the actor. Under all the palaver and braggadocio, fired at us in volleys of vertiginous rapidity, there was a rich vein of satire, and a grain of truth as well as sentiment. I learned to admire the author for turning out the simplest, most archaic dialogue, and yet entertaining and holding us by its inner meaning. . . .

This was a great conquest for the dramatist over one Englishman who had begun in quandary over "The Show-Off" as so much drivel. But he, and such others as Arnold Bennett, when they found the casual dialogue unerringly shaded in its middle-class commonplaceness, soon wondered how and why there came from this dialogue such slants of satire, such human applications away from West Philadelphia, such human inclusions as *Aubrey Piper*.

The play has run for over a year in New York; the London company, after a five weeks' engagement, was brought back and sent to Chicago, where houses are repeating the success of New York. Critics, with sweeping enthusiasm, are saying that Kelly has changed the pattern of comedy, has brought it back to its significant richness from which it had been heretofore taken by those American dramatists who had simply interpreted it as a merry thing of noisy situation. There is nothing strident about "The Show-Off", though it has many of the outward signs of the old comedy: eccentricity of outward character, seemingly hackneyed plot. But what makes the play luminous is the completeness with which the playwright sees through his characters, the significant handling of their petty psychologies, their commonplace reactions, until out of it comes that thing which is life itself, which is not merely West Philadelphia, not something particular, but something universal and bigger and more tragic and more ironically humorous than *Aubrey Piper*: something of world character.

This effect is not gained by any chance trick on the part of the dramatist: it is due, first of all, to an excellent power he has of characterizing, not by trickery — even though *Piper's* laugh is an accessory no less valuable to the stage than it is true to life — but from the inside out, so arranging his commonplace doings of commonplace people that every move will enrich the human material he deals with. Read the first long play with which Mr. Kelly broke from vaudeville into the legitimate — "The Torch-Bearers" — and this method declares itself. It is a valuable gift, one which will carry the dramatist a far way.

In "The Show-Off" *Piper* is the central point; while the whole play is a transcript of life — the author would have it so — this life acts and reacts and is acted upon by the presence of the big bluff who talks "bunk." We laugh at him, but he is one of the tragedies of the democratic idea; we get to like *Aubrey*, but he is still the menace that comes out of a mediocre education; he wins out in the end, through his characteristic bluff, and in his successful issue there is a whole commentary on American life. It is monumentally splendid, this irony of Kelly: an irony that holds the interest through the characteristically American good-humored way we have of laughing at our own foibles and of believing they are the other fellow's. The London critics seem to have been waiting, in the play, for what they call "drama" — probably for what other American plays had accustomed them to look for — the much-talked-of "punch." One critic said: "The play is much more successful when it is comedy than when it is drama." But American drama has stood too long by this slogan of "punch", and the refreshing thing about the work of George Kelly so far — even in his little vaudeville sketches — is that he makes his characters stand up and live or fall by their own little philosophies. *Aubrey* is true to himself to the end. He is not, like Miss Crothers's *Willie*, in "Expressing Willie", at any moment abased by the contempt others show him. He is all-sufficient, and the good-natured all-sufficiency of him gives us a feeling that, though we pity him, we somehow pity him quite as much for his innocuous conceit as for the tragedy of his insufficiency which is helped out — so the world runs — by the accidentals of life.

George Kelly came to the theatre by way of the stage. He had been ensnared away from civil engineering and architecture, and had won in New York some attention as a juvenile actor. Then he went on the road, and in due course found himself a great success on the vaudeville stage in a one-act satire, "Woman Proposes." A vaudeville audience is far different from the audience of the legitimate theatre; the methods of writing for it, of interpreting for it are of an entirely different nature. Kelly seemed to sense this, and it was not long before he was appearing in one-act pieces of his own which, on the Keith and Orpheum circuits, became headliners, with runs approximating two years each. These sketches are all in print: "Finders-Keepers", "The Flattering Word", "Smarty's Party", "The Weak Spot", and "Poor Aubrey" — the latter being the one-act beginning of "The Show-Off."

These little sketches show the complete way in which Kelly on all occasions observes details, and brings them to valuable account. They show that he has in mind a central theme, usually caught and expressed in one speech which he takes as the guiding motive of his play and prints as a foreword to the play itself. One can detect a surety in the handling of detail that shows how completely Kelly knows his theatre, not only on the stage but in front of the footlights. He has, since the beginning, directed his own dramas; he has, so we learn, been eagerly sought by the leading managers as director of their own productions. He understands the economy of attention, the necessity for driving home points of character. With the skill of the trained stage-manager, he can handle any amount of detail, get his effects, and still never lose the thread of his more important purpose. "The Torch-Bearers" is an excellent study of the focussing of multifarious details, multifarious characters on the main satire — which has to do with effete drama societies and the human stuff that constitutes them. Kelly delights in this satire : there is a diabolical pleasure apparent in his plays, as healthful as it is enlightening — a delight which comes from a higher source than mere drama expediency.

I am not saying that Mr. Kelly disregards dramatic effectiveness ; I am not saying that he does not at times resort to dramatic expediency. He knows his theatre too well not to make use of every "point" at his command. His structure, however, is not a technical one predominantly : it is one that comes through an unerring movement of character. I have talked with him about this ; I have heard from him ideas concerning new plays and have seen the way his mind works. We live in a world where not a thing we do but affects our little world. Kelly views his stage in this way. Character is not alone the laying on of identifying colors : it is a growth ; it is a contrast by reason of the way it affects other characters and modifies them ; it is a pulsating back and forth, a give and take, high lights and shadows due to the passing of some other persons near. Kelly, by his method, does not endow his people with identifying marks — unless those identifying marks are of the character itself, like *Aubrey's* toupee. They are already endowed, and it is this which makes them act as they do. "The Show-Off" is a success because of its substance. "The Torch-Bearers" has the same quality. The little vaudeville sketches too.

The student of drama will find much profit in noting the expansion of "The Show-Off" from the one-act skit, "Poor Aubrey." An analysis of this expansion will do quite as much good as the reading of books on technique which so often state propositions without proving them. It will reveal Kelly's method : which is an unusual one in the American Theatre, and one on which we bank highly. A man who writes for the theatre cannot show that persistent pursuit of character, — based on an observation which, on all sides, both masculine and feminine, is so acute — without making a far claim to attention. His sense of humor is abundant ; his satire is profound ; his observation acute ; his stage control astounding. With these at his command, Mr. Kelly should do much for American comedy in the near future.

THE SHOW–OFF

A TRANSCRIPT OF LIFE IN THREE ACTS

———

By GEORGE KELLY

CAST OF CHARACTERS

As first produced at the Playhouse Theatre, New York, on February 4th, 1924.

CLARA	Juliette Crosby
MRS. FISHER	Helen Lowell
AMY	Regina Wallace
FRANK HYLAND	Guy D'Ennery
MR. FISHER	C. W. Goodrich
JOE	Lee Tracy
AUBREY PIPER	Louis John Bartels
MR. GILL	Francis Pierlot
MR. ROGERS	Joseph Clayton

THE SHOW–OFF

ACT I

After a slight pause a door out at the left is heard to close, and then CLARA *comes in carrying a fancy box of candy. She glances about the room and crosses to the kitchen-door at the right.*

CLARA. Anybody out there? [*She crosses back again towards the left, laying the box of candy on the center-table as she passes. Upon reaching the parlor-doors, at the left, she opens them and calls into the parlor*] You in there, Mom? [MRS. FISHER *can be heard coming down the stairs.* CLARA *turns, with a glance toward the hall-door, and moves over to the mirror above the mantelpiece.* MRS. FISHER *appears in the hall-door and glances in at* CLARA]

MRS. FISHER. Oh, it's *you*, Clara. [*She peers out into the hall*]

CLARA. Where is everybody?

MRS. FISHER. I thought I heard that front-door open.

CLARA. Where are they all?

MRS. FISHER [*moving towards the parlor-door*]. Your Pop's gone over to Gillespie's for some tobacco: I don't know where Joe is. [*She glances into the parlor, then turns and kisses* CLARA. CLARA *moves down to the chair at the left of the center-table and* MRS. FISHER *moves over to the kitchen-door at the right*] I don't know how you can stand that fur on you, Clara, a night like this.

CLARA. It's rather cool out.

MRS. FISHER [*calling out through the kitchen-door*]. You out there, Joe?

CLARA [*sitting down*]. He isn't out there.

MRS. FISHER [*turning around to the cellar-door at her left*]. He must be around here somewhere; he was here not two minutes ago, when I went upstairs. [*Opening the cellar-door and calling down*] You down there, Joey?

JOE [*from the cellar*]. Yes.

MRS. FISHER. All right. [*Closes the cellar-door*]

JOE. What do you want?

MRS. FISHER [*turning to the cellar-door again*]. What?

[JOE *and* CLARA, *speaking together*]

JOE. What do you want?

CLARA. He sez, "What do you want?"

MRS. FISHER [*opening the cellar-door again*]. I don't want anything; I was just wonderin' where you were. [*She closes the cellar-door and comes a step or two forward, fastening an old-fashioned brooch that she wears on the front of her dress*] He spends half his time down in that cellar foolin' with that old radio thing. He sez he can make one himself, but I sez, "I'll believe it when I see it."

CLARA. There's some of that candy you like.

MRS. FISHER [*crossing to the center-table*]. Oh, did you bring me some more of that nice candy? [*Beginning to untie the ribbon around the candy*] I never got a taste of that last you brought.

CLARA. Why not?

MRS. FISHER. Why, — Lady Jane took it away with her down to the office, and never brought it back. She sez the girls down there et it. I sez, "I guess you're the girl that et it." She sez she didn't, but I know she did.

CLARA. Well, I hope you'll keep that out of sight, and don't let her take that too.

MRS. FISHER [*opening the candy*]. Oh, she won't get her hands on this, I can promise you that. Let her buy her own candy if she's so fond of it.

CLARA [*opening the "Delineator"*]. She won't *buy* much of *anything*, if she can get hold of it any *other* way.

MRS. FISHER. Oh, isn't that lovely! Look Clara — [*Tilting the box of candy towards* CLARA] Don't that look nice?

CLARA. Yes, they do their candy up nice.

MRS. FISHER [*gingerly picking up the cover of lace paper*]. That looks just like Irish point lace, don't it? [CLARA *nods yes*] I think I'll put that away somewhere, — in a book or something. My, look at all the colors — look Clara — did you ever see so many colors?

CLARA. It's pretty, isn't it?

MRS. FISHER. It's beautiful —. seems a pity to spoil it. Do you want a bit of it, Clara?

CLARA. Not now, Mom.

MRS. FISHER. I think I'll take this pink one here. I *like* the pink ones. [*She picks up the box and the lid and moves around to the chair at the right of the table*] Mind how they all have this little fancy paper around them. You'd wonder they'd bother, wouldn't you? — just for a bit of candy. [*She tastes the candy and chews, critically*] That's nice candy, isn't it?

CLARA. Yes, *I* like bonbons.

MRS. FISHER [*sitting down*]. I do too — I think I like them better than most anything. [*Putting the box of candy down on the table*] I'm sorry these are not all bonbons.

CLARA [*looking up from the "Delineator"*]. They *are* all bonbons — [*Her Mother looks at her*] There's nothing else in there.

MRS. FISHER. Oh, are they! — I thought only the pink ones were the bonbons.

CLARA. No, they're all bonbons.

MRS. FISHER. Well, that's lovely. I can eat any one of them I like, then, can't I? [*She sits back in her chair and rocks and chews*] How is it you're not home to-night, Clara?

CLARA. Frank had to go to a dinner of some kind at the Glenwood Club; so I thought I'd stay in town and get something. He said he might call for me here around eight o'clock. I was in anyway about my lamp.

MRS. FISHER [*rocking*]. Men are always going to dinners somewhere. Seems to me they can't talk about anything unless they've got a dinner in front of them. It's no wonder so many of them are fat.

CLARA [*turning a page of the "Delineator"*]. Where's Amy, — upstairs?

MRS. FISHER. Yes, she's gettin' dressed. I was just hookin' her when you came in.

CLARA. Is she going out?

MRS. FISHER. I don't know whether she is or not, — I didn't hear her say.

[*Leaning a bit towards* CLARA, *and lowering her voice*] But it's Wednesday night, you know.

CLARA. Is that fellow still coming here?

MRS. FISHER. Oh, right on the dot — such as he is. Sunday nights too now, as well as Wednesdays. It looks like a steady thing. And you never in your life heard anybody talk so much Clara — I don't know how she stands him. Your Pop can hardly stay in the room where he is. I believe in my heart that's the reason he went over to Gillespie's to-night — so he wouldn't be listenin' to him.

CLARA. Doesn't she take him into the parlor?

MRS. FISHER. She does, yes; but she might just as well leave him out here; for he's not in there five minutes till he's out here again — talkin' about Socialism. That's all you hear, — Socialism — and capital and labor. You'd think he knew somethin' about it. And the Pennsylvania Railroad. He's always talkin' about that, too. That's where he works, you know. I don't know what he does down there. He sez himself he's head of the freight department; but as I sez to our Joe, I sez, "I don't know how *he* can be head of *anything*, from the talk of him." Joe sez he thinks he's a nut. And your Pop told him right to his face last Sunday night — that he didn't know the meanin' of the *word* Socialism. [*She checks herself and gets up*] I'd better not be talkin' so loud, — he's apt to walk in on us. [*She moves up towards the hall-door and glances out*] He's a great joker, you know — That's what he did last Sunday night. [*Coming forward again to a point above the center-table*] I never got such a fright in my life. Your Pop and me was sittin' here talkin', just the way we are now, when, all of a sudden, I glanced up, and there he was, — standin' in the doorway there, doin' this [*She points her forefinger and thumb at* CLARA *and wriggles her thumb.* CLARA *laughs faintly*] — as though he was a bandit, you know. Well, — I thought the breath'd leave my body. Then he sez, "Haha! — that's the time I fooled you!" I don't know how long he'd been standin' there. But, as luck'd have it, we wasn't talkin' about him at the time: altho we *had* been talkin' about him not five minutes before. I don't know whether he heard is or not, for I don't know how long he'd been standin' there. I hope he did: t'd just be the price of him, for bein' so smart. [*With a glance toward the hall-door, and speaking very confidentially*] But, you know, what'd kill you, Clara, you can't say a *word* about him in front of her. [CLARA *moves*] Oh, not a word. No matter what he sez, she thinks it's lovely. When Joe told her here the other night he thought he was a nut, she just laughed, and said that Joe was jealous of him — because *he* could express himself and *he* couldn't. [CLARA *smiles*] You never *heard* such talk. And, you know, Clara, *I* think he wears a wig. [CLARA *laughs*] I do, honestly. And our Joe sez he thinks he does too. But when I asked *her* about it here one mornin', I thought she'd take the head right off me. You never *seen* anybody get themselves into such a temper. She sez, "It's a lie," she sez, "he *don't* wear a wig." She sez, "People always say somethin' like that about a fellow that makes a good appearance." But, *I* think he does, just the same; and the first chance I get I'm goin' to take a good look. [*She moves around to her chair again, at the right of the table*] He often sits right here, you know, under this light, while he's talkin'; [*Selecting another piece of candy*] and I'm goin' to look close the very first chance I get. [*She sits down*] *I* can tell a wig as good as anybody. [*She rocks and looks straight out, chewing*] She won't make a liar out of me.

AMY [*from the head of the stairs*]. Mom, did you see anything of that blue bar-pin of mine?

MRS. FISHER [*calling back to her*]. Which blue bar-pin?

AMY. Well now, how many blue bar-pins have I got?

MRS. FISHER. I don't know how many you've got, and I don't care! [*Turning back again and speaking rather to herself*] So don't be botherin' me about it. [*Calling up to* AMY *again*] If you can't find it, go look for it. [*She resumes her rocking and her chewing*] She thinks all she's got to do is come to the head of them stairs and holler and everybody'll jump. — But she'll get sadly left. — I've got somethin' else to do besides waitin' on her. [*She takes another bite of candy, and turns casually to* CLARA] Did you *get* your lamp yet?

CLARA. No, that's what I was in town to-day about. The girl sez they haven't been able to match the silk till yesterday.

MRS. FISHER. I wish I could get somethin' done to that one of mine there in the parlor; the wire's right out through the silk in two places.

CLARA. Why doesn't Amy take it in some day [MRS. FISHER *makes a sound of amusement*] — when she's going to work?

MRS. FISHER. Why don't she! It's all Amy can do to take *herself* into work these days. I've almost got to *push* her out the door every morning.

CLARA. Couldn't she take it over at lunch-time?

MRS. FISHER. She sez she hasn't time at lunch-time.

CLARA. Oh, she has so time.

MRS. FISHER. Of course she has.

CLARA. It's only at Ninth and Chestnut, and she's at Eighth.

MRS. FISHER. That's what I told her. I sez, "I bet if it was somethin' for yourself you'd have plenty of time." [*Leaning towards* CLARA] But, you know, — what *I* think, Clara — *I* think she's meetin' this fellow at lunch-time. Because in the mornin's here she stands fixin' herself there in front of that glass till it's a wonder to me she don't drop on the floor. And whenever you see them gettin' very particular that way all of a sudden — there's somethin' in the wind. I sez to her the other mornin', when she was settlin' herself there till I got tired lookin' at her, I sez, "You must be goin' to see him to-day, ain't you?" And she sez, "He must be on your mind, isn't he?" "No," I sez, "but by the looks of things, I think he's on yours. And," I sez, "maybe after you get him you won't think he was worth all the bother you went to." Because, you know, Clara, she don't know a *thing* about him; except that he works in the Pennsylvania freight office — I believe he *did* tell her that much. But *she* don't know whether he works there or not. He could tell her anything; and she'd believe it [*Taking another bite of candy and settling herself in her chair*] — before she'd believe me.

CLARA. That's where he works [*Her Mother looks at her sharply*] — at the Pennsylvania freight office.

MRS. FISHER. How do you know?

CLARA. Frank knows him.

MRS. FISHER. Frank Hyland?

CLARA. Yes, — he sez he eats his lunch at the same place, there at Fifteenth and Arch.

MRS. FISHER. And, does he say he knows him?

CLARA. Yes. He sez he's seen him around there for a long time. I've often heard him speak of him, but I didn't know it was the same fellow. Frank always called him Carnation Charlie. He sez he's always got a big carnation in his buttonhole.

MRS. FISHER [*tapping the table conclusively*]. That's the one; he's always got it on when he comes here, too.

CLARA. Frank sez he's never seen him without it.

MRS. FISHER. I haven't either. And I believe in my heart, Clara, that's what's turned her head. [CLARA *smiles*] You often see things like that, you know. The worst fool of a man can put a carnation in his coat or his hat over one eye, and half a dozen sensible women'll be dyin' about him.

CLARA. Well, Frank sez this fellow's absolutely *crazy*.

MRS. FISHER. That's what your Father sez.

CLARA. He sez they kid the life out of him down around the restaurant there.

MRS. FISHER. Well, he don't know who Frank Hyland *is*, does he?

CLARA. No, Frank didn't tell him. He sez he just happened to get talking to him the other day and he mentioned that he was calling on a girl up this way named Fisher. So then Frank found out what his right name was, and when he came home he asked me about him.

MRS. FISHER. Well, is he sure it's the same fellow?

CLARA. He told him his name was Piper.

MRS. FISHER [*with finality*]. That the name — Aubrey Piper. I don't know where he got the Aubrey from; *I* never heard of such a name before, did you?

CLARA. Yes, I've heard the name of Aubrey.

MRS. FISHER [*rocking*]. Well, I never did. Sounds to me more like a place than a name. [AMY *can be heard coming down the stairs*] Here she comes. [*She snatches up the box of candy and puts it under her apron*]

CLARA. Don't say anything, now.

MRS. FISHER. It'd be no use. [*Trying to be casual*] What color are you havin' your lamp-shade made, Clara?

AMY [*hurrying in at the hall-door*]. Mom, you *must* have seen something of that bar-pin of mine; I can't find it anywhere. [*She tosses a beaded bag onto the center-table and turns to the mantel-piece and looks for the bar-pin*]

MRS. FISHER [*abstractedly*]. I saw a pin of yours in one of the drawers in the buffet there a few days ago, I don't know whether it's there yet or not.

AMY [*hurrying across to the buffet at the right*]. How's it *you're* not home tonight, Clara? [*She starts to rummage in the buffet-drawers*]

CLARA [*casually*]. I had my dinner in town.

AMY. Is that parlor all right, Mom?

MRS. FISHER. Certainly it's all right.

AMY. Well, did you side it?

MRS. FISHER [*sharply*]. Certainly I sided it.

AMY. All right, Mom, don't make a speech about it.

MRS. FISHER [*considerably ruffled*]. No, but you'd think the way she sez it that I sat here all day with my two hands as long as each other. [AMY *finds the pin and slams the drawer shut, leaving various ends of tape and pieces of lace hanging out. Then she starts back towards the mirror over the mantelpiece*] Did you find it?

AMY [*disrespectfully*]. Yes.

MRS. FISHER [*rising, still holding the candy under her apron, and stepping over to the buffet*]. It's a wonder you wouldn't leave these drawers the way you found them. She does that every time she goes near this buffet. [*She puts the various odds and ends back into the drawers and closes them*] She's in such a great rush lately.

AMY [*settling herself at the mirror*]. Isn't that a new dress on you, Clara?

CLARA. Yes.

MRS. FISHER [*coming back to her chair*]. I'd like to see the kind of house you'll keep.

AMY. Well, I hope it won't be anything like this one, I'll tell you that.

MRS. FISHER [*stopping halfway to her chair*]. Oh, go easy, lady! You might be very glad to have half as good, if you live long enough. [*Continuing to her chair, and looking keenly at* CLARA's *dress*] I thought I hadn't seen that dress on you before. [*She sits down*]

CLARA. No, I only got it last week.

MRS. FISHER. Stand up there till I see it. [CLARA *gets up and takes a couple of steps towards the left, pulling down her skirt, then turns around to her left and faces her Mother.* AMY *comes down to the center-table, looking sharply at* CLARA'S *dress*]

CLARA. I got it at a sale in Strawbridge's.

[AMY *opens her beaded purse on the table and looks at herself critically in the little inside mirror; then adds a touch of powder*]

MRS. FISHER. It's a nice length.

CLARA. I didn't have to have a thing touched on it.

MRS. FISHER. That's what I was tellin' you about the other day, Amy. — Do you see the way that dress hangs?

AMY. Yeh.

MRS. FISHER [*speaking directly to* CLARA]. There was a dress on Queen Mary in last Sunday's Ledger that I was sayin' to Amy I thought'd look good on me. And it had all buttons up and down the front, the way that has.

CLARA [*coming back to her chair*]. A lot of the new dresses are made that way.

MRS. FISHER. How much was it?

CLARA [*sitting down*]. Forty-two seventy-five.

[AMY *starts to polish her nails*]

MRS. FISHER [*turning away, with a lift of her eyes to Heaven*]. You must have plenty of money.

AMY. Mom, where'd you put those roses I brought home?

MRS. FISHER. They're out there in the dining-room. [AMY *starts towards the right*] I put them in some water. [AMY *goes out; and* MRS. FISHER *rocks for a second or two; then she turns and calls after* AMY] I think it's time you lit the light in that parlor, Amy, if that fellow of yours is comin' here tonight. [*She rocks a little bit more, then turns casually to* CLARA] What time is it by your watch there, Clara? [*With a glance toward the mantelpiece at the back*] That old clock of ours is stopped again.

CLARA [*looking at her wrist-watch*]. Quarter past eight.

MRS. FISHER [*getting up suddenly*]. I must tell her. [*The box of candy lands on the floor*] My God, there goes the candy! Pick that up, Clara, I can't stoop; and put it out of sight. [*Going towards the door up at the right*] It's a wonder I didn't do that while she was in here. [*Calling out after* AMY] Amy!

AMY. Yes?

MRS. FISHER. Clara sez it's a quarter past eight by her watch; — you'd better get some kind of a light in that parlor if that fellow's comin'. [*She moves back towards her chair, then speaks in a very subdued tone to* CLARA] She brings flowers home with her from the city now, every night he's coming. She must have flowers for him in the parlor. [*She sits down*] I told her, I sez, "I bet it'd be a long time before you'd bring any flowers home from the city to me."

CLARA. That's another new dress on *her* to-night, isn't it?

MRS. FISHER [*straightening the magazines on the table*]. She's had it about a week.

CLARA. What's she getting so many new dresses for lately?

MRS. FISHER. Heaven knows, I don't.

CLARA. That's the fourth I've seen on her since Easter.

MRS. FISHER. Tryin' to make him think she's rich, I guess. I told her the other night she might not get so many after she gets him.

AMY [*entering from the right, carrying a vase of roses, and crossing directly to the parlor-doors at the left*]. You need another box of matches out there, Mom.

MRS. FISHER. Is that box of matches gone already?

AMY. Pretty near. [*She goes into the parlor*]

MRS. FISHER. I swear I don't know where all the matches go to; — seems to me all I do is buy matches. [AMY *strikes a match in the parlor*] Be careful of them lace curtains there, now, Amy, if you're goin' to light that lamp. [*The lamp is lit in the parlor; and* AMY *closes the parlor-doors*]

CLARA [*rising and handing her Mother the box of candy, which she has been holding since she picked it up from the floor*]. I think I'll go, before he comes.

MRS. FISHER [*rising*]. You'd better, unless you want to be here all night. [CLARA *moves up to the looking-glass over the mantelpiece, and* MRS. FISHER *crosses to the buffet with the candy*] For if he ever starts talkin', you'll never get out. [*She puts the candy into one of the drawers, then starts across towards the hall-door, up at the left*] You wouldn't mind, you know, if he'd stay in there in the parlor; — but the minute ever he hears a voice out here, he's out like a jumpin'-jack. [AMY *can be heard coughing out in the hallway, and, as* MRS. FISHER *passes* back of CLARA, CLARA *half turns and suggests with a movement of her hand that* AMY *might overhear her*] Oh, he's not here yet; you'd know it if he was. [*She peers keenly out into the hallway, then turns and tiptoes back to* CLARA, *and speaks in a very low tone*] She stands out there in the vestibule until she sees him get off the trolley, then she comes in and lets him ring, so he won't think she's been waitin' for him. [*She tiptoes back and peers out into the hallway again, and* CLARA *moves over to the right, adjusting her neck-piece.* MRS. FISHER *comes back to the center-table*] You never seen anybody so crazy about a fellow.

CLARA. Well, I think somebody ought to tell her about him, Mom.

MRS. FISHER [*folding the ribbon and the paper from the candy-box*]. What's the good of tellin' her; — she'd only give you a look if you said anything about him.

CLARA. Well, I'd say it anyway, whether she gave me a look or not; for, remember what I'm telling you, Mom, it's *you* that'll have them on your hands if she takes him. [*Her Mother looks at her sharply*]

MRS. FISHER. *I'll* have them on my hands?

CLARA [*turning to her Mother*]. Well now, who else *will*, Mom? You couldn't leave her out on the street; and that's exactly where she'll land if she takes *him;* for you know how long Amy could get along on a hundred and fifty dollars a month.

MRS. FISHER. Takes more than that to keep herself, never name a house and a husband.

CLARA. Well, that's exactly what he gets, for he's only a clerk down there.

MRS. FISHER. He told her he was the head of the department.

CLARA. He's a clerk, Mom, — like a hundred others down there: Frank knows what he does.

MRS. FISHER [*moving a step or two nearer to* CLARA]. Well, why don't *you* say something to her, Clara?

CLARA. Now, you know how much attention she'd pay to anything I'd say.

MRS. FISHER [*with measured definiteness*]. She won't pay any attention to what anybody sez.

CLARA. Especially if she knew it was Frank Hyland that said it.

MRS. FISHER. She thinks everybody's jealous of him; and jealous of *her* because she's gettin' him. So let her

get him. If she makes her bed, let her lie in it.

CLARA [*looking straight out*]. Well, that's the trouble, Mom; it isn't always the person that makes the bed that lies *in it.* — Very often somebody else has to lie in it.

MRS. FISHER [*turning back to the table*]. Well, it'll be nobody around here, I can promise you that.

CLARA [*turning to the buffet-mirror*]. Maybe not.

MRS. FISHER. No maybe about it.

CLARA. But you know what *you* are, Mom, where Amy's concerned.

MRS. FISHER [*taking a step towards* CLARA]. Why, don't be silly, Clara. Do you think your Father'd be listenin' to that rattle-brain here every night?

CLARA [*turning and speaking directly to her Mother*]. He has to listen to him now, doesn't he — or go out, as he did to-night. [*The front-door closes. They both turn and glance in the direction of the hallway*] Maybe this is Frank now. [*There is a slight pause, then* FRANK HYLAND *comes in, and comes forward to the center-table*]

MRS. FISHER. Hello, Frank.

HYLAND. Hello, Mother. Hello, Clara. [*He puts his hat down on the table*]

CLARA. I was just going; I thought maybe you weren't coming.

HYLAND [*looking at his watch*]. I couldn't get away from there until nearly eight o'clock.

MRS. FISHER. Frank, — Clara sez you know this fellow that's comin' to see our Amy.

HYLAND. Who, Piper?

MRS. FISHER. Yes — the one that does so much talkin'.

HYLAND. Yes, I know him. [*He moves to the left and sits down on the arm of the Morris-chair*]

MRS. FISHER. I think he's crazy, Frank; [HYLAND *makes a sound of amusement*] I do, honestly; and Pop and Joe sez they think he is, too.

CLARA. Mom sez he told Amy he was head of the freight department, Frank.

MRS. FISHER. He did, honestly, Frank; and she believes him. But Clara sez *you* say he's only a clerk down there.

CLARA. That's all he is, Mom.

MRS. FISHER. He isn't head of the freight department, is he, Frank? [FRANK *sits looking away off, dreamily*]

CLARA. Frank —

HYLAND [*turning*]. I beg your pardon, what did you say, dear?

MRS. FISHER. He isn't head of the freight department down there, is he?

HYLAND. No, he's just one of the clerks.

MRS. FISHER [*turning to* CLARA]. Now, you see that — and she'd only laugh at you if you told *her* that. [*Turning back to* HYLAND] How much do them freight-clerks get a month, Frank? [HYLAND *is gazing out of the window at the left*]

CLARA. Frank, Mom is talking to you.

HYLAND [*turning*]. Oh, I beg your pardon, what did you say, Mother?

MRS. FISHER. I say, how much do them freight-clerks get a month?

HYLAND. Why, — about a hundred and forty or fifty dollars, — I don't know exactly; but not any more than that. [*His eyes wander to the window again*]

MRS. FISHER. What are we goin' to do about it, Frank? — It looks like a steady thing. He comes Wednesday and Sunday nights now — and if she ever takes him, she'll be the poorest woman in this city. You know how our Amy spends money. [*Turning to* CLARA] She's got seven pairs of shoes up in that hall-closet.

HYLAND [*abstractedly*]. Amy certainly does let her money fly. [MRS. FISHER *gives him a stoney look*]

MRS. FISHER. Well, if she does she earns it. She might as well have a good time now while she's young; — God knows what's ahead of her. [*The front door-bell rings, — a series of funny little taps*] Here he is now, I know his ring. [*She steps up to the mantelpiece and glances out into the hallway*]

CLARA [*turning towards the kitchen-door*]. We'll go out the side-door. Come on, Frank. [HYLAND *rises and picks up his hat from the table, as he crosses below it*]

HYLAND. Good-night, Mother. [MRS. FISHER *is too occupied with her interests out in the hallway*] Do you want to go to a picture, Clara?

CLARA [*going out at the right*]. I don't care.

HYLAND [*following her*]. It's only about twenty after eight. [*He glances at his watch*]

CLARA. We can get the second show at Broad and Columbia Avenue.

MRS. FISHER [*following them out*]. Frank, I wish you'd talk to Amy some time, and tell her what you told me; she won't believe *me*.

HYLAND. I don't suppose she'd believe me, either, Mother.

AUBREY [*out at the front-door*]. Right on the job!

AMY. Hello!

AUBREY. The pride of old West Philly! [*He laughs a bit, boisterously*]

AMY. I'll take your hat, Aubrey.

AUBREY. Anything to please the ladies. [*The front-door closes*] The boy rode off with many thanks, and many a backward bow. [*He laughs again, rather wildly.* MRS. FISHER *tiptoes into the room from the right and stands listening, keenly*] Do you know, I think I'll have to get hold of an airship somewhere, Amy, to come out here to see you.

AMY. It *is* quite a trip for you, isn't it?

AUBREY. Just one shining hour and a half, if you say it quick; by the little old Brill special. And how is the Mother? [MRS. FISHER's *face hardens, and a door closes. Then she tiptoes over to the double-doors at the left and listens.* AUBREY's *voice can be heard fairly distinctly from beyond the doors*] Say, Amy — wasn't that hold-up in last night's paper somewhere out this way?

AMY. Yes, it was right over here on Erie Avenue.

[MR. FISHER *appears in the hall-door and stands, looking with amusement at his wife. He takes an old pipe and tobacco-pouch from the pocket of his knit-jacket and starts to fill the pipe*]

AUBREY. A doctor's house, wasn't it?

AMY. Yes, Doctor Donnelly's. They got nearly two thousand dollars.

AUBREY. I don't believe that, Amy.

AMY. Why not?

AUBREY. I don't believe there's that much money *in* North Philadelphia. [*He roars with laughter*]

[MR. FISHER *gives his wife a little dig in the ribs and makes a sound like a startled cat. She starts violently smothering a little shriek*]

MRS. FISHER. Oh, you frightened me! [MR. FISHER *continues to the center-table and sets his newspaper down*]

MR. FISHER. You ought to be pretty nearly frightened to death by this time, oughtn't you? [*He replaces the tobacco-pouch in his pocket*]

MRS. FISHER. Well, it's no wonder I'd be.

MR. FISHER. You've been jumpin' that way ever since I knew you.

MRS. FISHER. Well, what do you come pussy-footin' in that way for, when you know how nervous I am?

MR. FISHER. I didn't come pussy-footin' in at all.

MRS. FISHER. You did so, or I'd have heard you.

MR. FISHER. You *would* have heard me, if you weren't so busy listenin' to somethin' that's none of your business.

MRS. FISHER. Well, it'll be somethin' of my business if you go spillin' any of that dirty old tobacco on my nice new table-cloth, I tell you that. [*She resumes her listening at the door, and* MR. FISHER *brushes the tobacco from the table-cloth*]

MR. FISHER. I'm not spillin' any of it. [*There's a burst of laughter from* AUBREY *in the parlor, and* MR. FISHER *looks toward the parlor-door*] Who's in there — Windy? [MRS. FISHER *nods, yes, and the old man moves down at the right of the center-table, picking up the newspaper and reaching into his vest-pocket for his spectacles*] What's he doin', laughin' at some more of them West Philadelphia jokes of his? [*He sits down to read, in the chair at the right of the table, and* MRS. FISHER *comes tiptoeing towards the chair at the left of the table*]

MRS. FISHER [*in a lowered tone*]. He was astin' Amy about that robbery over at Doctor Donnelly's yesterday mornin'; and when she told him the bandits got away with nearly two thousand dollars, he said it couldn't be true, because there wasn't that much money *in* North Philadelphia.

MR. FISHER [*with mock laughter*]. Ha! Ha! Ha!

MRS. FISHER [*returning to the parlor-doors to listen*]. Shush! [*There's a Ha! Ha! Ha! from the parlor from* AUBREY, *and the old man looks quickly and distrustfully in that direction.* AUBREY *continues to laugh*]

MR. FISHER [*settling himself to read*]. I'll bet there wouldn't have to be much money up this way to be more than *he's* got.

[*There's a sound of hammering in the cellar.* MRS. FISHER *hurries across to the cellar-door*]

AUBREY [*in the parlor*]. You know, I discovered tonight, Amy, that I can save a full fifteen minutes on this trip over here, by transferring up Twenty-ninth to the Lehigh Avenue car, instead of going on in and up Nineteenth.

MRS. FISHER [*opening the cellar-door and calling down, in a subdued voice*]. Joe! Stop that hammering down there, we can't hear our ears up here. [*The old man gives a hard chuckle.* MRS. FISHER *tip-toes back towards the parlor-doors, looking at her husband stonily*] What ails *you?*

AMY [*in the parlor*]. It *is* hard to get out here, unless you use the Park trolley. I hear some people say that's a great deal quicker. [MRS. FISHER *listens keenly again with her ear against the parlor-door*]

AUBREY. I don't know how you ever found this place.

AMY. I don't know how *you* ever found West Philadelphia.

AUBREY. Lot of people think they haven't found it *yet.* [*He bursts into violent laughter*] Lost somewhere between the Schuylkill River and Darby. [*He laughs some more. The old man looks piercingly over his spectacles at his wife*]

MR. FISHER [*almost shouting*]. Come away from there, Josie! [MRS. FISHER *is startled almost to death. She places her hand on her bosom and moves away from the door towards the center of the room*] Don't be listenin' to that damned blatherskite.

MRS. FISHER [*trying to be casual*]. I wasn't listen' to him; — I was just seein' what he was sayin'. [*She moves up to the little stand between the hall-door and the mantelpiece and picks up her knitting-bag.* AMY *is very much amused at something* AUBREY *has just said in the parlor.* MRS. FISHER *glances toward the parlor-doors, then comes down to her husband's right, and, with another glance toward the door, speaks very confidentially*] He was astin' Amy how she ever found this part of town to live in; and she was astin' him how *he* ever found West Philadelphia. He sez West Philadelphia ain't *been* found yet, — that it's lost somewhere between the Schuylkill River and Darby. [*She moves over to the arm-chair at the right, in front of the window, and sits down*]

MR. FISHER. I wish to God *he'd* get lost some night, somewhere between here and the Schuylkill River.

MRS. FISHER [*taking the needles and the pink wool out of the knitting-bag*] What'd kill you, too, you know, he always dies laughin' whenever he gets off one of them bum jokes.

MR. FISHER. Somebody's got to laugh.

AUBREY [*from the parlor*]. Ha! Ha! That's the time I fooled you, Amy! Leave it to me to put it right over the plate. [AMY *has quite a laughing fit in the parlor. Her Mother looks narrowly toward the parlor-doors until* AMY *has finished laughing*]

MRS. FISHER. He's got Amy laughin' now, too. [*She commences to knit; and there is a slight pause. Then she glances at the clock on the mantelpiece*] That old clock has stopped again, Neil.

MR. FISHER [*without moving*]. Needs fixin'.

MRS. FISHER. It's *been* fixed twice, — don't do no good. [*There is a pause, and* MRS. FISHER *sighs*] I think it's terrible lonesome not to hear the clock — it's too still in a room. — It always sounds to me like soap-bubbles meltin'.

MR. FISHER. H'm — here's a fellow here's been left a quarter of a million dollars, and he won't take it.

MRS. FISHER [*sharply*]. What's the matter with him?

MR. FISHER. Nothin' at all's the matter with him — he just won't take it.

MRS. FISHER [*resuming her knitting*]. He mustn't be in his right mind, poor boy. I wisht somebody'd leave *me* a quarter of a million dollars.

MR. FISHER. You wouldn't know what to do with it if they did.

MRS. FISHER. Well, I know *one* thing I'd do with it; and that'd be to have somethin' done to that old heater of ours downstairs, and not be freezin' to death all *next* winter, the way I was last. [AUBREY *laughs in the parlor.* MRS. FISHER *glances toward the parlor-doors; then shifts her knitting*] Every sweater I start I swear it'll be the last — and then I start right in on another. [*She gives a faint little laugh and looks at her husband; but he's reading; so she subsides and continues to knit. Suddenly she stops and rests her knitting in her lap, and thinks; then turns to* MR. FISHER] Well now, what becomes of money like that, Neil, that people won't take?

MR. FISHER [*squinting at her over his glasses*]. What'd you say?

MRS. FISHER. I say, what becomes of money that people won't take that way?

MR. FISHER [*resuming his paper*]. Why, nothing at all becomes of it; — they just come and get it. [*She looks at him steadily*]

MRS. FISHER. Who does?

MR. FISHER. The people that won't take it. [MRS. FISHER *is puzzled for a second*]

MRS. FISHER [*resuming her knitting*]. Well, I'll bet if they left it to *me* they wouldn't have to come and take it.

MR. FISHER [*looking at her again with a shade of irritation*]. Who wouldn't have to come and take it?

MRS. FISHER [*losing her temper*]. Why, the people that won't take it!

MR. FISHER. What are you talkin' about, Josie, do you know?

MRS. FISHER. Yes, I do know very well what I'm talkin' about! — but I don't think *you* do.

MR. FISHER. Let me read this paper, will you?

MRS. FISHER [*knitting rapidly*]. Go ahead and read it! — I'm sure I don't want to talk to you. It was you that started talkin' to me — readin' about that young man that took the money. [JOE *comes up from the cellar, carrying some kind of a radio-arrangement on a flat base-board and a screw-driver*] Joe, I'm goin' to have that light took out of that cellar, if you don't stop spendin' all your time down there.

JOE [*holding his work under the table-lamp to look at it closely*]. You don't want me hammerin' up here, do you?

MRS. FISHER. I don't want you hammerin' anywhere. I want you to go out at night and get some air, and not be cooped up in that dusty old cellar. [*There's a violent burst of laughter from* AUBREY *in the parlor.* JOE *glances towards the parlor-doors, then turns, with something of distress in his expression, to his Mother*]

JOE. Who's *in* there — the Pennsylvania Railroad?

MRS. FISHER. Yes, and he's got about as much sense as yourself.

JOE [*moving around to the chair at the left of the center-table and sitting down*]. You won't say that when you're sittin' here listenin' to the Grand Opera. [*He starts to tighten the small screws in the base-board*]

MRS. FISHER. I won't be listenin' to it, don't fret — I got somethin' else to do besides listenin' to a lot of dagoes singin'.

MR. FISHER [*looking over at* JOE'S *radio-arrangement*]. What is it?

MRS. FISHER. He sez when he gets that radio-thing finished, I can sit here and listen to the Grand Opera.

MR. FISHER [*resuming his paper*]. What's that, them singin' people?

MRS. FISHER. Yes — them that goes away up high, you know — that Clara has on her victrola.

[*The parlor-door opens, and* AMY *comes out, walking on air*]

AMY. Oh, it's all right if you let it run for a minute. [*She crosses to the right to the kitchen-door, glancing at herself in the mantelpiece-mirror as she pauses*]

MRS. FISHER. What's the matter?

AMY. Nothing; Aubrey wants a drink of water. [*She goes out at the right*]

MRS. FISHER [*with a significant sound*]. Oh.

AUBREY [*coming out of the parlor*]. Stay right where you are, folks, right where you are. [*He moves to the mirror over the mantelpiece*] Just a little social attention, — going right out again on the next train. [*He surveys himself critically in the mirror, touching his tie and toupé gingerly.* MRS. FISHER *gives him a smouldering look, and* JOE *looks at his Father.* AUBREY *turns from the mirror, and indicates his reflection with a wide gesture*] There you are, Mother! Any woman's fancy, what do you say? Even to the little old carnation. [*He gives the table a double tap with his knuckles, then laughs, and moves up towards the kitchen-door, and calls out to* AMY] Come on, Amy, step on the United Gas out there; customer in here waiting for the old aqua pura. [*Moving down to* MR. FISHER'S *right*] Man's got to have something to drink — how about it, Pop? [*He gives* MR. FISHER *a slap on the right shoulder*] You'll stay with me on that, won't you? [*He laughs and moves up to the mirror again. Old man* FISHER *is very much annoyed*] Yes, sir. [*Coming forward again at the right*] I want to tell those of you who have ventured out this evening, that this is a very pretty little picture of domestic felicity. [*He laughs a little and looks from one to the other, patronizingly; but nobody pays the slight-*

est attention to him] Father reading, — Mother knitting; [MRS. FISHER *withers him with a quick look*] But then, Mama is *always* knitting. [*She knits rapidly and* AUBREY *laughs, and moves up and across back of the table*] And little Tommy Edison over here, working eighteen hours a day to make the rich man richer and the poor man poorer. [*He gives* JOE *a tap on the back, then moves back again towards* MR. FISHER] What about it, Popcorn? [*Slaps him on the back*] Shake it up! Right or raving?

MR. FISHER [*starting to his feet violently*]. God damn it, let me alone! And keep your hands to yourself. [*He crosses below the center-table and up to the hall-door*] I never saw such a damn pest in my life! [*He goes up the stairs bristling with rage, and muttering to himself.* AUBREY *is vastly amused. He leans on the back of* MR. FISHER'S *chair and roars with laughter*]

AUBREY. Sign on the dotted line! And little old Popsy-Wopsy getting sore and going to leave us flat. [*He laughs again considerably; then turns to* MRS. FISHER] Nevertheless, and notwithstanding, Mrs. Fisher, I'd like to mention that the kid from West Philadelphia is giving the growing boy the said and done. [*He indicates* JOE *with a waving gesture.* AMY *comes in from the right with a glass of water. He turns and acknowledges her with even a wider gesture*] And there she is herself, and not a moving picture. [AMY *extends the glass of water, laughing, and with a touch of self-consciousness*] Blushing as she gave it, looking down — at her feet so bare, and her tattered gown. [AMY *giggles, and her Mother looks sharply at* AMY'S *shoes.* AUBREY *takes the glass of water and turns to* MRS. FISHER] How's that, Mother Fisher? Can't beat that little old Willie Shakespeare, can you? No, sir, — I'd like to tell the brothers that that little old Shakespeare party shook a wicked spear. [*He laughs at his own comedy, and* AMY *is immeasurably delighted*] Well, here's laughter, ladies! and, [*turning to* JOE] Mr. Marconi, — my best regards to you. [*He drinks*]

AMY. I'm afraid it's not very cold. [*He just raises his hand, signifying that it's perfectly satisfactory*]

MRS. FISHER. Why didn't you let it run?

AMY. I did, but it doesn't seem to get any colder.

AUBREY [*handing the glass back to* AMY]. Very nice indeed. And a sweeter draught, from a fairer hand was never quaffed.

AMY [*flipping her hand at him*]. Oh, you! [*She goes out at the right again with the empty glass*]

AUBREY [*laughing a bit*]. Thank you very much. [*He turns and moves across above the table towards* JOE, *drawing a gaily-bordered handkerchief from his breast-pocket and touching it to his lips*] Yes, sir, Mr. Joseph, I want to tell you you're wasting time; for when you're all through, they'll offer you twenty cents for it, and sell it for twenty million. [*He punctuates this last remark with a series of patronizing taps on* JOE'S *back*] — Take it or leave it — sign on the dotted line. [*He taps his knuckles on the table, and moves back again to* MRS. FISHER'S *left*] Yes, sir, — that's exactly what they did to little old yours truly here. Twenty Lincoln Anacondas, for a formula that would have solved the greatest problem before the Industrial Chemical world to-day. [AMY *comes in from the right, and, looking at* AUBREY *wonderingly, moves across towards the left.* AUBREY *moves forward and across in front of the table towards* JOE] A formula to prevent the rusting of iron and steel. [JOE *gets up and moves up and around above the table towards the kitchen-door at the right*] A solution of Vanadium and Manganese, to be added to the metal in its molten state; [JOE *stops and looks back at him*] instead of applied externally as they have been doing.

JOE. What did you say, Aubrey?

AUBREY. I said, a simple combination of chemical elements, to be added to the metal in its *molten* state, instead of applied externally as they have been doing.

[JOE *and* AUBREY, *speaking together*]

JOE [*speaking to his Mother*]. Mom, do you know anything about that little screw-driver with the black handle?

AUBREY. But, — simply because it was discovered by a working-man — that they saw they couldn't buy —

MRS. FISHER. Do you mean the one you fixed the sewing machine with?

[JOE *and* AUBREY, *speaking together*]

JOE. Yes, that little short one with the black handle.

AUBREY. They gave it the swinging door. [AMY *moves over to the parlor-doors*]

[MRS. FISHER *and* AUBREY, *speaking together*]

MRS. FISHER. I think I saw it on the shelf out there, over the sink. And now, don't go upsettin' everything out there.

AUBREY. They'd rather go on paying a million dollars a year [JOE *goes out, and* AUBREY *follows him to the kitchen-door*] — to paint their steel and iron structures throughout the country, than pay *me*.

MRS. FISHER. Do you see it, Joe?

AUBREY [*coming down to* MRS. FISHER'S *left*]. And do you know *why*, Mrs. Fisher?

JOE [*answering his Mother from the kitchen*]. No!

AUBREY. Then, I'll tell you. Because I work for my living. That's the said and done on the whole business. [MRS. FISHER *starts to put her things into the knitting-bag, preparatory to getting up*] Keep them poor and get them married; and then, [*he looks away off*] as my darling old Mother used to say, "You've got them on their beams and hinges."

MRS. FISHER [*getting up*]. I don't see that anybody's tryin' to make anybody get married if they don't want to. [*She passes up to the kitchen-door, putting her knitting-bag on the buffet as she goes*]

AUBREY [*following her up*]. But they *do* want to, Mrs. Fisher, — but the capitalist wants to stop them.

MRS. FISHER [*turning at the kitchen-door and speaking directly to him*]. Well, I guess it'd be just as well to stop *some* of 'em. [*She goes out*]

AUBREY [*calling after her through the kitchen-door*]. Ah, don't go back on little old William Jennings Bryan, Mother Fisher. Life, liberty and the pursuit of happiness, you know. [*He turns and comes forward at the right again, laughing a little*] Sign on the dotted line.

AMY [*trying to conceal her temper*]. Come on in here, Aubrey.

AUBREY [*starting towards her*]. Yes, sir, Amy, I want to tell you it's the poor man that gets it every time. I put a question up to Secretary Mellon, in a letter six weeks ago — that absolutely stumped him, because I haven't had a line from him since. [AMY *is smiling into his eyes. He passes in front of her and goes into the parlor. The curtain commences to descend slowly.* AMY *looks darkly toward the kitchen-door, and stamps her foot with temper; then follows* AUBREY *into the parlor*] I simply asked him to what extent his proposed program of Income Tax Revision would affect the great American Railroad Employé. [*The curtain is down*]

THREE HOURS PASS

THE CURTAIN RISES AGAIN

MRS. FISHER *is sitting at the right of the table asleep, her knitting lying in her lap; and* JOE, *sitting at the left of the table, is endeavoring to pass the tip of a wire through a small eyelet on the base-board.* AMY *starts to play the piano in the parlor; and, after the usual introduction,* AUBREY *begins to sing, "Rocked in the Cradle of the Deep", in a heavy bass voice.*

AUBREY [*singing*].
"Rocked in the cradle of the deep,
I lay me down, — in peace to sleep —
Secure I rest upon the wave,
For Thou alone —
[MRS. FISHER *starts slightly and wakens.* JOE *glances at her.* AUBREY *continues*]
has the power to save."
MRS. FISHER. Where'd you put it? What? Did you say something? [AUBREY *continues to sing*]
JOE. Not a thing, Mom.
MRS. FISHER [*brushing back her hair*]. I must have been dozin'.
JOE. You've been dead.
MRS. FISHER. What?
JOE. Since half-past nine. [MRS. FISHER *becomes conscious of* AUBREY *singing*]
MRS. FISHER. What time is it now, Joe? [*The singing becomes louder, and* MRS. FISHER *rises, with her eyes fastened on the parlor-door*] Is that him singin' in there?
JOE [*reaching into his belt-pocket for an Ingersoll watch*]. The old Scientific American himself. A quarter of twelve.
MRS. FISHER. My God! what's he startin' to sing at this hour for! [*She steps to the buffet at the right and puts her knitting-bag into one of the drawers*]
JOE. Talent should never be suppressed at any time, Mother.
MRS. FISHER. It's a wonder Amy wouldn't have sense enough to stop him. [*She slams the buffet-drawer shut, and starts across towards the parlor-doors*] I never saw a man yet that didn't think he could sing. Put that thing away,

now, Joe, you've been at it long enough. And see that that back is locked. I don't think Amy has any idea what time it is or she'd shut him up.
JOE. Let the young man express himself. [*He gets up and crosses below the table towards the right, and up to the kitchen-door*]
MRS. FISHER. Oh, I wouldn't care if he bawled his head off, as far as I'm concerned — I'd be glad if he did; but I don't want him to waken your Father. [*She steps up to the hall-door and listens, at the foot of the stairs*] And that's what he'll be doin' the first thing you know, and then the fat'll be in the fire for sure. [AUBREY *reaches a high note, and* JOE *and his Mother stand looking at each other. Then* JOE *bursts out laughing*] Ain't that terrible, Joe? Do you think I ought to tell Amy what time it is?
JOE. No, give the boy a chance. [AUBREY *finishes on a high note and holds it*] Hurray! [AUBREY *can be heard applauding himself.* JOE *applauds, also*]
MRS. FISHER [*frantically, and going toward* JOE]. Shush, Joe!
JOE [*going out through the door at the right*]. Sign on the dotted line!
MRS. FISHER. Don't encourage him, for God's sake, Joe, he's bad enough as it is.
MR. FISHER [*shouting from the head of the stairs*]. Josie!
MRS. FISHER [*rushing back towards the hall-door on her tiptoes*]. Yes?
MR. FISHER. What the devil's goin' on down there! Do you know what time it is?
MRS. FISHER [*trying to pacify him*]. Why, Joe was just cuttin' up here a minute ago.
MR. FISHER. What's Amy playin' the piano for, at this time of the night?
MRS. FISHER [*trying not to be heard in the parlor*]. Why, her and Joe was just foolin' —
MR. FISHER. Damn funny kind of foolin', at this time of night! The neighbors'll be wonderin' what kind of a house we're keepin' here!
MRS. FISHER. Well, they've stopped now, Neil.
MR. FISHER. Well, tell them to see that it's *kept* stopped! And get them lights out down there and go to bed! It's nearly twelve o'clock.

[MRS. FISHER *turns and looks at the parlor-doors. Then there's a burst of wild laughter from* AUBREY. *This decides* MRS. FISHER. *She steps resolutely towards the doors with the ostensible purpose of opening them, but, before she can reach the knob, the door is yanked open from the inside, and* AMY *steps out, looking resentfully at her*]

AMY. What's the matter?

MRS. FISHER [*a trifle disconcerted*]. Why, — a — I was just comin' to tell you to be sure and put them lights out; I'm just goin' up — it's nearly twelve o'clock.

AUBREY [*thrusting his head and shoulders out through the door*]. I am also just about to take my reluctant leave, Mrs. Fisher.

MRS. FISHER . [*trying to be polite*]. Well, I don't want to hurry you, but —

AUBREY. In fact, the recent outburst was in the nature of a farewell concert. [*He bursts into a wild laugh and draws back into the parlor; and* MRS. FISHER, *with a series of frantic gestures, intended to convey to* AMY *the imminence of her Father at the head of the stairs, steps back out of the range of the parlor-door.* AMY *makes an impatient movement of her body, and stamps her foot, then flounces into the parlor and slams the door*] The little old song at twilight, you know, Mother Fisher — to soothe the savage breast. [*He gives vent to another gale of laughter; and* MRS. FISHER *stands petrified, expecting to hear her husband again*]

MRS. FISHER [*as* AUBREY'S *laugh subsides*]. The damn fool! [*She crosses to the right to the kitchen-door and calls out to* JOE] Joe!

JOE. Yeh?

MRS. FISHER. You'd better bring Gypsy Queen in and put her in the laundry there; she was shiverin' when I opened the door this mornin'. I think it's too cold for her on that back porch yet a while. [*She moves a little back towards the center of the room*]

JOE [*out at the right*]. Come on in here, Gypsy! Come on. [*He whistles*]

MRS. FISHER [*turning around to her left and looking back toward the kitchen-door*]. Ain't she there?

JOE. I don't see her.

MRS. FISHER [*calling in a high voice*]. Where are you, Gypsy?

JOE. Here she is. Come on in here, Gypsy! Come on! That's the old gypsy kid. [*The door out at the right closes*]

MRS. FISHER [*going a step nearer the kitchen-door*]. Go into that laundry there, Gypsy.

JOE. Come back here, Gypsy!

MRS. FISHER. Make her go in there, Joe.

JOE [*stamping his foot*]. Gypsy!

MRS. FISHER [*stamping her foot at the kitchen-door*]. Go back there, Gypsy! You bad girl! And go into that laundry this minute —

JOE. There she goes.

MRS. FISHER. And don't let me hear a sound out of you when you get in there either, or I'll come right straight out and give you what I gave you last Sunday afternoon. [*A door closes*] You better put the ketch on that door, Joe, or she'll be pushin' it open again; she wants to lay out here on this rug. [*Going nearer to the door again, and calling*] Now, you remember what I told you, Gypsy; and don't let me have to speak to you again. [*Turning and moving across the room to the left*] Your Father has her spoiled. [*A door out in the hallway at the left opens, and* AMY *can be heard laughing.* MRS. FISHER *stops dead in the middle of the room and listens*]

AUBREY [*calling from the hallway*]. Good-night, Mrs. Fisher. [MRS. FISHER *turns and darts back into the cellar-alcove at the right*]

AMY [*in the hallway*]. I guess she's gone up, Aubrey.

AUBREY [*coming in at the hall-door, poising on one toe, hat and cane in hand, and looking about the room*]. Montreal, Mother. [MRS. FISHER *flattens herself against the wall at the head of the cellar-stairs, and listens with a stoney expression*]

AMY. I don't think she's in there, Aubrey.

AUBREY. And silence was her answer. [*He laughs wildly, turns, and starts out into the hallway again*] Right you are, Amy — [*Glancing up the stairs*] On the right side she is sleeping. [*He goes laughing out into the hallway*]

JOE [*coming in from the kitchen, mimicking* AUBREY'S *laugh*]. Ha! Ha! Ha! [*He passes his Mother without seeing her*]

MRS. FISHER [*coming out of the alcove*]. Shush! Don't let him hear you, Joe. [JOE *turns and looks at his Mother, then continues across to the left to the hall-door*]

JOE. Is he goin'?

MRS. FISHER [*following* JOE *to the center of the room*]. At last! [JOE *glances out into the hallway*] Don't let him see you, now, Joe, or we'll have him here for another hour.

JOE [*starting up the stairs*]. I'm goin' to bed.

MRS. FISHER. Joe!

JOE [*leaning back and looking*]. What?

MRS. FISHER. Come here! [AMY *can be heard giggling in the hallway.* JOE *comes back to his Mother*]

JOE. What?

MRS. FISHER [*very confidentially*]. What was that he was sayin' here to-night, about discoverin' something to keep rust out of iron and steel?

JOE [*very much amused*]. Wasn't that a scream.

MRS. FISHER. That's what *you're* always talkin' about, ain't it?

JOE. Yes, I was talkin' to *him* about it one night here, while he was waitin' for Amy to come down; and he's forgot where he heard it.

MRS. FISHER. Can you imagine!

JOE. I was wonderin' if you were gettin' that to-night.

MRS. FISHER. No, it never struck me till afterwards.

JOE [*with a shade of seriousness*]. Did you get what he said tonight, Mom?

MRS. FISHER. Now, you know I never pay any attention to what *he* sez.

JOE [*turning away laughing*]. He's a bird. [*He goes to the hall-door and looks out into the hall*]

MRS. FISHER. Don't let him see you, now, Joe.

JOE. The vestibule-door's shut. [*He goes up the stairs. His Mother follows him to the hall-door*]

MRS. FISHER. You'd better close that window at the head of your bed, Joe, and not have it blowin' in on you all night. [*She glances out into the hall-way, then steps to the parlor-door, opens it quietly and glances in, and starts across towards the right. The front-door closes out in the hallway, then the vestibule-door.* MRS. FISHER *glances over her right shoulder toward the hallway, then continues to the kitchen-door. Just as she reaches the kitchen-door and glances out, the parlor-door is flung open and* AMY *comes in. She takes a couple of steps towards the middle of the room, then stands still, looking bitterly at her Mother.* MRS. FISHER *speaks without looking at her*] Did you put that light out in there?

AMY [*in a quiet rage*]. That was a *nice* trick you people did tonight! [*Her Mother turns and looks at her*]

MRS. FISHER. What?

AMY. Everybody walking out of the room, while Aubrey was talking.

MRS. FISHER. What did you *want* us to do, sit here all night listenin' to him?

AMY. You wouldn't have *had* to sit here all night listening to him; he was only in here five minutes.

MRS. FISHER [*moving back towards the center-table*]. That's no thanks to him; he'd have been here till mornin' if somebody didn't do somethin'.

AMY [*swinging to the mirror over the mantelpiece*]. I was never so mortified in my life.

MRS. FISHER [*standing above the center-table*]. Oh, don't waste your sympathy, Amy! He don't have to have anybody listen to him; he'd talk to the wall if there wasn't anybody else around.

AMY [*coming forward at her Mother's right*]. What did Pop get into such a temper about?

MRS. FISHER [*getting mad*]. Because he hit him on the back!

AMY. That was a lot to get mad about.

MRS. FISHER. Well, he's always hittin' *somebody!* — on the back — or the shoulder — or someplace else. And your Father *said* the next time he did it he'd walk out of the room! — He can't say two words *together* without hittin' somebody someplace.

AMY. Well, I'll bet you won't get a chance to insult him *again*, Mom, I'll tell you that. [*She flounces down to the arm-chair at the extreme right*]

MRS. FISHER. Then, let him stop his silly talk! and he won't get insulted. Sign on the dotted line! every two minutes. And talkin' about Shakespeare. [*She crosses to the parlor-door*] What kind of goin' on is that for a sensible man. [*She slams the parlor-door shut, and moves up to the hall-door to listen for* MR. FISHER] It's no wonder our Joe sez he's a nut!

AMY. Oh, everybody's a nut with the people around here!

MRS. FISHER [*coming back towards the center-table*]. Oh, it ain't only the people around here that sez it; everybody that knows him sez it. [AMY *makes a sound of derisive amusement*] You needn't laugh, for it's true.

AMY [*turning sharply to her Mother*]. Who do *you* know that knows him?

MRS. FISHER. I know Frank Hyland. [AMY *is puzzled for the fraction of a second*]

AMY. You mean Clara's *husband?*

MRS. FISHER. Yes, I mean Clara's *husband.*

AMY. Oh, don't make up a lie, Mom! Frank Hyland never saw Aubrey Piper.

MRS. FISHER. Oh, didn't he!

AMY. No, he didn't.

MRS. FISHER. Well now, my lady, you're so smart, he knows him better than you do.

AMY. I don't believe it.

MRS. FISHER. Doesn't matter whether you believe it or not, he knows him just the same; he's been lookin' at him for years, down at that restaurant at Fifteenth and Arch, where he eats his lunch. And he sez he's as crazy as a *bass*-singer.

AMY [*whirling on her Mother*]. I suppose that's what Clara was here to tell you, was it?

MRS. FISHER. What does it matter *who* was here to tell it, Amy, if it's true.

AMY [*stepping up close to her Mother*]. Well now, listen, Mom, I want to tell you something right now! You tell our Clara for me the next time you see her, to mind her own damn business — [*She taps the back of the chair twice with her knuckles, emphasizing the words "damn" and "business"*] as far as Aubrey Piper is concerned.

MRS. FISHER [*before* AMY *has finished speaking*]. Oh, don't fly into a temper, if anybody speaks to you! [*She turns and crosses hurriedly to the hall-door to listen*]

AMY [*stamping her foot*]. Well then, don't speak to me about things that *put* me in a temper!

MRS. FISHER. You're not frightenin' anybody around here. [*She looks up the stairs and listens*]

AMY. No, and nobody around here is frightening *me*, either — Our Clara took who *she* wanted. And I guess you took who *you* wanted. [MRS. FISHER *moves steadily forward at the left to a point in front of the lower left-hand corner of the center-table*] And if I want Aubrey Piper I'll take *him!*

MRS. FISHER [*taking* AMY'S *tone*]. Well, take him then! — and the sooner the better; for it's a pity to spoil two houses with you. [*She leans forward a little on the table and speaks with a steady precision*] Only remember this, Amy, — if you *do* take him, — be sure that you keep him — and that — he — keeps

— you. [AMY *looks at her keenly*] And don't be comin' around here cryin' for your *Pop* to keep you.

AMY [*with a sound of amused derision, and flouncing down to the arm-chair at the right*]. Don't make me laugh.

MRS. FISHER. You can laugh all you like; there's a lot of that kind of laughin' goin' on these days. But they change their tune as soon as the rent begins to come due; and it's the Mothers and Fathers that has to listen to the changed tune. But nothin'll do but they'll get married.

AMY [*pinning her Mother with a quick look*]. *You* got married, didn't you?

MRS. FISHER. Yes I did.

AMY [*turning away again*]. Well —

MRS. FISHER. To a man that was able to keep me.

AMY [*back to her Mother again*]. And how do *you* know that Aubrey Piper wouldn't be able to keep *his* wife?

MRS. FISHER. Because I know what he *earns;* — [*She strikes the table with her fist*] and it isn't enough.

AMY [*stamping her foot*]. Oh, don't go making up things, Mom! — You don't know anything *about* what he earns.

MRS. FISHER [*with measured emphasis*]. He earns a hundred and fifty dollars a month and not a penny more, for Frank Hyland sez so.

AMY. What does Frank Hyland know about it?

MRS. FISHER. He knows what he does! — His business takes him in there all the time.

AMY. And what does he say he does?

MRS. FISHER. Why, he sez he's a clerk, of course, — [AMY *makes a sound of amusement*] like a hundred others down there.

AMY. That shows how much he knows about it.

MRS. FISHER. But I suppose he told you he *owns* the Pennsylvania Railroad.

AMY. Well, I'd take his word before I'd take Frank Hyland's. [*Her Mother looks at her narrowly, and there is a pause*]

MRS. FISHER [*significantly*]. Why would you take *his* word before you would take Frank Hyland's?

AMY. Well, why shouldn't I?

MRS. FISHER [*losing her temper*]. Because he's a fool! — of a blatherskite.

AMY. That's only your opinion, Mom.

MRS. FISHER. It's the opinion of everybody that ever listened to him.

But you'd believe *him* before you'd believe the word of a steady sensible man.

AMY. I don't know anything about Frank Hyland.

MRS. FISHER. You know he's been your brother-in-law for five years; and what do you know about this other clown?

AMY. Well, what do you *want* to know about him?

MRS. FISHER. *I* don't want to know *anything* about him; I *know* all I want to know about him. But before I'd get the name of havin' a fellow comin' to see *me* steady, there's a few things I'd want to know about him, I'll tell you that. [*She turns away and takes a step towards the back of the room*]

AMY. I've told you where he lives and where he works, — what else do you want to know about him?

MRS. FISHER. There's no use talkin' to you, Amy.

AMY. No, and there's no use talking to you, either.

MRS. FISHER [*turning to her sharply*]. This fellow's got you so crazy mad about him, that I believe you'd take him if you knew he had a wife and family somewhere, and not two cents in his pocket. [*She moves towards the mantelpiece at the back, removing her spectacles*]

AMY. Well, I guess we'd get along some way even if I did.

MRS. FISHER. All right.

AMY. Everybody else does.

MRS. FISHER [*turning upon AMY in a rage, and wiping the glasses in her apron*]. That's the kind of talk that leaves them livin' in garrets! And back at their jobs ten days after the weddin'.

AMY. Oh, you talk as though everybody that was married was starving to death.

MRS. FISHER [*lifting the glasses toward AMY with a quiet, knowing gesture*]. There are ways of starvin' to death, Amy, besides not gettin' enough to eat. [*With a change to great shrewdness of tone and manner*] And the funny part of it is, Amy, — like a lot of others, you're very shrewd about money while you're at home, as far as what you give your Mother and Father is concerned; but the minute some clown, with a flower in his coat and patent-leather shoes, winks at you, you seem to forget there's such a thing in the world as a ton of coal. [*Crossing suddenly above the table towards* AMY *in quite a surge of temper*] And

then it's just as Clara sez, it's your *people* that has to come to the rescue.

AMY [*furiously*]. I wish I'd been here while she was talking! I bet I'd a told her a thing or two!

MRS. FISHER. Oh, you needn't try to turn it onto Clara; — she wasn't talkin' at all.

AMY [*stamping her foot*]. She *must* have been talking!

MRS. FISHER. She simply asked me where you were! — and I told her you were gettin' dressed — that this fellow was comin' here to-night: so then she told me that Frank Hyland knew him, and where he worked, and what he got and all about him. [*She turns away and moves to the left. There is a slight pause*]

AMY [*half crying*]. I'd just take him for *spite* now. [MRS. FISHER *comes to a stop, and turns slowly — and looks at her*]

MRS. FISHER. Well, let me tell *you*, Amy — the day a girl that's used to spendin' money the way you do, takes a thirty-five-dollar-a-week man, — the only one she's spitin' is herself. [*She moves slowly to the mantelpiece at the back and puts her glasses down definitely, then turns and starts to remove her apron*] There'll be no more permanent waves after that — [*she rolls her apron up*] you can make up your mind to that. [*She flings the rolled apron onto the sofa at the right of the mantelpiece, and commences to unfasten the old-fashioned brooch in the front of her house-dress*] Nor fifty-five dollar beaded dresses, neither.

AMY [*in a crying temper*]. Well, I'd never bother anybody around here if I needed anything, I'll tell you that.

MRS. FISHER. Maybe you won't.

AMY. I won't, — you needn't worry.

MRS. FISHER [*with a bitter levelness*]. Time'll *tell* that, Lady Jane; I've heard the likes of you before. [*She detaches the brooch and goes to the hall-door, glances out into the hallway, then turns and looks back at* AMY] Put out that light and go to bed, it's twelve o'clock. [*She goes up the stairs.* AMY *stands for a second, fuming, over at the right; then she swings suddenly to the middle of the room and stops, with her hands on her hips, irresolute. Then she comes forward and stands above the table, thinking. As she clasps her hands together she becomes conscious of the ring in her hand. She tiptoes to the hall-door, stands listening for a second, then looks up. Then she hurries back to the center-table, looks at the ring, slides it onto the third finger of her left hand and holds it so that the diamond will catch the light from the chandelier. But, the reflection is evidently unsatisfactory; so, with a furtive glance toward the hall-door, she shifts her position to a point nearer the table-lamp and holds her hand so that the ring will reflect that light. The curtain commences to descend slowly; and she stands, holding her hand at arm's length, lost in the melting wonder of her engagement ring*]

THE CURTAIN IS DOWN

ACT II

SCENE. — *Same as preceding Act, six months later, about five-thirty on a Monday afternoon.* MRS. FISHER *is sitting in the arm-chair below the buffet, over at the right, listening in on the radio. Suddenly the front-door closes with a bang, and she starts, and looks in the direction of the hall-door.* AUBREY *bounces into the room, very much done up, with the traditional carnation, as usual, and comes forward, putting his hat down on the table.*

AUBREY. Hello, Mother — Amy here? [*He steps to the mirror at the back and gives himself a critical touch here and there*]

MRS. FISHER [*commencing to remove the listeners*]. Our Amy?

AUBREY. Yes, have you seen anything of her?

MRS. FISHER [*rising*]. No, I haven't seen anything of her. [*She places the listeners on the buffet, and signs off*]

AUBREY [*turning from the glass*]. Wonder where she is?

MRS. FISHER. Isn't she home?

AUBREY. No, I just came by there.

MRS. FISHER [*picking up her knitting-bag from the buffet*]. She hasn't been here today.

AUBREY. She was saying this morning she thought she'd go out looking for a house today; I suppose she hasn't got back yet. [*He gives the chair at the left of the center-table a double tap with his cane as he crosses down to the window at the left*] I wanted to take her out to the Automobile Show tonight; I got the loan of Harry Albright's car.

MRS. FISHER [*moving to the chair at the right of the center-table*]. Did you say she was out lookin' for a house?

AUBREY [*moving back, towards her*]. Yes, we've got to get out of that place we're in. The LePage printing people have bought the whole block: they're going to put up a new building there.

MRS. FISHER [*standing with her hand on the back of the chair*]. How soon do you have to get out?

AUBREY. Soon as we can find a place, I suppose. I understand they want to begin tearing down there about the first of the year.

MRS. FISHER. I'm afraid you won't find it so easy to get a place as reasonable as that again in a hurry. [*She sits down*]

AUBREY. I don't *want* a place as reasonable as that, if I can get something better. [*He plants himself at the left of the table and looks away off, with a dreamy narrowing of his eyes, and balancing himself on his toes*] I want a home — something with a bit of ground around it — where I can do a bit of tennis in the evening — [*he makes a couple of leisurely passes at an imaginary tennis-ball*] if I feel like it.

MRS. FISHER [*beginning to knit on a green sweater*]. Well, if you do you'll pay for it.

AUBREY. That is exactly what I expect to do, Mother Fisher, not giving you a short answer, — that is exactly what I expect to do. [*He gives the table a double tap with the cane*] But, I want what I'm paying for, I'll tell you that. No more of the old first-of-the-month business for this bambino. He's all washed up, and signed on the dotted line. [*He moves up to the mirror at the back*]

MRS. FISHER. They're not puttin' up any more houses, from what I can hear.

AUBREY. Be yourself, now, Mother Fisher, be yourself.

MRS. FISHER. Well, where *are* they?

AUBREY. You ought to go out along the Boulevard some Sunday, — see what they're doing out there.

MRS. FISHER. Well, there's no danger of you goin' out along the Boulevard, except for a walk.

AUBREY [*moving to the hall-door and glancing out into the hallway*]. Lot of people out that way, Mother.

MRS. FISHER. Well, if there is they're payin' more than you're able to pay.

AUBREY. Man's got to live somewhere, Mother. [*He swings forward to the window down at the left, and stands whistling to the canary*]

MRS. FISHER. Well, if he's wise, he'll live where he's able to pay for it; — unless he wants to be breakin' up half a dozen times a year — like a lot of them are doin'. Makin' a big show. Buyin' ten thousand dollar houses, and puttin' fifty dollars down on them. [*He turns to her*] Besides, you haven't got any furniture for a house, even if you got one — unless you want to be sittin' on the floor.

AUBREY. The matter of furniture nowadays, Little Mother, is a very inconsequential item, from what I can gather.

MRS. FISHER. You ought to price it sometime when you're in the city, and see how unconsequent it is.

AUBREY [*settling himself for a golf shot, using his cane for a club*]. I've investigated the matter very thoroughly, Mrs. Fisher, and I find that there are at least fifteen first-class establishments right here in this city that will furnish a man's house from garret to garage, and give him the rest of his life to pay for it. [*He hits the imaginary golf-ball, and pretends to follow it straight out with his eyes*]

MRS. FISHER. They'd need to give some of them the rest of their lives, at the rate they're goin' now.

AUBREY. Give the growing boy a chance, Mrs. Fisher, give the growing boy a chance. You know what Mr. L. D. Brophy of the American Can Company said in the September number of the American Magazine, don't you?

MRS. FISHER. No, I don't.

AUBREY. Well, I'll tell you. [MRS. FISHER *shifts her knitting, giving him a wearied glance*] He said, "I would say, to that innumerable host of young men, standing on the threshold of life, uncertain, and, mayhap, dismayed — as they contemplate the stress of modern industrial competition, 'Rome was not built in a day.'" Those were his very words, I wouldn't kid you, and I think the old boy's got it right, if you ask me. [*He moves up to the hall-door again and glances out*]

MRS. FISHER. What are *you* goin' out to the Automobile Show for?

AUBREY [*turning and coming forward again*]. Repeat the question, Mrs. Fisher, if you please.

MRS. FISHER. I say, what are you goin' out to the *Automobile* Show for?

AUBREY [*coming to a point above the center-table*]. Ha! Married five months ago today, Mother; got to celebrate the happy event. Besides, one never knows what a day will bring, in the way of an opportunity to satisfy a long-felt want. And since she knocks but once — [*he taps his cane on the table, causing* MRS. FISHER *to start slightly*] at each man's door, the kid here doesn't want to miss his chance by any uncertainty as to just what choo-choo he prefers. [MRS. FISHER *turns with an annoyed expression, to find him pointing at her with his forefinger and thumb. He laughs at her annoyance*] Well, got to run along now, Mother, and see if Amy's back at the house yet. [*He picks up his hat from the table and starts for the hall-door*]

MRS. FISHER. What'll I'll tell her if she comes here after you're gone?

AUBREY [*stopping at the door*]. Why, tell her I've got the loan of Harry Albright's car, and I want her to see that new Jordan Six that I was telling her about, out at the Show. And that I'll be at Childs' at Fifteenth and Chestnut until eight o'clock. [*He looks at his Ingersoll*]

MRS. FISHER. Fifteenth and Chestnut?

AUBREY. That's the said and done, Mother. [*He laughs boisterously*] The old Café Infanté. [*He laughs again*] Olive oil, Mother. [*He goes out the hall-door, breaking into another laugh, and in a second the front-door closes with a bang, causing* MRS. FISHER *to start again, and look irritatedly toward the hall-door. Then she resumes her knitting. The parlor-door opens and* AMY *drifts in, and starts across towards the chair at the left of the table*]

AMY. Hello! [MRS. FISHER *starts again*]

MRS. FISHER. Oh, you frightened me, Amy — walkin' in that way like a ghost! When did you come in?

AMY [*sitting down, with a wearied air*]. A couple of minutes ago — I've been in the parlor.

MRS. FISHER. Why, your man just left here, didn't you see him?

AMY. No, I heard him when I came in — I went in the parlor.

MRS. FISHER. He's lookin' for you — He sez he wants you to go to some kind of an Automobile Show with him.

AMY. I know; I don't want to go; I'm too tired.

MRS. FISHER. What's he doin' about his supper?

AMY. I told him this morning to get something in town; I knew I wouldn't be home till late. [MRS. FISHER *resumes her knitting; and there is a slight pause*]

MRS. FISHER. He sez you've got to get out of that place you're in.

AMY. Yes, they're going to tear those houses down. That's what I was doing today — looking around for someplace.

MRS. FISHER. Did you see anything?

AMY. I saw a couple of places that were fair, but they want too much money.

MRS. FISHER. I'm afraid that's what you'll find, Amy, wherever you go.

AMY. Thirty-eight dollars a month — for a little two-story house — that didn't even have a front porch.

MRS. FISHER. Well, you're surely not lookin' for a house, Amy, are you?

AMY. Yes, if I can find one.

MRS. FISHER. And have you any idea what they're askin' for houses these days?

AMY. Well, Aubrey sez he *will* not live in rooms any longer.

MRS. FISHER. What the devil does it matter *what he* sez! He don't know what he's sayin' half the time, anyway. It's *you* that has to stretch the money, and it'll only go so far; and the money that *he* gets won't cover any forty-dollar rents, you can make up your mind to that right now, before you go any further. And that's what you'll be asked to pay, Amy, remember I'm tellin' you.

AMY. He doesn't want to pay rent — he wants to buy.

MRS. FISHER. What on, thirty-two dollars a week?

AMY. He sez he can put it into a new building society that he heard about, over in Frankford.

MRS. FISHER. Wouldn't he have to pay the building society?

AMY. Well, he wouldn't have to pay it all at once.

MRS. FISHER. There'd be more onces than he'd be able to meet. I thought *you* had a *little* sense, but you're nearly as bad as him.

AMY. No, but you talk awfully silly, Mother; you'd think everybody that was married was livin' out in the street.

MRS. FISHER. That's where a good many of them would be livin', Amy, only that somebody belongin' to them is givin' them a hand. Money'll only go so far, and I've been keepin' house too long not to know just how far that far is. Nobody can tell *me*.

AMY. There was a girl down in our office that was married, just before I was married, and the fellow she married didn't even get as much money as Aubrey gets; he got about twenty-five a week — he was a guard in the Corn Exchange Bank; and *they* bought a house, out in Kensington, and they say it's beautiful.

MRS. FISHER. She's back at her job, though, isn't she?

AMY [*with reluctant admission*]. She never left her job.

MRS. FISHER. Well, — that's how she's doin' it. You told me yourself there were five girls in your office that have married within the last two years. Do you think they're hanging over books nine hours a day because they *like* it? And you haven't got any furniture even if you got a house.

AMY. Oh, you can always get furniture.

MRS. FISHER. You can if you pay for it. And I don't know how you expect to do all these wonders later on, when you find it so hard to make ends meet now, with only the rent of two rooms to pay for. You're everlastin' borrowin' from me as it is.

AMY. I always pay you, don't I?

MRS. FISHER. You do when you get it. But, that's not the point, Amy; it's that what you get one week don't last you till the next.

AMY. The reason I was short last week, Aubrey bought that new overcoat.

MRS. FISHER. And next week it'll be something else.

AMY. Well, a man can't be shabby, Mom, in a position like Aubrey's. He sez he's got nearly eighty clerks down there in his department; and he sez unless he sets some kind of an example of personal appearance, he sez there are some of them down there that'd come in in overalls.

MRS. FISHER [*laying her knitting on the table and looking keenly at* AMY]. How is it, Amy, that a girl like you — that was smart enough to keep books, has so little sense when it comes to what some man tells you? [AMY *looks at her Mother steadily*]

AMY. Who do you mean, Aubrey?

MRS. FISHER. Yes.

AMY. Why, what does he tell me that I have so little sense about?

MRS. FISHER. That he has eighty clerks under him.

AMY. So he has.

MRS. FISHER. And gets thirty-two dollars a week?

AMY. He gets thirty-two fifty. [MRS. FISHER *resumes her knitting, shaking her head hopelessly*] Well now, Mom, you know yourself what the Pennsylvania Railroad pays its men.

MRS. FISHER. I don't know what anybody pays anybody.

AMY. Well, the Pennsylvania Railroad is notorious. Aubrey sez that only that a couple of things haven't panned out just right with him, he'd have left them *long* ago. He sez they just try to break your spirit. He sez that's one of the main reasons why he pays so much attention to his clothes. — He sez he just wouldn't *please* them.

MRS. FISHER. How much did he pay for that overcoat?

AMY. Twenty-eight dollars. [MRS. FISHER *raises her eyes to Heaven*] Oh, he didn't have to pay it all at once; the man said on account of it being so near Christmas he could let it go till the first of February.

MRS. FISHER. I guess he'll be wantin' a suit, now, the first you know, to go with the overcoat.

AMY. No, his suit's all right, — yet a while. But this suit of mine is beginning to go; I've worn it till I'm tired looking at it.

MRS. FISHER. People can't *get* things so handy once they're married.

AMY. I thought I'd be able to put something away out of this week, toward a suit; but I don't know where the money went to : — it just seemed to go. Honestly, I had exactly *twelve cents* in my purse when Aubrey gave me his pay.

MRS. FISHER. I don't know what'll become of you, Amy, if ever you have a houseful of children to keep. [AMY *sits looking at nothing, with a rather troubled expression about the eyes, and her Mother continues to knit. Suddenly* AMY *bursts into tears.* MRS. FISHER *looks at her: then she gets up quietly, laying her knitting on the table, and crosses in front of the table to her — and lays her hand on her arm*] Now, there's no use a startin' that kind a thing, now, Amy; for it won't do you a bit of good. [*She continues across*]

AMY. I don't know what I'm going to do, Mom — I'm nearly crazy.

MRS. FISHER [*turning*]. I'll tell you what you're goin' to do, Amy, if you're a wise woman — You're goin' to realize that you're married; and that you've got some kind of a house to keep up; and just how much money you're goin' to get each week to keep it up *on;* and then suit your ideas accordin'. And if you don't, you'll have plenty of cryin' to do. And you'll have nobody to thank but yourself, for you had nothing but impudence for them that tried to tell you — how many beans made five. [*The front-door is heard to close*] I guess this is your Father. Go into the parlor there, and don't let him see you cryin'. [AMY *rises and steps quickly across and thru the parlor-doors at the left into the parlor; and* MRS. FISHER *crosses above the center-table to the buffet and puts her knitting into one of the drawers.* CLARA *appears in the hall-door*]

CLARA. What's the matter? [MRS. FISHER *turns and looks at her*]

MRS. FISHER. There's nothing at all the matter.

CLARA. What did Joe telephone me for?

MRS. FISHER. *Our* Joe, do you mean?

CLARA. Yes; Bertha said he telephoned the house about four o'clock and told her to tell me to come right over home as soon as I came in.

MRS. FISHER. Well, I'm sure *I* don't know what he'd want you for, Clara; he didn't leave any word with me for you this morning.

CLARA [*coming forward towards the center-table*]. I was over paying my Electric, and just got back; so I came right over; I thought maybe something was wrong here, and he was calling from next door.

MRS. FISHER. No, he hasn't been home here today. [CLARA *puzzles for a second, then tosses her purse onto the table*]

CLARA. I wonder what he wanted me for. [*She turns to the mirror at the back and touches her hat*]

MRS. FISHER. Is that girl at your house sure it was our Joe?

CLARA [*coming back to the table*]. She said it was; and I suppose she knows his voice, — she's often answered the 'phone when he's called. [*She picks up a book from the table and glances casually at it*]

MRS. FISHER. Well, maybe he wants to see you about something; I'd wait a while; he'll be here at six.

CLARA [*looking suddenly at her Mother*]. Maybe he's heard some news about that formula that those people are interested in.

MRS. FISHER [*coming over to the table*]. Oh, I guess he'll be an old man before he ever hears anything from that. [*She folds and settles various things on the table, and* CLARA *glances through the book. Then, as she moves over to settle the upper left-hand corner of the table-cover, she gives* CLARA *a little push*] Look out of my way, Clara, till I fix this cloth. [CLARA *just moves without looking up from the book*] That's a book Joe brought home last night: about that woman that was left up on the North Pole. He sez it's very nice. I've got to put those potatoes on, for your Father's supper; he'll be here around six. [*She moves to the door at the right*]

CLARA [*standing at the left of the table, still looking at the book*]. Did you know that Amy's got to get out of those rooms she's in?

MRS. FISHER [*from the kitchen*]. Yes.

CLARA. They're going to tear those houses down.

MRS. FISHER [*coming back into the room*]. So she was telling me.

CLARA [*moving to the chair at the left of the table*]. What's she going to do, [*tossing the book on to the table*] come in here to live? [*She sits down*]

MRS. FISHER. Now, that's a sensible question for you to ask, Clara; — you know how much she's comin' in here to live.

CLARA [*commencing to remove her gloves*]. I don't know where else she'll go, — with rents the way they are now; — unless she goes back to work.

MRS. FISHER. She'll have to look around.

CLARA. What good will it do her to look around — she certainly won't find anything as reasonable as where she is now: and when she's not able to pay that, how does she expect to pay any more? [*The parlor-door is whipped open and* AMY *is standing between the curtains looking tight-lipped at* CLARA]

AMY. How do *you* know I'm not able to pay my rent where I am?

MRS. FISHER [*moving towards the hall-door*]. Now, don't start a fight, Amy, your Pop'll be here any minute. [*She looks out into the hallway*]

AMY [*speaking to her Mother, and indicating* CLARA *with a gesture*]. No, but I'd like to know what business it is of hers whether I can pay my rent or not. I don't see that anybody's asking *her* to pay it for me.

CLARA [*very sure of her ground*]. It's a bit late in the day to talk that way, Amy; your husband's been to Frank Hyland *twice* already to pay it for you. [AMY *looks at her aghast, and* MRS. FISHER *comes forward between them*] It's time you quit this posing in front of me; *I* know how you're fixed better than you do yourself. [*She turns sharply away and flings her gloves onto the table*]

AMY [*almost crying*]. Now, do you hear that, Mom!

MRS. FISHER. Stop your talk, Amy! Do you want your Father to walk in and hear you?

AMY [*lowering her voice, but still speaking with angry rapidity*]. She sez that Aubrey Piper's been to Frank Hyland twice, for the loan of *our* rent.

CLARA. So he has.

AMY. You're a liar! [MRS. FISHER *gives her a slap on the back; and there is a vibrant pause. Then* AMY *moves down towards the window at the left and bursts out crying*]

MRS. FISHER [*with controlled excitement*]. Will you stop when I speak to you! [*There is a pause*] What kind of talk do you call that! [*She steps to the hall-door again and glances out into the hallway*]

AMY [*whirling again upon* CLARA]. Well, that's what she is! Aubrey Piper never asked Frank Hyland for a cent in his life.

CLARA. He's asked him a dozen times, and got it, too; till I put a stop to it.

MRS. FISHER [*coming forward again, and speaking with authority*]. Now, that'll do, Clara! — I don't want to hear another word — out of either one of you — I had enough of that when the two of you were at home.

AMY. Well, I'll make her prove what she sez about Aubrey Piper, just the same!

CLARA. It's very easily proved. Just come over to the house some night and I'll show you a few of his letters.

AMY. What do you do, open them?

CLARA. I do now, yes, — since I found out who they're from.

MRS. FISHER [*keenly*]. Do you mean to tell me, Clara, that he's writin' to Frank Hyland for money?

AMY. No, he doesn't do anything of the kind, Mom, that's another of her lies!

MRS. FISHER [*before* AMY *has finished speaking*]. I'm not talkin' to you, Amy.

AMY. She just makes those things up.

CLARA. I make them *up!*

AMY [*crying*]. Yes!

CLARA. And I've got at least twelve letters right in my bureau-drawer this minute that he's written within the last two months.

MRS. FISHER. What does he write letters for?

CLARA. For money — so he can pay seven dollars for a seat out at the football game — as he did Thanksgiving afternoon, — Frank saw him there.

MRS. FISHER. Why don't he just ast Frank Hyland for the money when he sees him, instead of writin' to him?

CLARA. I suppose he thinks a written request is more appropriate, coming from one of the heads of the Pennsylvania Railroad.

MRS. FISHER. How much does he ast for, when he asts him?

CLARA. There was one a couple of weeks ago, for three hundred. [AMY *makes a sound of bitter amusement, and turns away*]

MRS. FISHER [*aghast*]. Three hundred dollars?

CLARA. That's what the letter said. [MRS. FISHER *turns and looks at* AMY]

MRS. FISHER. What would he have wanted three hundred dollars for, Amy?

AMY. Oh, ask her, Mom; she's good at making them up. [*She sweeps towards the parlor-doors*]

MRS. FISHER [*taking a step or two after her*]. Oh, you wouldn't believe it, even if it was true, if it was against him.

AMY. Well, I wouldn't believe *her*, anyway. [AMY *slams the parlor-door with a bang*]

MRS. FISHER [*raising her voice*]. You wouldn't believe your own Mother, — never name your sister. [*She turns to* CLARA] She flew at *me* like a wild-cat, when I told her he wore a wig. I guess she knows it herself by this time.

CLARA. She's for *him*, Mom; and the sooner you get that into your head the better.

MRS. FISHER [*moving towards the right, above the table*]. I know very well she is, you needn't tell me. And she'd turn on everyone belongin' to her for him. The idea of askin' anybody for three hundred dollars. [*She continues towards the kitchen-door, fuming; then turns*] I suppose he wanted to buy an automobile or something. That's where he is tonight, out at the Automobile

Show — and not two cents in his pocket — like a lot of others that'll be out there I guess — And I'll bet he'll be doin' more talk out there than them that'll buy a dozen cars.

CLARA. I think that's what he *did* want the money for.

MRS. FISHER. It wouldn't surprise me, — the damned fool. [*She steps to the mantelpiece and glances out into the hallway*] It'd be fitter for him to be thinkin' about gettin' a house to live in.

CLARA. He doesn't think he *needs* to think about that; he thinks he's coming in here.

MRS. FISHER [*turning sharply, on her way back to the kitchen-door*]. Comin' in here *to live*, do you mean?

CLARA. That's what he told Frank, the day before yesterday.

MRS. FISHER. Well, he's very much mistaken if he does, I can tell you that. I'd like to be listenin' to that fellow seven days in the week. I'd rather go over and live with your Aunt Ellie in Newark.

CLARA [*rising, and picking up her gloves from the table*]. Well, that's about what you'll have to do, Mom, if you ever let them in on you. [*She stands looking straight out, unfastening her neck-piece*]

MRS. FISHER. I won't let them in on me, don't fret. Your Father 'ud something to say about that.

CLARA [*slipping off her neck-piece*]. Pop may not always be here, Mom. [*She turns around to her left and moves to a point above the table, and puts her fur and gloves down*]

MRS. FISHER. Well, I'll be here, if he isn't; and the furniture is mine. And there's very little danger of my walkin' off and leavin' it to any son-in-law. [*The front-door closes*] I guess this is your Pop now, and I haven't even got the kettle on. [*She hurries out at the right.* CLARA *glances at the hall-door, and* JOE *appears in it, and stands for the fraction of a second, irresolute*]

JOE. Where's Mom?

CLARA. Out in the kitchen, — why?

JOE [*motioning to her, causing the paper to drop from his hand*]. Come here, — don't let her hear you. [CLARA *steps towards him, with a shade of apprehension in her face and manner*] Listen, Clara — Pop had some kind of a stroke this afternoon at his work.

CLARA. *Pop did?*

Joe. They found him layin' in front of one of the boilers.

Clara. Oh, my God!

Joe. I tried to get you on the 'phone about four o'clock.

Clara. I know — I came right over as soon as I came in.

Joe. *You* better tell Mom. [*He starts for the stairs, and* Clara *turns towards the kitchen-door*]

Clara [*turning sharply back again*]. Joe!

Joe [*stopping abruptly on the first step of the stairs*]. What?

Clara. Where's Pop now?

Joe. They took him to the Samaritan Hospital. I just came from there — they telephoned me to the office.

Clara. Well, is he very bad?

Joe. *I* think he's done.

Clara. Oh, don't say that, Joe!

Joe. That's what the Doctor at the Hospital sez. — He hasn't regained consciousness since three o'clock. So you'd better tell Mom to get her things on and go right down there. I've got to change my clothes; I went right up there from work. [*He starts up the stairs; and* Clara *moves vaguely towards the kitchen-door. She stops and stands looking toward the kitchen in a controlled panic of indecision. Then, abruptly she whirls round and steps quickly back to the hall-door*]

Clara [*in a subdued voice*]. Joe!

Joe. What?

Clara. That Samaritan Hospital's at Broad and Ontario, isn't it?

Joe. Yes. [*She turns slowly and looks out, irresolute. Then she stoops down abstractedly and picks up the newspaper that* Joe *dropped. The parlor-door opens sharply and* Amy *stands looking at her apprehensively. Their eyes meet*]

Amy. What is it? [Mrs. Fisher *appears in the door at the right, drying an agate-ware plate*]

Mrs. Fisher. Wasn't that your Pop that came in, Clara? [Clara *makes a deft, silencing gesture with her left hand to* Amy, *and moves towards the center-table*]

Clara. No, it wasn't, Mom, it was the boy with the paper.

Mrs. Fisher [*coming further into the room to see the clock*]. I wonder what's keepin' him; he's late to-night. [Clara *leans against the center-table, keeping her face averted from her Mother*] He's nearly always here before this. [*She moves back again towards the kitchen*]

Amy [*crossing quickly down to* Clara's *left*]. What is it, Clara?

Mrs. Fisher [*turning and looking at* Clara]. What's the matter with her? [Clara *tries to control her feelings*]

Amy. I don't know what's the matter with her, Mom! Something Joe just told her — he's just gone upstairs.

Mrs. Fisher [*coming forward apprehensively at* Clara's *right*]. What is it, Clara, — somethin' about your Father? Is that what you're cryin' for?

Amy. Why don't you tell her, Clara?

Mrs. Fisher. Go to the foot of the stairs, Amy, and call Joe. [Amy *steps towards the foot of the stairs*] Something's happened to your Father, I know it.

Clara [*moving a step or two towards her Mother*]. Now, it's nothing to get upset about, Mom; he just took a little spell of some kind at his work this afternoon, and they had to take him to the hospital. [Amy *comes forward eagerly, and crosses to a point below the table*] Joe just came from there, and he sez we'd better get our things on right away and go down there. [Mrs. Fisher *sways a step forward, letting the agate-ware plate slide from her hands to the floor.* Amy *steps towards her Mother, lifting the chair from the right of the table and guiding her Mother into it*] Here, sit down here, Mom.

Mrs. Fisher [*slightly dazed*]. What is it she's sayin' happened to your Father, Amy? [Amy *passes back of the chair to her Mother's right, and* Clara *comes to her left*]

Clara. Now, it's nothing to get excited about, Mom; it might be just a little heart-attack or something that he took. [*She takes the towel from her Mother's hand and hands it to* Amy] Put this over there. [Amy *turns to the buffet*]

Mrs. Fisher. There was never anything the matter with your Father's heart, Clara.

Clara. Well, it's pretty hot in there where he works, you know that. [Mrs. Fisher *shakes her head up and down, knowingly*] And men at Pop's age are always taking little spells of some kind.

Mrs. Fisher [*with a long, heavy sigh*]. Ah, I guess it's a stroke, Clara.

Clara. It might not be, Mom, you can't tell.

Mrs. Fisher. That's how his two brothers went, you know.

CLARA. Amy, you'd better go to the telephone next door and tell Frank Hyland I won't be home. [AMY *hurries across towards the hall-door, and* CLARA *follows her, continuing her instructions*] If he isn't home yet, tell Bertha to tell him to come right down to the Samaritan Hospital as soon as he comes. And tell Johnny Harbison to go to the corner for a taxi. [*The front-door closes after* AMY, *and* CLARA *steps back to her Mother's side*]

MRS. FISHER. Is that where your Father is, Clara, the Samaritan Hospital?

CLARA. Yes; it's right down there near where he works, at Broad and Ontario.

MRS. FISHER [*starting to cry*]. Your poor Father — I wonder what happened to him. [CLARA *reflects her Mother's sentiment*]

CLARA [*picking up the plate*]. Now, there's no use looking on the dark side of it already, Mom.

MRS. FISHER. No, but me gettin' his supper out there, and him not comin' home to it at all. And maybe *never* comin' home to it again, Clara, for all we know.

CLARA. He'll be home again, Mom — Pop is a strong man. [*She puts the plate on the buffet*]

MRS. FISHER [*suddenly*]. I guess he's dead, now, and you're not tellin' me.

CLARA [*coming to her Mother's left*]. He isn't dead, Mom; I'd have told you if he was.

MRS. FISHER. What did Joe say?

CLARA. Just what I told you; that he'd had a spell of some kind.

MRS. FISHER. Well, why didn't he tell me! What's he doin' upstairs, anyway?

CLARA. He's changing his clothes; he's got to go right back down there again.

MRS. FISHER. He's cryin' I guess. You know, it'll kill our poor Joe, Clara, if anything happens to your Father.

CLARA. He sez we'd better go right down there, too, Mom; so you'd better go upstairs and fix yourself up a bit. Give me your apron.

MRS. FISHER [*rising and commencing to remove her apron*]. I don't know whether I'll be able to dress myself now or not; my hands are like lead.

CLARA. You don't need to get all dressed up, Mom — just put on your black-silk waist; that skirt's good

enough. [*She goes towards the door a the right with the apron and goes out*]

MRS. FISHER [*taking the comb from the back of her head and commencing to comb her hair*]. Well, I'm not goin down there lookin' like a dago woman

CLARA [*coming quickly in again*] Nobody'll see you in the dark. [*Sh picks up the plate and towel from the buffe and straightens the runner*]

MRS. FISHER [*moving aimlessly abou in front of the mantelpiece*]. It won't be dark in the *hospital;* unless somethin happens to the lights. [CLARA *goes ou again*] Put that gas out under them potatoes, Clara, I just lit it. And you'd better pick up this room a bit while I'm upstairs, you don't know who might be comin' here if they hear about you Father. [*She stops and looks helplessly about the room*] Oh, dear, Oh, dear, Oh, dear! I don't know what I'm doin' [CLARA *comes in again*] Take all them papers off that table, Clara, and put them in the kitchen.

CLARA [*crossing to the table and folding and gathering up the various papers*]. You'd better bring your umbrella down with you, Mom, when you go up, — it looked like rain when I came in.

MRS. FISHER. Oh, and I let our Amy take my rubbers the last day she was here, and she *never* brings anything back.

CLARA [*taking the papers out into the kitchen*]. You won't need rubbers.

MRS. FISHER. Oh, I get all my feet wet, when I don't have rubbers. [*She is facing the hall-door, fastening the old-fashioned brooch at her throat.* AUBREY *frames himself in the door, with a bandage around his head, and looking a bit battered*] My God, what happened to *you,* now!

AUBREY [*coming forward at the left, removing his hat*]. It's beginning to rain. [*He places his hat and cane on the table, and stands in front of the table removing his gloves*]

MRS. FISHER [*following him with her eyes*]. Never mind the rain, the rain didn't do that to you. [*She comes forward at his left.* CLARA *comes in and stands over near the door at the right, looking at him*] I guess you ran into somebody, didn't you?

AUBREY [*with a shade of nonchalance*]. Don't get excited, Mother, — just a little misunderstanding on the part of the traffic-officer.

MRS. FISHER. You don't mean to

tell me that you ran into a traffic-officer! [CLARA *comes forward at the right*]

AUBREY. Control, now, Little Mother, I assure there is no occasion for undue solicitation. [*He turns and sees* CLARA] Good evening, Mrs. Hyland.

CLARA. Hello! What happened to your head?

MRS. FISHER. You look like a bandit.

AUBREY. The veriest trifle, Mrs. Hyland — just a little spray from the wind-shield.

MRS. FISHER. Where's the car you borrowed? Smashed, I guess, ain't it?

AUBREY. The car I borrowed, Mother Fisher, is now in the hands of the bandits of the law. The judicial gentlemen, who have entered into a conspiracy with the regulators of traffic — to collect fines from motorists — by ordering them to go one way — and then swearing that they told them to go another.

MRS. FISHER. Never mind your fancy talk, we've heard too much of that already! I want to know who you killed, — or what you did run into; for I know you ran into somethin'. And where's the automobile that someone was fool enough to lend you?

AUBREY. The automobile, Little Mother, is perfectly safe — parked and pasturing — in the courtyard of the Twenty-second and Hunting Park Avenue Police Station.

MRS. FISHER. Did you get arrested, too?

AUBREY. I accompanied the officer as far as the station-house, yes; and I told them a few things while I was there, too, about the condition of traffic in this city.

MRS. FISHER. I guess they told you a few things, too, didn't they?

AUBREY. Beg pardon?

MRS. FISHER [*starting abruptly for the hall-door*]. Never mind; you're welcome.

CLARA. You'd better change your shoes, Mom; you can't go down there with those.

MRS. FISHER [*pointing toward the cellar-door*]. See if my long black coat's in the cellar-way there. [CLARA *goes quickly to the cellar-door, opens it, and looks for the coat*] That fellow's got me so upset I don't know what I'm doin'. [*She goes out the hall-door and to her left, up the stairs.* AUBREY *moves over to the chair at the right, where* MRS. FISHER *collapsed, and sits down, — quite ruffled*

in his dignity. CLARA *closes the cellar-door and, with a glance toward the hall-door, comes quickly forward at* AUBREY'S *left*]

CLARA. What did they do, fine you, Aubrey?

AUBREY. They were all set to fine me; but when I got through with them they didn't have a leg to stand on. So they tried to cover themselves up as gracefully as possible, by trumping up a charge against me of driving an automobile without a license.

CLARA. What did they do, take the automobile *away* from you?

AUBREY. Nothing of the sort; they simply complied with the usual procedure in a case of this kind — which is to release the defendent on bond, pending the extent of the victim's injuries.

CLARA. Was there somebody injured?

AUBREY. The traffic-cop that ran into me, yes.

CLARA. For God's sake, couldn't you find anybody but the traffic-cop to run into!

AUBREY. I did not run into him, Mrs. Hyland — you don't understand the circumstances of the case.

CLARA. Well, I understand this much about them — that they can give you ten years for a thing like that. And it'd just serve you right if they did, too. Borrowin' people's automobiles, and knowing no more about running them than I do. [*She turns away to her right and moves across above the table towards the hall-door*]

AUBREY. No time like the present to learn, Mrs. Hyland.

CLARA [*turning to him sharply*]. Well, you'll very likely have plenty of time, from now on, — if that officer is seriously injured. [*She continues over and down to the window at the left, where she draws the drape aside and looks anxiously down the street for the taxi*]

AUBREY. He was faking a broken arm around there when I left — But it's a wonder to me the poor straw-ride wasn't signed on the dotted line; for he ran head on right into me.

CLARA [*crossing back towards him, in front of the Morris-chair*]. Was *he* in a car, too?

AUBREY. No, he was jay-walking — trying to beat me to the crossing, after giving me the right of way.

CLARA. Where did this thing happen?

AUBREY. Broad and Erie Avenue, I wouldn't kid you.

CLARA. Did they take the cop to the hospital?

AUBREY. Yes, we took him over there in the car.

CLARA. Did they let *you* run it?

AUBREY. Repeat the question, Mrs. Hyland.

CLARA. You heard me, — I don't need to repeat it. And take that silly-looking bandage off your head, before Amy sees you; and don't frighten the life out of her. [*She steps up to the hall-door and glances out*] She's got enough to worry her now without looking at you.

[AUBREY *rises, and, detaching the hand-kerchief from around his head, moves across to a point above the center-table*]

AUBREY. Is my wife here?

CLARA. She's next door, telephoning, yes; and she'll be back in a minute. [*Coming forward a step or two at the left*] Pop just had a stroke of some kind at his work this afternoon, Joe just told us.

AUBREY. What are you doing, kidding me?

CLARA [*starting to cry*]. No, of course I'm not kidding you! What would I be kidding you about a thing like that for? [*She crosses down and across in front of the center-table. The front-door closes*]

AUBREY. Where is he now?

CLARA. They took him to the Samaritan Hospital; we're just going down there.

[AMY *appears in the hall-door, and stands looking questioningly at* AUBREY]

AMY. What's the matter, Aubrey? [*He turns and looks at her*]

AUBREY [*extending his arm and hand in a magnificent gesture*]. Well! [AMY *comes forward to her husband*] The old kid herself!

AMY. What is it, Aubrey?

AUBREY [*taking her in his arms*]. Nothing in the world but this, Baby. [*He kisses her affectionately*]

CLARA. Did you get Frank on the 'phone, Amy? [MRS. FISHER *can be heard hurrying down the stairs*]

AMY [*crossing above* AUBREY *and speaking directly to* CLARA]. He wasn't home yet; I told the girl to tell him as soon as he came in.

MRS. FISHER [*coming through the hall-door, and tossing her little knit-jacket onto the small stand at the left of the mantelpiece*]. Clara, is that automobile-cab here yet?

CLARA. It'll be here in a minute, Mom.

MRS. FISHER. What do you think of this fellow, Amy, — runnin' wild through the city breakin' policemen's bones! We didn't have enough trouble without that — with your poor Father layin' dead for all we know, — down in the Jewish hospital. [*She starts to cry and steps down to the window at the left to look out for the taxicab*] It's enough to make a body light-headed.

CLARA. Where's your coat, Mom?

MRS. FISHER [*turning to her*]. Isn't it there in the cellar-way?

CLARA. No, I just looked.

MRS. FISHER [*going up to the hall-door*]. It must be upstairs. Joe!

AMY [*at* AUBREY'S *right*]. I thought you were out at the Automobile Show, Aubrey.

MRS. FISHER [*at the foot of the stairs*]. Listen, Joe —

AUBREY. I had a little mix-up at Broad and Erie Avenue.

AMY. You didn't get hurt, did you? [MRS. FISHER *and* AUBREY, *speaking together*]

MRS. FISHER. Throw down my long black coat; you'll find it on a hook there in the hall-closet. [*She starts for the buffet*]

AUBREY. Nothing but a scratch or two, here on my forehead, from the glass in the wind-shield. Just a little shake-up.

MRS. FISHER [*stopping and turning sharply at the right of the center-table*]. He nearly killed a traffic-officer! — That's how much of a little shake-up it was. [*She continues to the buffet, where* CLARA *is standing*] Get out of my way, Clara, till I get a clean handkerchief out of here. [*She pushes* CLARA *out of her way and opens the left-hand drawer of the buffet and rummages for a handkerchief.* CLARA *passes across in front of the center-table to the window at the left*]

AMY. You *didn't*, Aubrey, did you?

AUBREY. Certainly not, Amy — your Mother's raving. [MRS. FISHER *finds the handkerchief, slams the drawer shut and turns*]

MRS. FISHER. The man's in the hospital! — I don't know what more you want. [*The big black coat lands at the foot of the stairs with a thud, causing* MRS. FISHER *to start nervously; then she hurries across at the back towards the hall-door, tucking the folded handkerchief at her waist]*

AMY. Is he, Aubrey?

AUBREY. Do you think I'd be here, Kid, if he was?

MRS. FISHER [*on the way over*]. You wouldn't be here, only that someone was fool enough to bail you out; instead of lettin' you stay in where you couldn't be killin' people. [CLARA *has stepped up to the foot of the stairs and picked the coat up immediately it fell, and now stands holding it for her Mother to put on; but* MRS. FISHER *disregards her, going straight out to the foot of the stairs and calling shrilly up to* JOE] Joe, why don't you tell a body when you're goin' to throw a thing down that way, and not be frightenin' the life out of people? [*She comes back into the room again and* CLARA *assists her.* AMY *stands above the center-table looking wide-eyed at* AUBREY, *who sways forward at the left, and, crossing below the center-table to the chair at the right, where he has been previously seated, sits down*]

CLARA. Aren't you going to put on another waist, Mom?

MRS. FISHER. No, this one is good enough — I'll keep the coat buttoned up. Put that collar inside.

AMY [*in a lowered tone*]. Are you out on bail, Aubrey?

AUBREY. They always bail a man in a case like this, Amy; they've got my car on their hands.

MRS. FISHER [*buttoning the coat, and moving to the mirror over the mantelpiece*]. Get my hat, will you, Clara?

CLARA [*starting for the hall-door*]. Where is it, upstairs?

MRS. FISHER. No, it's in the parlor there, inside the top of the Victrola. [CLARA *comes back and goes into the parlor*]

AMY. Why didn't you bring the car back with you, Aubrey? — That fellow might want it tomorrow.

AUBREY. I'll have it for him all right; I've got to call around there for it Monday morning at ten o'clock. [MRS. FISHER *turns sharply from her primping at the mirror*]

MRS. FISHER. I guess you've got to go down there to a hearing Monday morning at ten o'clock, — [AMY *turns and looks at her Mother*] and pay your fine! [*Speaking directly to* AMY] I guess that's the automobile he's got to call for.

[CLARA *hurries out of the parlor brushing the dust off an old black hat, with a bunch of cherries on it*]

CLARA. I'd better go out and get a whisk-broom and dust this, Mom.

MRS. FISHER [*turning to her nervously*]. No, never mind, it's good enough, give it to me.

CLARA [*crossing below her Mother, to the right*]. Your coat needs dusting. [*She takes a whisk-broom from a hook just inside the kitchen-door*]

AMY. How much did they fine you, Aubrey?

AUBREY. They didn't fine me at all.

MRS. FISHER [*settling her hat*]. They'll do that Monday.

AUBREY. Time'll tell that, Mother Fisher.

[CLARA *hurries back and starts brushing her Mother's coat*]

MRS. FISHER. And you'll pay it, too, or go to jail; and it'ud just be the price of you.

AUBREY. They didn't seem very anxious to do any fining today, after I got through telling it to them.

MRS. FISHER. Am I all right, Clara?

AUBREY. I took a slam at the Pennsylvania Railroad, too, while I was at it.

MRS. FISHER. You're always takin' slams at somethin'; that's what's leavin' you under bail right now. Are you ready, Clara? [*She hurries to the foot of the stairs*]

CLARA [*hurrying back to the kitchen with the whisk-broom*]. Yes, I'm ready.

AUBREY. Never mind about that, Mother Fisher.

MRS. FISHER [*calling up the stairs*]. Are you goin' down there with us, Joe?

JOE [*from upstairs*]. Comin' right down.

[MRS. FISHER *comes in to the mantelpiece and picks up her gloves.* CLARA *hurries in from the kitchen again to the center-table and picks up her neck-piece and gloves*]

AUBREY. Only don't be surprised if you hear of a very quiet little shake-up very soon — in the Department of Public Safety.

MRS. FISHER. Are you warm enough with that coat, Clara?

CLARA. Yes, I'm all right. How about the umbrella?

MRS. FISHER. I think it's out there in the hall-rack; look and see. [CLARA *hurries out into the hallway, and* MRS. FISHER *stands putting on her gloves.* AMY *crosses to* AUBREY'S *left*]

AMY [*very quietly*]. How much bail did they put you under, Aubrey?

AUBREY. One thousand berries, Amy. [MRS. FISHER *looks over at them keenly*]

AMY. A thousand dollars!

AUBREY. That's regulation — [AMY *turns and gives her Mother a troubled look, and* MRS. FISHER *moves forward at the left to a point where she can see* AUBREY] A little chicken-feed for the stool-pigeons.

MRS. FISHER. Did *he* say they put him under a thousand dollars' bail?

AUBREY. That's what I said, Mrs. Fisher, one thousand trifles — I wouldn't kid you.

MRS. FISHER. You wouldn't kid anybody that'd listen to you for five minutes. And who did you get to *go* a thousand dollars bail *for* you?

AUBREY. Don't be alarmed, Little Mother, — I saw that the affair was kept strictly within the family.

MRS. FISHER. Who do you mean?

AUBREY. Your other son-in-law — was kind enough to come forward.

[CLARA *hurries in from the hallway with the umbrella, and comes forward at the extreme left*]

MRS. FISHER. Clara's husband!

AUBREY. That's the gentleman, Mrs. Fisher, — Mr. Francis X. Hyland.

MRS. FISHER [*helplessly*]. My God! [*She turns around to her right till she locates* CLARA] Do you hear that, Clara?

CLARA. What?

MRS. FISHER. He got Frank Hyland to go his bail for a thousand dollars.

CLARA [*looking bitterly at* AUBREY]. What did you do, write him another letter?

AUBREY. That was not necessary, Mrs. Hyland, not giving you a short answer. Your husband was fortunate enough to see the whole affair from the trolley-car. He was just returning from his business, and happened to be on the trolley-car that ran into me.

MRS. FISHER. How many more things ran into you, — besides traffic-cops and trolley-cars! I suppose a couple of the buildin's ran into you too, didn't they?

[JOE *hurries in from the hall-door buttoning his overcoat*]

JOE. Are you ready, Mom?

CLARA [*going up to the hall-door*]. Yes, we're ready. [JOE *comes forward at the extreme left, looking questioningly from one to the other.* CLARA *goes out into the hall*]

AUBREY. You'll find out all about that Monday morning, Mrs. Fisher.

MRS. FISHER [*moving up towards the hall-door*]. Well, see that nothin' else runs into you between now and Monday.

JOE. What's the matter?

MRS. FISHER. We don't want Frank Hyland losin' any thousand-dollar bills on account of you.

JOE. What's happened, Mom?

MRS. FISHER [*turning to* JOE, *and pointing at* AUBREY *with a wide gesture*]. Why, this crazy Jack here's been runnin' into everything in the city but ourselves; and he got himself arrested; and Frank Hyland had to bail him out for a thousand dollars. [*She starts to cry*]

JOE. What were you doin', Aubrey, joy-ridin'?

MRS. FISHER. No! — he was trolley-ridin', — and traffic-cop-ridin', — and every other kind of ridin', — in an automobile that he borrowed.

CLARA [*hurrying in from the hallway*]. I think I see that taxi coming, Mom.

MRS. FISHER [*starting towards the hall-door*]. Come on here, Joe. [JOE *crosses up at the left of the center-table to the mirror over the mantelpiece, looking disapprovingly at* AUBREY. AUBREY *rises and strolls over to a point in front of the center-table*] How do we get down there, Clara?

CLARA. Right down Erie Ave.

AUBREY. Too bad I left that car down there at the Station House, I could have run you down there. [*They all turn and look at him; and* MRS. FISHER, *with poison in her right eye, moves forward at the left of the center-table, with a level, ominous slowness*]

MRS. FISHER. *You* wouldn't run me down there, — don't fret — not if you had a thousand cars. There's enough of us in the hospital as it is. [AUBREY *simply regards her from a great height*] And don't you come down there neither; — for you'd only start talkin', and that'd finish Pop quicker than a stroke. [*There's a startling hoot from the taxicab horn outside, which almost throws* MRS. FISHER *from her balance*]

CLARA [*going out*]. Come on, Joe.

JOE [*following her out*]. Ain't you comin' down to the hospital, Amy?

MRS. FISHER [*going out*]. No, you'd better stay here, Amy, — there'd better be some one of us here — or that fellow'll be runnin' into somethin' else. You ought to have somethin' heavier on you than that fur, Clara. [AUBREY *sits down at the left of the center-table*]

CLARA [*in the hallway*]. I'm all right, we'll be down there in a few minutes.

MRS. FISHER. Have you got your coat buttoned up good, Joe? [*The front-door closes after them. AUBREY turns from the hall-door, where she has been standing, seeing them out, and comes forward to the back of the chair at the left of the center-table, where AUBREY is sitting*]

AMY. Where's your toupé, Aubrey? [*Touching the sticking-plasters on his forehead*]

AUBREY. In my pocket here.

AMY [*stroking his hair*]. Is your head hurting you?

AUBREY [*reaching for her hand and drawing it down over his left shoulder*]. Not a bit, Honey — just a couple of little scratches. [*He kisses her hand. She raises her eyes and looks straight ahead, with a troubled expression*]

AMY. Aubrey, what do you think they'll do to you down there Monday?

AUBREY. Now, don't you worry about that, Sweetheart; I'll be right there if they try to pull anything. [*She moves over thoughtfully towards the upper right-hand corner of the center-table. Then a new thought occurs to her, and she turns her head and looks at him narrowly*]

AMY. You hadn't had anything to drink, had you, Aubrey?

AUBREY [*looking at her quickly*]. Who, me?

AMY. I mean I thought somebody might have treated you or something.

AUBREY [*making a statement*]. *I* had a glass of Champagne six months ago with a friend of mine in his suite at the Ritz-Carlton Hotel, and I haven't had a drink of anything since.

AMY. You better take off your overcoat, Aubrey; we'll have to stay here till they get back. [*He gets up and commences to remove the overcoat*]

AUBREY. Yes, I guess we will. — I wonder how your Father is.

AMY [*taking the overcoat from him*]. Pretty bad I guess, — or they wouldn't have sent for Joe. [*She takes the coat up to the sofa at the right of the mantelpiece, and AUBREY takes a huge cigar from his vest-pocket and feels for a match*] I'll get you a match, Aubrey. [*She goes out into the kitchen, and AUBREY moves to a point above the center-table, biting the tip of his cigar*]

AUBREY. I thought I had some here, but I guess I haven't. Did they send for Joe?

AMY. Yes, they telephoned for him, to the place where he works.

AUBREY. Your Mother said it was a stroke.

AMY [*entering with some matches*]. I guess that's what it is, too; his two brothers died that way.

AUBREY [*taking the matches from her*]. I'm sorry to hear that, Amy. But, you mustn't worry, now, Kid.

AMY. It isn't only that I'm worried about, Aubrey; — I'm thinking about you — Monday. [*She takes hold of the lapels of his coat and almost cries*]

AUBREY [*putting his arm around her*]. Now, listen to me, Baby — you know I'd tell you, don't you, if there was anything to worry about.

AMY. But, they're getting awfully strict in this city; there's been so many automobile accidents lately.

AUBREY. They're only strict, Honey, when a man's driving under the influence of liquor. [*There's a slight pause, and AMY thinks hard*]

AMY. What if that traffic-cop is hurt bad, Aubrey?

AUBREY. It'd only be a fine for reckless driving, even if they could prove it *was* reckless driving; and *I* can prove it was the copper's fault. [*Detaching himself from her*] So they'll very likely be *apologizing* to me around there Monday morning, instead of fining me. [*He moves across and down to the window at the left, — with ever so slight a touch of swagger*]

AMY. Oh, I wouldn't care if they only fined you, Aubrey; because I could go back to work until it was paid.

AUBREY [*looking out the window*]. You'll never go back to work, Kid, while I'm on the boat.

AMY. I wouldn't mind it, Aubrey.

AUBREY. Not while you're *my* wife, Amy. [*He half turns to her, with considerable consequence*] I'd rather leave the Pennsylvania Railroad *flat;* and go out and take one of the jobs that have been offered me where they pay a man what he's worth.

AMY. You don't think they might

do anything else to you, do you, Aubrey?

AUBREY [*turning to her*]. Oh, they might try to take away my license.

AMY. You haven't *got* a license, have you?

AUBREY [*turning back to the window*]. No, I neglected to attend to it this year.

AMY. They can fine you for that, can't they?

AUBREY. Driving an automobile without a license, you mean?

AMY. Yes.

AUBREY. Sure — they can fine you for anything unless you know how to beat them to it. [*He strikes the match on the arm of the Morris-chair at his right.* AMY *rests her hands on the center-table, and looks straight out, wretchedly*]

AMY [*tonelessly*]. What is it they send them to prison for, Aubrey? [*He is just holding the lighted match to the cigar, and, consequently, is unable to answer her immediately. The front door-bell rings. She glances apprehensively in the direction of the hall-door, then meets his eyes*] I wonder who that is.

AUBREY [*tossing the burnt match into the window at his left*]. Do you want me to answer it?

AMY. I wish you would, Aubrey; it might be something about Pop. [*He crosses in front of the Morris-chair and up at the left of the center-table to the mirror over the mantelpiece, where he stands settling his tie and vest.* AMY *turns to the couch and gathers up his coat, then steps forward to the center-table and picks up his hat and the bandage that he took off his head*]

AUBREY [*touching the plasters on his forehead*]. Does my head look all right?

AMY [*glancing at him, as she goes towards the hooks at the head of the cellar-stairs*]. Yes, it's all right, Aubrey.

AUBREY. Wait a minute — [*He steps to her side and takes the carnation from the buttonhole of his overcoat, then steps back to the mirror and fixes it in his sack-coat*]

AMY. Hurry up, Aubrey. [*The door-bell rings again*]

AUBREY [*going out into the hallway*]. All right — all right.

[AMY *hangs the overcoat and hat up, then turns, opens the cellar-door, and tosses the bandage down the cellar-stairs. Then she crosses quickly to a point in front of the mantelpiece and listens intently*]

GILL [*at the front-door*]. Good evenin'.

AUBREY. Good evening, sir.

GILL. Is this where Mr. Fisher lives?

AUBREY. This is Mr. Fisher's residence, yes, sir. What can I do for you?

GILL. Why, I got some things of his here that the boss ast me to leave.

AUBREY. Oh, just step inside for a minute. Getting a little colder I think. [*The front-door closes*]

GILL. Well, we can look for it any time, now.

AUBREY. Will you just step in this way, please? [AUBREY *enters from the hallway*] There's a gentleman here, Amy, with some things belonging to your Father. Just come right in. [AUBREY *comes forward a few steps at the left; and* GILL *enters*]

GILL. Good evenin'.

AMY. Good evening.

AUBREY. This is my wife, Mrs. Piper.

GILL [*nodding*]. How do you do. [AMY *nods*]

AUBREY. Mrs. Piper is Mr. Fisher's daughter. The rest of the folks have gone down to the hospital.

GILL. I see. [*Turning to* AMY] Have you *heard* anything from the hospital yet?

AMY. Not yet, no.

AUBREY. We didn't know anything about it at all, till fifteen minutes ago.

GILL. It's too bad.

AUBREY. Those hospitals won't tell you anything.

AMY. Do you work with my Father?

GILL. No, ma'am, I'm a twister on the second floor. But, one of the machinist's-helpers that works with your Father knows I live out this way, so he ast me to stop by with these things on me way home. [*He crosses towards* AMY, *with a hat and overcoat, and a more or less discolored lunch-box*]

AMY [*taking the things*]. Thanks ever so much.

GILL. There's just the overcoat and hat, and his lunch-box.

AMY. Thanks.

GILL. McMahon sez if he comes across anything else he'll let me know.

AMY [*crossing to the sofa with the things*]. No, I don't imagine there's anything else.

GILL. If there is, I'll bring it up.

AMY. Well, that's very nice of you; I'm ever so much obliged to you. [*She comes back towards* GILL]

AUBREY. Who is this McMahon?

GILL. He's one of the machinist's-helpers down there.

AUBREY. I see.

AMY. Were you there when my Father was taken sick?

GILL. No, ma'am, I wasn't. I don't think there was anybody there, to tell you the truth. McMahon sez he was talkin' to him at a quarter of three, and he sez when he came back from the annex at three o'clock, he found Mr. Fisher layin' in front of number five.

AUBREY [*with a suggestion of professionalism*]. Very likely a little touch of Angina Pectoria. [GILL *looks at him*]

GILL. The doctor down there sez he thought it was a stroke.

AUBREY. Same thing.

AMY. Won't you sit down, Mr. — a —

GILL. No, thank you, ma'am, I can't stay; I've got to get along out home. [*There's a rapping out at the right. They all look in the direction of the kitchen*]

AMY. Oh, I guess it's Mrs. Harbison — I'll go. [*She goes out at the right*]

AUBREY [*crossing above* GILL *towards the right*]. Don't stand out there talking, now, Amy, with nothing around you. [*Surveying himself in the buffet-mirror at the right*] Do you live up this way, Governor?

GILL. No, sir, I live out Richmond way.

AUBREY. I see.

GILL. I take number thirty-two over Allegheny Avenue.

AUBREY [*turning and moving over towards the center-table*]. Too bad my car's laid up, I could run you out there.

GILL. Oh, that's all right; the trolley takes me right to the door.

AUBREY. I had to turn it in Thursday to have the valves ground.

AMY [*appearing in the kitchen-door*]. I'm wanted on the telephone, Aubrey; I'll be right in. Will you excuse me for a minute?

GILL. That's all right, ma'am; I'm goin' right along meself.

AUBREY. Very likely some word from the Hospital.

GILL. I hope it ain't any bad news.

AUBREY. Well, you've got to be prepared for most anything, Governor, when a man gets up around the old three-score mark.

GILL. That's true, a lot of them push off about that age.

AUBREY. Especially when a man's worked hard all his life.

GILL. Yes, I guess Mr. Fisher's worked pretty hard.

AUBREY. Not an excuse in the world for it, either. — I've said to him a thousand times if I've said to him once, "Well, Pop, when are you going to take the big rest?" "Oh," he'd say, "I'll have lots of time to rest when I'm through." "All right," I'd say, "go ahead; only let me tell you, Pop, you're going to be through ahead of schedule if you don't take it soon."

GILL. Well, I guess it comes pretty hard on a man that's been active all his life to quit all of a sudden.

AUBREY. Well, he wouldn't have to quit exactly. — I mean, he's a handy man; he could putter around the house. There are lots of little things here and there that I'm not any too well satisfied with. [*He glances around the room*]

GILL. Is Mr. Fisher's wife livin'?

AUBREY. Yes, she's here with us too.

GILL. Well, that makes it nice.

AUBREY. Well, it's a pretty big house here; so when I married last June, I said, "Come ahead, the more the merrier." [*He laughs a little*]

GILL. 'Tis a pretty big house this.

AUBREY. Yes, they don't make them like this anymore, Governor. Put up by the McNeil people out here in Jenkintown.

GILL. Oh, yes.

AUBREY. They just put up the twenty of them — kind of sample houses — ten on that side and ten on this. Of course, these on this side have the southern exposure, — so a man's got to do quite a bit of wire-pulling to get hold of one of these.

GILL. You've got to do some wire-pullin' to get hold of *any* kind of a house these days.

AUBREY. Well, I have a friend here in town that's very close to the city architect, and he was able to fix it for me.

GILL [*glancing toward the window, at the left*]. It's a nice street.

AUBREY. Nice in summer.

GILL. I was surprised when I saw it, because when I ast a taxicab-driver down here where it was, he said he never heard of it.

AUBREY [*looking at him keenly*]. Never heard of Cresson Street?

GILL. He said not.

AUBREY [*with pitying amusement*]. He must be an awful straw-ride.

GILL. I had to ast a police officer.

AUBREY. Well, I'll tell you, Governor, — I don't suppose they have many *calls* for taxicabs out this way. You see, most everybody in through here has his own *car*.

GILL. I see.

AUBREY. Some of them have a half dozen, for that matter. [*He laughs, a bit consequentially*]

GILL [*starting for the parlor-doors*]. There certainly is plenty of them knockin' around.

AUBREY. All over the ice. [AUBREY *indicates the hall-door*] This way, Governor.

GILL [*turning towards the hall-door*]. Oh, excuse me.

AUBREY [*moving towards the hall-door*]. Those doors go into the parlor.

GILL. I see. [*He turns at the hall-door*] A fellow was tellin' me over here in the cigar store that there was quite a smash-up about a half hour ago down here at Broad and Erie Avenue.

AUBREY. That's so?

GILL. He sez there was some *nut* down there runnin' into everything in sight. He sez he even ran into the traffic-cop; and broke his arm. Can you imagine what they'll *do* to that guy, knockin' the traffic-cop down!

AUBREY. What was the matter with him, was he stewed?

GILL. *No,* — the fellow in the cigar store sez he was just a *nut*. He sez they didn't know where he got hold of this car; he sez it didn't belong to him. I guess he picked it up somewhere. They took it away from him and pinched him. [*Starting to go out*] So I guess he won't be runnin' into anything else for a while.

AUBREY [*following him out*]. Traffic's in pretty bad shape in this town right now.

GILL. Certainly is. Why, a man's not safe walkin' along the sidewalk, these days. I hope your wife'll hear some good news.

AUBREY. Well, while there's life there's hope, you know.

GILL. That's right. No use lookin' on the dark side of things.

[AMY *enters from the right, with a wide-eyed, wan expression, and comes slowly down to the center-table*]

AUBREY. Where do you get your car, Governor?

GILL. Why, I can get one right at the corner here, and transfer.

AUBREY. Oh, that's right, so you can. Well, we're ever so much obliged to you.

GILL. Don't mention it.

AUBREY. Good-night, sir.

GILL. Good-night. [*The door closes*]

AUBREY [*coming in from the hall-door*]. When did *you* come in, Amy? [*He stops to look at himself in the mantelpiece-mirror*]

AMY [*without turning*]. I came in the side-door; I thought that man'd be still here.

AUBREY [*coming down to her*]. Well, Kid, what's the good word?

AMY [*breaking down*]. Aubrey, Pop is dead. [*She buries her face in the lapel of his coat. He takes her in his arms, looks straight ahead, and there is a long pause — during which* AMY *cries hard*]

AUBREY. Don't let it get you, Honey — you have nothing to regret; and nothing to fear. The Kid from West Philly'll never go back on you, — you know that, don't you, Baby? [*She continues to cry*] You know that, don't you, Amy? [*She doesn't answer him*] Amy.

AMY. What?

AUBREY. You know I'm with you, don't you?

AMY. Yes. [*He kisses her hair affectionately*]

AUBREY. Don't cry, Honey; the old man's better off than we are. He knows all about it now. [*He kisses her again; then detaches himself and moves over and down at the left of the center-table*]

AMY. What do you think we ought to do, Aubrey?

AUBREY. There's nothing at all that you can do that I can see, Sweetheart; except to sit tight till the folks get back. They'll be down there themselves in a few minutes, and they'll know all about it.

AMY. They said that Pop died at a quarter of six.

AUBREY. Was that the Hospital on the telephone?

AMY. Yes.

AUBREY [*moving up to a point above the center-table again*]. Something we ought to have in here, Amy; a telephone — not be letting the whole neighborhood in on our business. [AMY *leans on the back of the chair at the right and cries softly*] Now, pull yourself together, Sweetheart. [*He crosses to her and puts his arm around her shoulders*]

AMY. This is where Pop always used

to sit in the evening. — It'll seem funny not to see him here anymore. [*She breaks down again*]

AUBREY [*after a slight pause*]. The old gent had to go sometime. [*He passes back of her, comes forward at the right and stands, looking at the tip of his cigar*] Your Mother'll have you and me to comfort her now. [*He strolls across below the center-table and stops, thinking profoundly.* AMY *sinks down on the chair dejectedly*]

AMY. I don't know how Mom'll keep this house going now, just on Joe's pay.

AUBREY. Why don't you say something to your Mother about letting *us* come in here? She'll need a man in the house. And my salary 'ud cover the rent.

AMY. Mom doesn't have to pay rent, Aubrey, — she owns this house. Pop left it to her. He made his will out the week after we were married. [AUBREY *looks at her keenly*] *Clara* got him to do it.

AUBREY. Who's the executor, do you know?

AMY. Clara is. [AUBREY *nods comprehendingly*]

AUBREY [*looking away off*]. Too bad your Father didn't make *me* the executor of that will; — I could have saved him a lot of money. [*He replaces the cigar in his mouth*]

AMY. I suppose he thought on account of Clara being the oldest.

AUBREY. I wonder why your Father never *liked* me.

AMY. Pop never said he didn't like you, Aubrey.

AUBREY. I always tried to be clubby with him. I used to slap him on the back whenever I spoke to him.

AMY. Pop was always very quiet.

AUBREY. And the Kid from West Philly had too much to say. Well, — forgive and forget. — It's all over now. — And the old man can be as quiet as he likes. [AMY *cries again, and there is a pause.* AUBREY *stands smoking*]

AMY [*pulling herself together and getting up*]. You haven't had anything to eat tonight yet, have you, Aubrey?

AUBREY [*coming out of his abstraction, and sauntering up at the left of the center-table*]. Don't worry about me, Sweetheart.

AMY [*going to the buffet-drawer at the right for an apron*]. I'll get you something.

AUBREY. It'll be all the same at the finish, — whether I've had my dinner or not. [*He rests his fist on the table, throws his head back, and looks to the stars*] "Sic transit gloria mundi." And we never get used to it. [*He moves across to the upper right-hand corner of the center-table*] The paths of glory lead but to the grave. [*He stops again, leans on the table and looks out and away off*] And yet we go on, — building up big fortunes — only to leave them to the generations yet unborn. Well, [*he moves forward to the chair at the right*] — so it goes. [*He sits down, throws one leg across his knee, and shakes his head up and down slowly*] And so it will *always* go, I suppose. "Sic transit gloria mundi."

AMY [*standing at his right*]. What does that mean, Aubrey, "Sic transit gloria mundi"?

AUBREY [*casually*]. It's an old saying from the French — meaning, "we're here to-day, and gone to-morrow."

AMY [*looking out, wretchedly*]. I'm worried about tomorrow, Aubrey. [*He looks at her*]

AUBREY. What are you worried about, Sweetheart?

AMY. I mean Monday.

AUBREY [*extending his hand towards her*]. Now, — "sufficient unto the day is the evil thereof ", — you know that, don't you, Baby? [*She takes his hand and moves over to the back of his chair*]

AMY. But, you didn't have a license, Aubrey. And if that traffic-officer should be seriously injured —

AUBREY. Don't you worry about that, Sweetheart; — we're here today; and if he's seriously injured, — we'll know all about it Monday. [*The curtain commences to descend slowly*] "Sic transit gloria mundi."

THE CURTAIN IS DOWN

ACT III

SCENE. — *Same as preceding Act — the following Monday, about four o'clock in the afternoon.* MRS. FISHER *is seated at the right of the center-table, in black, watching* MR. ROGERS, *the insurance agent, opposite her, writing on various papers.* CLARA, *also in mourning, is standing back of her Mother's chair, watching* MR. ROGERS.

ROGERS [*handing* MRS. FISHER *an insurance receipt*]. Now, will you just sign that, Mrs. Fisher. Right on that line there. [*He hands her his fountain-pen*]

Mrs. Fisher [*after a sincere attempt to write with the fountain-pen*]. It won't write.

Clara. Press on it a bit, Mom.

Mrs. Fisher. I *am* pressin' on it.

Rogers. Just let me have it a second, Mrs. Fisher. [*She hands him the pen*]

Mrs. Fisher. I never saw one of them fountain-pens yet that'd write.

Rogers [*holding the pen out and shaking it, in an attempt to force the ink forward*]. They cut up a little once in a while. [Mrs. Fisher *looks keenly to see if her carpet is being stained*]

Mrs. Fisher. I gave one to my son the Christmas before last, and it's been in that drawer there from that day to this.

Rogers [*handing her the pen again*]. There we are. I think you'll find that all right.

Mrs. Fisher. Right here?

Rogers. That's right. [*He commences to collect his papers*]

Mrs. Fisher [*writing*]. It's writin' now all right.

Rogers. It's usually pretty satisfactory. [*She hands him the receipt, and he hands her another*] And that one also, Mrs. Fisher, if you please.

Mrs. Fisher. In the same place?

Rogers. Yes; right on the dotted line. It's just a duplicate. [*She looks at him sharply, then signs it and hands it back to him; and he puts it into his wallet.* Mrs. Fisher *looks distrustfully at the point of the fountain-pen*]

Mrs. Fisher. Here's the pen.

Rogers. Thank you. [*He signs a check and looks at it*]

Mrs. Fisher [*half-turning towards the cellar-door*]. See if that cellar-door is closed, Clara, I feel a draught from somewhere. [Clara *goes and sees that the door is closed*]

Rogers [*handing a check*]. There you are, Mrs. Fisher, one thousand dollars.

Mrs. Fisher. Thank you. [Clara *comes forward again*]

Rogers [*collecting his things*]. That's the money we like to pay, Mrs. Fisher, and money we don't like to pay.

Mrs. Fisher. No, things are never very pleasant when this kind of money is bein' paid.

Rogers [*rising, and putting his wallet into his inside-pocket*]. Well, at least, it doesn't make things any less pleasant, Mrs. Fisher.

Mrs. Fisher [*rising*]. No, I'm sure I don't know what a lot of folks 'ud do without it.

Rogers. Pretty hard to make a good many of them see it that way, Mrs. Fisher.

Mrs. Fisher [*moving around to a point above the table*]. Yes, I guess we don't think much about trouble when we're not havin' it.

Rogers. Lot of people think they're never going to have trouble; [Mrs. Fisher *shakes her head knowingly*] and never going to need a dollar.

Mrs. Fisher. They're very foolish.

Rogers. Very foolish indeed.

Mrs. Fisher. Everybody'll have trouble if they live long enough.

Rogers. Yes, indeed.

Mrs. Fisher. Well now, what do I do with this check, Mr. Rogers?

Rogers. Why, you can deposit it if you like, Mrs. Fisher, or have it cashed — just whatever you like.

Clara. Frank'll get it cashed for you, Mom, downtown.

Mrs. Fisher. I'm not used to thousand-dollar checks, you know, Mr. Rogers.

Rogers. I'm not very used to them myself, Mrs. Fisher, except to pay them out to somebody else. [*He laughs a little*]

Mrs. Fisher. Well, will you take this, then, Clara, and give it to Frank Hyland?

Clara [*advancing*]. Yes; I'll give it to him tonight, Mom. [Rogers *moves to the window at the left and takes a paper from his pocket*]

Mrs. Fisher. Don't go layin it down somewhere, now, and forgettin' where you left it, — the way you're always doin' with your gloves.

Clara [*crossing to the buffet where her purse is lying*]. I'll put it in my purse here. [Mrs. Fisher *comes forward at the right of the Morris-chair*]

Rogers [*turning and coming back a little from the window*]. Oh, by the way, Mrs. Fisher — would you give this to your son-in-law, Mr. Piper? [*He hands her the paper*]

Mrs. Fisher. What is it?

Rogers. Why, it's a little explanation of some of the features of a very attractive *accident* policy that our company has brought out recently; — and I was talking to Mr. Piper about it the day I called for Mr. Fisher's policy. He seemed to be very much interested. In fact, I find that people are usually a little more susceptible to the advantages of a good insurance policy, when they actually see it being paid to somebody else. Now, that particular policy there — is a kind of combination of accident and life-insurance policy, — as well as disability and dividend features. In fact, we contend that there is no investment on the market today [CLARA *sits down in the arm-chair at the right window*] that offers the security or return that that particular policy described there does. The thing is really almost benevolent.

MRS. FISHER. How much is it for?

ROGERS. Why, we *have* them as low as ten thousand dollars; but the policy that Mr. *Piper* was most interested in, was one of our fifty-*thousand*-dollar policies. [CLARA *laughs faintly, and her Mother looks over at her*]

MRS. FISHER [*turning back to* ROGERS]. It's no wonder she's laughin', Mr. Rogers; for if you knew Mr. Piper as well as she knows him, you'd laugh too. He has just about as much notion of takin' out a fifty-thousand-dollar insurance policy as I have. And just about as much chance of payin' for it.

ROGERS. Why, he seemed very much interested, Mrs. Fisher.

MRS. FISHER. He was showin' off, Mr. Rogers, what he's always doin'. Why, that fellow don't make enough salary in six months — to pay one year's premium on a policy like this. So, if I was you, I'd just put this paper right back in my pocket, for you're only wastin' it to be givin' it to him.

ROGERS [*taking the paper*]. Seems rather funny that he'd talk about it at all, — I mean, if he had no idea of taking it.

MRS. FISHER. He never has any idea when *he* talks, Mr. Rogers — that's the reason he talks so much; it's no effort. That's the reason he's gettin' thirty-two dollars a week, down here in the Pennsylvania Freight Office. And it's a wonder to me they give him *that* much, after listenin' to him for five minutes.

ROGERS. It's particularly funny, because I spoke to Mr. Piper first about one of our ten-thousand-dollar policies; but he didn't seem to be interested in anything but the *fifty*-thousand-dollar life and *accident* policy.

MRS. FISHER. Well, I can under-

stand him being interested in the accident part of it, after last Monday. I suppose you heard about him runnin' into everything here last Monday evening, didn't you? Down here at Broad and Erie Avenue.

ROGERS. Oh, was that Mr. Piper?

MRS. FISHER. That was him. He ran into a traffic-cop, and broke his arm.

ROGERS. Yes, I saw that in the paper; but the name was spelled Pepper in my paper.

MRS. FISHER. Well, it was spelled Piper in our paper.

ROGERS. Well, what did they do about that, Mrs. Fisher?

MRS. FISHER. Why, he's down there today, at the Magistrate's, gettin' his hearin'. God knows what they'll do with him; for he didn't own the car he was drivin', and didn't have a license to drive it.

ROGERS. Well, that's very unfortunate.

MRS. FISHER. But, he'll very likely tire the magistrate out so with his talk, that the man'll discharge him just to get rid of him.

ROGERS [*laughing*]. I'm afraid Mr. Piper won't want to see *me* today when he comes back.

MRS. FISHER. He may not *be* back, for six months.

ROGERS [*starting for the hall-door*]. Oh, well, let's hope it won't be anything like that. Good afternoon, Mrs. Hyland.

CLARA [*rising*]. Good afternoon, Mr. Rogers.

[*He goes out into hallway*]

ROGERS. Good afternoon, Mrs. Fisher.

MRS. FISHER. Good afternoon, Mr. Rogers. [*Calling after him from the hall-door*] Will you close that vestibule-door tight after you, Mr. Rogers —

ROGERS. Yes, I will, Mrs. Fisher.

MRS. FISHER. This hallway gets awful cold when that vestibule-door isn't shut tight. [*A door closes in the hallway, then another door. And then* MRS. FISHER *turns, removing her glasses, and moves towards the mantelpiece*] I'm glad you were here; I don't understand them insurance papers. [*She puts her glasses on the mantelpiece*]

CLARA [*moving to the chair at the right of the center-table*]. What do you think you'll do with that money, Mom?

MRS. FISHER. Why, I think I'll just put it into a bank somewhere; everything is paid. And then I'll have something in my old days. [*She comes forward to the chair at the left of the center-table*]

CLARA. Do you want me to put the check right into the bank?

MRS. FISHER. No, — I want to see the money first. [*She sits down*] But, can you imagine that clown, Clara, takin' up that man's time talkin' about a fifty-thousand-dollar policy; and him in debt to his eyes.

CLARA [*sitting down*]. What does it matter, Mom; you can never change a man like Piper.

MRS. FISHER. No, but I hate to see him makin' such a fool of Amy; and of all of us, — with his name in all the papers, and the whole city laughin' at him.

CLARA. He doesn't mind that, he likes it.

MRS. FISHER. But, Amy's married to him, Clara, — that's the trouble.

CLARA. Amy doesn't mind it either, Mom, as long as it's Aubrey.

MRS. FISHER. Well, she ought to mind it, if she's got any pride.

CLARA [*looking straight ahead, wistfully*]. She's in love with him, Mom — she doesn't see him through the same eyes that other people do.

MRS. FISHER. You're always talkin' about love; you give me a pain.

CLARA. Well, don't you think she is?

MRS. FISHER. How do *I* know whether she is or not? I don't know anything about when people are in love; except that they act silly — most everybody that I ever knew that was. I'm sure *she* acted silly enough when she took *him*.

CLARA. She might have taken worse, Mom. [MRS. FISHER *looks at her; and* CLARA *meets the look*] He does his best. He works every day, and he gives her his money; and nobody ever heard of him looking at another woman.

MRS. FISHER. But, he's such a rattle-brain, Clara.

CLARA. Oh, there are lots of things that are harder to put up with in a man than that, Mom. I know he's terribly silly, and has too much to say, and all that, but, — I don't know, I feel kind of sorry for him sometimes. He'd so love to be important; and, of course, he never will be.

MRS. FISHER. Well, I swear I don't know how Amy stands the everlastin' talk of him. He's been here now only a week, and I'm tellin' you, Clara, I'm nearly light-headed. I'll be glad when they go.

CLARA. I'd rather have a man that talked too much than one of those silent ones. Honestly, Mom, I think sometimes if Frank Hyland doesn't *say* something I'll go out of my mind.

MRS. FISHER. What do you want him to say?

CLARA. Anything; just so I'd know he had a voice.

MRS. FISHER. He's too sensible a man, Clara, to be talkin' when he has nothin' to say.

CLARA. I don't think it's so sensible, Mom, never to have anything to say.

MRS. FISHER. Well, lot's of men are that way in the house.

CLARA. But there are usually children there, — it isn't so bad.

MRS. FISHER. Well, if Amy ever has any children, and they have as much to say as their Father, I don't know what'll become of her.

CLARA. She'll get along some way; people always do.

MRS. FISHER. Leanin' on somebody else, — *that's* how they get along.

CLARA. There are always the Leaners and the Bearers, Mom. But, if she's in love with the man she's married to, — and he's in love with her, — and there are children —

MRS. FISHER. I never saw a married woman so full of love.

CLARA. I suppose that's because I never had any of it, Mom. [*Her Mother looks over at her*]

MRS. FISHER. Don't your man love you? [CLARA *looks straight out, shaking her head slowly*]

CLARA. He loved someone else before he met me.

MRS. FISHER. How do you know?

CLARA. The way he talks sometimes.

MRS. FISHER. Why didn't he marry her?

CLARA. I think he lost her. I remember he said to me one time — "Always be kind, Clara, to anybody that loves you; for," he said, "a person always loses what he doesn't appreciate. And," he said, "it's a *terrible* thing to lose love." He said, "You never realize what it was worth until you've lost it." I think that's the reason he gives Piper a hand once in a while, — because he sees Amy's in love with him, and he wants to make it easy for her; because I have an idea he made it pretty hard for the woman that loved him. [MRS. FISHER *leans back and rocks slowly*]

MRS. FISHER. Well, a body can't have everything in this world, Clara. [*There is a pause: and* CLARA *touches her handkerchief to her eyes. Then the front-door closes softly, and* MRS. FISHER *gets up*] Maybe this is them now. [*She moves up to the hall-door.* AMY *comes in, looking wearied. She is in mourning*] What happened, Amy? [AMY *wanders down to the chair at left of table and sits down, and her Mother follows her down at the left*] Where's Aubrey Piper?

AMY. He's coming.

CLARA. Is Frank with him?

AMY. Yes.

MRS. FISHER. Where are they?

AMY. Aubrey stopped at the corner to get some cigars.

CLARA. What happened down there?

AMY. Oh, a lot of talk.

MRS. FISHER [*leaning towards her, solicitously*]. Are you sick?

AMY. No.

MRS. FISHER. Well, you look sick.

AMY. I have a headache; we had to wait there so long.

CLARA. Why don't you take off your hat? [AMY *starts to remove her hat*]

MRS. FISHER. Will I make you a cup of tea?

AMY. No, don't bother, Mom; I can get it myself.

MRS. FISHER [*going towards the right door*]. It won't take a minute. [AMY *takes her handkerchief from her bag.* CLARA *glances toward the right door*]

CLARA [*in a subdued tone*]. What did they do to Aubrey?

AMY [*confidentially*]. Fined him — a thousand dollars. Don't let Mom know. Recklessness, and driving without a license.

CLARA. Did Frank pay it?

AMY. Yes; I told him I'd be responsible for it.

CLARA. How can *you* ever pay him a thousand dollars, Amy?

AMY. I can go back to work for a while. I can always go back to the office. [CLARA *moves*] Well, it was either that or six months in jail. And Frank said we couldn't have that.

CLARA. Was there anybody there that we know?

AMY. I didn't see anybody.

CLARA. Was the traffic-cop there?

AMY. Yes, there were fourteen witnesses. The traffic-cop's arm was broken. The fellow that owned the car was there, too.

CLARA. When do you think you'll go back to work?

AMY [*after a troubled pause*]. As soon as I get settled. There's no use in my going back now; I'd only have to be leaving again pretty soon. [CLARA *looks at her*]

CLARA. Does Mom know?

AMY. No, I haven't told her. [*There is a pause.* CLARA *gets up; and, with a glance toward the kitchen-door, moves around and crosses towards the left, above the center-table. She stops back of* AMY's *chair and looks at her for a second compassionately; then she steps forward and lays her hand on her shoulder*]

CLARA. Don't worry about it, Amy. [*She moves towards the window at the left*] I wish to God it was me. [*There is a murmur of voices at the front-door; then* AUBREY's *laugh rings through the house.* AMY *rises quickly, picks up her hat from the table, and signifies to* CLARA, *with a gesture, that she will go into the parlor.* CLARA *moves across in front of the center-table*]

AUBREY [*entering, all dressed up, and with a little flourish of his cane to* CLARA]. Hello, Clara!

CLARA. Hello.

AUBREY [*hanging up his hat and cane on the hooks at the head of the cellar-stairs*]. Where's Amy?

CLARA. She's just gone in the parlor there.

[FRANK HYLAND *appears in the hall-door and comes forward to the chair at the left of the table*]

HYLAND. Hello! [AUBREY *crosses to the parlor, removing his gloves*]

AUBREY. You in there, Amy?

AMY. Yes. [*He goes into the parlor; and* CLARA *moves across above the center-table to* HYLAND's *left*]

CLARA. How is it you didn't go back to the office, Frank?

[AUBREY *hurries out of the parlor again and across to the hooks, removing his overcoat.* MRS. FISHER *appears in the kitchen-door, and stands, looking at him*]

HYLAND. It was so late when we got through down there I didn't think it was worth while.

AUBREY. Hello, Mother.

MRS. FISHER. I see you're back again. [*He hangs up his overcoat*]

AUBREY. Right on the job, Mother, — doing business at the old stand. [*He takes the carnation from the overcoat and fastens it in the sack-coat.* MRS. FISHER *comes forward at the right*]

HYLAND. Hello, Mother!

MRS. FISHER. Hello, Frank.

HYLAND. You're lookin' good, Mother.

MRS. FISHER. Well, I'm not feelin' good, Frank, I can tell you that.

HYLAND. What's the trouble?

MRS. FISHER. Why, I'm troubled to think of all the bother you've been put to in this business.

HYLAND. Don't worry about that, Mother — we've got to have a little bother once in a while.

MRS. FISHER. What did they do down there today, Frank?

HYLAND. Why, — they —

AUBREY [*coming forward, adjusting the carnation*]. I'll tell you what they *tried* to do.

MRS. FISHER. Oh, shut up, you! Nobody wants to hear what you've got to say about it at all. [CLARA *crosses above the Morris-chair and looks out the window at the left*]

AUBREY. Well, I *told* them down there what I had to say about it, whether they wanted to hear it or not. [*He goes up to the mirror at the back*]

MRS. FISHER. I guess they let you go just to get rid of you. [*He turns to his left and looks at her; then starts for the parlor-doors*]

CLARA. Why don't you take your coat off, Frank?

[AUBREY *goes into the parlor, looking back over his shoulder at his Mother-in-law, who has not taken her eyes off him*]

HYLAND [*looking at his watch*]. I've got to meet that fellow at North Philadelphia Station at four o'clock.

MRS. FISHER [*coming a step or two nearer to the table*]. What did they say to that fellow down there today, Frank?

HYLAND. Why, nothing very much, Mother — just a little reprimand, for driving without a license.

MRS. FISHER. Didn't they fine him at all, for breakin' that man's arm?

HYLAND. A little bit, not very much. — You see, that was more or less in the nature of an accident.

MRS. FISHER. How much was it?

HYLAND. Now, Mrs. Fisher, as Aubrey says, "It's all washed up, and signed on the dotted line." [*He laughs*]

MRS. FISHER. How much was it, Clara, do *you* know?

CLARA. He hasn't told me, Mom.

MRS. FISHER. Well, I'll bet you paid it, Frank, whatever it was; for I know he didn't have it. [*She sits at the right of the table*]

HYLAND [*rising*]. Well, you know, it's getting near Christmas, Mother — got to give some kind of a little present here and there.

MRS. FISHER. Well, I don't think it's right that you should have to be goin' around payin' for that fellow's mistakes.

HYLAND [*standing up a bit toward the hall-door, putting on his gloves*]. That's about all any of us is doin' in this world, Mother — payin' for somebody's mistakes — and somebody payin' for ours, I suppose.

MRS. FISHER. Well, it don't seem right to me.

HYLAND. Well, I'll tell you, Mother — when you've made a couple of mistakes that *can't* be paid for, why, then you try to forget about them by payin' for the kind that can. [*He makes a little pallid sound of amusement. And there is a pause.* MRS. FISHER *rocks back and forth*]

CLARA. Will you be home for dinner tonight, Frank?

HYLAND [*coming suddenly out of an abstraction*]. What'd you say?

CLARA. I say, will you be home for dinner tonight?

HYLAND [*picking up his hat from the table*]. I don't think so; I'll very likely have to go to dinner with *him*. [*He goes towards the hall-door*] Good-bye, Mother.

MRS. FISHER. Good-bye, Frank.

HYLAND [*going out into the hallway*]. Good-bye, dear. [CLARA *wanders up to the hall-door and looks out after him*]

CLARA. Good-bye. [*The vestibule-door is heard to close. And there is a significant pause; during which* CLARA *stands looking wistfully out into the hallway*]

MRS. FISHER [*rising, and moving to a point above the table*]. Listen, Clara. [CLARA *comes towards her*]

CLARA. What?

MRS. FISHER. Didn't he tell you how much they fined Aubrey?

CLARA. No, he didn't, Mom, really.

MRS. FISHER. Didn't *she* tell you, while I was out puttin' the tea on?

CLARA [*moving forward to the chair at the left of the table*]. Well now, what does it matter, Mom? You won't have to pay it. [*She sits down*]

MRS. FISHER. Well, I'll find out; it'll very likely be in the evening paper.

CLARA. Well, I wouldn't say anything to Amy about it, even if it is; she has enough to bother her now.

MRS. FISHER. Well, she brought it on herself if she has: — nobody could tell her anything.

CLARA. Well, there's nothing can be done by fighting with her, Mom.

MRS. FISHER [*with conviction*]. There's nothing can be done by *anything*, Clara, — when once the *main* thing is done. And that's the marriage. That's where all the trouble starts — gettin' married.

CLARA. If there were no marriages, Mom, there'd be no world.

MRS. FISHER [*moving around to the chair at the right of the table again*]. Oh, everybody sez that! — if there were no marriages there'd be no world.

CLARA. Well, would there?

MRS. FISHER. Well, what if there wouldn't? [*She sits down*] Do you think it'd be any worse than it is now? I think there'll be no world pretty soon, anyway, the way things are goin'. A lot of whiffets gettin' married, and not two cents to their names, and then throwin' themselves on their people to keep them. They're so full of love before they're married. You're about the only one I've *heard* talkin' about love *after* they were married. It's a wonder to me you have a roof over you; for they never have, with that kind of talk. Like the two in the parlor there — that has to *kiss* each other, every time they meet on the floor. [*She bristles for a second or two; and then there is a silence*]

CLARA [*quietly*]. Amy's going to have a child, Mom. [*Her Mother looks at her*]

MRS. FISHER. How do you know?

CLARA. She told me so.

MRS. FISHER [*softening a bit*]. Why didn't she tell me?

CLARA. I suppose she thought it'd start a fight.

MRS. FISHER [*indignant again*]. I don't know why it'd start a fight; I never fight with anybody; except him: and I wouldn't fight with *him* only for his impudence.

CLARA. Has Amy said anything to you about coming in here to live?

MRS. FISHER. She said something to me the night your Father was laid out, but I wasn't payin' much attention to her.

CLARA. I think you ought to let her come in here, Mom. [*Her Mother looks at her*] She'd be company for you, now that Pop is gone. And you don't know what day Joe might take a notion to get married.

MRS. FISHER. What's changed *your* ideas so much about lettin' her come in here? You were very much against it when she was married.

CLARA. I'd be against it now, if things around here were the way they were then. You didn't even own this house, Mom, when Amy was married: it was Pop's; and I knew if anything ever happened to him, and there was no will, — you might not find it so easy to order anybody out of it.

MRS. FISHER. It isn't that I'd mind lettin' Amy come in here, Clara, — but I wouldn't like to please him; for I know the first thing *I'd* know, he'd very likely be tellin' somebody that he'd let *me* come in. [CLARA *smiles faintly*] Oh, I wouldn't put it past him; he's told bigger lies than that. And if I ever found out that he said *that*, — he'd go out of here inside of five minutes, bag and baggage. [*The front door-bell rings*] See who that is, Clara. [*They rise; and* CLARA *goes out — into the hallway, and* MRS. FISHER *crosses below the table to the parlor-doors*] Are you in there, Amy? [*She opens the door*]

AMY. Yes; what is it, Mom?

MRS. FISHER. This kettle's boilin' out here, if you want a cup of tea.

AMY. All right, Mom, I'll be right out.

MRS. FISHER [*crossing to the kitchen-door*]. I'm goin' to make it right away, so you'd better come out if you want it hot. [*She goes out at the right*]

AMY [*coming out of parlor*]. Do you want a cup of tea, Aubrey? [*She crosses to the mirror over the mantelpiece and touches her hair*]

AUBREY [*coming out of the parlor*]. No, thanks, Honey, I don't care for any just now. [*He strolls to the hall-door, glances out, then moves to* AMY'S *side and puts his hands on her shoulders and kisses her affectionately. Then he pats her on the shoulder. She moves towards the kitchen-door*]

AUBREY [*patting her hand*]. Everything'll be all right, Kid. You know me. [*She goes out into the kitchen, and he settles himself at the mirror over the buffet at the right*]

CLARA [*in the hallway*]. Yes, I think it is myself. [*Appearing in the hall-door*] Just come right in, I'll call my Mother. Is she out in the kitchen, Aubrey?

AUBREY [*turning*]. Yes, she's getting some tea.

[GILL *appears in the hall-door*]

GILL. Well, you needn't bother, Ma'am, if she's busy. I just wanted to leave this watch.

AUBREY. How do you do.

GILL. How do you do. [CLARA *stops and looks back at the watch*]

AUBREY. And how is the young man?

GILL. I can't complain.

CLARA. Is that my Father's watch?

GILL. Yes, Ma'am. Are you Mr. Fisher's daughter?

CLARA. Yes. Close that door, Aubrey, will you? — I don't want Mom to see it. [*To* GILL] I'd rather my Mother wouldn't see it. [*She takes the watch, and* AUBREY *closes the kitchen-door*]

GILL. That's right.

CLARA. I believe she gave him this watch when they were married. [AUBREY *comes forward again, at right*]

GILL. Yes, it'd make her feel bad.

CLARA. Thanks ever so much.

GILL. McMahon didn't notice it when he was gettin' the rest of Mr. Fisher's things together.

CLARA. I see.

GILL. He said it was hangin' under the time-chart, back of number five.

AUBREY. This is the gentleman that brought Pop's lunch-box home.

CLARA. Oh, is that so?

GILL. I stopped by the day Mr. Fisher died.

CLARA. Did you work with my father?

GILL. No, Ma'am; I'm a twister; but I live out this way.

AUBREY. How is it you're not working today, Governor?

GILL. Mondays and Tuesdays is my earlies as a rule.

AUBREY. I see.

GILL. But the hunkies don't always get the stuff up to us. You got to keep right after them. Well, I guess I'll be gettin' along. [*He starts for the parlor-doors, then remembers that that is not the way out, and turns to his left towards the hall-door*]

CLARA. I'm ever so much obliged to you, for bringing this watch up.

GILL [*turning to her, at the hall-door*]. Oh, that's all right. I'm only sorry for the reason I have to do it.

CLARA. Yes, it was very sad.

GILL. Mr. Fisher was a hard-workin' man.

CLARA. I suppose he worked *too* hard, for his age.

GILL. Yes, I guess he did.

CLARA. You couldn't stop him, though.

GILL. No, that's what your brother-in-law here was sayin' the day I was here. He was tellin' me about all the times *he* tried to get him to quit, and take a rest. [AUBREY *turns to the buffet-mirror*] But, I guess when a man's worked as hard all his life as Mr. Fisher did, it ain't so easy for him to quit.

CLARA. No, I guess not.

GILL [*stepping a little forward again*]. I didn't know that was you, Mr. Piper, that was in that automobile smash-up that I was tellin' you about the day I was here.

AUBREY [*turning*]. That so?

GILL. I didn't know it till I saw your picture in the paper the next day.

AUBREY. What paper did you see it in?

GILL. I saw it in the *Record*.

AUBREY. Wasn't a very good picture of me, was it?

GILL. I knew it was you, though, the minute I saw it.

AUBREY. A friend of mine loaned me his car while mine was laid up, and something went wrong with the steer-gear.

GILL. How did you make out about that traffic-cop?

AUBREY. Oh, I squared that up all right.

CLARA. Where do you live up here, Mr. a —

GILL. I live out Richmond way. I'd like to get a house over this way more, on account of bein' a little nearer my work, but I don't see much chance.

CLARA. No, I don't know of any vacant houses around here right now.

GILL. No, your brother-in-law was tellin' me about the time *he* had gettin' hold of *this* one. [AUBREY *turns to the buffet-mirror again and smooths his toupé with considerable precision*] Well, I'll be gettin' along. [*He starts out into the hallway*]

CLARA [*with a bitter look over her shoulder at* AUBREY, *and following* GILL *out into the hallway*]. Well, thanks, ever so much, Mr. a — [*She puts the watch back of the statuette on the little stand at the left of the mantelpiece*]

GILL. Don't mention it.

CLARA. I'm sure Mother'll be glad to have this watch. [AUBREY *turns and looks after them. Then, with a glance toward the kitchen-door, he moves carefully to the mantelpiece and tries to see what is going on at the front-door*]

GILL. Yes; she might as well have it as one of them hunkies down there.

CLARA. Can you open it?

GILL. Yes, I got it. Good-bye.

CLARA. Good-bye; and thank you.

GILL. You're welcome. [*The front-door closes; and* AUBREY *glides hastily for the parlor-doors, in an attempt to avoid* CLARA; — *but just as he reaches the parlor-doors, she appears in the hall-door, and, with a quick glance toward the kitchen-door, comes forward to the back of the Morris-chair*]

CLARA. Come here, Aubrey, I want to talk to you. [*He turns towards her, with an attempt at nonchalance*] What do you mean by telling people that this is your house?

AUBREY. I didn't tell anybody it was my house.

CLARA. You *must* have told this man, or he wouldn't have said so.

AUBREY. What do you think I am, a liar?

CLARA. Yes, I do; one of the best I know.

AUBREY. Well, ask Amy what I said to him, she was here when I was talking to him.

CLARA [*before he has finished speaking*]. I don't have to ask anybody anything! — you were lying to him here to-day, right in front of me.

AUBREY [*with a shade of challenge in his manner*]. What'd I say?

CLARA. That you'd fixed the automobile thing up.

AUBREY. It's fixed up, isn't it?

CLARA. *You* didn't fix it up. [*There is a slight pause, during which* AUBREY, *his dignity considerably outraged, moves forward and crosses in front of her to the front of the center-table, where he stops.* CLARA *moves down at the right of the Morris-chair to a point near him*] You'd

have gone to jail for six months only for Frank Hyland. And telling this man that you tried to persuade Pop to stop working.

AUBREY [*over his left shoulder*]. So I did.

CLARA. When?

AUBREY. I didn't say it to him. But I told Amy he ought to stop. And I think he'd be right here to-day if he'd taken my advice.

CLARA. He wouldn't be right here to-day if he'd stopped expecting *you* to keep him. [*He moves further over to the right; and she follows him*] And now, listen to me, Aubrey; I want to talk seriously to you. You've made a lot of trouble for us since you've been in this family; and I want you to stop it. There's no reason my husband, because he happens to have a few dollars, should be going around paying *your* bills.

AUBREY [*half-turning to her*]. What do you want me to do?

CLARA. I want you to stop telling lies; for that's about all everything you do amounts to. Trying to make people believe you're something that you're not; — when if you'd just stop your talking and your showing-off, you *might* be the thing that you're trying to make them believe you are. [*She glances toward the kitchen-door, and then speaks to him again, in a slightly lower tone*] Your wife's going to have a child one of these days, Aubrey, and you want to pull yourself together and try to be sensible, like the man of a family *should* be. You're smart enough; — there's no reason why a fellow like you should be living in two rooms over a barber shop. I should think you'd have more respect for your wife. [*She turns and moves a few steps up towards the kitchen-door*]

AUBREY. A man doesn't stand much chance of getting ahead, Clara, when the boss has got a grudge against him.

CLARA [*turning sharply to her right, and moving to the upper right-hand corner of the center-table*]. Well, stop your silly talk, and get rid of that carnation, and the boss might get rid of his grudge. [*She glances toward the kitchen-door again, leans across the table towards him, and lowers her voice*] But, what I wanted to tell you was this, Aubrey, — I've asked Mom to let you and Amy come in here; and she sez she wouldn't mind it only that she knows that the first thing she'd *hear* is that you'd told someone that you'd taken *her* in. And, you see, that's exactly what you've done already, — to this man that brought the watch. If I told Mom that there'd be war.

AUBREY. Are you going to tell her?

CLARA [*with authoritative levelness*]. I'm going to put that up to you. And the very first time I hear that you've told anybody that this is *your* house, — I'll see to it that you'll get a house that *will* be your own. [AUBREY *smiles, a bit smugly, and looks at her out of the sides of his eyes*]

AUBREY. I guess your Mother 'ud have something to say about that, Clara.

CLARA [*with a measured evenness*]. Well, the only thing that needs to worry you, is what *I'll* have to say about it. [AUBREY'S *smugness begins to fade — into a questioning narrowness*] This is my house — Pop left it to me; so that Mom'ud always have a roof over her. For he knew how long she'd have it if Amy ever got round her. And if Amy ever got hold of it, he knew what she'd do if it ever came to a choice between you and Mom.

AUBREY. What are you doing, kidding me? [CLARA *holds his eyes steadily for a fraction of a second*]

CLARA. I'm giving you a tip; — see that you keep it to yourself. [AUBREY *withdraws his eyes slowly and looks straight out, weighing this new bit of intelligence carefully in his mind*] Be wise, now, Aubrey — you've got a chance to sit *in* here and live like a human being; and if you throw it away, you'll have nobody to blame but yourself. [*There is a sound at the front-door of a newspaper being thrown into the vestibule, and a man's voice says,* "Paper!" *Then the front-door is heard to close*] Open that door there, Mom'll be wondering what it's doing shut. [*She crosses up to the hall-door and goes out for the newspaper.* AUBREY *stands for a second thinking; and then* AMY *opens the kitchen-door and comes in. She glances about the room*]

AMY. Where's Clara, Aubrey?

AUBREY. I think she's out on the front porch. [AMY *glances toward the hall-door, then turns to her husband*] How are you feeling?

AMY. All right, I just had some tea. Listen, Aubrey, — [*She takes hold of the lapels of his coat*] Mom said we could come in here to live.

AUBREY. Yes, I got Clara to fix it up.

AMY. She said we could have *my* room.

AUBREY. Is it a front room?

AMY. No, it's that one at the head of the stairs.

AUBREY. Will we put that bureau of ours in there?

AMY. I think the one that's in there is better-looking. Let's go up and see. [*She starts up towards the hall-door*]

AUBREY [*following her*]. You look nice in black, Amy.

AMY [*glancing in the mantelpiece-mirror as she passes it*]. This is the dress that Clara gave me.

[CLARA *appears in the hall-door with the evening paper in her hand*]

CLARA. It's in the paper here about that trial today. [AMY *takes the paper*] Keep it out of sight and don't let Mom see it.

AMY [*going out the hall-door and to her left up the stairs*]. I'll take it upstairs. [CLARA *moves down towards the center-table, and* AUBREY *crosses above her towards the hall-door. As he passes her he excludes her with a look*]

AUBREY [*calling after* AMY *as he starts up the stairs*]. Has it got my picture in it? [CLARA *looks after him, rather hopelessly.* MRS. FISHER *comes in from the kitchen and moves down to the buffet at the right for her knitting-bag*]

MRS. FISHER. You goin' to stay here for supper to-night, Clara?

CLARA. Yes, I might as well, Mom; Frank won't be home. I think I'll run in next door and tell Bertha I won't be home. [*She starts towards the kitchen-door*]

MRS. FISHER [*crossing up to the mantelpiece for her spectacles*]. Yes, you'd better; she'll be expectin' you. Put somethin' around you.

CLARA [*stopping at the hooks at the head of the cellar-stairs*]. Is there something here?

MRS. FISHER. Put that old rain-coat of Joe's around you; it's good enough. [*She moves forward to the chair at the right of the center-table*] And go to the side-door, Clara; and don't be bringin' Mrs. Harbison to the front. [*She sits down and puts on her spectacles; and* CLARA *shakes the old raincoat out and puts it around her shoulders*] I told Amy she could have that side room upstairs.

CLARA. She might as well be using it, Mom.

MRS. FISHER. But I know I'm not goin' to hit it with *him*.

CLARA. Well, it's better to be fighting than lonesome, Mom. [*She goes out at the right, and* MRS. FISHER *takes a purple sweater that she's working on, out of the knitting-bag. A door out at the right closes after* CLARA. MRS. FISHER *commences to knit, when suddenly there is a shout of laughter from* AUBREY *upstairs.* MRS. FISHER *freezes instantly into a stoney stillness, and listens narrowly. There is another gale of laughter from* AUBREY, *and this decides* MRS. FISHER. *She puts her knitting back into the bag, very definitely, puts the bag on the table, gets up and marches resolutely across in front of the table and up to the hall-door. Just as she reaches the hall-door, with the ostensible purpose of reminding* AUBREY *that this is not his house, there is another roar from him.* AMY *can be heard laughing this time, also.* MRS. FISHER *subsides, and thinks. She appears to suddenly realize the futility of all remonstrances against the irresponsibility of* AUBREY; *and, after a thoughtful pause, to accept the situation. And as she moves back across the room, in front of the mantelpiece, to resume her chair at the right of the table, she seems a little older. Just as she reaches a point above the center-table, the front-door closes, with a bang. She starts nervously, and steps back to the mantelpiece to peer out into the hallway*]

MRS. FISHER. Is that you, Joe?

JOE [*from the hallway*]. Yes.

MRS. FISHER [*continuing to her chair at the right of the table*]. It's a wonder you wouldn't take the door off the hinges, and be done with it.

[JOE *hurries in from the hallway*]

JOE. How did they make out down there to-day, Mom? [*He tosses the evening paper onto the center-table, and continues on over and up to the hooks at the head of the cellar-stairs, to hang up his hat and overcoat*]

MRS. FISHER [*sitting down*]. Who do you mean, Aubrey Piper?

JOE. Yes. Are they back yet?

MRS. FISHER. They're upstairs.

JOE. What'd they do to him?

MRS. FISHER. They fined him.

JOE. How much?

MRS. FISHER [*taking her knitting out of the bag*]. I don't know; they wouldn't tell me. Frank paid it. But, I'll find out; it'll very likely be in the evening paper. [JOE *comes forward to the center-table*]

JOE [*picking up the paper from the table*]. It isn't in this paper, I looked.

MRS. FISHER. I'll find out.

JOE. But, there's something else in to-night's paper, Mom.

MRS. FISHER [*knitting*]. What?

JOE [*indicating a certain point on the paper*]. Just cast your eyes on this, right here.

MRS. FISHER [*looking casually*]. What is it?

JOE [*reading*]. "Philadelphia Youth Makes Important Chemical Discovery. Mr. Joseph Fisher of North Philadelphia Perfects Rust-Preventive Solution." [*He gives his Mother a squeeze and a kiss*]

MRS. FISHER [*startled, and giving him a little slap*]. Stop it, Joe! [*He laughs exultantly, strikes the palms of his hands together, and strides across above the table towards the left*] Did they buy the thing from you, Joe?

JOE [*turning to her, at the left of the center-table*]. One hundred thousand dollars, Mother! They signed for it this afternoon in the lawyer's office. [*He becomes aware that the shoe-lace of his right shoe is untied, and puts his foot up on the chair to tie it*]

MRS. FISHER [*leaning towards him*]. The Meyers and Stevens people?

JOE. Yeh. They sent for me to come over there this afternoon about two o'clock, so I knocked off and got hold of Farley right away, and we went over there. And they had the contracts all drawn up and everything.

MRS. FISHER. What did you say about a hundred thousand dollars, Joe?

JOE. That's what they paid for it this afternoon, on account; — [*He starts across above the center-table and up to the hooks again at the right, removing his coat*] then they're to market it for me from their laboratories, and give *me* half the net.

MRS. FISHER [*talking over her right shoulder*]. What's the net?

JOE [*hanging his coat up*]. Whatever's left after all expenses are paid. [MRS. FISHER *tries to encompass the situation*]

MRS. FISHER. I guess they'll see that there ain't much left, won't they?

JOE [*coming forward again to the center-table*]. Why, there'll be a fortune out of this thing, Mom. Have you any idea what a rust-preventive means as an industrial chemical problem? Why, they'll make a million dollars out of this, within the next five years. [*He moves over to the left, removing his tie*]

MRS. FISHER. Well, how much of that are you goin' to get, Joe?

JOE. I'll get the same as they get, that's the contract.

MRS. FISHER. A million dollars?

JOE. Easy, I got a hundred thousand today. [MRS. FISHER *shifts her eyes and tries to concentrate*]

MRS. FISHER. How many noughts is a hundred thousand?

JOE [*coming back to her left, taking a pencil from his vest-pocket*]. It's a one, [*He leans over the table and writes it on the margin of the newspaper*] and two noughts, and three more noughts. [MRS. FISHER *looks at it closely. JOE replaces the pencil in his pocket and moves across again towards the left*] They paid that today on account. I knew it was coming, though; their head chemist out at Bristol told me six weeks ago it was all set. I've got to go over there to their offices right away; they made an appointment for the newspaper and magazine people over there at five o'clock. [*He starts for the hall-door*] I've got to talk to them.

MRS. FISHER. Did they give you any of the money, Joe?

JOE [*stopping at the hall-door*]. A hundred thousand dollars, sure.

MRS. FISHER. Not in money though?,

JOE [*laughing and coming back towards the center-table*]. Not in dollar bills, no; they gave me a check for it.

MRS. FISHER. Where is it?

JOE. Farley has it in his safe, down in the office.

MRS. FISHER. How much do you have to give *him*, half of it?

JOE. No, he's not a partner, he's just my lawyer. I give him five per cent of all monies received. [*He moves forward at the left of the center-table*]

MRS. FISHER. How much will that be?

JOE. Well, that was five thousand dollars right off the bat, today. Pretty soft for that bird. When I first talked to him he wanted to stick me for ten per cent; but I nailed that quick; I knew what this was goin' to be worth.

MRS. FISHER. What are you goin' to do now, Joe, stop workin'?

JOE. No, of course not, I'm not goin' to stop working; I've got that oil-paint thing on the carpet, now.

MRS. FISHER. Well, won't you have to go to Washington or someplace?

JOE [*rolling his tie up on his finger, and stuffing it into his vest-pocket*]. No, that's all been attended to. But I'll tell you, Mom — I might go to Trenton.

MRS. FISHER. New Jersey?

JOE. Yes.

MRS. FISHER. Not to live, surely?

JOE. I might — till I put this oil-paint thing through.

MRS. FISHER. Well, I think you'd be very foolish, Joe, to go to Trenton at *your* age.

JOE [*removing his cuff-links and dropping them into his vest-pocket*]. Well, the Meyers and Stevens people made me a proposition this afternoon that looks pretty good. They've got one of the most perfectly equipped experimenting laboratories in the world, just outside of Trenton; and it's open day and night; and that's what I want. I'd have had this rust-preventive through six months sooner, if I could have had the use of a laboratory somewhere at night. So they want me to go up there on a salary, with a first look at anything I strike; but I didn't want to say anything till I talked to *you*.

MRS. FISHER. What do you mean?

JOE. I mean, I wouldn't like the idea of goin' away, and leavin' you alone in the house.

MRS. FISHER [*resuming her knitting*]. Oh, you go ahead, Joe, — if it's for your good. Never mind me, — I'll get along some way.

JOE. I don't like the idea of leavin' you here alone.

MRS. FISHER. Nearly every Mother is left alone, Joe, if she lives long enough. [JOE *looks straight out and thinks*]

JOE. I was wonderin', Mom, — why Amy couldn't come in here: she seems to be havin' a pretty tough time of it. [*There is a slight pause, during which* MRS. FISHER *knits*]

MRS. FISHER. She's *in* here already; and her man with her.

JOE. I mean, to stay.

MRS. FISHER. They're goin' to stay; — she can have that room at the head of the stairs. [*She stops knitting and thinks, looking steadily at the floor in front of her*] They'll have to live somewhere; and I guess it'll have to be here. It's just as our Clara said here one night, — I remember it as if it was yesterday. She said, "Remember what I'm telling you, Mom, — it's *you* that'll have them on your hands if she takes him." And I suppose that's true. She made her bed, — and I guess it's me that'll have to lie in it.

JOE [*starting up and across towards the hooks at the head of the cellar-stairs, to get a paper out of his coat-pocket*]. They want me to go to Trenton right away.

MRS. FISHER. What would you do, Joe, come home over Sundays?

JOE. Sure, it's only thirty-eight miles from here.

MRS. FISHER [*astonished*]. Is that all the further Trenton is from Philadelphia?

JOE [*starting across towards the left to the hall-door, removing his vest*]. That's all.

MRS. FISHER. It always seemed very far away to me. I guess it's the name.

JOE. I'm goin' up to get fixed up a bit before I go over to that office.

MRS. FISHER [*suddenly putting her knitting on the table, preparatory to getting up*]. Well, listen, Joe!

JOE [*stopping, with his foot on the first step of the stairs*]. What?

MRS. FISHER [*getting up and moving across in front of the center-table*]. Come here. [JOE *comes down to her left*] Don't say anything about this to him, Joe, or he'll be wantin' to go up and talk to the newspaper men, too. [JOE *laughs faintly, then looks away off and thinks*]

JOE. You know, Mom, — I kinda feel that there's somethin' comin' to that nut out of this thing.

MRS. FISHER. How do you mean?

JOE. *He* gave me an idea here one night.

MRS. FISHER [*seizing him suddenly by both arms*]. Well, for God's sake, don't tell *him* that, Joe! — or, as sure as you live, he'll be tellin' everybody that he done the whole thing.

JOE. You remember the night he was sayin' here about bein' at work on a solution for the prevention of rust in iron and steel?

MRS. FISHER. Yes.

JOE. Well, you know, I'd been tellin' him somethin' about it a week or so before —

MRS. FISHER. Yes, you told me.

JOE. While he was waitin' here for Amy one night.

MRS. FISHER. Yes.

JOE. Well, he forgot that night he was tellin' *me* about it that it was me that had been tellin' *him* about it; and he got it mixed.

MRS. FISHER. That's the way he does with everything.

JOE. And it was the way he got it mixed, Mom, that gave me the idea. *He* said, — that it was a combination of chemical elements to be added to the metal in its *molten state*, instead of applied *externally*, as they *had* been doin'. And I *landed* on it — the way Howe did when he dreamed of puttin' the eye in the point of the needle instead of the other end. That was exactly what *I'd* been doin' — applying the solution *externally* — in a mixture of paint. But the next day, I tried adding parts of it to the molten state of the metal, and it did the trick. Of course, he didn't know what he was sayin' when he said it —

MRS. FISHER. He never does.

JOE. And he didn't know anything about the solution-formula — But it was the way he got what I'd been tellin' him *twisted*, Mom, — that put the thing over.

MRS. FISHER. Well, that's no credit to him, Joe.

JOE. I know.

MRS. FISHER. He was only blowin' when he said it.

JOE. Sure.

MRS. FISHER. He don't know what a formula means. And I'd have told him where he heard it, too, if I'd been you.

JOE [*thoughtfully*]. I'd like to give him a little present of some kind. [*His Mother looks at him sharply*]

MRS. FISHER. What would you give him a present for?

JOE [*breaking into a little laugh*]. For makin' a mistake.

MRS. FISHER. That's all everybody's doin' around here, — givin' that fellow presents for makin' mistakes. That's what Frank Hyland said here to-day, when I ast him why he paid his fine. He said, "Oh, you've got to give a little present here and there once in a while." There's no use tryin' to be sensible anymore.

JOE. I'd like to give him *somethin'*. [*She looks at him again keenly, and thinks for a second*]

MRS. FISHER. I'll tell you what you can do, Joe, if you're so anxious to *give* him somethin'. — Find out what fine Frank Hyland paid for him this afternoon, and tell him you're goin' to give him that. But don't tell him what you're giving it to him *for*, Joe, or we won't be able to live in the house with him. And don't give him money, Joe; for he'd only be goin' from one room to another here in an automobile. And don't give it to her neither, Joe; for she'll only hand it right over to him. — Give it to me. [JOE *looks at her*] And I'll give it to them when I think they need it. [*A door closes out at the right; and* JOE *steps up towards the mantelpiece to look off*] That's Clara; she's been next door telephonin'. [*She turns to her left and picks up her knitting from the table and sits down again.* CLARA *comes in, slipping off the raincoat*]

JOE. Hello!

CLARA [*hanging the raincoat up on the hook*]. How's it you're home so early, Joe?

[AUBREY *enters from the hall-door, smoking a cigar*]

JOE. The long threatening has come at last!

CLARA [*coming forward, looking at him seriously*]. What?

JOE. The big news.

CLARA. The steel thing? [JOE *laughs*] Did they buy it, Joe?

JOE. One hundred thousand dollars! — first payment — they gave me the check this afternoon.

CLARA. Joe, you're not telling me the truth!

AUBREY [*coming forward*]. Something about the invention, Joe?

JOE. Hello, Aubrey!

CLARA [*coming down to her Mother's right*]. Did they, Mom?

[JOE *and* MRS. FISHER, *speaking together.*]

MRS. FISHER. So he sez.

JOE. They bought it this afternoon.

CLARA. Isn't that wonderful!

AUBREY [*extending his hand to* JOE]. Congratulations!

JOE [*laughing*]. Thanks.

AUBREY. So we put it over! [MRS. FISHER *poisons him with a look*]

JOE. To the tune of one hundred thousand clackers. [*He swings above* AUBREY *towards the hall-door*]

AUBREY [*turning and following him*]. No kidding?

JOE [*running up the stairs*]. The check's in the safe, down in the lawyer's office.

AUBREY [*calling up the stairs after him*]. Well, Kid, you know what I always told you!

[JOE *and* CLARA, *speaking together*]

JOE. Leave it to you to call the turn, Aubrey.

CLARA [*running up to the hall-door*]. Joe! Come here and tell us something about it.

JOE [*calling back*]. I've got to get dressed, Clara, I'll tell you about it later. [AUBREY *comes forward at the left, laughing; but suddenly he becomes conscious of* MRS. FISHER'S *left eye, and his laugh freezes into a detached gaze out the window at the left*]

MRS. FISHER [*speaking to* CLARA]. He's got to go down to see them people that bought the thing from him.

CLARA [*coming forward to the center-table*]. Why, what will Joe *do* with all that money, Mom?

MRS. FISHER [*knitting*]. Heaven knows, I don't.

CLARA. Have you any idea how much a hundred thousand dollars is?

MRS. FISHER. Joe sez it's a one and two noughts, and then three more noughts.

CLARA. Why, it's a fortune!

MRS. FISHER. Well, he brought it on himself; he'll have to tend to it; I'm sure I won't.

AUBREY [*coming towards the center-table from the left*]. If he's a *wise bird*, he'll let *me* handle that money for him. [MRS. FISHER *pins him with a look, and her knitting slides to her lap*] I could give him a couple of very fly tips on that.

MRS. FISHER [*with dangerous steadiness*]. He don't want *your* tips; nor your *taps* neither. We *know* about one tip *you* gave a man, and his arm has been in a sling ever since. [CLARA *picks up the "Delineator" from the table and moves over to the right to the buffet, to look at the styles*]

AUBREY. That's all right, Mrs. Fisher; but if he's a wise Bimbo, — he'll take the drooping left, [*he lowers the lid of his left eye, very mysteriously*] and I'll *double* that money for him, within the next two weeks; [MRS. FISHER *resumes her knitting*] and give him an extra pair of trousers.

MRS. FISHER. I guess he'd *need* an extra pair of trousers, if he was sittin' around waitin' for *you* to double his money for him.

AUBREY. Well, I'm telling you, Mother, — he's an awful strawride if he doesn't get in on some of that copper-clipping that those people are writing me about. [*She looks at him, hard*]

Mrs. Fisher. What is it, a copper mine this time?

Aubrey. 'Tain't a mine at all, — it's a mint.

Mrs. Fisher. What are they writin' to *you* about it for?

Aubrey. They're writing to everybody.

Mrs. Fisher. They must be. [*She resumes her knitting*]

Aubrey. Prospective Investors — They hear a man's got a few dollars laying around idle, and they get in touch with him.

Mrs. Fisher. Well, nobody's heard that you have any dollars layin' around idle, have they?

Aubrey [*with a touch of consequence*]. Oh, — I don't know, — they may have. [Mrs. Fisher *stops knitting and leans towards him, stonily, — her left elbow resting on the table*]

Mrs. Fisher. Listen, Boy, — if you've got any dollars layin' around idle, it'd be fitter for you to pay Frank Hyland the money he paid to keep you out of jail, than to be lookin' around for an investment for it — in some old copper mine, out in God-Knows-Where — that you don't know no more about than them that's writin' to you about it. [*She knits again, indignantly*]

Aubrey. I know a whole lot about this proposition, Mrs. Fisher; and so do a lot of other people. Why, — they say they can see enough copper in those rocks, right now, to keep this thing going for the next ten years.

Mrs. Fisher [*almost violently*]. They *shoot* that in there.

Aubrey. Shoot copper into solid rocks, eh?

Mrs. Fisher [*putting her knitting down on the table and picking up the newspaper that* Joe *has left there*]. That's what I said. [Aubrey *turns away, with a gesture of helplessness, and moves across in front of the Morris-chair to the window at the left*] I read all about just how they do it, in a magazine not two weeks ago. [*Looking at the paper*] Then they shoot a lot of letters to the likes of you, and you *shoot off* about it.

Amy [*entering hurriedly from the hall-door and coming forward to the center-table*]. Mom, is it true what Joe sez about the invention?

Mrs. Fisher [*looking sharply at something in the paper*]. Here it is in the paper. [Aubrey *moves across above the Morris-chair towards the center-table*]

Amy. Isn't that wonderful, Aubrey? [Aubrey *nods and smiles*]

Mrs. Fisher [*to* Clara]. I thought our Joe said it wasn't *in* here.

Clara [*moving a step or two from the buffet*]. What is it?

Amy [*leaning over her Mother's left shoulder, looking at the paper*]. What does it say, Mom?

Mrs. Fisher [*reading*]. Mad Motorist Fined One Thousand Dollars for Reckless Driving. [Aubrey *glides forward and crosses in front of the Morris-chair to the window at the left again.* Amy *straightens up and gives a distressed look at* Clara, *who suggests, with a nod, that she go into the kitchen*] Mr. Aubrey Piper, of 903 Lehigh Avenue, was arranged today before Magistrate Lister of the 22nd and Huntington Park Avenue Police Station, to answer to the charge of having diregarded traffic-signals at Broad Street and Erie Avenue last Monday evening; resulting in rather serious injuries to Mr. Joseph Hart, a traffic-officer. The defendent was fined one thousand dollars for reeklessness, disregard of traffic-signals, and operating an automobile without a license. [*She lowers the paper to her lap and looks at* Aubrey]

Aubrey [*turning from the window, and with a magnificent gesture*]. That's the law for you. [*He folds his arms and leans on the back of the Morris-chair, looking straight out*]

Mrs. Fisher. What do you think of that, Clara?

Clara [*moving to the arm-chair below the buffet at the right*]. Well, it's all over now, Mom — Frank paid it.

Mrs. Fisher. What did he pay it *for?*

Clara [*sitting down*]. Well, it was either that or go to jail, Mom; and you wouldn't want that, on account of Amy. [*She opens the "Delineator"*]

Mrs. Fisher. Well, Frank Hyland didn't have to pay it — [*She sits looking straight out, fuming*] Amy's got a Mother. [*Turning sharply to* Clara] And you take that thousand-dollar insurance check that I gave you and give it to him as soon as ever you see him. I don't want Frank Hyland goin' around payin' out thousand-dollar bills on account of this clown. [*She looks bitterly at* Aubrey, *who looks at her with an expression as though he were trying to come to some conclusion as to the most effectual means of putting her in her place*] It's bad enough for *me* to have to do it.

CLARA [*calling to* AMY]. Amy.

AMY [*from the kitchen*]. What?

CLARA. Come here a minute. [MRS. FISHER *puts the newspaper back onto the table and resumes her knitting.* AUBREY *strolls over and sits down at the left of the center-table, reaching for the newspaper which* MRS. FISHER *has just put down.* AMY *comes in from the kitchen*]

AMY. What?

CLARA. Here's that skirt I was telling you about. [AMY *comes forward to* CLARA'S *left and they look at a certain skirt in the "Delineator."* AUBREY *deposits some ashes from his cigar on the little tray on the table, then sits back, takes a pair of tortoiseshell rimmed glasses, with a black-tape attachment for over the ear, from his vest-pocket, and settles them on his nose. His Mother-in-law gives him a look*]

AUBREY. Was that Insurance man here to-day? [AMY *opens the left-hand drawer of the buffet and takes out a package of Life-Savers. She takes one herself, then offers* CLARA *one;* CLARA *takes it; and the two continue their discussion of the styles in the "Delineator"*]

MRS. FISHER. What do you want to know for?

AUBREY [*glancing over the evening paper*]. Nothing, — I was just wondering if he got around this way to-day. — Did he leave a paper here for me?

MRS. FISHER [*knitting*]. He *wanted* to; but I told him not to waste his time — [AUBREY *looks at her narrowly*] talkin' to *you* about fifty-thousand-dollar policies.

AUBREY. Well, what about it?

MRS. FISHER [*looking at him*]. Nothin' at *all* about it; only the man was laughin' up his sleeve at you.

AUBREY. Is that so?

MRS. FISHER. What else *could* he do? He knows you haven't the faintest idea of takin' out any such policy.

AUBREY. How do you know he does?

MRS. FISHER. Because he knows you're only a clerk; and that you don't get enough salary in *six months* — to pay one year's premium on a policy like that.

AUBREY. What were you doing, handing out a line of gab about my business?

MRS. FISHER [*quietly knitting again*]. You haven't got any business for anybody to hand out a line of gab about — that I ever heard of. [AMY *moves slowly across above the center-table towards the left, picking up a newspaper*]

AUBREY. Well, whether I have any line of business or not, it isn't necessary for you to be gabbing to perfect strangers about it.

MRS. FISHER [*getting mad*]. Then, you stop gabbin' to people about fifty-thousand-dollar policies! — On your thirty-two dollars a week. [*Turning to him furiously*] I told him *that*, too.

AMY [*touching* AUBREY *on the left shoulder, as she passes back of him*]. Keep quiet, Aubrey.

MRS. FISHER. So he'd know how much attention to pay to you the *next* time you start. [AMY *moves forward to the Morris-chair at the left and sits down*]

AUBREY. What else did you tell him?

MRS. FISHER. I told him the truth! — whatever I told him. — And I guess that's more than can be said for a whole lot *you* told him. [*She knits again*]

AUBREY [*resuming his paper*]. A man'ud certainly have a swell chance trying to make anything of himself around *this* hut. [MRS. FISHER *stops knitting, and leans her elbow on the table*]

MRS. FISHER. Listen, Boy, — any time you don't like this *hut*, you go right straight back to Lehigh Avenue to your two rooms over the dago barber shop. And I'll be glad to see your heels.

CLARA. Stop talking, Mom.

MRS. FISHER. Nobody around here's tryin' to stop you from makin' somethin' of yourself.

AUBREY. No, and nobody's trying to help me any, either; only trying to make me look like a *pin-head* — every chance they get.

MRS. FISHER. Nobody'll have to try very hard to make *you* look like a *pin-head;* your own silly talk'll do that for you, any time at all.

AUBREY. I suppose it's silly talk to try to make a good impression.

MRS. FISHER [*turning to him and speaking definitely*]. Yes; it's silly to try to make an impression of any kind; for the only one that'll be made'll be the right one, — and that'll make itself.

AUBREY. Well, if you were out in the world as much as *I* am, you'd very soon see how much easier it is for a fellow to get along — if people think he's got something.

MRS. FISHER. Well, anybody that-'ud listen to *you* very long'ud know you *couldn't* have very much.

AUBREY. Is that so.

MRS. FISHER [*tersely*]. You heard

me. [CLARA *rises and moves towards her Mother*]

AUBREY [*reaching over to dispose of some more cigar-ashes*]. People that are smart enough to be able to make it easier for you —

CLARA. Aubrey, — that'll do. [*He is silenced; and resumes his paper.* CLARA *shows her Mother a particular pattern in the "Delineator"*] Mom, that'd look good for that new black crepe de chine of yours, No. 18, there in the middle.

MRS. FISHER. But, I wouldn't want that bunch of fullness like that right there, Clara.

[JOE *enters hurriedly from the hall-door, wearing a clean shirt and collar, and with his face washed and hair combed*]

CLARA. Well, you're always saying you look too thin; and I think — Joe, tell me something about the invention.

JOE [*crossing quickly to the hooks at the right for his coat*]. They telephoned for me this afternoon about two o'clock, and I got hold of Farley and we went right over there. And they had the contracts all drawn up and everything.

CLARA [*having moved up towards the hooks with him*]. Well, did they really give you a hundred thousand dollars for it? [AUBREY *gets up and moves around and up to the upper left-hand corner of the table*]

JOE [*coming forward, putting on his coat*]. Check's in the safe, down in Farley's office.

AUBREY [*flicking some ashes from his cigar*]. Joe! — what do you think we ought to do with that money? [JOE *tries to hide his laughter, and steps down to his Mother's right; and* CLARA *comes forward and leans on the buffet*]

JOE. You know, it was a funny thing, Mom, — when I first talked to the Meyers and Stevens people, I was only to get *fifty* thousand dollars advance; and when I went up there to-day they had the contracts all made out for a *hundred* thousand.

AUBREY. And they're getting away with murder at that.

MRS. FISHER [*turning to him impatiently*]. Oh, keep still, you! — You don't know anything about this at all.

AUBREY. I made *them* think I knew something about it.

MRS. FISHER. You made *who* think?

AUBREY. The Meyers and Stevens people.

JOE. What are you talkin' about, Aubrey, do you know?

AUBREY. Certainly, I know what I'm talking about. *I* went to see those people, last Saturday afternoon, after you told me they'd talked to you.

JOE [*crossing towards him, to a point above the center-table*]. And, what'd you do up there?

AUBREY. Why, I told them, — that they'd have to double the advance, if they wanted to do business with us.

MRS. FISHER. And, what business was it of yours?

AUBREY. Well, — I'm Joe's guardian, ain't I?

MRS. FISHER. Who told you you were?

AUBREY. Well, — he's got to have somebody tend to his business, doesn't he? — He's only a lad.

MRS. FISHER. Well, he doesn't need *you* to tend to his business for him — He tended to his business long before he ever saw *you*.

AUBREY. He never landed a hundred thousand dollars, though, till he saw me, did he?

JOE. Well, what did you say to them, Aubrey?

AUBREY. Why, — I simply told them that your Father was dead, — and that I was acting in the capacity of *business*-adviser to you: and that, if this discovery of yours was as important as you had led me to believe it was, they were simply taking advantage of your youth by offering you fifty thousand dollars for it. And that I refused to allow you to negotiate further — unless they doubled the advance, market it at their expense, and one half the net — sign on the dotted line. [*He flicks more ashes from his cigar*]

JOE. Well, did they know who you were?

AUBREY. I told them — that I was head of the house here; [MRS. FISHER *grips the edge of the table, threateningly*] and that I was also connected with the Pennsylvania Railroad.

MRS. FISHER. It's too bad they didn't know what you do down there; and call your bluff.

AUBREY. I beat them to it; I called theirs first. [*He strolls towards the left, with a bit of swagger*]

JOE. Well, I certainly have to give you credit, Aubrey; that's the way the contract reads.

AUBREY [*strolling back again*]. I told

it to them ; and I told it to your lawyer, too.

JOE. I'll have to give you a little present of some kind out of this, Aubrey.

AUBREY [*dismissing the suggestion with a touch of ceremony*]. You'll not give *me* any present, Joe ; — give it to your Mother. [*He strolls over to the left again*] She'll need it more than I will. [*He comes forward at the left of the Morris-chair*] Amy, — have you got the financial page there?

AMY [*handing him the newspaper*]. Is this it, Aubrey?

AUBREY [*taking it*]. Thank you. [*He crosses in front of her to the chair at the left of the center-table and sits down. Amy gets up, looking at him wonderingly*]

AMY. Aubrey, you're wonderful !

AUBREY [*settling himself to look over the bond market*]. A little bit of bluff goes a long way sometimes, Amy.

AMY. Isn't he wonderful, Mom? [MRS. FISHER *prepares to resume her knitting*]

MRS. FISHER [*after a long sigh*]. God help *me*, from now on. [*The curtain descends slowly, with* AMY *standing lost in admiration of the wonder of* AUBREY. *When the curtain rises again* AUBREY *is reading,* MRS. FISHER *is knitting,* CLARA *is sitting reading the "Delineator", over on the arm of the arm-chair at the right,* JOE *is putting on his overcoat and hat at the mantelpiece-mirror, and* AMY *is sitting in the Morris-chair at the left, just looking at* AUBREY]

THE END OF THE PLAY

APPENDIX

BIBLIOGRAPHIES

THE bibliographies for a volume so largely contemporaneous, at this moment, as the present collection, cannot be over rigid or strict in choice of material. It is expected that the student will consult the current papers on the day following the dates of production; and that, where there is a London production, the same will hold true. It is also suggested that the Reader's Guides — cumulative indices — and the Dramatic Indexes be consulted, recording, as they do, the important critiques in the weeklies and monthlies. An excellent resumé of dramatic seasons, published yearly, was started by Burns Mantle in 1919–1920 (Boston: Small, Maynard & Co.). These should be consulted for the measurement of managerial activity in the theatre. These volumes not only record every production in New York, but give in outline, the plots, with generous inclusion of dialogue, of the ten best plays of the season, according to Mr. Mantle's judgment. There has been no attempt to be inclusive in this bibliography. There are so many available handbooks and collections of plays containing bibliographies, that the reader will find no difficulty in knowing the best that has been written about the various departments and movements of the modern theatre. I have indicated these bibliographies where necessary. Various comments are made under the separate divisions in the following list.

GENERAL REFERENCES

Consult the present Editor's "Representative Plays by American Dramatists" (New York: E. P. Dutton & Co., Vols. I and III, for further titles).

Carter, Huntly. "The New Spirit in Drama and Art." New York, 1912.

Clark, Barrett H. "A Study of the Modern Drama." New York: D. Appleton & Co. 1925. (A serviceable handbook. In the American section, see Thomas, Fitch, MacKaye, O'Neill. Consult also Clark's previous handbook, "The British and American Drama of To-day." New York: Henry Holt & Co. 1915. Notes on Belasco, Rachel Crothers, Josephine Preston Peabody. Also studies of Thomas, Fitch, and MacKaye.)

Dickinson, Thomas H. "Playwrights of the New American Theatre." New York: The Macmillan Co. 1925.

Dukes, Ashley. "The Youngest Drama." London: Benn. 1923. (Chicago, 1924.)

Eaton, Walter P. "Plays and Players: Leaves from a Critic's Scrapbook." Cincinnati: Stewart & Kidd. 1916. (Read the sections dealing with "What is a Good Play?" "The Man of Letters and the New Art of the Theatre", "What is Entertainment?")

667

Ford, James L. "Forty-odd Years in the Literary Shop." New York: E. P. Dutton & Co. 1921.

Glover, H. "Drama and Mankind." Boston: Small, Maynard & Co. 1924.

Goldberg, Isaac. "The Drama of Transition." Cincinnati: Stewart & Kidd. 1922.

Hapgood, Norman. "The Stage in America: 1897–1900." New York: The Macmillan Co. 1901.

Jourdain, Eleanor. "The Drama of Europe." New York, 1924.

MacMillan, Dougald. "Recent Tendencies in the Theatre." University of North Carolina, 1923. *Extension Bulletin*, Vol. 2, No. 12. Bibliography, pp. 27–28.

Mantle, Burns. "The Best Plays" series: Beginning the season 1919–1920. Boston: Small, Maynard & Co.

Moses, Montrose J. "The American Dramatist." (Revised edition.) Boston: Little, Brown, and Co. 1917.

Rockwell, E. T. "Study Course in the American One-Act Play." University of North Carolina. 1924.

Vernon, Frank. "The Twentieth-Century Theatre." Boston: Houghton Mifflin Co. (n.d.)

EXPRESSIONISM

Very little has been written on this subject in English. Especially is this so of the subject as it relates to the theatre. The German periodicals and theatre books deal more fully with this "new movement", though see the statement made by Barrett Clark in his "A Study of the Modern Drama" (Appleton, 1924), Index.

Bahr, Hermann. "Expressionismus." Munich, 1919.

Carter, Huntly. "The Theatre of Max Reinhardt." New York: Mitchell Kennerly. 1914. (See the same author's "The New Spirit in Drama and Art." New York, 1912.)

Cheney, Sheldon. "Expressionism." New York *Times Review and Magazine*, April 30, 1922. (Consult the Indexes of the principal New York newspapers under Expressionism. The term was defined by many critics, when they reviewed such plays as "The Adding Machine", "Beggar on Horseback", and "Processional.")

Cheney, Sheldon. "A Primer of Modern Art." New York: Boni & Liveright. 1924. (See also the same author's "The New Movement in the Theatre", New York, 1914; and "The Art Theatre", New York, 1917.)

Macgowan, Kenneth. "The Theatre of To-morrow." New York: Boni & Liveright. 1921.

Macgowan, Kenneth, and Robert Edmond Jones. "Continental Stagecraft." New York: Harcourt, Brace & Co. 1922.

Pfister, Oskar Robert. "Expressionism in Art. Its Psychological and Biological Basis." Translated by Barbara Low and M. A. Mügge. London, 1922.

The following magazine titles may be of interest:

"Chronique de l'art allemand sur l'expressionisme." L'amour de l'art. 1920. année 1, p. 222.

"Expressionism on the Stage." P. Henckels. *Theatre Arts Magazine*, Vol. 6, p. 112. April, 1922.

"Experiment on Broadway." Kenneth Macgowan. *Theatre Arts Magazine*, Vol. 7, pp. 175–185. July, 1923. (Consult the indexes of this magazine, and note the illustrations therein of Expressionistic style.)

"Expressionism, or, What You Will." H. Ould. *English Review*, Vol. 33, pp. 310–313. October, 1921.

"Expressionism: Good, Bad, and Indifferent." R. A. Parker. *Independent*, Vol. 110, pp. 270–272. April 14, 1923.

"Art as a Liberation." A. B. Walkley. *Arts and Decoration*, Vol. 17, pp. 380–382. September, 1922.

CHARLES H. HOYT

Mr. Hoyt was born in Concord, New Hampshire, July 26, 1860. He died in Charlestown, N. H., November 22, 1900. He was educated at the Boston Latin School and received an appointment to West Point. He failed to pass the physical examination at the Academy. He tried his hand as a Western stock raiser, served as reporter and dramatic critic on various newspapers, read law, was elected to the New Hampshire legislature, and became one of the successful dramatists in the theatre of the Eighteen-Nineties. There are many theatrical traditions about Hoyt. One was that he wrote "A Texas Steer" in five days, much after the fashion of Dion Boucicault: he started rehearsing the first act before the second was finished, playwright keeping just one act ahead of stage director. Another is that "A Trip to Chinatown", during the first five years of its life, made for Hoyt the sum of $500,000. A play of his, called "The Maid and the Moonshiner", was an immediate failure, and Hoyt is reported to have said that one reason for its non-success was that the title did not begin with the article "A." Very little has been written about Mr. Hoyt. Augustus Thomas mentions him in his "The Print of My Remembrance"; Norman Hapgood in "The Stage in America"; and so does Arthur Hornblow in the second volume of his "History of the Theatre in America" (Philadelphia: J. B. Lippincott Co. 1919).

The plays by Mr. Hoyt, which are in the New York Public Library, are as follows (the theatres, unless otherwise indicated, are in New York; the dates are not first performances):

"A Bunch of Keys; or, The Hotel." Newark, N. J., December 13, 1883.

"A Parlor Match." Bijou Theatre, September 19, 1893.

"A Rag Baby." Haverly's Theatre, Chicago, Ill., August 16, 1884.

"A Tin Soldier." Standard Theatre, May 3, 1886.

"A Hole in the Ground." 14th Street Theatre, September 12, 1887.

"A Brass Monkey." Bijou Theatre, October 15, 1888.

"A Midnight Bell." Bijou Theatre, March 5, 1889.

"A Trip to Chinatown." (Musical trifle.) Hoyt's Madison Square Theatre, November 9, 1891.

"A Texas Steer; or, Money Makes the Mare Go." Hoyt's Madison Square Theatre, January 8, 1894.

"A Temperance Town." Hoyt's Madison Square Theatre, September 18, 1894.

"A Milk White Flag: And its Battle-scarred Followers on the Field of Mars and in the Court of Venus. A Tribute to Our Citizen Soldiers by one who would gladly join the ranks if he knew how to dance." Hoyt's Theatre, October 8, 1894.

"A Black Sheep: And How It Came Out in the Wash." Hoyt's Theatre, January 6, 1896.

"A Contented Woman: A Sketch of the Fair Sex in Politics." Hoyt's Theatre, February 8, 1897.

"A Stranger in New York: Illustration of the Possible Adventures of." September 13, 1897 (and later transferred to Hoyt's Theatre).

"A Day and a Night in New York." Garrick Theatre, August 30, 1898.

"A Dog in a Manger."

"A Runaway Colt: A dalliance with facts, folks, and other things pertaining to the noble game of baseball." American Theatre, December 2, 1896.

DAVID BELASCO

DAVID BELASCO was born in San Francisco, Cal., July 25, 1853. He was the private secretary of Dion Boucicault. He was also an actor of no mean attainments. His California experience brought him in contact with most of the noted actors of his day. As a stage director and as a dramatist he began to win attention. He was at one time associated with James A. Herne. In the fall of 1882, he began his New York connection at the Madison Square Theatre, stage-managing Bronson Howard's "Young Mrs. Winthrop." At this time he won recognition for his stage realism. In 1885, began his association with Henry C. deMille. The two collaborated in such plays as "The Wife", "Lord Chumley", and "The Charity Ball" for the Lyceum Theatre, the successor in favor of the Madison Square Theatre, New York. The latter part of 1889, Mrs. Leslie Carter sought the direction of Mr. Belasco. In the early nineties, Belasco's activities were connected with those of Charles Frohman, and he wrote with Franklyn Files "The Girl I Left Behind Me" (January 16, 1893) for the opening of Frohman's Empire Theatre. His first independent success as a manager was in his own play, "The Heart of Maryland" (October 9, 1895), with Mrs. Leslie Carter. There followed such pieces as "Zaza" (January 9, 1899), "Madame Butterfly" (March 5, 1900), "The Auctioneer" (New Haven, Conn., September 9, 1901), "DuBarry" (Washington, December 12, 1901), "The Darling of the Gods" (New York, December 3, 1902), "The Music Master" (New York, September 26, 1904), "Adrea" (New York, January 11, 1905), "The Girl of the Golden West" (New York, November 14 1905), and so on. The list of original plays, collaborations with John Luther Long Richard Walton Tully and others, translations, adaptations, is a long one and is partly to be found in William Winter's "Life" of Mr. Belasco. "The Return of Peter Grimm" (New York, October 18, 1911) is the last play of Mr. Belasco's seen in New York. As a manager, however, he has been active in offering plays by native and foreign authors; and these productions have always shown the hand of Mr. Belasco giving final shape to materials. His stand against the theatrical trust is a significant part of theatre history. His attitude toward the "new" movement in the theatre is that of the uncompromising realist.

Baker, George Pierce. "Modern American Plays." New York: Harcourt, Brace & Co. 1920. Contains the text of "The Return of Peter Grimm."
Belasco, David. "The Theatre Through Its Stage Door." Edited by Louis V. De Foe. New York: Harper & Brothers. 1919.

Eaton, Walter P. "The American Stage of To-day." Boston: Small, Maynard & Co. 1908. ("Kisses and David Belasco.")

Eaton, Walter P. "Plays and Players: Leaves from a Critic's Scrapbook." Cincinnati: Stewart & Kidd. 1916. ("Belasco and Hypnotism" and "Bernstein and Belasco at their Best.")

Moses, Montrose J. "Representative Plays by American Dramatists." Vol. III. New York: E. P. Dutton & Co. 1921. (The text of "The Return of Peter Grimm." See introduction. Also "The Authors and their Plays", pp. 925–926. List of Belasco's Dramas. Also Individual Bibliographies, pp. 13–14.)

Quinn, A. H. "Representative American Plays." New York: The Century Co. 1917. Text of "Madame Butterfly" by Belasco and John Luther Long.

Winter, William. "The Life of David Belasco." 2 volumes. New York: Moffat, Yard & Co. 1918. (In "The Wallet of Time", by the same author, 2 vols., there are innumerable references to Belasco.)

AUGUSTUS THOMAS

Augustus Thomas was born in St. Louis, Missouri, January 8, 1859. He was a page boy in the 41st Congress, was in the freight department of the railroad, and earned a living with his pen as writer and illustrator on newspapers in St. Louis, Kansas City, and New York. In the early eighties he began his playwriting career. His varied activity in the theatre won for him the gold medal of the American Academy of Arts and Letters, of which he is a member.

Baker, George Pierce. "Modern American Plays." New York: Harcourt, Brace & Co. 1920. Text of "As a Man Thinks."

Cohen, Helen Louise. "Longer Plays by Modern Authors." New York: Harcourt, Brace & Co. 1922. Text of "The Copperhead."

Dickinson, Thomas H. "Chief Contemporary Dramatists." Boston: Houghton Mifflin Co. 1915. First Series. Text of "The Witching Hour."

Eaton, Walter P. "The American Stage of To-day." Boston: Small, Maynard & Co. 1908. ("The Witching Hour.")

Eaton, Walter P. "At the New Theatre and Others." Boston: Small, Maynard & Co. 1910. ("Mr. Thomas's New Birth.")

Eaton, Walter P. "Plays and Players: Leaves from a Critic's Scrapbook." Cincinnati: Stewart & Kidd. 1916. ("As Augustus Thomas Thinks.")

Moses, Montrose J. "Representative Plays by American Dramatists." Vol. III. New York: E. P. Dutton & Co. 1921. (Text of "In Mizzoura." See Introduction. Also "The Authors and Their Plays", pp. 921–922. List of Mr. Thomas's Dramas. Also Individual bibliographies, pp. 11–12.)

"One-Act Plays for Stage and Study." New York: Samuel French. 1924. Text of one-act play, "The Man Upstairs."

Quinn, A. H. "Representative American Plays." New York: The Century Co. 1917. Text of "The Witching Hour."

Thomas, Augustus. "The Print of My Remembrance." New York: Charles Scribner's Sons. 1922. (Mr. Thomas's Introductions to his plays, published by Samuel French, and his Introduction to Bronson Howard's "The Autobiography of a Play", issued by the Dramatic Museum of Columbia University, 1914, are of value.)

CLYDE FITCH

CLYDE FITCH was born on May 2, 1863, in Elmira, New York. He was a classmate of William Lyons Phelps at the Public High School of Hartford, Conn. Previous to his entering Amherst, in 1882, he went to Holderness, New Hampshire, where there was a boarding-school for boys. He began his career as a dramatist, when E. A. Dithmar, dramatic critic of the New York *Times*, recommended him to Richard Mansfield, who wished to have written for him a play based on the picturesque history of Beau Brummell. From that time to the day of his death, Clyde Fitch's career was the career of his plays. He died suddenly in France, at Chalôns-sur-Marne, September 4, 1909.

Archer, William. "Playmaking: A Manual of Craftsmanship." Boston: Small, Maynard & Co. 1912. Casual comment.

Baker, George Pierce. "Dramatic Technique." Boston: Houghton Mifflin Co. 1919. Casual comment.

Clark, Barrett H. "A Study of the Modern Drama." New York: D. Appleton & Co. 1925. Study and bibliography.

Cohen, Helen Louise. "Longer Plays by Modern Authors." New York: Harcourt, Brace & Co. 1922. Text of "Beau Brummell."

Dickinson, Thomas H. "Chief Contemporary Dramatists." Boston: Houghton Mifflin Co. 1915. First Series. Text of "The Truth."

Eaton, Walter P. "At the New Theatre and Others." Boston: Small, Maynard & Co. 1910. ("The Dramatist as a Man of Letters. The Case of Clyde Fitch.")

Fitch, Clyde. "The Play and the Public." The text of a lecture. See Memorial Edition of Clyde Fitch's Plays, Vol. IV.

Frohman, Daniel, and Isaac F. Marcosson. "Charles Frohman: Manager and Man." New York: Harper & Brothers. 1916.

Hamilton, Clayton. "Problems of the Playwright." New York: Henry Holt & Co. 1917. (See index for references. Mr. Hamilton's other volumes: "Studies in Stagecraft", "The Theory of the Theatre", and "Seen on the Stage" are likewise of use as revealing contemporary judgment of Thomas, Fitch, Belasco, and others.)

Hapgood, Norman. "The Stage in America: 1897–1900." New York: The Macmillan Co. 1901.

Marbury, Elizabeth. "My Crystal Ball." New York: Boni & Liveright. 1923.

Moses, Montrose J., and Virginia Gerson. "Clyde Fitch and His Letters." Boston: Little, Brown, and Co. 1924. (See likewise the Memorial Edition of Fitch's plays, issued by Little, Brown, and Co., in 1915.)

Moses, Montrose J. "Representative Plays by American Dramatists." Vol. III. New York: E. P. Dutton & Co. 1921. (Text of "The Moth and the Flame." See Introduction. Also "The Authors and Their Plays", p. 923. List of Fitch's Dramas. Also Individual bibliographies, pp. 12–13. The Editor has in preparation a new book, "The American Dramatist", which will contain thorough studies of Hoyt, Belasco, Fitch; and Thomas.)

Phelps, William Lyon. "Essays on American Dramatists." New York: The Macmillan Co. 1921.

Quinn, A. H. "Representative American Plays." New York: The Century Co. 1917. Text of "Her Great Match."

Skinner, Otis. "Footlights and Spotlights." Indianapolis: Bobbs-Merrill Co. 1924.

Thomas, Augustus. "The Print of My Remembrance." New York: Charles Scribner's Sons. 1922.

Wilson, Francis. "Francis Wilson's Life of Himself." Boston: Houghton Mifflin Co. 1924.

PERCY MACKAYE

MR. MACKAYE was born in New York City, March 16, 1875, and is the son of the dramatist, Steele MacKaye. He is a Harvard man, of the class of 1897. Since leaving college his life has been truly a steady devotion to his occupation, "poet and dramatist." It is as a dramatist that we represent him in this bibliography, omitting altogether his work in verse and in prose, outside the theatre. To his credit, the following plays are recorded, the dates being those of publication. The student is referred hereafter to a bibliography of dates of production.

Plays.

"The Canterbury Pilgrims." 1903.
"Fenris the Wolf." 1905.
"Jeanne d'Arc." 1906.
"Sappho and Phaon." 1907.
"Mater." 1908.
"The Scarecrow." 1908.
"Anti-Matrimony." 1910.
"A Garland to Sylvia." 1910.
"To-morrow." 1912.
"Yankee Fantasies: Five One-Act Plays." 1912.
"A Thousand Years Ago." 1914.
"Washington, the Man Who Made Us." 1918.
"This Fine-Pretty World." 1924.

Operas.

"The Immigrants." 1915.
"Sinbad, the Sailor." 1917.
"The Canterbury Pilgrims." 1916.
"Rip Van Winkle." 1919.

Communal Dramas (*Masques and Pageant-Rituals*).

"Saint-Gaudens Masque-Prologue" (In "Poems", 1909). Produced 1905.
The Gloucester Pageant: "The Canterbury Pilgrims." Produced 1909.
Pittsburgh Pageant: "A Masque of Labor." Produced July 4, 1910.
"Sanctuary: A Bird Masque." 1914. Produced 1913.
"St. Louis: A Civic Masque." 1914. Produced May 28, 1914.
"The New Citizenship: A Civic Ritual." 1915. Produced July 4, 1916.
"Caliban, by the Yellow Sands." 1916. Produced May 25, 1916.
"The Evergreen Tree: A Masque of Christmas Time, for Community Singing and Acting." 1917. Produced December 15, 1917.
"The Roll Call: A Masque of the Red Cross." 1918. Produced December, 1918.

"The Will of Song. A Dramatic Service of Community Singing." 1919.
Produced the same year.

"The Pilgrim and the Book." Written for the American Bible Society.
1920. Produced at the time of the Pilgrim Tercentenary.

Consult the following:

Crowley, Allister. "Percy MacKaye." *International*, Vol. 11, p. 47. 1917.

Dickinson, Thomas H. "Chief Contemporary Dramatists." First Series. Boston: Houghton Mifflin Co. 1915. (Text of "The Scarecrow." See MacKaye in Dickinson's latest book, "Playwrights of the New American Theatre.")

Eaton, Walter P. "The American Stage of To-day." Boston: Small, Maynard & Co. 1908. ("MacKaye's 'Sappho and Phaon.'")

MacKaye, Percy. "A Sketch of his Life, with Bibliography of His Works." Reprinted from the Twenty-fifth Anniversary Report of the Class of 1897, Harvard College, 1922.

In connection with MacKaye, see data on his father in Moses' "Representative Plays by American Dramatists." Vol. III. New York: E. P. Dutton & Co. 1921. Text of Steele MacKaye's "Paul Kauvar." Introduction, Bibliography and List of Plays. (See also Quinn's "Representative American Plays", containing the texts of Steele MacKaye's "Hazel Kirke" and Percy MacKaye's "The Scarecrow.")

—— "The Scarecrow; or, The Glass of Truth." A Tragedy of the Ludicrous. With an Introduction by the Author. New York: The Macmillan Co. 1908.

—— "The Playhouse and the Play." New York: The Macmillan Co. 1909.

—— "Steele MacKaye. Dynamic Artist of the American Theatre." *Drama*, No. 4, pp. 138–161. November, 1911. No. 5, pp. 153–173. February, 1915. See also Mr. MacKaye's article, "The Theatre of Ten Thousand." *Theatre Arts Magazine*, Vol. 7, pp. 116–126. 1923.

—— "The Civic Theatre." New York: Mitchell Kennerley. 1912.

—— "Community Drama." Boston: Houghton Mifflin Co. 1917.

—— "Plan for a National Council of the Theatre." *Theatre*, Vol. 27, pp. 203–204. April, 1918.

—— "Untamed America: A Comment on a Sojourn in the Kentucky Mountains." A reprint from the *Survey Graphic*, January, 1924.

Moses, Montrose J. "The American Dramatist." Boston: Little, Brown, and Co. 1917.

Thomas, Charles Swain. "The Atlantic Book of Junior Plays." Boston: The Atlantic Monthly Press. 1924. Text of "Kinfolk of Robin Hood."

JOSEPHINE PRESTON PEABODY

Plays by Mrs. Marks that are in print are as follows:

"Fortune and Men's Eyes." 1 act. Boston: Small, Maynard & Co. 1900. (Also an edition, Houghton Mifflin, 1900. See A. D. Dickinson's "Drama." Garden City, 1922. pp. 87–135.)

"Marlowe." 5 acts. Boston: Houghton Mifflin Co. 1901.

"The Piper." 4 acts. Boston: Houghton Mifflin Co. 1909. (Also in Thomas H. Dickinson's "Chief Contemporary Dramatists." Second Series. Boston: Houghton Mifflin Co. 1921.) The play was translated into French by Mlle. Henriette Orange-Colombier, into Swedish by Arvid Paulsen, into German by Margarethe Münsterberg.

"The Wolf of Gubbio." 3 acts. Boston: Houghton Mifflin Co. 1913.

"The Wings." 1 act. *Poet-Lore*, Vol. 25, pp. 352–369. 1914.

"The Chameleon." 3 acts. New York: Samuel French. 1917.

"Portrait of Mrs. W." 3 acts. Boston: Houghton Mifflin Co. 1922.

Eaton, Walter P. "Plays and Players: Leaves from a Critic's Scrapbook." Cincinnati: Stewart & Kidd. 1916. ("Playing the Piper.")

"Piper, The." Production at Stratford. A. F. Brown. *Bookman*, Vol. 57, pp. 263–266. May, 1923.

"Drift toward Fairyland." William Winter. *Harper's Weekly*, Vol. 55, p. 18. February 18, 1911.

"Play which won the Stratford Prize." A. Ruhl. *Collier's*, Vol. 46, p. 16. February 25, 1911.

"Reception in England." N. O. Barr. *Drama*, No. 1, pp. 176–186. February. 1911.

"Supernatural Plays." Clayton Hamilton. *Bookman*, Vol. 33, pp. 29–30. March, 1911.

Peabody, Josephine Preston. "America's Dramatic Poet." M. S. Stimpson. *New England Magazine*, N.S., Vol. 42, pp. 270–277. May, 1910.

"Author of 'The Piper.'" *Hampton*, Vol. 25, pp. 539–540. October, 1910.

"Miss Peabody and 'The Piper.'" J. Corbin. *Hampton*, Vol. 26, pp. 644–646. May, 1911.

"Neglected Stepchild of the Modern Stage." *Current Literature*, Vol. 49, pp. 435–436. October, 1910.

HARRY JAMES SMITH

Mr. Smith was born in New Britain, Connecticut, May 24, 1880. He was killed in a train and automobile collision, on March 16, 1918, near Murrayville, British Columbia. After general schooling, he entered Williams College in 1898. Following his graduation he was Assistant in the Biological Laboratory. After a year abroad (1903), he studied English at Harvard, and then went to Oberlin College for a short time in the English department. In 1906–1907 he was on the editorial staff of the *Atlantic Monthly*. Thereafter he gave his energy entirely to literature, the writing of novels, short stories and plays.

Consult the Periodical Index and Dramatic Index, under titles of plays for casual references. Samuel French published the following plays by Mr. Smith:

"Mrs. Bumpstead-Leigh." Produced at the Lyceum Theatre, New York, April 3, 1911.

"A Tailor-made Man." Produced at the Cohan and Harris Theatre, New York, August 27, 1917.

"The Little Teacher." Produced at the Playhouse, New York, February 4, 1918.

Interview. *Theatre Magazine*, Vol. 27, p. 230.

"Letters of Harry James Smith, The." With an Introduction by Juliet Wilbor Tompkins. Boston : Houghton Mifflin Co. 1919.

ROI COOPER MEGRUE AND WALTER HACKETT

Mr. Megrue was born in New York City, June 12, 1883. He was educated at Trinity School and Columbia University. He was for some time associated with Miss Elizabeth Marbury, one of the leading play brokers of the period of Clyde Fitch. Mr. Walter Hackett was born in Oakland, California, November 10, 1876. He has written many plays, a number of them in collaboration. Among the latter may be noted "The Regeneration" (1908) with Owen Kildare; and "The White Sister", with F. Marion Crawford.

Of Megrue's plays, Samuel French publishes the following :

"Under Cover." Cort Theatre, New York, October 26, 1914. This play was novelized by Wyndham Martin. (1914).

"It Pays to Advertise." George M. Cohan Theatre, New York, September 8, 1914.

"Under Fire." Hudson Theatre, New York, August, 1915. This play was novelized by R. Parker (1916).

"Seven Chances." George M. Cohan Theatre, New York, August 8, 1916.

"It Pays to Advertise" was given a London production. Others of Mr. Megrue's plays to be given London productions are :

"Potash and Perlmutter in Society." Queen's Theatre.

"Under Cover." Strand Theatre.

"Tea for Three." Haymarket Theatre.

Eaton, Walter P. "It Pays to Advertise." *American Magazine*, Vol. 79, p. 42. January, 1915. See also *McClure*, Vol. 44, p. 26. January, 1915.

Hamilton, Clayton. "Problems of the Playwright." New York : Henry Holt & Co. 1917.

"Megrue, Roi Cooper." Interview. *Theatre Magazine*, Vol. 20, pp. 276, 299. December, 1914. Sketch. *Green Book*, Vol. 10, pp. 930-931. November 19, 1916.

The Dramatic Indexes have notices of additional plays by Mr. Megrue :

"Double Cross." 1911.

"To Kill a Man." 1912.

"White Magic." From the novel by D. G. Phillips. 1912.

"The Neglected Lady." From the French of M. Maurey. 1914.

"Desperate Desmond." 1914.

"Abe and Mawruss" (with Montague Glass). 1915.

"Under Sentence" (with I. S. Cobb). 1916.

"Seven Chances." 1916.

"Where Poppies Bloom." (From Kistemaeker). 1918.

"Tea for Three." 1918.

"Honors Are Even." 1921.

JAMES FORBES

Mr. Forbes was born in Salem, Ontario, Canada. He became a naturalized citizen of the United States in 1892. He has been an actor, dramatic critic, press representative, general representative in a theatrical organization, and stage director. He brought to his playwriting, which he began in 1906, a thorough knowledge of the mechanics of the theatre.

Eaton, Walter P. "Plays and Players: Leaves from a Critic's Scrapbook." Cincinnati: Stewart & Kidd. 1916. (See "Holding the Mirror Up to Art", referring to "The Show Shop", given December 15, 1914.)

Forbes, James. "The Famous Mrs. Fair, and Other Plays." With an Introduction by Walter P. Eaton. New York: George Doran & Co. 1920. The plays in this volume, which include "The Chorus Lady" and "The Show Shop", are also published by Samuel French. "The Famous Mrs. Fair":

Photoplay by Frances Marion. Criticism: *Nation*, Vol. 117, pp. 636–637. December, 5, 1923. Fictionized by P. Andrews. *Motion Picture Magazine*, Vol. 25, pp. 61–65, 112. May, 1923.

EUGENE O'NEILL

Mr. O'Neill was born in New York City, October 16, 1888, son of the actor, James O'Neill. He was a student at Princeton, 1906–1907, and at Harvard, 1914–1915, where he studied dramatic technique under George P. Baker. But before then, he had varied business experience, had run away to sea, had acted with his father in a tabloid "Monte Cristo", and had served as reporter on a newspaper. Then, in 1914, he began writing plays. He has been awarded the Pulitzer Prize twice, for "Beyond the Horizon" (1920) and for "Anna Christie" (1922). He is a member of the American Institute of Arts and Letters. A Definitive Edition of his plays to date, in two volumes, has recently been issued (1925). The early editions of his plays are eagerly sought by book collectors. The following list is not complete:

1914. "Thirst and Other One-Act Plays." American Dramatists Series. Boston: The Gorham Press. Containing "Thirst", "The Web", "Warnings", "Fog", "Recklessness."

1916. "Before Breakfast." New York: Frank Shay.

1916. "Provincetown Plays. Series One." New York: F. Shay. "Bound East for Cardiff."

1917. *Smart Set*, Vol. 53, pp. 83–94, October. "The Long Voyage Home."

1918. *Smart Set*, Vol. 55, pp. 73–86. "The Moon of the Caribbees."

1919. "Representative One-Act Plays by American Authors." Edited by Margaret Mayorga. Boston: Little, Brown, and Co. 1919. Containing "In the Zone."

1920. "Gold." New York: Boni & Liveright.

1920. *Theatre Arts Magazine*, Vol. 4, pp. 41–56. "The Dreamy Kid."

1920. "Fifty Contemporary One-Act Plays." Edited by Frank Shay and Pierre Loving. Cincinnati: Stewart & Kidd. "Ile."

1921. "Provincetown Plays, selected by George Cram Cook and Frank Shay." With a foreword by Hutchins Hapgood. Cincinnati: Stewart & Kidd. "Bound East for Cardiff."

1922. "Contemporary One-Act Plays of 1921" (American). Cincinnati: Stewart & Kidd. "The Dreamy Kid."

1921. "The Moon of the Caribbees, and Six Other Plays of the Sea." New York: Boni & Liveright. Containing "Bound East for Cardiff", "The Long Voyage Home", "In the Zone", "Ile", "Where the Cross is Made", "The Rope."

1921. *Theatre Arts Magazine*, Vol. 5, pp. 29–59. "Emperor Jones."

1921. "The Emperor Jones, Diff'rent, The Straw." New York: Boni & Liveright.

1922. "The Hairy Ape, Anna Christie, The First Man." Boni & Liveright.

1923. "Beyond the Horizon." New York: Boni & Liveright.

1923. "Contemporary American Plays." Ed. by A. H. Quinn. New York: Charles Scribner's Sons. Containing "The Emperor Jones."

1924. "All God's Chillun Got Wings." *The American Mercury*, Vol. 1, pp. 131–148.

1924. "Unterm Karibischen Mond." Dramatische Studie. Translated by Gustaf Kauder. Berlin: Neue Rundschau, Jahrg. 35, Vol. 1, pp. 97–111.

Such plays as "Welded", "The Ancient Mariner" and "Desire under the Elms" are to be found in the Definitive Edition.

Boyd, Ernest. "Portraits: Real and Imaginary." New York: George H. Doran Co. 1924.

Clark, Barrett H. "A Study of the Modern Drama." New York: D. Appleton & Co. 1925.

Dickinson, Thomas H. "Playwrights of the New American Theatre." New York: The Macmillan Co. 1925.

Eaton, Walter P. "Eugene O'Neill." *Theatre Arts Magazine*, Vol. 4, pp. 286–289. 1920.

"Emperor Jones." *Nation* (Lewisohn), pp. 112, 189. February 2, 1921.

Hamilton, Clayton. "Conversations on Contemporary Drama." New York: The Macmillan Co. 1924. pp. 198–218.

"Horizon, Beyond the." Hamilton, Clayton. "Seen on the Stage." New York: Henry Holt & Co. 1920.

Macgowan, Kenneth. "The Theatre of To-morrow." New York: Boni & Liveright. 1921. (Casual reference also in "Continental Stagecraft." New York: Harcourt, Brace & Co. 1922.)

O'Neill, Eugene.

"A Broadway Philosopher." Jack Crawford. *Drama*, Vol. 12, pp. 117–118, 142. 1922.

"American Dramatist Abroad." *Living Age*, Vol. 314, p. 121. July 8, 1922.

"American Dramatist and Some Players." S. K. Ratcliffe. *New Statesman*, No. 17, p. 386. July 9, 1921.

Biographical. Alta M. Coleman. *Theatre*, Vol. 31, pp. 264, 302. April, 1920.

"Development of Eugene O'Neill." L. Lewisohn. *Nation*, Vol. 114, pp. 349–350. March 22, 1922.

"Early Days of Eugene O'Neill." New York *Times Magazine*. December 21, 1924.

"Estimate of Eugene O'Neill." S. Young. *New Republic*, Vol. 32, pp. 307–308. November 15, 1922.

"Eugene O'Neill." W. P. Eaton. *Theatre Arts Magazine*, No. 4, pp. 286–289. 1920.

"Eugene O'Neill As Realist." "Welded." Kenneth Macgowan. New York *Times*, March 23, 1924.

"Extraordinary Story of Eugene O'Neill." M. B. Mullett. *American Magazine*, Vol. 94, pp. 34–35. November, 1922.

"Home on the Dunes." J. M. Breese. *Country Life*, Vol. 45, pp. 72–76. November, 1923.

Interview. *Theatre*, Vol. 39, pp. 8–9, 60. June, 1924.

"Plays of Eugene O'Neill." E. A. Baughan. *Fortnightly*, Vol. 119, pp. 852–860. May, 1923.

"Plays of Eugene O'Neill." Andrew E. Marlow. *Dublin Magazine*, Vol. 1, pp. 401–409. 1923.

"The Rise of Eugene O'Neill." A. Woollcott. *Everybody's*, Vol. 43, p. 49. June, 1920.

Sayler, Oliver M. "Our American Theatre." New York: Brentano's. 1923. Chapter III: "Eugene O'Neill, the American Playwright", pp. 27–43. (A complete list of O'Neill's plays, to date, pp. 320–322.) See same writer's "Eugene O'Neill: Master of Naturalism." *Drama*, Vol. 11, pp. 189–190. March, 1921. "Real Eugene O'Neill." *Century*, Vol. 103, pp. 351–359. January, 1922.

Western Reserve University. Cleveland, Ohio. Studies by Members of the Faculty. Cleveland, 1923. *Bulletin*, Vol. 26, No. 8, August, 1923. A. F. White. "The Plays of Eugene O'Neill."

Wilde, Percival. "The Craftsmanship of the One-Act Play." Boston: Little, Brown, and Co. 1923.

RACHEL CROTHERS

Miss Crothers was born in Bloomington, Illinois, and received her education at the Illinois State Normal School. As teacher, actor, and writer, she has been connected with the theatre for some years. Her various plays are thus noted:

1902, April 3. "The Rector." Madison Square Theatre, New York.

1903, September. "Nora." Savoy Theatre, New York.

1904, March. "The Point of View." Manhattan Theatre, New York.

1906, October 17. "The Three of Us." Madison Square Theatre, New York.

1907, November 6. "The Coming of Mrs. Patrick." Madison Square Theatre, New York.

1908, October 5. "Myself, Bettina." Daly's Theatre, New York.

1910, February 8. "A Man's World." Comedy Theatre, New York.

1912, February 5. "The Herfords" ("He and She" — 1920). Plymouth Theatre. Boston, Mass.

1913, November 13. "Ourselves." Lyric Theatre. New York.

1914, January 5. "Young Wisdom." Criterion Theatre. New York.

1916, October 30. "Old Lady 31." Thirty-ninth Street Theatre, New York.

1918. "A Little Journey." Little Theatre. New York.

1919, March 31. "39 East." Broadhurst Theatre. New York.

1921, March 2. "Nice People." Klaw Theatre. New York.

1921. "Everyday."

1923, February 5. "Mary the Third." Thirty-ninth St. Theatre, New York.

1924, April 16. "Expressing Willie." Forty-eighth Street Theatre. New York.

"The Rector." New York: Samuel French. 1905. See also "One-Act Plays for Stage and Study." (New York: Samuel French. 1924.)

"A Man's World." Boston: R. G. Badger. *American Dramatists Series*. 1915.

"The Three of Us." New York: Samuel French. 1916.

"Mary the Third." "Old Lady 31." "A Little Journey." New York: Brentano's. 1923.

"Expressing Willie." "Nice People." "39 East." New York: Brentano's. 1924.

"39 East", "Mary the Third", and "Expressing Willie" are also published by Walter H. Baker Co., Boston, Mass.

"Peggy." *Scribner's Magazine*, Vol. 76, pp. 175–183. 1924.

Eaton, Walter P. "At the New Theatre and Others." Boston: Small, Maynard & Co. 1910. ("Miss Crothers Champions Her Sex.")

Mantle, Burns. "Nice People." In Abstract. "Best Plays." 1920–1921. Boston: Small, Maynard & Co. 1921.

Quinn, A. H. "Representative American Plays." New York: The Century Co. 1917. Text of "He and She." (See also same editor's "Contemporary American Plays." New York: Charles Scribner's Sons. 1923. Text of "Nice People.")

OWEN DAVIS

Mr. Davis was born in Portland, Maine, January 29, 1874. Attended the University of Tennessee and Harvard. Engaged in playwriting since 1898. "Who's Who" credits him with being the author of over 100 plays. "Icebound" was awarded the Pulitzer Prize in 1922. He is a member of the National Institute of Arts and Letters.

Autobiographical. *American Magazine*, Vol. 78, pp. 28–31, 77–80. September, 1914. Answers the question: "Why I Quit Writing Melodramas?"

"Recipe for Manufacturing Melodramas." *Current Opinion*, Vol. 57, p. 251. October, 1914.

Sketch. *Bookman*, Vol. 58, p. 231. October, 1923.

"Detour, The." Boston: Little, Brown, and Company. 1922.

"Icebound." Boston: Little, Brown, and Company. 1923.

GEORGE S. KAUFMAN AND MARC CONNELLY

Mr. Kaufman was born in Pittsburgh, Pennsylvania, November 16, 1889; Mr. Connelly in McKeesport, Pennsylvania, December 13, 1890. They have both had newspaper careers — have run humorous columns, been dramatic critics. Together they have written "Dulcy", "To the Ladies", "Merton of the Movies", "Helen of Troy, New York" and "Beggar on Horseback." Separately, they have written other plays and contributed lyrics to musical comedies.

Mr. Kaufman, with Miss Edna Ferber, wrote "Minick", just published (Doubleday, Page & Co. 1925).

Cohen, Helen Louise. "Longer Plays by Modern Authors." New York: Harcourt, Brace & Co. 1922. Text of "Dulcy." See Introduction.

"Dulcy." New York: G. P. Putnam's Sons. 1921. Also issued by Samuel French. 1923.

"To the Ladies." See Quinn, A. H. "Contemporary American Plays." New York: Charles Scribner's Sons. 1923. Also Samuel French. 1923.

"Beggar on Horseback." Suggested by "Hans Sonnenstoesser's hohlenfahrt", by Paul Apel. New York: Boni & Liveright. 1924.

"Merton of the Movies." Founded on a novel by H. L. Wilson. Given in London at the Shaftesbury Theatre.

ELMER L. RICE

Mr. Rice was born in New York City, September 28, 1892, was educated at High School and studied law. Connected at one time with various settlement dramatic societies.

"The Adding Machine." Foreword by Philip Moeller. Garden City: Doubleday, Page & Co. 1923. (Duncan Macdougall, in 1924, produced "The Adding Machine" at the Playbox Theatre, Sidney, Australia, and, in 1925, Fischer, of Berlin, has opened negotiations for the German rights.)

Dodge, W. P. Interview. *Strand*, Vol. 48, pp. 685–688. December, 1914.

Eaton, Walter P. Sketch. *American Magazine*, Vol. 79, pp. 42, 87. January, 1915. See also *McClure*, Vol. 44, pp. 18–21. January, 1915.

Hamilton, Clayton. "Problems of the Playwright." New York: Henry Holt & Co. 1917. ("Building a Play Backwards." Comments on "On Trial.")

GEORGE KELLY

Mr. Kelly was born at Falls of Schuylkill, one of the suburbs of the city of Philadelphia. When twenty-one, he won distinction as a juvenile actor, and four years thereafter entered vaudeville, writing his own plays. His career from then on has been bound up in his plays, all of which have been published.

"The Torch-Bearers." New York: American Library Service. 1923. Also in the French edition. 1924. (Preface by Kenneth Macgowan.)

"The Show-Off: A Transcript of Life." Boston: Little, Brown, and Company. 1924. (Preface by Heywood Broun.)

"The Flattering Word, and Other One-Act Plays." Boston: Little, Brown, and Co. 1925.

"Finders-Keepers." One act. In "Contemporary One-Act Plays of 1921" (American). Edited by Frank Shay. Cincinnati: Stewart & Kidd. 1922. (Now published by D. Appleton & Co. New York.)

"The Show-Off." Novelized by William Almon Wolff. Boston: Little, Brown, and Co. 1924. (The play was given in London, at the Queen's Theatre, October 20, 1924.)